POSTCARDS FROM

🖙 **Frommer's**®

Florida 2005

S0-AFE-801

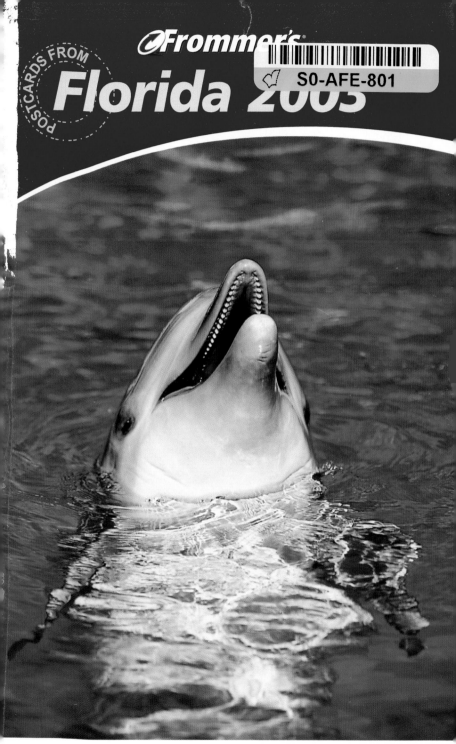

One *of the* playful residents of SeaWorld in Orlando. See chapter 12. © James Lemass/SeaWorld Florida.

"Houston, we have a problem . . ."
a U.S. Apollo astronaut suit on
display at the Kennedy Space
Center. See chapter 13.
© M. Timothy O'Keefe Photography.

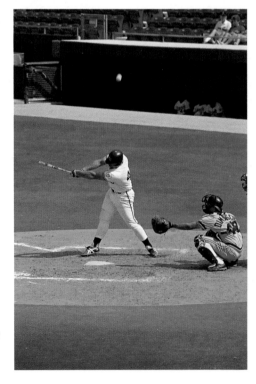

Every year, eager baseball fans
from across the country flock to
Florida for spring training. See
chapter 9. © M. Timothy O'Keefe
Photography.

Visit the house where "Papa" Hemingway wrote some of his most famous works and check out other Hemingway haunts while in Key West. See chapter 6. © Michael Ventura Photography.

Every year, millions of sunbathers head for the warm, pristine beaches of Florida. See chapter 1 for a list of the best beaches in the state. © Trevor Wood/Tony Stone Worldwide.

Warm weather and an abundance of marine life make Florida a year-round destination for anglers from throughout the world. © Mark Barrett/Silver Image Photography.

Traveling to orange groves allows visitors the chance to send some Florida sunshine back home. © Robert Holmes Photography.

Most everything in Miami's South Beach has an Art Deco feel, such as this trendy cafe. See chapter 5. © Michael Ventura Photography.

Parks and nature preserves in the Tampa Bay area are the best places to catch a glimpse of the Florida manatee. See chapter 11. © Stuart Westmorland/Tony Stone Images.

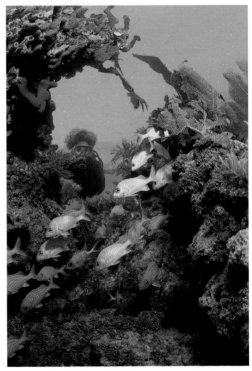

Biscayne National Park and the Florida Keys offer some of the best snorkeling and scuba diving in Florida. See chapters 6 and 7. © Stephen Frink Photography.

The Daytona International Speedway, known as the "World Center of Racing," is home to the Daytona 500—the world's best-known motor sports event. See chapter 13.
© Jamie Squire/Allsport.

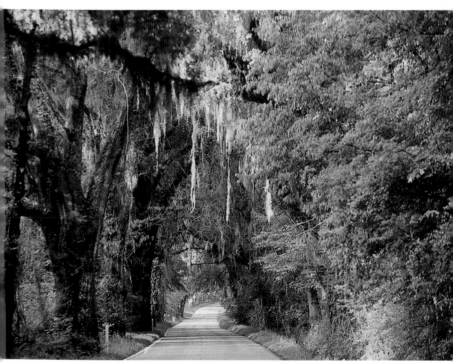

The picturesque and aptly named Canopy Road, located north of Tallahassee. See chapter 14.
© Robert Holmes Photography.

A bird's-eye view of the winding channels in Everglades National Park. See chapter 7.
© David Job/Tony Stone Images.

A New Star-Rating System & Other Exciting News from Frommer's!

In our continuing effort to publish the savviest, most up-to-date, and most appealing travel guides available, we've added some great new features.

Frommer's guides now include a new **star-rating system.** Every hotel, restaurant, and attraction is rated from 0 to 3 stars to help you set priorities and organize your time.

We've also added **seven brand-new features** that point you to the great deals, in-the-know advice, and unique experiences that separate travelers from tourists. Throughout the guide, look for:

Finds	Special finds—those places only insiders know about
Fun Fact	Fun facts—details that make travelers more informed and their trips more fun
Kids	Best bets for kids—advice for the whole family
Moments	Special moments—those experiences that memories are made of
Overrated	Places or experiences not worth your time or money
Tips	Insider tips—some great ways to save time and money
Value	Great values—where to get the best deals

We've also added a **"What's New"** section in every guide—a timely crash course in what's hot and what's not in every destination we cover.

Here's what the critics say about Frommer's:

"Amazingly easy to use. Very portable, very complete."

—*Booklist*

"Detailed, accurate, and easy-to-read information for all price ranges."
—*Glamour Magazine*

"Hotel information is close to encyclopedic."
—*Des Moines Sunday Register*

"Frommer's Guides have a way of giving you a real feel for a place."
—*Knight Ridder Newspapers*

Frommer's®

Florida

2003

by Lesley Abravanel, Bill Goodwin
& Jim and Cynthia Tunstall

Wiley Publishing, Inc.

Published by:

Wiley Publishing, Inc.

909 Third Ave.
New York, NY 10022

ISBN 0-7645-6662-8
ISSN 1044-2391

Editor: Kendra L. Falkenstein
Production Editor: Ian Skinnari
Cartographer: John Decamillis
Photo Editor: Richard Fox
Production by Wiley Indianapolis Composition Services

Front cover photo: Woman in red suit, floating in pool
Back cover photo: Universal Studios, Islands of Adventure, Incredible Hulk Coaster

For information on our other products and services or to obtain technical support,
please contact our Customer Care Department within the U.S. at 800-762-2974,
outside the U.S. at 317-572-3993 or fax 317-572-4002.

Wiley also publishes its books in a variety of electronic formats. Some content that
appears in print may not be available in electronic formats.

Manufactured in the United States of America

5   4   3   2   1

Contents

List of Maps

About the Authors

Lesley Abravanel is a freelance journalist and a graduate of the University of Miami School of Communication. When she isn't combing South Florida for the latest hotels, restaurants, and attractions, she is on the lookout for vacationing celebrities, about whom she writes in her weekly nightlife and gossip column, "Velvet Underground," for both the *Miami Herald* and its weekly entertainment newspaper, *Street*. She is a contributor to *Star Magazine* and the Miami correspondent for *Black Book Magazine* and is the author of *Frommer's South Florida* and *Frommer's Portable Miami*.

Bill Goodwin began his career as an award-winning newspaper reporter before serving as speechwriter and legal counsel for two U.S. senators. These days he spends as much time as possible exploring the ins and outs of other places with naturally hot air; he's also the author of *Frommer's South Pacific*.

Jim and Cynthia Tunstall have racked up plenty of waiting time in Walt Disney World lines so you won't have to. They were there when the Magic Kingdom opened in 1971, and in the three decades since that watershed moment, they've sampled virtually everything that's part of an Orlando vacation. Their many insider experiences allow them to separate the good from the bad and the ugly, and they give you the best ways to cut through the lines, the crowd, and the theme-park PR.

An Invitation to the Reader

In researching this book, we discovered many wonderful places—hotels, restaurants, shops, and more. We're sure you'll find others. Please tell us about them, so we can share the information with your fellow travelers in upcoming editions. If you were disappointed with a recommendation, we'd love to know that, too. Please write to:

Frommer's Florida 2003
Wiley Publishing, Inc. • 909 Third Ave. • New York, NY 10022

An Additional Note

Please be advised that travel information is subject to change at any time—and this is especially true of prices. We therefore suggest that you write or call ahead for confirmation when making your travel plans. The authors, editors, and publisher cannot be held responsible for the experiences of readers while traveling. Your safety is important to us, however, so we encourage you to stay alert and be aware of your surroundings. Keep a close eye on cameras, purses, and wallets, all favorite targets of thieves and pickpockets.

New! Frommer's Star Ratings & Icons

Every hotel, restaurant, and attraction listing in this guide has been ranked for quality, value, service, amenities, and special features using a star-rating scale. In country, state, and regional guides, we also rate towns and regions to help you narrow down your choices and budget your time accordingly. Hotels and restaurants in the Very Expensive and Expensive categories are rated on a scale of one (highly recommended) to three stars (exceptional). Those in the Moderate and Inexpensive categories rate from zero (recommended) to two stars (very highly recommended). Attractions, towns, and regions are rated according to the following scale: zero stars (recommended), one star (highly recommended), two stars (very highly recommended), and three stars (must-see).

In addition to the rating system, we also use seven icons to highlight insider information, useful tips, special bargains, hidden gems, memorable experiences, kid-friendly venues, places to avoid, and other useful information:

| Finds | Fun Fact | Kids | Moments | Overrated | Tips | Value |

The following abbreviations are used for credit cards:

AE	American Express	DISC	Discover	V	Visa
DC	Diners Club	MC	MasterCard		

FROMMERS.COM

Now that you have the guidebook to a great trip, visit our website at **www.frommers.com** for travel information on nearly 2,500 destinations. With features updated regularly, we give you instant access to the most current trip-planning information available. At Frommers.com, you'll also find the best prices on airfares, accommodations, and car rentals—and you can even book travel online through our travel booking partners. At Frommers.com, you'll also find the following:

- Online updates to our most popular guidebooks
- Vacation sweepstakes and contest giveaways
- Newsletter highlighting the hottest travel trends
- Online travel message boards with featured travel discussions

What's New in Florida

PLANNING YOUR TRIP TO FLORIDA Like most destinations, Florida saw its number of visitors plummet after the terrorist attacks on September 11, 2001. The industry has rebounded significantly, however, thanks in part to special discounts offered by **Visit Florida,** the state's official tourist information organization, on its website, www.flausa.com. You also can call ✆ **888/5-FLA-USA.**

Florida's state parks now have their own website at www.floridastate parks.org and a central camping reservations service (✆ **800/326-3521;** www.reserveamerica.com).

The no-frills carrier **AirTran** has discontinued service to Fort Walton Beach but is now flying to Pensacola and Tallahassee in northwest Florida.

Baseball **spring training** fans should note that the Montreal Expos and Minnesota Twins may be disbanded before the start of the 2003 season.

MIAMI For complete information on this region, see chapters 4 and 5.

A cash crop of luxury hotels, restaurants, and nightclubs has sprouted throughout Miami, though there are still plenty of deals to be found. And while the city remains a mostly seasonal destination, what used to be a completely somber summer in the city has been resurrected as a lively, cheaper, albeit much hotter, time to visit.

Accommodations The **Ritz-Carlton Key Biscayne** (455 Grand Bay Dr.; ✆ **800/241-3333**) is the first of three Ritz-Carltons to open in Miami. Two more locations, on South Beach (1 Lincoln Rd.) and in Coconut Grove (2700 Tigertail Ave.), were scheduled to open in mid-2002. To compete with the hauter-than-thou Delano Hotel on South Beach, the hyper-hip **Shore Club** (1901 Collins Ave.; ✆ **877/640-9500**) has officially opened, practically next door. The **Ritz Plaza** (1701 Collins Ave.; ✆ **305/534-3500**), taken over by W Hotels, has been resuscitated from its decrepit state into a revitalized stylish boutique hotel. **W South Beach** (✆ **877-W-HOTELS**) and its wing of oceanfront rooms is set to open in the fall of 2002. Miami's first **Four Seasons Hotel and Tower** on Brickell Avenue was set to open in the spring of 2002, with 63 stories, 1.5 million square feet, shops, and a spa.

Dining Proving its affection for things in the raw, Miami boasts two hot new sushi options. **Nobu,** a New York sushi import, opened (with Madonna's presence) at Shore Club (1901 Collins Ave., South Beach; ✆ **305/695-3100**) as did **Sushi Samba Dromo** (600 Lincoln Rd., at the corner of Pennsylvania Ave.; ✆ **305/673-5337**). A slew of trendy restaurant/lounge combos has also opened. **Kiss** (301 Lincoln Rd.; ✆ **305/695-4445**), a steakhouse-cum-cabaret attached to the Albion Hotel, puts the strip show in strip steak, while **Rumi** (330 Lincoln Rd.; ✆ **305/672-4353**) serves haute cuisine in the early hours before giving way to the A-list scenesters.

Sightseeing Even after Elián González was returned to his father's custody in Cuba, his relatives' Little Havana house remained a shrine. As a result, the house (**United in Elián House,** at 2319 NW 2nd St., Little Havana; no phone) is now a museum dedicated to the plight of Cubans in the United States. Also about to open as a museum dedicated to the Cuban Americans is downtown Miami's **Freedom Tower,** an Old-Spanish–style building (600 N. Biscayne Blvd.; ✆ **305/592-7768**) purchased by the Cuban American National Foundation. Work still continues on the **Miami Beach Cultural Park** in South Beach, which includes the new Arquitectonica-design home of the **Miami City Ballet,** the **Miami Beach Regional Library,** the **Bass Museum of Art,** and a sculpture garden. The Bass (✆ **305/673-7530**) has expanded and received a dramatically new look by world-renowned Japanese architect Arata Isozaki. Additions include triple the amount of exhibition space, an outdoor sculpture terrace, and a museum cafe. **The Vizcaya Museum and Gardens** has a new permanent orchid-display garden.

After Dark   At press time, the hottest nightspots are located on the still sizzling South Beach. However, over the causeway, a burgeoning nocturnal buzz is emanating from the once desolate area of **downtown Miami,** off of Biscayne Boulevard, thanks to cheaper rents and 24-hour liquor licenses. Among them, the former South Beach hot spot, The Living Room, has opened on NE 11th Street as **The Living Room Downtown.** South Beach's **Rain** (323 23rd St.; ✆ **786/295-9540**) has opened for the luxe and lithe lounge lizards, while an old hot spot, **Liquid** (1532 Washington Ave.; ✆ **305/531-9411**), has reopened under different ownership in a space formerly known as Shadow Lounge. The cavernous **Billboard Live** music and dance club debuted, featuring several bars, restaurants, and a recording studio at 1501 Collins Ave.

THE GOLD COAST   For complete information on this region, see chapter 8.

While the Gold Coast's beaches remain less congested than those in Miami, the area isn't impervious to development—especially when it comes to resorts, restaurants, and nightlife. Whereas the Gold Coast used to be a sleepy beachfront, today it's slowly en route to rivaling the liveliness of a big city like Miami.

Accommodations   Las Olas Boulevard's quaint **Riverside Hotel** (620 E. Las Olas Blvd., Fort Lauderdale; ✆ **800/325-3280**) has expanded its capacity to 217 rooms. Fort Lauderdale broke ground for the posh 132-suite **Atlantic** hotel/condo, managed by Starwood's Luxury Collection and set to debut in early to mid-2003. The Boca Raton Resort & Club (501 E. Camino Real; ✆ **800/327-0101**) unveiled its **Spa Palazzo,** a brand-new 30,000-square-foot Mediterranean-style spa with 22 treatment rooms as well as lap pools and indoor and outdoor lounges. West Palm Beach gets hip to the idea of the boutique hotel with **Hotel Biba** (320 Belvedere Rd.; ✆ **561/832-0094**), a very mod revamped motel turned hipster hangout. **The Boca Raton Resort & Club** opened its 112-unit Yacht Club wing on Feb. 1, 2002. The guest rooms overlook the Intracoastal Waterway, and personal butler service and a concierge lounge are provided for guests.

Dining   Boca Raton's new American restaurant **Zemi** (5050 Town Center Circle; ✆ **561/391-7177**) is drawing rave reviews for its chili-crusted shrimp. For the West Palm Beach wine-and-cheese set, the Hotel Biba's **Biba Bar** (320 Belvedere Rd.; ✆ **561/832-0094**) serves sleek portions of cheese and various *charcuterie*. And over at the ever-expanding City Place, star chef Mark Militello opened a branch of his successful New World chain, **Mark's City Place** (700 S. Rosemary Ave., West Palm Beach; © **561/514-0770**).

Shopping Fort Lauderdale's **Beach Place** (17 S. Fort Lauderdale Beach Blvd.) is receiving a face lift, transforming itself from a spring break–y hangout into something more upscale. West Palm Beach's **City Place** (222 Lakeview Ave.; © **561/835-0862**) is a $550 million outdoor Mediterranean-style complex featuring 78 stores (including Macy's and FAO Schwarz), a multiplex movie theater, and several restaurants such as Legal Seafoods and the Cheesecake Factory. It seems that something new is always opening here on a daily basis. The most recent places to sign on are New York City's **NV Lounge** and **Tsunami,** the Pan-Asian haute spot.

SOUTHWEST FLORIDA For complete information on this region, see chapter 10.

All telephone numbers in Fort Myers, Fort Myers Beach, Sanibel and Captiva Islands, Naples, and Marco Island all are now in **area code 239.** Boca Grande and Charlotte County remain in area code 941.

Fort Myers Formerly a branch of Shooters Waterfront Cafe USA, the popular riverside restaurant at the Holiday Inn Riverwalk & Marina is now the **Seahorse Restaurant,** with improved food and a curfew on its once-boisterous weekend parties. Also in downtown, Bavarian-born chef Peter Schmid has given up on his excellent **Peter's La Cuisine.**

Fort Myers Beach Calusa Coast Outfitters, one of the state's best environmental cruises, is no longer operating from Fort Myers Beach. **Palm Terrace Apartments** has a new website: www.palm-terrace.com.

Sanibel and Captiva Islands The visitor center at **J. N. ("Ding") Darling National Wildlife Refuge** is now open daily from 9am to 5pm from

November to April. It's still closed, however, on Fridays during the off-season. The refuge's wildlife drive also remains closed Friday year-round. **Tarpon Bay Recreation** no longer picks up guests for its naturalist-narrated tram tours at the refuge visitor center. Instead, you must board at Tarpon Bay. The **Hungry Heron,** Sanibel's best family restaurant, is now serving its popular weekend breakfast buffets year-round.

Naples The opening of **The Ritz-Carlton Golf Resort, Naples,** has added more luxury to this already swanky town. The 295-unit hotel adjoins the Greg Norman–designed Tiburon Golf Club, one of Florida's finest links. Sun-and-sand–loving guests can use the beach at The Ritz-Carlton, Naples, nearby. The obituary has been written for **Olde Naples Inn & Suites,** long one of the town's best values. On the restaurant scene, **Terra** has bitten the dust.

Marco Island Kayak tour operator **Osprey Adventures** has ceased operations. The inexpensive **Kahuna Restaurant** is now serving breakfast during the busy winter months.

THE TAMPA BAY AREA For complete information on this region, see chapter 11.

Tampa Despite the drop in tourism after 9/11, both **Busch Gardens Tampa Bay** and **Adventure Island** raised their admission prices—and probably will again before you get there. Call or check their websites for the latest.

St. Pete and Clearwater Beaches Don't expect to get your e-mail at St. Pete Beach's **Internet Outpost Cafe,** since it has gone out of business. Visitor information for the Crystal River area north of the beaches is now available from the **Citrus County Chamber of Commerce** (© **352/795-3149;** www.citruscountychamber. com).

Sarasota   The city's famous Ringling Museums and Asolo Theatre are now officially part of the **FSU Ringling Center for the Cultural Arts,** under the aegis of Florida State University. The phone numbers and website address remain the same.

The **Ritz-Carlton Sarasota** opened its 266 luxurious units on the downtown waterfront in 2001. It's not on the beach, but it is convenient to the FSU Ringling Center for the Cultural Arts and Sarasota's other performing-arts venues.

Among the St. Armands Circle restaurants, **Charley's Crab** has closed its doors for good.

WALT DISNEY WORLD & ORLANDO   For complete information on this region, see chapter 12.

Accommodations   Gaylord Palms (© **407/586-0000** or www.gaylord-palms.com) led the field of new arrivals with a spring 2002 debut. Its 1,400 rooms and public areas are decorated with flashes of St. Augustine, Key West, and the Florida Everglades. The show-stopper is a 4½-acre grand atrium.

Universal Orlando's **Royal Pacific,** a Loews hotel (© **407/363-8000** or www.universalorlando.com), is set to open around the time this guide reaches bookstores. Rack rates for its 1,000 units will be cheaper than Universal's other two hotels, the Portofino Bay and Hard Rock, but not as cut-rate as Disney's cardboard All-Star resorts.

Restaurants   Universal's Hard Rock Hotel now serves yummy but expensive steaks and seafood at **The Palm** (© **407/503-7256** or www.thepalm.com), the 23rd member of a chain launched 75 years ago in New York.

Exploring Walt Disney World   The economy has caused a lot of belt tightening around Mickeyville, but there have been a few new arrivals in the past year:

• Disney–MGM Studios continued upgrades with the addition of

Who Wants to Be a Millionaire—Play It! The attraction, which replaced **Doug Live,** is based on the Disney–ABC TV game show and offers contestants a chance to win prizes—but no millions.

• Animal Kingdom debuted **TriceraTop Spin,** a kids' ride that, like Magic Carpets of Aladdin, involves vehicles that circle a hub and move up and down, above the ground. **Primeval Whirl,** a carnival-style roller coaster, is set to debut in the summer of 2002.

The Disney parks also had some closings in 2001–02. These include the Magic Kingdom's **Mike Fink's Keel Boats** and, at least seasonally, **Timekeeper** and **Carousel of Progress.**

Exploring Beyond Disney   Like Disney, Universal Orlando and Sea-World have whittled hours, shows, and staff to make ends meet during lean times. These parks, too, have had only a few newcomers.

At Universal Studios Florida, Animal Actors Stage has been replaced by **Animal Planet Live!** The multimedia show stars a fox, a raccoon, and an Australian shepherd.

Discovery Cove has expanded its snorkeling and other areas. The park has also expanded the sticker price to $219 per person for the privilege of swimming with its dolphins. (The price, if you can skip the dolphin encounter, is $119.) In fairness, those tickets include a crowd limit of no more than 1,000 people per day, lunch, one week's admission to Sea-World, and chances to swim with or near other creatures of the deep and not so deep.

NORTHEAST FLORIDA   For complete information on this region, see chapter 13.

Cocoa Beach, Cape Canaveral & the Kennedy Space Center   The visitor complex at **John F. Kennedy Space Center** is no longer offering its Cape Canaveral Then & Now bus tours. The NASA Up Close tour still is the best way to see the space center. **King Rentals,** which handles condo and cottage rentals, is now at 102 W. Central Blvd., Cape Canaveral, FL 32920 (© **888/295-0934** or 321/784-5046; www.kingrentals.com).

Daytona Beach   Already the city's largest hotel, the **Adams Mark Daytona Beach** has added 306 oceanfront rooms and a huge new ballroom to its inventory. **McK's Dublin Station** no longer keeps wee hours. It now closes at 9pm Monday through Wednesday, 10pm Thursday through Saturday.

The new Ocean Walk Village area (on the beachfront, near Main Street Pier) continues to add new attractions, and its Ocean Walk Shoppes (upscale boutiques along with restaurants, a movie theater, and entertainment facilities) should be completed in early 2003.

The **Marine Science Center** opened in June of 2002, with exhibits on many subjects relating to marine life and a space dedicated to rehabilitating sick and injured sea turtles.

St. Augustine   The city's visitor center now shows "Struggle to Survive," a 42-minute video, about the Old City's beginnings (it costs $1 per person), while its free and useful orientation film is now 25 minutes long. Costumed interpreters no longer explain the city's history at the **Old St. Augustine Village Museum,** but they still do at **Colonial Spanish Quarter,** the new name of Spanish Quarter Village. The Radisson Ponce de León Golf & Conference Resort is now known as the **Ponce de León Hotel, Golf & Conference Resort.** Little has changed except its toll-free reservations number, which is now © **800/ 228-2821. Marineland** is presently receiving a facelift that should restore its facilities to their former glory.

Jacksonville   In addition to its existing downtown offices, the **Jacksonville and the Beaches Convention & Visitors Bureau** has a new visitor information office at 403 Beach Blvd. in Jacksonville Beach (© **904/242-0024**). It's open Monday through Saturday from 10am to 6pm. Also at the beaches, the **Sabal Palm Inn** has added a French restaurant, but **The Homestead** (long a bastion of Southern cooking) and the **Island Grille** have both gone to the restaurant graveyard.

Amelia Island   Aqua Explorers Dive Center has gone out of business.

NORTHWEST FLORIDA: THE PANHANDLE   For complete information on this region, see chapter 14.

Pensacola   Historic Pensacola Village is now open only Monday through Friday from 10am to 4pm. The **National Museum of Naval Aviation** has added a stomach-churning ride simulating the multi-G-force motion in the cockpit of a jet fighter. With the state's new camping reservations system in place, **Blackwater River State Park** now accepts advance reservations for its campsites.

Destin & Fort Walton Beach   Cafe New Orleans has thrown in the towel.

Apalachicola   The **Apalachicola Maritime Museum** has shut its doors for good, and the 1877-vintage schooner **Governor Stone** no longer cruises Apalachicola Bay. Nor does the stern-wheeler **Jubilee!** Also closed are **Apalachicola Tours** and the houseboat rental arm of **Benign Boat Works.**

Tallahassee   About Bikes, long a bike-rental fixture at the Tallahassee–St. Marks Historic Railroad State Trail, has lost its concession. **Killearn Country Club and Inn** no longer rents hotel rooms to the general public.

1

The Best of Florida

Every year millions of visitors escape bleak northern winters to bask in Florida's warmth, lured to the Sunshine State by the promise of clear skies and 800 miles (1,288km) of spectacular sandy beaches. A host of kid-pleasers, from Busch Gardens to Walt Disney World, makes this the country's most popular year-round family vacation destination.

Here you can choose from a wide array of accommodations, from deluxe resorts to mom-and-pop motels. You can visit remote little towns like Apalachicola or a megalopolis like Miami. Devour fresh seafood, from amberjack to oysters—and then work off those calories in such outdoor pursuits as bicycling, golfing, or kayaking. Despite overdevelopment in many parts of the state, Floridians have maintained thousands of acres of wilderness areas, from the little respite of Clam Pass County Park in downtown Naples to the magnificent Everglades National Park, which stretches across the state's southern tip.

Choosing the "best" of all this is a daunting task, and the selections in this chapter are only a rundown of some of the highlights. You'll find numerous other outstanding resorts, hotels, destinations, activities, and attractions described in the pages of this book. With a bit of serendipity, you'll come up with some bests of your own.

1 The Best Beaches

- **Virginia Key** (Key Biscayne): The producers of "Survivor" could feasibly shoot their show on this ultrasecluded, picturesque, and deserted key, where people go purposely not to be found. See p. 164.
- **Matheson Hammock Park Beach** (South Miami): This serene beach features an enclosed, man-made lagoon that is flushed naturally by the tidal action of the adjacent Biscayne Bay. Surrounded by the bay's warm, calm waters, the beach's backdrop is a tropical hardwood forest. See p. 166.
- **Lummus Park Beach** is world renowned, not necessarily for its pristine sands, but for its more common name of **South Beach,** on which seeing, being seen, and,

at times, the obscene, go hand in hand with the sunscreen and beach towels. The 12th Street section of this beach is the beach of choice for gay residents and travelers who come to show off just how much time they've spent in the gym, and, of course, catch up on the latest gossip and upcoming must-attend parties and events. Oftentimes, this beach is the venue for some of the liveliest parties South Beach has ever seen. See p. 164.
- **Haulover Beach,** nestled between the Intracoastal Waterway and the ocean, especially at the north end, is the place to be for that all-over tan. A gay, nude beach is also there, as is an area for nude volleyball. See p. 166.

- **Crandon Park Beach** in Miami is extremely popular for families with kids because of the shallow water created by a neighboring sandbar. Convenient parking, picnic areas, a winding boardwalk, and a multi-ethnic mix of families grilling, dancing, and relaxing are the benchmarks of this beach. See p. 164.
- **Bahia Honda State Park** (Bahia Honda Key): One of the nicest and most peaceful beaches in Florida, located amidst 635 acres of nature trails and even a portion of Henry Flagler's railroad. See p. 240.
- **John U. Lloyd Beach State Park** (Dania Beach): Unfettered by high-rise condominiums, T-shirt shops, and hotels, this wonderful beach boasts an untouched shoreline surrounded by a canopy of Australian pine to ensure complete seclusion. See p. 298.
- **Lover's Key State Park** (Fort Myers Beach): You'll have to walk or take a tram through a bird-filled forest of mangroves to this gorgeous, unspoiled beach just a few miles south of busy Fort Myers Beach. Although Sanibel Island gets all the accolades, the shelling here is just as good, if not better. See p. 388.
- **Cayo Costa State Park** (off Captiva Island): These days, deserted tropical islands with great beaches are scarce in Florida, but this 2,132-acre barrier strip of sand, pine forests, mangrove swamps, oak hammocks, and grasslands provides a genuine get-away-from-it-all experience. Access is only by boat from nearby Gasparilla, Pine, and Captiva Islands. See p. 413.
- **Naples Beach** (Naples): Many Florida cities and towns have beaches, but few are as lovely as the gorgeous strip that runs in front of Naples's famous Millionaires' Row.

You don't have to be rich to wander its length, peer at the mansions, and stroll on historic Naples Pier to catch a sunset over the gulf. See p. 418.
- **Caladesi Island State Park** (Clearwater Beach): Even though 3½-mile-long (6km) Caladesi Island is in the heavily developed Tampa Bay area, it has a lovely, relatively secluded beach with soft sand edged in sea grass and palmettos. Dolphins cavort in offshore waters. In the park itself, there's a nature trail, and you might see one of the rattlesnakes, black racers, raccoons, armadillos, or rabbits that live here. The park is accessible only by ferry from Honeymoon Island State Recreation Area off Dunedin. See p. 472.
- **Canaveral National Seashore** (Cape Canaveral): Midway between the crowded attractions at Daytona Beach and the Kennedy Space Center is a protected stretch of coastline 24 miles (39km) long, backed by cabbage palms, sea grapes, and palmettos. Its neighbor is the 140,000-acre Merritt Island National Wildlife Refuge, home to hundreds of Florida birds, reptiles, alligators, and mammals. Wooden boardwalks lead from a free parking lot to the huge expanse of soft brown sand and a few well-spaced picnic tables. See p. 583.
- **Gulf Islands National Seashore** (Pensacola): You could argue that all of Northwest Florida's gulf shore is one of America's great beaches—an almost-uninterrupted stretch of pure white sand that runs the entire length of the Panhandle, from Perdido Key to St. George Island. The Gulf Islands National Seashore preserves much of this natural wonder in its undeveloped state.

Florida

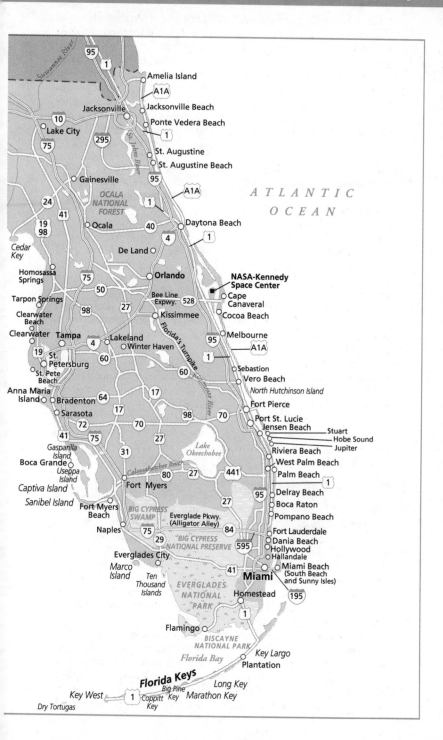

Suwannee River

95 1

Amelia Island

A1A

Jacksonville Jacksonville Beach

Ponte Vedra Beach

10 1

Lake City

295 St. Johns River

75 St. Augustine

St. Augustine Beach

Gainesville 95

A1A

24 OCALA NATIONAL FOREST 1 ATLANTIC

41 OCEAN

19 Ocala 40 Daytona Beach

98 4 1

Cedar Key De Land

Homosassa Springs 75

Tarpon Springs 50 Orlando NASA-Kennedy Space Center

98 27 Bee Line Expwy. 528 Cape Canaveral

Clearwater Kissimmee Cocoa Beach

Clearwater Beach Tampa Lakeland Melbourne

19 4 Winter Haven 95 A1A

St. Petersburg 60 1

St. Pete Beach 60 Sebastion

Anna Maria Island Bradenton 64 17 Vero Beach

Sarasota 17 North Hutchinson Island

72 98 70 Fort Pierce

41 75 27 Port St. Lucie

Gasparilla Island 31 Jensen Beach Stuart

Boca Grande Lake Okeechobee Hobe Sound

Useppa Island Caloosahatchee River Riviera Beach Jupiter

Captiva Island 80 27 441 West Palm Beach

Sanibel Island Fort Myers 27 Palm Beach 1

Fort Myers Beach BIG CYPRESS SWAMP 95 Delray Beach

Naples Everglade Pkwy. (Alligator Alley) Boca Raton

75 84 Pompano Beach

29 "BIG CYPRESS NATIONAL PRESERVE 595 Fort Lauderdale

Everglades City Dania Beach

Marco Island Hollywood

Ten Thousand Islands 41 Hallandale

EVERGLADES NATIONAL PARK Miami Beach (South Beach and Sunny Isles)

Miami

Homestead 195

Flamingo 1

BISCAYNE NATIONAL PARK

Florida Bay Key Largo

Plantation

Florida Keys Long Key

Big Pine Marathon Key

Key West 1 Coppitt Key

Dry Tortugas

Countless terns, snowy plover, black skimmers, and other birds nest along the dunes topped with sea oats. East of the national seashore and equally beautiful are Grayton Beach State Park near Destin and St. George Island State Park off Apalachicola. See p. 646.

- **St. Andrews State Park** (Panama City Beach): With more than 1,000 acres of dazzling white sand and dunes, this preserved wilderness demonstrates what Panama City Beach looked like before motels and condominiums lined its shore. Lacy, golden sea oats sway in gulf breezes and fragrant rosemary grows wild. The area is home to foxes, coyotes, and a herd of deer. See p. 676.

2 The Best Snorkeling

- **John Pennekamp Coral Reef State Park** (Key Largo): This is the country's first undersea preserve, with 188 square miles of protected coral reefs. The water throughout much of the park is shallow, so it's an especially great place for snorkelers to see an incredibly vibrant array of coral, including tree-sized elkhorn coral and giant brain coral. See p. 221.

- **Looe Key National Marine Sanctuary** (Bahia Honda State Park): With 5.3 square miles of gorgeous coral reef, rock ledges up to 35 feet (11m) tall, and a colorful and motley marine community, you may never want to come up for air. See p. 242.

- **Hutchinson Island:** Three popular artificial reefs off this island provide excellent scenery for divers of any level. The **USS Rankin,** sunk in 120 feet (36m) of water in 1988, lies 7 miles (11km) east-northeast of the St. Lucie Inlet. The 58-foot-deep (17m) **Donaldson Reef,** located due east of the Gilbert's House of Refuge Museum, consists of a cluster of plumbing fixtures sunk in 58 feet (17m) of water. The **Ernst Reef,** made from old tires, is a 60-foot (18m) dive located 4½ miles (7.5km) east-southeast of the St. Lucie inlet. Local dive shops have "tips" on the best spots, and rules and regulations for safe diving. See p. 357.

3 The Best Fishing

- **The Keys:** The Keys boast some world-class deep-sea fishing; the prize is such big-game fish as marlin, sailfish, and tuna. There's reef fishing as well, for "eating fish" like snapper and grouper, and backcountry fishing for bonefish, tarpon, and other "stalking" fish. Dozens of charter-fishing boats operate from Key West marinas and from other less-popular keys. Islamorada, in the Upper Keys, is the sport-fishing capital of the world. Anglers compete for trophy sailfish, marlin, wahoo, and kingfish at many annual big-money tournaments. Seven-Mile Bridge, linking the Middle and Lower Keys, is known as "the longest fishing bridge in the world"; it's also a favorite spot for local fishers who wait for barracuda, yellowtail, and dolphin to bite. See p. 223.

- **Lake Okeechobee:** Many visitors to the Treasure Coast come to fish, and they certainly get their fill off the miles of Atlantic shore and on the inland rivers. If you want to fish freshwater and nothing else, head for Lake Okeechobee, the state's largest lake, which is chock-full of good eating fish. It covers more than 467,000 acres; that's more than 730 square miles. At one time, the lake supported an enormous commercial fishing industry. Due to a commercial fishing-net ban, much of that industry has died off, leaving the sportfishers all the rich bounty of the lake. See p. 373.

- **Stuart:** Known as the "Sailfish Capital of the World," Stuart is an angler's haven. The fish bite all year, but peak months are December through March and June through July. Sailfishing is an art of its own—beginners need to learn to feel that exact moment to let the reel drag so that the fish run with the lure. See p. 356.

- **Boca Grande:** The deep, shadowy holes of Boca Grande Pass, between Gasparilla and Cayo Costa Islands off Fort Myers, harbor the mighty tarpon, the "silver king of the seas." Teddy Roosevelt and his rich buddies used to bag tarpon in these waters, and anglers from around the globe still compete every July in the World's Richest Tarpon Tournament. See p. 414.

- **Destin:** Florida's largest charter-boat fleet, with more than 140 vessels, is based in this Panhandle town, which calls itself the "World's Luckiest Fishing Village." Anglers here have landed championship catches of grouper, amberjack, snapper, mackerel, cobia, sailfish, wahoo, tuna, and blue marlin. See p. 663.

4 The Best Golf Courses

- **Biltmore Hotel** (Miami): The beautiful, rolling 18-hole golf course designed by Donald Ross and located at the majestic Biltmore Hotel in Coral Gables is open to the public and is a favorite of Bill Clinton. See p. 126.

- **Doral Golf Resort and Spa** (Miami): Four championship courses make the Doral one of Miami's best golf destinations. One course, the legendary Blue Monster course, is the site of the annual Doral-Ryder Open. See p. 123.

- **Turnberry Isle Resort and Club** (Aventura, North Miami Beach): These two courses by Robert Trent Jones are open only to guests but are among the city's best. See p. 125.

- **The Inn at Boca Teeca** (Boca Raton): For over 3 decades, this inn has been attracting golf fanatics who could care less about the small, but comfortable, rooms because they're too busy out on the superb 27-hole golf course at the Inn's Boca Teeca Country Club, open only to members and guests of the inn. See p. 324.

- **PGA National Resort & Spa** (Palm Beach): This rambling resort, the national headquarters of the PGA, is a premier golf destination, with five 18-hole courses on more than 2,300 acres. See p. 349.

- **Emerald Dunes Golf Course** (West Palm Beach): This gorgeous Tom Fazio–designed course (featuring 60 acres of water and stunning views of the ocean) is pricey but one of only a few in the area open to the public. See p. 332.

- **Champions Club at Summerfield** (Stuart): The best in the area, this rural, somewhat-challenging championship course was designed by Tom Fazio and built in 1994. It also offers great glimpses of wildlife amid the wetlands. See p. 357.

- **Lely Flamingo Island Club** (Naples): Designed by Robert Trent Jones Sr., Lely Flamingo's hourglass fairways and fingerlike bunkers present many challenges. It's part of a development that includes the Lely Mustang, a Lee Trevino–designed course that is more forgiving but still fun. See p. 419.
- **Tiburón Golf Club** (Naples): Greg Norman designed the 27 championship holes at this course to play like a British Open—but without the thick thatch rough. The course is now home to the luxurious Ritz-Carlton Golf Resort, Naples. See p. 420.
- **Naples Beach Hotel & Golf Club** (Naples): One of the state's oldest, this resort course is relatively flat, but small greens and masterful bunkers will test your skills. In addition, one of Florida's most charming resort hotels is across the street. See p. 424.
- **Mangrove Bay Golf Course** (St. Petersburg): One of the nation's top 50 municipal courses, the Mangrove Bay course hugs the inlets of Old Tampa Bay and offers 18-hole, par-72 play. Facilities include a driving range; lessons and golf-club rental are also available. See p. 464.
- **The Westin Innisbrook Resort** (Tarpon Springs): *Golfweek* has called Innisbrook's Copperhead Course, former home of the annual JCPenney Classic, number one in Florida. One thousand students a year go through Innisbrook's Golf Institute, and golfers from around the world come to play the 600 acres of courses. See p. 480.
- **Walt Disney World** (Orlando): The resorts surrounding the theme parks have 99 regulation holes that let you walk in the footsteps (and share the frustrations) of the game's greatest players.

Those with a shorter stroke can play the master miniature courses: Fantasia Gardens and Winter Summerland. See p. 572.
- **Ladies Professional Golf Association/LPGA International** (Daytona Beach): This "women-friendly" course has multiple tee settings, unrestricted tee times, a great pro shop, and state-of-the-art facilities. Designed by Rees-Jones, the older of the two courses here was chosen as one of the "Top Ten You Can Play" by *Golf Magazine*. See p. 593.
- **TPC at Sawgrass** (Ponte Vedra Beach, near Jacksonville): With 99 holes, Pete Dye's Tournament Players Club (TPC) at Sawgrass makes top-10 lists everywhere. The 17th hole, on a tricky island, is one of the most photographed holes in the world. See p. 625.
- **Ocean Hammock Golf Club** (Palm Coast, between Daytona Beach and St. Augustine): Opened in late 2000 with six of its holes actually skirting the Atlantic Ocean, this Jack Nicklaus–designed course is the first authentic seaside links built in Florida since the 1920s. See p. 612.
- **Amelia Island Plantation** (Amelia Island): This exclusive resort has three of the state's best courses. Long Point Club, designed by Tom Fazio, is the most beautiful and challenging. Pete Dye's Amelia Links is another oceanfront course. Both are open only to resort guests. See p. 638.
- **Marriott's Bay Point Resort Village** (Panama City Beach): Thirty-six holes of championship golf at this Marriott include the Lagoon Legends course, one of the country's most difficult. Nearby is The Hombre, an 18-holer where O. J. Simpson played a round right after his acquittal. See p. 682.

5 The Best Family Attractions

- **Parrot Jungle and Gardens** (Miami): Watch your head because flying above are hundreds of parrots, macaws, peacocks, cockatoos, and flamingos. Continuous suitable but cheesy shows star roller-skating cockatoos, card-playing macaws, and numerous stunt-happy parrots. There are also tortoises, iguanas, and a rare albino alligator on exhibit. See p. 192.

- **Sea Grass Adventures** (Miami): This is not your typical nature tour. With Sea Grass Adventures, you will be able to wade in the water on Key Biscayne with your guide and catch an assortment of sea life in the provided nets. At the end of the program, participants gather on the beach while the guide explains what everyone's just caught, passing the creatures around in miniature viewing tanks. See p. 192.

- **Miami Museum of Science and Space Transit Planetarium** (Miami): The Museum of Science features more than 140 hands-on exhibits that explore the mysteries of the universe. Live demonstrations and collections of rare natural-history specimens make a visit here fun and informative. Many of the demos involve audience participation, which can be lots of fun for willing and able kids and adults alike. See p. 172.

- **Busch Gardens Tampa Bay** (Tampa): Although the thrill rides, live entertainment, shops, restaurants, and games get most of the ink at this 335-acre family theme park, Busch Gardens also ranks among the top zoos in the country, with several thousand animals living in naturalistic environments. If you can get them off the roller coasters, the kids can find out what all those wild beasts they've seen on the Discovery Channel look like in person. See p. 439.

- **MOSI (Museum of Science and Industry)** (Tampa): One of the largest educational science centers in the Southeast, MOSI has more than 450 interactive exhibits in which the kids can experience hurricane-force winds, defy the laws of gravity, cruise the mysterious world of microbes, explore the human body, and more. They can also watch stunning movies in MOSIMAX, Florida's first IMAX dome theater. See p. 445.

- **Universal Studios Florida** (Orlando): Universal Orlando's original Florida park has many rides based on Hollywood blockbusters or cartoon heroes, such as Jaws and the Funtastic World of Hanna-Barbera. Kids can get slimed at Nickelodeon Studios or get thrilled by the pint-sized roller coaster and other fun in Woody Woodpecker's KidZone. See p. 560.

- **Walt Disney World's Magic Kingdom** (Orlando): Introduce your wee ones to many of the Disney characters at Mickey's Toontown Fair in the Magic Kingdom, Disney's premiere park. There's also a ton of fun on rides themed after Winnie the Pooh, Peter Pan, Dumbo, Cinderella, Aladdin, and Buzz Lightyear. Rides like Splash Mountain make sure older guests have fun, too. See p. 542.

- **Kennedy Space Center** (Cape Canaveral): Especially since the recent multimillion-dollar renovation and expansion, this family destination is a must-see. There is plenty to keep kids and parents busy for at least a full day, including interactive computer games,

IMAX films, and dozens of informative displays on the space program. Try to schedule a trip during a real launch; there are more than a dozen each year. See p. 581.

- **DAYTONA USA** (Daytona Beach): Opened in late 1996 on Daytona International Speedway grounds, this huge state-of-the-art interactive attraction is an exciting and fast-paced stop even for non-race fans. Kids can see real stock cars, go-karts, and motorcycles, and even participate in a pit stop on a NASCAR Winston Cup racecar. See p. 590.

6 The Best Offbeat Travel Experiences

- **Jimbo's** (Miami): Located at the very end of Virginia Key, in Key Biscayne, on the lagoon where they shot *Flipper*, Jimbo's has become the quintessential, albeit hard-to-find, South Florida watering hole, snack bar, and hangout for a wacky assortment of colorful characters from shrimpers and yachters to politicos. Dollar beers and excellent smoked fish are sold from a cooler, vacant shacks serve as backdrops for films, and visitors are able to test their skills in a game of bocce ball. See p. 155.

- **Columbus Day Regatta** (Miami): This unique observation of Columbus Day revolves around a so-called regatta in Biscayne Bay but always ends with participants stripping down to their bare, ahem, necessities and partying at the sandbar in the middle of the bay. There is a boat race at some point of the day, but most people are too preoccupied to notice. See p. 180.

- **People-Watching on South Beach and Worth Avenue** (Miami and Palm Beach): As cliché as the notion of people-watching may seem, it's never the same old scenario on Miami's neon-hued Riviera, where equally colorful locals and luminaries proudly prance as if every day was the Easter parade. In Palm Beach, titled nobility, bejeweled socialites, and an assortment of upper crusties put on the ritz on the city's version of Rodeo Drive. See p. 164 and 334.

- **Swimming with the Dolphins at the Dolphin Research Center** (Marathon): Of the four such centers in the continental United States, the Dolphin Research Center is the most impressive. With advanced reservations, you can splash around with dolphins in their natural lagoon homes. It's an amazing experience. See p. 224.

- **Underwater Stay at Jules' Undersea Lodge** (Key Largo): Submerge yourself in this single-room Atlantis-like hotel that offers a surprisingly comfortable suite 30 feet (9m) underwater. Don't worry, there's plenty of breathing room. See p. 231.

- **Fantasy Fest** (Key West): Mardi Gras takes a Floridian vacation as the streets of Key West are overtaken by wildly costumed revelers who have no shame and no parental guidance. This weeklong, hedonistic, X-rated Halloween party is *not* for children under 18. See p. 259.

- **Babcock Wilderness Adventures** (Fort Myers): Experienced naturalists lead "swamp buggy" tours through the Babcock Ranch, including the mysterious Telegraph Swamp, where alligators lounge in the sun. Although the Babcock Ranch is the largest cattle operation east of the Mississippi (with bison and quarter horses too), it is also a major wildlife preserve inhabited by countless birds and other creatures. See p. 383.

- **Swimming with the Manatees** (Crystal River, north of Clearwater): Some 300 manatees spend the winter in the Crystal River, and you can swim, snorkel, or scuba with them in the warmwater natural spring of Kings Bay, about 7 miles (11km) north of Homosassa Springs. It's not uncommon to be surrounded in the 72°F (21°C) water by 30 to 40 "sea cows," who nudge and caress you as you swim with them. See p. 465.

- **Dolphin Swims** (Orlando): Spend a big chunk of your day and budget at Discovery Cove, an all-inclusive park where visitors can take a 3-minute swim with a dolphin, among other things, for $199. See p. 567.

- **Surfing** (Orlando): Ride waves inland thanks to the machine-generated breakers at Typhoon Lagoon's main pool. See p. 556.

- **Learning to Surf the Big Curls at Cocoa Beach Surfing School** (Cocoa Beach): Even if you don't know how to hang ten, this school will get you riding the waves with the best of them. It offers equipment and lessons for all skill levels—beginner to pro—at these world-famous surf beaches. See p. 585.

7 The Best Small Towns

- **Sebastian:** Known as one of the last remaining fishing villages, Sebastian is located at the northern tip of the Treasure Coast region in Indian River County. The area's small-town feel and laid-back, relaxed atmosphere is one of its biggest draws. See p. 367.

- **Boca Grande** (Southwest Florida): Founded in the 1880s, this little village on Gasparilla Island retains the flavor of those Victorian times. Luxurious mansions coexist with simple homes of fishermen who guide rich folks in search of tarpon, just as their ancestors did a century ago. The du Ponts, Mellons, and Astors once arrived, for the wintertime "social season," at the town's railway depot, which has been restored and now houses shops and the Loose Caboose Restaurant and Ice Cream Parlor. See p. 414.

- **Olde Naples** (Naples): Started in 1886 as a real-estate development, the original part of Naples retains much of Old Florida's charm, with tree-lined streets dividing many of the original clapboard homes. With the houses on Millionaires' Row virtually hidden by dense foliage and with no high-rises in sight, Naples Beach seems far removed from today's modern city. See p. 420.

- **Tarpon Springs** (Tampa Bay Area): Tarpon Springs calls itself the "Sponge Capital of the World" because immigrants from Greece settled here in the late 1800s to harvest the sponges that grew in abundance offshore. Their descendants make Tarpon Springs a fascinating center of transplanted Greek culture. Sponges still arrive at the historic Sponge Docks, where a lively, carnival-like atmosphere and Greek cuisine prevail. Restored Victorian homes facing Spring Bayou also make this one of the most picturesque towns in the state. See p. 484.

- **Fernandina Beach** (Amelia Island): You can stay at two of Florida's ritziest resorts on Amelia Island, but the real charm here is in the quaint town of Fernandina Beach, where a 50-block area of

Victorian and Queen Anne homes is listed on the National Register of Historic Places. See p. 634.

- **Apalachicola** (Northwest Florida): Located at the mouth of the Apalachicola River, this gulf-shore town was a major cotton port before the Civil War, and a later timber boom resulted in the fine Victorian homes that still grace Apalachicola's uncurbed streets. It was here that Dr. John Gorrie invented the forerunner of the air conditioner, which revolutionized Florida's tourism industry. Today, the major industry is seafood, with famous Apalachicola oysters eaten fresh off the boats. See p. 685.

- **Pensacola** (Northwest Florida): One of America's oldest communities, Pensacola has preserved its Spanish, French, and English heritages in the Seville Historic District and Historic Pensacola Village. Spanish-named streets are bordered by both French-style wrought-iron balconies reminiscent of New Orleans and English colonial churches like those in Williamsburg, Virginia. See p. 644.

8 The Best Spas

- **Agua at The Delano Hotel** (Miami; © 800/555-5001 or 305/672-2000): One trip to this sublime, celebrity-saturated rooftop spa overlooking the Atlantic in a haute hotel and you'll feel like you're in heaven. Try the milk-and-honey massage and you'll understand. See p. 105.

- **The Spa at Turnberry Isle Resort and Club** (Miami; © 800/ 327-7028 or 305/936-2929): The Turnberry Spa, which has been renovated to the tune of $10 million, consists of three levels of deluxe pampering and includes aerobics and fitness classes, stress reductions, massage therapy, and a juice bar designed for complete rejuvenation. See p. 125.

- **The Ritz-Carlton Spa, Key Biscayne** (Key Biscayne; © 305/ 365-4223): This spa is a sublime, 20,000-square-foot West Indies colonial-style eden in which you can treat yourself to over 60 treatments including the Key Lime Coconut Body Scrub and the Everglades Grass Body Wrap in one of 21 treatment rooms. For a real splurge, the Fountain of Youth Balance treatment is a 6-hour indulgence featuring a facial, massage, manicure, pedicure, shampoo, styling, and lunch served on the oceanfront terrace. See p. 120.

- **Marriott's Harbor Beach** (Fort Lauderdale; © 800/222-6543 and 954/525-4000): This new $8-million, 24,000-square-foot European spa is the first full-service seaside facility of its kind in Fort Lauderdale. See p. 307.

- **PGA National Resort & Spa** (Palm Beach Gardens; © 800/ 633-9150 or 561/627-2000): This lauded golf resort provides the perfect pampering for sore golfers and bored nongolfers with its Mediterranean Spa featuring just about every treatment imaginable, including special ones for pregnant women. See p. 349.

- **Sanibel Harbour Resort & Spa** (Fort Myers; © 800/767-7777 or 239/466-2166): Many call this high-rise resort overlooking Sanibel Island the best spa value in the country. Regardless of the price, the spa obliges your every whim. Try the amazing Betar Bed, a suspended "bed of music" that floats you to a level where stresses disappear. There are also mud, algae, seaweed, and mineral wraps; Swiss showers; paraffin facials; and more. Day packages, makeovers, and men's sports packages are popular. The fitness center is also state-of-the-art. See p. 386.

- **Naples Beach Hotel & Golf Club** (Naples; © **800/237-7600** or 239/261-2222): A new spa adds complete relaxation to a stay at this venerable hotel, already one of Florida's most relaxing resorts. A deep-body massage followed by a milk-and-honey wrap will leave you on cloud nine, and a special wedding package will have you primed for the big day. See p. 424.
- **The Ritz-Carlton, Naples** (Naples; © **888/856-4372** or 239/598-3300): A new $50-million, full-service spa will leave you thoroughly relaxed before or after your stroll through the mangrove forest to the white-sand beach at one of Florida's finest luxury resorts. See p. 426.
- **Safety Harbor Resort and Spa** (Tampa Bay Area; © **800/237-0155** or 727/726-1161): Tucked away off the beaten track amid moss-draped oaks and cobblestone streets, Safety Harbor is the oldest continually running spa in the United States, and Florida's only spa built around natural healing springs—the feeling is very European. The Phil Green tennis school is also on the grounds, and many tennis programs are available. See p. 267.

9 The Best Luxury Resorts

- **Ritz-Carlton Key Biscayne** (Key Biscayne; © **800/241-3333** or 305/365-4500): In addition to the Ritz's consistently superior services and amenities, this British-colonial–style version of the Ritz rises above its casual Key Biscayne surroundings with a stellar view of the Atlantic Ocean, not to mention an equally impressive 20,000-square-foot spa. See p. 120.
- **Mandarin Oriental, Miami** (Brickell Key, Miami; © **305/913-8288**): The swank and stunning Mandarin Oriental features a waterfront location, residential-style rooms (most with balconies), superb service, and several upscale dining and bar facilities previously unknown to its nearby downtown Miami locale. See p. 122.
- **Ritz-Carlton** (South Beach; © **800/241-3333** or 786/276-4000): Taking the concept of swanky South Beach to a very literal level, the Ritz-Carlton South Beach may be a landmark building restored to its original 1950s Art Moderne style, but in terms of the hotel's standout service, amenities, and oceanfront, everything else is very much in the immediate present. See p. 106.
- **The Breakers** (Palm Beach; © **800/833-3141** or 561/655-6611): This stately, historic hotel epitomizes la dolce vita, Palm Beach–style, featuring expansive manicured lawns, an elegant lobby, the state's oldest and very scenic golf course, and impeccable service. See p. 337.
- **Ritz-Carlton Palm Beach** (Palm Beach; © **800/241-3333** or 561/533-6000): What better place for a Ritz-Carlton than in the city that defines the concept of ritzy? The ghosts of Rockefeller and co. are alive and well here in this Mediterranean-inspired outpost of the first-rate, well-respected hotel that's the quintessence of Palm Beach elegance. See p. 338.
- **Naples Beach Hotel & Golf Club** (Naples; © **800/237-7600** or 239/261-2222): A beachside setting on Millionaires' Row couldn't be better for carrying on

the hallowed-but-relaxed Old Florida traditions at this family-operated hotel. A championship 18-hole golf course, a tennis club, and a full-service spa are all on the premises. The beachside chickee hut bar is one of Florida's best sunset venues, and the dining room serves an exceptional, reasonably priced breakfast buffet. See p. 424.

- **The Ritz-Carlton Golf Resort, Naples** (Naples; ✆ **888/856-4372** or 239/593-2000): This luxurious new Mediterranean-style resort takes full advantage of the Greg Norman-designed Tiburon Golf Club. Guests here can use the beach and spa at The Ritz-Carlton, Naples, nearby. See p. 425.

- **The Ritz-Carlton, Naples** (Naples; ✆ **888/856-4372** or 239/598-3300): This opulent 14-story Mediterranean-style hotel at Vanderbilt Beach is a favorite of affluent guests, who like standard Ritz-Carlton amenities such as imported marble floors, antique art, Oriental rugs, Waterford crystal chandeliers, and afternoon British-style high tea. Guests relax in high-backed rockers on the verandas or unwind by the heated swimming pool set in a landscaped terrace, but they must walk through a narrow mangrove forest to reach the beach. See p. 426.

- **South Seas Resort** (Captiva Island; ✆ **800/CAPTIVA** or 239/472-5111): Built on what was once a 330-acre copra plantation, this exclusive spot is one of the best choices in Southern Florida for serious tennis buffs (22 courts with pro). Its gulf-side golf course is one of the most picturesque nine-holers anywhere. There are no high-rise buildings, just an assortment of luxury homes and condominiums, some with private pools and their own tennis courts. With three bedrooms or more, some units are ideal for families or couples who want to share the cost of a vacation. See p. 406.

- **Don CeSar Beach Resort & Spa** (St. Pete Beach; ✆ **800/282-1116,** 800/637-7200, or 813/360-1881): Dating back to 1928 and listed on the National Register of Historic Places, this "Pink Palace" tropical getaway is so romantic you may bump into six or seven honeymooning couples in one weekend. The lobby has classic high windows and archways, crystal chandeliers, marble floors, and original artworks. Most rooms have high ceilings and offer views of the gulf or Boca Ciega Bay. See p. 476.

- **Disney's Grand Floridian Resort & Spa** (Orlando; ✆ **407/934-7639**): This magnificent Victorian inn has an opulent five-story lobby complete with a Chinese Chippendale aviary. An orchestra plays big-band music every evening near Victoria & Albert's, the resort's five-star restaurant. See p. 514.

- **Hyatt Regency Grand Cypress Resort** (Orlando; ✆ **800/233-1234** or 407/239-1234): This standout has some impressive treats, including a half-acre pool with a dozen waterfalls and three spas, 12 tennis courts, a 45-hole Jack Nicklaus–designed golf course, and a 45-acre nature walk. All that adds up to luxury. See p. 521.

- **Amelia Island Plantation** (Amelia Island; ✆ **800/874-6878** or 904/261-6161): Set amidst magnolias, oak trees, and the Atlantic Ocean, this gracious resort is straight out of the Deep South. It's more rustic than the nearby Ritz, but it has excellent

THE BEST ROMANTIC HIDEAWAYS   19

hiking and biking paths, tennis, swimming, horseback riding, and boating. Golfers can enjoy exclusive use of two of the top courses in Florida. See p. 638 and "The Best Golf Courses," in section 4, earlier in this chapter.

- **The Ritz-Carlton Amelia Island** (© **800/241-3333** or 904/277-1100): Set on 13 acres of stunning beachfront, this Ritz-Carlton is more glitzy than its older neighbor, the Amelia Island Plantation, but it's also more relaxed than some of its siblings. You'll find all of the usual "Ritzy" first-class amenities as well as remarkable service. The Grill, the hotel's finest restaurant, is also one of the island's best. See p. 640.

10 The Best Romantic Hideaways

- **Hotel Place St. Michel** (Coral Gables; © **800/848-HOTEL** or 305/444-1666): This European-style hotel in the heart of Coral Gables is one of the city's most romantic options. The accommodations and hospitality are very Old World European, complete with dark wood-paneled walls, cozy beds, beautiful antiques, and a quiet elegance that seems startlingly out of place in trendy Miami. See p. 127.

- **Hotel Impala** (Miami Beach; © **800/646-7252** or 305/673-2021): During the heyday of 1990s excess, Miami Beach was known for the fabulous parties thrown by the eclectic designer Gianni Versace. The late Versace desired an intimate European-styled guesthouse that would please well-seasoned travelers, and the Impala is the result. His personal touch on this renovated Mediterranean inn is still evident, from the Greco-Roman frescos and friezes to an intimate garden that is perfumed with the scents from carefully hanging lilies and gardenias. See p. 109.

- **Little Palm Island** (Little Torch Key; © **800/343-8567**): Accessible only by boat, this private 5-acre island is not only remote, it's romantic, featuring no TVs, telephones, or faxes in the luxurious thatched cottages. See p. 243.

- **Marquesa Hotel** (Key West; © **800/869-4631** or 305/292-1919): Don't be fooled by the Marquesa's location on the heavily populated Key West: This charming B&B is in a wonderful world of its own, far enough from the tumult, yet close enough if you want it. See p. 262.

- **Island's End Resort** (St. Pete Beach; © **727/360-5023**). Sitting right on Pass-a-Grille, where the Gulf of Mexico meets Tampa Bay, this little all-cottage retreat is a great hideaway from the maddening crowds of St. Pete Beach. You won't have an on-site restaurant, bar, and other such amenities, but you can step from your cottage right onto the beach. And if you get the unit with two living rooms, you'll have a whirlpool tub and your own private gulf-side swimming pool. See p. 477.

- **Turtle Beach Resort** (Siesta Key, off Sarasota; © **941/349-4554**): Sitting beside the bay, this intimate little charmer began life years ago as a traditional Old Florida fishing camp, but today it's one of the state's most romantic retreats. It's a tightly packed little place, but high wooden fences surround each unit's private outdoor hot tub, and one-way mirror walls let you lounge in bed while passersby see only reflections of themselves. See p. 498.

- **Disney's Wilderness Lodge** (Lake Buena Vista; ℂ **407/934-7639**): This property is reminiscent of the lodge at Yellowstone. The geyser out back, the mammoth stone hearth in the lobby, the dining room's 340° view of Bay Lake, and the nightly electric water pageants are just a few of the reasons to stay here. Some guest rooms have patios or balconies overlooking the lake, woodlands, or a meadow. See p. 516.
- **Peabody Orlando** (Orlando; ℂ **800/732-2639** or 407/352-4000): This is the home of the famous mallards that trek through the lobby each morning accompanied by the music of John Philip Sousa. Even standard rooms are lavishly furnished. See p. 523.
- **The Lodge & Club at Ponte Vedra Beach** (Jacksonville; ℂ **800/243-4304** or 904/273-9500): Every unit at this intimate hotel in upscale Ponte Vedra Beach has a romantic seat built in front of its oceanview window, plus there's a big bathroom with a two-person tub and a separate shower. Gas fireplaces in most units add even more charm. One of the three swimming pools and

whirlpools here is reserved exclusively for couples. You can get married in the semicircular meeting room overlooking the Atlantic. See p. 629.
- **Henderson Park Inn** (Destin; ℂ **800/336-4853** or 850/837-4853): Nestled against the eastern edge of lovely Henderson Beach State Recreation Area, this Cape Hatteras–style bed-and-breakfast offers romantic escapes without screaming kids. The individually decorated rooms ooze Victorian charm, with high ceilings, fireplaces, Queen Anne furniture, and gulf views from private balconies. Some even have canopy beds. See p. 666.
- **Seaside** (near Destin; ℂ **800/277-8696** or 850/231-1320): If residents of Northwest Florida don't stay at the Henderson Park Inn for their getaways, they head for the romantic gulf-front cottages at Seaside. Built in the 1980s but evoking the 1880s, the Victorian-style village of Seaside (a short drive east of Destin) has several of the cozy cottages designed especially for honeymooners. See p. 670.

11 The Best Moderately Priced Accommodations

- **Abbey Hotel** (South Beach; ℂ **305/531-0031**): Off the beaten path, this '40s revival boutique hotel gives good reason to get off the main drag and revel in its quiet elegance. See p. 110.
- **Hotel Leon** (South Beach, ℂ **305/673-3767**): A true value, this charismatic and hip sliver of a property has won the loyalty of fashion industrialists and romantics alike. Built in 1929 and restored in 1996, the hotel still retains many original details such as facades, woodwork, and even fireplaces. See p. 111.

- **Pelican Hotel** (South Beach; ℂ **800/7-PELICAN** or 305/673-3373): Owned by the creative owners of the Diesel Jeans company, The Pelican is South Beach's only self-professed "toy-hotel," in which each of its 30 rooms and suites is decorated as outrageously as some of the area's more colorful drag queens. See p. 112.
- **Indian Creek Hotel** (Miami Beach; ℂ **800/491-2772** or 305/531-2727): A charming, Key West–style hotel that's full of character, the Indian Creek Hotel takes you back in time, with

period furnishings, attitude-free service, and a quaint pool and garden, completely lacking water slides, tiki huts, or calypso bands. See p. 118.

- **Townhouse** (South Beach; *©* **877/534-3800** or 305/534-3800): New York hipster Jonathan Morr decided to take matters into his own hands when he realized that Miami Beach had lost touch with the young bohemian bon vivants who gave the city its original cachet. His solution: this 67-room, five-story hotel, in which standard rooms started at just $99 during its opening in the fall of 2000. As with anything, the $99 rate proved too good to be true, elevating to a still-reasonable starting rate of $125. See p. 112.

- **Whitelaw Hotel** (South Beach; *©* **305/398-7000**): With a slogan that reads "clean sheets, hot water, and stiff drinks," the Whitelaw Hotel stands apart from the other boutique hotels with its fierce sense of humor, but it never compromises on the fabulous amenities found at some of the area's more serious properties. See p. 113.

- **Conch Key Cottages** (Marathon; *©* **800/330-1577** or 305/289-1377): This oceanfront hideaway offers rustic but immaculate and well-outfitted cottages that are especially popular with families. Each has a hammock, barbecue grill, and kitchen. See p. 232.

- **Banyan Marina Resort** (Fort Lauderdale; *©* **954/524-4430**): These fabulous waterfront apartments located on a beautifully landscaped residential island may have you vowing never to stay in a hotel again. See p. 309.

- **Hotel Biba** (West Palm Beach; *©* **561/832-0094**): The mod squad has adopted—and adapted—this '40s style motel into a Jetsonian, jet set hangout

that provides swank and sleek shelter from the upper-crusty hotels that surround it. See p. 340.

- **Best Western Pink Shell Beach Resort** (Fort Myers Beach; *©* **800/554-5454** or 239/463-6161): This popular, family-oriented spot fronting both the gulf and the bay has hotel rooms, suites, one- and two-bedroom apartments, and beach cottages. The pink-sided cottages make up for a lack of luxury with lots of 1950s-style character. Units in two mid-rise, gulf-front buildings have lovely views of Sanibel Island from their screened balconies. See p. 392.

- **Island's End Resort** (St. Pete Beach; *©* **727/360-5023**): A wonderful respite from the madding crowd, and a great bargain to boot, this little all-cottage hideaway sits right on the southern tip of St. Pete Beach, smack-dab on Pass-a-Grille, where the Gulf of Mexico meets Tampa Bay. You can step from the six contemporary cottages right onto the beach. One unit even has its own private swimming pool. See p. 477.

- **DoubleTree Guest Suites** (Lake Buena Vista; *©* **800/222-8733** or 407/934-1000): Children have their own check-in desk here, and all units have two rooms and beds for six. It's also next to Walt Disney World. See p. 519.

- **Best Western Lake Buena Vista Hotel** (Lake Buena Vista; *©* **800/348-3765** or 407/828-2424): This 12-acre, 18-story lakefront hotel is well kept and immaculate, with more-upscale rooms and public areas than you might expect at a Best Western. And it has a great location next to Walt Disney World. See p. 519.

- **Disney's Caribbean Beach Resort** (Lake Buena Vista; *©* **407/934-7639** or 407/934-3400):

Here's good value by Disney standards. Units on the 200-acre resort are grouped in five villages around a duck-filled lake. The welcoming rooms feature oak furniture and chintz bedspreads. There are also seven swimming pools, a 1½-mile (2.25km) promenade, and a festive food court. See p. 516.

- **Holiday Inn Family Suites Resort** (Lake Buena Vista; ☎ 877/387-5437 or 407/387-5437): The younger guests come first at this delightful resort, which offers special Kid Suites, but also offers suites especially themed for movie buffs and lovers, among others. See p. 522.
- **Casa Monica Hotel** (St. Augustine; ☎ 800/648-1888 or 904/827-1888): Built in 1888 as a luxury hotel, this Spanish-style building was gutted and restored to its previous elegance in 1998. Most

interesting of the guest quarters are suites installed in two tile-topped towers and a fortress-like central turret. One suite in the turret has a half-round living room with gun-port windows overlooking St. Augustine's historic district. See p. 614.
- **Gibson Inn** (Apalachicola; ☎ 850/653-2191): Built in 1907 as a seaman's hotel and gorgeously restored in 1985, this cupola-topped inn is such a brilliant example of Victorian architecture that it's listed on the National Register of Historic Inns. No two guest rooms are alike (some still have the original sinks in the sleeping area), but all are richly furnished with period reproductions. Grab a drink from the bar and relax in one of the high-backed rockers on the old-fashioned veranda. See p. 689.

12 The Best Seafood Restaurants

- **Joe's Stone Crab Restaurant** (South Beach; ☎ 305/673-0365): Open only during stone-crab season (Oct–May), this always-packed Miami institution knows how to reel in the crowds with the freshest, meatiest stone crabs and the essential accouterments that go with them, from creamed spinach to excellent sweet-potato french fries. See p. 133.
- **Fishbone Grille** (downtown Miami; ☎ 305/530-1915): Fish are flying in the open kitchen of this extremely popular, reasonably priced seafood joint. Whether you take yours grilled, blackened, or sautéed, the chefs here work wonders with fish in every size, shape, school, and color. Snapper, grouper, dolphin, tuna, sea bass, shrimp—you name it, they've got it. See p. 150.
- **Grillfish** (South Beach; ☎ 305/538-9908): From the beautiful

Byzantine-style mural and the gleaming oak bar, you'd think you were eating in a much more expensive restaurant. Thankfully, Grillfish still manages to pay the exorbitant South Beach rent by having a loyal following of locals who come for fresh, simple seafood in a relaxed but upscale atmosphere. See p. 138.
- **Big Fish** (downtown Miami; ☎ 305/373-1770): This hard-to-find, charismatic seafood shack on the Miami River is definitely a big fish in the little pond of downtown restaurants. With a spectacular riverfront setting, Big Fish has a terrific view of the Miami skyline and some of the freshest catch around. See p. 150.
- **Atlantic's Edge** (Islamorada; ☎ 305/664-4651): Of the many seafood restaurants in the Keys, this one is tops, with an innovative menu that includes some of

the freshest and tastiest fish around. It's also the most elegant offering in the Keys. See p. 235.

- **Marker 88** (Islamorada; ✆ **305/ 852-9315**): Bahamian conch, stone crabs from the Florida Bay, and shrimp from the West Coast are just some of the fresh items, innovatively prepared, at this Upper Keys institution. See p. 236.

- **Hobo's Fish Joint** (Coral Springs; ✆ **954/346-5484**): Huge portions of extremely fresh fish are prepared in well over a dozen ways at this steakhouse-style restaurant with wood floors and white tablecloths. Despite the fact that it's located away from the ocean in the utterly suburban enclave of Coral Springs, this joint is definitely worth a jaunt. See p. 313.

- **Sunfish Grill** (Pompano Beach; ✆ **954/788-2434**): Some argue that this is the best seafood restaurant on the entire Gold Coast, and we won't argue against them thanks to the chef/owner who buys seafood fresh from local fishermen and prepares it with stunning results. See p. 313.

- **Conchy Joe's Seafood** (Jensen Beach; ✆ **561/334-1130**): Known for fresh seafood and Old Florida hospitality, Conchy Joe's enjoys an excellent reputation that's far bigger than the restaurant itself. Dining is either indoors or on a covered patio overlooking the St. Lucie River. See p. 361.

- **Channel Mark** (Fort Myers Beach; ✆ **239/463-9127**): Every table looks out on a maze of channel markers on Hurricane Bay, and a dock with palms growing through it makes the Channel Mark a relaxing place for a waterside lunch. The atmosphere changes dramatically at night, when the relaxed tropical ambience is ideal for kindling romance.

Congenial owners Mike McGuigan and Andy Welsh put a creative spin on their seafood dishes, and their delicately seasoned crab cakes are tops. See p. 394.

- **Lobster Pot** (Redington Shores, near St. Pete Beach; ✆ **727/ 391-8592**): Here, owner Eugen Fuhrmann supplies the finest seafood dishes on the St. Pete and Clearwater Beaches. Among his amazing variety of lobster dishes is one flambéed in brandy with garlic, and the bouillabaisse is as authentic as any you'll find in the south of France. See p. 482.

- **Fulton's Crab House** (Lake Buena Vista; ✆ **407/934-2628**): Located in a riverboat replica, Fulton's has a nostalgic mood and an array of good seafood, though meals can get a bit pricey if you opt for stone or king crab. There's also an excellent wine list. See p. 534.

- **Back Porch** (Destin; ✆ **850/ 837-2022**): The food isn't gourmet at this cedar-shingled shack, whose long porch offers glorious beach and gulf views, but this is where charcoal-grilled amberjack originated. Today, you'll see it on menus throughout Florida. Other fish and seafood, as well as chicken and juicy hamburgers, also come from the coals. See p. 670.

- **Chef Eddie's Magnolia Grill** (Apalachicola; ✆ **850/653- 8000**): Chef Eddie Cass's pleasant restaurant occupies a small bungalow built in the 1880s that is still in possession of the original black cypress paneling in its central hallway. Nightly specials emphasize fresh local seafood and New Orleans–style sauces. Chef Eddie received more than 2,000 orders for his spicy seafood gumbo at a recent Florida Seafood Festival. See p. 690.

13 The Best Local Dining Experiences

- **Tantra** (South Beach; ✆ 305/672-4765): Edible nirvana is found in this culinary temple inspired by the Kama Sutra and entirely devoted to the senses with a grass floor, hookah pipes, and a sensual cuisine that's said to be an aphrodisiac. See p. 134.

- **BED** (South Beach; ✆ 305/532-9070): Eating in bed will never be the same once you've experienced this restaurant-cum-nightclub whose name stands for Beverage, Entertainment, and Dining, where the food is indeed served in beds and not on tables. See p. 130.

- **Big Fish** (downtown Miami; ✆ 305/373-1770): Located on the Miami River across from the spectacular Miami skyline, Big Fish is indeed just that, in a little pond—or river—whose scenic value is priceless. See p. 150.

- **Versailles** (Little Havana; ✆ 305/444-0240): This iconoclastic Cuban diner isn't as swanky as its palatial French namesake, but it is full of mirrors, through which you can view the colorful—and audible—Cuban clientele that congregates here for down-home cuisine and hearty conversation. See p. 150.

- **The Green Turtle Inn** (Islamorada; ✆ 305/664-9031): Tasty turtle chowder, campy pianist Tina Martin, and a handful of friendly, colorful locals contribute to this quintessential Keys landmark. See p. 237.

- **Islamorada Fish Company** (Islamorada; ✆ 800/258-2559 or 305/664-9271): We're not sure which is better—the view or the seafood—but whichever it is, it's a winning combination. See p. 238.

- **Blue Heaven** (Key West; ✆ 305/296-8666): What was once a well-kept secret in Key West's Bahama Village is now a popular eatery known for fresh food (it's some of the best in town) and a motley, bohemian crowd. See p. 268.

- **Mai Kai** (Fort Lauderdale; ✆ 954/563-3272): At this fabulous vestige of Polynesian kitsch, you're expected to forget you're in the middle of a tacky stretch of Fort Lauderdale and pretend you're somewhere in Hawaii or Tahiti as hula dancers and fire-eaters entertain and potent and sickly sweet cocktails are served in coconuts. See p. 317.

- **Taverna Opa** (Hollywood; ✆ 954/929-4010): Don't get nervous if you hear plates breaking when you enter this raucous, authentic Greek taverna situated directly on the Intracoastal Waterway—it's just the restaurant's lively waitstaff making sure your experience here is 100% Greek. See p. 315.

- **Cap's Place Island Restaurant** (Lighthouse Point; ✆ 954/941-0418): The only way to get to this rustic seafood restaurant, the former bootlegging and gambling hangout of Al Capone, is by boat, but don't be dismayed—it's not the least bit Disneyfied. Churchill, Roosevelt, Marilyn Monroe, and Sly Stallone have all indulged in this delicious taste of Old Florida. See p. 313.

- **Farmers Market Restaurant** (Fort Myers; ✆ 239/334-1687): The retail Farmers Market next door may be tiny, but the best of the cabbage, okra, green beans, and tomatoes ends up here at this simple eatery, frequented by everyone from business executives to truck drivers. The specialties of the house are Southern favorites like smoked ham hocks with a bowl of black-eyed peas. See p. 387.

- **Fourth Street Shrimp Store** (St. Petersburg; © 727/822-0325): The outside of this place looks like it's covered with graffiti, but it's actually a gigantic drawing of people eating. Inside, murals on two walls seem to look out on an early-19th-century seaport (one painted sailor permanently peers in to see what you're eating). This is the best and certainly the most interesting bargain in St. Petersburg. See p. 468.
- **Moore's Stone Crab** (Longboat Key, off Sarasota; © 941/383-1748): Located in Longbeach, the old fishing village on the north end of Longboat Key, this popular bay-front restaurant still looks a little like a packing house (it's an offshoot of a family seafood business), but the view of the bay (dotted with mangrove islands) makes a fine complement to stone crabs fresh from the family's own traps. See p. 502.
- **Pebbles** (Lake Buena Vista; © 407/827-1111): This local chain has a well-earned reputation for great food and drink without having a menu that prices itself off the planet. See p. 535.
- **Singleton's Seafood Shack** (Mayport/Jacksonville; © 904/246-4442): This rustic Old Florida fish camp has kept up with the times by offering fresh fish in more ways than just battered and fried. Yet it has still managed to retain the charming casualness of a riverside fish camp. Even if you don't want seafood, this spot is worth stopping at, if only for a feel of Old Florida. See p. 633.
- **Hopkins' Boarding House** (Pensacola; © 850/438-3979): There's a delicious peek into the past at this Victorian boardinghouse, surrounded by ancient trees and a wraparound porch with old-fashioned rocking chairs. Everyone eats family-style—at your elbow could be the mayor or a mechanic, for everyone in town dines here. Platters are piled high with seasonal Southern-style vegetables from nearby farms. In true boardinghouse fashion, guests bus their own dishes. See p. 656.
- **The Boss Oyster** (Apalachicola; © 850/653-9364): This rustic, dockside eatery is a good place to see if what they say about the aphrodisiac properties of Apalachicola oysters is true. The bivalves are served raw, steamed, or under a dozen toppings ranging from capers to crab meat. They'll even steam three dozen of them and let you do the shucking. Dine inside or at picnic tables on a screened dockside porch. See p. 689.

14 The Best Bars & Nightspots

- **Rose Bar at the Delano** (South Beach; © 305/672-2000): If every rose has its thorn, the thorn at this painfully chic hotel bar is the excruciatingly high-priced cocktails. Otherwise, the crowd here is full of the so-called glitterati, fabulati, and other assorted poseurs who view life through (Italian-made) rose-colored sunglasses. See p. 105.
- **Mac's Club Deuce** (South Beach; © 305/673-9537): Standing on its own amidst an oasis of trendiness, Mac's Club Deuce is the quintessential dive bar, with cheap drinks and a cast of characters ranging from your typical barfly to your atypical drag queen. See p. 205.
- **Tobacco Road** (downtown Miami; © 305/374-1198): Al

Capone used to hang out here when it was a speakeasy. Now, locals flock to this road-well-traveled place to hear live, local bands perform, as well as national acts such as George Clinton and the P-Funk All-Stars, Koko Taylor, and the Radiators. It's small, it's gritty, and it's meant to be that way, here at the proud owner of Miami's very first liquor license. See p. 210.

- **Upstairs at the Van Dyke Café** (South Beach; ℂ **305/534-3600**): Even though this jazz bar isn't located in a basement, but rather on the second floor of the Van Dyke Café, it resembles a classy speakeasy in which local jazz performers play to an intimate, enthusiastic crowd of mostly adults and sophisticated young things, who huddle at the small tables often until the wee hours. See p. 210.

- **La Covacha** (West Miami; ℂ **305/594-3717**): This hut, located virtually in the middle of nowhere, is the hottest Latin joint in the entire city. Do not wear silk here, as you *will* sweat. Friday is *the* night, so much so that the owners had to place a red velvet rope out front to maintain some semblance of order. See p. 211.

- **crobar** (South Beach; ℂ **305/ 531-8225**): With its intense, dance-heavy sound system, an industrially chic ambience, and huge crowds, this Chicago import has raised the bar on South Beach nightlife with crazy theme nights (the monthly Sex night is particularly, uh, stimulating), top-name deejays, and the occasional celebrity appearance. See p. 207.

- **Level** (South Beach; ℂ **305/ 532-1525**): The megastore of nightclubs, Level is a 40,000-square-foot space featuring four dance floors, three levels, five rooms, and nine bars. It's like a nocturnal video game, in which your status is determined by which level you can land on. See p. 207.

- **Nikki Beach Club** (South Beach; ℂ **305/538-1111**): What the Playboy Mansion is to Hollywood, the Nikki Beach Club is to South Beach. It's here where "Survivor" meets "The Brady Bunch in Hawaii," with a bit of St.-Tropez thrown in for taste. See p. 208.

- **Club Space** (downtown Miami; ℂ **305/577-1007**): This cavernous club, composed of several converted warehouses, is known for its 24-hour liquor license and its stellar roster of international celebrity dance and trance deejays. See p. 207.

- **Fox's Sherron Inn** (South Miami; ℂ **305/661-9201**): The spirit of Frank Sinatra is alive and well at this dark and smoky watering hole, which dates back to 1946. Everything down to the vinyl booths and the red lights makes Fox's a retro-fabulous dive bar. See p. 204.

- **Lola** (South Beach; ℂ **305/ 695-8697**): Lola redefines the neighborhood bar, striking the perfect balance between chill and chic. This bar, located away from the South Beach mayhem, is a showgirl in her own right—a swank, sultry lounge where people are encouraged to come as they are, leaving the attitude at home. See p. 205.

- **Duval Street** (Key West): South Florida's own version of Bourbon Street, Duval Street is party central with bars galore. See p. 248.

- **Clematis Street** (West Palm Beach): Until recently, nightlife in Palm Beach County was either an oxymoron or reserved for haughty private clubs on the island of Palm Beach. Thanks to a downtown revitalization, downtown West Palm now boasts a strip of its own with trendy restaurants, clubs, and bars. See p. 343.
- **Las Olas Boulevard/Riverwalk** (Fort Lauderdale): Moving off the beachfront strip and onto the more quaint (but no less calm) riverside, Fort Lauderdale now boasts its very own downtown nightlife scene with restaurants, bars, and clubs. See p. 317.
- **Biba Bar** (West Palm Beach; ✆ 561/832-0094): The harder to find, the hipper it is, so they say, which is why this dimly lit, loungey hotel bar is tucked away in the middle of this mod motor inn—a hangout for in-the-know locals and visitors. See p. 340.
- **The Dock at Crayton Cove** (Naples; ✆ 239/263-9940): Right on the City Dock, this lively pub is a perfect place for an open-air meal or libation while watching the action on Naples Bay. See p. 428.
- **CityWalk** (Orlando; ✆ 407/363-8000): This 12-acre entertainment complex is a collection of eateries and nighttime entertainment spots. It's also a haven for theme restaurant aficionados, featuring a Hard Rock Cafe, a NASCAR Café, a Motown Cafe, and an NBA-themed restaurant. Additionally, you'll find plenty of places to dance the night away to the sounds of jazz, reggae, hip-hop, and pop. See p. 576.
- **Pleasure Island** (Orlando; ✆ 407/934-7781): This 16-acre, all-in-one complex of clubs, restaurants, and shops runs the entertainment gamut from jazz to modern rock to dance music. Catch an improvisational comedy show or hustle along on the disco floor—there's something here for everyone. Big-name artists occasionally make special appearances on two outdoor stages, but a nightly fireworks display ensures that every night here ends with a bang. See p. 575.
- **Ocean Deck Restaurant & Beach Club** (Daytona Beach; ✆ 386/253-5224): Reggae rules at this hot, noisy, packed, and always-fun beach bar near Daytona Beach's municipal pier, the town's "happening" district. By contrast, the upstairs restaurant is suitable for children, and it has great ocean views to accompany its fine and inexpensive fare. See p. 600.
- **Seville Quarter** (Pensacola; ✆ 850/434-6211): In Pensacola's Seville Historic District, this restored antique brick complex with New Orleans–style wrought-iron balconies contains pubs and restaurants whose names capture the ambience: Rosie O'Grady's Goodtime Emporium, Lili Marlene's Aviator's Pub, Apple Annie's Courtyard, End o' the Alley Bar, Phineas Phogg's Balloon Works (a dance hall, not a balloon shop), and Fast Eddie's Billiard Parlor (which has electronic games for kids too). Live entertainment ranges from Dixieland jazz to Country and Western. See p. 658.
- **Flora-Bama Lounge** (Perdido Key, near Pensacola; ✆ 850/492-0611): This slapped-together gulf-side pub is almost a shrine to country music, with jam sessions

from noon until way past midnight on Saturdays and Sundays. Flora-Bama is the prime sponsor and a key venue for the Frank Brown International Songwriters' Festival during the first week of November. Take in the great gulf views from the Deck Bar. See p. 659.

- **Shuckums Oyster Pub & Seafood Grill** (Panama City Beach; ℂ **850/235-3214**):

"We shuck 'em, you suck 'em" is the motto of this extremely informal pub, which became famous when comedian Martin Short tried unsuccessfully to shuck oysters here during the making of an MTV spring-break special. The original bar is virtually papered over with dollar bills signed by old and young patrons who have been flocking here since 1967. See p. 684.

15 The Rest of the Best

- **Best Driving Route:** A1A, a gorgeous oceanfront route which runs north up Miami Beach, through Sunny Isles and Hollywood into Fort Lauderdale (starting at Ocean Dr. and First St. in Miami and merging onto Collins Ave. before running north), embodies the essence that is South Florida. From time-warped hotels steeped in Art Deco kitsch to multimillion-dollar modern highrises, A1A is one of the most scenic, albeit heavily trafficked, roads in all of Florida.

- **Best Place for People-Watching:** Lunchtime at News Café on Ocean Drive is the quintessential South Beach experience—lunching at News Café is more of a spectator sport than a dining experience. What the Big Mac is to McDonald's, people-watching is to News Café, whose Ocean Drive location is one of the best sidewalk spots from which to observe the wacky, colorful mix of pedestrians on parade. See p. 143.

- **Best Place to Hear a Moonlight Concert:** The Barnacle State Historic Site hosts once a month, on or near the full moon (except during July and Aug), a concert in the backyard of their charming 1908 Coconut Grove bungalow built on 5 acres of waterfront property. Listeners are welcome to picnic

and bask in this sublime setting for a mere $5. See p. 173.

- **Best Place to Learn the Salsa:** If the only salsa you're familiar with is the kind you put on your tacos, get over to Bongo's Cuban Café, the hottest salsa club north of Havana, where Miami's most talented salsa dancers will teach you how to move your two left feet in the right direction. See p. 206.

- **Best Dive Bar:** Jose Cuervo Underwater Bar. In May 2000, the legendary Tequila company celebrated Cinco de Mayo by submerging an actual, $45,000 fullsize bar and six stools about 200 yards off South Beach's First Street Beach. For expert divers, this bar is more than your average watering hole. See p. 182.

- **Best Place to Discover Your Inner Flipper:** The Dolphin Research Center will teach you how to communicate with and touch, swim, or play with the mammals at the nonprofit Dolphin Research Center in Marathon Key, home to a school of approximately 15 dolphins. See p. 224.

- **Best Cemetery:** The Key West Cemetery is funky, picturesque, and the epitome of the quirky Key West image, as irreverent as it is humorous. Headstones reflect residents' lighthearted attitudes toward life and death. I TOLD YOU

I WAS SICK is one of the more famous epitaphs, as is the tongue-in-cheek widow's inscription AT LEAST I KNOW WHERE HE'S SLEEPING TONIGHT. See p. 250.

- **Best Way to See the Everglades Without Breaking a Sweat:** Airboat rides through the outskirts of the Everglades are particularly wonderful, since the area is unfettered by jet skis, cruise ships, and neon bikinis. The Everglades are Florida's outback, resplendent in its swampy nature, which is best explored either by slow-moving canoes that really get you acquainted with your surroundings or via an airboat that can quickly navigate its way through the most stubborn of sawgrass, providing you with an up-close-and-personal (as well as fun) view of the land's inhabitants, from alligators and manatees to raccoons and Florida panthers. See p. 377.

- **Best Blending of Old South with the Modern Era:** There's as much Old South ambience in the state's capital, Tallahassee, as anywhere else in Florida. Here, you'll find 19th century homes nestled among towering pine trees and sprawling live oaks, historic plantations, ancient Native American settlement sites and mounds, gorgeous gardens, quiet parks with picnic areas, beautiful lakes and streams, and myriad outdoor activities as well as the state legislature, two powerful college football teams, and all the modern conveniences you could want. See p. 690.

2

Planning Your Trip to Florida

by Bill Goodwin

Whether you plan to spend a day, a week, 2 weeks, or longer in Florida, you'll need to make many "where," "when," and "how" choices *before* you leave home. This chapter explains how best to plan your trip.

1 The Regions in Brief

The first decision you'll have to make is where to go in Florida. You'll find ample sun, sea, and sand all along the 800 miles (1,288km) of shoreline here, but not every place in the Sunshine State is warm all the time. Many Florida beaches are lined with towering hotels and condominiums, whereas others are pristinely preserved in their natural states. You can spend your days in busy cosmopolitan cities or while them away in picturesque small towns steeped in history. You can take the kids to see Mickey Mouse, or you can find a romantic retreat far from the madding crowds. The choice is yours.

Here is a brief rundown of the state's regions to help get you started.

MIAMI & MIAMI BEACH Sprawling across the southeastern corner of the state, metropolitan Miami is a city with many distinct personalities and a vibrant, international flair. Here you will hear Spanish and many other languages, not to mention accents, spoken all around you, for this cosmopolitan area is a melting pot of immigrants from Latin America, the Caribbean, and, undeniably, the northeastern United States in particular. Cross the causeways and you'll come to the sands of Miami Beach, long a resort mecca and home to the hypertrendy South Beach, famous for its Art Deco architecture, electric nightlife, and celebrity sightings. See chapters 4 and 5 for more on the Miami area and p. 94 for descriptions of the different districts within Miami.

THE KEYS From the southern tip of the Florida mainland, U.S. 1 travels through a 100-mile-long (161km) string of islands stretching from Key Largo to the famous, laid-back "Conch Republic" of Key West, only 90 miles (145km) from Cuba and the southernmost point in the United States (it's always warm down here). While some of the islands are crammed with strip malls and tourist traps, most are dense with unusual species of tropical flora and fauna. The Keys don't have the best beaches in Florida, but the waters here—all in a vast marine preserve—offer the state's best scuba diving and snorkeling and some of its best deep-sea fishing. See chapter 6, "The Keys & The Dry Tortugas" for more information on this region.

THE EVERGLADES AND BISCAYNE NATIONAL PARK Encompassing more than 2,000 square miles and 1.5 million acres, Everglades National Park covers the entire southern tip of Florida. The park, along with nearby Big Cypress National Preserve, protects a unique and fragile "River of Grass" ecosystem teeming with wildlife that is best seen by canoe, by boat, or on long or short hikes. To the east of the Everglades is Biscayne National Park, preserving the northernmost living-coral reefs in the continental United States. See chapter 7 for more information on these parks.

THE GOLD COAST North of Miami, the Gold Coast is aptly named, for here are booming Hollywood and Fort Lauderdale and ritzy Boca Raton and Palm Beach—sun-kissed, sandy playgrounds of the rich and famous. Beyond its dozens of gorgeous beaches, the area offers fantastic shopping, entertainment, dining, boating, golfing, tennis, and many places to relax in beautiful settings. With some of the country's most famous golf courses and even more tennis courts, this area also attracts big-name tournaments. See chapter 8.

THE TREASURE COAST Despite gaining unprecedented numbers of new residents in recent years, the beach communities running from Hobe Sound north to Sebastian Inlet retain their small-town feel. In addition to a vast array of wildlife, the area has a rich and colorful history. Its name stems from a violent 1715 hurricane that sunk an entire fleet of treasure-laden Spanish ships. Excavators turned up hundreds of ancient coins in the 1950s and 1960s, and you'll still see treasure hunters prowling the beaches with metal detectors. The sea around Sebastian Inlet draws surfers to the largest swells in the state. See chapter 9 for more information on the Treasure Coast.

SOUTHWEST FLORIDA Ever since inventor Thomas Alva Edison built a home here in 1885, some of America's wealthiest families have spent their winters along Florida's southwest coast. They are attracted by the area's subtropical climate, shell-strewn beaches, and intricate waterways winding among 10,000-plus islands. Many charming remnants of Old Florida coexist with modern resorts in the sophisticated riverfront towns of Fort Myers and Naples and on islands like Gasparilla, Useppa, Sanibel, Captiva, and Marco. And thanks to some timely preservation, the area has many wildlife refuges, including the "backdoor" entrance to Everglades National Park. See chapter 10, "Southwest Florida."

THE TAMPA BAY AREA Halfway down the west coast of Florida lies Tampa Bay, one of the state's most densely populated areas. A busy seaport and commercial center, the city of Tampa is home to Busch Gardens Tampa Bay, which is both a major theme park and one of the country's largest zoos. Boasting a unique pier and fine museums, St. Petersburg's waterfront downtown is one of Florida's most pleasant. Most visitors elect to stay near the beaches skirting the narrow barrier islands running some 25 miles (40km) between St. Pete Beach and Clearwater Beach. Across the bay to the south lies Sarasota, one of Florida's prime performing-arts venues, the riverfront town of Bradenton, and another string of barrier islands with great beaches and resorts spanning every price range. See chapter 11 for more information.

WALT DISNEY WORLD & ORLANDO Walt Disney announced plans to build the Magic Kingdom in 1965, a year before his death and 6 years before the theme park opened, changing forever what was then a sleepy Southern town. In fact, Walt created a whole new world—if not universe—in central Florida. Today, in the new millennium, it seems that at least one full-scale theme park opens every year. Walt Disney World claims four distinct parks, two entertainment districts, enough hotels and restaurants to fill a small city, and several smaller attractions including water parks and miniature-golf courses. And then there are the rapidly expanding Universal Studios Orlando and SeaWorld, as well as many more non-Disney attractions. Orlando is Florida's most popular tourist destination, and its visitors have never had more options. See chapter 12.

NORTHEAST FLORIDA The northeast section of the state contains the oldest permanent settlement in America—St. Augustine, where Spanish colonists arrived and settled more than 4 centuries ago. Today, its history comes to life in a quaint historic district. St. Augustine is bordered to the north by Jacksonville, an up-and-coming sunbelt metropolis with miles of oceanfront beach and beautiful marine views along the St. Johns River. Up on the Georgia border, Amelia Island has two of Florida's finest resorts and its own historic town of Fernandina Beach. To the south of St. Augustine, Daytona Beach is the home of the Daytona International Speedway and is a spring-break mecca for the college crowd. Another brand of excitement is offered down at Cape Canaveral, where the Kennedy Space Center launches all manned U.S. space missions. See chapter 13.

NORTHWEST FLORIDA: THE PANHANDLE Historic roots run deep in Florida's narrow northwest extremity; and Pensacola's historic district, which blends Spanish, French, and British cultures, is a highlight of any visit to today's Panhandle. So, too, are the powdery, dazzlingly white beaches that stretch for more than 80 miles (129km) past the resorts of Pensacola Beach, Fort Walton Beach, Destin, and Panama City Beach. The Gulf Islands National Seashore has preserved much of this beach and its wildlife, and inland are state parks that offer some of the state's best canoeing adventures. All this makes the area a favorite summertime vacation destination for residents of neighboring Georgia and Alabama, with whom Northwest Floridians share many Deep South traditions. Sitting in a pine and oak forest just 30 miles (48km) from the Georgia line, the state capital of Tallahassee has a moss-draped, football-loving charm all its own. See chapter 14 for more information.

2 Visitor Information

Your best sources for detailed information about a specific destination in Florida are the **local visitor information offices.** They're listed under "Orientation" or "Essentials" in the following chapters.

Contact **Visit Florida,** P.O. Box 1100, Tallahassee, FL 32302-1100 (© **888/7-FLA-USA;** www.flausa.com), the state's official tourism marketing agent, for a free comprehensive guide to the state. Florida State Parks have a new website at www.floridastateparks.org. Visit Florida also operates **welcome centers** 16 miles (26km) west of Pensacola on I-10, 4 miles (6km) north of Jennings on I-75, 7 miles (11km) north of Yulee on I-95, and 3 miles (5km) north of Campbellton on U.S. 231. There's also a walk-in information office in the west foyer of the New Capitol Building in Tallahassee (see chapter 14).

Once you're here, you can call Visit Florida's 24-hour **tourist assistance hot line** (© **800/656-8777**) if you need help with lost travel documents, directions, emergencies, or references to attractions, restaurants, and shopping anywhere in the state. Hot-line operators speak several languages, including Spanish, French, German, Portuguese, Japanese, and Korean.

3 Money

How much money you spend on your Florida vacation will depend on your own desires and choices, and on the time of year you visit.

The state has a wide range of accommodations, from some of the country's most luxurious and expensive resorts to little mom-and-pop motels sitting right by the beach. If you can do without the luxuries, you needn't spend a fortune.

Tourism is Florida's biggest industry, and the economic law of supply and demand dictates that the prices of hotel rooms are highest during the seasons when tourists invade Florida: the winter months in the southern half of the state and during summertime up north.

See "When to Go," below, for details about Florida's high, low, and in-between seasons.

CREDIT CARDS & ATMS

The easiest way to pay for almost everything in Florida is with a credit card. MasterCard and Visa credit and debit cards are accepted almost everywhere. American Express, Diner's Club, and Discover cards also are accepted, although not as widely as MasterCard and Visa.

The best way to get cash while you're traveling in Florida is to use your debit or credit cards at **ATMs.** Of the big national banks, **First Union Bank** and **Bank of America** have offices with ATMs throughout Florida.

Most ATMs are linked to a national network that most likely includes your bank at home. **Cirrus** (© **800/424-7787;** www.mastercard.com/atm/) and **Plus** (© **800/843-7587;** www.visa.com/atms) are the two most popular networks; check the back of your ATM card to see which network your bank belongs to. Use the toll-free numbers to locate ATMs in your destination. Be sure to check your bank's

daily withdrawal limit and your credit limits before leaving home.

Also be sure to have your Personal Identification Number (PIN), which you will need to activate the cash withdrawal functions at all ATMs.

THEFT Almost every credit-card company has an emergency toll-free number you can call if your wallet or purse is stolen. Your own bank's customer-service number is on the back of your credit card; write it down and put it someplace where it isn't likely to be lost or stolen. If you do lose it, the toll-free information directory (© **800/555-1212**) will provide the number. Citicorp Visa's U.S. emergency number is © **800/336-8472.** American Express cardholders and traveler's check holders should call © **800/221-7282** for all money emergencies. MasterCard holders should call © **800/307-7309.**

The credit-card companies may be able to wire you a cash advance off your credit card immediately; in many places, they can deliver an emergency credit card in a day or two.

Odds are that if your wallet is gone, the police won't be able to recover it for you. However, after you realize that it's gone and you cancel your credit cards, it is still worth informing the police. Your credit-card company or insurer may require a police report number for reimbursements or to cancel any unauthorized charges.

If you need emergency cash over the weekend when all banks and American Express offices are closed (though you can always use ATMs if you still have your card), you can have money wired to you from **Western Union** (© **800/325-6000;** www.westernunion.com). You must present valid ID to pick up the cash at the Western Union office. However, in most countries, you can pick up a money transfer even if you don't have

> **Tips   Destination Florida—Red Alert Checklist**
>
> - Did you make sure your favorite attraction is open and did you make reservations for hotels, activities (baseball games, swimming with the dolphins, etc.), and more, if necessary?
> - If you purchased traveler's checks, have you recorded the check numbers and stored the documentation separately from the checks?
> - Did you pack your camera? If you packed film in your checked baggage, did you invest in protective pouches to shield film from airport x-rays?
> - Do you have a safe, accessible place to store money?
> - Did you bring your ID cards that could entitle you to discounts, such as AAA and AARP cards, student IDs, and so on?
> - Did you bring emergency drug prescriptions and extra glasses and/or contact lenses?
> - Do you have your credit card PINs?
> - If you have an E-ticket, do you have documentation?
> - Did you leave a copy of your itinerary with someone at home?

valid identification, as long as you can answer a test question provided by the sender. Be sure to let the sender know in advance that you don't have identification. If you need to use a test question instead of ID, the sender must take cash to his or her local Western Union office, rather than transferring the money over the phone or online.

4 When to Go

To a large extent, the timing of your visit will determine how much you'll spend—and how much company you'll have—once you get to Florida. That's because room rates can more than double during the high seasons, when countless visitors migrate to Florida.

The weather determines the high seasons (see "Climate," below). In subtropical Southern Florida, it's during the winter, from mid-December to mid-April. On the other hand, you'll be rewarded with incredible bargains if you can stand the heat and humidity of a South Florida summer between June and early September. In North Florida, the reverse is true: Tourists flock here during the summer, from Memorial Day to Labor Day.

Presidents' Day weekend in February, Easter week, Memorial Day weekend at the end of May, the Fourth of July, Labor Day weekend at the start of September, Thanksgiving, Christmas, and New Year's are busy throughout the state, and especially at Walt Disney World and the other Orlando area attractions, which can be packed anytime school's out (see chapter 12 for more information on these areas).

Northern and Southern Florida share the same "shoulder seasons": April and May and from September to November, when the weather is pleasant throughout Florida and hotel rates are considerably less than during the high seasons. If price is a consideration, these months of pleasant temperatures and fewer tourists are the best times to visit.

Average Temperatures in Selected Florida Cities (°F)

	Jan	Feb	Mar	Apr	May	June	July	Aug	Sept	Oct	Nov	Dec
Key West	69	72	74	77	80	82	85	85	84	80	74	72
Miami	69	70	71	74	78	81	82	84	81	78	73	70
Tampa	60	61	66	72	77	81	82	82	81	75	67	62
Orlando	60	63	66	71	78	82	82	82	81	75	67	61
Tallahassee	53	56	63	68	72	78	81	81	77	74	66	59

See the accommodations sections in the chapters that follow for specifics about the local high, shoulder, and off-seasons.

CLIMATE Northern Florida has a temperate climate, and even in the warmer southern third of the state, it's subtropical, not tropical. Accordingly, Florida sees more extremes of temperatures than, say, the Caribbean islands.

Spring (late Mar to May) sees warm temperatures throughout Florida, but it also brings tropical showers.

Summer runs from May to September in Florida, when it's hot and very humid throughout the state. If you're in an inland city during these months, you may not want to do anything too taxing when the sun is at its peak. Coastal areas, however, reap the benefits of sea breezes. Severe afternoon thunderstorms are prevalent during the summer heat (there aren't professional sports teams here named *Lightning* and *Thunder* for nothing), so schedule your activities for earlier in the day, and take precautions to avoid being hit by lightning during the storms.

Autumn (from about Sept–Nov) is a great time to visit—the hottest days are gone, and the crowds have thinned out. Unless a hurricane blows through, November usually is Florida's driest month. August through November is hurricane season here, but even if one threatens, the National Weather Service closely tracks the storms and gives ample warning if there's need to evacuate coastal areas.

Winter can get a bit nippy throughout the state, and sometimes downright cold in Northern Florida. Although snow is rare, a flake or two has been known to fall as far south as Miami. The "cold snaps" usually last only a few days in the southern half of the state, however, and daytime temperatures quickly return to the 70s.

For up-to-the-minute weather info, tune in to cable TV's Weather Channel, or click onto its website: www.weather.com.

FLORIDA CALENDAR OF EVENTS

January

Toyota Gator Bowl, Jacksonville. Two of the country's better college football teams battle it out in Alltel Stadium. © 904/798-1700; www. gatorbowl.com. Usually January 1.

Outback Bowl, Tampa. Two top college teams kick off at Houlihan's Stadium, preceded by a weeklong series of events. Call © 813/874-2695; www.outbackbowl.com. Usually January 1.

Epiphany Celebration, Tarpon Springs. After morning services at St. Nicholas Cathedral, young folks dive for the Epiphany cross in Spring Bayou. © 727/937-3540. First Saturday in January.

FedEx Orange Bowl Classic, Miami. Football fanatics flock down to the big Orange Bowl game (oddly taking place not at the Orange Bowl in seedy downtown, but at the much more savory

Pro Player Stadium) on New Year's Day, featuring two of the year's best college football teams. Tickets are available from March 1 of the previous year through the Orange Bowl Committee (© **305/371-4600**), but call early as they sell out quickly.

Key West Literary Seminar, Key West. Literary types get a good reason to put down the books and head to Key West. This annual 3-day event features a different theme every year, such as "The Memoir" or "Science Fiction," and a roster of incredible authors, writers, and other literary types such as Joyce Carol Oates, Barbara Ehrenreich, and Jamaica Kincaid. The event is so popular it sells out well in advance, so call early for tickets (available for individual lectures or events, or the entire 3-day conference). For information call © **888/293-9291** or visit www.keywestliteraryseminar.org.

Art Deco Weekend, South Beach. Gain a newfound appreciation for the Necco-wafered Art Deco buildings, Deco furniture, history, and fashion at this weekend-long festival of street fairs, films, lectures, and other events (© **305/672-2014**). Mid- to late January.

Royal Caribbean Golf Classic, Key Biscayne. Watch as pro golfers tee off for over $1 million at this tournament played on the scenic Crandon Park Golf Course. Call © **305/374-6180.** Late January.

Goodland Mullet Festival, Marco Island. Stan Gober's Idle Hour Seafood Restaurant in Goodland is mobbed during a massive party featuring the Buzzard Lope dance and the Best Men's Legs Contest. © **239/394-3041;** www.stansidle-hour.com. Mid-January.

Zora Neale Hurston Festival of the Arts and Humanities, Eatonville. A 4-day celebration of the author's life and works, held in the nation's first African-American municipality. Call © **800/352-3865** or 407/647-3307 for details. Usually last week in January.

February

Edison Pageant of Light, Fort Myers. This spectacular Parade of Lights tops off arts-and-crafts shows, pageants, and a 5K race. © **239/489-9314;** www.edisonfestival.org. First 2 weeks in February.

Gasparilla Pirate Fest, Tampa. Hundreds of boats and rowdy "pirates" invade the city and then parade along Bayshore Boulevard, showering crowds with beads and coins. © **813/353-8108;** www.gasparillapiratefest.com. Early February.

Everglades Seafood Festival, Florida City. What seems like schools of fish-loving people flock down to Florida City for a 2-day feeding frenzy, in which Florida delicacies from stone crab to gator tails are served from shacks and booths on the outskirts of this quaint Old Florida town. Free admission, but you pay for the food you eat, booth by booth (© **941/695-4100**). First full weekend in February.

Miami Film Festival. Though not exactly Cannes, the Miami Film Festival, sponsored by the Film Society of America, is an impressive 10-day celluloid celebration, featuring world premieres of Latin American, domestic, and other foreign and independent films. Actors, producers, and directors show up to plug their films and participate in Q&A sessions with the audiences. Call © **305/377-FILM.** Early to mid-February.

Speedweeks, Daytona. Nineteen days of events with a series of races that draw the top names in

NASCAR stock car racing, all culminating in the Daytona 500. All events take place at the Daytona International Speedway. Especially for the **Daytona 500,** tickets must be purchased even a year in advance. They go on sale January 1 of the prior year. © **904/253-7223;** www.daytonaintlspeedway. com. First 3 weeks of February.

Miami International Boat Show, Miami Beach. Agoraphobics beware, as this show draws a quarter of a million boat enthusiasts to the Miami Beach Convention Center. Some of the world's priciest mega-yachts, speedboats, sailboats, and schooners are displayed for purchase or for gawking. Call © **305/531-8410.** Mid-February.

Florida State Fair, Tampa. Despite all its development, Florida is still a major agricultural state. It celebrates this status at this huge annual exposition. Judged competitions, botanical gardens, crafts building, carny rides, and nationally known entertainers help make it fun. © **800/345-FAIR;** www.floridastate fair.com. Early to mid-February.

Mardi Gras at Universal Studios, Orlando. Authentic parade floats from New Orleans, stilt walkers, and traditional doubloons and beads thrown to the crowd add to the fun of this event, and all are included in the regular park admission. © **800/837-2273** or 407/363-8000; www.universalorlando. com. Mid-February.

Coconut Grove Arts Festival, Coconut Grove. Florida's largest art festival features over 300 artists, who are selected from thousands of entries. Possibly one of the most crowded street fairs in South Florida, the festival attracts art lovers, artists, and lots of college students who seem to think this event is the Mardi Gras of art fairs.

Call © **305/447-0401** for information. Presidents Day Weekend.

March

Bike Week, Daytona Beach. An international gathering of motorcycle enthusiasts draws a crowd of more than 200,000. In addition to major races held at Daytona International Speedway (featuring the world's best road racers, motorcrossers, and dirt trackers), there are motorcycle shows, beach parties, and the Annual Motorcycle Parade, with thousands of riders. © **800/854-1234** or 904/255-0981; www. officialbikeweek.com. First week in March.

Sanibel Shell Fair, Sanibel and Captiva Islands. A show of shells from around the world, which includes the sale of unusual shell art. © **239/472-2155;** www.sanibel-captiva.org. Begins first Thursday in March.

Spring Break, Daytona Beach, Miami Beach, Panama City Beach, Key West, and other beaches. College students from all over the United States and Canada flock to Florida for endless partying, wet T-shirt and bikini contests, free concerts, volleyball tournaments, and more. Tune into MTV if you can't be here. Call the local visitor information offices. Three weeks in March.

Calle Ocho Festival, Little Havana. What Carnivale is to Rio, the Calle Ocho Festival is to Miami. This 10-day extravaganza, also called Carnival Miami, features a lengthy block party spanning 23 blocks, live salsa music, parades, and, of course, tons of savory Cuban delicacies. Those afraid of mob scenes should avoid this party at all costs (© **305/644-8888**). Mid-March.

Grand Prix of Miami, Homestead. A little bit of Daytona in Miami, the Grand Prix is a premier racing event, attracting celebrities, Indy car drivers, and curious spectators who get a buzz off the smell of gasoline. Get tickets early, as this event sells out quickly. Call ✆ **305/250-5200.** Late March.

Winter Party, Miami Beach. Gays and lesbians from around the world book trips to Miami as far as a year in advance to attend this weekend-long series of parties and events benefiting the Dade Human Rights Foundation. Travel arrangements can be made through Different Roads Travel, the event's official travel company, by calling ✆ **888/ROADS-55,** ext. 510. For information on the specific events and prices, call ✆ **305/538-5908** or visit www.winterparty.com. Early March.

April

Bay Hill Invitational, Orlando. Hosted by Arnold Palmer and featuring Orlando-based golfers like Tiger Woods, this PGA Tour event is held at the Bay Hill Club, 9000 Bay Hill Blvd. Call ✆ **407/876-2429** or 407/876-2888 for details. Mid-March.

Springtime Tallahassee, Tallahassee. This is when the state capital welcomes abundant azaleas, camellias, and other blossoms. A don't-miss event for garden lovers. ✆ **850/224-5012;** www.springtimetallahassee.com. Runs 4 weeks from late March.

Festival of States, St. Petersburg. Since 1921, one of the South's largest civic celebrations offers national band competitions, three parades, concerts, sports, and more. ✆ **727/898-3654;** festivalofstates@aol.com. First full week in April.

Black College Reunion, Daytona Beach. Some 75,000 students from 115 predominantly African-American universities bring a sometimes-rowdy end to the spring-break season. ✆ **800/854-1234** or 904/255-0415; www.daytonabeach.com. Mid-April.

PGA Seniors Golf Championship, Palm Beach Gardens. This is the oldest and most prestigious of the senior golf tournaments in which aging swingers prove they've still got spunk in their swing. ✆ **561/624-8400.** Mid-April.

Epcot International Flower & Garden Festival, Orlando. This event showcases gardens, topiary characters, floral displays, speakers, and seminars. Call ✆ **407/824-4321** or visit www.disneyworld.com. Six weeks, beginning mid-April.

Sunfest, West Palm Beach. Sleepy downtown West Palm comes alive at the end of April for this street fair and concert, featuring big-name entertainment, food stands, a youth fair, and hordes of people. Admission charges are reasonable, but, unless there's someone performing who you must see, not always worth the price. Stick to the free nontented area on Clematis Street for excellent people-watching. ✆ **561/659-5992.** Late April.

Orlando International Fringe Festival. From sword swallowing to a 7-minute version of Hamlet, this 10-day festival presents over 100 acts. See drama, comedy, political satire, and experimental theater at various outdoor stages in downtown Orlando. Call ✆ **407/648-0077** for ticket information. Late April to early May.

May

Isle of Eight Flags Shrimp Festival, Amelia Island. This festival features a blessing of the fleet, the best-decorated shrimp boat contest, and tons of shrimp to eat. ✆ **800/2-AMELIA;** www.shrimpfestival.com. First weekend in May.

Florida Springfest, Pensacola. National rock, country, jazz, reggae, and pop musicians perform over 4 days, plus children's activities and more. ℭ **850/469-1069;** www. springfest.net. Mid-May.

Mayfest, Destin. This upscale arts-and-crafts festival attracts more than 20,000 people to look, buy, and sample fine cuisine at the Panhandle's ritziest resort. ℭ **850/837-6241;** www.destinchamber.com. Third full weekend in May.

June

Fiesta of Five Flags, Pensacola. This extravaganza commemorates the Spanish conquistador Tristan de Luna's arrival in 1559. ℭ **850/433-6512;** www.fiestaoffiveflags. org. First week in June.

Gay Weekend, Orlando. This weekend, grown out of the "Gay Day" that has been unofficially held at Walt Disney World since the early 1990s, attracts tens of thousands of gay and lesbian travelers to central Florida. Special events at other attractions, including Universal and SeaWorld, also cater to gay and lesbian travelers. You can get information at www.gayday.com. First weekend in June.

Billy Bowlegs Festival, Fort Walton Beach. A fleet of modern-day pirates captures the Emerald Coast in a rollicking, weeklong bash honoring notorious buccaneer William Augustus Bowles. A treasure hunt, parade, and carnival contribute to the festival's fun. ℭ **800/322-3319;** www.destin-fwb.com. First week of June.

Coconut Grove Goombay Festival, Coconut Grove. They may say it's better in the Bahamas, but that's questionable after you've attended Miami's own Bahamian bash, featuring lots of dancing in the streets, marching bands, scorching Caribbean temperatures, and the ever buzz-worthy and refreshing Goombay punch. ℭ **305/372-9966.** Early June.

Spanish Night Watch Ceremony, St. Augustine. Actors in period dress lead a torchlight procession through historic St. Augustine and reenact the closing of the city gates with music and pageantry. ℭ **800/ OLD-CITY;** www.visitoldcity.com. Third Saturday in June.

July

Pepsi 400, Daytona. A race marking the halfway point in the NASCAR Winston Cup Series for stock cars. Held at the Daytona International Speedway at 11am. ℭ **904/253-7223;** www.daytona intlspeedway.com. July 4.

World's Richest Tarpon Tournament, Boca Grande. Some $175,000 is at stake in the great tarpon waters off Southwest Florida. ℭ **941/964-0568;** www. bocagrandechamber.com. Second Wednesday and Thursday in July.

Lower Keys Underwater Music Fest, Looe Key. When you hear the phrase "the music and the madness," you may want to think of this amusing aural aquatic event in which boaters head out to the underwater reef at the Looe Key Marine Sanctuary, drop speakers into the water, and pipe in all sorts of music, creating a disco-diving spectacular. Considering the heat at this time of year, underwater is probably the coolest place for a concert. Call ℭ **800/872-3722.** Early July.

Blue Angels Air Show, Pensacola. World-famous navy pilots do their aerial acrobatics just 100 yards off Pensacola Beach. ℭ **800/874-1234** or 850/434-1234; www.visit pensacola.com or www.blueangels. navy.mil. Early July.

August

This month is possibly the most scorching, which is why event planners try to avoid it altogether. Your best bet? The beach, the pool, or anywhere with air-conditioning.

September

Labor Day Pro-Am Surfing Festival, Cocoa Beach. One of the largest surfing events on the East Coast draws pros and amateurs from around the country. There are also rock-and-roll bands and swimsuit contests. ✆ **800/927-9659;** www.space-coast.com. Labor Day weekend.

October

Destin Seafood Festival, Destin. The "World's Luckiest Fishing Village" cooks its bountiful catch in every style of cuisine imaginable. Also offered are arts, crafts, and music. This festival follows right after the Destin Fishing Rodeo, with 450 angler awards and giant dock parties. ✆ **850/837-6241;** www.destinchamber.com. First full weekend in October.

Biketoberfest, Daytona. Road-racing stars compete at the CCS Motorcycle Championship at Daytona International Speedway. There are also parties, parades, concerts, and more. ✆ **800/854-1235;** www. biketoberfest.org. Mid-October.

Clearwater Jazz Holiday, Clearwater. Top jazz musicians play for 4 days and nights at bay-front Coachman Park in this free musical extravaganza. ✆ **727/461-5200;** www.clearwaterjazz.com. Mid-October.

Columbus Day Regatta, Miami. On the day that Columbus discovered America, the party-hearty discover their fellow Americans' birthday suits, as this bacchanalia in the middle of Biscayne Bay encourages participants in this so-called regatta (there is a boat race at some point during the day, but most people are too preoccupied to notice) to strip down to their bare necessities and party at the sandbar in the middle of the bay. You may not need a bathing suit, but you will need a boat to get out to where all the action is. Consider renting one on Key Biscayne, which is the closest to the sandbar.

Halloween Horror Nights, Orlando. Universal Studios transforms its grounds for 19 nights into haunted attractions with live bands, a psychopath's maze, special shows, and hundreds of ghouls and goblins roaming the streets. The studio closes at dusk, reopening in a new macabre form at 7pm. Full admission is charged for the event, which is geared toward adults. ✆ **800/ 837-2273** or 407/363-8000; www. universalorlando.com. Mid-October through Halloween.

Mickey's Not-So-Scary Halloween Party, Orlando. At Walt Disney World, guests are invited to trick or treat in the Magic Kingdom, starting at 7pm. The party includes parades, storytelling, live music, and a bewitching fireworks display. Call ✆ **407/934-7639** for information; www.disneyworld. com. End of October.

Guavaween, Tampa. Ybor City's Latin-style Halloween celebration begins with the "Mama Guava Stumble," a wacky costume parade. The party also has all-night concerts from rock to reggae. ✆ **877/ 934-3782** or 813/248-3712; www.ybor.org. October 31.

Fantasy Fest, Key West. Mardi Gras takes a Floridian holiday as the streets of Key West are overtaken by wildly costumed revelers who have no shame and no parental guidance. This weeklong, hedonistic, X-rated Halloween party is not for children under 18. Make reservations in Key West early, as hotels tend to book up quickly during this event. Call *C* **305/296-1817.** Last week of October.

November

Frank Brown International Songwriters' Festival, Pensacola. Composers gather at the infamous Flora-Bama Lounge and other beach venues to perform their country-music hits. *C* **850/492-7664;** www.fbisf.com. First week in November.

Florida Seafood Festival, Apalachicola. Book a room at the Gibson Inn 5 years in advance of this huge chow-down in Florida's oystering capital. *C* **888/653-8011;** www.floridaseafoodfestival.com. First Saturday in November.

Miami Bookfair International, downtown Miami. Bibliophiles, literati, and some of the world's most prestigious and prolific authors descend upon downtown Miami for a week-long homage to the written word, which also happens to be the largest book fair in the United States. The weekend street fair is the most well attended of the entire event, in which regular folk mix with wordsmiths such as Tom Wolfe and Jane Smiley while indulging in snacks, antiquarian books, and literary gossip. All lectures are free, but they fill up quickly, so get there early. Call *C* **305/237-3258** for lecture schedules. Mid-November.

Blue Angels Homecoming Air Show, Pensacola. World-famous navy pilots do their aerial acrobatics just 100 yards off the beach. *C* **850/452-2311;** www.visit pensacola.com or www.blueangels. navy.mil. Second weekend in November.

American Sandsculpting Festival, Fort Myers Beach. Some 50,000

gather to sculpt or see the world's finest sand castles. *C* **800/782-9283** or 239/463-6451; www.fmbchamber.com. First weekend in November.

White Party Week, Miami and Fort Lauderdale. This week-long series of parties to benefit AIDS research is built around the main event, the White Party, which takes place at Villa Vizcaya and sells out as early as a year in advance. Philanthropists and celebrities such as Calvin Klein and David Geffen join thousands of white-clad mostly gay men (and some women) in what has become one of the world's hottest and hardest-to-score party tickets. Call *C* **305/667-9296** or visit www.whitepartyweek.com for a schedule of parties and events. Thanksgiving week.

Epcot International Food & Wine Festival, Orlando. Sip and savor the food and wines of 30 cultures. Events include wine tastings, seminars, and celebrity-chef cooking demonstrations. Call *C* **407/827-7200** or 407/824-4321 for ticket information.

December

Edison/Ford Winter Homes Holiday House, Fort Myers. Christmas music and thousands of lights hail the holiday season here. At the same time, candles create a spectacular Luminary Trail along the full length of Sanibel Island's Periwinkle Way. *C* **239/334-7419;** www.edison-ford-estate.com. First week of December.

Captiva Sea Kayak Classic, Captiva Island. Sea kayakers and surf skiers from around the nation depart from the beach in front of 'Tween Waters Inn for a series of races. *C* **239/472-5161;** www.sanibel-captiva.org. First weekend in December.

Christmas at Walt Disney World, Orlando. As you would imagine, all of the Disney properties get into the holiday spirit. In the Magic Kingdom, Main Street is lavishly decked out with lights and holly and an 80-foot (24m) glistening tree. Attend Mickey's Very Merry Christmas Party in the Magic Kingdom, and Holidays Around the World and the Candlelight Procession at Epcot. Call ✆ **407/824-4321** for holiday events, ✆ **407/934-7639** for special travel packages, or visit www.disney.com. Throughout December.

British Night Watch & Grand Illumination Ceremony, St. Augustine. Torchlight procession through the Spanish Quarter kicks off a month of Christmas festivities and the "Nights of Lights," in which 1.25 million twinkling bulbs bathe the Old City. ✆ **800/OLD-CITY**; www.visitoldcity.com. First Saturday in December; Nights of Lights to January 31.

The Citrus Bowl Parade, Orlando. This parade features lavish floats and high school bands in a nationally televised event. Reserved seats are $12, but you can watch along the route in downtown Orlando free. ✆ **800/297-2695** or 407/423-2476. Late December.

Winterfest Boat Parade, Fort Lauderdale. People who complain that the holiday season just isn't as festive in South Florida as it is in colder parts of the world haven't been to this spectacular boat parade along the Intracoastal Waterway. Forget decking the halls. At this parade, the decks are decked out in magnificent holiday regalia as they gracefully—and boastfully—glide up and down the water. If you're not on a boat, the best views are from waterfront restaurants or anywhere you can squeeze in along the water. Call ✆ **954/767-0686.** Mid-December.

5 Insurance, Health & Safety

TRAVEL INSURANCE AT A GLANCE

Check your existing insurance policies before you buy travel insurance to cover trip-cancellation, lost-luggage, medical-expenses, or car-rental insurance. You're likely to have partial or complete coverage. But if you need some, ask your travel agent about a comprehensive package. The cost of travel insurance varies widely, depending on the cost and length of your trip, your age and overall health, and the type of trip you're taking. Insurance for extreme sports or adventure travel, for example, will cost more than coverage for a cruise. Some insurers provide packages for specialty vacations, such as skiing or backpacking. More dangerous activities may be excluded from basic policies.

For information, contact one of the following popular insurers:

- **Access America** (✆ 800/284-8300); www.accessamerica.com/)
- **Travel Guard International** (✆ 800/826-1300; www.travel-guard.com)
- **Travel Insured International** (✆ 800/243-3174; www.travel insured.com)
- **Travelex Insurance Services** (✆ 800/228-9792; www.travelex-insurance.com)

TRIP-CANCELLATION INSURANCE (TCI)

There are three major types of trip-cancellation insurance—one, in the event that you pre-pay for a cruise or tour that gets canceled and you can't get your money back; a second when you or someone in your family gets

The Boys of Spring

Major-league baseball fans can watch the Florida Marlins in Miami and the Tampa Bay Devil Rays in St. Petersburg throughout their seasons April through September, but the entire state is a baseball hotbed from late February to the end of March, when many other teams tune up for the regular season with "Grapefruit League" exhibition games.

Most of Florida's spring-training stadiums are relatively small, so fans can see their favorite players up close; maybe even get a hand-shake or an autograph. Also, tickets are priced from $5 to $12, a bargain when compared with admission for regular-season games. Many games sell out by early March, so don't wait until you're in Florida to buy tickets.

The teams can move from year to year, so contact the **Florida Sports Foundation,** 2390 Kerry Forest Pkwy., Suite 101, Tallahassee, FL 32309 (**℃ 850/488-8347;** fax 850/922-0482; www.flasports.com), which usu-ally posts the Grapefruit League schedules on its website late in Janu-ary. The main office of **Major League Baseball,** 350 Park Ave., New York, NY 10022 (**℃ 212/339-7800;** www.mlb.com), is another place to find out where your favorite teams will be playing.

Here's where the teams played in 2002 (except for the Florida Mar-lins, who announced plans to relocate to Jupiter in 2003). See the out-door activities sections in subsequent chapters for specifics.

Atlanta Braves, Lake Buena Vista, near Orlando (**℃ 407/939-GAME;** www.braves.mlb.com); **Baltimore Orioles,** Fort Lauderdale (**℃ 954/ 776-1921;** www.orioles.mlb.com); **Boston Red Sox,** Fort Myers (**℃ 877/ 733-7699;** www.redsox.mlb.com); **Cincinnati Reds,** Sarasota (**℃ 941/954-4464;** www.reds.mlb.com); **Cleveland Indians,** Winter Haven (**℃ 863/293-3900;** www.indians.mlb.com); **Detroit Tigers,** Lake-land (**℃ 813/287-8844** or 407/839-3900; www.tigers.mlb.com); **Florida Marlins,** Jupiter (**℃ 305/930-HITS;** www.marlins.mlb.com); **Houston Astros,** Kissimmee, near Orlando (**℃ 407/933-2520;** www.astros.mlb. com); **Kansas City Royals,** Davenport (**℃ 868/424-2500;** www. royals.mlb.com); **Los Angeles Dodgers,** Vero Beach (**℃ 561/569-4900;** www.dodgers.mlb.com); **Minnesota Twins,** Fort Myers (**℃ 800/338-9467;** www.twins.mlb.com); **Montreal Expos,** Jupiter (**℃ 561/775-1818;** www.expos.mlb.com); **New York Mets,** Port St. Lucie (**℃ 561/871-2115;** www.mets.mlb.com); **New York Yankees,** Tampa (**℃ 813/879-2244;** www.yankees.mlb.com); **Philadelphia Phillies,** Clearwater (**℃ 727/ 442-8496;** www.phillies.mlb.com); **Pittsburgh Pirates,** Bradenton (**℃ 941/748-4610;** www.pirates.mlb.com); **St. Louis Cardinals,** Jupiter (**℃ 561/775-1818,** ext. 7; www.cardinals.mlb.com); **Tampa Bay Devil Rays,** St. Petersburg (**℃ 888/FAN-RAYS** or 727/825-3250; www. devilrays.mlb.com); **Texas Rangers,** Port Charlotte (**℃ 941/625-9500;** www.rangers.mlb.com); **Toronto Blue Jays,** Dunedin (**℃ 800/707-8269** or 813/733-0429; www.bluejays.mlb.com).

sick or dies, and you can't travel (but beware that you may not be covered for a pre-existing condition); and a third, when bad weather makes travel impossible. Some insurers provide coverage for events like jury duty; natural disasters close to home like floods or fire; or even the loss of a job. A few have added provisions for cancellations due to terrorist activities. Always check the fine print before signing on, and don't buy trip-cancellation insurance from the tour operator that may be responsible for the cancellation; buy it only from a reputable travel insurance agency. Don't overbuy. You won't be reimbursed for more than the cost of your trip.

MEDICAL INSURANCE

Most health insurance policies cover you if you get sick away from home—but check, particularly if you're insured by an HMO.

Some credit cards (American Express and certain gold and platinum Visa and MasterCards, for example) offer automatic flight insurance against death or dismemberment in case of an airplane crash if you charged the cost of your ticket to their card.

If you require additional insurance, try one of the following companies:

- **MEDEX International**, 9515 Deereco Rd., Timonium, MD 21093-5375 (© **888/MEDEX-00** or 410/453-6300; fax 410/453-6301; www.medexassist.com).
- **Travel Assistance International** (© **800/821-2828**; www.travel assistance.com), 9200 Keystone Crossing, Suite 300, Indianapolis, IN 46240 (for general information on services, call the company's Worldwide Assistance Services, Inc., at © **800/777-8710**).
- Scuba divers can sign up with **The Divers Alert Network** (DAN) (© **800/446-2671** or 919/684-8181; www.diversalert network.org).

The cost of travel medical insurance varies widely. Check your existing policies before you buy additional coverage. Also, check to see if your medical insurance covers you for emergency medical evacuation: If you have to buy a one-way same-day ticket home and forfeit your nonrefundable round-trip ticket, you may be out big bucks.

LOST-LUGGAGE INSURANCE

On domestic flights, checked baggage is covered up to $2,500 per ticketed passenger. On international flights (including U.S. portions of international trips), baggage is limited to approximately $9.07 per pound, up to approximately $635 per checked bag. If you plan to check items more valuable than the standard liability, you may purchase "excess valuation" coverage from the airline, up to $5,000. Be sure to take any valuables or irreplaceable items with you in your carry-on luggage. If you file a lost-luggage claim, be prepared to answer detailed questions about the contents of your baggage, and be sure to file a claim immediately, as most airlines enforce a 21-day deadline. Before you leave home, compile an inventory of all packed items and a rough estimate of the total value to ensure that you're properly compensated if your luggage is lost. You will be reimbursed only for what you lost, no more. Once you've filed a complaint, persist in securing your reimbursement; there are no laws governing the length of time it takes for a carrier to reimburse you. If you arrive at a destination without your bags, ask the airline to forward them to your hotel or to your next destination; they will usually comply. If your bag is delayed or lost, the airline may reimburse you for reasonable expenses, such as a toothbrush or a set of clothes, but the airline is under no legal obligation to do so.

Lost luggage may also be covered by your homeowner's or renter's policy. Many platinum and gold credit cards cover you as well. If you choose to purchase additional lost-luggage insurance, be sure not to buy more than you need. Buy in advance from the insurer or a trusted agent (prices will be much higher at the airport).

CAR-RENTAL INSURANCE (LOSS/DAMAGE WAIVER OR COLLISION DAMAGE WAIVER)

If you hold a private auto insurance policy, you probably are covered in the U.S., but not abroad, for loss or damage to the car, and liability in case a passenger is injured. The credit card you used to rent the card also may provide some coverage.

Car-rental insurance probably does not cover liability if you caused the accident. Check your own auto insurance policy, the rental company policy, and your credit-card agreement for the extent of coverage: Is your destination covered? Are other drivers covered? How much liability is covered if a passenger is injured? (If you rely on your credit card for coverage, you may want to bring a second credit card with you, as damages may be charged to your card and you may find yourself stranded with no money.)

Car-rental insurance costs about $20 a day.

THE HEALTHY TRAVELER

Florida doesn't present any unusual health hazards for most people. Folks with certain medical conditions such as liver disease, diabetes, and stomach ailments, however, should avoid eating raw **oysters,** which can carry a natural bacterium linked to severe diarrhea, vomiting, and even fatal blood poisoning. Cooking kills the bacteria, so, if in doubt, order your oysters steamed, broiled, or fried.

Florida has millions of **mosquitoes** and invisible biting **sand flies** (known as "no-see-ums"), especially in the coastal and marshy areas. Fortunately, neither insect carries malaria or other diseases. Keep these pests at bay with a good insect repellent.

It's especially important to protect yourself against **sunburn.** Don't underestimate the strength of the sun's rays down here, even in the middle of winter. Limit your exposure to the sun, especially during the first few days of your trip and, thereafter, from 11am to 2pm. Use a sunscreen with a high protection factor and apply it liberally. Remember that children need more protection than adults.

WHAT TO DO IF YOU GET SICK AWAY FROM HOME

If you worry about getting sick away from home, consider purchasing **medical travel insurance** and carry your ID card in your purse or wallet. In most cases, your existing health plan will provide the coverage you need. See the section on insurance earlier in this chapter for more information.

If you suffer from a chronic illness, consult your doctor before your departure. For conditions like epilepsy, diabetes, or heart problems, wear a **Medic Alert Identification**

Tips **Quick I.D.**

Tie a colorful ribbon or piece of yarn around your luggage handle, or slap a distinctive sticker on the side of your bag. This makes it less likely that someone will mistakenly appropriate it. And if your luggage gets lost, it will be easier to find.

Tag (© 800/825-3785; www.medic alert.org), which will immediately alert doctors to your condition and give them access to your records through Medic Alert's 24-hour hot line.

Pack **prescription medications** in your carry-on luggage, and carry prescription medications in their original containers. Also bring along copies of your prescriptions in case you lose your pills or run out.

And don't forget sunglasses and an extra pair of contact lenses or prescription glasses.

The United States **Centers for Disease Control and Prevention** (© 800/311-3435; www.cdc.gov) provides up-to-date information on necessary vaccines and health hazards by region or country. If you get sick, consider asking your hotel concierge to recommend a local doctor—even his or her own. You can also try the emergency room at a local hospital; many have walk-in clinics for emergency cases that are not life threatening. You may not get immediate attention, but you won't pay the high price of an emergency room visit (usually a minimum of $300 just for signing your name).

THE SAFE TRAVELER

While tourist areas in Florida are generally safe, you should always stay alert. This is particularly true in the large cities such as Miami, Orlando, Tampa, and St. Petersburg. It is wise to ask your hotel's front-desk staff or the city's or area's tourist office if you're in doubt about which neighborhoods are safe.

Remember also that hotels are open to the public, and in a large hotel, security may not be able to screen everyone entering. Always lock your room door. Don't assume that once inside your hotel you are automatically safe and no longer need to be aware of your surroundings.

DRIVING   A considerable amount of crime involves vehicles, so safety while driving is particularly important. Question your rental agency about personal safety, or ask for a brochure of traveler safety tips when you pick up your car. Obtain written directions from the agency, or a map with the route clearly marked, showing how to get to your destination.

Make sure that you have enough gasoline in your tank to reach your intended destination so that you're not forced to look for a service station in an unfamiliar and possibly unsafe neighborhood, especially at night. If you do drive off a highway into a doubtful neighborhood, leave the area as quickly as possible. If you have an accident in such a neighborhood, even on the highway, stay in your car with the doors locked until you assess the situation or until the police arrive. If you are bumped from behind on the street or are involved in a minor accident with no injuries and the situation appears to be suspicious, motion to the other driver to follow you. *Never* get out of your car in such situations. If you see someone on the road who indicates a need for help, do *not* stop. Take note of the location, drive on to a well-lighted area, and telephone the police by dialing © **911** from any telephone.

Park in well-lighted, well-traveled areas if possible. Always keep your car doors locked, whether attended or unattended. Look around you before you get out of your car, and never leave any packages or valuables in sight. If someone attempts to rob you or steal your car, do *not* try to resist the thief or carjacker—report the incident to the police department immediately.

6 Tips for Travelers with Special Needs

FOR TRAVELERS WITH DISABILITIES

Most disabilities shouldn't stop anyone from traveling. There are more resources out there than ever before.

AGENCIES/OPERATORS

- **Flying Wheels Travel** (© 800/ 535-6790; www.flyingwheels travel.com) offers escorted tours and cruises that emphasize sports and private tours in minivans with lifts.
- **Access Adventures** (© 716/889-9096), a Rochester, New York–based agency, offers customized itineraries for a variety of travelers with disabilities.
- **Accessible Journeys** (© 800/ TINGLES or 610/521-0339; www.disabilitytravel.com) caters specifically to slow walkers and wheelchair travelers and their families and friends.

ORGANIZATIONS

- **The Moss Rehab Hospital** (© 215/456-9603, www.moss resourcenet.org) provides friendly, helpful phone assistance through its **Travel Information Service.**
- **The Society for Accessible Travel and Hospitality** (© 212/ 447-7284, fax 212/725-8253; www.sath.org) offers a wealth of travel resources for all types of disabilities and informed recommendations on destinations, access guides, travel agents, tour operators, vehicle rentals, and companion services. Annual membership costs $45 for adults; $30 for seniors and students.
- **The American Foundation for the Blind** (© 800/232-5463; www.afb.org) provides information on traveling with Seeing Eye dogs.

PUBLICATIONS

- **Mobility International USA** (© 541/343-1284; www.miusa. org) publishes *A World of Options*, a 658-page book of resources, covering everything from biking trips to scuba outfitters, and a biannual newsletter, *Over the Rainbow*. Annual membership is $35.
- **Twin Peaks Press** (© 360/694-2462) publishes travel-related books for travelers with special needs.
- *Open World for Disability and Mature Travel* magazine, published by the Society for Accessible Travel and Hospitality (see above), is full of good resources and information. A year's subscription is $13 ($21 outside the U.S.).

FOR GAY & LESBIAN TRAVELERS

Florida is not without its intolerant contingent, but there are active gay and lesbian groups in most cities here. In fact, the editors of *Out and About*, a gay and lesbian newsletter, have described Miami's **South Beach** as the "hippest, hottest, most happening gay travel destination in the world." For many years that could also be said of **Key West**, which still is one of the country's most popular destinations for gays. **Fort Lauderdale**—where gays own more than 20 motels, 40 bars, and numerous other businesses—is definitely also on the gay-friendly map.

You can contact the **Gay, Lesbian & Bisexual Community Services of Central Florida**, 934 N. Mills Ave., Orlando, FL 32803 (© 407/ 425-4527 or 407/843-4297; www. glbcc.org), whose welcome packets usually include the latest issue of the *Triangle*, a quarterly newsletter (© 407/849-0099) dedicated to gay and lesbian issues, and a calendar of events pertaining to the gay and lesbian community. Although not a tourist-specific packet, it includes information and ads for the area's gay and lesbian clubs.

Watermark, P.O. Box 533655, Orlando, FL 32853 (© **407/481-2243;** fax 407/481-2246; www.watermarkonline.com), is a biweekly tabloid newspaper covering the gay and lesbian scene, including dining and entertainment options, in Orlando, the Tampa Bay area, and Daytona Beach.

Nationally, **The International Gay & Lesbian Travel Association** (IGLTA) (© **800/448-8550** or 954/776-2626; fax 954/776-3303; www.iglta.org) links travelers up with gay-friendly hoteliers, tour operators, and airline and cruise-line representatives. It offers monthly newsletters, marketing mailings, and a membership directory that's updated once a year. Membership is $150 yearly, plus a $100 administration fee for new members.

AGENCIES/OPERATORS

- **Above and Beyond Tours** (© **800/397-2681;** www.abovebeyondtours.com) offers gay and lesbian tours worldwide and is the exclusive gay and lesbian tour operator for United Airlines.
- **Now, Voyager** (© **800/255-6951;** www.nowvoyager.com) is a San Francisco–based gay-owned and operated travel service.
- **Olivia Cruises & Resorts** (© **800/631-6277** or 510/655-0364; http://oliviatravel.com) charters entire resorts and ships for exclusive lesbian vacations all over the world.

PUBLICATIONS

- **Out and About** (© **800/929-2268** or 415/644-8044; www.outandabout.com) offers guidebooks

and a newsletter 10 times a year packed with solid information on the global gay and lesbian scene.

- **Spartacus International Gay Guide** and **Odysseus** are good, annual English-language guidebooks focused on gay men, with some information for lesbians. You can get them from most gay and lesbian bookstores, or order them from **Giovanni's Room** bookstore, 1145 Pine St., Philadelphia, PA 19107 (© **215/923-2960;** www.giovannisroom.com).
- **Gay Travel A to Z: The World of Gay & Lesbian Travel Options at Your Fingertips,** by Marianne Ferrari (Ferrari Publications), is a very good gay and lesbian guidebook series.

FOR SENIORS

With one of the largest retired populations of any state, Florida offers a wide array of activities and benefits for seniors. Don't be shy about asking for discounts, but always carry some kind of identification, such as a driver's license, that shows your age/date of birth.

Major airlines offer coupons for domestic travel for seniors over 60. Typically, a book of four coupons costs less than $700, which means you can fly anywhere in the continental U.S. for under $350 round trip. In most cities, people over the age of 60 qualify for reduced admission to theaters, museums, and other attractions, as well as discounted fares on public transportation.

Members of **AARP** (formerly known as the American Association of Retired Persons), 601 E St. NW, Washington, DC 20049 (© **800/424-3410** or 202/434-2277; www.aarp.org), get discounts on hotels, airfares, and car rentals. AARP offers members a wide range of benefits, including *Modern Maturity* magazine and a monthly newsletter. Anyone over 50 can join.

The **Alliance for Retired Americans**, 8403 Colesville Rd., Suite 1200, Silver Spring, MD 20910 (© **301/578-8422;** www.retiredamericans.org), offers a newsletter six times a year and discounts on hotel and auto rentals; annual dues are $13 per person or couple. *Note:* Members of the former National Council of Senior Citizens receive automatic membership in the Alliance.

The **U.S. National Park Service** offers a **Golden Age Passport** that gives seniors 62 years or older lifetime entrance to all U.S. national park facilities for a one-time processing fee of $10, which must be purchased in person at any NPS facility that charges an entrance fee. Besides free entry, a Golden Age Passport also offers a 50% discount on federal-use fees charged for such facilities as camping, swimming, parking, boat launching, and tours. For more information, click onto www.nps.gov/fees_passes.htm or call © **888-GO-PARKS.**

AGENCIES/OPERATORS

- **Grand Circle Travel** (© **800/221-2610** or 617/350-7500; www.gct.com) offers package deals for the 50-plus market, mostly of the tour-bus variety, with free trips thrown in for those who organize groups of 10 or more.
- **Elderhostel** (© **877/426-8056;** www.elderhostel.org) arranges study programs for those aged 55 and over (and a spouse or companion of any age) in the U.S. and in more than 80 countries around the world. Most courses last 5 to 7 days in the U.S. (2–4 weeks abroad), and many include airfare, accommodations in university dormitories or modest inns, meals, and tuition.

- **Interhostel** (© **800/733-9753;** www.learn.unh.edu/interhostel), organized by the University of New Hampshire, also offers educational travel for seniors. On these escorted tours, the days are packed with seminars, lectures, and field trips, with sightseeing led by academic experts. **Interhostel** takes travelers 50 and over (with companions over 40), and offers 1- and 2-week trips, mostly international.

PUBLICATIONS

- *The Book of Deals* is a collection of more than 1,000 senior discounts on airlines, lodging, tours, and attractions around the country; it's available for $9.95 by calling © **800/460-6676.**
- *101 Tips for the Mature Traveler* is available from Grand Circle Travel (© **800/221-2610** or 617/350-7500; fax 617/346-6700).
- *The 50+ Traveler's Guidebook* (St. Martin's Press).
- *Unbelievably Good Deals and Great Adventures That You Absolutely Can't Get Unless You're Over 50* (Contemporary Publishing Co.).

FOR FAMILIES

Florida is a great family destination, with Walt Disney World leading the list of theme parks geared to young and old alike. Consequently, most Florida hotels and restaurants are willing if not eager to cater to families traveling with children. Many hotels and motels let children 17 and under stay free in their parents' room (be sure to ask when you reserve).

At the beaches, it's the exception rather than the rule for a resort not to have a children's activities program (some will even mind the youngsters while the parents enjoy a night off!).

Even if they don't have a children's program of their own, most will arrange babysitting services.

If you call ahead before dining out, you can find out whether restaurants have some facilities for children, such as booster chairs and low-priced kids' menus.

PUBLICATIONS

For a host of invaluable tips and other information, pick up copies of *The Unofficial Guide to Florida with Kids* and *The Unofficial Guide to Walt Disney World with Kids.*

WEBSITES

- **Family Travel Network** (www.familytravelnetwork.com) offers travel tips and reviews of family-friendly destinations, vacation deals, and thoughtful features such as "What to Do When Your Kids Are Afraid to Travel" and "Kid-Style Camping."
- **Travel with Your Children** (www.travelwithyourkids.com) is a comprehensive site offering sound advice for traveling with children.
- **The Busy Person's Guide to Travel with Children** (http://wz.com/travel/TravelingWithChildren.html) offers a "45-second newsletter" where experts weigh in on the best websites and resources for tips for traveling with children.

TRAVELING WITH PETS

Many of us wouldn't dream of going on vacation without our pets. Under the right circumstances, it can be a memorable experience. And these days, more and more lodgings and restaurants are going the pet-friendly route.

Many hotel and motel chains, such as Best Western, Motel 6, Holiday Inn, and Four Seasons–Regent Hotels, welcome pets. Policies vary, however, so call ahead to each hotel you plan to stay at to find out more about the rules.

An excellent resource is www.petswelcome.com, which dispenses medical tips, names of animal-friendly lodgings and campgrounds, and lists of kennels and veterinarians. Also check out *The Portable Petswelcome. com: The Complete Guide to Traveling with Your Pet* (Howell Book House), which features the best selection of pet travel information anywhere. Another resource is *Pets-R-Permitted Hotel, Motel & Kennel Directory: The Travel Resource for Pet Owners Who Travel* (Annenberg Communications).

If you plan to fly with your pet, the FAA has compiled a list of all requirements for transporting live animals at www.dot.gov/airconsumer/animals.htm. You may be able to carry your pet on board a plane if it's small enough to put inside a carrier that can slip under the seat. Pets usually count as one piece of carry-on luggage. Note that summer may not be the best time to fly with your pet: Many airlines will not check pets as baggage in the hot summer months. The ASPCA discourages travelers from checking pets as luggage at any time, as storage conditions on planes are loosely monitored and fatal accidents are not unprecedented. Your other option is to ship your pet with a professional carrier, which can be expensive. Ask your veterinarian whether you should sedate your pet on a plane ride or give it anti-nausea medication. Never give your pet sedatives used by humans.

Keep in mind that dogs are prohibited on hiking trails and must be leashed at all times on federal lands administered by the National Park Service (national parks and monuments). With a few exceptions,

Florida's state parks allow small pets but require that they be kept on leashes.

The sun in Florida can be blistering hot, so *never* leave your pet inside a parked car with the windows rolled up. It's a good idea never to leave a pet inside a hot car even with the windows rolled down for any length of time.

Make sure your pet is wearing a nametag with the name and phone number of a contact person who can take the call if your pet gets lost while you're away from home.

7 Getting There

BY PLANE

Most major domestic airlines fly to and from many Florida cities. Choose from **American** (℮ **800/433-7300;** www.aa.com), **Continental** (℮ **800/ 525-0280;** www. continental.com), **Delta** (℮ **800/221-1212;** www. delta-air.com), **Northwest/KLM** (℮ **800/225-2525;** www.nwa.com), **United** (℮ **800/241-6522;** www. united.com), and **US Airways** (℮ **800/428-4322;** www.usairways. com).

Of these, Delta and US Airways have the most extensive network of commuter connections within Florida (see "Getting Around," later in this chapter).

Several so-called no-frills airlines—low fares but few if any amenities—also fly to Florida. The biggest and best is **Southwest Airlines** (℮ **800/ 435-9792;** www.southwest.com), which has flights from many U.S. cities to Fort Lauderdale, Jacksonville, Orlando, and Tampa.

Others flying to Florida include **AirTran** (℮ **800/AIR-TRAN;** www.airtran); **American Trans Air** (℮ **800/435-9282;** www.ata.com); **Carnival Air** (℮ **800/824-7386**), an arm of the popular cruise line; **JetBlue** (℮ **800/538-2583;** www.jetblue. com); **MetroJet,** an arm of US Airways (℮ **800/888-638-7653;** www.flymetrojet.com); **Midway** (℮ **800/44-MIDWAY;** www. midwayair.com); **Midwest Express** (℮ **800/452-2022;** www.midwest express.com); **PanAm** (℮ **800/FLY-PANAM;** www.flypanam.com); **Spirit** (℮ **800/722-7117;** www.spiritair. com); and **Vanguard** (℮ **800/826-4827;** www.flyvanguard.com).

Internet resources such as **Travelocity** (www.travelocity.com) and **Microsoft Expedia** (www. expedia.com) make it relatively easy to compare prices and even purchase tickets. See "Planning Your Trip Online," later in this chapter.

FLYING FOR LESS: TIPS FOR GETTING THE BEST AIRFARE

There's no shortage of **discounted and promotional fares** to Florida. November, December, and January often see fare wars that can result in savings of 50% or more. Watch for advertisements in your local newspaper and on TV, call the airlines, or check out their websites (see "Planning Your Trip Online," later in this chapter).

If you call the airlines or a travel agent, ask for the lowest fares, and ask whether it's cheaper to book in advance, fly in midweek, or stay over a Saturday night. Don't stop at the 7-day advance purchase; ask how much the 14- and 30-day plans cost. Decide when you want to go before you call, since many of the best deals are non-refundable.

Passengers within the same airplane cabin are rarely paying the same fare. Business travelers who need to purchase tickets at the last minute, change their itinerary at a moment's notice, or get home for the weekend pay the premium rate. Passengers who can book their ticket long in advance, who can stay over Saturday night, or who are willing to travel on a Tuesday,

Wednesday, or Thursday after 7pm, will pay a fraction of the full fare. On many flights, even the shortest hops, the full fare is close to $1,000 or more, while a 7- or 14-day advance purchase ticket may cost less than half that amount. Here are a few other easy ways to save.

- Airlines periodically lower prices on their most popular routes. Check the travel section of your Sunday newspaper for advertised discounts or call the airlines directly and ask if any **promotional rates** or special fares are available. You'll almost never see a sale during the peak summer vacation months of July and August, or during the Thanksgiving or Christmas seasons; but in periods of low-volume travel, you should pay no more than $400 for a domestic cross-country flight. If your schedule is flexible, say so, and ask if you can secure a cheaper fare by staying an extra day, by flying midweek, or by flying at less-trafficked hours. If you already hold a ticket when a sale breaks, it may even pay to exchange your ticket, which usually incurs a $100 to $150 charge.

  Note: The lowest-priced fares are often nonrefundable, require advance purchase of 1 to 3 weeks and a certain length of stay, and carry penalties for changing dates of travel.

- **Consolidators**, also known as bucket shops, are a good place to find low fares. Consolidators buy seats in bulk from the airlines and then sell them back to the public at prices usually below even the airlines' discounted rates. Their small ads usually run in Sunday newspaper travel sections. And before you pay, request a confirmation number from the consolidator and then call the airline to confirm your seat. Be aware that bucket shop tickets are usually nonrefundable or rigged with stiff cancellation penalties, often as high as 50% to 75% of the ticket price. Protect yourself by paying with a credit card rather than cash. Keep in mind that if there's an airline sale going on, or if it's high season, you can often get the same or better rates by contacting the airlines directly, so do some comparison shopping before you buy. Also check out the name of the airline; you may not want to fly on some obscure Third World airline, even if you're saving $10. And check whether you're flying on a charter or a scheduled airline; the latter is more expensive but more reliable.

  Council Travel (℡ 800/226-8624; www.counciltravel.com) and **STA Travel** (℡ 800/781-4040; www.sta.travel.com) cater especially to young travelers, but their bargain-basement prices are available to people of all ages. **The TravelHub** (℡ 888/AIR-FARE; www.travelhub.com) represents nearly 1,000 travel agencies, many of whom offer consolidator and discount fares. Other reliable consolidators include **1-800-FLY-CHEAP** (www.1800flycheap.com); **TFI Tours International**

Tips **Canceled Plans**

If your flight is canceled, don't book a new fare at the ticket counter. Find the nearest phone and call the airline directly to reschedule. You'll be relaxing while other passengers are still standing in line.

> **Tips All About E-Ticketing**
>
> Only yesterday, **electronic tickets (E-tickets)** were the fast and easy ticket-free alternative to paper tickets. E-tickets allowed passengers to avoid long lines at airport check-in, all the while saving the airlines money on postage and labor. With the increased security measures in airports, however, an E-ticket no longer guarantees an accelerated check-in. You often can't go straight to the boarding gate, even if you have no bags to check. You'll probably need to show your printed E-ticket receipt or confirmation of purchase, as well as a photo I.D., and sometimes even the credit card with which you purchased your E-ticket. That said, buying an E-ticket is still a fast, convenient way to book a flight; instead of having to wait for a paper ticket to come through the mail, you can book your fare by phone or on the computer, and the airline will immediately confirm by fax or e-mail. In addition, airlines often offer frequent-flier miles as incentive for electronic bookings.

(© **800-745-8000** or 212/736-1140; www.lowestprice.com), which serves as a clearinghouse for unused seats; or "rebators" such as **Travel Avenue** (© **800/333-3335;** www.travelavenue.com) and the **Smart Traveller** (© 800/448-3338 in the U.S. or 305/448-3338), which rebate part of their commissions to you.

- Search **the Internet** for cheap fares. Great last-minute deals are available through free weekly e-mail services provided directly by the airlines. See "Planning Your Trip Online," later in this chapter, for more information.

- Join a travel club such as **Moment's Notice** (© 718/234-6295; www.moments-notice.com) or **Sears Discount Travel Club** (© 800/433-9383, or 800/255-1487 to join; www.travelersadvantage.com), which supply unsold tickets at discounted prices. You pay an annual membership fee to get the club's hot-line number. Of course, you're limited to what's available, so you have to be flexible.

- Join **frequent-flier clubs.** It's best to accrue miles on one program so that you can rack up free flights and achieve elite status faster. But it makes sense to open as many accounts as possible, no matter how seldom you fly a particular airline. It's free, and you'll get the best choice of seats, faster response to phone inquiries, and prompter service if your luggage is stolen, your flight is canceled or delayed, or if you want to change your seat.

NEW AIR-TRAVEL SECURITY MEASURES

In the wake of the terrorist attacks of September 11, 2001, the airline industry began implementing sweeping security measures in airports. Expect a lengthy check-in process and extensive delays. Although regulations vary from airline to airline, you can expedite the process by taking the following steps:

- **Arrive early.** Arrive at the airport at least 2 hours before your scheduled flight.

- **Try not to drive your car to the airport.** Parking and curbside access to the terminal may be limited. Call ahead and check.

- **Don't count on curbside check-in.** Some airlines and airports have stopped curbside check-in altogether, whereas others offer it on a limited basis. For up-to-date information on specific regulations and implementations, check with the individual airline.

- **Be sure to carry plenty of documentation.** A government-issued photo ID (federal, state, or local) is now required. You may need to show this at various checkpoints. With an E-ticket, you may be required to have with you printed confirmation of purchase, and perhaps even the credit card with which you bought your ticket (see "All About E-Ticketing," above). This varies from airline to airline, so call ahead to make sure you have the proper documentation. And be sure that your ID is **up-to-date:** An expired driver's license, for example, may keep you from boarding the plane altogether.

- **Know what you can carry on—and what you can't.** Travelers in the United States are now limited to one carry-on bag, plus one personal bag (such as a purse or a briefcase). The Transportation Security Administration (TSA) has also issued a list of newly restricted carry-on items; see the box "What You Can Carry On—and What You Can't."

- **Prepare to be searched.** Expect spot-checks. Electronic items, such as a laptops or cellphones, should be readied for additional screening. Limit the metal items you wear on your person.

- **It's no joke.** When a check-in agent asks if someone other than you packed your bag, don't decide that this is the time to be funny. The agents will not hesitate to call an alarm.

- **No ticket, no gate access.** Only ticketed passengers will be allowed beyond the screener checkpoints, except for those people with specific medical or parental needs.

Tips **What You Can Carry On—And What You Can't**

The Transportation Security Administration (TSA), the government agency that now handles all aspects of airport security, has devised new restrictions for carry-on baggage, not only to expedite the screening process but to prevent potential weapons from passing through airport security. Passengers are now limited to bringing just one carry-on bag and one personal item onto the aircraft (previous regulations allowed two carry-on bags and one personal item, like a briefcase or a purse). For more information, go to the TSA's website at www.tsa.gov. The agency has released an updated list of items passengers are not allowed to carry onto an aircraft:

Not permitted: knives and box cutters, corkscrews, straight razors, metal scissors, golf clubs, baseball bats, pool cues, hockey sticks, ski poles, ice picks.

Permitted: nail clippers, nail files, tweezers, eyelash curlers, safety razors (including disposable razors), syringes (with documented proof of medical need), walking canes and umbrellas (must be inspected first).

The airline you fly may have **additional restrictions** on items you can and cannot carry on board. Call ahead to avoid problems.

BY CAR

Florida is reached by **I-95** along the east coast, **I-75** from the Central states, and **I-10** from the west. **The Florida Turnpike,** a toll road, links Orlando, West Palm Beach, Fort Lauderdale, and Miami (it's a shortcut from Wildwood on I-75 north of Orlando to Miami). **I-4** cuts across the state from Cape Canaveral through Orlando to Tampa.

See "Getting Around," later in this chapter, for more information about driving in Florida and the car-rental firms operating here.

If you're a member, your local branch of the **American Automobile Association (AAA)** will provide a free trip-routing plan. AAA also has nationwide emergency road service for its members (📞 **800/AAA-HELP;** www.aaa.com).

BY TRAIN

Amtrak (📞 **800/USA-RAIL;** www. amtrak.com) offers train service to Florida from both the East and West Coasts. It takes some 26 hours from New York to Miami, 68 hours from Los Angeles to Miami, and Amtrak's fares aren't much less—if not more—than many of the airlines' lowest fares.

Amtrak's *Silver Meteor* and *Silver Star* both run twice daily between New York and either Miami or Tampa, with intermediate stops along the East Coast and in Florida. Amtrak's Thruway Bus Connections are available from the Fort Lauderdale Amtrak station and Miami International Airport to Key West; from Tampa to St. Petersburg, Treasure Island, Clearwater, Sarasota, Bradenton, and Fort Myers; and from Deland to Daytona Beach. From the West Coast, the *Sunset Limited* runs three times weekly between Los Angeles and Orlando. It stops in Pensacola, Crestview (north of Fort Walton Beach and Destin), Chipley (north of Panama City Beach), and Tallahassee. Sleeping accommodations are available for an extra charge.

If you intend to stop off along the way, you can save money with Amtrak's **Explore America** (or All Aboard America) fares, which are based on three regions of the country.

Amtrak's **Auto Train** runs daily from Lorton, Virginia (12 miles/ 19km south of Washington, D.C.), to Sanford, Florida (just northeast of Orlando). You ride in a coach while your car is secured in an enclosed vehicle carrier. You should make your train reservations as far in advance as possible.

8 Escorted & Package Tours

More than 120 travel companies offer hundreds of package tour options to the Sunshine State, particularly to Orlando and Miami. Quite often, these deals will result in savings not just on airfares but on hotels and other activities as well. You pay one price for a package that varies from one tour operator to the next. Airfare, transfers, and accommodations are always covered, and sometimes meals and specific activities are thrown in.

Before you start your search for the lowest airfare, therefore, you may want to consider booking your flight as part of a travel package, such as an escorted tour or a package tour. What you lose in adventure, you could gain in time and money saved when you book accommodations, and maybe even food and entertainment, along with your flight—but not necessarily.

PACKAGE TOURS FOR INDE-PENDENT TRAVELERS

Package tours are not the same thing as escorted tours. With a package tour, you travel independently but pay a group rate. Packages usually include airfare, a choice of hotels, and car rentals, and packagers often offer several options at different prices. In many cases, a package that includes airfare, hotel, and transportation to and from the airport will cost you less than just the hotel alone would have, had you booked it yourself. That's because packages are sold in bulk to tour operators—who resell them to the public at a cost that drastically undercuts standard rates.

RECOMMENDED PACKAGE TOUR OPERATORS

One good source of package deals is the airlines themselves. Most major airlines offer air/land packages, including **American Airlines Vacations** (© 800/321-2121; http:// aav1.aavacations.com), **Delta Vacations** (© 800/221-6666; www.delta vacations.com), **US Airways Vacations** (© 800/455-0123 or 800/ 422-3861; www.usairwaysvacations. com), **Continental Airlines Vacations** (© 800/301-3800; www.cool vacations.com), and **United Vacations** (© 888/854-3899; www.united vacations.com/).

Online Vacation Mall (© 800/ 839-9851; www.onlinevacationmall. com) allows you to search for and book packages offered by a number of tour operators and airlines. The **United States Tour Operators Association's** website (www.ustoa.com) has a search engine that allows you to look for operators that offer packages to a specific destination. Travel packages are also listed in the travel section of your local Sunday newspaper. **Liberty Travel** (© 888/271-1584; www. libertytravel.com), one of the biggest packagers in the Northeast, often runs full-page ads in Sunday newspapers. Or check ads in the national travel magazines such as *Arthur Frommer's Budget Travel Magazine, Travel & Leisure, National Geographic Traveler,* and *Condé Nast Traveler.*

THE PROS & CONS OF PACKAGE TOURS

Packages can save you money because they are sold in bulk to tour operators, who sell them to the public. They offer group prices but allow for independent travel. The disadvantages are that you're usually required to make a large payment up front; you may end up on a charter flight; and you have to deal with your own luggage and with transfers between your hotel and the airport, if transfers are not included in the package price. Packages often don't allow for complete flexibility or a wide

---

Tips **Saving with Golf & Tennis Packages**

Many Florida hotels and resorts and even some motels offer **golf and tennis packages,** which bundle the cost of room, greens and court fees, and sometimes equipment, into one price. These deals usually don't include airfare, but they do represent savings over paying for the room and golf or tennis separately. See the accommodations sections in the following chapters for hostelries offering special packages to their guests.

Summer, early fall, and the first 3 weeks of December are good times to search for discounted deals in Southern Florida. For example, the Naples Beach Hotel & Golf Club in Naples (p. 424) recently offered a bed-and-breakfast special for about $125 a night per room, including a full breakfast buffet, during September and December. Regular autumn room rates are more than twice that amount, without breakfast.

range of choices. For instance, you may prefer a quiet inn but have to settle for a popular chain hotel instead. Your choice of travel days may be limited as well.

QUESTIONS TO ASK IF YOU BOOK A PACKAGE TOUR

- What are the **accommodations choices** available and are there price differences? Once you find out, look them up in a Frommer's guide.
- What **type of room** will you be staying in? Don't take whatever is thrown your way. Request a no-smoking room, a quiet room, a room with a view, or whatever you fancy.
- Look for **hidden expenses.** Ask whether airport departure fees and taxes are included in the total cost.

ESCORTED TOURS (TRIPS WITH GUIDES)

Some people love escorted tours. They let you relax and take in the sights while a bus driver fights traffic for you and a guide explains what you're seeing. They spell out your costs up front, and they take you to the maximum number of sights in the minimum amount of time with the least amount of hassle.

For example, the very reputable **Tauck Tours** (© **800/468-2825;** fax 203/221-6828; www.tauck.com) recently offered an 11-day, 10-night escorted tour of Southern Florida beginning in Tampa and ending at Walt Disney World in Orlando. It included accommodations, most meals, bus transportation between the cities, most activities, and a guide, but not your airfare to join the tour in Tampa or to return home from Orlando. These "land" costs were about $2,750 to $3,000 per person, double occupancy ($3,750–$4,200 if you traveled alone). The hotels were all top-end, so this was a good deal, especially during the high winter season in South Florida.

THE PROS & CONS OF ESCORTED TOURS

If you book an escorted tour, most everything is paid for up front, so you deal with fewer money issues. They allow you to enjoy the maximum number of sights in the shortest time, with the least amount of hassle, as all the details are arranged by others. Escorted tours give you the security of traveling in a group and are convenient for people with limited mobility. Many escorted tours are theme tours, putting people together who share the same interest or activity (such as cooking or sailing).

On the downside, if you book an escorted tour you often have to pay a lot of money up front, and your lodging and dining choices are predetermined. Escorted tours can be jam-packed with activities, leaving little room for individual sightseeing, whim, or adventure. They also often focus only on the heavily touristed sites, so you miss out on the lesser-known gems. Plus, you may not always be happy rubbing suitcases with strangers.

QUESTIONS TO ASK IF YOU BOOK AN ESCORTED TOUR

- What is the **cancellation policy?** Do they require a deposit? Can they cancel the trip if they don't get enough people? Do you get a refund if they cancel? If *you* cancel? How late can you cancel if you are unable to go? When do you pay in full? *Note:* If you choose an escorted tour, think strongly about purchasing trip-cancellation insurance from an independent agency, especially if the tour operator asks you to pay up front. See the section on travel insurance, above.
- How busy is the **schedule?** How much sightseeing is planned each day? Is ample time allowed for relaxing or wandering solo?

- What is the **size** of the group? Generally, the smaller the group, the more flexible the itinerary, and the less time you'll spend waiting for people to get on and off the bus. Tour operators may be evasive about this, because they may not know the exact size of the group until everyone has made reservations; but they should be able to give you a rough estimate. Some tours have a minimum group size and may cancel the tour if they don't book enough people.
- What is included in the **price?** You may have to pay for transportation to and from the airport. A box lunch may be included in an excursion, but drinks might cost extra. Beer might be included, but wine might not. Can you opt out of certain activities, or does the bus leave once a day, with no exceptions? Are all your meals planned in advance? Can you choose your entree at dinner? Are tips included?
- What are the **names of the hotels** where you'll be staying? Once you've gotten the names, look them up in a Frommer's guide.
- What **type of room** will you be staying in? Don't take whatever is thrown your way. Request a no-smoking room, a quiet room, a room with a view, or whatever your fancy.
- What are the **demographics** of the group with whom you'll be traveling? What is the age range? What is the gender breakdown? Is this mostly a trip for couples?
- If you plan to be traveling alone, what is the **single supplement?** Will they find you a roommate at your request?

9 Planning Your Trip Online

Researching and booking your trip online can save time and money. Then again, it may not. It is simply not true that you always get the best deal online. Most booking engines do not include schedules and prices for budget airlines, and from time to time you'll get a better last-minute price by calling the airline directly, so it's best to call the airline to see if you can do better before booking online.

On the plus side, Internet users today can tap into the same travel-planning databases that were once accessible only to travel agents—and do it at the same speed. Sites such as **Frommers.com**, **Travelocity.com**, **Expedia.com**, and **Orbitz.com** allow consumers to comparison shop for airfares, access special bargains, book flights, and reserve hotel rooms and rental cars.

But don't fire your travel agent just yet. Although online booking sites offer tips and hard data to help you bargain shop, they cannot endow you with the hard-earned experience that makes a seasoned, reliable travel agent an invaluable resource, even in the Internet age. And for consumers with a complex itinerary, a trusty travel agent is still the best way to arrange the most direct flights to and from the best airports.

Still, there's no denying the Internet's emergence as a powerful tool in researching and plotting travel time. The benefits of researching your trip online can be well worth the effort.

Last-minute specials, such as weekend deals or Internet-only fares, are offered by airlines to fill empty seats. Most of these are announced on Tuesday or Wednesday and must be purchased online. They are only valid for travel that weekend, but some can be booked weeks or months in advance. Sign up for weekly e-mail alerts at airline websites or check mega-sites that compile comprehensive lists of last-minute specials, such as **Smarter Living** (smarterliving.com) or **WebFlyer** (www.webflyer.com).

Some sites, such as Expedia.com, will send you **e-mail notification** when a cheap fare becomes available to your favorite destination. Some will also tell you when fares to a particular destination are lowest.

TRAVEL PLANNING & BOOKING SITES

Keep in mind that because several airlines are no longer willing to pay commissions on tickets sold by online travel agencies, these agencies may either add a $10 surcharge to your bill if you book on that carrier—or neglect to offer those carriers' schedules.

The list of sites below is selective, not comprehensive. Some sites will have evolved or disappeared by the time you read this.

- **Travelocity** (www.travelocity.com or www.frommers.travelocity.com) and **Expedia** (www.expedia.com) are among the most popular sites, each offering an excellent range of options. Travelers search by destination, dates, and cost.
- **Orbitz** (www.orbitz.com) is a popular site launched by United, Delta, Northwest, American, and Continental airlines. (Stay tuned: At press time, travel-agency associations were waging an antitrust battle against this site.)
- **Qixo** (www.qixo.com) is another powerful search engine that allows you to search for flights and accommodations from some 20 airline and travel-planning sites (such as Travelocity) at once. Qixo sorts results by price.
- **Priceline** (www.priceline.com) lets you "name your price" for airline tickets, hotel rooms, and rental cars. For airline tickets, you

can't say what time you want to fly—you have to accept any flight between 6am and 10pm on the dates you've selected, and you may have to make one or more stopovers. Tickets are nonrefundable, and no frequent-flier miles are awarded.

SMART E-SHOPPING

The savvy traveler is armed with insider information. Here are a few tips to help you navigate the Internet successfully and safely.

- **Know when sales start.** Last-minute deals may vanish in minutes. If you have a favorite booking site or airline, find out when last-minute deals are released to the public. (For example, Southwest's specials are posted every Tuesday at 12:01am central time.)
- **Shop around.** If you're looking for bargains, compare prices on different sites and airlines—and against a travel agent's best fare. Try a range of times and alternative airports before you make a purchase.
- **Stay secure.** Book only through secure sites (some airline sites are not secure). Look for a key icon (Netscape) or a padlock (Internet Explorer) at the bottom of your web browser before you enter credit card information or other personal data.
- **Avoid online auctions.** Sites that auction airline tickets and frequent-flier miles are the number-one perpetrators of Internet fraud, according to the National Consumers League.
- **Maintain a paper trail.** If you book an E-ticket, print out a confirmation, or write down your confirmation number, and keep it safe and accessible—or your trip could be a virtual one!

Tips Easy Internet Access Away from Home

There are a number of ways to get your e-mail on the Web, using any computer.

- Your **Internet Service Provider (ISP)** may have a Web-based interface that lets you access your e-mail on computers other than your own. Just find out how it works before you leave home. The major ISPs maintain local access numbers around the world so that you can go online by placing a local call. Check your ISP's website or call its toll-free number and ask how you can use your current account away from home, and how much it will cost. Also ask about the cost of the service before you leave home. If you're traveling outside the reach of your ISP, you may have to check the *Yellow Pages* in your destination to find a local ISP.
- You can open an account on a free, Web-based **e-mail provider** before you leave home, such as Microsoft's **Hotmail** (hotmail.com) or **Yahoo! Mail** (mail.yahoo.com). Your home ISP may be able to forward your home e-mail to the web-based account automatically.
- Check out **www.mail2web.com**. This amazing free service allows you to type in your regular e-mail address and password and retrieve your e-mail from any web browser, anywhere, so long as your home ISP hasn't blocked it with a firewall.
- Call your hotel in advance to see whether Internet connection is possible from your room.

ONLINE TRAVELER'S TOOLBOX

Veteran travelers usually carry some essential items to make their trips easier. Following is a selection of online tools to bookmark and use.

- **Visa ATM Locator** (www.visa.com), for locations of Plus ATMs worldwide, or **MasterCard ATM Locator** (www.mastercard.com), for locations of Cirrus ATMs worldwide.
- **Intellicast** (www.intellicast.com) and **Weather.com** (www.weather.com). These sites give weather forecasts for all 50 states and for cities around the world.
- **Mapquest** (www.mapquest.com). This best of the mapping sites lets you choose a specific address or destination, and in seconds, it will return a map and detailed directions.

- **Cybercafes.com** (www.cybercafes.com) or **Net Café Guide** (www.netcafeguide.com/mapindex.htm). Locate Internet cafes at hundreds of locations around the globe. Catch up on your e-mail and log onto the Web for a few dollars per hour.

TOP GENERAL SITES FOR FLORIDA

Following are some of the best websites for Florida and its major metropolitan regions. For specific attractions, you will find Web addresses throughout this book.

Beach Directory
www.beachdirectory.com
This guide to beaches along Florida's Gulf Coast includes a virtual tour, maps, recommendations from "Dr. Beach," and a guide to restaurants and lodgings.

FLA USA
www.flausa.com

A product of Florida's official tourism bureau, this extensive website includes information on attractions, beaches, golfing, and water sports, as well as airport information, weather, and maps. The beach guide is nicely organized by region, and there's advice on Florida's natural attractions in the Activities section.

Florida Association of Convention and Visitors Bureaus
www.facvb.org

Links to more than a dozen bureaus throughout the state. Most of the sites include information on attractions, dining, lodging, and shopping.

Florida State Parks
www8.myflorida.com/communities/learn/stateparks

Though the home page is awkwardly designed (this is a government site, after all), you can find parks by clicking on "Parks Map" or "Park Index." From there you can learn about camping at each park, including information on fees, nearby attractions, and facilities.

See Florida
www.see-florida.com

A nicely organized guide to theme parks, marine attractions, museums, boating, fishing, and much more. See Florida includes guides to dozens of Florida cities and has advice for first-time visitors to the Sunshine State.

MIAMI

CitySearch: Miami
www.miami.citysearch.com

Reviews and listings for Miami arts and entertainment, restaurants, shopping, and attractions. Click on the calendar link for events recommended by the editors.

Miami Herald
www.miami.com

Miami's leading news source can give you a sense of what's going on in the city, but don't expect extensive entertainment listings.

Miami New Times
www.miaminewtimes.com

Miami's leading alternative weekly includes features and listings for music, theater, film, and more.

Sun-Sentinel: Showtime
www.sun-sentinel.com/showtime

A nice roundup of music, theater, sports, and dining choices for South Florida with coverage of local festivals and events. For hard news and weather, see www.sun-sentinel.com.

Time Out: Miami
www.timeout.com/miami

This site features reviews and listings for attractions, entertainment, restaurants, hotels, and shopping throughout the city. It also includes categories for kids and for gay/lesbian activities. Time Out is a lively guide with a youthful approach but has features for everyone.

Tropicool Miami (Miami Convention & Visitors Bureau)
www.miamiandbeaches.com

A nice site to get an overview of Miami and its beckoning beaches. The content is boosterish, but it's still informative.

WALT DISNEY WORLD & GREATER ORLANDO

Go2Orlando
www.go2orlando.com

Detailed practical information on attractions, dining, lodging, shopping, beaches, and recreation. Produced in conjunction with the *Orlando Sentinel,* Go2Orlando is a clean, well-organized place to browse. Planning tools include restaurant and hotel searches by area and price.

Orlando.com Vacation Guide
www.orlando.com/vacation

A well-organized roundup of attractions, events, and tips for planning your Orlando vacation. You'll also find dining, shopping, and lodging guides and can book a room through the site. Other sections cover nightlife, kids' activities, and outdoor recreation.

Orlando Sentinel
www.orlandosentinel.com
Everything you'd expect from a big-city newspaper—the online calendar, which includes listings for the arts, dining, attractions, and sports, is especially useful for visitors.

Orlando Weekly
www.orlandoweekly.com
Cutting-edge reviews and recommendations for arts, movies, music, and much more from Orlando's alternative weekly newspaper.

TAMPA & ST. PETERSBURG

City of St. Petersburg
www.stpete.org
A city roundup of what's going on in St. Pete. Though it's intended primarily for locals, the site has a nice calendar of events.

St. Petersburg Times
www.sptimes.com
Click on the A-Z Index, which lists arts, entertainment, and local activities, such as a guide to baseball spring training.

Tampa Bay CitySearch
www.tampabay.citysearch.com
Reviews and listings for arts and entertainment, restaurants, shopping, and attractions. Click on the calendar for events recommended by the editors.

Tampa Bay Online
www.tbo.com
Honest reviews from the *Tampa Bay Tribune* on dining, entertainment, and more. Search music listings based on type of club or type of music or find restaurants near your hotel.

Tampa Tribune
www.tampatrib.com
Get up-to-date on happenings around town-entertainment links are at the bottom of the page.

KEY WEST

Discover: Key West
http://key-west.com
A well-rounded guide to Key West, including an events calendar and extensive listings for attractions, sightseeing and eco-tours, theater, and art galleries. You'll also find a dining guide, lodging options, and sections on fishing and shopping.

Gay Key West Travel Guide
www.gaykeywestfl.com
A guide to gay-friendly lodgings, restaurants, and clubs in Key West.

10 Getting Around

Having a car is the best and easiest way to see Florida's sights, or just to get to and from the beach. Public transportation is available only in the cities and larger towns, and even there it may provide infrequent or even inadequate service. When it comes to getting from one city to another, cars and planes are the ways to go.

BY PLANE
The commuter arms of **Continental** (© **800/525-0280;** www.flycontinental.com), **Delta** (© **800/221-1212;** www.delta.com), and **US Airways** (© **800/428-4322;** www.usairways.com) provide extensive service between Florida's major cities and towns. Fares for these short hops tend to be reasonable.

Cape Air (© **800/352-0714;** www.flycapeair.com) flies between Key West, Fort Myers, and Naples, which means you can avoid backtracking to Miami from Key West if you're touring the state. (You can also take a boat between Key West and Fort Myers Beach, Naples, or Marco Island during the winter months; see p. 377.)

Two new small airlines are now providing in-state connections to the Keys. **Discover Air** (© **888/596-9247;** www.discoverair.com) flies between Orlando and Key West and

Florida Driving Times & Distances

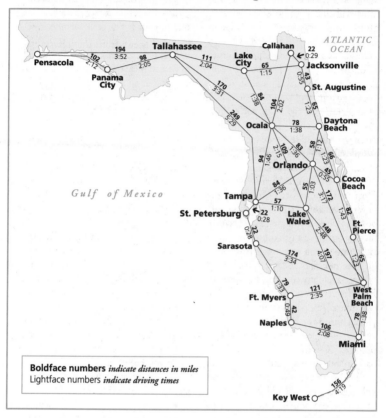

Pensacola • Panama City • Tallahassee • Lake City • Callahan • Jacksonville • St. Augustine • Ocala • Daytona Beach • Orlando • Cocoa Beach • Tampa • St. Petersburg • Lake Wales • Ft. Pierce • Sarasota • Ft. Myers • West Palm Beach • Naples • Miami • Key West

ATLANTIC OCEAN

Gulf of Mexico

Boldface numbers *indicate distances in miles*
Lightface numbers *indicate driving times*

Marathon, and **Paradise Aviation** (✆ **305/743-4222**) connects Fort Lauderdale with Marathon.

BY CAR

Jacksonville is about 350 miles (564km) north of Miami and 500 miles (805km) north of Key West, so don't underestimate how long it will take you to drive all the way down the state. The speed limit is either 65 miles per hour (105kmph) or 70 miles per hour (113kmph) on the rural interstate highways, so you can make good time between cities. Not so on U.S. 1, U.S. 17, U.S. 19, U.S. 41, and U.S. 301; although most have four lanes, these older highways tend to be

heavily congested, especially in built-up areas.

Every major car-rental company is represented here, including **Alamo** (✆ **800/327-9633**; www.goalamo. com), **Avis** (✆ **800/331-1212**; www.avis.com), **Budget** (✆ 800/527-0700; https://rent.drivebudget.com), **Dollar** (✆ 800/800-4000; www. dollarcar.com), **Enterprise** (✆ 800/325-8007; pickenterprise.com), **Hertz** (✆ 800/654-3131; www.hertz. com), **National** (✆ 800/227-7368; www.nationalcar.com), and **Thrifty** (✆ 800/367-2277; www.thrifty.com).

If you decide to rent a car, shop around and ask a lot of questions.

Reservations clerks are used to being asked for the lowest rate available, and most will find it in order to get your business. You may have to try different dates, different pickup and drop-off points, and different discount offers to find the best deal. It changes constantly. Also, if you're a member of any organization (AARP or AAA, for example), be sure to ask if you're entitled to discounts. It's not widely known, but members of **Costco Wholesale** stores get hefty discounts at Alamo, Avis, and Dollar.

Check the rental firms' websites. Most will automatically bring up the lowest available rate, and there are boxes to click if you are an association member or have a discount coupon or ID number. You can comparison shop on Internet sites such as **Travelocity** (www.travelocity.com) and **Microsoft Expedia** (www.expedia.com), which will make reservations for you once you've found the best deal.

State and local **taxes** will add as much as 20% to your final bill. You'll pay an additional $2.05 per day in statewide use tax, and local sales taxes will tack on at least 6% to the total, including the statewide use tax (the state is being sued over this tax-on-a-tax practice). Some airports add another 35¢ per day and as much as 10% in "recovery" fees. You can avoid the recovery fee by picking up your car in town rather than at the airport. Budget and Enterprise both have numerous rental locations away from the airports. But be sure to weigh the cost of transportation to and from your hotel against the amount of the fee.

Most of the companies pad their profits by selling **Loss/Damage Waiver** (LDW) insurance at $15 or more per day. Your automobile insurance carrier and credit-card companies may already provide coverage, so check with them before wasting your money on something you don't need.

Also, the rental companies will offer to refill your **gas** tank at "competitive" prices per gallon when you return. Gas is always less expensive in town, so fill up your vehicle on the way back to the airport if at all possible.

Competition is so fierce among Florida rental firms that most have now stopped charging **drop-off fees** if you pick up a car at one place and leave it at another. For example, I recently picked up a car at Tampa and dropped it off at Fort Myers for the same price I would have paid had I returned it to Tampa. Be sure to ask if there's a drop-off fee.

You must have a **valid credit card** (not a debit or check card) in your name, and most companies require you to be at least 25 years old to rent a car. Some also set maximum ages and may deny cars to anyone with a bad driving record. Ask about rental requirements and restrictions when you book in order to avoid problems when you get there.

Some packages are available that include airfare, accommodations, and a rental car with unlimited mileage. Compare these prices with the cost of booking airline tickets and renting a car separately to see if these offers are good deals.

BY TRAIN

You'll find that train travel isn't terribly feasible within Florida, and it's not much less expensive than flying, if at all. See "Getting There," earlier in this chapter, for Florida towns served by **Amtrak** (© **800/USA-RAIL;** www.amtrak.com).

BY BUS

See the "Essentials" and "Getting There" sections in the following chapters.

11 The Active Vacation Planner

Bird-watching, boating and sailing, camping, canoeing and kayaking, fishing, golfing, tennis—you name it, the Sunshine State has it. In fact, you'll find these activities almost everywhere you go in Florida. Of course, beach lovers and water-sports enthusiasts can indulge their passions almost anywhere along the state's lengthy coastlines. Merely head east or west, and you'll easily find plenty to do—or viewed another way, Florida's multitudinous water-sports operators will find you.

These and other activities are described in the outdoor activities sections of the following chapters, but here's a brief overview of some of the best places to move your muscles, with tips on how to get more detailed information.

The **Florida Sports Foundation,** 2390 Kerry Forest Pkwy., Suite 101, Tallahassee, FL 32309 (© **850/ 488-8347;** fax 850/922-0482; www. flasports.com), publishes free brochures, calendars, schedules, and guides to outdoor pursuits and spectator sports throughout Florida. I've noted some of its specific publications in the sections below.

For excellent color maps of state parks, campgrounds, canoe trails, aquatic preserves, caverns, and more, contact the **Florida Department of Environmental Protection,** Office of Communications, 3900 Commonwealth Blvd., Tallahassee, FL 32399 (© **850/488-2960;** www.dep.state. fl.us). Some of the department's publications are mentioned below.

ACTIVITIES A TO Z
BIKING & IN-LINE SKATING
Florida's relatively flat terrain makes it ideal for riding bikes and in-line skating. You can bike right into the **Everglades National Park** along the 38-mile-long (61km) Main Park Road, for example, and bike or skate from St. Petersburg to Tarpon Springs on the 47-mile-long (76km) converted railroad bed known as the **Pinellas Trail.** Many towns and cities have designated routes for cyclists, skaters, joggers, and walkers, such as the paved pathways running the length of Sanibel Island, the lovely Bayshore Boulevard in **Tampa,** and the bike lanes from downtown **Sarasota** out to St. Armands, Lido, and Longboat Keys. We've detailed all the many options in the following chapters.

BIRD-WATCHING With hundreds of both land- and sea-based species, Florida is one of America's best places for bird-watching—if you're not careful, pelicans will even steal your picnic lunch on the historic **Naples Pier.** The **J. N. ("Ding") Darling National Wildlife Refuge** is great for watching, and it shares Sanibel Island with luxury resorts and fine restaurants.

With its northeast Florida section now open, the **Great Florida Birding Trail** will eventually cover some 2,000 miles (3,220km) throughout the state. Fort Clinch State Park on Amelia Island and Merritt Island National Wildlife Refuge in Cape Canaveral are gateways to the northeast trail. Information is available from the Birding Trail Coordinator, Florida Fish & Wildlife Conservation Commission, 620 S. Meridian St., Tallahassee, FL 32399-1600 (© **850/922-0664;** fax 850/488-1961; www.floridabirding trail.com). You can download trail maps from their website.

Many of the state's wildlife preserves have gift shops that carry books about Florida's birds, including the *Florida Wildlife Viewing Guide,* in which authors Susan Cerulean and Ann Morrow profile 96 great parks, refuges, and preserves throughout the state. The guide is also available directly from the publisher, Falcon Press, at © **800/582-2665;** www.falconbooks.com.

BOATING & SAILING With some 1,350 miles (2,174km) of shoreline, it's not surprising that Florida is a boating and sailing mecca. In fact, you won't be anyplace near the water very long before you see flyers and other advertisements for rental boats and for cruises on sailboats. Many of them are mentioned in the following chapters.

The Moorings, the worldwide sailboat charter company, has its headquarters in Clearwater and its Florida yacht base nearby in St. Petersburg (© **800/437-7880** or 813/530-5424; www.moorings.com). From St. Pete, experienced sailors can take its bareboats as far as the Keys and the Dry Tortugas, out in the Gulf of Mexico.

Key West keeps gaining prominence as a world sailing capital. *Yachting* magazine sponsors the largest winter regatta in America here each January, and smaller events take place regularly.

Even if you've never hauled on a halyard, you can learn the art of sailing at **Steve and Doris Colgate's Offshore Sailing School,** headquartered at the South Seas Plantation Resort & Yacht Harbour on Captiva Island, with an outpost in St. Petersburg (www.offshore-sailing.com). The prestigious **Annapolis Sailing** has bases in St. Petersburg and on Marathon in the Keys (http://annapolissailing.com).

The free *Florida Boating & Fishing,* which has tips about safe boating in the state and is available from the **Florida Sports Foundation** (see the introduction to this section, above), is a treasure trove of regulations; locations of marinas, hotels, and resorts; marine products and services; and more, in magazine format.

CAMPING Florida is literally dotted with RV parks (if you own such a vehicle, it's the least-expensive way to spend your winters here). But for the best tent camping, look to Florida's national preserves and 110 state parks and recreation areas. Options range from luxury sites with hot-water showers and cable TV hookups to primitive island and beach camping with no facilities whatsoever.

Regular and primitive camping in **St. George Island State Park** near Apalachicola, in fact, is a birdwatcher's dream, and you'll be on one of the nation's most magnificent beaches. Equally great are the sands at **St. Andrews State Park** in Panama City Beach (with sites right beside the bay). Other top spots are **Fort DeSoto Park** in St. Pete Beach (more gorgeous bay-side sites), the remarkably preserved **Cayo Costa Island State Park** between Boca Grande and Captiva Island in Southwest Florida, **Canaveral National Seashore** near the Kennedy Space Center, **Anastasia State Park** in St. Augustine, **Fort Clinch State Park** on Amelia Island, and **Bill Baggs Cape Florida State Park** on Key Biscayne in Miami. Down in the Keys, the ocean-side sites in **Long Key State Park** are about as nice as it gets.

In all these popular campgrounds, reservations are essential, especially in the high seasons. All of Florida's state parks take bookings up to 11 months in advance.

The **Florida Department of Environmental Protection,** Division of Recreation and Parks, Mail Station 535, 3900 Commonwealth Blvd., Tallahassee, FL 32399-3000 (© **850/488-2960;** www.dep.state.fl.us), publishes an annual guide of tent and RV sites in Florida's state parks and recreation areas.

Pet owners note: Pets are permitted at some—but not all—state park beaches, campgrounds, and food service areas. Before bringing your animal, check with the department or with the individual parks to see if your pet will be allowed. And bring your rabies certificate, which is required.

For private campgrounds, the **Florida Association of RV Parks & Campgrounds,** 1340 Vickers Dr., Tallahassee, FL 32303 (✆ **850/ 562-7151;** fax 850/562-7179; www.floridacamping.com), issues an annual *Camp Florida* directory with locator maps and details about its member establishments throughout the state.

CANOEING & KAYAKING

Canoers and kayakers have almost limitless options here: picturesque rivers, sandy coastlines, marshes, mangroves, and gigantic Lake Okeechobee. Exceptional trails run through several parks and wildlife preserves, including **Everglades National Park,** the **J. N. ("Ding") Darling National Wildlife Refuge** on Sanibel Island, and the **Briggs Nature Center,** on the edge of the Everglades near Marco Island.

According to the Florida state legislature, however, the state's official "Canoe Capital" is the Panhandle town of **Milton,** on U.S. 90 near Pensacola. Up there, Blackwater River, Coldwater River, Sweetwater Creek, and Juniper Creek are perfect for tubing, rafting, and paddleboating, as well as canoeing and kayaking.

Another good venue is the waterways winding through the marshes between **Amelia Island** and the mainland.

Many conservation groups throughout the state offer half-day, full-day, and overnight canoe trips. For example, **The Conservancy of Naples** (✆ **239/262-0304;** www. conservancy.org) has a popular series of moonlight canoe trips through the mangroves, among other programs.

Based during the winter at Everglades City, on the park's western border, **North American Canoe Tours, Inc.** (✆ **239/695-4666** Nov–Apr, or 860/739-0791 May–Oct; www.evergladesadventures.com) offers weeklong guided canoe expeditions through the Everglades.

Thirty-six creek and river trails, covering 950 miles (1,530km) altogether, are itemized in the excellent free *Canoe Trails* booklet published by the **Florida Department of Environmental Protection,** Office of Communications, 3900 Commonwealth Blvd., Tallahassee, FL 32399 (✆ **850/488-2960;** www.dep.state. fl.us).

Specialized guidebooks include *A Canoeing and Kayaking Guide to the Streams of Florida:* Volume 1, *North Central Florida and Panhandle,* by Elizabeth F. Carter and John L. Eearch, and Volume 2, *Central and Southern Peninsula,* by Lou Glaros and Dough Sphar. Both are published by Menasha Ridge Press (www.menasha ridge.com).

ECO-ADVENTURES

If you don't want to do it yourself, you can observe Florida's flora and fauna on guided field expeditions—and contribute to conservation efforts while you're at it.

The **Sierra Club,** America's oldest and largest grassroots environmental organization, offers eco-adventures through its Florida chapters. Recent outings have included canoeing or kayaking through the Everglades, hiking the Florida Trail in America's southernmost national forest, camping on a barrier island, and exploring the sinkhole phenomenon in North Central Florida. You do have to be a Sierra Club member, but you can join at the time of the trip. Contact the club's national outings office at 85 Second St., Second Floor, San Francisco, CA 94105-3441 (✆ **415/ 977-5500;** www.sierraclub.org).

The Florida chapter of **The Nature Conservancy** has protected 578,000 acres of natural lands in Florida and presently owns and manages 36 preserves. For a small fee, you can join one of its field trips or work parties that take place periodically throughout the year; fees vary from year to year, event to event, so call for more information. Participants get a chance to learn about and even participate in the preservation of the ecosystem. For details of all the preserves and adventures, contact The Nature Conservancy, Florida Chapter, 222 S. Westmonte Dr., Suite 300, Altamonte Springs, FL 32714 (© **407/682-3664;** fax 407/682-3077; http://nature.org).

A nonprofit organization dedicated to environmental research, the **Earthwatch Institute,** 3 Clocktower Place, Suite 100 (P.O. Box 75), Maynard, MA 01754 (© **800/776-0188** or 617/926-8200; fax 617/926-8532; www.earthwatch.org), has excursions to survey dolphins and manatees around Sarasota and to monitor the well-being of the captive-raised whooping cranes that have been released in the wilds of Central Florida. Another research group, the **Oceanic Society,** Fort Mason Center, Building E, San Francisco, CA 94123 (© **800/326-7491** or 415/441-1106; fax 415/474-3395; www.oceanicsociety.org), also has Florida trips among its expeditions, including manatee monitoring in the Crystal River area north of Tampa.

FISHING In addition to the amberjack, bonito, grouper, mackerel, mahimahi, marlin, pompano, redfish, sailfish, snapper, snook, tarpon, tuna, and wahoo running offshore and in its inlets, Florida has countless miles of rivers and streams, plus about 30,000 lakes and springs stocked with more than 100 species of freshwater fish. Indeed, Floridians seem to fish everywhere: off canal banks and old bridges, from fishing piers and fishing fleets. You'll even see them standing alongside the Tamiami Trail (U.S. 41) that cuts across the Everglades—one eye on their line, the other watching for alligators.

We listed our favorite places to fish in chapter 1, but nearly every marina in Florida harbors charter boats. You don't have to pay them a small fortune to try your luck, for most ports also have party boats that take groups out to sea. You'll have lots of company, but their rates are reasonable, they provide the gear and bait, and you won't need a fishing license.

Anglers age 16 and older need fishing licenses for any other kind of saltwater or freshwater fishing, including lobstering and spearfishing. Licenses are sold at bait-and-tackle shops around the state.

The **Florida Department of Environmental Protection,** 3900 Commonwealth Blvd., Tallahassee, FL 32399-3000 (© **850/488-2960;** www.dep.state.fl.us), publishes the annual *Fishing Lines,* a free magazine with a wealth of information about fishing in Florida, including regulations and licensing requirements. It also distributes free brochures with annual freshwater and saltwater limits. And the **Florida Sports Foundation** (see the introduction to this section, above) publishes *Florida Fishing & Boating,* another treasure trove of information.

HIKING Although you won't be climbing any mountains in this relatively flat state, there are thousands of beautiful hiking trails in Florida. The ideal hiking months are October through April, when the weather is cool and dry and mosquitoes are less prominent. Like anywhere else, you'll find trails that are gentle and short and others that are challenging—some trails in the Everglades require you to wade waist-deep in water!

If you're venturing into the backcountry, watch out for gators, and don't ever try to feed them (or any wild animal). You risk getting bitten (they can't tell the difference between the food and your hand). You're also upsetting the balance of nature, since animals fed by humans lose their ability to find their own food. Most Florida snakes are harmless, but a few have deadly bites, so it's a good idea to avoid them all.

The **Florida Trail Association,** 5415 SW 13th St., Gainesville, FL 32608 (© **800/343-1882** or 352/378-8823; www.florida-trail.org), maintains a large percentage of the public trails in the state and puts out an excellent book packed with maps, details, and color photos.

For a copy of *Florida Trails,* which outlines the many options, contact Visit Florida (see "Visitor Information," earlier in this chapter). Another resource is *A Guide to Your National Scenic Trails,* Office of Greenways and Trails, Department of Environmental Protection, 3900 Commonwealth Blvd., Tallahassee, FL 32399 (© **850/488-2960;** www.dep.state.fl.us/gwt). You can also contact the office of **National Forests in Florida,** Woodcrest Office Park, 325 John Knox Rd., Suite F-100, Tallahassee, FL 32303 (© **850/942-9300;** www.southernregion.fs.fed.us/florida). And *Hiking Florida,* by M. Timothy O'Keefe (Falcon Press; www.falconbooks.com), details 132 hikes throughout the state, with maps and photos.

GOLF Florida is the unofficial golf capital of the United States—some would say the world—since the **World Golf Hall of Fame** is located near St. Augustine. This state-of-the-art museum and shrine is worth a brief visit even if you're not in love with the game.

One thing's for certain: Florida has more golf courses than any other state—more than 1,150 at last count and growing. We picked the best in chapter 1, but suffice it to say that you can tee off almost anytime there's daylight. The highest concentrations of excellent courses are in Southwest Florida around Naples and Fort Myers (more than 1,000 holes!), in the Orlando area (Disney alone has 99 holes open to the public), and in the Panhandle around Destin and Panama City Beach. It's a rare town in Florida that doesn't have a municipal golf course—even Key West has 18 great holes.

Greens fees are usually much lower at the municipal courses than at privately owned clubs. Whether public or private, greens fees tend to vary greatly depending on the time of year. You could pay $150 or more at a private course during the high season, but less than half that when the tourists are gone. The fee structures vary so much that it's best to call ahead and ask, and always reserve a tee time as far in advance as possible.

You can learn the game or hone your strokes at one of several excellent golf schools in the state. **David Ledbetter** has teaching facilities in Orlando and Naples, **Fred Griffin** is in charge of the Grand Cypress Academy of Golf at Grand Cypress Resort in Orlando, and you'll find **Jimmy Ballard**'s school at the Ocean Reef Club on Key Largo. The Westin Innisbrook Resort at Tarpon Springs has its **Innisbrook Golf Institute.** Amelia Island (near Jacksonville) is home to **Amelia Island Plantation Golf School.**

You can get information about most Florida courses, including current greens fees, and reserve tee times through **Tee Times USA,** P.O. Box 641, Flagler Beach, FL 32136 (© **800/374-8633,** 888/465-3567, or 904/439-0001; fax 904/439-0099; www.teetimesusa.com). This company also publishes a vacation guide that includes many stay-and-play golf packages.

Florida Golf, published by the **Florida Sports Foundation** (see the introduction to this section), lists every course in Florida. It's the state's official golf guide and is available from Visit Florida (see the "Visitor Information" section, earlier in this chapter).

Golfer's Guide magazine publishes monthly editions covering most regions of Florida; it is available free at all the local visitor centers and hotel lobbies, or you can contact the magazine at P.O. Box 5926, Hilton Head, SC 29938 (© **800/864-6101** or 843/842-7878; fax 843/842-5743; www.golfersguide.com). Northwest Florida is covered by *Gulf Coast Tee Time,* published by Tee Time LLC, 3 W. Garden St., Pensacola, FL 32501 (© **888/520-4300** or 850/435-4858; fax 850/435-7383; www.teetimeweb.com).

You can also get more information from the **Professional Golfers' Association (PGA),** 100 Ave. of the Champions, Palm Beach Gardens, FL 33418 (© **561/624-8400;** www.pga.com), or the **Ladies Professional Golf Association (LPGA),** 2570 Volusia Ave., Suite B, Daytona Beach, FL 32114 (© **904/254-6200;** www.lpga.com).

More than 700 courses are profiled in *Florida Golf Guide* by Jimmy Shacky (Open Roads Publishing; $19.95), available at bookstores.

SCUBA DIVING & SNORKELING Divers love the Keys, where you can see magnificent formations of tree-sized elkhorn coral and giant brain coral, as well as colorful sea fans and dozens of other varieties, sharing space with 300 or more species of rainbow-hued fish. Reef diving is good all the way from Key Largo to Key West, with plenty of tour operators, outfitters, and dive shops along the way. Particularly worthy are **John Pennekamp Coral Reef State Park** in Key Largo and **Looe Key National Marine Sanctuary** off Big Pine Key.

Skin Diver magazine picked Looe Key as the number-one dive spot in North America. Also, the clearest waters in which to view some of the 4,000 sunken ships along Florida's coast are in the Middle Keys and the waters between Key West and the Dry Tortugas. Snorkeling in the Keys is particularly fine between Islamorada and Marathon.

In Northwest Florida, the 100-fathom curve draws closer to the white, sandy Panhandle beaches than to any other spot on the Gulf of Mexico. It's too far north here for coral, but you can see brilliantly colored sponges and fish and, in Timber Hole, discover an undersea "petrified forest" of sunken planes, ships, and even a railroad car. And the battleship USS *Massachusetts* lies in 30 feet (9m) of water just 3 miles (5km) off Pensacola. Every beach town in Northwest Florida has dive shops to outfit, tour, or certify visitors.

In the Crystal River area, north of the St. Petersburg and Clearwater beaches, you can snorkel with the manatees as they bask in the warm spring waters of Kings Bay.

If you want to keep up with what's going on statewide, you can subscribe to *Florida Scuba News,* a monthly magazine published in Jacksonville (© **904/783-1610;** www.scubanews.com). You might also want to pick up a specialized guidebook. Some good ones include *Coral Reefs of Florida,* by Gilbert L. Voss (Pineapple Press; www.pineapplepress.com), and *The Diver's Guide to Florida and the Florida Keys,* by Jim Stachowicz (Windward Publishing).

TENNIS Year-round sunshine makes Florida great for tennis. There are some 7,700 places to play throughout the state, from municipal courts to exclusive resorts. Even some of the municipal facilities—Cambier Park Tennis Center in Naples leaps to mind—are equal to those at expensive resorts, and they're either free or close to it.

If you can afford it, you can learn from the best in Florida. **Nick Bollettieri** has sports academies in Bradenton. Safety Harbor Resort and Spa near St. Petersburg hosts the **Phil Green Tennis Program.** Amateurs can hobnob with the superstars at **ATP Tour International Headquarters** in Ponte Vedra Beach, near Jacksonville. **Mary Jo Fernandez** is affiliated with the **Arthur Ashe Tennis Center** at the Doral Golf Resort & Spa in Miami. And **Chris Evert, Robert Seguso,** and **Carling Basset** have their own center in Boca Raton.

The three hard courts and seven clay courts at the Key Biscayne Tennis Association, 6702 Crandon Blvd. (© **305/361-5263**), get crowded on weekends, since they're some of Miami's most beautiful. You'll play on the same courts as Lendl, Graf, Evert, McEnroe, and other greats; this is the venue for one of the world's biggest annual tennis events, the Nasdaq 100 Open (see p. 186). There's a pleasant, if limited, pro shop, plus many good pros. Only four courts are lit at night, but if you reserve at least 48 hours in advance, you can usually take your pick. They cost $6 per person per hour. The courts are open daily from 8am to 9pm.

Famous as the spot where Chris Evert got in her early serves, the **Jimmy Evert Tennis Center,** 701 NE 12th Ave. (off Sunrise Blvd.), Fort Lauderdale (© **954/828-5378**), has 18 clay and 3 hard courts (15 lighted). Her coach and father, James Evert, still teaches young players here, though he is very picky about whom he'll accept. Nonresidents of Fort Lauderdale pay $3.50 (singles) to $4.50 (doubles) per hour. Reservations are accepted after 2pm for the following day but cost an extra $3. Lights are also an extra $3 per hour and are available only for the clay courts.

Other top places to learn and play are **Amelia Island Plantation** on Amelia Island; **Colony Beach and Tennis Resort** on Longboat Key off Sarasota (which *Tennis* magazine picked as the number-two tennis resort in the nation); **Sanibel Harbour Resort & Spa** in Fort Myers, whose 5,500-seat stadium has hosted Davis Cup matches; **South Seas Plantation Resort & Yacht Harbour** on Captiva Island; and **The Registry Resort** in Naples.

12 Tips on Accommodations

Florida has such a vast array of accommodations—from rock-bottom roadside motels to some of the nation's finest resorts—that we can cover only the tip of the iceberg in this book. Whether you spend a pittance or a bundle depends on your budget and your tastes. But, to repeat a well-worn phrase, you can enjoy "champagne on a beer budget"—if you plan carefully.

The annual trip-planning guide published by the state's tourism promotion agency, *Visit Florida* (see "Visitor Information," earlier in this chapter), lists most hotels and motels in the state. It's particularly handy if you're taking your animal along, since it tells which accommodations accept pets.

Another excellent source is **Superior Small Lodgings** ✿, a national organization of quality hotels, motels, and inns. None of these properties has more than 75 rooms, and all have been inspected for cleanliness, quality, comfort, privacy, and safety. Contact the local tourist information offices for lists of members in their areas, or the **Florida Superior Small Lodging Association,** 1809 Silver Valley Court, Apopka, FL 32712 (© **407/880-1707;** fax 407/884-1301; www.SuperiorSmallLodging.com).

Many hotels and motels recommended in this book are members.

Inn Route, P.O. Box 6187, Palm Harbor, FL 34684 (© **800/524-1880;** fax 281/403-9335; www.florida-inns.com), publishes the *Inns of Florida,* which lists inns and bed-and-breakfasts throughout the state. Inn Route also inspects each property, thus ensuring the quality and cleanliness of its members.

At the inexpensive end, **Hostelling International/American Youth Hostels,** 735 15th St. NW, Suite 840, Washington, DC 20005 (© **202/783-6161;** www.hiayh.org), offers low-cost accommodations in Miami Beach, Key West, Florida City, Orlando, St. Augustine, and Clearwater Beach.

UNDERSTANDING HOTEL ROOM RATES

The rates quoted in this book are "rack" or "published" rates; that is, the highest regular rates charged by a hotel or motel at the time we researched this edition. Not long ago the rack rate was what you paid, unless you were part of a tour group or had purchased a vacation package. These days, however, most hotels give discounts to corporate travelers, government employees, seniors, automobile-club members, active-duty military personnel, and others. Most hotels don't advertise these discounted rates or even volunteer them at the front desk, so it's important to ask.

Computerized reservations systems also have permitted many larger properties to adjust their rates on an almost daily—if not hourly—basis, depending on how much business they anticipate having.

Many Florida hotels and motels offer weekly rates, which, as a general rule, will knock off the price of 1 night if you stay for 7.

Most also have free self-parking, but parking fees can run up the cost at some downtown and beachfront

hotels. We've indicated in the listings if a hotel or resort charges for parking; if no charge is given, parking is free.

TIPS FOR SAVING ON YOUR HOTEL ROOM

- **Don't be afraid to bargain.** Most rack rates include commissions of 10% to 25% for travel agents, which some hotels may be willing to reduce if you make your own reservations and haggle a bit. Always ask whether a room less expensive than the first one quoted is available, or whether any special rates apply to you. You may qualify for corporate, student, military, senior, or other discounts. Be sure to mention membership in AAA, AARP, frequent-flier programs, or trade unions, which may entitle you to special deals as well. Find out the hotel policy on children—do kids stay free in the room or is there a special rate?

- **Rely on a qualified professional.** Certain hotels give travel agents discounts in exchange for steering business their way, so if you're shy about bargaining, an agent may be better equipped to negotiate discounts for you.

- **Dial direct.** When booking a room in a chain hotel, compare the rates offered by the hotel's local line with that of the toll-free number. Also check with an agent and online. A hotel makes nothing on a room that stays empty, so the local hotel reservation desk may be willing to offer a special rate unavailable elsewhere.

- **Remember the law of supply and demand.** Resort hotels are most crowded and therefore most expensive on weekends, so discounts are usually available for midweek stays. Business hotels in downtown locations such as Tampa are busiest during the week, so you can expect discounts over the weekend. Avoid high-season

---

Tips Post 9/11 Discounts

In an effort to restore the state's tourism business in the wake of the September 11, 2001, terrorist attacks, Visit Florida is now offering special discounts on its website, www.flausa.com. Or you can call ℂ **888/5-FLA-USA** for more information.

---

stays whenever you can: planning your vacation just a week before or after official peak season can mean big savings.

- **Look into group or long-stay discounts.** If you come as part of a large group, you should be able to negotiate a bargain rate, since the hotel can then guarantee occupancy in a number of rooms. Likewise, if you're planning a long stay (at least 5 days), you might qualify for a discount. As a general rule, expect 1 night free after a 7-night stay.

- **Avoid excess charges.** When you book a room, ask whether the hotel charges for parking. Many hotels charge a fee just for dialing out on the phone in your room. Find out whether your hotel imposes a surcharge on local and long-distance calls. A pay phone, however inconvenient, may save you money, although many calling cards charge a fee when you use them on pay phones. Finally, ask about local taxes and service charges, which could increase the cost of a room by 25% or more.

- **Watch for coupons and advertised discounts.** Scan ads in your local Sunday newspaper travel section, an excellent source for up-to-the-minute hotel deals.

- **Consider a suite.** If you are traveling with your family or another couple, you can pack more people into a suite (which usually comes with a sofa bed), and thereby reduce your per-person rate. Remember that some places charge for extra guests.

- **Book an efficiency.** A room with a kitchenette allows you to shop for groceries and cook your own meals. This is a big money-saver, especially for families on long stays.

- Join hotel **frequent-visitor clubs,** even if you don't use them much. You'll be more likely to get upgrades and other perks.

- Many hotels offer **frequent-flier points.** Don't forget to ask for yours when you check in.

- **Investigate reservations services.** These outfits usually work as consolidators, buying up or reserving rooms in bulk, and then dealing them out to customers at a profit. You can get 10% to 50% off; but remember, these discounts apply to inflated rack rates that savvy travelers rarely end up paying. You may get a decent rate, but always call the hotel as well to see if you can do better.

Among the more reputable reservations services, offering both telephone and online bookings, are: **Accommodations Express** (ℂ 800/950-4685; www.accommodationsexpress.com); **Hotel Reservations Network** (ℂ 800/715-7666; www.hoteldiscounts.com or www.180096HOTEL.com); and **Quikbook** (ℂ **800/789-9887,** includes fax on demand service; www.quikbook.com). Online, try booking your hotel through **Frommers.com** (www.frommers.com). **Expedia** (www.expedia.com) features a "Travel Agent" that will also direct you to affordable lodgings.

CONDOMINIUMS, HOMES & COTTAGES

It may seem at first impression that many Florida beaches are lined with great walls of high-rise condominium buildings. That's not much of an overstatement, for the state literally has thousands upon thousands of condominium units. People actually live in many of them year-round, but others are for rent on a daily, weekly, or monthly basis. In addition, many private homes and cottages are for rent throughout Florida.

Be aware, however, that in Florida real estate and resort parlance, the word *villa* does not mean a luxurious house standing all by itself. Down here, "villa" means an apartment.

Some of the resorts listed in this book are actually condominium complexes operated as full-service hotels, but usually you'll have to do without such hotel amenities as on-site restaurants, room service, and even daily maid service. On the other hand, almost every condominium, home, and cottage has a fully equipped kitchen, and many have washers, dryers, and other such niceties of home, which means they can represent significant savings, especially if you're traveling with children or are sharing with another couple or family.

We have pointed out a few of the best condominium complexes in the "Where to Stay" sections of the following chapters, and we have named some of the **reputable real estate agencies** that have inventories of condominiums, private homes, and cottages to rent.

If you think a condominium will meet your needs, your best bet is to contact the rental agencies well in advance and request a brochure describing all the properties they represent, and their rates.

LANDING THE BEST ROOM

Somebody has to get the best room in the house. It might as well be you.

Always ask about a corner room. They're often larger and quieter, with more windows and light, and they often cost the same as standard rooms.

When you make your reservation, ask if the hotel is renovating; if it is, request a room away from the construction. Ask about no-smoking rooms, rooms with views, and rooms with twin, queen- or king-size beds. If you're a light sleeper, request a quiet room away from vending machines, elevators, restaurants, bars, and discos. Ask for one of the rooms that have been most recently renovated or redecorated. If you aren't happy with your room when you arrive, talk to the front desk. If they have another room, they may be willing to accommodate you. Join the hotel's frequent-visitor club; you may qualify for upgrades.

In resort areas, particularly in warm climates, there are some other questions to ask before you book a room:

- What's the view like? Cost-conscious travelers may be willing to pay less for a back room facing the parking lot, especially if they don't plan to spend much time in their room.
- Does the room have air-conditioning or just ceiling fans?
- Do the windows open?
- What is the noise level outside the room? If the climate is warm and nighttime entertainment takes place alfresco, you may want to find out when show time is over.
- What's included in the price? A so-called moderate hotel that charges for beach towels and chairs, and so on, may cost a lot more than a so-called expensive hotel that includes extras in the price.
- Is the hotel pool fresh or salt water? Is it heated?
- Are airport transfers included in the price?
- If it's off-season, will any facilities be shut down while you're there?

- If you're single, ask if there's a singles program. If it's off-season, inquire about the occupancy rate. (If you're with a partner and looking for quiet, an empty resort may be fine; but if you're single and looking for fun, you may want to find a place that's a little more bustling.)
- What programs are available for kids?
- How far is the room from the beach?
- What is the cancellation policy?

 ## FAST FACTS: **Florida**

American Express There are a number of American Express offices in Florida. Call Cardmember Services (℃ 800/528-4800; www.american express.com) for the location nearest you.

ATM Networks ATMs are as ubiquitous in Florida as the palm trees. Machines are found on nearly every street corner, main shopping area and, in most cases, supermarkets, and even in convenience stores.

Banks Banks are usually open Monday through Friday from 9am to 3 or 4pm, and most have automated teller machines (ATMs) for 24-hour banking. You won't have a problem finding a Cirrus or PLUS machine. See "Money," earlier in this chapter.

Emergencies To reach the police, ambulance, or fire department, dial ℃ 911 from any phone. No coins are needed. Emergency hot lines include **Crisis Intervention** (℃ **305/358-HELP** or 305/358-4357) and the **Poison Information Center** (℃ **800/282-3171**).

Liquor Laws You must be 21 to purchase or consume alcohol in Florida. This law is strictly enforced, so if you look young, carry some photo identification that gives your date of birth. Minors can usually enter bars where food is served but are not allowed to drink alcohol.

Newspapers/Magazines Most cities of any size have a local daily paper. The well-respected *Miami Herald* is generally available all over the state, with regional editions available in many areas. In the major cities, you can also find coin-operated boxes for *USA Today,* the *Wall Street Journal,* and the *New York Times.*

Safety Whenever you're traveling in an unfamiliar city, stay alert. Be aware of your immediate surroundings. Always lock your car doors and the trunk when your vehicle is unattended, and don't leave any valuables in sight. See "Insurance, Health & Safety" in section 5, earlier in this chapter for more information.

Taxes The Florida state sales tax is 6%. Many municipalities add 1% or more to that, and most levy a special tax on hotel and restaurant bills. In general, expect at least 9% to be added to your final hotel bill. There are also hefty taxes on rental cars here (see "Getting Around," earlier in this chapter).

Time The Florida peninsula observes Eastern Standard Time, but most of the Panhandle, west of the Apalachicola River, is on Central Standard Time, 1 hour behind the rest of the state.

Weather Hurricane season runs August through November. For an up-to-date recording of current weather conditions and forecast reports, call ℃ **305/229-4522.**

3

For International Visitors

by Bill Goodwin

Whether it's your first visit or your tenth, a trip to the United States may require an additional degree of planning. This chapter will provide you with essential information, helpful tips, and advice for the more common problems that some visitors encounter.

1 Preparing for Your Trip

ENTRY REQUIREMENTS

Immigration laws have been a hot political issue in the United States in recent years, and especially since the terrorist attacks of September 11, 2001, so it's wise to check at any U.S. embassy or consulate for current information and requirements. You can also plug into the U.S. State Department's Internet site at **www.state.gov**.

VISAS Canadians may enter the United States without passports or visas; you need only proof of residence.

The U.S. State Department has a **Visa Waiver Program** allowing citizens of certain countries to enter the United States without a visa for stays of up to 90 days. At press time these included Andorra, Australia, Austria, Belgium, Brunei, Denmark, Finland, France, Germany, Iceland, Ireland, Italy, Japan, Liechtenstein, Luxembourg, Monaco, the Netherlands, New Zealand, Norway, Portugal, San Marino, Singapore, Slovenia, Spain, Sweden, Switzerland, the United Kingdom, and Uruguay. Citizens of these countries need only a valid passport and a round-trip air or cruise ticket in their possession upon arrival. If they first enter the United States, they may also visit Mexico, Canada, Bermuda, and/or the Caribbean

islands and return to the United States without a visa. Canadian citizens may enter the United States without visas; they need only proof of residence.

If you're from any other country, you must have (1) a valid **passport** with an expiration date at least 6 months later than the scheduled end of your visit to the United States and (2) a **tourist visa,** which may be obtained without charge from the nearest U.S. consulate.

Obtaining a Visa To obtain a tourist visa, submit a completed application form with a 1½-inch-square photo and demonstrate binding ties to your residence abroad. If you cannot go in person, contact the nearest U.S. embassy or consulate for directions on applying by mail. Your travel agent or airline office may also be able to provide you with the visa application forms and instructions. The U.S. embassy or consulate where you apply will determine whether you receive a multiple- or single-entry visa and any restrictions regarding the length of your stay. This may take a few days or even weeks, so apply well in advance.

British subjects can obtain up-to-date visa information by calling the **U.S. Embassy Visa Information Line** (*C* **0891/200-290**) or the **London Passport Office** (*C* **0990/210-410** for recorded information).

Irish citizens can obtain up-to-date passport and visa information through the **Embassy of USA Dublin,** 42 Elgin Rd., Dublin 4, Ireland (© **353/ 1-668-8777**), or checking the visa website at www.usembassy.ie/ consulate/applications.html.

Australian citizens can obtain up-to-date passport and visa information by calling the **U.S. Embassy Canberra,** Moonah Place, Yarralumla, ACT 2600 (© **02/6214-5600**) or checking the website's visa page at www.usis-australia.gov/consular/ niv.html.

Citizens of **New Zealand** can obtain up-to-date passport and visa information by calling the **U.S. Embassy New Zealand,** 29 Fitzherbert Terr., Thorndon, Wellington, New Zealand (© **644/472-2068**), or getting the information directly from the website at http://usembassy.org.nz.

DRIVER'S LICENSES Foreign driver's licenses are generally recognized in the U.S., although you may want to get an international driver's license if your home license is not written in English.

MEDICAL REQUIREMENTS Unless you're arriving from an area known to be suffering from an epidemic (particularly cholera or yellow fever), inoculations or vaccinations are not required for entry into the United States. If you have a disease that requires treatment with narcotics or syringe-administered medications, carry a valid signed prescription from your physician to allay any suspicions that you may be smuggling narcotics (a serious offense that carries severe penalties in the U.S.).

For **HIV-positive visitors,** requirements for entering the United States are somewhat vague and change frequently. According to the latest publication of *HIV and Immigrants: A Manual for AIDS Service Providers,* the Immigration and Naturalization Service (INS) doesn't require a medical exam for entry into the United States, but INS officials may stop individuals because they look sick or because they are carrying AIDS/HIV medicine.

If an HIV-positive noncitizen applies for a non-immigrant visa, the question on the application regarding communicable diseases is tricky no matter which way it's answered. If the applicant checks "no," INS may deny the visa on the grounds that the applicant committed fraud. If the applicant checks "yes" or if INS suspects the person is HIV-positive, it will deny the visa unless the applicant asks for a special waiver for visitors. This waiver is for people visiting the United States for a short time, to attend a conference, for instance, to visit close relatives, or to receive medical treatment. It can be a confusing situation. For further up-to-the-minute information, contact the Centers for Disease Control's **National Center for HIV** (© **404/332-4559;** www.hivatis.org) or the **Gay Men's Health Crisis** (© **212/367-1000;** www.gmhc.org).

PASSPORT INFORMATION

Safeguard your passport in an inconspicuous, inaccessible place like a money belt. Make a copy of the critical pages, including the passport number, and store it in a safe place, separate from the passport itself. If you lose your passport, visit the nearest consulate of your native country as soon as possible for a replacement. Passport applications are downloadable from the Internet sites listed below.

Note that the International Civil Aviation Organization (ICAO) has recommended a policy requiring that *every* individual who travels by air have his or her own passport. In response, many countries are now requiring that children must be issued their own passport to travel internationally, where before those under 16 or so may have been allowed to travel on a parent or guardian's passport.

FOR RESIDENTS OF CANADA

You can pick up a passport application at one of 28 regional passport offices or most travel agencies. As of December 11, 2001, Canadian children who travel will need their own passport. However, if you hold a valid Canadian passport issued before December 11, 2001 that bears the name of your child, the passport remains valid for you and your child until it expires. Passports cost C$85 for those 16 years and older (valid 5 years), C$35 children 3 to 15 (valid 5 years), and C$20 children under 3 (valid for 3 years). Applications, which must be accompanied by two identical passport-sized photographs and proof of Canadian citizenship, are available at travel agencies throughout Canada or from the central **Passport Office, Department of Foreign Affairs and International Trade,** Ottawa, ON K1A 0G3 (© **800/567-6868;** www.dfait-maeci.gc.ca/passport). Processing takes 5 to 10 days if you apply in person, or about 3 weeks by mail.

FOR RESIDENTS OF THE UNITED KINGDOM

To pick up an application for a regular 10-year passport (the Visitor's Passport has been abolished), visit your nearest passport office, major post office, or travel agency. You can also contact the **London Passport Office** at © **0171/271-3000** or search its website at www.ukpa.gov.uk. Passports are £21 for adults and £11 for children under 16.

FOR RESIDENTS OF IRELAND

You can apply for a 10-year passport, costing 57€, at the **Passport Office,** Setanta Centre, Molesworth Street, Dublin 2 (© **01/671-1633;** www.irlgov.ie/iveagh). Those under age 18 and over 65 must apply for a 12€ 3-year passport. You can also apply at 1A South Mall, Cork (© **021/272-525)**

or over the counter at most main post offices.

FOR RESIDENTS OF AUSTRALIA

Apply at your local post office or passport office or search the government website at **www.dfat.gov.au/passports/.** Passports for adults are A$126 and for those under 18 are A$63.

FOR RESIDENTS OF NEW ZEALAND

You can pick up a passport application at any travel agency or Link Centre. For more info, contact the **Passport Office,** P.O. Box 805, Wellington (© **0800/225-050**). Passports for adults are NZ$80 and for those under 16 they're NZ$40.

CUSTOMS
WHAT YOU CAN BRING IN

Every visitor more than 21 years of age may bring in, free of duty, the following: (1) 1 liter of wine or hard liquor; (2) 200 cigarettes, 100 cigars (but not from Cuba), or 3 pounds of smoking tobacco; and (3) $100 worth of gifts. These exemptions are offered to travelers who spend at least 72 hours in the United States and who have not claimed them within the preceding 6 months. It is altogether forbidden to bring into the country foodstuffs (particularly fruit, cooked meats, and canned goods) and plants (vegetables, seeds, tropical plants, and the like). Foreign tourists may bring in or take out up to $10,000 in U.S. or foreign currency with no formalities; larger sums must be declared to U.S. Customs on entering or leaving, which includes filing form CM 4790. For more specific information regarding U.S. Customs, call your nearest U.S. embassy or consulate, or contact the **U.S. Customs** office at © **202/927-1770** or www.customs.ustreas.gov.

WHAT YOU CAN TAKE HOME

U.K. citizens returning from a non-EC country have a customs allowance of: 200 cigarettes; 50 cigars; 250 grams of smoking tobacco; 2 liters of still table wine; 1 liter of spirits or strong liqueurs (over 22% volume); 2 liters of fortified wine, sparkling wine, or other liqueurs; 60cc (ml) perfume; 250cc (ml) of toilet water; and £145 worth of all other goods, including gifts and souvenirs. People under 17 cannot have the tobacco or alcohol allowance. For more information, contact HM Customs & Excise, Passenger Enquiry Point, 2nd Floor Wayfarer House, Great South West Road, Feltham, Middlesex, TW14 8NP (℅ **0181/ 910-3744;** 44/181-910-3744 from outside the U.K.), or consult their website at www.open.gov.uk.

For a clear summary of **Canadian** rules, write for the booklet *I Declare,* issued by **Revenue Canada,** 2265 St. Laurent Blvd., Ottawa, ON K1G 4K3 (℅ **506/636-5064**). Canada allows its citizens a C$750 exemption, and you're allowed to bring back duty-free one carton of cigarettes, 1 can of tobacco, 40 imperial ounces of liquor, and 50 cigars. In addition, you're allowed to mail gifts to Canada valued at less than C$60 a day, provided they're unsolicited and don't contain alcohol or tobacco (write on the package "Unsolicited gift, under C$60 value"). All valuables should be declared on the Y-38 form before departure from Canada, including serial numbers of valuables you already own, such as expensive foreign cameras. *Note:* The $750 exemption can be used only once a year and only after an absence of 7 days.

The duty-free allowance in **Australia** is A$400 or, for those under 18, A$200. Personal property mailed back from the United States should be marked "Australian goods returned" to avoid payment of duty. Upon returning to Australia, citizens can bring in 250 cigarettes or 250 grams of loose tobacco, and 1,125ml of alcohol. If you're returning with valuable goods you already own, such as foreign-made cameras, you should file form B263. A helpful brochure, available from Australian consulates or Customs offices, is *Know Before You Go.* For more information, contact **Australian Customs Services,** GPO Box 8, Sydney NSW 2001 (℅ **02/9213-2000**).

The duty-free allowance for **New Zealand** is NZ$700. Citizens over 17 can bring in 200 cigarettes, or 50 cigars, or 250 grams of tobacco (or a mixture of all three if their combined weight doesn't exceed 250g); plus 4.5 liters of wine and beer, or 1.125 liters of liquor. New Zealand currency does not carry import or export restrictions. Fill out a certificate of export, listing the valuables you are taking out of the country; that way, you can bring them back without paying duty. Most questions are answered in a free pamphlet available at New Zealand consulates and Customs offices: *New Zealand Customs Guide for Travellers, Notice no. 4.* For more information, contact New Zealand Customs, 50 Anzac Ave., P.O. Box 29, Auckland (℅ **09/359-6655**).

HEALTH INSURANCE

Although it's not required of travelers, health insurance is highly recommended. Unlike many European countries, the United States does not usually offer free or low-cost medical care to its citizens or visitors. Doctors and hospitals are expensive, and in most cases will require advance payment or proof of coverage before they render their services. Policies can cover everything from the loss or theft of your baggage and trip cancellation to the guarantee of bail in case you're arrested. Good policies will also cover the costs of an accident, repatriation, or death. See "Insurance, Health & Safety" in chapter 2 for more information. Packages such as **Europ Assistance's "Worldwide Healthcare Plan"** are sold by European automobile clubs and travel agencies at attractive rates. **Worldwide Assistance Services**, Inc. (© **800/821-2828**; www.worldwideassistance.com) is the agent for Europ Assistance in the United States.

Though lack of health insurance may prevent you from being admitted to a hospital in nonemergencies, don't worry about being left on a street corner to die: The American way is to fix you now and bill the living daylights out of you later.

INSURANCE FOR BRITISH TRAVELERS Most big travel agents offer their own insurance and will probably try to sell you their package when you book a holiday. Think before you sign. **Britain's Consumers' Association** recommends that you insist on seeing the policy and reading the fine print before buying travel insurance. **The Association of British Insurers** (© **0171/600-3333**; www.abi.org.uk/) gives advice by phone and publishes *Holiday Insurance*, a free guide to policy provisions and prices. You might also shop around for better deals: Try **Columbus Direct** (© **0171/375-0011**; www.columbusdirect.net/) or, for students, **Campus Travel** (© **0171/730-2101**; www.campus travel.co.uk).

INSURANCE FOR CANADIAN TRAVELERS Canadians should check with their provincial health plan offices or call **Health Canada** (© **613/957-2991**; www.hc-sc.gc.ca/) to find out the extent of their coverage and what documentation and receipts they must take home in case they are treated in the United States.

MONEY

CURRENCY The U.S. monetary system is very simple: The most common **bills** are the $1 (colloquially, a "buck"), $5, $10, and $20 denominations. There are also $2 bills (seldom encountered), $50 bills, and $100 bills (the last two are usually not welcome as payment for small purchases). All the paper money was recently redesigned, making the famous faces adorning them disproportionately large. The old-style bills are still legal tender.

There are seven denominations of **coins:** 1¢ (1 cent, or a penny); 5¢ (5 cents, or a nickel); 10¢ (10 cents, or a dime); 25¢ (25 cents, or a quarter); 50¢ (50 cents, or a half dollar); the new gold "Sacagawea" coin worth $1; and, prized by collectors, the rare, older silver dollar.

Changing foreign currency in the United States is a hassle, so leave any currency other than U.S. dollars at home—it will prove more of a nuisance than it's worth. Even banks here may not want to change your home currency into U.S. dollars. The exceptions are the currency exchange desks in the Miami, Orlando, Tampa, and Fort Myers airports, and **Thomas Cook Foreign Exchange,** which changes foreign currency and sells commission-free foreign and U.S. traveler's checks, drafts, and wire transfers. Thomas Cook's Florida office is in Fort Lauderdale (© **800/287-7362**; www.us.thomas cook.com).

Traveler's checks denominated in U.S. dollars are readily accepted at most hotels, motels, restaurants, and large stores. Do not bring traveler's checks denominated in other currencies. Sometimes a passport or other photo identification is necessary. The three types of traveler's checks that are most widely recognized—and least likely to be denied—are **Visa, American Express,** and **Thomas Cook.** Be sure to record the numbers of the checks and keep that information in a safe place (not in your wallet or purse) in case they get lost or stolen.

American Express, Diners Club, Discover, MasterCard (EuroCard in Europe, Access in Britain, Chargex in Canada), and Visa (BarclayCard in

Britain) **credit and charge cards** are the most widely used form of payment in the United States. You should bring at least one with you—if for no other reason than to rent a car, since all rental companies require them.

Most **automated teller machines (ATMs),** located throughout Florida, will allow you to draw U.S. currency against your home bank and credit cards. When available, this is the easiest way to get U.S. dollars, and you get the bank's rate of exchange, normally better than you will receive at hotels and other businesses. Check with your bank before leaving home, and remember that you will need your personal identification number (PIN) to do so. See "Money," in chapter 2, for more information.

SAFETY
GENERAL SAFETY SUGGESTIONS
Although tourist areas are generally safe, U.S. urban areas tend to be less safe than those in Europe or Japan. You should always stay alert. This is particularly true of large American cities. If you're in doubt about which neighborhoods are safe, don't hesitate to make inquiries with the hotel front desk staff or the local tourist office.

Avoid deserted areas, especially at night, and don't go into public parks after dark unless there's a concert or similar occasion that will attract a crowd.

Avoid carrying valuables with you on the street, and keep expensive cameras or electronic equipment bagged or covered up when not in use. If you're using a map, try to consult it inconspicuously—or better yet, study it before you leave your room. Hold onto your pocketbook, and place your billfold in an inside pocket. In theaters, restaurants, and other public places, keep your possessions in sight.

Always lock your room door—don't assume that once you're inside the hotel you are automatically safe and no longer need to be aware of your surroundings. Hotels are open to the public, and in a large hotel, security may not be able to screen everyone who enters.

DRIVING SAFETY Driving safety is important too, especially given the highly publicized car-jackings of foreign tourists in Florida. Question your rental agency about personal safety and ask for a traveler-safety brochure when you pick up your car. Obtain written directions—or a map with the route clearly marked—from the agency showing how to get to your destination. (Many agencies now offer the option of renting a cellular phone for the duration of your car rental; check with the rental agent when you pick up the car.) And, if possible, arrive and depart during daylight hours.

If you drive off a highway and end up in a dodgy-looking neighborhood,

Speaking Your Language
You can call Visit Florida's 24-hour **tourist assistance hot line** (© 800/656-8777) if you need help with lost travel documents, directions, emergencies, or information about attractions, restaurants, and shopping anywhere in the state. Hot-line operators speak several languages, including Spanish, French, German, and Portuguese. The phone call is free.

In Orlando, **Walt Disney World** (© 407/2-DISNEY) has numerous services designed to meet the needs of foreign visitors, including personal translators and a special phone number (© 407/824-7900) to speak to someone in French, Spanish, German, and other languages.

leave the area as quickly as possible. If you have an accident, even on the highway, stay in your car with the doors locked until you assess the situation or until the police arrive. If you're bumped from behind on the street or are involved in a minor accident with no injuries, and the situation appears to be suspicious, motion to the other driver to follow you. Never get out of your car in such situations. Go directly to the nearest police precinct, well-lit service station, or 24-hour store. You may want to look into renting a cellphone on a short-term basis. One recommended wireless rental company is **InTouch USA** (② 800/872-7626; www.intouchusa.com).

Park in well-lit and well-traveled areas whenever possible. Always keep your car doors locked, whether the vehicle is attended or unattended. Never leave any packages or valuables in sight. If someone attempts to rob you or steal your car, don't try to resist the thief/carjacker. Report the incident to the police department immediately by calling ② **911.**

2 Getting to the U.S.

A number of U.S. airlines offer service from Europe and Latin America to Florida, including American, Delta, Northwest, and United (see "Getting There," in chapter 2). Many of the major international airlines, such as **British Airways** (www.british airways.com), **KLM Royal Dutch Airlines** (www.klm.com), and **Lufthansa** (www.lufthansa.com), also have direct flights from Europe to various Florida cities, either in their own planes or in conjunction with an American "partner" airline (Northwest/KLM, to name one such partnership). You can get here from Australia and New Zealand via **Air New Zealand** (www.airnz.com), **Qantas** (www.qantas.com), **American** (www.aa.com), and **United** (www.ual. com), with a change of planes in Los Angeles. Call the airlines' local offices or contact your travel agent, and be sure to ask about promotional fares and discounts.

From Great Britain, **Virgin Atlantic Airways** (② 800/662-8621 in the U.S., or 01/293-74-77-47 in the U.K.; www.virgin-atlantic.com) has attractive deals on its flights from London and Manchester to Miami and Orlando. From Germany, **LTU International Airways** (② 800/888-0200 in the U.S., 11/948-8466 in Germany; www.ltu.com) frequently has reduced fares to Miami, Orlando, and Fort Myers from Frankfurt, Munich, and Düsseldorf. From Johannesburg and Cape Town, **South African Airways** and **Delta Airlines** (www.delta.com) fly to Fort Lauderdale.

Canadians should check with **Air Canada** (② 800/776-3000; www.air canada.ca), which offers service from Toronto and Montreal to Miami, Tampa, West Palm Beach, Fort Lauderdale, and Fort Myers. Also ask your travel agent about **Air Transat** (② 800/470-1011; www.airtransat. com), which has wintertime charter flights to several Florida destinations.

AIRFARES Whichever airline you choose, always ask about **advance purchase excursion (APEX)** fares, which represent substantial savings over regular fares. Most require tickets to be bought 21 days prior to departure.

On the World Wide Web, the European Travel Network (ETN) operates a site at **www.discount-tickets.com**, which offers cut-rate prices on international airfares to the United States, accommodations, car rentals, and tours. Another site to click for current discount fares worldwide is **www.etn. nl/discount.htm#disco.**

IMMIGRATION & CUSTOMS CLEARANCE When you arrive in the U.S., getting through immigration control may take as long as 2 hours on

Travel Tip

Be sure to keep a copy of all your travel papers separate from your wallet or purse, and leave a copy with someone at home should you need it faxed in an emergency.

some days, especially summer weekends. Accordingly, you should make very generous allowances for delay in planning connections between international and domestic flights.

In contrast, travelers arriving by car or by rail from Canada will find border-crossing formalities to be more streamlined. And air travelers from Canada, Bermuda, and some places in the Caribbean can sometimes go through Customs and Immigration at the point of departure.

For further information, see "Getting There" in chapter 2.

3 Getting Around the U.S.

The United States is one of the world's largest countries, with vast distances separating many of its key sights. If you fly from Europe to New York, for example, you still have a trip of more than 1,350 miles (2,173km) to Miami. Accordingly, flying is the quickest and most comfortable way to get around the country.

BY PLANE   Some large airlines (for example, Northwest and Delta) offer travelers on their transatlantic or transpacific flights special discount tickets under the name **Visit USA,** allowing mostly one-way travel from one U.S. destination to another at very low prices. These discount tickets are not on sale in the United States and must be purchased abroad in conjunction with your international ticket. This system is the best, easiest, and fastest way to see the United States at a low cost. You should obtain information well in advance from your travel agent or the office of the airline concerned, since the conditions attached to these discount tickets can be changed without advance notice.

BY TRAIN   International visitors (excluding Canada) can also buy a **USA Railpass,** good for 15 or 30 days of unlimited travel on Amtrak (© **800/USA-RAIL;** www.amtrak. com). The pass is available through many foreign travel agents. Prices in 2002 for a 15-day pass were $295 off-peak, $440 peak; a 30-day pass costs $385 off-peak, $550 peak. With a foreign passport, you can also buy passes at some Amtrak offices in the United States, including locations in San Francisco, Los Angeles, Chicago, New York, Miami, Boston, and Washington, D.C. Reservations are generally required and should be made for each part of your trip as early as possible. Regional rail passes are also available.

BY BUS   Although bus travel is often the most economical form of public transit for short hops between U.S. cities, it can also be slow and uncomfortable—certainly not an option for everyone (particularly when Amtrak, which is far more luxurious, offers similar rates). **Greyhound/Trailways** (© **800/231-2222**), the sole nationwide bus line, offers an **International Ameripass** that must be purchased before coming to the United States, or by phone through the Greyhound International Office at the Port Authority Bus Terminal in New York City (© **212/971-0492**). The pass can be obtained from foreign travel agents and costs less than the domestic version. 2002

Important Note

In the United States, we drive on the **right side of the road** as in Europe, not on the left side as in the United Kingdom, Australia, New Zealand, and South Africa.

passes cost as follows: 4 days ($135), 7 days ($184), 10 days ($234), 15 days ($274), 21 days ($324), 30 days ($364), 45 days ($404), or 60 days ($494). You can get more info on the pass at www.greyhound.com, or by calling ✆ **212/971-0492** (14:00–21:00 GMT) and ✆ **402/330-8552** (all other times). In addition, special rates are available for seniors and students.

BY CAR   Unless you plan to spend the bulk of your vacation time in a city where walking is the best and easiest way to get around, the most cost-effective, convenient, and comfortable way to travel around the United States is by car. The interstate highway system connects cities and towns all over the country; in addition to these high-speed, limited-access roadways, there's an extensive network of federal, state, and local highways and roads. Some of the national car-rental companies include **Alamo** (✆ 800/327-9633; www.goalamo.com), **Avis** (✆ 800/ 331-1212; www.avis.com), **Budget**

(✆ 800/527-0700; https://rent. drivebudget.com), **Dollar** (✆ 800/ 800-4000; www.dollar.com), **Hertz** (✆ 800/654-3131; www.hertz.com), **National** (✆ 800/227-7368; www.nationalcar.com), and **Thrifty** (✆ 800/367-2277; www.thrifty.com).

If you plan to rent a car in the United States, you probably won't need the services of an additional automobile organization. If you're planning to buy or borrow a car, automobile-association membership is recommended. **AAA, the American Automobile Association** (✆ **800/ 222-4357**), is the country's largest auto club and supplies its members with maps, insurance, and, most important, emergency road service. The cost of joining runs from $63 for singles to $87 for two members, but if you're a member of a foreign auto club with reciprocal arrangements, you can enjoy free AAA service in America. See "Fast Facts: For the International Traveler," below, for more information.

4 Shopping Tips

The U.S. government charges very low duties when compared with the rest of the world, so you could get some excellent deals here on imported electronic goods, cameras, and clothing. Of course, it all depends on the value of your home currency versus the dollar, and how much duty you'll have to pay on your purchases when you get home.

Many computers and most other electronic equipment sold here use only 110- to 120-volt AC (60-cycle) electricity. You will need a transformer to use them at home if your power is

220 to 240 volts AC (50 cycles). Be sure to ask the salesperson if an item has a universal power adapter.

The national "discount" chain stores consistently offer some of our best shopping deals. For televisions, VCRs, radios, camcorders, computers, and other electronic goods, go to **Best Buy, Circuit City, Radio Shack,** or **The Wiz.** Best Buy also has a wide selection of music. **CompUSA, Computer City,** and **Micro Center** specialize in computer hardware, accessories, and software.

Our major department store chains are **Sears, Macy's, Saks Fifth Avenue, Lord & Taylor, Bloomingdale's,** and **JCPenney.** In Florida, you'll also find **Burdines, Jordan Marsh,** and **Dillard's** anchoring many shopping malls. You get real deals in department stores only during sales, when selected merchandise is marked down 25% or more. The **Marshall's** and **T.J. Maxx** chains carry name-brand clothing at department-store sale prices, but their stock tends to vary greatly from store to store.

Other popular sources for bargain shopping are **outlet malls,** in which manufacturers operate their own shops, selling directly to the consumer. Sometimes you can get very good buys at the outlets, especially when sales are going on. Most lingerie and china outlets have good prices when compared with those at department stores, but that's not necessarily the case with designer clothing. In addition, some manufacturers produce items of lesser quality so that they can charge less at their outlets, so inspect the quality of all merchandise carefully before buying. The main advantage to outlet malls is that if you are looking for a specific brand—Levi's jeans, for example—the company's outlet will have it.

You'll find national chain stores, department stores, and outlet malls throughout Florida. Many are listed under "Shopping" in the following chapters. You will also find listings for them in the local telephone directory.

SIZE CONVERSION CHART

Women's Clothing

American	4	6	8	10	12	14	16
French	34	36	38	40	42	44	46
British	6	8	10	12	14	16	18

Women's Shoes

American	5	6	7	8	9	10
French	36	37	38	39	40	41
British	4	5	6	7	8	9

Men's Suits

American	34	36	38	40	42	44	46	48
French	44	46	48	50	52	54	56	58
British	34	36	38	40	42	44	46	48

Men's Shirts

American	$14\frac{1}{2}$	15	$15\frac{1}{2}$	16	$16\frac{1}{2}$	17	$17\frac{1}{2}$
French	37	38	39	41	42	43	44
British	$14\frac{1}{2}$	15	$15\frac{1}{2}$	16	$16\frac{1}{2}$	17	$17\frac{1}{2}$

Men's Shoes

American	7	8	9	10	11	12	13
French	$39\frac{1}{2}$	41	42	43	$44\frac{1}{2}$	46	47
British	6	7	8	9	10	11	12

FAST FACTS: For the International Traveler

Automobile Organizations Auto clubs will supply maps, suggested routes, guidebooks, accident and bail-bond insurance, and emergency road service. The **American Automobile Association (AAA)** is the major auto club in the United States. If you belong to an auto club in your home country, inquire about AAA reciprocity before you leave. You may be able to join AAA even if you're not a member of a reciprocal club; to inquire, call AAA (© 800/222-4357; www.aaa.com). AAA is actually an organization of regional auto clubs; in Florida, look under "AAA Automobile Club South" in the White Pages of the telephone directory. AAA has a nationwide emergency road-service telephone number (© 800/AAA-HELP).

Automobile Rentals See "Getting Around," in chapter 2.

Currency & Currency Exchange See "Money," under "Preparing for Your Trip," earlier in this chapter.

Drinking Laws The legal age for purchase and consumption of alcoholic beverages is 21; proof of age is required and often requested at bars, nightclubs, and restaurants, so it's always a good idea to bring ID when you go out. On South Beach, in particular, the clubs and bars have become stricter since they raised the minimum age of entry from 18 to 21. Beer and wine can often be purchased in supermarkets, but liquor laws vary throughout the state.

Do not carry open containers of alcohol in your car or any public area that isn't zoned for alcohol consumption. The police can, and probably will, fine you on the spot. And nothing will ruin your trip faster than getting a citation for DUI ("driving under the influence"), so don't even think about driving while intoxicated.

Electricity Like Canada, the United States uses 110 to 120 volts AC (60 cycles), compared with 220 to 240 volts AC (50 cycles) in most of Europe, Australia, and New Zealand. If your small appliances use 220 to 240 volts, you'll need a 110-volt transformer and a plug adapter with two flat parallel pins to operate them here. Downward converters that change 220 to 240 volts to 110 to 120 volts are difficult to find in the United States, so bring one with you.

Embassies & Consulates All embassies are located in the nation's capital, Washington, D.C. Some consulates are located in Miami and are listed below. Travelers from other countries can get telephone numbers for their embassies and consulates by calling directory information in Washington, D.C. (© 202/555-1212).

In South Florida, the **Canadian Consulate** is located at 200 S. Bayshore Dr., Miami, FL 33131 (© 305/579-1600). The **British Consulate** is located at the Brickell Bay Tower, Suite 2110, 1001 S. Bayshore Dr., Coconut Grove, FL 33131 (© 305/374-1522). The **French Consulate** is located at 1 Biscayne Tower, Suite 1710, Miami, FL 33131 (© 305/372-9799); the **Italian Consulate** is located at 1200 Brickell Ave., Miami, FL 33131 (© 305/374-6322); the **Israeli Consulate** is located at 100 N. Biscayne Blvd., Miami, FL 33132 (© 305/925-9400); the **German Consulate** is located at 100 N. Biscayne Blvd., Suite 2200, Miami, FL 33132 (© 305/358-0290); the **Australian**

Consulate is located at 2525 SW Third Ave., Suite 208, Miami, FL 33129 (© 305/858-7633); and **Brazil's Consulate General** is located at 2601 S. Bayshore Dr., Suite 800, Coconut Grove, FL 33133 (© 305/285-6200).

Emergencies Call © **911** to report a fire, call the police, or get an ambulance anywhere in the United States. This is a toll-free call. (No coins are required at public telephones.)

If you encounter serious problems, contact the **Traveler's Aid Society International** (© **202/546-1127**; www.travelersaid.org) to help direct you to a local branch. This nationwide, nonprofit, social-service organization, geared to helping travelers in difficult straits, offers services that might include reuniting families separated while traveling, providing food and/or shelter to people stranded without cash, or even emotional counseling. If you're in trouble, seek them out.

Visit Florida, the state's tourist information agency, operates a 24-hour, multi-language **tourist assistance hot line** (© **800/656-8777**), which will give advice and information in case of an emergency.

Gasoline (Petrol) Petrol is known as gasoline (or simply "gas") in the United States, and petrol stations are known as both gas stations and service stations. Gasoline costs about half as much here as it does in Europe (about $1.55 per gallon or more), and taxes are already included in the printed price. One U.S. gallon equals 3.8 liters, or .85 Imperial gallons. A majority of gas stations in Florida are now actually convenience grocery stores with gas pumps outside. They do not service your automobile for you; all but a very few stations have self-service gas pumps.

Holidays Banks, government offices, post offices, and many stores, restaurants, and museums are closed on the following legal national holidays: January 1 (New Year's Day), the third Monday in January (Martin Luther King Jr. Day), the third Monday in February (Presidents Day, Washington's Birthday), the last Monday in May (Memorial Day), July 4 (Independence Day), the first Monday in September (Labor Day), the second Monday in October (Columbus Day), November 11 (Veterans' Day/Armistice Day), the last Thursday in November (Thanksgiving Day), and December 25 (Christmas). The Tuesday following the first Monday in November is Election Day and is a federal government holiday in presidential-election years (the next is in 2004).

Legal Aid The foreign tourist will probably never become involved with the American legal system. If you are "pulled over" for a minor driving infraction (for example, of the highway code, such as speeding), never attempt to pay the fine directly to a police officer; this could be construed as attempted bribery, a much more serious crime. Pay fines by mail, or directly into the hands of the clerk of the court. If accused of a more serious offense, say and do nothing before consulting a lawyer or your embassy or consulate. Here, the government must prove a person's guilt beyond a reasonable doubt, and everyone has the right to remain silent, whether he or she is suspected of a crime or actually arrested. If arrested, a person can make one telephone call to a party of his or her choice, and foreigners have a right to call their embassies or consulates.

Mail If you aren't sure what your address will be in the United States, mail can be sent to you, in your name, **c/o General Delivery** at the main post office of the city or region where you expect to be. You must pick up your mail in person and must produce proof of identity (driver's license, passport, and so on).

Generally to be found at intersections, **mailboxes** are blue with a red-and-white stripe and carry the inscription U.S. MAIL. If your mail is addressed to a U.S. destination, don't forget to add the five-digit postal code, or ZIP code, after the two-letter abbreviation of the state to which the mail is addressed (FL for Florida).

At press time, domestic postage rates were 23¢ for a postcard and 37¢ for a letter. For international mail, a first-class letter of up to one-half ounce costs 80¢ (60¢ to Canada and Mexico); a first-class postcard costs 70¢ (50¢ to Canada and Mexico); and a preprinted postal aerogramme costs 70¢.

Newspapers/Magazines All over Florida, you'll be able to purchase *USA Today*, our national daily, and the *Miami Herald*, one of the most highly respected dailies in the country. Every city has its own daily paper.

Taxes In the United States there is no value-added tax (VAT) or other indirect tax at the national level. However, every state, county, and city has the right to levy its own local tax on all purchases, including hotel and restaurant checks, airline tickets, and so on. For Florida's sales taxes, see "Fast Facts: Florida," in chapter 2.

Telephone, Telegraph & Fax The telephone system in the United States is run by private corporations, so rates, especially for long-distance service and operator-assisted calls, can vary widely. Generally, hotel surcharges on long-distance and local calls are astronomical, so you're usually better off using a **public pay telephone,** which you'll find clearly marked in most public buildings and private establishments as well as on the street. Convenience grocery stores and gas stations always have them. Many convenience groceries and packaging services sell **prepaid calling cards** in denominations up to $50; these can be the least-expensive way to call home. Many public phones at airports now accept American Express, MasterCard, and Visa credit cards. Local calls made from public pay phones in Florida cost 35¢.

Most **long-distance and international calls** can be dialed directly from any phone. For calls within the United States and to Canada, dial **1** followed by the area code and the seven-digit number. For other international calls, dial **011** followed by the country code, city code, and telephone number of the person you are calling.

Calls to area codes 800, 888, and 877 are toll-free. However, calls to numbers in area codes 700 and 900 (chat lines, bulletin boards, "dating" services, and so on) can be very expensive—usually a charge of 95¢ to $3 or more per minute, and they sometimes have minimum charges that can run as high as $15 or more.

For **collect (reversed-charge) calls** and for **person-to-person calls,** dial 0 (zero, *not* the letter O) followed by the area code and number you want; an operator will then come on the line, and you should specify that you are calling collect, or person-to-person, or both. If your operator-assisted call is international, ask for the overseas operator.

For local **directory assistance** ("information"), dial 411; for long-distance information, dial 1, then the appropriate area code and 555-1212.

Telegraph and telex services are provided primarily by Western Union (www.westernunion.com). You can bring your telegram into the nearest Western Union office (there are hundreds across the country) or dictate it over the phone (© **800/325-6000**). You can also quickly telegraph money, or have it telegraphed to you, over the Western Union system, but this service can cost as much as 15% to 25% of the amount sent.

Most hotels have **fax** machines available for guest use (be sure to ask about the charge to use one), and many hotel rooms are even wired for guests' fax machines. A less expensive way to send and receive faxes may be at stores such as **Mail Boxes Etc.** (© **800/789-4MBE**; www.mbe.com), a national chain of packing service shops (look in the Yellow Pages directory under "Packing Services"). Some Mail Boxes Etc. stores also have computers with Internet access for sending and receiving e-mail.

There are two kinds of telephone directories in the United States. The so-called **White Pages** list private and business subscribers in alphabetical order. The inside front cover lists emergency numbers for police, fire, ambulance, the Coast Guard, poison-control center, crime-victims hot line, and so on. The first few pages will tell you how to make long-distance and international calls, complete with country codes and area codes. Government numbers are usually found on pages printed on blue paper. Printed on yellow paper, the so-called **Yellow Pages** list all local services, businesses, industries, and churches and synagogues by type of activity, with an index at the front or back. The Yellow Pages also include city plans or detailed area maps, often showing postal ZIP codes and public-transportation routes.

Time The continental United States is divided into four **time zones:** Eastern Standard Time (EST), Central Standard Time (CST), Mountain Standard Time (MST), and Pacific Standard Time (PST). Alaska and Hawaii have their own zones. For example, noon in Miami (EST) is 11am in Pensacola (CST), 10am in Denver (MST), 9am in Los Angeles (PST), 8am in Anchorage (AST), and 7am in Honolulu (HST). Most of Florida observes Eastern Standard Time, though the Panhandle west of the Apalachicola River is on Central Standard Time (1 hour earlier than Tallahassee, Orlando, and Miami).

Daylight saving time is in effect from 2am on the first Sunday in April through 2am on the last Sunday in October. Daylight saving time moves the clock 1 hour ahead of standard time.

Tipping Tipping is so ingrained in the American way of life that the annual income tax of tip-earning service personnel is based on how much they should have received in light of their employers' gross revenues. Accordingly, they may have to pay tax on a tip you didn't actually give them.

Here are some rules of thumb:

In hotels, tip **bellhops** at least $1 per bag ($2–$3 if you have a lot of luggage) and tip the **chamber staff** $3 per day (more if you've left a disaster area for him or her to clean up, or if you're traveling with kids and/or pets). Tip the **doorman** or **concierge** only if he or she has provided you with some specific service (for example, calling a cab for you or obtaining difficult-to-get theater tickets). Tip the **valet parking attendant** $1 every time you get your car.

In restaurants, bars, and nightclubs, tip **service staff** 15% to 20% of the check, tip **bartenders** 10% to 15%, and tip **valet parking attendants** $1 per vehicle. Tip the **doorman** only if he has provided you with some specific service (such as calling a cab for you). Tipping is not expected in cafeterias and fast-food restaurants. Many restaurants on South Beach include a 15% tip in the check due to the enormous influx of European tourists who are not accustomed to tipping. Keep in mind that this amount is the *suggested* amount and can be adjusted, either higher or lower, depending on your assessment of the service provided. Because of this tipping-included policy, South Beach waitstaff are best known for their lax or inattentive service. Make sure to always read the bottom of your check to see if tipping is included. People tend to get ripped off because they assume the tip is not included.

Tip **cab drivers** 15% of the fare.

As for other service personnel, tip **skycaps** at airports at least $1 per bag and tip **hairdressers** and **barbers** 15% to 20%.

Tipping ushers at movies and theaters and tipping gas station attendants is not expected.

Toilets You won't find public toilets (euphemistically referred to here as "restrooms") on the streets in most U.S. cities, but they can be found in hotel lobbies, bars, restaurants, museums, libraries, department stores, railway and bus stations, and service stations. Note, however, that restaurants and bars in resorts or heavily visited areas may reserve their restrooms for the use of their patrons.

4

Getting to Know Miami

by Lesley Abravanel

There's much more to South Florida than the neon-hued nostalgia of *Miami Vice* and pink flamingos. In fact, what used to be a relatively sleepy beach vacation destination has awakened from its humid slumber, upped its tempo, and finally earned its place in the Palm Pilots of cutting-edge jetsetters worldwide. But don't be fooled by the hipper-than-thou, celebrity-drenched playground known as South Beach. While the chic elite do, indeed, flock to Miami's coolest enclave, it is surprisingly accessible to the average Joe, Jane, or José. For every Phillippe Starck–designed, bank-account-busting boutique hotel on South Beach, there's a kitschy, candy-coated Art Deco one that's much less taxing on the pockets. For each Pan-MediterAsian haute cuisinerie, there's always the down-home, no-nonsense Cuban bodega offering hearty food at ridiculously cheap prices.

Beyond the whole glitzy, *Access Hollywood*-meets-beach-blanket-bacchanalia-as-seen-on-TV, Miami has an endless number of sporting, cultural, and recreational activities to keep you entertained. Our sparkling beaches are beyond compare. Plus, there's excellent shopping and other nightlife activities that include ballet, theater, and opera.

Leave Miami, be it for the Keys, the Gold Coast, or the Treasure Coast, and you'll expose yourself not only to more UV rays, but to a world of cultural, historical, and sybaritic surprises where you can take in a spring baseball game, walk in the footsteps of Hemingway, get up close and personal with the area's sea life, soak up the serenity of unspoiled landscapes, and much more.

Forget what you've heard about South Florida being Heaven's Waiting Room. That slogan is as passé as the concept of Early Bird dinners (which you can still get—they just no longer define the region). In fact, according to some people, South Florida *is* heaven. So what are *you* waiting for?

1 Orientation

ARRIVING

Originally carved out of scrubland in 1928 by Pan American Airlines, **Miami International Airport (MIA)** has become second in the United States for international passenger traffic and tenth in the world for total passengers. Despite the heavy traffic, the airport is quite user-friendly and not as much of a hassle as you'd think. You can change money or use your ATM card at Nation's Bank of South Florida, located near the exit. Visitor information is available 24 hours a day at the **Miami International Airport Main Visitor Counter,** Concourse E, second level (© **305/876-7000**). Information is also available at **www.miami-airport.com**. Because MIA is the busiest airport in South Florida, travelers may want to consider flying into the less crowded **Fort Lauderdale–Hollywood**

International Airport (FLL) (✆ **954/359-1200**), which is closer to north Miami than MIA, or the **Palm Beach International Airport (PBI)** (✆ **561/ 471-7420**), which is about an hour and a half from Miami.

GETTING INTO TOWN

Miami International Airport is located about 6 miles (9.5km) west of downtown and about 10 miles (16km) from the beaches, so it's likely you can get from the plane to your hotel room in less than half an hour. Of course, if you're arriving from an international destination, it will take more time to go through Customs and Immigration.

BY CAR   All the major car-rental firms operate off-site branches reached via shuttles from the terminals. See "Getting Around," later in this chapter, for a list of major rental companies. Signs at the airport's exit clearly point the way to various parts of the city, but the car-rental firm should also give you directions to your destination. If you're arriving late at night, you might want to take a taxi to your hotel and have the car delivered to you the next day.

BY TAXI   Taxis line up in front of a dispatcher's desk outside the airport's arrivals terminals. Most cabs are metered, though some have flat rates to popular destinations. The fare should be about $20 to Coral Gables, $18 to downtown, and $24 to South Beach, plus tip, which should be at least 10% (add more for each bag the driver handles). Depending on traffic, the ride to Coral Gables or downtown takes about 15 to 20 minutes and to South Beach 20 to 25 minutes.

BY LIMO OR VAN   Group limousines (multipassenger vans) circle the arrivals area looking for fares. Destinations are posted on the front of each van, and a flat rate is charged for door-to-door service to the area marked.

  SuperShuttle (✆ **305/871-2000;** www.supershuttle.com) is one of the largest airport operators, charging between $10 and $20 per person for a ride within the county. Its vans operate 24 hours a day and accept American Express, MasterCard, and Visa. This is a cheaper alternative to a cab (if you are traveling alone or with one other person), but be prepared to be in the van for quite a while, as you may have to make several stops to drop passengers off before you reach your own destination. SuperShuttle also has begun service from Palm Beach International Airport to the surrounding communities. The door-to-door, shared-ride service operates from the airport to Stuart, Fort Pierce, Palm Beach, and Broward counties.

  Private limousine arrangements can be made in advance through your local travel agent. A one-way meet-and-greet service should cost about $50.

BY PUBLIC TRANSPORTATION   Public transportation in South Florida is a major hassle bordering on a nightmare. Painfully slow and unreliable, buses heading downtown leave the airport only once per hour (from the arrivals level), and connections are spotty at best. It could take about an hour and a half to get to South Beach. Journeys to downtown and Coral Gables are more direct. The fare is $1.25, plus an additional 25¢ for a transfer.

VISITOR INFORMATION

The most up-to-date information is provided by the **Greater Miami Convention and Visitor's Bureau,** 701 Brickell Ave., Suite 700, Miami, FL 33131 (✆ **800/ 933-8448** or 305/539-3000; fax 305/530-3113; www.tropicoolmiami.com).

  If you arrive at the Miami International Airport, you can pick up visitor information at the airport's main visitor counter on the second floor of Concourse E. It's open 24 hours a day.

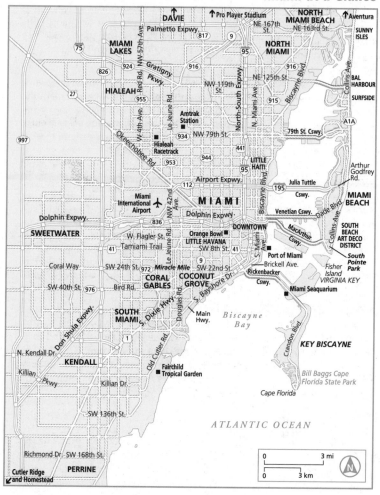

Always check local newspapers for special events during your visit. The city's only daily, the *Miami Herald,* is a good source for current-events listings, particularly the "Weekend" section in Friday's edition and the paper's entertainment weekly offshoot, *The Street,* available free every Friday in freestanding boxes anchored to city streets. Even better is the free weekly alternative paper, the *Miami New Times,* available in bright red boxes throughout the city.

Information on everything from dining to entertainment in Miami is available on the Internet at **www.miami.citysearch.com.**

CITY LAYOUT

Miami may seem confusing at first, but it quickly becomes easy to negotiate. The small cluster of buildings that makes up the downtown area is at the geographical heart of the city. In relation to downtown, the airport is northwest, the beaches are east, Coconut Grove is south, Coral Gables is west, and the rest of the city is north.

FINDING AN ADDRESS   Miami is divided into dozens of areas with official and unofficial boundaries. Street numbering in the city of Miami is fairly straightforward, but you must first be familiar with the numbering system. The mainland is divided into four sections (NE, NW, SE, and SW) by the intersection of Flagler Street and Miami Avenue. Flagler divides Miami from north to south and Miami Avenue divides the city from east to west. It's helpful to remember that avenues generally run north-south, while streets go east-west. Street numbers (1st St., 2nd St., and so forth) start from here and increase as you go farther out from this intersection, as do numbers of avenues, places, courts, terraces, and lanes. Streets in Hialeah are the exceptions to this pattern; they are listed separately in map indexes.

Getting around the barrier islands that make up Miami Beach is somewhat easier than moving around the mainland. Street numbering starts with 1st Street, near Miami Beach's southern tip, and increases to 192nd Street, in the northern part of Sunny Isles. Collins Avenue makes the entire journey, from head to toe of the island. As in the city of Miami, some streets in Miami Beach have numbers as well as names. When they are part of listings in this book, both name and number are given.

The numbered streets in Miami Beach are not the geographical equivalents of those on the mainland, but they are close. For example, the 79th Street Causeway runs into 71st Street on Miami Beach.

STREET MAPS   It's easy to get lost in sprawling Miami, so a reliable map is essential. The **Trakker Map of Miami** is a four-color accordion map that encompasses all of Dade County. The map is available at newsstands and shops throughout South Florida or online at **www.trakkermaps.com**.

Some maps of Miami list streets according to area, so you'll have to know which part of the city you are looking for before the street can be found. All the listings in this book include area information for this reason.

THE NEIGHBORHOODS IN BRIEF

South Beach—The Art Deco District South Beach's 10 miles (16km) of beach are alive with a frenetic, circus-like atmosphere and are center stage for a motley crew of characters, from eccentric locals, seniors, snowbirds, and college students to gender benders, celebrities, club kids, and curiosity-seekers: Individuality is as widely accepted on South Beach as Visa and Master-Card. Bolstered by a Caribbean-chic cafe society and a sexually charged, tragically hip nightlife, people-watching on South Beach (1st St.–23rd St.) is almost as good as a front-row seat at a Milan fashion show. Sure, the beautiful people do flock to South Beach, but the models aren't the only sights worth drooling over. The thriving Art Deco District within South Beach contains the largest concentration of Art Deco architecture in the world. In 1979, much of South Beach was listed in the National Register of Historic Places. The pastel-hued structures are supermodels in their own right—only these models improve with age.

Miami Beach In the fabulous '50s, Miami Beach was America's true Riviera. The stamping ground of choice for the Rat Pack and notorious mobsters such as Al Capone, its huge self-contained resort hotels were vacations unto themselves, providing a full day's worth of meals, activities, and entertainment. Then, in the 1960s and 1970s, people who fell in love with Miami began to buy apartments rather than rent hotel rooms. Tourism declined, the Rat Pack fled to Vegas, Capone disappeared, and many area hotels fell into disrepair.

However, since the late 1980s and South Beach's renaissance, Miami Beach (24th St. and up) has experienced a tide of revitalization. Huge beach hotels are finding their niche with new international tourist markets and are attracting large convention crowds. New generations of Americans are discovering the qualities that originally made Miami Beach so popular, and they are finding out that the sand and surf now come with a thriving international city.

Surfside, Bal Harbour, and **Sunny Isles** make up the north part of the beach (island). Hotels, motels, restaurants, and beaches line Collins Avenue and, with some outstanding exceptions, the farther north one goes, the cheaper lodging becomes. All told, excellent prices, location, and facilities make Surfside and Sunny Isles attractive places to stay, although they are still a little rough around the edges. However, a revitalization is in the works for these areas, and, while it's highly unlikely they will ever become as chic as South Beach, there is potential, especially as South Beach falls prey to the inevitable spoiler: commercialism. Keep in mind that beachfront properties are at a premium, so many of the area's moderately priced hotels have been converted to condominiums, leaving fewer and fewer affordable places to stay.

In exclusive and ritzy Bal Harbour, where well-paid police officers are instructed to ticket drivers who go above the 30 mph speed limit, few hotels remain amid the many beachfront condominium towers. Instead, fancy homes, tucked away on the bay, hide behind gated communities, and the Rodeo Drive of Miami (known as the Bal Harbour Shops) attracts shoppers who don't flinch at four-, five-, and six-figure price tags.

Note that **North Miami Beach,** a residential area near the Dade–Broward County line (north of 163rd St.; part of North Dade County), is a misnomer. It is actually northwest of Miami Beach, on the mainland, and has no beaches, though it does have some of Miami's better restaurants and shops. Located within North Miami Beach is the posh residential community of **Aventura,** best known for its high-priced condos, the Turnberry Isle Resort, and the Aventura Mall.

Note: South Beach, the historic Art Deco District, is treated as a separate neighborhood from Miami Beach.

Key Biscayne Miami's forested and secluded Key Biscayne is technically one of the first islands in the Florida Keys. However, this island is nothing like its southern neighbors. Located south of Miami Beach, off the shores of Coconut Grove, Key Biscayne is protected from the troubles of the mainland by the long Rickenbacker Causeway and its $1 toll.

Largely an exclusive residential community, with million-dollar homes and sweeping water views, Key Biscayne also offers visitors great public beaches, some top (read: pricey) resort hotels, and several good restaurants. Hobie Beach, adjacent to the causeway, is the city's premier spot for sailboarding and jet-skiing (see "Water Sports," in chapter 5). On the island's southern tip, Bill Baggs State Park has great beaches, bike paths, and dense forests for picnicking and partying.

Downtown Miami's downtown boasts one of the world's most beautiful cityscapes. Unfortunately, that's about all it offers. During the day, a vibrant community of students, businesspeople, and merchants makes its way through the bustling streets. Vendors sell fresh-cut pineapples and mangos while young consumers on shopping sprees lug bags and boxes. However, at night, downtown is desolate (except for NE 11th St, where there is a burgeoning nightlife scene) and not a place in which you'd want to get lost. The downtown area does have a mall (Bayside Marketplace, where many cruise passengers come to browse), some culture (Metro-Dade Cultural Center), and a few decent restaurants, as well as the new American Airlines Arena. Additionally, a downtown revitalization project is in the works, in which a cultural arts center, among other things, is expected to bring downtown back to life.

Design District With restaurants springing up between galleries and furniture stores galore, the Design District is, as locals say, the new South Beach, adding a touch of New York's SoHo to an area formerly known as downtown Miami's "Don't Go." The district, which is a hotbed for furniture-import companies, interior designers, architects, and more, has also become a player in Miami's ever-changing nightlife, with a cavernous nightclub/restaurant/production studio/recording studio/live music venue that has become hipster central for South Beach expatriates and artsy bohemian types. In anticipation of its growing popularity, the

district has also banded together to create an up-to-date website, www.designmiami.com, which includes a calendar of events and is chock-full of information. The district is loosely defined as the area bounded by NE 2nd Avenue, NE 5th Avenue East and West, and NW 36th Street to the South.

Biscayne Corridor From downtown near Bayside to the '70s, where trendy curio shops and upscale restaurants are slowly opening, Biscayne Boulevard is aspiring to reclaim itself as a safe thoroughfare where tourists can wine, dine, and shop. Previously known for sketchy, dilapidated 1950s- and '60s-era hotels that had fallen on hard times, residents fleeing the high prices of the beaches in search of affordable housing are renovating Biscayne block by block, trying to make this once-again famous boulevard worthy of a Sunday drive. With the trendy Design District immediately west of 36th and Biscayne by 2 blocks, there is hope for the area.

Little Havana If you've never been to Cuba, just visit this small section of Miami and you'll come pretty close. The sounds, tastes, and rhythms are very reminiscent of Cuba's capital city. Some even jokingly say you don't have to speak a word of English to live an independent life here—even street signs are in Spanish and English.

Cuban coffee shops, tailor and furniture stores, and inexpensive restaurants line "Calle Ocho" (pronounced *Ka*-yey *O*-choh), SW 8th Street, the region's main thoroughfare. Salsa and merengue beats ring loudly from old record stores while old men in *guayaberas* (loose fitting cotton or gauzy shirts, short sleeved, used to keep cool in Cuba and now a fashion statement in Miami) smoke cigars over their daily game of dominoes. The spotlight focused on the neighborhood during the Elián González situation in 2000, but the area was previously noted for the groups of artists and nocturnal types who have moved their galleries and performance spaces here, sparking a culturally charged neo-bohemian nightlife.

Coral Gables "The City Beautiful," created by George Merrick in the early 1920s, is one of Miami's first planned developments. This is not Levittown: The houses here were built in a Mediterranean style along lush, tree-lined streets that open onto beautifully carved plazas, many with centerpiece fountains. The best architectural examples of the era have Spanish-style tiled roofs and are built from Miami oolite, native limestone commonly called "coral rock." The Gables's European-flaired shopping and commerce center is home to many thriving corporations. Coral Gables also has landmark hotels, great golfing, upscale shopping, and some of the city's best restaurants, headed by world-renowned chefs.

Coconut Grove An arty, hippie hangout in the psychedelic '60s, Coconut Grove has given way from swirls of tie-dyes to the uniform color schemes of the Gap. Chain stores, theme restaurants, a megaplex, and bars galore make Coconut Grove a commercial success, but this gentrification has pushed most alternative types out. The intersection of Grand Avenue, Main Highway, and McFarlane Road pierces the area's heart. Right in the center of it all is CocoWalk and the Shops at Mayfair, filled with boutiques, eateries, and bars. Sidewalks here are often crowded, especially at night, when University of Miami students who frequent this adopted college town come out to play.

Southern Miami–Dade County To locals, South Miami is both a specific area, southwest of Coral Gables, and a general region that encompasses all of southern Dade County and includes Kendall, Perrine, Cutler Ridge, and Homestead. For the purposes of clarity, this book has grouped all these southern suburbs under the rubric "Southern Miami–Dade County." Similar attributes unite the communities: They are heavily residential and packed with strip malls amidst a few remaining plots of farmland. Tourists don't usually stay in these parts, unless they are on their way to the Everglades or the Keys. However, Southern Miami–Dade County contains many of the city's top attractions (see chapter 5), meaning that you're likely to spend some time here.

2 Getting Around

Officially, Dade County has opted for a "unified, multimodal transportation network," which basically means you can get around the city by train, bus, and taxi. However, in practice, the network doesn't work very well. Things may improve when the city completes its transportation center in 2005, but until then, unless you are going from downtown Miami to a not-too-distant spot, you are better off in a rental car or taxi.

With the exception of downtown Coconut Grove and South Beach, Miami is not a walker's city. Because it is so spread out, most attractions are too far apart to make walking between them feasible. In fact, most Miamians are so used to driving that they do so even when going just a few blocks.

BY PUBLIC TRANSPORTATION

BY RAIL   Two rail lines, operated by the **Metro-Dade Transit Agency** (© **305/770-3131** for information; www.co.miami-dade.fl.us/mdta/), run in concert with each other.

Metrorail, the city's modern high-speed commuter train, is a 21-mile (34km) elevated line that travels north-south, between downtown Miami and the southern suburbs. Locals like to refer to this semi-useless rail system as Metro*fail.* If you are staying in Coral Gables or Coconut Grove, you can park your car at a nearby station and ride the rails downtown. However, that's about it. There are plans to extend the system to service Miami International Airport, but until those tracks are built, these trains don't go most places tourists go, with the exception of Vizcaya in Coconut Grove. Metrorail operates daily from about 6am to midnight. The fare is $1.25.

Metromover, a 4½-mile (6.5km) elevated line, circles the downtown area and connects with Metrorail at the Government Center stop. This is a good way to get to Bayside (a waterfront marketplace; see p. 193) if you don't have a car. Riding on rubber tires, the single-car train winds past many of the area's most important attractions and shopping and business districts. You may not go very far, but you will get a beautiful perspective from the towering height of the suspended rails. System hours are daily from about 6am to midnight. The fare is 25¢.

BY BUS   Miami's suburban layout is not conducive to getting around by bus. Lines operate and maps are available, but instead of getting to know the city, you'll find that relying on bus transportation will acquaint you only with how it feels to wait at bus stops. In short, a bus ride in Miami is grueling. You can get a bus map by mail, either from the Greater Miami Convention and Visitor's Bureau (see "Visitor Information," earlier in this chapter) or by writing the Metro-Dade Transit System, 3300 NW 32nd Ave., Miami, FL 33142. In Miami, call © **305/770-3131** for public-transit information. The fare is $1.25.

BY CAR

Tales circulate about vacationers who have visited Miami without a car, but they are very few indeed. If you are counting on exploring the city, even to a modest degree, a car is essential. Miami's restaurants, hotels, and attractions are far from one another, so any other form of transportation is relatively impractical. You won't need a car, however, if you are spending your entire vacation at a resort, are traveling directly to the Port of Miami for a cruise, or are here for a short stay centered in one area of the city, such as South Beach, where everything is within walking distance and parking is a costly nightmare.

When driving across a causeway or through downtown, allow extra time to reach your destination because of frequent drawbridge openings. Some bridges open about every half-hour for large sailing vessels to make their way through the wide bays and canals that crisscross the city, stalling traffic for several minutes.

RENTALS   It seems as though every car-rental company, big and small, has at least one office in Miami. Consequently, the city is one of the cheapest places in the world to rent a car. Many firms regularly advertise prices in the neighborhood of $140 per week for their economy cars. You should also check with the airline you have chosen to get to Miami: There are often special discounts when you book a flight and reserve your rental car simultaneously. A minimum age, generally 25, is usually required of renters, while some rental agencies have also set maximum ages! A national car-rental broker, **Car Rental Referral Service** (© 800/404-4482), can often find companies willing to rent to drivers between the ages of 21 and 24 and can also get discounts from major companies as well as some regional ones.

National car-rental companies with toll-free numbers include **Alamo** (© 800/327-9633), **Avis** (© 800/331-1212), **Budget** (© 800/527-0700), **Dollar** (© 800/800-4000 or 800/327-7607), **Hertz** (© 800/654-3131), **National** (© 800/328-4567), and **Thrifty** (© 800/367-2277). One excellent company that has offices in every conceivable part of town and offers extremely competitive rates is **Enterprise** (© 800/325-8007). Call around and comparison-shop—car-rental prices can fluctuate more than airfares. For information on car-rental insurance, see "Getting There," in chapter 2.

Many car-rental companies also offer cellular phones or electronic map rentals. It might be wise to opt for these additional safety features (the phone will definitely come in handy if you get lost), although the cost can be exorbitant.

Finally, think about splurging on a convertible (at most companies, the price for convertibles is approximately 20% more). Not only are convertibles one of the best ways to see the beautiful surroundings, but they're also an ideal way to perfect a tan!

PARKING   Always keep plenty of quarters on hand to feed hungry meters. Or, on Miami Beach, stop by the chamber of commerce at 1920 Meridian Ave. or any Publix grocery store to buy a magnetic **parking card** in denominations of $10, $20, or $25. Parking is usually plentiful (except on South Beach and Coconut Grove), but when it's not, be careful: Fines for illegal parking can be stiff, starting at $18 for an expired meter and going way up from there.

In addition to parking garages, valet services are commonplace and often used. Expect to pay from $5 to $15 for parking in Coconut Grove and on South Beach's busy weekend nights.

BY TAXI

If you're not planning on traveling much within the city, an occasional taxi is a good alternative to renting a car. If you plan on spending your vacation within the confines of South Beach's Art Deco District, you might also want to avoid the parking hassles that come with renting your own car. Taxi meters start at $1.50 for the first quarter-mile and 25¢ for each additional one-eighth mile. There are standard flat-rate charges for frequently traveled routes—for example, Miami Beach's Convention Center to Coconut Grove will cost about $16.

Major cab companies include **Metro** (© 305/888-8888), **Yellow** (© 305/444-4444), and, on Miami Beach, **Central** (© 305/532-5555).

BY BIKE

Miami is a biker's paradise, especially on Miami Beach, where the hard-packed sand and boardwalks make it an easy and scenic route. However, unless you are a former New York City bike messenger, you won't want to use a bicycle as your main means of transportation.

For more information on bicycles, including where to rent the best ones, see chapter 5, "What to See & Do in Miami."

FAST FACTS: **Miami**

Airport See "Orientation," earlier in this chapter.

American Express You'll find American Express offices in downtown Miami at 100 N. Biscayne Blvd. (© **305/358-7350**); 9700 Collins Ave., Bal Harbour (© **305/865-5959**); and 32 Miracle Mile, Coral Gables (© **305/ 446-3381**). Offices are open weekdays from 9am to 5:30pm and Saturday from 9am to 5pm. To report lost or stolen traveler's checks, call © **800/ 221-7282.**

Area Code The original area code for Miami and all of Dade County was 305. That is still the code for older phone numbers, but all phone numbers assigned since July 1998 have the area code 786 (SUN). For all local calls, even if you're just calling across the street, you must dial the area code (305 or 786) first. Even though the Keys still share the Dade County area code of 305, calls to there from Miami are considered long distance and must be preceded by 1-305. (Within the Keys, simply dial the seven-digit number.) The area code for Fort Lauderdale is 954; for Palm Beach, Boca Raton, Vero Beach, and Port St. Lucie, it's 561.

Business Hours Banking hours vary, but most banks are open weekdays from 9am to 3pm. Several stay open until 5pm or so at least 1 day during the week, and many banks feature automated teller machines (ATMs) for 24-hour banking. Most stores are open daily from 10am to 6pm; however, there are many exceptions (noted in "Shopping," in chapter 5). As far as business offices are concerned, Miami is generally a 9-to-5 town.

Car Rentals See "Getting Around," above.

Climate See "When to Go" in chapter 2.

Dentists **A&E Dental,** 11400 N. Kendall Dr., Mega Bank Building (© **305/ 271-7777**), offers round-the-clock care and accepts MasterCard and Visa.

Doctors In an emergency, call an ambulance by dialing © **911** from any phone. The Dade County Medical Association sponsors a **Physician Referral Service** (© **305/324-8717**), weekdays from 9am to 5pm. **Health South Doctors' Hospital,** 5000 University Dr., Coral Gables (© **305/666-2111**), is a 285-bed acute-care hospital with a 24-hour physician-staffed emergency department.

Drugstores See "Pharmacies," below.

Embassies & Consulates See the "Fast Facts" section in chapter 3.

Emergencies To reach the police, ambulance, or fire department, dial © **911** from any phone. No coins are needed. Emergency hot lines include **Crisis Intervention** (© **305/358-HELP** or 305/358-4357) and the **Poison Information Center** (© **800/282-3171**).

Eyeglasses **Pearle Vision Center,** 7901 Biscayne Blvd. (© **305/754-5144**), can usually fill prescriptions in about an hour.

Hospitals See "Doctors," above.

Information See "Visitor Information," earlier in this chapter.

Liquor Laws Only adults 21 or older may legally purchase or consume alcohol in the state of Florida. Minors are usually permitted in bars, as long as the bars also serve food. Liquor laws are strictly enforced; if you look young, carry identification. Beer and wine are sold in most super-markets and convenience stores. The city of Miami's liquor stores are closed on Sundays. Liquor stores in the city of Miami Beach are open all week.

Lost Property If you lost something at the airport, call the **Airport Lost and Found** office (℗ 305/876-7377). If you lost something on the bus, Metrorail, or Metromover, call **Metro-Dade Transit Agency** (℗ 305/770-3131). If you lost something anywhere else, phone the **Dade County Police Lost and Found** (℗ 305/375-3366). You may also want to fill out a police report for insurance purposes.

Luggage Storage/Lockers In addition to the baggage check at Miami International Airport, most hotels offer luggage-storage facilities. If you are taking a cruise from the Port of Miami (see "Cruises & Other Caribbean Getaways" in chapter 5), bags can be stored in your ship's departure terminal.

Newspapers/Magazines The **Miami Herald** is the city's only English-lan-guage daily. It is especially known for its extensive Latin American cover-age and has a decent Friday "Weekend" entertainment guide. The most respected alternative weekly is the giveaway tabloid called **New Times,** which contains up-to-date listings and reviews of food, films, theater, music, and whatever else is happening in town. Also free, if you can find it, is **Ocean Drive,** an oversize glossy magazine that's limited on text (no literary value) and heavy on ads and society photos. It's what you should read if you want to know who's who and where to go for fun; it's avail-able at a number of chic South Beach boutiques and restaurants. It is also available on newsstands.

For a large selection of foreign-language newspapers and magazines, check with any of the large bookstores or try **News Café** at 800 Ocean Dr., South Beach (℗ 305/538-6397), or in Coconut Grove at 2901 Florida Ave. (℗ 305/774-6397). Adjacent to the **Van Dyke Café,** 846 Lincoln Rd., South Beach (℗ 305/534-3600), is a fantastic newsstand with magazines and newspapers from all over the world. Also check out **Eddie's Normandy,** 1096 Normandy Dr., Miami Beach (℗ 305/866-2026), and **Worldwide News,** 1629 NE 163rd St., North Miami Beach (℗ 305/940-4090).

Pharmacies **Walgreens Pharmacy** has dozens of locations all over town, including 8550 Coral Way (℗ 305/221-9271), in Coral Gables; 1845 Alton Rd. (℗ 305/531-8868), in South Beach; and 6700 Collins Ave. (℗ 305/861-6742), in Miami Beach. The branch at 5731 Bird Rd. at SW 40th Street (℗ 305/666-0757) is open 24 hours, as is **Eckerd Drugs,** 1825 Miami Gar-dens Dr. NE, at 185th Street, North Miami Beach (℗ 305/932-5740).

Photographic Needs **One Hour Photo,** in the Bayside Marketplace (℗ 305/377-FOTO), is pricey (about $17 to develop and print a roll of 36 pictures), but they're open Monday through Saturday from 10am to 10pm and Sunday from noon to 8pm. Walgreens or Eckerd (see above, under "Pharmacies") will develop film for the next day for about $6 or $7.

Police For emergencies, dial ℗ 911 from any phone. No coins are needed. For other matters, call ℗ 305/595-6263.

Post Office The **Main Post Office,** 2200 Milam Dairy Rd., Miami, FL 33152 ((℡ 305/639-4280), is located west of Miami International Airport. Conveniently located post offices include 1300 Washington Ave. in South Beach, and 3191 Grand Ave. in Coconut Grove. There is one central number for all post offices: ℡ 800/275-8777.

Radio On the AM dial, 610 (WIOD), 790 (WNWS), 1230 (WJNO), and 1340 (WPBR) are all talk. There is no all-news station in town, although 940 (WINZ) gives traffic updates and headline news in between its talk shows. WDBF (1420) is a good big-band station and WPBG (1290) features golden oldies. Switching to the FM dial, the two most popular R&B stations are WEDR/99 Jams (99.1) and Hot 105 (105.1). The best rock stations on the FM dial are WZTA (94.9), WBGG/Big 106 (105.9), and the progressive college station WVUM (90.5). WKIS (99.9) is the top country station. Top-40 music can be heard on WHYI (100.3) and classic disco on Mega 103 (103.5). WGTR (97.3) plays easy listening, WDNA (88.9) has the best Latin jazz and multiethnic sounds, and public radio can be heard either on WXEL (90.7) or WLRN (91.3).

Religious Services Miami houses of worship are as varied as the city's population and include St. Patrick Catholic Church, 3716 Garden Ave., Miami Beach (℡ 305/531-1124); Coral Gables Baptist Church, 5501 Granada Blvd. (℡ 305/665-4072); Temple Judea, 5500 Granada Blvd., Coral Gables (℡ 305/667-5657); Coconut Grove United Methodist, 2850 SW 27th Ave. (℡ 305/443-0880); Christ Episcopal Church, 3481 Hibiscus St. (℡ 305/442-8542); Plymouth Congregational Church, 3400 Devon Rd., at Main Highway (℡ 305/444-6521); Hindu Temple of South Florida, 12511 SW 112th Ave. (℡ 305/792-2494); Masjid Al-Ansar (Muslim), 5245 NW 7th Ave. (℡ 305/757-8741); and Buddhist Temple of Miami, 15200 SW 240th St. (℡ 305/245-2702).

Safety As always, use your common sense and be aware of your surroundings at all times. Don't walk alone at night, and be extra wary when walking or driving though downtown Miami and surrounding areas.

Reacting to several highly publicized crimes against tourists several years ago, both local and state governments have taken steps to help protect visitors. These measures include special highly visible police units patrolling the airport and surrounding neighborhoods and better signs on the state's most tourist-traveled routes.

Spas & Massage There are a number of great spa packages at some of the ritzier hotels, but those without spas often have relationships with on-call massage therapists, which can be arranged by asking the concierge to make an appointment for an in-room session. Popular day spas include the **Russian Turkish Baths,** 5445 Collins Ave. at the Castle Hotel (℡ 305/867-8316), otherwise known as "The Schvitz," where the old guard meets the new in eucalyptus-scented Turkish steam rooms and aroma baths bolstered by marble columns. **Some Like It Hot,** 841 Lincoln Rd., Miami Beach (℡ 305/532-8703), has expanded from a small second-floor salon into a full-service, 5,250-square-foot spa, offering massages, waxing, manicures, and a sublime signature hot-rock massage. **Le Spa Miami,** 150 8th St., Miami Beach (℡ 305/674-6744), is the newest day spa to hit the shores, exclusively using Lancôme products and featuring a laundry list of facials, body treatments, make-up applications, waxing, manicures, pedicures, and even photo shoots.

Taxes A 6% state sales tax (plus 0.5% local tax, for a total of 6.5% in Miami–Dade County [from Homestead to North Miami Beach]) is added on at the register for all goods and services purchased in Florida. In addition, most municipalities levy special taxes on restaurants and hotels. In Surfside, hotel taxes total 10.5%; in Bal Harbour, 9.5%; in Miami Beach (including South Beach), 11.5%; and in the rest of Dade County, a whopping 12.5%. In Miami Beach, Surfside, and Bal Harbour, the resort (hotel) tax also applies to hotel restaurants and restaurants with liquor licenses.

Taxis See "Getting Around," earlier in this chapter.

Time Zone Miami, like New York, is in the Eastern Standard Time zone. Between April and October, daylight saving time is adopted, and clocks are set 1 hour ahead. America's eastern seaboard is 5 hours behind Greenwich Mean Time. To find out what time it is, call ✆ **305/324-8811.**

Transit Information For Metrorail or Metromover schedule information, phone ✆ **305/770-3131** or surf over to **www.co.miami-dade.fl.us/mdta/.**

Weather Hurricane season runs August through November. For an up-to-date recording of current weather conditions and forecast reports, call ✆ **305/229-4522.** Also see the "When to Go" section in chapter 2.

3 Where to Stay in Miami

As much a part of the landscape as the palm trees, many of Miami's hotels are on display as if they were contestants in a beauty pageant. The city's long-lasting status on the destination A-list has given rise to an ever-increasing number of upscale hotels, and no place in Miami has seen a greater increase in construction than Miami Beach. Since the area's renaissance, which began in the late 1980s, the beach has turned what used to be a beachfront retirement home into a sand-swept hot spot for the Gucci and Prada set. Contrary to popular belief, however, the beach does not discriminate, and it's the juxtaposition of the chic elite and the hoi polloi that contributes to its allure.

While the increasing demand for rooms on South Beach means increasing costs, you can still find a decent room at a fair price. In fact, most hotels in the Art Deco District are less Ritz-Carlton than they are Holiday Inn, unless, of course, they've been renovated (many hotels in this area were built in the 1930s for the middle class). Unless you plan to center your vacation entirely in and around your hotel, most of the cheaper Deco hotels are adequate and a wise choice for those who plan to use the room only to sleep. Smart vacationers can almost name their price if they're willing to live without a few luxuries, such as an oceanfront view.

Many of the old hotels from the 1930s, 1940s, and 1950s have been totally renovated, giving way to dozens of "boutique" (small, swanky, and independently owned) hotels. Keep in mind that when a hotel claims that it was just renovated, it can mean that they've completely gutted the building—or just applied a coat of fresh paint. Always ask what specific changes were made during a renovation, and be sure to ask if a hotel will be undergoing construction while you're there. You should also find out how near your room will be to the center of the nightlife crowd; trying to sleep directly on Ocean Drive or Collins and Washington Avenues, especially during the weekend, is next to impossible, unless your lullaby of choice happens to include throbbing salsa and bass beats.

The best hotel options in each price category and those that have been fully upgraded recently are listed below. You should also know that along South Beach's Collins Avenue, there are dozens of hotels and motels—in all price categories—so there's bound to be a vacancy somewhere. If you do try the walk-in routine, don't forget to ask to see a room first. A few dollars extra could mean all the difference between flea and fabu.

While South Beach may be the nucleus of all things hyped and hip, it's not the only place with hotels. The advantage to staying on South Beach as opposed to, say, Coral Gables or Coconut Grove, is that the beaches are within walking distance, the nightlife and restaurant options are aplenty, and, basically, everything you would need is right there. However, staying there is definitely not for everyone. If you're wary, don't worry: South Beach is centrally located and only about a 15- to 30-minute drive from most other parts of Miami.

For a less expensive stay that's only a 10-minute cab ride from South Beach, Miami Beach proper (the area north of 23rd St. and Collins Ave. all the way up to 163rd St. and Collins Ave.) offers a slew of reasonable stays, right on the beach, that won't cost you your kids' college education fund.

For a less frenetic, more relaxed, and more tropical experience, the resorts on Key Biscayne exude an island feel, even though, if you look across the water, a cosmopolitan vibe beckons, thanks to the shimmering, spectacular Miami skyline.

Those who'd rather bag the beach in favor of shopping bags will enjoy North Miami Beach's proximity to the Aventura Mall as much as tan-o-holics are drawn to the sand on South Beach. And for Miami with an Old-World European flair, Coral Gables and its charming hotels and exquisite restaurants provide a more prim and proper, well-heeled perspective of Miami than the trendy boutique hotels on South Beach.

SEASONS & RATES   South Florida's tourist season is well defined, beginning in mid-November and lasting until Easter. Hotel prices escalate until about March, after which they begin to decline. During the off-season, hotel rates are typically 30% to 50% lower than their winter highs.

But timing isn't everything. In many cases, rates also depend on your hotel's proximity to the beach and how much ocean you can see from your window. Small motels a block or two from the water can be up to 40% cheaper than similar properties right on the sand.

Rates below have been broken down into two broad categories: winter (generally, Thanksgiving–Easter) and off-season (about mid-May to August). The months in between, the shoulder season, should fall somewhere in between the highs and lows, while rates always go up on holidays. Remember, too, that state and city taxes can add as much as 12.5% to your bill in some parts of Miami. Some hotels, especially those in South Beach, also tack on additional service charges, and don't forget that parking is a pricey endeavor.

PRICE CATEGORIES   The hotels below are divided first by area, then by price, using the following guidelines: **very expensive,** over $250; **expensive,** $180 to $250; **moderate,** $90 to $180; and **inexpensive,** below $90. Prices are based on published rates (or rack rates) for a standard double room during the high season. You should also check with the reservations agent, since many rooms are available above and below the category ranges listed below. Also ask about packages, since it's often possible to get a better deal than these "official" rates.

Most importantly, always call the hotel to confirm rates, which may be subject to change without notice because of special events, holidays, or blackout dates.

LONG-TERM STAYS If you plan to visit Miami for a month, a season, or more, think about renting a condominium apartment or a room in a long-term hotel. Long-term accommodations exist in every price category, from budget to deluxe, and in general are extremely reasonable, especially during the off-season. Check with the reservation services below, or write a short note to the chamber of commerce in the area where you plan to stay. In addition, many local real estate agents also handle short-term rentals (meaning less than a yr.).

RESERVATION SERVICES Central Reservation Service (© 800/ 950-0232 or 305/274-6832; www.reservation-services.com) works with many of Miami's hotels and can often secure discounts of up to 40%. It also gives advice on specific locales, especially in Miami Beach and downtown. During holiday time, there may be a minimum of a 3- to 5-day stay to use their services. Call for more information.

For bed-and-breakfast information throughout the state, contact **Florida Bed and Breakfast Inns** (© 800/524-1880; www.florida-inns.com).

SOUTH BEACH

Choosing a hotel on South Beach is similar to deciding whether you'd rather pay $1.50 for french fries at Denny's or $8.50 for the same fries—but let's call them *pomme frites*—in a pricey haute cuisinerie. Fortunately, for every chichi hotel in South Beach—and there are many—there are just as many moderately priced, more casual options.

Prices mentioned here are rack rates—that is, the price you would be quoted if you walked up to the front desk and inquired about rates. The actual price you will end up paying is usually less than this—especially if a travel agent makes the reservations for you. Many hotels on South Beach have stopped quoting seasonal and off-season rates and have, instead, chosen to go with a low-to-high rate representing the hotel's complete pricing range.

If status is important to you, as it is to many South Beach visitors, then you will be quite pleased with the number of haute hotels in the area, which are as popular as nightclubs and restaurants are on South Beach.

Art Deco hotels, while pleasing to the eye, may be a bit run-down inside. Par for the course on South Beach, appearances are at times deceiving.

VERY EXPENSIVE

The Delano ✦ *Overrated* Unless your name's Madonna or the equivalent, you will definitely feel like you are paying for the privilege of staying here. The Delano may not be the friendliest place, but it certainly is amusing to look at—with 40-foot sheer white billowing curtains hanging outside, mirrors everywhere, Adirondack chairs, and faux-fur-covered beds. The rooms are done up sanitarium style: sterile, yet toxically trendy, in pure white save for a perfectly crisp green Granny Smith apple in each room—the only freebie you're going to get here. A bathroom renovation recently took place in all of the rooms—but they remain small and spartan.

An attractive, white-clad staff looks as if they were handpicked from last month's *Vogue*. While they may sigh if you ask for something, eventually they'll get it for you. The gym here is great, but it costs $15 a day, even if you are a guest. The fantastic wading pool, thankfully, is free, but get out early to snag a chair. The Blue Door restaurant, formerly part-owned by Madonna, serves lots of attitude with its pricey haute cuisine; the lobby's **Rose Bar** is command central for the chic elite who don't flinch at paying in excess of $10 for a martini. The hotel's major saving grace is Agua, the rooftop spa, where, if you can afford it, an hour massage while overlooking the ocean is blissful.

1685 Collins Ave., South Beach, FL 33139. ℂ 800/555-5001 or 305/672-2000. Fax 305/532-0099. 209 units, 1 penthouse. Winter $325–$810 standard; $750–$2,000 suite; $2,000–$3,000 bungalow or 2-bedroom; $2,800–$3,000 penthouse. Off-season $245–$660 standard; $600–$2,000 suite; $940–$3,000 bungalow or 2-bedroom; $2,400–$3,000 penthouse. Additional person $35. AE, DC, DISC, MC, V. Valet parking $20. **Amenities:** 3 restaurants; bar; large outdoor pool; 24-hr. state-of-the-art David Barton gym; extensive watersports equipment; children's programs; concierge; business center; room service; in-room massage; same-day dry-cleaning and laundry service. *In room:* A/C, TV/VCR, minibar, hair dryer, CD player.

The Ritz-Carlton ✦✦✦   The luxe life comes to a congested and somewhat seedy corner of South Beach in the form of this beachfront, lushly landscaped Ritz-Carlton, slated to open in the fall of 2002, which has restored a landmark 1950s building to its original Art Moderne style and filled it with the hotel's signature five-star service. Far from ostentatious, the Ritz-Carlton's South Beach property moves away from gilded opulence in favor of the more soothing pastel-washed touches of Deco. Though South Beach is better known for its trendy boutique hotels, the Ritz-Carlton offers comfort to those who might prefer 100% cotton sheets and goose-down pillows to high-style minimalism.

With impeccable service, an impressive stretch of sand, and a world-class 13,000-square-foot spa and wellness center, the Ritz-Carlton kicks sand in the faces of some of the smaller hotels that think they're doing *you* a favor by allowing you to sleep there.

1 Lincoln Rd., South Beach, FL 33139. ℂ 800/241-3333 or 786/276-4000. Fax 786/276-4100. www.ritz carlton.com. 375 units. Winter $450–$690 double; off-season $245–$425 double. AE, DISC, MC, V. Valet parking $30. **Amenities:** 3 restaurants; outdoor heated pool; health club; spa; extensive water-sports rentals; children's program; 24-hr. business center; salon; 24-hr. room service; babysitting; overnight laundry service. *In room:* A/C, TV, dataport, minibar, coffeemaker, hair dryer, iron, safe.

The Shore Club ✦   Despite the fact that this newly opened, hyper-hip hotel is little more than a concrete canyon, a mod-version of the eerily deserted house in *The Shining*, it has been slowly making waves within the jet set and fabulatti thanks to one thing in particular: Florida's first ever Nobu sushi restaurant and cocktail lounge (a major hit in New York, Las Vegas, Paris, and London). The hotel's other restaurant, Sirena, also makes up for the hotel's somewhat trying-too-hard-to-be-hip lackluster vibe.

The Shore Club also boasts that 80% of its 325 rooms have an ocean view. Contrary to the cold, cavernous lobby, exquisite gardens draw guests toward the beach through courtyards and reflecting pools. Rooms are loaded with state-of-the-art amenities, not to mention 400-thread linen bedding, Mexican sandstone flooring in the bathroom with custom-designed glass, and an enclosed "wet area" with bathtub, shower, and teak bench. (Molton Brown bathroom amenities are worth bringing an extra bag for.) If you can't afford the penthouse or a poolside cabana, consider an Ocean View room, which is stellar in its own right, with its massive, two-nozzled shower-tub combo that's almost better than a day at the beach. If you are wondering whether to choose the always hip mainstay, the Delano, over this hotel, consider that The Shore Club is hardly as crowded, has little or no scene, and its rooms boast a bit more personality than the Delano's.

1901 Collins Ave., Miami Beach, FL 33139. ℂ 877/640-9500 or 305/695-3100. Fax 305/695-3299. www.shoreclubsouthbeach.com. 325 units, 8 cabanas. Winter $525–$775 double; $1,125 suite; $2,500 cabana. Off-season $425–$675 double; $1,025 suite; $1,500 cabana. AE, DC, MC, V. Valet parking $20.

Where to Stay in South Beach

Abbey Hotel **2**
Albion Hotel **9**
Aqua **12**
Banana Bungalow **1**
Beachcomber Hotel **16**
Brigham Gardens **14**
Clevelander **15**
Crest Hotel Suites **8**
The Delano **7**
The Hotel **26**
Hotel Astor **21**
Hotel Impala **17**
Hotel Leon **27**
Hotel Nash **19**
Loew's Hotel **11**
The Loft Hotel **22**
Park Washington Hotel **20**
Pelican Hotel **23**
Raleigh Hotel **5**
The Ritz-Carlton **10**
Royal Hotel **28**
The Shore Club **3**
The Tides **18**
Townhouse **4**
Villa Paradiso **13**
Villas at Caffé Milano **24**
Whitelaw Hotel **25**

Amenities: 3 restaurants, 4 bars; outdoor reflecting pools with poolside dataports; health club with steam room and outdoor equipment; spa; concierge; 24-hr. room service. *In room:* A/C, TV, fax, minibar, Intrigue System with digitally downloaded movies and high-speed Internet access, CD player, stereo.

The Tides ★★★ This 12-story Art Deco masterpiece is reminiscent of a gleaming ocean liner, with porthole windows and lots of stainless steel and frosted glass. Rooms are starkly white but much more luxurious and comfortable than those at the Delano. Also, all rooms are at least twice the size of a typical South Beach hotel room and have a view of the ocean. They feature king beds, spacious closets, large bathrooms, and even a telescope from which to view the vast ocean. The penthouses on the 9th and 10th floors are situated at the highest point on Ocean Drive, allowing for a priceless panoramic view of the ocean, the skyline, and the beach. Even if you can't afford it, you must ask for a tour of the Goldeneye Suite, a room suited for James Bond and his Bond girls, with hot tub in the middle, private deck, and high-tech toys. Although small, the freshwater pool is a welcome plus for those who aren't in the mood to feel the sand between their toes; but it really doesn't fit with the rest of the hotel, lacking in ambience and view (it overlooks an alley). The hotel's restaurant, Twelve Twenty, is an elegant, excellent, and pricey eatery with seating in the lobby. The Terrace is a less expensive outdoor cafe. The Tides is a place where celebrities like Ben Affleck, Jennifer Lopez, and Bono come to stay for some R&R, but you won't find gawkers or paparazzi lurking in the lobby, just an elegant clientele and staff who are respectful of people's privacy and desire for peace and quiet.

1220 Ocean Dr., South Beach, FL 33139. © **800/OUTPOST** or 305/604-5000. Fax 305/672-6288. www.islandoutpost.com. 45 units. Winter $525 suite; $3,000 penthouse. Off-season $375 suite; $2,000 penthouse. Additional person $15. AE, DC, DISC, MC, V. Valet parking $18. **Amenities:** 2 restaurants; lounge; bar; outdoor heated pool; small health club and discount at large nearby health club or yoga studio; concierge; secretarial services; 24-hr. room service; in-room massage; babysitting; laundry and dry-cleaning service; beach lounge service. *In room:* A/C, TV/VCR, minibar, hair dryer, iron, safe, stereo/CD player with selection of music, video rentals.

EXPENSIVE

The Hotel ★★★ Kitschy fashion designer Todd Oldham whimsically restored this 1939 gem (formerly the Tiffany Hotel) as he would have a vintage piece of couture. He laced it with lush, cool colors, hand-cut mirrors, and glass mosaics from his ready-to-wear factory, then added artisan detailing, terrazzo floors, and porthole windows. The small, soundproof rooms are very comfortable and incredibly stylish, though the bathrooms are a bit cramped. There's no need to pay more for an oceanfront view—go up to the rooftop, where the pool is located, and you'll see an amazing view of the Atlantic. The hotel's restaurant, Wish (see p. 135), is one of South Beach's best.

801 Collins Ave., South Beach, FL 33139. © **877/843-4683** or 305/531-2222. Fax 305/531-2222. www.the hotelofsouthbeach.com. 52 units. Winter $275–$405 double; off-season $215–$355 double. AE, DC, DISC, MC, V. Valet parking $18. **Amenities:** Restaurant; bar; pool bar; small pool; health club; concierge; business center; room service. *In room:* A/C, TV/VCR, dataport, minibar, coffeemaker, hair dryer, stereo system with CD and cassette players, Kiehl's products, video library.

Hotel Astor ★★★ Cozy-chic best describes this diminutive Deco hotel built in 1936. A 1995 renovation greatly improved on the original design of this simple three-story property, which has hosted the likes of Cameron Diaz and Madonna and continues to attract a lively local crowd to the small but sleek lobby bar. Though the hotel isn't as sceney (a la the Delano) as it once was, it's still a favorite spot for repeat visitors who wouldn't think of staying anywhere else.

Tips Hotel Dining

While travelers don't necessarily choose a hotel by its dining options, a number of Miami's best restaurants can be found inside hotels. Some of the city's most hailed cuisine can be had at the Delano's **Blue Door,** the Hotel Nash's **Mark's South Beach,** The Hotel's **Wish,** and the Mandarin Oriental's **Azul. Nobu,** a New York import at the Shore Club, is the primary reason why people go to that cavernous hotel. *Warning:* In some cases, your tab at these restaurants may be almost as high as the price of a room.

There is a small lap pool and a beautiful waterfall outside the bar area, but if you're looking to catch some sun, you may want to consider walking the 2 blocks to the beach because there are very few lounge chairs at the pool. The rooms are small but soothing, featuring plush and luxurious details—Belgian linens and towels, funky custom mood lighting with dimmer switches, and incredibly plush mattresses that are difficult to leave. I especially recommend the rooms overlooking the courtyard, for their views and for a bit more serenity than that which is afforded in rooms overlooking the street. Views are probably the worst thing about this hotel, as most rooms face the street or a neighboring seedy hotel. The hotel staff is known for its extreme attentiveness—especially Arturo, the hotel's "Cheers"-y bartender who actually knows everybody's names and their drinks of choice.

956 Washington Ave., South Beach, FL 33139. ⓒ 800/270-4981 or 305/531-8081. Fax 305/531-3193. www.hotelastor.com. 40 units. Winter $155–$420 double; off-season $110–$250 double. Additional person $30. AE, DC, MC, V. Valet parking $20. **Amenities:** Restaurant; 2 bars; small outdoor pool; access to nearby health club; 24-hr. concierge service; secretarial services; limited room service; in-room massage; babysitting; laundry and dry-cleaning service. *In room:* A/C, TV, dataport, minibar, fridge, hair dryer.

Hotel Impala ★★★ *Finds* This renovated Mediterranean inn is one of the area's best, and it's just beautiful, from the Greco-Roman frescos and friezes to an intimate garden that is perfumed with the scents from carefully hung lilies and gardenias. Rooms are extremely comfortable, with super-cushy sleigh beds, sisal floors, wrought-iron fixtures, imported Belgian cotton linens, wood furniture, and fabulous roomy bathrooms done up in stainless steel and coral rock. Adjacent to the hotel is Spiga, an intimate, excellent Italian restaurant that is reasonably priced. Enclaves like this one are rare on South Beach.

1228 Collins Ave., South Beach, FL 33139. ⓒ 800/646-7252 or 305/673-2021. Fax 305/673-5984. hotelimpala1@aol.com. 17 units. Winter $200–$400 double; off-season $169–$279 double. AE, DC, MC, V. Valet parking $18. No children under 16 permitted. **Amenities:** Restaurant; concierge; room service. *In room:* A/C, TV/VCR, dataport, hair dryer, stereo, CD player, complimentary videos.

Hotel Nash ★★★ Bridging the gap between the hyper-trendy and schlocky hotels often found on South Beach, the Hotel Nash is a rarity in that it boasts both style and substance. Located a block from the beach and behind the infamous Versace mansion, the Nash is housed in a 1930s Deco structure, which received an $11 million renovation. The result is a soothing, almost therapeutic hotel in which the scents of aromatherapy seep into every room and public space on the property. An aromatic indoor garden of jasmine, bougainvillea, star anise, and cypress, three tiny yet intimate pools—freshwater, saltwater, and mineral water—and possibly the best restaurant on the beach—Mark's South Beach—are permanent fixtures in this beautiful hotel. Rooms overlook either the city or the Versace mansion observatory. Ricky Martin chose the Nash's penthouse as the site to host a private dinner party. The best room in the house that's not a penthouse is the duplex suite, a tri-level room with sitting area downstairs, second-floor bedroom, and third-floor terrace.

1120 Collins Ave., Miami Beach, FL 33139. (*C*) **305/674-7800.** Fax 305/538-8288. www.hotelnash.com. 55 units. Winter $210–$255 double; $275–$625 suite; $775 duplex; $625–$1,600 penthouse. Off-season $180 double; $250–$480 suite; $780 duplex; $580–$1,100 penthouse. Rates change frequently. AE, DC, DISC, MC, V. Valet parking $16. **Amenities:** Restaurant; bar; 3 outdoor pools; water-sports equipment rental; car service. *In room:* A/C, TV/VCR or DVD, dataport, minibar, hair dryer, iron, safe, CD player.

Raleigh Hotel 🌟🌟 Upon entering the lobby of this oceanfront Art Deco hotel, you will feel like you've stepped back into the 1940s. Polished wood, original terrazzo floors, and an intimate martini bar add to the fabulous atmosphere that's favored by fashion photographers and production crews, for whom the hotel's fleur-de-lis pool is the favorite subject. In fact, one look at the pool and you'll expect Esther Williams to splash up in a dramatic, aquatic plié. Should you glance quickly inside the dimly lit lobby restaurant, the constantly changing Tiger Oak Room (last we checked, it was Mediterranean), you could swear Dorothy Parker and her fellow round-tablers took a detour from New York's Algonquin Hotel and landed here. Rooms are tidy and efficient (those overlooking the resplendent pool and ocean are the most peaceful), nothing too elaborate, but that's not why people stay here. It's the Raleigh's romantic Deco lure that has people skipping over from the chilly, antiseptic Delano a few blocks up for much needed warmth.

1775 Collins Ave., Miami Beach, FL 33139. (*C*) **800/848-1775** or 305/534-6300. Fax 305/538-8140. www.raleighhotel.com. 111 units. Winter $339–$769 double; off-season $209–$609 double. Rates are cheaper if booked on the hotel's website. AE, DC, DISC, MV, V. Valet parking $20. **Amenities:** Restaurant; bar; coffee bar; fantastic large outdoor pool; small open-air fitness center; concierge; business services; room service (24-hr. in winter, limited off-season); massage; overnight laundry service. *In room:* A/C, TV/VCR, dataport, minibar, fridge, safe, CD player.

MODERATE

Abbey Hotel 🌟🌟 *Finds* This charming, off-the-beaten-path '40s-revival boutique hotel is possibly the best deal on the entire beach. A haven for artists looking for quiet inspiration, the Abbey has recently undergone a $2.5 million renovation that restored its original Deco glory. Soft white-covered chairs and candles grace the lobby (which doubles as a chic Mediterranean-style restaurant), and the rooftop sun deck has been restored to its 1940s glamour as a bar and grill. Rooms are furnished with oversized earth-toned chairs and chrome beds that are surprisingly comfortable. It's extremely quiet at this hotel, as it is located in the midst of a sleepy residential neighborhood, but it's only 1 block from the beach and within walking distance of the Jackie Gleason Theater, the Convention Center, the Bass Museum of Art, and the Miami City Ballet.

300 21st St., Miami Beach, FL 33139. (*C*) **305/531-0031.** Fax 305/672-1663. www.abbeyhotel.com. 50 units. Winter $150–$225 double; $225 studio. Off-season $75–$150 double; $150 studio. AE, DC, DISC, MC, V. Off-site parking $17. Pets accepted with $500 deposit. **Amenities:** Restaurant; bar; exercise room; spa within a solarium; concierge; business center; room service; laundry and dry-cleaning service. *In room:* A/C, TV/VCR, dataport, hair dryer, iron, safe. Studios also have stereo with CD player, minibar, safe.

Aqua 🌟 *Value* It's been described as the Jetsons meets Jaws, but the Aqua isn't all Hollywood. Animated, yes, but with little emphasis on special effects and more on a friendly staff, Aqua is definitely a good catch for those looking to stay

---

Fun Fact **Desi Was Here**

During the Raleigh Hotel's opening-night white-tie ball in 1940, a sick band member was replaced by a then-unknown local drummer. You may have heard of him: Desi Arnaz.

---

in style without compromising their budget. Rooms are ultra-modern in an Ikea sort of way; in other words, cheap chic. There are apartment-like junior suites, suites, and a really fabulous penthouse, but the standard deluxe rooms aren't too shabby either, with decent-size bathrooms and high-tech amenities. It's a favorite amongst Europeans and young hipsters on a budget. This '50s-style motel has definitely been spruced up and its sun deck, courtyard garden, and small pool are popular hangouts for those who'd prefer to stay off the nearby sand. A small yet sleek lounge inside is a good place for a quick cocktail, breakfast, or a snack.

1530 Collins Ave., Miami Beach, FL 33139. © **305/538-4361**. Fax 305/673-8109. www.aquamiami.com. 50 units. Winter $125–$395; off-season $95–$295. Rates include European-style breakfast buffet. AE, DC, DISC, MC, V. Valet parking $18. **Amenities:** Cafe; bar; small pool. *In room:* A/C, TV, minibar, CD player, Web TV.

Crest Hotel Suites ★★ *Finds*   One of South Beach's best-kept secrets, the Crest Hotel is located next to the pricier, trendier Albion Hotel and features a quietly fashionable, contemporary, relaxed atmosphere with fantastic service. Built in 1939, the Crest was restored to preserve its Art Deco architecture, but the interior of the hotel is thoroughly modern, with rooms resembling cosmopolitan apartments. All suites have a living room/dining room area, kitchenette, and executive workspace. An indoor/outdoor cafe with terrace and poolside dining isn't besieged with trendy locals, but does attract a younger crowd. Crest Hotel Suites is conveniently located in the heart of the Art Deco Historic District, near all the major attractions. Around the corner from the hotel is Lincoln Road, with its sidewalk cafes, gourmet restaurants, theaters, and galleries. At press time, the Crest was about to open its second hotel, the South Beach Hotel, at 236 21st St.

1670 James Ave., Miami Beach, FL 33139. © **800/531-3880** or 305/531-0321. Fax 305/531-8180. www.cresthotel.com. Winter $155–$235 double; off-season $115–$175 double. Packages available and 10% discount offered if booked on website. AE, MC, V. **Amenities:** Restaurant; cafe; pool; laundry and dry-cleaning service. *In room:* A/C, TV, dataport, kitchenette, fridge, coffeemaker.

Hotel Leon ★★ *Finds*   A fabulous hotel without the fabulous attitude, the Hotel Leon is like a reasonably priced high-fashion garment found hidden on a rack full of overpriced threads. This charismatic sliver of a property has won the loyalty of fashion industrialists and romantics alike. Built in 1929 and restored in 1996, the hotel still retains many original details such as facades, woodwork, and even fireplaces (every room has one, not that you'll need to use it). The very central location 1 block from the ocean is a plus, especially since the Leon lacks a pool. Most of the spacious and stylish rooms are immaculate and reminiscent of a loft apartment; spacious bathrooms with large, deep tubs are especially enticing.

Wood floors and simple, pale furnishings are appreciated in a neighborhood where many others overdo the Art Deco motif. However, some rooms are dark and have not seen such upgrades (we have gotten complaints) and are to be avoided; do not hesitate to ask to change rooms. Service is warm, friendly, and accommodating. The lobby has an informal bar and restaurant, not to mention a large communal table at which guests—production crews, fashion photographers, Europeans, and young hipsters—tend to mix and mingle. Because its entrance is not directly on pedestrian-heavy Collins Avenue, the Hotel Leon remains one of South Beach's best-kept secrets.

841 Collins Ave., South Beach, FL 33139. ℂ **305/673-3767.** Fax 305/673-5866. www.hotelleon.com. 18 units. Winter $145–$245 suite; $395 penthouse. Off-season $100–$195 suite; $335 penthouse. Additional person $10. AE, DC, MC, V. Valet parking $18. "Well-behaved" pets accepted for $20 per night. **Amenities:** Restaurant and lobby bar; reduced rates at local gym; concierge; business services; room service (breakfast); massage; babysitting; laundry and dry-cleaning service. *In room:* A/C, TV, hair dryer, CD player.

Pelican Hotel ⭐⭐   Owned by the same creative folks behind the Diesel Jeans company, the Pelican is South Beach's only self-professed "toy-hotel," in which each of its 30 rooms and suites is decorated as outrageously as some of the area's more colorful drag queens. Each room has been designed daringly and rather wittily by Swedish interior decorator Magnus Ehrland, whose countless trips to antiques markets, combined with his wild imagination, have turned Room 309, for instance, into the "Psychedelic(ate) Girl," Room 201 into the "Executive Fifties" suite, and Room 313 into the "Jesus Christ Megastar" room. But the most popular room is the tough-to-score Room 215, or the "Best Whorehouse," which is said to have made even former Hollywood madam Heidi Fleiss red with envy. As South Beach is known for poseurs of all types, this hotel fits right in.

826 Ocean Dr., Miami Beach, FL 33139. ℂ **800/7-PELICAN** or 305/673-3373. Fax 305/673-3255. www. Pelicanhotel.com. Winter $170–$220 double; $240 oceanfront suite. Off-season $135–$155 double; $225 oceanfront suite. AE, DC, MC, V. Valet parking $16. **Amenities:** Restaurant; bar; access to area gyms; concierge; business services; same-day laundry and dry-cleaning service. *In room:* A/C, TV/VCR, dataport, fridge, hair dryer, iron, safe, stereo/CD player.

Royal Hotel ⭐⭐ *(Finds)*   There are several words to describe this mod, hipster hotel located in the heart of South Beach. Jetsonian, funkadelic, and, as the hotel proudly and aptly declares, "Barbarella at bedtime." What it really is, however, is truly different, in that the rooms' curvy, white plastic beds (less comfortable than chic) have headboards that double as bars! Designer Jordan Mozer of Barneys New York fame has managed to transform this historic Art Deco hotel into a trippy, 21st-century state-of-the-art facility. Chaise lounges are "digital" with attached computer and television. Italian marble, pastel colors, and large, newly tiled baths manage to successfully thwart a sterility that's all too common with many chic boutique hotels.

758 Washington Ave., Miami Beach, FL 33139. ℂ **888/394-6835** or 305/673-9009. Fax 305/673-9244. www.royalhotelsouthbeach.com. Winter $130–$240 double; off-season $120–$230 double. AE, DC, MC, V. Valet parking $20. **Amenities:** Bar; small swimming pool; concierge. *In room:* A/C, TV/VCR, dataport, fridge, hair dryer, iron, safe, stereo/CD player.

Townhouse ⭐⭐   New York hipster Jonathan Morr felt that Miami Beach had lost touch with the bon vivants who gave the city its original cachet, so he decided to take matters into his own hands. His solution: this 67-room, five-story hotel in which standard rooms started at just $99 during its opening in the fall of 2000. The $99 rate proved too good to be true, but even the revised starting rates of $195 during season and $125 off-season are still a great deal. The charm of this hotel is found in its clean and simple yet chic design with quirky details: exercise equipment that stands alone in the hallways, free laundry machines in the lobby, and a water bed–lined rooftop. Comfortable, shabby chic rooms boast L-shaped couches for extra guests (for whom you aren't charged). Though the rooms are all pretty much the same, consider the ones with the partial ocean view. The hotel's basement features the hot New York import, Bond St. Lounge.

150 20th St., South Beach, FL 33139. 🕐 **877/534-3800** or 305/534-3800. Fax 305/534-3811. www.town househotel.com. Winter $195–$225 double; $395 penthouse. Off-season $125–$155 double; $395 penthouse. Rates include Parisian-style breakfast. AE, MC, V. Valet parking $18. **Amenities:** Restaurant; bar; workout stations; bike rental; free laundry; rooftop terrace with water beds. *In room:* A/C, TV/VCR, dataport, fridge, hair dryer, safe, CD player.

Whitelaw Hotel ⭐⭐   With a slogan that reads "clean sheets, hot water, and stiff drinks," the Whitelaw Hotel stands apart from the other boutique hotels with a fierce sense of humor, but never compromises on its fabulous amenities. Only half a block from Ocean Drive, this hotel, like its clientele, is full of distinct personalities, pairing such disparate elements as luxurious Belgian sheets with shag carpeting to create a completely innovative setting. All-white rooms manage to be homey and plush and not at all antiseptic. Bathrooms are large and well stocked with just about everything you may have forgotten at home. Complimentary cocktails in the lobby every night from 8 to 10pm contribute to a very social atmosphere.

808 Collins Ave., Miami Beach, FL 33139. 🕐 **305/398-7000.** Fax 305/398-7010. www.whitelawhotel.com. Winter $175 double. Off-season $125 double; $145 suite. Rates include complimentary continental breakfast and free cocktails in the lobby from 8–10pm every night. AE, MC, DC, V. Parking $18. **Amenities:** Lounge; concierge; business services; laundry service; free airport pickup; complimentary passes to area nightclubs. *In room:* A/C, TV, dataport, minibar, hair dryer, safe, CD player.

INEXPENSIVE

Banana Bungalow   This hostel-like hotel is cheap, campy, and quintessentially Miami Beach. Popular with the MTV set, the Banana Bungalow is a redone 1950s two-story motel where it's always Spring Break. The hotel surrounds a pool and deck complete with shuffleboard, a small alfresco cafe serving cheap meals, and a tiki bar where young European travelers hang out. The best rooms face a narrow canal where motorboats and kayaks are available for a small charge. In general, rooms are clean and well kept, despite a few rusty faucets and chipped Formica furnishings. Guests in shared rooms need to bring their own towels. This is one of the only hotels in this price range with a private pool.

2360 Collins Ave., Miami Beach, FL 33139. 🕐 **800/746-7835** or 305/538-1951. Fax 305/531-3217. www.bananabungalow.com. 90 units. Winter $18–$20 per person in shared units; $95–$104 double. Off-season $16–$18 per person in shared units; $50–$60 double. MC, V. Free parking. **Amenities:** Cafe; bar; large pool; access to nearby health club; game room; coin-op laundry; theater. *In room:* A/C, TV, fridge.

Brigham Gardens ⭐⭐   In a prime location, this funky place, consisting of two buildings (Art Deco and Mediterranean) is a homey and affordable oasis run by a mother-daughter team that will make sure you feel like a member of the family. Because most rooms have full kitchens—you can also barbecue in the garden—you'll find many people staying for longer than a weekend. Room #12, in particular, is extremely charming and quiet, with cathedral ceilings, Art Deco decor, and views of the garden. When you enter the tropically landscaped garden, you'll hear macaws and parrots and see cats and lizards running through the bougainvillea. The tiny but lush grounds are framed by quaint Mediterranean buildings, which are pleasant, though in need of some improvements. A rooftop sun deck, with a view of the ocean, is the hotel's newest attraction, though the rooms are constantly being spruced up with funky artwork, furniture, and a colorful array of fresh paint.

1411 Collins Ave., South Beach, FL 33139. 🕐 **305/531-1331.** Fax 305/538-9898. www.brighamgardens. com. 23 units. Winter $100–$145 1-bedroom; off-season $70–$110 1-bedroom. Additional person $10. 10% discount on stays of 7 days or longer. Pets accepted for $6 a night. AE, MC, V. **Amenities:** Concierge; coin-op washers and dryers. *In room:* A/C, TV, dataport, kitchen, coffeemaker, microwave.

The Loft Hotel   A boutique hotel along the lines of the Aqua Hotel (though less whimsical, enticing, and airy-feeling), this renovated apartment building (which really gives you the feeling of staying in an apartment rather than a hotel) offers 20 suites, all surrounding a tidy, tropically landscaped garden. Rooms are especially spacious, with queen-size beds, breakfast room, conversation area, and hardwood or tile floors. Bathrooms are brand new and, for an old Art Deco building, pretty spacious. This hotel is popular with young, hip European types, just as the Aqua Hotel is, but there isn't that much difference between the two hotels other than the fact that The Loft's rooms have fully equipped kitchens while Aqua's rooms don't, and Aqua has a bar/restaurant while The Loft does not. Prices at The Loft are very reasonable, and the owners, who hail from Villa Paradiso, are extremely accommodating.

952 Collins Ave., Miami Beach, FL 33139. © 305/534-2244. Fax 305/538-1509. 57 units. Winter $149–$179 double; off-season $89–$129 double. AE, DC, MC, V. Valet parking $20. **Amenities:** On-site laundry; VIP passes to local nightclubs. *In room:* A/C, TV/VCR, kitchen, hair dryer.

Villa Paradiso ★★ *(Finds*   This guesthouse, like Brigham Gardens, is more like a cozy apartment house than a hotel. There's no elegant lobby or restaurant, but the amicable hosts, Lisa and Pascal Nicolle, are happy to give you a room key and advice on what to do. The recently renovated spacious apartments are simple but elegant—hardwood floors, French doors, and stylish wrought-iron furniture—and are remarkably quiet considering their location, a few blocks from Lincoln Road and all of South Beach's best clubs. Most have full kitchens or at least a fridge, and Murphy beds or foldout couches for extra friends. Bathrooms have recently been renovated with marble tile. All rooms overlook the hotel's pretty courtyard garden.

1415 Collins Ave., Miami Beach, FL 33139. © **305/532-0616.** Fax 305/673-5874. www.villaparadiso hotel.com. 17 units. Winter $100–$165 apartment; off-season $75–$129 apartment. Weekly rates are 10% cheaper. Additional person $10. AE, DC, MC, V. Parking nearby $12. Pets (including small "nonbarking" dogs) accepted for $10 with a $100 deposit. **Amenities:** Coin-op washers and dryers. *In room:* A/C, TV, kitchen, fridge, coffeemaker.

MIAMI BEACH: SURFSIDE, BAL HARBOUR & SUNNY ISLES

The area just north of South Beach, known as Miami Beach, encompasses Surfside, Bal Harbour, and Sunny Isles. Unrestricted by zoning codes throughout the 1950s, 1960s, and especially the 1970s, area developers went crazy, building ever-bigger and more brazen structures, especially north of 41st Street, which is now known as "Condo Canyon." Consequently, there's now a glut of medium-quality condos, with a few scattered holdouts of older hotels and motels casting shadows over the beach by afternoon.

VERY EXPENSIVE

Alexander All-Suite Luxury Hotel ★★★   This luxury hotel is a place Robin Leach would give his "champagne wishes and caviar dreams" approval rating. Just a few miles from either happening South Beach or ritzy Bal Harbour, the Alexander is pricey, but worth it for the size of the suites and the doting attention. The Alexander features spacious one- and two-bedroom mini-apartments with private balconies overlooking the Atlantic Ocean and Miami's Intracoastal Waterway. Each contains a living room, a fully equipped kitchen, *two* bathrooms (one with just a shower and the other with a shower/tub combo), and a balcony. The rooms are elegant without being pretentious and have every convenience you could want. The hotel itself is well decorated, with sculptures,

ACCOMMODATIONS ■
Alexander All-Suite
  Luxury Hotel **10**
Bay Harbor Inn and Suites **3**
Baymar Ocean Resort **5**
Beach House Bal Harbour **5**
Dezerland Beach Resort Hotel **6**
Eden Roc Renaissance
  Resort & Spa **11**
Fontainebleau Hilton **12**
Four Points Sheraton
  Miami Beach **13**
Indian Creek Hotel **17**
Newport Beachside
  Hotel & Resort **2**
The Palms South Beach **16**

DINING ◆
Atlantic Restaurant **5**
Baraboo **8**
Cafe Prima Pasta **9**
Cafe Ragazzi **4**
Christine Lee's **1**
Crystal Café **14**
Curry's **8**
The Forge Restaurant **15**
The Greek Place **4**
Lemon Twist **7**
Sheldon's Drugs **4**
Shula's Steak House **10**
Wolfie Cohen's Rascal House **1**

paintings, antiques, and tapestries, most of which were garnered from the Cornelius Vanderbilt mansion. An ongoing renovation to upgrade the suites promises to keep the Alexander on the forefront of modern luxury. Two oceanfront pools are surrounded by lush vegetation; one of these "lagoons" is fed by a cascading waterfall. Shula's Steakhouse, owned by former Dolphins football coach Don Shula, is open for lunch and dinner daily, and is a favorite of both meat eaters and Dolphins fans.

5225 Collins Ave., Miami Beach, FL 33140. ⓒ **800/327-6121** or 305/865-6500. Fax 305/341-6553. www.alexanderhotel.com. 150 units. Winter $325 1-bedroom suite; $470 2-bedroom suite. Off-season $250 1-bedroom suite; $370 2-bedroom suite. Additional person $35. Packages available. AE, MC, V. Valet parking $18. Very small pets accepted for a $250 nonrefundable deposit for cleaning the suite. **Amenities:** 2 restaurants; 2 bars; 2 large outdoor pools; small fitness center; Jacuzzi; sauna; water-sports equipment; concierge; car rental through concierge; business center and secretarial services; salon; limited room service; in-room massage; dry-cleaning and laundry service. *In room:* A/C, TV, VCR upon request, fax, dataport, kitchen, coffeemaker, hair dryer, radio.

Beach House Bal Harbour 🌟🌟🌟 *Finds*   The Beach House Bal Harbour is the closest thing the city has to a summer beach home—comfortable, unpretentious, and luxurious, yet decidedly low-key. In place of an elaborate hotel lobby, the public spaces of the Rubell-owned Beach House are divided into a series of intimate homey environments, from the wicker-furnished screened-in porch to the Asian-inspired Bamboo Room, with overstuffed Ralph Lauren leather couches and Japanese bric-a-brac. The 24-hour Pantry, inspired by Long Island's Sagaponack General Store, is packed with all the needs of the hotel's "unplugged" urban clientele.

The ultraspacious rooms (those ending in 04 are the most spacious) are literally brimming with the comforts of home. The Atlantic Restaurant offers a little of Nantucket in Miami, from Sheila Lukins, author of the best-selling *Silver Palate* cookbooks, who creates some delicious feasts (such as buttermilk fried chicken with Austin baked beans and homemade corn bread). The Seahorse Bar features a giant tank of—you guessed it—seahorses. The 200-foot private beach, hammock grove, and topiary garden are so lush, they're said to have caused several New York hipsters to renege on their summer shares in the Hamptons in favor of this Beach House.

9449 Collins Ave., Surfside, FL 33154. ⓒ **877/RUBELLS** or 305/535-8606. Fax 305/535-8602. www.rubell hotels.com. 170 units. Winter $215–$315 double; $245–$305 junior suite. Off-season $180–$210 double; $230–$270 junior suite. Year-round $800 1-bedroom suite. AE, DC, DISC, MC, V. Valet parking $15. **Amenities:** Restaurant; 24-hr. pantry; bar; heated pool; health club and spa; water-sports equipment; children's playground; business center. *In room:* A/C, TV, dataport, fridge, hair dryer, iron, stereo/CD player, wireless TV Web access.

Eden Roc Renaissance Resort and Spa 🌟🌟   Just next door to the mammoth Fontainebleau Hilton, this large Morris Lapidus–designed flamboyant hotel, opened in 1956, seems almost intimate by comparison. The hotel completed a top-to-bottom $24 million renovation in late 1999 and an $11 million renovation of the beachfront in 2001. The nautical Deco decor is a bit gaudy, but nonetheless reminiscent of Miami Beach's Rat-Packed glory days of the '50s. The 55,000-square-foot modern Spa of Eden has excellent facilities and exercise classes, including yoga. The big, open, and airy lobby is often full of name-tagged conventioneers and tourists looking for a taste of Miami Beach kitsch. The rooms, uniformly outfitted with purple and aquatic-colored interiors and retouched 1930s furnishings, are unusually spacious, and the bathrooms boast Italian marble baths. Because of the hotel's size, you should be able to negotiate

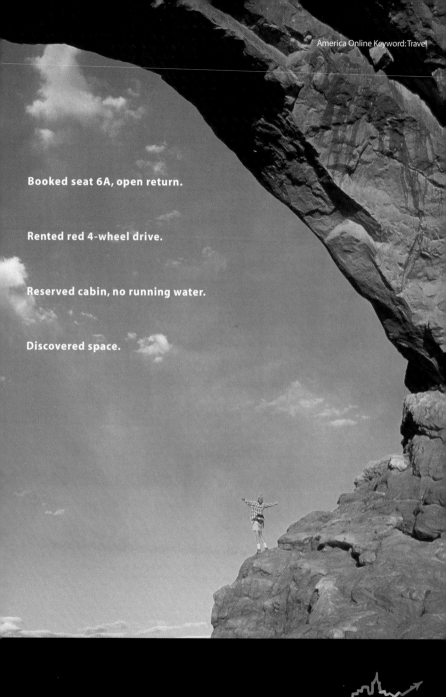

America Online Keyword: Travel

Booked seat 6A, open return.

Rented red 4-wheel drive.

Reserved cabin, no running water.

Discovered space.

ith over 700 airlines, 50,000 hotels, 50 rental car companies and
000 cruise and vacation packages, you can create the perfect get-
way for you. Choose the car, the room, even the ground you walk on.

Travelocity.com
A Sabre Company
Go Virtually Anywhere.

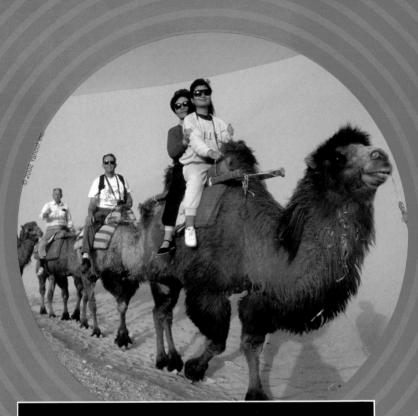

Book your air, hotel, and transportation all in one place.

Hotel or hostel? Cruise or canoe? Car?
Plane? Camel? Wherever you're going,
visit Yahoo! Travel and get total control
over your arrangements. Even choose
your seat assignment. So. One hump
or two? travel.yahoo.com

powered by COMPAQ

YAHOO!
Travel

a good rate unless there's a big event going on. Harry's Grille specializes in seafood and steaks. From Jimmy Johnson's, the poolside sports bar, patrons can watch swimmers through an underwater "porthole" window.

4525 Collins Ave., Miami Beach, FL 33140. ℂ **800/327-8337** or 305/531-0000. Fax 305/674-5568. www.edenrocresort.com. 349 units. Winter $299–$359 double; $369 suite; $2,500 penthouse. Off-season $159–$224 double; $310 suite; $1,500 penthouse. Additional person $15. Packages available. AE, DC, DISC, MC, V. Valet parking $20–$25. Pets under 20 lb. accepted for a $75 fee. **Amenities:** 2 restaurants; lounge; bar; 2 outdoor pools; squash courts; racquetball courts; basketball courts; health club and spa; water-sports equipment; concierge; tour desk; car-rental desk; business center; salon; limited room service; in-room massage; babysitting; laundry and dry-cleaning service; rock-climbing arena. *In room:* A/C, TV, VCRs for rent, dataport, kitchenettes in suites and penthouse, minibar, hair dryer.

Fontainebleau Hilton ★★ [overrtd] *Kids* In many ways, this is the quintessential Miami Beach hotel. Also designed by Morris Lapidus, who oversaw an expansion in 2000, this grand monolith symbolizes Miami decadence. Since its opening in 1954, the Fontainebleau has hosted presidents, pageants, and movie productions, including the James Bond thriller *Goldfinger.* This is where all the greats, including Sinatra and his pals, performed in their prime. Club Tropigala is reminiscent of Ricky Ricardo's Tropicana and features a Las Vegas–style floor show with dozens of performers and two orchestras. Rooms are luxurious and decorated in various styles from 1950s to ultramodern; bathrooms are done up in Italian marble a la Caesar's Palace. In 2001, the hotel underwent a $10 million food and beverage renovation, introducing the massive, cruise-ship-esque 150-seat Bleu View Mediterranean restaurant and cocktail lounge. Adding to the Fontainebleau's opulence is the 7,000-square-foot Cookie's World water park; the water slide and river-raft ride bring a bit of Disney to Deco-land, which, along with supervised children's activities, is catered toward (though not reserved for) the little ones.

4441 Collins Ave., Miami Beach, FL 33140. ℂ **800/HILTONS** or 305/538-2000. Fax 305/674-4607. www.fontainebleau.hilton.com. 1,206 units. Winter $289–$459 double; off-season $209–$329 double. Year-round $525–$1,300 suite. Additional person $30. Packages available. AE, DC, DISC, MC, V. Overnight valet parking $13. Pets accepted at no extra cost. **Amenities:** 7 restaurants (including 2 by the pool); 5 cocktail lounges; 2 large outdoor pools; 7 lighted tennis courts; state-of-the-art health club; 3 whirlpool baths; water-sports rentals; children's programs; game rooms; concierge; tour desk; car-rental desk; business center; shopping arcade; salon; room service; in-room massage; babysitting; laundry and dry-cleaning service. *In room:* A/C, TV, fax, dataport, minibar, coffeemaker, hair dryer, iron, safe.

MODERATE

Bay Harbor Inn and Suites ★★ Under the management of Johnson & Wales University, this thoroughly renovated inn is just moments from the beach, fine restaurants, and the Bal Harbour Shops. The inn comes in two parts: The more modern section overlooks a swampy river, a heated outdoor pool, and a yacht named *Celeste,* where guests eat a complimentary breakfast buffet. On the other side of the street, "townside," is the cozier, antiques-filled portion, where glass-covered bookshelves hold good beach reading. The rooms have a hodgepodge of wood furnishings (mostly Victorian replicas), while suites boast an extra half bathroom. You can often smell the aroma of cooking from the restaurant below, which is operated by students at Johnson & Wales Culinary Institute.

9660 E. Bay Harbor Dr., Bay Harbor Island, FL 33154. ℂ **305/868-4141.** Fax 305/867-9094. www.bay harborinn.com. 45 units. Winter $149–$239 double; $159–$279 suite. Off-season $80–$159 double; $95–$179 suite. Additional person $35. Rates include continental breakfast. AE, MC, V. Free parking and dockage space. **Amenities:** Restaurant; brunch room; bar; exercise room; concierge; business center; limited room service. *In room:* A/C, TV, dataport, minibar, hair dryer.

Four Points Sheraton Miami Beach ✿   Right on the Miami Beach board-walk, this chain hotel aspires to elegance with gaudy interiors inspired by the grandeur of ancient Greece. *Yikes!* A lobby of marble and rich mahogany goes against the grain of a typical South Beach hotel and only adds to this contrived, out-of-place decor. However, its location right on the beach is obviously a perk, as is its spacious rooms and good Sheraton-quality service. This hotel is not lux-ury, but it's not a bad choice if you're looking to be right on the beach and near the trendier, less ancient side of town.

4343 Collins Ave., Miami Beach, FL 33140. ✆ **800/525-6994** or 305/531-7494. Fax 305/532-2490. www.sheratonfourpoints.com. 216 units. Winter $199–$299 double; off-season $119–$199 double. AE, DC, DISC, MC, V. Valet parking $12.50. **Amenities:** Restaurant; bar; pool; exercise room; Jacuzzi; concierge; car-rental desk; business center; room service; same-day dry-cleaning service. *In room:* A/C, TV, dataport, cof-feemaker.

Indian Creek Hotel ✿✿ *Finds*   Located off the beaten path, the Indian Creek Hotel is a meticulously restored 1936 building featuring one of the beach's first operating elevators. It's also the most charming hotel in the area. Besides that, the service is impeccable. Because of its location facing the Indian Creek water-way and its lush landscaping, this place feels more like an old-fashioned Key West bed-and-breakfast than your typical Miami Beach Art Deco hotel. The rooms are outfitted in Art Deco furnishings, such as an antique writing desk, pretty tropical prints, and small but spotless bathrooms. All the rooms have been completely renovated. Just 1 short block from a good stretch of sand, the hotel is also within walking distance of shops and restaurants and has a landscaped pool area that is a great place to lounge in the sun. If you're looking for charm, friendly service, and peace and quiet, stay away from the South Beach hype and come here instead.

2727 Indian Creek Dr. (1 block west of Collins Ave. and the ocean), Miami Beach, FL 33140. ✆ **800/491-2772** or 305/531-2727. Fax 305/531-5651. www.indiancreekhotel.com. 61 units. Winter $140–$240 double; off-season $90–$150 double. Additional person $10. Group packages and summer specials available. AE, DC, DISC, MC, V. **Amenities:** Restaurant; bar; pool; concierge; car-rental desk; limited room service; laun-dry and dry-cleaning service. *In room:* A/C, TV/VCR, dataport, fridge in suites, hair dryer, CD player.

Newport Beachside Hotel & Resort *Value* *Kids*   This hotel is a great budget option, especially for young families who don't mind being away from the hus-tle and bustle of South Beach. The continental Newport Pub restaurant is very good and reasonably priced. The pool area is massive, which makes it great for kids. The hotel is situated directly on the beach, and for the aspiring angler, there is also a fishing pier out back. At night, by the poolside bar, a calypso band plays. Another plus is its location directly across the street from the R. K. Cen-tres, a destination for both tourists and residents, with shopping and restaurants, from fine dining to fast food. Guest rooms are comfortable and spacious, and most have ocean views and balconies.

16701 Collins Ave., Sunny Isles, FL 33160. ✆ **800/327-5476** or 305/949-1300. Fax 305/947-5873. www.newportbeachsideresort.com. 300 units. Winter $129–$299 double; off-season $95–$250 double. AE, DC, MC, V. Valet parking $5. **Amenities:** Restaurant; sports bar; massive outdoor pool; concierge; business center; babysitting. *In room:* A/C, TV, minibar, fridge, coffeemaker, hair dryer, iron, safe, microwave.

KEY BISCAYNE

Locals call it the Key, and, technically, Key Biscayne is the northernmost island in the Florida Keys even though it is located in Miami. A relatively unknown area until an impeached Richard Nixon bought a home here in the '70s, Key Biscayne, at 1.25 square miles, is an affluent but hardly lively residential and

Where to Stay in Key Biscayne, Downtown, West Miami, Airport Area, North Dade, Coral Gables & Coconut Grove

Biltmore Hotel **8**
Biscayne Bay Marriott **27**
Clarion Hotel & Suites **22**
David William Hotel **9**
Days Inn **5, 6**
Don Shula's Hotel
    and Golf Club **4**
Doral Golf Resort and Spa **1**
Grove Isle Club and Resort **18**
Hampton Inn **13**
Hotel Inter-Continental
    Miami **24**
Hotel Place St. Michel **7**
Hyatt Regency Coral Gables **10**
Hyatt Regency at Miami
    Convention Center **23**
JW Marriott Hotel **19**
Mandarin Oriental, Miami **25**
Mayfair House Hotel **14**
Miami International Airport
    Hotel **2**
Miami River Inn **21**
Mutiny Hotel **15**
Omni Colonnade Hotel **11**
Riviera Court Motel **12**
Ritz-Carlton Coconut Grove **16**
Ritz-Carlton Key Biscayne **31**
Sheraton Biscayne Bay Hotel **20**
Turnberry Isle
    Resort and Club **28**
Silver Sands Beach Resort **29**
Sonesta Beach Resort
    Key Biscayne **30**
Wyndham Grand Bay Hotel **17**
Wyndham Hotel Miami **26**
Wyndham Miami Airport **3**

recreational island known for its pricey homes, excellent beaches, and actor Andy Garcia, who makes his home here. The island is far enough from the mainland to make it feel semiprivate, yet close enough to downtown for guests to take advantage of everything Miami has to offer.

VERY EXPENSIVE

Ritz-Carlton Key Biscayne ★★★ *Kids* Described by some as an oceanfront mansion, the Ritz-Carlton takes Key Biscayne to the height of luxury with 44 acres of tropical gardens, a 20,000-square-foot European-style spa, and a world-class tennis center under the direction of tennis pro Cliff Drysdale. Decorated in British colonial style, the Ritz-Carlton looks as if it came straight out of Bermuda, with its impressive flower-laden landscaping. The Ritz Kids programs provide children ages 5 to 12 with fantastic activities, and the 1,200-foot (360m) beachfront offers everything from pure relaxation to fishing, boating, or windsurfing. Spacious and luxuriously appointed rooms are elegantly Floridian, featuring large balconies overlooking the ocean or the lush gardens. Unlike many behemoth hotels, the Ritz-Carlton is as much a part of the aesthetic value of the island as is its natural beauty, and its oceanfront Mediterranean-style restaurant, Aria, is exquisite. The best spa in Miami is also here, with 20,000 square feet of space that overlooks the Atlantic Ocean and features unheard-of treatments such as the Fountain of Youth Ocean Balance treatment (in which you attain total relaxation while floating in the water) and the Key Lime Coconut Body Scrub.

415 Grand Bay Dr., Key Biscayne, FL 33149. ℭ **800/241-3333** or 305/365-4500. Fax 305/365-4509. www.ritzcarlton.com. 402 units. Winter $440–$690 suite; off-season $215–$405 suite. AE, DC, DISC, MC, V. Valet parking (call for fees). **Amenities:** Restaurant; pool grill; spa cafe; 3 bars; 2 outdoor heated pools; tennis center w/lessons available; health club and spa; water-sports equipment; children's programs; 24-hr. room service; overnight laundry service. *In room:* A/C, TV, dataport, minibar, hair dryer, safe.

Silver Sands Beach Resort If Key Biscayne is where you want to be and you don't want to pay the prices of the Sonesta next door, consider this quaint one-story motel. Everything is crisp and clean, and the pleasant staff will help with anything you may need, including babysitting. But despite the name, it's certainly no resort. Except for the beach and pool, you'll have to leave the premises for almost everything else, including food. The well-appointed rooms are very beachy, sporting a tropical motif and simple furnishings. Oceanfront suites have the added convenience of full kitchens, with stoves and pantries. You'll sit poolside with an unpretentious set of Latin-American families and Europeans who have come for a long and simple vacation—and get it.

301 Ocean Dr., Key Biscayne, FL 33149. ℭ **305/361-5441.** Fax 305/361-5477. 56 units. Winter $149–$349 double. Off-season $129–$309 double. Additional person $30. Weekly rates available. AE, DC, MC, V. Free parking. **Amenities:** Medium-size pool; secretarial services; coin-op washers and dryers. *In room:* A/C, TV, VCR in some rooms, kitchenette, fridge, coffeemaker, microwave,.

Sonesta Beach Resort Key Biscayne ★★ *Kids* The Sonesta is an idyllic, secluded resort on Key Biscayne—like a souped-up summer camp. Families and couples alike love this place for its oceanfront location and its many high-caliber amenities, which make it almost impossible to want to venture off the property.

Each of the plush 292 rooms, also recently upgraded, has a private balcony or terrace. There are also 12 one- and two-bedroom suites as well as fully furnished three- and four-bedroom vacation homes, with private pools, adjacent to the main hotel. Room 828 is particularly appealing, with its sweeping views of the ocean, comfortable (to say the least) king bed, and top-floor location.

Known for having the best piña coladas in the entire city, the pool and beach bars are popular with locals and vacationers alike. The hotel's Two Dragons restaurant is good, featuring Chinese, Thai, and Japanese food. A fantastic, free, and fully supervised kids' program (ages 3–12) will actually allow parents to have a vacation of their own. Although you may not want to leave the lush grounds, Bill Baggs State Recreation Area and the area's best beaches are nearby and worth the trip. Travelers here are only about 15 minutes from Miami Beach and even closer to the mainland and Coconut Grove.

A new Sonesta Hotel & Suites just opened in Coconut Grove, at 2889 McFarlane Rd. (𝒞 **305/529-2828**). With 300 rooms, many of which overlook Biscayne Bay, it is much smaller (and, for now at least, much cheaper) than it's sprawling Key Biscayne sister and, thankfully, it brings a much needed additional option to the hotel-challenged Coconut Grove.350 Ocean Dr., Key Biscayne, FL 33149. 𝒞 **800/SONESTA** or 305/361-2021. Fax 305/361-3096. www.sonesta.com. 292 units. Winter $295–$465 double; $875–1,475 suite. Off-season $195–$285 double; $650–$1,000 suite. 15% gratuity added to food and beverage bills. Special packages available. AE, DC, DISC, MC, V. Valet parking $12. **Amenities:** 4 restaurants; 2 bars; lounge; outdoor heated Olympic-size pool; access to nearby golf; 7 tennis courts; fitness center; full service spa; 2 waterfront Jacuzzis; extensive water-sports equipment rental; bike and moped rental; children's programs; shuttle service to shopping and entertainment; business center; salon; limited room service; laundry and dry-cleaning service; sports court; sailing lessons. *In room:* A/C, TV, dataport, minibar, coffeemaker, hair dryer.

DOWNTOWN

If you've ever read Tom Wolfe's *Bonfire of the Vanities*, you may understand what downtown Miami is all about. If not, it's this simple: Take a wrong turn and you could find yourself in some serious trouble. Desolate and dangerous at night, downtown is trying to change its image, but it's a long, tedious process. Recently, however, part of the area has experienced a renaissance in terms of nightlife, with several popular dance clubs and bars opening up in the environs of NE 11th Street off Biscayne Boulevard. Most downtown hotels cater primarily to business travelers and pre- and post-cruise passengers. Although business hotels are expensive, quality and service are of a high standard. Look for discounts and packages for the weekend, when offices are closed and rooms often go empty. If you're the kind of person who digs an urban setting, you may enjoy downtown, but if you're looking for shiny, happy Miami, you're in the wrong place (for now). As of press time, the developer of the Ritz-Carlton on South Beach was about to close a deal with downtown's shoddy DuPont Plaza, located on the sketchier side of the Miami River, in which millions of dollars would be invested to revamp the decrepit property, upgrading it into a classy lower-end hotel. Keep your eyes on this area.

VERY EXPENSIVE

Hotel Inter-Continental Miami ⭐ This hotel presents a serious catch-22: It's got a front-row view of all of Miami Beach, Biscayne Bay, the Miami River, and the Atlantic Ocean, but it is also located in downtown Miami. If it's a view that you want, then you should stay here; but if you're more interested in location, you may want to reconsider.

With the decidedly threatening presence of the hyper-luxurious Mandarin Oriental just over the Brickell Bridge, the Inter-Continental had no choice but to keep up with the competition. A $34 million renovation has brought it up to speed, rendering it downtown proper's swankiest hotel. It boasts more marble than the Liberace Museum (both inside and out), but it is warmed by bold colors and a fancified Florida flavor. The five-story lobby features a marble centerpiece sculpture by Henry Moore and is topped by a pleasing skylight. Plenty of plants, palm trees, and eclectic furnishings also add charm and enliven the otherwise stark space. Perfectly designed for business travelers, each room is outfitted with a desk and Internet-ready telephone lines, but is not fabulous. They're really just swankier versions of the rooms in a typical chain hotel, albeit a little more frou-frou and elaborate, with marble bathrooms, upholstered seating areas, and sit-in windowsills. Some suites have fully equipped kitchenettes. Guests who stay in the Inter-Continental are big fish in the very small sea of desolate downtown Miami, but don't worry about your safety—this hotel is extremely secure.

100 Chopin Plaza, Miami, FL 33131. ✆ 800/327-3005 or 305/577-1000. Fax 305/577-0384. www.inter conti.com. 640 units. Winter $255–$335 double; off-season $150–$245 double. Year-round $550–$3,000 suite. Additional person $20. Weekend and other packages available. AE, DC, DISC, MC, V. Valet parking $17. **Amenities:** 3 restaurants; 2 lounges; Olympic-size outdoor heated pool; access to nearby golf course; spa; concierge; tour desk; car-rental desk; large business center; shopping arcade; salon and barbershop; room service; coin-op washers and dryers; laundry and dry-cleaning service. *In room:* A/C, TV/VCR, minibar, hair dryer, CD player.

Mandarin Oriental, Miami ★★★ Corporate big shots finally have a high-end luxury hotel to stay in while wheeling and dealing their way through Miami. Catering to business travelers, conventioneers, and the occasional leisure traveler who doesn't mind spending in excess of $500 a night for a room, the swank Mandarin Oriental features a waterfront location, residential-style rooms with Asian touches (most with balconies), and several upscale dining and bar facilities. The waterfront view of the city is the hotel's best asset, both priceless and absolutely stunning. Much of the hotel's staff was flown in from Bangkok and Hong Kong to demonstrate the hotel's unique brand of super-attentive Asian-inspired service. The hotel's two restaurants, the high-end Azul and the more casual Café Sambal, are up to Mandarin standards and are both wonderful, as is the 15,000-square-foot spa in which traditional Thai massages and Ayurvedic treatments are your tickets to nirvana.

500 Brickell Key Dr., Miami, FL 33131. ✆ 305/913-8288. Fax 305/913-8300. www.mandarinoriental.com. 329 units. $550–$575 double; $1,200–$4,000 suite. AE, DC, DISC, MC, V. Valet parking $24. **Amenities:** 2 restaurants; bar; outdoor pool; state-of-the-art health club; full-service spa; outdoor Jacuzzi; concierge; 24-hr. business center. *In room:* A/C, TV, dataport, minibar, hair dryer, iron, safe.

MODERATE

JW Marriott Hotel ★★ Located smack in the middle of the business-oriented Brickell Avenue near downtown Miami, the JW Marriott is a *really* nice Marriott catering mostly to business travelers, but located conveniently enough between Coconut Grove and South Beach that it isn't a bad choice for vacationers, either. A small but elegant lobby features the classy, appropriately named Drake's Power Bar. The buzz of business deals being sealed amidst clouds of cigar smoke contributes to the smoky, but not staid, atmosphere here. Rooms are equipped with every amenity you might need. A lovely outdoor pool, fitness center, sauna, and hot tub should become everybody's business at this hotel. Next door is the area's bustling brewery, Gordon Biersch, which attracts well-heeled, young professional types who gather for post-work revelry.

1111 Brickell Ave., Miami, FL 33131. ✆ 800/228-9290 or 305/374-1224. Fax 305/374-4211. www. marriott.com. Winter $219 deluxe room; $319 concierge room; $450 junior suite. Off-season $149 deluxe room; $189 concierge room; $350 junior suite. AE, DC, DISC, MC, V. Valet parking $18; self-parking $16. **Amenities:** 2 restaurants; bar; outdoor pool; health club; spa; sauna; concierge; tour desk; business center; laundry service. *In room:* A/C, TV, dataport (with free Internet access), minibar, coffeemaker, hair dryer, iron, safe.

Miami River Inn ★★★ *Finds*   The Miami River Inn, listed on the National Register of Historic Places, is a quaint country-style hideaway (Miami's *only* bed-and-breakfast!) consisting of four cottages smack in the middle of downtown Miami. In fact, it's so hidden that most locals don't even know it exists, which only adds to its panache. Every room has hardwood floors and is uniquely furnished with antiques dating from 1908. In one room, you might find a hand-painted bathtub, a Singer sewing machine, and an armoire from the turn of the 20th century, restored to perfection. Thirty-eight rooms have private baths—4 have a shower only, 6 have a tub only, and 28 have a splendid shower and tub combo. One- and two-bedroom apartments are available as well. In the foyer, you can peruse a library filled with books about old Miami, with histories of this land's former owners: Julia Tuttle, William Brickell, and Henry Flagler. It's close to public transportation, restaurants, and museums, and only 5 minutes from the business district.

118 SW South River Dr., Miami, FL 33130. (℃ 800/468-3589 or 305/325-0045. Fax 305/325-9227. www.miamiriverinn.com. 40 units. Winter $99–$229 double; off-season $69–$109 double. Rates include continental breakfast. Additional person $15. AE, DC, DISC, MC, V. Free parking. Pets accepted for $25 per night. **Amenities:** Small, lushly landscaped swimming pool; access to nearby YMCA facilities; Jacuzzi; babysitting; coin-op washers and dryers; laundry and dry-cleaning service. *In room:* A/C, TV, hair dryer, iron.

WEST MIAMI/AIRPORT AREA

As Miami continues to grow at a rapid pace, expansion has begun westward, where land is plentiful. Several resorts have taken advantage of the space to build world-class tennis and golf courses. While there's no sea to swim in, a plethora of facilities makes up for the lack of an ocean view.

EXPENSIVE

Doral Golf Resort and Spa ★   This recently renovated (to the tune of $40 million) 650-acre golf and tennis resort is in the middle of nowhere, but with all it's got, it really is a destination in itself. While the pamperings in the spa are nothing to sneer at, the next-door golf resort hosts world-class tournaments and boasts the Great White Course—the Southeast's first desert-scape course, designed by The Shark himself, Greg Norman. *Note:* Repeat guests usually book the season well in advance. The Blue Lagoon water park features two 80,000-gallon pools with cascading waterfalls, a rock facade, and the 125-foot Blue Monster water slide. Rooms here, like the hotel itself, are spacious, all with private balconies, many overlooking a golf course or garden. Much-needed renovations to the rooms reveal a plantation-style decor with lots of wicker and wood. Spacious bathrooms are done up in marble. Enhancements to the golf courses, spa suites, and driving range have also brought the resort up to speed with its competition. The spa's restaurant serves tasty, healthy fare—so good you won't realize it's health food, actually. For a spa or golf vacation, the Doral is an ideal choice. Otherwise, consider investing your money in a hotel that's better located.

4400 NW 87th Ave., Miami, FL 33178. (℃ 800/71-DORAL or 305/592-2000. Fax 305/594-4682. www.doral resort.com. 693 units. Winter $349 double; $439 suite; $565 1-bedroom suite; $909 2-bedroom suite. Off-season $155 double; $225 suite; $305 1-bedroom suite; $405 2-bedroom suite. Additional person $35. Golf and spa packages available. AE, DC, DISC, MC, V. Valet parking $15. **Amenities:** Restaurant; sports bar; 4 pools and a 125-ft. water slide; 5 golf courses and driving range; 10 tennis courts; health club and world-class spa; bike rental; concierge; business center; room service; babysitting; laundry and dry-cleaning service. *In room:* A/C, TV, dataport, minibar, coffeemaker, hair dryer, iron, safe, CD player.

Miccosukee Resort and Convention Center ⭐   Located on the edge of the Everglades, about 30 to 40 minutes west of the airport, the Miccosukee Resort is the closest thing South Florida's got to Las Vegas, but accommodations really are just a step above a Holiday Inn. The Miccosukee tribe was originally part of the lower Creek Nation, who lived in areas now known as Alabama and Georgia. Following the final Seminole War in 1858, the last of the Miccosukees settled in the Everglades. Following the lead set recently by many other Native American tribes, they built the resort to accumulate gambling revenue. Although many tourists go out to the resort solely to gamble, it also has expansive meeting and banquet facilities, spa services, great children's programs, entertainment, and excursions to the Florida Everglades. Guest rooms are standard, furnished with custom pieces made exclusively for the resort, but if you're here, you're not likely to spend that much time in your room.

500 SW 177th Ave. (at intersection with SW 8th St.), Miami, FL 33194. ℭ **877/242-6464** or 305/221-8623. Fax 305/221-8309. www.miccosukee.com. 302 units. Year-round $99 double; $125 suite; $325 presidential suite. All rooms sleep up to 4 people. AE, DC, DISC, MC, V. Free parking. **Amenities:** 3 restaurants, 24-hr. deli; indoor heated pool; state-of-the-art health club and spa; game room; 24-hr. room service; dry-cleaning and laundry service. *In room:* A/C, TV, dataport, minibar, coffeemaker, hair dryer, in-room movies; some suites have whirlpool and wet bar.

MODERATE

Don Shula's Hotel and Golf Club   Guests come to Shula's mostly for the golf, but there's plenty here to keep nongolfers busy, too. Opened in 1992 to much fanfare from the sports and business community, Shula's resort is an all-encompassing oasis in the middle of the planned residential neighborhood of Miami Lakes, complete with a Main Street and nearby shopping facilities—a good thing, since the site is more than a 20-minute drive from anything. The guest rooms, located in the main building or surrounding the golf course, are plain but pretty in typical, uninspiring Florida decor—pastels, wicker, and light wood. As expected, the hotel's Athletic Club features state-of-the-art equipment and classes, but costs hotel guests $10 per day or $35 per week. The award-winning Shula's Steak House and the more casual Steak House Two get high rankings nationwide. They serve huge Angus beef steaks and seafood, which can be worked off with a round of golf the next day.

Main St., Miami Lakes, FL 33014. ℭ **800/24-SHULA** or 305/821-1150. Fax 305/820-8190. 330 units. Winter $129–$289 suite; off-season $99–$209 suite. Additional person $10. Business packages available. AE, DC, MC, V. **Amenities:** 6 restaurants; 2 bars; 2 pools; 2 golf courses and a driving range; 9 tennis courts; health club; saunas; sporting courts. *In room:* A/C, TV/VCR.

Miami International Airport Hotel ⭐   I don't know of a nicer airport hotel, and you can't beat the convenience—it's actually in the airport at Concourse E. Every amenity of a first-class tourist hotel is here. The rooms are modern, clean, and spacious, with newly renovated furnishings, mattresses, fixtures, and carpeting. You might think you'd be deafened by the roar of the planes, but all of the rooms have been soundproofed and actually allow very little noise in. In addition, the hotel has modern security systems and is extremely safe.

Airport Terminal Concourse E (at the intersection of NW 20th St. and Le Jeune Rd.; P.O. Box 997510), Miami, FL 33299-7510. ℭ **800/327-1276** or 305/871-4100. Fax 305/871-0800. www.miahotel.com. 260 units. Winter $179–]$650 double; off-season $130–$270 double. Additional person $10. AE, DC, MC, V. Parking $10. **Amenities:** Restaurant; cocktail lounge; large rooftop pool; racquetball courts; well-equipped health club; Jacuzzi; sauna; concierge; tour desk; business center; salon; limited room service; laundry and dry-cleaning service. *In room:* A/C, TV, dataport, hair dryer, iron.

BARGAIN CHAINS

If you must stay near the airport, consider any of the dozens of moderately priced chain hotels. You'll find one of the cheapest and most recommendable options at either of the **Days Inn** locations at 7250 NW 11th St. or 4767 NW 36th St. (② **800/329-7466** or 305/888-3661), each about 2 miles (3.25km) from the airport. The larger property on 36th Street offers slightly cheaper rates with singles starting as low as $49. The 11th Street locale may charge more for weekends, but prices usually start at $70. Prices include free transportation from the airport.

A more luxurious option is the **Wyndham** at 3900 NW 21st St. (② **800/ 933-1100**), with rates from $100 to $225. There's also another location in downtown Miami at 1601 Biscayne Blvd. (② **800/WYNDHAM** or 305/ 374-0000). Rates there run from a high of $238 in season to $158 during the summer.

NORTH DADE

Turnberry Isle Resort & Club ★★★   One of Miami's classiest resorts (along the lines of the Mandarin Oriental), this gorgeous 300-acre compound, owned by the Mandarin Oriental Hotel group, has every possible facility for active guests, particularly golfers. You'll pay a lot to stay here—but it's worth it. The main attractions are two Trent Jones courses, available only to members and guests of the hotel. A new seven-story Jasmine wing looks like a Mediterranean village and is surrounded by tropical gardens that are joined by covered marble walkways to the other wings. Treat yourself to a "Turnberry Retreat" at the Turnberry Spa, which recently underwent a $10 million renovation. The spa comprises three levels of deluxe pampering and includes aerobics and fitness classes, stress reduction, massage therapy, and a juice bar designed for complete rejuvenation. Impeccable service from check-in to checkout consistently brings loyal fans back to this resort for more. Its location in the well-manicured residential and shopping area of North Miami Beach known as Aventura means you'll find excellent shopping and some of the best dining in Miami right in the neighborhood. Unless you're into boating, the higher-priced resort rooms (instead of the yacht club) are where you'll want to stay; you'll be steps from the spa facilities and the renowned Veranda restaurant. The well-proportioned rooms are gorgeously tiled to match the Mediterranean-style architecture. The huge bathrooms even have a color TV mounted within reach of the whirlpool bathtubs and glass-walled showers. The only drawback to this hotel is that you'll need to take a shuttle to the beach.

19999 W. Country Club Dr., Aventura, FL 33180. ② **800/327-7028** or 305/936-2929. Fax 305/933-6560. www.turnberryisle.com. 395 units. Winter $395–$495 double; $605–$1,200 suite; $3,000–$4,200 penthouse. Off-season $175–$275 double; $375–$730 suite; $2,500–$3,500 penthouse. AE, DC, DISC, MC, V. Valet parking $12; free self-parking. **Amenities:** 6 restaurants; numerous bars and lounges; 2 outdoor pools; 2 golf courses; 2 tennis complexes; state-of-the-art spa; extensive water-sports equipment rental; concierge; secretarial services; 24-hr. room service; babysitting. *In room:* A/C, TV/VCR, fax, dataport, minibar, fridge and coffeemaker on request, hair dryer, CD player.

CORAL GABLES

Translated appropriately as "City Beautiful," the Gables, as it's affectionately known, was one of Miami's original planned communities and is still among the city's prettiest, pedestrian-friendly, albeit preservation-obsessed, neighborhoods. Pristine with a European flair, Coral Gables is best known for its wide array of excellent upscale restaurants of various ethnicities, as well as a hotly contested (the quiet city didn't want to welcome new traffic) mega-shopping complex featuring upscale stores such as Nordstrom.

If you're looking for luxury, Coral Gables has a number of wonderful hotels, but if you're on a tight budget, you may be better off elsewhere. Two popular and well-priced chain hotels in the area are a **Holiday Inn** (℃ **800/327-5476** or 305/667-5611) at 1350 S. Dixie Hwy., with rates between $75 and $125, and a **Howard Johnson** (℃ **800/446-4656** or 305/665-7501) at 1430 S. Dixie Hwy., with rates ranging from $65 to $95. Both are located directly across the street from the University of Miami and are popular with families and friends of students.

VERY EXPENSIVE

Biltmore Hotel ★★★ A romantic sense of Old-World glamour combined with a rich history permeate the Biltmore as much as the pricey perfume of the guests who stay here. Built in 1926, it's the oldest Coral Gables hotel and a National Historical Landmark—one of only two operating hotels in Florida to receive that designation. Rising above the Spanish-style estate is a majestic 300-foot copper-clad tower, modeled after the Giralda bell tower in Seville and visible throughout the city. Over the years, the Biltmore has passed through many incarnations (including a post–World War II stint as a VA hospital), but it is now back to its original 1926 splendor. More intriguing than scary is the rumor that ghosts of wounded soldiers and even Al Capone, for whom the Everglades Suite is nicknamed, roam the halls here. But don't worry. The hotel is far from a haunted house. It is warm, welcoming, and extremely charming. Now under the management of the Westin Hotel group, the hotel boasts large Moorish-style rooms decorated with tasteful period reproductions and some high-tech amenities. The enormous lobby, with its 45-foot vaulted ceilings, makes a bold statement of elegance. Always a popular destination for golfers, including former President Clinton (who stays in the Al Capone suite), the Biltmore is situated on a lush, rolling 18-hole course that is as challenging as it is beautiful. The spa is fantastic and the enormous 21,000 square foot winding pool (surrounded by arched walkways and classical sculptures) is legendary—it's where a pre-*Tarzan* Johnny Weismuller broke the world's swimming record. Even if you don't stay at the Biltmore Hotel, definitely take a tour of it to learn about its fascinating history and mystery. Call ℃ **305/445-1926** for more information or see p. 179.

1200 Anastasia Ave., Coral Gables, FL 33134. ℃ **800/727-1926** or 305/445-1926; Westin 800/228-3000. Fax 305/442-9496. www.biltmorehotel.com. 275 units. Winter $339–$509; off-season $259–$479. Additional person $20. Special packages available. AE, DC, DISC, MC, V. Valet parking $14; free self-parking. **Amenities:** 5 restaurants; 2 bars; outdoor pool; 18-hole golf course; 10 lighted tennis courts; state-of-the-art health club; full-service spa; sauna; concierge; car rental through concierge; elaborate business center and secretarial services; salon; 24-hr. room service; babysitting; laundry and dry-cleaning service. *In room:* A/C, TV, VCR on request, fax, dataport, minibar, hair dryer, iron, safe; kitchenette in tower suite.

Hyatt Regency Coral Gables ★★ High on style, comfort, and price, this Hyatt is part of Coral Gables's Alhambra, an office-hotel complex with a Mediterranean motif. The building itself is gorgeous, designed with pink stone, arched entrances, grand courtyards, and tile roofs. Most recently, the pool and lobby were beautifully renovated. Inside you'll find overstuffed chairs on marble floors surrounded by opulent antiques and chandeliers. The large guest rooms are comfortable, if uninspired. A few rooms have balconies. Though the hotel fails to authentically mimic something much older and much farther away, it is attractive in its newness and an excellent place from which to admire the more historic properties in the neighborhood.

50 Alhambra Plaza, Coral Gables, FL 33134. ☎ **800/233-1234** or 305/441-1234. Fax 305/441-0520. www.hyatt.com. 242 units. Winter $340 double; off-season $254 double. Year-round $375–$1,800 1-bedroom suite; $575–$2,050 2-bedroom suite. Additional person $25. Packages and senior discounts available. AE, MC, V. Valet parking $14; self-parking $11. **Amenities:** Restaurant; bar; large outdoor heated pool; nearby golf course; health club; Jacuzzi; 2 saunas; concierge; business center; limited room service; in-room massage; babysitting; same-day laundry and dry-cleaning service. *In room:* A/C, TV, fax in some rooms, dataport, mini-bar, coffeemaker, hair dryer, iron, safe.

EXPENSIVE

David William Hotel ★★ This sister hotel to the Biltmore shares many of the same amenities without the Biltmore's price. You can even take a shuttle to the Biltmore to play a round of golf, enjoy the health club and spa, play tennis, or take a dip in the pool. The luxurious one- and two-bedroom suites are extremely spacious and have eat-in kitchens for extended stays. For a spectacular view of Miami, go up to the roof and have a drink by the pool. The hotel, which has undergone a recent external renovation, is directly across the street from the Granada Golf Course, less than 5 miles (8km) from the airport and only 20 minutes from Miami Beach. Donna's Bistro, a fusion restaurant with a homey feel, is spectacular. Executive chef Donna Wynter was the Chef de Cuisine at the Biltmore Hotel and has worked as a chef at New York's Tavern on the Green and Toscana Ristorante. If you want luxury without the price, this is your best alternative in the Gables.

700 Biltmore Way, Coral Gables, FL 33134. ☎ **800/757-8073** or 305/445-7821. Fax 305/913-1943. www.davidwilliamhotel.com. 116 units. Winter $249–$489 double; off-season $209–$269 double. AE, DISC, MC, V. Valet parking $9. **Amenities:** Restaurant; coffee shop; lounge; rooftop pool; limited room service; gourmet market. *In room:* A/C, TV, fax, kitchenette, minibar, coffeemaker, hair dryer, iron, safe.

Hotel Place St. Michel ★★★ This European-style hotel in the heart of Coral Gables is one of the city's most romantic options. The accommodations and hospitality are straight out of Old World Europe, complete with dark wood–paneled walls, cozy beds, beautiful antiques, and a quiet elegance that seems startlingly out of place in trendy Miami. Everything here is charming—from the brass elevator and parquet floors to the paddle fans. One-of-a-kind furnishings make each room special. Bathrooms are on the smaller side but are hardly cramped. All have shower/tub combos except for two, which have either or. If you're picky, request your preference. Guests are treated to fresh fruit baskets upon arrival and enjoy perfect service throughout their stay. The exceptional Restaurant St. Michel is a very romantic dining choice.

162 Alcazar Ave., Coral Gables, FL 33134. ☎ **800/848-HOTEL** or 305/444-1666. Fax 305/529-0074. www.hotelplacestmichel.com. 27 units. Winter $165 double; $200 suite. Off-season $125 double; $160 suite. Additional person $10. Rates include continental breakfast and fruit basket upon arrival. AE, DC, MC, V. Self-parking $7. **Amenities:** Restaurant; lounge; access to nearby health club; concierge; room service; laundry and dry-cleaning service. *In room:* A/C, TV, dataport, hair dryer, iron (available upon request).

INEXPENSIVE

Riviera Court Motel Besides the Holiday Inn down the road, this family-owned motel is the best discount option in the area. The comfortable and clean two-story property, dating from 1954, has a small pool and is set back from the road, so the rooms are all relatively quiet. Vending machines are the only choice for refreshments, but guests are near many great dining spots. You can also choose to stay in one of the efficiencies, which have fully stocked kitchens. For gossip mavens, this is the place where the pre-rehabilitated tennis star Jennifer Capriati was busted for drug possession many years ago.

5100 Riviera Dr. (on U.S. 1), Coral Gables, FL 33146. ✆ **800/368-8602** or 305/665-3528. 30 units. Winter $75–$88 double; off-season $68–$80 double. 10% discount for seniors and AAA members. AE, DC, DISC, MC, V. **Amenities:** Pool. *In room:* A/C, TV.

COCONUT GROVE

This waterfront village hugs the shores of Biscayne Bay, just south of U.S. 1 and about 10 minutes from the beaches. Once a haven for hippies, head shops, and arty bohemian characters, the Grove succumbed to the inevitable temptations of commercialism and has become a Gap nation, featuring a host of fun, themey restaurants, bars, a megaplex, and lots of stores. Outside of the main shopping area, however, you will find the beautiful remnants of old Miami in the form of flora, fauna, and, of course, water.

Also see the last paragraph of the Sonesta Beach Resort Key Biscayne listing, on p. 120, for a review of the new Sonesta Hotel & Suites Coconut Grove.

VERY EXPENSIVE

Grove Isle Club and Resort ✸✸✸ Hidden away in the bougainvillea and lushness of the Grove, the Grove Isle Resort is off the beaten path on its own lushly landscaped 20-acre island, just outside the heart of Coconut Grove. The isolated exclusivity of this resort contributes to a country club vibe, though, for the most part, the people here aren't snooty; they just value their privacy and precious relaxation time. Everyone dresses in white and pastels, and if they're not on their way to a set of tennis, they're not in a rush to get anywhere. You'll step into rooms that are elegantly furnished with mosquito-netted canopy beds and a patio overlooking the bay. You'll need to reserve early here—rooms go very fast. Baleen, a fantastic yet pricey haute cuisinerie, serves fresh seafood and other regional specialties in a spectacular, elegant dining room, or, better yet, outside on the water.

4 Grove Isle Dr., Coconut Grove, FL 33133. ✆ **800/88-GROVE** or 305/858-8300. Fax 305/854-6702. www.groveisle.com. 49 units. Winter $350–$495 suite; off-season $295–$475 suite. Rates include breakfast. Additional person $20. AE, DC, MC, V. Valet parking $15. **Amenities:** Large outdoor heated pool; 12 outdoor tennis courts; deluxe health club; water-sports rentals; concierge; secretarial services; salon; room service; in-room massage; babysitting; laundry and dry-cleaning service. *In room:* A/C, TV/VCR, dataport, minibar, hair dryer, iron, safe, video rental delivered to room for $5.

Ritz-Carlton Coconut Grove The third and smallest of Miami's Ritz-Carlton hotels, scheduled to open in fall 2002, promises to be the most intimate of its properties, surrounded by 2 acres of tropical gardens and overlooking Biscayne Bay and the Miami skyline. Decorated in an Italian Renaissance design, the hotel's understated luxury will be a welcome addition to an area known for its gaudiness. Expect the Ritz-Carlton standard of service and comfort.

2700 Tigertail Ave., Coconut Grove, FL 33133. ✆ **800/241-3333** or 305/644-4680. Fax 305/644-4681. www.ritzcarlton.com. 115 units. Winter $385–$750 double; off-season $245–$550 double. AE, DC, DISC, MC, V. Valet parking. **Amenities:** 2 restaurants; cigar bar; outdoor pool; health club; concierge; business center; 24-hr. room service. *In room:* A/C, TV, dataport, minibar, hair dryer.

Wyndham Grand Bay Hotel ✸✸✸ Grand in size and stature, the Grand Bay Hotel looks like it belongs in Acapulco with its ziggurat structure and tropical landscaping, but once you see the massive bright red sculpture/structure done by late Condé Nast editorial director Alexander Lieberman in the driveway, you know you're not in Mexico. Ultraluxurious, the Grand Bay is quietly elegant, and, as a result, has hosted the likes of privacy fanatics such as Michael Jackson. British singer George Michael filmed his "Careless Whisper" video here because of its sweeping views of Biscayne Bay. Rooms are superb, with views of the bay and the Coconut Grove Marina, and they're decorated in soft peach tones with a country French theme. Bathrooms are equally luxurious. Service is outstanding, and the clientele ranges from families to international jet-setters. Bice, a sublime Northern Italian restaurant, is the hotel's most popular dining option.

2669 S. Bayshore Dr., Coconut Grove, FL 33133. (✆ 800/327-2788 or 305/858-9600. Fax 305/858-1532. www.wyndham.com. 181 units. Winter $359–$400 suite. Off-season $279–$349 suite. Additional person $20. AE, DC, MC, V. Valet parking $16. **Amenities:** 4 restaurants; lounge serving afternoon tea; indoor heated pool and outdoor pool; 24-hr. health club; Jacuzzi; sauna; concierge; business center; babysitting. *In room:* A/C, TV, fax, dataport, minibar, coffeemaker, hair dryer, iron, safe, CD player.

MODERATE

Hampton Inn   This very standard chain hotel is a welcome reprieve in an area otherwise known for very pricey accommodations. The rooms are nothing exciting, but the freebies, like local phone calls, parking, in-room movies, breakfast buffet, and hot drinks around the clock, make this a real steal. Although there is no restaurant or bar, it is close to lots of both—only about half a mile to the heart of the Grove's shopping and retail area and about as far from Coral Gables. Rooms are brand new, sparkling clean, and larger than that of a typical motel. Located at the residential end of Brickell Avenue, it's a quiet, convenient location 15 minutes from South Beach and 5 minutes from Coconut Grove. If you'd rather save your money for dining and entertainment, this is a good bet.

2800 SW 28th Terrace (at U.S. 1 and SW 27th Ave.), Coconut Grove, FL 33133. (✆ 888/287-3390 or 305/448-2800. Fax 305/442-8655. www.Hampton-inn.com. 137 units. Winter $134–$154 double. Off-season $104–$124 double. Rates include continental breakfast buffet and local calls. AE, DC, DISC, MC, V. Free parking. **Amenities:** Large outdoor pool; Jacuzzi; exercise room. *In room:* A/C, TV, microwave on request.

4 Where to Dine in Miami

Don't be fooled by the plethora of superlean model types you're likely to see posing throughout Miami: Contrary to popular belief, dining in this city is as much a sport as the in-line skating on Ocean Drive. With over 6,000 restaurants to choose from, dining out in Miami has become a passionate pastime for locals and visitors alike. Our star chefs have fused Californian-Asian with Caribbean and Latin elements to create a world-class flavor all its own: *Floribbean.* Think mango chutney splashed over fresh swordfish or a spicy sushi sauce served alongside Peruvian ceviche.

Formerly synonymous with early-bird specials, Miami's new-wave cuisine, 10 years in the making, now rivals that of San Francisco—or even New York. Nouveau Cuban chef Douglas Rodriguez may have fled his Miami kitchen in favor of one in Manhattan, but other stellar chefs such as Mark Militello, Allen Susser, Norman van Aken, and Jonathan Eismann remain firmly planted in the city's culinary scene, fusing local ingredients into edible masterpieces. Indulging in this New World cuisine is not only high in calories, it's high in price. But if you can manage to splurge at least once, it'll be worth it.

Thanks to a thriving cafe society in both South Beach and Coconut Grove, you can also enjoy a moderately priced meal and linger for hours without having a waiter hover over you. In Little Havana, you can chow down on a meal that serves about six for less than $10. And since seafood is plentiful, it doesn't have to cost you an arm and a leg to enjoy the appendages of a crab or lobster. Don't be put off by the looks of our recommended seafood shacks in places such as Key Biscayne—oftentimes these spots get the best and freshest catches.

Whatever you're craving, Miami's got it—with the exception of decent Chinese food and a New York–style slice of pizza. If you're craving a scene with your steak, then South Beach is the place to be. Like many cities in Europe and Latin America, it is fashionable to dine late in South Beach, preferably after 9pm, sometimes as late as midnight. Service on South Beach is notoriously slow and arrogant, but it comes with the turf. (Of course, it is possible to find restaurants that defy the notoriety and actually pride themselves on friendly service.) On the mainland—especially in Coral Gables, and, more recently, downtown and on Brickell Avenue—you can also experience fine, creative dining without the pretense.

The biggest complaint when it comes to Miami dining isn't the haughtiness, but rather the dearth of truly moderately priced restaurants, especially in South Beach and Coral Gables. It's either really cheap or really expensive; the in-between somehow gets lost in the culinary shuffle. Quick-service diners don't really exist here as they do in other cosmopolitan areas. I've tried to cover a range of cuisines in a range of prices. But with new restaurants opening on a weekly basis, you're bound to find a savory array of dining choices on every budget.

Many restaurants keep extended hours in season (roughly Dec–Apr), and may close for lunch and/or dinner on Monday when the traffic is slower. Always call ahead, since schedules do change. Also, always look carefully at your bill—many Miami restaurants add a 15% gratuity to your total. Feel free to adjust it if you feel your server deserves more or less. If you want to picnic on the beach or pick up some dessert, check out the gourmet food shops, green markets, and bakeries listed under "Food" in chapter 5, beginning on p. 199.

SOUTH BEACH

The renaissance of South Beach (which started in the early '90s and is still continuing as classic cuisine gives in to mod-temptation by inevitably fusing with more chic, nouveau developments created by faithful followers and devotees of the Food Network school of cooking) has spawned dozens of first-rate restaurants. In fact, big-name restaurants from across the country have capitalized on South Beach's international appeal and opened, and continue to open, branches here with great success. A few old standbys remain from the *Miami Vice* days, but the flock of newcomers dominates the scene, with places going in and out of style as quickly as the tides.

The Lincoln Road area is packed with places offering good food and a great atmosphere. Since it's impossible to list them all, I recommend strolling and browsing. Most restaurants post a copy of their menu outside.

With very few exceptions, the places on Ocean Drive are crowded with tourists and priced accordingly. You'll do better to venture a little farther into the pedestrian-friendly streets just west of Ocean Drive.

VERY EXPENSIVE

BED ★★ ECLECTIC BED—that's Beverage. Entertainment. Dining—is one of the most gimmicky dining lounges to land in South Beach in a very long time. When you walk inside, you'll feel as if you've entered a Buddhist temple. An array of inviting mosquito-netted beds awaits diners. You'll rest your head against soft cushiony pillows. A deejay spins Euro mood music and some

Where to Dine in South Beach

0 — 1/4 mi
0 — 1/4 km

To Central Miami Beach ↗ 12

The Bass Museum of Art

COLLINS PARK

22nd St.
20th St.
19th St. 14 13

Dade Boulevard

Miami Beach Convention Center

18th St.

Jackie Gleason Theater of Performing Arts

17th St.

Venetian Causeway

BELLE ISLAND

Purdy Ave. 1 2

West Ave.
Bay Rd.

Dade Boulevard

Lincoln Rd. 5 6 7 9 8

Lincoln Road Mall 10

11

16th St.

James Ave.

Collins Ave. 15

16

15th St.

Española Way 17

18

Alton Rd.

Lenox Ave.
Michigan Ave.
Jefferson Ave.
Meridian Ave.

14th St.
Miami Beach Post Office 22
13th St. 23

21 20 19

12th St.

24 25

FLAMINGO PARK

11th St. 26
27

Beach Patrol Station

Pennsylvania Ave.
Washington Ave.
Ocean Dr.

Art Deco Welcome Center

10th St.

9th St.

Alton Rd.

8th St. 28
29
30 31

Michigan Ave.
Lenox Ave.

7th St. 32
34 33

6th St.

5th St. 35
4th St. 36
37

ATLANTIC OCEAN

LUMMUS PARK

3rd St.

2nd St.

Washington Ave.
Collins Ave.
Ocean Dr.

1st St. 38
39

Commerce St. 40

41 Biscayne St.

SOUTH POINTE PARK

Government Cut

FLORIDA

Miami Beach
Miami

Balan's **5**
BED **28**
Big Pink **38**
Bond St. Lounge **13**
China Grill **37**
11th Street Diner **27**
El Rancho Grande **11**
Escopazzo **23**
Front Porch Café **19**
Gaucho Room **16**
Grillfish **18**
Jeffrey's **7**
Joe Allen **2**
Joe's Stone Crab
   Restaurant **41**
Joia Restaurant and Bar **40**
Kiss **15**
Larios on the Beach **29**
La Sandwicherie **21**
L'Entrecote de Paris **36**
Lincoln Road Café **6**
Macaluso's **3**
Macarena **22**
Mama Vieja **12**
Mark's South Beach **26**
Nemo **39**
News Café **32**
Nobu **14**
Pacific Time **9**
Paninoteca **8**
Piola **4**
Pizza Rustica **30**
Puerto Sagua **33**
Shoji Sushi **39**
Sirena **14**
Spiga **24**
Sport Café **34**
Sushi Rock Café **20**
Sushi Samba Dromo **10**
Tambo **1**
Tantra **17**
Tuscan Steak **35**
Twelve Twenty **25**
Van Dyke Cafe **8**
Wish **31**

techno. You'll have no problem appreciating the taste and aroma of the exqui-site (and exquisitely priced) cuisine, featuring dishes such as macadamia nut–crusted swordfish with black-bean daikon-sprout salad and peanut sauce. For dessert, try the Ménage à Trois—peanut-butter mousse, homemade jam, and brittle all under a "blanket" of chocolate—or take a Roll in the Sack—an apple-cinnamon Swiss roll in a phyllo sack with vanilla ice cream. Beware of crumbs in the sheets, as they aren't always changed between customers, and for the agoraphobic, do not go to BED on a weekend night—it's a nightmare. This restaurant gets my approval for the stellar food, not as a night club-esque hangout.

929 Washington Ave., South Beach. ✆ **305/532-9070.** Fax 305/532-7757. Reservations required, accepted only on the day you plan to dine there. Main courses $32–$40. AE, DC, MC, V. Wed–Sun: first lay (no actual seats) 8:30pm; second lay 10:30pm. Lounge 11pm–3am.

China Grill ★★★ PAN-ASIAN   Unless your surname is Pacino, DeNiro, or Winfrey (you get the idea), you might find yourself digging a hungry hole to China Grill at the gauche hour of 6pm or the indigestion-inducing hour of mid-night. But with an incomparable albeit dizzying array of amply portioned dishes such as the outrageous crispy spinach, wasabi mashed potatoes, seared rare tuna in spicy Japanese pepper, broccoli rabe dumplings, lobster pancakes, and a sin-fully delicious dessert sampler complete with sparklers, this hub of South Beach flash is well worth the wait. In fact, the wait is part of the China Grill experi-ence. A coveted spot at the bar is headquarters for many of Miami's movers and shakers who come solely for the frenetic scene. On weekend nights, there's barely room to breathe. Keep in mind that China Grill is a family-style restaurant and that dishes are meant to be shared.

404 Washington Ave., South Beach ✆ **305/534-2211.** Reservations strongly recommended. Main courses $25–$59. AE, DC, M, V. Mon–Thurs 11:45am–midnight, Fri 11:45am–1am; Sat 6pm–1am; Sun 6pm–midnight.

Escopazzo ★★★ ITALIAN   Escopazzo means "crazy" in Italian, but the only sign of insanity in this primo Northern Italian eatery is the fact that it only seats 70. The wine bottles have it better—the restaurant's cellar holds 1,000 bottles of various vintages. Should you be so lucky to score a table at this romantic local favorite, you'll have trouble deciding between dishes that will have you swearing off the Olive Garden with your first bite. Among these, pappardelle with wild game and mushroom ragout, swordfish carpaccio, and braised leg of lamb with juniper berries, rosemary, and fennel. The hand-rolled pastas and risotto are near perfection. Eating here is like dining with a big Italian family—it's never boring (the menu changes five or six times a year), the service is excellent, and nobody's happy until you are blissfully full.

1311 Washington Ave., South Beach. ✆ **305/674-9450.** Reservations required. Main courses $18–$28. AE, MC, V. Mon, Tues, and Thurs 6pm–midnight; Fri–Sat 6pm–1am; Sun 6–11pm.

Gaucho Room ★★★ STEAK   This restaurant will set you back *mucho dinero,* but it is one of the best steakhouses in the city. The Gaucho Room is a stunning Argentinean dining room that serves prime aged meats with unparalleled serv-ice. Argentine rib eye is marinated in garlic, herbs, and olive oil before being grilled and served on butcher blocks. *Warning:* Those with lighter palates should probably request light seasoning on their food.

In the Loews Hotel, 1601 Collins Ave. (St. Moritz Bldg.), South Beach. ✆ **305/604-5290.** Reservations rec-ommended. Main courses $22–$52. AE, MC, V. Daily 7pm–1am.

Joe's Stone Crab Restaurant ★★ SEAFOOD Unless you grease the palms of one of the stone-faced maitre d's with some stone-cold cash, you'll be waiting for those famous claws for up to 2 hours—if not more. As much a Miami landmark as the beaches themselves, Joe's is a microcosm of the city, attracting everyone from T-shirted locals to a bejeweled Ivana Trump. Whatever you wear, however, will be eclipsed by a kitschy, unglamorous plastic bib that your waiter will tie on you unless you say otherwise. Open only during stone-crab season (Oct–May), Joe's reels in the crowds with the freshest, meatiest stone crabs and their essential accouterments: creamed spinach and excellent sweet-potato fries. The claws come in medium, large, or jumbo. Some say size doesn't matter; others swear by the jumbo (and more expensive) ones. Whatever you choose, pair them with a savory mustard sauce (a perfect mix of mayo and mustard) or hot butter. Not feeling crabby? The fried chicken and liver and onions on the regular menu are actually considered by many as far superior—they're definitely far cheaper—to the crabs. Oh yeah, and save room for dessert. The Key lime pie here is the best in town. If you don't feel like waiting, try Joe's Take Away, which is located next door to the restaurant—it's a lot quicker and just as tasty.

11 Washington Ave. (at Biscayne St., just south of 1st St.), South Beach. ✆ 305/673-0365, or 305/673-4611 for takeout. www.joesstonecrab.com. Reservations not accepted. Market price varies but averages $62.95 for a serving of jumbo crab claws, $38.95 for large claws. AE, DC, DISC, MC, V. Daily 11:30am–2:30pm; Sun–Thurs 5–10pm; Fri–Sat 5–11pm. Open mid-Oct to mid-May.

Kiss ★ STEAK This is not your grandfather's steakhouse. Sure, you can order the same New York strip as at, say, the Palm, but at Kiss, you can also get a strip show with your strip steak. Yes, Kiss is a high-style, high concept cabaret, with live entertainment that isn't necessarily as raw as you may like your meat, but it's certainly more sizzling than medium rare. The food is quite good here, especially the ridiculously priced Kiss exclusive magnum slow-roasted prime rib, served with a trio of sauces for $69.95, but you will be distracted by the circus-like atmosphere and cavalcade of club clowns who don't convene here for food, but for fanfare and, of course, lots of air kisses.

In the Albion Hotel, 301 Lincoln Rd., South Beach. ✆ **305/695-4445**. Reservations recommended. Main courses $22–$52. AE, MC, V. Mon–Thurs 7pm–1am; Fri–Sat 7pm–2am. Lounge open until 3am weekdays, 4am weekends. Closed Sun.

Mark's South Beach ★★★ NEW WORLD/MEDITERRANEAN Named after owner and chef Mark Militello, this is one of the best restaurants in all of Miami. A cozy, contemporary restaurant nestled in the basement of the quietly chic Hotel Nash, Mark's New World and Mediterranean-influenced menu changes nightly. What doesn't change is the consistency and freshness of the restaurant's exquisite cuisine. The roasted rack of Colorado lamb with semolina gnocchi is exceptional and worth every bit of cholesterol it may have. Crispy-skin yellowtail snapper with shrimp, tomato, black olives, oregano, and crumbled feta cheese is in a school of its own. Desserts, including an impressive cheese cart, are outrageous, especially the pistachio cake with chocolate sorbet. Unlike many South Beach eating establishments, the knowledgeable servers are here because of their experience in the restaurant—not modeling—business.

In the Hotel Nash, 1120 Collins Ave., South Beach. ✆ **305/604-9050**. Reservations recommended. Main courses $16–$38. AE, DC, DISC, MC, V. Sun–Thurs 7pm–11pm; Fri–Sat 7pm–midnight.

Nobu ★★★ SUSHI   When Madonna ate here, no one really noticed. Not because they were purposely trying not to notice, but because the real star at Nobu is the sushi. The raw facts: Nobu has been hailed as one of the best sushi restaurants in the world, with always-packed eateries in New York, London, and Los Angeles. The Omakase, or Chef's Choice—a multicourse menu entirely up to the chef for $70 per person and up—gets consistent raves. And although you won't wait long for your food to be cooked, you will wait forever to score a table here.

At the Shore Club Hotel, 1901 Collins Ave., South Beach. ✆ 305/695-3100. Reservations for parties of 6 or more. Main courses $10–$30. AE, MC, V. Sun–Thurs 6pm–12am; Fri–Sat 6pm–1am.

Pacific Time ★★★ PAN-ASIAN   Chef and co-owner (and former model) Jonathan Eismann was awarded the Robert Mondavi Award for Culinary Excellence in June 1994, and his restaurant, Pacific Time, has been recognized by *Bon Appétit* and *Esquire* magazines as one of America's "Best New Restaurants." Eismann's dishes are stunning hybrids of Chinese, Japanese, Korean, Vietnamese, Korean, Mongolian, and Indonesian flavors. One of the best dishes is the Mongolian lamb salad, which has a lightly sweet, earthy taste with a crunchy kick of onion. For a main course, the ever-changing menu offers many locally caught fish specialties such as Szechwan grilled mahimahi served on a bed of shredded shallots and ginger with a sweet sake-infused sauce and tempura-dunked sweet-potato slivers on the side. The famous chocolate bomb is every bit as decadent as they say, with hot bittersweet chocolate bursting from the cupcake-like center—order it as soon as you sit down. The wine list is quite extensive and includes red and white wines from Italy, France, the Napa Valley, Australia, Argentina, New Zealand, and South Africa. The restaurant's best deal is its pre-theater menu, a three-course dinner for only $34.

915 Lincoln Rd. (between Jefferson and Michigan aves.), South Beach. ✆ 305/534-5979. Reservations recommended. Main courses $23.50–$32. AE, DC, MC, V. Sun–Thurs 6–11pm; Fri–Sat 6pm–midnight.

Tantra ★★★ ECLECTIC   Marrakech meets Miami Beach in this truly original, outrageously priced exotic outpost devoted to the ancient Indian tantric philosophy of tempting the senses with all things pleasurable. Begin with your surroundings: a sultry interior of soft grass (yes, it's real; they resod weekly) and starry lights overhead. In the front room by the bar, there are low-lying couches and pillow-lined booths bolstered by drapes that can be closed for privacy. Belly dancers mix with cocktail waitresses singing the praises of Tantra's special aphrodisiac cocktails and offering you a puff of Turkish tobacco from the communal hookah pipe (they insist it's clean, but I'd be wary). A private VIP room off to the side features a hammock and a peaceful spiritual soundtrack.

Tantra serves a combination of Middle Eastern, Mediterranean, and Indian dishes that really are divine. Consider the Tantra Love Apple: a ripe tomato layered with Laura Chenel goat cheese and basil oil, garnished with pomegranate seeds; or perhaps Nine Jewel Indian Spiced Rack of Lamb. The $52 filet mignon is delicious, but its price tag borders on obscene.

Don't come to Tantra looking for a serene vibe to match the setting and menu. Tantra practically turns into a nightclub after dinner, attracting a crowd of celebrities and scenesters.

1445 Pennsylvania Ave. (at Española Way), South Beach. ✆ 305/672-4765. Reservations required. Main courses $24–$48. AE, DC, DISC, MC, V. Daily 7pm–5am. Late-night menu 1am to closing.

Tuscan Steak ★★★ ITALIAN/STEAK   This excellent Northern Italian restaurant, a member of the China Grill scion, is all about meat served Italian style, in large family-style portions. With a rich wood interior, the atmosphere is reminiscent of the dining room of a well-connected family—ornate and very loud. The house salad is a massive undertaking of the classic antipasto, filled with shredded slices of salami and pepperoni, chunks of mozzarella, and a delicate vinaigrette. Be sure to order the sautéed spinach with garlic and the onion mashed potatoes with whichever steak you choose. All steaks are big enough for at least three people to share. The house specialty is a delicious T-bone steak served with pungent garlic purée. On any given weekend night, reservations are secondary to being friends with the ultratanned host, so expect a long wait for a table. The bar is the only place to wait if you can find a spot there, and drinks are rather pricey. The background music is straight out of Studio 54 and so is the flashy crowd. Despite the long waits, after one meal here, you'll likely want to kiss the ring of the true boss of this culinary mob scene—the chef.

433 Washington Ave., South Beach. ✆ 305/534-2233. Reservations strongly recommended on weekends. Main courses $20–$65. Family-style meals are $50 per person, including appetizer and main course. AE, DISC, MC, V. Sun–Thurs 6pm–midnight; Fri–Sat 6pm–1am.

Twelve Twenty ★★★ AMERICAN PROGRESSIVE   Prepare to shell out a pretty penny for the very haute twist on American and international cuisine (portions are small and prices are big) that rolls out of this kitchen in the high and mighty Tides Hotel. The air of elegance (perhaps pickled by the scent of money) mixes with the fragrances of dishes such as the blue-prawn risotto with black trumpet mushrooms and curry and warm maple-and-bourbon-smoked salmon. For dessert, save room, because you will want to try the Baked Jamaica—a luscious concoction of coffee and banana-macadamia ice creams, English toffee fudge, cinnamon meringue, and dark rum crème Anglaise. Also worthy of dessert are the restaurant's signature Tropical Popsicle martinis such as the apricot-and-ginger version that comes complete with a mini Popsicle cum stirrer made of lychee; a pineapple-basil martini comes with a Guanabana Popsicle. Unlike the oft-harried atmospheres of other South Beach eateries, where scene serves as an aperitif, there really is no scene here other than a trickle of hotel guests who occasionally pass through the lobby. Despite its exposure, Twelve Twenty does offer a fair share of privacy, which is good for the number of business power meals it hosts.

In the Tides Hotel, 1220 Ocean Dr., South Beach. ✆ 305/604-5130. Reservations recommended. Main courses $26–$35. AE, MC, V. Sun–Thurs 7–11pm; Fri–Sat 7pm–midnight.

Wish ★★★ ECLECTIC/BRAZILIAN/FRENCH   Wish got its start as a haute vegetarian restaurant, located in the stylish Todd Oldham–designed The Hotel. It was, and still is, a terrific setting (request an outside table in the serene, umbrella-covered courtyard), but the foodies couldn't bear a meal without meat. First culinary whiz Andrea Curto came on board and redirected the meaty menu and then passed her whisk on to E. Michael Reidt, one of *Food & Wine* magazine's Ten Best New Chefs of 2001, whose own culinary wishes have come true in the form of fantastic French Brazilian cuisine. Two of Wish's finest are cachaca-marinated tuna over jicama-quinoa salad on spicy charred watermelon and pan-seared beef tenderloin on a truffled taro-root purée with stewed carrots and grilled asparagus.

In The Hotel, 801 Collins Ave., South Beach. ✆ 305/531-2222. Reservations recommended. Main courses $16–$32. AE, DC, DISC, MC, V. Daily 6–10:30pm.

EXPENSIVE

Joia Restaurant and Bar ★★ ITALIAN   Owned by Miami nightlife diva Ingrid Casares, famous for her friendship with Madonna, Joia exudes a cozy atmosphere of self-conscious camaraderie, with a few tables indoors and several outdoors in a large courtyard. On any given night you're bound to see celebrities such as Ben Stiller, Donald Trump, Rupert Everett, and, yes, Madonna. Without harping on the service too much (it's quite leisurely), the pasta here is among the freshest anywhere on the beach. The chef is a native Italian and he takes great pride in crafting the perfect pasta no matter who's eating it. There is a laundry list of appetizers, salads, and pastas. Recommended dishes include the *rigatoni al funghi*, a mushroom-lover's delight, with large tube pasta filled with shiitake and porcini mushrooms; the *gnocchi di zucca*, homemade potato and pumpkin dumplings in a tomato or cheese sauce; and the *bauletti di pollo al funghi*, a folded chicken breast stuffed with Fontina cheese, mushrooms, and sage. The wine list is also exquisite.

150 Ocean Dr., South Beach. ℭ 305/674-8871. Reservations recommended. Main courses $12–$30. AE, DC, DISC, MC, V. Daily noon–4pm; Sun–Thurs 6pm–midnight; Fri–Sat 6pm–1am.

Nemo ★★★ PAN-ASIAN   What Wolfgang Puck is to foodies on the West Coast, Nemo's chef, Michael Schwartz, is to Miami. Hailing from Puck's lauded Chinois in L.A., Schwartz's Pan-Asian cuisine is masterful. Located on the quickly developing South Beach area known as SoFi (for "south of Fifth Street"), Nemo is a funky, high-style eatery with an open kitchen and an outdoor courtyard canopied by trees and lined with an eclectic mix of model types, foodies, and Schwartz groupies. Among the reasons to eat in this restaurant, whose name is actually "omen" spelled backward: grilled Indian-spiced pork chop; grilled local mahi with citrus and grilled sweet-onion salad, kimchi glaze, basil and crispy potatoes; and an inspired dessert menu by Hedy Goldsmith that's not for the faint of calories. Seating inside is comfy-cozy but borders on cramped. On Sunday mornings, the open kitchen is converted into a buffet counter for the restaurant's unparalleled brunch. Be prepared for a wait, which tends to spill out onto the street.

100 Collins Ave., South Beach. ℭ 305/532-4550. Reservations recommended. Main courses $22–$36; Sun brunch $26. AE, MC, V. Mon–Fri noon–3pm and 7pm–midnight; Sun 11am–3pm and 6–11pm. Valet parking $10.

Shoji Sushi ★★★ SUSHI   Despite the sushi saturation on South Beach, Shoji stands apart from the typical sashimi and California roll routine with expertly prepared, exquisitely fresh, and *innovative* top-notch rolls. The sleek sister to its next-door neighbor Nemo, Shoji is known for its authentic Japanese box sushi technique, in which the sushi, rice, and ingredients are packed into a tidy, tasty cake that won't crumble into your lap. Among the rolls I can't seem to get enough of here are the hamachi jalapeño—cilantro, daikon sprout, asparagus, avocado, and jalapeños—and the spicy lobster roll, which consists of mango, avocado, scallion, shiso, salmon egg, and huge chunks of lobster. Wash it all down with the saketinis and my personal fave, the gingertini, which is made with ginger, vodka, triple sec, ginger ale, and pickled ginger juice.

100 Collins Ave., South Beach. ℭ 305/532-4245. Reservations recommended. Main courses $13–$21. AE, MC, V. Mon–Fri noon–3pm; daily 6pm–1am. Valet parking $10.

Sushi Samba Dromo ★★★ SUSHI/CEVICHE   It's Brazilian, it's Peruvian, it's Japanese, it's super sushi! This multinational New York City import is definitely sceneworthy: It's a hipster's paradise. This stylish, sexy restaurant charges a pretty penny for some exotic sushi rolls such as the $14.50 soft-shell crab roll, a tasty combo of chives, jalapeño, and crab, and the $11.50 South Asian roll with shrimp, tomato, cucumber, chives, cilantro, and onions. And while the sushi is top notch, the sashimi ceviches are even better. An assortment of four—your choice of lobster, salmon, yellowtail, tuna, and fluke—is somewhat of a deal at $27, considering the fact that separately each can run you from $9 to $13.50. Main plates are equally exceptional, and while they have the usual haute dishes of snapper and Chilean sea bass, I'd try the churrasco à Rio Grande, a divine assortment of meats served with rice, beans, collard greens, and chimichurri sauce. Sushi Samba Dromo is one of the area's newer places to be, be it for a sushi roll that may set you back your kid's college fund or a very potent Pisco Sour or sakegria. Come here for good food and an excellent scene.

600 Lincoln Rd., South Beach. ℂ 305/673-5337. Reservations recommended. Main courses $17–$27. AE, MC, V. Mon–Sun noon–2am.

Tambo ★★★ SUSHI/CEVICHE   Nikkei is not just a name for a financial index, though if it were, in the case of this large, stylish, and dimly lit restaurant, it would be sky high as far as cuisine is concerned. A hybrid of Japanese and Peruvian flavors, Tambo's Nikkei cuisine is exquisite. Skip the sushi here—there are too many other sushi restaurants in town to satisfy that craving—and go straight to the ceviches. Until Tambo, I was always very skeptical of the soupy mix of marinated, uncooked fish, sauces, and assorted ingredients. When I read the offerings on this menu, though, my eyes zoomed in on the Ceviche Timbo: fresh scallops marinated in lime juice, with red onion, orange, mango, ginger, garlic, cilantro, scotch bonnet, and choclo salsa criolla, and I knew I had to take the plunge. It was one of the best things my overworked palate has ever experienced. Fresh and bursting with flavor, it turned me into a ceviche convert. There's a total of 15 ceviches to choose from. I suggest the Degustación de Ceviches, a variety pack, if you will, of three ceviches. The gorgeous, meticulous, food-as-art presentation is worthy of a photo shoot, but don't spend too much time gawking; it tastes as good, if not better, as it looks.

1801 Purdy Ave./Sunset Harbor Dr., South Beach. ℂ 305/535-2414. Reservations accepted. Main courses $21–$30. AE, DC, DISC, MC, V. Mon–Sat 6:30pm–2:30am (kitchen open until 12:30am).

MODERATE

Balan's ★★ MEDITERRANEAN   Balan's provides undeniable evidence that the Brits actually do know a thing or two about cuisine. A direct import from London's hip Soho area, Balan's draws inspiration from various Mediterranean and Asian influences, labeling its cuisine "Mediterrasian." With a brightly colored interior straight out of a mod '60s flick, Balan's is a local favorite among the gay and arty crowds. The moderately priced food is rather good here—especially the sweet-potato soufflé with leeks and roasted garlic; fried goat cheese and portobello mushrooms; and the Chilean sea bass with roasted tomato. When in doubt, the restaurant's signature lobster club sandwich is always a good choice. Adding to the ambience is the restaurant's people-watching vantage point on Lincoln Road.

1022 Lincoln Rd. (between Lenox and Michigan), South Beach. ℂ 305/534-9191. Reservations not accepted. Main courses $8–$18. AE, DISC, MC, V. Sun–Thurs 8am–midnight; Fri–Sat 8am–1am.

Bond St. Lounge ★★ SUSHI   A New York City import, the sceney Bond St. Lounge is located in the basement of the shabby chic Townhouse Hotel and is packing in hipsters as tightly as the crab meat in a California roll. Despite its tiny size, Bond St. Lounge's superfresh nigiri and sashimi and funky sushi rolls such as the sun-dried tomato and avocado or the arugula crispy potato, are worth cramming in for. As the evening progresses, however, Bond St. becomes more of a bar scene than a restaurant, but sushi is always available at the bar to accompany your sake Bloody Mary.

Townhouse Hotel, 150 20th St., South Beach. ⓒ 305/534-3800. Reservations not accepted. Sushi $6–$12. AE, MC, V. Daily 6pm–2am.

Grillfish ★★ SEAFOOD   From the beautiful Byzantine-style mural and the gleaming oak bar, you'd think you were eating in a much more expensive restaurant, but Grillfish manages to pay the exorbitant South Beach rent with the help of a loyal local following who come for fresh, simple seafood in a relaxed but upscale atmosphere.

The servers are friendly and know the menu well. The barroom seafood chowder is full of chunks of shellfish, as well as some fresh whitefish fillets in a tomato broth. The small ear of corn, included with each entree, is about as close as you'll get to any type of vegetable offering besides the pedestrian salad. Still, at these prices, it's worth a visit to try some local fare including mako shark, swordfish, tuna, marlin, and wahoo. For the surf and turf lovers, Grillfish has taken the plunge into a meaty venture right next door, at Grillsteak (1438 Collins Ave., same hours, credit cards, price range, and reservation policy). The two get along with each other rather swimmingly.

1444 Collins Ave. (corner of Española Way), South Beach. ⓒ 305/538-9908. www.grillfish.com. Reservations for 6 or more only. Main courses $9–$26. AE, DC, DISC, MC, V. Sun–Thurs 6–11pm; Fri–Sat 6pm–midnight.

Jeffrey's ★★ *Finds* CONTINENTAL/BISTRO   Some say this is the most romantic restaurant on the beach; South Beach's gay crowd certainly seems to agree. Old-fashioned lace curtains and candlelight are a welcome respite from the glitz and chrome of the rest of the island. Most people don't even realize this restaurant exists. But don't think that means there are empty tables. Jeffrey's certainly has its fair share of regulars.

You can choose a succulent three-quarter-pound burger or try a hearty chicken breast marinated in balsamic sauce and served with freshly mashed sweet potatoes over spinach, on white-lace tablecloths. Some of the better seafood options include the conch fritters and the meaty crab cakes. Macadamia-encrusted tilapia is exceptional. Most desserts are tasty (there's an old-fashioned dessert cart to tempt you), but the homemade tarte tatin, a caramelly deep-dish apple tart, is delicious.

1629 Michigan Ave., South Beach. ⓒ 305/673-0690. Reservations highly recommended. Main courses $12–$24. AE, DC, MC, V. Tues–Sat 6–11pm; Sun 5–10pm. Closed Sept.

Joe Allen ★★ *Finds* AMERICAN   It's hard to compete in a city with haute spots everywhere you look, but Joe Allen, a restaurant that has proven itself in both New York and London, has stood up to the challenge by establishing itself off the beaten path in possibly the only area of South Beach that has managed to remain impervious to trendiness and overdevelopment. Located on the bay side of the beach, Joe Allen is nestled in an unassuming building conspicuously devoid of neon lights, valet parkers, and fashionable pedestrians. Inside, however, one discovers a hidden jewel: a stark yet elegant interior and no-nonsense, fairly priced, ample-portioned dishes such as meatloaf, pizza, fresh fish, and salads. The scene has a homey feel flavored by locals looking to escape the hype without compromising quality.

1787 Purdy Ave./Sunset Harbor Dr. (3 blocks west of Alton Rd.), South Beach. © 305/531-7007. Reservations recommended, especially on weekends. Main courses $14.50–$25. MC, V. Mon–Fri 11:30am–11:45pm; Sat–Sun noon–11:45pm.

Larios on the Beach ⭐ [overrtd] CUBAN   If you're a fan of singer Gloria Estefan, you will definitely want to check out this restaurant, which she and her husband Emilio co-own; if not, you may want to reconsider, as the place is an absolute mob scene, especially on weekends. The classic Cuban dishes get a so-so rating from the Cubans, but a better one from those who aren't as well versed in the cuisine. The portions here are larger than life, as are some of the restaurant's patrons, who come here for the sidewalk scenery and the well-prepared black beans and rice. Inside, the restaurant turns into a makeshift salsa club, with music blaring over the animated conversations and the sounds of English clashing with Spanish. Because of its locale on Ocean Drive, Larios is a great place to bring someone who's never experienced the Cuban culture or tasted its cuisine.

820 Ocean Dr., South Beach. © 305/532-9577. Reservations recommended. Main courses $8–$27. AE, MC, V. Sun–Thurs 11:30am–midnight; Fri–Sat 11:30am–2am.

L'Entrecote de Paris ⭐⭐ FRENCH   New York's got the Statue of Liberty and Miami's got L'Entrecote de Paris. We don't complain. Everything in this little piece of Paris, a classy, albeit recently expanded, little bistro, is simple. For dinner, it's either steak, chicken, or seafood—I'd stick to the steaks, particularly the house special, L'Entrecote's French steak, with all-you-can-eat french fries (or *pommes frites,* rather). The salmon looks like spa cuisine, served with a pile of bald steamed potatoes and a salad with simple greens and an unmatchable vinaigrette. The steak, on the other hand, is the stuff cravings are made of, even if you're not a die-hard carnivore. Its salty sharp sauce is rich but not thick, and full of the beef's natural flavor. I loved the *profiteroles au chocolat,* a perfect puff pastry filled with vanilla ice cream and topped with a dark bittersweet chocolate sauce. Most diners are very Euro and pack a petit attitude. Servers, however, are super-quick and professional, and almost friendly in a French kind of way, making up for the close quarters.

413 Washington Ave., South Beach. © 305/673-1002. Reservations recommended on weekends. Main courses $16–$24. DC, MC, V. Sun–Thurs 6:30pm–midnight; Fri–Sat 6pm–1am.

Macaluso's ⭐⭐⭐ ITALIAN   This restaurant epitomizes the Italians' love for—and mastery of—savory, plentiful, down-home Staten Island–style food. While the storefront restaurant is intimate and demure in nature, there's nothing delicate about the bold mix of flavors in every meat and pasta dish here. Catch the fantastic clam pie when in season—the portions are huge. Pricier items vary throughout the season, but will likely feature fresh fish handpicked by Chef (and owner) Michael, the Don of the kitchen, who is so accommodating he'll take special requests or even bring to your table a complimentary, signature meatball. If he doesn't, don't hesitate to ask you waiter for one, he'll be glad to bring it to you. Everyone will recommend perennial favorites such as the rigatoni and broccoli rabe. There are delicious desserts that range from homemade anisette cookies to Patricia Scott's pastries. The wine list is also good. The

Georges Dub[oe]uf Beaujolais at $22 a bottle is a steal, when you consider that it comes nicely chilled with slices of luscious Georgia peaches, which make a great and affordable dessert by themselves.

1747 Alton Rd., Miami Beach. ☎ 305/604-1811. Main courses $14–$28; pizza $8–$13. AE, MC, V. Tues–Sat 6pm–midnight; Sun 6–11pm. After 10:30pm only pies are served. Closed Mon.

Piola ★★ PIZZA   This hip Italian import miraculously transforms pizza from an eat-out-of-the-box-stuff-a-slice-into-your-mouth experience into a fun, sit-down meal that's hard to beat for the price, quality, and quantity. An unabridged menu of nearly 80 different kinds of pizzas-for-one that are really enough to share between two people is mind numbing and mouth watering. I suggest that you order several pizzas, depending on how many people you are dining with (two is more than enough for two, for example). Start with the quattro formaggio pizza—brie, Gorgonzola, Parmesan and mozzarella—and then consider a funkier version, say, smoked salmon and caviar. All pizzas are thin crusted and full of flavor. Waitstaff is extremely friendly, too, but be prepared for a lengthy wait, especially on weekend nights when the movie-going crowds next door spill over for a snack.

1625 Alton Rd., South Beach. ☎ 305/674-1660. Reservations accepted. $7–$15 main courses. AE, DC, MC, V. Daily 6pm–1am.

Spiga ★★ ITALIAN   This intimate Italian restaurant is cool without being pretentious, concentrating on the food rather than the fanfare that has become central to so many South Beach eateries. Like the hotel in which it resides, Spiga's atmosphere is wonderfully low-key, making it a quiet favorite with locals and some luminaries. The complimentary bruschetta with grilled eggplant, served to you at one of the few tables inside or out, is the first of many culinary treats. The garlicky gnocchi with tomato and basil is an incredible illustration of how simple doesn't have to mean bland. The pungent Gorgonzola polenta appetizer is a meal in itself, and the risotto with bay scallops is a rousing display of culinary precision. The place is vaguely reminiscent of a Florentine trattoria, and if you stop to listen, you'll notice the prevailing language here is, in fact, Italian.

Hotel Impala, 1228 Collins Ave., South Beach. ☎ 305/534-0079. Reservations accepted. $7–$20 main courses. AE, DC, MC, V. Daily 6pm–midnight.

Van Dyke Cafe ★ AMERICAN   The younger, jazzier sibling of Ocean Drive's News Café, the Van Dyke is similar in spirit and cuisine but different in attitude. Unlike the much scenier and much more touristy News Café, Van Dyke is a locals' favorite, at which people-watching is also premium, but attitude is practically nonexistent. Both cafes have nearly the same menu, with decent salads, sandwiches, and omelets, but the Van Dyke's warm, wood-floored interior, upstairs jazz bar, accessible parking, and intense chocolate soufflé make it a less taxing alternative. Also, unlike News, Van Dyke turns into a sizzling nightspot, featuring live jazz nearly every night of the week (a $5 cover charge is added to your bill if you sit at a table; the bar's free). Outside there's a vast tree-lined seating area.

846 Lincoln Rd., South Beach. ☎ 305/534-3600. Reservations recommended for dinner. Main courses $9–$17. AE, DC, MC, V. Daily 8am–2am.

MODERATE

Big Pink ★ *Kids* AMERICAN   Real Food for Real People is the motto to which this restaurant strictly adheres. Located on what used to be a gritty corner of Collins Avenue, Big Pink—owned by the folks at the higher-end Nemo—

is quickly identified by a whimsical Pippi Longstocking–type mascot on a sign outside. Scooters and motorcycles line the streets surrounding the place, which is a favorite among beach bums, club kids, and those craving Big Pink's comforting and hugely portioned pizzas, sandwiches, salads, and hamburgers. The fare is above average at best, and the menu is massive, but it comes with a good dose of kitsch, such as their "gourmet" spin on the classic TV dinner, which is done perfectly, right down to the compartmentalized dessert. Televisions line the bar area, and family-style table arrangement (there are several booths, too) promotes camaraderie among diners. Outdoor tables are available. Even picky kids will like the food here, and parents can enjoy the family-friendly atmosphere (not the norm for South Beach) without worrying if their kids are making too much noise.

157 Collins Ave., Miami Beach. ℂ 305/532-4700. Main courses $12.50–$19.95. AE, DC, MC, V. Sun and Thurs 8am–2am; Mon–Wed 8am–midnight; Fri–Sat 8am–5am.

11th Street Diner AMERICAN   Like many of Miami's residents, this retrodiner is a transplant from the Northeast. Uprooted from its 1948 Wilkes-Barre, Pennsylvania, foundation, the actual structure was dismantled and rebuilt on a bustling corner of Washington Avenue. It's a popular round-the-clock spot that attracts a friendly yet motley crew of locals, club kids, and curious tourists and is well known for its slow service and greasy diner fare. Come in for breakfast and you'll find bleary-eyed patrons chowing down after a night of partying.

1065 Washington Ave., South Beach. ℂ 305/534-6373. Items $8–$15. AE, MC. Daily 24 hr.

El Rancho Grande ★★ MEXICAN   Hidden just off Lincoln Road, El Rancho Grande was once a well-kept secret among devout Mexican food fanatics. It's not such a secret anymore. With a relatively restrained decor (clay pots, sponge-painted yellow walls), El Rancho Grande doesn't hold anything back when it comes to the cuisine. The Aztec Soup, a hot and spicy blend of chicken and tortilla strips, is some of the best I've had. Fresh, spicy salsa and expertly prepared, hugely portioned enchiladas, burritos, and fajitas are sensational. The scene is young and lively without being too rowdy. Margaritas are a little weak when frozen and better ordered on the rocks. Expect a wait at the small bar for your table, especially on weekends. Limited outdoor seating is available.

1626 Pennsylvania Ave., Miami Beach. ℂ 305/673-0480. Main courses $10–$19. AE, DC, MC, V. Daily 11am–11pm.

Front Porch Café ★ AMERICAN   Located in an unassuming, rather drearylooking Art Deco hotel, the Front Porch Café is a relaxed local hangout known for cheap breakfasts. While some of the wait staff might be a bit sluggish (many are bartenders or club kids by night), it seems that nobody here is in a rush. If you are, this is *not* the place for you. Enjoy home-style French toast with bananas and walnuts, omelets, fresh fruit salads, pizzas, and classic breakfast pancakes that put IHOP to shame. Front Porch Café is also known for its daily dose of local gossip, which flows as freely as the syrup.

In the Penguin Hotel, 1418 Ocean Dr., South Beach. ℂ 305/531-8300. Main courses $5–$16. AE, DC, DISC, MC, V. Daily 8:30am–10:30pm.

Mama Vieja ★ COLOMBIAN   This funky Colombian hangout looks like a total dive from the outside, but once inside you will want to dive right in to the supremely fresh national specialties such as *pargo rojo estofado a la mama vieja* (red snapper stuffed with a super-creamy and delicate seafood sauce in a rice base). Brightly painted walls and elevated porches look out onto a large-screen TV showing music videos from the old country. The walls and ceilings are decorated with hundreds of hats that have been donated by customers and signed in exchange for a free meal. Bring in an interesting hat and mention it to the server before placing your order so that he or she can bring you to the attention of the owner. All the dishes here are worth trying and are so reasonably priced that it's easy to order a lot. Try to save room for the milky sweet desserts and a good strong coffee—you'll need it if you want to dance it off after at Lola, the very popular, unpretentious hot spot next door. If not, there's live music here, too.

235 23rd St. (just west of Collins Ave.), South Beach. ⓒ 305/538-2400. Main courses $4.95–$14.95. AE, DC, DISC, MC, V. Daily noon–midnight. Closed Tues.

INEXPENSIVE

La Sandwicherie SANDWICHES   You can get mustard, mayo, or oil and vinegar on sandwiches elsewhere in town, but you'd be missing out on all the local flavor. This gourmet sandwich bar, open until the crack of dawn, caters to ravenous club kids, biker types, and the body artists who work in the tattoo parlor next door. For many people, in fact, no night of clubbing is complete without capping it off with a turkey sub from La Sandwicherie.

229 14th St. (behind the Amoco station), South Beach. ⓒ **305/532-8934.** Sandwiches and salads $6–$12. No credit cards. Daily 9am–5am. Delivery 9:30am–10pm.

Lincoln Road Café ✦ _Value_ CUBAN   A local favorite, this down-to-earth Cuban-accented cafe is very popular for its cheap breakfasts. For $6, you can indulge in a hearty portion of eggs any style, with bacon, ham, sausage, Cuban toast, and coffee. Lunch and dinner specials are delicious and very cheap as well; try the ubiquitous black beans and rice or a chicken fricassee with plantains. The few tables inside are usually passed up in favor of the several outdoors, but in the evenings the house is full inside and out, as talented Latin musicians perform out front.

941 Lincoln Rd., South Beach. ⓒ **305/538-8066.** Items $6–$11. AE, DC, MC, V. Daily 8am–midnight.

News Café ✦ AMERICAN   In the late '80s, South Beach pioneer Mark Soyka opened this cafe on a depressed, decrepit Ocean Drive, sparking what some now call the South Beach renaissance. The thriving News has become part of Miami history and it still draws locals onto what has become the most tourist-ridden street in the area. Whether you come by foot, blade, Harley, or Ferrari, you should wait for an outside table, which is where you need to be to fully appreciate the experience. Service is notoriously slow and often arrogant (perhaps because the tip is included), but the menu, while not newsworthy, has some fairly good items, such as the Middle Eastern platter of hummus, tahini, tabbouleh, and grape leaves; hamburgers; and omelets. If it's not too busy, you can enjoy a leisurely cappuccino outside; creative types like to bring their laptops and sit here all day (or all night—this place is open 24 hr. a day!). There's also an extensive collection of national and international newspapers and magazines at the in-house newsstand. News Café also opened another clone, Café Cardozo, at the Cardozo Hotel at 1300 Ocean Dr. on South Beach, in case 5 blocks is too much to walk to the original.

800 Ocean Dr., South Beach. ⓒ **305/538-6397.** Items $5–$20. AE, DC, MC, V. Open 24 hr.

Pizza Rustica ✦ PIZZA   Italians often scoff at the way Americans have mangled their recipe for pizza. But at Pizza Rustica, even the Italians marvel at these thin-crusted gourmet meals. This is the real deal—no thick, doughy, greasy concoctions here. Instead, Rustica features several delicious, huge slices of gourmet, authentically Tuscan-style pizza. Spinach and Gorgonzola cheese blend harmoniously with a brush of olive oil and garlic on a slate of the delicious, crispy dough. There's also a four-cheese, arugula, and rosemary-potato slice, among others. Check out their new location at 1447 Washington Ave. (between 8th and 9th sts.), South Beach (℃ **305/538-6009**).

863 Washington Ave., South Beach. ℃ **305/674-8244**. Slice $4. No credit cards. Daily 11am–6am.

Puerto Sagua ✩ CUBAN/SPANISH   This brown-walled diner is one of the only old holdouts on South Beach. Its steady stream of regulars ranges from *abuelitos* (little old grandfathers) to hipsters who stop in after clubbing. It has endured because the food is good, if a little greasy. Some of the less heavy dishes are a super-chunky fish soup with pieces of whole flaky grouper, chicken, and seafood paella, or marinated kingfish. Also good are most of the shrimp dishes, especially the shrimp in garlic sauce, which is served with white rice and salad.

This is one of the most reasonably priced places left on the beach for simple, hearty fare. Don't be intimidated by the hunched, older waiters in their white button shirts and black pants. Even if you don't speak Spanish, they're usually willing to do charades. Anyway, the extensive menu, which ranges from BLTs to grilled lobsters to yummy fried plantains, is translated into English. Hurry, before another boutique goes up in its place.

700 Collins Ave., South Beach. ℃ **305/673-1115**. Main courses $6–$24; sandwiches and salads $5–$10. AE, DC, MC, V. Daily 7:30am–2am.

Sport Café ✩ ITALIAN   When Sport Café first opened, way back when South Beach was still a fledgling in the trendoid business, it had a plain interior, wooden chairs, and a view of the parking lot. Televisions inside were tuned to soccer matches at all times—hence the name. The key to Sport's success was, and still is, its good, cheap, homemade Italian food—nothing fancy. Only now the cafe has moved up the block to a large corner space complete with private outdoor garden. The restaurant might have moved on to better digs, but one thing remains the same: The food is still great and the soccer matches continue to kick the crowd into a European-style frenzy. Try the nightly specials, especially when the owners' mother is cooking her secret lasagna.

560 Washington Ave., South Beach. ℃ **305/674-9700**. Reservations accepted for 4 or more. Main courses $5–$18; sandwiches and pizzas $6–$9. AE, MC, V. Daily noon–1am.

Sushi Rock Café ✩ SUSHI   Perhaps it has something to do with its campy name, but for some reason almost every rock star that comes to town makes a requisite stop here for a sushi fix. Aerosmith's Joe Perry and Steven Tyler ate here almost every night during their Miami-based recording sessions, and David Lee Roth has been spotted here more than once. Sushi Rock is known for a sporadically fresh assortment of sushi, hand rolls, and traditional Japanese cuisine, funky atmosphere, and hip late-night crowds. What diners are to hamburgers, Sushi Rock is to raw fish—it's always consistent but will never appear on any "best of" lists.

1351 Collins Ave. (at 14th St.), South Beach. ℃ **305/532-2133**. Items $4–$19. AE, DC, MC, V. Sun–Thurs noon–midnight; Fri–Sat 2pm–1am.

MIAMI BEACH, NORTH BEACH, SURFSIDE & BAL HARBOUR

The area north of the Art Deco District—from about 21st Street to 163rd Street—had its heyday in the 1950s when huge hotels and gambling halls blocked the view of the ocean. Now, many of the old hotels have been converted

into condos or budget lodgings, and the bay-front mansions have been renovated by and for wealthy entrepreneurs, families, and speculators. The area has
many more residents, albeit seasonal, than visitors. On the culinary front, the
result is a handful of superexpensive, traditional restaurants as well as a number
of value-oriented spots. (For a map of these restaurants, see p. 115.)

VERY EXPENSIVE

The Forge Restaurant ★★★ STEAK/AMERICAN   English oak paneling
and Tiffany glass suggest high prices and haute cuisine, and that's exactly what
you get at the Forge. Each elegant dining room possesses its own character and
features high ceilings, ornate chandeliers, and European artwork. The atmosphere is elegant but not too stuffy. On Wednesday night (the party night here),
however, it's pandemonium as the who's who of Miami society gather for dinner, dancing, and schmoozing. Like the rest of the menu, appetizers are mostly
classics, from Beluga caviar to baked onion soup to shrimp cocktail and escargot. When they're in season, order the stone crabs. For the main course, any of
the seafood, chicken, or veal dishes are recommendable, but the Forge is especially known for its award-winning steaks. Its wine selection is equally lauded—
ask for a tour of the cellar.

432 Arthur Godfrey Rd. (41st St.), Miami Beach. © 305/538-8533. Reservations required. Main courses
$21–$55. AE, DC, MC, V. Sun–Thurs 6pm–midnight; Fri–Sat 6pm–1am.

Shula's Steak House ★★ AMERICAN/STEAK   Climb a sweeping staircase
in the Alexander All-Suite Luxury Hotel and go through the glass hallway—
designed like an atrium, so exotic flora and fauna beckon from both within and
without—and you'll find yourself in this magnificent restaurant that has been
acclaimed as one of the greatest steakhouses in all of North America. If you're
feeling adventurous, try the 48-ounce club (you can get your name engraved on
a gold plaque if you can finish this absolutely *huge* piece of meat) or settle for
the 20-ounce Kansas City strip or the 12-ounce filet mignon. Fresh seafood
abounds when in season, and the oysters Rockefeller are a particularly good
choice. The entertaining staff is very knowledgeable. The restaurant also has the
"No Name Lounge," where live piano music, premium spirits, and cigar smoking are available.

There's another branch of Shula's at 7601 NW 154th St. (in Don Shula's Golf
Club off the Palmetto Expwy.; © **305/820-8102**) in West Dade.

In the Alexander Hotel, 5225 Collins Ave., Miami Beach. © 305/341-6565. Reservations recommended.
Main courses $18–$58. AE, DISC, MC, V. Daily 11am–3:30pm and 6–11pm. Free valet parking.

EXPENSIVE

Atlantic Restaurant ★★ AMERICAN   If you didn't know any better, you'd
think you were in Nantucket at this comfortable blue and white beach-style
restaurant designed to make you feel like you're eating in someone's guest-house
kitchen. The food, however, isn't your typical hamburger and hot dog on the
grill fare. Sure, you can get all-American mac and cheese, but the Atlantic's version comes with truffles. Thanks to the Beach House Bal Harbour's owner, Jennifer Rubell, Atlantic gets delightfully kitschy with special themed-dinner nights
such as the Clam Bake, in which a slew of fresh, all-you-can-eat seafood is yours
for the taking. Same goes for the Meat and Potatoes night. Brunches are particularly delicious here, too, as is the poolside and oceanfront seating.

In the Beach House Bal Harbour Hotel, 9449 Collins Ave., Bal Harbour. © 305/695-7930. Reservations recommended, required on weekends. Main courses $9.50–$22. AE, DC, MC, V. Daily 7am–11pm.

Baraboo ★★ *Kids* MEDITERRANEAN   Baraboo, a crowded eatery in up-and-coming North Beach, is named for the small Wisconsin town that served as the original winter quarters of the Ringling Brothers Circus. Strolling mimes and magicians work the room, entertaining—or harassing, at times—diners who are indulging in the Mediterranean fare. Kids will love the distractions but will probably not like the adult food very much. Though not necessarily a theme restaurant, if they took away the clowning around, Baraboo could be a serious restaurant, featuring excellent ravioli with spinach, ricotta, and egg yolk; potato-crusted sea bass with saffron-sage sauce; and roasted muscovy duck breast. If you prefer to remain outside the big top, there are several outdoor tables that will protect you from a wayward mime or magician.

7300 Ocean Terrace (at 73rd St. and Collins Ave.), North Beach. ✆ 305/867-4242. Reservations recommended, required on weekends. Main courses $9–$39.95. AE, MC, V. Daily 5:30pm–1am.

Christine Lee's ★★ CHINESE   This Cantonese restaurant is a 35-year-old Miami staple that serves excellent but overpriced Chinese steak, shrimp, and lobster sauce, and steak kew. Considering the dearth of good Chinese restaurants in Miami, this is a good choice if you absolutely *must* satisfy your cravings for Chinese, but it will definitely cost you more than it should.

17082 Collins Ave. (1 block south of the Rascal House, in the RK strip mall, directly on Collins Ave.), Sunny Isles. ✆ 305/947-1717. Reservations recommended. Main courses $6.95–$29. AE, DISC, MC, V. Daily 4–11pm; winter lunch 11am–3pm.

Crystal Café ★★★ CONTINENTAL/NEW WORLD   The setting is sparse, with a bottle of wine and Lucite salt and pepper grinders as the only centerpiece on each of the 15 or so tables. I promise you won't need the seasoning. Chef Klime has done it all with the help of his affable wife and a superb waitstaff. Enjoy his unique sparkle at this little-known hideaway, which attracts stars like Julio Iglesias and other in-the-know gourmands.

With approximately 30 entrees, including a few nightly specials, each is beautifully presented and perfectly prepared. The shrimp-cake appetizer, for example, is the size of a bread plate and rests on top of a small mound of lightly sautéed watercress and mushrooms. Surrounding the delicately breaded disc are concentric circles of beautiful sauces. The veal Marsala is served in a luscious brown sauce thickened not with heavy cream or flour but with delicate vegetable broth and a hearty mix of mushrooms. The osso buco (an Italian dish consisting of veal shangs stewed in white wine with tomatoes, garlic, minced veggies, and more) is a masterpiece.

726 41st St., Miami Beach. ✆ 305/673-8266. Reservations recommended on weekends. Main courses $11–$25. AE, DC, DISC, MC, V. Tues–Thurs 5–10pm; Fri–Sat 5–11pm.

MODERATE

Cafe Prima Pasta ★★ ITALIAN   Proving that good things do come in small packages, this tiny corner cafe's home cooking draws nightly hordes of carbo-craving diners who don't seem to mind waiting for a table for upwards of an hour, maybe more on weekends. The scent of garlic wafting into the street is guaranteed to kill any vampire, and it makes the wait for a table a bit more torturous. Other choice ingredients include the ripest, freshest tomatoes, the finest olive oil, mozzarella that melts in your mouth, and fish that puts some seafood restaurants to shame. The spicy garlic-and-oil dip that comes with the bread is hard to resist and will likely linger with you for days, like the memory of this fine meal. Though tables are packed in a bit, the atmosphere still manages to be romantic.

414 71st St. (half a block east of the Byron movie theater), Miami Beach. ℂ **305/867-0106.** Reservations not accepted. Main courses $9–$19; pastas $7–$9. No credit cards. Mon–Thurs noon–midnight; Fri noon–1am; Sat 1pm–1am; Sun 5pm–midnight.

Cafe Ragazzi ★★ ITALIAN This diminutive Italian cafe, with its rustic decor and a swift, knowledgeable waitstaff, enjoys great success for its tasty, simple pastas. The spicy puttanesca sauce with a subtle hint of fish is perfectly prepared. Also recommended is the salmon with radicchio. You can choose from many decent salads and carpacci, too. Lunch specials are a real steal at $7, including soup, salad, and daily pasta. Unlike Café Prima Pasta, Café Ragazzi is light on sceniness—people come here for the food only. Expect to wait on weekend nights.

9500 Harding Ave. (on the corner of 95th St.), Surfside. ℂ **305/866-4495.** Reservations accepted for 4 or more. Main courses $9–$18. MC, V. Mon–Fri 11:30am–3pm; daily 5:30–11pm.

Lemon Twist ★★ MEDITERRANEAN In addition to great Mediterranean fare, there is a twist to this place in the form of a complimentary shot of the eponymous house spirit (a lemon-vodka shot). But that comes after your meal. To start, you will receive a bowl of perfectly marinated olives, which can endanger your appetite, so go easy on them. A soothing, mellow interior makes for a romantic dining experience, or, if you prefer, outdoor tables are available (though the street is hardly as scenic). In between, expect friendly service and excellent meat and pasta dishes at terrific prices. Specialties such as spinach lasagna with smoked salmon and shank of lamb caramelized with whole garlic are savored by a savvy crowd that has likely escaped South Beach for this refreshing change of scenery.

908 71st St. (off the 79th St. Causeway), Miami Beach/Normandy Isle. ℂ **305/868-2075.** Reservations recommended on weekends. Main courses $9–$18. AE, MC, V ($25 minimum). Tues–Sun 5:30pm–midnight. Closed July 4 weekend.

Wolfie Cohen's Rascal House ★ DELI Open since 1954 and still going strong, this historic, nostalgic culinary extravaganza is one of Miami Beach's greatest traditions. Scooch into one of the ancient vinyl booths—which have hosted many a notorious bottom, from Frank Sinatra to mob boss Sam Giancana—and review the huge menu that's loaded with authentic Jewish staples. Consider the classic corned beef sandwich, stuffed cabbage, brisket, or potato pancakes. If you're lucky, the waitress will give you a wax-paper doggy bag to wrap up the leftover rolls and danish from your breadbasket. There is another Wolfie's in Boca Raton, at 2006 NW Executive Center Circle (ℂ **561/ 982-8899**).

17190 Collins Ave. (at 163rd St.), Sunny Isles. ℂ **305/947-4581.** Main courses $8–$30. AE, MC, V. Daily 7am–1am. There is another Wolfie Cohen's Rascal House in Boca Raton, at 2006 NW Executive Center Circle, Boca Raton, 561-982-8899.

INEXPENSIVE

Curry's _Value_ AMERICAN Established in 1937, this large dining room on the ocean side of Collins Avenue is one of Miami Beach's oldest, and kitschiest, restaurants. Neither the restaurant's name nor the tacky Polynesian wall decorations are indicative of its offerings, which are straightforwardly American and reminiscent of the area's heyday. Broiled and fried fish dishes are available, but the best selections, including steak, chicken, and ribs, come off the open charcoal grill perched by the front window. Prices are incredibly reasonable here, and include an appetizer, soup, or salad, as well as a potato or vegetable, dessert, and coffee or tea.

7433 Collins Ave., Miami Beach. ✆ 305/866-1571. Reservations accepted. Main courses (including appetizer and dessert) $10–$20. MC, V. Tues–Sun 4–10pm.

The Greek Place GREEK   This little hole-in-the-wall diner with sparkling white walls and about 10 wooden stools serves fantastic Greek and American diner-style food. Daily specials like *pastitsio*, chicken *alcyone*, and roast turkey with all the fixings are big lunchtime draws for locals working in the area. Typical Greek dishes like shish kebab, souvlaki, and gyros are cooked to perfection as you wait. Even the hamburger, prime ground beef delicately spiced and freshly grilled, is wonderful.

233 95th St. (between Collins and Harding Aves.), Surfside. ✆ 305/866-9628. Main courses $6–$7. No credit cards. Mon–Fri 10am–5pm; Sat 11am–3pm.

Sheldon's Drugs 🎈 *Value* AMERICAN   This typical old-fashioned drugstore counter was a favorite breakfast spot of Isaac Bashevis Singer. Consider stopping into this historic site for a good piece of pie and a side of history. According to legend, the author was sitting at Sheldon's eating a bagel and eggs when his wife got the call in 1978 that he had won the Nobel Prize for Literature. The menu hasn't changed much since then. You can get eggs and oatmeal and a good tuna melt. A blue-plate special might be generic spaghetti and meatballs or grilled frankfurters. The food is pretty basic, but you can't beat the prices.

9501 Harding Ave., Surfside. ✆ 305/866-6251. Main courses $4–$8; soups and sandwiches $2–$5. AE, DISC, MC, V. Mon–Sat 7am–9pm; Sun 7am–4pm.

NORTH MIAMI BEACH

Although there aren't many hotels in North Dade, the population in the winter months explodes due to the onslaught of seasonal residents from the Northeast. A number of exclusive condominiums and country clubs, including William's Island, Turnberry, and the Jockey Club, breed a demanding clientele, many of whom dine out nightly. That's good news for visitors, who can find superior service and cuisine at value prices.

VERY EXPENSIVE

Chef Allen's ★★★ NEW WORLD CUISINE   If anyone deserves to have a restaurant named after him, it's chef Allen Susser, winner of the esteemed James Beard Award for Best American Chef in the Southeast—the Academy Award of cuisine—and practically every other form of praise and honor awarded by the most discriminating palates. Chef Allen, the man, is royalty around here. Chef Allen, the restaurant, is his province, and foodies are his disciples. His platform? New World Cuisine and the harmony of exotic tropical fruits, spices, and vegetables. It is under Chef Allen's magic that ordinary Key limes and mangos reappear in the form of succulent salsas and sauces. A traditional antipasto is transformed into a Caribbean one, with papaya-pineapple barbeque shrimp, jerk calamari, and charred rare tuna. Whole yellowtail in coconut milk and curry sauce is a particularly spectacular entree. Unlike other restaurants where location is key, Chef Allen's, located in the rear of a strip mall, could be in the desert, and hordes of people would still make the trek.

19088 NE 29th Ave. (at Biscayne Blvd.), North Miami Beach. ✆ 305/935-2900. Reservations recommended. Main courses $22–$40. AE, DC, MC, V. Sun–Thurs 6–10pm; Fri–Sat 6–11pm.

Kids **Family-Friendly Restaurants**

Baraboo *(p. 145)* While the cuisine may be a bit funky for kids' palates, the wandering magicians and mimes are guaranteed to entertain the little ones, who will likely eat anything after the magician says "abracadabra."

Big Pink *(p. 140)* One of South Beach's only family-friendly sit-down restaurants, Big Pink is a fun, noisy restaurant with a comprehensive menu consisting of macaroni and cheese, hamburgers, and other comfort foods guaranteed to satisfy the pickiest kids.

Bubba Gump Shrimp Co. Named after the character from the motion picture *Forrest Gump,* this is a great place to bring the entire family on a lazy Sunday afternoon. You get to eat some good, moderately priced seafood, watch ships sail by on the bay, and shop at the Bayside Marketplace afterward. There's also a gift shop where you can buy Forrest Gump souvenirs, T-shirts, and caps. In Bayside Marketplace, 401 Biscayne Blvd. (at 4th Ave., north of the port of Miami); © **305/379-8866.**

Wilderness Grill Let the kids run wild in this noisy theme restaurant that serves as many sound effects as it does hamburgers. Shops at Sunset (57th and U.S. 1), 5701 Sunset Dr. #114; © **305/740-3033.**

EXPENSIVE

Lagoon ⭐ SEAFOOD/CONTINENTAL This old bay-front fish house has been around since 1936. Major road construction nearby should have guaranteed its doom years ago, but the excellent view and incredible specials make it a worthwhile stop. If you can disregard the somewhat dirty bathrooms and nonchalant service, you'll find the best-priced juicy Maine lobsters around.

Yes, it's true! Lobster lovers can get two 1½ pounders for $22.95. Try them broiled with a light buttery-seasoned coating. This dish is not only inexpensive but incredibly succulent, too. Side dishes include fresh vegetables, like broccoli or asparagus, as well as a huge baked potato, stuffed or plain.

488 Sunny Isles Blvd. (163rd St.), North Miami Beach. © **305/947-6661.** Reservations accepted. Main courses $12–$40; appetizers $6–$14. AE, MC, V. Daily 4:30–11pm. Happy hour daily 4:30–6pm.

INEXPENSIVE

Laurenzo's Café ⭐⭐ ITALIAN This recently expanded lunch counter in the middle of a chaotic grocery store has been serving delicious buffet lunches to the *paesanos* for years. New additions include an open kitchen and wood-burning pizza oven. A meeting place for the growing Italian population in Miami, the store has been open for more than 40 years. Daily specials usually include lasagna or eggplant parmigiana and two or three salad options. Also good are the rustic pizzas. Choose a wine from the vast selection and take your meal to go, or sit in the trellis-covered area amid busy shoppers buying their evening's groceries. You'll get to eavesdrop on some great conversations over your plastic tray of real Southern Italian–style cooking.

16385 W. Dixie Hwy. (south of the corner of 163rd St.), North Miami Beach. © **305/945-6381.** Main courses $4–$8; salads $2–$5. No credit cards. Mon–Fri 11am–7:30pm; Sat 11am–7pm; Sun 11am–4pm.

DOWNTOWN

Downtown Miami is a large, sprawling area divided by the Brickell Bridge into two distinct areas: Brickell Avenue and the bay-front area near Biscayne Boulevard. You shouldn't walk from one to the other—it's quite a distance and unsafe at night. Convenient Metromover stops do adjoin the areas, so for a quarter it's better to hop on the scenic sky tram (closed after midnight).

VERY EXPENSIVE

Azul ✸✸✸ GLOBAL FUSION   If there was an Epicurean version of the Academy Awards, this restaurant would win Best Director, hands down. Executive chef Michelle Bernstein, Miami's wunderkind in the kitchen, creates a tour de force of international cuisine, inspired by Caribbean, French, Argentine, Asian, and even American flavors. Like a stunning designer gown, the restaurant's decor, with its waterfront view, high ceilings, walls burnished in copper, and silk-covered chairs, is complemented by sparkling jewels—in this case, the food. The hamachi carpaccio appetizer is a sumptuous arrangement of yellowtail (imported from Japan), shaved fennel, mixed greens, and cucumber. Entrees, or "Plates of Resistance" as they're called here, include braised langoustine open-faced ravioli; ginger-lemon grass–glazed Chilean sea bass served with black rice, kimchi, and Napa cabbage; and chicken with red Thai curry. Desserts range from fruity to chocolatey and shouldn't be skipped.

At the Mandarin Oriental, 500 Brickell Key Dr., Miami. ✆ **305/913-8254**. Reservations strongly recommended. Main courses $24–$38. AE, DC, DISC, MC, V. Mon–Fri noon–3pm; Mon–Sat 7–11pm.

Capital Grille ✸✸ STEAK   This place reeks of power. Seated among wine cellars filled with high-end classics, the dark wood paneling, pristine white tablecloths, chandeliers, and marble floors all contribute to the clubby atmosphere. For an appetizer, start with the lobster and crab cakes. If you're not in the mood for beef or lobster, try the pan-seared red snapper and asparagus covered with Hollandaise. The wine cellars you're surrounded by are filled with about 5,000 bottles of wine—too extensive and rare to list. While some people prefer the more stalwart style and service of Morton's up the block, others find Capital to be a bit livelier. The food's pretty much the same between the two, though I find the steaks at Morton's to be a notch better; however, the atmosphere at the Capital Grille is *much* more inviting. Complimentary valet parking here as opposed to Morton's, which charges a fee, is another reason to visit this carnivorous capital.

444 Brickell Ave., Miami. ✆ **305/374-4500**. Reservations recommended. Main courses $21–$35. AE, DC, DISC, MC, V. Mon–Fri 11:30am–3pm; Mon–Thurs 5–10:30pm; Fri 5–11pm; Sat 6–11pm; Sun 5–10pm.

Morton's of Chicago ✸ STEAK   A private, club-like ambience, with dark wood, leather booths, and tablecloths, makes Morton's of Chicago the preferred spot for major business transactions and quiet, romantic dinners. A vast menu includes a wide variety of excellent steaks and an award-winning menu consisting of shrimp Alexander, oysters on the half shell, sea scallops with apricot chutney, swordfish medallions with béarnaise sauce, and a dense, hot Godiva chocolate cake that's out of this world. Private dining rooms are perfect to carry on clandestine conversations and romantic liaisons. The open kitchen is probably the only thing here that's not private. At lunchtime, the power is tangible as business deals are sliced and diced as often as the steak is. At night, the scene is more elegant, attracting older sophisticates and pre- and post-theater crowds.

1200 Brickell Ave., Miami. ✆ **305/400-9990**. Reservations recommended. Main courses $20–$30. AE, DC, MC, V. Mon–Fri 11:30am–11pm; Sat 2:30–11pm; Sun 2:30–10pm.

Porcao ★★ BRAZILIAN   The name sounds eerily like "pork out," which is what you'll be doing at this exceptional Brazilian *churrascaria* (a Brazillian-style restaurant devoted mostly to meat—it's the Portuguese translation of steakhouse). For about $30, you can feast on salads and meats *after* you sample the unlimited gourmet buffet, which includes such fillers as pickled quail eggs, marinated onions, and an entire prosciutto. Do not stuff yourself here, as the next step is the meaty part: Choose as much lamb, filet mignon, chicken hearts, and steaks as you like, grilled, skewered, and sliced right at your table. Side dishes also come with the meal, including beans and rice and fried yucca.

801 Brickell Bay Dr., Miami. ✆ **305/373-2777.** Reservations accepted. Prix fixe $31.50 per person, all you can eat. AE, DC, MC, V. Daily noon–midnight.

EXPENSIVE

Big Fish ★★ *Finds* SEAFOOD/ITALIAN   This scenic seafood shack on the Miami River is a real catch—if you can find it. Hard to locate, but well worth the search, Big Fish's remote location keeps many people biting. In fact, Big Fish added some Italian options to its all-seafood menu in the hopes of luring more people, and that worked, too. Big Fish has a sweeping view of the Miami skyline and some of the freshest catch around; the pasta served with it is only a starchy diversion. But the spectacular setting may be the real draw, right there on the Miami River where freighters, fishing boats, dinghies, and sometimes yachts slink by to the amusement of the faithful diners who no longer have to fish around for a charming, serene seafood restaurant. Beware of Friday nights, when Big Fish turns into a big happy hour scene.

55 SW Miami Ave. Rd. ✆ **305/373-1770.** Main courses $15–$28. AE, DC, MC, V. Daily 11am–11pm. Cross the Brickell Ave. Bridge heading south and take the first right on SW 5th St. The rd. narrows under a bridge. The restaurant is just on the other side.

MODERATE

5061 Eaterie & Deli ★ AMERICAN/FRENCH/DELI   This two-story, 1949 building on the up-and-coming 50s block of Biscayne Boulevard features a mind-numbing selection of generously portioned, uncomplicated cuisine (think American diner meets French bistro) with a lively, hip atmosphere to match. The urban industrial chic palette of muted tones, concrete floors, and subtle textures complements the leather sofas, animal-print recliners, and wooden chairs—all enhanced by an extensive menu and wine list. 5061 features a confusing selection of several types of fair-tasting cuisine—quiche, sandwiches, hamburgers, fish, pasta, salads—everything from cheese plates to cheeseburgers. Paté and terrine are also available and are made on site and are expertly prepared thanks to the fact that the restaurant's owner is Parisian. An open kitchen stretching 20 feet (6m) along the back wall creates a "set" emulating a live television cooking show, with the restaurant patrons serving as the studio audience. There's a large bar downstairs with an excellent wine list as well as a second-floor bookstore slash cafe in which only travel, food, and wine books are sold.

5061 Biscayne Blvd. (at 50th St.), Miami. ✆ **305/756-5051.** Main courses $9.95–$29.95. AE, DC, MC, V. Daily 10:30am–11:30pm; deli 6:30am–8:30pm daily.

Fishbone Grille ★★ SEAFOOD   Fish are flying in the open kitchen of this extremely popular, reasonably priced seafood joint. Whether you take yours grilled, blackened, or sautéed, the chefs here work wonders with super-fresh snapper, grouper, dolphin, tuna, sea bass, and shrimp, to name just a few. For nonfish eaters, there are delicious pizzas and an excellent New York strip steak.

Where to Dine in Downtown Miami, Little Havana, Key Biscayne, Coconut Grove & Coral Gables

Anokha **33**
Azul **13**
Baleen **19**
Bayside Seafood Restaurant and Hidden Cove Bar **17**
Bice **36**
Big Fish **9**
Biscayne Miracle Mile Cafeteria **28**
Brasserie Les Halles **28**
Bubba Gump Shrimp Co. **7**
Cafe Tu Tu Tango **34**
Caffe Abbracci **30**
Capital Grille **10**
Casa Juancho **21**
Christy's **27**
Daily Bread Marketplace **20**
Fishbone Grille **9**
5061 Eaterie & Deli **2**
Franz & Joseph's in the Grove **33**
Gordon Biersch Brewery Restaurant **14**
Granny Feelgood's **6**
House of India **25**
Hy-Vong **22**
Jimbo's **15**
Joe's Seafood **5**
John Martin's **29**
La Carretta **22**
La Cibeles Café **8**
La Esquina de Tejas Hondureña **4**
Latin American Cafeteria **31**
Le Bouchon du Grove **33**
Le Festival **23**
Meza Fine Art Gallery Café **30**
Miss Saigon Bistro **24**
Morton's of Chicago **14**
Norman's **26**
Oasis **18**
Oggi Café **1**
Ortanique on the Mile **29**

Paninoteca **29**
Paolo Luigi's **35**
Perricone's Marketplace **14**
Porcao **12**
Provence Grill **11**
Red Fish Grill **32**
The Red Lantern **33**

Rusty Pelican **16**
S&S Restaurant **3**
Señor Frogs **33**
Soyka Restaurant & Café **2**
Stefano's **18**
Tobacco Road **9**
Versailles **22**

All meals come with salad and a fantastic slab of jalapeño corn bread. The interior is plain and simple; the only thing elaborate is the long list of daily specials.

650 S. Miami Ave., Miami. ✆ 305/530-1915. Reservations recommended for 6 or more. Main courses $9–$20. AE, DC, DISC, MC, V. Mon–Thurs 11:30am–10pm; Fri 11:30am–11pm; Sat 5–11pm; Sun 5:30–9pm.

Gordon Biersch Brewery Restaurant CONTINENTAL Best known for its home-brewed lager beers and strict adherence to the 1516 German Purity Law (which mandates the use of only malt, hops, water, and yeast in the brewing process), Gordon Biersch is always buzzing with locals who cram into every bit of the restaurant's sprawling 10,800 square feet. The food, for a beer hall, is particularly good, but sometimes too exotic. There are the usual suspects—burgers and pizza—offset by heavier dishes such as chicken-and-andouille-sausage gumbo and cashew chicken stir-fry. A popular lunch place for local businesspeople, Gordon Biersch is absolutely packed and oppressive on Friday night, when happy hour turns into harassment hour.

1201 Brickell Ave. (next to the JW Marriott), Miami. ✆ 786/425-1130. Main courses $12–$20. AE, DC, MC, V. Sun–Thurs 11:30am–midnight; Fri–Sat 11:30am–2am.

Joe's Seafood ★ *Finds* SEAFOOD A good catch on the banks of the Miami River, Joe's Seafood (not to be confused with Joe's Stone Crab) has a great waterfront setting and a fairly simple, yet tasty menu of fresh fish cooked in a number of ways—grilled, broiled, fried or, the best in my opinion, in garlic or green sauce. Meals are quite the deal here, all coming with green salad or grouper soup and yellow rice or french fries. The complimentary fish spread appetizer is also a nice touch. Because of this, not to mention the great, gritty ambience that takes you away from neon, neo-Miami in favor of the old, sea-faring days, there's usually a wait for a table.

400–404 NW N. River Dr., Miami. ✆ 305/381-9329. Reservations not accepted. Main courses $13.95–$22.95. AE, DC, DISC, MC, V. Daily 11am–10pm.

Soyka Restaurant & Café ★ AMERICAN Brought to us by the same man who owns the News and Van Dyke Cafés in South Beach, Soyka is a much-needed addition (though it's easy to miss) to the seedy area known as the Biscayne Corridor. The motif inside is industrial chic, reminiscent of a souped-up warehouse you might find in New York. Lunches focus on burgers, sandwiches, and wood-fired oven pizzas. Dinners include simple fare such as an excellent, massive Cobb salad or more elaborate dishes such as the delicious turkey Salisbury steak. The bar area offers a few comfy couches and bar stools and tables on which to dine, if you prefer not to sit in the open dining room. A children's menu is available for both lunch and dinner. A lively crowd of bohemian Design District types, professionals, and singles gathers here for a taste of urban life. On weekends, the place is packed and very loud. Do not expect an after-dinner stroll around the neighborhood—it's still too dangerous for pedestrian traffic. Head over the causeway to South Beach and stroll there.

5556 NE 4th Court (Design District, off Biscayne Blvd. and 55th St.), Miami. ✆ 305/759-3117. Reservations recommended. Main courses $8–$26. AE, MC, V. Sun–Thurs 11am–11pm (bar open until midnight); Fri–Sat 11am–midnight (bar open until 1am). Happy hour Mon–Fri 4–7pm.

INEXPENSIVE

Latin American Cafeteria ★★ CUBAN The name may sound a bit generic, but this no-frills indoor-outdoor cafeteria has the best Cuban sandwiches in the entire city. They're big enough for lunch and a doggy-bagged dinner, too. Service is fast, prices are cheap, but be forewarned: English is truly a second language at this chain, so have patience. It's worth it.

9796 Coral Way, Miami. © **305/226-2393.** Main courses $5–$9. AE, MC, V. Daily 7:30am–11pm.

Perricone's Marketplace ⭐ ITALIAN   A large selection of groceries and wine, plus an outdoor porch and patio for dining, makes this one of the most welcoming spots downtown. Its rustic setting in the midst of downtown is a fantastic respite from city life. Sundays offer buffet brunches and all-you-can-eat dinners, too. But it's most popular weekdays at noon, when the suits show up for delectable sandwiches, quick and delicious pastas, and hearty salads.

15 SE 10th St. (corner of S. Miami Ave.), Miami. © **305/374-9693.** Sandwiches $6.95–$8.25; pastas $11.50–$16.95. AE, MC, V. Sun–Mon 7:30am–10:30pm; Tues–Sat 7:30am–midnight.

S&S Restaurant AMERICAN/DINER FARE   This tiny chrome-and-linoleum-counter restaurant in the middle of downtown looks like a truck stop. But locals have been coming back since it opened in 1938. Expect a wait at lunchtime while the mostly male clientele, from lawyers to linemen, waits patiently for huge quantities of old-fashioned fast food. Although the neighborhood has become pretty undesirable, the food—basic diner fare with some excellent stews and soups—hasn't changed in years. In addition to cheap breakfasts, the diner serves up some of the best comfort food in Miami.

1757 NE 2nd Ave., Miami. © **305/373-4291.** Main courses $5–$11. No credit cards. Mon–Fri 6am–4pm; Sat–Sun 6am–2 or 2:30pm (later on Heat game nights).

Tobacco Road AMERICAN   Miami's oldest bar is a bluesy Route 66–inspired institution favored by barflies, professionals, and anyone else who wishes to indulge in good and greasy bar fare—chicken wings, nachos, and so on—for a reasonable price in a down-home, gritty-but-charming atmosphere. The burgers are also good—particularly the Death Burger, a deliciously unhealthy combo of choice sirloin topped with grilled onions, jalapeños, and pepper jack cheese—bring on the Tums! Also a live music venue, the Road, as it is known by locals, is well traveled, especially during Friday's happy hour and Tuesday's lobster night, when 100 1¼-pound lobsters go for only $10.99 apiece.

626 S. Miami Ave. © **305/374-1198.** Main courses $7–$10. AE, DC, MC, V. Mon–Sat 11:30am–5am; Sun noon–5am. Cover charge $5 Fri–Sat night.

LITTLE HAVANA

The main artery of Little Havana is a busy commercial strip called Southwest 8th Street, or Calle Ocho. Auto-body shops, cigar factories, and furniture stores line this street, and on every corner there seems to be a pass-through window serving super-strong Cuban coffee and snacks. In addition, many of the Cuban, Dominican, Nicaraguan, Peruvian, and other Latin American immigrants have opened full-scale restaurants ranging from intimate candlelit establishments to bustling stand-up lunch counters.

EXPENSIVE

Casa Juancho ⭐⭐ SPANISH   A generous taste of Spain comes to Miami in the form of the cavernous Casa Juancho, which looks like it escaped from a production of *Don Quixote*. The numerous dining rooms are decorated with traditional Spanish furnishings and enlivened nightly by strolling Spanish musicians who tend to be annoying and expect tips—do not encourage them to play at your table; you'll hear them loud and clear from other tables, trust me. Try not to be frustrated with the older staff that doesn't speak English or respond quickly to your subtle glance—the food's worth the frustration. Your best bet is to order lots of *tapas*, small dishes of Spanish finger food. Some of the best include mixed seafood vinaigrette, fresh shrimp in hot garlic sauce, and fried calamari rings. A few entrees stand out, like roast suckling pig, baby eels in garlic and olive oil, and Iberian-style snapper.

2436 SW 8th St. (just east of SW 27th Ave.), Little Havana. ⓒ **305/642-2452.** Reservations recommended, but not accepted on Fri–Sat after 8pm. Main courses $15–$34; tapas $6–$8. AE, DC, DISC, MC, V. Sun–Thurs noon–midnight; Fri–Sat noon–1am.

MODERATE

Hy-Vong ★★ VIETNAMESE   A must in Little Havana, expect to wait hours for a table, and don't even think of mumbling a complaint. Despite the poor service, it's worth it. Vietnamese cuisine combines the best of Asian and French cooking with spectacular results. Food at Hy-Vong is elegantly simple and super-spicy. Appetizers include small, tightly packed Vietnamese spring rolls and kim-chi, a spicy, fermented cabbage. Star entrees include pastry-enclosed chicken with watercress cream-cheese sauce and fish in tangy mango sauce.

Enjoy the wait with a traditional Vietnamese beer and lots of company. Outside this tiny storefront restaurant, you'll meet interesting students, musicians, and foodies who come for the large, delicious portions.

3458 SW 8th St. (between 34th and 35th aves.), Little Havana. ⓒ **305/446-3674.** Reservations accepted for parties of 5 or more. Main courses $9–$19. AE, DISC, MC, V. Tues–Sun 6–11pm. Closed 2 weeks in Aug.

INEXPENSIVE

La Esquina de Tejas Hondureña ★★ *Value* CUBAN   Best known as the diner where Ronald Reagan ate during his 1983 campaign in Miami, La Esquina de Tejas Hondureña has gained a national reputation for its great food and low prices. There's a shrine dedicated to the former president in the "Presidential Quarters," and the menu even has his signed autograph and the presidential seal of approval. This Cuban restaurant was recently bought by Hondurans, who serve its excellent food in either a Cuban or Honduran style, depending on what you choose. For instance, if you order the traditional Cuban steak dish, *carne asada*, you can choose it if you want it prepared Cuban sytle (fried) or Honduran style (grilled). There is also a completely new Honduran menu to choose from, featuring tacos, enchiladas, and *baleadas* (flour tortillas with butter, refried beans, and cheese). You must try the *arroz a la marinera*, the Cuban version of Spanish paella. It's filled with clams, oysters, mussels, lobster, shrimp, squid, snapper, stone crab, and scallops cooked in fresh seafood broth. If you're not in the mood for seafood, try the *vaca frita*, a grilled, shredded flank steak served with moro rice (black beans cooked with white rice) and *maduros* (sweet, fried plantains). Another house specialty is the *masas de puerco fritas*, a pork tenderloin cut in chunks, roasted, and then quickly deep-fried and served with mojo, grilled onions, garlic, olive oil, and bitter orange. You won't regret a trip here.

101 SW 12th Ave., Little Havana. ⓒ **305/545-0337.** Daily specials $7–$15; appetizers 75¢–$5.50. AE, MC, V. Daily 8am–5pm.

Versailles ★★ CUBAN   Versailles is the meeting place of Miami's Cuban power brokers, who meet daily over *cafe con leche* to discuss the future of the exiles' fate. A glorified diner, the place sparkles with glass, chandeliers, murals, and mirrors meant to evoke the French palace. There's nothing fancy here—nothing French, either—just straightforward food from the home country. The menu is a veritable survey of Cuban cooking and includes specialties such as

Moors and Christians (flavorful black beans with white rice), *ropa vieja* (shredded beef stew), and fried whole fish. Whereas La Esquina de Tejas Hondureña is known more for its food and Ronald Reagan than its atmosphere, Versailles is the place to come for mucho helpings of Cuban kitsch. With its late hours, it's also the perfect place to come after spending your night in Little Havana.

3555 SW 8th St., Little Havana. (©) 305/444-0240. Soup and salad $2–$10; main courses $5–$20. DC, DISC, MC, V. Mon–Thurs 8am–2am; Fri 8am–3:30am; Sat 8am–4:30am; Sun 9am–1am.

KEY BISCAYNE

Key Biscayne has some of the world's nicest beaches, hotels, and parks, yet it is not known for great food. Locals, or "Key rats" as they're known, tend to go off-island for meals or takeout, but here are some of the best on-the-island choices.

EXPENSIVE

Rusty Pelican ⭐ SEAFOOD   The Pelican's private tropical walkway leads over a lush waterfall into one of the most romantic dining rooms in the city, located right on beautiful blue-green Biscayne Bay. The restaurant's windows look out over the water onto the sparkling stalagmites of Miami's magnificent downtown. Inside, quiet wicker paddle fans whirl overhead and saltwater fish swim in pretty tableside aquariums. The restaurant's surf-and-turf menu features conservatively prepared prime steaks, veal, shrimp, and lobster. The food is good, but the atmosphere—the reason why you're here—is even better, especially at sunset, when the view over the city is magical.

3201 Rickenbacker Causeway, Key Biscayne. (©) 305/361-3818. Reservations recommended. Main courses $16–$22. AE, DC, MC, V. Daily 11:30am–4pm; Sun–Thurs 5–11pm; Fri–Sat 5pm–midnight.

INEXPENSIVE

Bayside Seafood Restaurant and Hidden Cove Bar ⭐ *Finds* SEAFOOD   Known by locals as "the Hut," this ramshackle restaurant and bar is a laid-back outdoor tiki hut and terrace that serves pretty good sandwiches and fish platters on paper plates. A blackboard lists the latest catches, which can be prepared blackened, fried, broiled, or in a garlic sauce. The fish dip is wonderfully smoky and moist, if a little heavy on mayonnaise. Local fishers and yachties share this rustic outpost with equal enthusiasm and loyalty. A completely new air-conditioned area for those who can't stand the heat is a welcome addition, as are the new deck and spruced-up decor. But behind it all, it's nothing fancier than a hut—if it was anything else, it wouldn't be nearly as appealing.

3501 Rickenbacker Causeway, Key Biscayne. (©) 305/361-0808. Reservations accepted for 15 or more. Appetizers, salads, and sandwiches $4.50–$8; platters $7–$13. AE, MC, V. Daily 11:30am until closing (which varies).

Jimbo's *Finds* SEAFOOD   Locals like to keep quiet about Jimbo's, a ramshackle seafood shack that started as a gathering spot for fishermen and has since become the quintessential South Florida watering hole, snack bar, and hangout for those in the know. If ever Miami had a backwoods, this was it, right down to the smoldering garbage can, stray dogs, and chickens. Do *not* get dressed up to come here—you will get dirty. Go to the bathroom before you get here, too, because the Porta-Potties are absolutely rancid. Grab yourself a dollar can of beer (there's only beer, water, and soda, but you are allowed to bring your own choice of drink if you want) from the cooler and take in the view of the tropical lagoon where they shot *Flipper*. You may even see a manatee or two. Vacant shacks that served as backdrops for films such as *True Lies* surround this hidden enclave, which attracts everyone from shrimpers and politicians to well-oiled beach bums. Oddly enough, there's even a bocce court here, and the owner, Jimbo, may challenge you to a game. Play if you must, but word has it he never loses. Jimbo's smoked fish—marlin or salmon—is the best in town, but be forewarned: There are no utensils or napkins. When I asked for some, the woman said, "Lady, this is a place where you eat with your hands." I couldn't have said it better.

Off the Rickenbacker Causeway at Sewerline Rd., Virginia Key. ℂ **305/361-7026.** Smoked fish about $4. No credit cards. Daily 6am–6:30pm. Head south on the main rd. toward Key Biscayne, make a left just after the MAST Academy (there will be a sign that says VIRGINIA KEY), tell the person in the toll booth you're going to Jimbo's, and he'll point you in the right direction.

COCONUT GROVE

Coconut Grove was long known as the artists' haven of Miami, but the rush of developers trying to cash in on the laid-back charm of this old settlement has turned it into something of an overgrown mall. Still, there are several great dining spots both in and out of the confines of Mayfair or CocoWalk.

VERY EXPENSIVE

Baleen ✸✸✸ SEAFOOD/MEDITERRANEAN While the prices aren't lean, the cuisine here is worth every pricey, precious penny. Oversize crab cakes, oak-smoked diver scallops, and steakhouse-quality meats are among Baleen's excellent offerings. The lobster bisque is the best on Biscayne Bay. Everything here is a la carte, so order wisely, as it tends to add up quicker than you can put your fork down. The restaurant's spectacular waterfront setting makes Baleen a true knockout. Brunch is particularly noteworthy as well.

4 Grove Isle Dr. (in the Grove Isle Hotel), Coconut Grove. ℂ **305/858-8300.** Reservations recommended. Main courses $18–$34. AE, DC, MC, V. Sun–Wed 7am–10pm; Thurs–Sat 7am–11pm.

Bice ✸✸✸ ITALIAN Upon entering the dining room here, you feel as if you're sailing on a grand ocean liner, with several cozy tables and booths, high ceilings, and a glorious view of the hotel's sprawling waterfall and pool area. Knowledgeable and friendly servers complement the comprehensive Italian menu. Every appetizer sounds so good that it's almost impossible to decide. Beef carpaccio is a delight with hearts of palm and Reggiano cheese; a colorful grilled vegetable pyramid consists of gargantuan portions of meaty portobello mushrooms, fresh asparagus, and peppers with bursts of mouthwatering goat cheese lying within; Maryland crab cakes with the perfect hint of lemon are exceptional. For main courses, the pastas, homemade and extremely fresh, are eclipsed by a heavenly slab of Nebraska filet mignon with peppercorn sauce and a tower of french fries and onion rings. The veal chop is also sublime. For dessert, the crème brûlée and coffee gelato are delicious. Unlike many chichi restaurants, especially those found within swanky hotels, all dishes at Bice are generous in portion—huge actually—and the only thing stuffy about dining here is how you'll feel after indulging.

2669 S. Bayshore Dr. (in the Grand Bay Hotel), Coconut Grove. ℂ **305/860-0960.** Reservations recommended. Main courses $12–$37. AE, MC, V. Daily 7–11am; 11:30am–3pm and 6–11pm.

EXPENSIVE

Anokha ✸✸✸ INDIAN This is the best Indian restaurant in Miami. Anokha's motto is "a guest is equal to God and should be treated as such," and they do stick to it. The food here is from the gods, with fantastic tandooris, curries, and stews. The restaurant's location at the end of a quiet stretch of Coconut Grove is especially enticing because it prevents the throngs of pedestrians from overtaking what some people consider a diamond in the rough.

3195 Commodore Plaza (between Main Hwy. and Grand Ave.), Coconut Grove. ☎ 786/552-1030. Main courses $10–$30. AE, DC, MC, V. Tues–Sun 11:30am–10:30pm.

Le Bouchon du Grove ★★ FRENCH   This very authentic, exceptional bistro is French right down to the waitstaff, who may only speak French to you, forgetting that they are in the heart of Coconut Grove, USA. But it matters not. The food, prepared by an animated French (what else) chef, is superb. An excellent starter is the wonderful *gratinée Lyonnaise* (traditional French onion soup). Fish is brought in fresh daily; try the Chilean sea bass when in season (*filet de loup poele*). Though it is slightly heavy on the oil, it is delivered with succulent artichokes, tomato confit, and seasoned roasted garlic that is a gastronomic triumph. The *carre d'agneau roti* (roasted rack of lamb with Provence herbs) is served warm and tender, with an excellent amount of seasoning. There is also an excellent selection of pricey but doable French and American red and white wines.

3430 Main Hwy., Coconut Grove. ☎ 305/448-6060. Reservations recommended. Main courses $18–$25. AE, MC, V. Mon–Fri 10am–3pm; Mon–Thurs 5–11pm; Fri 5pm–midnight; Sat 8am–midnight; Sun 8am–11pm.

MODERATE

Paulo Luigi's ★ ITALIAN   Pauloluigi's serves rich dishes that include cold and hot appetizers, homemade soups and salads, pastas, and pizzas. Owners Paul and Lola Shalaj, restaurant entrepreneurs for the past 27 years, have gained and kept a large, devoted clientele with their tasty light Italian cuisine, generous portions, and friendly environment that has served as the perfect fine-dining hideaway for both local and national customers alike.

A favorite is the *jumbo rigatti rubino,* a chicken dish with a side of sausages, asparagus, and portobello mushrooms in light marinara sauce. There's also *chicken Marsala, linguine al frutti di mare* (for poultry and seafood lovers), and a special children's menu.

3324 Virginia St., Coconut Grove. ☎ 305/445-9000. Reservations recommended. Main courses $9–$17. AE, MC, V. Daily noon–4pm and 5–11pm; Fri–Sat 5pm–1am.

INEXPENSIVE

Cafe Tu Tu Tango ★ SPANISH/INTERNATIONAL   This restaurant in the bustling CocoWalk is designed to look like a disheveled artist's loft. Dozens of original paintings—some only half-finished—hang on the walls and on studio easels. Seating is either inside, among the clutter, or outdoors, overlooking the Grove's main drag. Flamenco and other Latin-inspired tunes complement a menu with a decidedly Spanish flair. Hummus spread on rosemary flat bread and baked goat cheese in marinara sauce are two good starters. Entrees include roast duck with dried cranberries, toasted pine nuts, and goat cheese, plus Cajun chicken egg rolls filled with corn, cheddar cheese, and tomato salsa. Pastas, ribs, fish, and pizzas round out the eclectic offerings, and several visits have proved each consistently good. Try the sweet, potent sangria and enjoy the warm, lively atmosphere from a seat with a view.

3015 Grand Ave. (on the second floor of CocoWalk), Coconut Grove. ☎ 305/529-2222. Reservations not accepted. Tapas $3–$9.50. AE, MC, V. Sun–Wed 11:30am–midnight; Thurs 11:30am–1am; Fri–Sat 11:30am–2am.

CORAL GABLES & ENVIRONS

Coral Gables is a foodie's paradise—a city in which you certainly won't go hungry. What Starbucks is to most major cities, excellent gourmet and ethnic restaurants are to Coral Gables, where there's a restaurant on every corner, and everywhere in between.

VERY EXPENSIVE

Christy's ★★ STEAK/AMERICAN Power is palpable at this elegant English-style restaurant where an ex-president could be sitting at one table and a rock star at another. But Christy's is the kind of place where conversations are at a hush and no one seems to care whom they're sitting next to. The selling point here, rather, is the corn-fed beef and calves' liver, not to mention the broiled lamb chops, prime rib of beef with horseradish sauce, teriyaki marinated filet mignon, and perfectly tossed Caesar salad. Baked sweet potatoes and a sublime blackout cake are also yours for the taking. For a little drama, order the cruise-ship-esque Baked Alaska. It livens up the staid place. Just like a fine wine or the typical Christy's customer, the meat here is aged a long time. A landmark since 1978, Christy's has thrived amid the comings and goings of neighboring nouveau Coral Gables restaurants. Located on a nondescript corner, you know you've arrived at the right place if you can count the Rolls Royces parked out front.

3101 Ponce de León Blvd., Coral Gables. ② 305/446-1400. Reservations recommended. Main courses $20–$35. AE, DC, MC, V. Mon–Thurs 11:30am–10pm; Fri 11:30am–11pm; Sat 5–11pm; Sun 5–10pm.

Le Festival ★★ FRENCH Le Festival's contemporary pink awning hangs over one of Miami's most traditional Spanish-style buildings, hinting at the unusual combination of cuisine and decor that awaits inside. The modern dining rooms, enlivened with New French features and furnishings, belie the traditional highlights of a well-planned menu.

Shrimp and crab cocktails, fresh patés, and an unusual cheese soufflé are star appetizers. Both meat and fish are either simply seared with herbs and spices or doused in wine and cream sauces. Dessert can be a delight if you plan ahead: Grand Marnier and chocolate soufflés are individually prepared and must be ordered at the same time as the entrees. There's also a wide selection of other homemade sweets. If you go on a Monday, you'll get a complimentary soufflé. Not a bad way to start the week.

2120 Salzedo St. (right above Alhambra Circle), Coral Gables. ② 305/442-8545. Reservations required for dinner. Main courses $30–$60. AE, DC, DISC, MC, V. Mon–Fri 11:45am–2:30pm; Mon–Thurs 6–10:30pm; Fri–Sat 6–11pm.

Norman's ★★★ NEW WORLD CUISINE *Gourmet* magazine called Norman's the best restaurant in South Florida, but many disagree: They think it's the best restaurant in the entire United States. Gifted chef and cookbook author Norman van Aken takes New World Cuisine (which, along with chef Allen Susser, he helped create) to another plateau with dishes that have landed him on such shows as the Discovery Channel's "Great Chefs of the South" and on the wish lists of gourmands everywhere. The open kitchen invites you to marvel at the mastery that lands on your plate in the form of pan-roasted swordfish with black-bean *muneta;* stuffed baby bell pepper in cumin-scented tomato broth with avocado *crema;* chargrilled New York strip steak with chimichurri sabayon, *pommes frites,* and Creole mustard–spiced caramelized red onions; plantain-crusted dolphin; or chicken and tiny shrimp paella with garbanzo beans and chorizo mojo, to name a few.

The staff is adoring and professional and the atmosphere is tasteful without being too formal. The portions are realistic, but still, be careful not to overdo it. You'll want to try some of the funky, fantastic desserts.

21 Almeria Ave. (between Douglas and Ponce de León), Coral Gables. ✆ **305/446-6767.** Reservations highly recommended. Main courses $22–$38. AE, DC, MC, V. Mon–Thurs 6–10:30pm; Fri–Sat 6–11pm. Bar opens at 5:30pm.

EXPENSIVE

Caffe Abbracci ★★ ITALIAN   You'll understand why this restaurant's name means "hugs" in Italian the moment you enter the dark, romantic enclave: Your appetite will be embraced by the savory scents of fantastic Italian cuisine wafting through the restaurant. The homemade black and red ravioli filled with lobster in pink sauce, risotto with porcini and portobello mushrooms, and the house specialty—grilled veal chop topped with tricolor salad—are irresistible and perhaps the culinary equivalent of a warm, embracing hug. A cozy bar and lounge was added recently to further encourage the warm and fuzzy feelings.

318 Aragon Ave. (1 block north of Miracle Mile, between Salzedo St. and Le Jeune Rd.), Coral Gables. ✆ **305/441-0700.** Reservations recommended for dinner. Main courses $16–$26.50; pastas $15.50–$19.50. AE, DC, MC, V. Mon–Fri 11:30am–3pm; Sun–Thurs 6–11:30pm; Fri–Sat 6pm–12:30am.

MODERATE

Brasserie Les Halles ★★ FRENCH   Known especially for its fine steaks and delicious salads, this very welcome addition to the Coral Gables dining scene became popular as soon as it opened in 1997 and has since continued to do a brisk business. The modest and moderately priced menu is particularly welcome in an area of overpriced, stuffy restaurants. For starters, try the mussels in white-wine sauce and the escargot. For a main course, the duck confit is an unusual and rich choice. Pieces of duck meat wrapped in duck fat are slow-cooked and served on salad frissé with baby potatoes with garlic. Service by the young French staff is polite but a bit slow. The tables tend to be a little too close, although there is a lovely private balcony space overlooking the long, thin dining room where large groups can gather.

2415 Ponce de León Blvd. (at Miracle Mile), Coral Gables. ✆ **305/461-1099.** Reservations recommended on weekends. Main courses $12.50–$22.50. AE, DC, DISC, MC, V. Daily 11:30am–midnight.

House of India ★ INDIAN   House of India's curries, kormas, and kabobs are very good, but the restaurant's well-priced all-you-can-eat lunch buffet is unsurpassed. All the favorites are on display, including tandoori chicken, naan, various meat and vegetarian curries, as well as rice and dal (lentils). This place isn't fancy and could use a good scrub-down (in fact, I've heard it described as a "greasy spoon"), but the service is excellent and the food is good enough to keep you from staring at your surroundings.

22 Merrick Way (near Douglas and Coral Way, 1 block north of Miracle Mile), Coral Gables. ✆ **305/444-2348.** Reservations recommended. Main courses $8–$17. AE, DC, DISC, MC, V. Daily 11:30am–3pm; Sun–Thurs 5–10pm; Fri–Sat 5–11pm.

John Martin's ★ IRISH PUB   Forest green and dark wood give way to a very intimate pub-like atmosphere in which local businesspeople and barflies alike come to hoist a pint or two. The menu offers some tasty British specialties (not necessarily an oxymoron!), such as bangers and mash and shepherd's pie as well as Irish lamb stew and corned beef and cabbage.

Of course, to wash it down, you'll want to try one of the ales on tap or one of the more than 20 single-malt scotches. The crowd is upscale and chatty, as is the young waitstaff. Check out happy hour on weeknights, plus the Sunday brunch with loads of hand-carved meats and seafood.

253 Miracle Mile, Coral Gables. ℂ **305/445-3777.** Reservations recommended on weekends. Main courses $9–$20; sandwiches and salads $5–$16. AE, DC, DISC, MC, V. Mon–Thurs 11:30am–midnight; Fri–Sat 11:30am–1am; Sun noon–10pm.

Ortanique on the Mile ★★ NEW WORLD CARIBBEAN You'll be greeted as you walk in by soft spider-like lights and canopied mosquito netting that will make you wonder whether you're on a secluded island or inside one of King Tut's temples. Chef Cindy Hutson has truly perfected her tantalizing New World Caribbean menu. For starters, an absolute must is the pumpkin bisque with a hint of pepper sherry. Afterward, move on to the tropical mango salad with fresh marinated Sable hearts of palm, julienne mango, baby field greens, toasted Caribbean candied pecans, and passion-fruit vinaigrette. For an entree, I recommend the pan-sautéed Bahamian black grouper marinated in teriyaki and sesame oil. It's served with an ortanique (an orange-like fruit) orange liqueur sauce and topped with steamed seasoned chayote, zucchini, and carrots on a lemon-orange boniato–sweet plantain mash. For dessert, try the chocolate mango tower—layers of brownie, chocolate mango mousse, meringue, and sponge cake, accompanied by mango sorbet and tropical-fruit salsa. Entrees may not be cheap, but they're a lot less than airfare to the islands, from where most, if not all, the ingredients used here hail.

278 Miracle Mile (next to Actor's Playhouse), Coral Gables. ℂ **305/446-7710.** Reservations requested. Main courses $11–$29. AE, DC, MC, V. Mon–Tues 6–10pm; Wed–Sat 6–11pm; Sun 5:30–9:30pm.

INEXPENSIVE

Biscayne Miracle Mile Cafeteria ★ *Value* AMERICAN Here you'll find no bar, no music, and no flowers on the tables—just great Southern-style cooking at unbelievably low prices. The menu changes, but roast beef, baked fish, and barbecued ribs are typical entrees, few of which exceed $5.

Food is picked up cafeteria style and brought to one of the many unadorned Formica tables. The restaurant is always busy. The kitschy 1950s decor is an asset in this last of the old-fashioned cafeterias, where the gold-clad staff is proud and attentive. Enjoy it while it lasts.

147 Miracle Mile, Coral Gables. ℂ **305/444-9005.** Main courses $3.50–$4.50. MC, V. Daily 11am–8:30pm.

Daily Bread Marketplace GREEK This place is great for takeout food and homemade breads. The falafel and gyro sandwiches are large, fresh, and filling. The spinach pie for less than $1 is also recommended, though it's short on spinach and heavy on pastry. Salads, including luscious tabbouleh, hummus, and eggplant, are also worth a go. To eat in or take out, the Middle Eastern fare here is a real treat, especially in an area so filled with fancy French and Cuban fare. Plus, you can pick up hard-to-find groceries such as grape leaves, fresh olives, couscous, fresh nuts, and pita bread. A South Beach location has opened at 840 1st St. at Alton Road (ℂ **305/673-2252**).

2400 SW 27th St. (off U.S. 1 under the monorail), Coral Gables. ℂ **305/856-0363** or 305/856-0366. Sandwiches and salads $3–$6. MC, V. Mon–Sat 8am–8pm; Sun 11am–5pm.

Miss Saigon Bistro ★★ VIETNAMESE Unlike Andrew Lloyd Webber's bombastic Broadway show, this Miss Saigon is small, quiet, and not at all flashy. Servers at this family-run restaurant—among them, Rick, the owners' son—will graciously offer to recommend dishes or even to custom-make something for you. The menu is varied and reasonably priced and the portions are huge—large enough to share. Noodle dishes and soup bowls are hearty and flavorful; caramelized prawns are fantastic, as is the whole snapper with lemongrass and ginger sauce. Despite the fact that there are few tables inside and a hungry crowd usually gathers outside in the street, they will not at all rush you through your meal, which is worth savoring.

146 Giralda Ave. (at Ponce de Le_n and 37th Ave.), Coral Gables. ℂ **305/446-8006.** Main courses $4–$17. AE, DC, DISC, MC, V. Mon–Thurs 11am–3pm and 5:30–10pm; Fri–Sat 5:30–11pm; Sun 5:30–10pm.

SOUTH MIAMI & WEST MIAMI

Though mostly residential, these areas nonetheless have several eating establishments worth the drive.

EXPENSIVE

Tropical Chinese ★★ CHINESE   This strip-mall restaurant way out there in West Miami–Dade is hailed as the best Chinese restaurant in the city. While the food is indeed very good—certainly more interesting than at your typical beef-and-broccoli shop—it still seems somewhat overpriced. Garlic spinach and prawns in a clay pot is delicious with the perfect mix of garlic cloves, mushrooms, and fresh spinach, but it's not cheap at $16.99. And unlike most Chinese restaurants, the dishes here are not large enough to share. Sunday-afternoon dim sum is extremely popular, and lines often snake around the shopping center.

7991 Bird Rd., West Miami. ℂ **305/262-7576.** Reservations highly recommended. Main courses $10–$25. AE, DC, MC, V. Mon–Fri 11:30am–10:30pm; Sat 11am–10:30pm; Sun 10:30am–10pm. Take U.S. 1 to Bird Rd. and go west on Bird, all the way down to 78th Ave. The restaurant is between 78th and 79th on Bird Rd. on the north side of the rd.

INEXPENSIVE

Crepe Maker Café ★ *Kids* CREPES/FRENCH   Create your own delicious crepes at this little French cafe. You can choose from ham, tuna, black olives, red peppers, capers, artichoke hearts, and pine nuts. Some of the best combinations include a Philly cheese steak with mushrooms and a classic cordon bleu. Delicious dessert crepes have ice cream, strawberries, peaches, walnuts, and pineapples. Enjoy your crepe fresh off the griddle at the counter or on a bar stool. The soups are also delicious. Kids can run around in a small play area, too.

8269 SW 124th St., South Miami. ℂ **305/233-4458** or 305/233-1113. Crepes $3–$7.50. No credit cards. Sun and Tues–Thurs 10:30am–8:30pm; Fri–Sat 10:30am–10:30pm. Crepe cart in CocoWalk Tues–Wed 4–10pm; Sun and Thurs 11am–11pm; Fri–Sat 11am–1am. Take U.S. 1 south to 124th St. and make a left. Restaurant is on the north side of the street, across from the park.

El Toro Taco Family Restaurant ★★★ *Finds* MEXICAN   Until I discovered this Mexican oasis in the midst of South Florida farmland, I'd never had good enough reason to leave my quasi-cosmopolitan confines in Miami for rural Homestead way down south. This 96-seat family-run restaurant has put major miles on my car since I first stumbled upon it a few years ago when I was lost and very hungry. Fabulous, and I mean fabulous, Mexican fare, from the usual tacos, enchiladas, and burritos drenched with the freshest and zestiest salsa this side of Baja, is what you'll find here in abundance. It may sound odd to travel from a big city with tons of restaurants to farm country for Mexican food, but trust me, it's so cheap and delicious, it's worth the trip.

1 S. Krome Ave., Homestead. ℂ **305/245-8182.** Main courses $1.39–$8.75. DISC, MC, V. Tues–Sun 11am–9pm. Take 836 W (Dolphin Expressway) toward Miami International Airport. Take Florida Turnpike S ramp toward Florida City/Key West. Take U.S. 41/SW 8th St. exit (#25) and turn left onto SW 8th St. Take SW 8th St. to Krome Ave. (⅕ mile/.5km) and turn left onto Krome Ave.

Kon Chau ⭐ CHINESE/DIM SUM   Don't be put off by the rather unappealing shopping center in which this cheap dim sum place is located. If you want fancy plastic chopsticks and fancy prices, go up the block to Tropical Chinese. If you want delicious dim sum at ridiculously low prices, Kon Chau is where you'll find it. A simple checklist allows you to choose as much of whatever you want, from savory steamed shrimp dumplings to airy pork buns, for as little as $1 a piece, all day long. They also have regular dishes if you don't want dim sum.

8376 Bird Rd., West Miami. ✆ **305/553-7799.** Items $1 and up. MC, V. Mon–Sat 11am–10pm; Sun 10am–10pm. Take Bird Rd. west to 83rd St. Restaurant is between 83rd and 84th sts. on the south side of the rd., in a Dunkin' Donuts shopping center.

Shorty's ⭐ BARBECUE   A Miami tradition since 1951, this honky-tonk of a log cabin is still serving some of the best ribs and chicken in South Florida. People line up for the smoke-flavored, slow-cooked meat that's so tender it seems to fall off the bone. The secret, however, is to ask for your order with sweet sauce. The regular stuff tastes bland and bottled. All the side dishes, including the coleslaw, corn on the cob, and baked beans, look commercial, but are necessary to complete the experience. This is a jeans and T-shirt kind of place, but you may want to wear an elastic waistband, as overeating is not uncommon.

9200 S. Dixie Hwy. (between U.S. 1 and Dadeland Blvd.), South Miami. ✆ **305/670-7732.** Main courses $5–$9. DISC, MC, V. Mon–Thurs 11am–10pm; Fri–Sat 11am–11pm.

Tea Room ⭐ ENGLISH TEA   Do stop in for a spot of tea at this recently rebuilt tearoom in historic Cauley Square off U.S. 1. The little lace-curtained room is an unusual sight in this heavily industrial area better known for its warehouses than its doilies.

Try one of the simple sandwiches, such as the turkey club with potato salad and a small lettuce garnish or onion soup full of rich brown broth and stringy cheese. Daily specials, such as spinach and mushroom quiche, and delectable desserts are a must before beginning your explorations of the old antiques and art shops in this little enclave of civility down south.

12310 SW 224th St. (at Cauley Sq.), South Miami. ✆ **305/258-0044.** Sandwiches and salads $7–$12; soups $3–$4. AE, DISC, MC, V. Mon–Sat 11am–4pm. Take 836 W (Dolphin Expwy.) toward Miami International Airport. Take Palmetto Expwy. S. ramp toward Coral Way. Merge onto 826 S. Follow signs to Florida Tpk. toward Homestead. Take Tpk. south and exit at Caribbean Blvd. (#12). Go about a mile on Caribbean Blvd. and turn left on S. Dixie Hwy. and then right at SW 224th St. Then turn left onto Old Dixie Hwy. and take a slight right onto SW 224th St. The restaurant is at Cauley Square Center.

What to See & Do in Miami

by Lesley Abravanel

If there's one thing Miami doesn't have, it's an identity crisis. In fact, it's the city's vibrant, multifaceted personality that attracts millions each year, from all over the world. South Beach may be on the top of many Miami to-do lists, but the rest of the city, a fascinating assemblage of multicultural neighborhoods, should not be overlooked or neglected. Once considered "God's Waiting Room," the Magic City now attracts an eclectic mix of old and young, celebs and plebes, American and international, and geek and chic with an equally varied roster of activities.

For starters, Miami boasts some of the most natural beauty there is, with blinding blue waters, fine, sandy beaches, and lush tropical parks. The city's human-made brilliance, in the form of Crayola-colored architecture, never seems to fade in Miami's unique Art Deco District. For cultural variation, you can also experience the tastes, sounds, and rhythms of Cuba in Little Havana.

As in any metropolis, however, there are areas that aren't as great as others. Downtown Miami, for instance, is in the throes of a major, albeit slow, renaissance, in which the sketchier, warehouse sections of the city are being transformed into hubs of all things hip. In contrast to this development, however, are the still poverty-stricken areas of downtown such as Overtown, Liberty City, and Little Haiti. While it's obvious to advise you to exercise caution when exploring the less-traveled parts of the city, we would also be remiss in telling you to bypass them completely.

Lose yourself in the city's nature and its neighborhoods, and, best of all, its people—a sassy collection of artists and intellectuals, beach bums and international transplants, dolled-up drag queens and bodies beautiful. No wonder celebrities love to vacation here—the spotlight is on the city and its residents. And unlike most stars, Miami is always ready for its close-up. With so much to do and see, Miami is a virtual amusement park that's bound to entertain all those who pass through its palm-lined gates.

1 Miami's Beaches

Perhaps Miami's most popular attraction is its incredible 35-mile (56.5km) stretch of beachfront, which runs from the tip of South Beach north to Sunny Isles and circles Key Biscayne and the numerous other pristine islands dotting the Atlantic. The characteristics of Miami's many beaches are as varied as the city's population: There are beaches for swimming, socializing, or serenity; for family, seniors, or gay singles; some to make you forget you're in the city, others darkened by huge condominiums. Whatever type of beach vacation you're looking for, you'll find it in one of Miami's two distinct beach areas: Miami Beach and Key Biscayne.

MIAMI BEACH'S BEACHES   Collins Avenue fronts more than a dozen miles of white-sand beach and blue-green waters from 1st to 192nd Streets. Although most of this stretch is lined with a solid wall of hotels and condos, beach access is plentiful. There are lots of public beaches here, wide and well maintained, complete with lifeguards, bathroom facilities, concession stands, and metered parking (bring lots of quarters). Except for a thin strip close to the water, most of the sand is hard-packed—the result of a $10 million Army Corps of Engineers Beach Rebuilding Project meant to protect buildings from the effects of eroding sand.

In general, the beaches on this barrier island (all on the eastern, ocean side of the island) become less crowded the farther north you go. A wooden boardwalk runs along the hotel side of the beach from 21st to 46th Streets—about 1½ miles (2.5km)—offering a terrific sun-and-surf experience without getting sand in your shoes. Aside from "The Best Beaches," listed below, Miami's lifeguard-protected public beaches include 21st Street, at the beginning of the boardwalk; 35th Street, popular with an older crowd; 46th Street, next to the Fontainebleau Hilton; 53rd Street, a narrower, more sedate beach; 64th Street, one of the quietest strips around; and 72nd Street, a local old-timers' spot.

KEY BISCAYNE'S BEACHES   If Miami Beach doesn't provide the privacy you're looking for, try Virginia Key and Key Biscayne. Crossing the Rickenbacker Causeway ($1 toll), however, can be a lengthy process, especially on weekends, when beach bums and tan-o-rexics flock to the Key. The 5 miles (8km) of public beach there, however, are blessed with softer sand and are less developed and more laid-back than the hotel-laden strips to the north.

THE BEST BEACHES
Here are my picks:

- **Best Party Beach:** In Key Biscayne, **Crandon Park Beach,** on Crandon Boulevard, is National Lampoon's *Vacation* on the sand. It's got a diverse crowd consisting of dedicated beach bums and lots of leisure-seeking families, set to a soundtrack of salsa, disco, and reggae music blaring from a number of competing stereos. With 3 miles (5km) of oceanfront beach, bathrooms, changing facilities, 493 acres of park, 75 grills, three parking lots, several soccer and softball fields, and a public 18-hole championship golf course, Crandon is like a theme park on the sand. Admission is $2 per vehicle. It's open daily from 8am to sunset.
- **Best Beach for People-Watching: Lummus Park Beach,** aka Glitter Beach, runs along Ocean Drive from about 6th to 14th Streets on South Beach. It's the best place to go if you're seeking entertainment as well as a great tan. On any day of the week, you might spy models primping for a photo shoot, nearly naked (topless is legal here) sun-worshippers avoiding tan lines, and an assembly line of washboard abs off of which you could (but shouldn't) bounce your bottle of sunscreen. Bathrooms and changing facilities are available on the beach, but don't expect to have a Cindy Crawford encounter in one of these. Most people tend to prefer using the somewhat drier, cleaner bathrooms of the restaurants on Ocean Drive.
- **Best Swimming Beach:** The **85th Street Beach,** along Collins Avenue, is the best place to swim away from the maddening crowds. It's one of Miami's only stretches of sand with no condos or hotels looming over sunbathers. Lifeguards patrol the area throughout the day and bathrooms are available, though they are not exactly the benchmark of cleanliness.

Miami Area Attractions & Beaches

Amelia Earhart Park **5**
American Airlines Arena **17**
American Police Hall of Fame
  and Museum **14**
Barnacle State Historic Site **31**
Bayfront Park **21**
Bayside Marketplace **20**
Bill Baggs Cape Florida State
  Recreation Center **40**
Biltmore Hotel **26**
CocoWalk **29**
Coral Castle **38**
Crandon Park Golf Course **35**
Diaspora Vibe Art Gallery **12**
Doral Park Golf and Country Club **10**
Fairchild Tropical Garden **39**
Fisher Island **23**
Freedom Tower **17**
GameWorks **34**
Golf Club of Miami **1**
Gulfstream Park **4**
Haulover Marina **8**
Haulover Park Beach **7**
Hialeah Park **9**
Historical Museum
  of Southern Florida **18**

IMAX Theatre at Sunset Place **34**
The Kampong **30**
Latin American Art Museum **25**
Lowe Art Museum **33**
Marjory Stoneman Douglas
  Biscayne Nature Center **36**
Miami Art Museum **19**
Miami Jai Alai Fronton **11**
Miami Metrozoo **38**
Miami Museum of Science and
  Space Transit Planetarium **33**
Miami Seaquarium **32**
Miami-Dade Cultural Center
  (Miami Art Museum &
  the Historical Museum
  of Southern Florida) **18**
Miccosukee Indian Gaming **38**
Monkey Jungle **38**
Museum of Contemporary Art
  (MOCA) **6**
National Hurricane Center **24**
Oleta River State Recreation Area **4**
Parrot Jungle and Gardens **37**
  (until fall 2002);
  22 (from winter of 2003)

Preston B. Bird and Mary Heinlein
  Fruit and Spice Park **38**
Pro Player Stadium **2**
Rubell Family Art Collection **13**
The Scott Rakow Youth Center **15**
Sea Grass Adventures **36**
Spanish Monastery Cloisters **3**
Tropical Park **28**
United in Eliàn House **16**
Venetian Pool **27**
The Vizcaya Museum and Gardens **38**
World Chess Hall of Fame and Sidney
  Samole Chess Museum **38**

- **Best Windsurfing Beach: Hobie Beach,** on the side of the causeway leading to Key Biscayne, is not really a beach, but an inlet with predictable winds and a number of places where you can rent windsurfers. Bathrooms are available.
- **Best Shell-Hunting Beach:** You'll find plenty of colorful shells at **Bal Harbour Beach,** Collins Avenue at 96th Street. There's also an exercise course and good shade—but no lifeguards, bathrooms, or changing facilities.
- **Best (Ahem) All-Around Tanning Beach:** For that all-over tan, head to **Haulover Beach,** just north of the Bal Harbour border, and join nudists from around the world in a top-to-bottom tanning session. Should you choose to keep your swimsuit on, however, there are changing rooms and bathrooms.
- **Best Surfing Beach: Haulover Beach Park,** just over the causeway from Bal Harbour, seems to get Miami's biggest swells. Go early to avoid getting mauled by the aggressive young locals prepping for Maui.
- **Best Scenic Beach: Matheson Hammock Park Beach,** at 9610 Old Cutler Rd. in South Miami (© **305/665-5475**), is the epitome of tranquillity, tucked away off of scenic Old Cutler Road in South Miami. And while it's scenic, it's not too much of a scene. It's a great beach for those seeking "alone time." Bathrooms and changing facilities are available.
- **Best Family Beach:** Because of its man-made lagoon, which is fed naturally by the tidal movement of the adjacent Biscayne Bay, the waters of **Matheson Hammock Park Beach** are extremely calm, not to mention safe and secluded enough for families to keep an eye on the kids.
- **Best Beach for Seculusion: Virginia Key on Key Biscayne,** where people go when they don't want to be found. It's also incredibly picturesque.

2 The Art Deco District

"You know what they used to say?" recalls Art Deco revivalist Dona Zemo, "Who's Art?" "You'd say, 'This is an Art Deco building,' and they'd say, 'Really, who is Art?' These people thought 'Art Deco' was some guy's name."

How things have changed. This guy Art has become one of the most popular Florida attractions since, well, that mouse Mickey. The district is roughly bounded by the Atlantic Ocean on the east, Alton Road on the west, 6th Street to the south, and Dade Boulevard (along the Collins Canal) to the north.

Simply put, Art Deco is a style of architecture that, in its heyday of the 1920s and '30s, used to be considered ultra-modern. Today, fans of the style consider it retro-fabulous. And while some people may not consider the style fabulous, it's undoubtedly retro. According to the experts, Art Deco made its debut in 1925 in an exposition in Paris in which it set a stylistic tone, with buildings based on early neoclassical styles with the application of exotic motifs like flora, fauna, and fountains based on geometric patterns. In Miami, Art Deco is marked by the pastel-hued buildings that line South and Miami Beaches. But it's a lot more than just color. If you look carefully, you will see the intricacies and impressive craftsmanship that went into each building back in the day, which, in Miami's case was the '20s, '30s, and '40s, and now, thanks to intensive restoration, today.

Most of the finest examples of the whimsical Art Deco style are concentrated along three parallel streets—Ocean Drive, Collins Avenue, and Washington Avenue—from about 6th to 23rd Streets.

To Central Miami Beach ↗

The Bass Museum of Art

22nd St.

COLLINS PARK

20th St.

19th St.

Dade Boulevard

Purdy Ave.

18th St.

Miami Beach Convention Center

17th St.

James Ave.

Venetian Causeway

Dade Boulevard

Lincoln Road Mall

BELLE ISLAND

Lincoln Rd.

Collins Ave.

Bay Rd.

West Ave.

Alton Rd.

HISTORIC ART DECO DISTRICT

16th St.

15th St.

Española Way

Alton Rd.

Michigan Ave.

Jefferson Ave.

Meridian Ave.

Lenox Ave.

14th St. Miami Beach Post Office

13th St.

Ocean Dr.

Biscayne Bay

West Ave.

12th St.

11th St.

Washington Ave.

FLAMINGO PARK

10th St.

9th St.

Pennsylvania Ave.

Beach Patrol Station

Art Deco Welcome Center

8th St.

7th St.

Michigan Ave.

6th St.

5th St.

4th St.

3rd St.

ATLANTIC OCEAN

2nd St.

1st St.

Commerce St.

Biscayne St.

LUMMUS PARK

Washington Ave.

Collins Ave.

Ocean Dr.

SOUTH POINTE PARK

Government Cut

FISHER ISLAND

0   1/4 mi
0   1/4 km

N

Art Center/South Florida **8**
Art Deco Welcome Center **19**
Bass Museum of Art **1**
Collins Park **3**
Colony Theater **6**
The Community Church **11**
Crunch **15**
Estefan Enterprises **20**
Fritz's Skate Shop **9**
Holocaust Memorial **4**
Jackie Gleason Theater
  of the Performing Arts **12**
Jose Cuervo Underwater Bar **23**
Lincoln Theater **10**
Lummus Park Beach **16**
Mermaid Sculpture **12**
Miami Beach Bicycle Center **21**
Miami Beach Botanical Garden **5**
Miami Beach Cultural Park **2**
Miami Beach Post Office **14**
Miami Beach Public Courts
  at Flamingo Park **13**
Miami Beach Regional Library **2**
Morris Lapidus Sculptures **12**
1928 Sterling Building **7**
Sanford L. Ziff Jewish Museum
  of Florida **22**
Versace Mansion **18**
Wolfsonian-Florida
  International University **17**

Finds Walking By Design

The Miami Design Preservation League offers several tours of Miami Beach's historic architecture, which all leave from The Art Deco Welcome Center, located at 1001 Ocean Dr. in Miami Beach. A self-guided audio tour (available 7 days a week, from 10am–4pm) turns the streets into a virtual outdoor museum, taking you through Miami Beach's Art Deco District at your own leisure, with tours in several languages for just $10 per person. Guided tours conducted by local historians and architects offer an in-depth look at the structures and their history. The 90-minute Ocean Drive and Beyond tour (offered every Sat at 10:30am) takes you through the district, pointing out the differences between Mediterranean Revival and Art Deco for $15 per person. If you're not blinded by neon, the Thursday-night Art Deco District Up-to-Date tour (leaving at 6:30pm) will whisk you around for 90 minutes, making note of how certain local hot spots were architecturally famous way before the likes of Madonna and co. entered them. Cost is $15. For more information on tours or reservations, call © **305/672-2014**.

After years of neglect and calls for the wholesale demolition of its buildings, South Beach got a new lease on life in 1979. Under the leadership of Barbara Baer Capitman, a dedicated crusader for the Art Deco region, and the Miami Design Preservation League, founded by Baer Capitman and five friends, an area made up of an estimated 800 buildings was granted a listing on the National Register of Historic Places. Designers then began highlighting long-lost architectural details with soft sherbet shades of peach, periwinkle, turquoise, and purple. Developers soon moved in, and the full-scale refurbishment of the area's hotels was under way.

Not everyone was pleased, though. Former Miami Beach commissioner Abe Resnick said, "I love old buildings. But these Art Deco buildings are 40, 50 years old. They aren't historic. They aren't special. We shouldn't be forced to keep them." But Miami Beach kept those buildings, and Resnick lost his seat on the commission.

Today, hundreds of new establishments—hotels, restaurants, and night-clubs—have renovated, or are in the process of renovating, these older, historical buildings and are moving in, putting South Beach on the cutting edge of Miami's cultural and nightlife scene.

EXPLORING THE AREA

If you're touring this unique neighborhood on your own, start at the **Art Deco Welcome Center,** 1001 Ocean Dr. (© **305/531-3484**), which is run by The Miami Design Preservation League. The only beachside building across from the Clevelander Hotel and bar, they give away lots of informational material including maps and pamphlets and run guided tours about the neighborhood. Art Deco books (including *The Art Deco Guide,* an informative compendium of all the buildings here), T-shirts, postcards, mugs, and other paraphernalia are for sale. It's open Monday through Saturday from 9am to 6pm, sometimes later.

Take a stroll along **Ocean Drive** for the best view of sidewalk cafes, bars, colorful hotels, and even more colorful people. Another great place for a walk is **Lincoln Road,** which is lined with boutiques, large chain stores, cafes, and funky art and antiques stores. The Community Church, at the corner of Lincoln Road and Drexel Avenue, is the neighborhood's first church and one of its oldest surviving buildings, dating from 1921.

3 Miami's Museum & Art Scene

Miami has never been known as a cultural mecca as far as museums are concerned. Though several exhibition spaces have made forays into collecting nationally acclaimed work, limited support and political infighting have made it a difficult proposition. Recently, however, things have changed as museums such as the Wolfsonian, the Museum of Contemporary Art, the Bass Museum of Art, and the Miami Art Museum have gotten on the bandwagon, boasting collections and exhibitions high on the list of art aficionados. It's now safe to say that world-class exhibitions start here. Listed below are the most lauded museums that have become a part of the city's cultural heritage, and as such, are as diverse as the city itself.

IN SOUTH BEACH

Work continues to proceed on the **Miami Beach Cultural Park,** which comprises a trio of arts buildings on Collins Park and Park Avenue (off Collins Ave.), bounded by 21st to 23rd Streets—the newly expanded Bass Museum of Art (see below), the new Arquitectonica-designed home of the Miami City Ballet, and the Miami Beach Regional Library, which broke ground in January 2001 and will have a special focus on the arts. Collins Park, the former site of the Miami Beach Library, will return to its original incarnation as an open space extending to the Atlantic, but it will also be the site of large sculpture installations and cultural activities planned jointly by the organizations that share the space.

Bass Museum of Art ★★★ The Bass Museum of Art has expanded and received a dramatically new look, rendering it Miami's most progressive art museum. World-renowned Japanese architect Arata Isozaki designed the magnificent new facility, which has triple the former exhibition space, and added an outdoor sculpture terrace, a museum cafe and courtyard, and a museum shop, among other improvements. In addition to providing space in which to show the permanent collection, exhibitions of a scale and quality not previously seen in Miami will now be featured at the Bass. The museum's permanent collection includes European paintings from the 15th to the early 20th centuries with special emphasis on Northern European art of the Renaissance and baroque periods, including Dutch and Flemish masters such as Bol, Flinck, Rubens, and Jordaens. In 2001 an art lab opened, making it possible for all aspiring artists to create their own masterpieces on computers for free or a nominal charge.

2121 Park Ave. (1 block west of Collins Ave.), South Beach. © 305/673-7530. www.bassmuseum.org. Admission $6 adults, $4 students and seniors, free for children 6 and under. Tues–Wed and Fri–Sat 10am–5pm; Thurs 10am–9pm; Sun 11am–5pm. Closed Mon.

Holocaust Memorial ★★★ This heart-wrenching memorial is hard to miss and would be a shame to overlook. The powerful centerpiece, Kenneth Triester's *Sculpture of Love & Anguish,* depicts victims of the concentration camps crawling up a giant, yearning hand, stretching up to the sky, marked with an Auschwitz number tattoo. Along the reflecting pool is the story of the Holocaust, told in cut-marble slabs. Inside the center of the memorial is a tableau that is one of the most solemn and moving tributes I've seen to the millions of Jews who lost their lives in the Holocaust. You can walk through an open hallway lined with photographs and the names of concentration camps and their victims. From the street, you'll see the outstretched arm, but do stop and tour the sculpture at ground level.

1933 Meridian Ave. (at Dade Blvd.), South Beach. © 305/538-1663. www.holocaustmmb.com. Free admission. Daily 9am–9pm.

Sanford L. Ziff Jewish Museum of Florida ✮ Chronicling over 230 years of Jewish heritage and experiences in Florida, the Jewish Museum presents a fascinating look at religion and culture through films, lectures, and exhibits such as "Mosaic: Jewish Life in Florida," which features over 500 photos and artifacts documenting the Jewish experience in Florida since 1763. The museum is housed in a former synagogue.

301 Washington Ave., South Beach. ✆ 305/672-5044. www.jewishmuseum.com. $5 adults, $4 seniors and students, $10 families. Free admission Sat. Tues–Sun 10am–5pm. Closed Mon and Jewish holidays.

Wolfsonian-Florida International University ✮✮✮ *Finds* Mitchell Wolfson Jr., heir to a family fortune built on movie theaters, was known as an eccentric, but I'd call him a pack rat. A premier collector of propaganda and advertising art, Wolfson was spending so much money storing his booty that he decided to buy the warehouse that was housing it. It ultimately held more than 70,000 of his items, from controversial Nazi propaganda to King Farouk of Egypt's match collection. Thrown in the eclectic mix are also zany works from great modernists such as Charles Eames and Marcel Duchamp. He then gave this incredibly diverse collection to Florida International University. The former 1927 storage facility has been transformed into a museum that is the envy of curators around the world. The museum is unquestionably fascinating and hosts lectures and rather swinging events surrounding particular exhibits.

1001 Washington Ave., South Beach. ✆ 305/531-1001. Admission $5 adults; $3.50 seniors, students with ID, and children 6–12; by donation Thurs 6–9pm. Mon, Tues, Fri, and Sat 11am–6pm; Thurs 11am–9pm; Sun noon–5pm.

IN & NEAR DOWNTOWN

American Police Hall of Fame and Museum This strange museum appeals mostly to those fascinated by police and their gadgetry. Once inside, you'll find a combination of reality and fantasy that's part thoughtful tribute, part Hollywood-style drama. Just past the car featured in the motion picture *Blade Runner* is a mock prison cell, in which visitors can take pictures of themselves pretending they're doing 5 to 10. Also on hand are execution devices, including a guillotine and an electric chair (whose controversial use was recently abolished in Florida). In the entry is a touching memorial to the more than 7,000 American police officers who have lost their lives in the line of duty. Even if you don't go inside, you can't miss the museum, which has a real police car attached to its facade. Unfortunately, at press time, it was announced that sometime in 2003, the museum would be moving out of Miami and up to Titusville, in central Florida. Call for information and to see whether the museum is still in Miami when you're there.

3801 Biscayne Blvd., Miami. ✆ 305/573-0070. www.aphf.org. Admission $12 adults, $9 seniors over 61, $6 children 11 and under, free for law-enforcement officers and family survivors. Daily 10am–5:30pm. Go north on U.S. 1 from downtown; it's the building with the police car affixed to its side. Parking in the back.

Diaspora Vibe Art Gallery ✮✮ This art complex, housed in an old bakery, is a funky artist hangout and is the home to some of the greatest artworks of Miami's diverse Caribbean, Latin American, and African-American cultures. The gallery has two seasons of shows, often focusing on emerging artists. During the winter, three artists are selected by the gallery to travel to and exhibit their works in Paris. On the last Friday of every month, May through October, the gallery holds its fabulous "Final Fridays." A new artist's work is spotlighted inside, while outside in the courtyard are live music performances and readings of poetry and folk tales. Delicious Caribbean cuisine is also served. The who's who of Miami's cognoscenti gather here to recharge their cultural batteries.

561 NW 32nd St., Studio 48 (Bakehouse Art Complex), Miami. ✆ 305/759-1110. www.diasporavibe.com. Free admission. "Final Fridays" events $15. Mon–Fri by appointment; Sat–Sun 1–6pm; Final Fridays events May–Oct last Fri of the month 7–11pm.

Latin American Art Museum   In addition to the permanent collection of contemporary artists from Spain and Latin America, this 3,500-square-foot museum hosts monthly exhibitions of works from Latin America and the Caribbean Basin. Usually, the exhibitions focus on a theme, such as international women or surrealism. It's not a major attraction, but worth a stop if you're interested in Latin American art. On the same block, you'll find great design stores and a few other galleries.

2206 SW 8th St., Little Havana. ✆ 305/644-1127. Free admission. Tues–Fri 11am–5pm; Sat 11am–4pm. Second Fri of every month, 6:30–10pm. Closed Aug and major holidays.

Lowe Art Museum ★★   Located on the University of Miami campus, the Lowe Art Museum has a dazzling collection of 8,000 works that includes American paintings, Latin American art, Navajo and Pueblo Indian textiles, and Renaissance and baroque art. Traveling exhibits such as *Rolling Stone* magazine's photo collection also stop here. For the most part, the Lowe is known for its collection of Greek and Roman antiquities, and, as compared to the more modern MOCA, Bass, and Miami Art Museum, features mostly European and international art hailing from ancient times.

University of Miami, 1301 Stanford Dr. (at Ponce de León Blvd.), Coral Gables. ✆ 305/284-3603. Admission $5 adults, $3 seniors and students with ID. Donation day is first Tues of the month. Tues, Wed, Fri, and Sat 10am–5pm; Thurs noon–7pm; Sun noon–5pm.

Miami Art Museum at the Miami-Dade Cultural Center ★★★   The Miami Art Museum (MAM) features an eclectic mix of modern and contemporary works by such artists as Eric Fischl, Max Beckmann, Jim Dine, and Stuart Davis. Rotating exhibitions span the ages and styles, and often focus on Latin American or Caribbean artists. There are also fantastic themed exhibits such as the Andy Warhol exhibit, which featured all-night films by the artist, make-your-own pop art, cocktail hours, and parties with local deejays. JAM at MAM is the museum's popular happy hour, which takes place the second Thursday of the month and is tied in to a particular exhibit. Almost as artistic as the works inside the museum is the composite sketch of the people—young and old—who attend these events.

The Miami-Dade Cultural Center, where the museum is housed, is a fortress-like complex designed by Phillip Johnson. In addition to the acclaimed Miami Art Museum, the center houses the main branch of the Miami-Dade Public Library, which sometimes features art and cultural exhibits, and the Historical Museum of Southern Florida, which highlights the fascinating history of the area. Unfortunately, the plaza onto which the complex opens is home to many of downtown Miami's homeless population, which makes it a bit off-putting but not dangerous.

101 W. Flagler St., Miami. ✆ 305/375-3000. Admission $5 adults, $2.50 seniors and students, free for children under 12. Tues–Fri 10am–5pm; third Thurs of each month 10am–9pm; Sat–Sun noon–5pm. Closed major holidays. From I-95 S, exit at Orange Bowl–NW 8th St. and continue south to NW 2nd St.; turn left at NW 2nd St. and go 1½ blocks to NW 2nd Ave.; turn right.

Miami Museum of Science and Space Transit Planetarium ★★ *Kids*
The Museum of Science features more than 140 hands-on exhibits that explore
the mysteries of the universe. Live demonstrations and collections of rare natural-history specimens make a visit here fun and informative. Many of the demos
involve audience participation, which can be lots of fun for willing and able
kids and adults alike. There is also a Wildlife Center with more than 175 live
reptiles and birds of prey. The adjacent Space Transit Planetarium projects
astronomy and laser shows as well as interactive demonstrations of upcoming
computer technology and cyberspace features. Call, or visit their website, for a
list of upcoming exhibits and laser shows.

3280 S. Miami Ave. (just south of the Rickenbacker Causeway), Coconut Grove. ⓒ **305/646-4200** for general information or 305/854-2222 for planetarium show times. www.miamisci.org. $10 adults, $8 seniors and
students, $6 children 3–12, free for children 2 and under; laser shows $6 adults, $3 seniors and children 3–12.
After 4:30pm, ticket prices are half price. 25% discount for AAA members. Ticket prices include entrance to
all museum galleries, planetarium shows, and the Wildlife Center. Museum of Science, daily 10am–6pm; call
for planetarium show times (last show is at 4pm weekdays and 5pm on weekends). Closed Thanksgiving and
Christmas Day.

Museum of Contemporary Art (MOCA) ★★★   MOCA boasts an impressive collection of internationally acclaimed art with a local flavor. It is also
known for its forward thinking and ability to discover and highlight new artists.
A high-tech screening facility allows for film presentations to complement the
exhibitions. You can see works by Jasper Johns, Roy Lichtenstein, Larry Rivers,
Duane Michaels, and Claes Oldenberg, plus there are special exhibitions by such
artists as Yoko Ono, Sigmar Polke, John Baldessari, and Goya. Guided tours are
offered in English, Spanish, French, Creole, Portuguese, German, and Italian.

770 NE 125th St., North Miami. ⓒ **305/893-6211.** Fax 305/891-1472. www.mocanomi.org. Admission $5
adults, $3 seniors and students with ID, free for children 12 and under. Tues by donation. Tues–Sat
11am–5pm; Sun noon–5pm. Closed major holidays and Mon.

Rubell Family Art Collection ★★★ *Finds*   This impressive collection, owned
by the Miami hotelier family, the Rubells, is housed in a two-story 40,000-
square-foot former Drug Enforcement Agency warehouse in a sketchy area
north of downtown Miami. The building looks like a fortress, which is fitting:
Inside is a priceless collection of more than a thousand works of contemporary
art, by the likes of Keith Haring, Damien Hirst, Julian Schnabel, Jean-Michel
Basquiat, Paul McCarthy, Charles Ray, and Cindy Sherman. But be forewarned:
Some of the art is extremely graphic and may be off-putting to some. The gallery
changes exhibitions twice yearly and there is a seasonal program of lectures,
artists' talks, and performances by prominent artists. As of press time, the gallery
was looking to move to a larger space nearby toward the end of 2002 to accommodate this ever-growing, ever-impressive collection.

95 NW 29th St. (on the corner of NW 1st Ave. near the Design District), Miami. ⓒ **305/573-6090.** Free
admission. Thurs–Sat 9am–9pm and by appointment.

4 Historic Homes & Sites

South Beach's well-touted Deco District is but one of many colorful neighborhoods that can boast dazzling architecture. The rediscovery of the entire Biscayne Corridor (from downtown to about 80th St. and Biscayne Blvd.) has
given light to a host of ancillary neighborhoods on either side that are filled with
Mediterranean-style homes and Frank Lloyd Wright gems. Coral Gables is home
to many large and beautiful homes, mansions, and churches that reflect

architecture from the 1920s, '30s, and '40s. Some of the homes, or portions of their structures, have been created from coral rock and shells. The Biltmore Hotel is also filled with history. See p. 179 for information on touring the hotel.

Barnacle State Historic Site ★★   The former home of naval architect and early settler Ralph Middleton Munroe is now a museum in the heart of Coconut Grove. It's the oldest house in Miami and it rests on its original foundation, which sits on 5 acres of hardwood and landscaped lawns. The house's quiet surroundings, wide porches, and period furnishings illustrate how Miami's first snowbird lived in the days before condo-mania and luxury hotels. Enthusiastic and knowledgeable state park employees offer a wealth of historical information to those interested in quiet, low-tech attractions like this one. Call for details on the fabulous monthly moonlight concerts during which folk, blues, or classical music is presented and picnicking is encouraged.

3485 Main Hwy. (1 block south of Commodore Plaza), Coconut Grove. © 305/448-9445. Fax 305/448-7484. Admission $1. Concerts $5, free for children under 10. Fri–Mon 9am–4pm. Tours Fri–Sun at 10 and 11:30am, and 1 and 2:30pm. From downtown Miami, take U.S. 1 south to 27th Ave., make a left, and continue to S. Bayshore Dr.; then make a right, follow to the intersection of Main Hwy., and turn left.

Coral Castle ★★ *Finds*   There's plenty of competition, but Coral Castle is probably the strangest attraction in Florida. In 1923, the story goes, a 26-year-old crazed Latvian, suffering from unrequited love of a 16-year old who left him at the altar, immigrated to South Miami and spent the next 25 years of his life carving huge boulders into a prehistoric-looking roofless "castle." It seems impossible that one rather short man could have done all this, but there are scores of affidavits on display from neighbors who swear it happened. Apparently, experts have studied this phenomenon to help figure out how the Great Pyramids and Stonehenge were built. Rocker Billy Idol was said to have been inspired by this place to write his song "Sweet Sixteen." An interesting 25-minute audio tour guides you through the spot, now in the National Register of Historic Places. Although Coral Castle is overpriced and undermaintained, it's worth a visit when in the area, which is about 37 miles (60km)/an hour from Miami.

28655 S. Dixie Hwy., Homestead. © 305/248-6345. www.coralcastle.com. Admission $9.75 adults, $6.50 seniors, $5 children 7–12. Daily 7am–9pm. Take 836 W (Dolphin Expwy.) toward Miami International Airport. Merge onto 826 S (Palmetto Expwy.) and take it to the Florida Turnpike toward Homestead. Take the 288th St. exit (#5) and then take a right on S. Dixie Hwy. and a left on SW 157th Ave. and then a sharp left back onto S. Dixie Hwy. Coral Castle is about ⅕ mile (.5km) down on the left side of the st.

Spanish Monastery Cloisters ★★★ *Finds*   Did you know that the alleged oldest building in the Western Hemisphere dates from 1133 and is located in Miami? The Spanish Monastery Cloisters were first erected in Segovia, Spain. Centuries later, newspaper magnate William Randolph Hearst purchased and brought them to America in pieces. The carefully numbered stones were quarantined for years until they were finally reassembled on the present site in 1954. It has often been used as a backdrop for movies and commercials and is a very popular tourist attraction.

16711 W. Dixie Hwy. (at NE 167th St.), North Miami Beach. © 305/945-1461. monastery@earthlink.net. Admission $5 adults, $2.50 seniors, $2 children 3–12. Mon–Sat 9am–5pm; Sun 1–5pm.

United in Elián House   It was only a matter of time. After Elián González was rescued from a raft off the coast of Fort Lauderdale in November 1999, he lived in this modest, now famous, Little Havana house with relatives for 5 months before being reunited with his father and returned to Cuba in a storm of controversy. For Cuban nationals, the house became a shrine and the boy became a symbol for their struggle. There are collages of Elián all over the house; there's also trash in the yard as if someone still actually lives there. Apparently there was no time to clean up before the throngs of curiosity seekers came and the place was turned into a museum. Visitors receive a sticker with "the picture" of when the boy was seized by federal marshals and returned to his father—a day of infamy in Cuban-American history. See where Elián lived, played, breathed, and ate. See Elián's toys. See where the international media camped out for 5 months. See where relatives cried for the cameras. You get the picture.

2319 NW 2nd St., Little Havana. No tel. Free admission. Sun 10am–6pm.

Venetian Pool ★★★ *Kids* Miami's most beautiful and unusual swimming pool, dating from 1924, is hidden behind pastel stucco walls and is honored with a listing in the National Register of Historic Places. Underground artesian wells feed the free-form lagoon, which is shaded by three-story Spanish porticos and features both fountains and waterfalls: It can be cold in the winter months. During summer, the pool's 800,000 gallons of water are drained and refilled nightly thanks to an underground aquifer, ensuring a cool, *clean* swim. Visitors are free to swim and sunbathe here, just as Esther Williams and Johnny Weissmuller did decades ago. For a modest fee, you or your children can learn to swim during special summer programs.

2701 DeSoto Blvd. (at Toledo St.), Coral Gables. ℂ **305/460-5356.** www.venetianpool.com. Admission and hours vary seasonally. Nov–Mar $5.50 13 and older, $2.50 children under 13; Apr–Oct, $8.50 13 and older, $4.50 children under 13. Children must be 38 in. tall to enter or provide proof of 3 years of age with birth certificate. Hr. are at least 11am–4:30pm, but are often longer. Call for more information.

The Vizcaya Museum and Gardens ★★★ Sometimes referred to as the "Hearst Castle of the East," this magnificent villa is more Gatsby-esque than anything else you'll find in Miami. It was built in 1916 as a winter retreat for James Deering, cofounder and former vice president of International Harvester. The industrialist was fascinated by 16th-century art and architecture and his ornate mansion, which took 1,000 artisans 5 years to build, became a celebration of that period. If you love antiques, this place is a dream come true, packed with European relics and works of art from the 16th to the 19th century. Most of the original furnishings, including dishes and paintings, are still intact. You will see very early versions of a telephone switchboard, central vacuum cleaning system, elevators, and fire sprinklers. A free guided tour of the 34 furnished rooms on the first floor takes about 45 minutes. The second floor, which consists mostly of bedrooms, is open to tour on your own. The spectacularly opulent villa wraps itself around a central courtyard. Outside, lush formal gardens, accented with statuary, balustrades, and decorative urns, front an enormous swath of Biscayne Bay. Definitely take the tour of the rooms, but immediately thereafter, you will want to wander and get lost in the resplendent gardens.

3251 S. Miami Ave. (just south of Rickenbacker Causeway), North Coconut Grove. ℂ **305/250-9133.** www.vizcayamuseum.com. Admission $10 adults, $5 children 6–12, free for children 5 and under. Villa daily 9:30am–5pm (ticket booth closes at 4:30pm); gardens daily 9:30am–5:30pm.

5 Nature Preserves, Parks & Gardens

The Miami area is a great place for outdoors types, with beaches, parks, nature preserves, and gardens galore. For information on South Florida's two national parks, the Everglades and Biscayne National Park, see chapter 7.

The **Amelia Earhart Park,** 401 E. 65th St., Hialeah (*©* **305/685-8389**), is the only real reason to travel to industrial, traffic-riddled Hialeah. The park has five lakes stocked with bass and bream for fishing; playgrounds; picnic facilities; and a big red barn that houses cows, sheep, and goats for petting and ponies for riding. There's also a country store and dozens of old-time farm activities like horseshoeing, sugar-cane processing, and more. Parking is free on weekdays and $3.50 per car on weekends. Open daily from 9am to sunset. To drive here, take I-95 north to the NW 103rd Street exit, go west to East 4th Avenue, and then turn right. Parking is 1½ miles (2.5km) down the street. Depending on traffic, Hialeah is about a half hour from downtown Miami.

At the historic **Bill Baggs Cape Florida State Park** ✿, 1200 Crandon Blvd. (*©* **305/361-5811**), at the southern tip of Key Biscayne, about 20 minutes from downtown Miami, you can explore the unfettered wilds and enjoy some of the most secluded beaches in Miami. There's also an historic lighthouse that was built in 1825, which is the oldest lighthouse in South Florida. The lighthouse was damaged during the Second Seminole War (1836) and again in 1861 during the Civil War. Out of commission for a while, in 1978, the U.S. Coast Guard restored it to working lighthouse condition. A rental shack rents bikes, hydrobikes, kayaks, and many more water toys. It's a great place to picnic, and a newly constructed restaurant serves homemade Latin food, including great fish soups and sandwiches. Just be careful that the raccoons don't get your lunch—the furry, black-eyed beasts are everywhere. Wildlife aside, however, Bill Baggs has been consistently rated as one of the top 10 beaches in the U.S. for its 1¼ miles (2km) of wide, sandy beaches and its secluded, serene atmosphere. Admission is $4 per car with up to eight people. Open daily from 8am to sunset. Tours of the lighthouse are available Thursday through Monday at 10am and 1pm. Arrive at least half an hour early to sign up—there is room for only 10 people on each. Take I-95 to the Rickenbacker Causeway and take that all the way to the end.

Fairchild Tropical Garden ✿✿✿, at 10901 Old Cutler Rd. in South Miami (*©* **305/667-1651;** www.ftg.org), is the largest garden of its kind in the continental United States. A veritable rain forest of both rare and exotic plants, as well as 11 lakes and countless meadows, are spread across 83 acres. Palmettos, vine pergola, palm glades, and other unique species create a scenic, lush environment. More than 100 species of birds have been spotted at the garden (ask for a checklist at the front gate), and it's home to a variety of animals. You should not miss the 30-minute narrated tram tour (tours leave on the hour 10am–3pm weekdays and 10am–4pm on weekends) to learn about the various flowers and trees on the grounds. There is also a museum, a cafe, a picnic area, and a gift shop with fantastic books on gardening, cooking, and edible gifts. The 2-acre rain-forest exhibit, Windows to the Tropics, will save you a trip to the Amazon. Expect to spend a minimum of 2 hours here.

Admission is $8 for adults, free for children 12 and under accompanied by an adult. Open daily, except December 25, from 9:30am to 4:30pm. Take I-95 south to U.S. 1, turn left onto Le Jeune Road, and follow it straight to the traffic circle; from there, take Old Cutler Road 2 miles (3.25km) to the park.

You might remember the pink flamingos at **Hialeah Park** ✿, 2200 E. 4th Ave., Hialeah (*©* **305/885-8000;** www.hialeahpark.com), from *Miami Vice.* This famous flamingo colony is the largest of its kind. The track (which no longer hosts races), listed on the National Register of Historic Places, is one of the most beautiful in the world, featuring old-fashioned stands and acres of immaculately manicured grounds. It is open to the public, for free, to tour around and see the spectacular grounds. Call before going as hours can be erratic.

Located on Biscayne Bay in Coconut Grove (4013 Douglas Rd.; www.ntbg.org/kampong.html), **The Kampong** ★★ is a 7-acre botanical garden featuring a stunning array of flowering trees and tropical fruit trees including mango, avocado, and pomelos. In the early 1900s, noted plant explorer David Fairchild traveled the world seeking rare plants of economic and aesthetic value that might be cultivated in the United States. In 1928, he and his wife, Marian (daughter of Alexander Graham Bell), built a two-story residence here (listed on the National Register of Historic Places) amid some of his collections, borrowing the Malaysian word *kampong* for his home in a garden. In the 1960s, the Fairchilds sold the Kampong to Catherine Hauberg Sweeney, who donated the property to the National Tropical Botanical Garden to promote and preserve this South Florida treasure. It's a must-see for those interested in horticulture. Tours are by appointment only, from Monday to Friday. For tour information, call ✆ **305/442-7169.** Admission is $10 a person. Take U.S. 1 to Douglas Road (SW 37th Ave.). Go east on Douglas Road for about a mile. The Kampong will be on your left.

Named after the late champion of the Everglades, the **Marjory Stoneman Douglas Biscayne Nature Center** ★, 6767 Crandon Blvd., Key Biscayne (✆ **305/361-6767;** www.biscaynenaturecenter.org), has just moved into a brand-new $4 million facility and offers hands-on marine exploration, hikes through coastal hammocks, bike trips, and beach walks. Local environmentalists and historians lead intriguing trips through the local habitat. Call to reserve a spot on a regularly scheduled weekend tour or program. Be sure to wear comfortable closed-toe shoes for hikes through wet or rocky terrain. Open daily from 10am to 7pm Memorial Day through Labor Day; daily from 10am to 4pm the rest of the year. Admission to the park is $4 per person; admission to the nature center is free. Call for weekend programs. To get there, take I-95 to the Rickenbacker Causeway exit (#1) and take the Rickenbacker Causeway all the way until it becomes Crandon Boulevard. The center is on the east side of the street (the Atlantic Ocean side). Driving time is about a 25 minutes from downtown Miami.

Because so many people are so focused on the beach itself, the **Miami Beach Botanical Garden,** 2000 Convention Center Dr., Miami Beach (✆ **305/673-7256**), remains, for the most part, a secret garden. The lush, tropical 4½-acre garden is a fabulous, all-natural retreat from the hustle and bustle of the silicone-enhanced city. Open Monday through Friday from 8:30am to 5pm, Saturday and Sunday from 9:30am to 5pm. Admission is free.

The **Oleta River State Recreation Area** ★★, 3400 NE 163rd St., North Miami (✆ **305/919-1846**), consists of 993 acres—the largest urban park in the state—on Biscayne Bay. The beauty of the Oleta River combined with the fact that you're essentially in the middle of a city makes this park especially worth visiting. With miles of bicycle and canoe trails, a sandy swimming beach, shaded picnic pavilions, and a fishing pier, Oleta River State Recreation Area offers visitors an outstanding outdoor recreational experience cloistered from the confines of the big city. Open daily from 8am to sunset. Admission for pedestrians and cyclists is $1 per person. By car: driver plus car costs $2; driver plus 1 to 7 passengers and car costs $4. Take 1-95 to exit 17 (S.R. 826 E.) and go all the way east until just before the causeway. The park entrance is on your right. Driving time from downtown Miami is about a half-hour.

A testament to Miami's unusual climate, the **Preston B. Bird and Mary Heinlein Fruit and Spice Park** ✿, 24801 SW 187th Ave., Homestead (© **305/ 247-5727**), harbors rare fruit trees that cannot survive elsewhere in the country. If a volunteer is available, you'll learn some fascinating things about this 30-acre living plant museum, where the most exotic varieties of fruits and spices—ackee, mango, Ugli fruits, carambola, and breadfruit—grow on strange-looking trees with unpronounceable names. There are also original coral-rock buildings dating back to 1912. An art festival here in January is among the park's most popular—and populated events.

The best part? You're free to take anything that *naturally* falls to the ground. You'll also find samples of interesting fruits and jellies made from the park's bounty as well as exotic ingredients and cookbooks in the gift store.

Admission to the spice park is $3.50 for adults and $1 for children under 12. It's open daily from 10am to 5pm; closed major holidays. Tours are included in the price of admission and are offered at 11am, and 1 and 2:30pm. Take U.S. 1 south, turn right on SW 248th Street, and go straight for 5 miles (8km) to SW 187th Avenue. The drive from Miami should take 45 minutes to an hour.

Tropical Park, 7900 SW 40th St. in West Miami (© **305/226-8315**), has it all. Enjoy a game of tennis and racquetball for a minimal fee, or swim and sun yourself on the secluded little lake. You can use the fishing pond for free, and they'll even supply you with the rods and bait. If you catch anything, however, you're on your own. Open daily from sunrise to sunset. Admission is free. To get there, go west on Bird Road until you reach the overpass for the Palmetto Expressway (826). The park is on the left side immediately after the overpass.

6 Sightseeing Cruises & Organized Tours

BOAT & CRUISE-SHIP TOURS

You don't need a boating license or a zillion-dollar yacht to explore Miami by boat. Thanks to several enterprising companies, boat tours are easy to find, affordable, and are an excellent way to see the city from a more liquid perspective.

Bay Escape ✿   This 1-hour air-conditioned cruise will take you past Millionaires' Row and the Venetian Islands for just $10. There's also a food stand and cash bar. The tours are bilingual.

Bayside Marketplace Marina, 401 Biscayne Blvd., downtown. © **305/373-7001.** All tickets $10 adults, children 12 and under sail free. Millionaires' Row tour daily 1, 3, 5, and 7pm. Evening party cruise (music and cash bar) Fri–Sat 9–11pm.

Heritage Miami II **Topsail Schooner**   This relaxing ride aboard Miami's only tall ship is a fun way to see the city, since it's on a schooner (as opposed to the other tour company's cruising boats), which gives you more of a feel of the water. The 2-hour cruise passes by Villa Vizcaya, Coconut Grove, and Key Biscayne and puts you in sight of Miami's spectacular skyline and island homes. Call to make sure the ship is running on schedule. On Friday, Saturday, and Sunday evenings, there are 1-hour tours to see the lights of the city, leaving at 6:30pm, for $10 per person.

Bayside Marketplace Marina, 401 Biscayne Blvd., downtown. © **305/442-9697.** Fax 305/442-0119. Tickets for day tours $15 adults, $10 children 12 and under. Sept–May only. Tours leave daily at 1:30, 4, and 6:30pm and Fri–Sun also at 9, 10, and 11pm.

Water Taxi ★★★ *Value* Not exactly a tour, per se, the Water Taxi is a cheap and fantastic way to see the city via local waterways. The two major routes run between Bayside Marketplace and the 5th Street Marina on South Beach; the second is basically a downtown water-shuttle service between the various hotels in downtown as well as the Port of Miami, the Hard Rock Cafe at Bayside, East Coast Fisheries, and Fisher Island. Cost is $7 one way, $12 round trip, and $15 for an all-day pass. The Bayside/South Beach trip is the best one to take because there aren't as many stops.

© 305/467-6677. www.watertaxi.com.

SIGHTSEEING TOURS

While there are several sightseeing tour operators in Miami, most, unfortunately, either don't speak English or are just plain shoddy. The following is the one we'd recommend:

Miami Nice Excursion Travel and Service ★ Pick your destination and the Miami Nice tours will take you to the Everglades, Fort Lauderdale, South Beach, the Seaquarium, Key West, Cape Canaveral, or wherever else you desire. The best trip for first-timers is the City Tour, a comprehensive tour of the entire city and its various neighborhoods. If you've got the time, you will definitely want to add on a side trip to the Everglades and/or Key West (though I suggest exploring the Everglades on your own). Included in most Miami trips is a fairly comprehensive city tour narrated by a knowledgeable guide. The company is one of the oldest in town.

18430 Collins Ave., Miami Beach. © 305/949-9180. www.miaminicetours.com. Tours are $29–$55 adults, $25 children. Daily 7am–10pm. Call ahead for directions to various pickup areas.

SPECIALIZED TOURS

In addition to those listed below, a great option for seeing the city is to take a tour led by **Dr. Paul George.** Dr. George is a history teacher at Miami-Dade Community College and a historian at the Historical Museum of Southern Florida. He also happens to be "Mr. Miami." There's a set calendar of tours, and all of them are fascinating to South Florida buffs. Tours focus on neighborhoods, such as Little Havana, Brickell Avenue, or Key Biscayne, and on themes, such as Miami cemeteries and the Miami River. The often long-winded discussions can be a bit much for those who just want a quick look around, but Dr. George certainly knows his stuff. The cost is $15 to $25; reservations are required (© **305/375-1621**). Tours leave from the Historical Museum at 101 W. Flagler St., downtown.

⸢ *Tips* Go Ahead, Act Like a Tourist!

The Miami Tourist Bus may sound like a savvy traveler's worst nightmare, but if you want to see the city London-style on a double-decker diesel bus *and* get a tan, this is your best bet. Running daily from Aventura to Miami's Kendall suburb, the bus allows unlimited hop-on/hop-off service at popular stops such as Sunset Place, CocoWalk, and Bayside, and has on-board commentary and history as you're being driven through the city. The bus also takes you through the Art Deco District and the tony Bal Harbour Shoppes, all for a $20 day pass. Weeklong passes are also available for $45. For more information, call © **305/573-8687** or log onto www.miamitouristbus.com.

Biltmore Hotel Tour ★★★ *Value*   Take advantage of these free Sunday walking tours to enjoy the hotel's beautiful grounds. The Biltmore is chock-full of history and mystery, including a few ghosts; go out there and see for yourself. In addition, there are also free weekly fireside sessions that are open to the public and presented by Miami Storytellers. Learn about the hotel's early days and rich stories of the city's past. These wonderful sessions are held in the main lobby by the fireplace and are accompanied by a glass of champagne. Call ahead to confirm.

1200 Anastasia Ave., Coral Gables. © 305/445-1926. www.biltmorehotel.com. Free admission. Tours depart on Sun at 1:30, 2:30, and 3:30pm. Call for times of storytelling sessions.

Coral Gables Art and Gallery Tour ★★★ *Value*   This is a fabulous and *free* event that draws art aficionados and the generally curious to sip wine and analyze the various works of art displayed in the many galleries of Coral Gables featuring American folk, African, Native American, and Latin art and photography. On the first Friday of every month, art lovers are shuttled to more than 20 galleries that participate in Gables Night. Pick up one from outside any of the galleries in the area. Most galleries are on Ponce de León Boulevard, between SW 40th and SW 24th streets. The vans run continuously from 7 to 10pm.

Various locations in Coral Gables. For more information, call Elite Fine Art (© 305/448-3800) or stop by any of the galleries in the area. Free. First Fri of the month 7–10pm.

Miami Design Preservation League ★★   On Thursday evenings and Saturday mornings, the Design Preservation League sponsors walking tours that offer a fascinating inside look at the city's historic Art Deco District. Tour-goers meet for a 1½-hour walk through some of America's most exuberantly "architectured" buildings. The league led the fight to designate this area a National Historic District and is proud to share the splendid locale with visitors. Also, see p. 166 for more information.

Art Deco Welcome Center, 1001 Ocean Dr., South Beach. © 305/672-2014. www.mdpl.org. Walking tours $10 per person. Tours leave Sat at 10:30am and Thurs at 6:30pm. Self-guided audio tours also available daily for $10. No reservations necessary. Call ahead for updated schedules.

Murder, Mystery, and Mayhem Bus Tour ★★★   Visit the past by video and bus to Miami-Dade's most celebrated crimes and criminals from the 1800s to the present. From the murder spree of the Ashley Gang to the most notorious murders and crimes of our century, including the murder of designer Gianni Versace, historian Paul George conducts a most fascinating 3-hour tour of scandalous proportions.

Leaves Sat at 10pm from the Dade Cultural Center, 101 W. Flagler St., Miami. Tickets $35. Advance reservations required; call © 305/375-1621.

Second Thursdays: Miami Beach Arts Night ★★★ *Value*   The artistic equivalent of a triathlon, this free cultural open house in Miami Beach takes place on the second Thursday of every month at various venues throughout the city. Hear a string quartet at an area church and then hop on the shuttle for a Haitian dance performance at the Miami Beach Recreation Center. A celebration of the arts, Second Thursdays are a wonderful way to explore the rich and diverse cultures that make the city such a fascinating melting pot.

Various venues. © 305/673-7600. www.2ndthursdays.com. Free. Second Thurs of every month 6–9pm.

7 Water Sports

There are many ways to get well acquainted with Miami's wet look. Choose your own adventure from the suggestions listed below.

BOATING

Private rental outfits include **Boat Rental Plus,** 2400 Collins Ave., Miami Beach (© **305/534-4307**), where 50-horsepower 18-foot powerboats rent for some of the best prices on the beach. There's a 2-hour minimum and rates go from $99 to $449, including taxes and gas. They also have great specials on Sundays. A $250 cash or credit-card deposit is required. Cruising is permitted only in and around Biscayne Bay. Ocean access is prohibited. Renters must be over 21. The rental office is at 23rd Street, on the inland waterway in Miami Beach. It's open daily from 10am to sunset. If you want a specific type of boat, call ahead to reserve. Otherwise, show up and take what's available.

Club Nautico of Coconut Grove, 2560 S. Bayshore Dr. (© **305/858-6258**), rents high-quality powerboats for fishing, water-skiing, diving, and cruising in the bay or ocean. All boats are Coast Guard equipped, with VHF radios and safety gear. Rates range from $199 for 4 hours and $299 for 8 hours, to as much as $419 on weekends. Club Nautico is open daily from 9am to 5pm (weather permitting). Other locations include the Crandon Park Marina, 4000 Crandon Blvd., Key Biscayne (© **305/361-9217**), with the same rates and hours as the Coconut Grove location; and the Miami Beach Marina, Pier E, 300 Alton Rd., South Beach (© **305/673-2502**), where rates range from $229 for 4 hours and from $299 for 8 hours. Nautico on Miami Beach is open daily from 9am to 5pm. For money-saving coupons, log on to www.boatrent.com.

JET SKIS/WAVERUNNERS

Don't miss a chance to tour the islands on the back of your own powerful watercraft. Bravery is, however, a prerequisite, as Miami's waterways are full of speeding jet skiers and boaters who think they're in the Indy 500. Many beachfront concessionaires rent a variety of these popular (and loud) water scooters. The latest models are fast and smooth. Try **Tony's Jet Ski Rentals,** 3601 Rickenbacker Causeway, Key Biscayne (© **305/361-8280**), one of the city's largest rental shops, located on a private beach in the Miami Marine Stadium lagoon. There are three models available accommodating up to three people. Rates range from $45 for a half hour to $80 for a full hour, depending on the number of riders. Tony's is open daily from 10:30am to 6:30pm.

KAYAKING

The laid-back **Urban Trails Kayak Company** rents boats at 10800 Collins Ave. in South Beach (© **305/947-1302**). The outfitters here give interested

---

A Whole New World

Every Columbus Day, Biscayne Bay becomes a veritable mob scene of boaters celebrating the discovery of another day off of work. The unofficial Columbus Day Regatta has become a tradition in which people take to the water for a day of boating, sunning, and, literally, the bare necessities, as they often strip down to their birthday suits in an eye-opening display of their appreciation for Columbus's discovery of the nude -er, new world.

explorers a map to take with them and quick instructions on how to work the paddles and boats. They also operate very scenic 4-hour guided tours through rivers with mangroves and islands as your destination—less than 10 people on the tour costs $45 per person; more than 10 people costs $35 per person. These must be booked in advance. Rates are $8 an hour, $20 for up to 4 hours, and $25 for over 4 hours. Tandems (for two people) are $12 an hour, $30 for up to 4 hours, and $35 for the day. Open daily from 9am to 5pm.

SAILING

You can rent sailboats and catamarans through the beachfront concessions desk of several top resorts, such as the Doral Golf Resort and Spa (p. 123).

Sailboats of Key Biscayne Rentals and Sailing School, in the Crandon Marina (next to Sundays on the Bay), 4000 Crandon Blvd., Key Biscayne (© **305/361-0328** days, 305/279-7424 evenings), can also get you out on the water. A 22-foot sailboat rents for $27 an hour or $81 for a half day. A Cat-25 or J24 is available for $35 an hour or $110 for a half day. If you've always had a dream to win the America's Cup but can't sail, the able teachers at Sailboats will get you started. They offer a 10-hour course over 5 days for $300 for one person or $400 for you and a buddy.

Shake-a-Leg, 2600 Bayshore Dr., Coconut Grove (© **305/858-5550**), is a membership-mostly sailing and boating organization that caters to the physically challenged by offering unique sailing programs specifically designed for those with physical disabilities. The program offers instructional lessons on kayaking and sailing and features certified instructors who will work with the student as they develop boating skills at their own pace. Shake-a-Leg members also welcome physically nondisabled volunteers for activities on and off the water. It costs $60 for nonmembers to rent a boat for 3 hours; free for volunteers and members of Shake-a-Leg. Open Wednesday through Sunday from 9am to 5pm.

SCUBA DIVING & SNORKELING

In 1981, the U.S. government began a wide-scale project designed to increase the number of habitats available to marine organisms. One of the program's major accomplishments has been the creation of nearby artificial reefs, which have attracted all kinds of tropical plants, fish, and animals. In addition, Biscayne National Park (see "Biscayne National Park," in chapter 7) offers a protected marine environment just south of downtown.

Several dive shops around the city offer organized weekend outings, either to the reefs or to one of over a dozen old shipwrecks around Miami's shores. Check "Divers" in the Yellow Pages for rental equipment and for a full list of undersea tour operators.

Diver's Paradise of Key Biscayne, 4000 Crandon Blvd. (© **305/361-3483**), offers two dive expeditions daily to the more than 30 wrecks and artificial reefs off the coast of Miami Beach and Key Biscayne. You can take a 3-day certification course for $399, which includes all the dives and gear. If you already have your C-card, a dive trip costs about $90 if you need equipment and only $35 if you bring your own gear. It's open Monday through Friday from 10am to 6pm and Saturday and Sunday from 8am to 6pm. Call ahead for times and locations of dives. For snorkeling, they will also set you up with equipment and maps on where to see the best underwater sights. Rental for mask, fins, and snorkel is $15.

> ### Finds Miami's Best Dive Bar
>
> In May 2000, Jose Cuervo Tequila company celebrated Cinco de Mayo—or, as their clever marketing staff deemed it, Sinko de Mayo—by submerging an actual, $45,000 full-size margarita bar and six stools about 200 yards offshore from Ocean Drive and 3rd Street. Known as the Jose Cuervo Underwater Bar, the bar is 8 feet (2.4m) high and made of concrete and steel, lying 20 feet (6m) below the ocean's surface. Now an official artificial reef, it's one of South Beach's coolest—and most hidden—wreck-reational watering holes.

South Beach Divers, 850 Washington Ave., Miami Beach (© **305/531-6110**), will also be happy to tell you where to go under the sea and will provide you with rental equipment as well for $30, which includes the mask, fins, and snorkel. They also do dive trips to Key Largo three times a week and do dives off Miami on Sundays at $95 for a two-tank dive.

WINDSURFING
Many hotels rent windsurfers to their guests, but if yours doesn't have a watersports concession stand, head for Key Biscayne. **Sailboards Miami,** Rickenbacker Causeway, Key Biscayne (© **305/361-SAIL**), operates out of big yellow trucks on Hobie Beach, the most popular windsurfing spot in the city. For those who've never ridden a board but want to try it, they offer a 2-hour lesson for $69 that's guaranteed to turn you into a wave warrior or you get your money back. After that, you can rent a board for $26 an hour or $38 for 2 hours. If you want to make a day of it, a 10-hour prepaid card costs $150. These cards require you to prepay, but they also reduce the price by about $70 for the day. You can use the card all year, until the time on it runs out. Open daily from 10am to 5:30pm. Make your first right after the tollbooth (at the beginning of the causeway—you can't miss it) to find the outfitters.

8 More Ways to Play, Indoors & Out

BIKING
The cement promenade on the southern tip of South Beach is a great place to ride. Biking up the beach (on either the beach or along the beach on a cement pathway—which is a lot easier!) is great for surf, sun, sand, exercise, and people-watching—just be sure to keep your eyes on the road, as the scenery can be most distracting. Most of the big beach hotels rent bicycles, as does the **Miami Beach Bicycle Center,** 601 5th St., South Beach (© **305/674-0150**), which charges $5 per hour or $14 per day. It's open Monday through Saturday from 10am to 7pm, Sunday from 10am to 5pm.

Bikers can also enjoy more than 130 miles (209km) of paved paths throughout Miami. The beautiful and quiet streets of Coral Gables and Coconut Grove (several bike trails are spread throughout these neighborhoods) are great for bicyclists. Old trees form canopies over wide, flat roads lined with grand homes and quaint street markers.

The terrain in Key Biscayne is perfect for biking, especially along the park and beach roads. If you don't mind the sound of cars whooshing by your bike lane, **Rickenbacker Causeway** is also fantastic, since it is one of the only bikeable inclines in Miami from which you get fantastic elevated views of the city and waterways. However, be warned that this is a grueling ride, especially going up the causeway. **Key Biking,** 61 Harbor Dr., Key Biscayne (© **305/361-0061**), rents mountain bikes for $5 an hour or $15 a day. It's open Monday through Friday from 10am to 7pm, Saturday from 10am to 6pm, and Sunday from 11am to 4pm.

If you want to avoid the traffic altogether, head out to **Shark Valley** in the Everglades National Park—one of South Florida's most scenic bicycle trails and a favorite haunt of city-weary locals. For more information, see chapter 7.

For a decent list of trail suggestions throughout South Florida, visit www.geocities.com/floutdoorzone/bike.html. *Biking note:* Children under the age of 16 are required by Florida law to wear a helmet, which can be purchased at any bike store or retail outlet selling biking supplies.

FISHING

Fishing licenses are required in Florida. If you go out with one of the fishing charter boats listed below, you are automatically accredited because the companies are. If you go out on your own, however, you must have a Florida fishing license, which costs $16.50. Call © **888/FISH-FLORIDA** for more information.

Some of the best surf casting in the city can be had at **Haulover Beach Park** at Collins Avenue and 105th Street, where there's a bait-and-tackle shop right on the pier. **South Pointe Park,** at the southern tip of Miami Beach, is another popular fishing spot and features a long pier, comfortable benches, and a great view of the ships passing through Government Cut, the deep channel made when the port of Miami was dug.

You can also do some deep-sea fishing in the Miami area. One bargain outfitter, the **Kelley Fishing Fleet,** at the Haulover Marina, 10800 Collins Ave. (at 108th St.), Miami Beach (© **305/945-3801**), has half-day, full-day, and night fishing aboard diesel-powered "party boats." The fleet's emphasis on drifting is geared toward trolling and bottom fishing for snapper, sailfish, and mackerel. Half-day and night fishing trips are $29 for adults and $20 for children up to 10 years old; full-day trips are $40 for adults and $25 for children; prices are $5 cheaper if you have your own rod. Daily departures are scheduled at 9am, and 1:45 and 8pm; reservations are recommended.

Also at the Haulover Marina is the charter boat *Helen C* (10800 Collins Ave.; © **305/947-4081**). Although there's no shortage of private charter boats here, Capt. Dawn Mergelsberg is a good pick, since she puts individuals together to get a full boat. Her *Helen* is a twin-engine 55-footer, equipped for big-game "monster" fish like marlin, tuna, dolphin fish, shark, and sailfish. The cost is $85 per person. Private, full-day trips are available for groups of six people per vessel and cost $800. Group rates and specials are also available. Sailings are scheduled for 8am to noon and 1 to 5pm daily; call for reservations. Children are welcome.

Key Biscayne offers deep-sea fishing to those willing to get their hands dirty and pay a bundle. The competition among the boats is fierce, but the prices are basically the same no matter which you choose. The going rate is about $400 to $450 for a half day and $600 to $700 for a full day of fishing. These rates are usually for a party of up to six, and the boats supply you with rods and bait as well as instruction for first-timers. Some will take you out to the Upper Keys if the fish aren't biting in Miami.

You might also consider the following boats, all of which sail out of the Key Biscayne marina and are in relatively good shape and nicer than most out there:

A Berry Good Time

South Florida's farming region has been steadily shrinking in the face of industrial expansion, but you'll still find several spots where you can get back to nature while indulging in a local gastronomic delight—picking your own produce at the "U-Pic-'Em" farms that dot South Dade's landscape. Depending on what's in season, you can get everything from fresh herbs and vegetables to a mélange of citrus fruits and berries. During berry season—January through April—it's not uncommon to see hardy pickers leaving the groves with hands and faces that are stained a tale-telling crimson and garnished with happy smiles. On your way through South Dade, keep an eye out for the bright red "U-Pic" signs.

There are also a number of fantastic fruit stands in the region. **Burr's Berry Farms,** 12741 SW 216th St. (© **305/251-0145**), located in the township of Goulds about an hour from downtown Miami, has created a sensation with its fabulous strawberry milkshakes. To get there, go south on U.S. 1 and turn right on SW 216th Street. The fruit stand is about 1 mile (1.5km) west. Open daily from 9am to 5:30pm.

For fresh fruit in a tasty pastry or tart, head over to **Knaus Berry Farm** at 15980 SW 248th St. (© **305/247-0668**), in an area known as the Redlands. Some people erroneously call this farm an Amish farm, but in actuality it's run by a sect of German Baptists. The stand offers items ranging from fresh flowers to homemade ice cream, but be sure to indulge in one of their famous homemade cinnamon buns. Be prepared to wait on a long line to stock up—people flock here from as far away as Palm Beach. Head south on U.S. 1 and turn right on 248th Street. The stand is 2½ miles (4km) farther on the left side. Open Monday through Saturday from 8am to 5:30pm.

Sunny Boy III (© *305/361-2217*), *Queen B* (© *305/361-2528*), and *L & H* (© *305/361-9318*). Call for reservations.

Bridge fishing in Biscayne Bay is also popular in Miami; you'll see people with poles over almost every waterway. But look carefully for signs telling you whether it's legal to do so wherever you are. Some bridges forbid fishing.

GAMBLING

Although gambling is technically illegal in Miami, there are plenty of loopholes that allow all kinds of wagering. Gamblers can try their luck at offshore casinos or on shore at bingo, jai alai, card rooms, horse tracks, dog races, and Native American reservations.

Especially popular is **Miccosukee Indian Gaming,** 500 SW 177th Ave. (off S.R. 41, in West Miami on the outskirts of the Everglades; © **800/741-4600** or 305/222-4600), where a touch of Vegas meets west Miami. This tacky casino isn't Caesar's Palace, but you can play tab slots, high-speed bingo (watch out for the serious blue-haired players who will scoff if you make too much noise or if you win before they do), and even poker (with a $10 maximum pot). With more than 85,000 square feet of playing space, the complex even offers overnight accommodations for those who can't get enough of the thrill and don't want to make the approximately 1-hour trip back to downtown Miami. Take the Florida Turnpike south toward Florida City/Key West. Take the SW 8th Street exit (#25) and turn left onto SW 8th Street. Drive for about 3½ miles (5.75km) and then turn left onto Krome Avenue. You can't miss the place—it's the only thing there!

Recently, many of Miami's sketchier gambling-cruise operators have been shut down. The classiest and most legit gambling cruise still in business is the *Casino Princesa,* which docks behind the Hard Rock Cafe in Bayside Marketplace. This 200-foot $15 million yacht has more than 200 slot machines, 32 tables, a restaurant, and four lounges in 10,000 square feet of gaming space on two decks. It's also a major bargain (unless, of course, you lose) at $10.95 per person. Ships sail for 4½ hours from 12:30 to 5pm daily and also from 7:30pm to midnight on weekend nights. They will also pick you up at your hotel. Call *©* **305/379-5825** for updated schedules.

GOLF

There are more than 50 private and public golf courses in the Miami area. Contact the **Greater Miami Convention and Visitor's Bureau** (*©* **800/933-8448;** www.miamiandbeaches.com) for a list of courses and costs.

The best hotel courses in Miami are found at the **Doral Golf Resort and Spa** (p. 123), home of the legendary Blue Monster course as well as the Gold Course, designed by Raymond Floyd; the Great White Shark Course; and the Silver Course, refinished by Jerry Pate.

Other hotels with excellent golf courses include the **Turnberry Isle Resort & Club** (p. 125), with two Robert Trent Jones–designed courses for guests and members, and the **Biltmore Hotel** ★★ (p. 126), which is my pick for best public golf course because of its modest greens fees and an 18-hole par-71 course located on the hotel's spectacular grounds. It must be good: Despite his penchant for privacy, former President Bill Clinton prefers teeing off at this course over any other in Miami!

Otherwise, the following represent some of the area's best public courses. **Crandon Park Golf Course,** formerly known as the Links, 6700 Crandon Blvd., Key Biscayne (*©* **305/361-9129**), is the number-one–ranked municipal course in the state and one of the top five in the country. The park is situated on 200 bay-front acres and offers a pro shop, rentals, lessons, carts, and a lighted driving range. The course is open daily from dawn to dusk; greens fees (including cart) are $86 per person during the winter and $45 per person during the summer. Special twilight rates are available.

One of the most popular courses among real enthusiasts is the **Doral Park Golf and Country Club,** 5001 NW 104th Ave., West Miami (*©* **305/ 591-8800**); it's not related to the Doral Hotel or spa. Call to book in advance, since this challenging, semi-private 18-holer is extrememly popular with locals.

(*Tips* **Par for the Course**

You can get information about most Florida courses, including current greens fees, and reserve tee times, through **Tee Times USA,** P.O. Box 641, Flagler Beach, FL 32136 (*©* **800/374-8633,** 888/465-3567, or 904/439-0001; fax 904/439-0099; www.teetimesusa.com). This company also publishes a vacation guide that includes many stay-and-play golf packages.

The course is open from 6:30am to 6pm during the winter and until 7pm during the summer. Cart and greens fees vary, so call ✆ **305/594-0954** for information.

Known as one of the best in the city, the **Golf Club of Miami,** 6801 Miami Gardens Dr., at NW 68th Avenue, North Miami (✆ **305/829-8456**), has three 18-hole courses of varying degrees of difficulty. You'll encounter lush fairways, rolling greens, and some history to boot. The west course, designed in 1961 by Robert Trent Jones and updated in the 1990s by the PGA, was where Jack Nicklaus played his first professional tournament and Lee Trevino won his first professional championship. The course is open daily from 6:30am to sunset. Cart and greens fees are $45 to $75 per person during the winter, and $20 to $34 per person during the summer. Special twilight rates are available.

Golfers looking for some cheap practice time will appreciate **Haulover Park Beach,** 10800 Collins Ave., Miami Beach (✆ **305/940-6719**), in a pretty bayside location. The longest hole on this par-27 course is 125 yards. It's open daily from 7:30am to 5:30pm during the winter, and until 7:30pm during the summer. Greens fees are $5 per person during the winter and $4 per person during the summer. Handcarts cost $1.40.

IN-LINE SKATING
Miami's consistently flat terrain makes in-line skating a breeze. Lincoln Road, for example, is a virtual skating rink as bladers compete with bikers and walkers for a slab of slate. But the city's heavy traffic and construction do make it tough to find long routes suitable for blading.

Because of the popularity of blading and skateboarding, the city has passed a law prohibiting skating on the west side (the cafe-lined strip) of Ocean Drive in the evenings as well as a law that all bladers must skate slowly and safely. Also, if you're going to partake in the sport, remember to keep a pair of sandals or sneakers with you, since many area shops won't allow you inside with skates on.

Despite all the rules, you can still have fun, and the following rental outfit can help chart an interesting course for you and supply you with all the necessary gear. In South Beach, **Fritz's Skate Shop,** 726 Lincoln Rd. Mall (✆ **305/532-1954**), rents top-quality skates, including safety pads, for $8 per hour, $24 per day, and $34 overnight. If you're an in-line skater newbie, an instructor will hold your hand for $25 an hour. The shop also stocks lots of gear and clothing.

TENNIS
Hundreds of tennis courts in South Florida are open to the public for a minimal fee. Most courts operate on a first-come, first-served basis and are open from sunrise to sunset. For information and directions, call the **City of Miami Beach Recreation, Culture, and Parks Department** (✆ **305/673-7730**) or the **City of Miami Parks and Recreation Department** (✆ **305/575-5256**).

Of the 590 public tennis courts throughout Miami, the three hard courts and seven clay courts at the **Key Biscayne Tennis Association,** 6702 Crandon Blvd. (✆ **305/361-5263**), are the best and most beautiful. Because of this, they often get crowded on weekends. You'll play on the same courts as Lendl, Graf, Evert, McEnroe, and other greats; this is also the venue for one of the world's biggest annual tennis events, the Nasdaq 100 Open. There's a pleasant, if limited, pro shop, plus many good pros. Only four courts are lit at night, but if you reserve at least 48 hours in advance, you can usually take your pick. They cost $6 per person per hour. The courts are open daily from 8am to 9pm.

Other courts are pretty run of the mill and can be found in most neighborhoods. I do, however, recommend the **Miami Beach public courts at Flamingo Park,** 1001 12th St. in South Beach (℡ **305/673-7761**), where there are 19 clay courts that cost $2.50 per person an hour during the day and $3 per person an hour at night. It's first-come, first-serve.

9 Spectator Sports

Check the *Miami Herald*'s sports section for a daily listing of local events and the paper's Friday "Weekend" section for comprehensive coverage and in-depth reports. For last-minute tickets, call the venue directly, since many season-ticket holders sell singles and return unused tickets. Expensive tickets are available from brokers or individuals listed in the classified sections of the local papers. Some tickets are also available through **Ticketmaster** (℡ **305/358-5885**).

BASEBALL

The **Florida Marlins** shocked the sports world in 1997 when they became the youngest expansion team to win a World Series, but then floundered as their star players were sold off by former owner Wayne Huizenga. As long as the rebuilding process continues and the Marlins continue to struggle, tickets are easy to come by. If you're interested in catching a game, be warned: The summer heat in Miami can be unbearable, even in the evenings.

Home games are held at the **Pro Player Stadium,** 2267 NW 199th St., North Miami Beach (℡ **305/626-7426**). Tickets range from $4 to $50. Box office hours are Monday through Friday from 8:30am to 6pm, Saturday from 8:30am to 4pm, and before games; tickets are also available through Ticketmaster. The team currently holds spring training in Melbourne, Florida.

BASKETBALL

The **Miami Heat** (℡ **305/577-HEAT** or 305/835-7000), now led by celebrity coach Pat Riley, made its NBA debut in November 1988 and their games remain one of Miami's hottest tickets. Courtside seats are full of visiting celebrities from Puff Daddy to Madonna. The season lasts from October to April, with most games beginning at 7:30pm. They play in the brand-new waterfront **American Airlines Arena** located downtown on Biscayne Boulevard. Tickets are $14 to $50. Box office hours are Monday through Friday from 10am to 4pm (until 8pm on game nights); tickets are also available through Ticketmaster.

FOOTBALL

Miami's golden boys are the **Miami Dolphins,** the city's most recognizable team, followed by thousands of "dolfans." The team plays at least eight home games during the season, between September and December, at **Pro Player Stadium,** 2267 NW 199th St., North Miami Beach (℡ **305/620-2578**). Tickets cost between $20 and $40. The box office is open Monday through Friday from 8:30am to 5:30pm; tickets are also available through Ticketmaster.

HORSE RACING

Located on the Dade–Broward County border in Hallandale (just north of North Miami Beach/Aventura) is **Gulfstream Park,** at U.S. 1 and Hallandale Beach Boulevard (℡ **305/931-7223;** www.gulfstreampark.com), South Florida's very own version of the Kentucky Derby, albeit not nearly as sceney. This horse track is a haven for serious gamblers and voyeurs alike. Large purses and important races are commonplace at this sprawling suburban course, and the track is typically crowded, especially during its amusing and entertaining concert series from January to April, which features has-beens and one-hit wonders such as Cindy Lauper, REO Speedwagon, and Bryan Adams on the front lawn for just $5. Call for schedules. Admission is $3 to the grandstand and $5 to the clubhouse; parking is free. January through March, post times are Wednesday through Monday at 1pm.

ICE HOCKEY
The young **Florida Panthers** (© **954/835-7000**) have already made history. In the 1994–95 season, they played in the Stanley Cup finals, and they have amassed a legion of fans who love them. Much to the disappointment of Miamians, they moved to a new venue in Sunrise, the next county north of Miami-Dade, more than an hour from downtown Miami. Call for directions and ticket information.

JAI ALAI
Jai alai, sort of a Spanish-style indoor lacrosse, was introduced to Miami in 1924 and is regularly played in two Miami-area frontons (the buildings in which jai alai is played). Although the sport has roots stemming from ancient Egypt, the game, as it's now played, was invented by Basque peasants in the Pyrenees Mountains during the 17th century.

Players use woven baskets, called *cestas,* to hurl balls, called *pelotas,* at speeds that sometimes exceed 170 mph. Spectators, who are protected behind a wall of glass, place bets on the evening's players. The Florida Gaming Corporation owns the jai alai operations throughout the state, making betting on this sport as legal as buying a lottery ticket.

The **Miami Jai Alai Fronton,** 3500 NW 37th Ave., at NW 35th Street (© **305/633-6400**), is America's oldest fronton, dating from 1926. It schedules 13 games per night, which typically last 10 to 20 minutes, but can occasionally go much longer. Admission is $1 to the grandstand, $5 to the clubhouse. There are year-round games on Monday and Wednesday through Saturday at 7pm and matinees on Monday, Wednesday, and Saturday at noon. This is the main location where jai alai is played in Miami. The other South Florida jai alai venue is in Dania, near the Fort Lauderdale–Hollywood International Airport. See p. 301 for more information on **Dania Jai Alai.**

 Jai Alai Explained

Jai alai originated in the Basque country of Northern Spain, where players used to use church walls as their courts. The game looks very much like lacrosse, actually, with rules very similar to handball or tennis. The game is played on a court with numbered lines. What makes the game totally unique, however, is the requirement that the ball must be returned in one continuous motion. The server must bounce the ball behind the serving line and with the basket, must hurl the ball to the front wall, with the aim being that, upon rebound, the ball will bounce between lines 4 and 7. If it doesn't, it is an under or over serve and the other team receives a point.

10 Cruises & Other Caribbean Getaways

Cruising has come a long way since the days of bingo, shuffleboard, and even the delusional *Love Boat.* Whether you prefer megaships with rock-climbing walls or a smaller, less elaborate ship that just sails you to your destination, a floating vacation can be a very enticing option for people traveling to South Florida. The proximity to the Caribbean makes a 3-, 4-, or 7-day cruise an excellent diversion from the hustle and bustle of the big city.

If you want to catch a weekend in the Caribbean while you're in South Florida but aren't enthralled with the idea of boat travel, there are a number of air packages available as well. Travel to Cuba is severely restricted from Miami (or anywhere in the United States) for all but those who have obtained licenses from the U.S. State Department (see details at www.destinationcuba.com/whocanvisit.htm), although many people choose to go there from Mexico, Jamaica, or the Bahamas.

The following sections aren't intended to be detailed descriptions of the cruising and package options available out of Miami and the Keys—that would fill up an entire book on its own—but they will give you a good overview of the cruising and package picture.

CRUISES

The Port of Miami is the world's busiest cruise-ship port, with a passenger load of close to 3 million annually. The popularity of these cruises shows no sign of tapering off, and the trend in ships is toward bigger, more luxurious liners. Usually all-inclusive, cruises offer value and simplicity compared to other vacation options. Most of the Caribbean-bound cruise ships sail weekly out of the Port of Miami. They are relatively inexpensive, can be booked without advance notice, and make for an excellent excursion.

The Port of Miami is very close to downtown Miami, but the most popular pre- and post-cruise destination in Miami is South Beach (about a 10-min. ride from the port), because of its proximity to the port and the fact that it's a relatively small (and walkable) area full of nightlife, beaches, hotels, and restaurants (see the South Beach sections of this book). If you're just looking for a quick overnight stay, your best bet may be one of the downtown-area hotels, which are closest to the port. The only two in the immediate area that I'd recommend, however, are The Hotel Inter-Continental Miami (p. 121), which is literally up the block from the port, or the Biscayne Bay Marriott. located about 5 minutes away. For food and shopping, Bayside Marketplace (p. 200) is within walking distance of the port. For other restaurants in this area, check the Downtown dining section of chapter 4, beginning on p. 149. Cabs are abundant at the port. A ride to the airport should cost about $25 and a ride to South Beach should be about $10.

All the shorter cruises (3 and 4 days) are well equipped for gambling. Their casinos open as soon as the ship clears U.S. waters—typically 45 minutes after leaving port. Usually, four full-size meals are served daily, with portions so huge they're impossible to finish. Games, movies, and other onboard activities ensure you're always busy. Passengers can board up to 2 hours before departure for meals, games, and cocktails.

There are dozens of cruises from which to choose—from 1-day excursions to a trip around the world. You can get a full list of options from the **Metro-Dade Seaport Department,** 1015 N. America Way, Miami, FL 33132 (© **305/371-7678**). It's open Monday through Friday from 8am to 5pm.

The cruise lines and ships listed below offer 3-, 4-, and 7-night cruises to the Caribbean, Key West, and other longer itineraries that often change. If you want more information, contact the individual line, or, for Bahamas cruises, call the **Bahamas Tourist Office,** 19495 Biscayne Blvd., Suite 809, Aventura, FL 33180 (© **305/932-0051**). All passengers must travel with a passport or proof of citizenship for reentry into the United States.

For detailed information on Caribbean cruises, pick up a copy of *Frommer's Carribean Cruises & Ports of Call.*

Carnival Cruise Lines (© **800/327-9501** or 305/599-2200; www.carnival. com) has 3- and 4-day cruises to Key West and the Caribbean as well as 7-day excursions that include stops in Mexico, Jamaica, and the Cayman Islands. Carnival's ships are appropriately known as Fun Ships, catering to a young, party-hearty crowd. There's also a smoke-free ship called the *Paradise.* Cruises usually depart from Miami Friday through Monday. Prices range from $400 to $3,000, not including port charges (lower rates are usually available, depending on season), which can be as high as $200 per person.

Cunard (© **800/528-6273** or 305/463-3000; www.cunardline.com), which moved here in late 1997, is known for its Old-World elegance and caters to an older, sophisticated crowd. If you're looking for Internet cafes and ice-skating rinks, Cunard isn't for you. This line's Miami ships include the legendary throwback from the halcyon days of the mighty luxe ocean liner, *Queen Elizabeth II,* as well as the *Queen Mary II.* Itineraries are usually at least 10 days long, though there are some that last 6 days, such as the jazz, fine arts, and big-band cruises. Prices start at $3,300 per person.

Norwegian Cruise Line (© **800/327-7030** or 305/436-0866; www.ncl. com) has four ships based in Miami during the winter months and usually one in the summer. NCL is known for having the most flexible dining setup at sea, with open seating and casual dress codes. A mixture of young and older crowds can be found on their ships. Ships go to Key West, the Bahamas, and the Western Caribbean. Its shortest cruises are 3 days; the longest—from Miami to France—is 15 days. Rates range from $199 per person for an inside cabin on the shortest cruises to $4,500 per person for the very best cabin on the transcontinental journey.

Royal Caribbean International (© **800/327-6700** or 305/539-6000; www.rccl.com), one of the premier lines in Miami, has about half a dozen ships departing Miami at any given time. The Port of Miami actually had to renovate three cruise terminals in 1999—at a price of $60 million—to accommodate Royal Caribbean's 142,000-ton ship *Voyager of the Seas,* which boasts an ice-skating rink and a rock-climbing wall, among other theme-park-like diversions. *Explorer of the Seas* and *Adventure of the Seas* are the line's second and third theme parks at sea, also featuring extreme sports and an assortment of high-tech activities. As a result, RCI caters to a young and old(er), active crowd as well as families with children. The line mostly offers Caribbean cruises and some Bahamas destinations. The *Legend of the Seas* and the *Splendor of the Seas* offer 3- and 4-night Bahamas trips as for as low as less than $100 per person, per day to as high as $7,500 per person for an 11-night cruise through the Caribbean.

FLIGHTS & WEEKEND PACKAGES

For those who want a quick getaway to the Caribbean without the experience of cruising, many airlines and hotels team up to offer extremely affordable weekend packages.

For example, the Bahamas' most entertaining and family-friendly resort, the **Atlantis** on Paradise Island (© **888/528-7155;** www.atlantis.com), is a tropical theme park offering extensive water sports plus an active casino. Reasonably priced 3-day packages start at about $390, depending on departure date. (It's generally cheaper to fly midweek.) Flights on **Continental Airlines** (© **800/ 786-7202**) depart at least twice daily from Miami International. You can also choose to stay in the company's other luxurious resorts: the **Paradise Beach Resort** or the **Ocean Club.** Book package deals through **Paradise Island Vacations** (© **800/722-7466**).

Other groups that arrange competitively priced packages include **American Flyaway Vacations,** operated by American Airlines (© **800/321-2121**); **Bahamas Air** (© **800/222-4262** or 305/593-1910); and **Chalks Ocean Airways** (© **305/371-8628**). Call for rates, since they vary dramatically throughout the year and also depend on what type of accommodations you choose. Keep your eye on the travel section of the *Miami Herald,* as well, as special deals and packages are almost always advertised.

11 Animal Parks

For a tropical climate, Miami's got a lot of nontropical animals to see, and we're not talking about the motorists on I-95. Everything from dolphins and alligators to lions, tigers, and bears call Miami home (most in parks, some in nature). Call the parks to inquire about discount packages or coupons, which may be offered at area retail stores or in local papers.

Miami Metrozoo ★★ *Kids* This 290-acre, sparsely landscaped complex (it was devastated by Hurricane Andrew) is quite a distance from Miami proper and the beaches—about 45 minutes—but worth the trip. Isolated and never really crowded, it's also completely cageless—animals are kept at bay by cleverly designed moats. This is a fantastic spot to take younger kids—the older ones seem bored and unstimulated here; there's a wonderful petting zoo and play area, and the zoo offers several daily programs designed to educate and entertain. Mufasa and Simba (of Disney fame) were modeled on a couple of Metrozoo's lions. Other residents include two rare white Bengal tigers, a Komodo dragon, rare koala bears, a number of kangaroos, and an African meerkat. The air-conditioned Zoofari Monorail tour offers visitors a nice overview of the park. An Andean Condor exhibit opened in 2000, and the zoo is always upgrading its facilities, including the impressive aviary. *Note:* The distance between animal habitats can be great, so you'll be doing *a lot* of walking here. For this reason, there are benches and shaded gazebos strategically positioned throughout the zoo so you can rest when you need to. Also, because the zoo can be miserably hot during summer months, plan these visits in the early morning or late afternoon. Expect to spend about 3 hours here.

12400 SW 152nd St., South Miami. © 305/251-0400. www.zsf.org. Admission $8.95 adults, $4.75 children 3–12. Daily 9:30am–5:30pm (ticket booth closes at 4pm). Free parking. From U.S. 1 south, turn right on SW 152nd St. and follow signs about 3 miles (5km) to the entrance.

Miami Seaquarium ★ *Kids* *Overrated* If you've been to Orlando's SeaWorld, you may be disappointed with Miami's version, which is considerably smaller and not as well maintained. It's hardly a sprawling seaquarium, but you will want to arrive early to enjoy the effects of its mild splash. You'll need at least 3 hours to tour the 35-acre oceanarium and see all four daily shows starring a number of showy ocean mammals. You can cut your visit to 2 hours if you limit your shows to the better, albeit corny, Flipper Show and Killer Whale Show. The highly regarded Water and Dolphin Exploration Program (WADE) allows visitors to touch and swim with dolphins in the Flipper Lagoon. The program costs $125 per person and is offered twice daily, Wednesday through Sunday. Children must be at least 52 inches tall to participate. Reservations are necessary for this program. Call © **305/365-2501** in advance for reservations.

4400 Rickenbacker Causeway (south side), en route to Key Biscayne. © **305/361-5705**. www.miami seaquarium.com. Admission $23.95 adults, $18.95 children 3–9, free for children under 3. Daily 9:30am–6pm (ticket booth closes at 4:30pm).

Monkey Jungle ★ *Overrated*   Personally, I think this place is disgusting. It reeks, the monkeys are either sleeping or in heat, and it's really far from the city, even farther than the zoo. But if primates are your thing and you'd rather pass on the zoo, you'll be in paradise. You'll see rare Brazilian golden lion tamarins and Asian macaques. There are no cages to restrain the antics of the monkeys as they swing, chatter, and play their way into your heart. Screened-in trails wind through acres of "jungle," and daily shows feature the talents of the park's most progressive pupils. People who go here are not monkeying around—many of the park's frequent visitors are scientists and anthropologists. Despite the smell, however, I must admit that I found myself thoroughly amused by the animal antics at the Orangutans' Asiatic Ape Exhibit. Newer exhibits include the Cameroon Jungle and the Lemurs of Madagascar. If you can stand the humidity, the smell, and the bugs (flies, mosquitoes, and so on), expect to spend about 2 hours here. The park's website sometimes offers downloadable discount coupons, so if you have Internet access, take a look before you visit.

14805 SW 216th St., South Miami. © **305/235-1611**. www.monkeyjungle.com. Admission $15.95 adults, $12.95 seniors and active-duty military, $9.95 children 4–12. Daily 9:30am–5pm (tickets sold until 4pm). Take U.S. 1 south to SW 216th St., or from Florida Turnpike, take exit 11 and follow the signs.

Parrot Jungle and Gardens ★★ *Kids*   This Miami institution will take flight from its current location in South Miami in the fall of 2002 and head north in the winter of 2003 to a new $46 million home on Watson Island, along the McArthur Causeway near Miami Beach. While the island will double as a protected bird sanctuary, the jungle's soon-to-be former digs in the heart of South Miami in a coral-rock structure built around 1900 are a lot more charming and kitschier. The new 18.6-acre park will feature an Everglades exhibit, a petting zoo, and several theaters, jungle trails, and aviaries. Watch your heads because flying above are hundreds of parrots, macaws, peacocks, cockatoos, and flamingos. Continuous shows star roller-skating cockatoos, card-playing macaws, and numerous stunt-happy parrots. There are also tortoises, iguanas, and a rare albino alligator on exhibit. The park's website sometimes offers downloadable discount coupons, so if you have Internet access, take a look before you visit.

Until the move: 11000 SW 57th Ave., Southern Miami–Dade County. © **305/666-7834**. After the move: 1111 Parrot Jungle Trail, Watson Island (on the north side of MacArthur Causeway/I-395). © **305/372-3822**. www.parrotjungle.com. Admission $15.95 adults, $13.95 seniors, $10.95 children 3–10. Daily 9:30am–6pm. Cafe opens at 8am. Take U.S. 1 south and turn left at SW 57th Ave., or exit Kendall Dr. from the Florida Turnpike and turn right on SW 57th Ave.

Sea Grass Adventures ★ *Value* *Kids*   Even better than the Seaquarium is Sea Grass Adventures, in which a naturalist from the Marjory Stoneman Douglas Biscayne Nature Center will introduce kids and adults to an amazing variety of creatures that live in the sea grass beds of the Bear Cut Nature Preserve near Crandon Beach on Key Biscayne. Not just a walking tour, you will be able to wade in the water with your guide and catch an assortment of sea life in nets provided by the guides. At the end of the program, participants gather on the beach while the guide explains what everyone's just caught, passing the creatures around in miniature viewing tanks. Call for available dates and reservations.

Marjory Stoneman Douglas Biscayne Nature Center, 6767 Crandon Blvd., Key Biscayne. ✆ 305/361-6767. $10 per person. Daily 10am–4pm.

12 Shopping

Miami is one of the world's premier shopping cities; more than 10 million visitors came here last year and they spent in excess of $13 billion. People come to Miami from all over—from Latin America to Hong Kong—in search of some products that are all-American (i.e. Levis, Nikes, etc.).

So if you're not into sunbathing and outdoor activities, or you just can't take the heat, you'll be in good company in one of Miami's many malls—and you are not likely to emerge empty-handed. In addition to the strip malls, Miami offers a choice of megamalls, from the upscale Shops at Sunset to the mammoth Aventura Mall to the ritzy Bal Harbour Shops (just to name a few).

Miami also offers more unique shopping spots, such as Bayside Marketplace, where you can buy such eclectic items as handcrafted tropical birds or jewelry made of precious stones, and Little Havana, where you can buy hand-rolled cigars and guayabera shirts.

You may want to order the Greater Miami Convention and Visitor's Bureau's "Shop Miami: A Guide to a Tropical Shopping Adventure." Although it is limited to details on the bureau's paying members, it provides some good advice and otherwise unpublished discount offers. The glossy little pamphlet is printed in English, Spanish, and Portuguese and provides information about transportation from hotels, translation services, and shipping. Call ✆ **800/283-2707** or 305/539-3034 for more information.

THE SHOPPING SCENE

Below, you'll find descriptions of some of the more popular retail areas, where many stores are conveniently clustered together to make browsing easier.

As a general rule, shop hours are Monday through Saturday from 10am to 6pm and Sunday from noon to 5pm. Many stores stay open late (until 9pm or so) 1 night of the week (usually Thurs). Shops in Coconut Grove are open until 9pm Sunday through Thursday and even later on Friday and Saturday nights. South Beach's stores also stay open later—as late as midnight. Department stores and shopping malls also keep longer hours, with most staying open from 10am to 9 or 10pm Monday through Saturday, and noon to 6pm on Sunday. With all these variations, call ahead to specific stores to find out what their hours are.

The 6.5% state and local sales tax is added to the price of all nonfood purchases. Food and beverages in hotels and restaurants are taxed via the resort tax, which is 3% in Miami/South Beach and Bal Harbour, 4% in Surfside, and 2% in the rest of Miami–Dade County

Most Miami stores can wrap your purchase and ship it anywhere in the world via United Parcel Service (UPS). If they can't, you can send it yourself, either through UPS (✆ **800/742-5877**) or through the U.S. Mail (see the "Post Office" section under "Fast Facts: Miami," in chapter 4).

SHOPPING AREAS

Most of Miami's shopping happens at the many megamalls scattered from one end of the county to the other; however, there is also some excellent boutique shopping and browsing to be done in the following areas (see "The Neighborhoods in Brief," in chapter 4, for more information about these areas):

AVENTURA   On Biscayne Boulevard between Miami Gardens Drive and the county line at Hallandale Beach Boulevard is a 2-mile (3.25km) stretch of major retail stores including Best Buy, Borders, Circuit City, Linens N' Things, Marshall's, Sports Authority, and more. Also here is the mammoth Aventura Mall, housing a fabulous collection of shops and restaurants.

CALLE OCHO   For a taste of "Little Havana," take a walk down 8th Street between SW 27th Avenue and SW 12th Avenue, where you'll find some lively street life and many shops selling cigars, baked goods, shoes, and furniture, and record stores specializing in Latin music. For help, take your Spanish dictionary.

COCONUT GROVE   Downtown Coconut Grove, centered on Main Highway and Grand Avenue and branching onto the adjoining streets, is one of Miami's most pedestrian-friendly zones. The Grove's wide sidewalks, lined with cafes and boutiques, can provide hours of browsing pleasure. Coconut Grove is best known for its chain stores (Gap, Banana Republic, etc.) and some funky holdovers from the days when the Grove was a bit more bohemian, plus excellent sidewalk cafes centered around CocoWalk and the Streets of Mayfair.

MIRACLE MILE (CORAL GABLES)   Actually only a half-mile long, this central shopping street was an integral part of George Merrick's original city plan. Today, the strip still enjoys popularity, especially for its bridal stores, ladies' shops, haberdashers, and gift shops. Recently, newer chain stores, like Barnes & Noble, Old Navy, and Starbucks, have been appearing on the Mile. **Merrick Park,** a mammoth, 850,000-square-foot upscale outdoor shopping complex between Ponce de León Boulevard and Le Jeune Road, just off the mile, opened in the fall of 2002 with Nordstrom, Neiman Marcus, Armani, and Yves St. Laurent on board, to name a few.

DOWNTOWN MIAMI   If you're looking for discounts on all types of goods—especially watches, fabric, buttons, lace, shoes, luggage, and leather—Flagler Street, just west of Biscayne Boulevard, is the best place to start. I wouldn't necessarily recommend buying expensive items here, as many stores seem to be on the shady side and do not understand the word *warranty.* However, you can still have fun here as long as you are a savvy shopper and don't mind haggling with people who may not have the firmest grasp on the English language. Most signs are printed in English, Spanish, and Portuguese; however, many shopkeepers may not be entirely fluent in English.

SOUTH BEACH ⍟   Slowly but surely, South Beach has come into its own as far as shopping is concerned. While the requisite stores—Gap, Banana Republic, and so on—have anchored here, several higher-end stores have also opened on the southern blocks of Collins Avenue, which has become the Madison Avenue of Miami. For the hippest clothing boutiques (including Armani and Armani Exchange, Ralph Lauren, Versace, Benetton, Agnes B, Guess?, Club Monaco, Kenneth Cole, and Nicole Miller, among others), stroll along this pretty strip of the Deco District.

For those who are interested in a little more fun with their shopping, consider South Beach's legendary Lincoln Road. This pedestrian mall, originally designed in 1957 by Morris Lapidus, recently underwent a multimillion-dollar renovation restoring it to its former glory. Here, shoppers find an array of clothing, books, tchotchkes, and art as well as a menagerie of sidewalk cafes flanked on one end by a multiplex movie theater and at the other by the Atlantic Ocean.

SHOPPING A TO Z
ANTIQUES/COLLECTIBLES

Miami's antiques shops are scattered in small pockets around the city. Many that feature lower-priced furniture can be found in North Miami, in the 1600 block of Northeast 123rd Street, near West Dixie Highway. About a dozen shops sell china, silver, glass, furniture, and paintings. But you'll find the bulk of the better antiques in Coral Gables and in Southwest Miami along Bird Road between 64th and 66th avenues and between 72nd and 74th avenues. For international collections from Bali to France, check out the burgeoning scene in the Design District centered on Northeast 40th Street west of 1st Avenue. Miami also hosts several large antiques shows each year. In October and November, the most prestigious one—the **Antique Show**—hits the Miami Beach Convention Center (© **305/754-4931**). Exhibitors from all over come to display their wares, including jewelry. There's also a decent monthly show at the **Coconut Grove Convention Center** (© **305/444-8454**). Miami's huge concentration of Deco buildings from the '20s and '30s makes this the place to find the best selections of Deco furnishings and decorations. A word to the serious collectors: Dania Beach, up in Broward County (see chapter 8), about half an hour from downtown Miami, is the best place for antiques (known as the antiques capital of South Florida), so you may want to consider browsing in Miami and shopping up there.

Architectural Antiques   A great place to browse—if you don't mind a little dust—this huge warehouse has an impressive stash of ironwork, bronzes, paintings, lamps, furniture, and sculptures, which have been salvaged from estates worldwide. Don't be surprised to find odd items, too, like an old British phone booth or a pair of gargoyles off an ancient church. 2500 SW 28th Lane (just west of U.S. 1), Miami. © **305/285-1330.** archantique@earthlink.net.

Modernism Gallery   Specializing in 20th-century furnishings from Gilbert Rohde, Noguchi, and Heywood Wakefield, this shop has some of the most beautiful examples of Deco goods from France and the United States. If they don't have what you're looking for, ask. They possess the amazing ability to find the rarest items. 1622 Ponce de León Blvd., Coral Gables. © **888/217-2760.**

Senzatempo *Finds*   If the names Charles Eames, George Nelson, and Gio Ponti mean anything to you, then this is where you'll want to visit. There's retro, Euro-fabulous designer furniture and decorative arts from 1930 to 1960, as well as collectible watches, timepieces, and clocks. 1655 Meridian Ave. (at Lincoln Rd.), South Beach. © **305/534-5588.** www.senzatempo.com.

BOOKS

Barnes & Noble *Kids*   With half a dozen outlets in the area (Aventura, South Miami, Kendall, etc.) and more on the way, this huge chain offers anything readers could ask for, including a comfortable cafe, a large children's section, and tons of magazines. Plus, the chain gives you a 10% discount on all best-sellers and has incredible closeout specials. They often schedule readings with noted authors, too. There are more than six locations in Miami, but this branch has an especially nice little scene, featuring local intellectuals, students, and professors from the nearby University of Miami. 152 Miracle Mile, Coral Gables. © **305/446-4152.** www.bn.com.

Books & Books   A dedicated following turns out to browse at this warm and wonderful little independent shop. Enjoy the upstairs antiquarian room, which specializes in art books and first editions. If that's not enough intellectual stimulation for you, the shop hosts free lectures from noted authors, experts, and personalities almost nightly, from Monica Lewinsky to Martin Amis. At another location (933 Lincoln Rd., South Beach; ✆ 305/532-3222), you'll rub elbows with tanned and buffed South Beach bookworms sipping cappuccinos at the Russian Bear Cafe inside the store. This branch stocks a large selection of gay literature and also features lectures. 265 Aragon Ave., Coral Gables. ✆ 305/442-4408. www.booksandbooks.com.

Kafka's Cyberkafe   Check your e-mail and surf the Web while you sip a latte or snack on a sandwich or pastry with friendly neighborhood regulars. This popular used bookstore also stocks a wide range of foreign and domestic magazines and caters to an international youth hostel–type crowd. 1464 Washington Ave., South Beach. ✆ 305/673-9669.

CIGARS

Although it is illegal to bring Cuban cigars into the United States, somehow, forbidden *Cohibas* show up at every dinner party and nightclub in town. Not that I condone it, but if you hang around the cigar smokers in town, no doubt one will be able to tell you where you can get some of the highly prized contraband. Be careful, however, of counterfeits, which are typically Dominican cigars posing as Cubans. Cuban cigars are illegal, and unless you go down a sketchy alley to buy one from a dealer (think of it as being as shady as a drug deal), you are going to be smoking Dominican ones.

The stores listed below sell excellent hand-rolled cigars made with domestic- and foreign-grown tobacco. Many of the *viejos* (old men) got their training in Cuba working for the government-owned factories in the heyday of Cuban cigars.

La Gloria Cubana   This tiny storefront shop employs about 45 veteran Cuban rollers who sit all day rolling the very popular torpedoes and other critically acclaimed blends. They're usually backordered, but it's worth stopping in: They will sell you a box and show you around. 1106 SW 8th St., Little Havana. ✆ 305/858-4162.

Mike's Cigars (Finds   Mike's recently moved to this new location, but it's one of the oldest and best smoke shops in town. Since 1950, Mike's has been selling the best from Honduras, the Dominican Republic, and Jamaica, as well as the very hot local brand, La Gloria Cubana. Many say it has the best prices, too. Mike's has the biggest selection of cigars in town and the employees speak English. 1030 Kane Concourse (at 96th St.), Bay Harbor Island. ✆ 305/866-2277. www.mikes cigars.com.

FASHION

Miami didn't become a fashion capital until—believe it or not—the pastel-hued, Armani-clad cops on *Miami Vice* had their close-ups on the tube. Before that, Miami was all about old men in white patent leather shoes and well-tanned women in bikinis. How things have changed! Miami is now a fashion mecca in its own right, with some of the same high-end stores you'd find on Rue de Fauborg St. Honore in Paris or Bond Street in London. You'll find all the chichi labels, including Prada and Gucci, right here at the posh Bal Harbour Shops.

For funkier frocks, South Beach is the place, where designers such as Cynthia Rowley, Betsey Johnson, and Giorgio Armani compete for window shoppers with local up-and-coming designers, some of whom design for drag queens and club kids only. The strip on Collins Avenue between 7th and 10th streets has become quite upscale, including such shops as Armani Exchange and Nicole Miller, along with the inescapable Gap and Banana Republic. Of course, there's also more mainstream (and affordable) shopping in the plethora of malls and outdoor shopping and entertainment complexes that are sprinkled throughout the city (see the section on malls later in this chapter).

Unisex

Agnes B This fabulous French import features unique women's, men's, and children's high fashion at high prices. If you don't have carte blanche, however, the best buy in the store is the one-of-a-kind Agnes B perfume, in a lovely heart bottle, for just $20. 640 Collins Ave., South Beach. (✆ 305/604-8705.

Base A beautiful store featuring one-of-a-kind clothing made in St. Vincent that's light, breezy, fashionable, and, of course, pricey. Keep on the lookout for excellent sales. 939 Lincoln Rd., South Beach. (✆ 305/531-4982.

Glitzy Tartz The name alone says it all. This outlandish boutique features everything you'd want if you were a go-go boy or girl, in vinyl, mesh, and lamé—all in several sizes way too tight, to accentuate the, uh, positive. 1251 Washington Ave., South Beach. (✆ 305/535-0068.

Island Trading Part of music mogul Chris Blackwell's empire, Island sells everything you'd need to wear in a tropical resort town: batik sarongs, sandals, sundresses, bathing suits, cropped tops, and more. Many of the unique styles are created on the premises by a team of young, innovative designers. 1332 Ocean Dr., South Beach. (✆ 305/673-6300.

Laundry Industry If you're color blind, from New York, or just can't be bothered with coordinating your colors, Laundry Industry is for you, with the chicest (and priciest) black-and-white–only threads for men and women this side of SoHo. 666 Collins Ave., South Beach. (✆ 305/531-2277.

Urban Outfitters It took a while for this urban outpost to hit Miami, but once it did, it became a favorite for the young hipster set, who favor T-shirts that say "Princess" instead of Prada. Cheapish, utilitarian, and funky, Urban Outfitters is an excellent place to pick up a pair of used jeans or some funky tchotchkes for your apartment. Two locations: 653 Collins Ave., South Beach. (✆ 305/535-9726; and Shops at Sunset, 5701 SW 72nd St., South Miami. (✆ 305/663-1536.

Women's

Alice's Day Off For beachwear, Alice's is the place. Season after season, you'll find pretty and flattering floral patterns and many flashy bikinis. If an itsy-bitsy bikini is not your style, Alice's also has a range of more modest cuts. Three locations: Miami International Mall, 1455 NW 107th Ave., Miami. (✆ 305/477-0393; Dadeland Mall, 7223 SW 88th St. Miami. (✆ 305/663-7299; and 5900 SW 72nd St., South Miami. (✆ 305/284-0301. www.alicesdayoff.com.

Belinda's This German designer makes some of the most beautiful and intricate teddies, nightgowns, and wedding dresses. The styles are a little too Stevie Nicks for me, but the creations are absolutely worth admiring. The prices are appropriately high. 827 Washington Ave., South Beach. (✆ 305/532-0068.

Betsey Johnson Wacky, spirited New York designer Betsey Johnson offers outrageous, funky, and very loud clothes for young women. 805 Washington Ave., South Beach. (℃ 305/673-0023. www.betseyjohnson.com.

Intermix Pretty young things can get all dolled up thanks to Intermix's fun assortment of hip women's fashions, from Stella McCartney's pricey rhinestone T-shirts to the latest jeans worn by everyone at the MTV Awards. 634 Collins Ave., South Beach. (℃ 305/531-5950.

La Perla The only store in Florida that specializes in superluxurious Italian intimate apparel. Of course, you could fly to Milan for the price of a few bras and a nightgown, but you can't find better quality. 9700 Collins Ave. (in the Bal Harbour Shops), Bal Harbour. (℃ 305/864-2070.

Place Vendome For cheap and funky club clothes from zebra-print pants to bright, shiny tops. Two locations: 934 Lincoln Rd., South Beach. (℃ 305/673-4005; and Aventura Mall, North Miami Beach. (℃ 305/932-8931.

Therapy Opened by Ellen Lansburgh, who ran successful shops in Aspen and New York that catered to a famous clientele, this intimate boutique offers one-of-a-kind pieces. The clothes, made of luxurious fabrics such as silk, taffeta, and tulle, are elegant and comfortable and are all the rage for the ladies-who-lunch crowd. 1065 Kane Concourse, Bay Harbor Islands. (℃ 305/861-6900.

Men's

Giorgio's One of the finest custom men's stores in Miami, Giorgio's features an extensive line of Italian suits and all the latest by Canelli. 208 Miracle Mile, Coral Gables. (℃ 305/448-4302.

La Casa de las Guayaberas *Finds* Miami's premier purveyor of the traditional yet retro-hip Cuban shirt known as the *guayabera*—a loose-fitting, pleated, button-down shirt—was founded by Ramon Puig, who emigrated to Miami over 40 years ago. He still uses the same scissors he did back then, only now he's joined by a team of seamstresses who hand-sew 20 shirts a day in all colors and styles. Prices range from $15 to $375. 5840 SW 8th St., Little Havana. (℃ 305/266-9683.

Wilke Rodriguez Miami designer Eddie Rodriguez is a Latin Hugo Boss, with high-fashion suits in linens and light wool blends made especially for warmer climates. Cool T-shirts, shorts, and jackets are also part of this line, which is a local status symbol for many of Miami's fashion-conscious males. Prices range from the high $50s for T-shirts to $275 and up for jackets. 801 Washington Ave., South Beach. (℃ 305/534-4030.

Accessories

SEE This fantastic eyewear store features an enormous selection of stylish specs all priced at $169, including your prescription. The staff is patient and knowledgeable. 921 Lincoln Rd., South Beach. (℃ 305/672-6622.

Simons and Green Fantastic sterling silver jewelry, leather goods, and other assorted high-end tchotchkes and gift items are what you'll find in this quaint mainstay on South Miami's Sunset Drive. 5842 Sunset Dr., South Miami. (℃ 305/667-1692.

Crybaby Like a shop straight off of Melrose in Los Angeles or Magazine Street in New Orleans, this funky, kitschy tchotchke store carries whimsical toys, accessories, gifts, and clothing bearing the likenesses of the queen of kitsch, Hello Kitty, and much more, made by neo-pop artists such as Paul Frank (whose work entails Julius the monkey!). 6669 Biscayne Blvd., Miami ((℃ 305/754-4279).

FOOD

There are dozens of ethnic markets in Miami, from Cuban bodegas to Jamaican import shops and Guyanese produce stands. Check the phone book under grocers for listings. I've listed a few of the biggest and best markets in town that sell prepared foods as well as staple items. On Saturday mornings, vendors set up stands loaded with papayas, melons, tomatoes, and citrus, as well as cookies, ice creams, and sandwiches, on South Beach's Lincoln Road.

Biga Bakery   You'll be happy to pay upwards of $6 a loaf when you sink your teeth into these inimitable old-world–style breads. Also, most of the locations have a to-die-for prepared-food counter serving up everything from chicken curry salad to hummus and pot pies. Pastries and cakes are as gorgeous as they are delicious. 305 Alcazar, Coral Gables. ✆ **305/446-2111.** Check the phone book for other locations.

Epicure   This is the closest thing Miami Beach has got to the famed Balducci's or Dean & DeLuca. Here, you'll find not only fine wines, cheeses, meats, fish, and juices, but some of the best produce, such as portobello mushrooms the size of a yarmulke. This neighborhood landmark is best known for supplying the Jewish residents of the beach with all their Jewish favorites, such as matzo ball soup, gefilte fish, and deli items. Prices are steep but generally worth it. The cakes in particular are rich and decadent, and a rather large one doesn't cost more than $10. 1656 Alton Rd., Miami Beach. ✆ **305/672-1861.**

Gardner's Market   Anything a gourmet or novice cook could desire can be found here. One of the oldest and best grocery stores in Miami, Gardner's now has three locations, all of which offer great takeout and the freshest produce. 7301 Red Rd., South Miami. ✆ **305/667-9953;** 8287 SW 124th St., Pinecrest. ✆ **305/255-2468;** 651 Brickell Key Dr., downtown. ✆ **305/371-3701.**

Joe's Takeaway   If you don't want to wait 2 hours to get your paws on Joe's Stone Crab's meaty claws, let Joe's, Miami's stone crab institution (p. 133), ship you stone crabs anywhere in the country, but only during the season, which runs from mid-October to mid-May. 227 Biscayne St., South Beach. ✆ **800/780-CRAB** or 305/673-0365.

La Brioche Doree   This tiny storefront off 41st Street is packed most mornings with French expatriates and visitors who crave the real thing. There are luscious pastries and breads, plus soup and sandwiches at lunch. No one makes a better croissant. 4017 Prairie Ave., Miami Beach. ✆ **305/538-4770.**

Laurenzo's Italian Supermarket and Farmer's Market   Anything Italian you want—homemade ravioli, hand-cut imported Romano cheese, plus fresh fish and meats—can be found here. Laurenzo's also offers one of the most comprehensive wine selections in the city. Be sure to see the neighboring store full of just-picked herbs, salad greens, and vegetables from around the world. A daily Farmer's Market is open from 7am to 6pm. Incredible daily specials lure thrifty shoppers from all over the city (see the review of the cafe on p. 148). 16385 and 16445 W. Dixie Hwy., North Miami Beach. ✆ **305/945-6381** or 305/944-5052.

JEWELRY

For name designers like Gucci and Tiffany & Co., go to the Bal Harbour Shops (see "Malls," below).

International Jeweler's Exchange   At least 50 reputable jewelers hustle their wares from individual counters at one of the city's most active jewelry centers. Haggle your brains out for excellent prices on timeless antiques from

Tiffany's, Cartier, or Bulgari, or on unique designs you can create yourself. 18861 Biscayne Blvd. (in the Fashion Island), North Miami Beach. ✆ 305/931-7032.

Seybold Building   Jewelers who specialize in an assortment of goods (diamonds, gems, watches, rings, etc.) gather here daily to sell diamonds and gold. With 300 jewelry stores located inside this independently owned and operated multilevel treasure chest, the glare is blinding as you enter. Here, you'll be sure to see handsome and up-to-date designs, but not too many bargains. 36 NE 1st St., downtown. ✆ 305/374-7922.

MALLS

There are so many malls in Miami and more being built all the time that it would be impossible to mention them all. What follows is a list of the biggest and most popular.

You can find any number of nationally known department stores including Saks Fifth Avenue, Macy's, Lord & Taylor, Sears, and JCPenney in the Miami malls listed below, but Miami's own is **Burdines,** at 22 E. Flagler St., downtown (✆ **305/835-5151**), and 1675 Meridian Ave. (just off Lincoln Rd.) in South Beach (✆ **305/674-6311**). One of the oldest and largest department stores in Florida, Burdines specializes in good-quality home furnishings and fashions.

Aventura Mall *Kids*   A multimillion-dollar makeover has made this spot one of the premier places to shop in South Florida. With more than 2.3 million square feet of space, this airy, Mediterranean-style mall has a 24-screen movie theater and more than 250 stores, including megastores JCPenney, Lord & Taylor, Macy's, Bloomingdale's, Sears, and Burdines. The mall offers moderate to high-priced merchandise and is extremely popular with families. A large indoor playground, Adventurer's Cove, is a great spot for kids, and the mall frequently offers activities and entertainment for children. There are numerous theme restaurants and a food court that eschews the usual suspects in favor of local operations. 19501 Biscayne Blvd. (at 197th St. near the Dade–Broward County line), Aventura. ✆ 305/935-1110. www.shopaventuramall.com.

Bal Harbour Shops   One of the most prestigious fashion meccas in the country, Bal Harbour offers the best-quality goods from the finest names. Giorgio Armani, Dolce & Gabbana, Christian Dior, Fendi, Joan & David, Krizia, Rodier, Gucci, Brooks Brothers, Waterford, Cartier, H. Stern, Tourneau, and many others are sandwiched between Neiman Marcus and a newly expanded Saks Fifth Avenue. Well-dressed shoppers stroll in a pleasant open-air emporium, featuring several good cafes, covered walkways, and lush greenery. Parking costs $1 an hour with a validated ticket. You can stamp your own at the entrance to Saks Fifth Avenue, even if you don't make a purchase. 9700 Collins Ave. (on 97th St., opposite the Sheraton Bal Harbour Hotel), Bal Harbour. ✆ 305/866-0311. www.balharbourshops.com.

Bayside Marketplace   A popular stop for cruise-ship passengers, this touristy waterfront marketplace is filled with the usual suspects of chain stores as well as a slew of tacky gift shops and carts hawking assorted junk in the heart of downtown Miami. The second-floor food court is stocked with dozens of fast-food choices and bars. Most of the restaurants and bars stay open later than the stores. There's Lomardi's Conga Bar, Dick's Last Resort, Hard Rock Cafe, Fat Tuesday, Sharkey's, and Let's Make a Daiquiri. Parking is $1 per hour. While we wouldn't recommend you necessarily drop big money at Bayside, you should go by just for the view (of Biscayne Bay and the Miami skyline) alone. In June you can watch the Opsail sailboat show, and in February, the Miami Sailboat Show, where sailboats dock in the area and make the view even nicer. Beware of the adjacent amphitheater known as Bayfront Park, which usually hosts large-scale concerts and festivals, causing major pedestrian and vehicle traffic jams. 401 Biscayne Blvd., downtown. ✆ 305/577-3344. www.baysidemarketplace.com.

CocoWalk   CocoWalk is a lovely outdoor Mediterranean-style mall with the usual fare of Americana: Gap, Banana Republic, etc. Its open-air–style architecture is inviting not only for shoppers but also for friends or spouses of shoppers who'd prefer to sit at an outdoor cafe while said shopper is busy in the fitting room. A multiplex movie theater is also here, which comes in handy when there are big sales going on and the stores are mobbed. 3015 Grand Ave., Coconut Grove. ✆ 305/444-0777. www.cocowalk.com.

Dadeland Mall   One of the county's first malls, Dadeland features more than 175 specialty shops, anchored by four large department stores: Burdines, JCPenney, Lord & Taylor, and Saks Fifth Avenue. Sixteen restaurants serve from the adjacent Treats Food Court. New retail stores are constantly springing up around this centerpiece of South Miami suburbia. If you're not in the area, however, the mall is not worth the trek. Additionally, many non-Spanish-speaking people are put off by Dadeland because of the predominance of Spanish-speaking store employees. 7535 N. Kendall Dr. (intersection of U.S. 1 and SW 88th St., 15 min. south of downtown), Kendall. ✆ 305/665-6226.

Dolphin Mall   As if Miami needed another mall, this $250 million megamall and amusement park rivals Broward County's monstrous Sawgrass Mills outlet. The 1.4-million-square-foot outlet mall features outlets such as Off 5th (Saks Fifth Avenue), plus several discount shops, a 28-screen movie theater, and, not to be outdone by the Mall of America in Minnesota, a roller coaster. Florida Turnpike at S.R. 836, West Miami. ✆ 305/365-7446.

The Falls   Traffic to this mall borders on brutal, but once you get there, you'll feel a slight sense of serenity. Tropical waterfalls are the setting for this outdoor shopping center with dozens of moderately priced and slightly upscale shops. Miami's first Bloomingdale's is here, as are Polo, Ralph Lauren, Caswell-Massey, and more than 60 other specialty shops. A recent renovation added Macy's, Crate & Barrel, Brooks Brothers, and Pottery Barn, among others. If you are planning to visit any of the nearby attractions, which include Metrozoo and Monkey Jungle, check with customer service for information on discount packages. 8888 Howard Dr. (at the intersection of U.S. 1 and 136th St., about 3 miles/5km south of Dadeland Mall), Kendall. ✆ 305/255-4570. www.shopthefalls.com.

Sawgrass Mills   Just as some people need to take a tranquilizer to fly, others need one to traipse through this mammoth mall—the largest outlet mall in the country. Depending on what type of shopper you are, this experience can either be blissful or overwhelming. If you've got the patience, it is worth setting aside a day to do the entire place. (See p. 305 for more information.) Though it's located in Broward County, it is a phenomenon that attracts thousands of tourists and locals sniffing out bargains. From Miami, buses run three times daily; the trip takes just under an hour. Call **Coach USA** (✆ **305/887-6223**) for exact pick-up points at major hotels. The price is $10 for a round-trip ticket. If you are driving, take I-95 north to 595 west to Flamingo Road. Exit and turn right, driving 2 miles (3.25km) to Sunrise Boulevard. You can't miss this monster on the left. Parking is free, but don't forget where you parked your car or you might spend a day looking for it. 12801 W. Sunrise Blvd., Sunrise (west of Fort Lauderdale). ✆ 954/846-2300. www.millscorp.com.

Shops at Sunset Place   Completed in early 1999 at a cost of over $140 million, this sprawling outdoor shopping complex offers more than just shopping. Visitors experience high-tech special effects, such as daily tropical storms (minus the rain) and the electronic chatter of birds and crickets. In addition to a 24-screen movie complex and an IMAX theater, there's a GameWorks (Steven Spielberg's Disney-esque playground for kids and adults), a Virgin Records store, and a NikeTown, as well as mall standards such as Victoria's Secret, the Gap, Urban Outfitters, Bebe, etc. 5701 Sunset Dr. (at 57th Ave. and U.S. 1, near Red Rd.), South Miami. ℂ **305/663-0482.**

Streets of Mayfair   This sleepy, desolate, labyrinthine shopping area conceals a movie theater, several top-quality shops, a bookstore, restaurants, art galleries, bars, and nightclubs. It was meant to compete with the CocoWalk shopping complex (just across the street), but its structure is very maze-like and though it is open air, it is not wide open like CocoWalk and pales in comparison to that more populated neighbor. 2911 Grand Ave. (just east of Commodore Plaza), Coconut Grove. ℂ **305/448-1700.**

MUSIC STORES

Blue Note Records (Finds)   Here for more than 18 years, Blue Note is music to the ears of music fanatics with a good selection of hard-to-find progressive and underground music. There are new, used, and discounted CDs and old vinyl, too. Call to find out about performances. Some great names show up occasionally. A second location features jazz and LPs only. 16401 NE 15th Ave., North Miami Beach. ℂ **305/940-3394.** For jazz/LPs: 2299 NE 164th St., North Miami Beach ℂ **305/354-4563.** www.bluenoterecords.com.

Casino Records Inc.   The young, hip salespeople here speak English and tend to be music buffs. This store has the largest selection of Latin music in Miami, including pop icons such as Willy Chirino, Gloria Estefan, Albita, and local boy Nil Lara. Their slogan translates to "If we don't have it, forget it." Believe me, they've got it. 1208 SW 8th St., Little Havana. ℂ **305/856-6888.**

Esperanto Music (Finds)   According to the experts, this independently owned record store boasts the city's best collection of Cuban and Latin music. 513 Lincoln Rd., Miami Beach. ℂ **305/534-2003.**

Revolution Records and CDs   Here you'll find a quaint and fairly well-organized collection of CDs, from hard-to-find jazz to original recordings of Buddy Rich. They'll search for anything and let you hear whatever you like. 1620 Alton Rd., Miami Beach. ℂ **305/673-6464.**

Yesterday and Today Records (Finds)   This is Miami's most unique and well-stocked store for vinyl—you know, the audio dinosaur that went out with the Victrola? Y & T, as it's known, is a collector's heaven, featuring every genre of music imaginable on every format. Chances are, you could find some eight-track tapes, too. 7902 NW 36th St., Miami. ℂ **305/468-0311.**

THRIFT STORES/RESALE SHOPS

Children's Exchange (Kids)   Selling everything from layettes to overalls, this pleasant little shop is chock-full of good Florida-style stuff for kids to wear to the beach and in the heat. 1415 Sunset Dr., Coral Gables. ℂ **305/666-6235.**

Douglas Gardens Jewish Home and Hospital Thrift Shop   Prices here are no longer the major bargain they once were, but for housewares and books, you can do all right. Call to see if they are offering any specials for seniors or students. 5713 NW 27th Ave., North Miami Beach. ✆ 305/638-1900.

Rags to Riches   This is an old-time consignment shop where you might find some decent rags, and maybe even some riches. Though not as upscale as it used to be, this place is still a good spot for costume jewelry and shoes. 12577 Biscayne Blvd., North Miami. ✆ 305/891-8981.

Red White & Blue *Finds*   Miami's best-kept secret is this mammoth thrift store that is meticulously organized and well stocked. You've got to search for great stuff, but it is there. There are especially good deals on children's clothes and housewares. 12640 NE 6th Ave., North Miami. ✆ 305/893-1104.

13 Miami After Dark

With all the hype, you'd expect Miami to have long outlived its 15 minutes of fame by now. But you'd be wrong. Miami's nightlife, especially in South Beach, is hotter than ever before—and still getting hotter.

Practically every club in the area has installed closely guarded velvet ropes to create an air of exclusivity. Don't be fooled or intimidated by them—*anyone* can go clubbing in the magic city, and throughout this chapter, I've provided tips to ensure you gain entry to the venue you want to go to.

South Beach is certainly Miami's uncontested nocturnal nucleus, but more and more diverse areas, such as the Design District, South Miami, and even Little Havana, are increasingly providing fun alternatives without the ludicrous cover charges, "fashionably late" hours of operation (things don't typically get started on South Beach until after 11pm), lack of sufficient self-parking, and outrageous drink prices that come standard in South Beach.

And while South Beach dances to a more electronic beat, other parts of Miami dance to a Latin beat—from salsa and merengue to tango and cha-cha. However, if you're looking for a less frenetic good time, Miami's bar scene offers something for everyone, from haute hotel bars to sleek, loungey watering holes.

If the possibility of a celebrity sighting doesn't fulfill your cultural needs, Miami also offers a variety of first-rate diversions in theater, music, and dance, including a world-class ballet under the aegis of Edward Villella, a recognized symphony, and a talented opera company.

For up-to-date listing information, and to make sure time hasn't elapsed for the club of the moment, check the *Miami Herald's* "Weekend" section, which runs on Friday, or the more comprehensive listings in *New Times,* Miami's free alternative weekly, available each Wednesday, or visit www.miami.citysearch.com online.

BARS & LOUNGES

There are countless bars in and around Miami, with the highest concentration on trendy South Beach. The selection listed here is a mere sample. Keep in mind that many of the popular bars—and the easiest to get into—are in hotels. For a clubbier scene, if you don't mind making your way through hordes of inebriated club kids, a stroll on Washington Avenue will provide you with ample insight into what's hot and what's not. Just hold onto your bags. It's not dangerous, but occasionally, a few shady types manage to slip into the crowd. Another very important tip when in a club: *Never put your drink down out of your sight*—there have been unfortunate incidents in which drinks have been spiked with illegal

Swank Hotel Bars

Long gone are the days of the old-school Holiday Inn lounges. In fact, some hotels seem to spend more money on their bars than they do on their bedding. That aside, hotel bar-hopping is very popular in Miami. Here's my list of the best:

Rose Bar at the Delano (p. 105) for seeing and being seen.

Lobby bar at the Hotel Astor, 956 Washington Ave., South Beach (② 305/672-1402), to bask in a flattering light with a sophisticated, not snotty, crowd.

Marlin Bar at the Marlin hotel, 1200 Collins Ave., South Beach (② 305/673-8373), to experience what is known as Caribbean chic.

Bond St. Lounge at the Townhouse hotel, 150 20th St., South Beach (② 305/534-3800), a New York import, is a tiny bar slash lounge that also serves food; it's known for excellent sushi and a hip, chic jet-set crowd.

Harry's American Bar at the Eden Roc Resort, 4525 Collins Ave., Miami Beach (② 305/674-5568), a throwback to the days of Miami Beach kitsch, when Liza, Sammy, and Frank were splashing around at the pool.

chemical substances. For a less hard-core, collegiate nightlife, head to Coconut Grove. Most require proof that you are over 21 to enter. Oh, yes, and when going out in South Beach, make sure to take a so-called disco nap, as things don't get going until at least 11pm. If you go earlier, be prepared to face an empty bar or club. Off of South Beach and in hotel bars in general, the hours are fashionably earlier, with the action starting as early as, say, 7pm.

Blue A very laid-back, very locals scene set to a sultry soundtrack of deep soul and house music has Miami's hipsters feeling the blues on a nightly basis from 10pm to 5am. Before you whip out the St. John's Wort, dive into this so-not-trendy-it's-trendy lounge, in which the pervasive color blue will actually heighten your spirits as an eclectic haze of models, locals, and lounge lizards gathers to commiserate in their dreaded trendy status. 222 Española Way (between Washington and Collins aves.), South Beach. ② 305/534-1009. No cover.

Clevelander If wet T-shirt contests and a fraternity party atmosphere are your thing, then this Ocean Drive mainstay is your kind of place. Popular with tourists and locals who like to pretend they're tourists, the Clevelander attracts a lively, sporty, adults-only crowd (the burly bouncers *will* confiscate fake IDs) who have no interest in being part of a scene, but, rather, taking in the very revealing scenery. A great time to check out the Clevelander is on a weekend afternoon, when beach Barbies and Kens line the bar for a post-tanning beer or frozen cocktail. 1020 Ocean Dr., South Beach. ② 305/531-3485. No cover.

Fox's Sherron Inn *Finds* The spirit of Frank Sinatra is alive and well at this dark and smoky watering hole that dates back to 1946. Everything down to the vinyl booths and the red lights make Fox's a retro-fabulous dive bar. Cheap drinks, couples cozily huddling in booths, and a seasoned staff of bartenders and barflies make Fox's the perfect place to retreat from the trenches of trendiness. Oh, and the food's actually good here, too. 6030 S. Dixie Hwy. (at 62nd Ave.), South Miami. ✆ 305/661-9201. No cover.

Laundry Bar   The only place in Miami where it's okay to let friends drink and dry. Laundry Bar features working washers, dryers, a fully stocked bar, and several other distractions to help make doing your laundry a fun rather than a dreaded chore. It's also one of the only bars on South Beach open from 7am to 5am daily. Thursdays seem to be laundry night on South Beach, when a deejay spins the best in house music. On Wednesdays and Fridays, a gospel diva (of the Astor Place restaurant's Gospel Brunch fame) sings live to an always packed and lively house. And although it's most popular with the gay community, Laundry Bar draws a mixed crowd; on weekends, the place is packed like an overloaded washing machine. Daily happy hours (5–7pm) with two-for-one drinks allow you to save your change for the washing machines. 721 Lincoln Lane (behind Burdines off Lincoln Rd.), South Beach. ✆ 305/531-7700. www.laundrybar.com. No cover.

Lola *Finds*   Lola redefines the neighborhood bar, striking the perfect balance between chill and chic. This bar, located away from the South Beach mayhem, is a showgirl in her own right—a swank, sultry lounge where people are encouraged to come as they are, leaving the attitude at home. Attracting a mixed crowd of gay, straight, young, and old(er), Lola reinvents itself each night with deejays spinning everything from retro '80s music to hard rock and classic oldies. On Tuesdays, the bar's most popular—and populated—night, it gets mobbed inside and outside, so they tend to keep a crowd at the ropes before letting them all in like cattle. 247 23rd St., South Beach. ✆ 305/695-8697. No cover.

Mac's Club Deuce   Standing on its own amidst an oasis of trendiness, Mac's Club Deuce is the quintessential dive bar, with cheap drinks and a cast of characters ranging from your typical barfly to your atypical drag queen. It's got a well-stocked jukebox, friendly bartenders, a pool table, and best of all, it's an insomniac's dream, open daily from 8am to 5am. 222 14th St., South Beach. ✆ 305/673-9537. No cover.

Purdy Lounge   With the exception of a wall of lava lamps, Purdy is not unlike your best friend's basement, featuring a pool table and a slew of board games such as Operation to keep the attention-deficit disordered from getting bored. Because it's a no-nonsense bar with relatively cheap cocktails (by South Beach standards), Purdy gets away with not having a star deejay or fancy bass-heavy Bose sound system. A CD player somehow does the trick. With no cover and no attitude, a line is inevitable, so be prepared to wait. Saturday night has become the preferred night for locals, while Friday-night happy hour draws a young professional crowd on the prowl. 1811 Purdy Ave./Sunset Harbor, South Beach. ✆ 305/531-4622. No cover.

Wet Willie's   With such telling drinks as "Call a Cab," this beachfront oasis is not the place to go if you have a long drive ahead of you. A well-liked pre- and post-beach hangout, Wet Willie's inspires serious drinking. Popular with the Harley Davidson set, tourists, and beachcombers, this bar is best known for its rooftop patio (get there early if you plan to get a seat) and its half-nude bikini beauties. 760 Ocean Dr., South Beach. ✆ 305/532-5650. No cover.

DANCE CLUBS, LIVE MUSIC, THE GAY & LESBIAN SCENE & LATIN CLUBS

DANCE CLUBS

Clubs are as much a cottage industry in Miami as is, say, cheese in Wisconsin. Clubland, as it's known, is not just a nocturnal theme park, but a way of life for some. On any given night in Miami, there's something going on—no excuses are needed to throw a party here. Short of throwing a glammy event for the grand opening of a new gas station, Miami is very party hearty, celebrating everything from the fact that it's Tuesday night to the debut of a hot new deejay. Within this very bizarre after-dark community, a very colorful assortment of characters emerges, from your (a)typical nine-to-fivers to shady characters who have reinvented themselves as hotshots on the club circuit. While this scene of seeing and being seen may not be your cup of Absolut, it's certainly never boring.

The club music played on Miami's ever-evolving social circuit is good enough to get even the most rhythmically challenged wallflowers dancing. To keep things fresh in clubland, local promoters throw one-nighters, which are essentially parties with various themes or motifs, from funk to fashion. Because these change so often, we can't possibly list them here. Word of mouth, local advertising, and listings in the free weekly *New Times,* www.miami.citysearch.com, or the "Weekend" section of the *Miami Herald* are the best ways to find out about these ever-changing events.

Before you get all decked out to hit the town as soon as the sun sets, consider the fact that Miami is a very late town. Things generally don't get started before 11pm. The Catch-22 here is that if you don't arrive on South Beach early enough, you may find yourself driving around aimlessly for parking, as it is very limited outside of absurd $20 valet charges. Municipal lots fill up quickly, so your best bet is to arrive on South Beach somewhat early and kill time by strolling around, having something to eat, or sipping a cocktail in a hotel bar. Another advantage of arriving a bit earlier than the crowds is that some clubs don't charge a cover before 11pm or midnight, which could save you a wad of cash over time. Most clubs are open every night of the week, though some are open only Thursday through Sunday and others are open only Monday though Saturday. Call ahead to get all of this information as up-to-date as possible: Things change very quickly around here. Cover charges are very haphazard, too. If you're not on the ubiquitous guest list (ask your concierge to put you on the list—he or she has the ability to do so, which won't help you with the wait to get in, but will eliminate the cover charge), you may have to fork over a ridiculous $20 to walk past the ropes. Don't fret, though. There are many clubs and bars that have no cover charge—they just make up for it by charging $13 for a martini! *Note:* As with anything on Miami's nocturnal circuit, call in advance to make sure that the dance club you're planning to go to hasn't become a video arcade.

Bongos Cuban Café Gloria Estefan's latest hit in the restaurant business pays homage to the sites, sounds, and cuisine of pre-Castro Cuba. Bongo's is a mammoth restaurant attached to the American Airlines Arena in downtown Miami. On Friday and Saturday after 11:30pm, it's transformed from a friendly family restaurant into the city's hottest 21-and-over salsa nightclub. Cover charge at that time is a hefty $20, but consider it your ticket to what happens to be an astounding show of some of the best salsa dancers in the city. Prepare yourself for standing room only. At the American Airlines Arena, 601 Biscayne Blvd., downtown Miami. ✆ 786/777-2100. Cover $20.

Tips Ground Rules: Stepping Out in Miami

- Nightlife on South Beach doesn't really get going until after 11pm. As a result, you may want to consider taking what is known as a disco nap so that you'll be fully charged until the wee hours.
- If you're unsure of what to wear out on South Beach, your safest bet will be anything black.
- Do *not* try to tip the doormen manning the velvet ropes. That will only make you look desperate and you'll find yourself standing outside for what will seem like an ungodly amount of time. Instead, try to land your name on the ever-present guest lists by calling the club early in the day yourself, or, better yet, having the concierge at your hotel do it for you. Concierges have connections. If you don't have connections and you find yourself without a concierge, then act assertive, not surly, at the velvet rope, and your patience will usually be rewarded with admittance. If all else fails—for men, especially—surround yourself with a few leggy model types and you'll be noticed quicker.
- Finally, have fun. It may look like serious business when you're on the outside, but once you're in, it's another story. Attacking clubland with a sense of humor is the best approach to a successful, memorable evening out.

Club Space Clubland hits the mainland with this cavernous downtown warehouse of a club. With over 30,000 square feet of dance space, you can spin around a la Stevie Nicks (albeit to a techno beat) without having to worry about banging into someone. However, after hours (around 2am), Club Space packs them in. While Saturday caters to a more homogeneous and gay crowd, Friday is a free-for-all. Conveniently, the club often runs shuttles from the beach. Call for more information, as it doesn't have a concrete schedule. 142 NE 11th St., Miami. ② 305/372-9378. Cover $0–$20.

crobar *(Finds)* Still haunted by the ghost of clubs past, the space formerly known as the Cameo Theatre is now possessed by the mod, millennial, industrial spirit that is crobar. With its intense, dance-heavy sound system, an industrially chic ambience, and crowds big enough to scare away any memories of a sadly abandoned Cameo, this Chicago import has raised the bar on South Beach nightlife with crazy theme nights (the monthly Sex Night is particularly, uh, stimulating), top-name deejays, and the occasional celebrity appearance. On Sunday, the club hosts an extremely popular gay night known as Anthem. (See "The Gay & Lesbian Scene," later in this chapter.) 1445 Washington Ave., South Beach. ② 305/531-8225. www.crobarmiami.com. Cover $25.

Level Overdone and some say overhyped, Level takes the notion of South Beach excess even further with its outlet mall–sized, 40,000-square-foot space featuring four dance floors, three levels, five rooms, and nine bars. Like a video game, your status here is determined by which level you can land on. If you befriend one of the club's owners, you may end up at the top. Leveling out the competition, this club has cornered the market on parties and events, throwing one nearly every night. Because it is the largest club on the beach, the velvet rope scene can be quite harassing, but if you call in advance, the accommodating staff will usually put you on the guest list, which means you don't have to pay the cover, though you will still have to wait in line. Friday night is a very popular gay night, while the rest of the week attracts a mixed crowd of straights, gays, and somewhere in betweens. Celebs love Level because it has so many VIP rooms. 1235 Washington Ave., South Beach. (*C*) 305/532-1525. www.levelnightclub.com. Cover $20–$30.

Liquid   Way back when, during South Beach's halcyon days, before Madonna became a mother and stopped her clubbing ways, Liquid was the Studio 54 of the south, and everyone who was anyone showed up here to show off. Then one of the club's owners was arrested for his alleged "family" connections and Liquid dried up. In late 2001, Liquid was resurrected by a completely new owner in a completely different space. Without Madonna, however, Liquid is just your generic dance club, just a ghost of a legend, which no one who experienced the original has any desire to visit. 1532 Washington Ave., South Beach. (*C*) 305/531-9411. Cover $10–$20.

Living Room Downtown   The downtown satellite of a now defunct South Beach club that was formerly the hautest of the hot (especially amongst European jet-setters), the Living Room Downtown is nearly as velvety chic as its original incarnation, only there's a twist: This one has a 24-hour liquor license. *Note:* This place is not for the weary. 60 NE 11th St., downtown. (*C*) 305/342-7421. Cover $10–$20.

Nikki Beach Club *(Finds)*   What the Playboy Mansion is to Hollywood, the Nikki Beach Club is to South Beach. This place is the product of local nightlife royalty Tommy Pooch and Eric Omores. Half-naked ladies and men actually venture into the daylight on Sundays (around 4pm, which is ungodly in this town) to see, be seen, and, at times, be obscene. At night, it's very Brady-Bunch-goes-to-Hawaii–seeming, with a sexy tiki hut/Polynesian theme style, albeit rated R. The Sunday-afternoon beach party is almost legendary and worth a glimpse—that is, if you can get in. This is not your equal-opportunity beach club. Egos are easily shattered, as surly doormen are known to reject those who don't drive up in a Ferrari. Also located within this bastion of hedonism is the super-hot **Pearl**, a mod-ish, 380-seat, orange-hued restaurant and lounge that features a Continental menu created by Nikki chef Brian Rutherford. But you'd do better to forget the food and go for the eye candy. 101 Ocean Dr., South Beach. (*C*) 305/538-1111. Cover $10–$20.

Opium Garden   Housed in the massive, open-air space formerly known as Amnesia, Opium Garden is a highly addictive nocturnal habit for those looking for a combination of sexy dance music, scantily clad dancers, and, for the masochists out there, an oppressive door policy in which two sets of velvet ropes are set up to keep those deemed unworthy out of this see-and-be-sceney den of inequity. 136 Collins Ave., South Beach. (*C*) 305/531-5535. Cover $10–$30.

Rain   A very minimalist dance club slash lounge, Rain is a great nightspot for many reasons. First and foremost, its location off the beachy path is ideal for

---

Impressions
Working the door teaches you a lot about human nature.
                                        —A former South Beach doorman

those who insist on clubbing and driving. Ample parking in the area definitely makes up for the fact that you'll pay upwards of $9 for a cocktail. Second, the music's great. Local deejay Mark Leventhal's Tuesday-night funkfest known as Home Cookin' is particularly fun and comes complete with a free barbecue. If you don't feel like dancing, outdoor and indoor lounging space is a-plenty. 323 23rd St., South Beach. ✆ 786/295-9540. Cover $10–$30.

Rumi   Named after a 13th-century Sufi mystic, South Beach's first upscale supper club is command central for hipsters hailing from all coasts. Designed by hot NYC designers Nancy Mah and Scott Kester, Rumi is an urbane oasis of reds, tans, and chocolates, reminiscent of the golden age of supper clubs of the '30s and '40s. This bi-level space features intimate lounge areas as well as private and public dining rooms, in which haute Florida-Caribbean cuisine is served until around 11pm, when the tables conspicuously disappear and give way to a neo-Zen-like stamping ground for South Beach's chic elite. Make sure to check out the queen-size Murphy bed that snaps down from the wall to make room for late-night lounging. As long as you can get past the velvet ropes (by either looking pretty, being on the guest list, or just getting the doorman on a good day), there is no cover to bask in this bastion of South Beach scene-dom. 330 Lincoln Rd., South Beach. ✆ 305/672-4353. www.rumimiami.com. No cover.

LIVE MUSIC

Unfortunately, Miami's live music scene is not thriving. Instead of local bands garnering devoted fans, local deejays are more admired, skyrocketing much more easily to fame—thanks to the city's lauded dance club scene. However, there are still several places that strive to bring Miami up to speed as far as live music is concerned. You just have to look—and listen—for it a bit more carefully. The following is a list of places you can, from time to time, catch some live acts, be it a deejay or an aspiring Nirvana.

Billboard Live   Affiliated with the national music industry magazine, this mammoth dance club, bar, recording studio, and live music venue is much cooler than its chain-ish name implies. Although at press time the live acts haven't necessarily been major headliners (Macy Gray was supposed to kick off a tour here, but then canceled with no reason), the acoustics in this multilevel club are exceptional, as is the Saturday-night deejayed dance scene and Sunday-afternoon mostly gay tea dance disco parties. The club's first-floor patio restaurant is also a great alternative to the thumping club vibe. 1501 Collins Ave., South Beach. ✆ 305/538-2251. Cover $0–$20.

Churchill's Hideaway *(finds)*   British expatriate Dave Daniels couldn't live in Miami without a true English-style pub, so he opened Churchill's Hideaway, the city's premier space for live rock music. Filthy and located in a rather unsavory neighborhood, Churchill's is committed to promoting and extending the lifeline of the lagging local music scene. A fun, no-frills crowd hangs out here. Bring earplugs with you, as it is deafening once the music starts. 5501 NE 2nd Ave., Little Haiti. ✆ 305/757-1807. Cover $0–$5.

Jazid *(finds)*   Smoky, sultry, and illuminated by flickering candelabras, Jazid is the kind of place where you'd expect to hear Sade's "Smooth Operator" on constant rotation. Instead, however, you'll hear live jazz (sometimes on acid), soul, and funk. Past surprise performers at Jazid include former Smashing Pumpkins frontman Billy Corgan. An eclectic mix of mellow folk convenes here for a much-necessary respite from the surrounding Washington Avenue mayhem. 1342 Washington Ave., South Beach. ✆ 305/673-9372. No cover.

Tobacco Road   Al Capone used to hang out here when it was a speakeasy. Now, locals flock here to see local bands perform, as well as national acts such as George Clinton and the P-Funk All-Stars, Koko Taylor, and the Radiators. Tobacco Road (the proud owner of Miami's very first liquor license) is small and gritty and meant to be that way. Escape the smoke and sweat in the backyard patio, where air is a welcome commodity. The downright cheap nightly specials, such as the $11 lobster on Tuesday, are quite good and are served until 2am; the bar is open until 5am. 626 S. Miami Ave. (over the Miami Ave. Bridge near Brickell Ave.), downtown. © 305/374-1198. Cover $5 Fri–Sat.

Upstairs at the Van Dyke Café (Finds   The café's jazz bar, located on the second floor, resembles a classy speakeasy in which local jazz performers play to an intimate, enthusiastic crowd of mostly adults and sophisticated young things, who often huddle at the small tables until the wee hours. 846 Lincoln Rd., Miami Beach. © 305/534-3600. Cover $3–$6 for a seat; no cover at the bar.

THE GAY & LESBIAN SCENE

Miami and the beaches have long been host to what is called a "first-tier" gay community. Similar to the Big Apple, the Bay Area, or LaLa land, Miami has had a large alternative community since the days when Anita Bryant used her citrus power to boycott the rise in political activism in the early '70s. Well, things have changed and Miami-Dade now has a gay-rights ordinance.

Newcomers intending to party in any bar, whether downtown or certainly on the beach, will want to check ahead for the schedule, as all clubs must have a gay or lesbian night to pay their rent. Miami Beach, in fact, is a capital of the gay circuit party scene, rivaling San Francisco, Palm Springs, and even the mighty Sydney, Australia, for tourist dollars.

Academy   Hordes of gay men (and some women) join the Academy at Level every Friday, when the dance floor is packed with wall-to-wall hard bodies. 1235 Washington Ave., South Beach. © 305/532-1525. Cover $20–$30.

Anthem   Sunday nights at crobar sing the gay anthem with this hyperpopular 1-nighter featuring Miami's own superstar deejay Abel. 1445 Washington Ave., South Beach. © 877/CRO-SOBE or 305/531-5027. Cover $25.

Cactus Bar & Grill   Somewhere, over the causeway, there is life beyond South Beach—that is, for Miami's gay society. Housed in a large two-story space, Cactus attracts a mix of unpretentious, professional, and very attractive men and women. There's something for everyone here, whether it's the indoor pool tables, the outdoor swimming pool, or drinks that are considerably cheaper than on South Beach. Friday-evening happy hours and Sunday-afternoon tea dances are a virtual cattle call, attracting hordes of folks looking to quench their thirst for fun at Miami's sprawling urban oasis. 2401 Biscayne Blvd., downtown. © 305/438-0662. No cover.

Loading Zone   A leather and Levi's bar known for its cruisability, pool tables, movies, and pitchers of beer. There's also an in-house leather store for the kinky shopper. Open daily 10pm to 5am. 1426 Alton Rd., South Beach. © 305/531-5623. Cover $15–$20.

1771   For those seeking liberation from the cookie-cutter mold of run-of-the-mill Saturday-night dance clubs, this place, formerly known as Salvation, is where you'll find it. Housed in an old warehouse, Salvation is spacious but always filled to capacity with shirtless, sweaty circuit boys dancing themselves into oblivion. Major deejays spin here, and, at times, divas sing here, such as

The Rhythm Is Gonna Get You

If you're feeling shy about hitting a Latin club because you fear your two left feet will stand out, show up Thursday and Friday nights at **Bongo's Cuban Café** (American Airlines Arena, 601 Biscayne Blvd., downtown Miami; © **786/777-2100**), where you'll see an amazing showcase of some of the city's best salsa dancers. And best of all, amateurs need not be intimidated! Thanks to the instructors at Latin Groove Dance Studios, there are people on hand to help you with your two left feet.

Bette Midler, who did a rare and ribald cabaret performance to an SRO audience. You can't blame the owners for charging $20 to get in when you see this bevy of beautiful boys. Open only on Saturday nights. 1771 West Ave., South Beach. © **305/673-6508.** Cover $20.

Score   There's a reason this Lincoln Road hotbed of gay social activity is called Score. In addition to the huge pick-up scene, Score offers a multitude of bars, dance floors, lounge-like areas, and outdoor tables in case you need to come up for air. Sunday afternoon tea dances are legendary here. 727 Lincoln Rd., South Beach. © **305/535-1111.** No cover.

Twist   One of the most popular bars (and hideaways) on South Beach, this recently expanded bar (which is literally right across the street from the police station) has a casual yet lively local atmosphere. 1057 Washington Ave., South Beach. © **305/538-9478.** No cover.

LATIN CLUBS
Considering that Hispanics make up a large part of Miami's population and that there's a huge influx of Spanish-speaking visitors, it's no surprise that there are some great Latin nightclubs in the city.

Plus, with the meteoric rise of the international music scene based in Miami, many international stars come through the offices of MTV Latino, SONY International, and a multitude of Latin TV studios based in Miami—and they're all looking for a good club scene on weekends. Most of the Anglo clubs also reserve at least 1 night a week for Latin rhythms.

Casa Panza *Finds*   This *casa* is one of Little Havana's liveliest and most popular nightspots. Every Tuesday, Thursday, and Saturday night, Casa Panza, in the heart of Little Havana, becomes the House of Flamenco, with shows at 8 and 11pm. You can either enjoy a flamenco show or strap on your own dancing shoes and participate in the celebration. Enjoy a fantastic Spanish meal before the show, or just a glass of sangria before you start stomping. Open until 4am, Casa Panza is a hot spot for young Latin club kids, and, occasionally, a few older folks who are so taken by the music and the scene that they've failed to realize that it's well past their bedtime. 1620 SW 8th St. (Calle Ocho), Little Havana. © **305/643-5343.** No cover.

La Covacha *Finds*   This hut, located virtually in the middle of nowhere (West Miami), is the hottest Latin joint in the entire city. Sunday features the best in Latin rock, with local and international acts. But the shack is really jumping on weekend nights when the place is open until 5am. Friday is *the* night here, so much so that the owners had to place a red velvet rope out front to maintain some semblance of order. It's an amusing sight—a velvet rope guarding a shack—but once you get in, you'll understand the need for it. Do not wear silk here, as you *will* sweat. 10730 NW 25th St. (at NW 107th Ave.), West Miami. ℭ 305/594-3717. Cover $0–$10.

Mango's Tropical Café Claustrophobic types do not want to go near Mango's. Ever. One of the most popular spots on Ocean Drive, this outdoor enclave of Latin liveliness shakes with the intensity of a Richter-busting earthquake. Welcome and *bienvenido;* Mango's is *Cabaret,* Latin style. Nightly live Brazilian and other Latin music, not to mention scantily clad male and female dancers, draw huge, gawking crowds in from the sidewalk. But pay attention to the music if you can: Incognito international musicians often lose their anonymity and jam with the house band on stage. Open daily from 11am to 5am. 900 Ocean Dr., South Beach. ℭ 305/673-4422. Cover $5–$15.

THE PERFORMING ARTS

Highbrows and culture vultures complain that there is a dearth of decent cultural offerings in Miami. What do locals tell them? Go back to New York! In all seriousness, however, in recent years Miami's performing arts scene has improved greatly. The city's Broadway Series features Tony Award–winning shows (the touring versions, of course), which aren't always Broadway caliber, but they are usually pretty good and not nearly as pricey. Local arts groups such as the Miami Light Project, a not-for-profit cultural organization that presents live performances by innovative dance, music, and theater artists, have had huge success in attracting big-name artists such as Nina Simone and Philip Glass to Miami. In addition, a burgeoning bohemian movement in Little Havana has given way to performance spaces that have become nightclubs in their own right.

THEATER

The **Actors' Playhouse** *(Kids*, a musical theater at the newly restored Miracle Theater at 280 Miracle Mile, Coral Gables (ℭ 305/444-9293; www.actors playhouse.org), is a grand 1948 Art Deco movie palace with a 600-seat main theater and a smaller theater/rehearsal hall that hosts a number of excellent musicals for children throughout the year. In addition to these two rooms, the Playhouse recently added a 300-seat children's balcony theater. Tickets run from $26 to $50.

The **Coconut Grove Playhouse,** 3500 Main Hwy., Coconut Grove (ℭ 305/442-4000; www.cgplayhouse.com), is also a former movie house, built in 1927 in an ornate Spanish rococo style. Today, this respected venue is known for its original and innovative staging of both international and local dramas and musicals. The house's second, more intimate Encore Room is well suited to alternative and experimental productions. Tickets run from $37 to $42.

The **Gables Stage** at the Biltmore Hotel, Anastasia Avenue, Coral Gables (ℭ 305/445-1119), stages at least one Shakespearean play, one classic, and one contemporary piece a year. This well-regarded theater usually tries to secure the rights to a national or local premiere as well. Tickets cost $22 and $28; $10 and $17 for students and seniors.

The **Jerry Herman Ring Theatre** is on the main campus of the University of Miami in Coral Gables (ℭ 305/284-3355). The University's Department of

Theater Arts uses this stage for advanced-student productions of comedies, dramas, and musicals. Faculty and guest actors are regularly featured, as are contemporary works by local playwrights. Performances are usually scheduled Tuesday through Saturday during the academic year. In the summer, don't miss "Summer Shorts," a selection of superb one-acts. Tickets sell for $5 to $20.

The **New Theater,** 65 Almeria Ave., Coral Gables (✆ **305/443-5909**), prides itself on showing world-renowned works from America and Europe. As the name implies, you'll find mostly contemporary plays, with a few classics thrown in for variety. Performances are staged Thursday through Sunday year-round. Tickets are $20 on weekdays, $25 weekends. If tickets are available on the day of the performance—and they usually are—students pay half price.

CLASSICAL MUSIC

In addition to a number of local orchestras and operas (see below), which regularly offer quality music and world-renowned guest artists, each year brings a slew of classical music special events and touring artists to Miami. The Concert Association of Florida (CAF) (✆ **305/532-3491**) produces one of the most important and longest-running series. Known for more than a quarter of a century for its high-caliber, star-packed schedules, CAF regularly arranges the best "serious" music concerts for the city. Season after season, the schedules are punctuated by world-renowned dance companies and seasoned virtuosi like Itzhak Perlman, Andre Watts, and Kathleen Battle. Since CAF does not have its own space, performances are usually scheduled in the Miami–Dade County Auditorium or the Jackie Gleason Theater of the Performing Arts (see the "Major Venues" section below). The season lasts October through April, and ticket prices range from $20 to $70.

Florida Philharmonic Orchestra   South Florida's premier symphony orchestra, under the direction of James Judd, presents a full season of classical and pops programs interspersed with several children's and contemporary popular music performances. The Philharmonic performs downtown in the Gusman Center for the Performing Arts and at the Miami–Dade County Auditorium (see the "Major Venues" section below). 1243 University Dr., Miami. ✆ **800/226-1812** or 305/476-1234. Tickets $15–$60. When extra tickets are available, students are admitted free on day of performance.

Miami Chamber Symphony   This professional orchestra is a small, subscription-series orchestra that's not affiliated with any major arts organizations and is therefore an inexpensive alternative to the high-priced classical venues. Renowned international soloists perform regularly. The season runs October through May, and most concerts are held in the Gusman Concert Hall, on the University of Miami campus. 5690 N. Kendall Dr., Kendall. ✆ **305/858-3500.** Tickets $12–$30.

New World Symphony   This organization, led by artistic director Michael Tilson Thomas, is a stepping stone for gifted young musicians seeking professional careers. The orchestra specializes in ambitious, innovative, energetic performances and often features renowned guest soloists and conductors. The symphony's season lasts from October to May, during which time there are many free concerts. 541 Lincoln Rd., South Beach. ✆ **305/673-3331.** www.nws.org. Tickets free–$58. Rush tickets (remaining tickets sold 1 hr. before performance) $20. Students $10 (1 hr. before concerts: limited seating).

OPERA

Florida Grand Opera Around for over 60 years, this company regularly features singers from top houses in both America and Europe. All productions are sung in their original language and staged with projected English supertitles. Tickets become scarce when Placido Domingo or Luciano Pavarotti (who made his American debut here in 1965) comes to town. The opera's season runs roughly from November to April, with five performances each week. A new multimillion-dollar headquarters for the opera is scheduled to open in mid-2004; until then, performances take place at the Miami–Dade County Auditorium and the Broward Center for the Performing Arts, about 40 minutes from downtown Miami. Box office: 1200 Coral Way, Southwest Miami. ℂ 800/741-1010. www.fgo.org. Tickets $19–$145. Student discounts available.

DANCE

Several local dance companies train and perform in the Greater Miami area. In addition, top traveling troupes regularly stop at the venues listed below. Keep your eyes open for special events and guest artists.

Ballet Flamenco La Rosa For a taste of local Latin flavor, see this lively troupe perform impressive flamenco and other styles of Latin dance on Miami stages. (They also teach Latin dancing—see the "The Rhythm Is Gonna Get You" box earlier in this chapter.) 13126 W. Dixie Hwy., North Miami. ℂ 305/899-7729. Tickets $25 at door, $20 in advance, $18 for students and seniors.

Miami City Ballet This artistically acclaimed and innovative company, directed by Edward Villella, features a repertoire of more than 60 ballets, many by George Balanchine, and has had more than 20 world premieres. The company moved into a new $7.5 million headquarters in January 2000—the Ophelia and Juan Jr. Roca Center at the Collins Park Cultural Center in Miami Beach. This three-story center features eight rehearsal rooms, a ballet school, a boutique, and ticket offices. The City Ballet season runs from September to April. Ophelia and Juan Jr. Roca Center, Collins Ave. and 22nd St., South Beach. ℂ 305/532-4880 or 305/532-7713 for box office. Tickets $17–$50.

MAJOR VENUES

The **Colony Theater,** on Lincoln Road in South Beach (ℂ 305/674-1026), which has become an architectural showpiece of the Art Deco District, is closing its doors for 16 months beginning in July 2002 for a $4.3 million renovation that will add wing and fly space, improve access for the disabled, and restore the lobby to its original art deco look.

At the **Miami–Dade County Auditorium,** West Flagler Street at 29th Avenue, Southwest Miami (ℂ 305/547-5414), performers gripe about the lack of space, but for patrons, this 2,430-seat auditorium is the only Miami space in which you can hear the opera—for now. A multimillion-dollar performing arts center downtown has been in the works for years (see below). For now, though, the Miami–Dade County Auditorium is home to the city's Florida Grand Opera, and it also stages productions by the Concert Association of Florida, many programs in Spanish, and a variety of other shows.

At the 1,700-seat **Gusman Center for the Performing Arts,** 174 E. Flagler Street, downtown Miami (ℂ 305/372-0925), seating is tight, and so is funding, but the sound is superb. In addition to hosting the Florida Philharmonic Orchestra and the Miami Film Festival, the elegant Gusman Center features pop concerts, plays, film screenings, and special events. The auditorium was built as the Olympia Theater in 1926, and its ornate palace interior is typical of that era, complete with fancy columns, a huge pipe organ, and twinkling "stars" on the ceiling.

Not to be confused with the Gusman Center (above), the **Gusman Concert Hall,** 1314 Miller Dr. at 14th Street, Coral Gables (© **305/284-6477**), is a roomy 600-seat hall that gives a stage to the Miami Chamber Symphony and a varied program of university recitals.

The elegant **Jackie Gleason Theater of the Performing Arts (TOPA),** located in South Beach at Washington Avenue and 17th Street (© **305/ 673-7300**), is the home of the Miami Beach Broadway Series, which has recently presented *Rent, Phantom of the Opera,* and *Les Misérables.* This 2,705-seat hall also hosts other big-budget Broadway shows, classical music concerts, and dance performances.

At press time, the city granted a budget in excess of $200 million for its official Performing Arts Center. Planned are a 2,400-seat ballet/opera house and a 2,000-seat concert hall for the Florida Philharmonic Orchestra, Florida Grand Opera, New World Symphony, Miami City Ballet, and a major concert series. Designed by world-renowned architect Cesar Pelli, it will be the focal point of a planned Arts, Media, and Entertainment District in mid-Miami. The complex will be wrapped in limestone, slate, decorative stone, stainless steel, glass curtain walls, and tropical landscaping, and is slated to be complete in mid-2004. For more information, check out their website at www.pacfmiami.org.

CINEMAS, THE LITERARY SCENE, SPECTATOR SPORTS & MORE
CINEMAS

In addition to the annual Miami Film Festival in February and other, smaller film events (See "Florida Calendar of Events," in chapter 2), Miami has nearly as many multiplex cinemas as it does palm trees. And for good reason. When it rains in Miami, what else is there to do besides go to the movies, a museum, or the mall? But if 40 screens of *Jurassic Park III* isn't your idea of a day at the movies, consider the following artsy theaters, known for playing lots of subtitled, foreign films as well as those that get bumped off the big screen by the *Jurassic Parks* of the celluloid world.

Absinthe Cinemateque, 235 Alcazar Ave., Coral Gables (© **305/446-7144**), is a small one-screen theater that shows good movies, often Spanish-language films, without the hustle and bustle of the crowded multiplexes. The Alcazar shows the more artsy of the major films as well as some obscure independents. Tickets are $6.

Astor Art Cinema, 4120 Laguna St. (© **305/443-6777**), is an oasis in the midst of a desert of Cineplex Odeons and AMCs in Coral Gables. This quaint double theater hosts foreign, classic, independent, and art films and serves decent popcorn, too. Tickets are $5.

The **Bill Cosford Cinema,** at the University of Miami, is located on the second floor of the memorial building off Campo Sano Avenue (© **305/ 284-4861**). This well-endowed little theater was recently revamped and boasts high-tech projectors, new air-conditioning, and a new decor. It sponsors independent films as well as lectures by visiting filmmakers and movie stars. Andy Garcia and Antonio Banderas are a few of the big names this theater has attracted. It also hosts the African American Film Festival, a Student Film Festival, and collaborations with the Fort Lauderdale Festival (a very small film festival). Admission is $5.

Warhol Redux?

Miami's **Artemis Performance Network** sets the stage for the city's creative types with eclectic venues and events dedicated to and showcasing the local arts community. A network of performing artists, visual artists, musicians, presenters, educators, and administrators, Artemis is backed by the support of the Miami–Dade County Cultural Affairs Council, among others. Responsible for turning Little Havana into a bohemian hangout, Artemis sponsors most of their events at a loft-like performance space simply known as PS 742, at 742 SW 16th Ave. in Little Havana (© 305/643-6611), in which events such as Surreal Saturdays (first Sat of every month) feature a funky roster of spoken-word, multimedia, and musical artists. Locals have compared the scene at PS 742 to that of New York City's East Village, around 1980.

The special effects at the IMAX Theatre at Sunset Place, 5701 Sunset Dr. in South Miami (© **305/663-4629**), will make you feel like you're part of the action.

The **Mercury Theatre,** Biscayne Boulevard at 55th Street, Miami (© **305/ 759-8809**), is the city's newest art-house cinema, showing classic and contemporary films from all over the world. Tickets are $8 or $6 for seniors and matinees.

THE LITERARY SCENE

Books & Books, in Coral Gables at 265 Aragon Ave. and in Miami Beach at 933 Lincoln Rd., hosts readings almost every night and is known for attracting such top authors as Colleen McCullough, Jamaica Kincaid, and Martin Amis. For details on their free readings, call © **305/442-4408.** (Also see p. 196 for more information on the shop.)

To hear more about what's happening on Miami's literary scene, tune into the "Cover to Cover" radio show, broadcast at 8pm on Mondays on public radio station WLRN (91.3 FM).

SPECTATOR SPORTS

For information on watching baseball, basketball, football, horse racing, ice hockey, and jai alai (many of these games are at night), please see the "Spectator Sports" section earlier in this chapter, beginning on p. 187.

VIDEO ARCADE

GameWorks *Kids* Steven Spielberg's SEGA GameWorks in the Shops at Sunset Place has become the hottest place for young adults to play. You'll see kids, gen-Xers, and baby boomers fighting off dinosaurs from *Jurassic Park,* racing in the Indy 500, swooshing down a snowy ski trail, throwing darts, and shooting pool in this sleek multilevel playground. The young at heart will find the perfect combination of vintage arcade games, high-tech videos, virtual-reality arenas, pool tables, food, and cocktails in this playground occupying more than 33,000 square feet. The GameWorks Grill serves up everything from gourmet salads to pizzas and burgers. Bring lots—and we mean lots—of change. 5701 Sunset Dr., South Miami. © **305/667-4263.** www.gameworks.com. Sun–Wed 11am–midnight; Thurs–Sat 11am–2am. Games 50¢–$5.

The Keys & The Dry Tortugas

by Lesley Abravanel

The drive from Miami to the Keys is a slow descent into an unusual but breathtaking American ecosystem: On either side of you, for miles ahead, lies nothing but emerald waters. (On weekends, however, you will also see plenty of traffic.) Strung out across the Atlantic Ocean like loose strands of cultured pearls, more than 400 islands make up this 150-mile-long (242km) chain of the Keys.

Despite the usually calm landscape, these rocky islands can be treacherous, as a series of tropical storms, hurricanes, and tornadoes reminded residents in the summer and fall of 1998 when millions of dollars of damage was inflicted. The exposed coast has always posed dangers to those on land as well as at sea.

When Spanish explorers Juan Ponce de León and Antonio de Herrera sailed amid these craggy, dangerous rocks in 1513, they and their men dubbed the string of islands "Los Martires" (The Martyrs), because they thought the rocks looked like men suffering in the surf. It wasn't until the early 1800s that rugged and ambitious pioneers, who amassed great wealth by salvaging cargo from ships sunk nearby, settled the larger islands (legend has it that these shipwrecks were sometimes caused by the "wreckers," who occasionally removed navigational markers from the shallows to lure unwitting captains aground). At the height of the salvaging mania (in the 1830s), Key West boasted the highest per capita income in the country.

However, wars, fires, hurricanes, mosquitoes, and the Depression took their toll on these resilient islands in the early part of this century, causing wild swings between fortune and poverty. In 1938, the spectacular Overseas Highway (U.S. 1) was finally completed atop the ruins of Henry Flagler's railroad (which was destroyed by a hurricane in 1935, leaving only bits and pieces still found today), opening the region to tourists, who had never before been able to drive to this seabound destination. These days, the highway connects more than 30 of the populated islands in the Keys. The hundreds of small, undeveloped islands that surround these "mainline" keys are known locally as the "backcountry" and are home to dozens of exotic animals and plants. Therein lie some of the most renowned outdoor sporting opportunities, from bonefishing to spear fishing and—at appropriate times of the year—diving for lobsters. To get to the backcountry, you must take to the water—a vital part of any trip to the Keys. Whether you fish, snorkel, dive, or just cruise, include some time on a boat in your itinerary; otherwise, you haven't truly seen the Keys.

Of course, people go to the Keys for the peaceful waters and the year-round warmth, but the sea and the teeming life beneath it are the main attractions here: Countless species of brilliantly colored fish can be found swimming above the ocean's floor, and you'll discover a stunning abundance of tropical and exotic plants, birds, and reptiles.

The warm, shallow waters (waters are deeper and rougher on the eastern/

Atlantic side of the Keys) nurture living coral that supports a complex, delicate ecosystem of plants and animals—sponges, anemones, jellyfish, crabs, rays, sharks, turtles, snails, lobsters, and thousands of types of fish. This vibrant underwater habitat thrives on one of the only living tropical reefs in the entire North American continent. As a result, anglers, divers, snorkelers, and water-sports enthusiasts of all kinds come to explore.

Heavy traffic has taken its toll on this fragile ecoscape, but conservation efforts are underway (traffic laws are strictly enforced on Deer Key, for example, due to deer crossings). In fact, environmental efforts in the Keys exceed those in many other high-traffic visitor destinations.

Although the atmosphere throughout the Keys is that of a laid-back beach town, don't expect to find many impressive beaches here, especially after the damaging effects of the tropical storms and hurricanes in 1998. Beaches are mostly found in a few private resorts, though there are some small, sandy beaches in John Pennekamp State Park, Bahia Honda State Park, and in Key West. One great exception is Sombrero Beach in Marathon (p. 222), which is well maintained by Monroe County and is larger and considerably nicer than other beaches in the Keys. Sombrero Beach features a beachfront park, picnic facilities, a playground, and a protected cove for children at the west end of the beach.

The Keys are divided into three sections, both geographically and in this chapter. The Upper and Middle Keys are closest to the Florida mainland, so they are popular with weekend warriors who come by boat or car to fish or relax in towns like Key Largo, Islamorada, and Marathon. Further on, just beyond the impressive Seven-Mile Bridge (which actually measures only 6½ miles [10km]), are the Lower Keys, a small, unspoiled swath of islands teeming with wildlife. Here, in the protected regions of the Lower Keys, is where you're most likely to catch sight of the area's many endangered animals—with patience, you may spot the rare eagle, egret, or Key deer. You should also keep an eye out for alligators, turtles, rabbits, and a huge variety of birds.

Key West, the most renowned—and last—island in the Lower Keys, is literally at the end of the road. The southernmost point in the continental United States (made famous by the Nobel Prize–winning Ernest Hemingway), this tiny island is the most popular destination in the Florida Keys, overrun with cruise-ship passengers and day-trippers, as well as franchises and T-shirt shops. More than 1.6 million visitors pass through each year. Still, this "Conch Republic" has a tightly knit community of permanent residents who cling fiercely to their live-and-let-live attitude—an atmosphere that has made Key West famously popular with painters, writers, and free spirits.

The last section in this chapter is devoted to the Dry Tortugas, a National Park, located 68 nautical miles (100km) from Key West.

⌜Tips **Don't Be Fooled**

Avoid the many "Tourist Information Centers" that dot the main highway. Most are private companies hired to lure visitors to specific lodgings or outfitters. You're better off sticking with the official, not-for-profit centers that are extremely well located and staffed.

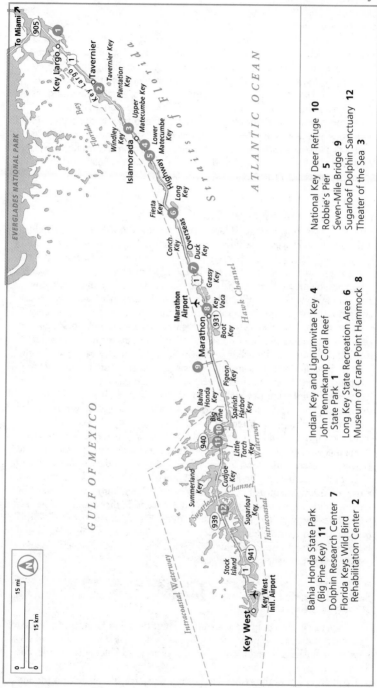

Bahia Honda State Park
(Big Pine Key) 11
Dolphin Research Center 7
Florida Keys Wild Bird
Rehabilitation Center 2

Indian Key and Lignumvitae Key 4
John Pennekamp Coral Reef
State Park 1
Long Key State Recreation Area 6
Museum of Crane Point Hammock 8

National Key Deer Refuge 10
Robbie's Pier 5
Seven-Mile Bridge 9
Sugarloaf Dolphin Sanctuary 12
Theater of the Sea 3

Moments **No Place Like Homestead**

On its own, there's not much to the waterfront shack that is Alabama Jack's. The bar serves beer and wine only, and the restaurant specializes in greasy bar fare. But this quintessential Old Floridian dive, located between Homestead and Key Largo, is a colorful must on the drive south. Hordes of Harley Davidson bikers, local Miamians, barflies, and anglers flock here with much devotion, and the views of the mangroves are spectacular. Pull up a bar stool, order a cold one, and take in the sights—in the bay and at the bar. To get there, pick up Card Sound Road (the old Rte. 1) a few miles after you pass Homestead, heading toward Key Largo. Alabama Jack's is on the right side and can't be missed. 5800 Card Sound Rd., Homestead. ℭ **305/248-8741.**

EXPLORING THE KEYS BY CAR

After you have gotten off the Florida Turnpike and landed on U.S. 1, which is also known as the Overseas Highway (see "Getting There," under "Essentials," below), you'll have no trouble negotiating these narrow islands, since it is the only main road connecting the Keys. The scenic, lazy drive from Miami can be very enjoyable if you have the patience to linger and explore the diverse towns and islands along the way. If you have the time, I recommend allowing at least 2 days to work your way down to Key West and 3 or more days once there.

Most of U.S. 1 is a narrow, two-lane highway, with some wider passing zones along the way. The speed limit is usually 55 miles (89km) per hour (35–45 mph [56–72kmph] on Big Pine Key and in some commercial areas). Despite the protestations of island residents, there has been talk of expanding the highway, but plans have not been finalized. Even on the narrow road, you can usually get from downtown Miami to Key Largo in just over an hour. If you're determined to drive straight through to Key West, allow at least 3½ hours. Weekend travel is another matter entirely: When the roads are jammed with travelers from the mainland, the trip could take upward of 5 to 6 hours (when there's an accident, traffic is at an absolute standstill). If at all possible, I strongly urge you to avoid driving anywhere in the Keys on Friday afternoons or Sunday evenings.

To find an address in the Keys, don't bother looking for building numbers; most addresses (except in Key West and parts of Marathon) are delineated by mile markers (MM), small green signs on the roadside that announce the distance from Key West. The markers start at number 127, just south of the Florida mainland. The zero marker is in Key West, at the corner of Whitehead and Fleming Streets. Addresses in this chapter are accompanied by a mile marker (MM) designation when appropriate.

1 The Upper & Middle Keys: Key Largo ✮✮ to Marathon ✮

58 miles (93km) SW of Miami

The Upper Keys are a popular, year-round refuge for South Floridians, who take advantage of the islands' proximity to the mainland. This is the fishing and diving capital of America, and the swarms of outfitters and billboards never let you forget it.

Key Largo, once called Rock Harbor but renamed to capitalize on the success of the 1948 Humphrey Bogart film (which wasn't actually filmed there), is the largest key and is more developed than its neighbors to the south. Dozens of chain hotels, restaurants, and tourist-information centers service the many water enthusiasts who come to explore the nation's first underwater state park, **John Pennekamp Coral Reef State Park,** and its adjacent marine sanctuary. **Isla morada,** the unofficial capital of the Upper Keys, offers the area's best atmosphere, food, fishing, entertainment, and lodging. It's an unofficial "party capital" for mainlanders seeking a quick tropical excursion. Here (Islamorada is actually composed of four islands), nature lovers can enjoy walking trails, historic explorations, and big-purse fishing tournaments. For a more tranquil, quieter, less party-hearty Keys experience, all other Keys besides Key West and Islamorada are better choices. **Marathon,** smack in the middle of the Florida Keys, is one of the most populated keys and is known as the heart of the Keys. It is part fishing village, part tourist center, and part nature preserve. This area's highly developed infrastructure includes resort hotels, a commercial airport, and a highway that expands to four lanes.

ESSENTIALS

GETTING THERE   From Miami International Airport (there is also an airport in Marathon), take Le Jeune Road (Northwest 42nd Ave.) to Route 836 west. Follow signs to the Florida Turnpike south (about 7 miles [11km]). The turnpike extension connects with U.S. 1 in Florida City. Continue south on U.S. 1. For a scenic option, weather permitting, take Card Sound Road south of Florida City, a backcountry drive that reconnects with U.S. 1 in upper Key Largo. The view from the Card Sound Bridge is spectacular and well worth the $1 toll.

If you're coming from Florida's west coast, take Alligator Alley to the Miami exit and then turn south onto the turnpike extension. The turnpike ends in Florida City, at which time you will be dumped directly onto the one-lane road, U.S. 1, that leads to the Keys. Have plenty of quarters (at least $10 worth, round-trip) for the tolls.

Greyhound (© **800/231-2222;** www.greyhound.com) has three buses leaving Miami for Key West every day, which also stop in Key Largo, Tavenier, Islamorada, Marathon, Big Pine Key, Cudjoe Key, Sugarloaf, and Big Coppit on their way south. Prices range up from about $13 to $32 one way and take between an hour and 40 minutes to 4 hours and 40 minutes, depending on how far south you're going. Seats fill quickly in season, so come early. It's first-come, first-served.

VISITOR INFORMATION   Make sure you get your information from official, not-for-profit centers. The **Key Largo Chamber of Commerce,** U.S. 1 at MM 106, Key Largo, FL 33037 (© **800/822-1088** or 305/451-1414; fax 305/451-4726; www.keylargo.org), runs an excellent facility, with free direct-dial phones and plenty of brochures. Headquartered in a handsome clapboard house, the chamber operates as an information clearinghouse for all of the Keys and is open daily from 9am to 6pm.

The **Islamorada Chamber of Commerce,** housed in an actual little red caboose, U.S. 1 at MM 82.5, P.O. Box 915, Islamorada, FL 33036 (© **800/322-5397** or 305/664-4503; fax 305/664-4289; www.islamoradachamber.com), also offers maps and literature on the Upper Keys.

You can't miss the big blue visitor center at MM 53.5, the **Greater Marathon Chamber of Commerce,** 12222 Overseas Hwy., Marathon, FL 33050 (© **800/262-7284** or 305/743-5417; fax 305/289-0183; www.floridakeysmarathon.com). Here, you can receive free information on local events, festivals, shows, attractions, dining, and lodging.

OUTDOOR SIGHTS & ACTIVITIES

Anne's Beach (at MM 73.5, on Lower Matecumbe Key, at the Southwest end of Islamorada) is really more of a picnic spot than a full-fledged beach, but die-hard suntanners still congregate on this lovely but tiny strip of coarse sand that was damaged beyond recognition during the series of storms in 1998. Plans are in place to reconstruct the boardwalk and huts, but at press time, work had not yet started.

A better choice for real beaching is **Sombrero Beach** ★★ in Marathon at the end of Sombrero Beach Road (near MM 50). This wide swath of uncluttered beachfront actually benefited from Hurricane George in September 1998, with generous deposits of extra sand and a face lift courtesy of the Monroe County Tourist Development Council. More than 90 feet (27m) of sand is dotted with palms, Australian Pines, and Royal Poincianas as well as with barbecue grills, clean bathrooms, and some brand new tiki huts for relaxing in the shade.

If you are interested in seeing the Keys in their natural state, before modern development, you must venture off the highway and take to the water. Two backcountry islands that offer a glimpse of the "real" Keys are **Indian Key** and **Lignumvitae Key** ★★★. Visitors come to these to relax and enjoy the islands' colorful birds and lush hammocks (elevated pieces of land above a marsh).

Named for the lignum vitae ("wood of life") trees found there, **Lignumvitae Key** supports a virgin tropical forest, the kind that once thrived on most of the Upper Keys. Over the years, human settlers imported "exotic" plants and animals to the Keys, irrevocably changing the botanical makeup of many backcountry islands and threatening much of the indigenous wildlife. Over the past 25 years, however, the Florida Department of Natural Resources has successfully removed most of the exotic vegetation from this key, leaving this 280-acre site much as it existed in the 18th century. The island also holds the Matheson House, a historic house built in 1919 that has survived numerous hurricanes. You can go inside the house, but this is interesting only if you have a hankering for coral rock, which the house is made out of. It's now a museum dedicated to the history, nature, and topography of the area. More interesting is actually seeing the area via the Botanical Gardens, which surround the house and are a state preserve. Lignumvitae Key has a visitor's center at MM 88.5 (© **305/664-2540**).

Indian Key, a much smaller island on the Atlantic side of Islamorada, was occupied by Native Americans for thousands of years before European settlers arrived. The 10-acre historic site was also the original seat of Dade County before the Civil War. Interestingly, from an archaeological standpoint, you can see the ruins of the previous settlement and tour the lush grounds on well-marked trails. Off Indian Key Fill, Overseas Highway, MM 79. To get information about Indian Key, call the Florida Park Service at © **305/664-4815** or check out www.dep.state.fl.us/parks/district5/indiankey/index.asp.

If you want to see both islands, plan to spend at least half a day. To get there, you can rent your own power boat at **Robbie's Rent-A-Boat,** U.S. 1 at MM 77.5 on the bay side (p. 222), on Islamorada. It's then a $1 admission fee to each island, which includes an informative hour-long guided tour by park rangers. This is a good option if you are a confident boater.

However, I also recommend taking Robbie's **ferry service.** A visit to one island costs $15, $10 for kids 12 and under, which includes the $1 park admission; trips to both islands cost $25 per person. (If you have time for only one island, make it Lignumvitae.) Not only is the ferry more economical, but it's easier to enjoy the natural beauty of the islands when you aren't negotiating the shallow reefs along the way. The runabouts, which carry up to six people, depart from Robbie's Pier Thursday through Monday at 9am and 1pm for Indian Key, and at 10am and 2pm for Lignumvitae Key. In the busy season, you may need to book as early as 2 days before departure. Call 🕿 **305/664-4815** for information from the park service or 🕿 **305/664-9814** for Robbie's.

Crane Point Hammock ★★ *Finds* *Kids* Crane Point Hammock is a little-known but worthwhile stop, especially for those interested in the rich botanical and archaeological history of the Keys. This privately owned 64-acre nature area is considered one of the most important historical sites in the Keys. It contains what is probably the last virgin thatch palm hammock in North America, as well as a rain-forest exhibit and an archaeological dig site with pre-Columbian and prehistoric Bahamian artifacts.

Also headquarters for the Florida Keys Land and Sea Trust, the hammock's impressive nature museum has simple, informative displays of the Keys' wildlife, including a walk-through replica of a coral-reef cave and life-size dioramas with tropical birds and Key deer. Kids can participate in art projects, see 6-foot-long iguanas, climb through a scaled-down pirate ship, and touch a variety of indigenous aquatic and landlubbing creatures.

5550 Overseas Hwy. (MM 50), Marathon. 🕿 **305/743-9100.** Admission $7.50 adults, $6 seniors over 64, $4 students, free for children under 6. Mon–Sat 9am–5pm; Sun noon–5pm.

Pigeon Key ★★ At the curve of the old bridge on Pigeon Key is an intriguing historical site that has been under renovation since late 1993. This 5-mile-long (8km) island was once the camp for the crew that built the old railway in the early part of the century, and later served as housing for the bridge builders. From here, your vista includes both the vestiges of Henry Flagler's old Seven-Mile Bridge as well as the one on which traffic presently soars, many old wooden cottages, and a truly tranquil stretch of lush foliage and sea. If you miss the shuttle tour from the Pigeon Key Visitor Center or would rather walk or bike to the site, it's about 2½ miles (4km). Either way, you may want to bring a picnic to enjoy after a brief self-guided walking tour of the Key and museum visit to what has become an homage to Flagler's railroad, featuring artifacts and photographs of the old bridge. There is also an informative 28-minute video of the island's history offered every hour starting at 10am. Parking is available at the Knight's Key end of the bridge, at MM 48, or at the visitor center at MM 47, on the ocean side.

East end of the 7-Mile Bridge near MM 47, Marathon. 🕿 **305/743-5999.** Open 9am–5pm; shuttle tours run every hr. 10am–4pm. Admission $8.50, $5 for children under 13. Price includes shuttle transportation from the visitor center.

Seven-Mile Bridge ★★★ A stop at the Seven-Mile Bridge is a rewarding and relaxing break from the drive south. Built alongside the ruins of oil magnate Henry Flagler's incredible Overseas Railroad, the "new" bridge (between MMs 40 and 47) is considered an architectural feat. The wide-arched span, completed in 1985 at a cost of more than $45 million, is impressive, and its apex is the highest point in the Keys. The new bridge and its now-defunct neighbor provide an excellent vantage point from which to view the stunning waters of the Keys. In the daytime, you may want to walk, jog, or bike along the scenic 4-mile (6.5km) stretch of old bridge, or join local anglers, who catch barracuda, yellowtail, and dolphin (the fish, not the mammal) on what is known as "the

---

Fun Fact Bridge Mix

The Seven-Mile Bridge is the longest fragmented (unconnected pieces) bridge in the world. Completed in 1985, it was constructed parallel to the original bridge, part of Henry Flagler's Florida East Coast Railroad, which served as the original link to the Lower Keys. Some people may recognize the remnants of the old bridge from the Arnold Schwarzenegger film *True Lies*. Others fearfully contemplate whether a wrong turn would lead them to the old bridge instead of the new one. Not to worry: The old bridge is closed to cars and has been transformed into the world's longest fishing pier.

---

longest fishing pier in the world." Parking is available on both sides of the bridge.

Between MMs 40 and 47 on U.S. 1. © 305/289-0025.

VISITING WITH THE ANIMALS

Dolphin Research Center ✮✮✮ *Kids*   If you've always wanted to touch, swim, or play with dolphins, this is the place to do it. Of the three such centers in the continental United States (all located in the Keys), the Dolphin Research Center is the most organized and informative. Although some people argue that training dolphins is cruel and selfish, this is one of the most respected of the institutions that study and protect the mammals. Knowledgeable trainers at the Dolphin Research Center will also tell you that the dolphins need stimulation and enjoy human contact. They certainly seem to. They nuzzle and seem to smile and kiss the lucky few that get to swim with them in the daily program. The "family" of 15 dolphins swims in a 90,000-square-foot natural saltwater pool carved out of the shoreline.

If you can't get into the swim program, you can still take the interesting hour-long walking tour of the facilities, sign up for a class in hand signals, or feed the dolphins from docks. Because the Dolphin Encounter swimming program is the most popular, reservations must be made at least 1 month in advance. The cost is $135 per person. If you're not brave enough to swim with the dolphins or you have a child under 12 (not permitted to swim with dolphins), try the Dolphin Splash program, in which participants stand on an elevated platform from which they can "meet and greet" the dolphins. A height requirement of 44 inches is enforced, and an adult must hold up children under the required height. Cost for this program is $75 per person; free for children under 3.

U.S. 1 at MM 59 (on the bay side), Marathon. © 305/289-1121. Swim with the Dolphins, $135 per person. Call on the first day of the month to book for the following month. Educational walking tours 5 times daily: 10 and 11am, and 12:30, 2, and 3:30pm. Admission $15 adults, $12.50 seniors, $10 children 4–12, free for children 3 and under. Daily 9:30am–4pm.

Florida Keys Wild Bird Center ✮   Wander through lush canopies of mangroves on narrow wooden walkways to see some of the Keys' most famous residents—the large variety of native birds, including broad-wing hawks, great blue and white herons, roseate spoonbills, white ibis, cattle egrets, and a number of pelicans. This not-for-profit center operates as a hospital for the many birds that have been injured by accident or disease. Visit at feeding time, usually about 3:30pm, when you can watch the dedicated staff feed the hundreds of hungry beaks.

U.S. 1 at MM 93.6, Bayside, Tavernier. ℂ 305/852-4486. fkwbc@reefnet.com. Donations suggested. Daily 8:30am–6pm.

Robbie's Pier ★★★ *Value*   One of the best and definitely one of the cheapest attractions in the Upper Keys is the famed Robbie's Pier. Here, the fierce steely tarpons, a prized catch for backcountry anglers, have been gathering for the past 20 years. You may recognize these prehistoric-looking giants that grow up to 200 pounds; many are displayed as trophies and mounted on local restaurant walls. To see them live, head to Robbie's Pier, where tens and sometimes hundreds of these behemoths circle the shallow waters waiting for you to feed them. Kayak tours promise an even closer glimpse.

U.S. 1 at MM 77.5, Islamorada. ℂ 305/664-9814. Admission $1. Bucket of fish $2. Daily 8am–5pm. Look for the Hungry Tarpon restaurant sign on the right after the Indian Key channel.

Theater of the Sea ★ *Kids*   Established in 1946, the Theater of the Sea is one of the world's oldest marine zoos. Recently refurbished, with newly paved walkways, landscaping, and an on-site photo service, the park's dolphin and sea lion shows are entertaining and informative, especially for children, who can also see sharks, sea turtles, and tropical fish. If you want to swim with dolphins and you haven't booked well in advance, this is the place you may be able to get into with just a few hours, or days, notice as opposed to the more rigid Dolphin Research Center (see above) in Marathon. (While the Dolphin Research Center is a legitimate, scientific establishment, this is more of a theme parky attraction. That's not to say the dolphins are mistreated, but it's just not as, say, educational and professional as it is at the Dolphin Research Center.) Theater of the Sea also permits you to swim with the sea lions and stingrays. Children under 5 are not permitted to participate. There are also 4-hour adventure and snorkel cruises, $60 for adults and $35 for children, in which you can learn about the history and ecology of the marine environment. The facility also serves as a haven for dozens of stray cats that have free run of the grounds and gift shop.

U.S. 1 at MM 84.5, Islamorada. ℂ 305/664-2431. www.theaterofthesea.com. Admission $17.75 adults, $11.25 children 3–12. Dolphin swim $135; sea lion swim $90; stingray swim $40 per person. Reservations a must. Daily 9:30am–5:45pm (ticket office closes at 4pm).

TWO EXCEPTIONAL STATE PARKS

One of the best places to discover the diverse ecosystem of the Upper Keys is in its most famous park, **John Pennekamp Coral Reef State Park** ★★★, located on U.S. 1 at MM 102.5, in Key Largo (ℂ 305/451-1202). Named for a former *Miami Herald* editor and conservationist, the 188-square-mile park is the nation's first undersea preserve: It's a sanctuary for part of the only living coral reef in the continental United States. The original plans for Everglades National Park included this part of the reef within its boundaries, but opposition from local homeowners made its inclusion politically impossible.

Because the water is extremely shallow, the 40 species of coral and more than 650 species of fish here are particularly accessible to divers, snorkelers, and glass-bottomed-boat passengers. To experience this park, visitors must get in the water—you can't see the reef from the shore. Your first stop should be the visitor center, which is full of educational fish tanks and a mammoth 30,000-gallon saltwater aquarium that re-creates a reef ecosystem. At the adjacent dive shop, you can rent snorkeling and diving equipment and join one of the boat trips that depart for the reef throughout the day. Visitors can also rent motorboats, sailboats, windsurfers, and canoes. The 2-hour glass-bottomed-boat tour is the best way to see the coral reefs if you don't want to get wet. Watch for the lobsters and other sea life residing in the fairly shallow ridge walls beneath the coastal waters. *But remember:* These are protected waters, so you can't remove anything from the water.

Canoeing around the park's narrow mangrove channels and tidal creeks is also popular. You can go on your own in a rented canoe or, in winter, sign up for a tour led by a local naturalist. Hikers have two short trails from which to choose: a boardwalk through the mangroves and a dirt trail through a tropical hardwood hammock. Ranger-led walks are usually scheduled daily from the end of November to April. Phone ⓒ **305/451-1202** for schedule information and reservations.

Park admission is $2.50 per vehicle for one occupant; for two or more, it is $4 per vehicle, plus 50¢ per passenger; $1.50 per pedestrian or bicyclist. On busy weekend days, there's often a line of cars to get into the park. On your way into the park, ask the ranger for a map. Glass-bottomed-boat tours cost $18 for adults and $10 for children 11 and under. Snorkeling tours are $25.95 for adults and $19.95 for children 17 and under, including equipment. Sailing and snorkeling tours are $31.95 for adults, $26.95 for children 17 and under, including equipment. Canoes rent for $10 per hour. For experienced boaters only, four different-sized reef boats (powerboats) rent for $27.50 to $50 per hour, with cheaper half-day and full-day rates available; call ⓒ **305/451-6325** for more information. A $400 deposit (and up depending on boat size, starting at a 22-ft. boat) is required. The park's boat rental is open daily from 8am to 5pm—the last boat rented is at 3pm; phone for tour and dive times. Reservations are recommended for all of the above. Also, see below for more options on diving, fishing, and snorkeling these reefs.

Long Key State Recreation Area ★★★, U.S. 1 at MM 68, Long Key (ⓒ **305/664-4815**), is one of the best places in the Middle Keys for hiking, camping, snorkeling, and canoeing. This 965-acre site is situated atop the remains of an ancient coral reef. At the entrance gate, ask for a free flyer describing the local trails and wildlife.

There are three nature trails that can be explored via foot or canoe: The Golden Orb Trail is a 40-minute walk through mostly just plants; the Layton Trail is a 15-minute walk along the bay; and the Long Key Canoe Trail glides along a shallow-water lagoon. Campsites are located along the Atlantic Ocean and the swimming, snorkeling, and saltwater fishing (license required) are top notch here. Educational programs on the aforementioned are available, too, for novices. Snorkeling is shallow and on the shoreline of the Atlantic Ocean. The nearest place to rent snorkeling equipment is Holiday Isle, 84001 U.S. 1, Islamorada (ⓒ **800/327-7070**).

The park's excellent 1½-mile (2.5km) canoe trail is also short and sweet, allowing visitors to loop around the mangroves in about an hour. You can rent canoes at the trail head for about $4 per hour. Long Key is also a great spot to stop for a picnic if you get hungry on your way to Key West.

Railroad builder Henry Flagler created the Long Key Fishing Club here in 1906, and the waters surrounding the park are still popular with game fishers. In summer, sea turtles lumber onto the protected coast to lay their eggs, all lined up on the coast. It's a big event, and educational programs are available to view this phenomenon.

Admission is $3.25 per car plus 50¢ per person (except for the Layton Trail, which is free). Open daily from 8am to sunset.

The 10 "Keymandments"

The Keys have always attracted independent spirits, from Ernest Hemingway and Tennessee Williams to Jimmy Buffett, Zane Grey, and local hero Mel Fisher. Writers, artists, and free thinkers have long drifted down here to escape.

Although you'll generally find a very laid-back and tolerant code of behavior in the Keys, some rules do exist. Be sure to respect the 10 "Keymandments" while you're here, or suffer the consequences.

- Don't anchor on a reef. (Reefs are alive.)
- Don't feed the animals. (They'll want to follow you home, and you can't keep them.)
- Don't trash our place (or we'll send Bubba to trash yours).
- Don't touch the coral. (After all, you don't even know them. Some pose a mild risk of injury as well.)
- Don't speed (especially on Big Pine Key, where deer reside and tar-and-feathering is still practiced).
- Don't catch more fish than you can eat. (Better yet, let them go. Some of them support schools.)
- Don't collect conch. (This species is protected by Bubba.)
- Don't disturb the bird nests. (They find it very annoying.)
- Don't damage the sea grass. (And don't even think about making a skirt out of it.)
- Don't drink and drive on land or sea. (There's absolutely nothing funny about it.)

WATER SPORTS FROM A TO Z

There are literally hundreds of outfitters in the Keys who will arrange all kinds of water activities, from cave dives to parasailing. If those recommended below are booked up or unreachable, ask the local chamber of commerce for a list of qualified members.

BOATING In addition to the rental shops in the state parks, you will find dozens of outfitters along U.S. 1 offering a range of runabouts and skiffs for boaters of any experience level. **Captain Pip's,** U.S. 1 at MM 47.5, Marathon (© **800/707-1692** or 305/743-4403), rents 18- to 24-foot motorboats with 90- to 225-horsepower engines for $130 to $225 per day. Overnight accommodations are available and include a free boat rental; 2-night minimum $220 to $255; weekly $1,190 to $1,890. Rooms are Key West comfortable and charming, with ceiling fans, tile floors, and pine paneling. But the best part about it is that every room comes with an 18- to 21-foot boat for your use during your stay.

Robbie's Rent-a-Boat, U.S. 1 at MM 77.5, Islamorada (© **305/664-9814**), rents 14- to 27-foot motorboats with engines ranging from 15 to 200 horsepower. Boat rentals are $70 to $205 for a half day and $90 to $295 for a full day.

CANOEING & KAYAKING I can think of no better way to explore the uninhabited, shallow backcountry on the Gulf side of the Keys than by kayak or canoe, since you can reach places big boats just can't get to because of their large draft. Sometimes manatees will even cuddle up to the boats, thinking them another friendly species.

Tips **Boat Choices**

For a more enjoyable time, ask for a sit-inside boat—you'll stay drier. Also, a fiberglass (as opposed to plastic) boat with a rudder is generally more stable and easier to maneuver.

Many area hotels rent kayaks and canoes to guests, as do the outfitters listed here. **Florida Bay Outfitters,** U.S. 1 at MM 104, Key Largo (© **305/451-3018**), rents canoes and sea kayaks for use in and around John Pennekamp Coral Reef State Park for $20 to $40 for a half day and $35 to $55 for a whole day. Canoes cost $25 for a half day and $35 for a whole day. At **Coral Reef Park Co.,** on U.S. 1 at MM 102.5, Key Largo (© **305/451-1621**), you can rent canoes and kayaks for $8 per hour, $28 for a half day; most canoes are sit-on-tops.

DIVING & SNORKELING   The **Florida Keys Dive Center,** on U.S. 1 at MM 90.5, Tavernier (© **305/852-4599**), takes snorkelers and divers to the reefs of John Pennekamp Coral Reef State Park and environs every day. PADI (Professional Association of Diving Instructors) training courses are also available for the uninitiated. Tours leave at 8am and 12:30pm and cost $25 per person to snorkel (plus $8 rental fee for mask, snorkel, and fins) and $59 per person to dive (plus an extra $20 if you need to rent all the gear).

At **Hall's Dive Center & Career Institute,** U.S. 1 at MM 48.5, Marathon (© **305/743-5929**), snorkelers and divers can choose to dive at Looe Key, Sombrero Reef, Delta Shoal, Content Key, and Coffins Patch. Tours are scheduled daily at 9am and 1pm. You will spend 1 hour at each of two sites per tour. If you mention this book, you will get a special discounted rate ($5–$10 off) of $30 per person to snorkel (additional gear is $11) and $40 per person to dive (tanks are $8.50 each).

With **SNUBA Tours of Key Largo** (© **305/451-6391;** www.pennekamp.com/sw/snuba.htm), you can dive down to 20 feet (6m) attached to a comfortable breathing apparatus that really gives you the feeling of scuba diving without having to be certified. You can tour shallow coral reefs teeming with hundreds of colorful fish and plant life, from sea turtles to moray eels. Reservations are required; call to find out where and when to meet. A 2- to 3-hour underwater tour (typically 1–4pm) costs $75, including all equipment. If you have never dived before, you may require a 1-hour lesson in the pool, which costs an additional $45.

FISHING   **Robbie's Partyboats & Charters,** on U.S. 1 at MM 84.5, Islamorada (© **305/664-8070** or 305/664-4196), located at the south end of the Holiday Isle Docks (see the Holiday Isle Resort in "Where to Stay," later in this chapter), offers day and night deep-sea and reef-fishing trips aboard a 65-foot party boat. Big-game fishing charters are also available, and "splits" are arranged for solo fishers. Party-boat fishing costs $25 for a half-day morning tour (rod and reel rental is $3); it's $15 extra if you want to go back out on an afternoon tour. Charters run $400 for a half day, $600 for a full day; splits begin at $65 per person. Phone for information and reservations.

Bud n' Mary's Fishing Marina, on U.S. 1 at MM 79.8, Islamorada (© **800/742-7945** or 305/664-2461), one of the largest marinas between Miami and Key West, is packed with sailors offering guided backcountry fishing charters.

This is the place to go if you want to stalk tarpon, bonefish, and snapper. If the seas are not too rough, deep-sea and coral fishing trips can also be arranged. Charters cost $500 to $550 for a half day, $750 to $800 for a full day; and splits begin at $125 per person.

The Bounty Hunter, 15th Street at Burdine's Marina, Marathon (✆ **305/743-2446**), offers full- and half-day outings. For 28 years, Captain Brock Hook's huge sign has boasted, "no fish, no pay:" You're guaranteed to catch something, or your money back! Choose your prey from shark, barracuda, sailfish, or whatever else is running. Prices are $400 for a half day, $500 for three-quarters of a day, and $600 for a full day. Rates are for groups of no more than six people.

SHOPPING

On your way to the Keys, you'll find an outlet center, the **Prime Outlets at Florida City** (✆ **305/248-4727**), at 250 E. Palm Dr. (where the Florida Turnpike meets U.S. 1), in Florida City. The center holds more than 60 stores, including Nike Factory Store, Bass Co. Store, Levi's, OshKosh, and Izod. Travelers can pick up a free discount coupon booklet called the "Come Back Pack" from the Customer Service Center. The outlet is open Monday through Saturday from 10am to 9pm, Sunday from 11am to 6pm.

The Upper and Middle Keys have no shortage of tacky tourist shops selling shells and T-shirts (the ubiquitous "beads and trinkets") and other hokey souvenirs, but for real Keys-style shopping, check out the weekend **flea markets.** The best, The Key Largo Storage/Flea Market, is held every Saturday and Sunday on the bay side at MM 103.5 (✆ **305/451-0677**). Dozens of vendors open their stalls from 9am until 4 or 5pm, selling every imaginable sort of antiques, T-shirts, plants, shoes, books, toys, and games, as well as a hearty dose of good old-fashioned junk. Also decent is the Grassy Key Flea Market, at MM 60, on the ocean side. The rest, however, are pretty schlocky.

A mecca for fishing and sports enthusiasts, **The World Wide Sportsman** (✆ **305/664-4615**) at MM 81.5, is not only the largest fishing store in the Keys, but also a meeting place for anglers from all over the world. Every possible gizmo and gadget, plus hundreds of T-shirts, hats, books, and gift items are displayed in its more than 25,000 square feet. The salespeople are knowledgeable and eager to help. Travel specialists can even arrange for charter trips and backcountry tours. The store is open daily from 7am until 8:30pm.

WHERE TO STAY

U.S. 1 is lined with chain hotels in all price ranges. In the Upper Keys, the best moderately priced option is the **Ramada Limited Resort & Casino** (✆ **800/**

Acquaint Yourself

Fans of stone crabs can get further acquainted with those seasonal crustaceans thanks to Keys Fisheries' 3-hour tours aboard 40- to 50-foot vessels, which leave from Marathon. The tour includes views of fishermen as they collect crabs from traps and process their claws. The $425 tour cost includes up to six passengers and up to 6 pounds of fresh claws iced for travel or prepared at a dockside restaurant. Stone crab season is from October 15 to May 15. Call ✆ **305/743-4353** or check the Web at www.keysfisheries.com for more information.

THE-KEYS or 305/451-3939) at MM 100, off of U.S. 1 in Key Largo, which has three pools and a casino boat and is just 3 miles (5km) from John Pennekamp Coral Reef State Park. Another good option in the Upper Keys is **Islamorada Days Inn**, U.S. 1 at MM 82.5 (© **800/DAYS-INN** or 305/664-3681). In the Middle Keys, the **Wellesley Inn** at 13351 Overseas Hwy., MM 54 in Marathon (© **305/743-8550**), also offers reasonably priced ocean-side rooms.

Since the real beauty of the Keys lies mostly beyond the highways, there is no better way to see this area than by boat. Why not stay in a floating hotel? Especially if you're traveling with a group, houseboats can be economical. To rent a houseboat, call Ruth and Michael Sullivan at **Smilin' Island Houseboat Rentals** (MM 99.5), Key Largo (© **305/451-1930**). Rates are from $750 to $1,350 for 3 nights. Boats accommodate up to six people.

For land options, consider the recommendations below.

VERY EXPENSIVE

Cheeca Lodge & Spa ★★★ *Kids*   Luxurious and relaxing Cheeca has been hosting celebrities, royalty, and politicians since its opening in 1949. Guests now enjoy the luxury of the Cheeca's freshly renovated and remodeled rooms. Each of the 203 units offers all the amenities of a world-class resort in a very laid-back setting. You may not feel compelled to leave the sprawling grounds, but it's good to know that the hotel is conveniently situated near the best restaurants and nightlife. Located on 27 acres of beachfront property (the 1,100-ft. palm-lined beach is truly idyllic), this rambling resort is known for its excellent sports facilities, including one of the only golf courses in the Upper Keys. All rooms are spacious and have small balconies. The nicer ones overlook the ocean and have large marble bathrooms. Rooms by the golf course have showers, not bathtubs, and overlook man-made lagoons. The Atlantic's Edge restaurant is one of the best in the Upper Keys (see "Where to Dine," later in this chapter). In May 2001, the state-of-the-art Avanyu health spa and fitness center opened. Children 6 to 12 can have their own customized vacation with Camp Cheeca's organized activities and events.

U.S. 1 at MM 82 (P.O. Box 527), Islamorada, FL 33036. © 800/327-2888 or 305/664-4651. Fax 305/664-2893. www.cheeca.com. 203 units. Winter $149–$650 double; $219–$1,600 suite. Off-season $129–$475 double; $189–$1,225 suite. AE, DC, DISC, MC, V. **Amenities:** 2 restaurants; 2 lounges (1 poolside); 3 outdoor heated pools; kids' pool; 9-hole, par-3 golf course; 6 lighted tennis courts; Jacuzzi; 5 hot tubs; access to nearby health club; water-sports equipment rental; bike rental; children's nature programs; concierge; tour desk; car-rental desk; room service; in-room massage; babysitting; dry-cleaning and laundry services; nature trails. *In room:* A/C, TV/VCR, dataport, kitchenette (in suites), minibar, coffeemaker, hair dryer, CD player.

Hawk's Cay Resort ★★★ *Kids*   Located on its own 60-acre island in the Middle Keys, this resort has a relaxed and casual island atmosphere. If it's recreation you're looking for, Hawk's Cay is far superior to the more luxurious Cheeca Lodge. It offers an impressive array of activities—sailing, fishing, snorkeling, and water-skiing to name a few—and the unique opportunity to swim in a special pool reserved for swimming with dolphins. (You'll need to reserve a spot well in advance for the dolphins—there's a waiting list.) The rooms are large and newly renovated, with island-style furniture, and each opens onto a private balcony with ocean or tropical views (pricing varies depending on the view). The large bathrooms are well appointed and have granite countertops. The clubhouse has an exercise room, whirlpool, and steam room. In addition to a lagoon and several pools for families, the resort boasts a secluded pool for adults only.

Organized children's activities, including special marine- and ecologically inspired programs, will keep your little ones busy while you relax.

61 Hawk's Cay Blvd. at MM 61, Duck Key, FL 33050. (℃) **888/814-9104** or 305/743-7000. Fax 305/743-5215. www.hawkscay.com. 176 units. Winter $240–$395 double; $445–$1,100 suite. Off-season $200–$325 double; $375–$1,000 suite. Packages available. AE, DC, DISC, MC, V. **Amenities:** 3 restaurants; lounge; outdoor heated pool; adults-only private pool; 18-hole putting course; nearby golf course (transportation available); 8 tennis courts (2 lighted); small exercise room; Jacuzzi; water-sports equipment rental; bike rental; children's programs ($25–$35 per child); game room; concierge; limited room service; in-room massage. *In room:* A/C, TV/VCR, fridge, iron, coffeemaker, hair dryer.

Westin Beach Resort ★★   In addition to a $3 million overhaul, the resort distinguishes itself by its secluded yet convenient location—it's set back on 12 private acres of gumbo-limbo and hardwood trees, making it invisible from the busy highway. Despite its hideaway location, the sprawling pink-and-blue four-story complex is surprisingly large: Two wings that face 1,200 feet (360m) of the Florida Bay flank a three-story atrium lobby. The large guest rooms all have private balconies overlooking either the bay or nature trails and are immaculate and fairly large—your typical, upscale-ish Westin room. The suites are twice the size of standard rooms with double-size balconies and better-quality wicker furnishings. Ten suites feature private spa tubs and particularly luxurious bathrooms with adjustable showerheads, bidets, and lots of room for toiletries.

U.S. 1 at MM 97, Key Largo, FL 33037. (℃) **800/728-2738**, 800/539-5274, or 305/852-5553. Fax 305/852-8669. www.keylargoresort.com. 200 units. Winter $189–$389; Jacuzzi suites start at $369. Off-season $109–$369; Jacuzzi suites start at $279. AE, DC, DISC, MC, V. **Amenities:** 2 restaurants; snack bar; 2 outdoor heated swimming pools; 2 lighted tennis courts; exercise room; Jacuzzi; water-sports equipment/rentals; bike rental; children's programs; concierge; secretarial services; 24-hr. room service; in-room massage; babysitting; dry-cleaning and laundry service; nature trails. *In room:* A/C, TV, dataport, minibar, coffeemaker, hair dryer, iron.

EXPENSIVE

Jules' Undersea Lodge ★★★ *(Finds)*   Staying here is certainly an experience of a lifetime—if you're brave enough to take the plunge. Originally built as a research lab in the 1970s, this small underwater compartment (which rests on pillars on the ocean floor) now operates as a two-room hotel. As expensive as it is unusual, Jules' is most popular with diving honeymooners. To get inside, guests swim 21 feet (6.25m) under the structure and pop up into the unit through a 4-by-6-foot "moon pool" that gurgles soothingly all night long. The 30-foot-deep (9m) underwater suite consists of two separate bedrooms that share a common living area. Room service will deliver your meals, daily newspapers, even a late-night pizza in waterproof containers at no extra charge.

51 Shoreland Dr., Key Largo, FL 33037. (℃) **305/451-2353.** Fax 305/451-4789. www.jul.com. 2 units. $250–$350 per person. Rates include breakfast and dinner as well as all equipment and unlimited scuba diving in the lagoon for certified divers. Packages available. AE, DISC, MC, V. From U.S. 1 S, at MM 103.2, turn left onto Transylvania Ave., across from the Central Plaza shopping mall. **Amenities:** Entertainment center; dining area. *In room:* A/C, phone, kitchenette.

Marriott Key Largo Bay Beach Resort ★★   While hardly quaint, this amenities-laden 17-acre complex has everything an active or resting traveler could want, including a private beach, a new European health spa, a small, nine-hole putting course, and tennis courts. All guests are also welcome to sail for free on a gambling cruise ship that anchors in international waters from 2pm until 2am daily. Rooms are decorated in a pleasant, if generic, tropical style, and most have balconies overlooking the stunning Florida Bay. The enormous suites can easily sleep a family of five, and all have large wraparound terraces and big sitting areas.

103800 Overseas Hwy. at MM 103, Key Largo, FL 33037. (*C*) **800/932-9332** or 305/453-0000. Fax 305/453-0093. www.marriottkeylargo.com. 153 units. Winter $289–$649; off-season $209–$449. AE, DC, MC, V. **Amenities:** Restaurant; snack bar; large outdoor pool; access to nearby tennis and racquetball courts; health center and spa; Jacuzzi; water-sports equipment/rentals; bike rental; children's programs; game room; concierge; business center; limited room service; in-room massage; babysitting; dry-cleaning and laundry services; nature trail. *In room:* A/C, TV, VCR on request, dataport, minibar, coffeemaker, hair dryer, iron, safe.

The Moorings ★★★ *(Finds)* Staying at The Moorings is more like staying at a secluded beach house than at a hotel. You'll never see another soul on this 18-acre resort if you choose not to. There isn't even maid service unless you request it. The romantic whitewashed units, from cozy cottages to three-bedroom houses, are spacious and modestly decorated. All have full kitchens (though there are 2 restaurants within walking distance), and most have washers and dryers. Some have CD players and VCRs; ask when you book. The real reason to come to this resort is to relax on the more than 1,000-foot beach (one of the only real beaches around). There are a hard tennis court, a few kayaks and windsurfers, but absolutely no motorized water vehicles in the waters surrounding the hotel, making it completely quiet and tranquil. There is no room service or restaurant (although Morada Bay across the street is excellent). This is a place for people who like each other a lot. Leave the kids at home unless they are extremely well behaved and not easily bored.

123 Beach Rd. near MM 81.5 on the ocean side, Islamorada, FL 33036. (*C*) **305/664-4708.** Fax 305/664-4242. www.themooringsvillage.com. 18 cottages. Winter daily $200–$250 small cottages; $475 1-bedroom house; $3,325–$7,875 weekly oceanfront house. Off-season daily $185–$225 small cottages; $375 1 bedroom house; $2,625–$6,650 weekly oceanfront house. 2-night minimum for smaller cottages; 1-week minimum for larger cottages. MC, V. **Amenities:** Large outdoor heated pool; tennis court; water-sports equipment rental. *In room:* A/C, TV, kitchen, coffeemaker, hair dryer.

MODERATE

Banana Bay Resort & Marina ★★ *(Finds)* It doesn't look like much from the sign-cluttered Overseas Highway, but when you enter the lush grounds of Banana Bay, you will realize you're in one of the most bucolic and best-run properties in the Upper Keys. Built in the early 1950s as a place for fishermen to stay during extended fishing trips, the resort is a beachfront maze of two-story buildings hidden among banyans and palms. The rooms are moderately sized, and many have private balconies where you can enjoy your complimentary coffee and newspaper every morning. Recent additions to the hotel include a recreational activity area with horseshoe pits, a bocce court, picnic areas with barbecue grills, and a giant lawn chessboard. The hotel's kitschy restaurant serves three meals a day, indoors or poolside. This resort is family friendly, but if you're looking for an adults-only resort, there's also a Banana Bay Resort in Key West ((*C*) **305/296-6925**) that doesn't allow children.

U.S. 1 at MM 49.5, Marathon, FL 33050. (*C*) **800/BANANA-1** or 305/743-3500. Fax 305/743-2670. www.bananabay.com. 60 units. Winter $125–$250 double; off-season $85–$175 double. Rates include continental breakfast. 3- and 7-night honeymoon and wedding packages available. AE, DC, DISC, MC, V. **Amenities:** Restaurant; 3 bars; pool; tennis courts; health club; Jacuzzi; water-sports rental; self-service laundromat; small beach and snorkel area; charter fishing; sailing and diving. *In room:* A/C, TV, dataport, fridge, hair dryer, iron.

Conch Key Cottages ★★ *(Finds)* Here's your chance to play castaway in the Keys. Occupying its own private microisland just off U.S. 1, Conch Key Cottages is a comfortable hideaway run by live-in owners Ron Wilson and Wayne Byrnes, who are constantly fixing and adding to their unique property. This is a place to get away from it all; the cottages aren't located close to much, except maybe one or two interesting eateries. The cabins, which were built at different times over the past 40 years, overlook their own stretch of natural, but very small, private beach and have a screened-in porch, cozy bedroom, bathroom, hammock, barbecue grill, and a two-person kayak. Request one of the two-bedroom cottages—especially if you are traveling with the family. They are the most spacious and are well designed, practically tailor-made for couples or families. On the other side of the pool are a handful of efficiency apartments (all with fully equipped kitchens) that are similarly outfitted but enjoy no beach frontage.

Near U.S. 1 at MM 62.3, Marathon, FL 33050. (C) **800/330-1577** or 305/289-1377. Fax 305/743-8207. www. conchkeycottages.com. 12 cottages. Dec 15–Sept 8 $110–$288; Sept 9–Dec 14 $74–$215. DISC, MC, V. **Amenities:** Pool; complimentary kayaks; laundry facilities. *In room:* A/C, TV, kitchen, coffeemaker, no phone.

Faro Blanco Marine Resort ✪   Spanning both sides of the Overseas High-way and all on waterfront property, this huge, two-shore marina and hotel complex offers something for every taste. Free-standing camp-style cottages with a small bedroom are the resort's least-expensive accommodations, but they are in dire need of rehabilitation. Old appliances and a musty odor make them the least-desirable units on the property. The houseboats are the best choice and value. Permanently tethered (so tightly moored, you hardly move at all, even in the roughest weather) in a tranquil marina, these white rectangular boats look like floating mobile homes and are uniformly clean, fresh, and recommendable, with four hotel rooms to each boat. They have colonial American-style furnishings, fully equipped kitchenettes, front and back porches, and water, water everywhere. The resort's condos have three bedrooms, two baths, and terraces. Finally, there are two unusual rental units located in a lighthouse on the pier. Circular staircases, unusually shaped immaculate rooms and showers, and nautical decor make it a unique place to stay, but some guests might find it claustrophobic.

1996 Overseas Hwy., U.S. 1 at MM 48.5, Marathon, FL 33050. (C) **800/759-3276** or 305/743-9018. Fax 305/ 866-5235. 123 units, 31 houseboats with 4 units each. Winter $89–$150 cottage; $109–$200 houseboat; $185 lighthouse; $267–$327 condo. Off-season $79–$119 cottage; $99–$178 houseboat; $145 lighthouse; $215–$263 condo. AE, DISC, MC, V. **Amenities:** 4 restaurants; 2 lounges; Olympic-size pool; fully equipped dive shop; barbecue and picnic areas; playground. *In room:* A/C, TV.

Holiday Isle Resort ✪   A huge resort complex encompassing five restaurants, several lounges, tiki huts, a large marina, many retail shops, and four distinct (if not distinctive) hotels, the Holiday Isle is one of the biggest resorts in the Keys. It attracts a spring-break kind of crowd year-round. Its Tiki Bar claims to have invented the rum runner drink (151-proof rum, blackberry brandy, banana liqueur, grenadine, and lime juice), and there's no reason to doubt it. Hordes of partiers are attracted to the resort's nonstop merrymaking, live music, and beachfront bars. As a result, some of the accommodations can be noisy. Rooms can be bare-bones budget to oceanfront luxury, as the broad range of prices reflects. Even the nicest rooms could use a good cleaning. El Captain and Harbor Lights, two of the least-expensive hotels on the property, are both austere. Like the other hotels here, rooms could use a thorough rehab. Howard Johnson, another Holiday Isle property, is a little farther from the action and a tad more civilized. If you plan to be here for a few days, choose an efficiency or a suite; both have kitchenettes.

U.S. 1 at MM 84, Islamorada, FL 33036. (C) **800/327-7070** or 305/664-2321. Fax 305/664-2703. www. holidayisle.com. 199 units. Winter $130–$290 double; $290–$420 suite. Off-season $110–$240 double; $240–$410 suite. AE, DISC, MC, V. **Amenities:** 5 restaurants; 12 bars; 3 outdoor heated pools; kids' pool; Jacuzzi; kids' programs; laundry facilities; water-sports equipment/rentals. *In room:* A/C, TV, fridge, hair dryer.

Kona Kai Resort & Gallery ★★   Unique to the Upper Keys, this little haven, with just 11 units, is both casual and elegant. Quaint rooms and complete suites dot the lushly landscaped 2-acre property, which boasts a large variety of native vegetation like palms, bougainvillea, and ferns, plus an impressive collection of fruit-bearing trees, such as carambola, passion fruit, banana, Key lime, guava, and coconut, which you can sample. An orchid house has over 250 beautiful flowers. Lounge chairs, hammocks, a Jacuzzi, and a compact beach are available for those who just want to relax (no phones in the rooms make relaxing imperative), while the owners will organize excursions to the Everglades, the backcountry, or wherever for the more adventurous. All the rooms are very private and simply furnished; bathroom amenities are fabulous, with lotions, soaps, and shampoos made from tropical fruits. For meals, you'll need to visit a nearby restaurant—there are three within walking distance and several more a short drive away. Smoking is not permitted in the rooms. An art gallery featuring work by American and international painters, photographers, and sculptors doubles as the property's office and lobby. Even if you are not staying here, stop in to see the artwork.

97802 Overseas Hwy. (U.S. 1 at MM 97.8), Key Largo, FL 33037. ℂ 800/365-7829 or 305/852-7200. Fax 305/852-4629. www.konakairesort.com. 11 units. Winter $196–$233 double; $257–$658 1- to 2-bedroom suite. Off-season $108–$129 double; $143–$433 1- to 2-bedroom suite. AE, DISC, MC, V. Closed Sept. Children under 16 not permitted. **Amenities:** Heated pool; tennis court; spa; Jacuzzi; water-sports equipment rental; concierge; in-room massage and facials; boat ramp/dockage. *In room:* A/C, TV, fridge, hair dryer; kitchen, VCR, CD player (suites only).

Lime Tree Bay Resort Motel   The Lime Tree Bay Resort is the only hotel in the tiny town of Layton (pop. 183). Midway between Islamorada and Marathon, the hotel is only steps from Long Key State Recreation Area. It's situated on a very pretty piece of waterfront graced with hundreds of mature palm trees and lots of other tropical foliage. Motel rooms and efficiencies have tiny bathrooms with standing showers but are clean and well maintained. The best deal is the two-bedroom bay-view cottage. The large living area with new fixtures and furnishings leads out to a large private deck where you can enjoy a view of the Gulf from your hammock. A full kitchen and two full bathrooms make it a comfortable space for six people. Fifteen efficiencies and suites have kitchenettes.

U.S. 1 at MM 68.5 in Layton, Long Key, FL 33001. ℂ 800/723-4519 or 305/664-4740. Fax 305/664-0750. www.limetreebayresort.com. 30 units. Winter $102–$235 double; off-season $79–$215 double. AE, DC, DISC, MC, V. **Amenities:** Restaurant; small outdoor pool; tennis court; Jacuzzi; water-sports equipment rental. *In room:* A/C, TV, dataport, kitchenette (in some units).

INEXPENSIVE

Bay Harbor Lodge ★   A small, simple retreat that's big on charm, the Bay Harbor Lodge is an extraordinarily welcoming place. The lodge is far from fancy, though it features new windows and paint, and the widely ranging accommodations are not created equal. The motel rooms are small and ordinary in decor, but even the least expensive is recommendable. The efficiencies are larger motel rooms with fully equipped kitchenettes. The oceanfront cottages are larger still, have full kitchens, and represent one of the best values in the Keys. The vinyl-covered furnishings and old-fashioned wallpapers won't win any design awards, but elegance isn't what the "real" Keys are about. The 1½ lush acres of grounds are planted with banana trees and have an outdoor heated pool and several small barbecue grills. A small beach is ideal for some quiet sunning and relaxation.

Guests are free to use the rowboats, paddleboats, canoes, kayaks, and snorkeling equipment. Bring your own beach towels.

97702 Overseas Hwy., U.S. 1 at MM 97.7 (off the southbound lane of U.S. 1), Key Largo, FL 33037. ✆ 800/ 385-0986 or 305/852-5695. www.thefloridakeys.com/bayharborlodge. 16 units. Winter $75–$165 double; $95–$165 cottage. Off-season $65–$95 double; $95–$105 cottage. MC, V. **Amenities:** Freshwater pool; water-sports equipment rental. *In room:* A/C, TV, fridge, coffeemaker, hair dryer, microwave.

Ragged Edge Resort ★★   This small oceanfront property's 11 units are spread out along more than half a dozen gorgeous, grassy waterfront acres. All are immaculately clean and comfortable, and most are outfitted with full kitchens and tasteful furnishings. There's no bar, restaurant, or staff to speak of, but the retreat's affable owner, Jackie Barnes, is happy to lend you bicycles or good advice on the area's offerings. A large dock attracts boaters and a good variety of local and migratory birds.

243 Treasure Harbor Rd. (near MM 86.5), Islamorada, FL 33036. ✆ 800/436-2023 or 305/852-5389. www. ragged-edge.com. 11 units. Winter $69–$189; off-season $49–$132. AE, MC, V. **Amenities:** Outdoor pool; free use of bikes; laundromat. *In room:* A/C, kitchen (most units), fridge, coffeemaker.

CAMPING

John Pennekamp Coral Reef State Park ★★   One of Florida's best parks (p. 225), Pennekamp offers 47 well-separated campsites, half of which are available by advance reservation, the rest distributed on a first-come, first-served basis. The tent sites are small but well equipped with bathrooms, hot water, and showers. Note that the local environment provides fertile breeding grounds for insects, particularly in the late summer, so bring insect repellant or you will be sorry. Two man-made beaches and a small lagoon nearby attract many large wading birds. Reservations are held until 5pm, and the park must be notified of late arrival by phone on the check-in date. Pennekamp opens at 8am and closes around sundown.

U.S. 1 at MM 102.5 (P.O. Box 487), Key Largo, FL 33037. ✆ 305/451-1202. 47 campsites. Reservations can be made in advance by calling Reserve America (✆ 800/326-3521). $24 (without electricity) to $26 (with electricity) per site. Park entry $4 per vehicle (50¢ for each additional person). Yearly permits and passes available. AE, DISC, MC, V. No pets.

Long Key State Park ★   The Upper Keys' other main state park is more secluded than its northern neighbor—and more popular. All sites are located ocean-side and surrounded by narrow rows of trees and nearby toilet and bathroom facilities. Reserve well in advance, especially in winter.

U.S. 1 at MM 67.5 (P.O. Box 776), Long Key, FL 33001. ✆ 305/664-4815. 60 oceanfront sites. $24–$26 per site for 1–4 people. $3.25 per vehicle. AE, DISC, MC, V. No pets.

WHERE TO DINE

Although not known as a culinary hot spot (though always improving), the Upper and Middle Keys do offer some excellent restaurants, most of which specialize in seafood. Often, visitors (especially those who fish) take advantage of accommodations that have kitchen facilities and cook their own meals. Some restaurants will even clean and cook your catch, for a fee.

VERY EXPENSIVE

Atlantic's Edge ★★★ SEAFOOD/REGIONAL   Ask for a table by the oceanfront window to feel really privileged at this restaurant, the most elegant in the Keys. Although the service and food are generally first rate, don't get dressed up—a sports coat for men will be fine but isn't necessary. You can choose from an innovative, varied menu, which offers several choices of fresh fish, steak, chicken, and pastas. The crab cakes, made with stone crab when in season, are the very best in the Keys; served on a warm salad of baby greens with a mild sauce of red peppers, they're the stuff cravings are made of. Other excellent dishes include a Thai-spiced fresh baby snapper and the vegetarian angel-hair pasta with mushrooms, asparagus, and peppers in a rich broth. Service can sometimes be less than efficient but is always courteous and professional.

In the Cheeca Lodge, U.S. 1 at MM 82, Islamorada. © 305/664-4651. Reservations recommended. Main courses $20–$36. AE, DC, DISC, MC, V. Daily 6–10pm.

EXPENSIVE

Barracuda Grill ★★ SEAFOOD Owned by Lance Hill and his wife, Jan (a former sous chef at Little Palm Island; see p. 243), this small, casual spot serves excellent seafood, steaks, and chops, but unfortunately, it's open only for dinner. Some of the favorite dishes are the Caicos Gold Conch and Mangrove Snapper and Mango. Try the Tipsy Olives appetizer, marinated in gin or vodka, to kick-start your meal. For fans of spicy food, try the red-hot calamari. Decorated with barracuda-themed art, the restaurant also features a well-priced American wine list with lots of California vintages.

U.S. 1 at MM 49.5 (bay side), Marathon. © 305/743-3314. Main courses $10–$26. AE, MC, V. Mon–Sat 6–10pm.

Marker 88 ★★★ SEAFOOD/REGIONAL An institution in the Upper Keys, Marker 88 has been pleasing locals and visitors for dinner since it opened in the early 1970s. Chef-owner Andre Mueller fuses tropical fruit and fish with such items as crab-meat stuffing, asparagus, tomatoes, lemons, olives, capers, and mushrooms to make the most delectable and innovative seafood dishes around. Taking full advantage of his island location, Andre offers dozens of seafood selections, including Keys lobster, Bahamas conch, Florida Bay stone crabs, Gulf Coast shrimp, and an impressive variety of fish from around the country. After you've figured out what kind of seafood to have, you can choose from a dozen styles of preparation. The Keys' standard style is meunière, which is a subtle, tasty sauce of lemon and parsley. Although everything looks tempting, don't overorder—portions are huge. The waitresses, who are pleasant enough, require a bit of patience, but the food—not to mention the spectacular Gulf views from the outdoor bar and tables—is worth it.

U.S. 1 at MM 88 (bay side), Islamorada. © 305/852-9315. Reservations suggested. Main courses $14–$33. AE, DC, DISC, MC, V. Tues–Sun 5–11pm. Closed in Sept.

Morada Bay Beach Cafe ★★ CARIBBEAN/AMERICAN This lovely bayside bistro offers super-fresh, innovative seafood as well as more basic offerings, such as chicken salads, fajitas, and hamburgers. Salads such as the Sunshine Salad are large and lavished with slices of avocado, mango, and tomato. When in season, delicious raw oysters are imported from Long Island. Fish dishes are always fresh and served in a number of styles; I like mine jerked with a peppery coating and nearly black finish. If you can't decide, share a few items from the tapas menu: jumbo shrimp cocktails, fried calamari, conch fritters, smoked fish dip, or a charcuterie of sausage and ham on country bread. Located at the same address is Pierre's Restaurant (© 305/664-3225), a New-World cuisine fine-dining restaurant that's a bit pricier (main courses $24–$37), but worth a splurge.

U.S. 1 at MM 81.6, Islamorada. © 305/664-0604. Reservations recommended for large groups. Main courses $17–$28. AE, DISC, MC, V. Daily 11:30am–10pm.

The Truth About Keys Cuisine

There are few world-class chefs in the Florida Keys, but that's not to say the food isn't great. Restaurants here serve very fresh fish and a few local specialties—most notably conch fritters and chowder, Key lime pie, and stone crab claws and lobster when they're in season.

Although a commercial net-fishing ban has diminished the stock of once-abundant fish in these parts, even the humblest of restaurants can be counted on to take full advantage of the gastronomic treasures of their own backyard. The Keys have everything a cook could want: the Atlantic and the Gulf of Mexico for impeccably fresh seafood; a tropical climate for year-round farm-stand produce (including great tomatoes, beans, berries, and citrus fruit), and a freshwater swamp for rustic delicacies such as alligator, frog legs, and hearts of palm.

Conch fritters and chowder are mainstays on most tourist-oriented menus. Because the queen conch was listed as an endangered species by the U.S. government in 1985, however, the conch in your dish was most likely shipped fresh-frozen from the Bahamas or the Caribbean.

Key lime pie consists of the juice of tiny yellow Key limes (a fruit unique to South Florida), along with condensed milk, all in a graham-cracker crust. Experts debate whether the true Key lime pie should have a whipped cream or a meringue topping, but all agree that the filling should be yellow, *never* green.

Another unique offering, the **Florida lobster,** is an entirely different species from the more common Maine variety and has a sweeter meat. It's also known as the "Spiney" lobster because of all the bumps on its shell. You'll see only the tails on the menu because the Florida lobster has no claws.

Stone crabs are even better—succulent, sweet, tender, and very meaty. They've been written about and talked about by kings, presidents, and poets. Although you'll find them on nearly every menu in season (Oct–May), consider buying a few pounds of jumbos at the fish store to take to the beach in a cooler. Don't forget to ask to have them cracked for you, and get a cup of creamy mustard sauce for dipping. Topped off with a cold bottle of champagne, there is no better meal. (You'll be glad to know that after their claws are harvested, the crabs grow new ones, thus ensuring a long-lasting supply of these unique delicacies.)

MODERATE

Green Turtle Inn ★★ SEAFOOD   The Green Turtle Inn was established in 1947 as a place where anglers and travelers to and from Key West could stop for local delicacies made from sea turtles harvested in local waters. It has become the quintessential Keys eatery, with a friendly, local flavor and delicious and *different* fare, such as turtle steaks, soups, and chowders. Alligator steak is also popular and, yes, it does taste like chicken. Campy house pianist Tina Martin has become somewhat of a local celebrity, but it's really the Turtle Chowder for which the Inn has become best known. The restaurant also has a cannery so you can take some of the chowder to your friends, who won't believe how good it is until they taste it for themselves.

U.S. 1 at MM 81.5, Islamorada. ✆ **305/664-9031.** Main courses $13.50–$21.95. AE, DISC, MC, V. Noon–10pm Tues–Sun.

Lazy Days Oceanfront Bar and Seafood Grill ✹ SEAFOOD/AMERICAN Opened in 1992, the Lazy Days quickly became one of the most popular restaurants around, mostly because of its large portions and lively atmosphere. Dining on the oceanfront outdoor veranda is highly recommended. Meals are pricier than the casual dining room would suggest, but the food is good enough and the menu varied. Steamed clams with garlic and bell peppers make a tempting appetizer. The menu focuses on—what else?—seafood, but you can also find good pasta dishes such as linguine with littleneck clams. Most main courses come with baked potato, vegetables, a tossed salad, and French bread, making appetizers redundant.

U.S. 1 at MM 79.9, Islamorada. ✆ **305/664-5256.** Main courses $11–$29.95. AE, DISC, MC, V. Wed–Sun 11:30am–10pm.

Lorelei Restaurant and Cabana Bar ✹✹ SEAFOOD/BAR FOOD   Don't resist the siren call of the enormous, sparkling roadside mermaid—you won't be dashed onto the rocks. This big old fish house and bar is a great place for a snack, a meal, or a beer. Inside, a good-value menu focuses mainly on seafood. When in season, lobsters are the way to go. For $20, you can get a good-size tail—at least a 1 pounder—prepared any way you like. Other fare includes the standard clam chowder, fried shrimp, and doughy conch fritters. Salads and soups are hearty and satisfying. For those tired of fish, the menu also offers a few beef selections. The outside bar has live music every evening, and you can order snacks and light meals from a limited menu that is satisfying and well priced.

U.S. 1 at MM 82, Islamorada. ✆ **305/664-4656.** Reservations not usually required. Main courses $12–$24. AE, DC, DISC, MC, V. Daily 7am–10:30pm. Outside bar serves breakfast 7–11am; lunch/appetizer menu 11am–9pm. Bar closes at midnight.

INEXPENSIVE

Calypso's ✹ SEAFOOD   The awning still bears the name of the former restaurant, Demar's, but the food here is all Todd Lollis's, an inspired young chef who looks like he might be more comfortable at a Grateful Dead concert than in a kitchen, but who turns out inventive seafood dishes in a casual and rustic waterside setting. If it's available, try the butter-pecan sauce over whatever fish is freshest. Don't miss the white-wine sangria, full of tangy oranges and limes and topped with a dash of cinnamon. The prices are surprisingly reasonable, but the service can be a little more laid-back than you're used to. The toughest part is finding the place. From the south, turn right at the blinking yellow lights near MM 99.5 to Ocean Bay Drive and then turn right. Look for the blue vinyl-sided building on the left.

1 Seagate Blvd. (near MM 99.5), Key Largo. ✆ **305/451-0600.** Main courses $9–$18. MC, V. Wed–Mon 11:30am–10pm; Fri–Sat until 11pm.

Islamorada Fish Company ✹✹ SEAFOOD   The original Islamorada Fish Company has been selling seafood out of its roadside shack since 1948. It's still the best place to pick up a cooler of stone crab claws in season (mid-Oct to Apr). Also great are the fried-fish sandwiches, served with melted American cheese, fried onions, and coleslaw. A few hundred yards up the road (at MM 81.6) is Islamorada Fish Company Restaurant & Bakery, the newer establishment, which looks like an average diner but has a selection of fantastic seafood and pastas. It's also the place for breakfast. Locals gather for politics and gossip as well as delicious grits, oatmeal, omelets, and homemade pastries.

U.S. 1 at MM 81.5 (up the street from Cheeca Lodge), Islamorada. ✆ **800/258-2559** or 305/664-9271. www. islamoradafishco.com. Reservations not accepted. Main courses $8–$27; appetizers $4–$7. DISC, MC, V. Sun–Thurs 11am–9pm; Fri–Sat 11am–10pm.

Time Out Barbecue ★★ BARBECUE   This barbecue joint serves up hot and hearty old-fashioned barbecue that is among the best around. According to management, the secret is in the slow cooking—more than 10 hours for the melt-in-your-mouth soft pork sandwich. Topped off with delicious, not-too-creamy coleslaw and sweet baked beans, any of the many offerings are worth a stop. You can grab a seat at the picnic table on the grassy lawn next to the Trading Post.

U.S. 1 at MM 81.5 (ocean side). ✆ **305/664-8911.** Sandwiches $4.25–$6; rib and chicken platters to share $7–$15. MC, V. Daily 11am–10pm.

THE UPPER & MIDDLE KEYS AFTER DARK

Nightlife in the Upper Keys tends to start before the sun goes down, often at noon, since most people—visitors and locals alike—are on vacation. Also, many anglers and sports-minded folk go to bed early.

Hog Heaven opened in the early 1990s, the joint venture of some young locals tired of tourist traps. Located at MM 85.3, just off the main road on the ocean side in Islamorada (✆ **305/664-9669**), it's a welcome respite from the neon-colored cocktail circuit. This whitewashed biker bar offers a waterside view and diversions that include big-screen TVs and video games. The food isn't bad, either. The atmosphere is cliquish since most patrons are regulars, so start up a game of pool or skeet to break the ice. Open 11am to 4am daily.

No trip to the Keys is complete without a stop at the **Tiki Bar at the Holiday Isle Resort,** U.S. 1 at MM 84, Islamorada (✆ **800/327-7070** or 305/664-2321). Hundreds of revelers visit this ocean-side spot for drinks and dancing at any time of day, but the live rock music starts at 8:30pm. (See "Where to Stay," above.) The thatched-roof Tiki Bar draws a high-energy but laid-back mix of thirsty people, all in pursuit of a good time. In the afternoon and early evening (when everyone is either sunburned, drunk, or just happy to be dancing to live reggae), head for **Kokomo's,** just next door. Kokomo's often closes at 7:30pm on weekends (5:30pm on weekdays), so get there early. For information, call the Holiday Isle Resort.

Locals and tourists mingle at the outdoor cabana bar at **Lorelei** (see "Where to Dine," above). Most evenings after 5pm, you'll find local bands playing on a thatched-roof stage—mainly rock and roll, reggae, and sometimes blues.

Woody's Saloon and Restaurant, on U.S. 1 at MM 82, Islamorada (✆ **305/664-4335**), is a lively, wacky, loud, gritty, raunchy, local legend of a place serving up mediocre pizzas and live bands almost every night. The house band, Big Dick and the Extenders, showcases a 300-pound Native American who does a lewd, rude, and crude routine of jokes and songs starting at 9pm, Tuesday through Sunday. He is a legend. By the way, don't think you're lucky if you are offered the front table: It's the target seat for Big Dick's haranguing. Avoid the lame karaoke performance on Sunday and Monday evenings. There's a small cover charge most nights. Drink specials, contests, and the legendary Big Dick keep this place packed until 4am almost every night. *Note:* This place is not for the faint of heart (or tact!), but more for those of the Howard Stern school of nightlife.

For a more subdued atmosphere, try the handsome stained-glass and mahogany-wood bar and club at **Zane Grey's** (on the second floor of World Wide Sportsman at MM 81.5). Outside, enjoy a view of the calm waters of the bay; inside, soak up the history of some real longtime anglers. It is open from 11am to 11pm, and later on weekends. Call to find out who is playing on weekends (© **305/664-4244**), when there is live entertainment and no cover charge.

2 The Lower Keys: Big Pine Key to Coppitt Key

128 miles (206km) SW of Miami

Unlike their neighbors to the north and south, the Lower Keys (including Big Pine, Sugarloaf, and Summerland) are devoid of rowdy spring-break crowds, boast few T-shirt and trinket shops, and have almost no late-night bars. What they do offer are the very best opportunities to enjoy the vast natural resources on land and water that make the area so rich. Stay overnight in the Lower Keys, rent a boat, and explore the reefs—it might be the most memorable part of your trip.

ESSENTIALS

GETTING THERE   See "Essentials," for the Upper and Middle Keys (p. 221) and continue south on U.S. 1. The Lower Keys start at the end of the Seven-Mile Bridge. There are also airports in Marathon and Key West.

VISITOR INFORMATION   The **Big Pine and Lower Keys Chamber of Commerce,** ocean side of U.S. 1 at MM 31 (P.O. Box 430511), Big Pine Key, FL 33043 (© **800/872-3722** or 305/872-2411; fax 305/872-0752; www.lower keyschamber.com), is open Monday through Friday from 9am to 5pm and Saturday from 9am to 3pm. The pleasant staff will help with anything a traveler may need. Call, write, or stop in for a comprehensive, detailed information packet.

WHAT TO SEE & DO

Once the centerpiece (these days, it's Big Pine Key) of the Lower Keys and still a great asset is **Bahia Honda State Park** ⭐, U.S. 1 at MM 37.5, Big Pine Key (© **305/872-2353**), which, even after the violent storms of 1998, has one of the most beautiful coastlines in South Florida. Bahia Honda (pronounced *Bah*-ya) is a great place for hiking, bird-watching, swimming, snorkeling, and fishing. The 524-acre park encompasses a wide variety of ecosystems, including coastal mangroves, beach dunes, and tropical hammocks. There are miles of trails packed with unusual plants and animals and a small, white beach. Shaded seaside picnic areas are fitted with tables and grills. Although the beach is never wider than 5 feet (1.5m) even at low tide, this is the Lower Keys' best beach area.

True to its name (Spanish for "deep bay"), the park has relatively deep waters close to shore, and they are perfect for snorkeling and diving. Easy offshore snorkeling here gives even novices a chance to lie suspended in warm water and simply observe diverse marine life passing by. Or else head to the stunning reefs at Looe Key, where the coral and fish are more vibrant than anywhere else in the United States. Snorkeling trips go from the Bahia Honda concessions to Looe Key National Marine Sanctuary (4 miles [6.5km] offshore). They depart twice daily March through September and cost $25.95 for adults, $20.95 for youths 6 to 14, and are free for children 5 and under. Call © **305/872-3210** for a schedule.

Admission to the park is $4 per vehicle (plus 50¢ per person), $1.50 per pedestrian or bicyclist, free for children 5 and under. If you are alone in a car, you'll pay only $2.50. Open daily from 8am to sunset.

The most famous residents of the Lower Keys are the tiny Key deer. Of the estimated 300 existing in the world, two-thirds live on Big Pine Key's **National Key Deer Refuge** ⟨★⟩. To get your bearings, stop by the rangers' office at the Winn-Dixie Shopping Plaza near MM 30.5 off U.S. 1. They'll give you an informative brochure and map of the area. The refuge is open Monday through Friday from 8am to 5pm.

If the office is closed, head out to the Blue Hole, a former rock quarry now filled with the fresh water that's vital to the deer's survival. To get there, turn right at Big Pine Key's only traffic light onto Key Deer Boulevard (take the left fork immediately after the turn) and continue 1½ miles (2.5km) to the observation-site parking lot, on your left. The half-mile **Watson Hammock Trail,** about a third of a mile past the Blue Hole, is the refuge's only marked footpath. Try coming out to the footpath in the early morning or late evening to catch a glimpse of these gentle, dog-size deer. There is an observation deck there from which you can watch and photograph the protected species. They are more active in cool hours and in cooler times of the year. Refuge lands are open daily from half an hour before sunrise to half an hour after sunset. Don't be surprised to see a lazy alligator warming itself in the sun, particularly in outlying areas around the Blue Hole. If you do see a gator, do not go near it, do not touch it, and do not provoke it. Keep your distance; and if you must get a photo, use a zoom lens. Also, whatever you do, do not feed the deer—it will threaten their survival. Call the **park office** (② **305/872-2239**) to find out about the infrequent free tours of the refuge, scheduled throughout the year.

OUTDOOR PURSUITS

BICYCLING   If you have your own bike, or your lodging offers a rental (many do), the Lower Keys are a great place to get off busy U.S. 1 to explore the beautiful back roads. On Big Pine Key, cruise along Key Deer Boulevard (at MM 30). Those with fat tires can ride into the National Key Deer Refuge.

BIRD-WATCHING   Bring your birding books. A stopping point for migratory birds on the Eastern Flyway, the Lower Keys are populated with many West Indian bird species, especially during spring and fall. The small, vegetated islands of the Keys are the only nesting sites in the United States for the great

---

Failed Ingenuity

The only man-made attraction in the Lower Keys is the **Sugarloaf Bat Tower,** off U.S. 1 at MM 17 (next to Sugarloaf Airport on the bay side). In a vain effort to battle the ubiquitous troublesome mosquitoes in the Lower Keys, developer Clyde Perkey built this odd structure to lure bug-eating bats. Despite his alluring design and a pungent bat aphrodisiac, his guests never showed. Since 1929, this wooden, flat-topped, 45-foot-high pyramid has stood empty and deserted, except for the occasional tourist who stops to wonder what it is. There is no sign or marker to commemorate this odd remnant of ingenuity. It's worth a 5-minute detour to see it. To get there, turn right at the Sugarloaf Airport sign and then right again onto the dirt road that begins just before the airport gate; the tower is about 100 yards (10m) ahead.

white heron and the white-crowned pigeon. They're also some of the very few breeding places for the reddish egret, the roseate spoonbill, the mangrove cuckoo, and the black-whiskered vireo. Look for them on Bahia Honda Key and the many uninhabited islands nearby.

BOATING Dozens of shops rent powerboats for fishing and reef exploring. Most also rent tackle, sell bait, and have charter captains available. **Bud Boats,** at the Old Wooden Bridge Fishing Camp and Marina, MM 30 in Big Pine Key (© 305/872-9165), has a wide selection of well-maintained boats. Depending on the size, rentals cost between $70 and $250 for a day, between $50 and $130 for a half day. Another good option is **Jaybird's Powerboats,** U.S. 1 at MM 33, Big Pine Key (© 305/872-8500). They rent for full days only. Prices start at $155 for a 19-footer.

CANOEING & KAYAKING The Overseas Highway (U.S. 1) touches on only a few dozen of the many hundreds of islands that make up the Keys. To really see the Lower Keys, rent a kayak or canoe—perfect for these shallow waters. **Reflections Kayak Nature Tours,** operating out of Parmer's Resort, on U.S. 1 at MM 28.5, Little Torch Key (© 305/872-2896), offers fully outfitted backcountry wildlife tours, either on your own or with an expert. The expert, Mike Wedeking, a former U.S. Forest Service guide, keeps up an engaging discussion describing the area's fish, sponges, coral, osprey, hawks, eagles, alligators, raccoons, and deer. The 3-hour tours cost $49 per person and include spring water, fresh fruit, granola bars, and use of binoculars. Bring a towel and sea sandals or sneakers.

FISHING A day spent fishing, either in the shallow backcountry or in the deep sea, is a great way to ensure yourself a fresh fish dinner, or you can release your catch and just appreciate the challenge. Whichever you choose, **Larry Threlkeld's Strike Zone Charters,** U.S. 1 at MM 29.5, Big Pine Key (© 305/ 872-9863), is the charter service to call. Prices for fishing boats start at $450 for a half day and $595 for a full day. If you have enough anglers to share the price, it isn't too steep. They may also be able to match you with other interested visitors.

HIKING You can hike throughout the flat, marshy Keys, on both marked trails and meandering coastlines. The best places to trek through nature are **Bahia Honda State Park** at MM 29.5 and **National Key Deer Refuge** at MM 30 (for more information on both, see "What to See & Do," above). Bahia Honda Park has a free brochure describing an excellent self-guided tour along the Silver Palm Nature Trail. You'll traverse hammocks, mangroves, and sand dunes and cross a lagoon. The walk (which is less than a mile) explores a great cross-section of the natural habitat in the Lower Keys and can be done in under half an hour.

SNORKELING & DIVING Snorkelers and divers should not miss the Keys' most dramatic reefs at the **Looe Key National Marine Sanctuary.** Here, you'll see more than 150 varieties of hard and soft coral—some, centuries old—as well as every type of tropical fish, including gold and blue parrotfish, moray eels, barracudas, French angels, and tarpon. **Looe Key Dive Center,** U.S. 1 at MM 27.5, Ramrod Key (© 305/872-2215), offers a mind-blowing 5-hour tour aboard a 45-foot catamaran with two shallow 1-hour dives for snorkelers and scuba divers. Snorkelers pay $22.50, and divers with their own equipment pay $35; on Wednesdays and Saturdays you can do a fascinating dive to the *Adolphus Busch Sr.,* a shipwreck sunk off Looe Key in 100 feet (30m) of water, for $40. Good-quality rentals are available. (See "What to See & Do," above, for other diving options.)

SHOPPING

Certainly not known for great shopping, the Lower Keys do happen to be home to many talented visual artists, particularly those who specialize in depicting their natural surroundings. The **Artists in Paradise Gallery,** on Big Pine Key in the Winn-Dixie Shopping Plaza, near MM 30.5, 1 block north of U.S. 1 at the traffic light (© **305/872-1828**), displays a changing selection of watercolors, oils, photos, and sculptures. This cooperative gallery displays the work of more than a dozen artists who share the task of watching the store. Hours are usually daily from 10am to 6pm.

WHERE TO STAY

There are a number of cheap, fairly unappealing fish shacks along the highway for those who want bare-bones accommodations. So far, there are no national hotel chains in the Lower Keys. For information on lodging in cabins or trailers at local campgrounds, see "Camping," below.

VERY EXPENSIVE

Little Palm Island ✦✦✦   This exclusive island escape—host to presidents and royalty—is not just a place to stay while in the Lower Keys; it is a destination all its own. Built on a private 5-acre island, it's accessible only by boat. Guests stay in thatched-roof duplexes amid lush foliage and flowering tropical plants. Many villas have ocean views and private sun decks with rope hammocks. Inside, the romantic suites have all the comforts and conveniences of a luxurious contemporary beach cottage, but without telephones, TVs, or alarm clocks. As if its location weren't idyllic enough, a new full-service spa recently opened on the island. Note that on the breezeless south side of the island, mosquitoes can be a problem, even in the winter. (So bring spray and lightweight, long-sleeved clothing.) Known for its innovative and pricey food, Little Palm also hosts visitors just for dinner or lunch. If you are staying on the island, opt for the full American plan, which includes three meals a day for about $140 per person. If you pay a la carte, you could spend that much just on dinner. At these prices, Little Palm appeals to those who aren't keeping track.

Launch is at the ocean side of U.S. 1 at MM 28.5, Little Torch Key, FL 33042. © **800/343-8567** or 305/872-2524. Fax 305/872-4843. www.littlepalmisland.com. 28 bungalows, 2 deluxe suites. Winter $795–$1,695 per couple. Off-season $695–$1,595 per couple. Rates include transportation to and from the island and unlimited (nonmotorized) water sports. Meal plans include 2 meals daily for $125 per person per day, 3 meals at $140 per person. AE, DC, DISC, MC, V. No children under 16. **Amenities:** Restaurant; bar; 2 pools (1 outdoor with small waterfall, 1 indoor); health club and spa; extensive water-sports equipment/rental; concierge; courtesy van from Key West or Marathon airport; ferry service to and from the mainland; limited room service; in-room massage; dry-cleaning and laundry services; jogging trail. *In room:* A/C, dataport, minibar, coffeemaker, hair dryer, Jacuzzi.

MODERATE

Deer Run Bed and Breakfast ✦✦ *(Finds)*   Located directly on the beach, Sue Abbott's small, homey, smoke-free B&B is a real find. One upstairs and two downstairs guest rooms are comfortably furnished with queen-size beds, good closets, and touch-sensitive lamps. Rattan and 1970s-style chairs and couches furnish the living room, along with 13 birds and three cats. Breakfast, which is served on a pretty, fenced-in porch, is cooked to order by Sue herself. The wooded area around the property is full of Key deer, which are often spotted on the beach as well. A hot tub overlooking the ocean is especially nice. Ask to use one of the bikes to explore nearby nature trails.

Long Beach Dr. (P.O. Box 431), Big Pine Key, FL 33043. ℭ 305/872-2015. Fax 305/872-2842. deerrunbb@aol. com. 3 units. Winter from $165 double; off-season from $95 double. Rates include full American breakfast. No credit cards. From U.S. 1 S, turn left at the Big Pine Fishing Lodge (MM 33); continue for about 2 miles (3km). No children under 16. **Amenities:** Jacuzzi; free use of bikes. *In room:* A/C, TV.

INEXPENSIVE

Parmer's Resort ★★ Parmer's, a fixture here for more than 20 years, is well known for its charming hospitality and helpful staff. This downscale resort offers modest but comfortable cottages, each of them unique. Some are waterfront, many have kitchenettes, and others are just a bedroom. Room 26, aka Wahoo, a one-bedroom efficiency, is especially nice, with a small sitting area that faces the water. Room 6, a small efficiency, has a kitchenette and an especially large bathroom. The rooms have been recently updated—and are consistently very clean. Many can be combined to accommodate large families. The hotel's waterfront location almost makes up for the fact that you must pay extra for maid service.

Barry Ave. (P.O. Box 430665), near MM 28.5, Little Torch Key, FL 33043. ℭ 305/872-2157. Fax 305/872-2014. www.parmersresort.com. 45 units. Winter $75–$220 double; from $105 efficiency. Off-season $55–$85 double; $75–$150 efficiency. Rates include continental breakfast. AE, DISC, MC, V. From U.S. 1, turn right onto Barry Ave. Resort is a half-mile down on the right. **Amenities:** Heated pool; bike rental; coin-op washers and dryers; boat ramp. *In room:* A/C, TV.

CAMPING

Bahia Honda State Park ★★★ (ℭ 305/872-2353; www.abfla.com/parks/BahiaHonda/bahiahonda.html) offers some of the best camping in the Keys. It is as loaded with facilities and activities as it is with campers. However, don't be discouraged by its popularity—this park encompasses more than 500 acres of land, 80 campsites spread throughout three areas, and six spacious and comfortable cabin units (fitting six people each) that were reconstructed between 2000 and 2001. Cabins hold up to eight guests and come complete with linens, kitchenettes, and utensils as well as a wraparound terrace, barbecue pit, and rocking chairs.

For one to four people, camping here costs about $25 per site without electricity and $26 with electricity. Depending on the season, cabin prices change: Prices range from $50 to $110. Additional people (over four) cost $6 each. MasterCard and Visa are accepted.

Another excellent value can be found at the **KOA Sugarloaf Key Resort** ★★, near MM 20. This ocean-side facility has 200 fully equipped sites, with water, electricity, and sewer, which rent for about $70 a night (no-hook-up sites cost about $38). Or pitch a tent on the 5 acres of lush waterfront property. This site is especially nice because of its private beaches and access to diving, snorkeling, and boating; and its grounds are nice and well maintained. The resort also rents travel trailers. The 22-foot Dutchman sleeps six and is equipped with eating and cooking utensils. It costs about $100 a day. More luxurious trailers go for $160 a day. All major credit cards are accepted. For details, write them at P.O. Box 420469, Summerland Key, FL 33042 (ℭ 800/562-7731 or 305/745-3549; fax 305/745-9889; www.koa.com).

WHERE TO DINE

There aren't many fine-dining options in the Lower Keys, with the exception of the Dining Room at Little Palm Island Resort, MM 285, Little Torch Key

(© 305/872-2551), in which you'll be wowed with gourmet French Caribbean fare that looks like a meal but eats like a vacation. You need to take a ferry to this chichi private resort island, on which you can indulge in the exquisite ocean-side restaurant, even if you're not staying over. If you don't have the chance to get there, try the following, worth a stop for those passing through.

MODERATE

Mangrove Mama's Restaurant SEAFOOD/CARIBBEAN   As the dedicated locals who come daily for happy hour will tell you, this is a true Lower Keys institution and a dive (the restaurant is a shack that used to have a gas pump as well as a grill) in the best sense of the word. Guests share the property with some miniature horses (out back) and stray cats. A handful of simple tables, inside and out, are shaded by banana trees and palm fronds. Fish is the menu's mainstay, although soups, salads, sandwiches, and omelets are also good. Grilled teriyaki chicken and club sandwiches are tasty alternatives to fish, as are meatless chef's salads and spicy barbecued baby-back ribs.

U.S. 1 at MM 20, Sugarloaf Key. © 305/745-3030. Main courses $10–$20; lunch $6–$9; brunch $5–$7. MC, V. Daily 11:30am–10pm (open at 11am in season).

Monte's SEAFOOD   Certainly nobody goes to this restaurant/fish market for its atmosphere: Plastic place settings rest on plastic-covered picnic-style tables in a screen-enclosed dining patio. But Monte's doesn't need great atmosphere, since it has survived for more than 20 years on its very good and incredibly fresh food. The day's catch may include shark, tuna, lobsters, stone crabs, or shrimp.

U.S. 1 at MM 25, Summerland Key. © 305/745-3731. Main courses $13–$17; lunch $6–$10. No credit cards. Mon–Sat 9am–10pm; Sun 10am–9pm.

INEXPENSIVE

Coco's Kitchen ★ CUBAN/AMERICAN   This tiny storefront has been dishing out black beans, rice, and shredded beef to fans of Cuban cuisine for more than 10 years. The owners, who are actually from Nicaragua, cook not only superior Cuban food but also some local specialties, Italian food, and Caribbean food. Specialties include fried shrimp, whole fried yellowtail, and Cuban-style roast pork (available only on Sat). The best bet is the daily special, which may be roasted pork or fresh grouper, served with rice and beans or salad and crispy fries. Top off the huge, cheap meal with a rich caramel-soaked flan.

283 Key Deer Blvd. (in the Winn-Dixie Shopping Center), Big Pine Key. © 305/872-4495. Main courses $6–$14.79; breakfast $2–$5. MC, V. Mon–Sat 7am–7:30pm. Turn right at the traffic light near MM 30.5. Stay in the left lane.

No Name Pub PUB FOOD/PIZZA   This funky old bar out in the boonies serves snacks and sandwiches until 11pm on most nights, and drinks until midnight. Pizzas are tasty—thick-crusted and super-cheesy. Try one topped with local shrimp, or consider a bowl of chili with all the fixings—hearty and cheap. Everything is served on paper plates. Locals hang out at the rustic bar, one of the Florida Keys' oldest, drinking beer and listening to a jukebox heavy with 1980s selections. The decor, if you can call it that, is basic—the walls and ceilings are plastered with thousands of autographed dollar bills.

¼ mile (.5km) south of No Name Bridge on N. Watson Blvd., Big Pine Key. © 305/872-9115. Pizzas $6–$18; subs $5. MC, V. 11am–11pm. Turn right at Big Pine's only traffic light (near MM 30.5) onto Key Deer Blvd. Turn right on Watson Blvd. At stop sign, turn left. Look for a small wooden sign on the left marking the spot.

THE LOWER KEYS AFTER DARK

Although the mellow islands of the lower Keys aren't exactly known for wild nightlife, there are some friendly bars and restaurants where locals and tourists gather to hang out and drink.

One of the most scenic is **Sandbar** (© **305/872-9989**), a wide-open breezy wooden house built on slender stilts and overlooking a wide channel on Barry Avenue (near MM 28.5). It attracts an odd mix of bikers and blue-hairs daily from 11am to 10pm and is a great place to overhear local gossip and colorful metaphors. Pool tables are the main attraction, but there's also live music some nights. The drinks are reasonably priced and the food isn't too bad, either. For another fun bar scene, see **No Name Pub,** listed above in "Where to Dine."

3 Key West ★★★

159 miles (256km) SW of Miami

There are two schools of thought on Key West—one is that it has become way too commercial, and the other is that it's still a place where one can go and not worry about being prim, proper, or even well groomed. I think it's a bizarre fusion of both—a fascinating look at small-town America in which people truly live by the (off)beat of their own drum, albeit one with a Gap and Banana Republic thrown in to bring you back to some reality. The locals, or "conchs" (pronounced *conks*), and the developers here have been at odds for years. This once low-key island has been thoroughly commercialized—there's a Hard Rock Cafe smack in the middle of Duval Street and thousands of cruise-ship passengers descend on Mallory Square each day. It's definitely not the seedy town Hemingway and his cronies once called their own. Or is it?

Laid-back Key West still exists, but it's now found in different places: the backyard of a popular guesthouse, for example, or an art gallery, a secret garden, or the hip hangouts of Bahama Village. Fortunately there are plenty of these, and Key West's greatest historic charm is found just off the beaten path. Don't be afraid to explore these residential areas, as conchs are notoriously friendly. In fact, exploring the side streets always seems to yield a new discovery of some sort. Of course, there are always the calm waters of the Atlantic and the Gulf of Mexico all around.

The heart of town offers party people a good time—that is, if your idea of a good time is the smell of stale beer, loud music, and hardly-shy revelers. Here, you'll find good restaurants, fun bars, live music, rickshaw rides, and lots of shopping. Key West is still very gay-centric, except during the time of spring break. Same-sex couples walking hand in hand are the norm here, and if you're not open minded and would prefer to avoid this scene, just look for the ubiquitous rainbow flag hanging outside of gay establishments and you'll know what to expect. For the most part, however, the scene is extremely mixed and colorful. If partying isn't your thing, then avoid Duval Street (the Bourbon St. of South Florida) at all costs. Instead, take in the scenery at a dockside bar or ocean-side Jacuzzi. Whatever you do, don't bother with a watch or tie—this is the home of the perennial vacation.

ESSENTIALS

GETTING THERE For directions by car, see "Essentials," for the Upper and Middle Keys (p. 221) and continue south on U.S. 1. When entering Key West, stay in the far-right lane onto North Roosevelt Boulevard, which becomes Truman Avenue in Old Town. Continue for a few blocks and you will find

Abaco Inn **41**
Alonzo's Oyster Bar **6**
Angelina Guest House **56**
Anthony's Cafe **42**
Antonia's **37**
Atlantic Shores Motel **46**
Audubon House & Tropical Gardens **51**
Bagatelle **31**
Bahama Mama's Kitchen **58**
Banana Cafe **43**
Big Ruby's **36**
Blue Heaven **58**
Cafe des Artistes **24**
Café Marquesa **22**
Captain Tony's Saloon **49**
Chelsea House **19**
Clinton Street Market **47**
The Crystal Room **42**
Cuba, Cuba! **40**
Curry Mansion Inn **33**
The Deli **23**
Diva's **28**
Durty Harry's **32**
801 Bourbon Bar **39**
El Siboney Restaurant **16**
Epoch **37**
Ernest Hemingway Home and Museum **59**
Fast Buck Freddie's **35**
Fausto's Food Palace **1, 28**
Flaming Maggie's **11**
The Florida Key Guesthouse **2**
Fort Zachary Beach **57**
The Grand **4**
Haitian Art Co. **3**
Half Buck Freddie's **18**
Harry S. Truman Little White House
    Museum **54**
Helio Gallery Store **12**
Hello Gorgeous **58**
Higgs Beach **5**
Hilton Key West Resort and Marina **30**
Island City House Hotel **10**

Jimmy Buffett's Margaritaville Cafe **35**
Key Lime Pie Co. **18, 49**
Key West Aloe **27**
Key West Aquarium **50**
Key West Cemetery **14**
Key West Cigar Factory **48**
Key West International Hostel
    & Seashell Motel **20**
Key West Island Bookstore **38**
Key West Lighthouse Museum **59**
Key West Museum of Art and History **53**
Key West Shipwreck Historeum **50**
La Pensione **15**
La Terraza de Marti (La-Te-Da) **42**
La Trattoria **35**
Louie's Backyard **25**
Mangia, Mangia **13**
Mangoes **28**
Marquesa Hotel **22**
Maskerville **58**
Mel Fisher Maritime Heritage Museum **52**
Number One Saloon **39**
Oasis **11**
Oldest House/Wrecker's Museum **34**
One Duval **30**
Pandemonium **40**
Pearl's Rainbow **44**
Pepe's **9**
Peppers of Key West **21**
Pier House Resort and Caribbean Spa **29**
PT's Late Night **16**
Reworx **40**
Sloppy Joe's **32**
Southernmost Point Guest House **45**
Tea by the Sea **46**
Turtle Kraals Wildlife Grill **7**
Wax **34**
Weatherstation Inn **55**
Westwinds Inn **8**
Wyndham Casa Marina Resort **17**
Wyndham Reach Resort **26**

yourself on **Duval Street** ✦, in the heart of the city. If you stay to the left, you'll also reach the city center after passing the airport and the remnants of historic houseboat row, where a motley collection of boats once made up one of Key West's most interesting neighborhoods.

Several regional airlines fly nonstop (about 55 min.) from Miami to Key West; fares are about $120 to $300 round-trip. **American Eagle, Continental, Delta,** and **US Airways Express** land at **Key West International Airport,** South Roosevelt Boulevard (© **305/296-5439**), on the southeastern corner of the island.

Greyhound (© **800/231-2222;** www.greyhound.com) has buses leaving Miami for Key West every day for about $30 to $32 one-way and $57 to $60 round-trip. Seats fill up in season, so come early. The ride takes about 4½ hours.

GETTING AROUND With limited parking, narrow streets, and congested traffic, driving in Old Town Key West is more of a pain than a convenience. Unless you're staying in one of the more remote accommodations, consider trading in the car for a bicycle. The island is small and as flat as a board, which makes it easy to negotiate, especially away from the crowded downtown area. Many tourists also choose to cruise by moped, an option that can make navigating the streets risky, especially since there are no helmet laws in Key West. So be careful and spend the extra few bucks to rent a helmet; hundreds of visitors are seriously injured each year.

Rates for simple one-speed cruisers start at about $8 per day (from $40 per week). Mopeds start at about $12 for 2 hours, $25 per day, and $100 per week. The best shops include **The Bicycle Center** at 523 Truman Ave. (© **305/294-4556**); the **Moped Hospital,** 601 Truman Ave. (© **305/296-3344**); and **Tropical Bicycles & Scooter Rentals** at 1300 Duval St. (© **305/294-8136**). **The Bike Shop,** 1110 Truman Ave. (© **305/294-1073**), rents mountain bikes for $12 per day ($60 per week). Cruisers go for $8 per day and $40 per week. A $150 deposit is required for cruisers, $250 for mountain bikes.

PARKING Parking in Key West's Old Town is particularly limited, but there is a well-placed **municipal parking lot** at Simonton and Angela Streets, just behind the firehouse and police station. If you have brought a car, you may want to stash it here while you enjoy the very walkable downtown part of Key West.

VISITOR INFORMATION The **Florida Keys and Key West Visitors Bureau,** P.O. Box 1147, Key West, FL 33041 (© **800/FLA-KEYS;** www.key west.com), offers a free vacation kit packed with visitor information. The **Key West Chamber of Commerce,** 402 Wall St., Key West, FL 33040 (© **800/527-8539** or 305/294-2587; www.keywestchamber.com), also offers both general and specialized information. The lobby is open daily from 8:30am to 6pm; phones are answered from 8am to 8pm. The **Key West Visitor Center** is the area's best for information on accommodations, goings-on, and restaurants; the number is © **800/LAST-KEY.** It's open weekdays from 8am to 5:30pm and weekends from 8:30am to 5pm. Gay travelers will want to call the **Key West Business Guild** (© **305/294-4603**), which represents more than 50 guest-houses and B&Bs in town, as well as many other gay-owned businesses (ask for its color brochure) or **Good Times Travel** (© **305/294-0980**), which will set up lodging and package tours on the island.

ORIENTATION A mere 2-by-4-mile island, Key West is simple to navigate, even though there is no real order to the arrangement of streets and avenues. As you enter town on U.S. 1 (also called Roosevelt Blvd.), you will see most of the moderately priced chain hotels and fast-food restaurants. The better restaurants, shops, and outfitters are crammed onto Duval Street, the main thoroughfare of Key West's Old Town. Surrounding streets contain many inns and lodges in picturesque Victorian/Bahamian homes. On the southern side of the island is the coral beach area and some of the larger resort hotels.

The area called Bahama Village has only recently become known to tourists. With several newly opened, trendy restaurants and guesthouses, this hippie-ish neighborhood, complete with street-roaming chickens and cats, is the most urban and rough you'll find in the Keys. You might see a few seedy drug dealings on street corners, but it's nothing to be overly concerned with: It looks worse than it is and resident business owners tend to keep a vigilant eye on the neighborhood. The area is actually quite funky and should be a welcome diversion from the Duvalian mainstream.

SEEING THE SIGHTS

Before shelling out big bucks for any of the dozens of worthwhile attractions in Key West, I recommend getting an overview on either of the two comprehensive island tours, **The Conch Tour Train** or the **Old Town Trolley** (see "Organized Tours," below). There are simply too many attractions and historic houses to list. I've highlighted my favorites below but encourage you to seek out others.

Audubon House & Tropical Gardens ★★ This well-preserved home, dating from the early 19th century, stands as a prime example of early Key West architecture. Named after renowned painter and bird expert John James Audubon, who was said to have visited the house in 1832, the graceful two-story home is a peaceful retreat from the bustle of Old Town. Included in the price of admission is a self-guided audio tour that lasts about half an hour and spotlights rare Audubon prints, gorgeous antiques, historical photos, and lush tropical gardens. With voices of several characters from the house's past, the tour never gets boring—although it is at times a bit hokey. Even if you don't want to spend the time and money to explore the grounds and home, check out the impressive gift shop, which sells a variety of fine mementos at reasonable prices.

205 Whitehead St. (between Greene and Caroline sts.). ⓒ **305/294-2116.** Admission $8.50 adults, $3.50 children 6–12. Daily 9:30am–5pm (last admission at 4:30pm). Discounts for students and AAA and AARP members.

Ernest Hemingway Home and Museum ★ Hemingway's particularly handsome stone Spanish Colonial house, built in 1851, was one of the first on the island to be fitted with indoor plumbing and a built-in fireplace, and it contains the first swimming pool built on Key West. The author owned the home from 1931 until his death in 1961, and he lived there with about 50 cats, whose descendants, including the famed six-toed cats, still roam the premises. It was during those years that the Nobel Prize winner wrote some of his most famous works, including *For Whom the Bell Tolls, A Farewell to Arms,* and *The Snows of Kilimanjaro.* Fans may want to take the optional half-hour tour, where you'll see rooms of his house with glass cabinets that store certain artifacts, books, and pieces of mail addressed to him. It's interesting (to an extent) and included in the price of admission. If you don't take the tour or have no literary interest in Hemingway, the admission price is really a waste of money. If you're feline phobic, beware: There are cats everywhere.

907 Whitehead St. (between Truman Ave. and Olivia St.). ⓒ **305/294-1136.** Fax 305/294-2755. www.hemingwayhome.com. Admission $9 adults, $5 children. Daily 9am–5pm. Limited parking.

Harry S Truman Little White House Museum ★★ President Harry Truman used to refer to the White House as the "Great White Jail." On temporary leave from the big house, Truman discovered the serenity of Key West and made his escape to what became known as the Little White House, which is open to the public for touring. The house is fully restored, and the exhibits document Truman's time in the Keys. Tours are every 15 minutes and last between 45 and 50 minutes. For fans of all things Oval Office–related, there's a presidential gift shop on the premises.

111 Front St. ℂ305/294-9911. www.trumanlittlewhitehouse.com. Admission $10 adults, $5 children under 12. Daily 9am–4:30pm.

Key West Cemetery ★★★ *Finds* This funky, picturesque cemetery is the epitome of the quirky Key West image, as irreverent as it is humorous. Many tombs are stacked several high, condominium style—the rocky soil made digging 6 feet under nearly impossible for early settlers. Headstones reflect residents' lighthearted attitudes toward life and death. I TOLD YOU I WAS SICK is one of the more famous epitaphs, as is the tongue-in-cheek widow's inscription AT LEAST I KNOW WHERE HE'S SLEEPING TONIGHT. There's a fun 1½-hour tour that's full of history and local lore, but if you want to save some money and just read the amusing inscriptions, it's free to walk through.

Entrance at the corner of Margaret and Angela sts. ℂ 305/294-WALK for tour reservations. Free admission. Tour $18 adults, $10 kids 12 and under. Daily dawn to dusk.

East Martello Museum and Gallery Adjacent to the airport, the East Martello Museum is located in a Civil War–era brick fort that itself is worth a visit. The museum contains a bizarre variety of exhibits that collectively do a thorough job of interpreting the city's intriguing past. Historical artifacts include model ships, a deep-sea diver's wooden air pump, a crude raft from a Cuban "boat lift," a supposedly haunted doll, a Key West–style children's playhouse from 1918, and a horse-drawn hearse. Exhibits illustrate the Keys' history of salvaging, sponging, and cigar making. After seeing the galleries (should take about 45 minutes to an hour), climb a steep spiral staircase to the top of a lookout tower for good views over the island and ocean. A member of the Key West Art and Historical Society, East Martello has two cousins, the Key West Museum of Art and History, 281 Front St. (ℂ **305/295-6616**) and the Key West Lighthouse Museum, 938 Whitehead St. (ℂ **305/294-0012**).

3501 S. Roosevelt Blvd. ℂ **305/296-3913**. Admission $6 adults, $4 seniors, $3 children 8–12, free for children 7 and under. Daily 9:30am–5pm (last admission is at 4pm).

Key West Aquarium ★★ *Kids* The oldest attraction on the island, the Key West Aquarium is a modest but fascinating exhibit. A long hallway of eye-level displays showcases dozens of varieties of fish and crustaceans. You'll see delicate sea horses swaying in the backlit tanks. Kids can touch sea cucumbers and sea anemones in a shallow tank in the entryway. If you can, catch one of the free guided tours, where you can witness the dramatic feeding frenzy of the sharks, tarpon, barracudas, stingrays, and turtles. Expect to spend about an hour to an hour and a half here.

1 Whitehead St. (at Mallory Sq.). ℂ **305/296-2051.** www.keywestaquarium.com. Admission $9 adults, $4.50 children 4–12, free for children under 4. Tickets are good for 2 consecutive days. Look for discount coupons at local hotels, at Duval St. kiosks, and from trolley and train tours. Daily 10am–6pm; tours at 11am and 1, 3, and 4pm.

Key West Lighthouse Museum When the Key West Lighthouse opened in 1848, many locals mourned. Its bright warning to ships signaled the end of a profitable era for wreckers, the pirate salvagers who looted reef-stricken ships. The story of this and other Keys lighthouses is illustrated in a small museum that was formerly the keeper's quarters. When radar and sonar made the lighthouse obsolete, it was opened to visitors as a tourist attraction. It's worth mustering the energy to climb the 88 claustrophobic steps to the top, where you'll be rewarded with magnificent panoramic views of Key West and the ocean.

938 Whitehead St. ℂ **305/294-0012.** Admission $8 adults, $4 children 7–12, free for children 6 and under. Daily 9:30am–5pm (last admission at 4:30pm).

Key West's Shipwreck Historeum You'll see more impressive artifacts at nearby Mel Fisher's museum, but for the morbidly curious, shipwrecks should rank right up there with car wrecks. For those of you who can't help but look, this museum is the place to be for everything you ever wanted to know about shipwrecks and more. See movies, artifacts, and a real-life wrecker, who will be more than happy to indulge your curiosity about the wrecking industry that

---

🌀 Going, Going, Gone: Where to Catch the Famous Key West Sunset

A tradition in Key West, the Sunset Celebration can be relaxing or overwhelming, depending on your vantage point. If you're in town, you must check out this ritual at least once. Every evening, locals and visitors gather at the docks behind Mallory Square (at the westernmost end of Whitehead St.) to celebrate the day gone by. Secure a spot on the docks early to experience the carnival of portrait artists, acrobats, food vendors, animal acts, and other performers trading on the island's Bohemian image. But the carnival atmosphere isn't for everyone: In season, the crowd can be overwhelming, especially when the cruise ships are in port. Also, hold onto your bags and wallets as the tight crowds make Mallory Square at sunset prime pick-pocketing territory.

A more refined choice is the Hilton's **Sunset Deck** (ℂ **305/294-4000**), a luxurious second-floor bar on Front Street, right next door to Mallory Square. From the civilized calm of a casual bar, you can look down on the mayhem with a drink in hand.

Also near the Mallory madness is the **Ocean Key Resort's** bar. This long open-air pier serves up drinks and decent bar food against a dramatic pink- and yellow-streaked sky. It's located at the very tip of Duval Street (ℂ **800/328-9815** or **305/296-7701**).

For the very best potent cocktails and great bar food on an outside patio or enclosed lounge, try **Pier House Resort and Caribbean Spa's Havana Docks** at 1 Duval St. (ℂ **305/296-4600**). There's usually live music and a lively gathering of visitors enjoying this island's bounty. The bar is right on the water and is a prime sunset-viewing spot.

preoccupied the early pioneers of Key West. Depending on your level of interest, you can expect to spend up to 2 hours here.

1 Whitehead St. (at Mallory Sq.). ℭ **305/292-8990.** Fax 305/292-5536. Admission $8 adults, $4 children 4–12. Shows daily every half-hour 9:45am–4:45pm.

Mel Fisher Maritime Heritage Museum ✦✦✦   This museum honors local hero Mel Fisher, whose death in 1998 was mourned throughout South Florida, and who, along with a crew of other salvagers, found a multimillion-dollar treasure trove in 1985 aboard the wreck of the Spanish galleon *Nuestra Señora de Atocha*. If you're into diving, pirates, and sunken treasures, check out this small, informative museum, full of doubloons, pieces of eight, emeralds, and solid-gold bars. A 1700 English merchant slave ship, the only tangible evidence of the transatlantic slave trade, is on view on the museum's second floor. A dated but informative film provides a good background for Fisher's incredible story.

200 Greene St. ℭ **305/294-2633.** Admission $7.50 adults, $3.75 children 6–12, free for children 5 and under. Daily 9:30am–5pm. Take U.S. 1 to Whitehead St. and turn left on Greene.

Memorial Sculpture Garden ✦   Installed in 1997, this impressive sculpture garden contains a large monument to the wreckers who made Key West rich more than a century ago. Also on display are 36 bronze busts of the island's most colorful leaders and characters: There's Harry Truman, Henry Flagler, and, of course, Ernest Hemingway, all mounted on elegant coral columns.

Front St., near Mallory Sq. Free admission.

Oldest House/Wrecker's Museum ✦   Dating from 1829, this old New England Bahama House has survived pirates, hurricanes, fires, warfare, and economic ups and downs. The 1½-story home was designed by a ship's carpenter and incorporates many features from maritime architecture, including portholes and a ship's hatch designed for ventilation before the advent of air-conditioning. Especially interesting is the detached kitchen building outfitted with a brick "beehive" oven and vintage cooking utensils. Although not a must-see on the Key West tour, history and architecture buffs will appreciate the finely preserved details and the glimpse of a slower, easier time in the island's life.

322 Duval St. ℭ **305/294-9502.** Admission $5 adults, $1 children 6–12, free for children 5 and under. Daily 10am–4pm.

Moments **A Great Escape**

Many people complain that Key West's quirky, quaint panache has been lost to the vulture of capitalism, evidenced by the glut of T-shirt shops and tacky bars. But that's not entirely so. For a quiet respite, visit the Key West Botanical Gardens, a little-known slice of serenity tucked between the Aqueduct Authority plant and the Key West Golf Course. The 11-acre gardens—maintained by volunteers and funded by donations—contain the last hardwood hammock in Key West, plus a colorful representation of wildflowers, butterflies, and birds. A genetically cloned tree is the latest addition to the gardens. Although the gardens received a terrible blow from the storms of 1998, the calm remains within them. Located at Botanical Garden Way and College Road, Stock Island. Free admission. Open daily from 8am to sunset. Follow College Road; then turn right just past Bayshore Manor.

Literary Key West

Counting Ernest Hemingway and Tennessee Williams among your denizens would give any city the right to call itself a literary mecca. But over the years, tiny Key West has been home—or at least home away from home—to dozens of literary types who are drawn to some combination of its gentle pace, tropical atmosphere, and lighthearted mood (not to mention its lingering reputation for an oft-ribald lifestyle). Writers have long known that more than a few muses prowl the tree-laden streets of Key West.

Robert Frost first visited Key West in 1934 and wintered here for the remainder of his life. In the early 20th century, writers like John Dewey, Archibald MacLeish, John Dos Passos, Wallace Stevens, and S.J. Perelman were drawn to the island.

Even as Key West boomed and busted and boomed again, and despite the island's growing popularity with world travelers, writers continued to move to Key West or visit with such regularity that they were deemed honorary "conchs." Novelists Phil Caputo, Tom McGuane, Jim Harrison, John Hershey, Alison Lurie, and Robert Stone were among these.

Of course, one of Key West's favorite sons also earned a spot in the annals of local literary history. Famous for his good-time, tropical-laced music, Jimmy Buffett was also a surprisingly well-received novelist in the 1990s. Although Buffett now makes the infinitely ritzier Palm Beach his Florida home, his presence is still felt in virtually every corner of Key West.

But it is Nobel Prize winner and avid outdoorsman Ernest Hemingway who is most identified with Key West. Much of the island has changed since he lived here from 1931 to 1961. Even the famous Sloppy Joe's bar, which Hemingway frequented mostly from 1933 to 1937, has changed locations (reportedly without closing—customers supposedly picked up their drinks and whatever else from the bar they could carry and brought it all down the block to the new location, and service resumed with barely a blink!). Fortunately, The Ernest Hemingway Home and Museum (p. 249) has been lovingly preserved. But perhaps to get the best feel for what Hemingway loved most about Key West, visit the docks at Garrison Bight. It is from there that Hemingway and his many famous (and infamous) friends and contemporaries departed for Caribbean ports of call and for sport upon the sea.

Key West pays homage to its literary legacy with the annual January Key West Literary Seminar. For information, call © **888/293-9291** or visit www.keywestliteraryseminar.org.

ORGANIZED TOURS

BY TROLLEY-BUS & TRAM   Yes, it's more than a bit hokey to sit on this 60-foot tram of yellow cars, but it's worth it—at least once. The city's whole story is packed into a neat, 90-minute package on the **Conch Tour Train,** which covers the island and all its rich, raunchy history. Operating since 1958, the trains are open-air, which can make the ride uncomfortable in bad weather. The "train's" engine is a propane-powered Jeep disguised as a locomotive. Tours depart from both Mallory Square and the Welcome Center, near where U.S. 1 becomes North Roosevelt Boulevard, on the less-developed side of the island. For more information, contact the **Conch** at © **305/294-5161**. The cost is $18 for adults, $9 for children 4 to 12, and free for children 3 and under. Daily departures are every half-hour from 9am to 4:30pm.

The **Old Town Trolley** is the choice in bad weather or if you are staying at one of the many hotels on its route. Humorous drivers maintain a running commentary as the enclosed tram loops around the island's streets past all the major sights. Trolleys depart from Mallory Square and other points around the island, including many area hotels. For details, call © **305/296-6688.** Tours are $18 for adults, $9 for children 4 to 12, and free for children 3 and under. Departures are daily every half-hour (though not always on the half-hour) from 9am to 4:45pm. Whichever you choose, these historic trivia-packed tours are well worth the price of admission.

BY AIR   Proclaimed by the mayor as "the official air force of the Conch Republic," **Island Airplane Tours,** at Key West Airport, 3469 S. Roosevelt Blvd. (© **305/294-8687**), offers windy rides in its open-cockpit 1940 Waco biplanes that take you over the reefs and around the islands. Thrill seekers—and only they—will also enjoy a spin in the company's S2-B aerobatics airplane, which does loops, rolls, and sideways figure-eights. Company owner Fred Cabanas was "decorated" in 1991, after he spotted a Cuban airman defecting to the United States in a Russian-built MIG fighter. Sightseeing flights cost $50 to $200, depending on the duration.

BY BOAT   The Pride of Key West, *Fireball,* at Zero Duval St. (© **305/ 296-6293;** fax 305/294-8704), is a 58-foot glass-bottomed catamaran that goes on both day (noon and 2 and 4pm) coral-reef tours and evening sunset cruises. Reef trips cost $25 per person; sunset cruises (4:30pm) are $30 per person and include snacks, sodas, and a glass of champagne. Kids sail for half price.

Schooner *Western Union* (© **305/292-9830;** www.schoonerwesternunion. **com**) was built in 1939 and served as a cable-repair vessel until it was designated the flagship of the city of Key West and began day, sunset, and charter sailings. Sunset sailings are especially memorable and include entertainment, cocktails, and a cannon fire. Prices vary.

OTHER TOURS   For a lively look at Key West, try a 2-hour tour of the island's five **most famous pubs.** It starts daily at 2:30pm, lasts 1½ hours, costs $21, and includes four drinks. Another fun tour is the 1-mile (1.5km), 90-minute **nightly ghost tour,** leaving at 8pm from the Holiday Inn La Concha, 430 Duval St. Cost is $18 for adults and $10 for children under 12. This spooky and interesting tour gives participants insight into many old island legends. The Key West Tour Association offers both tours. Finally, there's a cemetery tour (p. 250), which leaves daily at 10:30am (© **305/294-WALK**). It's creepy, spooky, and altogether kooky, as it approaches death with a sense of humor.

OUTDOOR PURSUITS

BICYCLING & MOPEDING   A popular mode of transportation for locals and visitors, bikes and mopeds are available at many rental outlets in the city (p. 248). Escape the hectic downtown scene and explore the island's scenic side streets by heading away from Duval Street toward South Roosevelt Boulevard and the beachside enclaves along the way.

Parrotheads on Parade

For Jimmy Buffett fans, or Parrotheads as they're also known, there's a fabulous tour that shouldn't be missed. **Trails of Margaritaville** (© **305/ 292-2040**) is an amusing 90-minute walking tour providing fans with an officially sanctioned peek at the stamping grounds of Buffett's carefree days in Key West back in the 1970s. Decked out in full Parrothead regalia—Hawaiian shirts and parrot hats—the informative and often hilarious guides lead you past the hangouts and other highpoints of Buffett's Key West, spinning yarns about the musician and Key West in general. The tour departs daily at 4pm from **Captain Tony's Saloon** (428 Greene St.), where Buffett used to hang out and perform, and ends at, you guessed it, Margaritaville Cafe on Duval Street. Tour tickets are $18 for adults, $15 for locals with ID, and $10 for children. Bring cash or traveler's checks; no credit cards accepted. Reservations are required at least 2 days in advance.

BEACHES   Unlike the rest of the Keys, you'll actually find a few small beaches here, although they don't compare with the state's wide natural wonders up the coast: A narrow, rocky beach is typical of the Key's beaches. Here are your options: **Smathers Beach,** off South Roosevelt Boulevard west of the airport; **Higgs Beach,** along Atlantic Boulevard between White Street and Reynolds Road; and **Fort Zachary Beach,** located off the western end of Southard Boulevard.

A magnet for partying teenagers, **Smathers Beach** is Key West's largest and most overpopulated beach. Despite the number of rowdy teens, the beach is actually quite clean and it looks lovely since its renovation in the spring of 2000. If you go early enough in the morning, you may notice some people sleeping on the beach from the night before.

Higgs Beach is a favorite among Key West's gay crowds, but what many people don't know is that beneath the sand is an unmarked cemetery of African slaves who died while waiting for freedom. Higgs has a playground and tennis courts and is near the minute Rest Beach, which is actually hidden by the White Street Pier.

Although there is an entrance fee ($3.75 per car, plus more for each passenger), I recommend the beach at **Fort Zachary,** since it also includes a great historical fort, a Civil War museum, and a large picnic area with tables, barbecue grills, bathrooms, and showers. Plus, large trees scattered across 87 acres provide shade for those who are reluctant to bake in the sun. Hurricane George damaged the vulnerable point in 1998, but replanting of native vegetation has made it even better than before.

DIVING   One of the area's largest scuba schools, **Dive Key West Inc.,** 3128 N. Roosevelt Blvd. (© **800/426-0707** or 305/296-3823; fax 305/296-0609; www.divekeywest.com), offers instruction on all levels and its dive boats take participants to scuba and snorkel sites on nearby reefs.

Wreck dives and night dives are two of the special offerings of **Lost Reef Adventures,** 261 Margaret St. (© **800/952-2749** or 305/296-9737). Regularly scheduled runs and private charters can be arranged. Phone for departure information.

Also see **Mosquito Coast Outfitters,** under "Kayaking," below.

FISHING   As any angler will tell you, there's no fishing like Keys fishing. Key West has it all: bonefish, tarpon, dolphin, tuna, grouper, cobia, and more. Sharks, too.

Step aboard a small exposed skiff for an incredibly diverse day of fishing. In the morning, you can head offshore for sailfish or dolphin (the fish, not the mammal), and then by afternoon, get closer to land for a shot at tarpon, permit, grouper, or snapper. Here in Key West, you can probably pick up more cobia— one of the best fighting and eating fish around—than anywhere else in the world. For a real fight, ask your skipper to go for the tarpon—the greatest fighting fish there is, famous for its dramatic "tail walk" on the water after it's hooked. Shark fishing is also popular.

You'll find plenty of competition among the charter-fishing boats in and around Mallory Square. You can negotiate a good deal at **Charter Boat Row,** 1801 N. Roosevelt Ave. (across from the Shell station), home to more than 30 charter-fishing and party boats. Just show up to arrange your outing, or call **Garrison Bite Marina** (✆ 305/ 292-8167) for details.

Tips   Reel Deals

When looking for the best deals on fishing excursions, know that the bookers from the kiosks in town generally take 20% of a captain's fee in addition to an extra monthly fee. You can usually save yourself money by booking directly with a captain or going straight to one of the docks.

The advantage of the smaller, more expensive charter boats is that you can call the shots. They'll take you where you want to go, to fish for what you want to catch. These "light tackles" are also easier to maneuver, which means you can go to backcountry spots for tarpon and bonefish, as well as out to the open ocean for tuna and dolphin. You'll really be able to feel the fish, and you'll get some good fights. Larger boats, for up to six or seven people, are cheaper and are best for kingfish, billfish, and sailfish. Consider Captain Vinnie Argiro's **Heavy Hitters Charters** (✆ 305/745-6665) if you want a light-tackle experience. For a larger boat, try Captain Henry Otto's 44-foot **Sunday,** docked at the Hyatt in Key West (✆ 305/294-7052).

The huge commercial party boats are more for sightseeing than serious angling, though you can get lucky and get a few bites at one of the fishing holes. One especially good deal is the **Gulfstream III** (✆ 305/296-8494), an all-day charter that goes out daily from 9:30am to 4pm. You'll pay $35, plus $3 for a rod and reel. It's $25 for kids under 12. This 65-foot party boat usually has at least 30 other anglers. Bring your own cooler or buy snacks on the boat. Beer and wine are allowed.

Serious anglers should consider the light-tackle boats that leave from **Oceanside Marina** (✆ 305/294-4676) on Stock Island, at 5950 Peninsula Ave., 1½ miles (2.5km) off U.S. 1. It's a 20-minute drive from Old Town on the Atlantic side. There are more than 30 light-tackle guides, which range from flatbed, backcountry skiffs to 28-foot open boats. There are also a few larger charters and a party boat that goes to the Dry Tortugas. Call for details.

For a light-tackle outing with a very colorful Key West flair, call **Captain Bruce Cronin** at ✆ 305/294-4929 or **Captain Kenny Harris** at ✆ 305/ 294-8843, two of the more famous (and pricey) captains working these docks for over 20 years. You'll pay from $550 for a full day, usually about 8am to 4pm, and from $400 for half a day.

GOLF   A relative newcomer in terms of local recreation, golf is gaining in popularity here as it is in many visitor destinations. The area's only public golf club is **Key West Golf Club** (© **305/294-5232**), an 18-hole course located at the entrance to the island of Key West at MM 4.5 (turn onto College Rd. to the course entrance). Designed by Rees Jones, the course has plenty of mangroves and water hazards on its 6,526 yards. It's open to the public and has a new pro shop. Call ahead for tee-time reservations. $140 per player, including cart.

KAYAKING   **Mosquito Coast Outfitters,** housed in a woodsy wine bar at 1017 Duval St. (© **305/294-7178**), operates a first-rate kayaking and snorkeling tour every day as long as the weather is mild. The tours depart at 9am sharp (and return around 3pm) and cost $45 per person. Included in the price are snacks, soft drinks, and a guided tour of the mangrove-studded islands of Sugar Key or Geiger Key just north of Key West. The tour is primarily for kayaking, but you will have the opportunity to get in the water for snorkeling, if you're interested.

SHOPPING

You'll find all kinds of unique gifts and souvenirs in Key West, from coconut postcards to Key lime pies. On Duval Street, T-shirt shops outnumber almost any other business. If you must get a wearable memento, be careful of unscrupulous salespeople. Despite efforts to curtail the practice, many shops have been known to rip off unwitting shoppers. It pays to check the prices and the exchange rate before signing any sales slips. You are entitled to a written estimate of any T-shirt work before you pay for it.

At Mallory Square is the **Clinton Street Market,** an overly air-conditioned mall of kiosks and stalls designed for the many cruise-ship passengers who never venture beyond this super-commercial zone. Amid the dreck are some delicious coffee and candy shops and some high-priced hats and shoes. There's also a free and clean restroom.

Once the main industry of Key West, cigar making is enjoying renewed success at the handful of factories that survived the slow years. Stroll through "**Cigar Alley**" (while on Green St., go 2 blocks west and you'll hit Cigar Alley, also known as Pirate's Alley), where you will find *viejitos* (little old men) rolling fat stogies just as they used to do in their homeland across the Florida Straits. Stop at the **Key West Cigar Factory,** at 308 Front St. (© **305/294-3470**), for an excellent selection of imported and locally rolled smokes, including the

---

(**Fun Fact**   **Conch If You Love Key West**

Ever wonder how Key West got the nickname The Conch Republic? In 1982, the U.S. Border Patrol set up a roadblock on U.S. 1 to search for illegal aliens and drugs. This maneuver effectively slowed passage from the Keys to the mainland and damaged the economy (albeit temporarily). In response, Key West mayor Dennis Wardlow collaborated with five businessmen and established the so-called Conch Republic, declaring Key West's independence from—and war on—the U.S. The roadblock was removed, but the moniker stuck.

famous El Hemingway. Remember, buying or selling Cuban-made cigars is illegal. Shops advertising "Cuban Cigars" are usually referring to domestic cigars made from tobacco grown from seeds that were brought from Cuba decades ago. To be fair, though, many premium cigars today are grown from Cuban seed tobacco—only it is grown in Latin America and the Caribbean, not Cuba.

If you are looking for local or Caribbean art, you will find nearly a dozen galleries and shops clustered on Duval Street between Catherine and Fleming Streets. You'll also find some excellent shops scattered on the side streets. One worth seeking out is the **Haitian Art Co.,** 600 Frances St. (© **305/296-8932**), where you can browse through room upon room of original paintings from well-known and obscure Haitian artists in a range of prices from a few dollars to a few thousand. Also, check out **Cuba, Cuba!** at 814 Duval St. (© **305/ 295-9442**), where you'll find paintings, sculpture, and photos by Cuban artists as well as books and art from the island.

A favorite stop in the Keys is the deliciously fragrant **Key West Aloe** at 524 Front St., between Simonton and Duval Streets (© **305/294-5592**). Since 1971, this shop has been selling a simple line of bath products, including lotions, shampoos, and soothing balms for those who want a reminder of the tropical breezes once they're back home. At the main shop (open until 8pm), you can find great gift baskets, tropical perfumes, and candies and cookies, too. In addition to frangipani, vanilla, and hibiscus scents, sample Key West for Men, a unique and alluringly musky bestseller.

For foodies, the **Key Lime Pie Co.** (© **305/294-6567**) is so popular for its pies, cookies, and pretty much anything you can think of made with Key lime (candles, soaps, lotions), that there are two on the tiny island. One is at 701 Caroline St. and the other is at 424 Greene St. From sweet to spicy, **Peppers of Key West** (© **305/295-9333**) at 602 Greene St. is a hot-sauce lover's heaven, with hundreds of variations of sauce, from brutally spicy to mild. Grab a seat at the tasting bar and be prepared to let your taste buds sizzle.

Literature and music buffs will appreciate the many bookshops and record stores on the island. **Key West Island Bookstore** (© **305/294-2904**) at 513 Fleming St. carries new, used, and rare books and specializes in fiction by residents of the Keys, including Hemingway, Tennessee Williams, Shel Silverstein, Ann Beattie, Richard Wilbur, and John Hersey. **Flaming Maggie's** (© **305/ 294-3931**) at 830 Fleming St. carries a wide selection of gay books. Both shops are open daily.

One of the area's newer and funkier shops is the combination museum and gift shop called **Reworx,** just behind the quirky gift gallery **Pandemonium** and the mosaic car at 825 Duval St. (© **305/294-0351**). (Actually, this is Pande-monium's number, but the owners are friends. For Reworx, ask for Valerie.) Mammoth functional art made from salvaged metal parts is on display, and smaller works from recycled material are on sale. Admission to the adjacent museum of industrial art from recycled items is $7 for adults, $5 for children aged 5 to 12, and well worth it.

Also worth checking out in the newly revitalized Bahama Village section of town are the shops along Petronia Street between Thomas and Whitehead Streets. Especially interesting is **Maskerville** (© **305/293-6937**), which sells a variety of feather-laden artwork from masks to lampshades. Just next door is **Hello Gorgeous,** at 315 Petronia St. (© **305/294-1770**), which carries unique clothing, shoes, and jewelry for women and impersonators (the name comes from one of Barbra Streisand's more memorable lines).

Off the beaten track at 814 Fleming St. (© **305/294-7901**) is the **Helio Gallery Store,** featuring locally made crafts and fine art.

For anything else, from bed linens to candlesticks to clothing, go to downtown's oldest and most renowned department store, **Fast Buck Freddie's,** at 500 Duval St. (© **305/294-2007**). For the same merchandise at reduced prices, try **Half Buck Freddie's** ✲, 726 Caroline St. (© **305/294-2007**), where you can shop for out-of-season bargains and "rejects" from the main store.

WHERE TO STAY

You'll find a wide variety of places to stay in Key West, from resorts with all the amenities to seaside motels, quaint bed-and-breakfasts, and clothing-optional guesthouses. Unless you're in town during Key West's most popular holidays—Fantasy Fest (around Halloween), where Mardi Gras meets South Florida for the NC-17 set, Hemingway Days (in July), where Papa is seemingly and eerily alive and well, and Christmas and New Year's—or for a big fishing tournament (many are held from Oct–Dec) or boat-racing tourney, you can almost always find a place to stay at the last minute. However, you may want to book early, especially in winter, when prime properties fill up and many require 2- or 3-night minimum stays. Prices at these times are also extremely high. Finding a decent room for under $100 a night is a real trick.

Another suggestion, and my recommendation, is to call **Vacation Key West** (© **800/595-5397** or 305/295-9500; www.vacationkw.com), which is a wholesaler that offers discounts of 20% to 30% and is skilled at finding last-minute deals. They represent mostly larger hotels and motels but can also place visitors in guesthouses. The phones are answered weekdays from 9am to 6pm and Saturday from 11am to 2pm. The **Key West Innkeepers Association,** P.O. Box 6172, Key West, FL 33041 (© **800/492-1911** or 305/292-3600), can also help find lodging in any price range from its dozens of members and affiliates.

Gay travelers will want to call the **Key West Business Guild** (© **305/294-4603**), which represents more than 50 guesthouses and B&Bs in town, as well as many other gay-owned businesses. Be advised that most gay guesthouses have a clothing-optional policy. One of the most elegant and popular ones is **Big Ruby's** (© **800/477-7829** or 305/296-2323; rates start at $145 for a double during peak season and $85 during off season) at 409 Applerouth Lane (a little alley just off Duval St.). A low cluster of buildings surrounds a lushly landscaped courtyard where a hearty breakfast is served each morning and wine is poured at dusk. The mostly male guests hang out by a good-sized pool, tanning in the buff. Also popular is **Oasis** at 823 Fleming St. (© **305/296-2131;** rates are $169–$229 in winter and $109–$169 in summer), which is super-clean and friendly, with a central location and a 14-seat hot tub.

Another luxurious property is **The Florida Key Guesthouse** at 412 Frances St. (© **305/296-4719;** rates are $225 in season and $125 during the off season), which is more romantic and traditionally decorated and welcomes many lesbian travelers as well. *Out and About* gave it a five-star rating. For women only, **Pearl's Rainbow,** 525 United St. (© **800/74-WOMYN** or 305/292-1450), is a large, fairly well-maintained guesthouse with lots of privacy and amenities, including two pools and two hot tubs. Rates in season range from $109 to $229.

VERY EXPENSIVE

Hilton Key West Resort and Marina ✪✪   Completed in fall 1996, this Hilton, which saw a light room renovation in 2001, is a truly luxurious addition to downtown's hotel scene, situated at the very end of Duval Street in the middle of all of Old Town's action. The sparkling rooms are large and well appointed, with all the modern conveniences. Choose a suite in the main building if you want a large Jacuzzi in your living room. Otherwise, the marina building has great views. The secluded beach is great for an escape from the Duval Street frenzy. Flagler's, the elegant indoor dining room, offers ample breakfasts and a huge Sunday brunch.

Hilton's gorgeous **Sunset Key Guest Cottages** ★★★, with whitewashed interiors, picture windows, and fabulous views, are located 100 yards offshore on Sunset Key and are accessible only by private launch. Check in at the Hilton and take a 10-minute cruise to the island, where there are no cars, only a gourmet grocery, restaurant, bar, and free-form tropical pool with whirlpool jets. Sunset guests also have access to all water sports at the Hilton. Cottages are equipped with full kitchens, high-tech entertainment centers, and one, two, or three massive bedrooms. For true luxe when staying in a cottage, consider hiring a private chef for a meal or two.

245 Front St. (at the end of Duval St.), Key West, FL 33040. © 800/221-2424 or 305/294-4000. Fax 305/294-4086. www.keywestresort.hilton.com. 215 units. Winter $299–$525 double; $375–$800 suite. Off-season $195–$425 double; $300–$800 suite. 37 Sunset Key Cottages, up to 5 people: Winter $575–$1,825; off-season $325–$1,095. Private chef: $75 per person plus additional chef/hotel fees, tax, and gratuities. AE, DC, DISC, MC, V. Self parking $7, valet parking $10. **Amenities:** 2 restaurants; pool bar; outdoor heated pool; health club; Jacuzzi; water-sports equipment/rental; bike rental; game room; concierge; business center; limited room service; in-room massage; dry-cleaning service; self-service laundry; full-service marina. *In room:* A/C, TV, dataport, minibar, coffeemaker, hair dryer, iron.

Pier House Resort and Caribbean Spa ★★   Pier House is one of the area's best resort choices, offering luxurious rooms, top-notch service, and a full-service spa. If you're looking for something a bit more intimate than the Wyndham Reach, Pier House is an ideal choice. Its location—at the foot of Duval Street and just steps from Mallory Docks—is the envy of every hotel on the island. Set back from the busy street, on a short strip of beach, this hotel is a welcome oasis of calm. The accommodations here vary tremendously, from relatively simple business-style rooms to romantic guest quarters complete with integrated stereo systems and whirlpool tubs. Their best waterfront suites and rooms have recently been renovated. Although every accommodation has either a balcony or a patio, not all overlook the water. My favorites, in the two-story spa building, don't have any view at all. But what they lack in scenery, they make up for in opulence; each well-appointed spa room has a sitting area and a huge Jacuzzi bathroom.

1 Duval St. (near Mallory Docks), Key West, FL 33040. © 800/327-8340 or 305/296-4600. Fax 305/296-9085. www.pierhouse.com. 142 units. Winter $245–$410 double; off-season $200–$355 double. AE, DC, MC, V. **Amenities:** 3 restaurants; 3 bars; heated swimming pool; full-service spa and fitness center; 2 Jacuzzis; sauna; water-sports equipment/rentals; moped/bike rental; concierge; limited room service; in-room massage; babysitting; laundry services; private beach. *In room:* A/C, TV, dataport, minibar, coffeemaker, hair dryer, iron.

Wyndham Casa Marina Resort ★★ *Kids*   Located on Kokomo Beach, Key West's largest private beach, the Casa Marina Resort (built in 1921) is one of the island's most desirable. The setting couldn't be more idyllic, and to further complement its surroundings, the hotel itself is luxurious with beamed ceilings, polished pine floors, and French Provincial furniture. Rooms are comfortable and soothing; the best ones are those with oceanfront balconies or French doors overlooking the oceanfront lawn. The pools are gorgeous, with stunning views of the Atlantic. Families love the Casa Marina for its Kid's Retreat, which runs Thursday through Sunday and offers full- and half-day programs ($35 full-day; $25 half-day), which consist of activities such as swimming, arts and crafts, and sports. Evening activities (movies, campfires, cookouts) are available for the whole family. In 2001, the hotel spent $2 million on renovating Flagler's, its 1920s-style surf-and-turf restaurant.

1500 Reynolds St., Key West, FL 33040. ✆ 800/626-0777 or 305/296-3535. www.casamarinakeywest.com. 311 units. Winter $269–$799; off-season $169–$799. AE, DC, DISC, MC, V. From Key West International Airport, go west on Roosevelt Blvd. 1 mile (1.5km) to Atlantic Blvd. and turn left. Go 1 mile (1.5km) to Reynolds St. and turn right. Hotel is on left. **Amenities:** 2 restaurants; 2 outdoor pools; lighted tennis court; exercise room; sauna; water-sports equipment/rental; bike/moped rental; children's programs; concierge; tour desk; courtesy airport transportation; massage; babysitting. *In room:* A/C, TV, coffeemaker, hair dryer.

Wyndham Reach Resort ★★ Unlike Wyndham's Casa Marina resort, the Reach is better suited to adults only and not families. The location here can be either a highlight or a drawback; it's a 5-minute walk away from the center of the Duval Street action. Supported by stilts that leave the entire ground floor for car parking, the hotel offers four floors of rooms designed around atriums. The wonderful guest rooms are large and feature tile floors and sturdy wicker furnishings. Each has a vanity area separate from the bathroom. The rooms are so nice, you can easily forgive the small closets and diminutive dressers. All have sliding glass doors that open onto balconies, and some have ocean views. The grounds are amply planted with palms and surround a small pool area. There's also a private pier for fishing and tanning. The protected waters are tame and shallow. For steak lovers, there's Shula's on the Beach, a Keys sibling to Miami's lauded Shula's Steak House.

1435 Simonton St., Key West, FL 33040. ✆ 800/874-4118, or 800/996-3426 for reservations. Fax 305/296-4633. www.wyndham.com/reachresort. 150 units. Winter $259–$469 single or double. Off-season $159–$369 single or double. AE, DC, DISC, MC, V. **Amenities:** 2 restaurants; bar; outdoor heated swimming pool; nearby tennis and golf; health club and spa; water-sports equipment/rental; bike rental; concierge; tour desk; business center; salon; room service; in-room massage; babysitting; dry cleaning. *In room:* A/C, TV, mini-bar, fridge, coffeemaker.

EXPENSIVE

Curry Mansion Inn ★★ *Finds* This wonderfully charismatic inn is the former home of the island's first millionaire, a once penniless Bahamian immigrant who made a fortune as a pirate. Owned today by innkeepers Al and Edith Amsterdam, the Curry Mansion is now on the National Register of Historic Places, but you won't feel like you're staying in a museum, but rather in a wonderfully warm home. Rooms are very sparsely decorated, with white wicker furniture, four-poster wooden beds, and pink walls, in which Key West minimalism meets Victorian. The pool, located in the house's courtyard, is open 24 hours for those who enjoy midnight swimming. The dining room is reminiscent of a Victorian dollhouse, with rich wood floors and furnishings and elegant table settings. Every morning there's a delicious European-style breakfast buffet; and at night, cocktail parties. There's also a really nice patio out back, on which, from time to time, there's live entertainment.

511 Caroline St., Key West, FL 33040. ✆ 800/253-3466 or 305/294-5349. Fax 305/294-4093. www.currymansion.com. 28 units. Winter $150–$375 double; off-season $130–$250 double. Rates include European breakfast buffet. AE, DC, MC, V. No children under 12. **Amenities:** Dining room; swimming pool; bike rental; concierge. *In room:* A/C, TV, minibar.

(*Fun Fact* **Did You Know?**

Rumor has it that the very first Key lime pie ever created was made at the turn of the 19th century in the Curry Mansion's kitchen by Mr. Curry's cook, Aunt Sally.

Island City House Hotel ★★   A small resort unto itself, the Island City House consists of three separate and unique buildings that share a common jun-glelike patio and pool. The first building, unimaginatively called the Island City House building, is a historic three-story wooden structure with wraparound verandas that allow guests to walk around the entire edifice on any floor. The warmly dressed, old-fashioned interiors here include wood floors and many antique furnishings. Many rooms have full-size kitchens. The tile bathrooms could use more counter space, and the room lighting isn't always perfect, but eccentricities are part of this hotel's charm.

The unpainted wooden Cigar House has particularly large bedrooms, similar in ambience to those in the Island City House. The Arch House is the least appealing of the three buildings, but still recommended. Built of Dade County pine, the Arch House's cozy bedrooms are furnished in wicker and rattan and come with small kitchens and bathrooms.

411 William St., Key West, FL 33040. ℭ 800/634-8230 or 305/294-5702. Fax 305/294-1289. www.islandcity house.com. 24 units. Winter $175–$315; off-season $115–$210. Rates include breakfast. AE, DC, DISC, MC, V. **Amenities:** Outdoor heated pool; Jacuzzi; access to nearby health club; bike rental; concierge; in-room massage; babysitting; dry-cleaning and laundry service; self-service laundromat. *In room:* A/C, TV, kitchen, coffeemaker, hair dryer.

Marquesa Hotel ★★★ *Finds*   The Marquesa offers the charm of a small his-toric hotel coupled with the amenities of a large resort. It encompasses four buildings, two swimming pools, and a three-stage waterfall that cascades into a lily pond. Two of the hotel's houses are luxuriously restored Victorian homes whose rooms are outfitted with extra-plush antiques and oversized contempo-rary furniture. The rooms in the two other, newly constructed, buildings are even more opulent; many have four-poster wrought-iron beds with bright floral spreads. The green-marble bathrooms in the new building are lush and spacious; those in the older building are also nice, but not nearly as huge and luxe. The decor is simple, elegant, and spotless. These are the only hotel rooms I have ever seen that I would love to have in my own home. The hotel also boasts one of Key West's most elegant restaurants, The Cafe Marquesa.

600 Fleming St. (at Simonton St.), Key West, FL 33040. ℭ 800/869-4631 or 305/292-1919. Fax 305/ 294-2121. www.marquesa.com. 27 units. Winter $260–$395 double; off-season $170–$285 double. AE, DC, MC, V. No children under 12. **Amenities:** Restaurant; 2 outdoor swimming pools (1 is heated); access to nearby health club; bike rental; concierge; limited room service. *In room:* A/C, TV, dataport, minibar, hair dryer.

Weatherstation Inn ★ *Finds*   Originally built in 1912 as a weather station, this beautifully restored and meticulously maintained two-story, Renaissance-style inn is located just 2 blocks from Duval Street. It's situated on the tropical grounds of the former Old Navy Yard, now an exclusive and very private gated community. Harry Truman, Eisenhower, and JFK all visited the station. Spacious and unclut-tered, each room is uniquely furnished to complement the interior architecture: hardwood floors, tall sash windows, and high ceilings. The large, modern bath-rooms are especially appealing. Enjoy a complimentary continental breakfast by the pool among the flowers. The staff is friendly and accommodating.

57 Front St., Key West, FL 33040. ℭ 800/815-2707 or 305/294-7277. Fax 305/294-0544. www.weather stationinn.com. 8 units. Winter $195–$315 double; off-season $150–$215 double. Rates include continental breakfast. AE, MC, V. **Amenities:** Outdoor pool; concierge. *In room:* A/C, TV, dataport, hair dryer.

MODERATE

Chelsea House ★   Despite its decidedly English name, the Chelsea House is "all American," a term that in Key West isn't code for "conservative." Chelsea

House caters to a mixed gay/straight clientele and displays its liberal philosophy most prominently on the clothing-optional sun deck. One of only a few guest-houses in Key West that offer TVs, VCRs, private bathrooms, and kitchenettes in each guest room, Chelsea House has a large number of repeat visitors. The apartments come with full kitchens and separate living areas, as well as palm-shaded balconies in back. The bathrooms and closets could be bigger, but both are adequate and serviceable. When weather permits, which is almost always, breakfast is served outside by the pool.

707 Truman Ave., Key West, FL 33040. ☎ **800/845-8859** or 305/296-2211. Fax 305/296-4822. www. chelseahousekw.com. 20 units. Winter $135–$245 double; off-season $85–$135 double. Rates include break-fast. AE, DC, DISC, MC, V. Private parking. Pets accepted, $15 per night. Children 17 and under not accepted. **Amenities:** Outdoor pool; access to nearby health club; bike rental; concierge. *In room:* A/C, TV/VCR, fax, kitchenette, fridge, hair dryer, iron.

La Pensione ★★ This classic bed-and-breakfast, located in the 1891 home of a former cigar executive, distinguishes itself from other similar inns by its extreme attention to details. The friendly and knowledgeable staff treats the stunning home and its guests with extraordinary care. The comfortable rooms all have air-conditioning, ceiling fans, king-size beds, and private bathrooms. Many also have French doors opening onto spacious verandas. Although the rooms have no phones or televisions, the distractions of Duval Street, only steps away, should keep you adequately occupied during your visit. Breakfast, which includes made-to-order Belgian waffles, fresh fruit, and a variety of breads or muffins, can be taken on the wraparound porch or at the communal dining table.

809 Truman Ave. (between Windsor and Margaret sts.), Key West, FL 33040. ☎ **800/893-1193** or 305/ 292-9923. Fax 305/296-6509. www.lapensione.com. 9 units. Winter from $178 double; off-season from $98 double. Rates include breakfast. 10% discount for readers who mention this book. AE, DC, DISC, MC, V. No children accepted. **Amenities:** Outdoor pool; access to nearby health club; bike rental. *In room:* A/C.

Southernmost Point Guest House ★★ *Finds* *Kids* One of the few inns that actually welcome children and pets, this romantic and historic guesthouse is a real find. The antiseptically clean rooms are not as fancy as the house's ornate 1885 exterior, but each is unique and includes some combination of basic beds and couches and a hodgepodge of furnishings, including futon couches, high-back wicker chairs, and plenty of mismatched throw rugs. Room 5 is best; situated upstairs, it has a private porch, an ocean view, and windows that let in lots of light. Every room has fresh flowers, a refrigerator, and a full decanter of sherry. Mona Santiago, the hotel's kind, laid-back owner, provides chairs and towels that can be brought to the beach, which is just a block away. Plus, guests can help themselves to free wine as they soak in the 14-seat hot tub. Kids will enjoy the swings in the backyard and the pet rabbits.

1327 Duval St., Key West, FL 33040. ☎ **305/294-0715.** Fax 305/296-0641. www.southernmostpoint.com. 6 units. Winter $105–$250; off-season $65–$165. Rates include breakfast. AE, MC, V. Pets accepted, $5 in summer, $10 in winter. **Amenities:** Garden pool; hot tub; laundry facilities; barbecue grills. *In room:* A/C, TV/VCR, coffeemaker, hair dryer, iron.

Westwinds Inn ★ A close second to staying in your own private, 19th-century clapboard, tin-roofed house is this tranquil inn located just 4 blocks from Duval Street in the historic Seaport district. Lush landscaping—banana stalks, mango, and Spanish Lime trees—keeps the inn extremely private and secluded, and at times, you do feel as if you're alone. And that's not a scary thing, it's absolutely fabulous. Two pools, one heated in the winter, are offset by alcoves, fountains, and the extremely well maintained whitewashed inn, which is actually composed of five separate houses. Rooms are Key West comfortable, with wicker furnishings and fans, and all have private bathrooms. Families are welcome, but children under 12 are not. All rooms are no-smoking.

914 Eaton St., Key West, FL 33040. ✆ **800/788-4150** or 305/296-4440. Fax 305/293-9031. www.westwinds keywest.com. 26 units. Winter $90–$150; off-season $70–$120. Rates include continental breakfast. DISC, MC, V. **Amenities:** 2 pools (1 heated); bike rental; self-service laundry. *In room:* A/C (some rooms have TVs and kitchenettes).

INEXPENSIVE

Abaco Inn ★ (*Value*)   This tidy little guesthouse is situated on a secluded lane just off Duval Street. Although there is no pool or view, the three simple but comfortable rooms are well stocked, immaculate, and charming. Each room has a sizeable private bath, queen bed, and a twin-size Murphy bed. Once the home of a cigar maker, the house dates from the early 1900s. Now it is owned and operated by George Fontana, a friendly and knowledgeable tour guide and writer. Look for his column on local characters in the *Key West Citizen*. You can't beat the price in this super-convenient location. No smoking is allowed on the property.

415 Julia St. (between Truman Ave. and Virginia St.), Key West, FL 33040. ✆ **800/358-6307** or 305/296-2212. Fax 305/295-0349. www.abaco-inn.com. 3 units. Winter from $99–$109 double; off-season from $69 double. 4-day minimum stay in season. Additional person $15 extra. AE, DISC, MC, V. **Amenities:** Bike rental; concierge. *In room:* A/C, TV, microwave, fridge, coffeemaker, hair dryer.

Angelina Guest House ★★   This youth hostel–type guesthouse is about the cheapest in town and conveniently located near a hot, hippie restaurant called Blue Heaven (see "Where to Dine," below). It is generally safe and full of character. The rooms are all furnished differently in a modest style, recently upgraded with new decor. Only three rooms do not have private baths. Two rooms have full kitchens, and one has a microwave and small refrigerator; there are no televisions or telephones. A gorgeous lagoon-style heated pool with waterfall and tropical landscaping was an excellent addition. Even better are the poolside hammocks—get out there early, they go quickly! Even though the Angelina is sparse, it's a great place to crash if you are on the cheap. Many repeat guests consider "this old house" their home away from home.

302 Angela St. (at the corner of Thomas St.), Key West, FL 33040. ✆ **888/303-4480** or 305/294-4480. Fax 305/272-0681. www.angelinaguesthouse.com. 15 units. Winter $75–$149; off-season $49–$95. Rates include continental breakfast. DISC, MC, V. **Amenities:** Outdoor heated pool; concierge. *In room:* A/C, hair dryer, iron.

The Grand ★★ (*Finds*)   Don't expect cabbies or locals to know about this well-kept secret, located in a modest residential section of Old Town, about 5 blocks from Duval Street. It's got almost everything you could want, including a very moderate price tag. Proprietor Elizabeth Rose goes out of her way to provide any and all services for her appreciative guests. All rooms have private bathrooms, air-conditioning, and private entrances. Room no. 2 on the backside of the house is the best deal; it's small, but it has a porch and the most privacy. Suites are a real steal, too. The large two-room units come with a complete kitchen. This place is undoubtedly the best bargain in town.

1116 Grinnell St. (between Virginia and Catherine sts.), Key West, FL 33040. ✆ **888/947-2630** or 305/294-0590. Fax 305/294-0477. www.thegrandguesthouse.com. 10 units. Winter $98–$188; off-season $88–$118. Rates include continental breakfast. AE, DISC, MC, V. **Amenities:** Bike/scooter rental; concierge. *In room:* A/C, TV/VCR, fridge.

Grand Key Resort ★ (*Finds*)   If you don't mind staying on the quiet "other" side of the island, a 10-minute cab ride away from Duval Street, the Grand Key Resort is an excellent choice, not to mention value. An ecologically conscious resort, Grand Key has been renovated with eco-sensitive materials as well as an interior created to conserve energy, reduce waste, and preserve the area's natural resources. Rooms are clean and comfortable, with some looking out onto the spacious pool area, which is surrounded by an unsightly empty lot of mangroves and marshes. The hotel's restaurant is also very good; but for excitement, you will need to look elsewhere.

3990 S. Roosevelt Blvd., Key West, FL 33040. © **888/310-1540** or 305/293-1818. Fax 305/296-6962. www. grandkeyresort.com. 216 units. Winter $179–$489; off-season $125–$420. Rates include continental breakfast. AE, DISC, MC, V. Free parking. **Amenities:** Restaurant; Tiki bar and lounge; pool; concierge; meeting rooms; limited room service. In room: A/C, TV/Web TV, dataport, minibar, coffeemaker, hair dryer, Sony PlayStation.

Key West International Hostel & Seashell Motel This well-run, affordable hostel is a 3-minute walk to the beach and to Old Town. Very busy with European backpackers, it's a great place to meet people. The dorm rooms are dark and sparse, but clean enough. The higher-priced motel rooms are a good deal, especially those equipped with full kitchens. The common-area room has been upgraded, and a two-bedroom suite has been added for those looking to upgrade a bit. Amenities include a pool table under a tiki roof, and bicycle rentals for $8 per day. There's also cheap food available for breakfast, lunch, and dinner, as well as discounted prices for snorkeling, diving, and sunset cruises.

718 South St., Key West, FL 33040. © **800/51-HOSTEL** or 305/296-5719. Fax 305/296-0672. www. keywesthostel.com. 100 units. Year-round members $19.50, nonmembers $22.50. Motel units $75–$105 in season; $55–$85 off season. MC, V. **Amenities:** Bike rental; kitchen. In room: A/C, TV, fridge, coffeemaker, hair dryer. Dorm rooms have only A/C.

WHERE TO DINE

With its share of the usual drive-through fast-food franchises (mostly up on Roosevelt Blvd.) and Duval Street succumbing to the lure of a Hard Rock Cafe, you might be surprised to learn that, over the years, an upscale and high-quality dining scene has begun to thrive in Key West. Wander Old Town or the newly spruced-up Bahama Village and browse menus after you have exhausted my list of picks below.

If you don't feel like venturing out, call **We Deliver** (© **305/293-0078**), a service that will bring you anything you want from any of the area's restaurants or stores for a small fee (between $3–$6). We Deliver operates between 3 and 11pm. If you are staying in a condominium or efficiency, you may want to stock your refrigerator with groceries, beer, wine, and snacks from the area's oldest grocer, **Fausto's Food Palace.** Open since 1926, there are now two locations: 1105 White St. and 522 Fleming St. The Fleming Street location will deliver (© **305/ 294-5221** or 305/296-5663). Fausto's has a $25 delivery minimum.

VERY EXPENSIVE

Cafe des Artistes ★★★ FRENCH Open for nearly 2 decades, the Cafe des Artistes' impressive longevity is the result of its winning combination of food and atmosphere. The fact that it was once part of a hotel built in 1935 by Al Capone's bookkeeper adds to its allure, but it's really the food that people come for. Traditional French meals benefit from a subtle tropical twist. Start with the duck-liver paté, made with fresh truffles and old cognac, or Maryland crab meat served with an artichoke heart and herbed-tomato confit. Ask about the escargot du jour. Nouvelle and traditional French entrees include lobster flambé with mango and basil, and wine-basted lamb chops rubbed with rosemary and ginger.

1007 Simonton St. (near Truman Ave.). © **305/294-7100.** Reservations recommended. Main courses $25–$38. AE, MC, V. Daily 6–11pm.

Café Marquesa ★★★ CONTEMPORARY AMERICAN   If you're looking for fabulous dining in Key West, this is the place. The intimate, 50-seat restaurant is something to look at, but it's really the food that you'll want to admire. Specialties include peppercorn-dusted, seared yellowfin tuna with saffron risotto; grilled Florida lobster tail and diver sea scallops with Thai basil sauce, black Thai rice, and Asian vegetables; and an almost perfect feta and pine nut–crusted rack of lamb with rosemary demi-glace, creamy polenta, and egg-plant caponata. If you're looking to splurge, financially and gastronomically, this is the place.

The Marquesa Hotel, 600 Fleming St. ✆ 305/292-1919. Reservations highly recommended. Main courses $20–$36. AE, DC, MC, V. Daily 7–11pm summer; 6–11pm winter. No smoking.

Louie's Backyard ★★ CARIBBEAN   Nestled amid blooming bougainvillea on a lush slice of the Gulf, Louie's remains one of the most romantic restaurants on earth. Famed chef Norman Van Aiken of Norman's in Miami brought his talents farther south and started what has become one of the finest dining spots in the Keys. As a result, this is one of the hardest places to score a reservation: Either call way in advance or hope that your hotel concierge has some pull. After dinner, sit at the dockside bar and watch the waves crash, almost touching your feet, while enjoying a cocktail at sunset. You can't go wrong with the fresh catch of the day, or any seafood dish, for that matter. The weekend brunches are also great. Even if you can't stay for dinner, go for lunch; this is one dining experience you won't want to miss.

700 Waddell Ave. ✆ 305/294-1061. Reservations highly recommended. Main courses $25–$30; lunch $8–$15. AE, DC, MC, V. Daily 11:30am–3pm and 6–10:30pm.

One Duval ★★★ CARIBBEAN   The waterfront setting of this restaurant at the Pier House Resort is beautiful, but you may be too distracted to notice the views when you taste the food, which executive chef Will Greenwood describes as New Calypso Harvest. One of the best restaurants in Key West, One Duval blends the ingredients of the Caribbean and Florida with an innovative twist. For starters, the crab meat stuffed in phyllo dough is outstanding, not to mention filling, and the goat-cheese souffle is rich and incredibly hedonistic. For main courses, the smoked cured pork chop with Captain Morgan spiced rum sauce is a best bet, as is the ponzu marinated yellowfin tuna tartare and avocado mousse timbale served in a macadamia-nut cilantro jus. The Key lime pie with meringue is a must have. Service is friendly and hyper-professional, and it's not the kind of restaurant they rush you out of. Eat first, then sit back and digest the views. You don't want to miss any of what this fine restaurant has to offer.

One Duval St. ✆ 305/296-4600. Reservations highly recommended. Main courses $25–$30. AE, DC, MC, V. Daily 6–10:30pm.

EXPENSIVE

Antonia's ★★ REGIONAL ITALIAN   The food is great, but the atmosphere is a bit fussy for Key West. If you don't have a reservation in season, don't bother. Still, if you are organized and don't mind paying high prices for dishes that go for much less elsewhere, try this old favorite. From the perfectly seasoned homemade focaccia to an exemplary crème brûlée, this elegant little standout is amazingly consistent. The menu includes a small selection of classics, such as *zuppa di pesce*, rack of lamb in a rosemary sauce, and veal Marsala. However, the way to go is with the nightly specials. You can't go wrong with any of the hand-made pastas. And the owners, Antonia Berto and Phillip Smith, travel to Italy every year to research recipes, so you can be sure you're getting an authentic taste of Italy in small-town Key West.

615 Duval St. ℂ 305/294-6565. Fax 305/294-3888. Reservations suggested. Main courses $20–$28; pastas $13–$18. AE, DC, MC, V. Daily 6–11pm.

Bagatelle ★★★ SEAFOOD/TROPICAL   Reserve a seat at the elegant second-floor veranda overlooking Duval Street's mayhem. From the calm above, you may want to start your meal with the excellent herb-and-garlic–stuffed whole artichoke or the sashimi-like seared tuna rolled in black peppercorns. Also recommended is a lightly creamy garlic-herb pasta topped with Gulf shrimp, Florida lobster, and mushrooms. The best chicken and beef dishes are given a tropical treatment: grilled with papaya, ginger, and soy.

115 Duval St. ℂ 305/296-6609. Reservations recommended. Main courses $14–$21; lunch $5–$10. AE, DISC, MC, V. Sun–Thurs 11:30am–10pm; Fri–Sat 11:30am–11pm.

La Trattoria ★ ITALIAN   Have a true Italian feast in a relaxed atmosphere. Each dish here is prepared and presented according to old Italian tradition and is cooked to order. The antipasti are scrumptious. Try the delicious baked bread-crumb–stuffed mushroom caps; they're firm yet tender. The stuffed eggplant with ricotta and roasted peppers is light and flavorful. Or have the seafood salad of shrimp, calamari, and mussels, fish-market fresh and tasty. The pasta dishes are also great: Try the *penne Venezia*, with mushrooms, sun-dried tomatoes, and crab meat, or the cannelloni stuffed with veal and spinach. For dessert, don't skip the homemade tiramisu; it's light yet full-flavored. The dining room is spacious but still intimate, and the waiters are friendly and informative. Before you leave, be sure to visit Virgilio's, the restaurant's very own cocktail lounge with live jazz until 2am.

524 Duval St. ℂ 305/296-1075. Pasta $10–$17; main courses $17–$22. AE, DC, DISC, MC, V. Daily 5:30–11pm.

Mangoes ★★★ FLORIBBEAN   This restaurant's large brick patio, shaded by overgrown banyan trees, is so alluring to passersby that it's packed almost every night of the week. Many people don't realize how pricey the meals can be here because, upon first glance, it looks like a casual Duval Street cafe, but both its prices and cuisine are a notch above casual. Appetizers include conch chowder laced with sherry, lobster dumplings with tangy Key-lime sauce, and grilled shrimp cocktail with spicy mango chutney. Spicy sausage with black beans and rice, crispy curried chicken, and local snapper with passion-fruit sauce are typical among the entrees, but the Garlic and Lime Pinks—a half pound of Key West pink shrimp seasoned and grilled with a roasted garlic and Key lime glaze—are the menu's best offering by far. The Cuban Coffee Pork is definitely a different take on roast pork, rubbed with Cuban coffee and grilled with a vanilla-bean butter sauce and banana–black currant chutney. Even though it is right on tourist-laden Duval Street, Mangoes enjoys a good reputation among locals and stands out from the rest of the greasy bar fare found there.

700 Duval St. (at Angela St.). ℂ 305/292-4606. Reservations recommended for parties of 6 or more. Main courses $12–$26; pizzas $10–$13; lunch $7–$14. AE, DC, DISC, MC, V. Daily 11am–midnight; pizza until 1am.

MODERATE

Alonzo's Oyster Bar ★ SEAFOOD   Alonzo's Oyster Bar offers good seafood in a casual setting. It's located on the ground floor of the A&B Lobster House at the end of Front Street in the marina. To start off your meal, try the steamed beer shrimp—tantalizingly fresh jumbo shrimp in a garlic, Old Bay, beer, and cayenne-pepper sauce. A house specialty is white clam chili, a delicious mix of tender clams, white beans, and potatoes served with a dollop of sour cream. An excellent entree is the pan-fried lobster cakes, served with sweet-corn mashed potatoes, chipotle gravy, and roasted-corn salsa. Alonzo's is the casual section of the A&B Lobster House; if you want to dress up, go upstairs for their "fine dining." The staff is cheerful and informative, and the service is very good.

231 Margaret St. ⓒ 305/294-5880. Appetizers $5–$8; main courses $11–$17. MC, V. Daily 11am–11pm.

Banana Café ★★★ *Finds* FRENCH   Although neither as elaborate as Café des Artistes nor quite as casual as Blue Heaven, Banana Café is open for three meals a day and benefits from a French country cafe look and feel. It's an upscale local eatery that's been discovered by savvy visitors on the less-congested end of Duval Street and kept its loyal clientele with affordable prices and delightful, light preparations. Banana Café's crepes are legendary on the island for breakfast or lunch, and fresh quality ingredients and a French-themed menu bring daytime diners back for the casual, classy, tropical-influenced dinner menu. Every Thursday night, there's live jazz.

1211 Duval St. ⓒ 305/294-7227. Main courses $4.79–$23; breakfast and lunch $2–$8.50. AE, DC, MC, V. Daily 8am–11pm.

Blue Heaven ★★ *Finds* SEAFOOD/AMERICAN/NATURAL   This little hippie-run gallery and restaurant has become the place to be in Key West—and with good reason. Be prepared to wait in line. The food here is some of the best in town, especially for breakfast. You can enjoy homemade granola, huge tropical-fruit pancakes, and seafood Benedict. Dinners are just as good and run the gamut from fresh-caught fish dishes to Jamaican-style jerk chicken, curried soups, and vegetarian stews. But if you're a neat freak, don't bother. Some people are put off by the dirt floors and roaming cats and birds, but frankly, it adds to the charm. The building used to be a bordello, where Hemingway was said to hang out watching cockfights. It's still lively here, but not *that* lively!

305 Petronia St. ⓒ 305/296-8666. Main courses $10–$30; lunch $6–$14; breakfast $5–$11. DISC, MC, V. Daily 8–11:30am, noon–3pm, and 6–10:30pm; Sun brunch 8am–1pm. Closed mid-Sept to early Oct.

Mangia, Mangia ★ *Value* ITALIAN/AMERICAN   Locals appreciate that they can get good, inexpensive food here in a town filled with tourist traps. Off the beaten track, in a little corner storefront, this great Chicago-style pasta place serves some of the best Italian food in the Keys. The family-run restaurant offers superb homemade pastas of every description, including one of the tastiest marinaras around. The simple grilled chicken breast brushed with olive oil and sprinkled with pepper is another good choice, as is the Picadillo Pasta—black-bean pasta shells smothered in a Cuban-inspired sauce with meat, tomatoes, olives, capers, and spices. You wouldn't know it from the glossy glass-front room, but there's a fantastic little outdoor patio dotted with twinkling pepper lights and lots of plants. You can relax out back with a glass of one of their excellent wines—they're said to have the largest selection in the Keys—or homemade beer while you wait for your table.

900 Southard St. (at Margaret St.). ⓒ 305/294-2469. Reservations not accepted. Main courses $9–$15. AE, MC, V. Daily 5:30–10pm.

Pepe's *Finds* AMERICAN   This old dive has been serving good, basic food for nearly a century. Steaks and Apalachicola Bay oysters are the big draw for regulars who appreciate the rustic barroom setting and historic photos on the walls. Look for original scenes of Key West in 1909, when Pepe's first opened. If the weather is nice, choose a seat on the patio under a stunning mahogany tree. Burgers, fish sandwiches, and standard chili satisfy hearty eaters. Buttery sautéed mushrooms and rich mashed potatoes are the best comfort food in Key West. Stop by early for breakfast, when you can get old-fashioned chipped beef on toast and all the usual egg dishes. In the evening, there are reasonably priced cocktails on the deck.

806 Caroline St. (between Margaret and Williams sts.). ✆ **305/294-7192**. Main courses $13–$22; breakfast $2–$9; lunch $5–$9. DISC, MC, V. Daily 6:30am–10:30pm.

Turtle Kraals Wildlife Grill ✿ *Finds* SOUTHWESTERN/SEAFOOD
You'll join lots of locals in this out-of-the-way converted warehouse with indoor and dockside seating that serves innovative seafood at great prices. Try the twin lobster tails stuffed with mango and crab meat or any of the big quesadillas or fajitas. Kids will like the wildlife exhibits and the very cheesy menu. Blues bands play most nights.

213 Margaret St. (corner of Caroline St.). ✆ **305/294-2640**. Main courses $10–$20. DISC, MC, V. Mon–Thurs 11am–10:30pm; Fri–Sat 11am–11pm; Sun noon–10:30pm. Bar closes at midnight.

INEXPENSIVE

Anthony's Cafe ✿ ITALIAN DELI/ROTISSERIE Although owned and operated by a Greek import, this rustic Italian-style trattoria is a welcome addition to an area crowded with more expensive and less delicious options. Fragrant roasted chicken and overstuffed sandwiches on fresh baked bread are the best choices. Also good are the many salads and daily specials.

1111 Duval St. (at Amelia St.). ✆ **305/296-8899**. Breakfast $2–$5; sandwiches and salads $5.50–$7 with a side; hot plates $8–$13. Cash only. Daily 8am–10pm.

Bahama Mama's Kitchen ✿✿ BAHAMIAN Sit outside under an umbrella and enjoy the authentic Bahamian dishes made from recipes that have been handed down through owner Corey's family for the past 150 years. Prepared fresh daily, all dishes are created with their special "Bahamian" seasonings. Try the coconut shrimp butterflied, soaked in coconut oil, battered with egg, and then rolled in fresh shredded coconut and deep-fried. The fresh catch of the day comes blackened, broiled, or fried and is served with island plantains, shrimp hash cakes, and crab rice. The service is good and the staff is friendly.

In the Bahama Village Market, 324 Petronia St. ✆ **305/294-3355**. Appetizers $4–$7; main courses $9–$13. MC, V. Daily 11am–10pm.

The Deli DINER/AMERICAN In operation since 1950, this family-owned corner eatery has kept up with the times. It's really more of a diner than a deli and has a vast menu with all kinds of hearty options, from meatloaf to yellow-tail snapper. The seafood options are pretty good. A daily selection of more than a dozen vegetables includes the usual diner choices of beets, corn, and coleslaw with some distinctly Caribbean additions, such as rice and beans and fried plantains. Most dinners include a choice of two vegetables and homemade biscuits or corn bread. Breakfasts are made to order and attract a loyal following of locals. The Deli also offers ice-cream sundaes and gourmet coffees.

531 Truman Ave. (corner of Truman Ave. and Simonton St.). ✆ **305/294-1464**. Full meals $7–$23; sandwiches $3–$8. DISC, MC, V. Daily 7:30am–10pm.

El Siboney Restaurant ✿ *Value* CUBAN For good, cheap Cuban food, stop at this corner dive that looks more like a gas station than a diner. Be prepared, however, to wait like the locals for succulent roast pork, Cuban sandwiches,

grilled chicken, and *ropa vieja* (a stew-like dish of beef, onion, garlic, and tomatoes), all served with heaps of rice and beans.

900 Catherine St. (at Margaret St.). ℂ **305/296-4184**. Main courses $5–$13. No credit cards. Mon–Sat
11am–9:30pm.

PT's Late Night ★ *Finds* AMERICAN   This place is worth knowing about not
only because it's one of the only places in town serving food past 10pm, but also
because it happens to serve good food at extremely reasonable prices. PT's is
more like a sports bar than a restaurant, and service can be a bit slow and
brusque, but you'll enjoy their heaping plates of nachos, sizzling fajitas served
with all the trimmings, and super-fresh salads—so big they can be a meal in
themselves.

920 Caroline St. (at the corner of Margaret St.). ℂ **305/296-4245**. Main courses $6.95–$14.95. DISC, MC,
V. Daily 11am–4am.

KEY WEST AFTER DARK

Duval Street is the Bourbon Street of Florida. Amid the T-shirt shops and
clothing boutiques, you'll find bar after bar serving neon-colored frozen drinks
to revelers who bounce from one to the next from noon till dawn. Bands and
crowds vary from night to night and season to season. Your best bet is to start at
Truman Avenue and head up Duval to check them out for yourself. Cover
charges are rare, except in gay clubs (see the "The Gay Scene" section below), so
stop into a dozen and see which you like. For the most part, Key West is a late-
night town, and bars and clubs don't close until around 3 or 4am.

Captain Tony's Saloon   Just around the corner from Duval's beaten path,
this smoky old wooden bar (see the "The Legend of Captain Tony" box, below)
is about as authentic as you'll find. It comes complete with old-time regulars
who remember the island before cruise ships docked here; they say Hemingway
drank, caroused, and even wrote here. The owner, Captain Tony Tarracino, a
former controversial Key West mayor—"immortalized" in Jimmy Buffett's "Last
Mango in Paradise"—has recently capitalized on the success of this once-quaint
tavern by franchising the place. 428 Greene St. ℂ **305/294-1838**.

Durty Harry's   This large complex features live rock bands almost every night.
You can wander to one of the many outdoor bars or head up to Upstairs at
Rick's, an indoor/outdoor dance club that gets going late. For the more racy singles or couples, there is also the Red Garter, a pocket-size strip club. The hawker
outside reminds couples, in case they've forgotten, that "the family that strips
together sticks together." 208 Duval St. ℂ **305/296-4890**.

Epoch   Until an arsonist put an end to the legend in 1995, this former gay
club was the place to dance to everything from techno to house and disco to reggae. Now expanded to include seven bars, an even bigger dance floor, a huge
outside deck overlooking Duval Street, and a new state-of-the-art sound system,
this is a better-than-ever choice for people of any orientation who can appreciate a good time. 623 Duval St. ℂ **305/296-8521**.

Jimmy Buffett's Margaritaville Cafe   This cafe, named after another Key
West legend, is a worthwhile stop. Although Mr. Buffett moved to glitzy Palm
Beach years ago, his name is still attracting large crowds. This kitschy restau-
rant/bar/gift shop features live bands every night—from rock to blues to reggae
and everything in between. The touristy cafe is furnished with plenty of Buffett
memorabilia, including gold records, photos, and drawings. The margaritas are

The Legend of Captain Tony

Captain Tony Tarracino, proprietor of Captain Tony's Saloon, 428 Greene St. (© 305/294-1838), was a Key West legend even before Jimmy Buffett immortalized him in "The Last Mango in Paris." Notwithstanding Mr. Buffett's influence, you won't find a cheeseburger-in-paradise at Captain Tony's, because they don't serve food. They do, however, serve mind-erasing cocktails and visions of old Key West. The walls and ceiling are adorned with, among other colorful things, old photos of the old Captain, a tombstone, an old horn, and a tree that actually grows out of the ceiling. The music is loud; the patrons louder.

The legendary Captain also happens to be the ex-mayor of Key West and everybody's favorite barkeep. If you really want a sublime experience, ask the crusty old Captain (if you're lucky enough to catch a glimpse of him, probably drinking out of a mug containing some sort of dark liquor) anything about love, life, or even libations and he'll be happy to indulge you with his off-the-cuff philosophies.

high priced but tasty, but the cheeseburgers aren't worth singing about. 500 Duval St. © 305/292-1435.

Sloppy Joe's   You'll have to stop in here just to say you did. Scholars and drunks debate whether this is the same Sloppy Joe's that Hemingway wrote about, but there's no argument that this classic bar's early 20th-century wooden ceiling and cracked-tile floors are Key West originals. There's live music nightly as well as a cigar room and martini bar. 201 Duval St. © 305/294-5717, ext. 10. www.sloppyjoes.com.

Wax   Wax oozes a cosmopolitan ambience, looking as if it were shipped down from New York, with its blood-red interior, very hip, loungey atmosphere, and excellent deejayed dance music. Though it has a more elegant atmosphere than any other place on the island, Wax's patrons (it's where all the locals go to avoid tourists) dress down. 422 Applerouth Lane. © 305/296-6667.

THE GAY SCENE

Key West's Bohemian live-and-let-live atmosphere extends to its thriving and quirky gay community. Since Tennessee Williams and before, Key West has provided the perfect backdrop to a gay scene unlike that of many large urban areas. Seamlessly blended with the prevailing culture, there is no "gay ghetto" in Key West, where alternative lifestyles are embraced and even celebrated.

Although restaurants and businesses welcome visitors without discrimination, nightlife *is* inevitably nightlife. In Key West, the best music and dancing can be found at the predominantly gay clubs. While many of the area's other hot spots are geared toward tourists who like to imbibe, the gay clubs are for those who want to rave, gay or not. Covers vary, but are rarely more than $10.

Two adjacent popular late-night spots are the **801 Bourbon Bar/One Saloon** (801 Duval St. and 514 Petronia St.; © 305/294-9349; www.801bourbon.com for both), featuring great drag and lots more disco. A mostly male clientele frequents this hot spot from 9pm until 4am. Another Duval Street favorite is **Diva's,** at 711 Duval St. (© 305/292-8500), where you might catch drag queens belting out torch songs or judges voting on the best package in the wet jockey shorts contest.

Sunday nights are fun at two local spots. **Tea by the Sea,** on the pier at the Atlantic Shores Motel (510 South St.; © 800/520-3559), attracts a faithful following of regulars and visitors alike. The clothing-optional pool is always an attraction. Show up after 7:30pm. Better known around town as La-Te-Da, **La Terraza de Martí,** the former Key West home of Cuban exile José Martí, at 1125 Duval St. (© **305/296-6706**), is a great spot to gather poolside for the best martini in town—but don't bother with the food. Just upstairs from there is **The Crystal Room** (© **305/296-6706**), with a high-caliber cabaret performance featuring the popular Randy Roberts in the winter.

4 The Dry Tortugas ★★

70 miles (113km) W of Key West

Few people realize that the Florida Keys don't end at Key West, since about 70 miles (113km) west of there is a chain of seven small islands known as the Dry Tortugas. As long as you have come this far, you might wish to visit them, especially if you're into bird-watching, which is their primary draw.

Ponce de León, who discovered this far-flung cluster of coral keys in 1513, named them "Las Tortugas" because of the many sea turtles, which still flock to the area during the nesting season in the warm summer months. Oceanic charts later carried the preface "dry" to warn mariners that fresh water was unavailable here. Modern intervention has made drinking water available, but little else.

These undeveloped islands make a great day trip for travelers interested in seeing the natural anomalies of the Florida Keys—especially the birds. The Dry Tortugas are nesting grounds and roosting sites for thousands of tropical and subtropical oceanic birds. Visitors will also find a historical fort, good fishing, and terrific snorkeling around shallow reefs.

GETTING THERE

BY BOAT   The **Yankee Fleet,** based in Key West (© **800/634-0939** or 305/294-7009), offers day trips from Key West for sightseeing, snorkeling, or both. Cruises leave daily for the 3-hour journey at 7:30am from the Land's End Marina at Margaret Street and travel to Garden Key. Breakfast is served on board. Once on the island, you can join a guided tour of Fort Jefferson or explore it on your own. Boats return to Key West by 7pm. Tours cost $109 per person, including breakfast, lunch, dinner, and snorkeling equipment; $69 for children 16 and under; $99 for seniors, students, and military personnel. Phone for reservations.

The **Sunny Days Catamarans' "Fast Cat"** (© **800/236-7937** or 305/292-6100) is faster, quieter, and more high-tech than the loud Yankee fleet, as well as a better value. Included in the $95 round-trip adult fare ($65 for children) is a continental breakfast and a buffet lunch with cold cuts, fresh veggies, fruits, salads, unlimited sodas and water, plus an island tour and a snorkeling excursion to a shipwreck in 5 to 20 feet (1.5–6m) of water. The high-speed power cat leaves Key West for Garden Key at 8am and returns by 6pm.

BY PLANE   **Seaplanes of Key West,** based at Key West Airport (© **800/950-2-FLY** or 305/294-0709), offers daily excursions. Weather permitting, flights depart at 8 and 10am, noon, and 2pm. The 40-minute trip at about 500 feet (150m) offers a great introduction to the Dry Tortugas. Fares, which include snorkeling equipment and a cooler for use on the island, start at $179 for adults, $129 for kids 12 and under, and $99 for kids 6 and under for a half day; and $305 for adults, $225 for kids 12 and under, and $170 for kids 6 and under for a full day. Bring a bathing suit, snorkeling equipment, and some snacks to enjoy on these remote and beautiful islands. If you want to stay overnight at Fort Jefferson, it costs $329 for adults, $235 for kids 12 and under, and $179 for kids 6 and under.

EXPLORING THE DRY TORTUGAS

Of the seven islands that make up the Dry Tortugas, Garden Key is the most visited, because it is where Fort Jefferson and the visitor center are located. Loggerhead Key, Middle Key, and East Key are open only during the day and are for hiking. Bush Key is for the birds—literally! It's a nesting area for birds only, though it is open from October to January for special excursions. Hospital and Long Keys are closed to the public.

Fort Jefferson, a huge six-sided 19th-century fortress, is built almost at the water's edge of Garden Key, giving the appearance that it floats in the middle of the sea. The monumental structure is surrounded by formidable 8-foot-thick (2.5m) walls that rise up from the sand to a height of nearly 50 feet (15m). Impressive archways, stonework, and parapets make this 150-year-old monument a grand sight. With the invention of the rifled cannon, the fort's masonry construction became obsolete and the building was never completed. For 10 years, however, from 1863 to 1873, Fort Jefferson served as a prison, a kind of "Alcatraz East." Among its prisoners were four of the "Lincoln Conspirators," including Samuel A. Mudd, the doctor who set the broken leg of fugitive assassin John Wilkes Booth. In 1935, Fort Jefferson became a national monument administered by the National Park Service. For more information about Fort Jefferson and the Dry Tortugas, call the **Everglades National Park Service** at © **305/242-7700** or visit www.fortjefferson.com. Fort Jefferson is open during daylight hours on Garden Key, and there is a self-guided trail that interprets the history of human presence in the Dry Tortugas while leading visitors through the fort.

OUTDOOR PURSUITS

BIRD-WATCHING   Bring your binoculars and your bird books: Bird-watching is *the* reason to visit this little cluster of tropical islands. The Dry Tortugas, uniquely situated in the middle of the migration flyway between North and South America, serve as an important rest stop for the more than 200 winged varieties that pass through here annually. The season peaks from mid-March to mid-May, when thousands of birds show up, but many species from the West Indies can be found here year-round.

DIVING & SNORKELING   The warm, clear, shallow waters of the Dry Tortugas produce optimum conditions for snorkeling and scuba diving. Four endangered species of sea turtles—the green, leatherback, Atlantic ridley, and hawksbill—can be found here, along with myriad marine species. The region just outside the seawall of Fort Jefferson is excellent for underwater touring; an abundant variety of fish, coral, and more live in just 3 or 4 feet (1–1.25m) of water.

FISHING   Fishing for snapper, tarpon, grouper, and other fish used to be popular here until July 2001, when a federal law closed off all fishing in a 90-square-mile tract of open ocean called The Tortugas North and a 61-square-mile tract of open ocean called The Tortugas South, which basically prohibits all fishing in order to preserve the dwindling population of fish (a result of commercial fishermen and environmental factors). Instead, head to Key West.

CAMPING

The rustic beauty of tiny Garden Key (the only island of the Dry Tortugas where campers are allowed to pitch their tents) is a camper's dream. Don't worry about sharing your site with noisy RVs or motor homes; they can't get here. The abundance of birds doesn't make it quiet, but camping here—a stone's throw from the water—is as picturesque as it gets. Picnic tables, cooking grills, and toilets are provided, but there are no showers. All supplies must be packed in and out. Sites are $3 per person per night and are available on a first-come, first-served basis. With only 10 sites, they book up fast. For more information, call the **National Park Service** (© **305/242-7700**).

The Everglades & Biscayne National Park

by Lesley Abravanel

Miami has been called the "gateway to the world," because its port leads the pack in passengers heading to the Caribbean and to Latin America. But tourists should also take some time out to see the wild plant and animal life in the swampy Everglades and the underwater treasures of Biscayne National Park.

1 A Glimpse of Everglades National Park ★ ★

35 miles (56km) SW of Miami

Before going, my conception of the Everglades was that it was one big swamp swarming with ominous creatures. For someone who'd rather endure an endless series of root canals than audition for a role on *Survivor* (the closest I'd ever been to nature was sleep-away camp), the Everglades may as well have been the *Never*glades. That is, until I finally decided to venture there. To my surprise, and contrary to popular belief, the Everglades isn't really a swamp at all, but one of the country's most fascinating natural resources. Imagine a shallow river of grass protected by canopies of lush mangroves and you've got the Everglades, where primitive wildlife peacefully coexists with awe-struck visitors.

For first-timers or those with dubious athletic skills, the best way to see the 'glades is probably via airboats, which actually aren't allowed in the park proper, but cut through the sawgrass on the park's outskirts, taking you past countless birds, alligators, crocodiles, deer, and raccoons. A walk on one of the park's many trails will provide you with a different vantage point: up-close interaction with an assortment of tame wildlife. But the absolute best way to see the 'glades is via canoe, where you can get incredibly close to nature. Whichever method you choose, I guarantee you will marvel at the sheer beauty of the Everglades. Despite the multitude of mosquito bites (the bugs seem to be immune to repellent—wear long pants and cover your arms, if possible), an Everglades experience will definitely contribute to a newfound appreciation for Florida's natural (and beautiful) wonderland.

This vast and unusual ecosystem is actually a shallow, 40-mile-wide (64km), slow-moving river. Rarely more than knee-deep, the water is the lifeblood of this wilderness, and the subtle shifts in water level dictate the life cycle of the native plants and animals. Most folks viewed the Everglades as a worthless swamp until Marjory Stoneman Douglas (who fought tirelessly to save this fragile resource until her death in 1998 at the age of 108) focused attention on the area with her moving and insightful book *The Everglades: River of Grass,* published in 1947.

In that same year, 1.5 million acres—less than 20% of the Everglades' wilderness—were established as Everglades National Park. At that time, few lawmakers understood how neighboring ecosystems relate to each other.

Everglades National Park

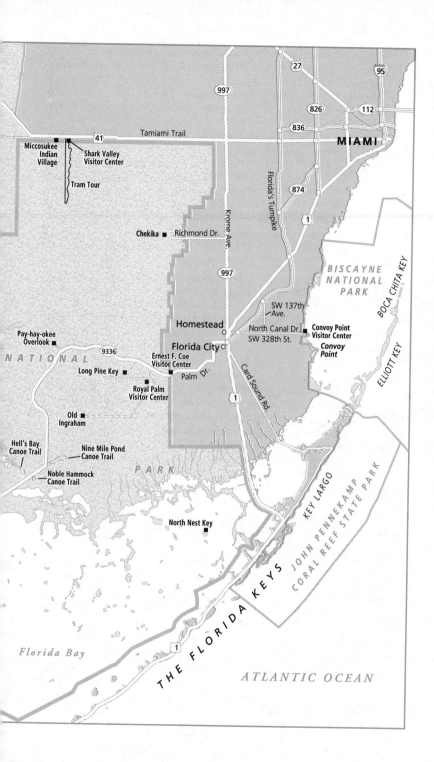

Miccosukee
Indian
Village

Shark Valley
Visitor Center

Tram Tour

Tamiami Trail

MIAMI

Chekika Richmond Dr.

Pay-hay-okee
Overlook

NATIONAL

9336

Long Pine Key

Ernest F. Coe
Visitor Center

Royal Palm
Visitor Center

Palm Dr.

Old
Ingraham

Homestead

Florida City

SW 137th
Ave.

North Canal Dr.
SW 328th St.

Convoy Point
Visitor Center

Convoy
Point

BISCAYNE
NATIONAL
PARK

BOCA CHITA KEY

ELLIOTT KEY

Card Sound Rd.

Florida's Turnpike

Krome Ave.

Hell's Bay
Canoe Trail

Nine Mile Pond
Canoe Trail

PARK

Noble Hammock
Canoe Trail

North Nest Key

KEY LARGO

JOHN PENNEKAMP
CORAL REEF STATE PARK

Florida Bay

THE FLORIDA KEYS

ATLANTIC OCEAN

Consequently, the park is heavily affected by surrounding territories and is at the butt end of every environmental insult that occurs upstream in Miami. Recently, environmental activists have succeeded in persuading politicians to enact legislation to clean up the pollution that has threatened this unusual ecosystem ever since the days when heavy industry—most notably the sugar industry—first moved into the area.

While there has been a marked decrease in the indigenous wildlife here, Everglades National Park nevertheless remains one of the few places where you can see dozens of endangered species in their natural habitat, including the swallowtail butterfly, American crocodile, leatherback turtle, southern bald eagle, West Indian manatee, and Florida panther.

> **Lazy River**
> It takes a month for 1 gallon of water to move through Everglades National Park.

Take your time on the trails, and a hypnotic beauty begins to unfold. Follow the rustling of a bush, and you might see a small green tree frog or tiny brown anole lizard, with its bright-red–spotted throat. Crane your neck to see around a bend and discover a delicate, brightly painted mule-ear orchid.

The slow and subtle splendor of this exotic land may not be immediately appealing to kids raised on video games and rapid-fire commercials, but they'll certainly remember the experience and thank you for it later. Meanwhile, you'll find plenty of dramatic fun around the park, such as airboat rides, alligator wrestling, and biking, to keep the kids satisfied for at least a day.

In the 1800s, before the southern Everglades were designated a national park, the only inhabited piece of this wilderness was a quiet fishing village called Flamingo. Accessible only by boat and leveled every few years by hurricanes, the mosquito-infested town never grew very popular. When the 38-mile-long (61km) road from Florida City was completed in 1922, many of those who did live here fled to someplace either more or less remote. Today, Flamingo is a center for visitor activities and is the main jumping-off point for backcountry camping and exploration. It is also now home to National Park Service and concessionaire employees and their families. Some 1,400 residents still live in this small enclave in the eastern section of the park, though the local agency governing the area has recently begun a buyout program so the area can be returned to its original state.

JUST THE FACTS

GETTING THERE & ACCESS POINTS Although the Everglades may seem overwhelmingly large and unapproachable, it's easy to get to the park's two main areas—the northern section, which is accessible via Shark Valley and Everglades City, or the southern section, accessible through the Ernest F. Coe Visitor Center, near Homestead and Florida City.

Northern entrances A popular day trip for Miamians, **Shark Valley,** a 13-mile (21km) paved road ending at an observation tower overlooking the pulsating heart of the Everglades, is the easiest and most scenic way to explore the Everglades. Just 25 miles (40km) west of the Florida Turnpike, Shark Valley is best reached via the Tamiami Trail, South Florida's pre-Turnpike, two-lane road, which cuts across the southern part of the state along the park's northern border. Roadside attractions (boat rides and alligator farms, for example) along the Trail are operated by the Miccosukee Indian Village and are fun and worth a quick stop. An excellent tram tour (leaving from the Shark Valley Visitor Center) goes deep into the park along a trail that's also terrific for biking. This is also the best way to reach the park's only accommodation (and full-service outfitters), the Flamingo Lodge. Shark Valley is about an hour's drive from Miami.

A little less than 10 miles (16km) west along the Tamiami Trail from Shark Valley, you'll discover the **Big Cypress National Preserve,** in which stretches of vibrant green cypress and pine trees make for a fabulous Kodak moment. If you pick up State Road 29 and head south from the Tamiami Trail, you'll hit a modified version of civilization in the form of Everglades City (where the Everglades meets the Gulf of Mexico) and see another entrance to the park and the **Gulf Coast Visitor Center.** From Miami to Shark Valley: Go west on I-395 to State Road 821 south (the Florida Tpk.). Take the U.S. 41/SW 8th Street (Tamiami Trail) exit. The Shark Valley entrance is just 25 miles (40km) west. To get to Everglades City, continue west on the Tamiami Trail and head south on State Road 29. Everglades City is approximately a 2½-hour drive from Miami, but because it is scenic, it may take longer if you stop or slow down to view your surroundings.

Southern entrance—via Homestead and Florida City   If you're in a rush to hit the 'glades and don't care about the scenic route, this is your best bet. Just southeast of Homestead and Florida City, off of State Road 9336, the southern access to the park will bring you directly to the Ernest F. Coe Visitor Center. Right inside the park, 4 miles beyond the Ernest F. Coe Visitor Center, is the Royal Palm Visitor Center, which is the starting point for the two most popular walking trails—Gumbo Limbo and Anhinga, on which you will witness a plethora of birds and wildlife roaming freely, unperturbed by their human voyeurs. If you go 13 miles (21km) west of the Ernest F. Coe Visitor Center, you will hit the Pa-hay-okee Overlook Trail, which is worth a trek across the boardwalk to reach the observation tower, over which vultures and hawks hover protectively amidst a resplendent, picturesque, bird's-eye view of the Everglades. From Miami to the southern entrance: Go west on I-395 to State Road 821 south (Florida Tpk.). The Turnpike will end in Florida City. Take your first right turn through the center of town (you can't miss it) and follow the signs to the park entrance on State Road 9336. The Ernest F. Coe Visitor Center is about 1½ hours from Miami.

VISITOR CENTERS & INFORMATION   General inquiries and specific questions should be directed to **Everglades National Park Headquarters,** 40001 S.R. 9336, Homestead, FL 33034 (© **305/242-7700**). Ask for a copy of *Parks and Preserves,* a free newspaper that's filled with up-to-date information about goings-on in the Everglades. Headquarters is staffed by helpful phone operators daily from 8:30am to 4:30pm. You can also try www.nps.gov/ever/visit/index.htm or www.florida-everglades.com.

Note that all hours listed are for the high season, generally November through May. During the slow summer months, many offices and outfitters keep abbreviated hours. Always call ahead to confirm hours of operation.

Thirty-eight miles (61km) from the main entrance, at the park's southern access, is the **Flamingo Visitor Center,** which offers natural-history exhibits and information on Flamingo's visitor services.

Especially since its recent expansion, the **Ernest F. Coe Visitor Center,** located at the Park Headquarters' entrance, west of Homestead and Florida City, is the best place for gathering information for your trip. In addition to information on tours and boat rentals, and free brochures outlining trails, wildlife, and activities, you will also find state-of-the-art educational displays, films, and interactive exhibits. A gift shop sells postcards, film, unusual gift items, an impressive selection of books about the Everglades, and a supply of your most important gear: insect repellent. The shop is open from 8am to 5pm daily.

The **Royal Palm Visitor Center,** a small nature museum located 3 miles (5km) past the park's main entrance, is a smaller information center. The museum is not great (there are displays with recorded messages interpreting the park's ecosystem), but the center is the departure point for the popular Anhinga and Gumbo Limbo Trails. Open daily from 8am to 4pm.

Knowledgeable rangers, who provide brochures and personal insight into the park's activities, also staff the **Shark Valley Visitor Center,** at the park's northern entrance, and the **Flamingo Visitor Center.** Both are open from 8:30am to 5pm.

ENTRANCE FEES, PERMITS & REGULATIONS   Permits and passes can be purchased only at the main park, Chekika, or Shark Valley entrance station.

Even if you are just visiting the park for an afternoon, you'll need to buy a 7-day permit, which costs $10 per vehicle. Pedestrians and cyclists are charged $5 each and $4 at Shark Valley.

An Everglades Park Pass, valid for a year's worth of unlimited admissions, is available for $20. U.S. citizens may purchase a 12-month Golden Eagle Passport for $65, which is valid for entrance into any U.S. national park. U.S. citizens aged 62 and older pay only $10 for a Golden Age Passport—that's valid for life. A Golden Access Passport is available free to U.S. citizens with disabilities.

Permits are required for campers to stay overnight either in the backcountry or in the primitive campsites. See "Camping & Houseboating in the Everglades," in "Where to Stay," later in this chapter.

Those who want to fish without a charter captain must obtain a standard State of Florida saltwater fishing license. These are available in the park at Flamingo Lodge or at any tackle shop or sporting goods store nearby. Nonresidents will pay $17 for a 7-day license or $7 for 3 days. Florida residents can get a fishing license good for the whole year for $14. Snook and crawfish licenses must be purchased separately at a cost of $2.

Charter captains carry vessel licenses that cover all paying passengers, but ask to be sure. Freshwater fishing licenses are available at various bait-and-tackle shops outside the park at the same rates as those offered inside the park. A good one nearby is **Don's Bait & Tackle,** located at 30710 S. Federal Hwy., in Homestead right on U.S. 1 (© **305/247-6616**). *Note:* Most of the area's freshwater fishing, limited to murky canals and artificial lakes near housing developments, is hardly worth the trouble when so much good saltwater fishing is available.

Firearms are not allowed anywhere in the park.

SEASONS   There are two distinct seasons in the Everglades: high season and mosquito season. High season is also dry season and lasts from late November to May. Despite the bizarre cold and wet weather patterns that El Niño brought in 1998, most winters here are warm, sunny, and breezy—a good combination for keeping the bugs away. This is the best time to visit because low water levels attract the largest variety of wading birds and their predators. As the dry season wanes, wildlife follows the receding water; and by the end of May, the only living things you are sure to spot will cause you to itch. The worst, called "no-see-ums," are not even swattable. If you choose to visit during the buggy season, be vigilant in applying bug spray.

Also, realize that many establishments and operators either close or curtail offerings in the summer, so always call ahead to check schedules.

RANGER PROGRAMS   More than 50 ranger programs, free with admission, are offered each month during high season and give visitors an opportunity to gain an expert's perspective. Ranger-led walks and talks are offered year-round from the Royal Palm Visitor Center, west of the main entrance, and at the Flamingo and Gulf Coast Visitor Centers, as well as the Shark Valley Visitor Center during the winter months. Park rangers tend to be helpful, well informed, and good-humored. Some programs occur regularly, such as Royal Palm Visitor Center's Glade Glimpses, a walking tour during which rangers point out flora and fauna and discuss issues affecting the Everglades' survival. These tours are scheduled at 12:30pm daily. The Anhinga Ambles, a similar program that takes place on the Anhinga Trail, starts at 10:30am or 3:30pm daily. Since times, programs, and locations vary from month to month, check a schedule, available at any of the visitor centers (see above).

SAFETY   There are many dangers inherent in this vast wilderness area. *Always* let someone know your itinerary before you set out on an extended hike. It's mandatory that you file an itinerary when camping overnight in the backcountry (which you can do when you apply for your overnight permit at either the Flamingo Visitor Center or the Gulf Coast Visitor Center). When you're on the water, watch for weather changes; severe thunderstorms and high winds often develop rapidly. Swimming is not recommended because of the presence of alligators, sharks, and barracudas. Watch out for the region's four indigenous poisonous snakes: diamondback and pygmy rattlesnakes, coral snakes (identifiable by their colorful rings), and water moccasins (which swim on the surface of the water). Again, bring insect repellent to ward off mosquitoes and biting flies. First aid is available from park rangers. The nearest hospital is in Homestead, 10 miles (16km) from the park's main entrance.

SEEING THE HIGHLIGHTS
Shark Valley, a 13-mile (21km) paved road (ideal for biking) through the Everglades, provides a fine introduction to the wonder of the Everglades, but don't plan on spending more than a few hours there. Bicycling or taking a guided tram tour (p. 285) are fantastic ways to see the park's highlights.

If you want to see a greater array of plant and animal life, make sure that you venture into the park through the main entrance, pick up a trail map, and dedicate at least a day to exploring from there.

Stop first along the Anhinga and Gumbo Limbo trails, which start right next to one another, 3 miles (5km) from the park's main entrance. These trails provide a thorough introduction to Everglades flora and fauna and are highly recommended to first-time visitors. Each of them is one-half mile (1km) round-trip. **Gumbo Limbo Trail** (my pick for best walking trail in the Everglades) meanders through a gorgeous shaded, junglelike hammock of gumbo limbo trees, royal palms, ferns, orchids, air plants, and a general blanket of vegetation, though it doesn't put you in close contact with much wildlife. **Anhinga Trail** is one of the most popular trails in the park because of its abundance of wildlife: There's more water and wildlife in this area of the park than in most parts of the Everglades, especially during dry season. Alligators, lizards, turtles, river otters, herons, egrets, and other animals abound, making this one of the best trails for seeing wildlife. Arrive early to spot the widest selection of exotic birds, like the Anhinga bird, the Trail's namesake, a large black fishing bird so accustomed to humans that many of them build their nests in plain view. Take your time—at

Island Hopping

Beginning at Marco Island and heading south into the Everglades, there are a whopping 10,000 islands, whose primary residents are the same red mangrove trees that can be found throughout the Everglades. Often called "walking trees" because of their roots, mangrove trees arch above the ground like crouched legs.

least an hour is recommended for each trail. Both are wheelchair accessible. If you treat the trails and modern boardwalk as pathways to get through quickly, rather than destinations to experience and savor slowly, you'll miss out on the still beauty and hidden treasures that await.

If you want to get closer to nature, a few hours in a canoe along any of the trails allows paddlers the chance to sense the park's fluid motion and to become a part of the ecosphere. Visitors who choose this option end up feeling more like explorers than merely observers. (See "Sports & Outdoor Activities," below.)

No matter which option you choose (and there are many), I strongly recommend staying for the 7pm program, available during high season at the Long Pine Key Amphitheater. This talk and slide show, given by one of the park's rangers, will give you a detailed overview of the park's history, natural resources, wildlife, and threats to its survival.

SPORTS & OUTDOOR ACTIVITIES

BIKING   The relatively flat 38-mile-long (61km) paved Main Park Road is great for biking because of the multitude of hardwood hammocks (treelike islands or dense stands of hardwood trees that grow only a few inches above land) and a dwarf cypress forest (stunted and thinly distributed cypress trees, which grow in poor soil on drier land), but Shark Valley is the best biking trail by far. Expect to spend 2 to 3 hours along either.

If the park isn't flooded from excess rain (which it often is, especially in spring), Shark Valley in Everglades National Park is South Florida's most scenic bicycle trail. Many locals haul their bikes out to the 'glades for a relaxing day of wilderness-trail riding. You'll share the flat, paved road only with other bikers and a menagerie of wildlife. (Don't be surprised to see a gator lounging in the sun or a deer munching on some grass. Otters, turtles, alligators, and snakes are common companions in the Shark Valley area.) There are no shortcuts, so if you become tired or are unable to complete the entire 15-mile (24km) trip, turn around and return on the same road.

Those who love to mountain bike, and who prefer solitude, might check out the **Southern Glades Trail,** a 14-mile-long (23km) unpaved trail opened in late 1998 that is lined with native trees and teeming with wildlife such as deer, alligators, and the occasional snake. The remote trail runs along the C-111 canal, off State Road 9336 and Southwest 217th Street.

You can rent bikes at the Flamingo Lodge, Marina, and Outpost Resort (see "Where to Stay," below) for $17 per 24 hours, $14 per full day, $8.50 per half day (any 4-hr. period), and $3 per hour. A $50 deposit is required for each rental. Rentals can be picked up from 7am and the bikes have to be returned by 5pm. Bicycles are also available from Shark Valley Tram Tours, at the park's Shark Valley entrance (© **305/221-8455**), for $4.75 per hour; rentals can be picked up anytime between 8:30am and 3pm and must be returned by 4pm.

BIRD-WATCHING   More than 350 species of birds make their homes in the Everglades. Tropical birds from the Caribbean and temperate species from North America can be found here, along with exotics that have blown in from more distant regions. Eco and Mrazek ponds, located near Flamingo, are two of the best places for birding, especially in early morning or late afternoon in the dry winter months. Pick up a free birding checklist from a visitor center (see "Just the Facts," earlier in this chapter), and ask there what's been spotted in recent days.

CANOEING   Canoeing through the Everglades may be one of the most serene, surprisingly diverse adventures you'll ever have. From a canoe (where you're incredibly close to the water level), your vantage point is priceless. Canoers in the Glades can co-exist with the gators and birds there in a way no one else can; they behave as if you are part of the ecosystem—something that can't happen on an airboat. A ranger-guided boat tour is your best bet and costs $19.95, plus a required deposit. As always, a ranger will help you understand the surroundings and give you an education on what you're seeing.

Everglades National Park's longest "trails" are designed for boat and canoe travel, and many are marked as clearly as walking trails. The **Noble Hammock Canoe Trail,** a 2-mile (3.25km) loop, takes 1 to 2 hours and is recommended for beginning canoers. The **Hell's Bay Canoe Trail,** a 3- to 6-mile (5–10km) course for hardier paddlers, takes 2 to 6 hours, depending on how far you choose to go. Park rangers can recommend other trails that best suit your abilities, time limitations, and interests.

You can rent a canoe at the Flamingo Lodge, Marina, and Outpost Resort (p. 286) for $40 for 24 hours, $32 per full day, $22 per half day (any 4-hr. period), and $8 per hour. They also have family canoes that rent for $12, $30, $40, and $50, respectively. Skiffs, kayaks, and tandem kayaks are also available. The concessionaire will shuttle your party to the trail head of your choice and pick you up afterward. Rental facilities are open daily from 6am to 8pm.

Overnight canoe rentals are available for $50 to $60. During ideal weather conditions (stay away during bug season!), you can paddle right out to the Gulf and camp on the beach. However, Gulf waters at beach sites can be extremely rough, and people in small watercraft such as a canoe should exercise caution.

You can also take a canoe tour from the Parks Docks on Chokoloskee Causeway on State Road 29, a half-mile (.75km) south of the traffic circle at the ranger station in Everglades City. Call Everglades National Park Boat Tours at ✆ **800/445-7724.**

FISHING   About one-third of Everglades National Park is open water. Freshwater fishing is popular in brackish **Nine-Mile Pond** (25 miles [40km] from the main entrance) and other spots along the Main Park Road, but because of the high mercury levels found in the Everglades, freshwater fishers are warned not to eat their catch. Before casting, check in at a visitor center, as many of the park's lakes are preserved for observation only. Fishing licenses are required. See "Just the Facts," earlier in this chapter.

Saltwater anglers will find snapper and sea trout plentiful. Charter boats and guides are available at Flamingo Lodge, Marina, and Outpost Resort (see "Where to Stay," later in this chapter). Phone for information and reservations.

MOTORBOATING   Motorboating around the Everglades seems like a great way to see plants and animals in remote habitats, and, indeed, is an interesting and fulfilling experience as you throttle into nature. However, environmentalists are taking stock of the damage motorboats (especially airboats) inflict on the delicate ecosystem. If you choose to motor, remember that most of the areas near land are "no wake" zones and that, for the protection of nesting birds, landing is prohibited on most of the little mangrove islands. Motorboating is allowed in certain areas such as Florida Bay, the backcountry toward Everglades City, and the Ten Thousand Islands area. In all the freshwater lakes, however, motorboats are prohibited if they're above 5 horsepower. There's a long list of restrictions and restricted areas, so get a copy of the park's boating rules from National Park Headquarters before setting out (see "Just the Facts," above).

The Everglades' only marina—accommodating about 50 boats with electric and water hookups—is the Flamingo Lodge, Marina, and Outpost Resort, in Flamingo. The well-marked channel to the Flamingo is accessible to boats with a maximum 4-foot (1.25m) draft and is open year-round. Reservations can be made through the marina store (© **941/695-3101,** ext. 304). Skiffs with 15-horsepower motors are available for rent. These low-power boats cost $90 per day, $65 per half day (any 5-hr. period), and $22 per hour. A $125 deposit is required.

ORGANIZED TOURS

AIRBOAT TOURS   Shallow-draft, fan-powered airboats were invented in the Everglades by frog hunters who were tired of poling through the brushes. Airboats cut through the sawgrass and are sort of like hydraulic boats in which at high enough speeds, the boat actually lifts above the sawgrass and into the air. And even though airboats are the most efficient (not to mention fast and fun!) way to get around, they are not permitted in the park (these shallow-bottom runabouts tend to inflict severe damage on animals and plants). Just outside the boundaries of the Everglades, however, you'll find a number of outfitters offering rides (if you choose to ride on one, you should consider bringing earplugs; these high-speed boats are loud).

Airboat rides are offered at the **Miccosukee Indian Village,** just west of the Shark Valley entrance on U.S. 41/the Tamiami Trail (© **305/223-8380**). Native American guides will take you through the reserve's swampy brushes at high speeds and stop along the way to point out alligators, native plants, and exotic birds. The price is $10. However, *be warned and advised:* we are not recommending this particular outfit over the many others you're sure to see along the way—they are merely the ones closest to the Shark Valley entrance. While the Miccosukee can offer excellent tours, we've also received complaints about both their tours (taking visitors along a canal instead of above the sawgrass) and their tour guides (not pointing out wildlife or talking much at all). Because the Miccosukee Indian Village is, essentially, a tourist spot, complete with a souvenir-laden shopping area, be wary of the fact that the airboat tours given here may not be 100 percent authentic.

Nevertheless, the ones offered by the reservation can be campy and kitschy fun—if you get a good guide. The situation isn't going to be any different anywhere else: As always, the quality of your tour is only going to be as good as the quality of your tour guide, and there's almost no way of judging that before you lay down your money and go. That said, the best boat rides in the Everglades seem to be in Everglades City and anywhere that's off the Indian Reservation.

The **Everglades Alligator Farm,** 4 miles (6.5km) south of Palm Drive on Southwest 192nd Avenue (© **305/247-2628**), offers half-hour guided airboat tours from 9am until 6pm daily. The price, which includes admission to the park, is $14.50 for adults, $8 for children.

MOTORBOAT TOURS   Both Florida Bay and backcountry tours are offered at the Flamingo Lodge, Marina, and Outpost Resort (see "Where to Stay," below). Florida Bay tours cruise nearby estuaries and sandbars, while six-passenger backcountry boats visit smaller sloughs. Passengers can expect to see birds and a variety of other animals (I once saw a raccoon and some wild pigs). Both are available in 1½- and 2-hour versions that cost an average of $16 for adults, $8 for children, free for under 6. Tours depart throughout the day, and reservations are recommended. There are also charter-fishing and sightseeing boats that can be booked through the resort's main reservation number (℡ **941/695-3101**).

TRAM TOURS   At the park's Shark Valley entrance, open-air tram buses take visitors on 2-hour naturalist-led tours that delve 7½ miles (12km) into the wilderness. At the trail's midsection, passengers can disembark and climb a 65-foot (20m) observation tower that offers good views of the 'glades, though the tower on the Pa-hay-okee trail is better. Visitors will see plenty of wildlife and endless acres of sawgrass. Tours run November through April only, daily from 9am to 4pm, and are sometimes stalled by flooding or particularly heavy mosquito infestation. Reservations are recommended from December to March. The cost is $9.30 for adults, $5.15 for children 12 and under, and $8.25 for seniors. For further information, contact the **Shark Valley Tram Tours** at ℡ **305/221-8455.**

SHOPPING

You won't find big malls or lots of boutiques in this area, although there is an outlet center nearby, the **Keys Factory Shops** (℡ **305/248-4727**), at 250 E. Palm Dr. (where the Florida Tpk. meets U.S. 1), in Florida City, with more than 60 stores, including Nike Factory Store, Bass Co. Store, Levi's, OshKosh, and Izod. You can pick up a free coupon booklet (called the "Come Back Pack") from the Customer Service Center, which includes coupons good for discounts at the outlet center. It's open Monday through Saturday until 9pm, Sunday until 6pm.

A necessary stop and a good place for a refreshment is one of Florida's best-known fruit stands: **Robert Is Here** (℡ **305/246-1592**). Robert has been selling his homegrown treats for nearly 40 years at the corner of Southwest 344th Street (Palm Dr.) and Southwest 192nd Avenue. Here, you'll find the freshest pineapples, bananas, papayas, mangos, and melons anywhere, as well as his famous shakes in unusual flavors like Key lime, coconut, orange, and cantaloupe. Exotic fruits, bottled jellies, hot sauces, and salad dressings are also available. This is a great place to pick up culinary souvenirs and sample otherwise unavailable goodies. Open daily from 8am to 7pm.

Along Tamiami Trail, there are several roadside shops hawking Native American handicrafts, including one at the **Miccosukee Indian Village** (℡ **305/ 223-8380**), just west of the Shark Valley entrance. At nearly every one of these shops, you'll find the same stock of feathered dream-catchers, stuffed alligator heads and claws, turquoise jewelry, and other trinkets. Be sure to take note of the unique, colorful, handmade cloth Miccosukee dolls.

WHERE TO STAY

The only lodging in the park proper is the Flamingo Lodge, a fairly priced and very recommendable option. However, there are a few hotels just outside the park that are even cheaper. A $45 million casino hotel (℡ **877/242-6464; www.miccosukee.com**) was built adjacent to the Miccosukee bingo and gaming hall on the northern edge of the park. And although bugs can be a major nuisance, especially in the warm months, camping is really the way to go in this very primitive environment, since it's the best way to fully experience South Florida's wilderness.

LODGING IN EVERGLADES NATIONAL PARK

Flamingo Lodge, Marina, and Outpost Resort ★★   The Flamingo Lodge is the only lodging actually located within the boundaries of Everglades National Park. This woodsy, sprawling complex offers rooms (overlooking the Florida Bay) in either a two-story simple motel or the lodge. Either option feels very much like being at summer camp, with a few more amenities. Rooms are your standard, cookie-cutter, motel-style rooms, with functional bathrooms. No luxury here, but it's nonetheless a comfort for those who'd rather not experience the great outdoors while they sleep. More interesting than the actual motel, however, are the visitors who crop up on the lawn—alligators, raccoons, and other nomadic creatures. The hotel is open year-round, although the restaurant (see "Where to Dine in and Around the Park," below) closes in the summer.

1 Flamingo Lodge Hwy., Flamingo, FL 33034. © **800/600-3813** or 941/695-3101. Fax 941/695-3921. www. flamingolodge.com. 127 units. Winter from $95 double, from $99–135 cottage, $110–$145 suite. Off-season $65–$79 double, $59 cottage, no concrete prices for suites. Rates for cottages or suites are for 1 to 4 people. Children under 18 stay free. Continental breakfast included in rates May–Oct. AE, DC, DISC, MC. Take Florida Tpk. south to Florida City; exit on U.S. 1. At 4-way intersection, turn right onto Palm Dr.; continue for 3 miles (5km) and turn left at Robert Is Here fruit stand. Turn right at the 3-way intersection. The park entrance is 3 miles (5km) ahead. Continue for about 38 more miles (61km) to reach lodge. **Amenities:** Waterside bar and restaurant; freshwater swimming pool; convenience store; bike, canoe, and kayak rentals; marina with boat tours; boat rentals; houseboat and fishing charters; coin-op washers and dryers. *In room:* A/C, TV in standard rooms and suites but not in cottages, kitchen in cottages and suites only.

CAMPING & HOUSEBOATING IN THE EVERGLADES

Campgrounds are available year round in Flamingo, Chekika, and Long Pine Key. All three have drinking water, picnic tables, charcoal grills, bathrooms, and tent and trailer pads. All welcome RVs, though there are no electrical hook-ups. Flamingo has cold-water showers; Chekika has free hot showers; and Flamingo offers hot showers for $3. Private ground fires are not permitted, but supervised campfire programs are conducted during winter months. Chekika campers must register before 5pm, after which time the gates are locked and only registered campers are allowed access. Long Pine Key and Flamingo are much more popular and require reservations in advance. Reservations may be made through the National Park Reservations Service at © **800/365-CAMP.** Campsites are $14 per night with a 14-day consecutive stay limit, 30 days a year maximum.

Camping is also available in the **backcountry** (those remote areas accessible only by boat, foot, or canoe—basically most of the park) year-round on a first-come, first-served basis. Campers must register with park rangers/get a free permit (see the section on "Safety," earlier in this chapter) in person or by telephone no less than 24 hours before the start of their trip. For more information, contact the Gulf Coast Visitor Center (© **941/695-3311**) or the Flamingo Visitor Center (© **941/695-2945**), which are the only two places that give out these permits. Once you have one, camping sites cost $10 for 1 to 6 people, $20 for 7 to 12 people, and $30 for more than 13 people. Campers can use only designated campsites, which are plentiful and well marked on visitor maps.

Many backcountry sites are *chickee huts*—covered wooden platforms (with toilets) on stilts. They're accessible only by canoe and can accommodate free-standing tents (without stakes). Ground sites are located along interior bays and rivers, and beach camping is also popular. In summer especially, mosquito repellent is necessary gear.

Houseboat rentals are one of the park's best-kept secrets. Available through the Flamingo Lodge, Marina, and Outpost Resort, motorized houseboats make it possible to explore some of the park's more remote regions without having to worry about being back by nightfall. You can choose from two different types of houseboats. The first, a 40-foot (12m) pontoon boat, sleeps six to eight people in a single large room that's separated by a central head (bathroom) and shower. There's a small galley (kitchen) that contains a refrigerator, stove, oven, and charcoal grill. Prices aren't cheap, unless you are with a good-sized group. It rents for between $340 and $475 for 2 nights (there is a 2-night min. in high season).

The newer, sleeker Gibson fiberglass boats sleep six and have toilets and showers, air-conditioning, electric stoves, and a full rooftop sun deck. These rent for $575 for 2 nights (the 2-night min. lasts all year long). With either boat, the 7th night is free when renting for a full week.

Boating experience is helpful but not mandatory, as the boats cruise up to only 6 miles per hour (10kmph) and are surprisingly easy to use. In-season, reservations should be made months in advance; call Ⓒ **800/600-3813** or 941/695-3101.

LODGING IN EVERGLADES CITY

Since Everglades City is 35 miles (56km) southeast of Naples and 83 miles (134km) west of Miami, many people choose to explore this western entrance to Everglades National Park, located off the Tamiami Trail, on State Road 29. An annual seafood festival held the first weekend in February is a major event that draws hordes of people. Everglades City (the gateway to the Ten Thousand Islands), where the 'glades meets the Gulf of Mexico, is the closest thing you'll get to civilization in South Florida's swampy frontier, with a few tourist traps—er, shops, a restaurant, and two bed-and-breakfasts (see below).

Ivey House B&B ★★ *Finds*   Housed in what used to be a recreational center for the men who built the Tamiami Trail, the Ivey House offers three types of accommodations. In the original house, there are 10 small rooms that share communal bathrooms (one each for women and men). One private cottage consists of two bedrooms, a full kitchen, a private bath, and a screened-in porch. The Ivey's new inn (opened in 2001) adds 17 rooms (with private bathrooms) that face a courtyard with a screened-in shallow "conversation" pool. During the summer, however, the mosquitoes are out in full force and a trip to the pool could leave you with multiple bites as it did me (screens or not). Bring bug spray!

Owners Sandee and David Harraden are extremely knowledgeable about the Everglades, and usually the guests are as well. A living-room area offers guests the opportunity to mingle. A typical continental breakfast is available from 7 to 9am only. Boxed lunches, stored in a cooler so you can bring them along for your Everglades excursions, are offered for $9.50 each. Dinners may be available by the time you go. Call to get more information. The Ivey House is closed in September. *Note:* No smoking in any of the buildings.

107 Camellia St., Everglades City, FL 34139. Ⓒ **941/695-3299.** Fax 941/695-4155. www.iveyhouse.com. 28 units. Winter $60–$85 main house (older rooms); $125–$155 cottage (2-night min.); $100 and up for 1 of the newer rooms. Off-season $50–$70 main house; $90–$105 cottage; $90 and up for newer rooms. MC, V. **Amenities:** Restaurant; small pool; free use of bikes; Everglades excursions available. *In room:* A/C (all rooms), TV, kitchen (cottage only), fridge (inn and cottage),.

On the Banks of the Everglades ★★★ *Finds*   This very cute bed-and-breakfast is right on the money, as far as kitsch is concerned. On the Banks of the Everglades is a fabulous retreat from the lush greenery of the swampy

Everglades to the even more lush greenery of money. Located in a building that was formerly the first bank established, in 1923, in Collier County, money is this place's premise, but it won't cost you too much to stay here. Rooms such as the Trust Room, the Checking Department, and the Stocks and Bond Room are clean and comfortable (though bathrooms are down the hall) and are all located on the floor where banking used to be done until 1962. All other rooms, such as the Mortgage Loan Department, Savings Department, and Dividends Department do have bathrooms. Perhaps the best things about the place, besides the congenial service, are that breakfast is served in the bank's fully restored vault and that original artifacts from the bank are still visible, such as the 3,000-pound cannonball safe. Unlike a real bank, however, the knowledgeable staff at the inn is happy to give free advice on what to do in the area.

201 W. Broadway, Everglades City, FL 34139. (C) 888/431-1977 or 941/695-3151. Fax 941/695-3335. www. banksoftheeverglades.com. 10 units, 6 with private bath. $85 (shared bath); $153–$160 (private bath). Rates include continental breakfast. AE, DISC, MC, V. Open Nov–June. **Amenities:** Free use of bikes; Everglades excursions available. In room: A/C, TV.

Rod & Gun Lodge   This rustic, old white clapboard house has plenty of history and all kinds of activities for sports enthusiasts, including a swimming pool, bicycle rentals, tennis center, and nearby boat rentals and private fishing guides. Sitting on the banks of the sleepy Barron River, the Rod & Gun Lodge was originally built as a private residence nearly 170 years ago, but Barron Collier turned it into a cozy hunting lodge in the 1920s. President Herbert Hoover vacationed here after his 1928 election victory, and President Harry S Truman flew in to sign Everglades National Park into existence in 1947 and stayed over as well. Other guests have included President Richard Nixon, Burt Reynolds, and Mick Jagger. The public rooms are beautifully paneled and hung with tarpon, wild boar, deer antlers, and other trophies. Guest rooms in this single-story building are unfussy but perfectly comfortable. Out by the swimming pool and riverbank, a screened veranda with ceiling fans offers a pleasant place for a libation. The excellent seafood restaurant serves breakfast, lunch, and dinner. The entire property is no-smoking. *Note:* No credit cards are accepted.

Riverside Dr. and Broadway (P.O. Box 190), Everglades City, FL 34139. (C) 941/695-2101. 17 units, all with bathroom (some with shower only). Winter $95 single or double; off-season $75 single or double. No credit cards. Closed after July 4 for the summer. **Amenities:** Restaurant; pool; tennis courts; bicycle rentals. In room: A/C, TV.

NEARBY IN HOMESTEAD & FLORIDA CITY

Homestead and Florida City, two adjacent towns that were almost blown off the map by Hurricane Andrew in 1992, have come back better than before. Located about 10 miles (16km) from the park's main entrance, along U.S. 1, 35 miles (56km) south of Miami, these somewhat rural towns offer several budget lodging options, including a handful of chain hotels. There is a **Days Inn** (© 305/245-1260) in Homestead and a **Hampton Inn** (© 800/426-7866 or 305/247-8833) right off the turnpike in Florida City. However, the best option is listed below.

Best Western Gateway to the Keys   This two-story standard motel offers contemporary style and comfort about 10 miles (16km) from the park's main entrance. A decent-size pool and a small spa make it an attractive option to some. Each identical standard room has bright, tropical bedspreads and oversize picture windows. The suites offer convenient extras like a microwave, a coffeemaker, an extra sink, and a small fridge. Clean and conveniently located, the only drawback is that in season, there is often a 3-day minimum stay requirement. You'd do best to call the local reservation line (© 305/246-5100) instead of the toll-free number—on several occasions, the hotel made an exception to the rule while the central reservation line was not able to do the same.

411 S. Krome Ave. (U.S. 1), Florida City, FL 33034. ℂ 800/528-1234 or 305/246-5100. Fax 305/242-0056. www.bestwestern.com. 114 units. Winter from $91–$109; off-season from $71–$89. Rates include continental breakfast. During races and the very high season, there may be a 3-night min. stay. AE, DC, DISC, MC, V. **Amenities:** Pool; spa; laundry and dry-cleaning. *In room:* A/C, TV, dataport, fridge, coffeemaker, hair dryer.

WHERE TO DINE IN & AROUND THE PARK

You won't find fancy nouvelle cuisine in this suburbanized farm country, but there are plenty of fast-food chains along U.S. 1 and a few old favorites worth a taste, listed below.

Here for nearly a quarter of a century, **El Toro Taco Family Restaurant** (p. 161) at 1 S. Krome Ave. (near Mowry Dr. and Campbell Dr.; ℂ **305/ 245-8182**) opens daily at 9:30am and stays crowded until at least 9pm most days. The fresh grilled meats, tacos, burritos, salsas, guacamole, and stews are all mild and delicious. No matter how big your appetite, it's hard to spend more than $12 per person at this Mexican outpost. Bring your own beer or wine.

Housed in a squat, one-story, windowless stone building that looks something like a medieval fort, the **Capri Restaurant,** 935 N. Krome Ave., Florida City (ℂ **305/247-1542**), has been serving hearty Italian-American fare since 1958. Great pastas and salads complement a full menu (portions are big) of meat and fish dishes. They serve lunch and dinner every day (except Sun) until 11pm.

The **Miccosukee Restaurant** (ℂ **305/223-8380**), just west of the Shark Valley entrance on the Tamiami Trail (U.S. 41), serves authentic pumpkin bread, fry bread, fish, and not-so-authentic Native American interpretations of tacos and fried chicken. It's worth a stop for brunch, lunch, or dinner.

In Everglades City, **The Oyster House** (ℂ **941/695-2073**) on Chokoloskee Causeway, State Road (the locals call it Highway) 29 South, is a large but homey seafood restaurant with modest prices, excellent service, and a fantastic view of the 10,000 islands. Try their hush puppies.

Once inside the Everglades, you'll want to eat at the only restaurant within the boundaries of this huge park, **The Flamingo Restaurant** (ℂ **941/ 695-3101**). Located in the Flamingo Lodge (see "Where to Stay," earlier in this chapter), this is a very civilized and affordable restaurant. Besides the spectacular view of Florida Bay and numerous Keys from the large, airy dining room, you'll also find fresh fish that is grilled, blackened, or deep-fried. Dinner entrees come with salad or conch chowder, steamed vegetables, black beans, and rice or baked potato. The large menu has something for everyone, including basic and very tasty sandwiches, pastas, burgers, and salads. A kids' menu offers standard choices like hot dogs, grilled cheese, or fried shrimp for less than $6. Prices are surprisingly moderate, with full meals starting at about $11 and going no higher than $22. You may need reservations for dinner, however, especially in season.

2 Biscayne National Park ✦

35 miles (56km) S of Miami, 21 miles (34km) E of Everglades National Park

With only about 500,000 visitors each year (mostly boaters and divers), the unusual Biscayne National Park is one of the least-crowded parks in the country. Perhaps that's because the park is a little more difficult than most to access—more than 95% of its 181,500 acres are underwater.

The park's significance was first formally acknowledged in 1968 when, in an unprecedented move (and against intense pressure from developers), President

Lyndon B. Johnson signed a bill to conserve the barrier islands off South Florida's east coast as a national monument—a protected status that's just a rung below national park. After being twice enlarged, once in 1974 and again in 1980, the waters and land surrounding the northernmost coral reef in North America became a full-fledged national park—the largest of its kind in the country.

To be fully appreciated, Biscayne National Park should be thought of more as a preserve than as a destination. I suggest using your time here to explore underwater life, of course, but also to relax.

The park consists of 44 islands, but only a few of them are open to visitors. The most popular one is **Elliott Key,** which has campsites and a visitor center plus freshwater showers (cold water only), restrooms, trails, and a buoyed swim area. It's located about 9 miles (15km) from **Convoy Point,** the park's official headquarters on land. During Columbus Day weekend, there is a very popular regatta in which a lively crowd of party people gathers—sometimes in the nude—to celebrate the long weekend. If you'd prefer to rough it a little more, the 29-acre island known as **Boca Chita Key,** once an exclusive haven for yachters, has now become a popular spot for all manner of boaters. Visitors can enjoy camping and tour the island's restored historic buildings, including the county's second-largest lighthouse and a tiny chapel.

The park's small mainland mangrove shoreline and keys are best explored by boat. Its extensive reef system is renowned by divers and snorkelers worldwide.

JUST THE FACTS

GETTING THERE & ACCESS POINTS Convoy Point, the park's mainland entrance, is located 9 miles (15km) east of Homestead. To reach the park from Miami, take the Florida Turnpike to the Tallahassee Road (SW 137th Ave.) exit. Turn left, then left again at North Canal Drive (SW 328th St.) and follow signs to the park. Another option is to rent a speedboat in Miami and cruise south for about an hour and a half. If you're coming from U.S. 1, whether you're heading north or south, turn east at North Canal Drive (SW 328th St.). The entrance is approximately 9 miles (15km) away. The rest of the park is accessible only by boat.

Most of Biscayne National Park is accessible only to boaters. Because of that, mooring buoys abound, since it is illegal to anchor on coral. When no buoys are available, boaters must anchor on sand or on the new docks surrounding the small harbor off of Boca Chita. Boats can also dock there overnight for $15. Even the most experienced boaters should carry updated nautical charts of the area, which are available at Convoy Point. The waters are often murky, making the abundant reefs and sandbars difficult to detect—and there are more interesting ways to spend a day than waiting for the tide to rise. There's a boat launch at adjacent Homestead Bayfront Park and 66 slips on Elliott Key, available free on a first-come, first-served basis.

Transportation to and from the visitor center to Elliot Key costs $24.95 round-trip per person and takes about an hour. This is a convenient option, ensuring that you don't get lost on some deserted island by boating there yourself. Call for a seasonal schedule (© **305/230-1100**).

VISITOR CENTERS & INFORMATION The **Convoy Point Visitor Center,** 9700 SW 328th St., Homestead, FL 33033-5634, at the park's main entrance (© **305/230-7275;** fax 305/230-1190; www.biscayne.national-park. com), is the natural starting point for any venture into the park without a boat.

In addition to providing comprehensive information about the park, on request, rangers will show you a short video on the park, its natural surroundings, and what you may see. Open Monday through Friday from 8:30am to 4:30pm and Saturday and Sunday from 8:30am to 5pm.

For information on transportation, glass-bottom boat tours, and snorkeling and scuba-diving expeditions, contact the park concessionaire, **Biscayne National Underwater Park, Inc.,** P.O. Box 1270, Homestead, FL 33030 (*𝒞* **305/230-1100;** fax 305/230-1120; captsaw@bellsouth.net). The company is open daily from 8:30am to 5pm and later in winter.

ENTRANCE FEES & PERMITS   Entering Biscayne National Park is free. There is a $15 per night overnight docking fee at both Boca Chita Key Harbor and Elliott Key Harbor ($7.50 per night for holders of Golden Age or Golden Access Passports). See p. 280 for information on fishing permits. Backcountry camping permits are free and can be picked up from the Convoy Point Visitor Center. For information on fees and permits, call the park ranger at *𝒞* **305/ 230-1144.**

SEEING THE HIGHLIGHTS

Since the park is primarily underwater, the only way to truly experience it is with snorkel or scuba gear. Beneath the surface of Biscayne National Park, the aquatic universe pulses with multicolored life: Bright parrotfish and angelfish, gently rocking sea fans, and coral labyrinths abound. See the "Snorkeling & Scuba Diving" section below for more information.

Afterward, take a picnic out to Elliott Key and taste the crisp salt air blowing off the Atlantic. Or, head to Boca Chita, an intriguing island that was once the private playground of wealthy yachters.

SPORTS & OUTDOOR ACTIVITIES

CANOEING & KAYAKING   Biscayne National Park offers excellent canoeing, both along the coast and across the open water to nearby mangroves and artificial islands that dot the longest uninterrupted shoreline in the state of Florida. Since tides can be strong, only experienced canoeists should attempt to paddle far from shore. If you do plan to go far, first obtain a tide table from the visitor center (see "Just the Facts," above) and paddle with the current. Free ranger-led canoe tours are scheduled every Saturday from 9am to noon; phone for information. You can rent a canoe at the park's concession stand; rates are $8 an hour or $22 for 4 hours. Kayakers will have to bring their own boats but are welcome to explore the same quiet routes. Call *𝒞* **305/230-1100** for reservations, information, ranger tours, and boat rentals.

FISHING   Ocean fishing is excellent year-round at Biscayne National Park; many people cast their lines right from the breakwater jetty at Convoy Point. A fishing license is required (see p. 280) for complete information). Bait is not available in Biscayne National Park but is sold in adjacent Homestead Bayfront Park. Stone crabs and Florida lobsters can be found here, but you're allowed to catch these only on the ocean side when they're in season. There are strict limitations on size, season, number, and method of take (including spear fishing) for both fresh- and saltwater fishing. The latest regulations are available at most marinas, bait-and-tackle shops, and the park's visitor centers. Or you can contact the **Florida Game and Fresh Water Fish Commission,** Bryant Building, 620 S. Meridian St., Tallahassee, FL 32399-1600 (*𝒞* **904/488-1960**).

Fun Fact   **Navigational Hazards**

Boca Chita Key's lighthouse was built by Honeywell Corporation tycoon Mark Honeywell, who owned the Key from 1937 through 1945, as a land-mark and navigational tool for his boat captain. Built out of coral rock with interior stairs designed to resemble something out of King Arthur's round-table days, the lighthouse was lit but never registered properly with the Lighthouse Service, which informed Honeywell that the lighthouse was not charted and, as a result, was considered a navigational hazard rather than a tool (since it was built on the western side of the island in the path of shallow reefs, boaters would have followed the beacon only to go aground). The lighthouse's lights were extinguished, leaving nothing more than a monument to Honeywell's belief in living by his own rules.

HIKING & EXPLORING   Since the majority of this park is underwater, hiking is not the main attraction here, but, nonetheless, there are some interesting sights and trails. At Convoy Point, you can walk along the 370-foot (111m) boardwalk and along the half-mile jetty that serves as a breakwater for the park's harbor. From there, you can usually see brown pelicans, little blue herons, snowy egrets, and a few exotic fish.

Elliott Key is accessible only by boat, but once you're there, you have two good trail options. True to its name, the Loop Trail makes a 1½-mile (2.5km) circle from the bay-side visitor center, through a hardwood hammock and mangroves, to an elevated ocean-side boardwalk. It's likely that you'll see purple and orange land crabs scurrying around the mangrove roots.

Reopened in 1998, Boca Chita Key was once the playground for wealthy tycoons, and it still offers the peaceful beauty that attracted elite anglers from cold climates. Many of the historical buildings are still intact, including an ornamental lighthouse, which was never put into use.

Take advantage of the tours, usually led by a park ranger and available every Sunday at 1pm. The tour, including the boat trip, takes about 3 hours. The price is $19.95 for adults and $9.95 for children. However, call in advance to see if the sea is calm enough for the boat trip—the boats won't run in rough seas.

SNORKELING & SCUBA DIVING   The clear, warm waters of Biscayne National Park are packed with colorful tropical fish that swim in the offshore reefs. If you don't have your own gear, or don't want to lug it to the park, you can rent or buy snorkeling and scuba gear at the full-service dive shop at Convoy Point. Rates are in line with dive shops on the mainland.

The best way to see the park from underwater is to take a snorkeling or scuba-diving tour operated by **Biscayne National Underwater Park, Inc.** (© **305/ 230-1100**). Snorkeling tours depart at 1:30pm daily, last about 3 hours, and cost $29.95 per person, including equipment. They also run weekend two-tank dives for certified divers. The price is $44.95 per person, including two tanks and weights. Reef dives depart on Saturdays and wall dives depart on Sundays. Make your reservations in advance. The shop is open daily from 9am to 5pm.

Before entering the water, be sure to apply waterproof sunblock—once you begin to explore, it's easy to lose track of time, and the Florida sun is brutal, even during winter.

SWIMMING   You can swim at the protected beaches of Elliott Key, Boca Chita Key, and adjacent Homestead Bayfront Park, but none of these match the width or softness of other South Florida beaches. Check the water conditions before heading into the sea: The strong currents that make this a popular destination for windsurfers and sailors can be dangerous, even for strong swimmers. Homestead Bayfront Park is really just a marina located next to Biscayne National Park, but it does have a beach and picnic facilities as well as fishing areas and a playground. It's located at Convoy Point, 9698 SW 328th St., Homestead (© **305/230-3033**).

GLASS-BOTTOM BOAT TOURS

If you prefer not to dive, the best way to see the sights is on a glass-bottom boat tour. **Biscayne National Underwater Park, Inc.** (© **305/230-1100**) offers daily trips to view some of the country's most beautiful coral reefs and tropical fish. Boats depart year-round from Convoy Point at 10am and stay out for about 3 hours. At $19.95 for adults, $17.95 for seniors, and $9.95 for children 12 and under, the scenic and informative tours are well worth the price. Boats carry fewer than 50 passengers; reservations are almost always necessary.

WHERE TO STAY

Besides campsites, there are no facilities available for overnight guests to this watery park. Most noncamping visitors come for an afternoon, on their way to the Keys, and stay overnight in nearby Homestead, where there are many national chain hotels and other affordable lodgings (p. 288).

CAMPING

Although you won't find hotels or lodges in Biscayne National Park, it does have some of the state's most pristine campsites. Since they are inaccessible by motor vehicle, you'll be sure to avoid the mass of RVs so prevalent in many of the state's other campgrounds. Sites are on Elliott Key and Boca Chita (also see p. 290) and can be reached only by boat. If you don't have your own, call © **305/230-1100** to arrange a drop-off. Transportation to and from the visitor center costs $21 per person. Boca Chita has only saltwater toilets; Elliot Key has fresh water, but is otherwise no less primitive. With a backcountry permit, available free from the Visitor Center, you can pitch your tent somewhere even more private. Ask for a map at the Visitor Center, and be sure to bring plenty of bug spray. Sites cost $10 a night for up to six persons staying in one or two tents.

Backcountry camping is allowed only on Elliot Key, which is a very popular spot (accessible only by boat) for boaters and campers. It is approximately 9 miles (15km) from Convoy Point Visitor Center and offers hiking trails, fresh water, boat slips, showers, and restrooms. While there, don't miss the Old Road, a 7-mile (11km) tropical hammock trail that runs the length of Elliott Key. This trail is one of the few places left in the world to see the highly endangered Schaus' swallowtail butterfly, recognizable by its black wings with diagonal yellow bands. They're usually out from late April to July.

The Gold Coast: Hallandale to the Palm Beaches

by Lesley Abravanel

Named not for the sun-kissed skin of the area's residents but for the gold salvaged from shipwrecks off its coastline, the Gold Coast embraces more than 60 miles (97km) of beautiful Atlantic shoreline—from the pristine sands of Jupiter in northern Palm Beach County to the legendary strip of beaches in Fort Lauderdale.

If you haven't visited the cities along Florida's southeastern coast in the last few years, you'll be amazed at how much has changed. Miles of sprawling grassland and empty lots have been replaced with luxurious resorts and high-rise condominiums. Taking advantage of their close proximity to Miami, the cities that make up the Gold Coast have attracted millions looking to escape crowded sidewalks, traffic jams, and the everyday routines of life.

Fortunately, amid all the building, much of the natural treasure of the Gold Coast remains. There are 300 miles (483km) of Intracoastal Waterway, not to mention Fort Lauderdale's Venetian-inspired canals. And the unspoiled splendor of the Everglades is just a few miles inland.

The most popular areas in the Gold Coast are Fort Lauderdale, Boca Raton, and Palm Beach. While Fort Lauderdale is a favored beachfront destination, Boca Raton and Palm Beach are better known for their country-club lifestyles and excellent shopping. Farther north is the quietly popular Jupiter, best known for spring training at the Roger Dean Stadium and for its former resident Burt Reynolds. In between these better-traveled destinations are a few things worth stopping for, but not much. Driving north along the coastline is one of the best ways to fully appreciate what the Gold Coast is all about—it's a perspective you certainly won't find in a shopping mall.

Tourists come here by the droves, but they aren't the only people coming; thousands of transplants, fleeing the increasing population influx in Miami and the frigid winters up North, have made this area their home. As a result, there has been a construction boom in the existing cities and even westward, into the swampy areas of the Everglades. More than 20 homes per day are being built in Broward County alone. There has also been a great revitalization of several downtown areas, including Hollywood, Fort Lauderdale, and West Palm Beach. These once-desolate urban centers have been spruced up and now attract more young travelers and families than ever before.

Unfortunately, like its neighbors to the south, the Gold Coast can be prohibitively hot and buggy in the summer. The good news is that bargains are plentiful in the summer months (May–Oct), when many locals take advantage of package deals and uncrowded resorts.

For the purposes of this chapter, the Gold Coast will consist of the towns of Hallandale, Hollywood, Pompano Beach, Fort Lauderdale, Dania, Deerfield, Boca Raton, Delray Beach, Boynton Beach, and the Palm Beaches.

EXPLORING THE GOLD COAST BY CAR

Like most of South Florida, the Gold Coast consists of a mainland and an adjacent strip of barrier islands. You'll have to check the maps to keep track of the many bridges that allow access to the islands where most of the tourist activity is centered. Interstate 95, which runs north-south, is the area's main highway. Farther west is the Florida Turnpike, a toll road that can be worth the expense since the speed limit is higher and it is often less congested than I-95. Also on the mainland is U.S. 1, which generally runs parallel to I-95 (to the east) and is a narrower thoroughfare mostly crowded with strip malls and seedy hotels.

I recommend taking Fla. A1A, a slow ocean-side road that connects the long, thin islands of Florida's whole east coast. Although the road is narrow, it is the most scenic and forces you into the relaxed atmosphere of these resort towns.

1 Broward County: Hallandale & Hollywood ✦ to Fort Lauderdale ✦✦

23 miles (37km) N of Miami

Until the 2000 presidential election fiasco, most people had never heard of Broward County. Less exposed than the highly hyped Miami, Broward County is a lot calmer and, according to some, a lot friendlier than the magic city. In fact, a friendly rivalry exists between residents of Miami–Dade County and those of Broward County. Miamians consider themselves more sophisticated and cosmopolitan than their northern neighbors who, in turn, dismiss the alleged sophistication as snobbery and actually prefer their own county's gentler pace.

With more than 23 miles (37km) of beachfront and 300 miles (483km) of navigable waterways, Broward County is also a great outdoor destination. Scattered amid the shopping malls, condominiums, and tourist traps is a beautiful landscape lined with hundreds of parks, golf courses, tennis courts, and, of course, beaches.

The City of Hallandale Beach is a small, peaceful oceanfront town located just north of Dade County's Aventura. Condos are the predominant landmarks in Hallandale, which is still pretty much a retirement community, although the revamped multimillion–dollar Westin Diplomat Resort is trying to revitalize and liven up the area. Just north of Hallandale is the more energetic, but not-yet-thriving, Hollywood.

Like many other small American towns, South Florida's city of Hollywood has been working on redeveloping its downtown area for years. Once a sleepy community wedged between Fort Lauderdale and Miami, Hollywood is now a bustling area of 1.5 million people belonging to an array of ethnic and racial identities: from white and African American, to people of Jamaican, Chinese, and Dominican descent. (*Money* magazine trumpeted the self-described "City of the Future" as having an ethnic makeup that mirrors what America will look like by the year 2022.)

A spate of redevelopment has made the pedestrian-friendly center along Hollywood Boulevard and Harrison Street, east of Dixie Highway, a popular destination for travelers and locals alike. Some predict Hollywood will be South Florida's next big destination—South Beach without the attitude, traffic jams, and parking nightmares. While the prediction is a dubious one, Hollywood is definitely awakening from its long slumber. Prices are a fraction of other tourist areas, and a quasi-bohemian vibe is apparent in the galleries, clubs, and restaurants that dot the new "strip." Its gritty undercurrent, however, prevents it from becoming too trendy.

Fort Lauderdale, and its well-known strip of beaches, restaurants, bars, and souvenir shops, has also undergone a major transformation. Once famous (or infamous) for the annual mayhem it hosted during spring break, this area is now attracting a more affluent, better-behaved yachting crowd.

In addition to beautiful wide beaches, the city, known as the Venice of America, has more than 300 miles (483km) of navigable waterways and innumerable canals, which permit thousands of residents to anchor boats in their backyards. Boating is not just a hobby here; it's a lifestyle. Visitors can easily get on the water, too, by renting a boat or simply hailing a moderately priced water taxi.

Huge cruise ships also take advantage of Florida's deepest harbor, Port Everglades, whose name is somewhat misleading because it is not part of the Florida Everglades. The seaport is actually located on the southeastern coast of the Florida peninsula, near the Fort Lauderdale–Hollywood International Airport on the outskirts of Hollywood and Dania Beach. Port Everglades is the second-busiest cruise-ship base in Florida after Miami and one of the top five in the world. For further information on cruises, see chapter 5, "What to See & Do in Miami," and consult *Frommer's Caribbean Cruises & Ports of Call.*

ESSENTIALS

GETTING THERE   If you're driving from Miami, it's a straight shot north to Hollywood or Fort Lauderdale. Visitors on their way to or from Orlando should take the Florida Turnpike to exit 53, 54, 58, or 62, depending on the location of your accommodations.

The **Fort Lauderdale–Hollywood International Airport** is small, easy to negotiate, and located just 15 minutes from both of the downtown areas it services.

Amtrak (℗ 800/USA-RAIL) stations are at 200 SW 21st Terrace (Broward Blvd. and I-95), Fort Lauderdale (℗ **954/587-6692**), and 3001 Hollywood Blvd., Hollywood (℗ **954/921-4517**).

VISITOR INFORMATION   The **Greater Fort Lauderdale Convention & Visitors Bureau,** 1850 Eller Dr., Suite 303 (off I-95 and I-595 east), Fort Lauderdale, FL 33316 (℗ **954/765-4466;** fax 954/765-4467; www.sunny.org), is an excellent resource for area information in English, Spanish, and French. I highly recommend calling them in advance to request a free comprehensive guide covering events, accommodations, and sightseeing in Broward County. In addition, once you are in town, you can call an **information line** (℗ **954/ 527-5600**) to get easy-to-follow directions, travel advice, and assistance from multilingual operators who staff a 'round-the-clock help line. Also available for brochures, information, and vacation packages in Fort Lauderdale are operators at Greater Than Ever Fort Lauderdale; ℗ **800/22-SUNNY.**

The **Greater Hollywood Chamber of Commerce,** 330 N. Federal Hwy. (on the corner of U.S. 1 and Taylor St.), Hollywood, FL 33020 (℗ **954/923-4000;** fax 954/923-8737), is open Monday through Friday from 8:30am to 5pm. Here you'll find the lowdown on all of Hollywood's events, attractions, restaurants, hotels, and tours.

BEACHES

The southern part of the Gold Coast, Broward County, has the region's most popular and amenities-laden beaches, which stretch for more than 23 miles (37km). Most do not charge for access, though all are well maintained. Here's a selection of some of the county's best from south to north.

Hollywood Beach, stretching from Sheridan Street to Georgia Street, is a major attraction in the city of Hollywood, a virtual carnival with a motley

Attractions & Where to Stay in Fort Lauderdale

Armadillo Cafe **28**
Banyan Marina Resort **20**
Bass Pro Shops Outdoor World **32**
Beach Place **15**
Blue Seas Courtyard **9**
Bonnet House **14**
Boomers **34**
Brasserie Las Olas **23**
Broward Mall **26**
Butterfly World **1**
Cap's Place Island Restaurant **2**
Courtyard Villa on the Ocean **10**
Creolina's **25**
Dania Jai Alai **33**
Darrel & Oliver's Cafe Maxx **3**
Dave & Busters **36**
Emerald Hills **35**
The Floridian Restaurant **21**
Fort Lauderdale Beach
Promenade **13**
Fort Lauderdale Stadium **7**

Galleria **13**
GameWorks **11**
Gulfstream Park **42**
Himmarshee Bar & Grille **25**
Hollywood Beach Broadwalk **37**
Hyatt Regency Pier Sixty-Six **19**
Indigo **21**
International Swimming Hall of Fame
and Aquatic Complex **16**
Jaxon's **21**
Jimmy Evert Tennis Center **22**
John U. Lloyd Beach State Park **31**
La Casa Del Mar **14**

Lago Mar Resort and Club **18**
Left Bank **21**
Lester's Diner **30**
Lord & Taylor Clearance Center **6**
Marina Bay Resort **29**
Mark's Las Olas **21**
Marriott's Harbor Beach **19**
Museum of Discovery & Science **24**
Orangebrook Golf Course **43**
Pillars Hotel **15**
Pompano Park Racing **4**
Riverside Hotel **21**
Ronny Dee Resort Motel **5**

Sawgrass Mills **11**
Sea Downs
(and the Bougainvillea) **38**
Stranahan House **20**
Sugar Reef **40**
Sunfish Grill **3**
Tarpon Bend **21**
Taverna Opa **39**
Traders Ocean Resort **8**
Tuscan Today Trattoria **12**
The Westin Diplomat
Resort & Spa **41**
Wyndham Resort and Spa **27**

assortment of young hipsters, big families, and sunburned French Canadians who dodge bicyclers and skaters along the rows of tacky souvenir shops, T-shirt shops, game rooms, snack bars, beer stands, hotels, and even miniature-golf courses. The 3-mile-long (5km) Hollywood Beach **Broadwalk,** modeled after Atlantic City's legendary boardwalk, is Hollywood's most popular beachfront pedestrian thoroughfare, a cement promenade that's 30 feet (9m) wide and stretches along the shoreline. Popular with runners, skaters, and cruisers, the broadwalk is also renowned as a hangout for thousands of retirement-age snow-birds who get together for frequent dances and shows at a faded outdoor amphitheater. Despite efforts to clear out a seedy element, the area remains a haven for drunks and scammers, so keep alert.

If you tire of the hectic diversity that defines Hollywood's broadwalk, enjoy the natural beauty of the beach itself, which is wide and clean. There are life-guards, showers, bathroom facilities, and public areas for picnics and parties.

The **Fort Lauderdale Beach Promenade,** along the beach, underwent a $26 million renovation, and it looks fantastic. It's especially peaceful in the mornings when there's just a smattering of joggers and walkers; but even at its most crowded on the weekend, the expansive promenade provides room for everyone. Note, however, that the beach is hardly pristine; it is across the street from an uninterrupted stretch of hotels, bars, and retail outlets. Also nearby is a mega-retail and dining complex, Beach Place, on Fla. A1A, midway between Las Olas Boulevard and Sunrise Boulevard (see "Shopping & Browsing," later in this chapter, for more information).

Just across the road, on the sand, most days you will find hard-core volley-ballers, who always welcome anyone with a good spike, and an inviting ocean welcoming swimmers of any level. The unusually clear waters are under the careful watch of some of Florida's best-looking lifeguards. Freshen up afterward in any of the clean showers and restrooms conveniently located along the strip. Pets have been banned from most of the beach in order to maintain the impres-sive cleanliness not commonly associated with such highly trafficked public beaches; a designated area for pets exists away from the main sunbathing areas.

Especially on weekends, parking along the ocean-side meters is nearly impos-sible to find. Try biking, skating, or hitching a ride on the water taxi instead. The strip is located on Fla. A1A, between SE 17th Street and Sunrise Boulevard.

Dania Beach's **John U. Lloyd Beach State Park,** 6503 N. Ocean Dr., Dania (© **954/923-2833**), is 251 acres of barrier island between the Atlantic Ocean and the Intracoastal Waterway, from Port Everglades on the north to Dania on the south. Its natural setting contrasts sharply with the urban development of Fort Lauderdale. Lloyd Beach, one of Broward County's most important nesting beaches for sea turtles, produces some 10,000 hatchlings a year. The park's broad, flat beach is popular for swimming and sunning. Self-guided nature trails are great for those who are too restless to sunbathe.

ACTIVE PURSUITS
BOATING Often called the "yachting capital of the world," Fort Lauderdale provides ample opportunity for visitors to get out on the water, either along the Intracoastal Waterway or on the open ocean. If your hotel doesn't rent boats, try **Bill's Sunrise Watersports,** 2025 E. Sunrise Blvd., Fort Lauderdale (© **954/ 462-8962**). They will outfit you with a variety of craft, including jet skis, WaveRunners, 13-foot (4m) Cigarette boats, 15-foot (4.5m) jet boats, and 8-foot (2.5m) powerboats, year-round. Bill's is open daily from 9am to 6pm. Rates start at $50 per half-hour for WaveRunners, $75 to $85 for boats (for 2 hr., with

Turtle Trail

In June and July, the John U. Lloyd beach is crawling with nature lovers who come for the spectacular Sea Turtle Awareness Program. Park rangers begin the evening with a lecture and slide show while scouts search the beach for nesting loggerhead sea turtles. If a turtle is located—plenty of them usually are—a beach walk is conducted, where participants can see the turtles nesting and, sometimes, hatching their eggs. The program begins at 9pm. Call ℂ **954/923-2833** for reservations. Comfortable walking shoes and insect repellent are recommended. The park entrance fee of $2 to $4 per carload applies.

a 2-hr. minimum), and $65 for parasailing solo, $120 for a tandem flight. Parasailing lasts about 1 hour and 15 minutes, with four flights a day taking off.

CRUISES   The **Jungle Queen,** 801 Sea Breeze Blvd. (3 blocks south of Las Olas Blvd. on Fla. A1A), in the Bahia Mar Yacht Center, Fort Lauderdale (ℂ **954/462-5596**), a Mississippi River–style steamer, is one of Fort Lauderdale's best-known attractions, cruising up and down the New River. All-you-can-eat dinner cruises and 3-hour sightseeing tours take visitors past Millionaires' Row, Old Fort Lauderdale, and the new downtown. Cruises depart nightly at 7pm and cost $29 for adults and $15 for children 12 and under. Sightseeing tours are scheduled daily at 10am and 2pm and cost $13.75 for adults and $8.75 for children 10 and under.

If you're interested in gambling, several casino-boat companies operate day cruises out of Port Everglades and offer blackjack, slots, and poker. **Discovery Cruise Lines** (ℂ **800/937-4477**) has daily cruises to the Bahamas, where you can gamble, eat, and party for 5 to 6 hours (you have about 3 hr. in the Bahamas to go to the Straw Market or to do even more gambling) for about $120. The price includes breakfast, lunch, and dinner, but drinks cost extra.

Sea Escape (ℂ **800/327-2005** or 954/453-3333) also launches daily casino cruises 13 times a week. But theirs don't travel more than a few miles offshore. These trips "to nowhere" depart Monday through Thursday from 11am to 4:30pm and 7:30pm to 12:30am. The party cruises offer buffet meals and full casinos for $30 to $40 per person. I'd recommend spending an additional $20 for a cabin (do not expect *Love Boat* luxe here), so you can stretch out and relax between hands. Even though the cruises don't go far from the coast, 5 or 6 hours is a long time to spend at sea, especially if the weather is rough. Evening cruises, which return at 1:30am on weekends, cost $48 and offer full buffet dinners and a Las Vegas–style show. Port charges are included, although you must pay a $3 departure tax and $2.65 passenger charge. This is one of the best deals you'll find. Sea Escape also has a new 2- and 3-night cruise option, where visitors can go to Nassau, the Bahamas, for as little as $199 per person with all meals included.

FISHING   Completed in 1999 at a cost of more than $32 million, the **IGFA (International Game Fish Association) World Fishing Center** at 300 Gulf Stream Way (ℂ **954/922-4212**) in Dania Beach is an angler's paradise. One of the highlights of this museum, library, and park is the virtual-reality fishing simulator, which allows visitors to actually reel in their own computer-generated catch. Also included in the 3-acre park are displays of antique fishing gear, record catches, famous anglers, various vessels, and a wetlands lab. To get a list

Kids Wild Things

Deerfield Island Park (on the ocean, 2 miles [3.25km] south of the Palm Beaches), surrounded by the Intracoastal Waterway and two canals, is accessible only by boat. The heavily wooded 56-acre site includes an 8½-acre mangrove swamp and is home to the gopher tortoise. The park also serves as a nesting place for squirrels, raccoons, and armadillos. Visitors can hike the park's two main trails, and the park is good for kids because it's an urban wilderness with a rustic Tom Sawyer-esque adventure feel. Picnic areas with grills and tables are available on a first-come, first-served basis, and there is also a small playground. A free boat shuttle transports visitors to the island hourly, but book early as the shuttle fills up quickly. Call for times and reservations. The shuttle takes off from the Sullivan Park boat dock. To get there from I-95, head east on Hillsboro Boulevard past Federal Highway and then north (left) on Riverview Road to the park. It's at 1720 Deerfield Island Park on Deerfield Beach. Open Wednesdays through Sundays from 9am to 5pm. For more information, call ✆ **954/360-1320.**

of local captains and guides, call **IGFA headquarters** (✆ **954/927-2628**) and ask for the librarian. Admission is $5 for adults, $4 for children between 3 and 12, and free for children under 3. On the grounds is also **Bass Pro Shops Outdoor World,** a huge multifloor retail complex situated on a 3-acre lake.

GAME PARKS   Boomers, at 1801 NW 1st St., east of I-95 between the Griffin and Sterling Road exits, in Dania, is good for kids during the day—at night, the park attracts a rowdy bunch of teenagers. The newest addition to the park is a 100-foot-high (30m), 3,200-foot-long (960m) wooden roller coaster (the thrills are high, but the lines are long). With a massive 24-hour video arcade, five challenging miniature-golf greens, go-carts and NASCAR racing, batting cages, and a huge sky coaster, this place provides exhaustive entertainment. Plan to spend all day or night. Call for prices and hours (✆ **954/921-1411**). Rides average $6.

For adults who love video games but can't deal with hordes of kids, there's **Dave & Busters** at 3000 Oakwood Blvd. in Hollywood, just off the Sheridan Street exit of I-95 (✆ **954/923-5505**). This 50,000-square-foot complex is basically an adult Chuck E. Cheese's—it features tons of video games, a full bar and sit-down restaurant, as well as a more casual spot with table service. On weekends, Dave & Busters is packed with young adults on dates and rowdy groups of guys of all ages. An admission of $3 is charged only on Friday and Saturday after 10pm. D&B's opens weekdays at 11am and weekends at 11:30am and usually closes by 1am.

GameWorks, the mega-arcade of Hollywood movie mogul Steven Spielberg, is located in the Sawgrass Mills outlet center (p. 305) and features a high-tech playground with video games that appeal to adults and kids, from virtual reality to arcade standards to interactive games, plus a restaurant and full bar.

GOLF   More than 50 golf courses in all price ranges compete for players. Some of the best include **Emerald Hills** at 4100 N. Hills Dr., Hollywood, just west of I-95 between Sterling Road and Sheridan Street. This beauty consistently lands on the "best of" lists of golf writers throughout the country. The 18th hole, on a two-tier green, is the challenging course's signature; it's surrounded by water and is more than a bit rough. The course is pricey—greens fees start at $75. Call ✆ **954/961-4000** for tee times. For one of Broward's best municipal challenges, try the 18-holer at the **Orangebrook Golf Course** at 400 Entrada Dr. in Hollywood (② **954/967-GOLF**). Built in 1937, this is one of the state's oldest courses and one of the area's best bargains. Morning and noon rates range from $21 to $33. After 2pm, you can play for less than $20, including a cart. Men must wear collared shirts to play here, and no spikes are allowed.

SCUBA DIVING   In Broward County, the best wreck dive is the *Mercedes I,* a 197-foot (59m) freighter that washed up in the backyard of a Palm Beach socialite in 1984 and was sunk for divers the following year off Pompano Beach. The artificial reef, filled with colorful sponges, spiny lobsters, and barracudas, is located 97 feet (29km) below the surface, a mile offshore between Oakland Park Boulevard and Sunrise Boulevard. Dozens of reputable dive shops line the beach. Ask at your hotel for a nearby recommendation or contact **Lauderdale Undersea Adventures,** 1525 S. Andrews Ave., Fort Lauderdale (② **954/462-3400**).

SPECTATOR SPORTS   Baseball fans can get their fix at the **Fort Lauderdale Stadium,** 5301 NW 12th Ave. (② **954/938-4980**), where the Baltimore Orioles play Spring Training exhibition games starting in early March; call ② **954/776-1921** for tickets. General admission is $6, a spot in the grandstand $9, kids 14 and under $3, and box seats $12. During the season, the Florida Marlins play just south of Hallandale at the **Pro Player Stadium** near the Dade–Broward County line. Call Ticketmaster for tickets (② **305/358-5885**), which range from $4 to $50. Tickets go on sale in January.

> **Fun Fact   Remnants of the Past**
>
> Any diving outfit in Jupiter Beach will take you to the spot where the remnants of a shipwreck from a 16th- or 17th-century Spanish galleon lie. Discovered in 1988 by Jupiter lifeguard Peter Leo, who on his morning swim came across an anchor and a cannon, the wreck has since produced 10 more cannons and over 10,000 gold and silver coins. However, should you come across more coins, you won't be able to throw them in your piggy bank—Leo owns the mining rights to the wreck. This is a more historic dive than the Mercedes, since it's an actual wreck and not one that was intentionally submerged for divers.

Pompano Park Racing, 1800 SW 3rd St., Pompano Beach (② **954/ 972-2000**), features parimutuel harness racing from October to early August. Grandstand admission is free; clubhouse admission is $2.

Jai alai, a sort of Spanish-style indoor lacrosse, was introduced to Florida in 1924 and still draws big crowds, who bet on the fast-paced action. Broward's only fronton, **Dania Jai Alai,** 301 E. Dania Beach Blvd. at the intersection of Fla. A1A and U.S. 1 (② **954/920-1511** or 954/426-4330), is a great place to spend an afternoon or evening.

Wrapped around an artificial lake, **Gulfstream Park,** at U.S. 1 and Hallandale Beach Boulevard, Hallandale (② **954/454-7000**), is pretty and popular. Large purses and important horse races are commonplace at this recently refurbished suburban course, and the track is often crowded. It hosts the Florida Derby each March. Call for schedules. Admission is $3 to the grandstand and $5 to the clubhouse. Parking is free. From January 3 to March 15, post times are Wednesday through Monday at 1pm, and the doors open at 11am. Many weekends feature live concerts by well-known musicians.

In the sport of ice hockey, the young Florida Panthers (© **954/835-7000**) have already made history. In the 1994–95 season, they played in the Stanley Cup finals, and the fans love them. They play in Sunrise at the **National Car Rental Center** at 2555 NW 137th Way. Tickets range from $14 to $100. Call for directions and ticket information.

TENNIS   There are hundreds of courts in Broward County, and plenty are accessible to the public. Many are at resorts and hotels. If one's not at yours, try one of these.

Famous as the spot where Chris Evert got in her early serves, the **Jimmy Evert Tennis Center,** 701 NE 12th Ave. (off Sunrise Blvd.), Fort Lauderdale (© **954/ 828-5378**), has 18 clay and 3 hard courts (15 lighted). Her coach and father, James Evert, still teaches young players here, though he is very picky about whom he'll accept. Nonresidents of Fort Lauderdale pay $3.50 (singles) to $4.50 (doubles) per hour. Reservations are accepted after 2pm for the following day but cost an extra $3. Lights are also an extra $3 per hour and are available only for the clay courts.

At the **Marina Bay Resort,** 2175 S.R. 84, west of I-95 in Fort Lauderdale (© **954/791-7600**), visitors can play for free on any one of nine hard courts on a first-come, first-served basis. Three are lighted at night.

SEEING THE SIGHTS

Museum of Discovery & Science ★★ *Kids*   This museum's high-tech, interactive approach to education proves that science can equal fun. Adults won't feel as if they're in a kiddie museum, either. During the week, school groups meander through the cavernous two-story modern building. Kids 7 and under enjoy navigating their way through the excellent explorations in the "Discovery Center." Florida Ecoscapes is particularly interesting, with a living coral reef, bees, bats, frogs, turtles, and alligators. Most weekend nights, you'll find a diverse crowd ranging from hip high-school kids to 30-somethings enjoying a rock film in the IMAX 3-D theater, which also shows short, science-related, super-size films daily. Out front, see the 52-foot-tall (16m) "Great Gravity Clock," located in the museum's atrium, the largest kinetic-energy sculpture in the state. Call for changing exhibits.

401 SW 2nd St., Fort Lauderdale. © 954/467-6637. www.mods.org. Museum admission (includes admission to 1 IMAX film) $13 adults, $12 seniors, $11 children 3–12. Mon–Sat 10am–5pm; Sun noon–6pm. Movie theaters stay open later. From I-95, exit on Broward Blvd. E. Continue to SW 5th Ave.; turn right, garage on right.

Billie Swamp Safari ★   Billie Swamp Safari is an up-close-and-personal view of the Seminole Indians' 2,200-acre Big Cypress Reservation. There are daily tours into reservation wetlands, hardwood hammocks, and areas where wildlife (seemingly strategically placed deer, water buffalo, bison, wild hogs, ornery ostriches, rare birds, and alligators) reside. Tours are provided aboard swamp buggies, customized motorized vehicles specially designed to provide visitors with an elevated view of the frontier while comfortably riding through the wetlands and cypress heads. For the more adventurous, you may want to take a fast-moving airboat ride or trek through a nature trail. Airboat rides run about 20 minutes and are $8 less than the 1-hour long swamp buggy tours. A stop at an alligator farm reeks of Disney, but the kids won't care. You can also stay overnight in a native tiki hut if you're really looking to immerse yourself in the culture.

Big Cypress Reservation, 1½-hr. drive west of Fort Lauderdale. © 800/949-6101. Free admission. Boat tours $10–$20. Daily 8am–8pm. Airboats depart every 30 min.; last ride at 4:30pm.

One If by Land, Taxi If by Sea

Plan to spend at least an afternoon or evening cruising Fort Lauderdale's 300 miles (483km) of waterways in the only way you can: by boat. The **Water Taxi of Fort Lauderdale** (© **954/467-6677**) is one of the greatest innovations for water lovers since those cool Velcro sandals. A trusty fleet of older port boats serves the dual purpose of transporting and entertaining visitors as they cruise through "The Venice of America."

Taxis operate on demand and also along a fairly regular route, carrying up to 48 passengers. If you stay at a hotel on the route, you can be picked up at your hotel, usually within 15 minutes of calling, and then be shuttled to any of the dozens of restaurants, bars, and attractions on or near the waterfront. If you aren't sure where you want to go, ask one of the personable captains, who can point out historic and fun spots along the way.

For a day cruise with the kids, make a stop at the Museum of Discovery & Science, where you can catch an IMAX film or just enjoy the current educational exhibits. Then, if you are up for a walk, head across the 3-mile-long (5km) Riverwalk, a scenic, palm-lined walkway along the New River where you can enjoy your picnic lunch; or try one of the restaurants dotting the way to Las Olas Boulevard and the Las Olas Riverfront. When you are ready for some shopping or a sit-down meal, reboard and head to Beach Place at Las Olas Boulevard and Cortez Street in the heart of Fort Lauderdale's most famous "strip." Stop for refreshments at Casablanca Café (3049 Alhambra St.; © **954/ 764-3500**), an oceanfront American restaurant located in a beautiful historic home.

In the evening, the water taxi is ideal for bar-hopping—no worrying about parking or choosing a designated driver. Make your first stop at Shooters, where professionals, boaters, and tourists share the large, lively patio for a popular happy hour from 5 to 7pm on weekdays. Right next door is Bootlegger's, featuring more than 70 beers at an outside bar. Later debark at O'Hara's, in the downtown section of Las Olas Boulevard (see "The Hollywood & Fort Lauderdale Area After Dark" section later in this chapter), where you'll hear a great mix of live jazz and blues.

Starting daily from 10am, boats usually run until midnight, and until 2am on weekends, depending on the weather. The cost is $7.50 per person per trip, $14 round-trip, and $16 for a full day. Children under 12 ride for half price and free on Sundays. Opt for the all-day pass; it's worth it.

Bonnet House ★★★ This historic 35-acre plantation home and estate, accessible by guided tour only, will provide you with a fantastic glimpse of old South Florida. Built in 1921, the sprawling two-story waterfront home (surrounded with formal tropical gardens) is really the backdrop of a love story, which the very chatty volunteer guides will share with you if you ask. Some have actually lunched with the former resident of the house, the late Evelyn Bartlett, the wife of world-acclaimed artist Frederic Clay Bartlett. The worthwhile 1¼-hour tour brings you quirky people, whimsical artwork, lush grounds, and interesting design. Inquire about the literary walks and science workshops, which are offered regularly on the grounds.

900 N. Birch Rd. (1 block west of the ocean, south of Sunrise Blvd.), Fort Lauderdale. ✆ 954/563-5393. www.bonnethouse.org. Admission $9 adults, $8 seniors, $7 students under 18, free for children 6 and under. Tours Wed–Fri 10am–1:30pm; Sat–Sun 12:30–2:30pm.

Butterfly World *Kids*   One of the world's largest butterfly breeders, Butterfly World cultivates more than 150 species of these colorful and delicate insects. In the park's walk-through, screened-in laboratory, visitors can see thousands of caterpillars and watch newborn butterflies emerge from their cocoons and flutter around as they learn to fly. Depending on how interested you are in these winged beauties, you may want to allow from 1 to 2 hours to tour the gardens and the well-stocked gift shop. There's also a new, separate aviary dedicated to lorikeets (the "clowns" of the bird world, because they are quite animated and very colorful), which offers visitors the opportunity to hand-feed the birds.

Tradewinds Park S., 3600 W. Sample Rd., Coconut Creek (west of the Florida Tpk.). ✆ 954/977-4400. www. butterflyworld.com. Admission $13.95 adults, $8.95 children 4–12, free for children 3 and under. Mon–Sat 9am–5pm; Sun 1–5pm; last admission at 4pm. Directions: From I-95, exit at Sample Rd. and head west until you reach Tradewinds Park on the south side of Sample Rd.. Enter the park and the butterfly house is inside, straight ahead, about ⅓ mile (.5km).

International Swimming Hall of Fame and Aquatic Complex ✫   Olympic diver Greg Louganis dove here, and you will want to take your best Olympic plunge, too, when you see the two very inviting 10-lane, 50-meter pools. Fortunately you can, for just $3, so bring your bathing suit. For inspiration, take in a swim flick (featuring Esther Williams and other aquatic stars) at the complex's theater or visit the comprehensive exhibition of medals, photos, and other memorabilia of swimming contests past.

1 Hall of Fame Dr., Fort Lauderdale. ✆ 954/462-6536, or 954/828-4580 for the pool. $3 for museum, $3 for pool. Family rate $5. Museum open daily from 9am–7pm. Pool open daily 8am–4pm; closed late Dec to mid-Jan.

Stranahan House ✫✫✫   In a town whose history is younger than many of its residents, visitors may want to take a minute to see Fort Lauderdale's very oldest standing structure and a prime example of classic "Florida Frontier" architecture. Built in 1901 by the "father of Fort Lauderdale," Frank Stranahan, this house once served as a trading post for Seminole trappers, who came here to sell pelts. It's been a post office, town hall, and general store and now is a worthwhile little museum of South Florida pioneer life, containing turn-of-the-last-century furnishings and historical photos of the area. It is also the site of occasional concerts and social functions. Call for details.

335 SE 6th Ave. (Las Olas Blvd. at the New River Tunnel), Fort Lauderdale. ✆ 954/524-4736. www.stranahan house.com. Admission $5 adults, $3 students and children. Wed–Sat 10am–4pm; Sun 1–4pm. Tours are on the hr.; last tour at 3pm. Accessible by water taxi.

SHOPPING & BROWSING

It's all about malls in Broward County. And while most of the best shopping is located within Fort Lauderdale proper, there are other areas in the county also worth browsing.

Dania is known as the Antique Capital of the South because within 1 square mile of Federal Highway, the city has over a hundred dealers selling everything from small collectibles to fine antiques. **R. Cook & Co.,** 44 N. Federal Hwy.

(© 954/922-1118), for instance, deals in vintage Louis Vuitton, plus exotic skins once owned by Ernest Hemingway (who was an avid sportsman and hunter), and antique scientific instruments, among other things. **Louis Kleinman Collectibles,** 60 N. Federal Hwy. (© 954/920-2801), boasts a large collection of china, including Limoges porcelain pillboxes. **Iris Fields of Dania,** 60 N. Federal Hwy. (© 954/926-5658), features a fabulous collection of antique perfume bottles. **Daddy's Inc.,** 19 N. Federal Hwy. (© 954/920-4001), has a huge selection of Tiffany lamps, furniture, watercolors, silver, and gold.

For bargain mavens, there's a strip of "fashion" stores on Hallandale Beach Boulevard's "Schmatta Row," east of Dixie Highway and the railroad tracks, where off-brand shoes, bags, and jewelry are sold at deep discounts. Hollywood Boulevard also offers some interesting shops, with everything from Indonesian artifacts to used and rare books, leather bustiers, and handmade hats. Dozens of shops line the pedestrian-friendly strip just west of Young Circle. The art galleries are clustered along Harrison Street, just east of Dixie Highway.

The area's only beachfront mall, **Beach Place,** is in Fort Lauderdale on Fla. A1A just north of Las Olas Boulevard. The recipient of a $1.6 million face lift in 2001, this 100,000-square-foot giant sports the usual chains like Sunglass Hut, Limited Express, Banana Republic, and Gap, as well as lots of popular bars and restaurants. While it used to be all the rage with the spring break set, Beach Place is now aiming for a much more upscale clientele, adding many new higher-end stores and restaurants.

Other more traditional malls include the upscale **Galleria,** at Sunrise Boulevard near the Fort Lauderdale Beach, and **Broward Mall,** west of I-95 on Broward Boulevard, in Plantation.

If you are looking for unusual boutiques, especially art galleries, head to trendy **Las Olas Boulevard** (located west of A1A and a block east of Federal Hwy./U.S. 1, off of SE 8th St.), where there are hundreds of shops with alluring window decorations (like kitchen utensils posing as modern art sculptures) and intriguing merchandise such as mural-size oil paintings.

On the edge of the Arts and Science District is **Las Olas Riverfront,** a retail complex with 260,000 square feet of restaurants, clothing stores, arcades, and a multiplex movie theater.

Lord & Taylor has a little-known clearance center where discounts on new clothing for women, kids, and men can be as much as 75%. If you can handle open dressing rooms, overstuffed racks, and surly sales help, the Lord & Taylor Clearance Center is a great find at 6820 N. University Dr. in Tamarac. You may want to call © 954/720-1915 to find out about special events, when prices are lowered even further.

The Fort Lauderdale Swap Shop, 3291 W. Sunrise Blvd. (© 954/791-SWAP), is one of the world's largest flea markets. I think it's rather schlocky, actually. In addition to endless acres of vendors hawking everything from electronics to underwear, there's a miniature amusement park, a 13-screen drive-in movie theater, weekend concerts, and even a free daily circus complete with elephants, horse shows, high-wire acts, and clowns.

The monster of all outlet malls is **Sawgrass Mills,** 12801 W. Sunrise Blvd., Sunrise (© 800-FL-MILLS or 954/846-2350; fax 954/846-2312). Since the most recent expansion, completed in mid-1999, which added more than 30 new designer outlet stores, this behemoth (shaped like a Florida alligator) now holds more than 300 shops, kiosks, a 24-screen movie theater, and many restaurants and bars, including a Hard Rock Cafe. Make sure you note which section you parked in, as it is nearly impossible to locate your car in the equally mammoth, labyrinthine parking lot. The enclosed area covers nearly 2.5 million square feet over 50 acres—there's no way to see it all in a day. Wear your most comfortable shoes, or buy an extra pair while you're there! Stores include Donna Karan Company Store, Levi's Outlet, Sunglass Hut, Ann Taylor Loft, and Barney's New York, all selling goods at between 20% and 80% below retail. Label-conscious shoppers are especially impressed with Off Fifth, the Saks Fifth Avenue outlet store, and Last Call, the Neiman Marcus clearance center. You may want to invest in a coupon booklet ($5), which entitles you to even greater discounts at many of the mall's stores and restaurants as well as area attractions. A booklet is good for up to a year and can be turned in for an updated booklet at no charge. To get there, take I-95 to I-595 west to the Flamingo Road exit, turn right, and drive 2 miles (3.25km) to Sunrise Boulevard; you will see the large complex on the left. From the Florida Turnpike, exit Sunrise Boulevard west.

Fishing enthusiasts won't want to miss **Bass Pro Shops Outdoor World** (200 Gulfstream Way, Dania Beach; © **954/929-7710**), a sprawling retail complex just west of I-95, where you can buy anything from yachts to lures.

WHERE TO STAY

The Fort Lauderdale beach has a hotel or motel on nearly every block, and they range from the run-down to the luxurious. Both the **Howard Johnson** (© **800/ 327-8578** or 954/563-2451), at 700 N. Atlantic Blvd. (on Fla. A1A, south of Sunrise Blvd.), and the **Days Inn** (© **800/329-7466** or 954/462-0444), at 435 N. Atlantic Blvd. (Fla. A1A), offer clean ocean-side rooms starting at about $150.

In Hollywood, where prices are generally cheaper, the **Holiday Inn** at 101 N. Ocean Blvd. (© **954/921-0990**) operates a full-service hotel right on the ocean. With prices starting at around $110 in season and discounts for AAA members, it's a great deal. **Howard Johnson** (© **800/423-9867** or 954/925-1411) has a good location right on the beach at 2501 N. Ocean Dr. (I-95 to Sheridan St. east to Fla. A1A south).

Extended Stay America/Crossland Economy Studios (© **800/398-7829**) has four super-clean properties in Fort Lauderdale and offers year-round rates as low as $49 a night and $159 per week. The studios are designed with business travelers in mind. Each includes free local calls, a dataport, a kitchenette, a recliner, and a well-lit desk.

Especially for rentals for a few weeks or months, call **Florida Sunbreak** (© **800-SUNBREAK**). Or call the **South Florida Hotel Network** (© **800/ 538-3616**) for help in finding small inns and lodges in any price range. Also, check out the annual list of small lodgings compiled by the **Greater Fort Lauderdale Convention & Visitors Bureau** (© **954/765-4466**). It is especially helpful for those looking for privately owned, charming, and affordable lodgings.

VERY EXPENSIVE

Hyatt Regency Pier Sixty-Six ★★ Located on 22 tropical acres on the Intracoastal Waterway, this resort is best known for its world-class marina and its rooftop lounge that spins every 66 minutes. If you experience vertigo after sitting in the revolving lounge, an invigorating body- or skin-care treatment at the hotel's intimate, private, exquisite European Spa LXVI will help relocate your sense of balance. Equally invigorating are the hotel's recreational amenities, which include a sprawling three-pool complex with a 40-person hydrotherapy pool, tennis courts, and an aquatic center complete with every water sport imaginable. The hotel's California Cafe is a popular, eclectic eatery. After a recent renovation, the tropical-style rooms are spruced up with cherrywood furnishings and bathrooms with marble floors and granite vanities. All rooms have balconies with views of the Intracoastal and the hotel's lushly landscaped gardens. Designer suites come with Jacuzzi, wet bar, living room, dining room, and exceptional views.

2301 SE 17th St. Causeway, Fort Lauderdale, FL 33316. ☎ 800/233-1234 or 954/525-6666. Fax 954/728-3541. www.hyatt.com. 380 units. Winter $289 double; off-season $229 double. Year-round from $1,000 suite. AE, DC, DISC, MC, V. Valet parking $10; self-parking $8 a day. **Amenities:** 3 restaurants; 3 bars; 2 swimming pools; 2 lighted clay tennis courts; spa; water-sports equipment/rental; bike rental; children's center/programs; concierge; tour desk; courtesy car; business center; shopping arcade; salon; 24-hr. room service; babysitting; dry-cleaning and laundry services; self-service laundry. *In room:* A/C, TV, dataport, minibar, coffeemaker, hair dryer.

Marriott's Harbor Beach ⚝⚝⚝   This resort is loaded with the same amenities as Pier Sixty-Six but with a more secluded setting, located on 16 oceanfront acres just south of Fort Lauderdale's "strip." Everything in this place is huge—from the guest rooms and suites to the 8,000-square-foot swimming pool to the $8 million 24,000-square-foot European spa. A huge 1999 renovation added a bit more personality to the formerly stale guest rooms and suites. Accommodations now feature marble, deep crown molding, and all-new bathrooms with granite vanities, Italian marble flooring, and wraparound mirrors. A revamped lobby affords sweeping ocean views. All rooms open onto private balconies overlooking either the ocean or the Intracoastal Waterway. The hotel's 3030 Ocean is an excellent seafood restaurant and raw bar; Riva, a Mediterranean-style, oceanfront eatery is also top notch. Return guests include many convention groups and families who enjoy the space and the great location off the beaten strip.

3030 Holiday Dr., Fort Lauderdale, FL 33316. ☎ 800/222-6543 or 954/525-4000. Fax 954/766-6193. www.marriottharborbeach.com. 659 units. Winter $259–$429 double; off-season $99–$279 double. Year-round from $600 suite. AE, DC, DISC, MC, V. Valet parking $10. From I-95, exit on I-595 east to U.S. 1 N.; proceed to SE 17th St.; make a right and go over the Intracoastal bridge past 3 traffic lights to Holiday Dr.; turn right. **Amenities:** 4 restaurants; 2 bars; outdoor heated pool; 5 clay tennis courts; health club; European-style spa; extensive water-sports equipment; bike rental; children's center and programs; game room; concierge; tour desk; courtesy car; business center; salon; 24-hr. room service; in-room massage; babysitting; laundry services and self-service laundry. *In room:* A/C, TV, dataport, minibar, coffeemaker, hair dryer.

The Westin Diplomat Resort & Spa   In its day, the Hollywood Diplomat was a swanky affair, an oceanfront playground attending to a host of celebs that included Sinatra and Co. The new Diplomat, which opened in February 2002, was built on the site of the original to the tune of $600 million.

This is a 1,060-room full-service beach resort that's loaded with amenities. The hotel's main building is a 39-story oceanfront tower (with adjacent conference center) surrounded by 8 acres of man-made lakes. A gorgeous bridged, glass-bottomed swimming pool with cascading waterfalls, private cabanas, and a slew of water sports and activities adds a tropical touch. Rooms are a cross between a subtle boutique hotel and an Art Deco throwback, with dark woods, hand-cut marble and, most impressive, the 10-layer Heavenly Bed, a Westin trademark, with custom-designed pillow-top mattresses and a very cushy down blanket (crank up the A/C!). Dining options are resort-like in quantity and quality. A fine-dining steakhouse is very elegant looking, and several more casual options are available. A South Beach–style nightclub is also on site—convenient, considering there is no nightlife in the surrounding area unless you go north to downtown Hollywood or south to South Beach. At press time, construction on the hotel's shopping and entertainment complex across the street was still ongoing.

The Diplomat's Country Club and Spa opened in March 2000 and is modeled after an Italian villa, with 60 luxurious guest rooms, yacht slips, a 155-acre golf course, and a world-class spa and tennis club. The 30,000-square-foot spa has 17 treatment rooms, a spa pool, a spa menu, and an extensive selection of treatments.

Although the hotel is attached to a newly built, massive convention center, the Diplomat is so mammoth that you may never come into contact with the name-tagged conventioneers sharing the hotel with you.

3555 S. Ocean Dr. (Fla. A1A), Hollywood, FL 33019. ℂ **800/327-1212** or 954/457-2000. www.diplomatresort. com. 1,060 units. Winter $285–$370; off-season $195–$315. AE, DC, DISC, MC, V. Valet parking $16. **Amenities:** 8 restaurants, 3 lounges; 2 pools; golf course; 10 clay tennis courts; health club and spa; water-sports equipment/rental. *In room:* A/C, TV/Web TV, fax, dataport, minibar, coffeemaker, hair dryer.

Wyndham Resort and Spa ✹   This resort couldn't be any more remote, not to mention a long way from any water or beaches; but if you're looking for a purely spa and/or golf vacation—for which there are many packages available—it's not a bad choice. Located in an unoriginal planned community known as Weston, the resort is located on a man-made lake and golf course. Rooms are spacious and bathrooms are huge, all overlooking the lake or golf course.

250 Racquet Club Rd., Fort Lauderdale, FL 33326. ℂ **800/996-3426** or 954/389-3300. Fax 954/384-6878. www.wyndham.com. 496 units. Winter from $209–$289; off-season $134–$249. Golf and spa packages (with or without meals) $265–$305 per person based on double occupancy. AE, DC, DISC, MC, V. Valet parking $8. From I-95, exit at I-595, driving west to 136th Ave. (S.R. 84); turn left to Bonaventure Blvd. Make a right to Racquet Club Rd. From W. I-75, exit 12 (Arvida Pkwy.), continue west to Weston Blvd.; turn right and proceed to Saddle Club Rd. Turn left to Bonaventure Blvd.; make a right to Racquet Club Rd. **Amenities:** 4 restaurants (nutritionist services available); 2 bars; 5 swimming pools; 2 championship golf courses; 15 lighted tennis courts; spa; Jacuzzi; sauna; children's programs; concierge; tour desk; business center; 24-hr. room service; in-room massage; dry-cleaning and laundry service; courtesy car. *In room:* A/C, TV, dataport, kitchenette in some suites, minibar, coffeemaker, hair dryer.

EXPENSIVE

Lago Mar Resort and Club ✹✹✹ *Kids*   A charming lobby with a rock fireplace and saltwater aquarium sets the tone of this utterly inviting resort, a casually elegant piece of Old Florida that occupies its own little island between Lake Mayan and the Atlantic. Lago Mar guests have access to the broadest and best strip of beach in the entire city, not to mention the wonderful bougainvillea-lined, 9,000-square-foot swimming lagoon. Lago Mar is very family oriented, with lots of facilities and supervised activities for children, especially during spring break and Christmas vacations. Service is spectacular. The rooms and suites have Mediterranean or Key West influences and are well appointed—but it's likely you won't be spending much time inside. As of January 2002, a full-service spa will offer a wide array of pampering treatments and steam rooms; and a 1,000-square-foot exercise facility may come in handy after you indulge in the hotel's Northern Italian restaurant, Acquario, which is worth a visit even if you don't stay here.

1700 S. Ocean Lane, Fort Lauderdale, FL 33316. ℂ **800/524-6627** or 954/523-6511. Fax 954/524-6627. www.lagomar.com. 212 units. Winter $195 double; from $295 suite. Off-season $100–$135 double; from $135 suite. AE, DC, MC, V. Free valet parking. From Federal Hwy. (U.S. 1), turn east onto SE 17th St. Cause-way; turn right onto Mayan Dr.; turn right again onto S. Ocean Dr.; turn left onto Grace Dr.; then left again onto S. Ocean Lane to the hotel. **Amenities:** 4 restaurants; cocktail lounge; wine room; outdoor pool and lagoon; 2 tennis courts; exercise room; water-sports equipment rental; children's programs during holiday periods; game room; concierge; tour desk; business center; 24-hr. room service; dry-cleaning and laundry serv-ices. *In room:* A/C, TV, dataport, hair dryer; kitchenette, coffeemaker in some units.

Pillars Hotel ✹✹✹ *Finds*   It took me a while to discover this hotel and, appar-ently, that's exactly the point. One of Fort Lauderdale's best-kept secrets, if not the best, Pillars Hotel transports you from the neon-hued flash and splash of Fort Lauderdale's strip and takes you to a two-story British Colonial, Caribbean-style retreat tucked away on the bustling Intracoastal Waterway. With just 23 rooms, you feel as if you have the grand house all to yourself, albeit with white-tablecloth room service, an Eden-istic courtyard with free-form pool, lush landscaping, access to a water taxi, and signing privileges at nearby restaurants and spa. Rooms are luxurious and loaded with amenities such as private-label bath products, ultra-plush bedding and, if you're so inclined, a private masseuse to iron out your personal kinks. Upon arrival, you will be greeted with a welcome cocktail, and there's always free iced tea at the pool in case you're thirsty. A library area, with grand piano and over 500 books and videos, is at your disposal as is pretty much anything you request here. The quintessential Fort Lauderdale retreat, the Pillars is the zenith of Fort Lauderdale accommodations. There are four suites and all rooms are no-smoking.

111 N. Birch Rd., Fort Lauderdale, FL 33304. ✆ **954/467-9639.** Fax 954/763-2845. www.pillarshotel.com. 23 units. Winter $189–$259 double; $279–$389 suite. Off-season $119–$199 double; $189[nd[$349 suite. AE, DC, DISC, MC, V. Complimentary off-street parking. **Amenities:** Waterfront pool; 24-hr. concierge; business services; 24-hr. room service; same-day laundry service; signing privileges at Max's Beach Place restaurant; water-taxi service; preferred rates at beachfront and downtown health clubs. *In room:* AC, TV/VCR, dataport, minibar, hair dryer, iron, safe.

Riverside Hotel ✪✪   A touch of New Orleans hits Fort Lauderdale's popular Las Olas Boulevard in the form of this charming, six-story 1936 hotel. There's no beach here, but the hotel is located on the sleepy and scenic New River, capturing the essence of that ever-elusive Old Florida. Guest rooms are a bit nicer than the public areas (outfitted in Mexican tile and wicker furnishings) and are spacious and well maintained. Details like intricately tiled bathrooms and old-style furniture enhance the charm of the otherwise stark building. The best rooms face the New River, but it's hard to see the water past the parking lot and trees. Twelve rooms offer king-size beds with mirrored canopies and flowing drapes. There are also seven elegantly decorated suites with wet bars and French doors that lead to private balconies. The hotel has two restaurants worth trying: Indigo, a fantastic Asian/Indonesian restaurant in the hotel lobby (see "Where to Dine," below), and the Grill Room, for Old World elegance.

620 E. Las Olas Blvd., Fort Lauderdale, FL 33301. ✆ **800/325-3280** or 954/467-0671. Fax 954/462-2148. www.riversidehotel.com. 217 units. Winter $179–$369 suite; off-season $124–$339 suite. Special packages are available. Discount for online bookings. AE, DC, MC, V. Valet parking $8–$10. From I-95, exit onto Broward Blvd.; turn right onto Federal Hwy. (U.S. 1), then left onto Las Olas Blvd. **Amenities:** 2 restaurants; outdoor pool; concierge; secretarial services; limited room service; babysitting; dry-cleaning and laundry services. *In room:* A/C, TV, dataport, minibar, fridge, coffeemaker, hair dryer, iron.

MODERATE

Banyan Marina Resort ✪✪   These fabulous waterfront apartments, located on a beautifully landscaped residential island, may have you vowing never to stay in a hotel again. They're intimate, charming, *and* reasonably priced. Built around a stunning 75-year-old banyan tree, the Banyan Marina Resort is located directly on the active canals halfway between Fort Lauderdale's downtown and the beach. When available, you'll choose between one- and two-bedroom apartments, which have been recently renovated. All are comfortable and spacious, with French doors, full kitchens, and living rooms. The best part of staying here, besides your gracious and knowledgeable hosts, Dagmar and Peter Neufeldt, is that the convenient water taxi will find you here and take you anywhere you want to be, day or night. There is a small outdoor heated pool and a marina for those with boats in tow. Since 1998, the Neufeldts have been honored by a local campaign to enhance the area, Broward Beautiful, winning first place for the past 3 years in a row in the category of small multifamily dwellings.

111 Isle of Venice, Fort Lauderdale, FL 33301. (C) **954/524-4430.** Fax 954/764-4870. www.banyanmarina. com. 10 units. Winter $95–$250 apt.; off-season $60–$170 apt. Weekly and monthly rates available. MC, V. Free parking. From I-95, exit Broward Blvd. E.; cross U.S. 1 and turn right on SE 15th Ave. At the first traffic light (Las Olas Blvd.), turn left. Turn left at the third island (Isle of Venice). **Amenities:** Restaurant; pool; dock. *In room:* A/C, TV, dataport, kitchen, coffeemaker, hair dryer.

Courtyard Villa on the Ocean ★★ Nestled between a bunch of larger hotels, this small, eight-room historic hotel offers a romantic getaway right on the beach. It recently underwent a complete renovation, adding 19th-century antique reproduction furnishings to its charmed setting. Courtyard Villa offers spacious oceanfront efficiencies with private balconies, larger suites overlooking the pool, and full two-bedroom apartments. Rooms are plush, with chenille bedspreads and carved four-poster beds; fully equipped kitchenettes are an added convenience. The tiled bathrooms have strong, hot showers to wash off the beach sand. Room #8 is especially nice, with French doors that open to a private balcony overlooking the ocean. Relax in the hotel's unique heated pool/spa or on the second-floor sun deck. You can also swim off the beach to a living reef just 50 feet (15m) offshore. Scuba-diving instruction is available on premises.

4312 El Mar Dr., Lauderdale-by-the-Sea, FL 33308. (C) **800/291-3560** or 954/776-1164. Fax 954/491-0768. www.courtyardvilla.com. 10 units. Winter $159 double; $250 2-bedroom. Off-season $105 double; $150 2-bedroom. Rates include full breakfast. AE, MC, V. Pets under 35 lbs. are accepted with a $200 deposit; must be caged while outside; no pit bulls, Dobermans, or Rottweilers. **Amenities:** Outdoor heated pool; Jacuzzi; free use of bikes; limited room service; scuba instruction; free laptop use with Internet service. *In room:* A/C, TV/VCR, kitchenette, coffeemaker, hair dryer.

La Casa Del Mar ★★ *Finds* The 10 theme rooms in this Spanish-Mediterranean bed-and-breakfast, situated right on the beach, are splendid, with private baths and each decorated in a motif inspired by an artist (such as Monet), regional style (such as Southwestern), or star (Judy Garland). Enjoy exquisite personal service by the English- and German-speaking co-owners. A delicious, home-cooked buffet-style breakfast is served in the main house but can be enjoyed outdoors under a mango tree in the resplendent garden. The swimming pool is large for such a small accommodation and is a great place to mingle at a late-afternoon wine-and-cheese party with the other guests, who range from young couples to savvy European travelers. Best of all, it's a deal and a pretty well-kept secret.

3003 Granada St., Fort Lauderdale, FL 33304. (C) **954/467-2037.** Fax 954/467-7439. www.lacasadelmar. com. 10 units. Winter $110–$145; off-season $80–$100. Rates include breakfast. AE, MC, V. **Amenities:** Outdoor pool. *In room:* A/C, TV/VCR, fridge.

Traders Ocean Resort ★ Located directly on the beach, this recently renovated hotel is not luxurious; but its service is superb, amenities are plentiful, and its atmosphere is completely conducive to a most relaxing vacation. Rooms are large and comfortable, and many feature ocean views. An outdoor tiki bar, often with live entertainment, provides further encouragement to unwind. The hotel attracts a mostly mature crowd, but if it's a tranquil vacation you're after, Traders may make a loyal customer out of you, regardless of your age.

1600 S. Ocean Blvd., Lauderdale-by-the-Sea, FL 33062. (C) **800/325-5220** or 954/941-8400. Fax 954/ 941-1024. www.tradersresort.com. 93 units. Winter $95–$239; off-season $79–$139. AE, DC, DISC, MC, V. **Amenities:** Restaurant; lounge; Tiki bar; freshwater heated outdoor pool; extensive water-sports equipment/rental; shuffleboard; volleyball; concierge; massage. *In room:* A/C, TV.

INEXPENSIVE

Blue Seas Courtyard ⭐ *(Finds*) This 1940s motel will take you back to the days of Old Florida, thanks to a careful restoration and renovation. Rooms are large and bright, with full kitchens, huge bathrooms, terra-cotta tiles, Haitian and Peruvian art, and Southwest and Danish furnishings. Outside are a brick pool, flowing fountains, and lounges and tables facing the gardens or even the ocean, which is just a block away.

4525 El Mar Dr., Lauderdale-by-the-Sea, FL 33308. [tel **877/225-8373** or 954/772-6337. Fax 954/772-6337. www.blueseascourtyard.com. 12 units. Winter $64–$94; off-season $60–$69. Free parking. MC, V. **Amenities:** Heated pool; access to nearby tennis court; nearby children's playground; coin laundry. *In room:* A/C, TV.

Ronny Dee Resort Motel ⭐ The good news is that this family-owned motel is just 100 yards from the beach and extremely affordable. The bad news is that it's located on busy Fla. A1A. Popular with European guests, this two-story yellow motel is wrapped around a central swimming pool; its guest rooms are wood-paneled (suburban style) and filled with an eclectic mix of furniture. A new coat of paint and new flooring helped to spruce up the place recently. It's clean but not overflowing with all the creature comforts of other chain motels.

717 S. Ocean Blvd., Pompano Beach, FL 33062. ℂ **954/943-3020.** Fax 954/783-5112. 35 units. Winter $49–$72 double; from $390 efficiency. Off-season $35–$41 double; from $249 efficiency. AE, MC, V. From I-95, exit Atlantic Blvd. E. to Fla. A1A N. **Amenities:** Outdoor heated pool; game room. *In room:* A/C, TV, dataport, fridge.

Sea Downs (and the Bougainvillea) ⭐⭐ This bargain accommodation is often booked months in advance by returning guests who want to be directly on the beach without paying a fortune. The hosts of this super-clean 1950s motel, Claudia and Karl Herzog, live on the premises and keep things running smoothly. Renovations completed in 1997 have replaced bathroom fixtures, and many rooms have been redecorated here and at the Herzogs' other even less expensive property next door, the 11-unit Bougainvillea. Guests at both hotels share the Sea Downs' pool.

2900 N. Surf Rd., Hollywood, FL 33019. ℂ **954/923-4968.** Fax 954/923-8747. www.seadowns.com or www. bougainvilleahollywood.com. 12 units. Winter $80–$135 daily; $511–$875 weekly. Off-season $52–$99 daily; $315–$651 weekly. No credit cards. From I-95, exit Sheridan St. E. to Fla. A1A and go south; drive ½ mile (.75km) to Coolidge St.; turn left. **Amenities:** Freshwater outdoor pool; concierge; laundry facilities. *In room:* A/C, TV, dataport, kitchen, fridge, coffeemaker.

WHERE TO DINE

It took a while for a more sophisticated, varied Epicurean scene to reach these shores, but Fort Lauderdale, and to some extent Hollywood, finally has several fine restaurants. Increasingly, ethnic options are joining the legions of surf-and-turferies that have dominated the area for so long. **Las Olas Boulevard** has so many eateries that the city has put a moratorium on the opening of new restaurants on the 2-mile-long (3.25km) street.

VERY EXPENSIVE

Darrel & Oliver's Cafe Maxx ⭐⭐ FLORIDIAN/NEW WORLD Despite its bleak location in an unassuming storefront, Darrel & Oliver's Cafe Maxx is one of the best restaurants in Broward County. When it opened in 1984, it was the first restaurant to have an open kitchen, and what a stir that caused! Now, instead of focusing on the kitchen, it's what comes out of it that's a marvel. Consider pecan-crusted chicken breasts with honey-lime–roasted sweet potatoes, caramelized apples and onion; sweet-onion–crusted yellowtail snapper with Madeira sauce; or a macadamia-pesto–crusted veal chop.

2601 E. Atlantic Blvd., Pompano Beach. ✆ **954/782-0606.** Fax 954/782-0648. Reservations recommended. Main courses $18–$39. AE, DC, DISC, MC, V. Mon–Thurs 5:30–10:30pm; Fri–Sat 5:30–11pm; Sun 5:30–10pm. From I-95, exit at Atlantic Blvd. E. The restaurant is 3 lights east of Federal Hwy.

Left Bank ★★★ FRENCH Regulars complain that the usually brilliant Provençal cuisine at the Left Bank has suffered now that Jean-Pierre Brehier has joined the celebrity-chef bandwagon. I think they just miss him—Brehier's sous chefs handle his menu like pros. Compared with other chefs who flee the galley for the Food Network, Brehier is still very much devoted to his own kitchen. Left Bank provides an elegant, romantic atmosphere that's bolstered by dark woods and large murals—perfect for Valentine's Day or an anniversary. Skip the Japanese-influenced seared tuna and Thai-peanut Chilean sea bass and go totally French with the French onion soup and grilled baby veal rack with grilled shrimp, herb-potato mash, and Cabernet sauce; or the herb-crusted roasted filet mignon with blue-cheese–stuffed red potatoes and Cabernet sauce. Jackets are not required here, but are recommended.

214 SE Sixth Ave. (north of Las Olas Blvd.), Fort Lauderdale. ✆ **954/462-5376.** Reservations strongly recommended. Main courses $25–$33. AE, DC, MC, V. Sun, Tues–Thurs 5:30–9:30pm; Fri–Sat 5:30–10pm. Closed Mon.

Mark's Las Olas ★★★ NEW WORLD CUISINE Before star chef Mark Militello hit Las Olas Boulevard, there was really no reason to dine here. However, once he opened the doors to his sleek, modern restaurant, he opened the eyes and mouths of discriminating Fort Lauderdale gourmands to his excellent New World cuisine. Grilled spiny lobster, with applewood-smoked bacon-conch sauce, sweet plantain mash, and conch fritters, is possibly the best item on the menu. If the kitchen is out of it—they tend to run out quickly— everything else on the menu, from the tuna pizza to the wood-oven–roasted salmon, is delicious. Save room for a chocolate dessert—any one will do.

1032 E. Las Olas Blvd., Fort Lauderdale. ✆ **954/463-1000.** Reservations suggested. Main courses $14–$30. Mon–Fri 11:30am–2:30pm; Mon–Thurs 6–10:30pm; Fri–Sat 6–11pm; Sun 6–10pm. AE, DC, MC, V.

EXPENSIVE

Armadillo Cafe ★★★ SOUTHWESTERN The city of Davie may be best known for farmland and rodeos, but it's also celebrated for this outstanding Southwestern restaurant, which attracts city slickers from all over South Florida. The Armadillo recently moved from its strip-mall digs to a much larger space to accommodate all the foodies who flock here in search of porcini-dusted sea bass and lobster quesadillas, among other things. At press time, a more casual off-shoot, Armadillo Cafe 2.0, was slated to open, offering light meals, lunch, and dinner.

3400 S. University Dr., Davie. ✆ **954/791-5104.** Reservations essential. Main courses $16.95–$28.95. AE, DC, DISC, MC, V. Mon–Thurs 5–10pm; Fri–Sun 5–11pm.

Himmarshee Bar & Grille ★ AMERICAN Located on a popular street of bars frequented by Fort Lauderdale's young professionals, Himmarshee Bar & Grille is known for its cool scene and its cuisine. A mezzanine bar upstairs is ideal for people-watching; outdoor tables, if you can score one, are tight but strategically situated in front of all the street's action. On Friday and Saturday nights, in particular, it's difficult to get a table here. However, if you can deal with cramming into the bar, it's worth a cocktail or two. The wine list is particularly impressive, and the grilled sirloin burger with creamy basil Gorgonzola is a delicious meal in itself for only $7.50.

210 SW 2nd St. (south of Broward Blvd., west of U.S. 1), Fort Lauderdale. ℂ **954/524-1818.** Reservations recommended. Main courses $12–$24. AE, MC, V. Mon–Fri 11:30am–2:30pm; Sun–Thurs 6–10:30pm; Fri–Sat 6–11:30pm.

Hobo's Fish Joint ★★ SEAFOOD   Huge portions of extremely fresh fish are prepared in more than a dozen ways at this steak-house–style restaurant with wood floors and white tablecloths. Despite the fact that it's located away from the ocean in the utterly suburban enclave of Coral Springs, this joint is worth the trip. Some even say it's the best seafood in Broward County. I say it's a tough call between here and the Sunfish Grill (see below). See for yourself with the littleneck clams in garlic bouillon or Chilean sea bass oreganato on a bed of orzo.

10317 Royal Palm Blvd. (at Coral Springs Dr.), Coral Springs. ℂ **954/346-5484.** Reservations for 6 or more. Main courses $17–$27. AE, MC, V. Mon–Thurs 5:30–9:30pm; Fri–Sat 5:30–10:30pm; Sun 5:30–9pm. From I-95, exit at Commercial Blvd., go west to University Dr., turn right and then about a mile up, take a left on Royal Palm Blvd.

Sunfish Grill ★★★ SEAFOOD   Unlike its fellow contemporary seafood restaurants, the Sunfish Grill chooses to focus on fish, not fusion. Chef Anthony Sindaco doesn't want to be a star, either. He'd prefer to leave the spotlight on his fantastic fish dishes, which are possibly the freshest in town thanks to the fact that he buys his fish at local markets and often from well-known local fishermen who appear at his back door with their catches of the day. The shrimp bisque cappuccino is a deliciously rich soup served in a demitasse cup—because it's that rich. Conch fritters are purely spectacular, not full of filler. Chilean sea bass, expertly cooked with roasted fennel, saffron potatoes, and a caramelized-onion broth is wonderful, but the best thing in my opinion was the seared tuna resting on a bed of mushroom and oxtail ragout with garlic mashed potatoes. It's not your typical Japanese-style seared tuna. It's better. In fact, almost everything is better than most seafood restaurants at the Sunfish Grill.

2771 E. Atlantic Blvd., Pompano Beach. ℂ **954/788-2434.** Reservations accepted. Main courses $17–$28. AE, MC, V. Mon–Thurs 6–9:30pm; Fri–Sat 6–10:30pm. Closed Sun.

MODERATE

Brasserie Las Olas ★ AMERICAN   This is the News Café of Fort Lauderdale, owned by the same man who spread the News and its uncomplicated cafe cuisine in Miami way back when. Located on the bottom floor of an office building and just over the bridge from the Broward County Courthouse, the Brasserie is a big power-lunch spot, with high ceilings and high noise levels. Food is simple, from pizza to pasta, with some comfort food thrown into the mix. The calves' liver with caramelized onions and the balsamic-marinated pork chop are excellent choices if pizza with Gorgonzola and bacon sound too simple for you. Desserts and coffees are plenty, and just like its Miami sibling, the Brasserie won't frown if you just prefer to order a cappuccino rather than an entire meal.

333 Las Olas Blvd., Fort Lauderdale. ℂ **954/779-7374.** Reservations accepted for groups of 6 or more. Main courses $8–$17. AE, DC, DISC, MC, V. Mon–Fri 11am–11pm; Sat–Sun 9am–11pm.

Cap's Place Island Restaurant ★★★ (Finds) SEAFOOD   Opened in 1928 by a bootlegger who ran in the same circles as gangster Meyer Lansky, this barge-turned-restaurant is one of South Florida's best-kept secrets. Although it's no longer a rum-running restaurant and gambling casino, its illustrious past (FDR and Winston Churchill dined here together, too) landed it a coveted spot on the National Register of Historic Places. To get there, you have to take a ferryboat, provided by the restaurant. The ride across the Intracoastal is not long and it definitely adds to the Cap's Place experience. And the food's good, too! Traditional seafood dishes such as Florida or Maine lobster, clams linguine, clams casino, and oysters Rockefeller will take you back to the days when a soprano was thought to be just an opera singer.

2765 NE 28th Court, Lighthouse Point. ✆ 954/941-0418. Reservations accepted. Main courses $20–$25. MC, V. Daily 5:30pm–midnight. To get to Cap's Place motor launch from I-95, exit at Copan's Rd. and go east to U.S. 1 (Federal Hwy.). At NE 24th St., turn right and follow the double lines and signs to the Lighthouse Point Yacht Basin and Marina (8 miles [13km] north of Fort Lauderdale). From there, follow a Cap's Place sign pointing you to the shuttle.

Creolina's ★★ CREOLE   You'll find authentic Louisiana Creole cuisine at this small but very popular restaurant, situated along the Riverwalk. Try the shrimp jambalaya with shrimp sausage and vegetables in a rich brown Cajun sauce served over rice, or the crayfish étouffée with crayfish tail simmered in a mellow Cajun sauce served over rice. The mashed potatoes are homemade, and the delicious fresh-squeezed lemonade is made daily. There is also a terrific New Orleans Sunday brunch. Ask to sit in sassy Rosie's section.

209 SW 2nd St., Fort Lauderdale. ✆ 954/524-2003. Appetizers $4–$9; main courses $13–$18. AE, MC, V. Tues–Fri 11am–2:30pm and 5–10pm; Fri–Sat 5–11pm; Sun–Mon 5–9pm.

Indigo ★★ SOUTHEAST ASIAN/ECLECTIC   It seems a little strange to chow down on Southeast Asian food in an utterly New Orleans–style hotel, but this is South Florida—the wackier, the better. This not-so-traditional meal begins with a basket of pappadoms, puffy naan bread, and shrimp-puff bread. Next might be a super-rich grilled vegetable cassoulet au gratin and a fried-rice dish with shallots, corn, and asparagus; or pizzas baked on top of nan covered with such toppings as onions, shiitake mushrooms, goat cheese, spinach, eggplant, garlic, curried tomato, and pine nuts. Particularly good is the meaty soy and portobello mushroom combination wrapped in fluffy puff pastry and served with a delicate broccoli sauce. Sounds like a lot of activity going on in one dish, but like the restaurant itself, somehow it all works.

In the Riverside Hotel, 620 E. Las Olas Blvd., Fort Lauderdale. ✆ 954/467-0671. Reservations accepted for groups of 6 or more. Main courses $12–$22. AE, DC, DISC, MC, V. Daily 7am–9:45pm.

Sugar Reef ★★ FRENCH VIETNAMESE   I could go on about the restaurant's priceless, unobstructed ocean view, but the menu of Mediterranean, Caribbean, and French-Vietnamese dishes is just as outstanding. A pleasant tropical decor is bolstered by the fresh air wafting in from the Atlantic through the open windows. Seafood bouillabaisse in green curry and coconut broth and pork loin Benedict—layers of jerk-spiced pork and hollandaise sauce—are among the restaurant's most popular dishes. The restaurant puts a savory spin on duck, roasted and topped with sweet-chile-and-papaya salsa. This is not a restaurant you'd expect to find on a beach boardwalk, which makes it all the more delightful.

600 N. Surf Rd. (on the broadwalk just north of Hollywood Blvd.), Hollywood. ✆ 954/922-1119. Reservations accepted for groups of 6 or more. Main courses $10–$24; sandwiches and salads $4–$9. AE, DISC, MC, V. Mon 4–10:30pm; Tues–Thurs 11am–10:30pm; Fri–Sun 11am–11pm (sometimes later in winter).

Tarpon Bend ★★ SEAFOOD/AMERICAN   This restaurant is one of the few places where the fishermen still bring the fish to the back door. The oysters from the raw bar are shucked to order and are incredible. Try the house specialty "smoked fish dip"—a kingfish smoked on premises. The steamed clambake, with half a Maine lobster, clams, potatoes, mussels, and corn on the cob is scrumptious and served in its own pot. Also try some of the homemade side dishes. For chocolate lovers, the chocolate brownie sundae is a must. There's live entertainment Wednesday through Saturday and a full bar.

200 SW 2nd St., Fort Lauderdale. ☎ **954/523-3233**. Reservations accepted for groups of 6 or more. Main courses $12–$15. AE, MC, V. Mon–Thurs 11:30am–1am; Fri–Sat 11:30am–3am.

Tuscan Today Trattoria ★★ *Finds* ITALIAN   For classic Tuscan food in a charming atmosphere, Tuscan Today is something you should not put off until tomorrow. Inspired by the peasant origins of the original trattoria, the restaurant consistently turns out outstanding pizzas and flavorful meat and fish from a cus-tomized wood-burning brick oven imported from Tuscany. A reasonable and excellent wine list provides you with a difficult choice in two affordable price ranges: $18.75 and $22.50. Artichokes steamed in white-wine broth provide a flavorful balance between garlic and sun-dried tomatoes. Grilled thin-crusted pizzas are prepared as the Italians prefer them—light on sauce and cheese but heavy on flavor. For pasta lovers, the powerful but surprisingly light gnocchi with spinach is a good way to go. And if you order a meat or fish entree, be sure to try the rosemary roasted potatoes.

1161 N. Federal Hwy., Fort Lauderdale. ☎ **954/566-1716**. Reservations accepted for groups of 6 or more. Main courses $8.95–$14.95. AE, DC, DISC, MC, V. Sun–Thurs 11am–10pm; Fri–Sat 11am–11pm.

INEXPENSIVE

The Floridian Restaurant ★ *Value* AMERICAN/DINER   The Floridian has been filling South Florida's diner void for over 63 years, serving breakfast, lunch, and dinner, 24/7. It's especially busy on weekend mornings when locals and tourists come in for huge omelets, fresh oatmeal, sausage, and biscuits.

1410 E. Las Olas Blvd., Fort Lauderdale. ☎ **954/463-4041**. Fax 954/761-3930. Sandwiches $3–$7; breakfast combos $3.50–$8; hot platters $7–$14. No credit cards. Open 24 hr.

Jaxon's ★ *Kids* ICE CREAM   South Florida's best and only authentic old-fashioned ice cream parlor and country store attracts sweet teeth from all over the area looking to satisfy their cravings with an unabridged assortment of homemade ice cream served any which way. Kids love the place because of the candy store in the front of the restaurant, and adults love it for its pre–Ben and Jerry's authenticity. For the calorie-conscious, the sugar-free and fat-free versions are pretty good. Jaxon's most famous everything-but-the-kitchen-sink sundae features countless scoops and endless toppings.

128 S. Federal Hwy., Dania Beach. ☎ **954/923-4445**. Sundaes $2.75–$7.95. AE, DISC, MC, V. Mon–Thurs 11:30am–11pm; Fri–Sat 11:30am–midnight; Sun noon–11pm.

Lester's Diner ★ AMERICAN   Since 1968, Lester's Diner has been serving swarms of hungry South Floridians large portions of great greasy-spoon fare until the wee hours. Try the eggs Benedict and the 14-ounce "cup" of classic coffee, or sample one of Lester's many homemade desserts. The place serves breakfast 24 hours a day and is a Fort Lauderdale institution that attracts locals, after-club crowds, city officials, and a generally motley, friendly crew of hungry people craving no-nonsense food served by seasoned waitresses, whose beehive hairdos only contribute to the campy atmosphere.

250 State Rd. 84, Fort Lauderdale. ☎ **954/525-5641**. Main courses $5–$12. AE, MC, V. Open 24 hr.

Taverna Opa ★★ *Value* GREEK   Don't get nervous if you hear plates break-ing when you enter this raucous, authentic Greek taverna situated directly on the Intracoastal Waterway—it's just the restaurant's lively staff making sure your experience here is 100% Greek. Delicious *meze* (appetizers), including a large

Greek salad with hunks of fresh feta cheese, moist and savory stuffed grape leaves, and grilled calamari, are offered at ridiculously cheap prices. All the food is appetizers that are to be shared by the table. You should order a lot of them to get the full experience of the restaurant. When you've had enough ouzo, you may want to consider hopping up on one of the tables and dancing to the jacked-up Greek music. If not, don't worry; the waiters usually wind up on the tabletop, encouraging diners to shout the restaurant's name, "Opa!" making sure you don't forget it. You won't. *Note:* Taverna Opa did so well here in Hollywood that it opened another restaurant on the Intracoastal Waterway in Fort Lauderdale (3051 NE 2nd Ave.; ✆ **954/567-1630**) in April 2002. A South Beach property is slated as well.

410 N. Ocean Dr., Hollywood. ✆ **954/929-4010.** Reservations accepted weekdays only. Appetizers $2.95–$10. AE, DC, DISC, MC, V. Open daily from 4pm "until the ouzo runs out."

THE HOLLYWOOD & FORT LAUDERDALE AREA AFTER DARK

Fort Lauderdale no longer mimics the raucous antics of *Animal House* as far as nightlife and partying are concerned. It has gotten hip to the fact that an active nightlife is vital to the city's desires to distract sophisticated, savvy visitors from the magnetic lure of South Beach. And while Fort Lauderdale is no South Beach, it has vastly improved the quality of nightlife throughout the city by welcoming places that wouldn't dare host wet-T-shirt and beer-chugging contests. It also lacks the South Beach attitude, which is part of the attraction.

Hollywood's nightlife seems to be in the throes of an identity crisis, touting itself as the next South Beach, while at the same time hyping its image as an attitude-free nocturnal playground. Here's the real deal: At press time, Hollywood nightlife was barely awake, with the exception of a few bars and one struggling dance club. If you're looking for a quiet night out, it's probably your best bet. But don't come too late—after midnight, the city is absolutely deserted.

For information on clubs and events, pick up a free copy of Fort Lauderdale's weekly newspaper *City Link* or the Fort Lauderdale edition of the *New Times.*

Beach Place This outdoor shopping and entertainment complex, modeled after Coconut Grove's hugely successful CocoWalk, landed on the legendary "strip" with several franchised bars and restaurants. It's the beachy version of a mall and is popular with a very young set at night. The view overlooking the ocean makes it worth a stop for a drink. No cover charge. Hours vary depending on the establishment. Some places are open until 2 or 3am, others close around 11pm. 17 S. Fort Lauderdale Beach Blvd., Fort Lauderdale. ✆ **954/760-9570.**

Chili Pepper David Bowie, who rarely gives concerts anymore, played here: not on South Beach, but right in the heart of downtown Fort Lauderdale. And what a coup that was. Since Bowie, there've been tons of Billboard-charting, mostly alternative musicians who have made Chili Pepper a requisite stop on touring itineraries. 200 W. Broward Blvd., east of I-95, Fort Lauderdale. ✆ **954/525-0094.** Weds–Sat 10pm–3am. Cover varies from $0–$20.

The Culture Room If you consider rock and heavy metal to be culture, visit the Culture Room and bang your head to local bands. 3045 N. Federal Hwy. (at the corner of Oakland Park Blvd.), Fort Lauderdale. ✆ **954/564-1074.** Daily 8pm–3am. Cover varies.

Elbo Room Formerly spring break central, the Elbo Room has actually managed to maintain its rowdy and divey reputation by serving up frequent drink specials and live bands. 241 S. Atlantic Blvd. on the corner of Las Olas Blvd. and Fla. A1A., Fort Lauderdale. ✆ **954/463-4615.** Daily 10am–2am. No cover.

Mai Kai *(Moments)* Immerse yourself in this fabulous vestige of Polynesian kitsch: hula dancers, fire-eaters, and potent (and sickly sweet) drinks served in coconuts. The food, which draws an ambiguous line between Chinese, Polynesian, and other forms of Asian cuisine, is tasty enough but definitely overpriced. No matter; it's bound to get cold as you watch the hilarious show, which includes everything from Tahitian classics to Polynesian versions of American hits. Trippy and undeniably fun, a trip to Mai Kai is a must. *Note:* The cocktails cost almost as much as a meal. 3599 N. Federal Hwy. (between Commercial and Oakland Park Blvds.), Fort Lauderdale. ✆ **954/563-3272.** Daily 5pm–midnight. Reservations required. Shows (2 nightly) are $9.95 for adults; free for children 12 and under.

O'Hara's What used to be a mediocre jazz club has turned into a premier venue for excellent, live R&B, pop, and funk music. Two locations: 1905 Hollywood Blvd., Hollywood (✆ **954/925-2555;** 24-hr. Jazz & Blues Hot Line ✆ 954/524-2801); and 722 E. Las Olas Blvd., Fort Lauderdale (✆ **954/524-1764**).

The Parrot Fort Lauderdale's most famous—and fun—dive bar, The Parrot is a local's and out-of-towner's choice for an evening of beer (16 kinds on tap), bonding, and browsing of the bar's virtual gallery of photos of almost everyone who's ever imbibed here since its opening in 1970. 911 Sunrise Lane, Fort Lauderdale. ✆ **954/563-1493.** Sun–Thurs 11am–2am; Fri–Sat 11am–3am. No cover.

Riverwalk You'll find this outdoor shopping and entertainment complex located in the heart of downtown Fort Lauderdale on the sleepy yet scenic New River—as a result of its river site, it's got more charm than most such complexes. In fact, if you've got a boat, you can sail here and anchor away until you're ready to move on. A host of bars, restaurants, and shops, not to mention a high-tech virtual reality arcade, The Escape, and a multiplex cinema, are enough to keep you occupied for at least a few hours. On weekends, this place is packed. 400 SW 2nd St. (along the New River from NE 6th Ave. to SW 6th Ave.), Fort Lauderdale.

Rush Street Known for its ice-cream flavors of martinis, from chocolate to Key lime, Rush Street is a sleek bar, with two dance floors, that attracts a young

---

 ***Where the Boys Are:* Gay Fort Lauderdale**

While South Beach is a magnet for the so-called circuit boys—gay men who party on a continual, ritualistic basis—Fort Lauderdale has more of a low-key, small-town scene similar to, say, Provincetown. Here, local gay-owned and -operated bars, clubs, and restaurants are the places of choice for those who find South Beach's scene too pretentious, superficial, and drug infested. The Fort Lauderdale neighborhood of Wilton Manors is the hub of gay life, but there is a smattering of gay establishments throughout the city.

   The Copa, located at 2800 S. Federal Hwy. (east on I-595, near the airport; ✆ **954/463-1507**), is the hottest gay spot north of South Beach—the granddaddy of Fort Lauderdale's gay club scene. Patrons of **Cathode Ray** call this bar their "Cheers." It's located at 1105 E. Las Olas Blvd. (✆ **954/462-8611**). **Georgie's Alibi** is Wilton Manors' most popular gay bar. Find it at 2266 Wilton Dr., Wilton Manors (✆ **954/565-2526**). Two great dance clubs are the **Coliseum** (2520 S. Miami Rd.; ✆ **954/832-0100**) and **The Saint** (1000 W. S.R. 84; ✆ **954/525-7883**).

professional crowd. 220 SW 2nd St., Fort Lauderdale. ℂ **954/522-6900.** Open daily 4pm–4am. No cover.

Shooters This waterfront bar is quintessential Fort Lauderdale. Inside, you'll find nautical types, families, and young professionals mixed in with a good dose of sunburned tourists enjoying the live reggae, jazz, or Jimmy Buffett–style tunes with the gorgeous backdrop of the bay and marinas all around. 3033 NE 32nd Ave., Fort Lauderdale. ℂ **954/566-2855.** Mon–Fri 11:30am–2am; Sat 11:30am–3am; Sun 10am–2am. No cover.

2 Boca Raton ⨯⨯ & Delray Beach ⨯

26 miles (42km) S of Palm Beach, 40 miles (64km) N of Miami, 21 miles (34km) N of Fort Lauderdale

Boca Raton is one of South Florida's most expensive, well-maintained cities— home to ladies who lunch and SUV-driving yuppies. The city's name literally translates as "rat's mouth," but you'd be hard-pressed to find rodents in this area's fancy digs.

If you're looking for funky, wacky, and eclectic, look elsewhere. Boca is a lux-urious resort community and, for some, the only place worth staying in South Florida. Although Jerry Seinfeld's TV parents retired to the fictional Del Boca Vista, Boca's just too pricey to be a retirement community. With minimal nightlife, entertainment in Boca is restricted to leisure sports, excellent dining, and upscale shopping. The city's residents and vacationers happily comply.

Delray Beach, named after a suburb of Detroit, grew up completely separate from its southern neighbor. This sleepy yet starting-to-awaken beachfront com-munity was founded in 1894 by a Midwestern postmaster who sold off 5-acre lots through Michigan newspaper ads. Because of their close proximity, Boca and Delray can easily be explored together. Budget-conscious travelers would do well to eat and sleep in Delray and dip into Boca for sightseeing and beaching only. The 2-mile (3.25km) stretch of beach here is well maintained and crowded, but not mobbed. Delray's "downtown" area is confined to Atlantic Avenue, which is known for casual to chic restaurants, quaint shops, and art galleries. Compared to Boca, Delray is much more laid back, hardly as chichi, and more like a cute little beach town than the sprawling, swanky, suburban feel emitted by Boca.

ESSENTIALS

GETTING THERE Like the rest of the cities on the Gold Coast, Boca Raton and Delray are easily reached from I-95 or the Florida Turnpike. Both the Fort Lauderdale–Hollywood International Airport and the Palm Beach International Airport are about 20 minutes away. Amtrak (ℂ **800/USA-RAIL;** www.amtrak.com) trains make stops in Delray Beach at an unattended station at 345 S. Congress Ave.

VISITOR INFORMATION Contact or stop by the **Palm Beach County Convention and Visitors Bureau,** 1555 Palm Beach Lakes Blvd., Suite 800, West Palm Beach, FL 33401 (ℂ **800/554-PALM** or 561/233-3000; fax 561/471-3990; www.palmbeachfl.com). They're open Monday through Friday from 8:30am to 5:30pm and have excellent coupons and discounts. On weekdays from 8:30am until at least 4pm, stop by **The Greater Boca Raton Chamber of Commerce** at 1800 N. Dixie Hwy., 4 blocks north of Glades Road (ℂ **561/395-4433;** fax 561/392-3780; www.bocaratonchamber.com), Boca Raton, FL 33432, for information on attractions, accommodations, and events in the area.

Where to Stay & Dine in Boca Raton & Delray Beach

Also, try the **Greater Delray Beach Chamber of Commerce** (© **561/ 278-0424;** fax 561/278-0555; www.delraybeach.com) at 64 SE 5th Ave., half a block south of Atlantic Avenue on U.S. 1, Delray Beach, FL 33483; but I recommend the Palm Beach County Convention and Visitors Bureau since it has information on the entire county.

BEACHES & ACTIVE PURSUITS

BEACHES   Thankfully, Florida had the foresight to set aside some of its most beautiful coastal areas for the public's enjoyment. Many of the area's best beaches are located in state parks and are free to pedestrians and bikers, though most do charge for parking. Among the beaches I recommend are Delray Beach's **Atlantic Dunes Beach,** 1600 S. Ocean Blvd., a 7-acre developed beach with lifeguards, restrooms, changing rooms, and a family park area; Boca Raton's **South Beach Park,** 400 N. Ocean Blvd., with 1,670 feet (501m) of beach, 25 acres, lifeguards, picnic areas, restrooms, showers, and 955 feet (287m) of developed beach south of the Boca Inlet, for an admission charge of $7 on weekdays and $9 on weekends. The two beaches below are also very popular.

The **Delray Beach Public Beach,** on Ocean Boulevard at the east end of Atlantic Avenue, is one of the area's most popular hangouts. Weekends especially attract a young and good-looking crowd of active locals and tourists. Regular volleyball, Frisbee, and paddleball games make for good entertainment. Refreshments, snack shops, bars, and restaurants are just across the street. Families enjoy the protection of lifeguards on the clean, wide beach. Gentle waters make it a good swimming beach, too. Restrooms and showers are available, and there's limited parking at meters along Ocean Boulevard.

Spanish River Park Beach, on North Ocean Boulevard (Fla. A1A), 2 miles (3.25km) north of Palmetto Park Road in Boca Raton, is a huge 95-acre oceanfront park with a half-mile-long (.75km) beach complete with lifeguards as well as a large grassy area, making it one of the best choices for picnicking. Facilities include picnic tables, grills, restrooms, showers, and a bi-level 40-foot (12m) observation tower. You can walk through tunnels under the highway to access nature trails that wind through fertile grasslands. Volleyball nets are ocean-side and always have at least one serious game going on. The park is open from 8am to 8pm. Admission is $8 for vehicles on weekdays and $10 on weekends and major holidays. Also, read about Red Reef Park under "Scuba Diving & Snorkeling," below.

GOLF   This area has plenty of good courses. The best ones, that are not located in a gated community, are found at the **Boca Raton Resort & Club** (p. 323) and **The Inn at Boca Teeca** (p. 324). Another great place to swing your clubs is at the **Deer Creek Golf Club** in Deerfield Beach, 2801 Country Club Blvd., Deerfield Beach (© **954/421-5550**), a 300-plus-yard driving range where a large bucket of balls costs $7 and a small one costs $4. Rates at the Deer Creek Golf Club are seasonal and range from $45 to $125. However, from May to October or November, about a dozen private courses open their greens to visitors staying in Palm Beach County hotels. This "Golf-A-Round" program is free or severely discounted (carts are additional), and reservations can be made through most major hotels. Ask at your hotel, or contact the **Palm Beach County Convention and Visitors Bureau** (© **561/471-3995**) for information on which clubs are available for play.

The semiprivate, 18-hole, par-61 course at the **Boca Raton Executive Country Club,** 7601 E. Country Club Blvd. (© **561/997-9410**), is usually open to the public and is an excellent choice for those looking to improve their game in a professional setting. A driving range is on the property as well as a restaurant and a pro shop, where you can rent clubs. If you like, take lessons from a PGA pro. Greens fees are $20 per person.

The **Boca Raton Municipal Golf Course,** 8111 Golf Course Rd. (© **561/ 483-6100**), is the area's best public golf course. There's an 18-hole, par-72 course covering approximately 6,200 yards as well as a 9-hole, par-30 course. There's a snack bar and a pro shop where clubs can be rented. Greens fees are $11 to $14 for 9 holes and $19 to $25 for 18 holes. Ask for special summer discount fees.

SCUBA DIVING & SNORKELING **Moray Bend,** a 58-foot (17m) dive spot located about three quarters of a mile (1km) off Boca Inlet, is the area's most popular. It's home to three moray eels that are used to being fed by scuba divers. The reef is accessible by boat from **Force E Dive Center,** 877 E. Palmetto Park Rd., Boca Raton (© **561/368-0555**). Phone for dive times. Dives cost $40 to $45 per person.

Red Reef Park, 1400 N. Ocean Park Blvd. (© **561/393-7974**), a fully developed 67-acre oceanfront park in Boca Raton, has good swimming and year-round lifeguard protection. There's snorkeling for beginners around the rocks and reefs that lie just off the beach in 2 to 6 feet (.5–1.75m) of water. The park also has restrooms and a small picnic area with grills and tables. Located a half-mile (.75km) north of Palmetto Park Road, it is open daily from 8am to 10pm. You pay only if you drive in. It's $8 per car during the week or $10 on weekends.

TENNIS The snazzy **Delray Beach Tennis Center,** 201 W. Atlantic Ave. (© **561/243-7360;** www.delraytennis.com), has 14 lighted clay courts and 5 hard courts available by the hour. Phone for rates and reservations.

The 17 public lighted hard courts at **Patch Reef Park,** 2000 NW 51st St. (© **561/997-0881;** www.ci.boca-raton.fl.us/parks/Patchreef.cfm), are available by reservation. The fee for nonresidents is $5.75 per person per hour. Courts are available Monday through Saturday from 7:30am to 10pm and Sunday from 7:30am to dusk; you can phone ahead to see if a court is available. To reach the park from I-95, exit at Yamato Road West and continue past Military Trail to the park.

SEEING THE SIGHTS

Boca Raton Museum of Art ★★ In addition to a relatively small but well-chosen permanent collection that's strongest in 19th-century European oils, the museum stages a wide variety of temporary exhibitions by local and international artists. Lectures and films are offered on a fairly regular basis, so call ahead for details.

Mizner Park, 501 Plaza Real, Boca Raton. © 561/392-2500. www.bocamuseum.org. Admission $8 adults, $6 seniors, $4 students, free for children under 12. Additional fees may apply for special exhibits and performances. Free on Wed except during special exhibitions. Tues, Thurs, and Sat 10am–5pm; Wed and Fri 10am–9pm; Sun noon–5pm. Closed Mon.

Daggerwing Nature Center ★ Seen enough snowbirds? Head over to this 39-acre swampy splendor where birds of another feather reside, including herons, egrets, woodpeckers, and warblers. The park's trails come complete with a soundtrack provided by songbirds hovering above (watch your head). The park's Night Hikes will take you on a nocturnal wakeup call for owls at 6pm. Bring a flashlight.

S. County Regional Park, 11200 Park Access Rd., Boca Raton. © 561/488-9953. Free admission. Tues–Fri 1–4:30pm; Sat 9am–4:30pm. Call for tour and activity schedule.

Gumbo Limbo Environmental Complex ★★★ If manicured lawns and golf courses aren't your idea of communing with nature, then head to Gumbo Limbo. Named for an indigenous hardwood tree with continuously shedding bronze bark, the 20-acre complex protects one of the few surviving coastal hammocks, or forest islands, in South Florida. Visitors can walk through the hammock on a ½-mile-long (.75km) elevated boardwalk that ends at a 40-foot (12m) observation tower, from which you can see the Atlantic Ocean, the Intracoastal Waterway, and much of Boca Raton. From mid-April to September, sea turtles come ashore here to lay their eggs.

1801 N. Ocean Blvd. (on Fla. A1A between Spanish River Blvd. and Palmetto Park Rd.), Boca Raton. ✆ 561/338-1473. Fax 561/338-1483. Free admission. Mon–Sat 9am–4pm; Sun noon–4pm.

International Museum of Cartoon Art ★ *Kids* This extensive collection of cartoon art spans the decades and styles in its glitzy home in Mizner Park. In a gorgeous 52,000-square-foot gallery space, cartoon fans can see prints, frames, moving pictures, and books by some of the world's greatest cartoonists, including many by the museum's late founder, Mort Walker (of *Beetle Bailey* fame). A fantastic gift shop offers posters, books, and lots of memorabilia.

201 Plaza Real at Mizner Park, Boca Raton. ✆ 561/391-2200. www.cartoon.org. Donation requested. Wed–Sun 10am–5pm.

Morikami Museum and Japanese Gardens ★★★ Slip off your shoes and enter into a serene Japanese garden that dates from 1905, when an entrepreneurial farmer, Jo Sakai, came to Boca Raton to build a tropical agricultural community. The Yamato Colony, as it was known, was short-lived; by the 1920s only one tenacious colonist remained: George Sukeji Morikami. But Morikami was quite successful, eventually running one of the largest pineapple plantations in the area. The 200-acre Morikami Museum and Japanese Gardens (a stroll through the garden is actually ⅞ mile [1.25km]), which opened to the public in 1977, was Morikami's gift to Palm Beach County and the State of Florida. The park section, dedicated to the preservation of Japanese culture, is constructed to appeal to all the senses. An artificial waterfall that cascades into a koi- and carp-filled moat; a small rock garden for meditation; and a large bonsai collection that includes miniature maple, buttonwood, juniper, and Australian pine trees are all worth contemplation. There's also a cafe with a Japanese- and Asian-inspired menu if you want to stay for lunch.

4000 Morikami Park Rd., Delray Beach. ✆ 561/495-0233. www.morikami.org. Museum $8 adults, $7 seniors, $5 children 6–18, free for members and children 5 and under. Museum Tues–Sun 10am–5pm; gardens Tues–Sat 10am–5pm. Closed major holidays.

SHOPPING & BROWSING

Even if you don't plan to buy anything, a trip to Boca Raton's **Mizner Park** is essential for capturing the essence of the city. Like Main Street in a small town, Mizner is the place to see and be seen, where Rolls-Royces and Ferraris are parked curbside, freshly coifed women sit amidst shopping bags at outdoor cafes, and young movers and shakers make evening plans on their constantly buzzing cellphones. Beyond the human scenery, however, Mizner Park is scenic in its own right with beautiful landscaping. It's really an outdoor mall, with 45 specialty shops, seven good restaurants, and a multiplex. Each shop front faces a grassy island with blue and green gazebos, potted plants, and garden benches. Mizner Park is located on Federal Highway (between Palmetto Park Rd. and Glades Rd.; ✆ 561/362-0606).

Boca's **Town Center Mall,** located on the south side of Glades Road, just west of I-95, has seven huge department stores, including the state's only Nordstrom as well as Bloomingdale's, Burdines, Lord & Taylor, and Saks Fifth Avenue. Add to that the hundreds of specialty shops, an extensive food court, and a range of other restaurants, and you have the area's most comprehensive shopping center.

A lifeless, overrated area, but good enough for a quick stroll, is the more artsy community of Delray Beach, known by many as Pineapple Grove. Here, along Atlantic Avenue, especially east of Swinton Avenue, you'll find a few antiques shops, clothing stores, and art galleries shaded by palm trees and colorful awnings. Pick up the "Downtown Delray Beach" map and guide at almost any of the stores on this strip, or call ☎ **561/278-0424** for more information.

WHERE TO STAY

A number of national chain hotels worth considering include a moderately priced **Holiday Inn Highland Beach Oceanside** at 2809 S. Ocean Blvd., on Fla. A1A, southeast of Linton Boulevard (☎ **800/234-6835** or 561/278-6241). Although you won't find rows of cheap hotels as in Fort Lauderdale and Holly-wood, a handful of mom-and-pop motels have survived along Fla. A1A between the towering condominiums of Delray Beach. Look along the beach just south of Atlantic Boulevard. Especially noteworthy is the pleasant little two-story, shingle-roofed **Bermuda Inn** at 64 S. Ocean Blvd. (☎ **561/276-5288**).

Even more economical options can be found in Deerfield Beach, Boca's neighbor, south of the county line. A number of beachfront efficiencies offer great deals, even in the winter months. Try the **Panther Motel and Apartments** at 715 S. A1A (☎ **954/427-0700**). This clean and convenient motel has rates starting as low as $40, although in season you may have to book for a week at a time. Weekly rates in season start at $457.

If you are looking for something more private or for longer than just a few days, you may want to call a reservations service for help. **Palm Beach Accommodations** (☎ **800/543-SWIM**) handles rentals for a few weeks or months.

VERY EXPENSIVE

Boca Raton Resort & Club ★★ *(Kids*   This famous and often-photographed property shows that Boca's country-club lifestyle is alive and well. Built in 1926 by Addison Mizner, the posh resort now comprises three oddly matched buildings: the original, more traditional building; the somewhat drab, pink 27-story Tower; and the more modern, airier Beach Club, which is accessible by a water shuttle. Everything at this resort, which straddles the Intracoastal Waterway and encompasses over 350 acres of land, is fully at your fingertips but may sometimes require a little effort to reach it. The amenities here cannot be beat. The resort features two 18-hole championship golf courses, a $10-million Tennis and Fitness Center, indoor basketball and racquetball courts, a 25-slip marina with full fishing and boating facilities, and a private beach with various water-sports equipment for rent. With a choice of 10 places to dine, five pools to swim in, and an excellent children's program, the resort is ideal for families. Upon check-in, see if Harry the bellman is available to take you to your room—he's been at the resort for over 46 years and has a photographic memory of the hotel's previous guests, from Joseph Cotton and Charlton Heston to Bill Gates, who became a partner in the hotel after spending enough time there.

501 E. Camino Real (P.O. Box 5025), Boca Raton, FL 33431. ☎ **800/327-0101** or 561/395-3000. Fax 561/447-3183. www.bocaresort.com. 963 units, 120 golf villas. Winter $400–$750 double; off-season $175–$450 double. Reasonable seasonal packages available. AE, DC, DISC, MC, V. From I-95 N., exit onto Palmetto Park

Rd. E. Turn right onto Federal Hwy. (U.S. 1), and then left onto Camino Real to the resort. **Amenities:** 10 restaurants, 6 bars; 5 pools; 2 18-hole championship golf courses; 34 tennis courts; Mediterranean spa; 3 fitness centers; indoor basketball court; 4 indoor racquetball courts; water-sports equipment/rental; extensive children's programs; concierge; business center; 24-hr. room service; laundry; 25-slip marina with full fishing and boating. *In room:* A/C, TV, minibar, hair dryer.

MODERATE

The Inn at Boca Teeca ★★★   For over 3 decades, this inn has been attracting golf fanatics who could care less about the small but comfortable rooms because they're too busy out on the superb 27-hole golf course at the Inn's Boca Teeca Country Club, open only to members and guests of the Inn. For the golf widow(er)s, however, most of the rooms in this three-story building have balconies or patios from which to watch or signal their significant others that it's time for dinner.

5800 NW 2nd Ave., Boca Raton, FL 33487. ℂ 561/994-0400. Fax 561/998-8279. 46 units. Winter $140 and up; off-season $80–$120. AE, DC, MC, V. **Amenities:** Restaurant; small pool; golf course; 6 tennis courts; fitness center. *In room:* A/C, TV.

Radisson Bridge Resort of Boca Raton ★★   Not as pricey as the Boca Raton Resort, this resort nevertheless does feature priceless water views and is an excellent choice for the money. All guest rooms have balconies with views of the Intracoastal or the Atlantic, and some corner suites have both. Its popular outdoor waterfront restaurant, Watercolors, is the only place in the city to dine on the water. The restaurant and lounge at the top of the hotel behold gorgeous panoramic views. Just a 5-minute walk to the beach, this Radisson bridges the gap between ultra-pricey and ultra-schlocky area hotels.

999 E. Camino Real, Boca Raton, FL 33432. ℂ 800/333-3333 or 561/368-9500. Fax 561/362-0492. www. radisson.com. 121 units. Winter $209–$299; off-season $109–$189. Some rates include breakfast. AE, DC, MC, V. **Amenities:** 2 restaurants; outdoor heated pool; health club and spa; water-sports equipment/rental; bike rental; concierge. *In room:* A/C, TV, coffeemaker, hair dryer.

Spanish River Resort ★★★ *Finds*   An especially good value for those staying longer than a few days, this pleasant, family-oriented property offers fully furnished condominiums half a block from a popular beach and within walking distance of Delray's best shops, restaurants, and galleries. The 11-story Mediterranean-style building has lighted tennis courts, a large outdoor pool, and lovely oceanview balconies from the fourth floor and above. Apartments are spacious and outfitted with fully equipped kitchens. All units also have pullout queen-size sofa beds and, incredibly, there is no additional charge for extra guests. A one-bedroom unit can comfortably fit four or five people; a two-bedroom unit can easily accommodate six. Cots and rollaway beds are available at a minimum charge. Compared with many of the run-down 1950s motels in the area, this moderately priced, well-maintained tower is a real find.

1111 E. Atlantic Ave., Delray Beach, FL 33483. ℂ 800/543-SWIM or 561/243-7946. Fax 561/276-9634. 75 units. Winter $150 studio; $350 2-bedroom. Off-season from $98 studio; $228 2-bedroom. Free 6th and 7th nights with weekly booking. AE, DISC, MC, V. **Amenities:** Restaurant; outdoor pool; lighted tennis courts. *In room:* A/C, TV.

Sundy House ★★   Most locals know the Sundy House as an impeccably restored 1902 home, which is command central for one of the area's best Sunday brunches. But unless you take a post-meal stroll through the beautiful tropical gardens (ask for a tour if you want to learn about the 5,000 plants, fruits, herbs, and spices, some of which are used in the hotel's restaurant), you may miss the fact that there are nine modern and luxe guest accommodations for those who want to make a meal into a memorable overnight stay. The Sundy House prefers to call itself a residential inn, with rooms resembling very plush one- and two-bedroom apartments decorated in a very colorful, very tasteful Caribbean-meets-mod style with amazing bathrooms, gorgeous views of the garden, and high-tech amenities that may rival those found in your own living room. The only frivolous amenities, in my opinion, are the full kitchens, because nobody should cook when they can stroll past the waterfalls and gazebos and indulge in a fantastic meal at the American-Caribbean–influenced Sundy House restaurant.

106 S. Swinton Ave., Delray Beach, FL 33444-3656. ✆ **561/272-5678.** Fax 561/272-1115. www.sundyhouse. com. 9 units. Winter $250–$375 1- or 2-bedroom; off-season $175–$275 1- or 2-bedroom. Honeymoon cottage $500. 2-night min. AE, DC, DISC, MC, V. Free parking. **Amenities:** Restaurant; pool; concierge. *In room:* A/C, TV/VCR/DVD, full kitchens, CD player, washer/dryer.

INEXPENSIVE

Ocean Lodge ✦ Situated around a small heated pool and sun deck, this two-story motel is a particularly well-kept accommodation in an area of run-down or overpriced options. The large rooms offer furnishings and decor that are clean but a bit impersonal. A recent renovation that added modern Formica and floral wallpaper lifts this a notch above a basic motel. Ask for a room in the back, since the street noise can be a bit loud, especially in season. The bonus is that you are across the street from the ocean and in one of Florida's most upscale resort towns.

531 N. Ocean Blvd. (just north of Palmetto Park Rd. on Fla. A1A), Boca Raton, FL 33432. ✆ **800/STAY-BOCA** or 561/395-7772. Fax 561/395-0554. 18 units. Winter $99–$125 double; off-season $75–$99 double. AE, MC, V. **Amenities:** Pool. *In room:* A/C, TV.

Shore Edge Motel Another relic of the 1950s, this motel has been recently spiffed up with new landscaping and some redecorating and is a good choice, especially because of its location—across the street from a public beach, just north of downtown Boca Raton. It's the quintessential South Florida motel: a small, pink, single-story structure surrounding a modest swimming pool and courtyard. Although the rooms are on the small side, they're very neat and clean. The higher-priced accommodations are larger and come with full kitchens.

425 N. Ocean Blvd. (on Fla. A1A, north of Palmetto Park Rd.), Boca Raton, FL 33432. ✆ **561/395-4491.** Fax 561/ 347-8759. 16 units. Winter $85–$99 double; off-season $55–$65 double. AE, MC, V. **Amenities:** Pool. *In room:* A/C, TV.

WHERE TO DINE

Boca Raton, and its surrounding area, is the kind of place where you discuss dinner plans at the breakfast table. Nightlife in Boca means going out to a restaurant. But who cares? These are some of the best restaurants in South Florida.

VERY EXPENSIVE

La Vieille Maison ✦✦✦ FRENCH The luxurious setting, a Mediterranean-inspired home filled with a variety of antique French furnishings and paintings, gives you the feeling of walking into a small château. Culinarily speaking, however, this place is a castle. Begin with lobster bisque, gratin of escargot with fennel and pistachio nuts, or pan-seared foie gras—each is equally delectable. It's difficult to choose from the many enticing entrees, which range from red snapper in black- and green-olive potato crust to medallions of beef, lamb, and venison over three sauces. You'll surely have to try at least a few of the gorgeous cheeses the server offers after your main course—the most extensive selection I've seen in this country. The lemon crepe soufflé with raspberry sauce is the dessert of choice—remember to order it early.

770 E. Palmetto Park Rd., Boca Raton. ⓒ 561/391-6701 or 561/737-5677. Reservations recommended. Main courses $18–$50; fixed-price dinners $42 and $68. AE, DC, DISC, MC, V. Daily 6–9:30pm (call for seating times).

New York Prime ★★★ *Finds* STEAKHOUSE Forget Morton's and Smith & Wollensky. This South Florida outpost of a South Carolina–based chain is the prime spot for carnivores looking to satisfy their cravings for big, succulent steaks. Fish dishes are also available, including lobsters ranging from 3 to 13 pounds. But the price of excess does not come cheap. In fact, the restaurant brazenly states its case on the menu: "We strive to be the Mercedes of steak houses by offering the very best . . . but you can't drive a Mercedes for the same price as a Buick." To me, this is more like the DeLorean of steak houses—a rare find.

2350 Executive Center Dr., Boca Raton. ⓒ **561/998-3881.** Reservations recommended. Main courses $22.50–$64. AE, MC, V. Daily 5–11pm.

EXPENSIVE

Max's Grille ★★ AMERICAN Max's Grille is a very popular, very good option in Mizner Park, but you will inevitably wait to be seated. With a large exhibition kitchen that occupies the entire back wall of the restaurant, those lucky enough to score a table can watch as their yellowfin tuna steak or filet mignon is seared on a flaming oak grill. There's also a large selection of chicken, meatloaf, pastas, and main-course salads.

404 Plaza Real, in Mizner Park, Boca Raton. ⓒ **561/368-0080.** Reservations accepted for 6 or more. Main courses $14–$26; pastas $10.95–$16.95. AE, DC, DISC, MC, V. Lunch Mon–Sat 11:30am–3pm. Dinner Mon–Thurs 5–10:30pm, Fri–Sat 5–11pm. Sun brunch/dinner 11:30am–10pm.

32 East ★★ NEW AMERICAN The menu changes every day at this very popular people-watching outpost of tasty, contemporary American food that has finally added a little hip to the Delray Beach dining scene. Delicious items have included rigatoni with braised lamb shank and oregano; thinly cut steak on roasted-garlic polenta; and grilled salmon with arugula purée and olive tapenade.

32 E. Atlantic Ave., Delray Beach. ⓒ **561/276-7868.** Reservations recommended. Main courses $10–$16. AE, DC, MC, V. Sun–Thurs 5:30–10pm; Fri–Sat 5:30–11pm; bar until 2am.

Uncle Tai's ★★★ CHINESE Not your average egg roll and lo mein kind of place, Uncle Tai's, Boca's best upscale Chinese restaurant, offers a savory spin on classics such as garlic chicken and duck with plum sauce. A family-run restaurant, Uncle Tai's is the product of Wen Dah Tai, a man who studied with the master chefs in China, Japan, and the Philippines. Tai wants to make sure you will emerge from his restaurant fully satisfied, and will even go the extra mile to discourage you from ordering a dish that's less suited to Western palates, having been created for the restaurant's many Chinese diners.

5250 Town Center Circle (between Glades and Palmetto Park rds.), Boca Raton. ⓒ **561/368-8806.** Reservations suggested. Main courses $12–$32. AE, DISC, MC, V. Daily 11:30am–2:30pm and 5–10pm.

Zemi ★★★ NEW AMERICAN Possibly the best privately owned restaurant to be attached to a mall, Zemi is a sleek and chic neo-American restaurant that's a favorite with the ladies-who-lunch set, the Boca scenesters, and foodies alike. Chili-crusted shrimp with manchego cheese, roasted garlic, sun-dried tomatoes, lemon oil, and cilantro; grilled pork T-bone in a pear-ginger compote; and the marinated, grilled skirt steak with vegetable hash and crispy onions are all so good that even the size-2 set of mall rats would be happy to go up a half size for a taste.

5050 Town Center Circle, in the Boca Center, Boca Raton. ℂ **561/391-7177**. Reservations accepted for groups of 6 or more. Main courses $18–$28. AE, DC, DISC, MC, V. Lunch Mon–Fri 11:30am–2:30pm. Dinner Mon–Thurs, Sun 6–10pm, Fri–Sat 6–11pm.

MODERATE

Bistro Zenith 🏵 NEW AMERICAN   At the height of innovative cuisine, Bistro Zenith's consistently changing menu keeps local foodies coming back for its tasty offerings of traditional American dishes graced with Oriental, Mediterranean, or Southwestern influences served in a high-tech atmosphere. During its Southwestern phase, Zenith hit a new high with a fantastic Grand Canyon chicken with red beans, ancho chili sauce, rice, corn tortillas, and Tex-Mex–corn and cilantro oil.

Regency Court, 3011 Yamato Rd., Boca Raton. ℂ **561/997-2570**. Reservations recommended. Main courses $9–$15. AE, MC, V. Lunch Mon–Fri 11:30am–2:30pm. Dinner Sun–Thurs 5:30–10pm, Fri–Sat 5:30–11pm.

Mario's of Boca 🏵 ITALIAN   This extremely popular, bustling Italian bistro keeps Boca's biggest mouths busy with massive portions of great homemade Italian food. The garlic rolls and the pizza are especially worth piping down for. If you're really hungry, there's an all-you-can-eat buffet 7 days a week.

2200 Glades Rd. (between 19th St. and Sheridan Way), Boca Raton. ℂ **561/392-5595**. Reservations not accepted. Main courses under $15. AE, MC, V. Mon–Thurs 11:30am–10pm; Fri–Sat 11:30am–11pm; Sun noon–9:30pm.

INEXPENSIVE

Baja Cafe 🏵 MEXICAN   A jeans and T-shirt kind of place with wooden tables, Baja Cafe serves fantastic Mexican food at even better prices. It's located right by the Florida East Coast Railway tracks, so don't be surprised if you feel a little rattling. Live music and entertainment in the evening make this place a hot spot for an unpretentious crowd.

201 NW 1st Ave., Boca Raton. ℂ **561/394-5449**. No reservations. Main courses $6–$10. No credit cards. Mon–Thurs 11:30am–10:30pm; Fri–Sat 11:30am–11pm; Sun 5–10pm.

The Tin Muffin Cafe 🏵 BAKERY/SANDWICH SHOP   Popular with the downtown lunch crowd, this excellent storefront bakery keeps them lining up for big sandwiches on fresh bread, plus muffins, quiches, and good homemade soups like split-pea or lentil. The curried-chicken sandwich is stuffed with oversize chunks of only white meat doused in a creamy curry dressing and fruit. There are a few cafe tables inside and even one outside on a tiny patio. Be warned, however, that service is forgivably slow and parking is a nightmare. Try parking a few blocks away at a meter on the street.

364 E. Palmetto Park Rd. (between Federal Hwy. and the Intracoastal Bridge), Boca Raton. ℂ **561/392-9446**. Sandwiches and salads $6.50–$10.95. No credit cards. Mon–Fri 11am–5pm; Sat 11am–4pm.

Tom's Place 🏵🏵 *Finds* BARBECUE   There are two important factors in a successful barbecue: the cooking and the sauce. Tom and Helen Wright's no-nonsense shack wins on both counts, offering flawlessly grilled meats paired with well-spiced sauces. Beef, chicken, pork, and fish are served soul-food style, with your choice of two sides such as rice with gravy, collard greens, black-eyed peas, coleslaw, or mashed potatoes. Signed celebrity photographs decorate the walls.

7251 N. Federal Hwy., Boca Raton. ℂ **561/997-0920**. Reservations not accepted. Main courses $8–$15; sandwiches $5–$6; early-bird special $7.95. AE, MC, V. Tues–Thurs 11:30am–9:30pm; Fri 11:30am–10pm; Sat noon–10pm.

BOCA RATON & DELRAY BEACH AFTER DARK
THE BAR, CLUB & MUSIC SCENE
South Ocean Boulevard and Atlantic Avenue in Delray Beach are slowly but surely getting hip to nightlife—though they are still a far cry from the Fort Lauderdale "strip." In Boca Raton, Mizner Park is the nucleus of a makeshift nightlife, with restaurants masking themselves as nightclubs or, at the very least, very sceney bars, such as **Gigi's Tavern,** 346 Plaza Real, in Mizner Park (✆ **561/ 368-4488**), and **Mark's Mizner Park,** 344 Plaza Real (✆ **561/395-0770**).

Boston's on the Beach   This is a family restaurant with a somewhat lively bar scene. It's a good choice for post-sunbathing, super-casual happy hours Monday through Friday from 4 to 8pm, or for live reggae on Monday. With two decks overlooking the ocean, Boston's is an ideal place to mellow out and take in the scenery. 40 S. Ocean Blvd., Delray Beach. ✆ 561/278-3364. Daily 7am–2am. No cover.

Dakotah 624   Creative cocktails such as the Kissing Cousin (Southern Comfort, Fris vodka, lime juice, and triple sec) and its own line of cigars attract a hip, young clientele to this vaguely Southwestern-style bar on the beach. 270 E. Atlantic Ave., Delray Beach. ✆ 561/274-6244. Mon–Wed 4pm–1am; Thurs–Sat 4pm–2am; Sun 4–11pm. No cover.

Gatsby's   This always-busy bar is singles central, featuring big-screen TVs, microbrews, and martinis. Thursday-night college nights are especially popular, as are Friday happy hours. 5970 SW 18th St., Boca Raton. ✆ 561/393-3900. Mon–Fri 4pm–2am; Sat–Sun 6pm–4am. No cover.

Mezzanotte   The Mezzanotte on South Beach's Washington Avenue used to be the place for a bacchanalian funfest. Then the place went from crazy to closed. The good times have traveled north to this Boca offshoot, where a well-tanned, glitzy crowd of young and old let their hair (or toupees) down, especially on weekends. 150 E. Palmetto Park Rd., Boca Raton. ✆ 561/361-0111. Sun–Thurs 5–10pm; Fri–Sat 5pm–2am. No cover.

Radius   This big, noisy techno-trance warehouse west of the highway attracts a range of big-haired girls and macho guys with gold chains. It's Boca's only attempt at a clubby nightlife and, if you don't mind dancing with a really young crowd, it can be amusing depending on your sense of humor. If you can, try to have your hotel concierge put you on the "list" so you won't have to shell out $20 or more for this nocturnal gamble. 7000 W. Palmetto Park Rd. (at the SW corner of Powerline Rd. in the Bank of America building), Boca Raton. ✆ 561/392-3747. Thurs–Sun 9pm–5am. Cover varies $5–$20.

THE PERFORMING ARTS
For details on upcoming events, check the *Boca News* or the *Sun-Sentinel,* or call the **Palm Beach County Cultural Council** information line at ✆ **800/ 882-ARTS.** During business hours, a staffer can give details on current performances. After hours, a recorded message describes the week's events.

The **Florida Symphonic Pops,** a 70-piece professional orchestra, performs jazz, swing, rock, big band, and classical music throughout Boca Raton. For nearly 50 years, this ever-growing musical force has entertained audiences of every age. Call ✆ **561/393-7677** for a schedule of concerts.

Boca's best theater company is the **Caldwell Theatre,** and it's worth checking out. Located in a strip shopping center at 7873 N. Federal Hwy., this equity showcase does well-known dramas, comedies, classics, off-Broadway hits, and new works throughout the year. Prices are reasonable (usually $29–$38).

Full-time students with ID will be especially interested in the little-advertised "Student Rush." When available, tickets are sold for $5 to those who arrive at least an hour in advance. Call © **561/241-7432** for details.

3 Palm Beach ✶✶ & West Palm Beach ✶

65 miles (105km) N of Miami, 193 miles (311km) E of Tampa, 45 miles (72km) N of Fort Lauderdale

Palm Beach County encompasses cities from Boca Raton in the south to Jupiter and Tequesta in the north. But it is Palm Beach, the small island town across the Intracoastal Waterway, which has been the traditional winter home of America's aristocracy—the Kennedys, the Rockefellers, the Pulitzers, the Trumps, titled socialites, and plenty of CEOs. For a real-time perspective on what it means to put on the ritz, there is no better place than Palm Beach, where teenagers cruise around in their parents' Rolls-Royces and socialites, seen only in society publications, seem to jump out of the glossy pages and into an even glossier, glitzier real life. It's really something to be seen, despite the fact that some may consider it all over the top and, frankly, obscene. But it is not only a city of upscale resorts and chic boutiques. In fact, Palm Beach holds some surprises, from a world-class art museum to one of the top bird-watching areas in the state.

Across the water from Palm Beach proper, or the "island" as locals call it, is downtown West Palm Beach, which is where everybody else lives. Clematis Street is the area's nightlife hub, with a great selection of bars, clubs, and restaurants. City Place is West Palm's version of Mizner Park; shops, restaurants, and other entertainment options liven up this once-dead area of West Palm. In addition to good beaching, boating, and diving, you'll find great golf and tennis throughout the county.

Note: Palm Beach's population swells from 20,000 in the summer to 40,000 in the winter. Book early if you plan to visit during the winter months.

ESSENTIALS

GETTING THERE   If you're driving up or down the Florida coast, you'll probably reach the Palm Beach area by way of I-95. Exit at Belvedere Road or Okeechobee Boulevard and head east to reach the most central part of Palm Beach.

Visitors on their way to or from Orlando or Miami should take the Florida Turnpike, a toll road with a speed limit of 65 miles per hour (105kmph). Tolls are pricey, though; you may pay upward of $9 from Orlando and $4 from Miami. If you're coming from Florida's west coast, you can take either State Route 70, which runs north of Lake Okeechobee to Fort Pierce, or State Route 80, which runs south of the lake to Palm Beach.

All major **airlines** fly to the Palm Beach International Airport, at Congress Avenue and Belvedere Road (© **561/471-7400**). **Amtrak** (© **800/USA-RAIL;** www.amtrak.com) has a terminal in West Palm Beach, at 201 S. Tamarind Ave. (© **561/832-6169**).

⌐ Fun Fact **So That's How It Got Its Name**

In 1878, the Spanish brigantine *Providencia,* bound from Trinidad to Cadiz with a cargo of coconuts, washed ashore on an unknown island. The strewn coconuts propagated and caused a wild growth of palm trees. That island, of course, was Palm Beach.

GETTING AROUND   Although a car is almost a necessity in this area, a recently revamped public transportation system is extremely convenient for getting to some attractions in both West and Palm Beach. **Palm Tran** underwent a major expansion in late 1996, increasing service to 32 routes and more than 140 buses. The fare is $1 for adults and 50¢ for children ages 3 to 18, seniors, and riders with disabilities. Free route maps are available by calling © **561/233-4-BUS.** Information operators are available from 6am to 7pm, except Sunday.

In downtown West Palm, free shuttles from City Place to Clematis Street operate Monday through Friday from 9am until 4pm, with plans to expand operations to evenings and weekends too. Allegedly, the shuttles come every 5 minutes, but I'd count on them taking longer. Look for the bubble-gum–pink minibuses throughout downtown. Call © **561/833-8873** for more details.

For a more nostalgic route, consider the stately wicker chariots that run in the downtown area, especially on weekends and during special events. Rates vary according to the time of day but average $1 to $2 per block, plus a per-person charge of $1. Call © **561/835-8922** for pickup or information.

VISITOR INFORMATION   The **Palm Beach County Convention and Visitors Bureau,** 1555 Palm Beach Lakes Blvd., Suite 204, West Palm Beach, FL 33401 (© **800/554-PALM** or 561/471-3995; www.palmbeachfl.com), distributes an informative brochure and will answer questions about visiting the Palm Beaches. Ask for a map as well as a copy of its "Arts and Attractions Calendar," a day-to-day guide to art, music, stage, and other events in the county.

BEACHES & ACTIVE PURSUITS

BEACHES   Public beaches are a rare commodity here in Palm Beach. Most of the island's best beaches are fronted by private estates and are inaccessible to the general public. However, there are a few notable exceptions, including **Midtown Beach,** east of Worth Avenue, on Ocean Boulevard, between Royal Palm Way and Gulfstream Road, which boasts more than 100 feet (30m) of undeveloped beach. This newly widened sandy coast is now a centerpiece and a natural oasis in a town dominated by commercial glitz. There are no restrooms or concessions here, although a lifeguard is on duty until sundown. About 1½ miles (2.25km) north of there, near Dunbar Street, is a popular hangout for locals, who prefer it to Midtown Beach because of the relaxed and serene atmosphere. Parking is available at meters along Fla. A1A. At the south end of Palm Beach, there's a less-popular but better-equipped beach at **Phipps Ocean Park.** On Ocean Boulevard, between the Southern Boulevard and Lake Avenue Causeways, is a large and lively public beach encompassing more than 1,300 feet (390m) of groomed and guarded oceanfront. With picnic and recreation areas, as well as plenty of parking, the area is especially good for families.

BIKING   Rent anything from an English single-speed to a full-tilt mountain bike at the **Palm Beach Bicycle Trail Shop,** 223 Sunrise Ave. (© **561/659-4583**). The rates are $8 an hour, $20 a half day (9am–5pm), or $26 for 24 hours and include a basket and lock (not that a lock is necessary in this fortress of a town). The most scenic route is called the Lake Trail, running the length of the island along the Intracoastal Waterway. On it, you'll see some of the most magnificent mansions and grounds and will enjoy the views of downtown West Palm Beach as well as some great wildlife.

GOLF   There's good golfing in the Palm Beaches, but many of the private-club courses are maintained exclusively for the use of their members. Ask at your hotel, or contact the **Palm Beach County Convention and Visitors Bureau**

Where to Dine in Palm Beach & West Palm Beach

The Sport of Kings

The posh Palm Beach Polo and Country Club is one of the world's premier polo grounds and hosts some of the sport's top-rated players. Even if you're not a sports fan, you must attend a match at this field, which is actually on the mainland in an area called Wellington. Rest assured, however, that the spectators, and many of the players, are pure Palm Beach. After all, a day at the pony grounds is one of the only good reasons to leave Palm Beach proper.   Don't worry, you need not be a Vanderbilt or a Kennedy to attend—matches are open to the public and are surprisingly affordable.

Even if you haven't a clue as to how the game is played, you can spend your time people-watching. Stargazers have spotted Prince Charles, Sylvester Stallone, Tommy Lee Jones, Bo Derek, and Ivana Trump, among others, in recent years. Dozens of lesser-known royalty, and just plain old characters, keep box seats or chalets right on the grounds.

Incidentally, the point of polo is to keep the other team from getting the ball through your goal. The fast-paced game is divided into six chukkers—like an inning in baseball—each 7 minutes long. There are 3-minute breaks between chukkers, except at half time, which lasts 10 minutes. The whole thing is narrated by a British chap who sounds as though he walked off a Monty Python set.

Dress is casual; a navy or tweed blazer over jeans or khakis is a standard for men, while neat-looking jeans or a pantsuit is the norm for women. On warmer days, shorts and, of course, a polo shirt are fine, too.

General admission is $6 to $10; box seats cost $10 to $36. Matches are held throughout the week. Schedules vary, but the big names usually compete on Sunday at 3:30pm from January to April.

The fields are located at 11809 Polo Club Rd., Wellington, 10 miles (16km) west of the Forest Hill Boulevard exit of I-95. Call ℂ **561/ 793-1440** for tickets and a detailed schedule of events.

(ℂ **561/471-3995**) for information on which clubs are currently available for play. In the off-season, some private courses open their greens to visitors staying in a Palm Beach County hotel. This "Golf-A-Round" program offers free greens fees (carts are additional); reservations can be made through most major hotels.

The best hotel for golf in the area is the **PGA National Resort & Spa** (p. 349; ℂ **800/633-9150**), which features a whopping 90 holes of golf.

One of the state's best courses that is open to the public is **Emerald Dunes Golf Course** ⚑, 2100 Emerald Dunes Dr. in West Palm Beach (ℂ **561/ 687-1700**). Designed by Tom Fazio, this dramatic 7,006-yard, par-72 course was voted "One of the Best 10 You Can Play" by *Golf* magazine. It is located just off the Florida Turnpike at Okeechobee Boulevard. Bookings are taken up to 30 days ahead. Fees start at $130, including carts.

The **Palm Beach Public Golf Course,** 2345 S. Ocean Blvd. (ℂ **561/ 547-0598**), a popular public 18-hole course, is a par-54. The course opens at 8am and runs on a first-come, first-served basis. Club rentals are available. Greens fees start at $20 per person.

SCUBA DIVING   Year-round warm waters, barrier reefs, and plenty of wrecks make South Florida one of the world's most popular places for diving. One of the best-known artificial reefs in this area is a vintage Rolls-Royce Silver Shadow, which was sunk offshore in 1985. Nature has taken its toll, however, and divers can no longer sit in the car, which has been ravaged by time and saltwater.

Call either of the following outfitters for gear and excursions: **Ocean Sports Scuba Center,** 1736 S. Congress Ave., West Palm Beach (© 561/641-1144) or **Jim Abernaethy's Scuba Adventures,** at 2116 Avenue B. in Riviera Beach (© 561/691-5808).

TENNIS   There are hundreds of tennis courts in Palm Beach County. Wherever you are staying, you are bound to be within walking distance of one. In addition to the many hotel tennis courts (see "Where to Stay," below), you can play at **Currie Park,** 2400 N. Flagler Dr., West Palm Beach (© 561/835-7025), a public park with three lighted hard courts. They are free and available on a first-come, first-served basis.

WATER SPORTS   Call the **Seaside Activities Station** (© 561/835-8922) to arrange sailboat, jet-ski, bicycle, kayak, water-ski, and parasail rentals.

SEEING THE SIGHTS

Flagler Museum ★★★   The Gilded Age is preserved in this luxurious mansion commissioned by Standard Oil tycoon Henry Flagler as a wedding present to his third wife. *Whitehall,* also known as the "Taj Mahal of North America," is a classically columned Edwardian-style mansion containing 55 rooms, including a Louis XIV music room and art gallery, a Louis XV ballroom, and 14 guest suites outfitted with original antique European furnishings. Out back, climb aboard "The Rambler," Mr. Flagler's private restored railroad car. Allow at least 1½ hours to tour the stunning grounds and interior. School and group tours are available, but, for the most part, this is a self-guided museum.

One Whitehall Way (at Cocoanut Row and Whitehall Way), Palm Beach. © 561/655-2833. www.flagler.org. Admission $8 adults, $3 children ages 6–12. Tues–Sat 10am–5pm; Sun noon–5pm.

Norton Museum of Art ★★★   Since a 1997 expansion doubled the Norton's space, the museum has gained even more prominence in the art world. It is world famous for its prestigious permanent collection and top temporary exhibitions. The museum's major collections are divided geographically. The American galleries contain major works by Edward Hopper, Georgia O'Keeffe, and Jackson Pollock. The French collection contains Impressionist and post-Impressionist paintings by Cézanne, Degas, Gauguin, Matisse, Monet, Picasso, Pissarro, and Renoir. And the Chinese collection contains more then 200 bronzes, jades, and ceramics, as well as a collection of monumental Buddhist sculptures. Allow about 2 hours to see this museum, depending on your level of interest.

1451 S. Olive Ave., West Palm Beach. © 561/832-5196. Fax 561/659-4689. www.norton.org. Admission $6 adults, $2 ages 13–21, free for children 12 and under. Mon–Sat 10am–5pm; Sun 1pm–5pm Closed Mon (May–Oct) and all major holidays. Take I-95 to exit 52 (Okeechobee Blvd. E.). Travel east on Okeechobee to Dixie Hwy., then south ½ mile (.75km) to the Norton. Parking may be accessed through entrances on Dixie Hwy. and S. Olive Ave.

Playmobil Fun Park ★★ *Kids*   In a child's mind, it doesn't get any better than this. The 17,000-square-foot Playmobil Fun Park is housed in a replica castle and loaded with themed areas for imaginative play: a medieval village, a Western town, a fantasy dollhouse, and more. Plus, there are two water-filled tables on which kids can play with the Playmobil boats. Tech-minded kids could get

Unreal Estate

No trip to Palm Beach is complete without at least a glimpse of Mar-A-Lago, the stately residence of Donald Trump, the 21st century's answer to Jay Gatsby. In 1985, Trump purchased Mar-A-Lago, the former estate of cereal heiress Marjorie Merriweather Post, for what was considered a meager $8 million (for a fully furnished beachfront property of this stature, it was a relative bargain, actually), to the great consternation of locals, who feared that he would turn the place into a casino. Instead, Trump, who resides in a portion of the palace, opened the house to the public—for a price, of course—as a tony country club (membership fee: $100,000). Infinitely more interesting than any of Trump's other real estate acquisitions, Mar-A-Lago, Spanish for "from sea to lake," has a history that's priceless.

Built as Post's vacation home in 1923, Mar-A-Lago eventually became the heiress's primary residence, which she shared with her second husband, E.F. Hutton. Together they lived in utter opulence, throwing gala events and lavish dinner parties on a nightly basis. The dining room, with 27 different china patterns and at least 4,000 pieces of silver, was modeled after the Chigi Palace in Rome. Other rooms captured various styles, including Venetian and Norwegian. The exterior, done in a Hispano-Moresque style, featured a massive collection of Spanish tile for the rooftops.

When Post died in 1973, she bequeathed Mar-a-Lago to the U.S. government for use in housing presidents and traveling dignitaries. Because the maintenance was in excess of $1 million a year, the government eventually returned the estate to the Post Foundation. Enter the Donald, who, to everyone's surprise, restored the home to its original glory, saying, "Some people collect artworks . . . I collect great homes."

While there are currently no tours open to the public, you can glimpse the gorgeous manse as you cross the bridge from West Palm Beach into Palm Beach. Its website (www.pbol.com/maralago/tour.html) offers photos, a calendar of events, and more details than you'd ever care to know. 1100 S. Ocean Blvd., Palm Beach; ✆ **561/833-2466.**

bored, but toddlers (and up to age 5 or so) will love this place. You *could* spend hours here and not spend a penny, but parents beware: Everything is available for purchase.

8031 N. Military Trail, Palm Beach Gardens. ✆ **800/351-8697** or 561/691-9880. Fax 561/691-9517. www.playmobil.com. Admission $1. Mon–Sat 10am–6pm; Sun noon–5pm. From I-95, go north to Palm Beach Lakes Blvd.; then west to Military Trail. Turn left, and the park is about a mile down on the right.

NATURE PRESERVES & ATTRACTIONS

Lion Country Safari ✿ *Kids* More than 1,300 animals on this 500-acre preserve are divided into their indigenous regions, from the East African preserve of the Serengeti to the American West. Elephants, wildebeest, ostriches, American bison, buffalo, watusi, pink flamingos, and many other more unusual species roam the preserve. When I visited, most of the lions were asleep; when they are awake, they travel freely throughout the cageless grassy landscape. In fact, you're the one who's confined in your own car without an escort (no convertibles allowed). You're given a detailed informational pamphlet with photos and descriptions and are instructed to obey the 15-mile-per-hour (24kmph) speed limit—unless you see the rhinos charge (a rare occasion), in which case you're encouraged to floor it. To drive the loop takes just over an hour, though you could make a day of just watching the chimpanzees play on their secluded islands. Included in the admission price is Safari World, an amusement park with paddleboats, a carousel, miniature golf, and a nursery for baby animals born in the preserve. Picnics are encouraged, and camping is available (call for reservations). The best time to go is late afternoon right before the park closes, when they herd up all the animals; plus, it's much cooler then, so the lions are more active.

Southern Blvd. W. at S.R. 80, West Palm Beach. ✆ 561/793-1084, or 561/793-9797 for camping reservations. www.lioncountrysafari.com. Admission $16.95 adults, $14.95 seniors, $12.95 children 3–9, free for children under 3. Van rental is $8 per hr. Daily 10am–5:30pm (last vehicle admitted at 4:30pm). From I-95, exit on Southern Blvd. Go west for about 18 miles (29km).

Palm Beach Zoo at Dreher Park ✿   If you want animals, go to Lion Country Safari. Unlike big-city zoos, this intimate 23-acre park is more like a stroll in the park than an all-day excursion. It features about 500 animals representing more than 100 different species. A special monkey exhibit and petting zoo are favorites with kids. Stroller and wagon rental available. Allow at least 2 hours to see all of the sights here.

1301 Summit Blvd. (east of I-95 between Southern Blvd. and Forest Hill Blvd.). ✆ 561/547-WILD. Fax 561/585-6085. www.palmbeachzoo.org. Admission $7.50, $6 seniors, $5 children 3–12, free for children under 3. Daily 9am–5pm. Closed Thanksgiving.

Rapids Water Park ✿ *Kids*   It may not be on the same grand scale as the theme parks in Orlando, but Rapids is a great way to cool off on a hot day. There are 12 acres of water rides, including a children's area and miniature-golf course.

6566 N. Military Trail, West Palm Beach (1 mile [1.5km] west of I-95 on Military between 45th St. [exit 54] and Blue Heron Blvd. [exit 55] in West Palm Beach). ✆ 561/842-8756. www.rapidswaterpark.com. Admission $17–$24 per person; free for ages 2 and under. Open mid-Mar to Sept. Mon–Fri 10am–5pm; Sat–Sun 10am–6pm.

SHOPPING & BROWSING

No matter what your budget is, be sure to take a stroll down Worth Avenue, "the Rodeo Drive of the South" and a window-shopper's dream. Between South Ocean Boulevard and Cocoanut Row, there are more than 200 boutiques, posh shops, art galleries, and upscale restaurants. If you want to fit in, dress as if you were going to an elegant luncheon and not to the mall down the street.

Despite the presence of the usual suspects (**Gucci, Chanel, Armani, Hermès, Louis Vuitton,** among others), Worth Avenue is not impervious to the mainstream. **Victoria's Secret, Limited Express,** and several other chains have sneaked in here too, but so have a good number of unique boutiques. **History Buff,** 32 Via Mizner (✆ 561/366-8255), is a virtual museum, selling every genre of original historical autographs, some dating back to the 1600s, as well as vintage signed photos, first-edition books, and memorabilia. A similar store is **Paper Treasures,** at 217 Worth Ave. (✆ 561/835-1891), an autograph gallery with a priceless collection of John Hancocks, including those of Joe DiMaggio, Mickey Mantle, Andrew Jackson, Abraham Lincoln, Howard Hughes, and hundreds more, all displayed in beautiful frames. For privileged feet, **Stubbs & Wooton,** 323 Worth Ave. (✆ 561/655-4105), sells velvet slippers that are a favorite of the loofahed locals. **The Purple Turtle,** 150 Worth Ave. (✆ 561/655-1625) in the Esplanade shopping promenade, sells designer clothes for infants, including Baby Dior and Baby Armani. For rare and estate jewelry, **Richter's of Palm Beach,** 224 Worth Ave. (✆ 561/655-0774), has been specializing in priceless gems since 1893. Just off Worth Avenue, at 374 S. County Rd., is the **Church Mouse** (✆ 561/659-2154), a great consignment/thrift shop with antique furnishings and tableware as well as lots of good castaway clothing and shoes, all reasonably priced. This shop usually closes for 2 months during the summer. Call to be sure.

City Place, 222 Lakeview Ave., West Palm Beach (✆ 561/835-0862), is a $550 million, Mediterranean-style shopping, dining, and entertainment complex that's responsible for revitalizing what was once a lifeless downtown West Palm Beach. Among the 78 mostly-chain stores are **Macy's, FAO Schwarz, Benetton,** which has an in-line skating track inside, **Armani Exchange, Pottery Barn,** and **SEE** eyewear. Restaurants include a Ghirardelli ice cream shop, Legal Seafoods, City Cellar Wine Bar and Grill, and Cheesecake Factory. Best of all is the Muvico Parisian, a 20-screen movie theater where you can wine and dine while watching a feature.

Elsewhere, Downtown West Palm Beach has a scant number of interesting boutiques along Clematis Street. In addition to a large and well-organized bookstore, **Clematis Street Books,** at 206 Clematis (✆ 561/832-2302), there are a few used-record stores, clothing shops, and several art galleries.

The **Palm Beach Outlet Center,** at 5700 Okeechobee Blvd. (3 miles [5km] west of I-95), West Palm Beach, is the most elegant outlet mall I have ever seen. Upscale clothing, luggage, and shoes are offered at bargain prices in lushly decorated surroundings. The fully enclosed mall also sports a food court.

WHERE TO STAY

The island of Palm Beach is the epitome of *Lifestyles of the Rich and Famous,* oozing with glitz, glamour, and the occasional scandal. Royalty and celebrities come to winter here, and there are plenty of lavishly priced options to accommodate them. Happily, there are also a few special inns that offer reasonably priced rooms in elegant settings. But the more modest places to lay your straw hat are mostly surrounding the island.

A few of the larger hotel chains operating in Palm Beach include the **Palm Beach Marriott/Fairfield Inn and Suites,** at 2870 S. Ocean Blvd. (✆ 800/654-2000 or 561/582-2581), which is across the street from the beach. Also beachside is the pricey **Palm Beach Hilton,** at 2842 S. Ocean Blvd. (✆ 800/433-1718 or 561/586-6542). An excellent and affordable alternative right in the middle of Palm Beach's commercial section is a condominium that operates as a hotel, too: the **Palm Beach Hotel,** at 235 Sunrise Ave. (between County Rd. and Bradley Place, across the street from the Publix supermarket; ✆ 561/659-7794). With winter prices starting at about $105, this clean and comfortable accommodation is a great option for those looking for the rare bargain in Palm Beach.

In West Palm Beach, the chain hotels are mostly located on the main arteries close to the highways and a short drive from the activities in downtown. They include a **Best Western,** 1800 Palm Beach Lakes Blvd. (✆ 800/331-9569 or 561/683-8810), and, just down the road, a **Comfort Inn,** 1901 Palm Lakes

Blvd. (© **800/221-2222** or 561/689-6100). Farther south is the **Parkview Motor Lodge,** 4710 S. Dixie Hwy., just south of Southern Boulevard (© **561/ 833-4644**). This 28-room, single-story motel is the best of the many motels along Dixie Highway (U.S. 1). With rates starting at $50 for a room with television, air-conditioning, and telephone, you can't ask for more.

For other options, try Palm Beach Accommodations (© **800/543-SWIM**).

VERY EXPENSIVE

Brazilian Court ★★★   This elegant, Old-World Palm Beach Mediterranean-style hotel dates back to the 1920s and almost looks like a Beverly Hills bungalow. The rooms, renovated in 1997, are spacious, albeit a bit blasé, but the marble bathrooms are beautiful and modern. Service is doting, though a bit aloof—you won't always be received by smiling faces, but you will get whatever you want. There's even room service exclusively for pets (you know the type: held hostage in Mummy's Gucci bag). A large hotel by Palm Beach standards (The Breakers notwithstanding), Brazilian Court is sprawled over half a block and features fountains and private courtyards.

301 Australian Ave., Palm Beach, FL 33480. © 800/552-0335 or 561/655-7740. Fax 561/655-0801. www.braziliancourt.com. 103 units. Winter $335–$875; off-season $165–$525. Special packages available. AE, DC, DISC, MC, V. **Amenities:** Restaurant; private dining room (up to 12); bar (see "The Palm Beaches After Dark," below); heated outdoor pool; exercise room; spa treatments; concierge; salon; 24-hr. room service; library. *In room:* A/C, TV, coffeemaker, hair dryer, iron.

The Breakers ★★★   This 140-acre beachfront hotel is what Palm Beach is all about. Elaborate, stately, and resplendent in all its Italian-Renaissance–style glory, it's where old money mixes with new money, and the Old World gives way, albeit reluctantly, to a bit of modernity (note the hotel's recent elimination of the jackets-required rule). The Breakers consists of a seven-story building with a frescoed lobby and long, majestic hallways reminiscent of a palace. The indulgent Oceanfront Spa and Beach Club features a spectacular oceanview fitness center (makes workouts a lot less grueling), four oceanfront pools, cabanas, and saunas. Rooms were modernized a bit, but remain elegant, not sterile, with plush furnishings, huge bathrooms, and views of the ocean or the hotel's magnificently manicured grounds. A revamp of Florida's oldest existing golf course, led by Brian Silva, transformed The Breakers Ocean Course into a 6,200-yard, championship-level par 70.

1 S. County Rd., Palm Beach, FL 33480. © 800/833-3141, 888/BREAKERS, or 561/655-6611. Fax 561/ 659-8403. www.thebreakers.com. 560 units. Winter $420–$3,000; off-season $270–$1,950. Special packages available. AE, DC, DISC, MC, V. Valet parking $17. From I-95, exit Okeechobee Blvd. E., head east to S. County Rd., and turn left. **Amenities:** 5 restaurants; 3 bars; 4 outdoor pools; golf course; 14 tennis courts; health club and spa; water-sports equipment (including scuba and sailing); bike rental; children's programs; game rooms; concierge; business center; shopping arcade; salon; 24-hr. room service; in-room massage; babysitting; dry-cleaning and laundry services; croquet; shuffleboard; beach volleyball courts. *In room:* A/C, TV, minibar, hair dryer, Internet access, CD player.

Four Seasons Resort Palm Beach ★★   Built in 1989 at the edge of Palm Beach's downtown district, this elegant resort has quickly gained accolades from around the world. An incredibly hospitable staff works hard to be sure this beachfront gem lives up to its reputation. The elegant marble lobby is replete with hand-carved European furnishings, grand oil paintings, tapestries, and dramatic flower arrangements—though I did feel like I was in a museum, unable to touch anything. The rooms are spacious with private balconies and lavish bathrooms with color TVs. The full-service spa is excellent, and you will be remiss if you go without experiencing the incredible oceanview massage at the poolside cabanas. The main dining room, known simply as The Restaurant, serves one of the best dinners (Southeastern regional cuisine) in Palm Beach. Executive Chef Hubert Des Marais is one of *Food & Wine* magazine's Ten Best New Chefs. Two other less-formal restaurants, including a pool bar and grill, round out the dining options.

2800 S. Ocean Blvd., Palm Beach, FL 33480. © **800/432-2335** or 561/582-2800. Fax 561/547-1557. www.fourseasons.com. 210 units. Winter $395–$695 double; from $1,500 suite. Off-season $275–$595 double; from $870 suite. AE, DC, DISC, MC, V. Valet parking $18. From I-95, take 6th Ave. exit east and turn left onto Dixie Hwy. Turn east onto Lake Ave. and north onto S. Ocean Blvd., and the hotel is just ahead on your right. Pets under 20 pounds accepted. **Amenities:** 3 restaurants; lounge; outdoor heated pool; 3 tennis courts; spa; water-sports rentals; bike rental; children's programs; concierge; business center; salon; 24-hr. room service; in-room massage; babysitting; dry-cleaning and laundry services; cooking classes weekly. *In room:* A/C, TV/VCR, dataport, minibar, fridge, hair dryer, iron.

Ritz-Carlton Palm Beach ★★★   If The Breakers is too mammoth for your tastes, consider the Ritz-Carlton. A lot warmer than the Four Seasons, the Ritz, though hyper-luxurious, manages to lack pretension. Located on a beautiful beach in a tiny town about 8 miles (13km) from Palm Beach's shopping and dining area, the Ritz-Carlton's location is a plus for those who seek privacy but may be a drawback for those interested in the activity of "town." It is so discreet, in fact, that Palm Beach's luminaries often escape here for a rare weekend or night of anonymity. The hotel's French 18th- and 19th-century antique furnishings give no hint that the property is not yet even 10 years old. Each room has a private balcony and at least a glimpse of the ocean below. All are spacious, while the large marble bathrooms are extremely inviting. The elegant dining room serves continental-style dinners in ornate surroundings. Other restaurants on the property include a grill, for dinner only; a casual restaurant, open all day; and a poolside cafe and bar. Cocktails are also served in the lobby lounge, where you can often find live entertainment. Afternoon tea is served daily but is best Wednesday through Saturday when a jazz trio entertains.

100 S. Ocean Blvd., Manalpan, FL 33462. © **800/241-3333** or 561/533-6000. Fax 561/540-4999. www. ritzcarlton.com. 270 units. Winter $395–$820; $3,150 suite. Off-season $285–$725; $2,700 suite. AE, DISC, MC, V. Valet parking $15. From I-95, take exit 45, heading east. After 1 mile (1.5km), turn left onto Federal Hwy. (U.S. 1). Continue north for about a mile and turn right onto Ocean Ave. Cross the Intracoastal Waterway; turn right onto Fla. A1A. **Amenities:** 4 restaurants; bar; outdoor pool; health club; Jacuzzi; sauna; water-sports equipment/rental; bike rental; children's center/programs; concierge; business center; salon; 24-hr. room service; in-room massage; dry-cleaning and laundry services. *In room:* A/C, TV, dataport, minibar, hair dryer.

EXPENSIVE

Chesterfield Hotel ★★★   Reminiscent of an English country manor, the Chesterfield Hotel in all its flowery, Laura Ashley–inspired glory is a magnificent, charming hotel with exceptional service to rival that of the Ritz. Warm and inviting, the Chesterfield is one of the only places in South Florida in which the idea of a fireplace (there's one in the hotel's library) doesn't seem ridiculous. Traditional English tea is served every afternoon, with fresh-baked scones, petit fours, and sandwiches. Rooms are decorated with bright fabrics and wallpaper and antiques. The roomy marble bathrooms are stocked with an array of luxurious toiletries. A small heated pool and courtyard are nice, and the beach is only 3 blocks away, but the real action is inside. At night, the hotel's retro-elegant Leopard Lounge (see "The Palm Beaches After Dark," below) serves decent continental cuisine but is better as a later-night hangout for live music, schmoozing, and staring at the local cognoscenti.

363 Cocoanut Row, Palm Beach, FL 33480. ⓒ **800/243-7871** or 561/659-5800. Fax 561/659-6707. www. redcarnationhotels.com. 65 units. Winter $309–$350 single or double; off-season $139–$230 single or double. Rollaway bed $15 extra. Packages available. AE, DC, DISC, MC, V. Free valet parking. From I-95, exit onto Okeechobee Blvd. E., cross the Intracoastal Waterway, and turn right onto Cocoanut Row. **Amenities:** Restaurant; lounge; small heated swimming pool; access to nearby health club; Jacuzzi; bike rental; concierge; business center; 24-hr. room service; in-room massage; babysitting; dry-cleaning service. *In room:* A/C, TV, VCR on request, dataport, hair dryer.

Plaza Inn ★★   This three-story, family-run bed-and-breakfast–style inn located 1 block from the beach is as understated and luxurious as the guests it hosts. From the simple and elegant flower arrangements in the marble lobby to the well-worn period antiques haphazardly placed throughout, the Plaza Inn, whose exterior was renovated in 2001, has the look of studied nonchalance. The courtyard, with its waterfalls and pool, and the intimate piano bar are just two examples of the inn's infinite charms. A small staff is remarkably hospitable and knowledgeable about the island's inner workings. Each uniquely decorated room is dressed with quality furnishings, several with carved four-poster beds, hand-crocheted spreads, and lace curtains. The bathrooms, renovated in 2000, are lovely if quite small, and the wall-mounted air conditioners can be noisy when they are needed in the warm months. Choose a corner room or one overlooking the small pool deck for the best light. It's a tough call to decide which is better— the Plaza Inn or the Chesterfield, but the Plaza, unlike the Chesterfield, does include a full breakfast in the price of the room.

215 Brazilian Ave., Palm Beach, FL 33480. ⓒ **800/233-2632** or 561/832-8666. Fax 561/835-8776. www. plazainnpalmbeach.com. 48 units. Winter $225–$375; off-season $105–$195. Rates include breakfast. AE, MC, V. From I-95, exit onto Okeechobee Blvd. E. and cross the Intracoastal Waterway. Turn right onto Cocoanut Row; then left onto Brazilian Ave. Small pets permitted. **Amenities:** Restaurant; lounge; heated outdoor pool; exercise room; Jacuzzi; access to nearby health club ($15 per day); bike rental; concierge; secretarial services; limited room service; in-room massage; babysitting; dry-cleaning and laundry services. *In room:* A/C, TV, dataport, fridge, coffeemaker, hair dryer on request.

MODERATE

The Colony ★★   The sign outside of this Palm Beach mainstay should read ROXANNE PULITZER SLEPT HERE. She did, actually, for quite a while after her 7-week marriage went bust. For years, The Colony has been a favorite hangout— hideout, perhaps—for assorted old timers, socialites, and mysterious luminaries. Beyond that, The Colony is a Georgian-style hotel known for its attentive staff, floral-decorated rooms and, unfortunately, really small bathrooms. The 39 suites and apartments, not to mention the seven two-bedroom villas with Jacuzzis, are much more lavish—and lavishly priced.

155 Hammon Ave., Palm Beach, FL 33480. ⓒ **800/521-5525** or 561/655-5430. Fax 561/659-8104. www. thecolonypalmbeach.com. 64 units, 19 suites, 7 villas. Winter $290–$695; off-season $130–$495. AE, DC, MC, V. From I-95, exit onto Okeechobee Blvd. E. and cross the Intracoastal Waterway. Turn right on S. County Rd.; then left onto Hammon Ave. **Amenities:** Restaurant; bar; heated Florida-shaped pool; spa; concierge; limited seasonal room service. *In room:* A/C, TV, dataport, hair dryer.

Palm Beach Historic Inn ★★   Built in 1923, the Palm Beach Historic Inn is an area landmark located within walking distance of Worth Avenue, the beach, and several good restaurants. The small lobby is filled with antiques, books, magazines, and an old-fashioned umbrella stand, all of which add to the homey feel of this intimate bed-and-breakfast. In your room, wine, fruit, snacks, tea, and cookies ensure that you won't go hungry—never mind the excellent continental breakfast that is brought to you daily. All the rooms are on the second floor, are uniquely decorated, and feature hardwood floors, down comforters,

Egyptian cotton linens, fluffy bathrobes, and plenty of good-smelling toiletries. Gone are the frills, floral prints, sheer curtains, and plethora of lace that once made this inn feel like staying at your grandmother's house. What you'll find here, thanks to new innkeepers who took over in July 2001, is a casual elegance that's comfortable for everyone. In addition, a baby grand piano and guitars for the musically inclined, as well as videotapes to keep the kids entertained, have been added to the hotel's amenities.

365 S. County Rd., Palm Beach, FL 33480. ✆ **561/832-4009.** Fax 561/832-6255. www.palmbeachhistoric inn.com. 13 units. Winter $150–$325; off-season $95–$175. Rates include continental breakfast. Children stay free in parents' room. AE, MC, V. Small pets accepted. No smoking. *In room:* A/C, TV/VCR, fridge, hair dryer.

INEXPENSIVE

Beachcomber Apartment Motel ★★   It's not just the bright pink building that makes this two-story beachfront motel stand out. For more than 35 years, the Beachcomber has been bringing sanity to pricey Palm Beach by offering a good standard of accommodation at reasonable prices. Squeezed between beachfront high-rises, the motel is located on a 300-foot (90m) private beach, adjacent to Lake Worth Beach and a short drive from Worth Avenue shops and local attractions. Every room has two double beds, large closets, and distinctive green-and-white tropical-style furnishings; some have kitchenettes. The most expensive have balconies overlooking the ocean. The bathrooms are basic, and amenities are limited to towels and soap.

3024 S. Ocean Blvd., Palm Beach, FL 33480. ✆ **800/833-7122** or 561/585-4646. Fax 561/547-9438. 45 units. Winter $95–$250; off-season $55–$130. AE, DISC, MC, V. From I-95, exit 10th Ave. N. Head east to Federal Hwy. and turn right. Continue to Lake Ave. and turn left. Go over bridge and turn right at first traffic light. **Amenities:** Large pool; coin-operated laundry. *In room:* A/C, TV.

Hibiscus House ★★ *Finds*   Inexpensive bed-and-breakfasts are rare in Southeast Florida, making the Hibiscus House, one of the area's firsts, a true find. Located a few miles from the coast in a quiet residential neighborhood, this 1920s-era B&B is filled with handsome antiques and tapestries in luxurious fabrics. Every room has its own private terrace or balcony. The Red Room has a fabulous new bathroom with Jacuzzi. The backyard, a peaceful retreat, has been transformed into a tropical garden, complete with heated swimming pool and lounge chairs. Also, there are plenty of pretty areas for guests to enjoy inside; one little sitting room is wrapped in glass and is stocked with playing cards and board games. *Beware:* Breakfast portions are enormous. The gourmet creations are as filling as they are beautiful. Ask for any special requests in advance; owners Raleigh Hill and Colin Rayer will be happy to oblige.

501 30th St., West Palm Beach, FL 33407. ✆ **800/203-4927** or 561/863-5633. Fax 561/863-5633. www.hibiscushouse.com. 8 units. Winter $105–$260 double; off-season $75–$180 double. Rates include breakfast. AE, MC, V. From I-95, exit onto Palm Beach Lakes Blvd. E. and continue 4 miles (6.25km). Turn left onto Flagler Dr. and continue for about 20 blocks. Then turn left onto 30th St. Pets accepted. **Amenities:** Heated pool; concierge. *In room:* A/C, TV, hair dryer.

Hotel Biba ★★ *Finds*   As West Palm Beach came into its own as far as nightlife is concerned, it was only a matter of time before a hip boutique hotel made its appearance in the historic El Cid neighborhood, located 1 mile (1.5km) from City Place and nightlife-heavy Clematis Street. The very cool Hotel Biba answers the call for an inexpensive, chic hotel that young hipsters can call their own. A word of advice, however: The hotel is not exactly soundproof. Rooms may be cloistered by fence and gardens, but they are still extremely close to a major thoroughfare. Try to ask for one that's on the quieter Belvedere Road as opposed to those facing South Olive Avenue. Housed in a renovated Colonial-style 1940s motor lodge, Biba has been remarkably updated on the inside by *de rigueur* designer Barbara Hulanicki and features a sleek and chic lobby with the requisite hip hotel bar, the Biba Bar; a gorgeously landscaped outdoor pool area with Asian gardens; and a reflection pond. Rooms are equally fabulous, with private patios, mosaic-tile floors, custom-made mahogany furniture, Egyptian cotton linens, down pillows, exquisite bathroom products, and high-tech amenities. The bold color schemes mix nicely with the high-fashion crowd that convenes here.

320 Belvedere Rd., West Palm Beach, FL 33405. ℂ 561/832-0094. Fax 561/833-7848. www.hotelbiba.com. 43 units. Year-round rates $79–$179. **Amenities:** Restaurant; lounge; outdoor pool; concierge. *In room:* A/C, TV, dataport, hair dryer, CD player.

WHERE TO DINE

Palm Beach has some of the area's swankiest restaurants. Thanks to the development of downtown West Palm Beach, however, there is also a great selection of trendier, less expensive spots. Dress here is slightly more formal than in most other areas of Florida: Men wear blazers, and women generally put on modest dresses or chic suits when they dine out, even in the oppressively hot days of summer.

VERY EXPENSIVE

Cafe l'Europe ✦✦✦ FRENCH/CONTINENTAL One of Palm Beach's finest and most popular, this award-winning, romantic, luxurious, and formal restaurant gives you good reason to get dressed up. The enticing appetizers, served by a superb staff, might include Chinese spring rolls, baked goat-cheese salad with raspberry-walnut dressing, poached salmon, or chilled gazpacho with avocado. Main courses run the gamut from sautéed potato-crusted Florida snapper to lamb chops to roast Cornish game hen. Seafood dishes and steaks in sumptuous but light sauces are always exceptional.

331 S. County Rd. (at the corner of Brazilian Ave.), Palm Beach. ℂ 561/655-4020. Reservations recommended. Main courses $18–$34. AE, DC, DISC, MC, V. Tues–Thurs noon–2:30pm and 5:45–10:30pm; Fri–Sat noon–2:30pm and 5:45pm–1am; Sun 6–10:30pm.

Mark's CityPlace ✦✦✦ NEW AMERICAN Star chef Mark Militello of Mark's Las Olas and South Beach fame has traveled on his high-speed culinary meteor and landed at West Palm's bustling entertainment and dining complex to the delight of foodies in Palm Beach. A Militello specialty, pizza, is cooked in wood-burning ovens, which churn out trendy versions of the thin-crusted classic, such as shrimp, pesto, fontina cheese, and sun-dried tomatoes. The sushi bar here is, frankly, out of place, since this is not a sushi restaurant. Entrees range from risotto with wild mushroom and truffle oil to an outstanding black-peppercorn–crusted, seared yellowfin tuna. For dessert, try the double-chocolate bread pudding with white-chocolate-chip ice cream.

700 S. Rosemary Ave., West Palm Beach. ℂ 561/514-0770. Reservations recommended. Main courses $17–$38. AE, DC, MC, V. Mon–Thurs 5–11pm; Fri–Sat 5pm–midnight; Sun 5–10:30pm.

EXPENSIVE

Amici ✦ *Overrated* ITALIAN This is one of those restaurants in which the scene is tastier than the cuisine. An upper-crusty Palm Beach set tends to convene here and consistently rave about what can only be considered above-average, overpriced Italian food. The best item on the entire menu is gnocchi with white truffle oil, fontina cheese, and spinach. Everything else is fairly standard: grilled sandwiches, pastas with rustic sauces, pizzas, grilled shrimp, and fish. Despite its less than stellar food, it's always crowded and very noisy.

288 S. County Rd. (at Royal Palm Way), Palm Beach. ☎ **561/832-0201.** Reservations strongly recommended on weekends. Main courses $18–$27; pastas and pizzas $8–$19. AE, DC, MC, V. Mon–Thurs 11:30am–3pm and 5:30–10:30pm; Fri–Sat 11:30am–3pm and 5:30–11pm; Sun 5:30–10:30pm.

Bice Restaurant ★★ ITALIAN   Bice's Northern Italian cuisine far surpasses that of Amici's, but as far as atmosphere is concerned, the air in here is a bit haughty, bordering on rude. Servers and diners alike seem to have noticeable attitudes, but you'll forget all that with one bite of the juicy veal cutlet with tomato salad or the *pasta e fagioli* (pasta with beans).

313½ Worth Ave., Palm Beach. ☎ **561/835-1600.** Reservations essential. Main courses $20–$32. AE, DC, MC, V. Daily 11am–10pm.

Galaxy Grille ★ NEW AMERICAN   Stargazing is certainly at a premium at this Deco-inspired Palm Beach hot spot known for a stellar clientele and a menu to match it. Two favorites include a superb horseradish-encrusted yellowtail snapper and an even better grilled swordfish with fresh tomato, black olives, grilled polenta, garlic, and escarole.

350 S. County Rd., Palm Beach. ☎ **561/833-9909.** Reservations recommended. Main courses $27–$38. AE, DC, MC, V. Daily 5–11pm.

MODERATE

Big City Tavern ★★ AMERICAN   If the Palm Beach–proper dining scene is too stuffy for you, head over the bridge to Clematis Street, downtown West Palm's hub of urban chic, where you will find this yuppie enclave of brick and pressed tin in which people-watching is at a premium. Despite its all-American appearance, Big City Tavern offers a varied menu, including coconut shrimp tempura with a salmon inside-out sushi roll and a delicious bowl of littleneck clams in wine broth with roasted garlic and escarole. On weekends, the Tavern is mobbed, so be prepared for a long wait that's best spent at the action-packed bar.

224 Clematis St., West Palm Beach. ☎ **561/659-1853.** Reservations suggested. Main courses $7.95–$28. AE, MC, V. Mon–Fri 11am–11pm; Sat 6pm–1am; Sun 6–10pm.

Rhythm Café ★ *Finds* ECLECTIC AMERICAN   This funky hole-in-the-wall is where those in the know come to eat some of West Palm Beach's most laid-back gourmet food. On the handwritten, photocopied menu (which changes daily), you'll always find a fish specialty accompanied by a hefty dose of greens and garnishes. Also reliably outstanding is the sautéed medallion of beef tenderloin, served on a bed of arugula with a tangy rosemary vinaigrette. Salads and soups are a great bargain, since portions are relatively large and the display usually spectacular. The kitschy decor of this tiny cafe comes complete with vinyl tablecloths and a changing display of paintings by local amateurs. Young, handsome waiters are attentive but not solicitous. The old drugstore where the restaurant recently relocated features an original 1950s lunch counter and stools.

3800 S. Dixie Hwy., West Palm Beach. ☎ **561/833-3406.** Reservations recommended on weekends. Main courses $12–$31. AE, DISC, MC, V. Tues–Sat 6–10pm. Sun (Dec–Mar) 5:30–9pm. Closed in early Sept. From I-95, exit east on Southern Blvd. Go 1 block north of Southern Blvd.; restaurant on the right.

INEXPENSIVE

Green's Pharmacy ★ *Value* AMERICAN   This neighborhood corner pharmacy offers one of the best meal deals in Palm Beach. Both breakfast and lunch are served coffee-shop style either at a Formica bar or at plain tables placed on a black-and-white checkerboard floor. Breakfast specials include eggs and omelets served with home fries and bacon, sausage, or corned-beef hash. At lunch, the grill serves burgers and sandwiches, as well as ice-cream sodas and milkshakes to a loyal crowd of pastel-clad Palm Beachers.

151 N. County Rd., Palm Beach. ✆ 561/832-0304. Fax 561/832-6502. Breakfast $2–$5; burgers and sandwiches $3–$6; soups and salads $2–$7. AE, DISC, MC, V. Mon–Sat 7am–5pm; Sun 7am–3pm.

John G's ⭐ AMERICAN   This coffee shop is the most popular in the county. For decades, John G's has been attracting huge breakfast crowds; lines run out the door (on weekends, all the way down the block). Stop in for some good, greasy-spoon–style food served in heaping portions right on the beachfront. This place is known for fresh and tasty fish and chips and its selection of creative omelets and grill specials.

10 S. Ocean Blvd., Lake Worth. ✆ 561/585-9860. www.johngs.com. Reservations not accepted. Breakfast $3–$8.50; lunch $5–$14. No credit cards. Daily 7am–3pm. From the Florida Tpk., take the Lake Worth exit and head toward the ocean.

TooJay's DELI   This simple and predictable restaurant and takeout spot is a favorite with locals and out-of-towners who want a good old-fashioned deli. It is so popular, in fact, that TooJay's now has more than eight locations throughout South Florida. This is no Carnegie Deli, but by South Florida deli standards, the food is excellent. All the classic sandwiches are available: hot pastrami, roast beef, turkey, chicken, chopped liver, egg salad, and more. Comfort food in the form of huge portions of stuffed cabbage, chicken pot pie, beef brisket, and sautéed onions and chicken livers is sure to satisfy.

313 Royal Poinciana Plaza (3 miles [5km] east of I-95, off exit 52A), Palm Beach. ✆ 561/659-7232. Reservations not accepted. Main courses $9–$13; lunch $6–$10. AE, DC, MC, V. Daily 8am–9pm.

THE PALM BEACHES AFTER DARK
THE BAR, CAFE & MUSIC SCENE

A decade-old project to revitalize downtown West Palm Beach has finally become a reality, with **Clematis Street** at its heart. Artist lofts, sidewalk cafes, bars, restaurants, consignment shops, and galleries dot the street from Flagler Drive to Rosemary Avenue, creating a hot spot for a night out, especially on weekends, when yuppies mingle with stylish Euros and disheveled artists. Every Thursday night is a mob scene of 20- and 30-somethings who come out for "Clematis by Night." Each week features a different rock, blues, or reggae band plus an art show. Vendors sell food and drinks, and the street's bars and restaurants are packed. It is a bit raucous at times, but fun. Minors unaccompanied by their guardians are not permitted in the downtown area around Clematis Street after 10pm on weeknights and after 11pm on weekend nights. Otherwise, most of the nightspots listed below are open until about 3 or 4am.

Over the bridge, it's a completely different world. Palm Beach is much quieter and better known for its rather private society balls and estate parties. With the exception of some restaurants that are more of a scene—**Ta-boo, Amici,** and **Galaxy Grille**—Palm Beach nightlife is more likely to entail sipping port at one of the finer hotels like The Breakers, The Colony, the Ritz-Carlton, the Four Seasons, or the Chesterfield.

West Palm Beach

Bliss Lounge   With its techno music and VIP rooms, this West Palm club seems like it belongs in the velvet-roped world of South Beach. 313 Clematis St. ✆ 561/833-1444. Tues–Sat. $7 cover. No cover before midnight.

E.R. Bradley's   What used to be a swank saloon on the island of Palm Beach is now a very casual, friendly indoor/outdoor bar in downtown West Palm,

---

Fun Fact **Equal Gambling Rights**

E.R. Bradley's is named for a legendary Palm Beach gambler and horse racer who opened the first casino to ever allow women to gamble.

---

attracting a mixed crowd. The later-night bar scene is a real draw. If you are hungry, try the "crab bomb," Maryland lump crabmeat baked in a light cream sauce with steamed vegetables. 104 Clematis St. © 561/833-3520. Sun–Wed 8am–3am; Thurs–Sat 8am–4am. No cover.

Liquid Room Former South Beach hot spot Liquid may have evaporated (and subsequently reopened by name alone, in a new space that's not nearly as haute as the original) from the scene, but this Clematis Street location, which shares the building with Bliss (located upstairs), is flowing with Palm Beach club kids who revel in the fact that they finally have a chic, celebrity-saturated dance club to call their own. 313 Clematis St. © 561/655-2332. Thurs–Sat. $10 cover.

Lost Weekend I'm not sure whether it's the local artist displays, the pool tables, or the more than 200 beers from around the world sold here, but for some reason, many of Palm Beach's hipsters love losing themselves in this place, which is actually quite nice. 115 S. Olive Ave. © 561/832-3452. Tues–Fri from 4:30pm. No cover.

Monkey Club This tacky yet trendy Caribbean-inspired dance club is 7,500 square feet of wall-to-wall, well-dressed revelers. Theme nights are popular here, from ladies' nights to the classier version of the wet-T-shirt contest—the Miss Hawaiian Tropic Model Search. 219 Clematis St. © 561/833-6500. Cover up to $10.

Respectable Street Café This is one of the premier live music venues in South Florida. In addition to the requisite deejays, this grungy bar features an impressive lineup of alternative music acts. The cafe's plain store-front exterior belies its funky, high-ceilinged interior decorated with large black booths, psychedelic wall murals, and a large checkerboard-tile dance floor. 518 Clematis St. © 561/832-9999. Wed–Sat 9pm–4am. Cover varies.

Palm Beach

Brazilian Court Bistro and Rio Bar Despite its location in the ritzy Brazilian Court Hotel's bistro, the bar here is surprisingly laid-back and unpretentious, featuring a mostly older crowd of couples and, at times, swinging singles. 301 Australian Ave. © 561/655-7740. 7am–10:30pm.

The Leopard Lounge *Finds* *The Flintstones* meet *Dynasty* at this spotty lounge in the Chesterfield Hotel, in which the carpeting, tablecloths, and waitstaff's waistcoats are all in leopard print. There's live music every night from Cole Porter to swing. The crowd's a bit older here, but younger couples and a celebrity or two often find their way here, which makes for an amusing scene. 363 Cocoanut Row. © 561/659-5800. 6pm–2am.

Ta-boo Ta-boo is reminiscent of an upscale TGI Fridays (with food that's about on the same level)—one that caters to a well-heeled crowd—with lots of greenery, a fireplace, and a somewhat cheesy Southwestern decor. But make no mistake, Ta-boo is not about the food: This stellar after-dinner spot is where bejeweled socialites spill out of fancy cars to show off their best Swarovski and salsa. Just find somewhere else to eat first. 221 Worth Ave., Palm Beach. © 561/ 835-3500. Sun–Thurs 11:30am–11pm; Fri–Sat 11:30am–1am.

GAMBLING

The *Palm Beach Princess* (© **800/841-7447** or 561/845-7447) is a small cruise ship (421 ft./126m) offering reasonably priced casino gambling cruises out of the Port of Palm Beach (U.S. 1 between 45th St. and Blue Heron Blvd.) every day and evening. Choose from craps, roulette, poker, blackjack, and slots. Cruises include a large buffet with average food like spaghetti and meatballs, chicken, Greek salad, and vegetables; best is the prime rib at the carving board. Five-hour cruises sail daily at 12:30pm (returning at 5:30pm) and 7pm (returning at 12:30am). Friday and Saturday evening cruises leave at 7pm and return at 1am. Sunday cruises sail from 11am to 5pm and 6 to 11pm. Prices during the week are $30 per person; on weekends, it's $35 per person. If your birthday is in the month you plan to sail, you'll pay $20. AAA discounts are available.

THE PERFORMING ARTS

With a number of dedicated patrons and enthusiastic supporters of the arts, this area happily boasts many good venues for those craving culture. Check the *Palm Beach Post* or the *Palm Beach Daily News* for up-to-date listings and reviews.

The **Raymond F. Kravis Center for the Performing Arts,** 701 Okeechobee Blvd., West Palm Beach (© **561/832-7469;** www.kravis.org), is the area's largest and most active performance space. With a huge curved-glass facade and more than 2,500 seats in two lushly decorated indoor spaces, plus a new outdoor amphitheater, The Kravis, as it is known, stages more than 300 performances each year. Phone or check their website for a current schedule of Palm Beach's best music, dance, and theater.

4 Jupiter ✱ & Northern Palm Beach County ✱

20 miles (32km) N of Palm Beach, 81 miles (130km) N of Miami, 60 miles (97km) N of Fort Lauderdale

While Burt Reynolds is Jupiter's hometown hero (and Celine Dion just built a sprawling manse there, too), the true stars of quaint Jupiter are the beautiful beaches. In the springtime, you can also catch a glimpse of the St. Louis Cardinals and the Montreal Expos during their spring training seasons. North Palm Beach County's other towns—Tequesta, Juno Beach, North Palm Beach, Palm Beach Gardens, and Singer Island—are inviting for tourists who want to enjoy the many outdoor activities that make this area so popular with retirees, seasonal residents, and families.

ESSENTIALS

GETTING THERE   The quickest route from West Palm Beach to Jupiter is on the Florida Turnpike or the sometimes-congested I-95. You can also take a slower but more scenic coastal route, U.S. 1 or Fla. A1A. Since Jupiter is so close to Palm Beach, it's easy to fly into the **Palm Beach International Airport** (© **561/471-7420**) and rent a car there. The drive should take less than half an hour.

VISITOR INFORMATION   A **Visitor Information Center** is located between I-95 and the Florida Turnpike at 8020 Indiantown Rd. in Jupiter (© **561/575-4636;** www.jupiterfloridausa.com) and is open from 9am to 6pm daily.

BEACHES & ACTIVE PURSUITS

BASEBALL   The **Roger Dean Stadium,** 4751 Main St. (© **561/775-1818**), hosts spring training for both the St. Louis Cardinals and the Montreal Expos, along with minor-league action from Florida's state league, the Hammerheads. Tickets range in price from $6 to $18. Call for schedules and specific ticket information.

BEACHES The farther north you head from populated Palm Beach, the more peaceful and pristine the coast becomes. Just a few miles north of the bustle, castles and condominiums give way to wide open space and public parkland. There are dozens of recommendable spots. Following are a few of the best.

John D. MacArthur Beach is a spectacular beach that preserves the natural heritage of the subtropical coastal habitat that once covered Southeast Florida. This state park has a remarkable 4,000-square-foot Nature Center with exhibits, displays, and a video interpreting the barrier island's plant and animal communities. Dominating a large portion of Singer Island, the barrier island just north of Palm Beach, this beach has lengthy frontage on both the Atlantic Ocean and Lake Worth Cove. The beach is great for hiking, swimming, and sunning. Bathrooms and showers are available. To reach the park from the mainland, cross the Intracoastal Waterway on Blue Heron Boulevard and turn north on Ocean Boulevard.

Jupiter Inlet meets the ocean at **Dubois Park,** a 29-acre beach that is popular with families. The shallow waters and sandy shore are perfect for kids, while adults can play in the rougher swells of the lifeguarded inlet. A footbridge leads to **Ocean Beach,** an area popular with windsurfers and surfers. There's a short fishing pier and plenty of trees shading barbecue grills and picnic tables. Visitors can also explore the Dubois Pioneer Home, a small house situated atop a shell mound built by the Jaega Indians. Built from cypress, the home was built in 1898 by Harry Dubois, a citrus worker, as a wedding gift to his wife Susan, whose pictures are still in the house. You will see an original butter churn and pump sewing machine in the living room, and the dining room and bedroom are almost straight out of *Little House on the Prairie.* The park entrance is on Dubois Road, about a mile south of the junction of U.S. 1 and Fla. A1A.

BIKING Rent a bike from **Raleigh Bicycles of Jupiter,** at 103 U.S. 1, Unit F1 (© **561/746-0585**). Prices start at $15.50 per day and $49.50 per week. Bike enthusiasts will enjoy exploring this flat and uncluttered area. North Palm Beach has hundreds of miles of smooth, paved roads. Loggerhead Park in Juno Beach or Fla. A1A along the ocean also has great trails for starters. You'll find many more scenic routes over the bridges and west of the highway.

CANOEING You can rent a boat at several outlets throughout northern Palm Beach County, including **Canoe Outfitters,** 8900 W. Indiantown Rd. (west of I-95), North Jupiter (© **561/746-7053**), which provides access to one of the area's most beautiful natural waterways. Canoers start at Riverbend Park along an 8-mile (13km) stretch of Intracoastal Waterway, where the lush foliage supports dozens of exotic birds and reptiles. Keep your eyes open for the gators, who love to sunbathe on the shallow shores of the river. You'll end up, exhausted, at Jonathan Dickinson Park about 5 or 6 hours later. A pamphlet describing local flora and fauna is available for $1. Trips run Wednesday through Sunday and cost $40 per person for a double canoe with guide.

CRUISES Several sightseeing cruises offer tours of the magnificent waterways that make up northern Palm Beach County. Water taxis conduct daily narrated tours through the scenic waters. One interesting excursion that will take you past the mansions of the rich and famous, and possibly past the manatees swimming off the port of Palm Beach, departs from **Panama Hatties** at PGA Boulevard and the Intracoastal Waterway. Prices are $17 for adults and $9 for children under 12 for the 1½-hour ride. Call © **561/775-2628.** The *Manatee Queen*, 1065 N. Ocean Blvd. (at the Crab House), Jupiter (© **561/744-2191**), is a 40-foot (12km) catamaran with bench seating for up to 49 people. Two-hour tours of Jupiter Island depart daily at 2:30pm, passing Burt Reynolds' and Perry Como's former mansions, among other spots of historical and natural interest. Reservations are highly recommended, especially in season; call for the current schedule of offerings. Prices start at $17 for adults and $10 for children. Bring your own lunch or purchase chips and sodas at the mini-snack bar.

FISHING   Before you leave, send for an information-packed fishing kit with details on fish camps, charters, and tournament and tide schedules, distributed by the **West Palm Beach Fishing Club** (© **561/832-6780**). The cost is $10 and well worth it. Allow at least 4 weeks for delivery.

Once in town, several outfitters along U.S. 1 and Fla. A1A have vessels and equipment for rent if your hotel doesn't. One of the most complete facilities is the **Sailfish Marina & Resort,** 98 Lake Dr. (off Blue Heron Blvd.), Palm Beach Shores (© **561/844-1724**). Call for equipment, bait, guided trips, or boat rentals.

GOLF   Even if you're not lucky enough to be staying at the **PGA National Resort & Spa,** you may still be able to play on their award-winning courses. If you or someone in your group is a member of another golf or country club, have the head pro write a note on club letterhead to Jackie Rogers at PGA (see "Where to Stay," below) to request a play date. Be sure the pro includes his PGA number and contact information. Allow at least 2 weeks for a response. Also, ask about the Golf-A-Round program, where selected private clubs open to nonmembers for free or discounted rates. Contact the **Palm Beach County Convention and Visitors Bureau** (© **561/471-3995**) for details.

Plenty of other great courses dot the area, including the **Golf Club of Jupiter,** 1800 Central Blvd., Jupiter (© **561/747-6262**), where a well-respected 18-hole, par-70 course is situated on more than 6,200 yards featuring narrow fairways and fast greens. Fees are $55 until noon, $45 after noon, and $25 after 3pm, and include a mandatory cart. The course borders I-95.

HIKING   In an area that's not particularly known for extraordinary natural diversity, **Blowing Rocks Preserve** has a terrific hiking trail along a dramatic limestone outcropping. You won't find hills or scenic vistas, but you will see Florida's unique and varied tropical ecosystem. The well-marked mile-long trail passes oceanfront dunes, coastal strands, mangrove wetlands, and a coastal hammock. The preserve, owned and managed by The Nature Conservancy, also protects an important habitat for West Indian manatees and loggerhead turtles. Located along South Beach Drive (Fla. A1A), north of the Jupiter inlet, the preserve is about a 10-minute drive northeast of Jupiter. Free guided tours are available Fridays and Sundays at 11am, and no reservations are necessary. From U.S. 1, head east on S.R. 707 and cross the Intracoastal Waterway to the park. Admission is free, but a $3 per-person donation is requested. For more information, contact the Preserve Manager, Blowing Rocks Preserve, P.O. Box 3795, Tequesta, FL 33469 (© **561/744-6668**).

SCUBA DIVING & SNORKELING   Year-round warm, clear waters make northern Palm Beach County great for both diving and snorkeling. The closest coral reef is located a quarter-mile from shore and can easily be reached by boat. Three popular wrecks are clustered near each other, less than a mile offshore of the Lake Worth Inlet at about 90 feet (27m). The best wreck, however, is the 16th or 17th century Spanish galleon discovered by lifeguard Peter Leo just off

Discovering a Remarkable Natural World

North Palm Beach is well known for the giant sea turtles that lay their eggs on the county's beaches from May to August. These endangered marine animals return here annually, from as far away as South America, to lay their clutches of about 115 eggs each. Nurtured by the warm sand, but targeted by birds and other predators, only about one or two babies from each nest survive to maturity.

Many environmentalists recommend that visitors take part in an organized turtle-watching program (rather than going on their own) to minimize disturbance to the turtles. The Jupiter Beach Resort (see "Where to Stay," below) and the Marinelife Center of Juno Beach (see below) both sponsor free guided expeditions to the egg-laying sites from May to August. Phone for times and reservations.

Just south of Jupiter, in Juno Beach, is the **Marinelife Center of Juno Beach,** in Loggerhead Park, 14200 U.S. 1, Juno Beach (© 561/ 627-8280). Combining a science museum and nature trail, the small Marinelife Center is dedicated to the coastal ecology of northern Palm Beach County. Hands-on exhibits teach visitors about wetlands and beach areas, as well as offshore coral reefs and the local sea life. Visitors are encouraged to walk the center's sand-dune nature trails, all of which are marked with interpretive signs. This is one place in which you're guaranteed to see live sea turtles year-round. During high breeding season (June and July), the center conducts narrative walks along a nearby beach. Reservations are a must. The booking list opens on May 1 and is usually full by midmonth. Admission to the center is free, though donations are accepted. Open Tuesday through Saturday from 10am to 4pm and Sunday from noon to 3pm.

Jupiter Beach (p. 301 for more information). If your hotel doesn't offer dive trips, call the **South Florida Dive Headquarters,** 23141 Lyons Rd., Boca Raton (© **800/771-DIVE** or 561/627-9558); or **Seafari Dive and Surf,** 75 E. Indiantown Rd., Suite 603, Jupiter (© **561/747-6115**).

TENNIS In addition to the many hotel tennis courts (see "Where to Stay," below), you can swing a racquet at a number of local clubs. The **Jupiter Bay Tennis Club,** 353 U.S. 1, Jupiter (© 561/744-9424), has seven clay courts (three lighted) and charges $12 per person per day. Reservations are highly recommended.

More-economical options are available at relatively well-maintained municipal courts. Call for locations and hours (© **561/966-6600**). Many are available free on a first-come, first-served basis.

A HISTORIC LIGHTHOUSE

Jupiter Inlet Lighthouse ★ Completed in 1860, this redbrick structure is the oldest extant building in Palm Beach County. Still owned and maintained by the U.S. Coast Guard, the lighthouse is now home to a small historical museum, located at its base. The Florida History Museum sponsors tours of the lighthouse, enabling visitors to explore the cramped interior, which is filled with artifacts and photographs illustrating the rich history of the area. A 15-minute video explains the various shipwrecks, Indian wars, and other events that helped shape this region. Helpful volunteers are eager to tell colorful stories to highlight the 1-hour tour.

500 S.R. 707, Jupiter. ✆ **561/747-8380.** Admission $5. Sun–Wed 10am–4pm (last tour departs at 3:15pm). Children must be 4 feet (1.25m) or taller to climb. No open-backed shoes.

SHOPPING

Northern Palm Beach County may not have the glitzy boutiques of Worth Avenue, but it does have an impressive indoor mall, the **Gardens of the Palm Beaches,** at 3101 PGA Blvd., where you can find large department stores including **Bloomingdale's, Burdines, Macy's,** and **Saks Fifth Avenue,** as well as more than 100 specialty shops. A large, diverse food court and fine sit-down restaurants in this 1.3-million-square-foot facility make this shopping excursion an all-day affair. Call ✆ **561/775-7750** for store information.

WHERE TO STAY

The northern part of Palm Beach County is much more laid-back and less touristy than the rest of the Gold Coast. Here, there are relatively few fancy hotels or attractions.

VERY EXPENSIVE

Jupiter Beach Resort ★★   The only resort located directly on Jupiter's beach, this unpretentious retreat is popular with families and seems a world away from the more luxurious resorts just a few miles to the south. The lobby and public areas have a Caribbean motif, accented with green marble, arched doorways, and chandeliers. The simple and elegant guest rooms are furnished in a comfortable island style, and every room has a private balcony with ocean or sunset views looking out over the uncluttered beachfront. A thorough refurbishing in the mid-1990s is responsible for the resort's increasing popularity. In fact, it is so popular that it is being gradually converted into a time-share property. Excursions are available to top-rated golf courses in the area.

5 N. Fla. A1A, Jupiter, FL 33477. ✆ **800/228-8810** or 561/746-2511. Fax 561/747-3304. www.jupiterbeach resort.com. 153 units. Winter $170–$450; off-season $97–$205. AE, DC, DISC, MC, V. Valet parking $5. From I-95, take exit 59A, going east to the end of Indiantown Rd. at A1A. Jupiter Beach Resort is at this intersection on the ocean. **Amenities:** Restaurant; 2 bars; pool; tennis court; exercise room; extensive water-sports equipment/rental; bike rental; children's programs; concierge; business center; room service; in-room massage; dry-cleaning service. *In room:* A/C, TV, dataport, minibar, coffeemaker, iron, and VCR (for a $10 additional charge). Suites have kitchenettes.

PGA National Resort & Spa ★★★   This rambling resort, the national headquarters of the PGA, is a premier golf vacation spot—but its top-rated Mediterranean spa could be a destination in itself. With five 18-hole courses on more than 2,300 acres, golfers and other sports-minded travelers will find plenty to keep them occupied—croquet, tennis, sailing, a health and fitness center, and the sublime spa. Constant updating has kept the grounds and buildings in like-new condition. In 2000, the lobby and all rooms were completely renovated. The par-72 Champion Course, redesigned in 1990 by Jack Nicklaus, is the resort's most valuable asset. More than 100 sand bunkers and plenty of water on 6,400-square-foot greens keep golfers of all levels alert. Watch out for hole 16. Rooms are spacious and comfortable, with immense bathrooms. This is not a beach resort, however. Six outdoor therapy pools known as "Waters of the World" are surrounded by mineral pools, which are so sublime, they make the

> ### (Fun Fact Burt Reynolds Slept Here
>
> Although there's no sign saying, "Welcome to Jupiter, Home of Burt Reynolds," there may as well be. You see, for a time, Reynolds was the ruler of this South Floridian planet, with a park, a museum, a theater, and a ranch that, in better times, all bore his name. Born in Waycross, Georgia, Reynolds grew up in West Palm Beach, where his half-Cherokee father was police chief. While attending Florida State University in Tallahassee, Reynolds injured his knee and lost all hopes of pursuing a pro-football career. That's when he turned to acting. But beyond *Gunsmoke, Deliverance, Smokey and the Bandit,* and that legendary centerfold in *Cosmopolitan,* Reynolds' star faded and the former sex symbol quietly retreated to Jupiter in the early 1980s, where he opened his dinner theater and, later, the Burt Reynolds Ranch, which featured a wedding chapel, the Burt Reynolds Petting Farm, and a Hall of Fame, among other things. The restaurant went into foreclosure, and the ranch was sold after Reynolds declared bankruptcy in 1996. Today, the only thing still bearing Reynolds' name is the Burt Reynolds Park, 805 U.S. 1. But the legend still lives on. No matter which chapter of his life he's currently on—11 or otherwise—Reynolds will always be responsible for bringing a bit of Hollywood to the little town of Jupiter.

ocean look like a kiddie pool. Don Shula's award-winning steak house and restaurant is the hotel's best and most popular restaurant.

400 Ave. of the Champions, Palm Beach Gardens, FL 33418. ⓒ 800/633-9150 or 561/627-2000. Fax 561/622-0261. www.pga-resorts.com. 339 units. Winter $319–$389 double; from $489 suite. Off-season $129–$169 double; from $249 suite. Children 16 and under stay free in parents' room. Special packages available. AE, DC, DISC, MC, V. From I-95, take exit 57B (PGA Blvd.) going west and continue for approximately 2 miles (3.25km) to the resort entrance on the left. **Amenities:** 6 restaurants and lounges; 9 swimming pools; 5 18-hole tournament courses plus the PGA National's Academy of Golf; 19 clay tennis courts; Mediterranean spa; water-sports equipment/rentals; concierge; car-rental desk; salon; room service; laundry; babysitting; aerobics studio; 5 tournament croquet lawns; 5 indoor racquetball courts. *In room:* A/C, TV, dataport, minibar, hair dryer, safe.

MODERATE/INEXPENSIVE

Baron's Landing Motel & Apartments ⭐ *Value*   This charming family-run inn is a perfect little beach getaway. It's not elegant, but it is cozy. The single-story motel fronting the Intracoastal Waterway is often full in winter with snowbirds, who dock their boats at the hotel's marina for weeks or months at a time. Nearly all rooms, which are situated around a small pool, have small kitchenettes. Each unit has a funky mix of used furniture, and some have pullout sofas. Bathrooms have been remodeled. Considering that you're a few blocks from some of the most expensive real estate in the country, this is a good deal. Dock rentals are available.

18125 Ocean Blvd. (Fla. A1A at the corner of Clemens St.), Jupiter, FL 33477. ⓒ 561/746-8757. 8 units. Winter $75–$125 double; $1,350–$1,700 monthly. Off-season $45–$75 double; $700–$900 monthly. No credit cards. **Amenities:** Small pool. *In room:* A/C, TV, fax, dataport, kitchen, fridge, coffeemaker, iron.

Cologne Motel   A modest roadside motel, the Cologne is a well-maintained one-story building with a pool but very little in the way of amenities. The small rooms were updated in 1999 with modest but bright bedspreads and curtains, and the retiled bathrooms are small but clean. The area is safe if not scenic and only about a 5-minute drive to the beach. A more direct route by foot gets you there in about 15 minutes.

220 U.S. 1, Tequesta/Jupiter, FL 33469. © 561/746-0616. 9 units. Winter $70 double; off-season $36 double. Weekly rates available. AE, MC, V. **Amenities:** Pool. *In room:* A/C, TV, fridge, no phone.

WHERE TO DINE

In addition to all the national fast-food joints that line Indiantown Road and U.S. 1, you'll find a number of touristy fish restaurants serving battered and fried everything. There are only a few really exceptional eateries in North Palm Beach and Jupiter. Try those listed below for guaranteed good food at reasonable prices.

MODERATE

Athenian Cafe ★ *Finds* GREEK   Peter Papadelis and his family have been running this pleasant store-front cafe for more than a decade. Tucked in the corner of a strip mall, this place is a favorite with businesspeople, who stop in for a heaping portion of rich and meaty moussaka or a flaky spinach pie made fresh by Peter himself. You could make a meal of the thick and lemony Greek soup and the large, fresh antipasto. In a town replete with tourist-priced fish joints, this is a welcome alternative. Early-bird specials, served until 7pm, include many Greek favorites and broiled local fish with soup or salad, rice, vegetables, pita, dessert, and coffee or tea.

In the Chasewood Shopping Center, 6350 Indiantown Rd., Ste. 7, Jupiter. © 561/744-8327. Main courses $5–$16. AE, MC, V. Mon–Sat 11am–9pm; Sun 4–9pm in high season only.

Capt. Charlie's Reef Grill ★★ SEAFOOD/CARIBBEAN   The trick here is to arrive early, ahead of the crowd of local foodies who come for the more than a dozen daily local-catch specials prepared in dozens of styles. Imaginative appetizers include Caribbean chili, a rich chunky stew filled with fresh seafood; and a tuna spring roll big enough for two. The enormous Cuban crab cake is moist and perfectly browned without tasting fried and is served with homemade mango chutney and black beans and rice. Sit at the bar to watch the hectic kitchen turn out perfect dishes on the 14-burner stove. Somehow, the pleasant waitresses keep their cool even when the place is packed. In addition to the terrific seafood, this little dive offers an extensive, affordable wine and beer selection—more than 30 of each from around the world.

12846 U.S. 1 (behind O'Brian's and French Connection), Juno Beach. © 561/624-9924. Reservations not accepted. Main courses $9.95–$18.95. MC, V. Sun–Thurs 11:30am–9:30pm; Fri–Sat 11:30am–10pm.

Nick's Tomato Pie ★ ITALIAN   A fun, family restaurant, Nick's is a popular attraction that's known to bring folks even from Miami for a piece of this pie. With a huge menu of pastas, pizzas, fish, chicken, and beef, this cheery (and noisy) spot has something for everyone. On Saturday night, you'll see lots of couples on dates and some families leaving with takeout bags left over from the impossibly generous portions. The homemade sausage is a delicious treat, served with sautéed onions and peppers. The *pollo marsala*, too, is good and authentic.

1697 W. Indiantown Rd. (1 mile [1.5km] east of I-95, exit 59A), Jupiter. © 561/744-8935. Reservations accepted for groups of 6 or more. Main courses $12–$20; pastas $10–$15. AE, DC, DISC, MC, V. Mon–Thurs and Sun 5–10pm; Fri–Sat 5–11pm.

Sinclair's Ocean Grill & Rotisserie ★★ CARIBBEAN   As close to upscale as Jupiter gets, Sinclair's is the Jupiter Beach Resort's excellent restaurant overlooking the pool and featuring fresh, locally caught fish as well as an excellent filet mignon. Especially popular are the Sunday brunches.

Jupiter Beach Resort, 5 N. Fla. A1A © **561/745-7120.** Reservations recommended. Main courses $9.95–$18. AE, MC, V. Daily 6:30–11am, 11:30am–2:30pm, and 6–10pm.

JUPITER & NORTHERN PALM BEACH COUNTY AFTER DARK

With one notable exception, there just isn't much going on here after dark. However, **Club Safari,** 4000 PGA Blvd. (just east of I-95), in Palm Beach Garden's Marriott Hotel (© **561/622-8888**), has a hilarious Vegas-style safari-themed decor, with faux, albeit lifelike, animals positioned throughout the club. The huge, sunken dance floor is surrounded by vines and lanky potted trees. Nearby, a large Buddha statue blows steam and smoke while waving its burly arms in front of a young gyrating crowd. There is deejay music, a large video screen, and a modest cover charge on the weekends. Open nights, Wednesday through Sunday. For more options, check your hotel or do what most people do, go to West Palm Beach.

The Treasure Coast: Stuart to Sebastian

by Lesley Abravanel

The area north of Palm Beach is known as the Treasure Coast for the same reason that the area from Fort Lauderdale to Palm Beach is known as the Gold Coast—it was the site of a number of shipwrecks that date back over 300 years, which led to the discovery of priceless treasures in the water (some historians believe that treasures from these sunken vessels *still* lie buried deep beneath the ocean floor).

The difference, however, is that while the Gold Coast is a bit, well, tarnished as far as development is concerned, the Treasure Coast remains, for the most part, an unspoiled, quiet natural jewel. Miles of uninterrupted beaches and aquamarine waters attract swimmers, boaters, divers, anglers, and sun worshippers who love to dip, dive, and surf. If you love the great outdoors and prefer a more understated environment than hyper-developed Miami and Fort Lauderdale, the Treasure Coast is a real find.

For hundreds of years, Florida's east coast was a popular stopover for European explorers, many of whom arrived from Spain to fill coffers with gold and silver. Rough weather and poor navigation often took a toll on their ships, but in 1715, a violent hurricane stunned the northeast coast and sank an entire fleet of Spanish ships laden with gold. Although Spanish salvagers worked for years to collect the lost treasure, much of it remained buried beneath the shifting sand. Workers hired to excavate the

area in the 1950s and 1960s discovered centuries-old coins under their tractors.

Today, you can still see shipwrecks and incredible barrier reefs in St. Lucie County, which can be reached from the beaches of Fort Pierce and Hutchinson Island. On these same beaches, you'll also find an occasional treasure hunter trolling the sand with a metal detector, alongside swimmers and sunbathers who come to enjoy the stretches of beach that extend into the horizon. The sea, especially around Sebastian Inlet, is a mecca for surfers, who find some of the largest swells in the state.

Along with the pleasures of the talcum-powder sands, the Treasure Coast also offers great shopping, entertainment, clubbing, sporting, and numerous other opportunities to take a reprieve from the hubbub of the rat race. Visitors to this part of South Florida should not miss the extensive array of wildlife, which includes the endangered West Indian manatee, loggerhead and leatherback turtles, tropical fish, alligators, deer, and exotic birds. For sports enthusiasts, there are boundless sporting opportunities here—from golf and tennis to polo, motorcar racing, the New York Mets during their spring training, and the best freshwater fishing around.

The downtown areas of the Treasure Coast have been experiencing a rebirth in the past few years, along with the influx of unprecedented numbers of new residents. Fortunately, the area's growth has occurred at a reasonable pace so that the neighborhoods have been able to retain their small-town feel. The result is a batch of freshly spruced-up accommodations, shops, and restaurants from Stuart to Sebastian.

Southern Martin County's well-to-do Hobe Sound, in particular, is a Treasure Coast hot spot with its pristine beaches, Banyan tree–canopied streetscapes, one-of-a-kind antiques shops, and art galleries. Hobe Sound rests at the front door of the Gold Coast and the back door of the Treasure Coast, and it has immediate access to the Atlantic Ocean and the Intracoastal Waterway. Real estate here is at a premium, with million-dollar waterfront mansions lining the shores.

For the purposes of this chapter, the Treasure Coast runs roughly from Hobe Sound in the south to the Sebastian Inlet in the north, encompassing some of Martin, St. Lucie, and Indian River Counties and all of Hutchinson Island.

TREASURE COAST ESSENTIALS
GETTING THERE
Since virtually every town described in this chapter runs along a straight route along the Atlantic Ocean, I've given all directions below.

BY PLANE The **Palm Beach International Airport** (© 561/471-7420), located about 35 miles (56km) south of Stuart, is the closest gateway to this region if you're flying. See the "Getting Around" section on Palm Beach in chapter 8 for complete information. If you are traveling to the northern part of the Treasure Coast, **Melbourne International Airport,** off U.S. 1 in Melbourne (© 407/723-6227), is less than 25 miles (40km) north of Sebastian and about 35 miles (56km) north of Vero Beach.

BY CAR If you're driving up or down the Florida coast, you'll probably reach the Treasure Coast via I-95. If you are heading to Stuart or Jensen Beach, take exit 61 (Rte. 76/Tanner Hwy.) or 62 (Rte. 714); to Port St. Lucie or Fort Pierce, take exit 63 or 64 (Okeechobee Rd.); to Vero Beach, take exit 68 (S.R. 60); to Sebastian, take exit 69 (County Rd.).

You can also take the Florida Turnpike; this toll road is the fastest (but not the most scenic) route, especially if you're coming from Orlando. If you are heading to Stuart or Jensen Beach, take exit 133; to Fort Pierce, take exit 152 (Okeechobee Rd.); to Port St. Lucie, take exit 142 or 152; to Vero Beach, take exit 193 (S.R. 60); to Sebastian, take exit 193 to State Route 60 east and connect to I-95 north.

If you are staying in Hutchinson Island, which runs almost the entire length of the Treasure Coast, you should check with your hotel or see the listings below to find the best route to take.

Finally, if you're coming directly from the west coast, you'll probably take State Route 70, which runs north of Lake Okeechobee to Fort Pierce, located just up the road from Stuart.

BY RAIL Amtrak (© 800/USA-RAIL; www.amtrak.com) stops in West Palm Beach at 201 S. Tamarind Ave., and in Okeechobee at 801 N. Parrot Ave., off U.S. 441 north.

BY BUS Greyhound buses (© 800/231-2222; www.greyhound.com) service the area with terminals in Stuart, at 1308 S. Federal Hwy.; in Fort Pierce, at 7005 Okeechobee Rd. (© 561/461-3299); and in Vero Beach, at U.S. 1 and State Route 60 (© 561/562-6588).

The Treasure Coast

Dodgertown **4**
Elliott Museum **14**
Environmental Learning Center **3**
Florida Oceanographic Coastal Center **14**
Gilbert's House of Refuge Museum **13**
Hale Indian River Groves **8**
Harbor Branch Oceanographic Institution **10**
Horizon Outlet Center **5**

Hutchinson Island Marriott **15**
Indian River Citrus Museum **7**
Indian River Mall **6**
McKee Botanical Garden **9**
McLarty Treasure Museum **1**
Mel Fisher's Treasure Museum **2**
Savannahs Recreation Center **12**
UDT-SEAL Museum **11**

GETTING AROUND

A car is a necessity in this large and rural region. Although heavy traffic is not usually a problem here, on the smaller coastal roads, like A1A, expect to travel at a slow pace, usually between 25 and 40 miles (40–64km) an hour.

1 Hobe Sound ✸✸✸, Stuart (North Hutchinson Island ✸✸ & Jensen Beach

Once just a stretch of pineapple plantations, the towns of Martin County, which include Hobe Sound, Stuart, and Jensen Beach, still retain much of their rural character. Dotted between citrus groves and mangroves are modest homes and an occasional high-rise condominium. Although the area is definitely still seasonal (with a distinct rise in street and pedestrian traffic beginning after the Christmas holidays), the atmosphere is pure small town. Even in historic downtown Stuart, the result of a successful, ongoing restoration, expect the store fronts to be dark and the streets abandoned after 10pm.

The Producers

During the land boom in the 1920s, big plans were made for Hobe Sound by the Olympia Improvement Corporation. The company would create a columned, trellised town in the style of a Greek village, one in which movies could be produced. Hobe Sound was renamed Picture City, and street names came straight from Greek mythology: Zeus Crescent, Saturn, Mercury, Mars, Olympus, and Athena. When the boom collapsed in 1928 after a devastating hurricane, the celluloid dreams for Picture City were shattered. The town's old name of Hobe Sound was restored, but the street names remain, as do the cement streetlights on Dixie Highway.

ESSENTIALS

The **Stuart/Martin County Chamber of Commerce,** 1650 S. Kanner Hwy., Stuart, FL 34994 (© 800/524-9704 or 561/287-1088; fax 561/220-3437), is the region's main source for information. The **Jensen Beach Chamber of Commerce,** 1901 NE Jensen Beach Blvd., Jensen Beach, FL 34957 (© 561/334-3444; fax 561/334-0817), also offers visitors information about its simple beachfront town.

BACK TO NATURE: THE BEACHES & BEYOND

BEACHES   Hutchinson Island, located in Stuart, is one of the most popular beach destinations of the Treasure Coast, located just north of Palm Beach on the Atlantic Ocean. 70 miles (113km) of excellent beaches and laid-back, Old Florida ambience make for an idyllic frozen-cocktail-on-the-beach resort vacation.

The best of them is **Bathtub Beach,** on North Hutchinson Island. Here, the calm waters are protected by coral reefs, and visitors can explore the region on dune and river trails. Pick a secluded spot on the wide stretch of beach, or enjoy marked nature trails across the street. Facilities include showers and toilets open during the day. To reach Bathtub Beach from the northern tip of Hutchinson Island, head east on Ocean Boulevard (Stuart Causeway) and turn right onto MacArthur Boulevard. The beach is about a mile ahead on your left, just north of the Hutchinson Island Marriott Beach Resort and Marina. Parking is plentiful.

CANOEING   **Jonathan Dickinson State Park** (see "Wildlife Exploration: From Gators to Manatees to Turtles," below) is the area's most popular for canoeing. The route winds through a variety of botanical habitats. You'll see lots of birds and the occasional manatee. Canoes cost $6 per hour and can be rented through the concession located in the back of the park. The concession (© 561/746-1466) is open Monday through Friday from 9am to 5pm and Saturday and Sunday from 8am to 5pm.

FISHING   Several independent charter captains operate on Hutchinson Island and Jensen Beach. One of the largest operators is the **Sailfish Marina,** 3565 SE St. Lucie Blvd., in Stuart (© 561/221-9456), which maintains half a dozen charter boats for fishing excursions year-round. Also on-site are a bait-and-tackle shop and a knowledgeable, helpful staff. Other reputable charter operators include **Hungry Bear Adventures, Inc.,** docked at Indian River Plantation Marriott Resort, 4730-1 SE Teri Place in Stuart (© 561/283-8034; fishing@tci.net); and **Bone Shaker Sportfishing,** 3585 SE St. Lucie Blvd., in Stuart (© 561/286-5504; veejay4842@aol.com).

GOLF   Try the **Champions Club at Summerfield,** on U.S. 1, south of Cove Road in Stuart (② **561/283-1500**), a somewhat challenging championship course designed by Tom Fazio. This rural course, the best in the area, offers great glimpses of wildlife amid the wetlands. Winter greens fees are around $60, and carts are mandatory. Reservations are a must and are taken 4 days in advance.

SCUBA DIVING & SNORKELING   Three popular artificial reefs off Hutchinson Island provide excellent scenery for both novice and experienced divers. The **USS *Rankin*** lies 7 miles (11km) east-northeast of the St. Lucie Inlet. The Rankin is a 459-foot (138m) ship that lays on its port side in 80 feet (24m) of water. This ship was used in World War II for troop transportation and was sunk in 1988. Deck hatches on the wreck are open and allow exploration. Inside, there are thousands of Atlantic Spiny oysters and a cannon is attached to the bow. The 58-foot-deep **Donaldson Reef** consists of a cluster of steel tanks and barrels sunk in 58 feet (17m) of water to create the artificial reef. It's located due east of the Gilbert's House of Refuge Museum (see below). The **Ernst Reef,** made from old tires, is a 60-foot (18m) dive located 4½ miles (7km) east-southeast of the St. Lucie inlet. Local dive shops have "tips" on the best

Wildlife Exploration: From Gators to Manatees to Turtles

One of the most scenic areas on this stretch of the coast is **Jonathan Dickinson State Park** ⚲, 12 miles (19km) south of Stuart at 16450 S. Federal Hwy. (U.S. 1), Hobe Sound (② **561/546-2771**). The park intentionally receives less maintenance than other, more meticulously maintained parks so that it will resemble the rough-around-the-edges, wilderness-like environment of hundreds of years ago, before Europeans started chopping, dredging, and "improving" the area. Dozens of species of Florida's unique wildlife, including alligators and manatees, live on the park's more than 11,300 acres. Bird-watchers will also be delighted by glimpses of rare and endangered species such as the bald Eagle, the Florida scrub-jay, and the Florida sandhill crane, which still call this park home. You can rent canoes from the concession stand to explore the Loxahatchee River on your own. Admission is $3.25 per car of up to eight adults. Day hikers, bikers, and walkers pay $1 each. The park is open from 8am until sundown. See "Where to Stay," below, for details on camping.

Close to Jonathan Dickinson State Park is **Hobe Sound Wildlife Refuge,** on North Beach Road off State Route 708, at the north end of Jupiter Island (② **561/546-6141**). This is one of the best places to see sea turtles that nest on the shore in the summer months, especially in June and July. Because it's home to a large variety of other plant and animal species, the park is worth visiting at other times of year as well. Admission is $4 per car, and the preserve is open daily from sunrise to sunset. Exact times are posted at each entrance and change seasonally.

For turtle walks on Hutchinson Island, call ② **877/375-4386.** These walks take place from May 22 to July 22 at 9pm, Friday and Saturday. Reservations are necessary and should be made well in advance, as walks are limited to 50 people. Reservations are accepted as of May 1.

spots and rules and regulations for safe diving. **The Donald F. Welton Scuba Repair Shop** (© 561/225-9717; dfwelton@aol.com) in Jensen Beach is a great place for information.

SEEING THE SIGHTS

Balloons Over Florida ★★★ *(Finds)* For a lofty view of Martin County's wildlife, take a hot-air balloon ride above the animals' natural habitat. Two fully licensed and insured balloons and pilots will take a maximum of four people up, up, and away for about an hour, depending on wind and weather conditions. After you've landed, drink in the sights over a glass of complimentary champagne and a continental breakfast. A certificate of flight is given to each passenger as a souvenir.

Tours begin at approximately 6:30am from a takeoff point to be determined. © 561/334-9393. $150 per person, including continental breakfast and champagne.

Elliott Museum ★★ A treasure trove of wacky artifacts that really personify Americana, the Elliott Museum is a rich tribute to inventors, sports heroes, and collectors. The museum was created by the son of turn-of-the-20th-century inventor Sterling Elliott to display the genius of the American spirit. Among the bizarre things you'll see here are displays of an apothecary, ice-cream parlor, barbershop, other old-fashioned commercial enterprises, and an authentic hand-carved miniature circus. Sports fans will appreciate the baseball memorabilia—a half-million dollars' worth—including an autographed item from every player in the Baseball Hall of Fame.

A gallery of patents and models of machines, invented by the museum's founder, Harmon Parker Elliott, and his son, provides an intriguing glimpse into the business of tinkering. Their collection of restored antique cars is also impressive. Expect to spend at least an hour seeing the highlights.

825 NE Ocean Blvd. (north of Indian River Plantation Resort), Hutchinson Island, Stuart. © 561/225-1961. Admission $6 adults, $2 children 6–13, free for children 5 and under. Daily 10am–4pm.

Florida Oceanographic Coastal Center ★★ This is a nature lover's Disney World. Opened by the South Florida Oceanographic Society in late 1994, this 44-acre site (surrounded by coastal hammock and mangroves) is its own little ecosystem and serves as an outdoor classroom, teaching visitors about the region's flora and fauna. The modest main building houses saltwater tanks and wet and dry "discovery tables" with small indigenous animals. The incredibly eager staff of volunteers encourages visitors to wander the lush, well-marked nature trails.

890 NE Ocean Blvd. (across the street from the Elliott Museum), Hutchinson Island, Stuart. © 561/225-0505. www.fosusa.org. Admission $6 adults, $3 children 3–12, free for children under 3. Mon–Sat 10am–5pm; Sun noon–4pm.

Gilbert's House of Refuge Museum ★ Gilbert's, the oldest structure in Martin County, dates from 1875, when it functioned as one of 10 rescue centers for shipwrecked sailors. After undergoing a thorough rehabilitation to its original condition along the rocky shores, the house now displays marine artifacts and turn-of-the-20th-century lifesaving equipment and photographs and is worth a quick visit to get a feel for the area's early days.

301 SE MacArthur Blvd. (south of Indian River Plantation resort), Hutchinson Island, Stuart. © 561/225-1875. Admission $4 adults, $2 children 6–13, free for children 5 and under. Daily 10am–4pm.

A BOAT TOUR

The *Loxahatchee Queen* ★★★, a 35-foot (11m) pontoon boat (© 561/746-1466) in Jonathan Dickinson State Park in Hobe Sound, makes daily tours of the area's otherwise inaccessible backwater, where curious alligators, manatees, eagles, and tortoises often peek out to see who's in their yard. Try to catch the 2-hour tour, given Wednesday through Sunday as the tide permits, when it includes a stop at Trapper Nelson's home. Known as the "Wildman of Loxahatchee," Nelson lived in primitive conditions on a remote stretch of the water in a log cabin he built himself, which is preserved for visitors to see. Tours leave four times daily at 9 and 11am, and 1 and 3pm and cost $12 for adults, $7 for children 6 to 12, and free for children 5 and under. See the "Wildlife Exploration: From Gators to Manatees to Turtles" box for more information on the park.

SHOPPING

Downtown Stuart's historic district, along Flagler Avenue between Confusion Corner and St. Lucie Avenue, offers shoppers diversity and quality in a small old-town setting. Shops offer a range of goods: antique bric-a-brac, old lamps and fixtures, books, gourmet foods, furnishings, and souvenirs. For bargains, check out the **B & A Flea Market** (© **561/288-4915**), the Treasure Coast's oldest and largest flea market.

WHERE TO STAY

Although the area boasts some beautiful beaches, the bulk of the hotel scene is downtown, where the nicer (and more reasonably priced) accommodations can be found among the shops and restaurants. There are, however, a few excellent beachfront hotels and inns. One of the bigger hotel chains in the area is the **Holiday Inn.** Its recently renovated, stunning beachfront property is at 3793 NE Ocean Blvd., on Hutchinson Island in Jensen Beach (© **800/992-4747** or 561/225-3000). Rates in season range from $130 to $180. Holiday Inn also has a downtown location at 1209 S. Federal Hwy. (© **561/287-6200**). This simple two-story building on a busy main road is kept in very good shape and is convenient to Stuart's downtown historic district. Rates range from $99 to $140.

VERY EXPENSIVE

Hutchinson Island Marriott Beach Resort and Marina ✯✯✯ This sprawling 200-acre compound offers many diversions for active (or not-so-active) vacationers, and families in particular. After a $6 million renovation in 1998, this is definitely Hutchinson Island's best resort, occupying the lush grounds of a former pineapple plantation. Activities include tennis, golfing, boating, sport-fishing (especially for sailfish), scuba diving, and other water sports.

A complete room renovation occurred in 2000, and in 2001 the hotel's beach building was completely redone. Some rooms overlook the Intracoastal and the resort's marina, while others face the ocean or the gardens. All are generously sized and have fully equipped kitchens.

In the summer months, be sure to sign up for a "turtle watch," so you can watch turtles crawl onto the sand to lay their eggs. Another great activity, offered at an extra cost, is a sightseeing cruise along the St. Lucie and Indian Rivers.

555 NE Ocean Blvd., Hutchinson Island, Stuart, FL 34996. © **800/775-5936** or 561/225-3700. Fax 561/225-0003. www.marriott.com/marriott/pbiir. 298 units. Winter $209–$399; off-season $99–$349. AE, MC, V. From downtown Stuart, take E. Ocean Blvd. over 2 bridges to NE Ocean Blvd.; turn right. Pets accepted with a $50 deposit. **Amenities:** Restaurant; coffee shop; lounge; 4 large pools; 18-hole golf course; 13 tennis courts; fitness center and spa; extensive water sports; bike rental; children's programs; game room; concierge; on-property transportation; limited room service; babysitting; laundry and dry-cleaning services. *In room:* A/C, TV, dataport, kitchenette, minibar, coffeemaker, hair dryer.

CAMPING

There are comfortable campsites (rustic cabins or sites for your tent or camper) in **Jonathan Dickinson State Park** in Hobe Sound (see the "Wildlife Exploration: From Gators to Manatees to Turtles" box earlier in this chapter). The River Camp area of the park offers the benefit of the nearby Loxahatchee River, while the Pine Grove site has beautiful shade trees. There are concession areas for daytime snacks and 135 campsites with showers, clean restrooms, water, optional electricity, and an open-fire pit for cooking. Overnight rates in the winter are $18 without electricity, $20 with electricity. In the summer, rates are about $14 for four people.

For a more cushy camping experience, reserve a wood-sided cabin with a furnished kitchen, a bathroom with shower, heat and air-conditioning, and an outdoor grill. Bring your own linens. Cabins rent for $65 and up a night and sleep four people comfortably, six if your group is really into togetherness. Call ℂ **561/ 546-2771** Monday through Friday from 9am to 5pm, well in advance, to reserve a spot. A $50 key deposit is required.

WHERE TO DINE
EXPENSIVE

Eleven Maple Street ✪✪✪ AMERICAN   The most highly rated restaurant in Jensen Beach, Eleven Maple Street occupies a lovely little house. Dining is both indoors and out, in any one of a series of cozy dining rooms or on a covered patio surrounded by gardens. Interesting dishes not typically found in these parts of Florida include the wood grilled venison with French green lentils, broccoli rabe, caramelized turnip, hazlenut and white bean puree with grilled tomato sauce; and the braised Moulard duck leg with wood grilled Oregon quail, Tuscan cabbage, butternut squash, and chestnut tart with a balsamic pear reduction. The restaurant also uses organically grown produce from its own garden (when available) and poultry and meats that are farm raised and free of chemical additives.

11 Maple St., Jensen Beach. ℂ 561/334-7714. Reservations recommended. Main courses $17.50–$30. MC, V. Wed–Sun 6–10pm. Head east on Jensen Beach Blvd. and turn right after the railroad tracks.

Flagler Grill ✪✪ AMERICAN/FLORIDA REGIONAL   In the heart of historic downtown, this seemingly out-of-place Manhattan-style bistro serves up classics with a twist. The dishes are not so unusual as to alienate the conservative pink-shirted golfers who frequent the place, yet they're fresh and light enough to quench the appetites of the more adventurous—for example, Maryland jumbo lump crab meat and rock shrimp cake served with a Key-lime aioli and spicy Cajun aioli. For main courses, the grilled double-stuffed pork chop filled with pecan-apple corn bread stuffing with cranberry-orange chutney, fresh vegetables, and smashed garlic potatoes gives literal meaning to the term "comfort food." You *will* want to seek comfort in an expanding wasteband after that one! The menu changes every few weeks, so see what your server recommends. It's hard to go wrong with any of the many salads, pastas, fishes, or delectable beef choices. The desserts, too, are worth the calories. Ask the bartender to make you the Big Apple martini—apple vodka, apple schnapps, and a wedge of apple—dessert with a kick! No smoking is allowed in the restaurant or bar.

47 SW Flagler Ave. (just before the Roosevelt Bridge), downtown Stuart. ℂ 561/221-9517. Reservations strongly suggested in season. Main courses $18–$28. AE, DC, DISC, MC, V. Winter daily 5–10pm. Off-season Tues–Sat 5:30–9:30pm. Lounge and bar open to 11:30pm. Special sunset menu offered from 5–6pm.

MODERATE

Black Marlin ⚘ FLORIDA REGIONAL   Although it sports the look and feel of a dank English pub, the Black Marlin offers full Floridian flavor. The salmon BLT is typical of the dishes here—grilled salmon on a toasted bun topped with bacon, lettuce, tomato, and coleslaw. Designer pizzas are topped with shrimp, roasted red peppers, and the like; and main dishes, all of which are served with vegetables and potatoes, include a lobster tail with honey-mustard sauce, and a charcoal-grilled chicken breast served on radicchio with caramelized onions.

53 W. Osceola St., downtown Stuart. ℂ 561/286-3126. Reservations not accepted. Salads and sandwiches $4–$8; full meals $9–$24. AE, MC, V. Mon–Thurs 5–10pm; Fri–Sat 5–11pm (the bar is open later).

Conchy Joe's Seafood ⚘⚘ *Finds* SEAFOOD   Known for fresh seafood and Old Florida hospitality, Conchy Joe's enjoys an excellent reputation that's far bigger than the restaurant itself. Dining is either indoors, at red-and-white cloth-covered tables, or on a covered patio overlooking the St. Lucie River. The restaurant features a wide variety of freshly shucked shellfish and daily-catch selections that are baked, broiled, or fried. Beer is the drink of choice here, though other beverages and a full bar are available. Conchy Joe's has been the most active place in Jensen Beach since it opened in 1983. The large bar is especially popular at night and during weekday happy hours.

3945 NE Indian River Dr. (½ mile [.75km] from the Jensen Beach Causeway), Jensen Beach. ℂ 561/334-1130. Reservations not accepted. Main courses $12–$20. AE, DISC, MC, V. Daily 11:30am–2:30pm and 5–10pm.

INEXPENSIVE

Bubba's Fish Camp ⚘⚘ *Finds* SEAFOOD/SOUTHERN   As you would imagine from its name, Bubba's is an ultracasual spot designed to resemble an Old-Florida fish camp. Don't miss the great crawfish gumbo, corn bread, catfish, creamy spinach, hush puppies, or fried green tomatoes. They have a sort of early-bird special, starting at 4pm, where you'll find bargain deals on hearty Southern classics like meatloaf, baked Virginia ham with red-eye gravy, fried chicken, and pork chops. Each includes a choice of delicious side dishes. Locals and highway travelers line up outside the screened porch to get into this rustic eatery. The wait is usually 20 minutes to half an hour, but it's worth it, especially for a very interesting look at the colorful locals and visitors.

421 S. Federal Hwy. (at the south side of Roosevelt Bridge), Stuart. ℂ 561/220-3747. Full meals $8–$10. AE, MC, V. Daily 4–10pm and later on weekends. Call about weekend breakfasts.

Nature's Way Cafe ⚘ HEALTH FOOD   This lovely dining room has dozens of little tables, a few bar stools, and some sidewalk seating, too. A sort of health-food deli, Nature's Way excels in serving quick and nutritious meals such as huge salads, vegetarian sandwiches, and frozen yogurts. Try some of the homemade baked goods. Sit outside on quaint Osceola Street or ask them to pack your lunch for you to take to the beach.

25 SW Osceola St., in the Post Office Arcade, Stuart. ℂ 561/220-7306. Sandwiches and salads $4–$7; juices and shakes $1–$3. No credit cards. Mon–Fri 10am–4pm; Sat 11am–3pm.

STUART & JENSEN BEACH AFTER DARK

The nightlife on the Treasure Coast may as well be called Night*dead,* because there really isn't any! This is not a place to come if you are looking for active nightlife. That said, Stuart and Jensen Beach are the closest you get to nightlife in the entire region, where local restaurants serve as the centers of after-dark happenings. "Night" ends pretty early here, even on the weekends. The bar at the Black Marlin (see "Where to Dine," above) is popular with locals and out-of-towners alike.

No list of Jensen nightlife would be complete without mention of Conchy Joe's Seafood (see "Where to Dine," above), one of the region's most active spots. Inside, locals chug beer and watch a large-screen TV, while outside on the water-front patio, live bands perform a few nights a week for a raucous crowd of dancers. Happy hours, weekdays from 3 to 6pm, draw large crowds with low-priced drinks and snacks. No cover.

In a strip mall just outside of downtown, you'll find pickup trucks as far as the eye can see parked outside the **Rock 'n' Horse,** 1580 S. Federal Hwy. (U.S. 1), Stuart (© **561/286-1281**). It's a real locals' Country-and-Western spot and the only real late-night spot in town. Cover varies.

The centerpiece of Stuart's slowly expanding cultural offerings is the newly restored **Lyric Theater** at 59 SW Flagler Ave. (© **561/286-7827**). This beauti-ful 1920s-era, 600-seat theater hosts a variety of shows, readings, concerts, and films throughout the year.

2 Port St. Lucie & Fort Pierce

Port St. Lucie and Fort Pierce (two Old Florida towns, reminiscent of pre-Neon, pre-condo-maniacal Florida, which are sleepy, different worlds when compared to the Gold Coast and Miami) thrive on sport-fishing. A seemingly endless row of piers juts out along the Intracoastal Waterway and the Fort Pierce Inlet for both river and ocean runs. Here visitors can also dive, snorkel, beachcomb, and sunbathe in an area that has been left untouched by the overdevelopment that has altered its neighbors to the south and north.

Most sightseeing takes place along the main beach road (the strip across from the Ocean/A1A). Driving along Fla. A1A on Hutchinson Island, you'll discover several secluded beach clubs interspersed with 1950s-style homes, a few small inns, grungy raw bars, and a few high-rise condominiums. Much of this island is government owned and kept undeveloped for the public's enjoyment.

ESSENTIALS
The **St. Lucie County Chamber of Commerce,** 2200 Virginia Ave., Fort Pierce, FL 34982 (© **561/595-9999**), is the region's main source of informa-tion. There's another branch at 1626 SE Port St. Lucie Blvd., in Port St. Lucie. Both spots are open Monday through Friday from 9am to 5pm.

BEACHES & NATURE PRESERVES
North Hutchinson Island's beaches are the most pristine in this area. You won't find restaurants, hotels, or shopping; instead, spend your time swimming, surf-ing, fishing, and diving. Most of the beaches along this stretch of the Atlantic Ocean are private, but thankfully, the state has set aside some of the best areas for the public.

Fort Pierce Inlet State Recreation Area (© **561/468-3985**) is a stunning 340-acre park with almost 4,000 feet (1,200m) of sandy shores that were once the training ground for the original Navy frogmen. A short nature trail leads through a canopy of live oaks, cabbage palms, sea grapes, and strangler figs. The western side of the area has swamps of red mangroves that are home to fiddler crabs, osprey, and a multitude of wading birds. Jack Island State Preserve, in the State Recreation Area, is popular with bird-watchers and offers hiking and nature trails. Jutting out into the Indian River, the mangrove-covered peninsula contains several marked trails, varying in distance from a half-mile to over 4 miles (.75–6km). The trails go through mangrove forests and lead to a short observation tower.

The best beach in the recreation area, called Jetty Park, lies in the northern part of the state recreation area. Families enjoy the picnic areas and barbecue grills. There are restrooms and outdoor showers, and lifeguards look after swimmers.

The park is located at 905 Shorewinds Dr., north of Fort Pierce Inlet. To get there from I-95, take exit 66 east (Rte. 68) and turn left onto U.S. 1 north; in about 2 miles (3.25km), you will see signs to Fla. A1A and the North Bridge Causeway. Turn right on A1A and cross over to North Hutchinson Island. Admission is $3.25 per vehicle, and the park is open daily from 8am to sunset.

SPECTATOR SPORTS & OUTDOOR PURSUITS

BASEBALL   The **New York Mets** hold spring training in Port St. Lucie from late February to the end of March at the **Thomas J. White Stadium,** 525 NW Peacock Blvd. (© **561/871-2115**). Tickets for spring training exhibition games and practices cost $10 to $15. From April to August, their farm team, the Port St. Lucie Mets, plays home games in the stadium.

FISHING   The **Fort Pierce City Marina,** 1 Ave. A, Fort Pierce (© **561/464-1245**), has more than a dozen charter captains who keep their motors running for anglers anxious to catch a few. Brochures available at the marina list all the privately owned charter operators, who organize trips on an as-desired basis. The price usually starts at $150 per person for half-day tours, depending on the season.

GOLF   The most notable courses in Port St. Lucie are at the **PGA Golf Club at the Reserve** (© **561/467-1300**), at 1916 Perfect Dr. The club's first of three 18-hole public golf courses opened in January 1996 and was designed by Tom Fazio; another course was designed by Pete Dye. The South Course, a classic Old Florida–style course, is set on wetlands, offers views of native wildlife, and is the most popular. The center also offers lessons for amateurs. The club is open from 7am to 6pm daily. Greens fees are usually under $45; after 2pm, $25. Reserve at least 9 days in advance.

SEEING THE SIGHTS

Harbor Branch Oceanographic Institution ★★   Harbor Branch is a working nonprofit scientific institute that studies oceanic resources and welcomes visitors on regularly scheduled tours. The first stop is the J. Seward Johnson Marine Education Center, which houses institute-built submersibles that are used to conduct marine research at depths of up to 3,000 feet (900m). A video details current research projects, and several large aquariums simulate the environments of the Indian River Lagoon and a saltwater reef. Tourists are then shuttled by minibus to the Aqua-Culture Farming Center, a research facility that contains shallow tanks growing seaweed and other oceanic plants. The 90-minute Lagoon Wildlife Tour, on a pontoon boat, examines the Indian River Lagoon and is a fascinating tour. The bus tour of the 600-acre campus is $10 and leaves Monday through Saturday at 10am, noon, and 2pm. The boat tours are Monday through Saturday at 10am and 1 and 3pm and cost $19 for adults, $12 for children 6 to 12.

5600 U.S. 1 N., Fort Pierce. © **800/333-4264** or 561/465-2400. www.hboi.edu. Admission $10 adults, $6 children 6–12, free for children 5 and under. Mon–Fri 8am–5pm; Visitor Center Gift Shop Mon–Sat 9am–5pm. Arrive at least 20 min. before tour.

Savannahs Recreation Area ★★★ *(Finds)* A 550-acre former reservoir, Savannahs is one of the most interesting places in these parts—it's a veritable wilderness, with botanical gardens, nature trails, campsites, a petting zoo, and scenery reminiscent of the Florida Everglades, but in a much more contained environment.

1400 E. Midway Rd., Fort Pierce. ℂ 561/464-7855. Admission $1 per car. Daily 8am–6pm.

UDT-SEAL Museum (Underwater Demolition Team Museum) Florida is full of unique museums, but none is more curious than the UDT-SEAL Museum, an interesting tribute to the secret forces of the U.S. Navy frogmen and their successors, the SEAL teams. Chronological displays trace the history of these clandestine divers and detail their most important achievements. The best exhibits are those of the intricately detailed equipment used by the navy's most elite members. Expect to spend about an hour here, depending on your level of interest.

3300 N. S.R. A1A, Fort Pierce. ℂ 561/595-5845. Admission $4 adults, $1.50 children 6–12, free for children 5 and under. Mon–Sat 10am–4pm; Sun noon–4pm. Closed Mon in off-season.

WHERE TO STAY

The Port St. Lucie mainland is pretty run-down, but there are a number of inexpensive hotel options on scenic Hutchinson Island that are both charming and well priced. Probably the best option is the **Hampton Inn** (ℂ **800/426-7866** or 561/460-9855), 2831 Reynolds Dr., which is relatively new and beautifully maintained. However, if you want to be closer to the water, try the **Days Inn Hutchinson Island,** 1920 Seaway Dr. (ℂ **800/325-2525** or 561/461-8737), a small motel that sits along the Intracoastal inlet and is simple but very well kept.

Budget travelers will be glad to know about the **Edgewater Motel and Apartments,** 1160 Seaway Dr. (next door to and under the same ownership as the Dockside–Harborlight Inn and Resort), Fort Pierce (ℂ **800/286-1745** or 561/468-3555). Motel rooms start at less than $60 in high season, and efficiencies are also available from $80. Guests can enjoy a private pool, shuffleboard courts, and a nearby fishing pier.

EXPENSIVE

Club Med–Sandpiper ★★ *(Kids)* A former Hilton Hotel, the 400-acre Sandpiper resort was purchased by Club Med in 1985 and marketed to Europeans looking for a Florida getaway. They come in droves (Americans, too) with all the kids and nannies for a sunny, active vacation with lavish meals, from buffets to sit-downs, for a reasonable prepaid price. The drawback is that guests are 20 minutes from the nearest beach. The buildings could use a major overhaul, but there are plenty of diversions on the grounds, such as golf and tennis, and water-skiing, sailing, and boating on the Indian River. There's even a circus school. The rooms are sparse and small, but not uncomfortable. Because most of the activities here are outdoors, you probably won't spend much time inside anyway.

3500 SE Morningside Blvd., Port St. Lucie, FL 34952. ℂ **800/CLUB-MED** or 561/335-4400. Fax 561/398-5101. www.clubmed.com. 338 units. Winter $170–$280 per person, based on double occupancy. Off-season $150–$275 per person, based on double occupancy. Special rates available for children. Rates include 3 meals per day. AE, MC, V. From U.S. 1 S., turn left onto Westmoreland Blvd. Make another left onto Pine Valley Rd.; the resort entrance is straight ahead. **Amenities:** 2 restaurants; bar; 4 pools; 3 golf courses; 19 tennis courts (9 are lighted); fitness center; water-sports equipment; game rooms; coin-op washers and dryers. *In room:* A/C, TV, hair dryer.

MODERATE

Dockside–Harborlight Inn and Resort ⭐ Fronting the Intracoastal Waterway, the Harborlight is a great choice for boating and fishing enthusiasts, offering 15 boat slips and two private fishing piers. The hotel itself carries on the nautical theme with pierlike wooden stairs and rope railings. While not exactly captain's quarters, the rooms, which are simply decorated with pastel colors and small wall prints, are attractive, especially since a thorough renovation was completed in 1999. Higher-priced rooms have either waterfront balconies or small kitchenettes. Rooms are straight out of Rooms to Go, albeit with a bit of a nautical flair, with wood headboards and wicker.

1160 Seaway Dr., South Hutchinson Island, FL 34949. ℂ 800/286-1745 or 561/468-3555. Fax 561/489-9848. 64 units. www.docksideinn.com. Winter $65 standard rooms, $79–$130 efficiencies. Off-season $49–$89 standard rooms and efficiencies. AE, DC, DISC, MC, V. From I-95, exit at 66A east to U.S. 1 north to Seaway Dr. **Amenities:** 2 outdoor heated pools; self-service laundry; 5 lighted fishing docks; boat dockage; grilling areas. *In room:* A/C, TV, dataport, minibar, coffeemaker; higher-priced rooms have kitchenettes.

Mellon Patch Inn ⭐⭐ *Finds* The Mellon Patch offers just four bright rooms in what looks like a single-family house. Each room has a large bathroom and sturdy, soundproof walls, making it very quiet. The public living room is nicer than any of the small guest rooms: It's designed with a two-story vaulted ceiling, a fireplace, and lots of windows that overlook the Indian River. A gourmet breakfast that might include chocolate-chip pancakes or spinach soufflé is served here each morning. The best part is that there are free tennis courts and a public beach across the street. The inn is no-smoking, and children aren't allowed.

3601 N. Fla. A1A, North Hutchinson Island, FL 34949. ℂ 561/461-5231. Fax 561/464-6463. www.mellon patchinn.com. 4 units. $85–$150 double year-round. Rates include breakfast. AE, DISC, MC, V. *In room:* A/C, TV.

Villa Nina Island Inn ⭐⭐ *Finds* A more private option just down the road from the Mellon Patch is Villa Nina, in another simple but new home on 8 acres of the river's edge. Although it's more private, the silence is not nearly as heavy here as it is at the Mellon Patch. In fact, the atmosphere is rather cheery and extremely romantic. Innkeepers Nina and Glenn Rappaport live in the main house and have built riverfront rooms along the back, each with a private entrance and either a fully equipped kitchen or a kitchenette. Riverfront rooms are very homey, with comfortable beds and private baths. Enjoy breakfast poolside or delivered to your room (you may also opt out of breakfast for a $10 nightly savings). Possibly the best deal—and best room—in the Inn is the Grand View Suite, with high ceilings, a massive sitting area, sweeping views of the river and pool, floor-to-ceiling windows, breakfast nook, and marble shower, all for $165 off-season and $195 during high season. Smoking is not permitted anywhere in the inn.

On this stunning 8-acre property, you can use canoes and rowboats for river rides. A nearby shipwreck site makes for an excellent diving excursion. The hotel rents snorkeling and diving gear.

The nearby **Sterling Casino Lines Cruise ship** welcomes inn guests with free shuttle service from Vero Beach (ℂ **800/ROLL-7-11**).

3851 N. S.R. A1A, North Hutchinson Island, FL 34949. ℂ and fax 772/467-8673. www.villanina.com. 5 units. Winter $115–$195; off-season $95–$165. DISC, MC, V. **Amenities:** Outdoor heated pool; canoe and snorkel rental; bike rental; free laundry facilities; private beach access. *In room:* A/C, TV, kitchen or kitchenette, minibar (in most rooms), fridge, coffeemaker.

WHERE TO DINE

There are a number of good seafood restaurants in the Fort Pierce and St. Lucie area, but it's also easy to drive to Stuart for more diverse dining options. See section 1 of this chapter for recommendations in Stuart.

MODERATE

Mangrove Mattie's ★★ SEAFOOD   A rustic restaurant on the Fort Pierce Inlet, Mangrove Mattie's is the best place for outdoor dining, with its priceless location—right on the inlet, affording panoramic views of the Atlantic—and excellent fresh seafood. Weekday happy hours (4–7pm) are especially popular, thanks to the view and the free buffet.

1640 Seaway Dr., Fort Pierce. ℂ 561/466-1044. Reservations accepted. Main courses $11–$18. AE, DISC, MC, V. Daily 11:30am–10pm.

P.V. Martin's ★★ SEAFOOD/AMERICAN   This relatively elegant eatery with an eclectic American menu is as funky as it gets in Fort Pierce. The wood floors, beamed ceilings, tiled tabletops, and rattan chairs would be nice anywhere, but here diners enjoy them as they look out through floor-to-ceiling windows onto sweeping ocean vistas. At night, the room is warmed by a huge central stone fireplace, and on weekends there's live entertainment in the adjacent bar. Surf 'n' turf dinners run the gamut from crab-stuffed shrimp and grouper baked with bananas and almonds to Brie- and asparagus-stuffed chicken breast and barbecued baby-back ribs. An excellent selection of appetizers includes escargots in mushroom caps and a succulent fried softshell crab (available in season). Be sure to try the lively Sunday champagne brunch.

5150 N. S.R. A1A, North Hutchinson Island. ℂ 561/569-0700. Reservations recommended. Main courses $11–$20. AE, MC, V. Mon–Sat 5–10pm; Sun 10:30am–8pm.

Theo Thudpucker's Raw Bar and Seafood Restaurant ★ SEAFOOD   Located in a little building by the beach and wallpapered with maps and newspapers, Thudpucker's is a straightforward chowder bar. There's not much more to the dining room than one long bar and a few simple tables. Chowder and stews, often made with sherry and half-and-half, make excellent starters or light meals. The most recommendable (and filling) dinner dishes are sautéed scallops, deviled crabs, and deep-fried Okeechobee catfish.

2025 Seaway Dr., Fort Pierce. ℂ 561/465-1078. Reservations not accepted. Main courses $12–$29. MC, V. Mon–Thurs 11:30am–9:30pm; Fri–Sat 11:30am–11pm; Sun 1–9:30pm.

PORT ST. LUCIE/FORT PIERCE AFTER DARK

ArtWalk, a monthly event to showcase the downtown galleries, restaurants, and shops of Fort Pierce, takes place the second Wednesday of every month from 5 to 8pm and costs $5 per person, beginning in front of downtown's Sunrise Theater (ℂ 561/466-3880). All galleries are usually open to the public for this event, and they supply free beverages and cheese. The **Friday Fest Street Festival** occurs on the first Friday of every month at the Historic Downtown Riverfront in Fort Pierce and is free of charge, featuring live music and refreshments for sale. The **St. Lucie Blues Club,** 338 Port St. Lucie Blvd. (ℂ 561/873-1111), features live jazz, blues, and rock music Tuesday through Sunday nights. Reservations are recommended.

3 Vero Beach ⨍ & Sebastian ⨍⨍

Old Florida is thriving in these remote and tranquil villages. Vero Beach, known for its exclusive and affluent winter population, and Sebastian, known as one of the last remaining fishing villages, are located at the northern tip of the Treasure Coast region in Indian River County. These two beach towns are populated with folks who knew Miami and Fort Lauderdale in the days before massive high-rises and overcrowding. They appreciate the area's small-town feel, and that's exactly the area's appeal for visitors: a laid-back, relaxed atmosphere, friendly people, and friendlier prices.

A crowd of well-tanned surfers from all over the state descends on the region, especially the Sebastian Inlet, to catch some of the state's biggest waves. Other water-sports enthusiasts enjoy the area's fine diving and windsurfing. Anglers are also in heaven here, and in spring, baseball buffs can catch some action from the L.A. Dodgers as they train in exhibition games.

ESSENTIALS

The **Indian River County Tourist Council,** 1216 21st St., Vero Beach, FL 32961 (⨍ **561/567-3491;** fax 561/778-3181; www.vero-beach.fl.us/chamber), will send visitors an incredibly detailed information packet on the entire county (which includes Vero Beach and Sebastian), with a full-color map of the area, a comprehensive listing of upcoming events, a hotel guide, and more.

BEACHES & OUTDOOR ACTIVITIES

BEACHES   You'll find plenty of free and open beachfront along the coast—most are uncrowded and are open from 7am until 10pm.

South Beach Park, on South Ocean Drive, at the end of Marigold Lane, is a busy, developed, lifeguarded beach with picnic tables, restrooms, and showers. It's known as one of the best swimming beaches in Vero Beach and attracts a young crowd that plays volleyball and Frisbee in a tranquil setting. A nicely laid-out nature walk takes you into beautiful secluded trails.

At the very north tip of the island, **Sebastian Inlet** ⨍ has flat, sandy beaches with lots of facilities, including kayak, paddleboat, and canoe rentals; a well-stocked surf shop; picnic tables; and a snack shop. The winds seem to stir up the surf with no jetty to stop their swells, to the delight of surfers and boarders, who get here early to catch the big waves. Campers enjoy fully equipped sites in a woody area. Admission to the Sebastian Inlet State Recreation Area, 9700 S. Fla. A1A, Melbourne, is $3.25 per car and $1 for those who walk or bike in.

FISHING   Captain Jack Jackson works 7 days a week out of **Vero's Tackle and Sport-Shop,** 57–59 Royal Palm Point (⨍ **561/567-6550**), taking anglers on his 25-foot (7.5m) boat for private river excursions (all equipment is provided). Half-day jaunts on the Indian River cost $250 for two people (the minimum required for a charter), tackle, rigs, and everything included; $50 extra for a third person. You can either bring your own food and drinks or purchase food from the shop.

Many other charters, guides, party boats, and tackle shops operate in this area. Consult your hotel for suggestions, or call the Vero Beach Chamber of Commerce (⨍ **561/567-3491**) for a list of local operators.

GOLF   Hard-core golfers insist that of the dozens of courses in the area, only a handful are worth their plot of grass.

Set on rolling hills with uncluttered views of sand dunes and sky, the **Sandridge Golf Club** (© 561/770-5000), at 5300 73rd St., Vero Beach, offers two par-72 18-holers. The Dunes is a long course with rolling fairways, and the newer Lakes course has lots of water. Both charge $38, including a cart. Weekends cost $32 after noon. A small snack bar sells drinks and sandwiches. Reservations are recommended and are taken 2 days in advance.

Although less challenging, the **Sebastian Municipal Golf Course** (© 561/ 589-6800), at 1010 E. Airport Dr., is a good 18-hole par-72. It's scenic, well maintained, and a relative bargain. Greens fees are $35.31 per player with a cart, and about half that if you want to play 9 holes after 1:30pm.

Also, see "Dodgertown," below.

SURFING See Sebastian Inlet details under "Beaches," above. Also consider the beach north of the Barber Bridge (S.R. 70), where waves are slightly gentler and the scene less competitive, and Wabasso Beach, Fla. A1A and County Road 510, a secluded area near Disney's resort (see below) where lots of teenage locals congregate, especially when the weather gets rough.

TENNIS Many of the tennis courts around Vero Beach and Sebastian are at hotels and resorts, which do not allow nonguests to use their courts. Instead, try **Riverside Racket Complex,** 350 Dahlia Lane, at Royal Palm Boulevard at the east end of Barber Bridge in Vero Beach (© 561/231-4787). This popular park has 10 hard courts (6 lighted) that can be rented for $3.21 per person per hour, and two racquetball courts, also with reasonable rates. Reservations are accepted up to 24 hours in advance. Nature trails are also on the premises.

SEEING THE SIGHTS

Environmental Learning Center ★★ (Kids) The Indian River is not really a river at all, but a large brackish lagoon that's home to a greater variety of species than any other estuary in North America—it has thousands of species of plants, animals, fish, and birds, including 36 species on the endangered list. The privately funded Environmental Learning Center was created to protect the local habitat and educate visitors about the Indian River area's environment. Situated on 51 island acres, the center features a 600-foot (180m) boardwalk through the mangroves and dozens of hands-on exhibits that are geared to both children and adults. There are live touch-tanks, exhibits, and microscopes for viewing the smallest sea life up close. The best thing to do here is join one of the center's interpretive canoe trips, offered by reservation only ($10 for adults, $5 for children).

255 Live Oak Dr. (just off the 510 Causeway), Wabasso Island (a 51-acre island sitting in the middle of the Indian River Lagoon). © 561/589-5050. www.elcweb.org. Free admission. Tues–Fri 10am–4pm; Sat 9am–noon; Sun 1–4pm.

Indian River Citrus Museum The tiny Indian River Citrus Museum exhibits artifacts relating to the history of the citrus industry, from its initial boom in the late 1800s to the present; a small grove displays several varieties. The gift shop sells clever citrus-themed gift items, along with, of course, ready-to-ship fruit.

2140 14th Ave., Vero Beach. © 561/770-2263. Admission $1 donation. Tues–Fri 10am–4pm.

McKee Botanical Garden ★★ This impressive 18-acre attraction was originally opened in 1932 and featured a virtual jungle of orchids, exotic and native trees, monkeys, and birds. After years of neglect, it was placed on the National Register of Historic Places in 1998. It underwent a top-to-bottom overhaul that was completed in February 2000, and you can now again experience the full charms of this little Eden.

350 U.S. 1, Vero Beach. ℂ **561/794-0601.** Fax 561/794-0602. www.mckeegarden.org. Admission $6 adults, $5 seniors, $3.50 children 5–12. Tues–Sat 10am–5pm; Sun noon–5pm.

McLarty Treasure Museum ⭐ If you're unconvinced about why this area is called the Treasure Coast, then this is a must-see. Erected on the actual site of a salvaging camp from a 1715 shipwreck, this quaint little museum is full of interesting history. It may not have the vast treasures of the nearby Mel Fisher museum (see below), but it does offer a very engaging 45-minute video describing the many aspects of treasure hunting. You'll also see household items salvaged from the Spanish fleet and dioramas of life in the 18th century.

13180 N. Fla. A1A, Sebastian Inlet State Recreation Area, Vero Beach. ℂ **561/589-2147.** Admission $1, free for children under 6. Daily 10am–4:30pm.

Mel Fisher's Treasure Museum ⭐⭐ This museum (where you can see millions of dollars of treasures from the doomed Spanish fleet that went down in 1715) is truly priceless. Although not as extensive as the museum in Key West (p. 252), this exhibit includes gold coins, bars, and Spanish artifacts that are worth a look. Also, the preservation lab shows how the goods are extricated, cleaned, and preserved.

1322 U.S. 1, Sebastian. ℂ **561/589-9874.** www.melfisher.com. Admission $5 adults, $4 seniors over 55, $1.50 children 6–12, free for children 5 and under. Mon–Sat 10am–5pm; Sun noon–5pm.

DODGERTOWN

Vero is the winter home of the **Los Angeles Dodgers** (at least for the time being; there's been talk of a move), and the town hosts the team in grand style. The 450-acre compound, Dodgertown, at 3901 26th St. (ℂ **561/569-4900**) encompasses Spring Training Camp, two golf courses, a conference center, a country club, a movie theater, a recreation room, citrus groves, and a residential community. It is a city unto its own for baseball fanatics and retirees. You can watch afternoon exhibition games during the winter (usually between mid-Feb and the end of Mar) in the comfortable 6,500-seat outdoor stadium. Even if the game sells out, you can sprawl on the lawn for just $5. The stadium has never turned away an eager fan. Even when spring training is over, you can still catch a game; the Dodgers' farm team, the Vero Beach Dodgers, has a full season of minor-league baseball in summer.

Admission to the complex is free; tickets to games are $12 for a reserved seat, and the complex is open daily from 9am to 5pm; game time is usually 1pm. From I-95, take the exit for State Route 60 east to 43rd Avenue and turn left; continue to 26th Street and turn right.

SHOPPING

Ocean Boulevard and Cardinal Drive are Vero's two main shopping streets. Both are near the beach and are lined with specialty boutiques, including antiques and home-decorating shops.

If you want to send fruit back home, the local source is **Hale Indian River Groves,** 615 Beachland Blvd. (ℂ **800/562-4502;** www.halegroves.com), a shipper of local citrus and jams since 1947, with four locations in Vero Beach. The grove is closed 2 to 3 months a year, usually from summer through early fall, depending on the crops; the season generally runs from November to Easter.

The **Horizon Outlet Center,** at State Route 60 and I-95, Vero Beach (ℂ **877/GO-OUTLET** or 561/770-6171), contains more than 80 discount stores selling name-brand shoes, kitchenware, books, clothing, and more. The center is open Monday through Saturday from 9am to 8pm and Sunday from 11am to 6pm.

Indian River Mall (© 561/770-6255), 6200 20th St. (S.R. 60, about 5 miles [8km] east of I-95), is a monster mall with all the big national chains (Gap, Structure, and Victoria's Secret) as well as several department stores. It's open Monday through Saturday from 10am to 9pm and Sunday from noon to 6pm.

WHERE TO STAY
You can choose from accommodations on the mainland or on the beach. As you might expect, the beachfront accommodations are a bit more expensive—but, I think, worth it. A great spot to know, especially if you are planning to fish, is **Captain Hiram's** (see "Fishing," above, and also "Vero Beach & Sebastian After Dark," below), where there are four clean and cozy rooms available adjacent to the restaurant and overlooking the water. Rates are between $80 and $110.

Comfortable and inexpensive chain options near the Vero Beach Outlet Center off State Route 60 include a **Holiday Inn Express** (© 800/465-4329 or 561/567-2500), which opened in June 1998, and a slightly older **Hampton Inn** (© 800/426-7866 or 561/770-4299). Rates for both run between $70 and $80 and include breakfast and free local phone calls.

EXPENSIVE
Disney's Vero Beach Resort ★★★ (Kids)   Situated on the tip of 71 acres of pristine beaches, this Disney time-share resort is reminiscent of a turn-of-the-last-century Florida beach community. The resort takes advantage of its setting by offering exciting children's programs, such as canoe adventures, poolside miniature golf, campfire tales, a trip to a working cattle ranch, and stargazing from a powerful telescope. The best part is a large pool designed like a lagoon with a two-story winding slide that elicits squeals of delight from kids and adults alike. The beach is also an attractive option. Rooms are bright and spacious, many with balconies. The resort offers reservation-only Disney character breakfasts on select days and is less than 2 hours away from Walt Disney World.

9250 Island Grove Terrace, Vero Beach, FL 32963. © 800/359-8000 or 561/234-2000. Fax 561/234-2030. http://dvc.disney.go.com/disneyvacationclub/intro. 112 units, 60 cottages. Winter from $290 oceanview double, from $355 and up for villas, from $920 cottages (sleep up to 12). Off-season from $170 oceanview double, from $239 villas. AE, MC, V. From I-95 take exit 69 (512 going east); turn right onto County Rd. 510 heading east. Turn right again onto S. Fla. A1A. **Amenities:** 2 restaurants; bar; large pool; miniature golf; 2 lighted tennis courts; health club; Jacuzzi; sauna; water-sports equipment/rental; extensive children's programs; game room and sports areas; concierge; tour desk; business center; room service; babysitting; laundry service; dry-cleaning. In room: A/C, TV.

MODERATE
Driftwood Resort ★★ (Finds)   Originally planned in the 1930s as a private estate by eccentric entrepreneur Waldo Sexton, the Driftwood was opened to the public in the late '30s after several travelers stopped by to inquire about renting a room here, since it was the largest property in Vero Beach and people assumed it was an attraction or, at least, a hotel. All of the guest rooms were renovated in 2000, and each is unique. Some feature terra-cotta–tiled floors and lighter furniture, while others have a more rustic feel with hardwoods and antiques. Some of the rooms contain Jacuzzis, and all are equipped with full kitchens. Two of the best rooms at the Driftwood are the Captain's Quarters, which overlook the ocean with a private staircase to the pool, and the town house located in the breezeway building, featuring a spiral staircase as well as living room and

bedroom views of the ocean. The resort is listed on the National Register of Historic Places and, to say the least, has lots of quirky charm.

3150 Ocean Dr., Vero Beach, FL 32963. ☎ **561/231-0550.** Fax 561/234-1981. www.thedriftwood.com. 100 units. Winter $110–$180 double; off-season $75–$130 double. AE, DISC, MC, V. **Amenities:** 2 outdoor heated pools; dry-cleaning service. *In room:* A/C, TV, kitchen (in most 1-bedroom and all 2-bedroom units), coffeemaker, Jacuzzi in some rooms.

Islander Inn ⭐   This is one of the most comfortable and welcoming inns in the area. Well located in downtown Vero Beach, this small, quaint Key-West-meets-Old-Florida–style motel is just a short walk to the beach, restaurants, and shops. Every breezy guest room has a small refrigerator, either a king-size bed or two double beds, paddle fans, wicker furniture, and vaulted ceilings, and opens onto a pretty courtyard and sparkling pool. Efficiencies have full kitchens.

3101 Ocean Dr., Vero Beach, FL 32963. ☎ **800/952-5886** or 561/231-4431. 16 units. Winter $105–$120 double; off-season $72–$99 double. Efficiencies cost $10 extra. AE, MC, V. **Amenities:** Cafe; pool. *In room:* A/C, TV.

INEXPENSIVE

Davis House Inn ⭐⭐   Each of the dozen rooms in this contemporary three-story B&B has a private entrance. The rooms are large and clean, although somewhat plain, and each has a king-size bed, a pullout sofa, and a small kitchenette, making the rooms popular with long-term guests. The bathrooms are equally ample and have plenty of counter space. Guests will find a large wooden deck for sunbathing and a sunny second-floor breakfast room. The inn is a bit out of the way but is within walking distance of some nearby restaurants; the beach is a 10-minute drive.

607 Davis St., Sebastian, FL 32958. ☎ **561/589-4114.** Fax 561/589-1722. 12 units. Winter $69–$79 double; off-season $50–$69 double. 7-night min. in Feb. Weekly and monthly rates available. AE, DISC, MC, V. From I-95, take exit 69, heading east to Indian River Dr. and turn left. Go 1¼ miles (2km) to Davis St.; turn left. **Amenities:** Coin-op washers and dryers. *In room:* A/C, TV.

Sea Turtle Inn & Azalea Lane Apartments ⭐   This two-part property offers the best value on the beach (just 2 blocks from the ocean). The 1950s motel and an adjacent apartment building have been fully renovated and outfitted with understated but efficient furnishings. You won't find any fancy amenities (or even a phone, for that matter, unless you request one), but its price and location make up for what it lacks in frills. The properties share a small pool and sun deck. Book early, especially in season, since it fills up quickly with long-term visitors.

835 Azalea Lane, Vero Beach, FL 32963. ☎ **561/234-0788.** Fax 561/234-0717. www.vero-beach.fl.us/seaturtle. 20 units. Winter $79–$109 double; off-season $59–$89 double. Weekly and monthly rates available. MC, V. From I-95, go east on S.R. 60 (about 10 miles [16km]) to Cardinal Dr.; turn right onto Azalea Lane. **Amenities:** Small pool; bike rental; laundry facilities. *In room:* A/C, TV, small fridge, coffeemaker.

CAMPING

The Vero Beach and Sebastian area of the Treasure Coast area is popular with campers, who can choose from nearly a dozen camping locations throughout.

If you aren't camping at the scenic and very popular **Sebastian Inlet** (see "Beaches," earlier in this chapter), then try the **Vero Beach KOA RV Park,** 8850 U.S. 1, Wabasso (☎ **561/589-5665**). This 120-site campground is 2 miles (3.25km) from the ocean and the Intracoastal Waterway and a quarter-mile (.5km) from the Indian River, a big draw for fishing fanatics. There's access to running water and electricity, as well as showers, a shop, and hookups for RVs. Rates range from $20 to $24 per site, and $19 for tents. To get there, take I-95 to exit 69 east; at U.S. 1, turn left.

WHERE TO DINE

EXPENSIVE

Chez Yannick ★★★ FRENCH/CONTINENTAL Excellent cooking, a comprehensive wine list, and white-glove service complement the crystal and gilded decor at this French standout. Excellent starters include a succulent sliced duckling breast, cream of lobster soup, and hearts-of-palm salad with a slightly spicy vinaigrette. Some items, like lobster and shrimp in a cognac-dill sauce, are available as either an appetizer or an entree. Other main courses include beef tenderloin stuffed with Gorgonzola cheese and sautéed soft-shell crabs. Desserts might include profiteroles with ice cream and chocolate or raspberry sauce, crème caramel, chocolate-mousse pie, or raspberry sorbet.

1605 S. Ocean Dr., Vero Beach. © 561/234-4115. Reservations recommended. Main courses $15–$30; fixed-price dinner $19–$21 available in the off-season. AE, MC, V. Mon–Sat open at 6pm; closing time varies based on last reservation.

MODERATE

Black Pearl Brasserie and Grill ★★ CONTINENTAL This sophisticated brasserie may seem out of place in this beachy town, but it happens to be one of Vero Beach's trendiest spots. The restaurant's small list of appetizers includes salads, chilled sweet-potato vichyssoise, crispy fried-chicken fingers with mango dipping sauce, and grilled oysters with tangy barbecue sauce. Equally creative main courses are uniformly good. Don't miss their signature dish, an onion-crusted mahimahi with caramel-citrus glaze. Both this original, unassuming restaurant and its newer counterpart, The **Black Pearl Riverfront**, at 4445 N. Fla. A1A (© **561/234-4426**), serve fantastically fresh and inventive food. The riverfront location is more formal and serves only dinner, starting at 5pm.

2855 Ocean Dr., Vero Beach. © **561/234-7426**. Fax 561/234-9074. Reservations recommended. Main courses $12–$21. AE, DC, DISC, MC, V. Mon–Sun 11:30am–10pm; Sun brunch 10:30am–2pm.

Ocean Grill ★★ *Finds* AMERICAN The Ocean Grill attracts its faithful devotees with its simple but rich cooking and its stunning locale, right on the ocean's edge; ask for a table along the wall of windows that open onto the sea. This huge and handsome old-timer specializes in steaks and seafood. Try stone crab claws when they are in season, or the house shrimp scampi baked in butter and herbs and served with a tangy mustard sauce, or any of the big servings of meats. I especially recommend the Cajun Ribeye—the béarnaise sauce is delightfully jolting on the taste buds. (It'll wake you up from your Vero Beach slumber, that's for sure!) Dinners are uniformly good. The only tacky element of this place is the gift shop.

1050 Sexton Plaza (by the ocean at the end of S.R. 60), Vero Beach. © **561/231-5409**. Reservations accepted only for large parties. Main courses $17–$30. AE, DC, DISC, MC, V. Mon–Fri 11:30am–2:30pm and 5:30–10pm; Sat–Sun 5:30–10pm. Closed Thanksgiving, Superbowl Sunday, and July 4.

INEXPENSIVE

Beachside Restaurant at the Palm Court Resort ★ *Value* AMERICAN/ DINER For a great big, cheap American breakfast with an ocean view, this is the place to go. You can get omelets, home fries, cream chipped beef, corned-beef hash, pancakes, Belgian waffles, and even grits. Friendly waitresses also serve lunch and dinner in the comfy wooden booths. The best dishes, like chili, fried chicken, and steaks, are hearty and delicious. No smoking.

3244 Ocean Dr., Vero Beach. © **561/234-4477**. Breakfast $2–$5; full dinners $8.95 and up. AE, DC, DISC, MC, V. Mon–Sat 6am–9pm; Sun 6am–1:30pm.

Nino's Cafe ✦ ITALIAN   This little beachside cafe looks like a stereotypical pizza joint, complete with fake brick walls, murals of the Italian countryside, and red-and-white checked tablecloths. The atmosphere is pure cheese and so is much of the food—pizza and Parmigiana dishes are smothered in the stuff. Still, the thin crust and fresh toppings make the pizza here a cut above the rest. Entrees and pastas are also tasty.

1006 Easter Lily Lane (off Ocean Dr., next to Humiston Park), Vero Beach. ℂ 561/231-9311. Main courses $9–$12.95. No credit cards. Mon–Thurs 11am–9pm; Fri–Sat 11am–10pm; Sun 4–9pm.

VERO BEACH & SEBASTIAN AFTER DARK

More than half the residents in this area are retirees, so it shouldn't be a surprise that even on weekends, this town retires relatively early. Hotel lounges often have live music and a good bar scene, especially in high season, and sometimes stay open as late as 1am, if you're lucky. For beachside drinks, go to the Driftwood Resort. See "Where to Stay," above.

A mostly 30-something and younger crowd goes to **Bombay Louie's** in Vero Beach, at 398 21st St. (ℂ 561/978-0209), where a deejay spins dance music after 9pm from Wednesday to Saturday. Vero Beach is also known as an artsy enclave, hosting galleries such as **The Art Works,** 2855 Ocean Dr., Vero Beach (ℂ 561/231-4688), and the **Bottalico Gallery,** 3121 Ocean Dr., Vero Beach (ℂ 561/231-0414). **The Civic Arts Center** at Riverside Park is a hub of culture, including the Riverside Theatre (ℂ 561/231-6990), the Agnes Wahlstrom Youth Playhouse (ℂ 561/234-8052), and the Center for the Arts (ℂ 561/231-0707), known for films and an excellent lecture series.

In Sebastian, you'll find live music every weekend (and daily in season) at **Captain Hiram's,** 1606 N. Indian River Dr. (ℂ 561/589-4345), a salty outdoor restaurant and bar on the Intracoastal Waterway that locals and tourists love at all hours of the day and night. The feel is tacky Key West, complete with a sand floor and thatched-roof bar.

North of the inlet, head for the tried-and-true **Sebastian Beach Inn** (SBI to locals), 7035 S. Fla. A1A (ℂ 321/728-4311), for live music on the weekends. Jazz, blues, or sometimes rock-and-roll starts at 9pm on Friday and Saturday. On Sunday, it's old-style reggae after 2pm. The inn is open daily for drinks from 11am until anywhere from midnight to 2am.

4 A Side Trip Inland: Fishing at Lake Okeechobee ✦✦✦

60 miles (97km) SW of West Palm Beach

Many visitors to the Treasure Coast come to fish, and they certainly get their fill of it off the miles of Atlantic shore and on the inland rivers. But if you want to fish freshwater and nothing else, head for "The Lake"—**Lake Okeechobee,** that is. The state's largest, it's chock-full of good eating fish. Only about a 1½-hour drive from the coast, it makes a great day or weekend excursion.

Okeechobee comes from the Seminole Indian word for "big water"—and big it is. The lake covers more than 467,000 acres; that's more than 730 square miles. At one time, the lake supported an enormous commercial fishing industry, but due to a commercial fishing-net ban, much of that industry has died off, leaving the rich bounty of the lake (especially bass) to the sport-fishers.

As you approach the lake area, you'll notice a large levy surrounding its circumference. This was built after two major hurricanes killed hundreds of area residents and cattle. In an effort to control future flooding, the Army Corps of

Engineers, which had already built a cross-state waterway, constructed a series of locks and dams. The region is now safe from the threat of floods, but the ecological results of the flood control have not been as positive. The bird and wildlife population suffered dramatically, as did the southern portion of the Everglades, which relied on the down flow of water from the lake to replenish and clean the entire ecosystem. In early 2001, 30,000 acres of the lake's bottom caught fire due to a severe drought or, some say, arson. Drought had reduced the lake's depth to below 11 feet (3.25m), provoking officials to impose water restrictions. Surprisingly, however, experts say the fire was beneficial for the lake. High water levels had previously prevented fire, which is a part of the natural cycle of the lake, and surrounding torpedo grass threatened to take over the marshes where native fish tend to swim. The fire brought with it the hope that now that the grass has been burned, the fish and the native plants will return to the lake. In early 2002, the water levels had returned to very close to normal.

ESSENTIALS

GETTING THERE   From Palm Beach, take I-95 south to Southern Boulevard (U.S. 98 west) in West Palm Beach, which merges with State Route 80 and State Route 441. Follow signs for State Route 80 west through Belle Glade to South Bay. In South Bay, turn right onto U.S. 27 north, which leads directly to Clewiston.

VISITOR INFORMATION   Contact the **Clewiston Chamber of Commerce,** 544 W. Sugarland Hwy., Clewiston, FL 33440 (© **863/983-7979;** www.clewiston.org), for maps, business directories, and the names of numerous fishing guides throughout the area. In addition, you might contact the **Pahokee Chamber of Commerce,** 115 E. Main St., Pahokee, FL 33476 (© **561/ 924-5579;** fax 561/924-8116; www.pelinet.net/pahokee); they'll send a complete package of magazines, guides, and accommodations listings.

For an excellent map and a brief history of the area, contact the **U.S. Army Corps of Engineers,** Natural Resources Office, 525 Ridgelawn Rd., Clewiston, FL 33440 (© **863/983-8101;** fax 863/983-8579). It is open weekdays from 8am to 4:30pm.

OUTDOOR PURSUITS

FISHING   See the "Going After the Big One" box, below.

SKY DIVING   Besides fishing, the biggest sport in Clewiston is jumping out of planes, due to the area's limited air traffic and vast areas of flat, undeveloped land. **Air Adventures** (© **800/533-6151** or 863/983-6151) operates a year-round program from the Airglades Airport. If you've never jumped before, you can go on a tandem dive, where you'll be attached to a "jumpmaster." For the first 60 seconds, the two of you free-fall, from about 12,500 feet (3,750m). Then, a quick pull of the chute turns your rapid descent into a gentle, balletlike cruise to the ground, with time to see the whole majestic lake from a privileged perspective. Dive packages start at $165; group rates start at $150.

WHERE TO STAY

If you aren't camping (see below), book a room at the **Clewiston Inn** ★★, 108 Royal Palm Ave., Clewiston (© **800/749-4466** or 863/983-8151). Built in 1938, this Southern plantation–inspired hotel is the oldest in the Lake Okeechobee region. Its 52 rooms are simply decorated and nondescript. The lounge area sports a 1945 mural depicting the animals of the region. Double rooms start at $99 a night; suites begin at $129. All have air-conditioning and TVs.

Going After the Big One

Fishing on Lake Okeechobee is a year-round affair, though the fish tend to bite a little better in the winter, perhaps for the benefit of the many snowbirds who flock here (especially in Feb and Mar). RV camps are mobbed almost year round with fish-frenzied anglers who come down for weeks at a time for a decent catch.

You'll need a fishing license to go out with a rod and reel. It's a simple matter to apply. The chamber of commerce and most fishing shops can sign you up on the spot. The cost for non-Florida residents for 7 days is $16.50 or $31.50 for the year.

You can rent, charter, or bring your own boat to Clewiston; just be sure to schedule your trip in advance. You don't want to show up during one of the frequent fishing tournaments only to find you can't get a room, campsite, or fishing boat. All tournaments are held at Roland Martin's marina (see below). For more information on tournaments, log on to their website at www.rolandmartinmarina.com.

There are several marinas where you can rent or charter boats. If it's your first time on the lake, I suggest chartering a boat with a guide who can show you the lake's most fertile spots and help you handle your tackle. **Roland Martin**, 920 E. Del Monte (© **863/983-3151**), is the one-stop spot where you can find a guide, tackle, rods, bait, coolers, picnic supplies, and a choice of boats. Rates for a guided fishing tour are $200 for a half day and $300 for a full day for one to two people. You need a fishing license, which is available there for $17. They also have boat rentals: A 16-foot (5m) johnboat is $40 for half a day and $60 for a full day with a $40 deposit.

Another reputable boat-rental spot is **Angler's Marina**, 910 Okee-chobee Blvd. (© **800/741-3141** or 863/983-BASS). Rentals for a 14-footer (4.25m) start at $40 for a half day, for a maximum of four people. A full day is $60. If you want a guide, rates start at $150 (for two people) for a half day, though in the summer (June–Oct), when it's slow, you can usually get a cheaper deal.

Another choice, especially if you're here to fish, is **Roland Martin,** 920 E. Del Monte (© **800/473-6766** or 863/983-3151), the "Disney of fishing." This RV park (no tent sites) offers modest motel rooms, efficiencies, condominiums, apartments, or campsites, with two heated pools, gift and marina shops, and a restaurant. The modern complex, dotted with prefab buildings painted in white and gray, is clean and well manicured. Rooms rent for $68 and efficiencies cost $88. Condominiums are about $150 a night with a 3-night minimum. RV sites are about $25 with TV and cable hookup.

CAMPING

During the winter, campers own the Clewiston area. Campsites are jammed with regulars, who come year after year for the simple pleasures of the lake and, of course, the warm weather. Every manner of RV, from simple pop-top Volkswagens to Winnebagos to fully decked-out mobile homes, finds its way to the many campsites along the lake. Also see Roland Martin, above.

Okeechobee Landings, U.S. 27 east ((C) **863/983-4144**), is one of the best; it has every conceivable amenity included in the price of a site. More than 250 sites are situated around a small lake, clubhouse, snack bar, pool, Jacuzzi, horseshoe pit, shuffleboard court, and tennis court. Full hookup includes a sewage connection, which is not the case throughout the county. RV spots are sold to regulars, but there are usually some spots available for rental to one-time visitors. Rates start at $24.50 a day or $150 weekly plus tax, including hookup. Year-round rates for trailer rentals, which sleep two people, start at $32 from Sunday to Thursday and from $37 on Friday and Saturday.

WHERE TO DINE

If you aren't frying up your own catch for dinner, you can find a number of good eating spots in town. At the **Clewiston Inn** (see "Where to Stay," above), you can get catfish, beef stroganoff, ham hocks, fried chicken, and liver and onions in a setting as Southern as the food. The dining room is open daily from 6am to 2pm and 5 to 9pm, and entrees cost $9 to $18. **L&L Restaurant,** 265 N. Devils Garden Rd. ((C) **941/983-6666**), is a good Spanish restaurant, with entrees ranging from $8 to $12. **Pinky's On the Green Pub,** Highway 80 ((C) **941/983-8464**), is a no-frills diner, with entrees under $8.

Southwest Florida

by Bill Goodwin

Thanks to a citizenry that has fought to protect both its history and its present-day environment, the southwest corner of Florida is one of the best parts of the state in which to discover remnants of Old Florida and enjoy the great outdoors.

Bordered on the east by the wild, wonderful Everglades and on the west by an intriguing island-studded coast, Southwest Florida traces its nature-loving roots to inventor and amateur botanist Thomas A. Edison, who was so enamored of it that he spent his last 46 winters in Fort Myers. His friend Henry Ford liked it, too, and built his own winter home next door. The world's best tarpon fishing lured President Teddy Roosevelt and his buddies to the 10,000 or so islands dotting this coast. Some of the planet's best shelling helped entice the du Ponts of Delaware to Gasparilla Island, where they founded the Nantucket-like village of Boca Grande. The unspoiled beauty of Sanibel and Captiva Islands so entranced Pulitzer Prize–winning political cartoonist J.N. "Ding" Darling that he campaigned to preserve many of those islands in their natural states. And the millionaires who built Naples enacted tough zoning laws that to this day make their town one of the most alluring in Florida.

Southwest Florida International Airport, on the eastern outskirts of Fort Myers, is this region's major airport (see "Essentials," in section 1, below). From here it's only 20 miles (32km) to Sanibel Island, 35 miles (56km) to Naples, or 46 miles (74km) to Marco Island. If you have a car, you can see the area's sights and participate in most of its activities easily from one base of operations.

EXCURSIONS TO THE EVERGLADES & KEY WEST You won't be in Southwest Florida for long before you see advertisements for excursions to the Everglades. Naples is only 36 miles (58km) from Everglades City, the "back door" to wild and wonderful Everglades National Park, so it's easy to combine a visit to the national park with your stay in Southwest Florida. See chapter 7 for full details about the Everglades.

You also can easily make a day trip to Key West from here by air or sea. **Cape Air** (© **800/352-0714;** www. flycapeair.com) shuttles its small planes several times a day between Key West and both Southwest Florida International Airport and Naples Municipal Airport. The same-day round-trip fare is about $180.

The **Key West Shuttle** (© **888/ 539-2628** or 239/732-7744; www. keywestshuttle.com) runs to Key West from both Fort Myers Beach and Marco Island November through May, departing in the morning, arriving in Key West about midday, and beginning the return voyage about 5pm. That will give you about 5 hours in Key West, so you may want to stay there overnight in order to more thoroughly explore the town. Round-trip fare is about $120 for adults, $80 for children 6 to 12. Contact the shuttle for schedules and reservations.

148 miles (238km) NW of Miami, 142 miles (229km) S of Tampa, 42 miles (68km) N of Naples

It's difficult to picture this pleasant city of broad avenues along the Caloosa-hatchee River as a raucous cow town, but that's exactly what Fort Myers was just a few years before inventor Thomas Alva Edison came here in 1885 to regain his health after years of incessant toil and the death of his wife. Today, the city's prime attractions are the homes Edison and Henry Ford built on the banks of the Caloosahatchee. Edison planted lush tropical gardens around the two homes and royal palms in front of the properties along McGregor Boulevard, once a cow trail leading from town to the docks at Punta Rassa. Now lining McGregor Boulevard for miles, the trees give Fort Myers its nickname: The City of Palms.

Like most visitors to the area, you'll probably opt to stay near the sands at nearby Fort Myers Beach or on Sanibel or Captiva Islands (see sections 2 and 3, later in this chapter), but drive into Fort Myers at least to visit the Edison and Ford homes and have a riverside lunch. You also can venture inland and observe incredible numbers of wildlife in their river and swamp habitats, including those at the Babcock Ranch, largest of the surviving cattle producers and now a major game preserve.

ESSENTIALS

GETTING THERE   This entire region is served by **Southwest Florida International Airport** (© 239/768-1000; www.swfia.com), on Daniels Parkway east of I-75. You can get here on **Air Canada** (© 800/776-3000), **AirTran** (© 800/247-8726), **America West** (© 800/235-9292), **American** (© 800/433-7300), **American Trans Air** (© 800/225-2995), **Continental** (© 800/525-0280), **Delta** (© 800/221-1212), **JetBlue** (© 800/538-2583), **LTU International** (© 800/888-0200), **Midwest Express** (© 800/452-2022), **Northwest/KLM** (© 800/225-2525), **Royal** (© 800/667-7692), **Spirit** (© 800/772-7117), **Sun Country** (© 800/359-5786), **United** (© 800/241-6522), and **US Airways** (© 800/428-4322).

The two baggage-claim areas have information booths (with maps) and free phones to various hotels in the region.

Alamo (© 800/327-9633), **Avis** (© 800/331-1212), **Budget** (© 800/527-0700), **Dollar** (© 800/800-4000), **Enterprise** (© 800/325-8007), **Hertz** (© 800/654-3131), **National** (© 800/CAR-RENT), and **Thrifty** (© 800/367-2277) have rental cars here.

Vans and taxis are available at a booth across the street from the baggage claim. The maximum fares for one to three passengers are $26 to downtown Fort Myers, $38 to Fort Myers Beach, $40 to $47 to Sanibel Island, $60 to Captiva Island, $60 to Naples, and $75 to Marco Island. Each additional passenger pays $8.

Amtrak provides bus connections between Fort Myers and its nearest station, in Tampa (© **800/USA-RAIL;** www.amtrak.com). The Amtrak buses arrive and depart the **Greyhound/Trailways** bus station, 2275 Cleveland Ave. (© **800/231-2222;** www.greyhound.com).

VISITOR INFORMATION   For advance information about Fort Myers, Fort Myers Beach, and Sanibel and Captiva Islands, contact the **Lee Island Coast Visitor and Convention Bureau,** 2180 W. 1st St., Suite 100, Fort Myers, FL 33901 (© **800/237-6444** or 239/338-3500; fax 239/334-1106; www.lee islandcoast.com).

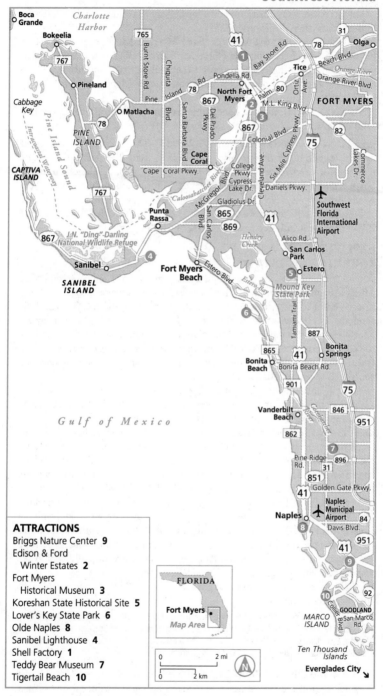

Southwest Florida

Charlotte Harbor

Boca Grande

Bokeelia

765

767

41

1

31

78

Olga

Pineland

Pine Island Rd.

78

Pondella Rd.

Tice

Beach Blvd.

Orange River

Orange River Blvd.

FORT MYERS

Cabbage Key

PINE ISLAND

78

Matlacha

867

North Fort Myers

Palm

80

M.L. King Blvd.

Ortiz Ave.

Chiquita Blvd.

Santa Barbara Blvd.

Del Prado Pkwy.

2

867

3

82

Colonial Blvd.

75

Commerce Lakes Dr.

CAPTIVA ISLAND

Intracoastal Waterway

Pine Island Sound

767

Cape Coral

College Pkwy.

Cypress Lake Dr.

Six Mile Cypress Pkwy.

Cleveland Ave.

Cape Coral Pkwy.

Caloosahatchee River

McGregor Blvd.

Gladiolus Dr.

Daniels Pkwy.

Southwest Florida International Airport

867

J.N. "Ding" Darling National Wildlife Refuge

Punta Rassa

865

869

41

Hendry Creek

Alico Rd.

San Carlos Park

4

Sanibel

San Carlos Blvd.

Fort Myers Beach

Estero Blvd.

5

Estero

SANIBEL ISLAND

Estero Bay

Mound Key State Park

6

Tamiami Trail

887

865

41

Bonita Springs

Bonita Beach

Bonita Beach Rd.

75

901

Gulf of Mexico

Vanderbilt Beach

Cocohatchee River

846

951

862

7

896

Pine Ridge Rd.

31

851

41

Golden Gate Pkwy.

Naples Municipal Airport

Naples

8

Davis Blvd.

84

951

41

9

92

10

GOODLAND

MARCO ISLAND

Collier Blvd.

San Marco Rd.

Ten Thousand Islands

Everglades City

ATTRACTIONS
Briggs Nature Center **9**
Edison & Ford
  Winter Estates **2**
Fort Myers
  Historical Museum **3**
Koreshan State Historical Site **5**
Lover's Key State Park **6**
Olde Naples **8**
Sanibel Lighthouse **4**
Shell Factory **1**
Teddy Bear Museum **7**
Tigertail Beach **10**

FLORIDA

Fort Myers
Map Area

0   2 mi
0   2 km

Volunteers staff information booths in the baggage-claim areas at Southwest Florida International Airport.

Once you're here, the **Greater Fort Myers Chamber of Commerce** (© **800/366-3622** from outside Florida, or 239/332-3624; fax 239/332-7276; www.fortmyers.org) has a walk-in visitor center at the corner of Edwards Drive and Lee Street on the downtown waterfront. Open Monday through Friday from 9am to 4:30pm.

There's also an information booth at the Edison and Ford Winter Estates (see "Exploring the Area," below).

GETTING AROUND   LeeTran (© **239/275-8726;** www.rideleetran.com) operates public buses. System maps are available from the Greater Fort Myers Chamber of Commerce (see "Visitor Information," above). There's no public bus service to Sanibel and Captiva Islands, but you can connect to the Fort Myers Beach trolleys (see "Getting Around," in section 2, below).

For a taxi, call **Yellow Cab** (© **239/332-1055**), **Bluebird Taxi** (© **239/275-8294**), or **Admiralty Taxi** (© **239/275-7000**).

EXPLORING THE AREA
TOURING THE ESTATES

Edison and Ford Winter Estates ★★   Thomas Edison and his second wife, Mina, brought their family to this Victorian retreat—they called it Seminole Lodge—in 1886 and wintered here until the inventor's death in 1931. Mrs. Edison gave the 14-acre estate to the city of Fort Myers in 1947, and today it's Southwest Florida's top historic attraction. It looks exactly as it did during Edison's lifetime. Costumed actors portraying the Edisons, the Fords, and their friends such as Harvey Firestone give "living history" accounts of how the wealthy lived in those days.

An avid amateur botanist, Edison experimented with the exotic foliage he planted in the lush tropical gardens surrounding the mansion (he turned goldenrod into rubber and used bamboo for light-bulb filaments). Some of his light bulbs dating from the 1920s still burn in the laboratory where he and his staff worked on some of his 1,093 inventions. The monstrous banyan tree that shades the laboratory was 4 feet (1m) tall when Harvey S. Firestone presented it to Edison in 1925; today it's the largest banyan in Florida. A museum displays some of Edison's inventions, as well as his unique Model-T Ford, a gift from friend Henry Ford. In 1916 Ford and his wife, Clara, built **Mangoes,** their bungalow-style house, next door, so they could winter with the Edisons. Like Seminole Lodge, Mangoes is furnished as it appeared in the 1920s. The Fords' home is not as interesting as the Edisons', but when you go to the Edison House, you have no choice but to go through the Ford House, too, since the only way to see either one is on a guided tour, which includes both.

Allow an extra hour here to take a scenic ride on the river in a replica of Edison's electric boat *Reliance.*

2350 McGregor Blvd. © **239/334-3614** for a recording, or 239/334-7419. www.edison-ford-estate.com. Admission $12 adults, $6 children 6–12, free for children 5 and under. Boat rides $4 per person. Homes open Mon–Sat 9am–4pm; Sun noon–4pm (1½-hr. tours of both homes depart continuously). Boat rides Mon–Fri 9am–3pm (weather permitting). Closed Thanksgiving, Christmas Eve, Christmas Day.

OTHER DOWNTOWN ATTRACTIONS
A good way to explore downtown Fort Myers during the winter season is on a leisurely, 2-hour guided walking tour hosted by the **Fort Myers Historical**

Museum, 2300 Peck St., at Jackson Street (© **239/332-5955;** www.city ftmyers.com/attractions/historical.htm). The tours are held on Wednesday from 10am to noon and cost $5 a head. Reservations are required.

The historical museum itself is housed in the restored Spanish-style depot served by the Atlantic Coast Line from 1924 to 1971. Inside you'll see exhibits depicting the city's history from the ancient Calusa peoples and the Spanish conquistadors to the first settlers, including the remains of a P-39 Aircobra, which helps explain the town's role in training fighter pilots in World War II. Outside stands a replica of an 1800s "cracker" home and the *Esperanza,* the longest and one of the last of the plush Pullman private cars. Admission is $6 for adults, $5.50 for seniors, $3 for children 3 to 12, free for kids under 3. Open Tuesday through Saturday from 9am to 4pm.

The Georgian Revival **Burroughs Home,** 2505 1st St., at Fowler Street (© **239/332-6125;** www.cityftmyers.com/Attractions/burroughs.htm), was built on the banks of the Caloosahatchee River in 1901 by cattleman John Murphy and later sold to the Burroughs family. You must take a 30-minute tour; they usually are given from mid-October to mid-May, Tuesday through Friday, on the hour from 11am to 3pm and by appointment off-season, but call ahead any time of year. Admission is $6 for adults, $3 for children 3 to 12, free for children under 3.

Rather than have the kids go stir-crazy on a rainy day, head for the **Imaginarium,** 2000 Cranford Ave., at Martin Luther King Jr. Boulevard (© **239/ 337-3332;** www.cityftmyers.com/Attractions/imaginarium.htm), a hands-on museum in the old city water plant. A host of toylike exhibits explains basic scientific principles such as gravity and the weather. Admission is $6 for adults, $5.50 for seniors, and $3 for children 3 to 12. Open Tuesday through Saturday from 10am to 5pm, Sunday noon to 5pm. Closed Thanksgiving and Christmas.

A NEARBY HISTORICAL ATTRACTION

Koreshan State Historic Site Worth a 15-mile (24km) drive south of downtown Fort Myers if you're into canoeing or quirky gurus, these 300 acres on the narrow Estero River were home to the Koreshan Unity Movement (pronounced Ko-*RESH*-en), a sect led by Chicagoan Cyrus Reed Teed. The Koreshans, who believed that humans lived *inside* the earth and—ahead of their time—that women should have equal rights, established a self-sufficient settlement here in 1894. You can visit their garden and several of their buildings, plus view photos from their archives. Canoeists will find marked trails winding down the slow-flowing river to **Mound Key,** an islet made of the shells discarded by the Calusa Indians (see "Canoeing & Kayaking" under "Enjoying the Outdoors," below). There's also a picnic and camping area with 60 wooded sites for tents or RVs. For information, contact the park superintendent at P.O. Box 7, Estero, FL 33928.

U.S. 41 at Corkscrew Rd., Estero (15 miles [24km] south of downtown Fort Myers). ℂ 239/992-0311. www.floridastateparks.org/district4/koreshan. Admission $3.25 per vehicle, $1 pedestrians or bikers; tours $1 adults, 50¢ children. Canoes $3 an hr., $15 per day. Camping, winter $16; off-season $10. Park daily 8am–sunset; settlement buildings daily 8am–5pm; 1-hr. tours Sat–Sun 1pm. From I-75, take Corkscrew Rd. (exit 19), go 2 miles (3.25km) west, and cross U.S. 41 into site.

AN OLD-FASHIONED TRAIN RIDE

Train and murder-mystery aficionados will enjoy a ride on the **Seminole Gulf Railway** (ℂ 800/736-4853 or 239/275-8487; www.semgulf.com), the original railroad that ran between Fort Myers and Naples. Today it chugs on daytime sightseeing trips and evening dinner-murder mystery excursions south to Bonita Springs and north across the river. Call for the schedule and for reservations, which are required for the dinner trips. The trains depart Fort Myers from its Colonial Station, a small coral-colored building on Colonial Boulevard at Metro Parkway. The Bonita Springs station is on Old U.S. 41 at Pennsylvania Avenue.

SHOPPING

A kitschy tourist attraction, **The Shell Factory,** 5 miles (8km) north of the Caloosahatchee River Bridge on U.S. 41 (ℂ 888/4-SHELLS or 239/995-2141; www.shellfactory.com), not only carries one of the world's largest collections of shells, corals, sponges, and fossils, but also has bumper-boat rides, a light show, a gallery of African art, a small zoo, and two restaurants. Inside the store, entire sections are devoted to shell jewelry and shell lamps, and many items here cost under $10, some under $1. Open daily from 10am to 6pm.

Outlet shoppers will find a large Levi's store among other major-brand shops at the **Sanibel Tanger Factory Stores,** on the way to the beaches at the junction of Summerlin Road and McGregor Boulevard (ℂ 888/SHOP-333 or 239/454-1616; www.tangeroutlet.com). Another Levi's store, plus Brooks Brothers, Donna Karan, Dockers, Fila, Nike, Reebok, Maidenform, Nautica, OshKosh B'Gosh, and many more stores are at the much larger **Miromar Outlets,** on Corkscrew Road at I-75 in Estero (ℂ 239/948-3766; www.miromar.com), about halfway between Fort Myers and Naples. Both outlet malls are open Monday through Saturday from 10am to 9pm, Sunday from 11am to 6pm.

"Buggy" Rides Through a Mysterious Swamp

One of the easiest and most informative ways to see Southwest Florida's abundant wildlife is on a "swamp buggy" ride with **Babcock Wilderness Adventures** ★★, 8000 S.R. 31, Punta Gorda, about 11 miles (18km) northeast of Fort Myers (☎ **800/500-5583** or 239/338-6367; www.babcockwilderness.com). Experienced naturalists lead 90-minute tours through the Babcock Ranch, the largest contiguous cattle operation east of the Mississippi River and home to countless birds and wildlife as well as domesticated bison and quarter horses.

Unlike most wildlife tours in the region, this one covers five different ecosystems, from open prairie to cypress swamp. Admission is $17.95 for adults, $9.95 for children 3 to 12. The tours usually leave on the hour between 9am and 3pm November through April, from 9am to noon May through October. Reservations are required, so call ahead. Three-hour off-road bicycle tours cost $35 for adults and $30 for children 10 to 14. Reservations are required at least 3 days in advance.

ENJOYING THE OUTDOORS

CANOEING & KAYAKING   The area's slow-moving rivers and quiet, island-speckled inland waters offer fine canoe and kayak ventures; you'll visit with birds and manatees along the way. Two popular local venues are the winding waterways around Pine Island west of town and the Estero River south of Fort Myers. The Estero River route is an official Florida canoe trail and leads 3½ miles (5.5km) from U.S. 41 to Estero Bay, which is itself a state aquatic preserve (see the introduction to section 2). Near the mouth of the river lies **Mound Key State Archeological Site,** one of the largest Calusa shell middens. Scholars believe that this mostly artificial island dates back some 2,000 years and was the capital of the Calusa chief who ruled all of South Florida when the Spanish arrived. There's no park ranger on the key, but signs explain its history.

Koreshan State Historic Site, half a mile south of the bridge at the intersection of U.S. 41 and Corkscrew Road (☎ 239/992-0311), rents canoes (see "A Nearby Historical Attraction," above). Less than a mile from the site, **Estero River Tackle & Canoe Outfitters,** 20991 S. Tamiami Trail (U.S. 41), Estero, at the Estero River bridge (☎ 239/992-4050; www.all-florida.com/swestero.htm), has guided historic and nature tours (call for schedule and prices) and rents canoes and kayaks at prices ranging from $18 to $30 a day. Open daily from 7am to 6pm.

In addition to its cruises mentioned below, **Tropic Star Cruises,** based at Knight's Landing marina, 16499 Porto Bello in Bokeelia on Pine Island (☎ 239/283-0015; www.tropicstarcruises.com), rents kayaks and has guided tours over 18 miles (29km) of paddling trails. Rentals cost $35 a day for single-seaters, $45 for doubles. Call for schedule and prices of guided tours. The company also has a ferry service to Cayo Costa State Park, where it rents kayaks (see "Nearby Island Hopping," in section 3, below).

CRUISES J. C. Boat Cruises (© 239/334-7474; www.floridatravel.com/ jccruises) presents a variety of year-round cruises on the Caloosahatchee River and its tributaries, including lunch and dinner voyages on the sternwheeler *Captain J. P.* The 3-hour Everglades Jungle Cruise is a good way to observe the area's wildlife, with lots of manatees to be seen from November to April. Once a week a full-day cruise goes all the way up the Caloosahatchee to Lake Okeechobee and back. The ticket office is at the downtown Fort Myers City Yacht Basin, Edwards Drive at Lee Street, opposite the chamber of commerce. Prices range from $14 to $75 for adults. Schedules change and advance reservations are required.

If you're headed out to Cabbage Key, Cayo Costa State Park, or Boca Grande (see "Nearby Island Hopping," in section 3, later in this chapter), **Tropic Star Cruises** (© 239/283-0015; www.tropicstarcruises.com) are a faster way to get there from Fort Myers than driving to Captiva Island and taking a boat from there. Tropic Star's all-day nature cruises on Pine Island Sound depart from Knight's Landing marina, 16499 Porto Bello in Bokeelia on Pine Island, daily at 9:30am. They include a stop at Cayo Costa and Cabbage Key and cost $25 for adults, $15 for kids under 12. The company also runs daily ferries to Cayo Costa State Park ($20 for adults, $15 for children 3–12) and to Boca Grande ($25 adults, $15 for kids 3–12). The ferries take less than 30 minutes to cross the sound. Call for departure times.

Much more luxurious, the sleek, 100-foot-long (30m) yacht *Sanibel Harbour Princess* (© 239/466-2128) goes on sunset dinner cruises from its base at Sanibel Harbour Resort & Spa (see "Where to Stay," below). Evening cruises start at $35 for adults, $27 for children, depending on the season. A 2-hour Sunday-brunch cruise during winter costs $31.50 for adults, $20.15 for children. Call ahead for departure times and reservations.

GOLF & TENNIS For an excellent rundown of Southwest Florida golf courses, pick up a free copy of *Golfer's Guide,* available at the visitor information centers and many hotel lobbies, or on the Internet at www.golfersguide. com. See "The Active Vacation Planner," in chapter 2, for information about subscribing or ordering the current edition. And don't forget that you can call **Tee Times USA** (© 800/374-8633 or 888/465-3356; www.teetimesusa.com) and book starting times at Florida courses.

Although it looks like an exclusive private enclave, the **Fort Myers Country Club,** McGregor Boulevard at Hill Avenue (© 239/936-2457), actually is a municipal course. Designed in 1917 by Donald Ross, it's flat and uninteresting by today's standards, but it's right in town. A steak-and-seafood restaurant now occupies the fine old clubhouse. The city's other municipal course is the more challenging **Eastwood Golf Club,** on Ortiz Avenue between Colonial Boulevard and Dr. Martin Luther King Jr. Boulevard in the eastern suburbs (© 239/ 275-4848). Greens fees at both range from about $30 in summer to $55 during winter. Nonresidents must book tee times at least 24 hours in advance.

Other area courses open to the public include the Tom Fazio–designed **Gateway Golf & Country Club,** on Daniels Parkway east of the airport (© 239/ 561-1010), and the two nationally acclaimed **Pelican's Nest** courses in Bonita Springs (© 239/947-4600).

SPECTATOR SPORTS While many Major League baseball teams have jumped around Florida for their **spring training,** the Boston Red Sox and the Minnesota Twins have worked out in Fort Myers for years. The **Boston Red Sox**

play at the 6,500-seat City of Palms Park, at Edison Avenue and Broadway (© **877/733-7699** or 239/334-4799; www.redsox.mlb.com). The **Minnesota Twins** work out at the 7,500-seat William Hammond Stadium in the Lee County Sports Complex on Six Mile Cypress Parkway between Daniels Parkway and Metro Parkway (© **800/338-9467** or 239/768-4200; www.twins.mlb.com). The Twins' minor-league affiliate, the **Fort Myers Miracle** (© **239/768-4210;** www.miraclebaseball.com), play in the stadium April through August.

The **Texas Rangers** hold their spring training at Charlotte County Stadium (© **941/625-9500;** www.rangers.mlb.com), about an hour's drive north of Ft. Myers. To get there from Ft. Myers, take I-75 north to exit 31 and go south on Kings Highway (Fla. 769); then take an immediate right on Veterans Boulevard (Fla. 776) to the stadium on the left.

The **Florida Everblades** (© **239/948-7825;** www.floridaeverblades.com) play minor-league professional hockey October through March at TECO Arena, at exit 19 off I-75 in Estero.

WHERE TO STAY

As in the rest of Southern Florida, room rates here are highest, and reservations essential, during winter, from mid-December to April. Even the chain hotels and motels along U.S. 41 in Fort Myers—most brands are represented along this busy thoroughfare—charge premium rates then. During the off-season, they drop by as much as 50% or more.

If you can't get a room at the properties mentioned below, the **Lee Island Coast Visitor and Convention Bureau** operates a free reservation service (© **800/733-7935**) covering many more accommodations in Fort Myers, Fort Myers Beach, and Sanibel and Captiva Islands.

A few blocks from the Edison and Ford homes, Jim Haas's **The Li-Inn Sleeps Bed & Breakfast,** 2135 McGregor Blvd., at Clifford Street (© **239/332-2651;** fax 239/332-8922; www.cyberstreet.com/users/li-inn/li-inn.html), has five comfortable rooms, all with private bathroom, in a charming wooden house built a century ago in North Fort Myers. The building was later split in two, floated across the river, and nailed back together. Almost twice the size of the others, "Therese" is the choice unit here. Rates range from $95 to $115 in winter, $65 to $85 off-season, including full breakfast.

The 25-story, 416-unit **Ramada Inn & Suites at Amtel Marina,** 2500 Edwards Dr., at Fowler Street (© **800/833-1620** or 239/337-0300; fax 239/ 337-1530; www.amtelmarinahotel.com), is downtown Fort Myers's only large hotel.

Many business travelers opt for the Art-Deco **Quality Inn Historic District,** 2431 Cleveland Ave. (U.S. 41), at Edison Ave. (© **800/998-0466** or 239/332-3232). Its location, a 2-block walk to the Boston Red Sox training facility and a short drive to the Edison and Ford homes, is a plus for vacationers, too. Minor-league hopefuls stay here during baseball spring training, so you could meet a future major-leaguer.

All hotel bills in Southwest Florida are subject to a 9% tax.

The only campground with tent sites near here is at **Koreshan State Historic Site** (p. 382).

Baymont Inn & Suites *Value* Like most members of this small chain, this modern, four-story establishment offers good value with relatively large rooms equipped with many extras, including easy chairs and large desks. It is centrally situated near the Courtyard by Marriott (see below). Rooms are entered from exterior walkways, so there are no balconies or patios. Your pet can stay with you here for an additional fee. The hotel's one suite has a full kitchen.

2717 Colonial Blvd., Fort Myers, FL 33907. ℂ **800/301-0200** or 239/275-3500. Fax 239/275-5426. www.baymontinns.com. 123 units. Winter $120 double; off-season $80–$95 double. Rates include continental breakfast and local phone calls. AE, DC, DISC, MC, V. Pets accepted ($25 fee). **Amenities:** Outdoor pool. *In room:* A/C, TV, coffeemaker, hair dryer, iron.

Courtyard by Marriott ⭐   This member of the exceptionally comfortable hotel chain designed for business travelers is situated 4 miles (6.5km) south of downtown and 10 miles (16km) north of the beach. The hotel surrounds a landscaped courtyard with swimming pool. The marble lobby features a fireplace and dining area serving breakfast only. The sizable rooms all have patios or balconies, sofas or easy chairs, and rich mahogany writing tables and chests of drawers.

4455 Metro Pkwy. (at the corner of Colonial Blvd.), Fort Myers, FL 33901. ℂ **800/321-2211** or 239/275-8600. Fax 239/275-7087. 149 units. Winter $119–$179 double; off-season $80–$110 double. Weekend rates available. AE, DC, DISC, MC, V. **Amenities:** Heated outdoor pool; exercise room with whirlpool; coin-op washers and dryers. *In room:* A/C, TV, dataport, coffeemaker, hair dryer, iron.

Fairfield Inn By Marriott *Value*   About halfway between downtown and the beaches, this 1999-vintage Marriott property is one of the best budget choices here. Although it's right in the middle of the U.S. 41 action—many chain restaurants and stores are within an easy walk—it sits far enough from the highway to escape the noise. Although sparsely equipped, the rooms are spacious and have writing desks and easy chairs.

7090 Cypress Terrace (off U.S. 41 a block south of Daniels Pkwy.), Fort Myers, FL 33907. ℂ **800/228-2800** or 239/437-5600. Fax 239/437-5616. 104 units. Winter $79–$119 double; off-season $64 double. Rates include continental breakfast and local phone calls. AE, DC, DISC, MC, V. **Amenities:** Heated outdoor pool; whirlpool; exercise room. *In room:* A/C, TV.

Holiday Inn Riverwalk & Marina   This islandlike riverside hotel is a convenient base from which to explore the nearby Edison and Ford Winter Estates and other downtown attractions. The L-shaped building wraps around an attractively landscaped pool area. A riverfront building known as La Marina holds the Seahorse Restaurant (see "Where to Dine," below), which has live music Friday and Saturday nights. The bands stop playing by 11pm, but you should ask for a room at the front of the property, which will be far enough removed from the action to escape most of the noise. Some of these have Jacuzzi tubs and small patios. Other units here lack both patios and balconies.

2220 W. 1st St. (at Euclid Ave.), Fort Myers, FL 33901. ℂ **800/HOLIDAY** or 239/334-3434. Fax 239/334-3844. 145 units. Winter $139–$189 double; off-season $99–$129 double. Weekend rates available. AE, DC, DISC, MC, V. **Amenities:** Restaurant (International); bar; outdoor adult and children's pools; activities desk; salon with massage; limited room service; coin-op washers and dryers; reading room. *In room:* A/C, TV, coffeemaker, fridge, hair dryer, iron.

Sanibel Harbour Resort & Spa ⭐⭐   This secluded, sports-oriented resort overlooks San Carlos Bay and Sanibel Island from Punta Rassa, next to the Sanibel Causeway (a complimentary shuttle takes guests to the island's beaches and to a bike-rental shop three times a day). A waterside cupola-topped pavilion evokes the turn-of-the-20th-century resort that once stood on this point, but the 11-story main hotel (240 rooms) and the boutique-style **Inn at Sanibel Harbour** (107 rooms) nearby are both modern and luxurious throughout. All of the hotel rooms and most of the condominium apartments have wonderful water and island views from their balconies, including spectacular sunsets over Sanibel. A large, attractive pool and sunning complex sit by the water, but don't be disappointed by the quality of the beach here—this is the bay and not the Gulf, after all, so stay over on the islands if a great beach is among your top priorities. But if tennis is your game, the resort has 13 lighted courts and a 5,000-seat stadium that has hosted Davis Cup matches.

17260 Harbour Pointe Rd., Fort Myers, FL 33908. ℂ 800/767-7777 or 239/466-4000. Fax 239/466-2150. www.sanibel-resort.com. 417 units, including 70 condo apts. Winter $299–$399 double; $349–$449 suite; $469–$649 condo apt. Off-season $159–$299 double; $209–$349 suite; $249–$419 condo apt. $10 per unit per day resort benefits fee. Packages available. AE, DC, DISC, MC, V. Free self-parking; valet parking $10. Take the last exit off Summerlin Rd. before the Sanibel Causeway toll plaza. **Amenities:** 5 restaurants (Mediterannean, Floribbean, steaks and seafood, deli, pubfare), 2 bars; 6 heated outdoor pools; 13 tennis courts; health club and spa; water-sports equipment/rentals; concierge; activities desk; business center; 24-hr. room service; laundry and dry-cleaning service. *In room:* A/C, TV, kitchen (condos only), minibar (main building only), fridge, coffeemaker, hair dryer, iron.

WHERE TO DINE

Fort Myers' main commercial strip, Cleveland Avenue (U.S. 41), has most national fast-food and family chain restaurants, especially near College Parkway.

Farmers Market Restaurant ★★ *Finds* SOUTHERN Cabbage, okra, green beans, and tomatoes at the retail Farmers Market next door provide the fodder for some of the best country-style cooking in Florida at this plain and simple restaurant frequented by everyone from business executives to truck drivers. Specialties are beef and pork barbecue from the tin smokehouse out by Edison Avenue, plus other Southern favorites like country-fried steak, fried chicken livers and gizzards, and smoked ham hocks with a bowl of lima beans. Yankees can order fried chicken, roast beef, or pork chops, and they can have hash browns instead of grits with their big breakfast. No alcohol is served, nor is smoking permitted.

2736 Edison Ave. (at Cranford Ave.). ℂ 239/334-1687. Breakfast $3–$7.50; sandwiches $3–$6; meals $7.50. No credit cards. Mon–Sat 6am–8pm; Sun 6am–7pm.

Sasse il Pizzaiuolo ★★ *Finds* CONTINENTAL/ITALIAN In a small shopping strip north of the Edison Mall, Michael and Karen Gavala's informal, often noisy spot offers one of the area's most unusual and reasonably priced dining experiences. Aromas waft from Michael's wood-fired oven in the open kitchen, from which come enormous slabs of pizzalike bread (served with seasoned olive oil for dipping). The selections change daily, although you can usually count on braised lamb shank served over polenta, and veal scaloppini stuffed with prosciutto, roasted peppers, and mozzarella. It's all of a quality rarely found at these prices, and the portions are so huge that most patrons carry home doggie bags. Note that reservations are not accepted (and preference is sometimes given to regulars), so be prepared to wait for a table, especially on weekends. We have gotten complaints about the service here, though we've never had a bad experience.

3651 Evans Ave., in Carrell Corner shopping center (between Carrell Rd. and Winkler Ave.). ℂ 239/278-5544. Reservations not accepted. Main courses $8–$18. No credit cards. Tues–Fri 11:30am–1:15pm; Wed–Sat 5:30–8:15pm.

Seahorse Restaurant ★ INTERNATIONAL In the La Marina part of the Holiday Inn Riverwalk & Marina, this restaurant's sliding-glass walls opening to a riverside deck makes it the most attractive place in town for taking a relaxing, alfresco lunch break while seeing the sights or for watching the sun set over the Caloosahatchee. Best bet at lunch is the reliable fried, blackened, or grilled grouper sandwich. At dinner the cuisine switches to a mix of styles, from grilled fish and steaks to scallops in a Thai spicy green-curry sauce.

At Holiday Inn Riverwalk & Marina, 2220 W. First St. (at Euclid Ave.). ℂ **239/334-2727.** Reservations accepted. Main courses $10–$24; salads and sandwiches $7.50–$10; Sun brunch $15 adults, $6 children under 11. AE, DC, DISC, MC, V. Daily 7am–10pm (bar open later); Sun brunch 10am–2pm.

Oasis Restaurant AMERICAN   A fine place for breakfast before touring the nearby Edison and Ford homes, Bonnie Grunberg and Tammie Shockey's narrow storefront spot also appeals to local professionals who don't mind sitting elbow to elbow while recovering from a night at Shooters Waterfront Cafe USA (just behind this shopping center) with a "hangover" omelet chock-full of bacon, cheese, peppers, tomatoes, and onions.

In Edison-Ford Sq., 2222 McGregor Blvd. (at Euclid Ave.). ℂ **239/334-1566.** Breakfast $3–$6; sandwiches, burgers, and salads $4–$6. No credit cards. Mon–Fri 8am–3pm; Sat–Sun 7am–2pm.

FORT MYERS AFTER DARK

For entertainment ideas and schedules, consult the daily *News-Press* (www.news-press.com), especially Friday's "Gulf Coasting" section. Also be on the lookout for *Happenings,* a tabloid-size entertainment guide distributed free at the visitor information offices and in some hotel lobbies. Tickets for most events are available from **Ticketmaster** (ℂ **239/334-3309**).

The city's showcase performing-arts venue is the **Barbara B. Mann Performing Arts Hall** ⋆, 8099 College Pkwy., at Summerlin Road (ℂ **800/440-7469** or 239/481-4849 for tickets; www.bbmannpah.com), on the campus of Edison Community College. It features world-famous performers and Broadway plays.

Originally a downtown vaudeville playhouse, the 1908-vintage **Arcade Theater,** 2267 1st St., between Bay and Hendry Streets (ℂ **239/332-6688**), presents a variety of performances.

2 Fort Myers Beach ⋆⋆

13 miles (21km) S of Fort Myers, 28 miles (45km) N of Naples, 12 miles (19km) E of Sanibel Island

Often overshadowed by trendy Sanibel and Captiva Islands to the north and ritzy Naples to the south, down-to-earth Fort Myers Beach, which occupies all of skinny Estero Island, offers just as much sun and sand as its affluent neighbors, both a half-hour drive away, but at more moderate prices.

Droves of families and young singles flock to the busy intersection of San Carlos Boulevard and Estero Boulevard, an area so packed with bars, beach-apparel shops, restaurants, and motels that the locals call it "Times Square." That Coney Island image certainly doesn't apply to the rest of Estero Island, where old-fashioned beach cottages, manicured condominiums, and quiet motels beckon couples and families in search of more sedate vacations. In fact, promoters of the southern end of the island say that they're not in Fort Myers Beach; they're on Estero Island. It's their way of distinguishing their part of town from congested Times Square.

Narrow Matanzas Pass leads into broad Estero Bay, which separates the island from the mainland. While the pass is the area's largest commercial fishing port (when they say "fresh off the boat" here, they aren't kidding), the bay is an official state aquatic preserve inhabited by a host of birds as well as manatees, dolphins, and other sea life. Nature cruises go forth onto this lovely protected bay, which is dotted with islands.

A few miles south of Fort Myers Beach, a chain of pristine barrier islands includes unspoiled **Lover's Key,** a state park where a tractor-pulled tram runs through a mangrove forest to one of Florida's best beaches.

ACCOMMODATIONS
Best Western Pink Shell
  Resort **2**
Diamond Head All Suite
  Beach Resort **6**
Edison Beach House
  All Suite Hotel **3**
Holiday Inn Gulfside **10**
Island House Motel **3**
Outrigger Beach Resort **9**
Palm Terrace Apartments **7**
Sandpiper Gulf Resort **8**

DINING
Channel Mark **1**
Francesco's Italian Deli **11**
Gulf Shore Grill **4**
Loggerheads **11**
Pappa Mondo Ristorante
  Italiano **5**
The Fish House **11**

ESSENTIALS

GETTING THERE   See section 1 on Fort Myers, earlier in this chapter, for information about Southwest Florida International Airport, car-rental firms, Amtrak's trains, and Greyhound/Trailways bus service to the area.

VISITOR INFORMATION   You can get advance information from the Lee Island Coast Visitor and Convention Bureau (see "Essentials," in section 1, earlier in this chapter) and from the **Fort Myers Beach Chamber of Commerce,** 17200 San Carlos Blvd., Fort Myers Beach, FL 33931 (© **800/782-9283** or 239/454-7500; fax 239/454-7910; www.fmbchamber.com), which provides free information, sells a detailed street map for $2, and operates a visitor welcome center on the mainland portion of San Carlos Boulevard just south of Summerlin Road. The chamber is open Monday through Friday from 8am to 5pm, Saturday from 10am to 5pm, Sunday from 11am to 5pm.

GETTING AROUND   Estero Island is absolutely inundated with traffic during the peak winter months, but you can get around on the **Beach Trolley,** which operates every 15 minutes daily from 7am to 9:30pm along the full length of Estero Boulevard from Bowditch Regional Park at the north end south to Lover's Key. It operates year-round. During the winter, the **Beach Park & Ride Trolley** runs daily from 6:30am to 9:30pm between Summerlin Square Shopping Center, on the mainland at Summerlin Road and San Carlos Boulevard, to Bowditch Regional Park. Rides on both trolleys cost 25¢ per person. Ask your hotel staff or call **LeeTran** (© **239/275-8726;** www.rideleetran.com) for more information.

For a cab, call **Local Motion Taxi** (© **239/463-4111**).

There are no bike paths per se here, although many folks ride along the paved shoulders of Estero Boulevard. A variety of rental bikes, scooters, and in-line skates are available at **Fun Rentals,** 1901 Estero Blvd. at Ohio Avenue (✆ **239/463-8844**), and **Scooters, Inc.,** 1698 Estero Blvd. at Avenue E (✆ **239/463-1007**). Charges start at $40 a day for one-passenger scooters, $14 a day for bikes.

HITTING THE BEACH

A prime attraction for both beachgoers and nature lovers is the gorgeous **Lover's Key State Park** ★★★, 8700 Estero Blvd. (✆ **239/463-4588;** www.florida stateparks.org/district4/loverskey), on the totally preserved Lover's Key, south of Estero Island. Although the highway runs down the center of the island, access to this unspoiled beach from the parking lot is restricted to footpaths or a tractor-pulled tram through a bird-filled forest of mangroves. The beach itself is known for its multitude of shells. There are bathhouses with outdoor showers, and a snack shop. The park is open daily from 8am to sunset. Admission is $4 per vehicle with two to eight occupants, $2 for vehicles with a single occupant, and $1 for pedestrians and bicyclists. No alcohol is allowed, nor are pets permitted on the beach or in the water (you must keep them on a leash elsewhere in the park). A branch of Tarpon Bay Recreation on Sanibel Island (see section 3, below), **Kayak Shack** (✆ **239/765-1880;** www.loverskey.net) provides kayak and canoe rentals for $20 a half day, $35 for a full day; and bicycles for $5 for a half day, $10 for a full day. Kayak Shack also offers 2- and 3-hour guided paddling tours to Mound Key and the back bays, starting at $25 (reservations are essential).

On Estero Island, **Lynn Hall Memorial Park** features a fishing pier and beach in the middle of Times Square. It has changing rooms, restrooms, and one of the few public parking lots in the area; the meter costs 75¢ per hour, but keep it fed—there's a $32 fine if your time runs out. At the island's north end, **Bowditch Regional Park** has picnic tables, cold-water showers, and changing rooms. It has parking only for drivers with disabilities permits, but it's the turn-around point for the Beach Connection Trolley.

Several beach locations are hotbeds of parasailing, jet skis, sailboats, and other beach activities. **Times Square,** at the intersection of San Carlos Boulevard and Estero Boulevard, and the **Best Western Beach Resort,** about one quarter mile (.5km) north, are popular spots on Estero's busy north end. Other hotbeds are **Diamond Head All Suite Beach Resort** (see "Where to Stay," below), just south of Times Square, and the **Junkanoo Beach Bar** in the middle beach area (see "Fort Myers Beach After Dark," later in this chapter). Down south, activities are centered at the **Holiday Inn** and the **Outrigger Beach Resort** (see "Where to Stay," below).

ENJOYING THE OUTDOORS

BOATING & BOAT RENTALS   Powerboats are available from the **Mid Island Marina** (✆ 239/765-4371), the **Fort Myers Beach Marina** (✆ 239/463-9552), the **Fish Tale Marina** (✆ 239/463-3600), the **Palm Grove Marina** (✆ 239/463-7333), and the **Summer Winds Marina** (✆ 239/454-6333). **Dockside Boat Rentals** (✆ 239/765-4433) rents them at the Best Western Pink Shell Beach Resort on Estero Island's northern end. Boats cost about $125 for half a day, $200 for a full day.

CRUISES   A good way to get out on the water and see some of this area's wildlife is on a nature cruise aboard the *Island Princess* (✆ **239/765-4433**), an open-air pontoon boat based at the Best Western Pink Shell Beach Resort marina on the north end of the island (see "Where to Stay," below). The boat usually goes on 1½-hour nature cruises Monday through Saturday afternoons. Prices are $12.50 for adults, $7 for children. The *Island Princess* also has bay fishing trips departing at 9am on Monday, Wednesday, Friday, and Saturday ($25 adults, $22.50 children) and shelling trips at 9am on Tuesday and Thursday ($25 adults, $12 children). Call ahead for reservations, which are required, and to learn what time the afternoon nature cruises depart.

FISHING   You can surf-cast, throw your line off the pier at Times Square, or venture offshore on a number of charter-fishing boats here. The staff at **Getaway Marina,** 18400 San Carlos Blvd., about half a mile north of the Sky Bridge (© 239/466-3600), is very adept at matching clients with skilled charter-boat skippers. Expect to spend about $600 a day for a full day's fishing for up to 6 persons.

No reservations are required on "party boats" that take groups out. Operating year-round, the *Great Getaway* and *Great Getaway II* (© 239/466-3600) sail from the Getaway Marina, about half a mile north of the bridge. The *Island Lady* (© 239/482-2005) is docked at Fisherman's Wharf, virtually under the San Carlos Island end of the Skyway Bridge. They all depart between 8 and 9:30am; charge between $30 and $50 per person, depending on the length of the voyage; and have air-conditioned lounges with bars. Call for details and reservations.

SCUBA DIVING & SNORKELING   Scuba diving is available at **Seahorse Scuba,** 15600 San Carlos Blvd. (© 239/454-3111; www.seahorsescuba.com). Two-tank dives start at $59. In business since 1989, the company also teaches diver-certification courses.

The live-aboard dive boat *Ultimate Getaway,* based at Getaway Marina, 18400 San Carlos Blvd. (© 239/466-3600; fax 239/644-7529; www. ultimategetaway.net), makes 4-day voyages to the Dry Tortugas (70 miles [113km] west of Key West). This 100-foot (30m) vessel carries a maximum of 20 divers and is equipped with a dive platform, chase boat, and TV/VCR. Trips cost about $500 per person, including meals, beer, air, and weights, but bring your own regulator, mask, and fins. Reservations are essential.

WHERE TO STAY

The hostelries recommended below are removed from the crowds of Times Square, but three chain motels offer comfortable accommodations right in the center of the action: **Ramada Inn** (© 800/544-4592 or 239/463-6158), **Days Inn** (© 800/544-4592 or 239/463-9759), and **Howard Johnson Inn** (© 800/544-4592 or 239/463-9231). The mid-rise **Best Western Beach Resort** (© 800/336-4045 or 239/463-6000) is one-fourth mile (.5km) north, just far enough to escape the noise but still have a lively beach.

Sunstream Resorts, 6640 Estero Blvd., Fort Myers Beach, FL 33931 (© 800/625-4111; fax 239/463-3060; www.sunstream.com), manages three "condominium hotels" here, including the plush **Casa Playa,** 510 Estero Blvd. (© 800/569-4876 or 239/765-0510; www.casaplayaresort.com), and the **Lover's Key Beach Club & Resort,** 8771 Estero Blvd. (© 877/798-4879 or 239/765-1040; www.loverskey.com), both of which opened in 2000. The latter and **The Grand View Resort,** 8701 Estero Blvd. (© 239/765-4422), are on the north end of Lover's Key. The 60 spacious apartments in the older, 16-story **Pointe Estero Island Resort,** 6640 Estero Blvd. (© 239/765-1155), all have whirlpool bathtubs and screened balconies with gorgeous gulf or bay views. The less expensive **Santa Maria,** 7317 Estero Blvd. (© **239/765-6700**), is on the bay side of the island.

For information about rate seasons, see "Where to Stay," in section 1 of this chapter.

For campers, the somewhat-cramped **Red Coconut RV Resort,** 3001 Estero Blvd. (© **239/463-7200;** fax 239/463-2609; www.redcoconut.com), has sites for RVs and tents both on the gulf side of the road and right on the beach. They start at $40 a night during winter, $25 off-season.

EXPENSIVE

Best Western Pink Shell Beach Resort ★★ Not to be confused with the nearby Best Western Beach Resort, this popular, family-oriented establishment fronts both the gulf and the Matanzas Pass from its perch on Estero's quiet northern end. It has efficiencies, suites, and one- and two-bedroom fully equipped apartments in three mid-rise, gulf-front buildings with lovely views of Sanibel Island from screened balconies. The standard efficiencies are the least-expensive units here. Sailboats and nature and sightseeing cruises pick up guests at the bay-side marina, which rents boats and bikes. The scenic Hungry Pelican Cafe, on a covered deck overlooking the channel, is a great spot for breakfast or lunch.

275 Estero Blvd., Fort Myers Beach, FL 33931. © **800/554-5454** or 239/463-6181. Fax 239/481-4947. www.pinkshell.com. 208 units. Winter $175–$449 condo or cottage; off-season $135–$309 condo or cottage. Packages and weekly rates available. AE, DC, DISC, MC, V. **Amenities:** Restaurant (American); bar; 4 heated outdoor pools; lighted tennis courts; water-sports equipment rental; bike rental; babysitting; laundry service; coin-op washers and dryers. *In room:* A/C, TV, kitchen, coffeemaker, hair dryer, iron.

Diamond Head All Suite Beach Resort ★ Opened in 1999, this luxurious, 12-story, beachside building sports large, comfortable one-bedroom apartments. Sliding-glass doors lead from both the living quarters and the bedroom to screened balconies. The beachfront apartments are the choice, but every unit has a view (spectacular from the upper floors). There's a full-service restaurant indoors, and Cabana's Beach Bar provides libation and light lunches beside the pool. An urbane lounge bar has live music after dark during the winter season.

2000 Estero Blvd. (at Palm Ave.), Fort Myers Beach, FL 33931. © **888/765-5002** or 239/765-7654. Fax 239/765-1694. www.diamondheadfl.com. 124 units. Winter $209–$295 double; off-season $158–$179 double. AE, DISC, MC, V. **Amenities:** 2 restaurants (American); 2 bars; heated outdoor pool; exercise room; Jacuzzi; water-sports equipment rental; children's program; game room; limited room service; laundry service; coin-op washers and dryers. *In room:* A/C, TV, kitchen, coffeemaker, hair dryer, iron.

Edison Beach House All Suite Hotel ★★ No standardized list of amenities does justice to this intimate, five-story beachside inn, for when owner Larry Yax built it in 1999, he equipped every unit as if he were going to live in it. The light and airy units all have a balcony, a ceiling fan, a fully equipped kitchen (look for your complimentary bag of popcorn in the microwave oven), a writing desk stocked with office supplies, and a linen closet packed with extra towels. Most of the bathrooms have a combo washer-dryer. The freshly laundered bedspreads provided each new guest are but one example of the premium Larry puts on cleanliness. The beachfront units have the best view, but much more romantic are the "A" suites, whose queen-size beds are almost surrounded by windows formed by a turret on one corner of the building—as in, you fall asleep and wake up to a panoramic view spanning from gulf to bay.

830 Estero Blvd., Fort Myers Beach, FL 33931. ✆ **800/399-2511** or 239/463-1530. Fax 239/765-9430. www.edisonbeachhouse.com. 24 units. Winter $225–$295 double; off-season $95–$175 double. AE, DC, DISC, MC, V. **Amenities:** Heated outdoor pool; laundry service. *In room:* A/C, TV, dataport, kitchen, coffeemaker, hair dryer, iron.

MODERATE

Holiday Inn Gulfside   Built by the shifting sands, the slowly emerging Little Estero Island (actually a peninsula) has left the surf a considerable distance from this conventional two-story motel, the center of beach activity on Estero's south end. Guests need not walk far, however, to a courtyard swimming pool, tiki bar, and a grill serving lunches and snacks. Beachfront suites are the choice accommodation here. Otherwise, you're better off paying a little more for a room facing the central courtyard rather than one looking out on the parking lots. They're all entered from common walkways running the length of the building, but you will get two plastic patio chairs to call your own out there. The shops and restaurants of Santini Marina Plaza are a short walk away.

6890 Estero Blvd., Fort Myers Beach, FL 33931. ✆ **800/465-4329** or 239/463-5711. Fax 239/463-7038. www.holidayinnfmb.com. 103 units. Winter $155–$265 double; $315–$460 suite. Off-season $105–$155 double; $280 suite. AE, DC, DISC, MC, V. **Amenities:** 2 restaurants (American); 2 bars; outdoor pool; 2 lighted tennis courts; water-sports equipment rental; game room; business center; shopping arcade; salon; limited room service; coin-op washers and dryers. *In room:* A/C, TV, dataport, kitchen (suites only), fridge (some rooms), coffeemaker, hair dryer, iron, safe.

Outrigger Beach Resort   Well known for its beachside tiki bar, this clean, pleasant motel has been owned and operated by the same family since 1965. Their "garden efficiencies" in the original building have the feel of small cottages, with excellent ventilation through both front and rear windows and doors opening to backyard decks. Other buildings here are two-story blocks containing motel-style rooms and efficiencies, which have views of the large parking lot. The **beachside bar** is one of the best places in Fort Myers Beach to watch the sun set.

6200 Estero Blvd., Fort Myers Beach, FL 33931. ✆ **800/749-3131** or 239/463-3131. Fax 239/463-6577. www.outriggerfmb.com. 144 units. Winter $115–$215 double; off-season $85–$185 double. AE, MC, V. **Amenities:** Restaurant (American); bar; heated outdoor pool; small exercise room; Jacuzzi; water-sports equipment rental; game room; coin-op washers and dryers; concierge-level rooms. *In room:* A/C, TV, kitchen, coffeemaker, hair dryer.

Sandpiper Gulf Resort   The units at this quiet, family-oriented gulf-side motel all have living and sleeping areas, full kitchens, convertible sofas, and overlook either the gulf or a courtyard. Steps lead from the pool directly to the beach. Some suites are in two- or three-story buildings arranged in a U, with the flattened ends right on the beach; others are in the Sandpiper II, a palm-fronted mid-rise with its own heated pool next door. All suites are identical, but those facing directly onto the beach are more expensive. Restaurants are nearby.

5550 Estero Blvd., Fort Myers Beach, FL 33931. ✆ **800/584-1449** or 239/463-5721. Fax 239/765-0039. www.sandpipergulfresort.com. 63 units. Winter $152–$206 double; off-season $85–$115 double. DISC, MC, V. **Amenities:** Heated outdoor pool; Jacuzzi; water-sports equipment rental; bike rental; coin-op washers and dryers. *In room:* A/C, TV, dataport, kitchen, coffeemaker, hair dryer, iron.

INEXPENSIVE

Island House Motel ⭐ *Value*   Sitting on stilts in the Old Florida fashion, but with modern furnishings, Ken and Sylvia Lachapelle's clapboard-sided Island House Motel enjoys a quiet location along a bay-side channel, directly across the boulevard from the Best Western Beach Resort and within walking distance of busy Times Square. Four of their units have screened porches; all have kitchens and ceiling fans. Ken and Sylvia maintain an open-air lounge with a small library beneath one of the units. They also provide free beach chairs and bikes. Book as early as possible for February and March. The Lachapelles also operate the three-story **Edgewater Inn,** less than a block away at 781 Estero Blvd. (same phone, fax, and website). The two one-bedroom and four two-bedroom apartments there all have screened lanais. They are available on a weekly basis during winter, for 3-day minimum stays off-season.

701 Estero Blvd., Fort Myers Beach, FL 33931. © 800/951-9975 or 239/463-9282. Fax 239/463-2080. www.edgewaterfmb.com. 5 units. Winter $119–$139 double; off-season $59–$79 double. Rates include local phone calls. Weekly rates available. MC, V. **Amenities:** Heated outdoor pool; access to nearby health club; coin-op washers and dryers. *In room:* A/C, TV, kitchen, coffeemaker, hair dryer, iron.

Palm Terrace Apartments ★ *(Value)*   Many European guests stay in these comfortable, well-maintained apartments about midway down the beach. In fact, between them, husband-and-wife owners Deborah Bowers and Peter Piazza speak fluent German and French and passable Italian. Their smaller, less-expensive units are on the ground level, with sliding-glass doors opening to a grassy yard, but even these units have cooking facilities including microwave ovens. Most units are upstairs, with screened porches or decks overlooking a courtyard with a heated swimming pool, a shuffleboard court, and a charcoal grill for barbecuing. Public access to the beach is across Estero Boulevard. There's no daily maid service, but you'll have an ample supply of clean linens.

3333 Estero Blvd., Fort Myers Beach, FL 33931. © 800/320-5783 or 239/765-5783. Fax 239/765-5783. www.palm-terrace.com. 9 units. Winter $89–$132 double; off-season $49–$81 double. 3-day min. stay required in winter. Weekly rates available. AE, DISC, MC, V. **Amenities:** Heated outdoor pool; access to nearby health club; coin-op washers and dryers. *In room:* A/C, TV/VCR, dataport, kitchen, coffeemaker.

WHERE TO DINE

The busy area around Times Square has fast-food joints to augment several local restaurants catering to the beach crowds. The pick is the moderately priced **Beach Pierside Grill,** directly on the beach at the foot of Lynn Hall Memorial Pier (© **239/765-7800**), a lively pub with bright-blond wood trim and vivid fabric colors reminiscent of establishments in Miami's South Beach. It all opens onto a large beachside patio with dining at umbrella tables, outstanding sunsets, and live bands playing at night. The reasonably priced fare is a catch-all of conch fritters, shrimp and fish baskets, burgers, and seafood main courses. They take reservations—a plus in this busy area. Food is served daily from 11am to 11pm.

MODERATE

Channel Mark ★★ SEAFOOD   Maryland-style crab cakes, delicately seasoned with Old Bay spice in true Maryland fashion, are enough to make this the beach's best place for seafood. Nestled by the "Little Bridge" leading onto San Carlos Island's northern end, every table here looks out on a maze of channel markers on Hurricane Bay. A dock with palms growing through it makes this a tranquil place for a waterside lunch. At night, a relaxed tropical ambience is ideal for kindling romance. The adjacent lounge offers the same menu and has live entertainment on weekends.

19001 San Carlos Blvd. (at the north end of San Carlos Island). © 239/463-9127. Reservations recommended on major holidays; not accepted other times. Main courses $10–$21. AE, DISC, MC, V. Sun–Thurs 11am–10pm; Fri–Sat 11am–11pm.

Gulf Shore Grill SEAFOOD/AMERICAN   On the southern fringes of Times Square, this old clapboard building offers splendid views of the gulf and the beach. It began life in the 1920s as the Crescent Beach Casino and has seen various incarnations as a bathhouse, gambling casino, dance hall, and rooming house. These days, an extensive salad bar accompanies traditional Florida-style main courses such as baked grouper imperial, grilled mahimahi, and shrimp wrapped in bacon and coated with honey. This is one of the best breakfast spots on the beach, with choices ranging from biscuits under sausage gravy to eggs served on a muffin under Alaskan crab meat and a charon sauce. The kitchen also provides the pub fare for **The Cottage Bar,** an open-air drinking establishment next door (it's open daily 11am–2am).

1270 Estero Blvd. (on the beach at Ave. A). ℂ **239/463-9951.** Reservations recommended for dinner. Main courses $13–$25; breakfast $4–$11; sandwiches and burgers $6–$13. AE, DISC, MC, V. Daily 8am–3pm and 5–10pm.

Loggerheads SEAFOOD/AMERICAN   The motto "The Local's Nest" accurately describes this friendly storefront restaurant, the best bet on the island's south end. Charter-boat captains and other locals congregate around a big square bar on one side of the knotty-pine–accented dining room. The menu offers a wide range of appetizers, big salads, sandwiches, burgers, and main course options from both land and sea. Grouper prepared in a number of satisfying if not spectacular ways leads the main courses, but you can order traditionally fried, grilled, broiled, or blackened seafood plus pastas, steaks, ribs, and jerk chicken.

In Santini Marina Plaza, 7205 Estero Blvd. (at Lennel Rd.). ℂ **239/463-4644.** Reservations recommended on weekends. Sandwiches and burgers $7–$8; main courses $12–$18. AE, DISC, MC, V. Sun–Thurs 11am–11pm; Fri–Sat 11am–midnight.

Pappa Mondo Ristorante Italiano ★★ (Value) NORTHERN ITALIAN Pasquale Riso (he's the chef) and Andrea Mazzonetto hail from Italy, and the fare they present in their attractive dining room—or out on their roadside patio—is authentic old-country cooking. They make everything from scratch— you can watch them producing pasta at a big machine behind a large picture window. Especially tasty is the ravioli, either ricotta-and-cheese topped with butter and sage sauce, or stuffed with veal and served with a light cream sauce tinged with balsamic vinegar.

1821 Estero Blvd. (at Ohio Ave.). ℂ **239/765-9660.** Reservations recommended. Main courses $11–$16. AE, MC, V. Daily 3:30–10pm. Closed Christmas.

INEXPENSIVE

The Fish House SEAFOOD   You'll find the beach's least-expensive outdoor dining at the dockside tables of this no-frills friendly pub. You'll also see charter-boat skippers slaking their thirst at a large wooden bar occupying about half the open-air but screened dining room. Go for the fried or grilled grouper and other fish the captains have just landed. Sandwiches are available all day, including a tasty grouper version.

7225 Estero Blvd. (at Fish Tale Marina, behind Santini Marina Plaza). ℂ **239/765-6766.** Sandwiches $6.50–$9; main courses $7–$20. AE, DISC, MC, V. Winter daily 11am–11pm. Off-season daily 11am–10pm. Closed Thanksgiving, Christmas.

Francesco's Italian Deli & Pizzeria ★ ITALIAN   Wonderful aromas of baking pizzas, cannoli, breads, cookies, and fabulous calzones waft from this

New York–style Italian deli. Order at the counter over a chiller packed with fresh deli meats, Italian sausage, and cheeses; then devour your goodies at tables inside or out on the covered walkway, or take them to the beach for a picnic. You can also take "heat-and-eat" meals of spaghetti, lasagna, eggplant parmigiana, manicotti, and ravioli to your hotel or condominium oven. Shelves are loaded with Italian wines, pastas, butter cookies, and anisette toast.

In Santini Marina Plaza, 7205 Estero Blvd. (at Lennel Rd.). © **239/463-5634.** Subs and sandwiches $5.50–$8; pizzas $12–$14; ready-to-cook meals $9–$11. No credit cards. Mon–Sat 8am–7pm.

FORT MYERS BEACH AFTER DARK

To find out what's going on while you're here, pick up copies of the daily *News-Press* (www.news-press.com) and of the *Beach Bulletin* and the *Fort Myers Beach Observer,* two local tabloid newspapers. They're available at the chamber of commerce (see "Essentials," earlier in this chapter).

The area around Times Square is always active, every day during winter and on weekends off-season. In the very heart of Times Square, at the foot of Lynn Hall Memorial Pier, the **Beach Pierside Grill,** 1000 Estero Blvd. (© **239/765-7800**), has live entertainment on its beachside patio. Facing due west, **Jimmy's Beach Bar,** in the Days Inn at 1130 Estero Blvd. (© **239/463-9759**), has live music nightly for the "best sunsets on the island" (actually, you can say that of all the beachside establishments here). It's not directly on the beach, but locals in the know head for the rooftop bar at **The Beached Whale,** 1249 Estero Blvd. (© **239/463-5505**), which supplies free chicken wings during their nightly happy hour. Rock and reggae music is played downstairs for nighttime dancing.

Away from the crowds in the "middle beach" area, the **Junkanoo Beach Bar,** under Anthony's on the Gulf, 3040 Estero Blvd. (© **239/463-2600**), attracts a more affluent crowd for its bohemian-style parties that run from 11:30am to 1:30am daily. Live bands here specialize in reggae and other island music. The menu offers inexpensive subs, sandwiches, burgers, and pizzas, and a concessionaire rents beach cabanas and water-sports toys, making it a good place for a lively day at the beach.

On Sunday afternoons, revelers jam the docks for the famous outdoor reggae parties at **The Bridge Waterfront Restaurant,** 708 Fisherman's Wharf (© **239/765-0050**), which is under the Sky Bridge on San Carlos Island.

3 Sanibel & Captiva Islands ★★★

14 miles (23km) W of Fort Myers, 40 miles (64km) N of Naples

Sanibel and Captiva are unique in Florida. Here you will find none of the neon signs, amusement parks, and high-rise condominiums that clutter most beach resorts in the state. Indeed, Sanibel's main drag, Periwinkle Way, runs under a canopy of whispery pines and gnarled oaks so thick they almost obscure the small signs for chic shops and restaurants. This wooded ambience is the work of local voters, who have saved their trees and tropical foliage, limited the size and appearance of signs, and permitted no building higher than the tallest palm and no WaveRunner or other noisy beach toy within 300 yards of their gorgeous, shell-strewn beaches. I had been to Sanibel many times before I saw an aerial photo of the island and realized that its southern shore is lined with hotels and condominiums. The foliage disguises the buildings that well.

Furthermore, more than half of the two islands is preserved in its natural state as wildlife refuges. Here you can ride, walk, bike, canoe, or kayak through the J.N. ("Ding") Darling National Wildlife Refuge, one of Florida's best.

ACCOMMODATIONS ■
Beachview Cottages **34**
Best Western Sanibel
  Island Beach Resort **33**
Buttonwood Cottages **22**
Captiva Island Inn
  Bed & Breakfast **5**
Casa Ybel Resort **31**
Gulf Breeze Cottages **29**
Island Inn **32**
Jensen's On the Gulf **5**
Palm View Motel **28**
Sanibel Inn **27**
Sanibel's Seaside Inn **25**
Song of the Sea **26**
South Seas Resort **1**
Sundial Beach Resort **32**
Tarpon Tale Inn **24**
'Tween Waters Inn **6**

ATTRACTIONS ●
Bailey-Matthews
  Shell Museum **10**
J.N. (Ding) Darling
  National Wildlife
  Refuge **8**
Sanibel Historical Village
  & Museum **14**
Sanibel Lighthouse **23**
Sanibel/Captiva
  Conservation
  Foundation **9**
Tarpon Bay Recreation **11**

DINING ◆
The Bubble Room **2**
Captiva Sunshine Cafe **2**
Grandma Dot's
  Seaside Saloon **20**
The Green Flash **4**
Hungry Heron **13**
Jacaranda **18**
Jerry's Family
  Restaurant **16**
The Lazy Flamingo II **19**
Lighthouse Cafe **21**
Mad Hatter **7**
McT's Shrimp House
  & Tavern **17**
Morgan's Forest **30**
Mucky Duck **3**
R.C. Otter's Island Eats **2**
Sanibel Cafe **12**
The Timbers Restaurant
  & Fish Market **12**

Legend says that Ponce de León named the larger of these two barrier islands "San Ybel," after Queen Isabella of Spain. Another legend claims that Captiva's name comes from the captured women kept here by the infamous pirate Jose Gaspar. The modern era dates from 1892, when a few farmers settled on the islands. One of them, Clarence Chadwick, started an unsuccessful Key lime and copra plantation on Captiva; many of his towering coconut palms still stand, adding to that skinny island's tropical luster.

ESSENTIALS

GETTING THERE   See "Getting There," in section 1 of this chapter, for information about air, train, bus, and rental-car services. The Amoco station at 1015 Periwinkle Way, at Causeway Road, is the Sanibel agent for **Enterprise Rent-a-Car** (✆ **800/325-8007** or 239/395-3880).

VISITOR INFORMATION   The Sanibel–Captiva Islands Chamber of Commerce, 1159 Causeway Rd., Sanibel Island, FL 33957 (✆ **239/472-1080;** fax 239/472-1070; www.sanibel-captiva.org), maintains a visitor center on Causeway Road as you drive onto Sanibel from Fort Myers. The chamber gives away an island guide and sells a detailed street map for $3. Other books are for sale, including comprehensive shelling guides and a helpful collection of menus from the islands' restaurants. There are phones for making hotel and condominium reservations (check the brochure racks for discounts during summer and Dec). Open Monday through Saturday from 9am to 7pm, Sunday from 10am to 5pm.

GETTING AROUND Neither Sanibel nor Captiva has public transportation. **No parking** is permitted on any street or road on Sanibel. Free beach parking is available on the Sanibel Causeway. Other municipal lots either are reserved for local residents or have a 75¢ hourly fee. Accordingly, many residents and visitors get around by bicycle (see "More Ways to Enjoy the Outdoors," below).

If you need a cab, call **Sanibel Taxi** (© **239/472-4160**).

PARKS & NATURE PRESERVES

Named for the *Des Moines Register* cartoonist who was a frequent visitor here and who started the federal Duck Stamp program, the outstanding **J.N. ("Ding") Darling National Wildlife Refuge** ☆☆☆, on Sanibel-Captiva Road, is home to alligators, raccoons, otters, and hundreds of species of birds. Occupying more than half of Sanibel Island, this 6,000-plus–acre area of mangrove swamps, winding waterways, and uplands has a 2-mile (3.25km) boardwalk nature trail and a 5-mile (8km), one-way **Wildlife Drive.** The visitor center shows brief videos about the refuge's inhabitants every half-hour and sells a map keyed to numbered stops along the Wildlife Drive. The best times for viewing the wildlife are early morning, late afternoon, and at low tide (tables are posted at the visitor center and are available at the chamber of commerce). Mosquitoes and "no-see-ums" (tiny, biting sand flies) are especially prevalent at dawn and dusk, so bring repellent.

Admission to the visitor center is free. The Wildlife Drive costs $5 per vehicle, $1 for hikers and bicyclists (free to holders of current federal Duck Stamps and National Park Service access passports). The visitor center is open from November to April, daily from 9am to 5pm; off-season, daily from 9am to 4pm. The center is open on federal holidays January through May, closed on holidays the rest of the year. The Wildlife Drive is open all year, Saturday through Thursday from 1 hour after sunrise to 1 hour before sunset.

For more information, contact the refuge at 1 Wildlife Dr., Sanibel Island, FL 33957 (© **239/472-1100**).

You'll get a lot more from your visit by taking a naturalist-narrated tram tour given by **Tarpon Bay Recreation,** at the north end of Tarpon Bay Road (© **239/472-8900;** www.tarponbay.com). The tours last 2 hours and cost $10 for adults, $5 for children 12 and under. Schedules are seasonal, so call ahead.

Tarpon Bay Recreation also offers a variety of guided **canoe and kayak tours,** with an emphasis on the historical, cultural, and environmental aspects of the refuge (call for the schedule and reservations, which are required). It also rents canoes, kayaks, and small boats with electric trolling motors (see "More Ways to Enjoy the Outdoors," below).

A short drive from the visitor center, the nonprofit **Sanibel/Captiva Conservation Foundation,** 3333 Sanibel-Captiva Rd. (© **239/472-2329;** www.sccf.org), maintains a nature center, a native plant nursery, and 4½ miles (7.25km) of nature trails on 1,100 acres of wetlands along the Sanibel River. You can learn more about the islands' unusual ecosystems through environmental workshops, guided 1½-hour trail walks, beach walks, and a 2-hour natural-history boat cruise (call for seasonal schedules and reservations). Various items are for sale, including native plants and publications about the islands' birds and other wildlife. Admission is $3 for adults, free for children 16 and under. The nature center is open November 15 to April 14, Monday through Friday from 8:30am to 4pm, Saturday 10am to 3pm; off-season, Monday through Friday 8:30am to 3pm.

Also nearby, the **Clinic for the Rehabilitation of Wildlife (C.R.O.W.),** 3883 Sanibel-Captiva Rd. (© **239/472-3644;** www.crowclinic.org), is dedicated to the care of sick, injured, or orphaned wildlife. Tours of the facility usually take place year-round Monday through Friday at 11am, Sunday at 1pm, but call to make sure. Tours cost $3 per person.

HITTING THE BEACH: SHELLING & SEA LIFE

BEACHES   Sanibel has four public beach-access areas with metered parking: the eastern point around **Sanibel Lighthouse,** which has a fishing pier; **Gulfside City Park,** at the end of Algiers Lane, off Casa Ybel Road; **Tarpon Bay Road Beach,** at the south end of Tarpon Bay Road; and **Bowman's Beach,** off Sanibel-Captiva Road. **Turner Beach,** at Blind Pass between Sanibel and Captiva, is highly popular at sunset since it faces due west; there's a small free parking lot on the Captiva side, but parking on the Sanibel side is limited to holders of local permits. All except Tarpon Bay Road Beach have restrooms. *Be forewarned:* Although nude bathing is illegal, the end of Bowman's Beach near Blind Pass often sees more than its share of bare straight and gay bodies.

Another popular beach on Captiva is at the end of Andy Rosse Lane in front of the Mucky Duck Restaurant. It's the one place here where you can rent motorized water-sports equipment (see "More Ways to Enjoy the Outdoors," below), but you'll have to use the Mucky Duck's restrooms. There's limited free parking just north of here, at the end of Captiva Drive (go past the entrance to South Seas Resort to the end of the road).

SHELLING   Sanibel and Captiva are famous for their seashells, and local residents and visitors alike can be seen in the "Sanibel stoop" or the "Captiva crouch" while searching for some 200 species.

Before you start scouring the beaches, visit the impressive **Bailey-Matthews Shell Museum** ★★, 3075 Sanibel-Captiva Rd. (© **888/679-6450** or 239/395-2233; www.shellmuseum.org), the only museum in the United States devoted solely to saltwater, freshwater, and land shells (yes, snails are included). Shells from as far away as South Africa surround a 6-foot (2m) globe in the middle of the main exhibit hall, thus showing their geographic origins. A spinning wheel–shaped case identifies shells likely to wash up on Sanibel. Other exhibits are devoted to shells in tribal art, fossil shells found in Florida, medicinal qualities of various mollusks, the endangered Florida tree snail, and "sailor's Valentines"—shell craft made by natives of Barbados for sailors to bring home to their loved ones. The upstairs library attracts serious malacologists—for the uninitiated, those who study mollusks—and a shop purveys clever shell-themed gifts. The museum is open Tuesday through Sunday from 10am to 4pm; admission is $5 adults, $3 children 8 to 16, free for children under 8.

The months from February to April, or after any storm, are the prime times of the year to look for whelks, olives, scallops, sand dollars, conch, and many other varieties of shells. Low tide is the best time of day. The shells can be sharp, so wear Aqua Socks or old running shoes whenever you go walking on the beach.

Tips **Don't Take Live Shells**

Florida law prohibits taking live shells from the beaches, and federal regulations prevent them from being removed from the J.N. ("Ding") Darling National Wildlife Refuge.

With so many residents and visitors scouring Sanibel, you may have better luck finding that rare shell on the adjacent shoals and nearby islands, such as Upper Captiva and Cayo Costa (see "Nearby Island Hopping," later in this chapter). **Captiva Cruises** ★★ (© **239/472-5300;** www.captivacruises.com) has shelling trips from the South Seas Resort on Captiva daily at 9am and noon. They cost $35 for adults, $17.50 for children. Reservations are required. Captiva Cruises also has popular dolphin-watching and wildlife cruises, with narration by a naturalist from the Sanibel-Captiva Conservation Foundation, daily from 4 to 5:30pm. These cost $20 for adults, $10 for kids. All of Captiva Cruises' boats are air-conditioned and have restrooms and snack bars.

At least 15 charter-boat skippers also offer to take guests on shelling expeditions to these less-explored areas. Their half-day rates are about $200 for up to four people, so get up a group to go. Several operate from the **'Tween Waters Inn Marina** (© **239/472-5161**) on Captiva, including **Capt. Mike Fuery** (© **239/472-1015,** or 239/994-7195 on his boat). Others are based at **Jensen's Twin Palms Marina,** on Captiva (© **239/472-5800**), and at the **Sanibel Marina,** on North Yachtsman Drive, off Periwinkle Way east of Causeway Boulevard (© **239/472-2723**). They all distribute brochures at the chamber of commerce visitor center (see "Essentials," above) and are listed in the free tourist publications found there.

MORE WAYS TO ENJOY THE OUTDOORS

BICYCLING, WALKING, JOGGING & IN-LINE SKATING   Paved bicycle paths follow alongside most major roads, including the entire length of Periwinkle Way and along Sanibel-Captiva Road to Blind Pass, making Sanibel a paradise for cyclists, walkers, joggers, and in-line skaters. And you can walk or bike the 5-mile (8km), one-way nature trail through the J.N. ("Ding") Darling National Wildlife Refuge.

The chamber of commerce visitor center has bike maps, as do Sanibel's rental firms: **Finnimore's Cycle Shop,** 2353 Periwinkle Way (© **239/472-5577**); **The Bike Rental,** 2330 Palm Ridge Rd. (© **239/472-2241**); **Billy's Rentals,** 1470 Periwinkle Way (© **239/472-5248**); **Boats, Bikes & Beach Stuff,** 2427 Periwinkle Way (© **239/472-8717**); and **Tarpon Bay Recreation,** at the north end of Tarpon Bay Road (© **239/472-8900**). On Captiva, **Jim's Bike & Skate Rentals** on Andy Rosse Lane (© **239/472-1296**) rents bikes and beach equipment. Bike rates range from $3 per hour to $15 a day for basic models. Both Finnimore's and Jim's also rent in-line skates.

There are no bike paths on Captiva, where trees alongside the narrow roads can make for dangerous riding.

BOATING & FISHING   On Sanibel, rental boats and charter-fishing excursions are available from **The Boat House** at the Sanibel Marina, on North Yachtsman Drive (© **239/472-2531**), off Periwinkle Way east of Causeway Road. **Tarpon Bay Recreation,** at the north end of Tarpon Bay Road (© **239/472-8900**), rents boats with electric trolling motors and tackle for fishing.

On Captiva, check with **Sweet Water Rentals** at the 'Tween Waters Inn Marina (© **239/472-6376**), **Jensen's Twin Palms Marina** (© **239/472-5800**), and **McCarthy's Marina** (© **239/472-5200**), all on Captiva Road. Rental boats cost about $125 for half a day, $200 for a full day.

Many **charter-fishing captains** are docked at these marinas. Half-day rates are about $300 for up to four people. The skippers leave free brochures at the chamber of commerce visitor center (see "Essentials," above), and they're also listed in the free tourist publications found there.

CANOEING & KAYAKING   As noted under "Parks & Nature Preserves," above, **Tarpon Bay Recreation** (✆ 239/472-8900; www.tarponbay.com) has guided canoe and kayak trips in the J.N. ("Ding") Darling National Wildlife Refuge. Do-it-yourselfers can rent canoes and kayaks here. They cost $20 for the first 2 hours, $5 for each additional hour. **Captiva Kayak Co./WildSide Adventures,** based at McCarthy's Marina (✆ 877/395-2925 or 239/395-2925; www.captivakayak.com), rents canoes and kayaks on Captiva, as does **'Tween Waters Inn Marina** (✆ 239/472-5161).

Naturalist, avid environmentalist, and former Sanibel mayor Mark "Bird" Westall of **Canoe Adventures** ★★ (✆ 239/472-5218; fax 239/472-6833) takes visitors on guided canoe trips through the wildlife refuge and on the Sanibel River. His excursions are timed for low tide and cost $40 for adults, $20 for children under 18. He will tailor shorter trips to accommodate children or anyone else not up to 2½ to 3 hours in a canoe. Naturalist **Brian Houston** leads kayaking trips from 'Tween Waters Inn Marina on Captiva, but make your reservations at Tarpon Bay Recreation on Sanibel (✆ 239/472-8900). Brian also charges $40 per person. **Captiva Kayak Co./WildSide Adventures,** based at McCarthy's Marina on Captiva (✆ 877/395-2925 or 239/395-2925; www.captivakayak.com), has both day and night back-bay ecology trips for $35 for adults, $25 for teenagers, $20 for children (add $10 to each price for night trips). They will customize tours, including camping on Cayo Costa (see "Nearby Island Hopping," below) for advanced kayakers. Reservations are essential with all these operators.

GOLF & TENNIS   Golfers may view a gallery of wild animals while playing the 5,600-yard, par-70, 18-hole course at the **Dunes Golf and Tennis Club,** 949 Sandcastle Rd., Sanibel (✆ 239/472-2535; www.dunesgolfsanibel.com), whose back nine runs across a wildlife preserve. Call a day in advance for seasonal greens fees and a tee time. The Dunes also has seven tennis courts.

You can also play nine water-bordered holes at **Beachview Golf Club,** 1100 Par View Dr. (✆ 239/472-2626). The **South Seas Resort** has tennis courts and a nine-hole golf course, but they're for guests only.

SAILING   If you want to learn how to sail, noted yachties Steve and Doris Colgate have a branch of their **Offshore Sailing School** at the South Seas Resort (✆ 888/454-9002 or 239/472-5111, ext. 7141; www.offshore-sailing.com). You can either learn to sail or polish your skills here. Clinics ranging from half a day to a full week are available. Also ask about their popular women-only, father/son, and mother/daughter programs.

Also based on Captiva, two sailboats take guests out on the waters of Pine Island Sound: the *Adventure* (✆ 239/472-6300 or 239/472-4386) and the *New Moon* (✆ 239/395-1782). They cost $95 per hour with a 2-hour minimum. Reservations are required.

Do-it-yourselfers can rent small sailboats from **Captiva Kayak Co./WildSide Adventures,** based at McCarthy's Marina (✆ 877/395-2925 or 239/395-2925; www.captivakayak.com). Prices range from $25 to $55 an hour, depending on the size of the craft.

WATER SPORTS   Sanibel may prohibit motorized water-sports equipment on its beaches, but Captiva doesn't. **Yolo Watersports** (✆ 239/472-9656) offers parasailing and WaveRunner rentals on the beach in front of the Mucky Duck Restaurant, at the gulf end of Andy Rosse Lane on Captiva.

MORE TO SEE & DO

Worth a brief stop after you've done everything else here, the **Sanibel Historical Village & Museum,** 950 Dunlop Rd. (© **239/472-4648**), includes the 1913-vintage Rutland home and the 1926 versions of Bailey's General Store (complete with Red Crown gasoline pumps), the post office, and Miss Charlotta's Tea Room. Displays highlight the islands' prehistoric Calusa tribal era, as well as old photos from pioneer days, turn-of-the-20th-century clothing, and a variety of other memorabilia. Open November through May, Wednesday through Saturday from 10am to 4pm; from June to mid-August, Wednesday through Saturday from 10am to 1pm. Admission is by $3 donation.

At the east end of Periwinkle Way, the **Sanibel Lighthouse** has marked the entrance to San Carlos Bay since 1884. The lightkeepers used to live in the cottages at the base of the 94-foot (151m) tower. The now-automatic lighthouse isn't open to visitors, but the grounds and beach are.

The best way to get the lay of the land and learn all about the islands' history is on a 2-hour **Sanibel Island Eco-History Trolley Tour,** staged by Adventures in Paradise (© **239/472-8443;** www.adventureinparadiseinc.com). They depart the chamber of commerce (see "Essentials," earlier in this chapter) Monday through Saturday at 10:30am and 1pm and cost $18 for adults, $15 for children, and are free for kids 3 and under. Call for reservations.

In addition to its other trips, **Captiva Cruises** (© **239/472-5300;** www. captivacruises.com) goes out daily on sunset cruises from the South Seas Resort on Captiva. These cost $17.50 for adults, $10 for children. Call for daily departure times and reservations.

SHOPPING

If you have no luck at the beach hunting for shells, several Sanibel shops sell thousands of them. **Sanibel Sea Shell Industries,** 905 Fitzhugh St. (© **239/472-1603**), has one of the largest collections, with more than 10,000 shells in stock. **She Sells Sea Shells** has two locations: 1157 Periwinkle Way near Causeway Road (© **239/472-6991**) and 2422 Periwinkle Way near the island's center (© **239/472-8080**). Others include **Neptune's Treasures Shell Shop,** in the Tree Tops Center, 1101 Periwinkle Way opposite the Dairy Queen (© **239/472-3132**), which also has a good collection of fossils.

You can burn up a rainy day and lots of credit at Sanibel's numerous upscale boutiques carrying expensive jewelry, apparel, and gifts. Many are in **Periwinkle Place** and **Tahitian Gardens,** the main shopping centers along Periwinkle Way. The larger Periwinkle Place sports mostly high-end men's and women's clothiers, while Tahitian Gardens has some excellent gift shops, including the **Audubon Nature Store** (© **239/395-2020**), which carries gifts and books with a wildlife theme, and **The Cheshire Cat** (© **239/472-3545**), offering nature toys and other unique items for kids.

More than a dozen Sanibel galleries feature original works of art; pick up a gallery guide at the chamber of commerce visitor center (see "Essentials," earlier in this chapter). On Captiva, the treehouselike **Jungle Drums,** on Andy Rosse Lane (© **239/395-2266**), has the area's most unique collection of wildlife art.

Founded in 1899, **Bailey's General Store** is still going strong at the corner of Periwinkle Way and Tarpon Bay Road (© **239/472-1516**), with a supermarket, deli, salad bar, hardware store, beach shop, shoe repair, and Western Union all under one roof.

Bailey's General Store is open daily from 7am to 9pm. Most other shops are open Monday through Saturday from 9am to 6pm, Sunday from noon to 5pm.

WHERE TO STAY

Sanibel & Captiva Central Reservations, Inc. (✆ 800/325-1352 or 239/472-0457; fax 239/472-2178; www.sanibel-captivarent.com) and **1-800-SANIBEL** (✆ 800/726-4235 or 239/472-1800; fax 239/395-9690; www.1-800-sanibel.com) are reservations services that will book you into most condominiums and cottages here.

In general, Sanibel and Captiva room and condominium rates are highest during the shelling season, February through April. January is usually somewhat less expensive. But note that most rates fall drastically during the off-season. Don't hesitate to ask for a discount or special deal then. Since most properties on the islands are geared to 1-week vacations, you can also save by purchasing a package deal if you're staying for 7 nights or longer.

The islands' sole campground, the **Periwinkle Trailer Park,** 1119 Periwinkle Way, Sanibel Island (✆ **239/472-1433**), is so popular it doesn't even advertise. No other camping is permitted on either Sanibel or Captiva.

SANIBEL ISLAND
Very Expensive

Best Western Sanibel Island Beach Resort ⚲   One of only two chain properties here, this excellently managed motel boasts spacious rooms, efficiencies, and apartments whose screened balconies face either the beach or a lawn festooned with palms, pink hibiscus, orange trees, a swimming pool, tennis courts, and white Adirondack chairs for lounging. Choice units are on the beach end of the building.

3287 W. Gulf Dr. (at St. Kilda Rd.), Sanibel Island, FL 33957. ✆ **800/645-6559** or 239/472-1700. Fax 239/472-5032. www.bwsanibel.com. 45 units. Winter $249–$465 double; off-season $135–$295 double. AE, DC, DISC, MC, V. **Amenities:** Heated outdoor pool; tennis courts; free use of bikes; coin-op washers and dryers. *In room:* A/C, TV, kitchen, coffeemaker, hair dryer, iron.

Casa Ybel Resort ⭐⭐⭐   One of the best resorts on Sanibel, this all-condo property sits beside the beach on the historic site of the island's first beachfront hotel, the Thistle Lodge. The present-day Casa Ybel's turn-of-the-20th-century central building houses a restaurant of that name, where both guests and nonguests can enjoy wonderful cuisine and magnificent gulf views. Reflecting Thistle Lodge, the swimming pool in front of the restaurant is one of Florida's most picturesque. In four-story, gray buildings on the island's most beautifully landscaped grounds, the spacious one- and two-bedroom condominiums all have screened porches facing the gulf. With upstairs bedrooms, the town house–style units provide more privacy than most condominiums on Sanibel. Complimentary daily maid service is provided in the one-bedroom units, but it costs $35 a day in the two-bedroom condominiums.

2255 W. Gulf Dr., Sanibel Island, FL 33957. ✆ **800/276-4753** or 239/472-3145. Fax 239/472-2109. www.casaybelresort.com. 114 units. Winter $315–$495 condo; off-season $220–$315 condo. Packages and weekly rates available. AE, DISC, MC, V. **Amenities:** Restaurant (American); bar; heated outdoor pool; tennis courts; Jacuzzi; water-sports equipment rental; bike rental; children's programs; concierge; massage; babysitting; laundry service. *In room:* A/C, TV, kitchen, coffeemaker, hair dryer, iron.

Sanibel Inn ⭐⭐ *Kids*   A back-to-nature theme prevails at this beachside inn, in both the room decor and the grounds planted with native Florida foliage specifically designed to attract butterflies and hummingbirds. In fact, back-to-nature children's programs make this a great choice for eco-friendly families. The inn offers attractively furnished hotel rooms and fully equipped two-bedroom, two-bathroom condominium apartments (the latter are some of Sanibel's most luxurious). All units have screened porches.

937 E. Gulf Dr., Sanibel Island, FL 33957. ℂ **800/237-1491** or 239/472-3181. Fax 239/472-5234. www. sanibelinn.com. 96 units. Winter $329–$539 double; off-season $175–$275 double. Packages available. AE, DC, DISC, MC, V. **Amenities:** Restaurant (Italian); bar; heated outdoor pool; tennis courts; access to nearby health club; water-sports equipment rental; bike rental; children's programs; limited room service; babysitting; laundry service. *In room:* A/C, TV, dataport, kitchen, fridge, coffeemaker, hair dryer, iron.

Sanibel's Seaside Inn ★★   This comfortable and friendly Key West–style establishment enjoys a tranquil location near the island's southeastern tip. The duplex, 1960s-style cottages are spacious, brightly furnished one-bedroom apartments, but if you can do without a kitchen, the choice units here are the beachfront hotel rooms, whose screened porches face the gulf. All units have ceiling fans and open-air balconies or decks. No smoking indoors.

541 E. Gulf Dr., Sanibel Island, FL 33957. ℂ **800/831-7384** or 239/472-1400. Fax 239/472-6518. www.seasideinn.com. 32 units. Winter $299–$408 double; off-season $169–$285 double. Rates include continental breakfast. Packages available. AE, DC, DISC, MC, V. **Amenities:** Heated outdoor pool; access to nearby health club; sauna; free use of bikes; babysitting; coin-op washers and dryers. *In room:* A/C, TV/VCR, dataport, kitchen (some units), fridge, coffeemaker, hair dryer, iron.

Song of the Sea ★★   Popular with Europeans, this beachside inn offers motel-like efficiencies and one-bedroom suites with plantation-style shutters behind sliding-glass doors opening to screened porches. Don't expect a lot of extra space in the suites, whose bedrooms are barely large enough to hold their king-size beds. A pathway leads next door to the Sanibel Inn (see above), where guests can use the facilities. An extensive continental breakfast is served in the public building and eaten at umbrella tables on a brick patio. Guests get discounts on the facilities at the Sundial Beach Resort (see below).

863 E. Gulf Dr., Sanibel Island, FL 33957. ℂ **800/231-1045** or 239/472-2220. Fax 239/472-8569. 30 units. www.songofthesea.com. Winter $229–$449 double; off-season $159–$305 double. Rates include continental breakfast. Packages available. AE, DC, DISC, MC, V. **Amenities:** Heated outdoor pool; access to nearby health club; Jacuzzi; free use of bikes; babysitting; coin-op washers and dryers. *In room:* A/C, TV, fax, dataport, kitchen, minibar, fridge, coffeemaker, hair dryer, iron.

Sundial Beach Resort ★★ *Kids*   The largest resort on Sanibel, this condominium complex lacks intimacy but has lots to keep families occupied, from a palm-studded, beachside pool area to a complimentary marine biology program and a small ecology center with a touch tank. The one-, two-, and three-bedroom condominiums are housed in two- and three-story buildings (as high as they get on Sanibel) and have screened balconies overlooking the beach or tropically landscaped gardens. Among several dining options here, the award-winning **Windows on the Water** dining room offers glorious gulf views at breakfast, lunch, and dinner; master chefs put on a show as they prepare delicious steak, chicken, and seafood dishes right by your table in **Noopie's Japanese Seafood & Steakhouse,** where dinner reservations are required (ℂ **239/ 395-6014**). Overlooking the pool and the gulf, the relaxing Beaches Grill & Bar is popular at sunset and has entertainment nightly.

1451 Middle Gulf Dr., Sanibel Island, FL 33957. ℂ **800/237-4184** or 239/481-3636. Fax 239/481-4947. www.sundialresort.com. 275 units. Winter $209–$650 condo apt.; off-season $155–$350 condo apt. Packages available. AE, DC, DISC, MC, V. **Amenities:** 4 restaurants (American, Japanese); 2 bars; 5 heated outdoor pools; 12 tennis courts; exercise room; Jacuzzi; water-sports equipment rental; bike rental; children's programs; game room; concierge; activities desk; business center; limited room service; massage; babysitting; laundry service; coin-op washers and dryers. *In room:* A/C, TV/VCR, kitchen, coffeemaker, hair dryer, iron.

Moderate

Island Inn ★★   It's difficult to get accommodations here during the peak winter season, but it's worth trying because this classic beach resort has been in business for more than a century. Its original central building houses a bright, genteel dining room, a spacious lounge, and a library brightly furnished with old-style bentwood and wicker sofas and chairs. This is the kind of place where guests dress for dinner—jackets and collared shirts required, ties recommended for men at dinner—and seating is assigned (some guests have had the same table for years). This main building looks out over a sandy, South Pacific–like yard to the Gulf. Although neither charming in an Old Florida sense nor luxurious by today's standards, the cottages and motel rooms (with or without kitchens) are modern and comfortable. Most have screened porches or balconies.

3111 W. Gulf Dr., Sanibel Island, FL 33957. ✆ **800/851-5088** or 239/472-1561. Fax 239/472-0051. www.islandinnsanibel.com. 57 units, including 9 cottages. Winter (including breakfast and dinner) $175–$425 double; off-season (no meals) $110–$215 double. AE, DISC, MC, V. **Amenities:** Restaurant (American); bar; small heated outdoor pool; tennis court; croquet area; coin-op washers and dryers. *In room:* A/C, TV, kitchen (some units), fridge, coffeemaker, hair dryer, iron.

Tarpon Tale Inn ★ *Finds*   Owners Dawn and Joe Ramsey preside over this low-slung gray building in the "Old Sanibel" neighborhood, the island's first settlement where the ferries from Fort Myers used to dock near the lighthouse. White walls and tile floors make their comfortable units bright; French doors lead to gardens dense with seagrape, palm, and ficus trees, which provide privacy for a large outdoor hot tub. Three of their five units have separate bedrooms, while two other "deluxe studios" actually are two-bedroom suites. All units have shower-only bathrooms. Continental breakfast makings are delivered the night before.

367 Periwinkle Way, Sanibel Island, FL 33957. ✆ **239/472-0939.** Fax 239/472-6202. www.tarpontale.com. 5 units. Winter $119–$210 double; off-season $79–$159 double. Rates include continental breakfast. AE, DC, DISC, MC, V. Some pets accepted ($30 fee); call first. **Amenities:** Jacuzzi; free use of bikes; coin-op washers and dryers; *In room:* A/C, TV/VCR, kitchen, coffeemaker, hair dryer and iron on request, no phone.

Inexpensive

Palm View Motel   In a quiet residential area less than a block from the Holiday Inn Beach Resort and Morgan's Forest restaurant, this little property is one of Sanibel's few inexpensive motels. The best choices here are the spacious, well-ventilated one- and two-bedroom apartments, but even the smaller efficiencies have kitchens and separate living and sleeping areas. You'll have to do without a phone in your room, but you can bring your pet. There's a hot tub in the backyard.

706 Donax St., Sanibel Island, FL 33957. ✆ **239/472-1606.** Fax 239/472-1606. www.palmviewmotel.com. 5 units. Winter $145–$185 efficiency and apts.; off-season $85–$135 efficiency and apts. Weekly rates available. MC, V. Pets accepted ($10 per day). **Amenities:** Jacuzzi; bike rental; free guest laundry. *In room:* A/C, TV, kitchen, coffeemaker, hair dryer, iron, no phone.

CAPTIVA ISLAND

Captiva Island Inn Bed & Breakfast ★   This B&B complex sits virtually surrounded by restaurants, art galleries, and boutiques along Captiva's block-long commercial street. That can make it a bit too busy for some eyes and ears, but it has its charms. Two suites in the Key West–style main building open to porches overlooking the lane, while four Dutch clapboard cottages sit out back on the fringes of a gravel parking lot (you get just enough yard here for hammocks and a gas grill). The ceiling in one cottage that once housed aviator Charles Lindbergh has clouds painted against a blue sky. It and the rest of the units have ceiling fans, kitchens, large bathrooms, queen-size sofa beds in their living rooms, cool tile floors, and designer bed linens (including down comforters for the occasional chilly night). Some rooms have only showers in their bathrooms. Guests get free use of bicycles and towels and chairs for the beach (a block away) and get a complimentary full breakfast at R.C. Otter's Island Eats across the lane.

11509 Andy Rosse Lane (P.O. Box 848), Captiva Island, FL 33924. ℂ 800/454-9898 or 239/395-0882. Fax 239/395-0862. www.captivaislandinn.com. 7 units. Winter $220–$260 double; off-season $130–$150 double. Rates include full breakfast. AE, DISC, MC, V. **Amenities:** Access to nearby health club; free use of bikes. *In room:* A/C, TV, kitchen, fridge, coffeemaker.

South Seas Resort ★★★ *Kids* Formerly Clarence Chadwick's 330-acre copra plantation, this exclusive establishment is the premier property on these two islands. It's one of the best choices in southern Florida for serious tennis buffs; its gulf-side golf course is one of the most picturesque nine-holers anywhere; and its two marinas host scuba-dive operators. The resort occupies all of Captiva's northern third, making it ideal if you want to step from your luxury house or condominium right onto 2½ miles (4km) of gorgeous beach. The resort is so spread out along the shore that a free trolley shuttles back and forth through the mangrove forests.

Most accommodations are so-called villas (actually condominium apartments), but there are a great variety of offerings, including luxury homes with private pools and their own tennis courts (many are occupied exclusively by their owners; watch for famous folks wandering about). With three bedrooms or more, some units are ideal for families or couples who want to share the cost of a vacation. The least-expensive (and least-inspired) units are the "Harbourside" hotel rooms at the yacht basin and marina near the island's northern tip, the jumping-off point for Captiva Cruises and Steve and Doris Colgate's Offshore Sailing School. Next up are the "Bayside Villas" and "Beachside Villas"—condominium apartments in three-story buildings near the main-gate area and its shops and restaurants. Whatever type of living space you choose, by all means inquire about package deals, which can result in significant savings for stays of 3 nights or more.

Outside the main gate, Chadwick's Shopping Center includes restaurants, high-fashion boutiques, jewelry stores, and gift shops, all open to the public, but the resort's no-cash, charge-to-your-room policy prevents gate-crashers from entering the resort proper.

P.O. Box 194, Captiva Island, FL 33924. ℂ 800/CAPTIVA or 239/472-5111. Fax 239/481-4947. www.south-seas-resort.com. 660 units. Winter $260–$370 double; $350–$1,800 condo or house. Off-season $169–$240 double; $165–$1,300 condo or house. $8 per person per day added to room bills, 18%–20% to food and bar bills, in lieu of tipping. Packages available. AE, DC, DISC, MC, V. **Amenities:** 3 restaurants (American); 2 bars; 18 heated outdoor pools; 9-hole golf course; 18 tennis courts; health club; Jacuzzis; water-sports equipment rental; bike rental; children's programs; game room; concierge; activities desk; business center; shopping arcade; salon; limited room service; massage; babysitting; laundry service; coin-op washers and dryers. *In room:* A/C, TV, dataport (some units), kitchen (larger units only), coffeemaker, hair dryer, iron.

'Tween Waters Inn ★★ Wedged between the gulf beach and the bay on the narrowest part of Captiva, this venerable establishment was the regular haunt of cartoonist J.N. ("Ding") Darling. Anne Morrow Lindbergh also dined here often while writing *A Gift from the Sea.* Just as Darling preserved the islands' wildlife, the 'Tween Waters has saved the cottages he stayed in. Situated in a sandy palm grove, these pink shiplap buildings have been upgraded but still capture Old Florida. Some face the gulf; others, the bay. Themed to honor their famous guests, they range in size from the bay-side honeymoon cottage with barely enough room for its king-size bed and a tiny kitchen to a three-bedroom, two-bath house. The spacious hotel rooms and apartments are in three modern buildings on stilts; they all have screened balconies facing the gulf or the bay.

The Old Captiva House restaurant appears very much as it did in Ding Darling's days (note his cartoons adorning the dining room walls), and The Canoe & The Kayak restaurant provides inexpensive lunches on its bay-side deck. The popular Crow's Nest Lounge has live entertainment and provides snacks and light evening meals from 9pm to 1am.

Charter captains dock at the full-service marina.

P.O. Box 249, Captiva Island, FL 33924. (Ⓒ) **800/223-5865** or 239/472-5161. Fax 239/472-0249. www.tween waters.com. 138 units. Winter $195–$250 double; $220–$560 suites; $115–$425 cottage. Off-season $160–$240 double; $215–$420 suites; $110–$335 cottage. Rates include continental breakfast. Packages available. AE, DC, MC, V. Pets accepted in some units ($15 per day). **Amenities:** 2 restaurants (Regional); 2 bars; outdoor pool; 3 tennis courts; exercise room; Jacuzzi; water-sports equipment rentals; bike rentals; coin-op washers and dryers. *In room:* A/C, TV, dataport, kitchen (suites and cottages), fridge, coffeemaker, hair dryer, iron (suites only), safe.

COTTAGES

The islands have several Old Florida–style cottages that offer charming and often less expensive alternatives to hotels and condominiums. Some of the best are members of the **Sanibel-Captiva Small Inns & Cottages Association.** You can contact the association (via its website only) at www.sanibelsmallinns.com for a complete listing of properties.

Sitting between two condominium complexes off Middle Gulf Drive, **Gulf Breeze Cottages** ★★, 1081 Shell Basket Lane, Sanibel Island, FL 33957 (Ⓒ **800/ 388-2842** or 239/472-1626; www.gbreeze.com), is a collection of clapboard cottages separated from the beach by a lawn with covered picnic area and outdoor shower. One two-story building is divided into four efficiencies (the pick is no. 7, with a two-way view of the gulf from its big picture windows). Rates are $215 to $350 a day in winter, $115 to $230 a day off-season.

With only one monstrous mansion standing between them and a narrow bay beach near Sanibel Lighthouse, **Buttonwood Cottages** ★, 1234 Buttonwood Lane, Sanibel Island, FL 33957 (Ⓒ **887/395-COTTAGE** or 239/395-9061; fax 239/395-2620; www.buttonwoodcottages.com), are less expensive options at $125 to $220 a day in winter, $75 to $160 off-season. Remodeled and equipped with many modern amenities, the five units occupy two long cottages built on stilts. Four of them have screened porches, with two overlooking a lushly tropical backyard sporting two hammocks and two hot tubs. The Lighthouse Cafe (see "Where to Dine," below) is around the corner.

Barely updated since the 1950s are the 32 pink clapboard structures at **Beachview Cottages,** 3325 W. Gulf Dr., Sanibel Island, FL 33957 (Ⓒ **800/ 860-0532** or 239/472-1202; fax 239/472-4720; www.beachviewsanibel.com). None of the cottages has a phone, and some have shower-only bathrooms. There's a heated outdoor swimming pool here. Winter rates are $169 to $269 a day, off-season $125 to $195 a day.

On Captiva, **Jensen's On the Gulf,** P.O. Box 460, Captiva Island, FL 33924 (Ⓒ **239/472-4684;** www.jensen-captiva.com), has cottages as well as homes, apartments, and studios ranging from $210 to $550 a day in winter, $140 to $385 a day off-season. **Jensen's Twin Palm Resort & Marina,** P.O. Box 191, Captiva Island, FL 33924 (Ⓒ **239/472-5800;** same website), on the bay side near the Andy Rosse Lane dining district, has cottages ranging from $120 to $190 a day during winter, from $105 to $130 a day off-season.

WHERE TO DINE

No restaurant can survive on these affluent islands without serving good food, so you're assured of getting a fine meal wherever you go. Oddly, only a handful of restaurants offer dining with water views.

SANIBEL ISLAND

Much of the "help" on this affluent island dines at **Jerry's Family Restaurant,** 1700 Periwinkle Way at Casa Ybel Road (℗ 239/472-9300), which offers wholesome and inexpensive diner fare (ingredients come fresh from the adjacent Jerry's Supermarket). Both the restaurant and the supermarket are open daily from 6am to 11pm. Breakfast is served from 6am to 4pm, and you can usually get a table quickly here (which can't be said of Sanibel's other popular breakfast spots).

You'll find very reasonably priced pub fare at Sanibel's sports bars, such as **The Lazy Flamingo II** (see below) and **Sanibel Grill,** 703 Tarpon Bay Rd., near Palm Ridge Road (℗ 239/472-3128), which actually serves as the bar for Timbers, the fine seafood restaurant next door (see below).

For picnics at Sanibel's beaches or on a canoe, the deli and bakery in **Bailey's General Store,** at Periwinkle Way and Tarpon Bay Road (℗ 239/472-1516), carries a gourmet selection of breads, cheeses, and meats. **Huxter's Deli and Market,** 1203 Periwinkle Way, east of Donax Street (℗ 239/472-6988), has sandwich fixings and "beach box" lunches to go.

Very Expensive

Mad Hatter ★★ ECLECTIC   One of Sanibel's best choices for a romantic special dinner, this gulf-front restaurant has only 12 tables, but each has a view that's perfect at sunset. The ever-changing eclectic menu features flavors from around the world, such as Thai-style peanut sauce over a seared, sesame-encrusted yellowfin tuna steak. The jumbo shrimp Wellington is a fascinating twist on the classic beef dish, and the stuffed crab served with a lobster volute is another winner.

6467 Sanibel-Captiva Rd., at Blind Pass. ℗ 239/472-0033. Reservations highly recommended. Main courses $25–$35. AE, MC, V. Dec 15–Jan 31 daily 5–9pm. Feb 1–Easter Sun–Mon 5–9:30pm, Tues–Sat 11:30am–2pm and 5–9:30pm. Easter–May 31 daily 5–9:30pm. June 1–Dec 14 Mon–Sat 5–9:30pm. Closed Sept after Labor Day.

Moderate

Jacaranda SEAFOOD/PASTA/STEAKS   With live music nightly, the Patio Lounge attracts an affluent over-40 crowd to this friendly and casual restaurant named for the purple-flowered jacaranda tree. Although the Jacaranda is best known as a local gathering spot, it has received several dining awards. Fresh fish is well prepared here, or you can choose certified Angus steaks or prime rib. The linguine with a dozen littleneck clams tossed in a piquant red or white clam sauce is consistently excellent. For dessert, the gooey turtle pie—ice cream, caramel, fudge sauce, chopped nuts, and whipped cream—will send you away stuffed.

1223 Periwinkle Way (east of Donax St.). ℗ 239/472-1771. Reservations recommended. Main courses $16–$30. AE, MC, V. Daily 5–10pm. Lounge daily 4pm–12:30am. Closed Christmas.

McT's Shrimp House & Tavern SEAFOOD   Shrimp reigns at this casual Old Florida–style establishment, where you'll see a line outside at 4pm waiting for the early-bird specials served to the first 100 persons in the door. Everyone else gets to view the daily catch displayed in a chiller case, including the night's shrimp ready for the chef to prepare in one of at least a dozen ways, from

steamed to fried in a coconut-and-almond batter. There are also grouper and
swordfish, plus steaks and chicken for the land-minded, but stick to the shrimp
here (see below for the Timbers Restaurant & Fish Market, which does a much
better job of cooking fish). McT's Tavern offers an extensive choice of appetizers and light dinners.

1523 Periwinkle Way (at Fitzhugh St.). ✆ **239/472-3161.** Main courses $13–$22; early-bird specials $10.
AE, DC, DISC, MC, V. Shrimp House daily 4:45–10pm. McT's Tavern daily 4pm–midnight. Closed Thanksgiving,
Christmas.

Morgan's Forest *Kids* SEAFOOD   The kids will love dining in this miniature
jungle patterned after the Rainforest Cafes elsewhere. Almost hidden among all
the foliage are mechanical but lifelike moving jaguars, monkeys, birds, and a
huge python entangled in vines above the bar. Squawking bird sounds, strobe-
lightning bolts followed by claps of thunder, and an occasional faux fog rolling
across the floor add to the Amazonian ambience. The owner of Fort Myers
Beach's excellent Channel Mark restaurant is in charge here, which means that
your taste buds will be as entertained as your eyes and ears. The fine crab cakes
are the pick of a menu otherwise accented with South- and Central-American
seasonings. Obviously, there's a children's menu.

1231 Middle Gulf Dr., at the Holiday Inn Beach Resort. ✆ **239/472-3351.** Main courses $14–$23. AE, DC,
DISC, MC, V. Mon–Sat 7–11am and 5–10pm; Sun 7am–noon and 5–10pm.

The Timbers Restaurant & Fish Market ★★ SEAFOOD/STEAK   This
casual upstairs restaurant, with bamboo railings, oversized canvas umbrellas, and
paintings of tropical scenes through faux windows, consistently is Sanibel's best
place for fresh fish and aged beef hot off the charcoal grill. In the fish market out
front, you can view the catch and have the chef charcoal-grill or blacken it to
order. The steaks, cut on the premises, are the island's best. You can order a drink
from the adjoining Sanibel Grill sports bar and wait for a table outside on the
shopping center's porch.

703 Tarpon Bay Rd. (between Periwinkle Way and Palm Ridge Rd.). ✆ **239/472-3128.** Main courses
$15–$23; early birds get $2.50 off regular price. AE, MC, V. Winter daily 4:30–9:30pm; off-season daily
5–9:30pm.

Inexpensive

Grandma Dot's Seaside Saloon SEAFOOD   One of Sanibel's most popular
lunch spots, this open-air but screened cafe on the docks of Sanibel Marina offers
excellent salads (try the seafood Caesar) and fine sandwiches plus a few main
courses led by broiled grouper in a sauce of lemon, dill, butter, and white wine.

At Sanibel Marina, 634 N. Yachtsman Dr. ✆ **239/472-8138.** Reservations not accepted. Main courses
$6–$23; salads and sandwiches $6–$12. MC, V. Daily 11:30am–7:30pm.

Hungry Heron ★★ *Kids* AMERICAN   This tropically decorated eatery is
Sanibel's most popular family restaurant. There's something for everyone on the
huge, tabloid-size menu—from hot and cold appetizers and overstuffed "sea-
wiches" to pasta and steamed shellfish. And if the 255 regular items aren't

enough, there's a list of nightly specials. Seafood, steaks, and stir-frys from a sizzling skillet are popular with local residents, who bring the kids here for fun and a children's menu. An all-you-can-eat breakfast buffet on Saturday and Sunday mornings is an excellent value.

In Palm Ridge Place, 2330 Palm Ridge Rd. (at Periwinkle Way). © **239/395-2300.** Reservations not accepted, but call for preferred seating. Main courses $9–$18; sandwiches, burgers, snacks $6–$11; weekend breakfast buffet $9 adults, $5 children under 10. AE, DISC, MC, V. Mon–Fri 11am–9pm; Sat–Sun 7:30am–9pm (breakfast buffet to 11am Sat, to noon Sun).

The Lazy Flamingo II *Value* SEAFOOD/PUB FARE   T-shirts and shorts or jeans are the dress code at this friendly pub that always seems packed by the young and young-at-heart, who flock here for reasonably priced food, a wide choice of beers iced down in a huge box behind the bar, and sports TVs. Some of that beer is used to steam shrimp and a finger-stinging collection of oysters, clams, and spices known as "The Pot." Best pick, however, is grouper from the charcoals, as either a main course or a sandwich. The flamingo-pink menu also has an array of sandwiches, burgers, fish platters, and very spicy "Dead Parrot Wings." Fillet your own catch, and the chef will cook it to order for you. Happy-hour prices prevail whenever football games are on the TVs. A sister institution, the **Lazy Flamingo I,** 6520-C Pine Ave., at Sanibel-Captiva Road, a quarter mile (.5km) south of Blind Pass (© **239/472-5353**), has the same menu and hours.

1036 Periwinkle Way, west of Causeway Blvd. © **239/472-6939.** Reservations not accepted. Main courses $11–$15; sandwiches and snacks $5–$9. Cook your catch $8. AE, DISC, MC, V. Daily 11:30am–1am.

Lighthouse Cafe ★ *Value* AMERICAN   Decorated with photos and drawings of lighthouses, this casual storefront establishment located appropriately near the Sanibel Lighthouse dishes up breakfast omelets that are meals in themselves, especially the ocean frittata containing delicately seasoned scallops, crab meat, shrimp, broccoli, and fresh mushrooms, and crowned with an artichoke heart and creamy Alfredo sauce. Seafood Benedict is another unusual offering. Interesting sandwiches are served after 11am. Reasonably priced cafe-style dinners are served during winter only.

In Seahorse Shops, 362 Periwinkle Way (at Buttonwood Lane, east of Causeway Rd.). © **239/472-0303.** Call ahead to get on waiting list. Main courses $10–$15; breakfast $3.50–$7.50; sandwiches and salads $4.50–$8.50. MC, V. Mid-Dec to Easter daily 7am–3pm and 5–9pm. Easter to mid-Dec daily 7am–3pm.

Sanibel Cafe ★ *Value* AMERICAN   Seashells are the theme at Lynda and Ken Boyce's pleasant cafe, whose tables are museum-like glass cases containing delicate fossilized specimens from the Miocene and Pliocene epochs. Fresh-squeezed orange and grapefruit juice, Danish Havarti omelets, and homemade muffins and biscuits highlight the breakfast menu (eggs Benedict and fruit-filled waffles are served until closing). Lunch features specialty sandwiches; shrimp, Greek, and chicken-and-grape salads made with a very light, fat-free dressing; and a limited list of main courses such as grilled or blackened chicken breast. At dinner they add homemade meatloaf, crunchy grouper, and certified Angus steaks. Fatten up on Lynda's homemade red-raspberry jam, apple or cherry crisps, and terrific Key lime pie.

In the Tahitian Gardens Shops, 2007 Periwinkle Way. © **239/472-5323.** Call ahead for preferred seating. Main courses $7.50–$17; breakfast $3.50–$9; salads, sandwiches, and burgers $4.50–$13. MC, V. Daily 7am–9pm.

CAPTIVA ISLAND

Big deli sandwiches and picnic fare are available at the **Captiva Island Store,** Captiva Road at Andy Rosse Lane (© **239/472-2374**), and the gourmet-oriented **C. W.'s Market and Deli,** at the entrance to the South Seas Resort (© **239/472-5111**). The beach is a block from these stores.

The Bubble Room ★★ *Kids* STEAK/SEAFOOD   The gaudy bubble-gum pink, yellow, purple, and green exterior of this amusing restaurant is only a prelude to the 1930s, 1940s, and 1950s Hollywood motif inside. The dining rooms are adorned with a collection of puppets, statues of great movie stars, toy trains, thousands of movie stills, and antique jukeboxes that play big band–era tunes. The menu carries on the cinematic theme: prime ribs Weissmuller, Eddie Fisherman filet of fresh grouper, and Henny Young-One boneless breast of young chicken. Both adults and children are attracted to this expensive but fun establishment, where the portions are huge. For lighter appetites, the "Tiny Bubble" sampler includes a salad, a choice of appetizer, and a dessert.

15001 Captiva Rd. (at Andy Rosse Lane). © **239/472-5558**. Reservations not accepted, but call for preferred seating. Main courses $17–$30. AE, DC, DISC, MC, V. Daily 11:30am–2:30pm and 5–10pm. Closed Christmas.

Captiva Sunshine Cafe ★ ECLECTIC   This friendly, open-kitchen cafe has only 12 tables—five of them inside, seven on the shopping center's porch—but the food is worth the close quarters. Everything except the bread is prepared on the premises; all of it is available for takeout. Specialties are steak, fish, and shrimp from a wood-fired grill. The portions are as big as the prices are high here; in fact, appetizers such as black beans and rice can make a meal for lighter appetites. Various desserts are offered daily; the apple crisp is a winner.

In Captiva Village Square, Captiva Rd. at Laika Lane. © **239/472-6200**. Reservations recommended. Main courses $23–$33; burgers $10. AE, MC, V. Daily 11:30am–3:30pm and 5–9pm.

The Green Flash ★ SEAFOOD   You can't miss this restaurant, which sits at the infamous "curve" where Captiva Road takes a sharp turn to the north. You won't see the real "green flash" as the sun sets here, because this modern building looks eastward across Pine Island Sound, but it does make for a nice view at lunch. And seeing the full moon turn the sound into glistening silver is worth having at least an evening drink here. The overall quality of the cuisine is very good, and the prices are very reasonable for Captiva. Start with oysters Rockefeller or shrimp bisque. Both are house specialties, as is the garlicky grouper "café de Paris" and salmon with a dill-accented béarnaise sauce.

15183 Captiva Rd. © **239/472-3337**. Reservations recommended. Main courses $13–$22. AE, DC, DISC, MC, V. Daily 11:30am–3:30pm and 5:30–9:30pm (bar open 11:30am–9:30pm).

Mucky Duck ★ SEAFOOD/PUB FARE   A Captiva institution since 1976, this lively, British-style pub is the only place on either island here where you can dine right by the beach. If you don't get a real seat with this great view, the humorous staff will gladly roll a fake window over to appease you. The menu offers a selection of fresh seafood items, plus English fish and chips, steak-and-sausage pie, and a ploughman's lunch. There's a vegetarian platter. No smoking is allowed inside. You can't make a reservation, but you can order drinks, listen to live music (Mon–Sat), and bide your wait at beachside picnic tables out front (come early for sunset).

Andy Rosse Lane (on the gulf). © **239/472-3434**. Reservations not accepted. Lunch $5.50–$11; dinner main courses $13–$18.50. AE, DC, DISC, MC, V. Mon–Sat 11am–2:30pm and 5–9:30pm.

R. C. Otter's Island Eats ★★ (Value) AMERICAN Occupying an old clapboard-sided island cottage, this Key West–style cafe brings informality and good, inexpensive food to Captiva. In contrast to the island's 15 or so formal haute-cuisine restaurants, you can dine here in your bare feet and not spend a fortune for an excellent breakfast, snack, lunch, or full meal. The tables are covered with wrapping paper, and rolls of paper towels substitute for napkins. The choice seats are under ceiling fans on the front porch or beneath umbrellas on the brick patio. In hot weather you can opt for the air-conditioned dining room, whose walls are adorned with the works of local artists. The wide-ranging menu includes salads, hot dogs, burgers, sandwiches, stir-fries, meatloaf, country-fried steak, broiled fish, and soft-shell crabs, plus delicious nightly specials. The island's best breakfasts are equally varied, from bacon and eggs to a seafood quesadilla. Musicians perform out in the yard every day, and you could find yourself dancing on the front porch.

11506 Andy Rosse Lane. ℂ **239/395-1142**. Reservations not accepted, but call for preferred seating. Main courses $10–$20; breakfast $6–$12; salads, sandwiches, burgers $6–$12. AE, DISC, MC, V. Daily 7:30am–10pm (breakfast to 11:30am).

SANIBEL & CAPTIVA ISLANDS AFTER DARK

You won't find glitzy nightclubs on these family-oriented islands, but night owls do have some fun places to roost at the resorts and restaurants mentioned above. Here's a brief recap:

ON SANIBEL The Sundial Beach Resort's **Beaches Bar & Grill,** 1451 Middle Gulf Dr. (ℂ **239/472-4151**), features entertainers during dinner, then live bands for dancing from 9pm on. The **Patio Lounge,** in the Jacaranda, 1223 Periwinkle Way (ℂ **239/472-1771**), attracts an affluent crowd of middle-agers and seniors to its live music every evening. **McT's Tavern,** 1523 Periwinkle Way (ℂ **239/472-3161**), has darts, video games, and a large-screen TV for sports fans. The **Sanibel Grill,** 703 Tarpon Bay Rd. (ℂ **239/472-4453**), and the two **Lazy Flamingo** branches (see "Where to Dine," above) are other popular sports bars.

The Pirate Players, a group of professional actors, perform Broadway dramas and comedies from November to April, in Sanibel's state-of-the-art, 150-seat **J. Howard Wood Theatre,** 2200 Periwinkle Way (ℂ **239/472-0006;** www.thewoodtheatre.com). The **Old Schoolhouse Theater,** 1905 Periwinkle Way (ℂ **239/472-6862;** www.oldschoolhousetheater.com), complements its neighbor by offering Broadway musicals and revues from December to April. Call for the current schedule and prices.

ON CAPTIVA Local songwriters perform their works nightly at **R. C. Otter's Island Eats,** 11500 Andy Rosse Lane (ℂ **239/395-1142**). The **Crow's Nest Lounge,** in the 'Tween Waters Inn, on Captiva Road (ℂ **239/472-5161**), is Captiva's top nightspot for dancing. **Chadwick's Lounge,** at the entrance to the South Seas Resort (ℂ **239/472-5111**), has a large dance floor and music from 9pm on.

NEARBY ISLAND HOPPING

Sanibel and Captiva are jumping-off points for island-hopping boat trips to barrier islands and keys teeming with ancient legends and Robinson Crusoe–style beaches. You don't have to get completely lost out there, however, because several islets have comfortable inns and restaurants. The trip across shallow Pine Island Sound is itself a sightseeing adventure, with playful dolphins surfing on the boats' wakes and a variety of cormorants, egrets, frigate birds, and (in winter) rare white pelicans flying above or lounging on sandbars between meals.

Captiva Cruises (© 239/472-5300; www.captivacruises.com) has daily trips from the South Seas Resort on Captiva. One vessel goes daily to Cabbage Key, departing at 10:30am and returning at 3:30pm. It stops at Useppa Island going and coming Tuesday through Sunday. During the winter months, another goes to Boca Grande by way of Cayo Costa State Park, departing Tuesday through Saturday at 10:30am and returning at 4pm. These day trips cost $27.50 per adult, $15 for children to Cabbage Key or Useppa; $35 for adults, $17.50 for children to Boca Grande or Cayo Costa. Reservations are required.

From Pine Island off Fort Myers, you can take **Tropic Star Cruises'** daily ferry service (© **239/283-0015;** www.tropicstarcruises.com) to Cayo Costa (see "Cruises" in section 1).

CABBAGE KEY ★★

You never know who's going to get off a boat at 100-acre Cabbage Key and walk unannounced into the funky **Cabbage Key Inn** ★★, a rustic house built in 1938 by the son and daughter-in-law of mystery novelist Mary Roberts Rinehart. Ernest Hemingway liked to hang out here in the early days, and novelist John D. MacDonald was a frequent guest 30 years later. Today, you could find yourself rubbing elbows at the bar with the likes of Walter Cronkite, Ted Koppel, Sean Connery, or Julia Roberts. Singer and avid yachtie Jimmy Buffett likes Cabbage Key so much that it inspired his hit song "Cheeseburger in Paradise."

A path leads from the tiny marina across a lawn dotted with coconut palms to this white clapboard house that sits atop an ancient Calusa shell mound. Guests dine in the comfort of two screened porches and seek libations in the Rineharts' library-turned-bar, its pine-paneled walls now plastered with dollar bills left by visitors. The straight-back chairs and painted wooden tables show their age, but that's part of Cabbage Key's laid-back, don't-give-a-hoot charm.

In addition to the famous thick, juicy cheeseburgers so loved by Jimmy Buffett, the house specialties are fresh broiled fish and shrimp steamed in beer. Lunches range from $5 to $10; main courses at dinner, $15 to $25.

Most visitors come out here for the day, but if you want to stay overnight, the Cabbage Key Inn has six rooms and six cottages. The more expensive cottages, four of which have kitchens, are preferable to the rooms. Although the units have private bathrooms and air conditioners, they are very basic by today's standards, and some of their original 1920s furnishings have seen better days. Service for overnight guests can leave a lot to be desired, and there's no place on the islet to buy snacks or sundries. If you do decide to rough it, room rates are $89 single or double for rooms, $145 to $239 for cottages. For information or reservations, contact Cabbage Key Inn, P.O. Box 200, Pineland, FL 33945 (© **239/ 283-2278;** fax 239/283-1384; www.cabbage-key.com).

Captiva Cruises (© **239/472-5300;** www.captivacruises.com) goes to Cabbage Key daily from Captiva Island, charging $27.50 per adult, $15 for children (reservations are required). You can get here from Pine Island via **Tropic Star Cruises** (© **239/283-0015;** www.tropicstarcruises.com), which depart from Knight's Landing marina daily (see "Cruises" in section 1). Fares are $25 adults, $15 for children. Call for departure times. You can also get here from Pine Island with **Island Charters** (© **800/340-3321** or 239/283-1113).

CAYO COSTA ★★★

You can't get any more deserted than at **Cayo Costa State Park** ★★★ (pronounced *Kay*-oh *Cos*-tah), which occupies a 2,132-acre, completely unspoiled barrier island with miles of white-sand beaches, pine forests, mangrove swamps,

Fishing with the Bushes

Former President George Bush, present President George W. Bush, Florida Governor Jeb Bush—indeed, the entire Bush clan—like to retreat to **Boca Grande** ★★ for a little rest and relaxation every now and then. And well they should, for this charming village on Gasparilla Island is a head-of-state's kind of place. The du Ponts, the Astors, the Morgans, the Vanderbilts, and other moneyed folk started coming here in the 1920s and still turn the island into a Florida version of Nantucket during their winter "social season." In addition to the warm weather, the lure was then, and still is, some of the world's best tarpon fishing. Descendants of the watermen who were here first still guide the rich and famous. They live in modest homes on streets named Dam-If-I-Know, Dam-If-I-Care, and Dam-If-I-Will. You can see their backyards full of boats and fishnets, but high hedges hide the manicured "beachfronter" mansions over by the gulf.

You can explore the little village in a few hours on foot or on a bike rented from **Island Bike 'n' Beach,** 333 Park Ave. (✆ **941/964-0711**). The pink-brick **Railroad Depot,** at the corner of Park Avenue and 4th Street, has been restored to the turn-of-the-20th-century grandeur it enjoyed when the rich arrived by train. It now houses a cluster of upscale boutiques and the **Loose Caboose** restaurant and ice-cream parlor (✆ **941/964-0440**), where movie stars have been seen satiating their sweet teeth. **Banyan Street** (actually 2nd St.) is canopied with tangled banyan trees and is one of the prettiest places for a stroll. The **Johann Fust Community Library,** at Gasparilla Road and 10th Street (✆ **941/964-2488**), contains the extraordinary **Du Pont Shell Collection,** gathered by Henry Francis du Pont during nearly 50 years of combing the island's beaches. At the island's south end, **Boca Grande Lighthouse Museum and Visitor's Center** (✆ **941/964-0060**) occupies the wood-frame lighthouse that began marking the pass into Charlotte Harbor in 1890. Exhibits explain the island's history, its tarpon fishing, and its wildlife and seashells. The white-sand beaches of **Gasparilla Island State Recreation Area** (✆ **941/964-0375;** www.floridastateparks.org/district4/gasparillaisland) trim the lighthouse.

Captiva Cruises (✆ **239/472-5300**) has daily trips here during the winter season (see "Nearby Island Hopping, above"). The fare is $35 for adults, $17.50 for children, and reservations are required. *Tropic Star* cruises (✆ **239/283-0015;** www.tropicstarcruises.com) come here daily from Pine Island off Fort Myers (see "Cruises" in section 1, earlier in this chapter). Fares are $25 for adults and $15 for children. Call for departure times.

For more information, contact the **Boca Grande Area Chamber of Commerce,** 5800 Gasparilla Rd. (P.O. Box 704), Boca Grande, FL 33921 (✆ **941/964-0568;** fax 239/964-0620; www.bocagrandechamber.com).

oak-palm hammocks, and grasslands. Other than natural wildlife, the only permanent residents here are park rangers.

Day-trippers can bring their own supplies and use a picnic area with pavilions. A free tram carries visitors from the sound-side dock to the gulf beach. The state maintains 12 very basic cabins and a primitive campground on the northern end of the island near Johnson Shoals, where the shelling is spectacular. Cabins cost $20 a day, and campsites are $13 a day all year. For camping or cabin reservations call © **800/326-3521** or go to www.reserveamerica.com. There's running water on the island but no electricity.

The park is open daily from 8am to sundown. There's a $1-per-person honor-system admission fee for day visitors. You can rent single-seat kayaks for $35 a day, $45 a day for two-seaters; for reservations, call the *Tropic Star* on Pine Island (© **239/283-0015;** www.tropicstarcruises.com).

For more information contact **Cayo Costa State Park,** P.O. Box 1150, Boca Grande, FL 33921 (© **941/964-0375;** www.floridastateparks.org/district4/cayocosta). Office hours are Monday through Friday from 8am to 5pm.

UPPER (NORTH) CAPTIVA

Cut off by a pass from Captiva, its northern barrier-island sibling is occupied by the upscale resort of **North Captiva Island Club,** P.O. Box 1000, Pineland, FL 33945 (© **800/576-7343** or 239/395-1001; fax 239/472-5836; www.north captiva.com). Despite the development, however, about 750 of the island's 1,000 acres are included in a state preserve. The club rents accommodations ranging from efficiencies to luxury homes. There's scheduled water-taxi service from **Jensen's Twin Palms Marina** on Captiva (© **239/472-5800**), or you can get here from Matson Marine on Pine Island with **Island Charters** (© **800/340-3321** or 239/283-1113). Both charge $25 per person round-trip.

USEPPA ISLAND

Useppa was a refuge of President Theodore Roosevelt and his tarpon-loving industrialist friends at the turn of the 20th century. New York advertising magnate Barron G. Collier bought the island in 1906 and built a lovely wooden home overlooking Pine Island Sound. His mansion is now the **Collier Inn,** where day-trippers and overnight guests can partake of lunches and seafood dinners in a country-club ambience. They can also visit the **Useppa Museum,** which explains the island's history and displays 4,000-year-old Calusa artifacts. Admission is by $2 donation.

The Collier Inn is the centerpiece of the **Useppa Island Club,** an exclusive development with more than 100 luxury homes, all in the clapboard-sided, tin-roofed style of Old Florida. For information, rates (all on the modified American plan), and reservations, contact **Collier Inn & Cottages,** P.O. Box 640, Bokeelia, FL 33922 (© **888/735-6335** or 239/283-1061; fax 239/283-0290; www.useppa.com).

4 Naples ✦✦✦

42 miles (68km) S of Fort Myers, 106 miles (171km) W of Miami, 185 miles (298km) S of Tampa

Because its wealthy residents are accustomed to the very best, Naples is easily Southwest Florida's most sophisticated city. Indeed, its boutiques and galleries are at least on a par with those in Palm Beach or Beverly Hills. And yet Naples has an easygoing friendliness to everyone who comes to enjoy its long, magnificent beach.

Naples was born in 1886, when a group of 12 Kentuckians and Ohioans bought 8,700 acres fronted by a gorgeous beach, laid out a town, and started selling lots. They built a pier and the 16-room Naples Hotel, whose first guest was President Grover Cleveland's sister Rose. She and other notables soon built a line of beach homes known as "Millionaires' Row." Today that area is known as Olde Naples and is carefully protected by its modern residents. Despite a recent building boom that has expanded the city to the north and east, the original ·ettlement still retains the air of that time a century ago.

Although high-rise buildings now line the beaches north of the old town, the newer sections of Naples still have their charm, thanks to Ohio manufacturer Henry B. Watkins Sr. In 1946, Watkins and his partners bought the old hotel and all the town's undeveloped land and laid out the Naples Plan, which created the very wealthy but environmentally conscious city you see today.

About 4 miles (6.25km) north of Olde Naples, Vanderbilt Beach has a more traditional beach-resort character than the historic district. Lined with a mix of two-story, 1960s-style motels and high-rise hotels and condominiums, the main beach here sits like an island of development between two preserved areas: Delnor-Wiggins Pass State Park to the north, and a county reserve fronting the expensive Pelican Bay golf-course community to the south.

ESSENTIALS

GETTING THERE   Most visitors arrive at the **Southwest Florida International Airport,** 35 miles (56km) north of Naples in Fort Myers (see "Getting There," under "Essentials," in section 1). **Naples Municipal Airport,** on North Road off Airport-Pulling Road (© 239/643-6875; www.flynaples.com), is served by the commuter arms of **American** (© 800/433-7300) and **United/US Airways** (© 800/428-4322), which means you'll have to change planes in Miami, Tampa, or Orlando. Taxis await all flights outside the small terminal building. **Avis** (© 800/331-1212), **Budget** (© 800/527-0700), **Hertz** (© 800/654-3131), and **National** (© 800/CAR-RENT) have booths at the airport. **Enterprise** (© 800/325-8007) is in town.

VISITOR INFORMATION   The most comprehensive source of information is the **Naples Area Chamber of Commerce,** which maintains a visitor center at 895 5th Ave. S. (at U.S. 41), Naples, FL 34102 (© **239/262-6141;** fax 239/435-9910; www.napleschamber.org). The center has a host of free information and phones for making hotel reservations, and it sells a detailed street map for $2. By mail, it will send you a free list of accommodations and other basic information, or you can order a complete Naples vacation packet for $8 ($12 to Canada and other countries) and the street map for $5. The visitor center is open Monday through Saturday from 9am to 5pm.

GETTING AROUND   The **Naples Trolley** (© **239/262-7300;** www.naplestrolleytours.com) clangs around 25 stops between the Naples Trolley General Store and Welcome Center, 1010 6th Ave. S. at 10th Street South (2 blocks west of Tin City in Olde Naples), and Vanderbilt Beach Monday through Saturday from 8:30am to 5:15pm and Sunday from 10:15am to 5:15pm. Daily fares are $16 for adults, $7 for children 4 to 12, free for children under 4, with free reboarding. Schedules are available in brochure racks in the lobbies of most hotels and motels. The drivers provide narration, so the entire loop makes a good 2-hour sightseeing tour.

For taxis, call **Yellow Cab** (© **239/262-1312**), **Checker Cab** (© **239/455-5555**), **Maxi Taxi** (© **239/262-8977**), or **Naples Taxi** (© **239/775-0505**).

Naples

ACCOMMODATIONS ■
Hotel Escalante **10**
Inn by the Sea **15**
Lighthouse Inn Motel **1**
Naples Beach Hotel &
  Golf Club **9**
Park Shore Resort **5**
The Registry Resort **2**
The Ritz-Carlton Golf Resort,
  Naples **1**
The Ritz-Carlton, Naples **1**
Trianon Old Naples **13**
Vanderbilt Inn Naples **1**

ATTRACTIONS ●
Caribbean Gardens **6**
Delnor-Wiggins Pass
  State Park **1**
The Conservancy's Naples
  Nature Center **7**
Naples Museum of Art **3**
Old Marine Marketplace at
  Tin City **12**
Teddy Bear Museum **4**
Vanderbilt Beach **1**

DINING ◆
Bistro 821 **11**
Chop's City Grill **11**
The Dock at Crayton Cove **16**
First Watch **8**
Old Naples Pub **15**
Silver Spoon American Cafe **3**
Tommy Bahama's Tropical
  Cafe **15**
Yabba Island Grill **11**
Zoë's **11**

Clam Bay
Seagate Dr.
Pine Ridge Rd.
West Blvd
Granada Blvd.
Neapolitan Wy.
Blvd. N.
Crayton Rd.
Park
Venetian Bay
Gulf Shore
Solano Rd.
9th St. N.
Anchor Rode Dr.
Ohio Dr.
Outer Doctors Bay
Crayton
Harbour Dr.
Wedge Dr.
Mooring Line Dr.
Spring Line Dr.
Golden Gate
Pkwy
Banyan Blvd.
Lowdermilk Park & Public Beach
7th Ave. N.
GULF OF MEXICO
OLDE NAPLES
9th St. St.
Central Ave.
3rd St.
5th Ave. S.
8th Ave. S.
Broad Ave. S.
Naples Pier
Ave. S.
15th Ave. S.
18th Ave. S.
Naples Bay

Goodlette Frank Rd. N.
Tamiami Trail N.
Gulf Shore Blvd. N.
County Rd.
Airport Rd.
Naples Municipal Airport
Terminal
North Rd.
Davis Blvd.

FLORIDA
Naples ●

⊠ Post Office
⚑ Golf Course
Ⓟ Police Station

HITTING THE BEACH

Unlike many Florida cities where you have to drive over to a barrier island to reach the beach, this city's beach is right in Olde Naples. And rather than being fronted by tall condominium buildings, here, the mansions along Millionaires' Row form the backdrop. Access to the gorgeous white sand is at the gulf end of each avenue, although parking in the neighborhood can be precious. Try the metered lots on 12th Avenue South near the **Naples Pier,** the town's most popular beaching spot (see "Exploring the Town," below), where there are also restrooms and a food concession. Families gather on the beach north of the pier, while local teens congregate on the south side.

Also popular with families, lovely **Lowdermilk Park,** on Millionaires' Row at Gulf Shore Boulevard and North Banyan Boulevard, has a pavilion, restrooms, showers, a refreshment counter, professional-quality volleyball courts (the area's best players practice here), a duck pond, and picnic tables. There's metered parking, so bring quarters. A few blocks farther north is another metered parking lot with beach access beside the Naples Beach Hotel & Golf Resort, 851 Gulf Shore Blvd. N., at Golf Drive.

Nature lovers head to the Pelican Bay development north of the historic district and the popular **Clam Pass County Park** ★★ (℃ 239/353-0404). A free tram takes you along a 3,000-foot (900m) boardwalk winding through mangrove swamps and across a back bay to a beach of fine white sand. It's a strange sight, what with high-rise condominiums standing beyond the mangrove-bordered backwaters, but this actually is a miniature wilderness. Some 6 miles (10km) of canoe and kayak trails—with multitudes of birds and an occasional alligator—run from Clam Pass into the winding streams. The beach pavilion here has a bar, restrooms with foot showers only, picnic tables, and beach equipment rentals, including one- and two-person kayaks and 12-foot (3.75m) canoes. Entry is from a metered parking lot beside The Registry Resort at the end of Seagate Drive. There's a $3-per-vehicle parking fee. You can push, but not ride, bicycles on the boardwalk.

At Vanderbilt Beach, about 4 miles (6.25km) north of Olde Naples, the **Delnor-Wiggins Pass State Park** ★★★, at the west end of Bluebill Avenue–111th Avenue North (℃ 239/597-6196; www.floridastateparks.org/district4/delnor-wiggins), has been listed among America's top 10 stretches of sand. It has bathhouses, a boat ramp, and the area's best picnic facilities. A concessionaire sells hot dogs, sandwiches, and ice cream and rents beach chairs, umbrellas, kayaks, canoes, and snorkeling gear. Fish viewing is great over a small reef under 12 feet (3.75m) of water about 50 yards offshore. Fishing from the beach is excellent here, too. Rangers provide nature tours throughout the year, with the most interesting during the Loggerhead turtle nesting season from June to October (call or check the website for the schedule).

The area is open daily from 8am to sunset. Admission is $2 per vehicle with one occupant, $4 for vehicles with two to eight occupants, and $1 for pedestrians and bikers. To get here from Olde Naples, go north on U.S. 41 about 4 miles (6.25km) and take a left on 111th Avenue, which turns into Bluebill Avenue before reaching the beach. Note that 111th Avenue is known as Immokalee Road east of U.S. 41.

OTHER OUTDOOR ACTIVITIES

BOATING   Powerboat and WaveRunner rentals are available from **Naples Watersports,** at the Old Naples Seaport, 10th Avenue South at 10th Street South in Olde Naples (℃ 239/435-9595); from **Club Nautico,** at the Boat

Haven Marina, 1484 E. Tamiami Trail (© **239/774-0100**), on the east bank of the Gordon River behind Kelly's Fish House; and from **Port-O-Call Marina,** also behind Kelly's Fish House (© **239/774-0479**).

CRUISES   The Gordon River and Naples Bay from the U.S. 41 bridge on 5th Avenue South to the gulf are prime territory for sightseeing, dolphin-watching, and sunset cruises. The double-decked *Double Sunshine* (© **239/263-4949;** www.ladybrett.com) sallies forth onto the river and bay daily from Tin City, where it has a ticket office. The 1½-hour cruises usually leave at 10am, noon, 2pm, and an hour before sunset. They cost $23 for adults, $11.50 for children under 12.

The *Sweet Liberty* (© **239/793-3525;** www.sweetliberty.com), a 53-foot (85km) sailing catamaran, makes 3-hour morning shelling cruises to Keewaydin Island. The vessel then spends the afternoon on 2-hour sightseeing cruises (you'll usually see dolphins playing in the river on this one) and 2-hour sunset cruises on Naples Bay before docking at Boat Haven Marina on the east side of the Gordon River Bridge. Shelling cruises cost $35 for adults, $15 for children; sightseeing and sunset cruises cost $25 for adults, $15 for children.

For a good deal more luxury, the 83-foot (25m) *Naples Princess* (© **800/ 728-2970** or 239/649-2275; www.naplesprincesscruises.com) has narrated breakfast, lunch, and sunset dinner cruises from Port-O-Call Marina, on the eastern shore of the Gordon River. With extensive buffets, the sightseeing, lunch, sunset, and dinner cruises are good values at $23, $28, $28.50, and $42 per person, respectively. Call for schedules and reservations.

FISHING   The locals like to fish from the **Naples Pier** (see "Exploring the Town," below). The pier has tables on which to clean your catch, but watch out for the ever-present pelicans, which are master thieves. You can buy tackle and bait from the local marinas (see "Boating," above). The pier is open around the clock, and admission is free. No fishing license is required.

The least expensive way for singles, couples, and small families to fish without paying for an entire boat is on the 45-foot (14m) *Lady Brett* (© **239/ 263-4949;** www.ladybrett.com), which makes two daily trips from Tin City for $50 for adults, $45 for kids under 12. Rod, reel, bait, and fishing license are included, but bring your own drinks and lunch. Its sister boat, the *Captain Paul,* goes on half-day backcountry fishing trips, departing daily at 9am. These cost $45 for adults, $40 for children.

A number of charter boats are based at the marinas mentioned under "Boating," above; call or visit them for booking information and prices.

GOLF   Naples has an extraordinary number of fine golf courses for a city its size. Most are out in the suburbs, but not the flat but challenging 18 holes at the **Naples Beach Hotel & Golf Club** 🏌🏌 (see "Where to Stay," below), which are right in the middle of town. Nonguests can play here, but call ahead for a tee time.

Two of the best-known courses are **Lely Flamingo Island Club** 🏌🏌 and the **Lely Mustang Golf Club,** both on U.S. 41 between Naples and Marco Island (© **800/388-GOLF** or 239/793-2223). Robert Trent Jones Sr. designed the Lely Flamingo course, and its hourglass fairways and fingerlike bunkers present many challenges. Designed by Lee Trevino, the Lely Mustang course is more forgiving but still fun. Former PGA Tour player Paul Trittler has his golf school at these courses. You'll pay a price here in winter, when 18-hole fees are about $135 at Lely Flamingo and $150 at Lely Mustang, including cart and range balls, but they drop progressively after Easter to about $40 and $50, respectively, in the muggy summer months.

Boyne South, on U.S. 41 between Fla. 931 and Fla. 92 (© **239/732-5108**), is another winner, with lots of wildlife inhabiting its many lakes (a 16-foot [5m] alligator reportedly resides near the 17th hole). There are a driving range, practice facility, and restaurant; instruction is available. Wintertime fees are about $70, but in the off-season they drop to $45 or less. Tee times are taken up to 4 days in advance.

Another local favorite is the player-friendly **Hibiscus Golf Club,** a half mile east of U.S. 41 off Rattlesnake Hammock Road in East Naples (© **239/ 774-0088**). A pro shop and teaching professional are available. Fees are about $70 in winter, cart included, dropping to about $30 in summer.

At the intersection of Vanderbilt Beach and Airport-Pulling Roads, the Greg Norman-designed 27 championship holes at the **Tiburón Golf Club** ★★, 2620 Tiburón Dr. (© **877/WCI-PLAY** or 239/594-2040), play like a British Open course—but without the thick-thatch rough. Fees reach $200 in winter but drop as low as $70 in summer. The course is home to the **Rick Smith Golf Academy** (© **877/464-6531** or 239/593-1111) and The Ritz-Carlton Golf Resort, Naples (see "Where to Stay," later in this section).

The area also has several other courses worth playing, most described in the Naples–Fort Myers edition of the *Golfer's Guide* available at the chamber of commerce visitor center (or check the magazine's website at www.golfers guide.com). On the Web, www.naplesgolf.com is a good source of information about area courses.

SCUBA DIVING   Kevin Sweeney's **SCUBAdventures,** 971 Creech Rd., at Tamiami Trail (© **239/434-7477;** www.scubadventureslc.com), which also has a base on Marco Island (see section 5, later in this chapter), takes divers into the gulf, teaches diver-certification courses, and rents water-sports equipment.

TENNIS   In Olde Naples, the city's **Cambier Park Tennis Center** ★★, 755 8th Ave. S., at 9th Street South (© **239/434-4694;** www.cambiertennis.com), is one of the country's finest municipal facilities. In fact, it matches those found at many luxury resorts. Play on its 12 lighted clay courts costs $10 for 90 minutes. Book at the pro shop upstairs in the modern building, which has restrooms but no showers. The shop is open Monday through Friday from 8am to 9pm, Saturday and Sunday from 8am to 5pm.

WATER SPORTS   **Good Times Rental,** 1947 Davis Blvd. (© **239/ 775-7529**), rents WaveRunners, Windsurfers, skim boards, snorkeling gear, and other beach equipment. Hobie Cats and windsurfers can also be rented on the beach at the **Naples Beach Hotel & Golf Club,** 851 Gulf Shore Blvd. N. (© **239/261-2222**), and at **Clam Pass County Park,** at the end of Seagate Drive (© **239/353-0404**). See "Hitting the Beach," above, for more about Clam Pass.

EXPLORING THE TOWN
OLDE NAPLES ★★★

Its history may go back only to 1886, but the beach skirting **Olde Naples** still has the charm of that Victorian era. The heart of the district lies south of 5th Avenue South (that's where U.S. 41 takes a 45° turn). The town docks are on the bay side, the glorious **Naples Beach** along the gulf. Laid out on a grid, the tree-lined streets run between many houses, some dating from the town's beginning, and along Millionaires' Row between Gulf Shore Boulevard and the beach. With these gorgeous homes virtually hidden in the palms and casuarinas, Naples

Beach seems a century removed from the high-rise condominiums found farther north.

The **Naples Pier,** at the gulf end of 12th Avenue South, is a focal point of the neighborhood. Built in 1888 to let steamers land potential real-estate customers, the original 600-foot-long (180m), T-shaped structure was destroyed by hurricanes and damaged by fire. Local residents have rebuilt it because they like strolling its length to catch fantastic gulf sunsets—and to get a glimpse of Millionaires' Row from the gulf side. The pier is now a state historic site. It's open 24 hours a day, but parking in the nearby lots is restricted between 11pm and 7am.

Nearby, **Palm Cottage,** 137 12th Ave. S., between 1st Street and Gordon Drive (© **239/261-8164**), was built in 1885 by one of Naples's founders, *Louisville Courier-Journal* publisher Walter Haldeman, as a winter retreat for his chief editorial writer. After World War II, its socialite owners hosted many galas attended by Hollywood stars such as Hedy Lamarr, Gary Cooper, and Robert Montgomery. One of the few remaining Southwest Florida houses built of tabby mortar (made by burning shells), Palm Cottage today is the home of the Naples Historical Society, which maintains it as a museum filled with authentic furniture, paintings, photographs, and other memorabilia. Tours are given during winter, Monday through Friday from 1 to 3:30pm. Adult admission is $5, free for children.

Near the Gordon River Bridge on 5th Avenue South, the old corrugated waterfront warehouses are now a shopping-and-dining complex known as the **Old Marine Marketplace at Tin City,** which tourists throng to and local residents assiduously avoid during the winter months.

MUSEUMS & ZOOS

Caribbean Gardens ⭐ *Kids*   A family favorite once headed by the late Colonel Larry Tetzlaff, a noted animal collector and wildlife filmmaker, this 52-acre, environmentally conscious zoo features a variety of animals and birds, including a fascinating community of monkeys living free on their own islands. You can see them on a boat safari through the spectacular tropical gardens. Kids especially will be captivated by "Safari Canyon," in which zookeepers display animals while wildlife programming appears on TV screens mounted in the rocks of a simulated canyon. Everyone gets to handle some of the animals and reptiles at the "Scales & Tails" area. The presentations are set up to keep you and the kids busy throughout the full day it will take to ingest it all. A Subway branch sells sandwiches, and there are picnic facilities on the premises.

1590 Goodlette-Frank Rd. (at Fleischmann Blvd.). © **239/262-5409.** www.caribbeangardens.com. Admission $14.95 adults, $9.95 children 4–15, free for children 3 and under. Daily 9:30am–4:30pm. Closed Easter, Thanksgiving, Christmas.

Naples Museum of Art   If anything's a sign of the emerging sophistication of a sleepy seaside town, it's the appearance of this three story, 30,000-square-foot art museum, attached to the Naples Philharmonic Center for the Arts. The first full-scale art museum in Southwest Florida, the Naples Museum of Art features an impressive 15 different galleries, highlighting paintings, sculptures, and drawings, with major permanent collections concentrating on both the American Modern and Ancient Chinese genres. Touring shows and exhibitions bring a welcome element of eclecticism to the museum, whose very structure, including a 90-foot (27m) by 45-foot (14m) glass dome and 14-foot (4.25m) entrance gates, is a dramatic work of art on its own. Tuesdays through Saturdays October through May, there are free guided tours at 11am and 2pm.

5833 Pelican Bay Blvd. (at West Blvd.). ℂ **941/597-1900**. www.thephil.org. Admission $6 adults, $3 students. Tues–Sat 10am–4pm; Sun noon–4pm. Closed Mondays, Memorial Day, July 4, Thanksgiving Day, Christmas Eve, Christmas Day, New Year's Eve, New Year's Day, and closed for the season mid-July to Sept.

Teddy Bear Museum *Kids* Another family favorite, this entertaining museum contains 3,000-plus examples of stuffed bears from around the world. They're displayed descending from the rafters in hot-air balloons, attending board meetings, sipping afternoon tea, and even doing bear things like hibernating.

2511 Pine Ridge Rd. (at Airport-Pulling Rd.). ℂ **800/365-2327** or 239/598-2711. www.teddymuseum.com. Admission $6 adults, $4 seniors, $2 children 4–12, free for children under 4. Tues–Sat 10am–5pm. Closed New Year's Day, July 4, Thanksgiving, Christmas.

A NATURE PRESERVE

You can experience Southwest Florida's abundant natural life without leaving town at **The Conservancy's Naples Nature Center** ✦, 14th Avenue North, east of Goodlette-Frank Road (ℂ **239/262-0304;** www.conservancy.org), one of two preserves operated by The Conservancy of Southwest Florida (see the Briggs Nature Center on p. 432. There are nature trails and an aviary with bald eagles and other birds. You can take 45-minute guided boat rides on the hour, between 9am and 3pm, weather permitting. The naturalist guides will explain the vegetation along the upper reaches of the Gordon River, and you may see some wildlife—including an occasional monkey escapee from Caribbean Gardens next door (see "Museums & Zoos," above). You can also rent canoes and kayaks and see the area by yourself. An excellent nature store carries gift items. Admission fees of $7.50 for adults and $2 for children 3 to 12 (free for children under 3) include the boat rides. Canoes and kayaks cost $13 for 2 hours, $5 for each additional hour. The center is open year-round Monday through Saturday from 9am to 4:30pm. Closed July 4, Labor Day, Thanksgiving, Christmas Eve, and Christmas Day.

SHOPPING

Two blocks of **3rd Street South** ✦✦, at Broad Avenue, is the Rodeo Drive of Naples. This glitzy collection of jewelers, clothiers, and art galleries may be too rich for many wallets, but the window shopping here is unmatched. Be sure to pick up a free brochure from the chamber of commerce visitor center (see "Essentials," earlier in this chapter); it lists the merchants and has a map of the area.

Nearby, the **5th Avenue South** ✦ shopping area, between 3rd and 9th Streets South, has seen a renaissance in recent years and is now Naples's hottest dining spot. The avenue is longer and a bit less chic than 3rd Street South, with stockbrokerages and real-estate offices thrown into the mix of boutiques and antiques dealers.

Also in Olde Naples, the **Old Marine Marketplace at Tin City,** 1200 5th Ave. S., at the Gordon River (ℂ **239/262-4200**), has 50 boutiques selling everything from souvenirs to avant-garde resort wear and imported statuary. There are more boutiques in the **Dockside Boardwalk,** a half block west on 6th Avenue South.

Even the malls in Naples have their charms. The **Village at Venetian Bay,** 4200 Gulf Shore Blvd., at Park Shore Drive (ℂ **239/261-0030**), evokes images of its Italian namesake, with 50 canal-side shops featuring high-fashion men's and women's clothiers and fine-art galleries. Ornate Mediterranean architecture and a tropical waterfall highlight the open-air **Waterside Shops at Pelican Bay,**

Seagate Drive at North Tamiami Trail (U.S. 41; © **239/598-1605**), where the anchor stores are Saks Fifth Avenue and Jacobson's. There's a huge Barnes & Noble bookstore across Seagate Drive.

Discount shoppers can head to **Prime Outlets Naples,** on Fla. 951 about a mile south of U.S. 41 on the way to Marco Island (© **888/545-7196** or 239/775-8083; www.primeoutlets.com). The 43 shops are open from 10am to 8pm Monday through Saturday, 11am to 6pm Sunday.

WHERE TO STAY

Branches of most chain hotels sit along U.S. 41, but these tend to be of higher quality and better value than their counterparts elsewhere in Southwest Florida. The **Hilton Naples & Towers,** 5111 Tamiami Trail N. (© **800/HILTONS** or 239/430-4900; fax 239/430-4901; www.naples.hilton.com), north of Olde Naples near the Waterside Shops at Pelican Bay, is luxurious, but since it's not on the beach, it attracts mainly business travelers and groups. It also contains a Don Shula's Steak House.

One of the most reasonably priced of the town's many condominium complexes, **Park Shore Resort,** 600 Neapolitan Way, Naples, FL 34103 (© **800/548-2077** or 239/263-2222; fax 239/263-0946; www.parkshorefl.com), has 156 attractive one- and two-bedroom condominiums surrounding an artificial lagoon with waterfalls cascading on its own island. Guests can walk across a bridge to the artificial island, where they can swim in the heated pool, barbecue on gas grills, or order a meal from the restaurant or a drink from the bar. There's once-a-day complimentary transport to the beach. The condominiums range from $153 to $239 in winter but drop to $89 to $119 off-season.

One of the biggest condominium-rental agents here is **Bluebill Properties,** 26201 Hickory Blvd., Bonita Springs, FL 33923 (© **800/237-2010** or 239/992-6620; www.naplesvacation.com).

I have organized the accommodations below geographically: in Olde Naples and north of the historic district, including Vanderbilt Beach.

IN OLDE NAPLES
Very Expensive
Hotel Escalante ★★   On the western end of the 5th Avenue shopping district and 2 blocks from the beach, this boutique hotel is perfect for singles or couples who want convenience, no crowds, and a bit of pampering. The Escalante seems smaller and more intimate than most properties with 65 units. The large rooms and spacious one-bedroom suites are in eight one- and two-story buildings spread out over most of a city block (this was an apartment hotel until being gutted and rebuilt in 2000). The cottagelike suites have private patios opening to lush courtyards with walkways of old brick from Chicago, fountains from France, and 300 species of tropical plants from around the world. All units are luxuriously appointed, and the bathrooms have two hand basins, ample vanity space, and big showerheads (the majority have walk-in showers as opposed to tubs). Special services include lunch served on the beach, a day spa with facials and massage, an evening wine reception, and an honor bar and complimentary cookies in the library.

290 5th Ave. S., Naples, FL 34102. © 877/GULF-INN or 239/659-3466. Fax 239/262-8748. www.hotel escalante.com. 65 units. Winter $250–$400; off-season $165–$300. Rates include continental breakfast and evening wine reception. AE, DC, DISC, MC, V. **Amenities:** Bar; heated outdoor pool; exercise room; day spa; Jacuzzi; sauna; 24-hr. room service; massage; laundry service. *In room:* A/C, TV, dataport, minibar, fridge, coffeemaker, hair dryer, iron.

Naples Beach Hotel & Golf Club ★★★ *Kids* In contrast to The Ritz-Carlton, Naples, and The Registry Resort (see below), which could be anywhere, this charming resort definitely belongs in Olde Naples. In fact, the beachside setting on Millionaires' Row couldn't be better for carrying on the friendly and relaxed Old Florida ambience installed by Henry B. Watkins a half century ago and carried on by his family today. This is also Southwest Florida's only resort with its own 18-hole golf course, tennis center, and full-service spa right on the premises. The spa, golf club, and a restaurant are in a stunning new building across Gulf Shore Boulevard from reception. Since the hotel predates the city's strict historic-district zoning laws, it also has Olde Naples's only restaurants and bar directly on the beach. Of these, the **Sunset Beach Bar** is one of the region's most famous beachside open-air bars and is always crammed as the sun sets over the gulf and when live bands perform on Sunday afternoons during the winter season. Facing the gulf, the semicircular Everglades Dining Room emphasizes traditional Florida cuisine, offers a reasonably priced breakfast buffet to guests and nonguests alike, and has live entertainment and dancing Tuesday through Saturday night in winter. Complimentary afternoon tea is served in the lobby lounge, and guests can hang shopping lists on their doorknobs at night for the staff to deliver breakfast goodies from the Seminole Store, which sells inexpensive pastries, pizzas, salads, and sandwiches.

Rooms and suites are in several buildings spread over lush gardens hung with more than 5,000 orchids. The least expensive are in the Florida Wing, a two-story relic from 1948, whose recently updated rooms and suites open to a long, railing-enclosed porch with views across a manicured lawn to the swimming pool by the gulf. Units in the Tower are over the main dining room and directly across the boulevard from the golf course, tennis center, and spa. The Watkins Wing houses the most spacious suites here. Rooms in the Penthouse Wing, removed from the action at the north end of the property, directly face the beach and are the best choice for couples, especially during holidays and the summer, when many families stay here (the clientele is mostly couples at other times).

851 Gulf Shore Blvd., Naples, FL 33940. ℃ 800/237-7600 or 239/261-2222. Fax 239/261-7380. www.naplesbeachhotel.com. 318 units. Winter $225–$385 double; $315–$525 suite. Off-season $175–$225 double; $250–$310 suite. Packages available. AE, DC, DISC, MC, V. **Amenities:** 4 restaurants (all American); 2 bars; heated Olympic-size outdoor pool; 18-hole golf course; 6 tennis courts; full-service spa; water-sports equipment rental; bike rental, children's programs; game room; concierge; activities desk; limited room service; salon; massage; babysitting; laundry service. *In room:* A/C, TV, dataport, hair dryer, iron.

Expensive

Trianon Old Naples ★ Constructed in 1998 in a quiet residential neighborhood, this elegant Mediterranean-style building, with a classical European interior, offers convenience and comfort without a lot of frills. The spacious rooms are equipped with Ritz-Carlton–quality furniture, including mahogany armoires, chairs, and writing desks. All have seating areas and extra-large bathrooms. Some units have balconies large enough for chairs, but others are for standing only. There's no restaurant here, but continental breakfast is served on silver in a refined lounge, where coffee and tea are available all day, and the staff will arrange for meals to be delivered from local restaurants. Champagne and port are served at a wine bar in the evenings.

955 7th Ave. S., Naples, FL 34102. ℃ 877/482-5228 or 239/437-9600. Fax 239/261-0025. www. trianon.com. 58 units. Winter $160–$280 double; off-season $85–$190 double. Rates include continental breakfast. AE, DC, DISC, MC, V. **Amenities:** Heated outdoor pool; laundry service. *In room:* A/C, TV, dataport, fridge (in some units), coffeemaker, hair dryer, iron.

Moderate

Inn by the Sea ☆   Listed in the National Register of Historic Places, this bed-and-breakfast, 2 blocks from the beach in the heart of Olde Naples, was built in 1937 as a boardinghouse by Alice Bowling, one of Naples's first schoolteachers and a grocer and entrepreneur to boot. The Federal-style house still has much of its original pine floors and pine or cypress ceilings and woodwork. With windows on three sides, the Sanibel on the ground floor is the lightest and airiest unit here, while the Bokeelia suite is the most romantic, with its bed set at an angle in one corner. The upstairs suites have assigned bathrooms, but you'll have to cross the hallway to get to them. Bikes, beach chairs, and towels are provided; in season, guests are served oranges from the backyard tree. You'll have to do without a phone or TV in your room here.

287 11th Ave. S., Naples, FL 34102. ✆ **800/584-1268** or 239/649-4124. Fax 239/434-2842. www.innbythe sea-bb.com. 5 units, 3 with bathroom. Winter $149–$189 double; off-season $94–$114 double. Rates include continental breakfast. AE, DISC, MC, V. Children 10 and under not accepted. **Amenities:** Access to nearby health club; free use of bikes. *In room:* A/C, hair dryer, no phone.

NORTH OF OLDE NAPLES
Very Expensive

The Registry Resort ☆☆   This sports-minded luxury high-rise is not directly on the beach: Guests must ride the free Clam Pass County Park shuttle along a 3,000-foot (900m) boardwalk through mangroves to the Gulf (see "A Nature Preserve," earlier in this chapter). Once there, they can charge lounge chairs, cabanas, water-sports equipment rentals, and drinks to their rooms. To compensate for the lack of a beachside setting, the resort recently installed a big outdoor complex with two swimming pools with water slide and waterfall. Plus, there is a 15-court tennis center, one of the main draws here. Inside its architecturally nondescript modern tower, the Registry radiates a more relaxed ambience than the traditional Ritz-Carlton, but none of the Old-Florida charm of its other chief rival, the Naples Beach Hotel & Golf Club (see above). Dining here is at least on a par with The Ritz-Carlton, with the magnificent **Lafite** dining room offering some of the city's finest French cuisine (open nightly during winter, only on Fri and Sat evenings off-season). The multilevel Club Zanzibar nightclub has dancing to deejay music every night. There's a full-service spa here, too.

475 Seagate Dr., Naples, FL 34103. ✆ **239/597-3232** or 800/247-9810. Fax 239/597-3147. www.registry resort.com. 424 units, including 29 suites. Winter $395–$475 double; $460–$715 suite. Off-season $160–$395 double; $205–$450 suite. $12-per-day resort amenities fee. Packages available. AE, DC, DISC, MC, V. From Olde Naples, go about 1½ miles (2.25km) north on U.S. 41 and turn left on Seagate Dr. Hotel is on right. **Amenities:** 6 restaurants (French, American); 4 bars; 5 heated outdoor pools; access to golf course; 15 tennis courts; health club; spa; Jacuzzi; sauna; water-sports equipment rentals; bike rental; children's programs; game room; concierge; business center; salon; 24-hr. room service; massage; babysitting; laundry service. *In room:* A/C, TV, fax, dataport, minibar, kitchen (some suites), coffeemaker, hair dryer, iron.

The Ritz-Carlton Golf Resort, Naples ☆☆☆   This Mediterranean-style resort opened in 2001 at the 27-hole, Greg Norman–designed Tiburón Golf Club, in an exclusive residential enclave at the intersection of Vanderbilt Beach and Airport-Pulling Roads. This is a golf-lover's version of its sister resort, The Ritz-Carlton, Naples (see below), and guests here can use the spa, beach, and other facilities at its older sibling, a 5-minute drive away. Each of the spacious, luxuriously appointed guest units here has a private balcony overlooking the gorgeously landscaped course. The units are high-tech marvels, with two phone lines, high-speed Internet access, and large safes with built-in electrical outlets (for recharging your laptop and cellphone while out on the links). Fine Italian-accented dining is available both indoors and out in Lemonia, the resort's signature restaurant, while a grill by the large outdoor pool provides lighter fare. The resort has extensive meeting space, so expect lots of corporate duffer company here.

2600 Tiburón Drive, Naples, FL 34109. ⓒ 888/856-4372 or 239/593-2000. Fax 239/254-3300. www.ritz carlton.com. 295 units. Winter $479–$729 double, $829–$1,649 suite. Off-season $229–$489 double; $389–$1,099 suite. Packages available. AE, DC, DISC, MC, V. From Olde Naples, go north 3½ miles (5.75km) on U.S. 41. Turn right on Vanderbilt Beach Rd. (C.R. 862), to Airport-Pulling Rd. Hotel is on left. **Amenities:** 2 restaurants (Italian, American); 2 bars; heated outdoor pool; 27-hole golf course; 4 tennis courts; health club; Jacuzzi; sauna; bike rentals; children's programs; game room (billiards, cards); concierge; business center; 24-hr. room service; massage; babysitting; laundry service; concierge-level rooms; *In room:* A/C, TV, dataport, minibar, hair dryer, iron, safe.

The Ritz-Carlton, Naples ★★★ This opulent 14-story Mediterranean-style hotel, one of Florida's finest, is a favorite among affluent guests who like standard Ritz-Carlton amenities such as imported marble floors, antique art, Oriental rugs, Waterford crystal chandeliers, British-style afternoon tea, and a staff that starts fawning over you from the moment you arrive. Still, it lacks the wonderful Old Florida charm of the Naples Beach Hotel & Golf Club (see above). Nor is it as close to the beach, for guests must walk through a narrow mangrove forest to reach the sands. The beach here is part of a public park, but the hotel has staff out there to answer phones, deliver drinks and snacks, and rent cabanas, boats, and other toys (only towels, chairs, and ice water are complimentary). The plush, fully equipped guest rooms and suites overlook the gulf, but not all have balconies. The **Dining Room,** the hotel's signature restaurant, prepares seafood with an Asian flair, while the wood-paneled **Grill Room** is a beef emporium reminiscent of a British private club. Together, they serve some of Naples's finest and most expensive cuisine. The Club turns into a nightclub with dancing after 10pm. A $50 million, 51,000-square-foot full-service spa offers a host of pampering treatments. Guests here can play the golf course and use the other amenities at The Ritz-Carlton Golf Resort, Naples (see above).

280 Vanderbilt Beach Rd., Naples, FL 34108. ⓒ 888/856-4372 or 239/598-3300. Fax 239/598-6690. www.ritzcarlton.com. 463 units. Winter $449–$899 double; $769–$969 suite. Off-season $200–$439 double; $365–$625 suite. AE, DC, DISC, MC, V. Valet parking $18; self-parking $10 in winter, free off-season. From Olde Naples, go north 3½ miles (5.75km) on U.S. 41. Turn left on Vanderbilt Beach Rd. (C.R. 862), to hotel on left. **Amenities:** 5 restaurants (French, American); 2 bars; 5 heated outdoor pools; access to golf course; 4 tennis courts; spa; Jacuzzi; sauna; water-sports equipment rental; bike rental; children's programs; game room; concierge; business center; salon; 24-hr. room service; massage; babysitting; laundry service. *In room:* A/C, TV, dataport, minibar, hair dryer, iron.

Expensive

Vanderbilt Inn Naples ★ Cheerful tropical decor in the accommodations and public areas sets the tempo for a casual, fun vacation at this two-story motel right on Vanderbilt Beach, where you can go parasailing and rent boats and water-sports equipment. Nature lovers can walk along the beach and into Delnor-Wiggins Pass State Park next door (see "Hitting the Beach," earlier in this section). The 16 efficiencies (with kitchens) on the ends of the building open to the beach. About half of the standard motel-style rooms face a magnificently landscaped courtyard with a kidney-shaped swimming pool surrounded by a brick terrace, while the other, less-expensive units open to parking lots. Although the rooms are entered from exterior walkways, their big windows are darkly tinted to provide privacy. A thatch-roof bar and full-service outdoor restaurant serve lunches and dinners by the beach and draw a crowd for sunset happy hour. Another restaurant turns lively when bands play on Friday and Saturday nights. Kids 13 and under dine free when accompanied by adults here.

11000 Gulf Shore Dr., Naples, FL 34108. ℂ 800/643-8654 or 239/597-3151. Fax 239/597-3099. www. vanderbiltinn.com. 147 units. Winter $205–$350 double; off-season $110–$210 double. Weekly rates available. AE, DC, DISC, MC, V. From Olde Naples, go 4 miles (6.25km) north on U.S. 41; take a left on 111th Ave. (which becomes Bluebill Ave.) to hotel on left. **Amenities:** 2 restaurants (American); 2 bars; heated outdoor pool; Jacuzzi; water-sports equipment rental; business center; limited room service; laundry service. *In room:* A/C, TV, dataport, kitchen (efficiencies only), coffeemaker, hair dryer, iron.

Inexpensive

Lighthouse Inn Motel   A relic from decades gone by, Judy and Buzz Dugan's no-frills but spotlessly clean motel sits across the street from other more expensive gulfside properties on Vanderbilt Beach and within walking distance of The Ritz-Carlton, Naples. The efficiencies and apartments are simple, with freshly painted cinder-block walls and small kitchens. The one kitchenless room has a small fridge and coffeemaker, but note: No unit has a telephone, and four of them have shower-only bathrooms. Most guests take advantage of weekly and monthly rates in winter, when it's heavily booked. The Dugans also operate Buzz's Lighthouse Cafe next door, a pleasant place for an inexpensive dockside breakfast, lunch, or dinner.

9140 Gulf Shore Dr. N., Naples, FL 34108. ℂ 239/597-3345. Fax 239/597-5541. 15 units. Winter $105 double; $110 efficiency; $120 apt. Off-season $49 double; $59 efficiency; $69 apt. MC, V. From Olde Naples, go 3½ miles (5.75km) north on U.S. 41; take a left on Vanderbilt Beach Rd. (C.R. 862). Turn right on Gulf Shore Dr. to hotel on right. **Amenities:** Restaurant (American); bar; heated outdoor pool. *In room:* A/C, TV, kitchen, fridge, coffeemaker, no phone.

WHERE TO DINE

If this is your first time here, you may opt to have a lunch or dinner at the touristy **Old Marine Marketplace at Tin City,** on the Gordon River at 5th Avenue South, where the **Riverwalk Fish & Ale House** (ℂ 239/262-2734) specializes in moderately priced seafood and steaks. Like its sibling, The Dock at Crayton Cove (see below), it's a fun establishment with dockside seating.

Naples's beaches are ideal for picnics. In Olde Naples, you can get freshly baked breads and pastries, prepackaged gourmet sandwiches, and fruit plates at **Tony's Off Third,** 1300 3rd St. S. (ℂ 239/262-7999). **Wynn's on Fifth,** 745 5th Ave. S. (ℂ 239/261-0901), between 8th Street and Park Street South, has high-quality deli items, prepackaged sandwiches, salads, takeout meals, and gourmet pastries at very reasonable prices. Both have a few sidewalk tables and are fine places for coffee or a snack while window-shopping on 3rd and 5th Avenues South.

IN OLDE NAPLES
Expensive

Chop's City Grill ★★ STEAKS/SEAFOOD   Wonderful aromas waft from the open kitchen at the rear of this urbane bistro. Aged, top-quality steaks and lamb chops are the house specialties, either chargrilled to perfection and served with thick onion rings and mashed potatoes, or peppered and served with a blackberry and cabernet-wine sauce. Fresh fish from the grill is another good choice. Asian influences appear here, too, such as sea scallops "shocked" in a wok with Thai curry sauce and served over noodles with wild mushrooms and stir-fried vegetables.

837 5th Ave. S. (between 8th and 9th sts. S.). ℂ 239/262-4677. Reservations recommended. Main courses $17–$30. AE, DC, DISC, MC, V. Daily 5:30–10pm.

Zoë's ★★ ECLECTIC   This slightly Art-Deco bistro draws a lively crowd of young professionals who preen at the big bar to one side or at a raised, English pub–style drinking table (you can dine at the table, too, which is handy if you're traveling alone since you're sure to get into conversations with your fellow guests). The eclectic menu changes every week or so to take advantage of fresh produce. Meatloaf, macaroni and cheese, and pot roast are regulars. They sound on the menu like those your mother made, but they're seasoned as lively as Zoë's patrons. If they're offered, opt for the pecan-crusted sea bass or the seared, sesame-coated yellowfin tuna served with a cucumber relish, a horseradish-tinged mayonnaise drizzle, and spicy soba noodles. Zoë's turns into a high-energy nightclub on Friday and Saturday nights.

720 5th Ave. S. (between 7th and 8th sts. S.). ℭ **239/261-1221.** Reservations recommended. Main courses $15–$34. AE, MC, V. Sun–Thurs 5–10pm; Fri–Sat 5–10:30pm (music and dancing Fri–Sat 11pm–2am).

Moderate

Bistro 821 ★ FUSION   This noisy bistro launched the dining revitalization along 5th Avenue South and is still an excellent choice for Mediterranean-influenced Fusion cuisine. A bench covered in bright print fabric runs down one side of this storefront to a bar and open kitchen in the rear. Although the quarters are too close for private conversations, small spotlights hanging from the ceiling romantically illuminate each table. The house specialty is rotisserie chicken, and a daily risotto leads a menu featuring penne pasta in a vodka sauce, and a seasonal vegetable plate with herb couscous. There's sidewalk dining here, too.

821 5th Ave. S. (between 8th and 9th sts. S.). ℭ **239/261-5821.** Reservations recommended. Main courses $13–$26. AE, DC, MC, V. Daily 5–10:30pm.

The Dock at Crayton Cove ★ *(Value)* SEAFOOD   Located right on the City Dock, this lively pub is the best place in town for an open-air meal or a cool drink while watching the boats go back and forth across Naples Bay. The chow ranges from hearty chowders by the mug to seafood with a Floribbean fare, with Jamaican-style jerk shrimp thrown in for spice; main courses are moderately priced. Grilled seafood Caesar salad and a good selection of sandwiches, hot dogs, and other pub-style fare also appear on the menu. "Margarita madness" happy hour and a half-price raw bar (don't miss the steamed mussels with French bread for dipping the garlic sauce) run daily from 9:30 to 11:30pm. The "Great Dock Canoe Race" draws thousands on the second Saturday in May.

12th Ave. S. (at the City Dock in Olde Naples). ℭ **239/263-9940.** Reservations not accepted. Main courses $11–$26; sandwiches $9–$13. AE, DISC, MC, V. Daily 11am–midnight.

Tommy Bahama's Tropical Cafe ★★ CARIBBEAN   You walk through a thatch gateway into this lively, island-style pub—an incongruous sight in the middle of the staid 3rd Street South shopping enclave. Diners gather on a large front patio under shade trees, where a musician performs, or inside, where a large back-wall mural creates a Polynesian scene. An open kitchen and service bar are on one side of the dining room, a real bar dispensing drinks on the other. In between, round-backed cane chairs and classic ceiling fans add to the exotic mood. Although the Jamaican pork, salmon St. Croix, and other Caribbean-style cuisine don't quite live up to the ambience, you'll have too much fun here to care whether or not it's gourmet—and the huge portions will satisfy any appetite. They don't appear on the dinner menu, but sandwiches are served if you ask for them (the meal-size grouper sandwich is a bargain at $10).

1220 3rd St. S. (between 12th and 13th aves. S.). ℭ **239/643-6889.** Reservations recommended. Main courses $17–$27; sandwiches $8–$14. AE, MC, V. Winter daily 11am–11pm; off-season daily 11am–10pm.

Yabba Island Grill ★★ *Value* CARIBBEAN   Naples's most reasonably priced chic restaurant, this lively joint re-creates a raucous Caribbean beachside bar in the middle of the 5th Avenue South dining district. The chow is as lively as Yabba's pastel color scheme, with most items providing a riot of flavors from across the Caribbean. I'll come back here for the St. Croix Sizzler, a terrific combination of small lobster tail, a chunk of mahimahi, and mussels over a bed of peppers, onions, and a sweet mango-curry sauce. Also worthy of a repeat: the Monsoon salad consisting of grilled chicken breast, hearts of palm, candied pecans, and mushrooms under a warm bacon-and-berry vinaigrette and topped with crispy onion rings.

711 5th Ave. S. (between 8th St. S. and Park Ave. S.). © 239/262-5787. Reservations recommended. Main courses $10–$24; sandwiches $8–$10. AE, DISC, MC, V. Daily 4:30–11pm (bar to 2am Fri–Sat).

Inexpensive

First Watch *Value* AMERICAN   Just like its siblings elsewhere in Florida, this shop is a favorite local haunt for breakfast, late brunch, or a midday meal. You may have to wait for a table, but once seated, a young staff will provide quick and friendly service. The menu leans heavily on healthy selections, but you can get your cholesterol from a sizzling skillet of fried eggs served over layers of potatoes, vegetables, and melted cheese. Lunch features large salads, sandwiches, and quesadillas. In addition to the dining room, there's more seating at umbrella tables in the shopping center's courtyard.

In Gulf Shore Square, 1400 Gulf Shore Blvd. (at Banyan Rd.). © 239/434-0005. Most items $3.50–$8. AE, DISC, MC, V. Daily 7am–2:30pm. Closed Christmas.

Old Naples Pub ★★ *Value* AMERICAN/PUB FARE   You would never guess that the person sitting next to you at the bar here is very, very rich, so relaxed is this small, somewhat-cramped pub in the middle of the fabulous 3rd Street South shops. Diners fortunately find more room at tables on the shopping center's patio. Inside, the pine-paneled walls are hung with trophy fish, a dartboard, and old newspaper clippings about Naples. The menu features very good pub fare (and at extraordinarily inexpensive prices for Olde Naples), including homemade soups, nachos, burgers, and sandwiches ranging from charcoal-grilled bratwurst to fried grouper. Only six main courses are offered: platters with New York strip steak, grilled tuna, the catch of the day, fried grouper or clam strips, and baby-back ribs. Best bets are the chicken salad with grapes and walnuts, and the burgers, steaks, and fish from the charcoal grill. You can catch live entertainment here nightly during winter, Wednesday through Saturday off-season.

255 13th Ave. S. (between 3rd and 4th sts. S.). © 239/649-8200. Main courses $11–$15; salads, sandwiches, and burgers $5–$9. AE, DISC, MC, V. Mon–Sat 11am–10pm; Sun noon–9pm.

North of Olde Naples

Silver Spoon American Cafe *Value* AMERICAN/ITALIAN/SOUTHWEST   Even though this chic member of the American Cafe chain is in the swanky Waterside Shops complex, it is one of Naples's best dining bargains. It flaunts sophisticated black-and-white high-tech decor and has large window walls overlooking the mall action. Thick sandwiches are served with french fries, spicy pecan rice, or black beans. The tomato-basil soup is worth a try, and the bruschetta appetizer—served on toasted French bread—is nearly a full meal in itself. Gourmet pizzas and pasta dishes also are popular, especially with the after-theater crowds from the nearby Philharmonic Center for the Arts. The less-expensive main courses such as Cajun or herb-grilled chicken are both tasty and an excellent value. Shoppers love to do lunch here, so come early or be prepared for a wait.

In the Waterside Shops at Pelican Bay, 5395 N. Tamiami Trail (at Seagate Dr.). ℂ **239/591-2123.** Reservations not accepted, but call ahead for preferred seating. Main courses $9.50–$15; pizza and pasta $8–$12; soups, salads, and sandwiches $7–$9. AE, DC, DISC, MC, V. Sun–Thurs 11am–10pm; Fri–Sat 11am–11pm. From Olde Naples, go north on U.S. 41 and left on Seagate Dr. right into shopping center. Go right at dead end to restaurant on left.

NAPLES AFTER DARK

For entertainment ideas, check the *Naples Daily News* (www.naplesnews.com), especially the "Neapolitan" section in Friday's edition.

PERFORMING ARTS   Known locally as "The Phil," the impressive **Philharmonic Center for the Arts** ✦✦, 5833 Pelican Bay Blvd., at West Boulevard (ℂ **800/597-1900** or 239/597-1900; www.thephil.org), is the home of the Naples Philharmonic, but its year-round schedule is filled with cultural events, concerts by celebrated artists and internationally known orchestras, and Broadway plays and shows aimed at children and families. Call or check the website for its seasonal calendar.

A fine local theater group, the **Naples Players,** holds their winter-season performances in the new Sugden Community Theatre, 701 5th Ave. S. (ℂ **239/ 263-7990;** www.naples.net/presents/theatre). Tickets can be hard to come by, so call well in advance.

THE CLUB & BAR SCENE   The restaurants and bistros along 5th Avenue South are popular watering holes, especially for young professional singles who make this their "meat market" on Friday nights. **Zoë's,** 720 5th Ave. S. (ℂ **239/ 261-1221;** see "Where to Dine," above), turns into a high-energy nightclub Friday and Saturday from 10:30pm to 2am. Nearby, **McCabe's Irish Pub,** 699 5th Ave. S. (ℂ **239/403-7170**), features traditional Irish music nightly.

In the 3rd Street South shopping area, **Old Naples Pub,** 255 13th Ave. S. (ℂ **239/649-8200**), has live music nightly during winter, Wednesday through Saturday nights off-season. See "Where to Dine," above.

The **Old Marine Marketplace at Tin City,** comprised of the restored waterfront warehouses on 5th Avenue South on the west side of the Gordon River, comes alive during the winter when visitors flock to its shops and the **Riverwalk Fish & Ale House** (ℂ **239/262-2734**), which has live entertainment during the season.

Some of the hotels mentioned earlier in this section have entertainment throughout the year. The beachside "chickee hut" bar at the **Naples Beach Hotel & Golf Club** (ℂ **239/261-2222**) is always popular, has live entertainment many nights, and is *the* place to go on Sunday afternoon and early evening. So is the beachside bar at the **Vanderbilt Inn Naples** (ℂ **239/597-3151**).

5 Marco Island

15 miles (24km) SE of Naples, 53 miles (85km) S of Fort Myers, 100 miles (161km) W of Miami

Captain William Collier would hardly recognize Marco Island if he were to come back from the grave today. No relation to Collier County founder Barron Collier, the captain settled his family on the north end of this island, the largest of Florida's Ten Thousand Islands, back in 1871. He traded pelts with the Native Americans, caught and smoked fish to sell to Key West and Cuba, and charged fishermen and other guests $2 a day for a room in his home. A few turn-of-the-20th-century buildings still stand here, but Captain Collier would be shocked to come across the high-rise bridge to the island and see it now sliced by man-made canals and virtually covered by resorts, condominiums, shops, restaurants, and winter homes. These are the products of an extensive real-estate development begun in 1965, which means that Marco lacks any of the charm found in Naples and on Sanibel and Captiva Islands. Much of the sales effort here was aimed at the northeastern states, so the island smacks more of New York and Massachusetts than of the laid-back Midwestern style of its neighbors.

Marco's top attractions are its crescent-shaped beach and access to the nearby waterways running through a maze of small islands, its excellent boating and fishing, and the island's proximity to thousands of acres of wildlife preserves.

ESSENTIALS

GETTING THERE   See sections 1 and 4, above, for information about the **Southwest Florida International Airport** and the **Naples Municipal Airport,** respectively, and about Amtrak's train service and Greyhound/Trailways buses to those cities.

VISITOR INFORMATION   The **Marco Island Area Chamber of Commerce,** 1102 N. Collier Blvd., Marco Island, FL 34145 (© **800/788-6272** or 239/394-7549; fax 239/394-3061; www.marcoislandchamber.org), provides free information about the island. A message board and a phone are located outside for making hotel reservations even when the office is closed. The chamber is open Monday through Friday from 9am to 5pm and Saturday from 10am to 3pm during winter.

GETTING AROUND   **Marco Island Trolley Tours** (© **239/394-1600**) makes four complete loops around the island from 10am to 3:15pm Monday through Saturday. The conductors sell tickets and render an informative narration about the island's history. Daily fare is $16 for adults, $7 for children 11 and under, with free reboarding. The entire loop takes about 1 hour and 45 minutes.

Enterprise Rent-a-Car (© 800/325-8007 or 239/642-4488) has an office here. For a cab, call **A-Action Taxi** (© 239/394-4400), **Classic Taxi** (© 239/394-1888), or **A-Okay Taxi** (© 239/394-1113).

Depending on the type, rental bicycles cost $5 an hour to $65 a week at **Scootertown,** 845 Bald Eagle Dr. (© **239/394-8400;** www.islandbikeshop.com), north of North Collier Boulevard near Olde Marco. Scooters cost about $50 for 24 hours.

HITTING THE BEACH & OTHER OUTDOOR ACTIVITIES

BEACHES   The sugar-white Crescent Beach curves for 3½ miles (5.75km) down the entire western shore of Marco Island. Its southern 2 miles (3.25km) are fronted by an unending row of high-rise condominiums and hotels, but the northern 1½ miles (2.25km) are preserved in **Tigertail Public Beach** (© **239/642-8414**). There are restrooms, cold-water outdoor showers, a children's playground, a water-sports rental concessionaire, and a snack bar. The park is at the end of Hernando Drive. It's open daily from dawn to dusk. There's no admission charge to the beach, but parking in the lot costs $3 per vehicle.

The beaches in front of the Marriott, Hilton, and Radisson resorts have parasailing, windsurfing, and other water-sports activities, all for a fee.

If you're not staying at the big resorts, Collier County maintains a $3-per-vehicle parking lot and access to the developed beach on the southern end of the island, on Swallow Avenue at South Collier Boulevard.

OUTDOOR ACTIVITIES **Marco River Marina,** 951 Bald Eagle Dr. (© **239/394-2502;** www.marcoriver.com), is the center for boat rentals, fishing, and cruises. Operating from a booth on the marina's dock, **Sunshine Tours** (© **239/642-5415**) will book offshore fishing charters and arrange back-bay fishing ($47 adults, $37 kids under 10), shelling excursions to the small islands ($37 adults, $27 children under 10), sunset cruises ($30 adults, $15 children under 10), and dinner cruises ($49 per person). The back-bay fishing trips go at high tide, the shelling trips at low tide, so call for the schedule and reservations.

SCUBAdventures has a base at 845 Bald Eagle Dr. (© **239/389-7889**) in Olde Marco. Two-tank dives range from $65 to $85 depending on distance offshore.

Naples's Lely and Boyne South golf courses are a short drive away (see "Other Outdoor Activities," in section 4, earlier in this chapter). The closest public courses are the **Marco Shores Golf Club,** 1450 Mainsail Dr. (© **239/394-2581**), and **Marriott's Golf Club at Marco** (© **239/353-7061**), both in the marshlands off Fla. 951 north of the island. A sign at the Marriott's course ominously warns: PLEASE DON'T DISTURB THE ALLIGATORS. Fees range from about $120 in winter down to $75 in summer.

A NATURE PRESERVE

Operated by The Conservancy and part of the Rookery Bay National Estuarine Research Reserve, the **Briggs Nature Center** ⚑, on Shell Island Road, off Fla. 951 between U.S. 41 and Marco Island (© **239/775-8569**), has a half-mile boardwalk through a pristine example of Florida's disappearing scrublands, home to the threatened scrub jays and gopher tortoises. Rangers lead a variety of nature excursions (call for the seasonal schedule), and there is a self-guided canoe trail, with canoes for rent from Tuesday to Saturday mornings (you must return them by 1pm) at $13 for the first 2 hours, $5 for each additional hour. The center is open Monday through Saturday from 9am to 4:30pm. Admission to the boardwalk is $7.50 for adults, $3 for children 3 to 12, free for children under 3. For more information, contact **The Conservancy of Southwest Florida,** 1450 Merrihue Dr., Naples, FL 34102 (© **239/262-0304;** fax 239/ 262-0672; www.conservancy.org).

WHERE TO STAY

There are no chain hotels on Marco Island other than the large Marriott, Hilton, and Radisson properties listed below, which stand in a row along Crescent Beach on the island's southwestern corner. **Century 21 First Southern Trust** (© **800/ 523-0069** or 239/394-7653; fax 239/394-8048; www.c21marco.com) is one of the largest agents representing rental property owners.

As elsewhere in South Florida, the high season here is from mid-December to mid-April. Rates drop precipitously in the off-season.

Boat House Motel *Value*   One of the best bargains in these parts, this comfortable little motel sits beside the Marco River in Olde Marco, on the island's northern end. The rooms are in a two-story, lime-green-and-white building that ends at a wooden dock with a small heated swimming pool, lounge furniture, picnic tables, and barbecue grills. Two rooms on the end have their own decks, and all open to tiny courtyards. Bright paint, ceiling fans, and louvered shutters add a tropical ambience throughout. The one-bedroom condominiums next door open to a riverside dock, upon which is built a two-bedroom cottage named "The Gazebo," whose peaked roof is supported by umbrella-like spokes from a central pole. Olde Marco restaurants are a short stroll away.

1180 Edington Place, Marco Island, FL 34148. © 800/528-6345 or 239/642-2400. Fax 239/642-2435. www.theboathousemotel.com. 25 units. Winter $99–$155 double; $170–$260 apt. or cottage. Off-season $63–$130 double; $125–$220 apt. or cottage. MC, V. Pets accepted ($15 fee plus $5 per day). **Amenities:** Heated outdoor pool; coin-op washers and dryers. In room: A/C, TV, fridge, iron.

Marco Island Hilton Beach Resort ★★   About half the size of the nearby Marco Island Marriott Resort & Golf Club (see below) but nevertheless a group-oriented hotel, this 11-story beachside tower overlooks the gulf and a courtyard with a multi-angled swimming pool wrapped around four coconut palms. The spacious units have curved balconies angled to give water views. One-bedroom units have cooking facilities. One kitchen here serves two outlets: the elegant Sandcastles for dinner and the adjacent Paradise Cafe for casual breakfasts, lunches, and dinners. The Beach Club by the pool serves lunches, snacks, and drinks. Sandcastles Lounge has a piano bar with nightly entertainment.

560 S. Collier Blvd., Marco Island, FL 34145. © 800/HILTONS or 239/394-5000. Fax 239/394-8410. www.marcoisland.hilton.com. 298 units. Winter $199–$359 double; off-season $89–$189 double. $9 per unit per day resort amenities fee (includes local calls). Packages available. AE, DC, DISC, MC, V. **Amenities:** 2 restaurants (American); 2 bars; heated outdoor pool; 3 tennis courts; exercise room; Jacuzzi; sauna; water-sports equipment rental; children's programs; game room; concierge; activities desk; business center; salon; limited room service; massage; babysitting; laundry service; concierge-level rooms. In room: A/C, TV, dataport, kitchen (suites only), minibar, fridge, coffeemaker, hair dryer, iron.

Marco Island Marriott Resort & Golf Club ★★ (Kids)   One of the biggest resorts on Florida's Gulf Coast, this deluxe hotel attracts large conventions but is also popular with families (it's one of the few North American resorts to have won the National Parenting Center's seal of approval). The sprawling complex has two nine-story towers and two A-frame public wings forming two beachfront courtyards with swimming pools, bars, and water-sports centers. Luxuriously furnished and decorated, the spacious accommodations range from hotel rooms to two-bedroom suites. All have balconies or patios with indirect views of the gulf. Golfers can play the resort's 18-hole championship golf course, which is on the mainland.

400 S. Collier Blvd., Marco Island, FL 34145. © 800/438-4373 or 239/394-2511. Fax 239/642-2672. www.marcomarriottresort.com. 797 units. Winter $275–$385 double; from $520 suite. Off-season $149–$340 double; from $320 suite. Packages available. AE, DC, DISC, MC, V. Valet parking $11; free self-parking. **Amenities:** 5 restaurants (American, Italian); 4 bars; 3 heated outdoor pools; golf course; 1 tennis court; exercise room; Jacuzzi; water-sports equipment rental; children's programs; game room; concierge; activities desk; car-rental desk; business center; shopping arcade; salon; limited room service; massage; babysitting; laundry service; concierge-level rooms. In room: A/C, TV, dataport, minibar, fridge, coffeemaker, hair dryer, iron.

Radisson Suite Beach Resort ★ (Kids)   Although it lacks the extensive amenities of the Marriott and Hilton resorts, units at this 11-story beachside resort are perfect for families, with one- and two-bedroom apartments with fully equipped kitchens and dining areas (some have two bathrooms). The 55 hotel rooms have microwave ovens and coffeemakers. All units have screened balconies. A Pizza Hut Express is on the premises, and a small store provides limited groceries, wine, and beer. A recreation center keeps the kids busy.

600 S. Collier Blvd., Marco Island, FL 34145. © 800/333-3333 or 239/394-4100. Fax 239/394-0419. www.marcobeachresort.com. 269 units. Winter $275 double; $315–$525 suite. Off-season $155–$165 double; $185–$295 suite. Packages available. AE, DC, DISC, MC, V. Free self-parking; valet parking $8. **Amenities:** 2 restaurants (American); 2 bars; heated outdoor pool; exercise room; Jacuzzi; water-sports equipment rental; children's programs; game room; concierge; limited room service; babysitting; laundry service. In room: A/C, TV, dataport, kitchen (apartments only), fridge, coffeemaker, hair dryer, iron.

WHERE TO DINE

Cafe de Marco ⚘⚘ SEAFOOD   Purveyor of some of the island's finest cuisine, this homelike establishment at the Marco Village shops was originally constructed as housing for maids at Captain William Collier's Olde Marco Inn. The chef specializes in excellent treatments of fresh seafood, from your choice of shrimp or fresh baked fish with mushrooms, seasoned shallots, and garlic butter to his own luscious creation of seafood and vegetables combined in a lobster sauce and served over linguine. If your waistline can stand it, finish with a Cafe Puff, an almond praline ice-cream ball rolled in chocolate cookie crumbs, placed in a puff pastry shell, and served with whipped cream. Early-bird specials here are a very good value. You can dine inside or on a screened patio.

244 Palm St., Olde Marco. ✆ 239/394-6262. Reservations recommended. Main courses $16–$30; early-bird specials $13. Minimum charge $13 per adult, $4.50 per child. AE, MC, V. Winter daily 5–10pm. Off-season Mon–Sat 5–10pm. Early-bird specials 5–6pm.

Kahuna Restaurant AMERICAN   With fanciful Hawaiian themes high-lighted by a small steaming volcano and a big mural of porpoises playing under-water on one wall, Kahuna is the least-expensive choice here. You can sit outside in the shopping center's parking lot or inside at colored booths and round tables under ceiling fans. The burgers are some of Marco's best (there's a condiment bar with a variety of fixings). Main courses include several fried seafood selections, baked crab cakes, and charcoal-grilled tuna, but your best bet should be a nightly special such as salmon in a light dill sauce. Don't expect gourmet dining here, but the quality is good for the price.

1035 N. Collier Blvd., in Town Center Mall (at Bald Eagle Dr.). ✆ 239/394-4300. Reservations not accepted. Main courses $8.50–$15; sandwiches and burgers $3.50–$7.50; breakfast $3–$8. MC, V. Winter daily 8:30am–9pm. Off-season daily 11:30am–9pm.

Kretch's ⚘⚘ *Value* SEAFOOD/CONTINENTAL   Noted pastry chef Bruce Kretschmer rules this shopping-center roost, Marco's best all-around restaurant. Bruce has created a sinfully rich seafood strudel by combining shrimp, crab, scal-lops, cheeses, cream, and broccoli in a flaky Bavarian pastry and serving it all under a lobster sauce. It's available in appetizer or main course–size portions. Cholesterol counters can choose from broiled or charcoal-grilled fish, shrimp, Florida lobster tail, steaks, or lamb chops. Bruce's popular "Mexican Friday" lunches feature delicious tacos and other inexpensive south-of-the-border selections. Sunday is home-cooking night during winter, with chicken and dumplings, Yankee pot roast, and braised lamb shanks.

527 Bald Eagle Dr. (south of N. Collier Blvd.). ✆ 239/394-3433. Reservations recommended in winter. Main courses $14–$25. DISC, MC, V. Mon–Fri 11am–3pm and 5–9pm; Sat–Sun 5–9pm. Closed Sun off-season and Easter, July 4, Thanksgiving, Christmas Eve, Christmas Day.

Snook Inn SEAFOOD   The choice dinner seats at this Old Florida establish-ment are in an enclosed dock right beside the scenic Marco River, but for lunch or libation head to the dockside Chickee Bar, a fun place anytime but especially at sunset. Live entertainment is featured out there both day and night during the winter season, nightly the rest of the year. Although seafood is the specialty, tasty steaks, chicken, burgers, and sandwiches are among the choices. Even the sand-wiches come with a trip to the salad bar at dinner, making them a fine bargain. Bring a filet of that fish you caught today and the chef will cook it for you. Call A-Okay Taxi (see "Essentials," above) for a free ride from anywhere on Marco Island.

1215 Bald Eagle Dr. (at Palm St.), Olde Marco. © 239/394-3313. Reservations not accepted. Main courses $11.50–$20.50; sandwiches $8–$10; cook-your-catch $11. AE, DC, DISC, MC, V. Daily 11am–4pm and 4:30–10pm. Closed Thanksgiving, Christmas.

MARCO ISLAND AFTER DARK

To find out what's going on, check the *Naples Daily News* (www.naplesnews. com), especially the "Neapolitan" section in Friday's edition and its weekly "The Marco Islander" section, available at the chamber of commerce (see "Essentials," above).

It's not after dark, but one of the biggest parties in Florida takes place every Sunday afternoon at **Stan's Idle Hour Seafood Restaurant,** on County Road 892 in Goodland (© **239/394-3041**), where owner Stan Gober—an Ernest Hemingway look-alike—plays host and fires up the barbecue grills; bands crank up country music for dancing the "Buzzard Lope"; and men compete to see who has the best legs. Stan's Goodland Mullet Festival, always the weekend before the Super Bowl, is the mother of all parties.

Marco Island's much tamer but nevertheless entertaining version is the **Snook Inn** (see the "Where to Dine" section above), where bands play out in the dockside Chickee Bar.

Much more sedate are the lounges in the **Marriott and Hilton resorts** (see "Where to Stay," above), which provide pianists every evening.

Everyone turns out for free outdoor entertainment at the **Mission San Marco Plaza** shopping center, South Collier Boulevard at Winterberry Drive, every Tuesday night year-round, and at the **Town Center Mall,** at North Collier Boulevard and Bald Eagle Drive, every Thursday night.

The Tampa Bay Area

by Bill Goodwin

Many families visiting Orlando's theme parks eventually drive an hour west on I-4 to another major kiddie attraction, Busch Gardens Tampa Bay. But this area shouldn't be a mere side trip from Disney World, for Florida's central west coast is an exciting destination unto itself.

The city of Tampa is the commercial center of Florida's west coast—a major seaport and a center of banking, high-tech manufacturing, and cigar making (half a billion drugstore stogies a year). You can come downtown during the day to see the sea life at the Florida Aquarium and stroll through the Henry B. Plant Museum, housed in an ornate, Moorish-style hotel built a century ago to lure tourists to Tampa. A short (soon to be trolley) ride will take you from downtown Tampa to Ybor City, the historic Cuban enclave, which is now an exciting entertainment and dining venue.

Two bridges and a causeway will whisk you westward across Old Tampa Bay to St. Petersburg, Pinellas Park, Largo, Clearwater, Dunedin, and other cities on the Pinellas Peninsula, one of Florida's most densely packed urban areas. Over here on the bay front, lovely downtown St. Petersburg is famous for wintering seniors, a shopping and dining complex built way out on a pier, and the world's largest collection of Salvador Dalí's surrealist paintings.

Keep driving west and you'll come to a line of barrier islands where St. Pete Beach, Clearwater Beach, and other gulf-side communities boast 28 miles (45km) of sunshine, surf, and white sand.

Heading south, I-275 will take you across the mouth of Tampa Bay to Sarasota and to another chain of barrier islands that stretches 42 miles (68km) along the coast south of Tampa Bay. One of Florida's cultural centers, affluent Sarasota is the gateway to St. Armands and Longboat Keys, two playgrounds of the rich and famous, and to Lido and Siesta Keys, both attractive to families of more modest means.

1 Tampa

200 miles (322km) SW of Jacksonville, 85 miles (137km) SW of Orlando, 254 miles (409km) NW of Miami

Even if you stay at the beaches 20 miles (32km) to the west, you should consider driving into Tampa to see its sights. If you have children in tow, they may *demand* that you go into the city so they can ride the rides and see the animals at Busch Gardens. Once there, you can also educate them (and yourself) at the Florida Aquarium and the city's other fine museums. Additionally, historic Ybor City has the bay area's liveliest nightlife.

Tampa was a sleepy little port when Cuban immigrants founded Ybor City's cigar industry in the 1880s. A few years later, Henry B. Plant put Tampa on the tourist map by building a railroad into town and constructing the bulbous minarets over his garish Tampa Bay Hotel, now a museum named in his honor. During the Spanish-American War, Teddy Roosevelt trained his Rough Riders here and walked the Ybor City streets with Cuban revolutionary José Martí. A land boom in the 1920s gave the city its charming, Victorian-style Hyde Park suburb, now a gentrified redoubt for the baby boomers just across the Hillsborough River from downtown.

Today's downtown skyline is the product of the 1980s and 1990s booms, when banks built skyscrapers and the city put up an expansive convention center, a performing-arts center, and the Ice Palace, a 20,000-seat bay-front arena that is home to professional hockey's Tampa Bay Lightning. The renaissance hasn't been as rapid as planned, given the recent economic recession, but it is continuing into the 21st century with redevelopment of the seaport area east of downtown. There the existing Florida Aquarium and the Garrison Seaport Center (a major home port for cruise ships bound for Mexico and the Caribbean) are being joined by office buildings, apartment complexes, and a major shopping-and-dining center known as Channelside at Garrison Seaport.

You won't want to spend your entire Florida vacation in Tampa, but everything it offers does add up to a fast-paced, modern city on the go.

ESSENTIALS

GETTING THERE **Tampa International Airport** (✆ **813/870-8770;** www.tampaairport.com), 5 miles (3.5km) northwest of downtown Tampa, is the major air gateway to this area (**St. Petersburg–Clearwater International Airport** has limited service; see section 2, "St. Petersburg," later in this chapter). Most major and many no-frills airlines serve Tampa International, including **Air Canada** (ⓒ 800/268-7240 in Canada, 800/776-3000 in the U.S.), **AirTran** (ⓒ 800/AIR-TRAN), **America West** (ⓒ 800/235-9292), **American** (ⓒ 800/433-7300), **British Airways** (ⓒ 800/247-9297), **Canadian Airlines International** (ⓒ 800/426-7000), **Cayman Airways** (ⓒ 800/422-9626), **Condor German Airlines** (ⓒ 800/524-6975), **Continental** (ⓒ 800/525-0280), **Delta** (ⓒ 800/221-1212), **JetBlue** (ⓒ 800/538-2583), **Lufthansa** (ⓒ 800/824-6200), **MetroJet** (ⓒ 800/428-4322), **Midway** (ⓒ 800/446-4392), **Midwest Express** (ⓒ 800/452-2022), **Northwest/KLM** (ⓒ 800/225-2525), **Southwest** (ⓒ 800/435-9792), **Spirit** (ⓒ 800/722-7117), **Tango** (ⓒ 800/315-1390), **United** (ⓒ 800/241-6522), and **US Airways** (ⓒ 800/428-4322).

Alamo (ⓒ 800/327-9633), **Avis** (ⓒ 800/331-1212), **Budget** (ⓒ 800/527-0700), **Dollar** (ⓒ 800/800-4000), **Enterprise** (ⓒ 800/325-8007), **Hertz** (ⓒ 800/654-3131), **National** (ⓒ 800/CAR-RENT), and **Thrifty** (ⓒ 800/367-2277) all have rental-car operations here.

The **Limo/SuperShuttle** (ⓒ **800/282-6817** or 727/527-1111; www.super-shuttle.com) operates van services between the airport and hotels throughout the Tampa Bay area. Fares for one person range from $9 to $27, depending on where you go in the bay area. **Taxis** are plentiful at the airport; the ride to downtown Tampa takes about 15 minutes and costs $11 to $15.

Amtrak trains arrive downtown at the **Tampa Amtrak Station,** 601 Nebraska Ave. N. (ⓒ **800/USA-RAIL;** www.amtrak.com).

VISITOR INFORMATION   Contact the **Tampa Bay Convention and Visitors Bureau,** 400 N. Tampa St., Tampa, FL 33602-4706 (ⓒ **800/826-8358** or 813/342-4077; fax 813/229-6616; www.visittampabay.com), for advance information. Once you're downtown, head to the bureau's **visitor information center** at the corner of Ashley Drive and Madison Street (ⓒ **813/223-1111**). It's open Monday through Saturday from 9am to 5pm.

Operated by the Ybor City Chamber of Commerce, the **Centro Ybor Museum and Visitor Information Center,** in Centro Ybor, 1600 E. 8th Ave. (between 16th and 17th sts. E.), Tampa, FL 33605 (ⓒ **877/934-3782** or 813/248-3712; fax 813/242-0398; www.ybor.org), distributes information and has exhibits about the area's history. A 7-minute video will help get you oriented with this area—an 8-block stretch of Seventh Avenue. The center is open Monday through Saturday from 10am to 6pm, Sunday from noon to 6pm.

GETTING AROUND   Like most other Florida destinations, it's virtually impossible to see Tampa's major sights and enjoy its best restaurants without a car. You can get around downtown via the free **Uptown-Downtown Connector Trolley,** which runs north-south between Harbor Island and the city's North Terminal bus station on Marion Street at I-275. The trolleys run every 10 minutes from 6am to 6pm Monday through Friday. Southbound they follow Tampa Street between Tyler and Whiting streets, and Franklin Street between Whiting Street and Harbor Island. Northbound trolleys follow Florida Avenue from the Ice Palace to Cass Street. It's operated by the Hillsborough Area Regional Transit/HARTline (ⓒ 813/254-HART; www.hartline.org), the area's transportation authority, which also provides scheduled **bus service** between downtown Tampa and the suburbs. Pick up a route map at the visitor information center (see above).

The situation will get much better when the **TECO Line Street Car System,** a new but old-fashion streetcar system, complete with overhead power lines, begins hauling passengers between downtown and Ybor City via the Ice Palace, Channelside, Garrison Seaport, and the Florida Aquarium. Plagued by delays, the system at press time was expected to begin operating in late 2002. Check with the visitor center or call HARTline to find out if indeed it is running, and if so, its schedule and fares. In the meantime, you'll have to drive or take a taxi from downtown to Ybor City.

Taxis in Tampa don't normally cruise the streets for fares, but they do line up at public loading places, such as hotels, the performing-arts center, and bus and train depots. If you need a taxi, call **Tampa Bay Cab** (© 813/251-5555), **Yellow Cab** (© 813/253-0121), or **United Cab** (© 813/253-2424). Fares are 95¢ at flag fall, plus $1.50 for each mile.

EXPLORING THE THEME & ANIMAL PARKS

Adventure Island *Kids*   If the summer heat gets to you before one of Tampa's famous thunderstorms brings late-afternoon relief, you can take a waterlogged break at this 25-acre outdoor water theme park near Busch Gardens Tampa Bay (see below). You can also frolic here during the cooler days of spring and fall, when the water is heated. The Key West Rapids, Tampa Typhoon, Gulf Scream, and other exciting water rides will drench the teens, while other, calmer rides are geared toward younger kids. There are also places to picnic and sunbathe, a games arcade, a volleyball complex, and an outdoor cafe. If you forget to bring your own, a surf shop sells bathing suits, towels, and suntan lotion.

10001 Malcolm McKinley Dr. (between Busch Blvd. and Bougainvillea Ave.). © 813/987-5600. www.4adventure.com. *Note:* Admission and hours vary from year to year so call ahead, check the website, or get a brochure at the visitor center. Admission at least $25.95 adults, $23.95 children 3–9, plus tax; free for children 2 and under. Combination tickets with Busch Gardens Tampa Bay (1 day each) $59.95 adults, $49.95 children 3–9, free for children under 3. Website sometimes offers discounts. Parking $4. Mid-Mar to Labor Day daily 10am–5pm; Sept–Oct Fri–Sun 10am–5pm (extended hours in summer and on holidays). Closed Nov to late Feb. Take exit 33 off I-275 and go east on Busch Blvd. for 2 miles (3.25km). Turn left onto McKinley Dr. (N. 40th St.) and entry is on right.

Busch Gardens Tampa Bay ★★ *Kids*   Although its heart-stopping thrill rides get much of the ink, this venerable theme park (it predates Disney World) ranks among the largest zoos in the country. It's a don't-miss attraction for children, who can see, in person, all those wild beasts they've watched on the *Animal Planet*—and they'll be closer to them here than at Disney's Animal Kingdom in Orlando (see chapter 12). Here, several thousand animals live in naturalistic environments and help carry out the park's overall African theme. Most authentic is the 80-acre plain, strongly reminiscent of the real Serengeti of Tanzania and Kenya, upon which zebras, giraffes, and other animals actually graze. Unlike the animals on the real Serengeti, however, the grazing animals have nothing to fear from lions, hyenas, crocodiles, and other predators, which are confined to enclosures—as are hippos and elephants.

The park has eight areas, each of which has its own theme, animals, live entertainment, thrill rides, kiddie attractions, dining, and shopping. A Skyride cable car soars over the park, offering a bird's-eye view of it all. Turn left after the main gate and head to **Morocco,** a walled city with exotic architecture, craft demonstrations, a sultan's tent with snake charmers, and an exhibit featuring alligators and turtles. The Moorish-style Moroccan Palace Theater features an ice show, which many families consider to be the park's best entertainment for both adults

Tampa & St. Petersburg

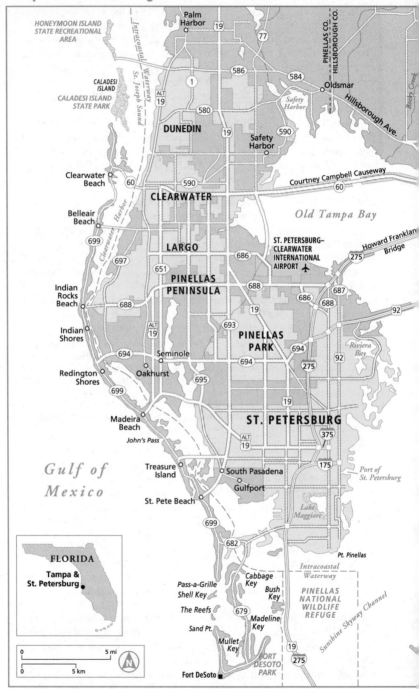

HONEYMOON ISLAND
STATE RECREATIONAL
AREA

Intracoastal Waterway

St. Joseph Sound

CALADESI
ISLAND

CALADESI ISLAND
STATE PARK

Palm
Harbor

19

77

586

584

PINELLAS CO.
HILLSBOROUGH CO.

1

ALT
19

580

Oldsmar

Hillsborough Ave.

DUNEDIN

19

Safety
Harbor

590

Safety
Harbor

Rocky Creek

Clearwater
Beach

60

CLEARWATER

590

Courtney Campbell Causeway

60

Old Tampa Bay

Belleair
Beach

699

Clearwater Harbor

LARGO

ST. PETERSBURG–
CLEARWATER
INTERNATIONAL
AIRPORT

Howard Franklin
Bridge

275

697

651

686

Indian
Rocks
Beach

688

PINELLAS
PENINSULA

688

687

686

688

92

693

19

Indian
Shores

ALT
19

PINELLAS
PARK

*Riviera
Bay*

694

Seminole

694

694

92

Redington
Shores

Oakhurst

695

275

699

19

Madeira
Beach

ST. PETERSBURG

John's Pass

375

*Gulf of
Mexico*

ALT
19

175

Treasure
Island

South Pasadena

*Port of
St. Petersburg*

Gulfport

St. Pete Beach

*Lake
Maggiore*

699

682

Pt. Pinellas

*Intracoastal
Waterway*

FLORIDA

Tampa &
St. Petersburg

Pass-a-Grille
Shell Key

Cabbage
Key

Bush
Key

PINELLAS
NATIONAL
WILDLIFE
REFUGE

Sunshine Skyway Channel

The Reefs

679

Madeline
Key

Sand Pt.

Mullet
Key

19

FORT
DESOTO
PARK

275

Fort DeSoto

0   5 mi
0   5 km

N

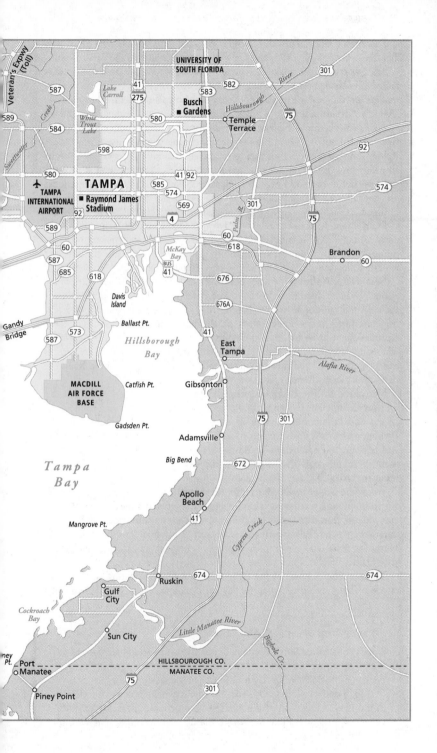

and children. Here you can also attend a song-and-dance show in the Marrakech Theater. Overlooking it all is the Crown Colony Restaurant, the park's largest.

After watching the snake charmers, walk eastward past Anheuser-Busch's fabled Clydesdale horses to **Egypt,** where you can visit King Tut's tomb with its replicas of the real treasures and listen to comedian Martin Short narrate "Akbar's Adventure Tours," a wacky simulator that "transports" one and all across Egypt via camel, biplane, and mine car. The whole room moves on this ride, which lasts only 5 minutes—much less time than the usual wait to get inside. Youngsters can dig for their own ancient treasures in a sand area. Adults and kids over 53 inches tall can ride Montu, the tallest and longest inverted roller coaster in the world with seven upside-down loops. Your feet dangle loose on Montu, so make sure your shoes are tied tightly and your lunch has had time to digest.

From Egypt, walk to the **Edge of Africa,** the most unique of the park's eight areas, and the home of most of the large animals. Go immediately to the Expedition Africa Gift Shop and see if you can get on one of the park's zoologist-led wildlife tours (see the "How to See Busch Gardens" box, below).

Next stop is **Nairobi,** the most beautiful part of the park, where you can see gorillas and chimpanzees in the Myombe Reserve in a lush area that replicates their natural rain-forest habitat. Nairobi also has a baby animal nursery, a petting zoo, turtle and reptile displays, an elephant exhibit (alas, the magnificent creatures seem to be bored to the point of madness), and Curiosity Caverns, where bats, reptiles, and small mammals that are active in the dark are kept in cages (it's the most traditional zoolike area here). The entry to Rhino Rally, the park's new safari adventure, is at the western end of Nairobi.

Next, head to **The Congo,** highlighted by rare white Bengal tigers that live on Claw Island. The Congo is also home to two roller coasters: the Kumba, the largest and fastest roller coaster in the southeastern United States; and the Python, which twists and turns for 1,200 feet (360m). You will get drenched—and refreshed on a hot day—by riding the Congo River Rapids (you're turned loose in round boats that float down the swiftly flowing "river"). There are bumper cars and kiddie rides here, too.

From The Congo, walk south into **Stanleyville,** a prototype African village, with a shopping bazaar, orangutans living on an island, and the Stanleyville Theater, usually featuring shows for children. Two more water rides are here: the Tanganyika Tidal Wave (you'll come to a very damp end) and the Stanley Falls Flume (an aqua version of a roller coaster). Serving ribs and chicken, the picnic-style Stanleyville Smokehouse has some of the best chow in the park.

The next stop is **Land of the Dragons,** the most entertaining area for small children. They can spend an entire day enjoying a variety of play elements in a

---

(Tips **If You Need Another Day**

Once you're inside Busch Gardens Tampa Bay and decide you really need more time to see the park, you can buy a **Next-Day Ticket,** which lets you back in on the following day for about $13 per person.

Also, if you're going to Orlando, Busch Gardens Tampa Bay is included in the five-park version of the **FlexTicket,** which also gives admission to Universal Studios Florida, SeaWorld, Islands of Adventure, and Wet 'n' Wild for $169.95 for adults and $134.95 for children 3 to 9.

How to See Busch Gardens

You can save a few dollars and avoid waiting in long lines by buying your tickets to Busch Gardens Tampa Bay at the privately owned **Tampa Bay Visitor Information Center,** opposite the park at 3601 E. Busch Blvd., at North Ednam Place (© **813/985-3601;** fax 813/985-7642; www.hometown.aol.com\tpabayinfoctr). Owner Jim Boggs worked for the park for 13 years and gives expert advice about how to get the most out of your visit. He sells discounted tickets to Busch Gardens, Adventure Island, and other attractions; and he will book hotel rooms and car rentals for you, often at a discount. The center is open Monday through Saturday from 10am to 5:30pm, Sunday from 10am to 2pm.

Arrive early and allow at least a day to see the park. Try not to come when it's raining, since some rides may not operate. Bring comfortable shoes; and, remember, you will get wet on some of the rides, so wear or bring appropriate clothing (shops near the rides sell inexpensive plastic ponchos). There are lockers throughout the park where you can stash your gear. Don't be surprised if the park's security staff asks to search your bags before they'll let you enter the main gate.

As soon as you're through the turnstiles, pick up a copy of a park map and the day's activity schedule, which tells what's showing and when at the 14 different entertainment venues in the park. Then take a few minutes to carefully plan your time—it's a big park with lots to see and do. Busch Gardens continues to grow, so be on the lookout for new attractions.

Although you'll get close to Busch Garden's predators, hippos, and elephants in their glass-walled enclosures, the only way to get out on the plain among the grazers is on a tour. The best is a **VIP Animal Adventure Tour,** on which you'll roam the plains in the company of a zoologist. These 1-hour excursions cost a pricey $75 per person (in addition to the park's entry fee) and usually leave about 1:30pm daily. The tours can fill up fast, and you can't call ahead for reservations, so as soon as you enter the park, go to the Expedition Africa Gift Shop, opposite the Crown Colony Restaurant in the Edge of Africa, to reserve a spot. Another (though less attractive) alternative is the 30-minute, zoologist-led **Serengeti Safari Special Tours,** in which you ride out among the grazers on the back of a flatbed truck. These are worth an extra $30 per person regardless of age. You can make reservations for the morning tour at the Expedition Africa Gift Shop, but the midday and afternoon tours are first-come, first-served. Note that children under 5 are not allowed on either tour.

fairy-tale setting, plus just-for-kids rides. The area is dominated by Dumphrey, a whimsical dragon who interacts with visitors and guides children around a three-story treehouse with winding stairways, tall towers, stepping stones, illuminated water geysers, and an echo chamber.

The next stop is **Bird Gardens,** the park's original core, offering rich foliage, lagoons, and a free-flight aviary for hundreds of exotic birds, including golden and American bald eagles. Be sure to see the Florida flamingos and Australian koalas.

Next, take a break at the **Hospitality House,** which offers piano entertainment and free samples of Anheuser-Busch's famous beers. You must be 21 to imbibe (there's a limit of two free mugs per seating), but soft drinks are also available.

If your stomach can take another hair-raising ride, the last stop is at **Gwazi,** the park's pair of old-fashioned wooden roller coasters named the Lion and the Tiger, which start simultaneously and whiz within a few feet of each other six times as they roar along at 50 miles per hour (81kmph). Since the coasters rise to "only" 90 feet (27m; that's low compared to the park's other thrillers), most family members can give them a go. In Gwazi's "Water Wars," participants shoot water-filled balloons at each other with big slingshots. It's a soaking way to end your visit.

You can exchange foreign currency in the park, and interpreters are available.

Note: You can get here from Orlando via shuttle buses, which pick up at area hotels between 8:00 and 10:15am for the 60-minute ride, with return trips starting at 5pm and continuing until the park closes. Round-trip fares are $5 per person. Call © **800/511-2450** for schedules, pickup locations, and reservations.

3000 E. Busch Blvd. (at McKinley Dr./N. 40th St.). © **888/800-5447** or 813/987-5283. www.buschgardens. com. *Note:* Admission and hours vary so call ahead, check website, or get brochure at visitor centers. Admission at least $49.95 adults, $40.95 children 3–9, plus tax; free for children 2 and under. Annual pass $84.95 adults, $74.95 children 3–9, plus tax. Combination season pass with Adventure Island $115. Website sometimes offers discounts. Daily 10am–6pm (extended hours to 7 and 8pm in summer and on holidays). Parking $7. Take I-275 north of downtown to Busch Blvd. (exit 33) and go east 2 miles (3.25km). From I-75, take Fowler Ave. (exit 54) and follow the signs west.

The Florida Aquarium ★★ *Kids* See more than 5,000 aquatic animals and plants that call Florida home at this entertaining and informative aquarium. The exhibits follow a drop of water from the pristine springs of the Florida Wetlands Gallery, through a mangrove forest in the Bays and Beaches Gallery, and out onto the Coral Reefs, where an impressive 43-foot-wide (13m), 14-foot-tall (4.25m) panoramic window lets you look out to schools of fish and lots of sharks and stingrays. Also worth visiting are the "Explore a Shore" playground to educate the kids, a deep-water exhibit, and a tank housing moray eels. You can also go out on the bay to look for birds and sea life on 90-minute Dolphin Quest cruises in the *Bay Spirit,* a 64-foot (19m) diesel-powered catamaran.

701 Channelside Dr. © 813/273-4000. www.flaquarium.net. Admission $15 adults, $12 seniors, $10 children 5–13, free for children under 5. Dolphin Quest $18 adults, $17 seniors, $13 children 5–13, free for children under 5. Combination aquarium admission and Dolphin Quest $30 adults, $26 seniors, $20 children 5–13, free for children under 5. Website sometimes offers discounts. Parking $4. Daily 9:30am–5pm. Dolphin Quest Mon–Fri 2pm, Sat–Sun 1 and 3pm. Closed Thanksgiving, Christmas.

Lowry Park Zoo *Kids* Watching 2,000-pound manatees, komodo dragons, and rare red pandas makes this a worthwhile excursion after the kids have seen the plains of Africa at Busch Gardens. With lots of greenery, bubbling brooks, and cascading waterfalls, this 24-acre zoo displays animals in settings similar to their natural habitats. Other major exhibits include a Florida wildlife display, an Asian Domain, a Primate World, an Aquatic Center, a free-flight aviary with a birds-of-prey show, an Australian-themed children's zoo (as in kangaroos and wallabies), a hands-on Discovery Center, and an endangered-species carousel ride.

1101 W. Sligh Ave. © 813/935-8552 or 813/932-0245 for recorded information. www.lowryparkzoo.com. Admission $9.50 adults, $8.50 seniors, $5.95 children 3–11, free for children 2 and under. Daily 9:30am–5pm. Closed Thanksgiving, Christmas. Take I-275 to Sligh Ave. (exit 31) and follow the signs.

VISITING THE MUSEUMS

Henry B. Plant Museum ★★   Originally built in 1891 by railroad tycoon Henry B. Plant as the 511-room Tampa Bay Hotel, this ornate building alone is worth a short trip across the river from downtown to the University of Tampa campus. Its 13 silver minarets and distinctive Moorish architecture, modeled after the Alhambra in Spain, make this National Historic Landmark a focal point of the Tampa skyline. Although the building itself is the highlight of a visit, don't skip its contents: art and furnishings from Europe and the Orient; and exhibits that explain the history of the original railroad resort, Florida's early tourist industry, and the hotel's role as a staging point for Teddy Roosevelt's Rough Riders during the Spanish-American War.

401 W. Kennedy Blvd. (between Hyde Park and Magnolia Aves.). ✆ 813/254-1891. www.plantmuseum.com. Admission free; suggested donation $5 adults, $2 children 12 and under. Tues–Sat 10am–4pm; Sun noon–4pm. Closed Thanksgiving, Christmas Eve, and Christmas Day. Take Kennedy Blvd. (Fla. 60) across the Hillsborough River.

MOSI (Museum of Science and Industry) ★ *Kids*   A great place to take the kids on a rainy day, MOSI is the largest science center in the Southeast and has more than 450 interactive exhibits. You can step into the Gulf Hurricane and experience 74 mile-per-hour (199kmph) winds, defy the laws of gravity in the unique *Challenger* space experience, cruise the mysterious world of microbes in LifeLab, and explore the human body in The Amazing You. If your heart's up to it, you can ride a bicycle across a 98-foot-long (29m) cable suspended 30 feet (9m) up in the air above the lobby (don't worry: you'll be harnessed to the bike). You can also watch stunning movies in Florida's first IMAX dome theater. Outside, trails wind through a 47-acre nature preserve with a butterfly garden.

4801 E. Fowler Ave. (at N. 50th St.). ✆ 813/987-6300. www.mosi.org. Admission $13.95 adults, $11.95 seniors, $9.95 children 2–12, free for children under 2. Admission includes IMAX movies. Daily 9am–5pm or later. From downtown, take I-275 north to the Fowler Ave. E. exit. Take this 2 miles (3.25km) to museum on right.

Tampa Museum of Art   Located on the east bank of the Hillsborough River next to the round NationsBank building (locals facetiously call it the "Beer Can"), this fine-arts complex offers eight galleries with changing exhibits ranging from classical antiquities to contemporary Florida art. There's also a 7-acre riverfront park and sculpture garden. Call or check the website for the schedule of temporary exhibits.

600 N. Ashley Dr. (at Twiggs St.), downtown. ✆ 813/274-8130. www.tampamuseum.com. Admission $5 adults, $4 seniors, $3 children 6–18 and students with identification cards, free for children under 6, by donation Thurs 5–8pm and Sat 10am–noon. Tues–Wed and Fri–Sat 10am–5pm; Thurs 10am–8pm; Sun 1–5pm. Parking 90¢ per hour. Take I-275 to exit 25 (Ashley Dr.).

YBOR CITY

Northeast of downtown, the city's historic Latin district takes its present name from Don Vicente Martinez Ybor (*Ee*-bore), a Spanish cigar maker who arrived here in 1886 via Cuba and Key West. Soon his and other Tampa factories were producing more than 300,000 hand-rolled stogies a day.

It may not be the cigar capital of the world anymore, but Ybor is the happening part of Tampa and it's one of the best places in Florida to buy hand-rolled cigars. It's not on a par with New Orleans's Bourbon Street, Washington's Georgetown, or New York's SoHo, but good food and great music do dominate the scene, especially on weekends when the streets bustle until 4am. Live-music offerings run the gamut from jazz and blues to indie rock.

Quacking Around

A fun way to tour downtown and Ybor City is with **Duck Tours of Tampa Bay** (© 813/432-3825; www.ducktoursoftampabay.com), which uses refurbished World War II amphibious "Ducks." Now equipped with bench seats under canopies, these bright yellow half-truck, half-boat vehicles pick up at the company's "Quack Shack" at Newk's Cafe, 514 Channelside Dr., opposite the Ice Palace, Wednesday through Sunday from 11am to 5pm. The narrated 1-hour, 20-minute excursions go on land through Ybor City, then on the river back to downtown. They cost $18.50 for adults, $16.50 for seniors, $9.95 for children 3 to 12, plus tax. Kids under 3 ride free. Call for the schedule and reservations, which are a good idea on weekends and holidays. The company also has land-sea tours in St. Petersburg (see "Organized Tours" in section 2, below).

At the heart of it all is **Centro Ybor,** a new dining-shopping-entertainment complex sprawling between 7th and 8th avenues and 16th and 17th streets (© 813/241-4545; www.thecentroybor.com). Here you'll find a multiscreen cinema, a comedy club, several restaurants, a large open-air bar, and several mall regulars such as Victoria's Secret and American Eagle Outfitters. The Ybor City Chamber of Commerce has its visitor center here (see "Essentials," earlier in this chapter), and the Ybor City State Museum's gift shop is here as well (see below).

Check with the visitor center about **walking tours** of the historic district. **Ybor City Ghost Walks** (© 813/242-4660) will take you to the spookier parts of the area beginning at 4pm Thursday and Saturday. They cost $10 per person and are by reservation only.

Even if you're not a cigar smoker, you'll enjoy a stroll through the **Ybor City State Museum** ★, 1818 9th Ave., between 18th and 19th streets (© 813/247-6323; www.ybormuseum.org or www.floridastateparks.org/district4/yborcitymuseum), housed in the former Ferlita Bakery (1896–1973). You can take a self-guided tour around the museum to see a collection of cigar labels, cigar memorabilia, and works by local artisans. Admission is $2 per person. Depending on the availability of volunteer docents, admission includes a 15-minute guided tour of **La Casita,** a renovated cigar worker's cottage adjacent to the museum; it's furnished as it was at the turn of the last century. The museum is open daily from 9am to 5pm, but the best time to visit is between 11am and 3pm, when you can take a guided tour of La Casita. Better yet, plan to catch the cigar-rolling demonstrations Friday through Sunday from 10am to 3pm.

Housed in a 100-year-old, three-story former cigar factory, **Ybor City Brewing Company,** 2205 N. 20th St., facing Palm Avenue (© 813/242-9222), produces Ybor Gold and other brews, none with preservatives. Admission of $3 per person includes a tour of the brewery and a taste of the end result. Tours are usually given Monday through Friday at 11am, noon, and 1pm.

ORGANIZED TOURS

Swiss Chalet Tours, 3601 E. Busch Blvd. (© 813/985-3601; www.hometown.aol.com\tpabayinfoctr), opposite Busch Gardens in the privately run Tampa Bay Visitor Information Center (see the "How to See Busch Gardens" box, above), operates guided bus tours of Tampa, Ybor City, and environs. The 4-hour tours of Tampa are given from 10am to 2pm daily, with a stop for lunch at the Columbia Restaurant in Ybor City. They cost $40 for adults and $35 for children. The full-day tours of both Tampa and St. Petersburg give a good overview of the two cities and the beaches; these cost $70 for adults and $65 for children. Reservations are required at least 24 hours in advance; passengers are picked up at major hotels and various other points in the Tampa/St. Petersburg area. They can also book bus tours to Orlando, Sarasota, Bradenton, and other regional destinations (call for schedules, prices, and reservations).

OUTDOOR ACTIVITIES & SPECTATOR SPORTS

BIKING, IN-LINE SKATING & JOGGING   Bayshore Boulevard, a 7-mile-long (11km) promenade, is famous for its sidewalk right on the shores of Hillsborough Bay and is a favorite for runners, joggers, walkers, and in-line skaters. The route goes from the western edge of downtown in a southward direction, passing stately old homes in Hyde Park, a few high-rise condominiums, retirement communities, and houses of worship, ending at Ballast Point Park. The view from the promenade across the bay to the downtown skyline is unmatched here (Bayshore Boulevard also is great for a drive).

FISHING   One of Florida's best guide services, **Light Tackle Fishing Expeditions,** 6105 Memorial Hwy., Suite 4 (© **800/972-1930** or 813/963-1930; www.leftcoastfishing.com), offers private sport-fishing trips for tarpon, redfish, cobia, trout, and snook. Call for prices, schedule, and required reservations.

GOLF   Tampa has three municipal golf courses where you can play for about $30, a relative pittance when compared with fees at the privately owned courses here and elsewhere in Florida. The **Babe Zaharias Municipal Golf Course,** 11412 Forest Hills Dr., north of Lowry Park (© **813/631-4374**), is an 18-hole, par-70 course with a pro shop, putting greens, and a driving range. It is the shortest of the municipal courses, but its small greens and narrow fairways present ample challenges. Water provides obstacles on 12 of the 18 holes at **Rocky Point Municipal Golf Course,** 4151 Dana Shores Dr. (© **813/673-4316**), located between the airport and the bay. It's a par-71 course with a pro shop, a practice range, and putting greens. On the Hillsborough River in north Tampa, the **Rogers Park Municipal Golf Course,** 7910 N. 30th St. (© **813/ 673-4396**), is an 18-hole, par-72 championship course with a lighted driving and practice range. All the courses are open daily from 7am to dusk, and lessons and club rentals are available.

You can book starting times and get information about these and the area's other courses by calling **Tee Times USA** (© **800/374-8633;** www.teetimes usa.com).

If you want to do some serious work on your game, the **Arnold Palmer Golf Academy World Headquarters** is at Saddlebrook Resort, 5700 Saddlebrook Way, Wesley Chapel, 12 miles (19km) north of Tampa (© **800/729-8383** or 813/973-1111; www.saddlebrookresort.com). Half-day and hourly instruction is available as well as 2-, 3-, and 5-day programs for adults and juniors. You have to stay at the resort or enroll in the golf program to play at Saddlebrook. See "Where to Stay," below, for more information about the resort.

Walk This Way
Bayshore Boulevard's 7-mile-long (11km) promenade is reputed to be the world's longest continuous sidewalk.

SPECTATOR SPORTS National Football League fans can catch the **Tampa Bay Buccaneers** at the modern, 66,000-seat Raymond James Stadium, 4201 N. Dale Mabry Highway, at Dr. Martin Luther King Jr. Boulevard (✆ **813/ 879-2827;** www.buccaneers.com) August through December.

The National Hockey League's **Tampa Bay Lightning** play in the Ice Palace, beginning in October (✆ **813/301-6500;** www.tampabaylightning.com).

New York Yankees fans can watch the Boys in Blue during baseball spring training from mid-February to the end of March at Legends Field (✆ **813/ 879-2244** or 813/875-7753; www.yankees.mlb.com), opposite Raymond James Stadium. This scaled-down replica of Yankee Stadium is the largest spring-training facility in Florida, with a 10,000-seat capacity. The club's minor-league team, the **Tampa Yankees** (same phone and website), plays at Legends Field April through August.

The only thoroughbred racecourse on Florida's west coast, **Tampa Bay Downs,** 11225 Racetrack Rd., Oldsmar (✆ **800/200-4434** in Florida, or 813/ 855-4401; www.tampadowns.com), is the home of the Tampa Bay Derby. Races are held from December to May, and the track presents simulcasts year-round. Call for post times.

TENNIS Players at all levels can sharpen their games at the **Hopman Tennis Program,** at the Saddlebrook Resort (p. 453). You must be a member or a guest to play here.

SHOPPING

Hyde Park and Ybor City are two areas of Tampa worth some window shopping, perhaps sandwiched around lunch at one of their fine restaurants (see "Where to Dine," later in this chapter).

CIGARS Ybor City no longer is a major producer of hand-rolled cigars, but you can still watch artisans making stogies at the **Gonzales y Martinez Cigar Factory,** 2025 7th Ave., in the Columbia Restaurant building (✆ **813/ 247-2469**). Gonzales and Martinez are recent arrivals from Cuba and don't speak English, but the staff does at the adjoining **Columbia Cigar Store** (it's best to enter here). Rollers are on duty Monday through Saturday from 10am to 6pm.

You can stock up on fine domestic and imported cigars at **El Sol,** 1728 E. 7th Ave. (✆ **813/247-5554**), the city's oldest cigar store; **King Corona Cigar Factory,** 1523 E. 7th Ave. (✆ **813/241-9109**); and **Metropolitan Cigars & Wine,** 2014 E. 7th Ave. (✆ **813/248-3304**).

SHOPPING CENTERS **Old Hyde Park Village,** 1507 W. Swann Ave., at South Dakota Avenue (✆ **813/251-3500;** www.oldhydeparkvillage.com), is a terrific alternative to cookie-cutter suburban malls. Walk around little shops in the sunshine and check out Hyde Park, one of the city's oldest and most historic neighborhoods at the same time. The cluster of 50 upscale shops and boutiques is set in a village layout. The selection includes Williams-Sonoma, Pottery Barn, Banana Republic, Brooks Brothers, Crabtree & Evelyn, Godiva, and Anthropologie, to name a few. There's a free parking garage on South Oregon Avenue behind Jacobson's department store. Most shops are open Monday through Saturday from 10am to 7pm, Sunday from noon to 5pm.

The centerpiece of the downtown seaport renovation, the huge new mall known as **Channelside at Garrison Seaport,** on Channelside Drive between the

Garrison Seaport and the Florida Aquarium (© 813/223-4250; www.channel side.com), has stores, restaurants, a dance club, a games arcade, and a multiscreen cinema with an IMAX screen. It opened in 2001 and was still a work in progress when we went to press.

In Ybor City, the new **Centro Ybor,** on 7th Avenue East at 16th Street (© 813/242-4660; www.thecentroybor.com), is primarily a dining and entertainment complex, but you'll find a few national stores here such as American Eagle, Birkenstock, and Victoria's Secret.

WHERE TO STAY

I've organized the accommodations listings below into three geographic areas: near Busch Gardens, downtown, and Ybor City. If you're going to Busch Gardens, Adventure Island, Lowry Park Zoo, and the Museum of Science and Industry (MOSI), the motels near Busch Gardens are much more convenient than those downtown, about 7 miles (11km) to the south. The downtown hotels are geared to business travelers, but staying there will put you near the Florida Aquarium, the Tampa Museum of Art, the Henry B. Plant Museum, the Tampa Bay Performing Arts Center, scenic Bayshore Boulevard, and the dining and shopping opportunities in the Channelside and Hyde Park districts. Staying in Ybor City will put you within walking distance of numerous restaurants and the city's hottest nightspots.

The Westshore area, near the bay west of downtown and south of Tampa International Airport, is another commercial center, with a wide range of national chain hotels catering to business travelers and conventioneers. It's convenient to Raymond James Stadium and the New York Yankees' spring-training complex. Check with your favorite chain for a Westshore-Airport location.

Room rates at most hotels in Tampa vary little from season to season. This is especially true downtown, where the hotels do a brisk convention business all year round. Hillsborough County adds 12% tax to your hotel room bill.

NEAR BUSCH GARDENS

The nearest chain motel to the park is **Howard Johnson Hotel Near Busch Gardens Maingate,** 4139 E. Busch Blvd. (© 800/444-5656 or 813/988-9191), an older property that was extensively renovated and reopened in 1999. It's 1½ blocks east of the main entrance.

A bit farther away, the 500-room **Embassy Suites Hotel and Conference Center,** 3705 Spectrum Blvd., facing Fowler Avenue (© 800/EMBASSY or 813/977-7066; fax 813/977-7933), is the plushest and most expensive establishment near the park. Almost across the avenue stands **LaQuinta Inn & Suites,** 3701 E. Fowler Ave. (© 800/NU-ROOMS or 813/910-7500; fax 813/910-7600). Side-by-side just south of Fowler Avenue are editions of **AmeriSuites,** 11408 N. 30th St. (© 800/833-1516 or 813/979-1922; fax 813/979-1926), and **DoubleTree Guest Suites,** 11310 N. 30th St. (© 800/222-TREE or 813/971-7690; fax 813/972-5525).

Tips **Ask About Busch Gardens Tickets**

Many Tampa hotels combine tickets to major attractions like Busch Gardens in their packages, so always ask about special deals.

Tampa

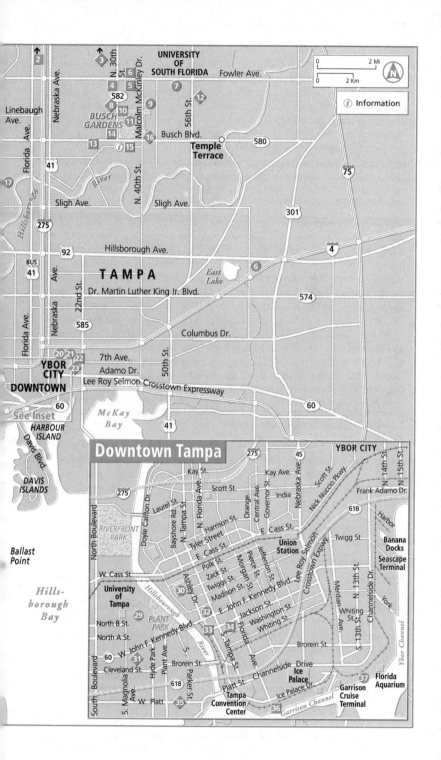

N. 30th St.

Nebraska Ave.

↑ 2

◆ 3

6

UNIVERSITY
OF
SOUTH FLORIDA   Fowler Ave.

Malcolm McKinley Dr.

4

5

582

8

10

11

14

13

ⓘ 15

BUSCH
GARDENS

16

Linebaugh
Ave.

Florida Ave.

9

7

12

56th St.

Busch Blvd.

Temple
Terrace

580

75

17

Hillsborough River

41

Sligh Ave.

N. 40th St.

Sligh Ave.

301

275

92

BUS
41

TAMPA

Dr. Martin Luther King Jr. Blvd.

East
Lake

6

574

4

22nd St.

Nebraska Ave.

585

Columbus Dr.

Florida Ave.

20 21

22

23

7th Ave.

Adamo Dr.

50th St.

YBOR
CITY

DOWNTOWN

Lee Roy Selmon Crosstown Expressway

60

See Inset

HARBOUR
ISLAND

60

McKay
Bay

41

Davis Blvd.

DAVIS
ISLANDS

2 Mi

0   2 Km

ⓘ Information

N

Downtown Tampa

YBOR CITY

275

45

Kay St.

Kay Ave.

Scott St.

India

Scott St.

Frank Adamo Dr.

N. 14th St.

N. 15th St.

275

North Boulevard

RIVERFRONT
PARK

Doyle Carlton Dr.

Bayshore Rd.

Laurel St.

N. Tampa St.

Harrison St.

Tyler Street

E. Cass St.

Florida Ave.

Orange

Central Ave.

Governor St.

Nebraska Ave.

Scott St.

Nick Nuccio Pkwy.

618

Harbor

E. Cass St.

Union
Station

Twigg St.

Banana
Docks

Seascape
Terminal

Ballast
Point

Hills-
borough
Bay

W. Cass St.

University
of
Tampa

29

PLANT
PARK

North B St.

North A St.

60

31

Cleveland St.

W. John F. Kennedy Blvd.

Hyde Park Ave.

Plant Ave.

Ashley Dr.

Hillsborough River

30

Polk St.

Zack St.

Twiggs St.

Madison St.

32

33

Pierce St.

Morgan St.

Jefferson St.

E. John F. Kennedy Blvd.

Jackson St.

34

Washington St.

Whiting St.

Florida

S. Tampa St.

Lee Roy Selmon

Crosstown Expwy

Meridian Ave.

Whiting

N. 13th St.

S. 13th St.

Channelside Dr.

Ybor Channel

York

Brorein St.

37

Florida
Aquarium

South Boulevard

S. Magnolia Ave.

618

Brorein St.

Parker St.

W. Platt

35

Platt St.

Tampa
Convention
Center

Channelside Drive

Ice Palace Dr.

36

Garrison Channel

Ice
Palace

Garrison
Cruise
Terminal

Baymont Inn & Suites *Value* Fake banana trees and a parrot cage welcome guests to the terra-cotta–floored lobby of this comfortable and convenient member of the small chain of cost-conscious but amenity-rich motels. All rooms are spacious and have ceiling fans and desks. Rooms with king beds also have recliners, business rooms sport dataport phones and extra-large desks, and the suites have refrigerators and microwave ovens. Outside, a courtyard with an unheated swimming pool has plenty of space for sunning. There's no restaurant on the premises, but plenty are within walking distance.

9202 N. 30th St. (at Busch Blvd.), Tampa, FL 33612. © 800/428-3438 or 813/930-6900. Fax 813/930-0563. www.baymontinns.com. 146 units. Winter $84–$109 double; off-season $79–$99 double. Rates include continental breakfast and local phone calls. AE, DC, DISC, MC, V. **Amenities:** Outdoor pool; game room; coin-op washers and dryers. *In room:* A/C, TV, dataport, fridge, coffeemaker, hair dryer, iron.

Best Western All Suites Hotel ★★ *Value* This three-story all-suites hotel is the most beachlike vacation venue you'll find close to the park. The product of hands-on owner John Ruzic, whimsical signs lead you around a lush tropical courtyard with heated pool, hot tub, and a lively, sports-oriented tiki bar. The bar can get noisy before closing at 9pm, and ground-level units are musty, so ask for an upstairs suite away from the action. Suite living rooms are well equipped and separate bedrooms have narrow screened patios or balconies. Great for kids, 11 "family suites" have bunk beds in addition to a queen-size bed for parents. Another 28 suites are especially equipped for business travelers (but are great for couples, too) with ergonomic chairs at big writing desks with speakerphones.

Behind Busch Gardens, 3001 University Center Dr. (faces N. 30th St. between Busch Blvd. and Fowler Ave.), Tampa, FL 33612. © 800/786-7446 or 813/971-8930. Fax 813/971-8935. www.thatparrotplace.com. 150 units. Winter $99–$159 suite for 2; off-season $79–$99 suite for 2. Rates include hot and cold breakfast buffet. AE, DC, DISC, MC, V. **Amenities:** Restaurant (breakfast and dinner only); bar; heated outdoor pool; access to nearby health club; Jacuzzi; game room; limited room service; laundry service; coin-op washers and dryers. *In room:* A/C, TV, dataport, fridge, coffeemaker, hair dryer, iron.

Red Roof Inn Less than a mile west of Busch Gardens, this is the best low-budget choice close to the park. Most of the rooms in the pleasant two-story building are away from the busy boulevard, but make sure to request one toward the rear of the building to avoid the road noise. Although in-room amenities are scarce, the units are spacious for the price.

2307 E. Busch Blvd. (between 22nd and 26th sts.), Tampa, FL 33612. © 800/THE-ROOF or 813/932-0073. Fax 813/933-5689. 108 units. Winter $60–$85 double; off-season $40–$76 double. Rates include local phone calls. AE, DC, DISC, MC, V. **Amenities:** Heated outdoor pool; Jacuzzi; sauna. *In room:* A/C, TV, dataport.

DOWNTOWN TAMPA

Hyatt Regency Tampa ★ Although this Hyatt lost its place as downtown's premier hotel to the new Tampa Marriott Waterside (see below), it still attracts the corporate crowd. It's just off the Franklin Street pedestrian mall. The spacious, contemporary rooms lack balconies, and the higher office towers that now surround the hotel restrict views from the windows. Office workers congregate at the Avanzare restaurant for inexpensive light lunches.

2 Tampa City Center (corner of Tampa and E. Jackson sts.), Tampa, FL 33602. © 800/233-1234 or 813/225-1234. Fax 813/273-0234. 521 units. $249–$274 double. Weekend packages available in summer. AE, DC, DISC, MC, V. Valet parking $12. **Amenities:** 2 restaurants (American); bar; heated outdoor pool; exercise room; Jacuzzi; concierge; business center; limited room service; laundry service; coin-op washers and dryers; concierge-level rooms. *In room:* A/C, TV, dataport, coffeemaker, hair dryer, iron.

Radisson Riverwalk Hotel ★ Sitting on the east bank of the Hillsborough River, this six-story hotel was completely remodeled in 1998. Half the rooms face west and have views from their balconies of the Arabesque minarets atop the Henry B. Plant Museum across the river—quite a scene at sunset. They cost more but are much preferable to units on the east side of the building, which face downtown's skyscrapers and don't have balconies. Beside the river, the Ashley Drive Grill serves indoor-outdoor breakfasts and lunches, then turns to fine dining in the evenings. The Boulanger bakery and deli, open from 5am to midnight, purveys fresh pastries, soups, sandwiches, and snacks.

200 N. Ashley Dr. (at Jackson St.), Tampa, FL 33602. (*) 800/333-3333 or 813/223-2222. Fax 813/221-5929. 282 units. Winter $219–$239 double; off-season $129–$179 double. AE, DC, DISC, MC, V. Valet parking $8, self-parking $7. **Amenities:** 2 restaurants (American/deli); bar; heated outdoor pool; exercise room; access to nearby health club; sauna; concierge; limited room service; laundry service; coin-op washers and dryers; concierge-level rooms. *In room:* A/C, TV, dataport, coffeemaker, hair dryer, iron.

Tampa Marriott Waterside 🏆🏆 This luxurious 22-story hotel occupies downtown's most strategic location—beside the river and between the Tampa Convention Center and the Ice Palace. Opening to a riverfront promenade, the towering, three-story lobby is large enough to accommodate the many conventioneers drawn to the two neighboring venues and the hotel's own 50,000 square feet of meeting space. The third floor has a fully equipped spa, modern exercise facility, and outdoor heated pool. About half of the guest quarters have balconies overlooking the bay or city (choice views are high up on the south side). Although spacious, the regular rooms are dwarfed by the 720-square-foot suites.

700 N. Florida Ave. (at Ice Palace Dr.), Tampa, FL 33602. (*) 800/228-9290 or 813/221-4900. Fax 813/221-0923. 717 units. $205–$265 double. AE, DC, DISC, MC, V. Weekend rates available. Valet parking $12; no self-parking. **Amenities:** 3 restaurants (American); 3 bars; heated outdoor pool; health club; spa; Jacuzzi; concierge; activities desk; car-rental desk; business center; salon; limited room service; massage; babysitting; laundry service; coin-op washers and dryers; concierge-level rooms. *In room:* A/C, TV, fax, dataport (with high-speed Internet), fridge, coffeemaker, hair dryer, iron.

YBOR CITY

Hilton Garden Inn This modern, four-story hotel stands just 2 blocks north of the heart of Ybor City's dining and entertainment district. A one-story brick structure in front houses the bright lobby, a comfy relaxation area with fireplace, a dining area providing cooked and continental breakfasts, and a small pantry selling beer, wine, soft drinks, and frozen dinners. You can heat up the dinners in your comfortable guest room's microwave oven or store them in your fridge. Since Hilton's "Garden" hotels are aimed primarily at business travelers (they compete with Marriott's Courtyards), your room also will have a large desk and two phones. If you opt for a suite, you'll have a separate living room and a larger bathroom than in the regular units.

1700 E. 9th Ave. (between 17th and 18th sts.), Tampa, FL 33605. (*) 800/HILTONS or 813/769-9267. Fax 813/769-3299. 95 units. $99–$199 double. AE, DC, DISC, MC, V. **Amenities:** Restaurant (breakfast only); heated outdoor pool; exercise room; Jacuzzi; business center; laundry service; coin-op washers and dryers. *In room:* A/C, TV, dataport (with high-speed Internet), fridge, coffeemaker, hair dryer, iron.

A NEARBY SPA & SPORTS RESORT

Saddlebrook Resort–Tampa Set on 480 rolling acres, Saddlebrook is off the beaten path (30 min. north of Tampa International Airport) and is a landlocked condominium development. If you're not going to Orlando or are not very interested in spas, tennis, golf, or all of the above, I would recommend any hotel on the beach over this one. But if those things do interest you (and you don't mind not being on the beach), treat yourself to complete spa treatments, join the pros at the Hopman Tennis Program, or perfect your swing at the

Arnold Palmer Golf Academy (see "Outdoor Activities & Spectator Sports," earlier in this chapter). In this condominium development, you'll stay in privately owned hotel rooms or one-, two-, or three-bedroom suites. Much more appealing than the rooms, the suites have kitchens and a patio or balcony overlooking lagoons, cypress and palm trees, and the resort's two 18-hole championship golf courses.

5700 Saddlebrook Way, Wesley Chapel, FL 33543. (C) **800/729-8383** or 813/973-1111. Fax 813/973-4504. www.saddlebrookresort.com. 800 units. Winter $185–$197 per person; off-season $120–$132 per person. Rates include breakfast and dinner. Packages available. AE, DC, DISC, MC, V. Valet parking $10; free self-parking. Take I-75 north to Fla. 54 (exit 58); go 1 mile (1.5km) east to resort. **Amenities:** 3 restaurants (American); 2 bars; heated outdoor pool; 2 golf courses; 45 tennis courts; health club; spa; Jacuzzi; sauna; massage; bike rental; concierge; activities desk; car-rental desk; business center; limited room service; children's activities program; laundry service; coin-op washers and dryers. *In room:* A/C, TV, dataport, kitchen, minibar, fridge, coffeemaker, hair dryer, iron.

WHERE TO DINE

As with the hotels, I have organized the restaurants below by geographic area: near Busch Gardens, in or near Hyde Park (across the Hillsborough River from downtown), and in Ybor City. Although Ybor City is better known, Tampa's trendiest dining scene is along South Howard Avenue—"SoHo" to the locals— between West Kennedy Boulevard and the bay in affluent Hyde Park.

NEAR BUSCH GARDENS

You'll find the national fast-food and family restaurants east of I-275 on Busch Boulevard and Fowler Avenue.

Cafe Don José SPANISH/AMERICAN   It's not nearly on a par with Columbia in Ybor City (see below), but this Spanish-themed restaurant is among the best there is within a short drive of Busch Gardens. High-back chairs, dark wood floors, and Spanish posters and paintings set an appropriate scene for the house specialties of traditional paella (allow 30 min. for preparation) and Valencia-style rice dishes. Don José also offers non-Spanish fare such as chateaubriand and red snapper baked in parchment.

11009 N. 56th St. (in Sherwood Forest Shopping Center, ¼ mile [.5km] south of Fowler Ave.). (C) **813/ 985-2392**. Main courses $13–$22. AE, DC, MC, V. Mon–Fri 11:30am–4:30pm and 5–10pm; Sat 5–10pm.

Mel's Hot Dogs *(Kids)* AMERICAN   Catering to everyone from businesspeople on a lunch break to hungry families craving inexpensive all-beef hot dogs, Mel Lohn's red-and-white cottage offers everything from "bagel-dogs" to bacon/cheddar Reuben-style hot dogs. All choices are served on a poppy-seed bun and can be ordered with french fries and a choice of coleslaw or baked beans. Even the decor is dedicated to wieners: The walls and windows are lined with hot-dog memorabilia. And just in case hot-dog mania hasn't won you over, there are a few alternative choices (chicken, beef and veggie burgers, and terrific onion rings).

4136 E. Busch Blvd., at 42nd St. (C) **813/985-8000**. Most items under $7. No credit cards. Sun–Thurs 11am–8pm; Fri–Sat 11am–9pm.

Ristorante Francesco 🏀 NORTHERN ITALIAN   Gregarious owner Francesco "Frankie" Murchesini patrols the tables in the hottest dining spot in North Tampa (as witnessed by the photos of famous patrons adorning the walls). When not playing his harmonica to celebrate someone's birthday, Frankie's making sure everyone is enjoying his delicious *cernia portofino* (grouper in a brandy sauce with shrimp) and other Northern Italian dishes. His sister makes the pasta, which shows up in more traditional fare such as seafood over linguini *pestatore* with a choice of marinara or white-wine sauce. Be sure to start with half a Caesar salad.

In La Place Village Shopping Center, 1441 E. Fletcher Ave. (between 14th and 15th sts.). ✆ 813/971-3649. Reservations recommended. Main courses $10–$27. AE, DC, DISC, MC. V. Mon–Fri 11:30am–2:30pm and 5:30–10pm; Sat 5:30–10pm; Sun 5–9pm.

Shells ★ *Value* SEAFOOD   You'll see Shells restaurants in many parts of Florida, and with good reason, for this casual, award-winning chain consistently provides excellent value. They all have virtually identical menus, prices, and hours. Particularly good are the spicy Jack Daniel's buffalo shrimp and scallop appetizers. Main courses range from the usual fried seafood platters to pastas and charcoal-grilled shrimp, fish, steaks, and chicken.

11010 N. 30th St. (between Busch Blvd. and Fowler Ave.). ✆ 813/977-8456. Main courses $9–$20 (most $10–$12). AE, DISC, MC, V. Sun–Thurs 11:30am–10pm; Fri–Sat 11:30am–11pm.

HYDE PARK
Expensive

Bern's Steak House ★★ STEAKHOUSE   The exterior of this famous steakhouse looks like a factory. Inside, however, you'll find eight ornate dining rooms with themes like Rhône, Burgundy, and Irish Rebellion. Their atmospheres are perfect for meat lovers, for here you order and pay for expertly charcoal-grilled steaks of perfectly aged beef according to the thickness and weight (the 60-oz., 3-in.-thick Porterhouse can feed four adults). The phone book–size wine list offers more than 7,000 selections, with many available by the glass.

Upstairs, the dessert quarters have 50 romantic booths paneled in aged California redwood, which can privately seat from 2 to 12 guests each. All of these little chambers are equipped with phones for placing your order and closed-circuit TVs for watching and listening to a resident pianist. The dessert menu offers almost 100 delicious selections, plus some 1,400 after-dinner drinks. It's possible to reserve a booth for dessert only, but preference is given to those who dine.

The big secret here is that steak sandwiches are available at the bar but are not mentioned on the menu. Smaller versions of the chargrilled steaks served in the dining rooms, they come with a choice of french fries or crispy onion rings. Add a salad and you have a terrific meal for about half the price of the least-expensive main course.

1208 S. Howard Ave. (at Marjory Ave.). ✆ 800/282-1547 within Florida or 813/251-2421. Reservations recommended. Main courses $17–$58.50; sandwiches $9. AE, DC, DISC, MC, V. Daily 5–11pm. Closed Christmas. Valet parking $4.

Le Bordeaux ★★ TRADITIONAL FRENCH   Located in a converted home, this romantic bistro's authentic French fare is some of the region's best. French-born chef/owner Gordon Davis offers seating in the living room–style main dining room of this converted house, which was expanded to include a plant-filled conservatory. His blackboard menu changes daily, but usually features traditional French favorites such as rack of lamb, cassoulet, and magret of duck. Part of the establishment is the lounge-style Left Bank Jazz Bistro, featuring live jazz Thursday through Saturday from 9pm to 1am.

1502 S. Howard Ave. (2 blocks north of Bayshore Blvd.). ✆ 813/254-4387. Reservations recommended. Main courses $15–$27. AE, DC, MC, V. Sun and Tues–Thurs 5:30–10pm; Fri–Sat 5–11pm.

Dining on the Bay

One of the newest additions to Tampa's dining scene is the 180-foot-long (54m) **StarShip Dining Yacht** (© 877/744-7999 or 813/223-7999; www.starshipdining.com), which makes 2-hour lunch and dinner cruises from the Channelside out onto Tampa Bay. The ship's four dining rooms serve exceptional cruise fare from a kitchen overseen by executive chef Jayson Polanski, who has done stints at some of Tampa's better restaurants. A house band plays during dinner and then moves to the top deck for dancing under the stars. Lunch cruises cost $30 per person with a meal, $16 for sightseers. Dinner cruises range from $50 during the week to $60 on weekends, whether you dine onboard or not. Call for the schedule and reservations.

Moderate

Mise en Place ★★ ECLECTIC   Look around at all those happy, stylish people soaking up the trendy ambience, and you'll know why chef Marty Blitz and his wife, Maryann, have been among the culinary darlings of Tampa since 1986. They present the freshest of ingredients, with a creative menu that changes weekly. Main courses often include fascinating choices such as Creole-style mahimahi served with chili cheese grits and a ragout of black-eyed peas, andouille sausage, and rock shrimp.

In Grand Central Place, 442 W. Kennedy Blvd. (at S. Magnolia Ave., opposite the University of Tampa). © 813/254-5373. Reservations recommended. Main courses $16–$27; tasting menu $35. AE, DC, DISC, MC, V. Tues–Thurs 11:30am–2:30pm and 5:30–10pm; Fri 11:30am–2:30pm and 5:30–11pm; Sat 5–11pm.

Inexpensive

Bella's Italian Cafe ★ *Value* ITALIAN   Creative dishes and very reasonable prices make this sophisticated yet informal cafe one of SoHo's most popular neighborhood hangouts. Although you can order the homemade pasta under traditional Bolognese or Alfredo sauces, the stars here feature the tasty likes of blackened chicken in a creamy tomato sauce over fettuccine, or shrimp and scallops in a roasted tomato sauce over bow-tie pasta. Finish off with the house version of tiramisu. Local professionals flock to the friendly bar during two-for-one happy hours nightly from 4 to 7pm and from 11pm until closing. The open kitchen provides only appetizers, salads, pizzas, and desserts after 11pm.

1413 S. Howard Ave. (at Mississippi Ave.). 850/254-3355. Reservations not accepted. Main courses $7–$12; pizza $6.50–$8.50. AE, DC, DISC, MC, V. Mon–Tues 11:30am–11:30pm; Wed–Thurs 11:30am–12:30am; Fri 11am–1:30am; Sat 4pm–1:30am; Sun 4–11:30pm.

Cactus Club *Value* AMERICAN SOUTHWEST   You can definitely taste the freshness at this Texas roadhouse–style cantina in the middle of the Old Hyde Park Village shops, because all ingredients except the beans come straight from the market. My favorite dish is the "fundido"—a spicy casserole of marinated fajita-style chicken strips and sautéed vegetables topped with melted Jack cheese, with beans and rice on the side. Other offerings are more traditional: tacos, enchiladas, chili, sizzling fajitas, hickory-smoked baby-back ribs, Jamaican jerk chicken, burgers, quesadillas, enchiladas (including vegetarian versions), sandwiches, and smoked chicken salad. The lively Cactus Cantina bar is another favorite neighborhood watering hole. Dine inside or outside, but get here early at lunchtime—it's usually packed.

In Old Hyde Park Village shopping complex, 1601 Snow Ave. (south of Swann Ave.). ✆ 813/251-4089. Reservations not accepted. Main courses $6.50–$14; burgers and sandwiches $7–$8. AE, DC, MC, V. Sun–Thurs 11:30am–10pm; Fri–Sat 11:30am–11pm.

The Colonnade SEAFOOD   Local couples and families have been flocking to this rough-hewn, shiplap place since 1935, primarily for the great view of Hillsborough Bay across Bayshore Boulevard. The food is a bit on the Red Lobsterish side, but the vista from the window tables more than makes up for any shortcomings in the fresh seafood: grouper prepared seven ways, crab-stuffed flounder, Maryland-style crab cakes, even wild Florida alligator as an appetizer. Prime rib, steaks, and chicken are also available.

3401 Bayshore Blvd. (at W. Julia St.). ✆ 813/839-7558. Reservations accepted only for large parties. Main courses $8–$20 (most $11–$15). AE, DC, DISC, MC, V. Sun–Thurs 11am–10pm; Fri–Sat 11am–11pm.

Four Green Fields IRISH/AMERICAN   Just across the bridge from the downtown convention center, America's only thatched-roof Irish pub may be surrounded by palm trees instead of potato fields, but it still offers the ambience and tastes of Ireland. Staffed by genuine Irish immigrants, the large room with a square bar in the center smells of Bass and Harp ales. The Gaelic stew is predictably bland, but the salads and sandwiches are passable. The live Irish music Thursday through Saturday nights and on Sunday afternoon draws a crowd ranging from post-college to early retirees.

205 W. Platt St. (between Parker St. and Plant Ave.). ✆ 813/254-4444. Reservations accepted. Main courses $9.50–$15; sandwiches $6–$7. AE, MC, V. Daily 11am–3am.

YBOR CITY
Moderate

Cafe Creole and Oyster Bar ★★ *Value* CREOLE/CAJUN   Resembling a turn-of-the-last-century railway station, this brick building dates from 1896 and was originally known as El Pasaje, the home of the Cherokee Club, a gentlemen's hotel and private club with a casino and an opulent decor with stained-glass windows, wrought-iron balconies, Spanish murals, and marble bathrooms. Today it's home to Tampa's best Creole and Cajun restaurant. Specialties include exceptionally prepared Louisiana crab cakes, oysters, blackened grouper, and jambalaya. If you're new to bayou cuisine, try the Creole sampler. Dine inside or out.

1330 9th Ave. (at Avenida de Republica de Cuba/14th St.). ✆ 813/247-6283. Reservations not accepted, but call for preferred seating. Main courses $10.50–$18. AE, DC, DISC, MC, V. Mon–Thurs 11:30am–10pm; Fri 11:30am–11:30pm; Sat 5–11:30pm.

Columbia ★★ SPANISH   Dating from 1905, this hand-painted tile building occupies an entire city block in the heart of Ybor City. Tourists flock here to soak up the ambience, and so do the locals because it's so much fun to clap along during fire-belching Spanish flamenco floor shows Monday through Saturday at 7 and 9:30pm. You can't help coming back time after time for the famous Spanish bean soup and original "1905" salad. The *paella a la valenciana* is outstanding, with more than a dozen ingredients from gulf grouper and gulf pink shrimp to calamari, mussels, clams, chicken, and pork. Lighter appetites can choose from a limited menu of tapas, including "Cuban caviar" (actually a spicy black-bean dip). The decor throughout is graced with hand-painted tiles, wrought-iron chandeliers, dark woods, rich red fabrics, and stained-glass windows. You can breathe your own fumes in the Cigar Bar.

2117 E. 7th Ave. (between 21st and 22nd Sts.). © 813/248-4961. Reservations recommended. Main courses $14–$23. AE, DC, DISC, MC, V. Mon–Thurs 11am–10pm; Fri–Sat 11am–11pm.

Inexpensive

Carmine's Restaurant & Bar CUBAN/ITALIAN/AMERICAN Bright blue poles hold up an ancient pressed-tin ceiling above this noisy corner cafe. It's not the cleanest joint in town, but a great variety of loyal local patrons gather here for genuine Cuban sandwiches—smoked ham, roast pork, Genoa salami, Swiss cheese, pickles, salad dressing, mustard, lettuce, and tomato on a crispy submarine roll. There's a vegetarian version too, and the combination half-sandwich and choice of black beans and rice or a bowl of Spanish soup made with sausages, potatoes, and garbanzo beans all make a hearty meal for just $6 at lunch, $7 at dinner. Main courses are led by Cuban-style roast pork, thin-cut pork chops with mushroom sauce, spaghetti with a blue-crab tomato sauce, and a few seafood and chicken platters.

1802 E. 7th Ave. (at 18th St.). © 813/248-3834. Reservations not accepted. Main courses $7–$17; sandwiches $4–$8. No credit cards. Mon–Tues 11am–11pm; Wed–Thurs 11am–1am; Fri–Sat 11am–3am; Sun 11am–6pm.

Ovo Cafe ★ INTERNATIONAL This cafe, popular with the business set by day and the club crowd on weekend nights, features a melange of sophisticated offerings. Pierogies and pasta pillows come with taste-tempting sauces and fillings, and there are several creative salads and unusual individual-size pizzas. Strawberries or blackberries and a splash of liqueur cover the thick waffles. Portions are substantial, but be careful of the strictly a la carte pricing here. The big black bar dispenses a wide variety of martinis, plus some unusual liqueur drinks.

1901 E. 7th Ave. (at 19th St.). © 813/248-6979. Reservations strongly recommended Fri–Sat. Main courses $10–$15; sandwiches $7–$8.50; pizza $8.50–$10. AE, DC, DISC, MC, V. Mon–Tues 11am–3pm; Wed–Thurs 11am–10pm; Fri–Sat 11am–1am.

TAMPA AFTER DARK

The Tampa/Hillsborough Arts Council maintains an **Artsline** (© **813/229-ARTS**), a 24-hour information service providing the latest on current and upcoming cultural events. Racks in many restaurants and bars have copies of *Weekly Planet* (www.weeklyplanet.com), *Focus,* and *Accent on Tampa Bay,* three free publications detailing what's going on in the entire bay area. And you can also check the "Baylife" and "Friday Extra" sections of the *Tampa Tribune* (www.tampatrib.com) and the Thursday "Weekend" section of the *St. Petersburg Times* (www.sptimes.com). The visitor center usually has copies of the week's newspaper sections (see "Essentials," earlier in this chapter).

THE CLUB & MUSIC SCENE Ybor City is Tampa's favorite nighttime venue by far. All you have to do is stroll along 7th Avenue East between 15th and 20th streets, and you'll hear music blaring out of the clubs. The avenue is packed with people, a majority of them high schoolers and early 20-somethings, on Friday and Saturday from 9pm to 3am, but you'll also find something going on from Tuesday to Thursday and even on Sundays. The clubs change names and character frequently, so you don't need names, addresses, or phone numbers; your ears will guide you along 7th Avenue East. With all of the sidewalk seating, it is easy to judge what the clientele is like in any given place and make your choice from there.

> **Tips** **Careful Where You Park**
>
> Parking can be scarce during nighttime in Ybor City, and the area has seen an occasional robbery late at night. Play it safe and use the municipal parking lots behind the shops on 8th Avenue East or the new parking garages near Centro Ybor, on 7th Avenue East at 16th Street.

The center of the action these days is **Centro Ybor,** on 7th Avenue East at 16th Street (© 813/242-4660; www.thecentroybor.com), the district's large new dining-and-entertainment complex. The restaurants and pubs in this family-oriented center tend to be considerably tamer than many of those along 7th Avenue, at least on non-weekend nights. You don't have to pay to listen to live music in the center's patio on weekend afternoons.

THE PERFORMING ARTS   With a prime downtown location on 9 acres along the east bank of the Hillsborough River, the huge **Tampa Bay Performing Arts Center** ★, 1010 N. MacInnes Place next to the Tampa Museum of Art (© 800/955-1045 or 813/229-STAR; www.tampacenter.com), is the largest performing-arts venue south of the Kennedy Center in Washington, D.C. Accordingly, this four-theater complex is the focal point of Tampa's performing-arts scene, presenting a wide range of Broadway plays, classical and pop concerts, operas, cabarets, improv, and special events.

A sightseeing attraction in its own right, the restored **Tampa Theatre,** 711 Franklin St. (© 813/223-8981; www.tampatheatre.org), between Zack and Polk streets, dates from 1926 and is on the National Register of Historic Places. It presents a varied program of classic, foreign, and alternative films, as well as concerts and special events.

The 66,321-seat **Raymond James Stadium,** 4201 N. Dale Mabry Hwy. (© 813/673-4300; www.raymondjames.com/stadium), is frequently the site of headliner concerts. The **USF Sun Dome,** 4202 E. Fowler Ave. (© 813/974-3111; www.sundome.org), on the University of South Florida campus, hosts major concerts by touring pop stars, rock bands, jazz groups, and other contemporary artists.

Ticketmaster (© 813/287-8844) sells tickets to most events and shows.

2 St. Petersburg ★

20 miles (32km) SW of Tampa, 289 miles (465km) NW of Miami, 84 miles (135km) SW of Orlando

On the western shore of the bay, St. Petersburg stands in contrast to Tampa, much like San Francisco compares to Oakland in California. Whereas Tampa is the area's business, industrial, and shipping center, St. Petersburg was conceived and built almost a century ago primarily for tourists and wintering snowbirds. Here you'll find one of the most picturesque and pleasant downtowns of any city in Florida, with a waterfront promenade and the famous, pyramid-shaped Pier offering great views across the bay, plus quality museums, interesting shops, and a few good restaurants.

Away from downtown, the city pretty much consists of strip malls dividing residential neighborhoods, but plan at least to have a look around the charming bay-front area. If you don't do anything else, go out on The Pier and take a pleasant stroll along Bayshore Drive.

ESSENTIALS

GETTING THERE **Tampa International Airport,** approximately 16 miles (26km) northeast of St. Petersburg, is the prime gateway for the area (see "Essentials," in section 1, earlier in this chapter). At press time, only **Pan Am** (℃ **800/FLY-PANAM;** www.flypanam.com) had year-round scheduled service to **St. Petersburg–Clearwater International Airport,** on Roosevelt Boulevard (Fla. 686) about 10 miles (16km) north of downtown St. Petersburg (℃ **727/ 535-7600**). The Canadian carrier **Air Transat** (℃ **877/872-6728;** www.air-transat.com) flies here during the winter months. **Amtrak** (℃ **800/USA-RAIL;** www.amtrak.com) has bus connections from its Tampa station to downtown St. Petersburg (see "Getting There," in section 1, above).

VISITOR INFORMATION For advance information about both St. Petersburg and the beaches (see section 3, below), contact the **St. Petersburg/Clearwater Area Convention & Visitors Bureau,** 14450 46th St. N., Clearwater, FL 34622 (℃ **800/345-6710,** or 727/464-7200 for advance hotel reservations; fax 727/464-7222; www.FloridasBeach.com for information specific to the beaches).

Once you get here, head to the **St. Petersburg Area Chamber of Commerce,** 100 2nd Ave. N. (at 1st St.), St. Petersburg, FL 33701 (℃ **727/821-4069;** fax 727/895-6326; www.stpete.com). Across the street from the BayWalk shopping-and-dining complex, this downtown main office and visitor center is open Monday through Friday from 8am to 5pm, Saturday from 10am to 4pm, and Sunday from noon to 4pm. Ask for a copy of the chamber's visitor guide, which lists hotels, motels, condominiums, and other accommodations.

Also downtown, there are **walk-in information centers** on the first level of The Pier and in the lobby of the Florida International Museum (see "Seeing the Top Attractions," below).

The chamber also operates the **Suncoast Welcome Center** (℃ **727/ 573-1449**), on Ulmerton Road at exit 18 southbound off I-275 (there's no exit here for northbound traffic). The center is open daily from 9am to 5pm except New Year's Day, Easter, Thanksgiving, and Christmas.

GETTING AROUND You can see everything on the very pink **Downtown Trolleys** (℃ 727/571-3440), which run out to the end of The Pier and past all of the downtown attractions every 30 minutes from 11am to 5pm daily except Thanksgiving and Christmas. Rides cost 50¢ per person.

The **Pinellas Suncoast Transit Authority/PSTA** (℃ 727/530-9911; www.psta.net) operates regular bus service throughout St. Petersburg and the rest of the Pinellas Peninsula. Rides cost $1.25 for adults, 60¢ for seniors, and 75¢ for students.

If you need a cab, call **Yellow Cab** (℃ 727/821-7777) or **Independent Cab** (℃ 727/327-3444). Fares are $1.50 at flag fall, plus 20¢ for each ½ mile.

SEEING THE TOP ATTRACTIONS

Florida Holocaust Museum ⋆ This thought-provoking museum has exhibits about the Holocaust, including a boxcar used to transport human cargo to the Auschwitz death camp in Poland. Its main focus, however, is to promote tolerance and understanding in the present. It was founded by Walter P. Loebenberg, a local businessman who escaped Nazi Germany in 1939 and fought with the U.S. Army in World War II.

55 5th St. S. (between Central Ave. and 1st Ave. S.). ℃ **727/820-0100.** www.flholocaustmuseum.org. Admission $6 adults, $5 seniors and colleges students, $2 children under 18. Mon–Fri 10am–5pm; Sat–Sun noon–5pm. Closed Easter, Rosh Hashanah, Yom Kippur, Thanksgiving, and Christmas.

Downtown St. Petersburg

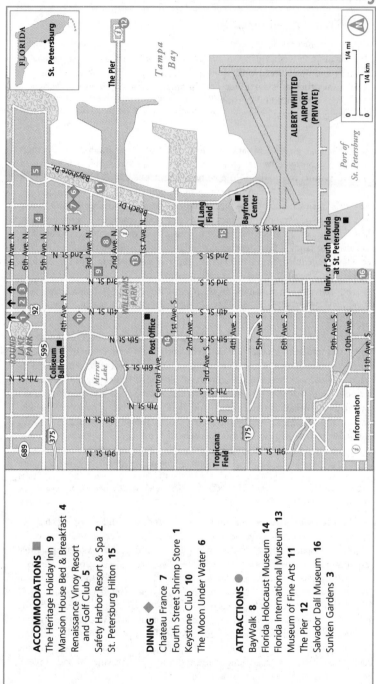

ACCOMMODATIONS ■

The Heritage Holiday Inn **9**
Mansion House Bed & Breakfast **4**
Renaissance Vinoy Resort
and Golf Club **5**
Safety Harbor Resort & Spa **2**
St. Petersburg Hilton **15**

DINING ◆

Chateau France **7**
Fourth Street Shrimp Store **1**
Keystone Club **10**
The Moon Under Water **6**

ATTRACTIONS ●

BayWalk **8**
Florida Holocaust Museum **14**
Florida International Museum **13**
Museum of Fine Arts **11**
The Pier **12**
Salvador Dali Museum **16**
Sunken Gardens **3**

Fun Fact **Open-Air Mail**

St. Petersburg residents don't have to go inside to get mail out of their boxes at St. Petersburg's open-air **Post Office,** at the corner of 1st Avenue North and 4th Street North. Built in 1917, this granite, arcaded Spanish Colonial structure is a popular local landmark and is often photographed by those enchanted by its charm.

Florida International Museum ★★ Housed in the former Maas Brothers Department Store, long an area landmark, this excellent museum attracted 600,000 visitors from around the world when it opened its first exhibition in 1995, and the success has continued. Its outstanding exhibit on the Cuban Missile Crisis was such a smash hit that it's now permanent—and well worth seeing even if the two temporary exhibits don't catch your fancy. On the other hand, they very well could, since the museum is associated with—and gets some of its staff on loan from—the Smithsonian Institution in Washington, D.C. Call to see what's scheduled during your visit. Allow at least 3 hours to tour all three exhibitions. There's an excellent museum store here.

100 2nd St. N. (between 1st and 2nd aves. N.). ✆ 877/535-7469 or 727/822-3693. www.floridamuseum. org. Admission to all exhibits $12 adults, $11 seniors, $6 children 6–18, free for children under 6. Mon–Sat 9am–5pm; Sun noon–5pm (last entry 4pm daily).

Museum of Fine Arts ★★ Resembling a Mediterranean villa on the waterfront, this museum houses an excellent permanent collection of European, American, pre-Colombian, and Far Eastern art, with works by such artists as Fragonard, Monet, Renoir, Cézanne, and Gauguin. Other highlights include period rooms with antiques and historical furnishings, plus a gallery of Steuben crystal, a new decorative-arts gallery, and world-class rotating exhibits. The best way to see it all is on a free, guided tour, which takes about 1 hour. Ask about classical-music performances from October to April.

255 Beach Dr. NE (at 3rd Ave. N.). ✆ 727/896-2667. www.fine-arts.org. Admission Tues–Sat $6 adults, $5 seniors, $2 students, free for children under 6. Admission free on Sun (donation suggested). Admission includes guided tour. Tues–Sat 10am–5pm; Sun 1–5pm. Winter, third Thurs of each month 10am–9pm. Guided tours Tues–Sat 11am, 1, 2, and 3pm; Sun 1 and 2pm. Closed New Year's Day, Martin Luther King, Jr. Day, Thanksgiving, Christmas.

The Pier ★ *Kids* The Pier is a festive waterfront dining-and-shopping complex overlooking Tampa Bay. Originally built as a railroad pier in 1889, today it's capped by a spaceshiplike inverted pyramid offering five levels of shops, three restaurants, a tourist information desk, an observation deck, catwalks for fishing, boat docks, miniature golf, boat and water-sports rentals, sightseeing boats, and a food court, plus an aquarium and **Great Explorations** (✆ 727/821-8992; www.greatexplorations.org), a hands-on children's museum offering a variety of exhibits—great for a rainy day or for kids who've overdosed on the sun and need to cool off indoors. Cruise boats often operate from The Pier during the winter months, and you can rent fishing gear and drop your line into the bay all year. There's valet parking at the end of the pier, or you can park on land and ride a free trolley out to the complex.

800 2nd Ave. NE. ✆ 727/821-6443. www.stpete-pier.com. Free admission to all the public areas and decks; donations welcome at the Pier Aquarium. Great Explorations $4, $2 seniors, free for children under 3. Valet

parking $6; self-parking $3. Pier Mon–Thurs 10am–9pm; Fri–Sat 10am–10pm; Sun 11am–7pm. Aquarium Mon–Sat 10am–8pm; Sun 11am–6pm. Great Explorations Mon–Sat 10am–8pm; Sun 11am–6pm. Shops and restaurant hours vary.

Salvador Dalí Museum ★★★   This starkly modern museum houses the world's most comprehensive collection of works by the renowned Spanish surrealist—and for art lovers is reason enough to visit downtown St. Petersburg. It includes oil paintings, watercolors and drawings, and more than 1,000 graphics, plus posters, photos, sculptures, objets d'art, and a 5,000-volume library on Dalí and surrealism. Reynolds Morse, an Ohio plastics engineer, and his wife, Eleanore, discovered the Catalonian artist and began collecting his works in 1943. They moved the collection here in 1980.

1000 3rd St. S. (near 11th Ave. S.). ✆ 727/823-3767. www.salvadordalimuseum.org. Admission $10 adults, $7 seniors, $5 students, free for children 10 and under. Thurs 5–8pm 50% discount. Mon–Sat 9:30am–5:30pm; Thurs 9:30am–8pm; Sun noon–5:30pm. Closed Thanksgiving, Christmas.

Sunken Gardens   Dating back to 1935, this former tourist attraction is now operated as a 7-acre botanical garden by the City of St. Petersburg. It contains a vast array of 5,000 plants, flowers, and trees; plus a butterfly aviary; a display of snakes, spiders, and scorpions; and a rain-forest information center. There's a daily wildlife show. Call for a schedule of exhibits and tours.

1825 4th St. N. (between 18th and 19th Aves. NE). ✆ 813/896-3186. www.stpete.org/sunken.htm. Admission $7 adults, $5 seniors, $3 children 3–12, free for children 2 and under. Wed–Sun 10am–4pm.

ORGANIZED TOURS

The only organized tours of St. Petersburg—and they are pretty good ones—are with **Duck Tours of Tampa Bay** (✆ **727/432-3825;** www.ducktoursoftampa bay.com), which has 1½-hour tours of downtown and the nearby waterways using reconditioned World War II amphibious "Ducks." The vehicles depart from The Pier daily from 11am to 5pm. The narrated tours cost $18.50 for adults, $16.50 for seniors, and $9.95 for children 3 to 12, plus tax. Kids under 3 are free. The same company has tours of Tampa (see the "Quacking Around" box in section 1, above).

OUTDOOR ACTIVITIES & SPECTATOR SPORTS

You can get up-to-the-minute recorded information about the city's sports and recreational activities by calling the **Leisure Line** (✆ 727/893-7500).

BIKING, IN-LINE SKATING & HIKING   With miles of flat terrain, the St. Petersburg area is ideal for bikers, in-line skaters, and hikers. The **Pinellas Trail** is especially good, since it follows an abandoned railroad bed 47 miles (76km) from St. Petersburg north to Tarpon Springs and from there to Tampa. It crosses the bay via the old Gandy Bridge (which runs alongside the newer Gandy Bridge), now known as the **Friendship TrailBridge** (✆ 813/289-4400). The

---

Tips Car Smarts

You can spend a small fortune in a parking garage or in feeding the meters in St. Petersburg, but you can cut costs substantially by parking at The Pier ($3 all day) and taking The Looper, the city's trolley service, which operates between The Pier and all major downtown attractions. See "Getting Around" in this section.

2½-mile-long (4km) bridge is open to hikers, bikers, bicyclists, fishers, and in-line skaters, but be careful going up and down the steep center span, especially if you're on skates. The **St. Pete trail head** is on 34th Street South (U.S. 19) between 8th and Fairfield Avenues south. It's packed on the weekends. Free strip maps of the trail are available at the St. Petersburg Area Chamber of Commerce (see "Visitor Information," above).

GOLF　One of the nation's top 50 municipal courses, the **Mangrove Bay Golf Course** ⚐⚐, 875 62nd Ave. NE (© **727/893-7797**), hugs the inlets of Old Tampa Bay and offers 18-hole, par-72 play. Facilities include a driving range; lessons and golf-club rental are also available. Fees are about $25 in winter, slightly lower off-season.

In Largo, the **Bardmoor Golf Club,** 7919 Bardmoor Blvd. (© **727/ 397-0483**), is often the venue for major tournaments. Lakes punctuate 17 of the 18 holes on this par-72 championship course. Lessons and rental clubs are available, as is a Tom Fazio–designed practice range. Call the clubhouse for seasonal greens fees. The course is open daily from 7am to dusk.

Call **Tee Times USA** (© **800/374-8633;** www.teetimesusa.com) to reserve times at these and other area courses.

If you want to take up golf or sharpen your game, TV "Golf Doctor" Joe Quinzi hosts his **Quinzi Golf Academy** (© **727/725-1999**) at the Safety Harbor Resort and Spa (see "Where to Stay," later in this chapter). His school offers personalized instruction and clinics.

SAILING　Both Steve and Doris Colgate's **Offshore Sailing School** (© **800/ 221-4326** or 941/454-1700; www.offshore-sailing.com) and the **Annapolis Sailing School** (© **800/638-9192** or 727/867-8102; www.annapolissailing. com) have operations here. Various courses lasting from 2 days to a week are offered. Contact the schools for prices and schedules.

SPECTATOR SPORTS　St. Petersburg has always been a baseball town, and **Tropicana Field,** a 45,000-seat domed stadium alongside I-175 between 9th and 16th Streets (© **727/825-3100;** www.stpete.org/dome.htm), is the home of the American League **Tampa Bay Devil Rays** (© **888/FAN-RAYS** or 727/825-3250; www.devilrays.mlb.com). The baseball season runs April through September. Call or check the website for schedule and ticket information. The Devil Rays move outdoors to Florida Power Park at Al Lang Field, on 2nd Avenue South at 1st Street South, for their spring-training games from mid-February to the end of March.

The **Philadelphia Phillies** play their spring-training season at Jack Russell Stadium, 800 Phillies Dr., in nearby Clearwater (© **727/442-8496** or 215/436-1000; www.phillies.mlb.com). Their minor-league affiliate, the **Clearwater Phillies** (© **727/441-8638;** www.clearwaterphillies.com), plays in the stadium April through August. The **Toronto Blue Jays** do their spring thing at Grant Field, 373 Douglas Ave. in Dunedin (© **800/707-8269** or 813/733-9302; www.bluejays.mlb.com), which also is home to their minor-league affiliate, the **Dunedin Blue Jays** (© **727/733-9302;** www.dunedinblue jays.com), April through August.

TENNIS　You can learn to play or hone your game at the **Phil Green Tennis Academy** at Safety Harbor Resort and Spa (see "Where to Stay," later in this chapter).

Mermaids & Manatees

Drive north of St. Petersburg for an hour on congested U.S. 19, and you'll come to one of Florida's original tourist attractions, the famous **Weeki Wachee Springs Water Park** (© **800/678-9335** or 352/596-2062; www.weekiwachee.com). "Mermaids" have been putting on acrobatic swimming shows here every day since 1947. It's a sight to see them doing their dances in waters that come from one of America's most prolific freshwater springs, pouring some 170 million gallons of 72°F (22°C) water a day into the river. There's more than mermaids here; you can take a Wilderness River Cruise across the Weeki Wachee River and send the kids on the flume ride at **Buccaneer Bay,** the water-park part of the attraction. Admission is $15.95 for adults, $11.95 for children 3 to 10. Kids under 3 get in free. The spring is open daily from 10am to 3pm in winter, to 4 or 5pm in spring and fall, to 6pm in the hot summer months (call for precise times and special shows). The water park is open from March to mid-autumn, daily from 10am to 5pm. You can also rent canoes (© **352/597-0360**).

From Weeki Wachee, travel 21 miles (34km) north to the **Homosassa Springs Wildlife State Park,** 4150 S. Suncoast Blvd. (U.S. 19) in Homosassa Springs (© **352/628-5343;** www.floridastateparks.org/district2/ homosassasprings). The highlight here is a floating observatory where visitors can "walk" underwater and watch manatees in a rehabilitation facility, as well as thousands of fresh- and saltwater fish. You'll also see deer, bear, bobcats, otters, egrets, and flamingos along unspoiled nature trails. The park is open daily from 9am to 5:30pm (last ticket sold at 4pm). Admission is $7.95 for adults and $4.95 for children 3 to 12, plus tax, and includes a 20-minute narrated boat ride. Kids under 3 get in free.

About 7 miles (11km) north of Homosassa Springs, some 300 manatees spend the winter in Crystal River, and you can **swim or snorkel with the manatees** ⭐ in the warm-water natural spring of Kings Bay. **American Pro Diving Center,** 821 SE Hwy. 19, Crystal River, FL 34429 (© **800/291-DIVE** or 352/563-0041; fax 352/563-5230; www.american prodive.com), offers daily swimming and snorkel tours. Early mornings are the best time to see the manatees, so try to take the 6:30am departure. The trips range from about $30 to $50 per person. Call for the schedule and reservations. American Pro Diving also rents cottages on the Homosassa River.

Baseball fans won't want to miss the **Ted Williams Museum & Hitters Hall of Fame,** 2455 N. Citrus Hills Blvd., off C.R. 486 west of Hernando (© **352/527-6566;** www.twmuseum.com). Built in the shape of a baseball diamond, the museum holds the great hitter's personal memorabilia, including his two Triple Crown batting titles. It's open Tuesday through Sunday from 10am to 4pm. Admission is $9 adults, $1 for children.

For more information about the area, contact the **Citrus County Chamber of Commerce,** 28 NW Hwy. 19, Crystal River, FL 34428 (© **352/ 795-3149;** fax 352/795-4260; www.citruscountychamber.com). The chamber's visitor center is open Monday through Friday from 8:30am to 4:30pm, Saturday from 9am to 1pm.

SHOPPING

The Pier, at the end of 2nd Avenue Northeast (see "Seeing the Top Attractions," earlier in this chapter), houses more than a dozen boutiques and craft shops; but nearby Beach Drive, running along the waterfront, is one of the most fashionable downtown strolling and shopping venues. Here you'll find the **Glass Canvas Gallery,** at 4th Avenue Northeast (© 727/821-6767), featuring a dazzling array of glass sculpture, tableware, art, and craft items by 250 local, national, and international artists. Also at 4th Avenue Northeast is **P. Buckley Moss** (© 727/894-2899), a museum-grade store carrying the works of the individualistic artist best known for her portrayal of the Amish and the Mennonites. The works include paintings, graphics, figurines, and collector dolls. **Red Cloud,** between 1st and 2nd avenues (© 727/821-5824), is an oasis for Native American crafts, including jewelry, headdresses, and art.

Downtown's new commercial showplace is **BayWalk** (© 727/895-9277; www.baywalklive.com), an open-air shopping, dining, and entertainment complex bordered by 1st and 2nd streets and 2nd and 3rd avenues North. It has branches of Ann Taylor, Chico's, Sunglass Hut, and a few other mall stores, plus some small boutiques.

Central Avenue is another shopping area, featuring the **Gas Plant Antique Arcade,** between 12th and 13th Streets (© 727/895-0368), the largest antiques mall on Florida's west coast, with more than 100 dealers displaying their wares. (Downtown has several antiques-and-collectibles dealers; get a list and map from the chamber of commerce.) The **Florida Craftsmen Gallery,** at 5th Street (© 727/821-7391; www.floridacraftsmen.net), is a showcase for the works of more than 150 Florida artisans and craftspeople specializing in jewelry, ceramics, woodwork, fiber works, glassware, paper creations, and metalwork.

WHERE TO STAY

The **St. Petersburg/Clearwater Area Convention & Visitors Bureau** (see "Essentials," earlier in this chapter) operates a free **reservations service** (© 800/345-6710), through which you can book rooms at most hotels and motels in both St. Petersburg and at the beaches. The bureau also publishes a brochure that lists members of its Superior Small Lodgings program; all establishments have fewer than 50 rooms and have been inspected and certified for cleanliness and value.

Other than the Renaissance Vinoy Resort and Golf Club (see below), the only chain hotel downtown is the **St. Petersburg Hilton,** 333 1st St. S., between 3rd and 4th avenues South (© 800/HILTONS or 727/894-5000; fax 727/823-4797; www.stpetehilton.com), a 15-story business and convention hotel within steps of the Salvador Dalí Museum, Florida Power Park at Al Lang Field, and the Bayfront Center's theaters. Otherwise, views from the upper-floor rooms are its main draw for casual travelers.

VERY EXPENSIVE

Renaissance Vinoy Resort and Golf Club ★★   Built as the grand Vinoy Park in 1925, this elegant Spanish-style establishment reopened in 1992 after a total and meticulous $93 million restoration that made it once again the city's finest hotel. Dominating the northern part of downtown, it overlooks Tampa Bay and is within walking distance of The Pier, Central Avenue, museums, and other attractions. All the guest rooms, many of which enjoy lovely views of the bay front, offer the utmost in comfort and include three phones, an additional

TV in the bathroom, and bath scales. Some rooms in the original building have standing-room-only balconies; so if you need enough room to sit outside, request a balconied unit in the new Tower wing (some of these have whirlpool tubs, too). Overlooking the bay, the Mediterranean-style **Marchand's Grille** is the city's most elegant dining room and serves some of the best steaks and chops in town.

501 5th Ave. NE (at Beach Dr.), St. Petersburg, FL 33701. © **800/HOTELS-1** or 727/894-1000. Fax 727/822-2785. www.renaissancehotels.com. 360 units. Winter $239–$429 double; off-season $139–$369 double. Packages available. AE, DC, DISC, MC, V. Valet parking $12; self-parking $8. **Amenities:** 4 restaurants (Mediterranean, American); 2 bars; 2 heated outdoor pools (connected by a waterfall); Jacuzzi; golf course; 12 tennis courts; health club and spa; concierge; activities desk; car-rental desk; business center; salon; 24-hr. room service; massage; laundry service; coin-operated washers and dryers; concierge-level rooms. *In room:* A/C, TV, dataport, minibar, coffeemaker, hair dryer, iron.

MODERATE

The Heritage Holiday Inn ✹   No ordinary Holiday Inn, the Heritage dates from the early 1920s, and although significantly updated, it still retains the ambience of an old-fashioned hotel, with tall double-hung windows and hard-wood floors that creak as you walk down the long central hallway. A sweeping veranda, French doors, and a tropical courtyard help attract an eclectic clientele, from business travelers to seniors. The furnishings include period antiques and brass beds. Some one-bedroom suites have sofa beds, two televisions, two phones, and two bathrooms.

234 3rd Ave. N. (between 2nd and 3rd Sts.), St. Petersburg, FL 33701. © **800/283-7829** or 727/822-4814. Fax 727/823-1644. www.sixcontinentshotels.com. 71 units. $100–$140 double. AE, DC, DISC, MC, V. **Amenities:** Restaurant (steaks); bar; heated outdoor pool; Jacuzzi; limited room service; laundry service. *In room:* A/C, TV, dataport, coffeemaker, hair dryer, iron.

Mansion House Bed & Breakfast ✹   Mirror images of each other, these two Arts-and-Crafts–style houses separated by a landscaped courtyard were built between 1901 and 1912. The comfortable living room in the main house, which has 6 of the 10 units here, opens to a sun room, off which a small screened porch provides mosquito-free lounging and the only place where guests can smoke. Both houses have upstairs front parlors with TVs, VCRs, and libraries. Tall, old-fashioned windows let lots of light into the attractive guest rooms. The pick of the litter is the "Pembroke" room, upstairs over the carriage house. It has a four-poster bed with mosquito netting, and its residents have their own whirlpool in an outdoor screened hut. The brick courtyard between the two houses (there's a heated swimming pool and Jacuzzi out there) is a popular spot for weddings, receptions, and other functions.

105 5th Ave. NE (at 1st St. NE.), St. Petersburg, FL 33701. © **800/274-7520** or 727/821-9391. Fax 727/821-6909. www.mansionbandb.com. 10 units (all with bathroom). $99–$220 double. Rates include full breakfast. AE, DC, DISC, MC, V. **Amenities:** Heated outdoor pool; access to nearby health club; Jacuzzi; bicycle rentals; laundry service. *In room:* A/C, TV, dataport, hair dryer.

A NEARBY SPA

Safety Harbor Resort and Spa ✹✹ *Value*   Hernando de Soto thought he had found Ponce de León's fabled Fountain of Youth when in 1539 he happened upon five mineral springs in what is now Safety Harbor on the western shore of Old Tampa Bay (see the "Tampa & St. Petersburg" map, above). You may not recover your youth at this venerable spa, which has been in operation since 1926 and got a face lift in 1998, but you will be rejuvenated with such services as massage and hydrotherapy and a full menu of fitness classes from boxing to yoga.

The mineral springs enable it to offer acclaimed water-fitness programs, and this a good place to work on your games at the Quinzi Golf Academy and the Phil Green Tennis Academy (see "Outdoor Activities & Spectator Sports," earlier in this chapter). The sprawling complex of beige stucco buildings with Spanish-tile roofs sits on 22 waterfront acres in the sleepy town of Safety Harbor, north of St. Petersburg. Moss-draped Safety Harbor has a charming small-town ambience, with a number of shops and restaurants just outside the spa's entrance. Given the reasonable off-season room rates and special packages available, this is one of Florida's better spa values.

105 N. Bayshore Dr., Safety Harbor, FL 34695. (℧ **888/BEST-SPA** or 727/726-1161. Fax 727/724-7749. www.safetyharborspa.com. 193 units. Winter $209–$229 double; off-season $139–$159 double. Packages available. AE, DC, DISC, MC, V. Valet parking $8; free self-parking. Pets accepted ($35-per-night charge). **Amenities:** 2 restaurants (American); bar; heated indoor and outdoor pools; golf course; 9 tennis courts; full-service spa; bicycle rentals; concierge; activities desk; car-rental desk; business center; limited room service; laundry service; coin-op washers and dryers. *In room:* A/C, TV, dataport (with high-speed Internet), coffeemaker, hair dryer, iron.

WHERE TO DINE

Don't overlook the food court at **The Pier,** where the inexpensive chow is accompanied by a very rich, but quite free, view of the bay. Among The Pier's restaurants is a branch of Tampa's famous **Columbia** (℧ **727/822-8000**). Downtown also has an offshoot of Ybor City's **Ovo Cafe,** at 515 Central Ave. (℧ **727/895-5515**). See "Where to Dine," in section 1, earlier in this chapter, for details about Columbia and Ovo Cafe.

EXPENSIVE

Chateau France ✹✹ CLASSICAL FRENCH   Chef Antoine Louro provides St. Petersburg's finest cuisine and most romantic setting in this charming pink Victorian house built in 1910. He specializes in French classics such as homemade paté, Dover sole meunière, filet mignon au poivre, coq au vin, orange duck, and a rich seafood bouillabaisse. Fresh baby vegetables, Gruyère-cheese potatoes, and Antoine's special Eiffel Tower salad accompany all main courses. The wine list is excellent, as are the bananas flambé and crêpes Suzette.

136 4th Ave. N. (between Bayshore Dr. and 1st St. N.). (℧ 727/894-7163. Reservations recommended. Main courses $20–$30. AE, DC, DISC, MC, V. Daily 5–11pm.

MODERATE

Keystone Club ✹ STEAKS/PRIME RIB   Resembling an exclusive men's club, this cozy restaurant's forest-green walls accented by dark wood and etched glass create an atmosphere that's reminiscent of a Manhattan-style chophouse. But women are also welcome to partake of the beef, which is king here. Specialties include roast prime rib, New York strip steak, and filet mignon. Seafood also makes an appearance, with fresh lobster and grouper at market price.

320 4th St. N. (between 3rd and 4th aves. N.). (℧ 727/822-6600. Reservations recommended. Main courses $12–$24. AE, DC, DISC, MC, V. Mon–Thurs 4:30–9pm; Fri–Sat 4:30–10pm.

INEXPENSIVE

Fourth Street Shrimp Store ✹✹ *Value* SEAFOOD   If you're anywhere in the area, don't miss at least driving by to see the colorful, cartoonlike mural on the outside of this eclectic establishment just north of downtown. On first impression it looks like graffiti, but it's actually a gigantic drawing of people eating. Inside, it gets even better, with paraphernalia and murals on two walls making the main dining room seem like a warehouse with windows that look out on an early-19th-century seaport (one painted sailor permanently peers in to see what you're eating). You'll pass a seafood market counter when you enter, from which comes the fresh namesake shrimp, the star here. You can also pick from grouper, clam strips, catfish, or oysters fried, broiled, or steamed, all served in heaping portions. This is the best and certainly the most interesting bargain in town.

1006 4th St. N. (at 10th Ave. N.). © 727/822-0325. Main courses $5–$14; sandwiches $2.50–$7. MC, V. Daily 11am–9pm.

The Moon Under Water ASIAN/MIDDLE EASTERN/AMERICAN Tables on the veranda or sidewalk in front of this pub are a great place to take a break during your downtown stroll. The British Raj rules supreme inside the darkly paneled dining room with its slowly twirling ceiling fans and plethora of colonial artifacts, including obligatory pith helmets. Your taste buds are in for a treat here, because the bill of fare covers a number of former British outposts, including America (burgers and Philly cheese steaks), but the emphasis here is on mild, medium, or blazing-hot Indian curries—with a recommended Irish, British, or Australian beer to slake the resulting thirst. For lighter fare, consider Mideastern tabbouleh. There's live music on weekend evenings.

332 Beach Dr. NE (between 3rd and 4th aves.). © 727/896-6160. Main courses $7.50–$17; sandwiches and salads $6–$8. AE, DC, DISC, MC, V. Sun–Thurs 11:30am–11pm; Fri–Sat 11:30am–midnight. Closed New Year's Day, Thanksgiving, Christmas.

ST. PETERSBURG AFTER DARK

Good sources of nightlife information are the Thursday "Weekend" section of the *St. Petersburg Times* (www.sptimes.com), the "Baylife" and "Friday Extra" sections of the *Tampa Tribune* (www.tampatrib.com), and the *Weekly Planet* (www.weeklyplanet.com), a tabloid available at the visitor information offices and in many hotel and restaurant lobbies.

The heart of downtown's nighttime scene is **BayWalk** (© 727/895-9277; www.baywalklive.com), downtown's new shopping-dining-entertainment complex bordered by 1st and 2nd streets and 2nd and 3rd avenues North. There, a 20-screen cinema and several restaurants and bars will keep you busy.

THE CLUB & MUSIC SCENE   A historic attraction as well as an entertainment venue, the Moorish-style **Coliseum Ballroom,** 535 4th Ave. N. (© 727/892-5202; www.stpete.org/coliseum.htm), has been hosting dancing, big bands, boxing, and other events since 1924 (it even made an appearance in the 1985 movie *Cocoon*). Come out and watch the town's many seniors doing the jitterbug just like it was 1945 again! Call for the schedule and prices.

PERFORMING-ARTS VENUES   The **Bayfront Center,** 400 1st St. S. (© 727/892-5767 or 727/892-5700 for recorded information), houses the 8,100-seat Bayfront Arena (www.stpete.org/bayfront.htm) and the 2,000-seat Mahaffey Theater (www.stpete.org/mahaffey.htm). The schedule includes a variety of concerts, Broadway shows, big bands, ice shows, and circus performances. **Ticketmaster** (© 813/287-8844) sells tickets to most events and shows.

Tropicana Field, 1 Stadium Dr. (© 727/825-3100; www.stpete.org/dome.htm), has a capacity of 50,000 for major concerts, but it also hosts a variety of smaller events when the Devil Rays aren't playing baseball.

3 St. Pete & Clearwater Beaches ★★

If you're looking for sun and sand, you'll find plenty of both on the 28 miles (45km) of slim barrier islands that skirt the gulf shore of the Pinellas Peninsula. With some one million visitors coming here every year, don't be surprised if you have lots of company. But you'll also discover quieter neighborhoods geared to families, and some of the nation's finest beaches, which are protected from development by parks and nature preserves.

At the southern end of the strip, St. Pete Beach is the granddaddy of the area's resorts: Visitors started coming here a century ago, and they haven't quit. Today, St. Pete Beach is heavily developed and often overcrowded during the winter season. If you like high-rises and mile-a-minute action, St. Pete Beach is for you. But even here, Pass-a-Grille, on the island's southern end, is a quiet residential enclave with eclectic shops and a fine public beach.

A more gentle lifestyle begins just to the north on the 3½-mile-long (6km) Treasure Island. From there, you cross famous John's Pass to Sand Key, a 12-mile-long (19km) island occupied by primarily residential Madeira Beach, Redington Shores, Indian Shores, Indian Rocks Beach, and Belleair Beach. Finally the road crosses a soaring bridge to Clearwater Beach, whose silky sands attract active families and couples.

If you like your great outdoors unfettered by development, the jewels here are Fort Desoto Park, south of St. Pete Beach at the mouth of Tampa Bay, and Caladesi Island State Park, north of Clearwater Beach. They are consistently rated among America's top beaches. Sand Key Park, looking at Clearwater Beach from the southern shores of Little Pass, which separates Clearwater Beach from Belleair Beach, is one of Florida's finest local beach parks.

ESSENTIALS

GETTING THERE   See "Getting There," in section 1, for information about getting to the beaches.

VISITOR INFORMATION   See "Visitor Information," in section 2, for the St. Petersburg/Clearwater Area Convention & Visitors Bureau and the St. Petersburg Area Chamber of Commerce. The bureau's website at www.Floridas-Beach.com has information specific to the beaches.

Once you're here, you can get beach information at the **Gulf Beaches of Tampa Bay Chamber of Commerce,** 6990 Gulf Blvd. (at 70th Ave.), St. Pete Beach, FL 33706 (℗ **800/944-1847** or 727/360-6957; fax 727/360-2233; www.gulfbeaches-tampabay.com). The chamber is open Monday through Friday from 9am to 5pm.

For advance information about Clearwater Beach, contact the **Clearwater Regional Chamber of Commerce,** 1130 Cleveland St., Clearwater, FL 33755 (℗ **727/461-0011;** fax 727/449-2889; www.clearwater.org). You can also walk into the **Clearwater Visitor Information Center,** on Causeway Boulevard in the lobby of the Clearwater Beach Marina Building (℗ **727/462-6531**). It's open Monday through Saturday from 9am to 5pm, Sunday from 1 to 5pm.

GETTING AROUND   The **Pinellas Suncoast Transit Authority/PSTA** (℗ **727/530-9911**) operates a motorized trolley service along Gulf Boulevard (Fla. 699) between the Hurricane Restaurant in St. Pete Beach and the Sheraton Sand Key Resort, where it connects with the **Jolly Trolley** (℗ **727/445-1200**), which continues on Gulf Boulevard through Clearwater Beach. The PSTA trolley runs daily, every 20 minutes between 5am and 10pm, to midnight on Friday

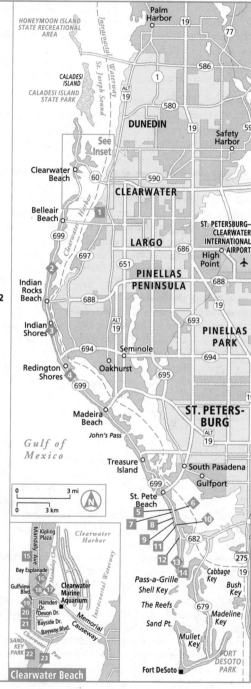

ACCOMMODATIONS ■

Beach Haven **11**
Belleview Biltmore
  Resort & Spa **1**
Best Western
  Beachfront Resort **7**
Best Western Sea
  Stone Resort **21**
Clearwater Beach Hotel **15**
Don CeSar Beach
  Resort & Spa **12**
Island's End Resort **14**
Radisson Suite Resort
  on Sand Key **23**
Sheraton Sand Key Resort **22**
Sun West Beach Motel **20**
TradeWinds Island
  Grand Resort **8**
TradeWinds Sirata
  Beach Resort **9**
Travelodge St. Pete Beach **5**

DINING ◆

Beachside Grill **4**
Bob Heilman's
  Beachcomber **18**
Bobby's Bistro
  & Wine Bar **17**
Crabby Bill's **10**
Frenchy's Original Cafe **16**
Guppy's **2**
Hurricane **13**
Lobster Pot **4**
The Salt Rock Grill **3**
Seafood & Sunsets
  at Julie's **19**
Skidder's Restaurant **6**

and Saturday. Rides cost $1, or you can buy a daily pass for $3. One-ride fares on the Jolly Trolley are 50¢ per person, 25¢ for seniors. Call the trolleys for schedules, or pick up printed copies at the Gulf Beaches of Tampa Bay Chamber of Commerce (see "Visitor Information," above).

Along the beach, the major cab company is **BATS Taxi** (© 727/367-3702). Fares are $1.50 at flag fall, plus 20¢ for each ½ mile.

HITTING THE BEACH

This entire stretch of coast is one long beach, but since hotels, condominiums, and private homes occupy much of it, you may want to sun and swim at one of the area's public parks. The very best are described below, but there's also the fine **Pass-a-Grille Public Beach,** on the southern end of St. Pete Beach, where you can watch the boats going in and out of Pass-a-Grille Channel and slake your thirst at Hurricane restaurant (see "Where to Dine," later in this chapter). This and all other Pinellas County public beaches have metered parking lots, so bring a supply of quarters. There are public restrooms along the beach.

The fine **Sand Key Park** ♠, on the northern tip of Sand Key facing Clearwater Beach, sports a wide beach and gentle surf and is relatively off the beaten path in this commercial area. It's great to go out for a morning walk or jog here. The park is open from 8am to dark and has restrooms. Admission is free, but the parking lot has meters. For more information, call © 727/464-3347.

Clearwater Public Beach (also known as Pier 60) has beach volleyball, watersports rentals, lifeguards, restrooms, showers, and concessions. The swimming is excellent, and there is a fishing pier with a bait-and-tackle shop, plus a children's playground. Gated municipal parking lots here cost $1 per hour or $7 a day. The lots are right across the street from Clearwater Beach Marina, a prime base for boating, cruises, and other waterborne activities (see "Outdoor Activities," below). A somewhat-less-crowded spot in Clearwater Beach is at the gulf end of Bay Esplanade.

CALADESI ISLAND STATE PARK ♠♠♠

Occupying a 3½-mile-long island north of Clearwater Beach, **Caladesi Island State Park** boasts one of Florida's top beaches—a lovely, relatively secluded stretch with fine, soft sand edged in sea grass and palmettos. Dolphins often cavort in the waters offshore. In the park itself is a nature trail, where you might see one of the rattlesnakes, black racers, raccoons, armadillos, or rabbits that live here. A concession stand, a ranger station, and bathhouses (with restrooms and showers) are available. Caladesi Island is accessible only by ferry from **Honeymoon Island State Recreation Area,** which is connected by Causeway Boulevard (Fla. 586) to Dunedin, north of Clearwater.

You'll first have to pay the admission to Honeymoon Island: $4 per vehicle with two to eight occupants, $2 per single-occupant vehicle, $1 for pedestrians and bicyclists. Beginning daily at 10am, the ferry (© 727/734-1501) departs Honeymoon Island every hour on winter weekdays, every 30 minutes on summer weekdays, and every 30 minutes on weekends year-round. Round-trip rides cost $7.50 for adults, $3.50 for kids.

Neither Caladesi nor Honeymoon allows camping, but pets are permitted in the inland parts of the island and on South Beach (bring a leash and use it at all times).

The two parks are open daily from 8am to sunset and are administered by Gulf Islands Geopark, 1 Causeway Blvd., Dunedin, FL 34698 (© 727/469-5942; www.floridastateparks.org/district4/caladesiisland and www.florida stateparks.org/district4/honeymoonisland).

To really get to know the islands, go with Linda Taylor of **It's Our Nature, Inc.** (© 727/441-2599; www.itsournature.com), on one of her guided walks of Honeymoon (usually at 9:30am Wed) and Caladesi (10am on Thurs). They last about 2 hours and cost $15 for adults, $8 for children, plus park admission and ferry fare. Call for reservations, which are required, and for information about Linda's kayak tours and other guided walks.

FORT DESOTO PARK ★★

South of St. Pete Beach at the very mouth of Tampa Bay, **Fort Desoto Park** encompasses all of Mullet Key, set aside by Pinellas County as a 900-acre bird, animal, and plant sanctuary. Besides the stunning white-sugar sand, it is best known for a Spanish-American War–era fort, which has a museum (open daily 9am–4pm). Other diversions include great fishing from piers, large playgrounds for kids, and 4 miles (6.5km) of trails winding through the park for in-line skaters, bicyclists, and joggers. Park rangers conduct nature and history tours, and you can rent canoes and kayaks to explore the winding mangrove channels along the island's bay side. The park has both changing rooms and restrooms.

Sitting by itself on a heavily forested island, the park's **campground** ★★ is one of Florida's most picturesque (many sites are beside the bay). It's such great camping that the 233 tent and RV sites usually are sold out, especially on weekends, so it's best to reserve well in advance. But, there are a few catches: You must appear in person no more than 30 days in advance at the campground office, at 631 Chestnut St. in Clearwater, or at 150 5th St. N. in downtown St. Petersburg. You must pay when you make your reservation in cash or by traveler's check (no credit cards). You must reserve for at least 2 nights, but you can stay no more than 14 nights in any 30-day period. Sites cost $33.30 a night January through July, $23.31 a night the rest of the year. All sites have water and electricity hookups.

Admission to the park is free. It's open daily from 8am to dusk, although campers and persons fishing from the piers can stay later. To get here, take the Pinellas Byway (50¢ toll) east from St. Pete Beach and follow Fla. 679 (35¢ toll) and the signs south to the park. For more information, contact the park at 3500 Pinellas Byway, Tierra Verde, FL 33715 (© 727/582-2267; www.fortdesoto.com).

OUTDOOR ACTIVITIES

BOATING, FISHING & OTHER WATER SPORTS　You can indulge in parasailing, boating, deep-sea fishing, wave running, sightseeing, dolphin watching, water-skiing, and just about any other waterborne diversion your heart could desire here. All you have to do is head to one of two beach locations: **Hubbard's Marina,** at John's Pass Village and Boardwalk (© 727/393-1947; www.hubbardsmarina.com), in Madeira Beach on the southern tip of Sand Key; or **Clearwater Beach Marina,** at Coronado Drive and Causeway Boulevard (© 800/772-4479 or 727/461-3133), which is at the beach end of the causeway leading to downtown Clearwater. Agents in booths there will give you the schedules and prices (they are approximately the same at both locations), answer any questions you have, and make reservations if necessary. Go in the early morning to set up the day's activities, or in the afternoon to book the next day's.

CRUISES　The top nature cruise here is the **Sea Life Safari** ★★ (© 727/462-2628), operated by the Clearwater Marine Aquarium (see "Attractions on Land," below). These 2½-hour "sea-life safaris" are more like field trips than pleasure cruises. Aquarium biologists go along to explain what they pull up in trawl nets (don't worry: They throw it all back). You'll also see birds and other wildlife on a visit to a bird sanctuary islet. Dolphin sightings are likely, too. The cruises are well worth $14.50 for adults, $9.50 for kids 3 to 12. You can combine the cruise with aquarium admission and save $3. Call for the schedule and to reserve. Also ask about sunset nature cruises from mid-April to mid-October.

Hubbard's Sea Adventures, based at John's Pass Village and Boardwalk in Madeira Beach (© 727/398-6577), offers a 2-hour dolphin-watching excursion daily at $12 for adults, $6 for kids under 12, but its best outings are cruises to fascinating **Egmont Key State Park** 🔆 on historic Egmont Key at the mouth of Tampa Bay (www.floridastateparks.org/district4/egmontkey). This uninhabited island is the site of a lighthouse, of now-crumbling Fort Dade (built in 1900 during the Spanish-American War but abandoned long ago), and of threatened gopher tortoises. Sea turtles also come ashore here to nest. You can go snorkeling and shelling here, so bring your swimsuit (snorkeling gear is available). The half-day cruises leave from St. Pete Beach Tuesday through Sunday and cost $35 for adults, $25 for children.

Another popular cruise target is lovely **Shell Key,** one of Florida's last completely undeveloped barrier islands. Shell Key is great for bird-watchers, who could spot a remarkable 88 different species, including some of North America's rarest shorebirds. Hubbard's Shell Key beachcombing trips usually depart at 9am Monday through Saturday, for $20 adults, $10 kids. You can rent beach chairs, umbrellas, snorkeling gear, and other equipment once you get there. Call to confirm the schedule and make reservations, which are recommended.

You can also get there on the **Shell Key Shuttle,** Merry Pier, on Pass-a-Grille Way at the eastern end of 8th Avenue in southern St. Pete Beach (© 727/ 360-1348; www.shellkeyshuttle.com). Boats leave daily at 10am, noon, and 2pm. Prices are $12 for adults, $6 for children 12 and under. The ride takes 15 minutes, and you can return on any shuttle you wish.

The most unusual outings here are with **Captain Memo's Pirate Cruise,** at Clearwater Beach Marina (© 727/446-2587; www.captmemo.com), which sails the *Pirate's Ransom,* a reproduction of a pirate ship with a pirate crew, on 2-hour daytime "pirate cruises," as well as sunset and evening champagne cruises.

Two paddle-wheel riverboats operate here: The *Show Queen* has lunch, sunset dinner, and Sunday-brunch cruises from Clearwater Beach Marina (© 800/ 772- 4479 or 727/461-3113; www.showqueen.com). The *Starlite Princess* does likewise from 3400 Pasadena Ave. S. (© 800/444-4814 or 727/462-2628; www.starlitecruises.com), at the eastern side of the Corey Causeway linking St. Pete Beach to the mainland. Call for prices, schedules, and reservations.

SCUBA DIVING   You can dive on reefs and wrecks with **Dive Clearwater,** P.O. Box 3594, Clearwater, FL 33767 (© 800/875-3483 or 727/443-6731; www.diveclearwater.com), which also operates the live-aboard boat *Plunger V.* Call for schedule and prices.

ATTRACTIONS ON LAND

Clearwater Marine Aquarium ★★ *(Kids)*   This little jewel of an aquarium on Clearwater Harbor is very low-key and friendly; it's dedicated to the rescue and rehabilitation of marine mammals and sea turtles. Exhibits include otters, sea turtles, sharks, stingrays, mangroves, and sea grass.

249 Windward Passage, Clearwater Beach. © 888/239-9414 or 727/441-1790. www.cmaquarium.org. Admission $8.75 adults, $5.25 children 3–11, free for children 2 and under. Mon–Fri 9am–5pm; Sat 9am–4pm; Sun 11am–4pm. The aquarium is off the causeway between Clearwater and Clearwater Beach; follow the signs.

John's Pass Village and Boardwalk Casual and charming, this Old Florida fishing village on John's Pass consists of a string of simple wooden structures topped by tin roofs and connected by a 1,000-foot (300m) boardwalk. Most of the buildings have been converted into shops, art galleries, restaurants, and saloons. The focal point is the boardwalk and marina, where many water sports are available for visitors (see "Outdoor Activities," above). If you don't go out on the water, this is a great place to have an alfresco lunch—**Sculley's** (℃ **727/393-7749**) is the best restaurant here—and watch the boats go in and out of the pass.

12901 Gulf Blvd. (at John's Pass), Madeira Beach. ℃ **800/944-1847** or 727/397-1511. www.johnspass.com. Free admission. Shops and activities daily 9am–6pm or later.

Suncoast Seabird Sanctuary ⭐ At any one time, there are usually more than 500 sea and land birds living at this sanctuary, from cormorants, white herons, and birds of prey to the ubiquitous brown pelican. The nation's largest wild-bird hospital, dedicated to the rescue, repair, recuperation, and release of sick and injured wild birds, is also here.

18328 Gulf Blvd., Indian Shores. ℃ **727/391-6211**. www.seabirdsanctuary.org. Free admission, donations welcome. Daily 9am–dusk. Free tours Wed and Sun 2pm.

SHOPPING

John's Pass Village and Boardwalk, on John's Pass in Madeira Beach (see "Attractions on Land," above), has an unremarkable collection of beach souvenir shops, but the atmosphere makes it worth a stroll. The pick of the lot is the **Bronze Lady** (℃ **727/398-5994**), featuring the world's largest collection of works by the late comedian-artist Red Skelton, best known for his numerous clown paintings. The shops are open daily from 9am to 6pm or later.

If you're in the market for one-of-a-kind hand-hammered jewelry, try **Evander Preston Contemporary Jewelry,** 106 8th Ave., Pass-a-Grille (℃ **727/ 367-7894**), a unique gallery/workshop housed in a 75-year-old building in Pass-a-Grille's 1-block-long 8th Avenue business district. Check out the golden miniature train with diamond headlight (it's not for sale). Open Monday through Saturday from 10am to 5:30pm. There's also a branch in the TradeWinds Island Grand Resort (see "Where to Stay," below).

Among the shops in St. Pete Beach's Corey Landings Area, the town's original business strip along 75th Street east of Gulf Boulevard, **The Shell Store** (℃ **727/360-0586**) specializes in corals and shells, with an on-premises mini-museum illustrating how they live and grow. There's a good selection of shell home decorations, shell hobbyist supplies, shell art, planters, and jewelry. The store is open Monday through Saturday from 9:30am to 5pm.

WHERE TO STAY

St. Pete Beach and Clearwater Beach have national chain hotels and motels of every name and description. You can also use the St. Petersburg/Clearwater Convention & Visitors Bureau's free **reservations service** (℃ **800/345-6710**) to book rooms at most of them. The **St. Petersburg Area Chamber of Commerce** lists a wide range of hotels, motels, condominiums, and other accommodations in its annual visitor guide (see "Essentials," in section 2), and it publishes a brochure listing all members of its Superior Small Lodgings program.

As is the case throughout Florida, there are more short- and long-term rental condominiums here than there are hotel rooms. Many of them are in highrise buildings right on the beach. Among local rental agents, **JC Resort Management,** 17200 Gulf Blvd., North Redington Beach, FL 33708 (℃ **800/**

535-7776 or 727/397-0441; fax 727/397-8894; www.jcresort.com), has many from which to choose, while **Resort Rentals,** 9524 Blind Pass Rd., St. Pete Beach, FL 33707 (© **800/293-3979** or 727/363-3336; fax 727/360-5086; www.resort-realty.com), specializes in luxury rental properties.

ST. PETE BEACH
Very Expensive

Don CeSar Beach Resort & Spa ★★★   This Moorish-style "Pink Palace" was built to be a grand hotel (it's on the National Register of Historic Places), but its scheduled 1928 opening was derailed when Florida real estate went bust. The federal government used it as a rest-and-recreation center for soldiers during World War II and as an office building until 1967. Developer William Bowman Jr. bought it in 1972 and restored it to its intended glory. Today it appeals to a wide range of clientele, from groups to families, from honeymooning couples to local ladies taking treatments in the full-service spa. Sitting majestically on 7½ acres of beachfront, the landmark sports a lobby of classic high windows and archways, crystal chandeliers, marble floors, and original artwork. Extensively renovated in 2000, some of the 275 rooms under the minarets of the original building may seem rather small by today's standards, but they have high windows and offer views of the gulf or Boca Ciega Bay. Some but not all of them have balconies. If you want more room but less charm, the resort has 70 spacious luxury condominiums in The Don CeSar Beach House, a mid-rise building three quarters of a mile (1.25km) to the north (there's 24-hr. complimentary transportation between the two).

3400 Gulf Blvd. (at 34th Ave./Pinellas Byway), St. Pete Beach, FL 33706. © **800/282-1116,** 800/637-7200, or 727/360-1881. Fax 727/367-6952. www.doncesar.com. 347 units. Winter $288–$428 double; $304–$699 suite. Off-season $209–$329 double; $251–$505 suite. $10 per person per day resort fee. Packages available. AE, DC, DISC, MC, V. Valet parking $10, free self-parking. **Amenities:** 4 restaurants (American); 3 bars; 2 heated outdoor pools; exercise room; spa; Jacuzzi; water-sports equipment rental; children's programs; game room; concierge; business center; shopping arcade; salon; 24-hr. room service; massage; babysitting; laundry service; coin-op washers and dryers. *In room:* A/C, TV, dataport, minibar, hair dryer, iron.

Expensive

TradeWinds Island Grand Resort ★★ (Kids)   Don't be dismayed by the outward appearance of this six- and seven-story, concrete-and-steel monstrosity, for underneath and beside it runs a maze of brick walkways, patios, and lily ponds connected by ¼ mile (.5km) of streams. Many of the guest units, which look out on the gulf or the 18 acres of grounds, have up-to-date kitchens or kitchenettes, and most have private balconies. Choice units directly face the gulf, but note that like its sister property, the TradeWinds Sirata Resort, this hotel has a great variety of accommodations; so consult with the reservation clerk when booking. Although the resort draws large meetings and conventions, it's a big hit with families, too, especially Europeans, all of whom appreciate the children's program, ice-cream parlor, Pizza Hut outlet, and summer packages. One of the four heated swimming pools is reserved for adults, and there's lots more to keep grownups busy, such as the libation offered by a unique Florida crackerhouse–style beachside bar floating on one of the lily ponds and the live entertainment nightly in another pub.

5500 Gulf Blvd. (at 55th Ave.), St. Pete Beach, FL 33706. © **800/237-0707** or 727/562-1212. Fax 727/562-1222. www.justletgo.com. 577 units. Winter $314–$599 double; off-season $197–$519 double. Resort amenities fee of $12 per day per unit covers most activities. Packages available summer and fall. AE, DC, DISC, MC, V. Valet parking $6; free self-parking. **Amenities:** 4 restaurants (American); 4 bars; 4 heated outdoor pools; 4 tennis courts; health club; Jacuzzi; sauna; water-sports equipment rental; children's programs; game room; concierge; car-rental desk; business center; salon; limited room service; massage; babysitting; laundry service; coin-op washers and dryers. *In room:* A/C, TV, dataport, kitchen, fridge, coffeemaker, hair dryer, iron.

TradeWinds Sirata Beach Resort ★★ A ton of money was spent a few years ago to completely renovate this older property and bring it up to second-tier status here, almost on a par with its sister hotel, the TradeWinds Island Grand Resort, but well below the Don CeSar Beach Resort and Spa. A yellow-and-green Old Florida–style facade now disguises the eight-story main building, which houses hotel rooms and one-bedroom suites upstairs (upper-level units have nice views) and a convention center. Some guest rooms in this two-story building face the courtyard, but the choice quarters here are its gulf-side rooms, the only units with patios or balconies opening directly onto the beach. The most spacious units are efficiencies and one-bedroom suites in two long, two-story buildings; they all have kitchenettes, but they look out primarily on parking lots.

5300 Gulf Blvd. (at 53rd Ave.), St. Pete Beach, FL 33706. © 800/237-0707 or 727562-1212. Fax 727/562-1222. www.justletgo.com. 380 units, including 170 suites. Winter $175–$399 double; off-season $145–$327 double. Resort amenities fee of $12 per day per unit covers most activities. AE, DC, DISC, MC, V. **Amenities:** 2 restaurants (seafood/steaks); 2 bars; 3 heated outdoor pools; exercise room; Jacuzzi; watersports equipment rental; children's programs; game room; concierge; business center; limited room service; babysitting; laundry service; coin-op washers and dryers. *In room:* A/C, TV, dataport, kitchen, fridge, coffeemaker, hair dryer, iron.

Moderate

Best Western Beachfront Resort Two long, gray buildings flank a courtyard with a heated swimming pool at this beachside property popular with young families. Furnished in dark woods and rich tones, most of the guest rooms have picture-window views of the courtyard. They open to wide exterior walkways, but each room has its own plastic chairs and drink table out there. About half of the units are efficiencies with kitchenettes. Jimmy B.'s beach bar is a fine place for a sunset cocktail and for evening entertainment, including beachside bonfires on Saturdays in winter.

6200 Gulf Blvd. (at 62nd Ave.), St. Pete Beach, FL 33706. © 800/544-4222 or 727/367-1902. Fax 727/367-4422. www.bestwesternstpetebeach.com. 102 units. Winter $168–$228 double; off-season $108–$168 double. Rates include continental breakfast. AE, DC, DISC, MC, V. **Amenities:** Restaurant (American); 2 bars; 2 heated outdoor pools; access to nearby health club; water-sports equipment rentals; game room; laundry service. *In room:* A/C, TV, kitchen, fridge, coffeemaker, hair dryer, iron.

Island's End Resort ★★ *Value* A wonderful respite from the maddening crowd, and a great bargain to boot, this little all-cottage hideaway sits right on the southern tip of St. Pete Beach, smack-dab on Pass-a-Grille, where the Gulf of Mexico meets Tampa Bay. You can step from the six contemporary cottages right onto the beach. And since the island curves sharply here, nothing blocks your view of the emerald bay. Strong currents run through the pass, but you can safely swim in the gulf or grab a brilliant sunset at the Pass-a-Grille public beach, just one door removed. Linked to each other by boardwalks, the comfortable one- or three-bedroom cottages have dining areas, living rooms, VCRs, and fully equipped kitchens. You will love the one monstrous unit with two living rooms (one can be converted to sleeping quarters), two bathrooms (one with a whirlpool tub and separate shower), and its own private bay-side swimming pool. Maid service on request.

1 Pass-a-Grille Way (at 1st Ave.), St. Pete Beach, FL 33706. © 727/360-5023. Fax 727/367-7890. www.islandsend.com. 6 units. Winter $125–$235 cottage; off-season $87–$235 cottage. Weekly rates available. Complimentary breakfast served Tues, Thurs, Sat. MC, V. **Amenities:** Coin-op washers and dryers. *In room:* A/C, TV, kitchen, coffeemaker, hair dryer, iron.

Travelodge St. Pete Beach This U-shaped beachfront complex of one- and two-story units is a favorite with cost-conscious families traveling on package tours from Canada and the United Kingdom. All units were completely renovated in 1999. Some open to the surrounding parking lots; much more preferable are those facing a landscaped central courtyard with pool and large sunning area. About half have refrigerators. On the premises is a branch of the very good and very inexpensive Shells seafood restaurant (p. 455). An indoor lounge and a lively beach bar offer light refreshments. The water-sports shack here offers parasailing equipment rentals and also services the Best Western Beachfront Resort next door (see above).

6300 Gulf Blvd. (at 63rd Ave.), St. Pete Beach, FL 33706. ✆ 800/237-8918 or 727/367-2711. Fax 727/367-7068. 200 units. Winter $104–$144 double; off-season $80–$112 double. AE, DC, DISC, MC, V. **Amenities:** Restaurant (American); 2 bars; heated outdoor pool; water-sports equipment rental; game room; coin-op washers and dryers. *In room:* A/C, TV, fridge, coffeemaker, hair dryer, iron.

Inexpensive

Beach Haven ✿ (Value) Nestled on the beach between two high-rise condominiums, these low-slung, pink-with-white-trim structures look from the outside like the early 1950s motel they once were. But Jone and Millard Gamble, who used to own this motel and still have the charming Island's End Resort (above), replaced the innards and installed bright tile floors, vertical blinds, pastel tropical furniture, and many modern amenities, including VCRs and refrigerators. Five of the original quarters remain as motel rooms (with shower-only bathrooms), but the others are linked to make 12 one-bedroom units and 1 two-bedroom unit, all with kitchens. The top choice is the one-bedroom suite with sliding-glass doors opening to a tiled patio beside an outdoor heated pool. There's also a sunning deck with lounge furniture by the beach. You don't get maid service on Sunday or holidays, and the rooms and bathrooms are 1950s smallish; but every unit here is bright, airy, and comfortable.

4980 Gulf Blvd. (at 50th Ave.), St. Pete Beach, FL 33706. ✆ 727/367-8642. Fax 727/360-8202. www.beach havenvillas.com. 18 units. Winter $90–$147 double; off-season $58–$122 double. AE, DISC, MC, V. **Amenities:** Heated outdoor pool; coin-op washers and dryers; concierge-level rooms. *In room:* A/C, TV, dataport, kitchen, coffeemaker, hair dryer, iron.

CLEARWATER BEACH
Moderate

Best Western Sea Stone Resort Located just across the street from the gulf in Clearwater Beach's busy south end, the Sea Stone is a six-story building of classic Key West–style architecture, containing 43 one-bedroom suites, each with a kitchenette and a living room. The living-room windows of the suites look across external walkways to the harbor. A few steps away, the older five-story Gulfview Wing offers 65 standard motel rooms, the least-expensive choices here.

445 Hamden Dr. (at Coronado Dr.), Clearwater Beach, FL 33767. ✆ 800/444-1919, 800/528-1234, or 727/441-1722. Fax 727/441-1680. www.seastoneresort.com. 106 units. Winter $89–$179 double; off-season $59–$115 double. AE, DC, DISC, MC, V. **Amenities:** Restaurant (American); bar; heated outdoor pool; Jacuzzi; coin-op washers and dryers. *In room:* A/C, TV, kitchen, fridge, coffeemaker, hair dryer, iron.

Clearwater Beach Hotel ✿ Besides the great beach location, you'll enjoy easy access to many nearby shops and restaurants from this Old Florida–style structure, built in 1986 to replace an old wooden hotel. The resort has been owned and operated by the same family since the 1950s and attracts a mixed clientele. Directly on the gulf, the complex consists of the six-story main building and two contemporary motel-style wings. Some rooms have balconies, and the efficiencies in the wings have kitchenettes. Offering French cuisine, the formal dining room is romantic at sunset and offers great views of the gulf, while the nautically themed lounge has entertainment nightly. A bar provides snacks and libations beside an outdoor heated swimming pool.

500 Mandalay Ave. (at Baymont St.), Clearwater Beach, FL 33767. ℂ 800/292-2295 or 727/441-2425. Fax 727/449-2083. www.clearwaterbeachhotel.com. 157 units. Winter $159–$269 double; off-season $115–$209 double. AE, DC, MC, V. Free valet parking. **Amenities:** Restaurant (French); bar; heated outdoor pool; access to nearby health club; limited room service; concierge; laundry service. *In room:* A/C, TV, kitchen (efficiencies only), fridge, coffeemaker.

Radisson Suite Resort on Sand Key *Kids*   You'll see the beauty of Sand Key from the suites in this boomerang-shaped, 10-story, all-suites hotel located across the boulevard from the Sheraton Sand Key Resort (see below). Although the resort sits on the bay and not the gulf, it has a large swimming pool complex next to the water, and the beach and beautiful Sand Key Park are short walks or trolley rides away. The resort has a good children's program, and the whole family will enjoy exploring the adjacent boardwalk with 25 shops and restaurants, including a branch of Ybor City's excellent Columbia (see "Where to Dine" in section 1). Each suite has a bedroom with a balcony offering water views, as well as a complete living room with a sofa bed, a wet bar, and an entertainment unit. Like the Sheraton Sand Key Resort, this hotel has many European visitors during the summer months, so room rates do not drop appreciably throughout the year.

1201 Gulf Blvd., Clearwater Beach, FL 33767. ℂ 800/333-3333 or 727/596-1100. Fax 727/595-4292. www.radissonsandkey.com. 220 units. $169–$339 suite. Packages available. AE, DC, DISC, MC, V. **Amenities:** 2 restaurants (American); 2 bars; heated outdoor pool; golf course; exercise room; Jacuzzi; sauna; children's programs; game room; car-rental desk; business center; shopping arcade; limited room service; massage; babysitting; laundry service; coin-op washers and dryers. *In room:* A/C, TV, dataport, minibar, coffeemaker, hair dryer, iron.

Sheraton Sand Key Resort ✦   Away from the honky-tonk of Clearwater, this nine-story Spanish-look hotel on 10 acres next to Sand Key Park is a big favorite with water-sports enthusiasts and groups. It's only a 150-yard walk across the broad beach in front of the hotel to the water's edge. The moderately spacious guest rooms here all have traditional dark wood furniture and balconies or patios with views of the gulf or the bay. The exercise room here is on the top floor, rendering great workout views.

1160 Gulf Blvd., Clearwater Beach, FL 33767. ℂ 800/325-3535 or 727/595-1611. Fax 727/596-8488. www.sheratonsandkey.com. 390 units. $135–$240 double. AE, DC, DISC, MC, V. **Amenities:** 2 restaurants (American); 2 bars; 24-hr. convenience store; heated outdoor pool; 3 tennis courts; exercise room; Jacuzzi; sauna; water-sports equipment rental; children's programs (summer only); game room; concierge; business center; limited room service; babysitting; laundry service; concierge-level rooms. *In room:* A/C, TV, dataport, coffeemaker, hair dryer, iron.

Inexpensive

Sun West Beach Motel *Value*   Sitting among several small motels a 2-block walk from the beach, Scott and Judy Barrows's simple one-story establishment dates from 1954, but it's well maintained, overlooks the bay, and has a fishing/boating dock and a heated bay-side pool and sun deck. All units, which face the bay, the pool, or the sun deck, were recently upgraded and have tropical-style furnishings, which make the place seem more modern than it is. The four motel rooms have small refrigerators, the 10 efficiencies have kitchens, and a few suites have separate bedrooms. The biggest and best unit is the Bayside Suite, which has vaulted ceilings, a steam room in its bathroom, and a fully equipped kitchen.

409 Hamden Dr. (at Bayside Dr.), Clearwater Beach, FL 33767. ℂ 727/442-5008. Fax 727/461-1395. 15 units. Winter $63–$99 double; off-season $44–$70 double. MC, V. **Amenities:** Heated outdoor pool; access to nearby health club; coin-op washers and dryers. *In room:* A/C, TV, kitchen (some units), fridge, coffeemaker.

Tips **Cheap Bunks for the Young-at-Heart**

The young and young-at-heart can find an inexpensive bed at **Clearwater Beach International Hostel**, 606 Bay Esplanade (℃ and fax **727/433-1211;** www.clearwaterbeachhostel.com), in a predominately residential neighborhood a short walk north of the busy beach area. There's a swimming pool, communal kitchen, TV lounge with hundreds of videos to watch, canoes and other toys to borrow, and bicycles to rent. The hostel's 33 dorm beds rent for $13 a night, while four private rooms range from $34 to $57. MasterCard and Visa credit cards are accepted. Reservations are strongly advised during the winter and summer months. The hostel is affiliated with both Hostelling International and American Youth Hostels.

TWO NEARBY GOLF RESORTS

Belleview Biltmore Resort & Spa   The Gulf Coast's oldest operating tourist hotel, this gabled clapboard structure was built in 1896 by Henry B. Plant as the Hotel Belleview to attract customers to his Orange Belt Railroad. Sited on a bluff overlooking the bay, it's the largest occupied wooden structure in the world. Today it attracts mostly groups and serious golfers (guests can play at the adjoining Belleview Country Club, an 18-hole, par-72 championship course), but there's no denying its Victorian charm and old-fashioned ambience—once you get past the out-of-place glass-and-steel foyer added by more recent owners. Historic tours are given daily (call for schedule and prices). The creaky hallways lead to several shops and a museum explaining the hotel's history. The hotel provides complimentary shuttle service to the country club and to Clearwater Beach.

25 Belleview Blvd., Clearwater, FL 33756. ℃ **800/237-8947** or 727/373-3000. Fax 727/441-4173 or 727/443-6361. www.belleviewbiltmore.com. 240 units. Winter $119–$229 double; off-season $89–$199 double. AE, DC, DISC, MC, V. Valet parking $3; free self-parking. Resort is 1 mile (1.5km) south of downtown on Belleview Blvd., off Alt. U.S. 19. **Amenities:** Restaurant (American); 2 bars; heated indoor and outdoor pools; golf course; 4 tennis courts; health club; Jacuzzi; sauna; concierge; business center; shopping arcade; salon; limited room service; babysitting; laundry service. *In room:* A/C, TV, coffeemaker, hair dryer, iron.

The Westin Innisbrook Resort   *Golf Digest, Golf,* and other magazines pick this as one of the country's best places to play (provided you stay here, of course). Situated off U.S. 19 between Palm Harbor and Tarpon Springs, this 1,000-acre, all-condominium resort has 90 holes on championship courses that are more like the rolling links of the Carolinas than the usually flat courses found in Florida. Some golf magazines think the **Copperhead course** 🏌🏌, former home of the annual JCPenney Classic, is number one in Florida. If you want to learn, Innisbrook has the largest resort-owned and -operated golf school in North America, and it boasts a tennis center with instruction, too. It's similar to the sports-oriented Saddlebrook Resort near Tampa (p. 453), except that the courses are more challenging here and you're much closer to the beach. A free shuttle runs around the property, and another goes to the beach three times a day. Ranging in size from suites to two-bedroom models, the quarters are privately owned condos spread all over the premises. The focal points are the golf and tennis clubhouses, all of which have restaurants and bars: This place is not for serious beachgoers.

36750 U.S. 19 N., Palm Harbor, FL 34684. © **800/456-2000** or 727/942-2000. Fax 727/942-5577. www.westin-innisbrook.com. 700 units. Winter from $209 condo; off-season from $119 condo. Golf packages available. AE, DC, DISC, MC, V. **Amenities:** 7 restaurants (American/Italian); 7 bars; heated outdoor pools; 4 golf courses; 15 tennis courts; health club; Jacuzzis; sauna; children's programs; concierge; activities desk; car-rental desk; limited room service; massage; babysitting; laundry service; coin-op washers and dryers. *In room:* A/C, TV, dataport, minibar, kitchen, coffeemaker, hair dryer, iron.

WHERE TO DINE

I have grouped the restaurants by their geographic location: St. Pete Beach, including Pass-a-Grille; Indian Rocks Beach, including Madeira Beach, Reding-ton Beach, North Redington Beach, Redington Shores, and Indian Shores; and, finally, Clearwater Beach.

ST. PETE BEACH

Crabby Bill's *Kids* SEAFOOD   The least-expensive gulf-side dining here, this member of a small local chain sits right on the beach in the heart of the hotel district. There's an open-air rooftop bar, but big glass windows enclose the large dining room. They offer fine water views from picnic tables equipped with rolls of paper towels and buckets of saltine crackers, the better to eat the blue, Alaskan, snow, and stone crabs that are the big draws here. The crustaceans fall into the moderate price category or higher, depending on the market, but most other main courses, such as fried fish or shrimp, are inexpensive—and they aren't overcooked or overbreaded. The creamy smoked fish spread is a delicious appe-tizer, and you'll get enough to whet the appetites of at least two people. This is a very good place to feed the entire family.

5100 Gulf Blvd. (at 51st Ave.), St. Pete Beach. © **727/360-8858.** Main courses $7.50–$20; sandwiches $4.50–$7. AE, MC, V. Mon–Thurs 11:30am–10pm; Fri–Sat 11:30am–11pm; Sun noon–10pm.

Hurricane SEAFOOD   A longtime institution across the street from Pass-a-Grille Public Beach, this three-level gray Victorian building with white ginger-bread trim is a great place to toast the sunset, especially at the rooftop bar. It's more beach pub than restaurant; but the grouper sandwiches are excellent, and there's always fresh fish to be fried, broiled, or blackened, and shrimp and crab to be steamed. Downstairs you can dine inside the knotty-pine–paneled dining room or on the sidewalk terrace, where bathers from across Gulf Way are welcome (there's a walk-up bar for beach libation). The second-floor dining area also has seating on a wraparound veranda. You must be at least 21 years old to go up to the Hurricane Watch rooftop bar or to join the revelry when the second level turns into Stormy's Nightclub at 10pm Wednesday through Saturday.

807 Gulf Way (at 9th Ave.), Pass-a-Grille. © **727/360-9558.** Main courses $10–$18; sandwiches $7. AE, MC, V. Daily 8am–1am.

Skidder's Restaurant *Value* ITALIAN/GREEK/AMERICAN   A local favorite, this inexpensive family restaurant in the hotel district offers a full range of breakfast fare plus handmade pan pizzas (available to eat here or carry out), burgers and sandwiches, big salads, gyro and souvlaki platters, and Italian-style veal, fish, and chicken dishes (Italian-style grouper is a house specialty). A chil-dren's menu features burgers and spaghetti.

5799 Gulf Blvd. (at 60th Ave.), St. Pete Beach. © **727/360-1029.** Main courses $8–$16; breakfast $3–$6; sandwiches and burgers $3.50–$8; pizza $6–$16. AE, DC, DISC, MC, V. Daily 7am–11pm.

INDIAN ROCKS BEACH AREA

You'll find a bay-front edition of **Shells,** the fine and inexpensive local seafood chain, opposite the Lobster Pot (see below) on Gulf Boulevard at 178th Avenue in Redington Shores ((©️ **727/393-8990**). See "Where to Dine," in section 1, for more information about Shells' menu and prices, which are the same at all branches.

Beachside Grille ★ Finds SEAFOOD/RIBS   Locals don't mind waiting for the best seafood bargains on the beach at Lynne and Douglas Casey's tiny place (seven tables plus five seats at the bar) tucked into the rear of a two-story commercial building opposite the landmark Friendly Tavern. They are rewarded with a savory Louisiana seafood gumbo as a starter, then fresh-off-the-boat grouper or mahimahi grilled or blackened, salmon under a dill sauce, or grilled shrimp with a zesty fruit salsa. The smoky, falling-off-the-bone barbecued ribs justifiably have been voted the best on the beach. Chargrilled steaks and steamed shrimp and crab legs also appear. Main courses come with rice, sautéed vegetables, and a salad with the Caseys' superb pesto salad dressing—it's so good they sell it by the bottle. Try a pitcher of the homemade white or red sangria, another local favorite. You can order lunch to take to the beach (there's public access next door).

35 182nd Ave. (at Gulf Blvd., opposite Friendly Tavern), Redington Shores. ©️ 727/397-1865. Reservations not accepted. Main courses $10–$15; sandwiches and burgers $5–$7.50. AE, DISC, MC, V. Daily 11am–10pm. Closed Thanksgiving and Christmas.

Guppy's ★★ SEAFOOD   Locals also love this small bar and grill across from Indian Rocks Public Beach because they know they'll always get terrific chow (it's associated with the excellent Lobster Pot, below). You won't soon forget the salmon coated with potatoes and lightly fried, then baked with a creamy leek and garlic sauce; it's fattening, yes, but also a bargain at $10. Another good choice is lightly cooked tuna finished with a peppercorn sauce. The atmosphere is casual beach friendly, with a fun bar in the middle of it all. Try the famous upside-down apple-walnut pie topped with ice cream. You can dine outside on a patio beside the main road.

1701 Gulf Blvd. (at 17th Ave.), Indian Rocks Beach. ©️ 727/593-2032. Main courses $10–$18; sandwiches $6–$7. AE, DC, DISC, MC, V. Sun–Thurs 11:30am–10:30pm; Fri–Sat 11:30am–11pm.

Lobster Pot ★★★ SEAFOOD/STEAKS   Step into this weathered-looking restaurant near the beach and experience some of the finest seafood in the area. The prices are high, but the variety of Maine lobster dishes is amazing. The lobster Américaine is flambéed in brandy with garlic, and the bouillabaisse is as authentic as any you'd find in the south of France. In addition to lobster, there's a wide selection of grouper, snapper, salmon, swordfish, shrimp, scallops, crab, Dover sole, and steaks, most prepared with elaborate sauces. The children's menu here is definitely out of the ordinary: It features half a Maine lobster and a petite filet mignon.

17814 Gulf Blvd. (at 178th Ave.), Redington Shores. ©️ 727/391-8592. Reservations recommended. Main courses $15.50–$39.50. AE, DC, MC, V. Daily 4:30–10pm.

The Salt Rock Grill ★★ SEAFOOD/STEAKS   Affluent professionals and other gorgeous folk pack this waterfront restaurant, making it *the* place to see and be seen on the beaches. The big urbane dining room is built on three levels, thus affording every table a view over the creeklike waterway out back. And in warm, fair weather you can dine out by the dock or slake your thirst at the lively tiki bar (bands play out here on Sat and Sun during the summer). Anything from the wood-fired grill is excellent. Thick, aged steaks are the house specialties. You can get a good sampling with the mixed grill: small portions of filet mignon, pork tenderloin, a two-bone lamb chop, and dessert-sweet coconut shrimp. Pan-seared peppered tuna and salmon cooked on a cedar board lead the seafoods. You can avoid spending a fortune by showing up in time for the early-bird specials or by ordering the meatloaf topped with mashed potatoes and onion straws ($8) or the half-pound sirloin steak ($10).

19325 Gulf Blvd. (north of 193rd Ave.), Indian Shores. © 727/593-7625. Reservations strongly advised. Main courses $9–$36 (early-bird specials $8–$10). AE, DC, DISC, MC, V. Sun–Thurs 4–10pm; Fri–Sat 4–11pm (early-bird specials daily 4–5:30pm). Tiki bar open Sat–Sun 2pm.

CLEARWATER BEACH

Bob Heilman's Beachcomber ✮ AMERICAN   In a row of restaurants, bars, and T-shirt shops, Bob and Sherri Heilman's establishment has been popular with the locals since 1948. Each dining room here is unique: large models of sailing crafts create a nautical theme in one, a pianist makes music in a second, works of art create a gallery in the third, and booths and a fireplace make for a cozy fourth. The menu presents a variety of well-prepared fresh seafood and beef, veal, and lamb selections. If you tire of fruits-of-the-sea, the "back to the farm" fried chicken—from an original 1910 Heilman family recipe—is incredible. The Beachcomber shares valet parking and an extensive wine collection with Bobby's Bistro & Wine Bar (see below).

447 Mandalay Ave. (at Papaya St.). © 727/442-4144. Reservations recommended. Main courses $13–$29. AE, DC, DISC, MC, V. Mon–Sat 11:30am–11pm; Sun noon–10pm.

Bobby's Bistro & Wine Bar ✮ AMERICAN   Son of Bob Heilman's Beachcomber, this chic bistro draws a more urbane crowd than its parent. A wine-cellar theme is amply justified by the real thing: a walk-in closet with several thousand bottles kept at a constant 55°F. Walk through and pick your vintage, then listen to jazz while you dine inside at tall, bar-height tables or outside on a covered patio. The chef specializes in gourmet pizzas on homemade focaccia crust (as a tasty appetizer), plus charcoal-grilled veal chops, filet mignon, fresh fish, and monstrous pork chops with caramelized Granny Smith apples and a Mount Vernon mustard sauce. Everything's served a la carte here, so watch your credit card. On the other hand, there's an affordable sandwich menu featuring the likes of bronzed grouper and chicken with a spicy Jack cheese.

447 Mandalay Ave. (at Papaya St., behind Bob Heilman's Beachcomber). © 727/446-9463. Reservations recommended. Main courses $8–$22; sandwiches and pizzas $6–$10. AE, DC, DISC, MC, V. Sun–Thurs 5–11pm; Fri–Sat 5pm–midnight, bar later.

Frenchy's Original Café SEAFOOD   Popular with locals and visitors in the know since 1981, this casual pub makes the best grouper sandwiches in the area and has all the awards to prove it. The sandwiches are fresh, thick, juicy, and delicious. The atmosphere is pure Florida casual style. There can be a wait during winter and on weekends all year round. For a similarly relaxed setting, directly on the beach, **Frenchy's Rockaway Grill,** at 7 Rockaway St. (© 727/446-4844), has a wonderful outdoor setting, and it keeps a charcoal grill going to cook fresh fish.

41 Baymont St. © 727/446-3607. Sandwiches and burgers $5–$7.50. AE, MC, V. Mon–Thurs 11:30am–11pm; Fri–Sat 11:30am–midnight; Sun noon–11pm.

The Sponge Capital of the World ★★

One of Florida's most fascinating small towns and a fine day trip from Tampa, St. Petersburg, or the beaches (it's 30 miles [48km] north of St. Petersburg, 23 miles [37km] west of Tampa, and 13 miles [21km] north of Clearwater), **Tarpon Springs** calls itself "the Sponge Capital of the World." Greek immigrants from the Dodecanese Islands settled here in the late 19th century to harvest sponges, which grew in abundance offshore. By the 1930s, Tarpon Springs was producing more sponges than any other place in the world. A blight ruined the business in the 1940s, but the descendants of those early immigrants stayed on. Today they compose about a third of the population, making Tarpon Springs a center of transplanted Greek culture.

Sponges still arrive at the historic **Sponge Docks,** on Dodecanese Boulevard. With a lively, carnival-like atmosphere, the docks are a great place to spend an afternoon or early evening, poking your head into shops selling sponges and other souvenirs while Greek music comes from the dozen or so family restaurants purveying authentic Aegean cuisine. You can also venture offshore from here, because booths on the docks hawk sightseeing and fishing cruises. Make your reservations as soon as you get here; then go sightseeing ashore or grab a meal at one of the multitudinous Greek restaurants facing the dock while waiting for the next boat to shove off. Your Tarpon Springs experience would be incomplete without taking a Greek meal here in one of the clean, inviting, authentic, and inexpensive Greek restaurants that line the Sponge Docks.

Seafood & Sunsets at Julie's ★ (Value) SEAFOOD   A Key West–style tradition takes over Julie Nichols's place at dusk as both locals and visitors gather at sidewalk tables or in the rustic upstairs bar to toast the sunset over the beach across the street. The predominantly seafood menu features fine and very reasonably priced renditions of charcoal-broiled mahimahi with sour cream, Parmesan, and herb sauce; bacon-wrapped barbecued shrimp on a skewer; broiled, fried, or blackened fresh Florida grouper; and flounder stuffed with crab meat. Everything is cooked to order here, so come prepared to linger over a cold drink.

351 S. Gulfview Blvd. (at 5th St.). (C) **727/441-2548.** Main courses $10–$20; salads and sandwiches $6–$10. AE, MC, V. Daily 11am–10pm.

THE BEACHES AFTER DARK
If you haven't already found it during your sightseeing and shopping excursions, the restored fishing community of **John's Pass Village and Boardwalk,** on Gulf Boulevard at John's Pass in Madeira Beach, has plenty of restaurants, bars, and shops to keep you occupied after the sun sets. Elsewhere, the nightlife scene at the beach revolves around rocking bars that pump out music until 2am. All of the places listed in this section are bars that have live music—and since Florida law requires that bars must serve food, they're also restaurants.

Pass-a-Grille has the popular, always-lively lounge at **Hurricane,** on Gulf Way at 9th Avenue, opposite the public beach (p. 481).

You also can visit the tin-roofed **Spongeorama** (no phone; open daily 10am–5pm), a museum dedicated to sponges and sponge divers that sells a wide variety of sponges (they'll ship your purchase home) and shows a 30-minute video several times a day about sponge diving. Admission is free. A scuba diver feeds sharks three times a day in the **Coral Sea Aquarium** (© 727/938-5378; open Mon–Sat 10am–5pm, Sun noon–5pm), at the western end of the boulevard. Admission is $4.75 adults, $4 seniors, $2.75 for children 3 to 11, free for kids under 3.

South of the docks, the **Downtown Historic District** sports turn-of-the-last-century commercial buildings along Tarpon Avenue and Pinellas Avenue (Alt. U.S. 19). On Tarpon Avenue west of Pinellas Avenue, you'll come to the Victorian homes overlooking **Spring Bayou.** This creek-side area makes for a delightfully picturesque stroll.

The **Tarpon Springs Chamber of Commerce,** 11 E. Orange St., Tarpon Springs, FL 34689 (© 727/937-6109; fax 727/937-2879; www.tarpon-springs.com), has an information office on Dodecanese Boulevard at the Sponge Docks, which is open Tuesday through Sunday from 10:30am to 4:30pm.

To get to Tarpon Springs from Tampa or St. Petersburg, take U.S. 19 north and turn left on Tarpon Avenue (C.R. 582). From Clearwater Beach, take Alt. U.S. 19 north through Dunedin. The center of the historic downtown district is at the intersection of Pinellas Avenue (Alt. U.S. 19) and Tarpon Avenue. To reach the Sponge Docks, go 10 blocks north on Pinellas Avenue and turn left at Pappas' Restaurant onto Dodecanese Boulevard.

On Treasure Island, **Beach Nutts,** on West Gulf Boulevard at 96th Avenue (© 727/367-7427), is perched atop a stilt foundation, like a wooden beach cottage, on the Gulf of Mexico. The music ranges from Top 40 to reggae and rock. Up on the northern tip of Treasure Island, **Gators on the Pass** (© 727/367-8951) claims to have the world's longest waterfront bar, with a huge deck overlooking the waters of John's Pass. The complex also includes a no-smoking sports bar and a three-story tower with a top-level observation deck for panoramic views of the Gulf of Mexico. There's live music, from acoustic and blues to rock, most nights.

In Clearwater Beach, the **Palm Pavilion Grill & Bar,** on the beach at 18 Bay Esplanade (© 727/446-6777), has live music Tuesday through Sunday nights during winter and on weekends in the off-season. Nearby, **Frenchy's Rockaway Grill,** at 7 Rockaway St. (© 727/446-4844), is another popular hangout.

If you're into laughs, **Coconuts Comedy Club,** at the Howard Johnson motel, Gulf Boulevard at 61st Avenue in St. Pete Beach (© 727/360-5653), has an ever-changing program of live stand-up funny men and women. Call for the schedule, performers, and prices.

For a more highbrow evening, go to the Clearwater mainland and the 2,200-seat **Ruth Eckerd Hall,** 1111 McMullen-Booth Rd. (© 727/791-7400; www.rutheckerdhall.com), which hosts a varied program of Broadway shows, ballet, drama, symphonic works, popular music, jazz, and country music.

4 Sarasota ★★★

52 miles (84km) S of Tampa, 150 miles (242km) SW of Orlando, 225 miles (362km) NW of Miami

Far enough away from Tampa Bay to have an identity very much its own, Sarasota is one of Florida's cultural centers. In fact, many retirees spend their winters here because there's so much to keep them entertained and stimulated, including the Van Wezel Performing Arts Hall and the FSU Center for the Performing Arts, home of the annual Asolo Theatre Festival. Sarasota also has an extensive array of first-class resorts, restaurants, and upscale boutiques.

Offshore, more than 40 miles (64km) of gloriously white beaches fringe a chain of long, narrow barrier islands stretching from Tampa Bay to Sarasota. To the south, **Siesta Key** is a residential enclave popular with artisans and writers and is home to Siesta Village, this area's funky, laid-back, and often-noisy beach hangout. Shielded from the gulf by **Lido Key,** which has a string of affordable hotels attractive to family vacationers, **St. Armands Key** sports one of Florida's ritziest shopping and dining districts, while adjacent **Longboat Key** is one of the country's swankiest islands.

ESSENTIALS

GETTING THERE   You probably will get a less-expensive airfare by flying into **Tampa International Airport,** an hour's drive north of Sarasota (see "Essentials," in section 1, earlier in this chapter), and you could save even more since Tampa's rental-car agencies usually offer some of the best deals in Florida. If you don't rent a car, **Sarasota-Tampa Express** (© **800/326-2800** or 941/727-1344) provides bus connections for $22 per adult, $11 children. Call in advance for schedule and pickup locations.

If you decide to fly directly here, **Sarasota-Bradenton International Airport** (© **941/359-2770;** www.srq-airport.com), north of downtown, off University Parkway between U.S. 41 and U.S. 301, is served by **American Trans Air** (© 800/225-2995), **American** (© 800/433-7300), **Canada 3000** (© 800/993-4378), **Continental** (© 800/525-0280), **Delta** (© 800/221-1212), **Northwest/KLM** (© 800/225-2525), and **US Airways** (© 800/428-4322).

Alamo (© 800/327-9633), **Avis** (© 800/331-1212), **Budget** (© 800/527-0700), **Dollar** (© 800/800-4000), **Enterprise** (© 800/325-8007), **Hertz** (© 800/654-3131), and **National** (© 800/CAR-RENT) have car-rental offices here.

Diplomat Taxi (© **941/355-5155**) has a monopoly on service from the airport to hotels in Sarasota and Bradenton. Look for the cabs at the west end of the terminal outside baggage claim. Fares range from about $10 to downtown Sarasota to $35 to Longboat Key or Anna Maria Island.

Amtrak has bus connections to Sarasota from its Tampa station (© **800/USA-RAIL;** www.amtrak.com).

VISITOR INFORMATION   Contact the **Sarasota Convention and Visitors Bureau,** 655 N. Tamiami Trail (U.S. 41), Sarasota, FL 34236 (© **800/522-9799** or 941/957-1877; fax 941/951-2956; www.sarasotafl.org). The bureau and its helpful visitor center are in a blue pagoda-shaped building on Tamiami Trail (U.S. 41) at 6th Street. They're open Monday through Saturday from 9am to 5pm, Sunday from 11am to 3pm; closed holidays.

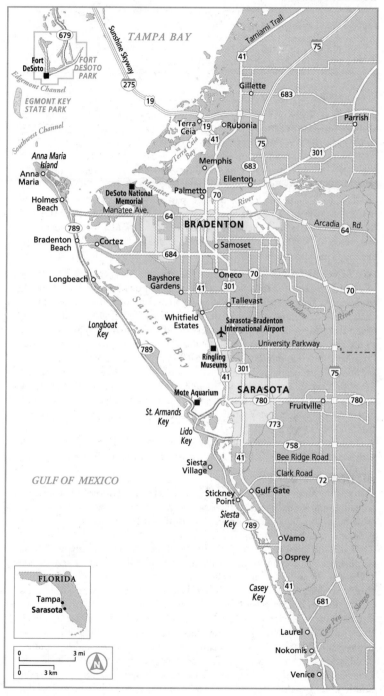

TAMPA BAY

Sunshine Skyway

679
Fort DeSoto
FORT DESOTO PARK
Edgemont Channel
EGMONT KEY STATE PARK
Southwest Channel

275
19

Gillette
41
75
683

Terra Ceia
19
Rubonia
41
75
301
Parrish

Memphis
683
Ellenton

Anna Maria Island
Anna Maria
Manatee River
Palmetto
70

Holmes Beach
DeSoto National Memorial
Manatee Ave.
64
BRADENTON
Arcadia Rd.
64

Bradenton Beach
Cortez
684
Samoset

Longbeach
Bayshore Gardens
Oneco
70
301
70

Sarasota Bay
41
301
Tallevast

Longboat Key
789
Whitfield Estates
Sarasota-Bradenton International Airport
Braden River

University Parkway
75

Ringling Museums
301
41

Mote Aquarium
SARASOTA
780
Fruitville
780

St. Armands Key
Lido Key
773

758
Bee Ridge Road

GULF OF MEXICO
Siesta Village
Clark Road
72

Stickney Point
Gulf Gate
41

Siesta Key
789
Vamo

Osprey

Casey Key
41
681

FLORIDA
Tampa
Sarasota

Laurel

Nokomis

0   3 mi
0   3 km
N

Venice

(*Fun Fact* **Soto's Sara**

Legend has it that Sarasota was named after the explorer Hernando de Soto's daughter, Sara—hence, Sara-sota.

You can get a packet of advance information about Bradenton and surrounding Manatee County from the **Greater Bradenton Area Convention and Visitors Bureau,** P.O. Box 1000, Bradenton, FL 34206 (© **800/4-MANATEE** or 941/729-9177; fax 941/729-1820; www.floridaislandbeaches.org).

If you're driving from the north via I-75, get off at U.S. 301 (exit 43) and head west to the **Manatee County Tourist Information Center** (© **941/729-7040**), where volunteers are on hand to answer your questions and sell you excellent road maps for less than you'll pay elsewhere. It's open daily from 8:30am to 5pm except Easter Sunday, Thanksgiving, the day after Thanksgiving, and Christmas Day. The office also has an information kiosk at **Prime Outlets,** across I-75, which is open Monday through Saturday from 10am to 6pm, Sunday from 11am to 6pm.

GETTING AROUND Operated by the Sarasota County Area Transit, or SCAT (© **941/316-1234;** www.co.sarasota.fl.us/public_works_scat/scat.asp), the **Sarasota Trolley** runs every 20 minutes from 9am to 5pm Monday through Friday, less frequently on Saturday. The Scenic Loop Trolley operates from Island Park, Bayfront at Ringling Boulevard, through downtown Sarasota, north to the FSU Ringling Center for the Cultural Arts, and out to St. Armands and Lido Keys (but not to Siesta or Longboat Keys). The Main Street Trolley goes from Island Park through downtown and eastward along Main Street. Fares are $1 on the Scenic Loop, 25¢ on the Main Street line, or you can buy a daily pass to both lines for $2. SCAT also operates regularly scheduled bus service. The Sarasota Convention and Visitors Bureau distributes route maps (see "Visitor Information," above).

Sarasota taxi companies include **Diplomat Taxi** (© 941/355-5155), **Green Cab Taxi** (© 941/922-6666), and **Yellow Cab of Sarasota** (© 941/955-3341).

HITTING THE BEACH

Many of the area's 40-plus miles (64km) of beaches are occupied by hotels and condominium complexes, but there are excellent public beaches as well. The area's most popular is **Siesta Key Public Beach,** with a picnic area, a 700-car parking lot, crowds of families, and quartz sand reminiscent of the blazingly white beaches in Northwest Florida. There's also beach access at **Siesta Village,** which has a plethora of casual restaurants and pubs with outdoor seating (see "Where to Dine," later in this chapter). More secluded and quiet is **Turtle Beach,** at Siesta Key's south end. It has shelters, boat ramps, picnic tables, and volleyball nets. Both beaches have bathroom facilities.

Unless you're staying on Longboat Key, you won't be able to hit the beach there, since luxury homes and condos block access to the gulf. However, do drive the length of Longboat Key and admire the luxurious homes and condominiums blocking access to the beach. Then, take a right off St. Armands Circle onto Lido Key and **North Lido Beach.** The south end of the island is occupied by **South Lido Beach Park,** with plenty of shade, making it a good spot for picnics and walks.

OUTDOOR ACTIVITIES & SPECTATOR SPORTS

BICYCLING & IN-LINE SKATING The flat terrain in this area makes for good in-line skating and for fine, though not challenging, bike riding. You can bike and skate from downtown Sarasota to Lido and Longboat Keys, since paved walkways/bike paths run alongside the John Ringling Causeway and then up Longboat Key. **Siesta Sports Rentals,** 6551 Midnight Pass Rd., in the South-bridge Mall just south of Stickney Point Bridge on Siesta Key (🕿 **941/346-1797;** www.siestasportsrentals.com), rents bikes of various sizes (including stroller attachments for kids), plus motor scooters, in-line skates, kayaks, and beach chairs and umbrellas. Bike rentals range from about $14 a day to $50 a week, while scooters go for $15 an hour, $50 a day, or $175 a week. The shop is open daily from 9am to 5pm.

BOAT RENTALS **All Watersports,** in the Boatyard Shopping Village, on the mainland end of Stickney Point Bridge (🕿 **941/921-2754**), rents personal watercraft such as jet skis, speedboats, runabouts, and bow riders. At the island end of the bridge, **C. B.'s Saltwater Outfitters,** 1249 Stickney Point Rd. (🕿 **941/349-4400**), and **Siesta Key Boat Rentals,** 1265 Old Stickney Point Rd. (🕿 **941/349-8880**), both rent runabouts, pontoon boats, and other craft. Bait and tackle are available at the marinas.

CRUISES The area's best nature cruises go forth from Mote Aquarium (see "Exploring the Area," below).

You can head over to Marina Jack's Marina, U.S. 41 at Island Park Circle, for 2-hour dolphin-watching, sightseeing, and sunset cruises around Sarasota's waterways aboard the 65-foot (20m), two-deck *Le Barge* (🕿 **941/366-6116;** www.lebargetropicalcruises.com). The dolphin-watching cruises run Tuesday, Thursday, and Saturday at 11am, while the other trips operate Tuesday through Sunday, with the sightseeing cruise at 2pm. Departure of the sunset cruises (with live music) changes with the time of sunset. The cruises cost $15 for adults and $10 for kids under 13. Snacks and libations are available for an extra charge, but credit cards are not accepted. Call for reservations.

That paddle-wheeler you see going up and down the bay is the *Seafood Shack Showboat,* operated by the Seafood Shack restaurant, 4110 127th St. W., in Cortez (🕿 **800/299-5048** or 941/794-5048). It has afternoon cruises to Sarasota Bay, Tampa Bay, and as far away as the Sunshine Skyway. Prices are $15 for adults, $13.50 for seniors, and $7.50 for children 4 to 11. The *Showboat* goes to a different destination each day, and its schedule is seasonal, so call a day ahead for the schedule. Reservations are not accepted.

FISHING Charter fishing boats dock at most marinas here. Check out **www.sarasotaboating.com** for a list. In downtown Sarasota, the **Flying Fish Fleet,** at Marina Jack's Marina, U.S. 41 at Island Park Circle (🕿 **941/366-3373;** www.flyingfishfleet.com), offers party-boat charter-fishing excursions, with bait and tackle furnished. Prices for half-day trips are $30 adults, $25 seniors, and $20 for kids 4 to 12. All-day voyages cost $45, $40, and $35, respectively. Call for the schedule. Charter boats also line up along the dock here.

GOLF The **Bobby Jones Golf Complex** ✦, 1000 Circus Blvd. (🕿 **941/365-GOLF**), is Sarasota's only municipal facility, but it has two 18-hole championship layouts—the American (par-71) and British (par-72) courses—and the 9-hole Gillespie executive course (par-30). Tee times are assigned 3 days in advance. Greens fees range from $25 to $35, including cart rental.

The semiprivate **Rolling Green Golf Club,** 4501 Tuttle Ave. (© **941/ 355-6620**), is an 18-hole, par-72 course. Facilities include a driving range, rental clubs, and lessons. Tee times are assigned 2 days in advance. Prices, including cart, are about $50 in winter, $30 off-season. Also semiprivate, the **Sarasota Golf Club,** 7820 N. Leewynn Dr. (© **941/371-2431**), is an 18-hole, par-72 course. Facilities include a driving range, lessons, club rentals, a restaurant, a lounge, and a golf shop. Fees, including cart, are about $45 in winter, $30 off-season.

If you have reciprocal privileges, **University Park Country Club,** west of I-75 on University Parkway (© **941/359-9999**), is Sarasota's only nationally ranked course.

Bradenton is home to the well-known **David Leadbetter Golf Academy,** 1414 69th Ave., at U.S. 41 (© **800/424-3542** or 941/739-2483; www.lead better.com), a part of the Nick Bollettieri Sports Academy (see "Tennis," below). Presided over by one of golf's leading instructors, this facility offers practice tee instruction, video analysis, scoring strategy, and more.

KAYAKING   Based at Mote Aquarium (see "Exploring the Area," below), **Sarasota Bay Explorers** ★★ (© **941/388-4200;** www.sarasotabayexplorers. com), uses a 38-foot (11m) pontoon boat to ferry both novice and experienced kayakers and their craft to a marine sanctuary, where everyone paddles through tunnels formed by mangroves. The paddling is easy and the waters are shallow. Experienced naturalists serve as guides. Wear swimsuits and tennis shoes or rubber-soled booties, and bring a towel and lunch. The 3-hour trips cost $50 for adults, $40 for children 5 to 17, free for kids under 5 (seats are provided for the youngsters). Reservations are required.

SAILING   Take a leisurely cruise on the waters of both Sarasota Bay and the Gulf of Mexico aboard the 41-foot (12m), 12-passenger sailboat *Enterprise,* docked at Marina Jack's Marina, U.S. 41 at Island Park Circle (© **888/ 232-7763** or 941/951-1833; www.sarasotaboating.com/sailingcharters.html). Cruises range from 2 hours for $35 per person to 4 hours for $55 a head, while sunset cruises cost $35 per person. Departure times vary, and reservations are required. **Siesta Key Sailing,** 1219 Southport Dr. (© **941/346-7245;** www.siestakeysailing.com), charges the same for similar cruises in a 42-foot (13m) Morgan Outlander sloop. Reservations are essential.

You can also get to historic Egmont Key, 3 miles (5km) off the northern end of Anna Maria Island at the mouth of Tampa Bay (see "Cruises," under "Outdoor Activities," in section 3, earlier in this chapter, for more information), on a 30-foot (9m) sloop-rigged sailboat with **Spice Sailing Charters** (© **941/ 778-3240**), based at the Galati Yacht Basin on Bay Boulevard on northern Anna Maria Island. The company also has sunset cruises. Call for schedule, prices, and reservations, which are required.

SPECTATOR SPORTS   **Ed Smith Stadium,** 2700 12th St., at Tuttle Avenue, east of downtown Sarasota (© **941/954-4464**), is the winter home of the **Cincinnati Reds** (© **941/955-6501;** www.cincinnatireds.com), who hold spring training here in February and March. From April to August, the stadium is home to the **Sarasota Red Sox** (© **941/365-4460,** ext. 2300; www. sarasox.com), a Class A minor-league affiliate of the Boston Red Sox.

The **Pittsburgh Pirates** (© **941/748-4610;** www.pirateball.com) do their February-through-March spring training at 6,562-seat McKechnie Field, 9th Street West and 17th Avenue West, south of downtown Bradenton.

The **Sarasota Polo Club,** 8201 Polo Club Lane, Sarasota (℃ **941/359-0000**), at Lakewood Ranch, a planned community midway between Sarasota and Bradenton, is the site of weekly polo matches November through March, on Sunday afternoons. General admission is $6, free for children under 13. Call for the schedule of matches.

TENNIS   The **Nick Bollettieri Sports Academy,** 5500 34th St. W. in Bradenton (℃ **800/872-6425** or 941/755-1000; www.bollettieri.com), is one of the world's largest tennis training facilities, with more than 70 championship courts and a pro shop. It's open year-round, and reservations are required for all activities.

WATER SPORTS   You'll find water-sports activities in front of the major hotels out on the keys (see "Where to Stay," later in this chapter). **Siesta Sports Rentals,** 6551 Midnight Pass Rd. on Siesta Key (℃ **813/346-1797;** www.siestasportsrentals.com), rents kayaks and sailboats, plus beach chairs and umbrellas. You can soar above the bay with **Siesta Parasail,** based at C. B.'s Saltwater Outfitters at the western end of the Stickney Point Bridge (℃ **877/591-0925** or 941/349-1900; www.siestaparasail.com).

EXPLORING THE AREA
IN SARASOTA

Art Center Sarasota   In addition to the marvelous John and Mable Ringling Museum of Art (see below), Sarasota is home to more than 40 art galleries and exhibition spaces, all open to the public year-round. A convenient artistic starting point is this downtown community art center, next to the Sarasota Convention and Visitors Bureau. It contains three galleries and a small sculpture garden, presenting the area's largest display of art by national and local artists, from paintings and pottery to sculpture, cartoons, jewelry, and enamelware. There are also art demonstrations and special events.

707 N. Tamiami Trail (at 6th St.). ℃ 941/365-2032. www.artsarasota.org. Admission free ($2 suggested donation). Tues–Sat 10am–4pm; Sun noon–4pm.

FSU Ringling Center for the Cultural Arts ★★★   By far the top attraction here, this 60-acre site is where showman and circus legend John Ringling and his wife, Mable, collected art and built houses on a grand scale. Now under the aegis of Florida State University, **The John and Mable Ringling Museum of Art** is the state's official art museum. It's filled with more than 500 years of European and American art, including one of the world's most important collections of grand 17th-century baroque paintings as well as collections of decorative arts and traveling exhibits. The old-master collection also includes five world-renowned tapestry cartoons by Peter Paul Rubens and his studio.

Built in 1925 and modeled after a Venetian palace, the Ringlings' 30-room palatial, bay-front winter residence **Ca'd'Zan** ("House of John" in the Venetian dialect) has been closed recently for a substantial restoration, but should be open

---

Tips   **How to See the Ringling Museums**

It's best to visit the FSU Ringling Center for the Cultural Arts on a weekday when you can take the two 1-hour guided tours (art museum and circus museum), which are included in the price of admission. Call ahead or check at the information desk as soon as you arrive for tour times. In between, explore the gardens and have lunch at The Banyan Cafe.

by the time you're reading this; even if it has not reopened, a visit to the museums should be on your Sarasota agenda. An 8,000-square-foot terrace leads down to the dock at which Mable Ringling moored her Venetian gondola.

The **Ringling Museum of the Circus** is devoted to circus memorabilia including parade wagons, calliopes, costumes, and colorful posters. The grounds also include a classical courtyard, a rose garden, a museum shop, and the historic **Asolo Theater,** a 19th-century Italian court playhouse, which the Ringlings moved here in the 1950s. It's now the centerpiece of the Florida State University Center for the Performing Arts. You'll need most of a day to see everything here.

5401 Bay Shore Rd. at N. Tamiami Trail (U.S. 41). ℭ **941/359-5700** or 941/351-1660 for recorded information. www.ringling.org. Admission $10 adults, $9 seniors, $5 out-of-state students, free for Florida students and all children 12 and under. Daily 10am–5:30pm. Closed New Year's Day, Thanksgiving, Christmas. From downtown, take U.S. 41 north to University Pkwy. and follow signs to museum.

Marie Selby Botanical Gardens ★★   A must-see for serious plant lovers, this peaceful retreat on the bay, just south of downtown, is said to be the only botanical garden in the world specializing in the preservation, study, and research of epiphytes; that is, "air plants" such as orchids. It's home to more than 20,000 exotic plants, including more than 6,000 orchids, as well as a bamboo pavilion, a butterfly and hummingbird garden, a medicinal plant garden, a waterfall garden, a cactus and succulent garden, a fernery, a hibiscus garden, a palm grove, two tropical food gardens, and a native shore-plant community. Selby's home and the Payne Mansion (both on the National Registry) are also located here.

811 S. Palm Ave. (south of U.S. 41). ℭ **941/366-5731.** www.selby.org. Admission $10 adults, $5 children 6–11, free for children 5 and under accompanied by an adult. Daily 10am–5pm. Closed Christmas.

Sarasota Classic Car Museum   There's more to this museum than its 90-plus classic and "muscle" autos, from Rolls-Royces and Pierce Arrows to the four cars used personally by circus czar John Ringling. Also here are more than 1,200 antique music boxes and several of Thomas Edison's early phonographs, including a 1909 diamond-tipped-needle model. Check out the Penny Arcade with antique games (with original prices), and grab a cone at the ice-cream and sandwich shop. In operation since 1953, this is now a nonprofit museum dedicated to preserving antique automobiles.

5500 N. Tamiami Trail (at University Pkwy.). ℭ **941/355-6228.** www.sarasotacarmuseum.org. Admission $8.50 adults, $7.65 seniors, $5.75 children 13–17, $4 children 6–12, free for children under 6. Daily 9am–6pm. Take U.S. 41 north of downtown; museum is 2 blocks west of the airport.

Sarasota Jungle Gardens (Kids   If you don't mind black Asian leopards, squirrel monkeys, and other animals going stir-crazy in cages, you and the kids should enjoy this commercial park's lush tropical vegetation, cool jungle trails, tropical plants, alligators and other reptiles, and exotic waterfowl, including a resident flock of pink flamingoes. Children like the petting zoo, pony rides, and bird and animal shows, too (call for a show schedule).

3701 Bay Shore Rd. ℭ **941/355-5305.** www.sarasotajunglegardens.com. Admission $10 adults, $9 seniors, $6 children 3–12, free for children 2 and under. Daily 9am–5pm. Closed Christmas. From downtown, take U.S. 41 north to Myrtle St., turn left, and go 2 blocks.

ON ST. ARMANDS KEY

Mote Aquarium ★★ (Kids   Kids get to touch cool stuff like a stingray (minus the stinger, of course) and watch sharks in the shark tank at this excellent aquarium. Part of the noted Mote Marine Laboratory complex, it is more broad-based than Tampa's Florida Aquarium, which concentrates primarily on local sea life. The kids won't believe all the sea-horse babies that come from the dad's pouch (one of Mother Nature's strange-but-true surprises), and they surely will gawk at a 35-foot-long (11m) deceased giant squid (it was 45 ft. long [14m] when alive). They can see manatees in the Marine Mammal Center, a block's walk from the aquarium. There are also many research-in-progress exhibits. Start by watching the aquarium's 12-minute film on the feeding habits of sharks; then allow at least 90 minutes to take in everything on land. Add another 2 hours to take a narrated sea-life encounter cruise with **The Sarasota Bay Explorers** (② 727/ **388-4200;** www.sarasotabayexplorers.com). These fun and informative cruises visit a deserted island, and the guides throw out nets and bring up sea life for inspection. It's a good idea to make reservations for the cruise a day in advance. This company has unusual kayaking adventures, too (see "Outdoor Activities & Spectator Sports," above).

1600 Ken Thompson Pkwy. (on City Island). ② 800/691-MOTE or 941/388-2541. www.mote.org. Admission $12 adults, $8 children 4–12, free for children under 4. Nature cruises $24 adults, $20 children 4–12, free for kids under 4. Combination aquarium-cruise tickets $30 adults, $25 children. Daily 10am–5pm. Nature cruises daily 11am, and 1:30 and 4pm. From St. Armands Circle, go north toward Longboat Key; turn right just before the Lido-Longboat bridge.

Pelican Man's Bird Sanctuary   Next to the Mote Aquarium (see above), this sanctuary and rehabilitation center treats more than 5,000 injured birds and other wildlife each year. It is home to more than 50 species of birds. Allow about 30 minutes to see it all, a few more to check out the gift shop with many bird-oriented items for sale.

1708 Ken Thompson Pkwy. ② 941/388-4444. www.pelicanman.org. Admission $4 adults, free for children 18 and under. Daily 10am–5pm.

IN & NEAR BRADENTON

DeSoto National Memorial   Nestled on the Manatee River, west of downtown, this park attracts history buffs by re-creating the look and atmosphere of the period when Spanish explorer Hernando de Soto landed here in 1539. It includes a restoration of de Soto's original campsite and a scenic half-mile nature trail that circles a mangrove jungle and leads to the ruins of one of the first settlements in the area. Start by watching a 21-minute film about de Soto in America. From December to March, park employees dress in 16th-century costumes and portray the way the early settlers lived, including demonstrations of cooking and the firing of an arquebus, one of the world's earliest firearms.

DeSoto Memorial Hwy. (north end of 75th St. W.). ② 941/792-0458. www.nps.gov/deso. Free admission. Daily 9am–5pm. Take Manatee Ave. (Fla. 64) west to 75th St. W. and turn right; follow the road to its end and the entrance to the park.

Milky-White Stallions

Horse lovers are drawn to the famous **Lipizzaner Stallions,** who do their spectacular leaps at the Ottomar Herrmann training grounds, 32755 Singletary Rd., Myakka City (② 941/322-1501), from late December to March (they tour the country the rest of the year). Members of a now-rare breed, the parents of these milky-white stallions were brought here from Austria in the 1960s by Colonel Ottomar Herrmann. Their *haute école* performances are straight from Vienna's famous Spanish Riding School. Call for schedule and directions. Admission is by donation.

Gamble Plantation   Situated northeast of downtown Bradenton, this is the oldest structure on the southwestern coast of Florida, and a fine example of an antebellum plantation home. Built over a 6-year period in the late 1840s by Major Robert Gamble, it was constructed primarily of "tabby mortar" (a mixture of oyster shells, sand, molasses, and water), with 10 rooms, verandas on three sides, 18 exterior columns, and eight fireplaces. Maintained as a state historic site, it includes a fine collection of 19th-century furnishings. Entrance to the house is by tour only, although you can explore the grounds on your own. The Prime Outlets Ellenton is a 5-minute drive from here via U.S. 301, so you can combine a plantation visit with some bargain hunting (see "Shopping," below).

3708 Patten Ave. (U.S. 301), Ellenton. (℗ 941/723-4536. www.floridastateparks.org/district4/gamble plantation. Free admission. Tours $4 adults, $2 children 6–12, free for children under 6. Thurs–Mon 9am–4:30pm; 30-min. guided house tour 9:30 and 10:30am, and 1, 2, 3, and 4pm. Take U.S. 301 north of downtown to Ellenton; the site is on the left, just east of Ellenton-Gillette Rd. (Fla. 683).

South Florida Museum and Parker Manatee Aquarium _Kids_   The star at this downtown complex is "Snooty," the oldest manatee born in captivity (1948) and Manatee County's official mascot. Snooty and his pal "Mo" live in the Parker Manatee Aquarium. The South Florida Museum tells the story of Florida's history, from prehistoric times to the present, including a Native American collection with life-size dioramas and a Spanish courtyard containing replicas of 16th-century buildings. (Fire recently damaged the museum's Bishop Planetarium, which is now closed.)

201 10th St. W. (on the riverfront, at Barcarrota Blvd.). (℗ 941/746-4131. www.southfloridamuseum.org. Admission $7.50 adults, $6 seniors, $4 children 5–12, free for children 4 and under. Jan–Apr and July Mon–Sat 10am–5pm; Sun noon–5pm. Rest of year Tues–Sat 10am–5pm; Sun noon–5pm. Closed New Year's Day, Thanksgiving, and Christmas. From U.S. 41, take Manatee Ave. west to 10th St. W. and turn right.

SHOPPING

Visitors come from all over the world to shop at **St. Armands Circle** 🌟🌟, on St. Armands Key. Wander around this outdoor circle of more than 150 international boutiques, gift shops, galleries, restaurants, and nightspots, all surrounded by lush landscaping, patios, and antiques. Pick up a map at the Sarasota Convention and Visitors Bureau (see "Essentials," earlier in this section). Many shops here are comparable to those in Palm Beach and on Naples's Third Avenue South, so check your credit-card limits—or resort to some great window shopping. I love to browse through **Global Navigator** (℗ **813/388-4515**), a travel-equipment and apparel shop that reminds me of Banana Republic when it carried really cool stuff (open daily 10am–10pm).

For discount shopping, the focal point of this area is the **Prime Outlets Ellenton,** on U.S. 301 at exit 43 off I-75 in Ellenton (℗ **941/723-1150**), about a 15-minute drive northeast of downtown Bradenton (turn left at the first stoplight east of I-75). This Spanish-style outdoor center has more than 100 factory and outlet stores. Shops are open Monday through Saturday from 10am to 9pm and Sunday from 11am to 6pm.

Tips   **Finding the Elusive Parking Space**

Parking on or near St. Armands Circle can be scarce, and if you _can_ find a spot, on-street parking is limited to 3 hours. Your best bets are the free, unrestricted lots on Adams Drive at Monroe and Madison drives.

WHERE TO STAY

The beaches here are virtually lined with condominiums, many of which are actually all-condominium projects operated as hotels. Among the rental agencies requiring stays of less than a month are **Argus Property Management,** 1200 Siesta Bayside, Sarasota, FL 34242 (© **800/237-2252** or 941/346-3499; fax 941/349-6156; www.argusmgmt.com), and **Florida Vacation Accommodations,** 4030 Gulf of Mexico Dr., Longboat Key, FL 34228 (© **800/237-9505** or 941/383-9505; fax 941/383-1830; www.vacationinfl.com).

The hotels below are organized by geographic region: In downtown Sarasota, on Lido Key, on Longboat Key, and on Siesta Key. The high season is from January to April. The hotel tax here is 9%.

DOWNTOWN SARASOTA

Most visitors stay out at the beaches, but cost-conscious travelers will find some good deals on the mainland, such as the **Best Western Midtown,** 1425 S. Tamiami Trail (U.S. 41), at Prospect St. (© **800/722-8227** or 941/955-9841; fax 941/954-8948; www.bwmidtown.com). This older but well-maintained motel is 2 miles (3.25km) in either direction from the main causeways leading to the keys. Winter rates are $119 for a double room, dropping to $79 off-season.

Downtown's top hotel prior to the opening of the new Ritz-Carlton (see below), the **Hyatt Sarasota,** 1000 Blvd. of the Arts (© **800/233-1234** or 941/953-1234; fax 941/952-1987), is adjacent to the Civic Center and the Van Wezel Performing Arts Hall and within walking distance of downtown shops and restaurants.

Most other national chain motels are near the airport, including a **Comfort Inn** (© **800/228-5150** or 941/355-7091), a **Days Inn** (© **800/329-7466** or 941/355-9271), and a **Hampton Inn** (© **800/336-9335** or 941/351-7734). All of recent vintage and thoroughly modern, they stand side-by-side on Tamiami Trail (U.S. 41) near the FSU Ringling Center for the Cultural Arts and the Asolo Center for the Performing Arts.

The Ritz-Carlton Sarasota ★★★ Downtown's swankiest digs opened in late 2001, just north of the Ringling Causeway and across a narrow creek from the Sarasota Quay shopping-and-dining complex (p. 504). The Ritz occupies the bottom 10 floors of an 18-story Mediterranean-style building (the top floors are private residencies). It sits perpendicular to the bay, so most of the spacious guest units have views looking across the water to the keys and the gulf. The rooms are luxuriously appointed in typical Ritz-Carlton fashion, including marble bathrooms. The hotel's four restaurants are led by Vernona, offering Mediterranean-influenced cuisine, while the Bay View Bar & Grill offers casual dining both indoors and out. The elegantly appointed lobby opens to a bay-side courtyard with a heated pool. There is no beach on site, but a shuttle will take you to Lido Key, where the hotel is planning to build its own private beach club. A full-service spa was also on the drawing board as we went to press.

1111 Ritz-Carlton Dr. (at Tamiami Trail/U.S. 41), Sarasota, FL 34236. © **800/241-3333** or 941/309-2000. Fax 941/309-2100. www.ritzcarlton.com. 266 units. Winter $395–$695 double; off-season $215–$535 double. AE, DC, DISC, MC, V. **Amenities:** 4 restaurants (Mediterranean/American); 3 bars; outdoor pool; golf course; 3 tennis courts; health club; Jacuzzi; sauna; children's programs; concierge; activities desk; car-rental desk; business center; 24-hr. room service; massage; babysitting; laundry service; concierge-level rooms. *In room:* A/C, TV, dataport, minibar, hairdryer, iron, safe.

ON LIDO KEY

Half Moon Beach Club ⚘ Near the south end of Lido, this two-story Art Deco–style hotel is right on the beach and less than half a block from South Lido Beach Park. The front of the building forms a circle around a small but very attractive courtyard with a heated pool and sunning area. From there, guests take a hallway through a motel-style block of spacious rooms to the beach, where they can rent cabanas and order drinks to be delivered from the bar inside. All units have balconies or patios; some have kitchenettes with microwave ovens, but only the four beachfront rooms have Gulf views.

2050 Ben Franklin Dr. (at Taft Dr.), Sarasota, FL 34236. ℂ 800/358-3245 or 941/388-3694. Fax 941/388-1938. www.halfmoon-lidokey.com. 85 units. Winter $144–$274 double; off-season $124–$194 double. AE, DC, DISC, MC, V. **Amenities:** Restaurant (American); bar; heated outdoor pool; water-sports equipment rental; bike rental; limited room service; coin-op washers and dryers. *In room:* A/C, TV, dataport, kitchen, fridge, coffeemaker, hair dryer, iron.

Holiday Inn Lido Beach Conveniently located at the north end of Lido, this modern seven-story hotel is within walking distance of St. Armands Circle. Unfortunately, the beach across the street (you'll have to dodge the traffic) isn't the best stretch of sand here. The motel-style bedrooms have balconies that face the gulf or the bay, and the rooftop restaurant and lounge offer panoramic views of the Gulf of Mexico.

233 Ben Franklin Dr. (at Thoreau Dr.), Sarasota, FL 34236. ℂ 800/HOLIDAY or 941/388-5555. Fax 941/388-4321. 135 units. Winter $180–$210 double; off-season $129–$210 double. AE, DC, MC, V. **Amenities:** Restaurant (American); 2 bars; heated outdoor pool; access to nearby health club; exercise room; water-sports equipment rental; bike rental; limited room service; babysitting; laundry service; coin-op washers and dryers; concierge-level rooms. *In room:* A/C, TV, dataport, fridge, coffeemaker, hair dryer, iron.

ON LONGBOAT KEY

Colony Beach & Tennis Resort ⚘⚘ Sitting 3 miles (5km) north of St. Armands Circle, this beachside facility is consistently rated one of the nation's finest tennis resorts. The beachside Colony Restaurant and swimming pool date from 1952 when this was a beach club, but today's accommodations are in modern, luxurious one- and two-bedroom condominium apartments complete with living rooms, dining areas, fully equipped kitchenettes, sun balconies, whirlpool tubs, and steam showers. The choice accommodations are three private cottages right on the superb beach (they also are the most expensive units). The condominiums are built around a 21-court tennis center, where a staff of professionals conducts highly acclaimed programs for both adults and children. The beachside Colony Restaurant offers fine continental cuisine for lunch and dinner (jackets requested for men at dinner).

1620 Gulf of Mexico Dr., Longboat Key, FL 34228. ℂ 800/4-COLONY or 941/383-6464. Fax 941/383-7549. www.colonybeachresort.com. 235 units. Winter $395–$675 suite; off-season $195–$370 suite. Packages available. AE, DC, DISC, MC, V. **Amenities:** 2 restaurants (continental/American); 2 bars; heated outdoor pool; 21 tennis courts; health club; Jacuzzi; sauna; water-sports equipment rental; bike rental; children's programs; game room; concierge; activities desk; car-rental desk; business center; salon; limited room service; massage; babysitting; laundry service; coin-op washers and dryers. *In room:* A/C, TV, kitchen, coffeemaker, hair dryer, iron.

Hilton Longboat Key Beach Resort ⚘ About 7½ miles (12km) north of St. Armands Circle, this five-story concrete building is more geared to couples than the nearby Holiday Inn Hotel & Suites (see below). Lush foliage and gardens and a charming gray wooden structure holding all of the public facilities help make up for the blandness of the guest-room building. In fact, the bar and pool area are pleasant areas for relaxing lunches or sunset cocktails even if you aren't staying here. Last refurbished in 1998, most of the bedrooms have a patio or narrow balcony. A few gulf-front rooms have larger balconies. Guests can ride a free shuttle to St. Armands Key.

4711 Gulf of Mexico Dr., Longboat Key, FL 34228. *©* **800/282-3046** or 941/383-2451. Fax 941/383-7979. www.hilton.com. 102 units. Winter $215–$305 double; $289–$309 suite. Off-season $155–$245 double; $229–$309 suite. Packages available. AE, DC, MC, V. **Amenities:** Restaurant (American); bar; heated outdoor pool; exercise room; water-sports equipment rental; bike rental; concierge; limited room service; laundry service; concierge-level rooms. *In room:* A/C, TV, dataport, minibar, coffeemaker, hair dryer, iron.

Holiday Inn Hotel & Suites *★* *(Kids)* Longboat Key's only family-oriented beachside motel is built around an indoor courtyard with a swimming pool, a whirlpool, a games area, and the island's only fast-food outlets (Pizza Hut, Nathan's Famous Hot Dogs, Mrs. Field's Cookies, and Seattle's Best Coffee). In addition, there's a restaurant with adjacent clubby bar plus a beachside snack bar. The enclosed area makes this a good respite on rainy days, during a cool snap, or when it's stiflingly hot outside. No matter what the weather's doing, there's plenty here to keep the kids busy. Extensively refurbished in 1999, most of the contemporary rooms and suites open to walkways overlooking the inside pool area; accordingly, the more expensive units with patios or balconies facing the beach are preferable.

4949 Gulf of Mexico Dr., Longboat Key, FL 34228. *©* **800/HOLIDAY** or 941/383-3771. Fax 941/383-7871. www.hilongboat.com. 146 units. Winter $206–$289 double; off-season $165–$289 double. AE, DC, DISC, MC, V. **Amenities:** 2 restaurants (American); 2 bars; heated indoor and outdoor pools; tennis courts; exercise room; Jacuzzi; sauna; water-sports equipment rental; bike rental; children's programs; game room; concierge; limited room service; babysitting; laundry service; coin-op washers and dryers. *In room:* A/C, TV, dataport, fridge, coffeemaker, hair dryer, iron.

The Resort at Longboat Key Club *★★* Part of a real-estate development on 410 acres at the southern end of Longboat Key, this award-winning condominium resort pampers the country-club set with upscale restaurants and a variety of recreational activities in a lush tropical setting. The spacious and luxurious rooms and suites all have private balconies overlooking either the Gulf of Mexico, a lagoon, or golf-course fairways. All have custom-designed furnishings and neoclassical decor, and all but 20 have full kitchens. Among several dining options here, the gulf-side Orchid's Restaurant has the feel of an informal but elegant supper club, serving classical Italian cuisine in a romantic setting by the gulf, while the adjacent Orchid's Lounge offers casual dining and live entertainment. Other choices are in the clubhouses at the resort's two golf courses and two tennis centers (all with instruction).

301 Gulf of Mexico Dr. (P.O. Box 15000), Longboat Key, FL 34228. *©* **800/237-8821** or 941/383-8821. Fax 941/383-0359. www.longboatkeyclub.com. 232 units. Winter $300–$435 double; $335–$1,120 suite. Off-season $175–$290 double; $210–$555 suite. Packages available. AE, DISC, MC, V. From St. Armands Key, take Gulf of Mexico Dr. north; take first left after bridge. **Amenities:** 5 restaurants (American/Italian); bars; heated outdoor pool; 2 golf courses (45 holes); 38 tennis courts; health club with spa treatments; Jacuzzi; sauna; water-sports equipment rental; bike rental; children's programs; concierge; activities desk; salon; limited room service; massage; babysitting; laundry service. *In room:* A/C, TV, dataport, kitchen, coffeemaker, hair dryer, iron.

ON SIESTA KEY

Captiva Beach Resort *★* *(Value)* Owners Robert and Jane Ispaso have substantially upgraded and improved this older property in the Stickney Point business district, about half a block from the beach on a narrow, closely packed circle populated by other small motels. Every one of the comfortable, sparkling-clean units here has some form of cooking facility, and some have separate living rooms with sleeper sofas. These are older buildings, so you'll find window air conditioners mounted through the walls, and shower-only bathrooms in some units. It's very popular with longer-term guests during winter. You'll get fresh towels daily but maid service only once a week. This and the circle's other motels share a common pool area, and guests get complimentary use of beach towels, chairs, and umbrellas. Several restaurants are a short walk away.

6772 Sara Sea Circle, Siesta Key, FL 34242. ✆ **800/349-4131** or 941/349-4131. Fax 941/349-8141. www.captivabeachresort.com. 20 units. Winter $130–$245; off-season $85–$180. Weekly and monthly rates available. AE, DISC, MC, V. **Amenities:** Heated outdoor pool; coin-op washers and dryers. *In room:* A/C, TV, kitchen, coffeemaker, hair dryer.

Turtle Beach Resort ★★★ On Siesta Key's south end, 2½ miles (4km) south of the Stickney Point Bridge, this intimate little bay-side charmer is one of Florida's most romantic retreats. It began life years ago as a ramshackle fishing camp, but owners Gail and Dave Rubinfeld renovated the five original clapboard cottages and added five more in a modern building. The complex is tightly packed; and although some units are very close to a small bay-side swimming pool, heavy tropical foliage provides a reasonable degree of privacy, and high wooden fences surround each unit's private outdoor hot tub. Sitting right on the bay, the two choice units also have one-way mirror walls, allowing guests to look out at the water in complete privacy, while passersby see only reflections of themselves. The cottages are done in various styles such as Caribbean and Nantucket, and have at least one bedroom each. Although they can accommodate small families, they are better suited as a terrific escape for couples. There's no restaurant on the grounds, but Ophelia's on the Bay is a seafood restaurant next door, once the old fishing camp's dining room, and all units have kitchens. Guests can use fishing poles, rowboats, kayaks, canoes, and paddle boats for free. No smoking is allowed inside the units.

9049 Midnight Pass Rd., Sarasota, FL 34242. ✆ **941/349-4554.** Fax 941/312-9034. www.turtlebeach resort.com. 10 units. Winter $265–$370 double; off-season $180–$230 double. Weekly rates available. AE, DISC, MC, V. Pets accepted at extra charge. **Amenities:** Outdoor pool; Jacuzzi; free water-sports equipment. *In room:* A/C, TV, kitchen, coffeemaker, hair dryer, iron.

WHERE TO DINE

The restaurants below are organized geographically: in downtown Sarasota, in Southside Village (the city's hottest new dining scene), on St. Armands Key (next to Lido Key), on Longboat Key, and on Siesta Key.

IN DOWNTOWN SARASOTA

Downtown's best breakfast spot is the local branch of **First Watch,** 1395 Main St., at Central and Pineapple avenues (✆ **941/954-1395**). Like its siblings in Naples (see "Where to Dine," in section 4 of chapter 10) and elsewhere, First Watch offers a wide variety of inexpensive breakfast and lunch fare. It's open daily from 7:30am to 2:30pm. If the wait's too long, walk south along Central Avenue; this block has several coffeehouses and cafes with sidewalk seating.

The local **Shells** seafood restaurant is at 7253 S. Tamiami Trail (U.S. 41), south of downtown in the vicinity of the Sarasota Square Mall (✆ **941/ 924-2568**). (See p. 455 for details about this inexpensive chain.) You'll also find most of the national chain fast-food and family restaurants nearby along U.S. 41.

Bijou Cafe ★★ INTERNATIONAL Chef Jean-Pierre Knaggs prepares award-winning cuisines from around the world in his cafe in the heart of the theater district. Although the more casual Michael's on East (see below) bistro draws a hefty after-theater crowd, this is the best place to dine within walking distance of the downtown entertainment venues. Jean-Pierre artfully presents the likes of prime veal Louisville (with crushed pecans and bourbon-pear sauce), pan-seared crab cakes served under a rémoulade and over a bed of fresh greens, and gently simmered lamb shanks with rosemary and garlic. His outstanding wine list has won accolades from *Wine Spectator* magazine.

1287 1st St. (at Pineapple Ave.). ℂ **941/366-8111.** Reservations recommended. Main courses $15–$30. AE, DC, MC, V. Mon–Sat 11:30am–2pm and daily 5–10pm. Closed Sun June–Dec. Free valet parking nightly in winter, on weekends off-season.

Marina Jack SEAFOOD/CONTINENTAL Overlooking the waterfront with a wraparound 270° view of Sarasota Bay and Siesta and Lido Keys, this establishment has spectacular water vistas and a carefree "on vacation" attitude, especially on the open-air raw-bar deck, which often is packed all afternoon on weekends and at sunset every day. The food is good but not the best in town, so come here for a relaxing, fun time. You may have to wait for a table or bar stool down on the deck, but be sure to make reservations if you want to have a meal in the upstairs dining room. Fresh local seafood is the star both upstairs and down—grilled grouper is your best bet. The downstairs lounge and raw bar also serves sandwiches and burgers.

In Island Park, Bayfront at Central Ave. ℂ **941/365-4232.** Reservations recommended in dining room. Dining room main courses $15–$30. Deck main courses $14–$17; sandwiches and salads $8–$11. AE, DISC, MC, V. Daily 11:30am–2am. Closed Christmas.

Michael's on East ⋆⋆ CREATIVE INTERNATIONAL   At the rear of the Midtown Plaza shopping center on U.S. 41 south of downtown, Michael Klauber's chic bistro is one of the top places here for fine dining and is the locals' favorite after-theater haunt. Huge cut-glass walls create three intimate dining areas, one a piano bar for pre- or after-dinner drinks. Prepared with fresh ingredients and a creative flair, the offerings here will tempt your taste buds. House specialties are the slightly spicy Louisiana-style crab cakes, pan-seared Chilean sea bass with couscous and artichoke hearts in a thyme-accented tomato coulis, and grilled duck breast with Napa cabbage, sweet potato, and smoked bacon in an apple-cider reduction.

1212 East Ave. S. (between Bahia and Prospect sts.). ℂ **941/366-0007.** Reservations recommended. Main courses $19–$36. AE, DC, DISC, MC, V. Winter Mon–Fri 11:30am–2pm; Sat 5:30–10pm; Sun 6–10pm. Off-season Mon–Fri 11:30am–2pm; Mon–Sat 6–10pm. Complimentary valet parking.

Patrick's AMERICAN/PUB FARE   With a semicircular facade, this up-scale, polished-oak and brass-rail sports bar offers wide-windowed views of downtown's main intersection. The menu offers very good pub fare: steaks and chops, burgers, seafood, pastas, small pizzas, salads, sandwiches, and omelets. Other entrees include broiled salmon with dill-hollandaise sauce, sesame chicken, and veal done three ways—piccata, Française, or Marsala. There's a good happy hour here Monday through Friday between 5 and 7pm.

1400 Main St. (at Pineapple Ave.). ℂ **941/952-1170.** Main courses $14–$21; sandwiches and burgers $7–$9. AE, DC, DISC, MC, V. Daily 11am–midnight; Sun brunch 11am–3pm. Closed Christmas.

Yoder's ⋆ *Value* AMISH/AMERICAN   Just 3 miles (5km) east of downtown is an award-winning, value eatery operated by an Amish family (Sarasota and Bradenton have sizable Amish communities and several other Amish restaurants). Evoking the Pennsylvania Dutch country, the simple dining room displays handcrafts, photos, and paintings celebrating the Amish way. The menu emphasizes plain, made-from-scratch cooking such as home-style meatloaf, baked and southern fried chicken, country-smoked ham, and fried filet of flounder.

Burgers, salads, soups, and sandwiches are also available. Leave room for Mrs. Yoder's traditional shoo-fly and other homemade pies, one of the biggest draws here. Neither alcohol nor smoking is allowed here.

3434 Bahia Vista St. (west of Beneva Rd.). ✆ **941/955-7771.** Main courses $6–$12; breakfast $2–$6; sandwiches and burgers $3–$6. No credit cards (ATM on premises). Mon–Sat 6am–8pm.

IN SOUTHSIDE VILLAGE

Sarasota's hottest dining spot is **Southside Village,** centered on South Osprey Avenue between Hyde Park and Hillview streets, about 15 blocks south of downtown. Here you'll find several hip restaurants, including Fred's and Pacific Rim (see below). The village landmark is **Morton's Gourmet Market** ✪, 1924 S. Osprey Ave. (✆ **941/955-9856**), which offers a multitude of deli items, specialty sandwiches, a ton of fresh salads, freshly baked pastries and desserts, and cooked meals dispensed from a cafeteria-style steam table. You dine picnic-fashion on sidewalk tables outside. Most ready-to-go items cost less than $7. Open Monday through Saturday from 8am to 8pm, Sunday from 10am to 5pm.

Fred's ✪ INTERNATIONAL   Directly across the avenue from Morton's Gourmet Market, Fred's is one of the city's biggest gathering places for single professionals, especially on Friday night. They have plenty of space to spread out in several dining rooms and bars, all accented with dark wood and etched glass. The fare, although often second on everyone's mind, consists of well-seasoned pizzas and main courses such as pan-seared tuna with Japanese noodles in a basil and lemon grass broth. There's even old-fashioned chicken pot pie and an open-face meatloaf sandwich with a wild mushroom ragout to clearly set it apart from your mother's. You can sample selections from the extensive wine list in a cigar-bar–style tasting room, then buy a bottle at the adjoining liquor store.

1917 S. Osprey Ave. (between Hyde Park and Hillview sts.). ✆ **941/364-5811.** Main courses $10–$28; pizza $8–$10. AE, DC, DISC, MC, V. Mon–Thurs 11am–10pm; Fri–Sat 11am–11:30pm; Sun 11am–9pm.

Pacific Rim ✪ *Value* JAPANESE/THAI   Sarasotans love this chic and very casual restaurant for exceptional cuisine at economical prices. Japanese influence is felt at the authentic sushi bar along one side of the dining room, while Thai spices make a strong impact on the regular menu. I found the chargrilled shrimp with Thai curry and coconut-milk sauce to be especially tasty, as was the combination of chicken and vegetables stir-fried in the wok. Here you can select your meat and vegetables separately from the sauce and the chefs will combine them on the grill, on the wok, or in the bowl (as in rice dishes).

In Hillview Centre, 1859 Hillview St. (between Osprey Ave. and Laurent Place). ✆ **941/330-8071.** Main courses $7.50–$15. AE, DISC, MC, V. Mon–Thurs 11:30am–2pm and 5–9pm; Fri 11:30am–2pm and 5–10pm; Sat 5–10pm.

ON ST. ARMANDS KEY

While the locals are hanging out in Southside Village, part-year residents and visitors flock to St. Armands Circle. Plan to spend at least one evening here, since the nighttime scene is like a fair, with everyone strolling around the circle, poking heads into a few stores that stay open after dark, and window-shopping the others. It's fun and safe, so come early and plan to stay late. See "Shopping," earlier in this chapter, for parking tips.

The circle has a branch of Tampa's famous **Columbia** (p. 457) between John Ringling Boulevard and John Ringling Parkway (✆ **941/388-3987**). The Spanish food is excellent, there's outdoor seating, and the Patio Lounge is one of the liveliest spots here for evening entertainment from Thursday to Sunday. Like its sibling in Naples (p. 428), the local edition of **Tommy Bahama's Tropical Cafe,** 300 John Ringling Blvd. (© **941/388-2888**), draws a lively crowd of young professionals to its moderately priced seafood. It's upstairs over Tommy Bahama's clothing store.

At night, you may wish to forgo an expensive dessert and wander over to the local branch of **Kilwin's,** 312 John Ringling Blvd. (© **941/388-3200**), for some gourmet chocolate, Mackinac Island fudge, or ice cream or yogurt in a home-made waffle cone. Enjoy your sweets on one of the sidewalk park benches—everyone else does.

Blue Dolphin Cafe _Value_ AMERICAN/DINER On the John Ringling Boulevard spoke of St. Armands Circle, this informal diner is the affluent area's best inexpensive place to have breakfast, and the owners, Jill and Rob Ball, are a font of free information, too. They serve standard breakfast fare as well as fresh crab or lobster benedict, raspberry pancakes, and pecan-peach waffles. Lunchtime highlights are homemade soups and grouper sandwiches. You can order breakfast anytime. The Blue Dolphin is open for dinner on Friday nights during the winter season, offering the likes of flaky-crust chicken pot pie, slow-roasted prime rib, and spicy crab cakes.

470 John Ringling Blvd. (1 block off St. Armands Circle). © 941/388-3566. Breakfast $4.50–$10; sandwiches, burgers, salads $5–$10. AE, DC, DISC, MC, V. Daily 7am–3pm.

Cafe l'Europe ★★ CONTINENTAL As its name implies, a European atmosphere prevails at this consistently excellent restaurant, the best place on the circle for fine dining. You can ask for a table out on the sidewalk, but brick walls and arches, dark woods, brass fixtures, pink linens, and hanging plants all lend an elegant ambience indoors. The menu offers selections ranging from a bouil-labaisse in a piquant pepper broth to veal tenderloin glazed with balsamic vine-gar and served with a rich blackberry-and-port-wine sauce. There's a wide choice of wines by the glass here, too.

431 St. Armands Circle (at John Ringling Blvd.). © 941/388-4415. Reservations recommended. Main courses $18–$36. AE, DC, DISC, MC, V. Daily 11am–3:30pm and 5–10pm.

Hemingway's ★ FLORIDIAN/CARIBBEAN For a casual spot with an eclectic Floribbean menu and a large bar with a friendly, laid-back Key West ambience, take the elevator or climb the winding stairs to this second-floor hide-away. Hemingway's is a charming and comfortable combination of good food and Old Florida tradition. You can dine inside or on one of two second-floor balconies.

325 John Ringling Blvd. (½ block off St. Armands Circle). © 941/388-3948. Reservations recommended on weekends. Main courses $16–$22. AE, DC, DISC, MC, V. Sun–Thurs 11:30am–10pm; Fri–Sat 11:30am–11pm.

Hungry Fox AMERICAN This upstairs restaurant is the only place on St. Armands Circle offering three inexpensive meals a day year-round. It's not much to look at inside, with marble-look tables and plastic lawn chairs, so wait for a table out on the veranda, especially next to the railing where you can oversee all the action down below. Breakfast, which is served until noon, offers everything from lox and bagels to Virginia ham and eggs. Sandwiches and salads appear at lunch, followed by steaks, chicken, pastas, and spicy jambalaya for dinner. Most items are a good value for the price, but stay away from anything cooked in the deep fryer.

419 St. Armands Circle (above Cha Cha Coconuts). © 941/388-2222. Main courses $11–$17; sandwiches, burgers, salads $4.50–$9; breakfast $4.50–$10. AE, DISC, MC, V. Mon–Sat 8am–9pm; Sun 8am–2:30pm.

ON LONGBOAT KEY

Euphemia Haye/The Haye Loft ✦✦✦ INTERNATIONAL This area's most extraordinary restaurant, the romantically lighted Euphemia Haye is best known for Chef Raymond Arpke's crispy roast duck filled with bread stuffing and accompanied by a tangy fruit sauce. His prime strip steak rolled in cracked peppercorns and served with an orange, brandy, and butter sauce is another winner, as are his shrimps in a delightful curry and coconut cream sauce. If all this sounds sweet, wait until you go upstairs to The Haye Loft, his casual dessert bar. Up here you can take your pick from fabulous pies topped with thick whipped cream or Ben & Jerry's ice cream. You can also sample the kitchen's offerings, for the loft has its own light-fare menu, including soups, appetizers, small pizzas, and sandwiches. If you're lucky, the night's special sandwich will be steak topped with Raymond's peppercorn sauce. Served open-face and garnished with a field-greens salad, it's a meal for just $9. Add a glass of superb wine and a slice of pie a la mode, and you've had a wonderful dinner for under $20.

5540 Gulf of Mexico Dr. (at Gulfbay Rd.). ℂ 941/383-3633. Reservations recommended downstairs, not accepted in The Haye Loft. Main courses $19.50–$37; sandwiches, pizzas, and salads $7–$9. DC, DISC, MC, V. Restaurant Sun–Thurs 5–10pm; Fri–Sat 5–10:30pm. Haye Loft daily 6pm–midnight.

Moore's Stone Crab SEAFOOD Located in Longbeach, the old fishing village on the north end of Longboat Key, this popular bay-front restaurant began in 1967 as an offshoot of a family seafood business established 40 years earlier. From the outside, in fact, it still looks a little like a packing house, but the view of the bay dotted with mangrove islands makes a fine complement to stone crabs fresh from the family's own traps from October 15 to May 15. Otherwise, the menu offers an incredibly large variety of seafood, most of it fried or broiled. Sandwiches and salads are served all day.

800 Broadway (at Bayside Dr.). ℂ 941/383-1748. Main courses $9–$23; sandwiches and salads $7–$13. AE, DISC, MC, V. Winter daily 11:30am–9:30pm. Off-season Mon–Fri 4:30–9:30pm; Sat–Sun 11:30am–9:30pm.

ON SIESTA KEY

Ocean Boulevard, which runs through **Siesta Village,** the area's funky, laid-back beach hangout, is virtually lined with restaurants and pubs. Most have outdoor seating and bars, which attract the beach crowd during the day. At night, rock-and-roll bands draw teenagers and college students to this lively scene.

Blasé Café ✦✦ _(Finds_ INTERNATIONAL One of Florida's most unusual restaurants, Ralph and Cindy Cole's super-casual establishment has tables indoors and a few under the cover of the Village Corner shopping center's walkway, but most are alfresco, on a wooden deck built around a palm tree in the center's asphalt parking lot. Never mind the cars pulling in and out virtually next to your chair: Ralph's food is so good that it draws droves of locals, who don't mind waiting for an umbrella table. This is the Siesta Key's best breakfast spot, offering Italian- and Louisiana-flavored frittatas as well as plain old bacon and eggs. Lunch sees burgers, big salads, and platters such as chicken Alfredo and Florentine crepes with shrimp. At night, Ralph puts forth the likes of pan-seared sushi-quality yellowfin tuna with tangy wasabi and pickled ginger. You can while away the rest of the evening in the wine bar, where the Coles have installed the original bar from the Don CeSar Beach Resort & Spa in St. Pete Beach. There's live music in there on weekends.

In Village Corner, 5263 Ocean Blvd. (at Calle Miramar), Siesta Village. ℂ 941/349-9822. Reservations recommended. Main courses $11–$22; breakfast and lunch $5–$9. MC, V. Mon–Thurs 8:30am–9:30pm; Fri–Sat 8:30am–10pm. Closed Mon June–Nov.

Turtles AMERICAN   With tropical overtones and breathtaking water vistas across from Turtle Beach, this informal restaurant on Little Sarasota Bay has tables both indoors and on an outside deck. Unique seafood offerings include snapper New Orleans and potato-encrusted mahimahi. You can't go wrong ordering grouper grilled, broiled, blackened, or fried. There's also a selection of pastas on the menu. The economical early-bird specials offer several choices ranging from a medium-sized portion of mahimahi to spicy Szechwan shrimp.

8875 Midnight Pass Rd. (at Turtle Beach Rd.). © 941/346-2207. Call for preferred seating. Main courses $11–$19; salads and sandwiches $7–$15; early-bird specials $9–$11. AE, DISC, MC, V. Mon–Sat 11:30am–9:30pm; Sun 10am–9pm. Early-bird specials daily 4–6pm.

SARASOTA AFTER DARK

The cultural capital of Florida's west coast, Sarasota is home to a host of performing arts, especially during the winter season. To get the latest update on what's happening any time of year, call the city's 24-hour **Artsline** (© 941/365-**ARTS**). Also check the "Ticket" section in Friday's *Herald-Tribune* (www.newscoast.com), the local daily newspaper; the Sarasota Convention and Visitors Bureau usually has copies (see "Essentials," earlier in this chapter).

THE PERFORMING ARTS   Located at the FSU Ringling Center for the Cultural Arts (p. 491), the Florida State University Center for the Performing Arts, 5555 N. Tamiami Trail (U.S. 41; © 800/361-8388 or 941/351-8000; www.asolo.org), presents the winter-through-spring **Asolo Theatre Festival** ✶✶✶. This annual program of ballet and Broadway-style musicals and drama is one of the state's finest. In addition to the Asolo Theatre, a 19th-century Italian court playhouse moved here from Asolo, Italy, in the 1950s by the Ringlings, the center uses the 487-seat Harold E. and Ethel M. Mertz Theatre, originally constructed in Scotland in 1900 and transferred piece by piece to Sarasota in 1987. The 161-seat Asolo Conservatory Theatre was later added as a smaller venue for experimental and alternative offerings. The complex is under the direction of Florida State University (FSU).

The city's other prime venue is the lavender, seashell-shaped **Van Wezel Performing Arts Hall** ✶✶✶, 777 N. Tamiami Trail (U.S. 41), at 9th Street (© 800/826-9303 or 941/953-3366; www.vanwezel.org). Recently renovated, it offers excellent visual and acoustic conditions and a wide range of year-round programming, including touring Broadway shows and visiting orchestras and dance troupes. Both it and the FSU Center host performances by the **Florida West Coast Symphony** (© 941/953-4252; www.fwcs.org), the **Jazz Club of Sarasota** (© 941/366-1552 or 941/316-9207; www.jazzclubsarasota.com), the **Sarasota Pops** (© 941/795-7677), and the **Sarasota Ballet** (© 800/361-8388 or 941/351-8000; www.sarasotaballet.org).

Downtown Sarasota's theater district is home to the **Florida Studio Theatre,** 1241 N. Palm Ave., at Cocoanut Avenue (© 941/366-9796; www.fst2000.org), which has contemporary performances from December to August, including a New Play Festival in May. Built in 1926 as the Edwards Theater, **The Opera House,** 61 N. Pineapple Ave., between Main and 1st Streets (© 941/953-7030; www.sarasotaopera.org), presents classical operas (in their original languages) as well as highbrow concerts. Next door to The Opera House, the **Golden Apple Dinner Theatre,** 25 N. Pineapple Ave. (© 941/366-5454), presents cocktails, dinner, and a professional Broadway-style show year-round. The professional, nonequity **Theatre Works,** 1247 1st St., at Cocoanut Avenue (© 941/952-9170), presents musical revues and other works all year.

THE CLUB & MUSIC SCENE You can find plenty of music to dance to on the mainland at **Sarasota Quay,** the downtown waterfront dining-shopping-entertainment complex on Tamiami Trail (U.S. 41) a block north of John Ringling Causeway. Just walk around this brick building and your ears will take you to the action. The laser sound-and-light crowd gathers at **In Extremis** (© **941/ 954-2008**), where a high-energy deejay spins Top-40 tunes for 20-somethings. Michael's Mediterranean Grill turns into **Anthony's After Dark** rocking disco at 10:30pm. An older but still energetic crowd dances to contemporary jazz at the **Downunder Jazz Bar** (© **941/951-2467**).

Over on St. Armands Circle, the Patio Lounge in **Columbia** restaurant (© **941/388-3987**) is one of the liveliest spots along the beach strip, featuring live, high-energy dance music Tuesday through Sunday evenings. And on Siesta Key, the pubs and restaurants along Ocean Boulevard in Siesta Village have noisy rock-and-roll bands entertaining a mostly young crowd, but you can retire to the pleasant confines of the wine bar at **Blasé Café** (© **941/349-9822**) for live jazz. See "Where to Dine," above, for more about these two restaurants.

Walt Disney World & Orlando

By Jim and Cynthia Tunstall

When Disney opened the Magic Kingdom in 1971, few imagined what Central Florida would be like 3 decades later. Today, it's bursting (and in some cases imploding) with newer, bigger, and better things for you to do.

Walt Disney World (WDW) has four theme parks, dozens of smaller attractions, tens of thousands of hotel rooms, scores of restaurants, a ton of bars and clubs, and two cruise ships.

When Universal Orlando, SeaWorld, and the marginal players add their share, well, it's pretty overwhelming.

Most of you don't have unlimited time and money, so it's our job to show you how to save both. Later in this chapter, you'll find the best deals on hotels, restaurants, attractions, and more. These tips will make your vacation easier to plan and more enjoyable and affordable to carry out.

1 Getting There

BY PLANE

THE MAJOR AIRLINES There are 35 scheduled airlines and as many charter companies serving the more than 30 million Orlando passengers each year. **Delta** (© 800/221-1212; www.delta-air.com) has more than 25% of the flights to and from Orlando International Airport. It offers service from 200 cities.

Other carriers include **Air Canada** (© 888/247-2262; www.aircanada.ca), **America West** (© 800/235-9292; www.americawest.com), **American** (© 800/433-7300; www.aa.com), **British Airways** (© 800/247-9297; www.britishairways.com), **Continental** (© 800/525-0280; www.continental.com), **Northwest** (© 800/225-2525; www.nwa.com), and **US Airways** (© 800/428-4322; www.usairways.com).

Several so-called no-frills airlines—low fares but no amenities—fly to Orlando. The biggest is **Southwest Airlines** (© 800/435-9792; www.southwest.com).

The best fares to Orlando International Airport are in November, December, and January. The airport is user-friendly and only 25 miles (40km) from Walt Disney World. **Mears Transportation** (© 407/423-5566) shuttles people to and from the airport. The vans run 24 hours a day, departing every 15 to 25 minutes. Round-trip fares are $23 to $27 for adults and $16 to $19 for children 4 to 11.

BY CAR

Orlando is 436 miles (702km) from Atlanta, 1,312 miles (2,112km) from Boston, 1,120 miles (1,803km) from Chicago, 1,170 miles (1,884km) from Dallas, and 1,088 miles (1,752km) from New York City.

From Atlanta, take I-75 south to the Florida Turnpike to I-4 west. From the Northeast, take I-95 south to I-4 west. From Chicago, take I-65 south to Nashville, I-24 south to I-75, and then south to the Florida Turnpike to I-4 west. From Dallas, take I-20 east to I-49, then south to I-10, east to I-75, and south to the Florida Turnpike to I-4 west.

BY TRAIN

Amtrak trains (© **800/872-7245;** www.amtrak.com) pull into stations in downtown Orlando (23 miles/37km from Walt Disney World) and Kissimmee (15 miles/24km from Disney). There are also stops in Winter Park (10 miles/16km north of downtown). Sanford (23 miles/37km northeast of downtown Orlando) is the end terminal for Amtrak's Auto Train.

PACKAGE TOURS

Orlando's packages can be a little confusing, partly because most offer different services. Start by looking at the ads in your Sunday newspaper's travel section.

If you're planning to spend all of your time in Mickeyville, contact the **Walt Disney World Travel Company** (© **800/828-0228;** www.disneyworld.com) for a wide assortment of packages available.

Universal Orlando packages can be booked at © **888/322-5537.** You can get online information at **www.universalorlando.com**.

For **SeaWorld,** call © **800/423-8368** or go to **www.seaworld.com**.

Airlines also offer packages. **Delta** (© **800/872-7786;** www.deltavacations. com), **Continental Airlines Vacations** (© **800/301-3800;** www.cool vacations.com), and **American Airlines Vacations** (© **800/321-2121;** www.aa.com) are three options.

American Express Travel (© **800/732-1991;** http://travel.american express.com/travel) has special deals for cardholders.

Other tour options include **Touraine Travel** (© **800/967-5583;** www. tourainetravel.com), which offers a variety of packages to Disney and Disney properties, Universal Orlando, and SeaWorld.

DISNEY ON THE HIGH SEAS

Subtle differences aside, Disney's ships—the *Magic* and *Wonder*—are nearly identical twins: 83,000 tons, 12 decks, 875 cabins, room for 2,400 guests, and some adults-only areas, but no casinos. Both have extensive kids and teen programs. There are also nurseries for 3-month- to 3-year-olds. Restaurants, shows, and other onboard activities are family oriented. A dine-around option lets you move among main restaurants (each ship has four). The *Magic* and *Wonder* depart from Port Canaveral on 3- to 7-day excursions; 7-day land-sea packages are also available. Prices range from $439 to $4,799 per adult, $229 to $999 for children 3 to 17, and $99 to $119 for children under 3, depending on the cabin level and length of trip (© **800/951-3532;** www.disneycruise.com).

VISITOR INFORMATION

The **Orlando/Orange County Convention & Visitors Bureau,** 8723 International Dr., Suite 101, Orlando, FL 32819 (© **407/363-5872;** www.orlandoinfo.com), can answer questions and send maps and brochures, such as the *Official Visitors Guide* and *Official Accommodations Guide*. The packet should reach you in 3 weeks and include the "Magicard," good for up to $500 in discounts on rooms, car rentals, attractions, and more. If you don't require a human voice, you can order by calling © **800/643-9492** or 800/551-0181.

For information about **Walt Disney World**—including vacation brochures and videos—write or call Walt Disney World, Box 10000, Lake Buena Vista, FL 32830-1000 (© **407/934-7639** or 407/824-2222; www.disneyworld.com).

For information about **Universal Orlando,** call © **800/837-2273** or 407/363-8000, surf over to **www.universalorlando.com**, or write to **Universal Orlando,** 1000 Universal Studios Plaza, Orlando, FL 32819.

You can obtain SeaWorld information online at **www.seaworld.com**.

Orlando

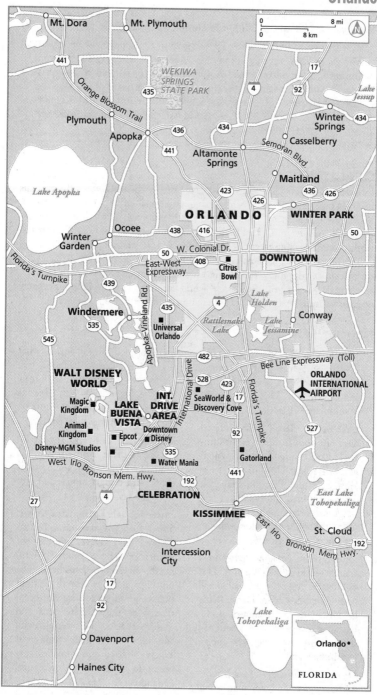

Mt. Dora

Mt. Plymouth

441

Orange Blossom Trail

WEKIWA
SPRINGS
STATE PARK

435

4

17

92

Lake
Jessup

Plymouth

436

434

Winter
Springs

434

Apopka

441

Altamonte
Springs

Semoran Blvd

Casselberry

Lake Apopka

423

426

Maitland

436

426

ORLANDO

WINTER PARK

Ocoee

438

416

50

Winter
Garden

50

W. Colonial Dr.

DOWNTOWN

Florida's Turnpike

East-West
Expressway

408

Citrus
Bowl

Lake
Holden

439

4

435

Windermere

Universal
Orlando

Rattlesnake
Lake

Lake
Jessamine

Conway

535

Apopka-Vineland Rd.

545

482

Bee Line Expressway (Toll)

WALT DISNEY
WORLD

528

ORLANDO
INTERNATIONAL
AIRPORT

Magic
Kingdom

LAKE
BUENA
VISTA

INT.
DRIVE
AREA

SeaWorld &
Discovery Cove

423

17

Florida's Turnpike

Animal
Kingdom

Downtown
Disney

Disney-MGM Studios

Epcot

92

527

West Irlo Bronson Mem. Hwy.

535

Gatorland

Water Mania

441

27

4

192

CELEBRATION

East Lake
Tohopekaliga

KISSIMMEE

St. Cloud

192

17

Intercession
City

East Irlo Bronson Mem. Hwy.

92

Lake
Tohopekaliga

Davenport

Orlando •

Haines City

FLORIDA

507

Tips Help for Guests with Disabilities

Walt Disney World's services are outlined in the *Guidebook for Guests with Disabilities,* which you can pick up at Guest Services near the front entrance to the parks, or call ✆ **407/824-4321** for answers to any questions regarding special needs. **Universal Orlando** distributes a *Disabled Guest Guidebook* at the Guest Services office just inside the main entrances (✆ **407/363-8000**). **SeaWorld** has a similar guide at Guest Services (✆ **407/351-3600**).

CITY LAYOUT

Interstate 4 runs diagonally across the state from Tampa to Daytona Beach. Exits from I-4 take you to Disney, SeaWorld, International Drive, Universal Orlando, Kissimmee, Lake Buena Vista, downtown Orlando, and Winter Park. *Note:* I-4 is woefully congested. It's best to use it during nonpeak hours, when tourists and workers aren't rushing to and from Orlando and the parks.

The Florida Turnpike crosses I-4 and links to I-75 to the north. U.S. 192, a major east-west highway, runs along Kissimmee's major motel area to U.S. 27, where it crosses I-4 near the Disney World entrance. The Bee Line Expressway goes east from I-4 past Orlando International Airport to Cape Canaveral.

NEIGHBORHOODS IN BRIEF

Walt Disney World   The empire, its big and little parks, resorts, restaurants, shops, and trimmings aren't in the city. They're southwest of municipal Orlando.

Lake Buena Vista   Disney's next-door neighbor is the home of "official" (but not Disney-owned) hotels. It's near Downtown Disney West Side and Pleasure Island. It offers tree-lined thoroughfares and free transportation throughout the realm, though it may take a while to get where you're going.

Celebration   Imagine living in a Disney world 365 days a year. This 4,900-acre town eventually will have thousands of residents living in Disney-dreamed homes. Celebration's downtown area is designed for tourists and includes shops, restaurants, and a hotel.

Downtown Disney   This is more a Disney *doo-wa-diddy* than a real

neighborhood; simply put, it's what WDW has taken to calling its two nighttime entertainment areas, Pleasure Island and West Side, as well as its shopping complex, Downtown Disney Marketplace.

Kissimmee   This once-sleepy city is a short drive from Mickey and more of a bargain, but some find it tacky, with budget motels and too, *too* many fast-food joints.

International Drive Area (Hwy. 536)   Can you say tourist mecca? Known as **I-Drive,** it's east of Disney and goes 10 miles (16km) north, nearly to Universal. The northern end has everything from bungee jumping and ice skating to dozens of theme restaurants and T-shirt shacks. The central and southern ends have numerous hotels. I-Drive also provides easy access to SeaWorld and Universal Orlando.

Downtown Orlando The downtown is northeast of Walt Disney World on I-4. It includes the Orlando Science Center, restaurants, hotels, and plenty of nightclubs.

Winter Park Just north of Orlando, Winter Park has a lot of upscale shops and restaurants along Park Avenue, but it's a bit too far north for hotels if you're spending much time at the Disney parks.

2 Getting Around

In a city that thrives on tourists, you won't find it difficult to get from point A to point B—especially if you have a car—but it can be slow. If you're traveling outside or between the tourist areas, avoid the 7-day-a-week rush hour (7–9am and 4–6pm) like the plague, which it is. Rush hours are bad anywhere, but commuter traffic here compounds the tourist traffic.

ON INTERNATIONAL DRIVE

I-Drive has two methods of transportation: Foot power (points of interest can be reasonably close together, but traffic can be deadly) and the **I-Ride Trolley** (© **866/243-7483;** www.iridetrolley.com), which stops about every 2 blocks. The trolley runs from 7am to midnight (75¢ adults, 25¢ seniors, children under 12 free; *exact change is required*). This is a great way to get around on this strip.

BY THE DISNEY TRANSPORTATION SYSTEM

If you plan to stay at and spend most of your time in Disney, there's a thorough, free transportation network that runs throughout the WDW complex.

Disney resorts and official hotels offer unlimited free transportation via bus, monorail, ferry, or water taxi to all WDW parks and properties 14 to 18 hours a day. You can get to Universal and other attractions, too, but you'll have to pay extra.

The pluses: The system is free; you can save on a rental car, insurance, and gas; and you don't have to pay for theme-park parking. The minuses: You're at the mercy of the schedule, which is often slow and *very* indirect.

BY SHUTTLE

Mears Transportation operates vans and buses that go to all of the theme parks, as well as Cypress Gardens, Kennedy Space Center, and Busch Gardens (yes, in Tampa), among others. Call © **407/423-5566** for rates.

BY TAXI

Taxis gather at resorts and smaller properties will call a cab for you. **Yellow Cab** (© **407/699-9999**) and **Ace Metro** (© **407/855-0564**) usually charge $2.50 for the first mile, $1.50 per mile thereafter.

 FAST FACTS: **Walt Disney World & Orlando**

American Express There's a Travel Service Office at Epcot's main gate. The one closest to Universal is **A Time to Travel**, 7512 Dr. Phillips Blvd. (© **407/ 345-1181**).

Babysitters Many Orlando hotels, including all of Disney's resorts, offer babysitting services, and several have good child-care facilities with counselor-supervised activity programs on the premises. Babysitting rates usually run $12 to $15 per hour for the first child and $1 per additional child, per hour.

Business Hours　Theme parks vary, depending on time of year. Most open at 8 to 10am and close at 6 to 7pm, later during summer and holidays, every day. Businesses are generally open 9am to 5pm, Monday through Friday.

Doctors and Dentists　There are basic first-aid centers in all of the theme parks. If you need to see a doctor while you're in Orlando, you can get a reputable referral from **Ask-A-Nurse** (© 407/870-1700). It's a free service. There's also a 24-hour, toll-free number for the **Poison Control Center** (© 800/282-3171). To find a dentist, call **Dental Referral Service** at © 888/343-3440 or go online to **www.dentalreferral.com**.

Disney offers in-room medical service 24 hours a day (© 407/238-2000). **Doctors on Call Service** (© 407/399-3627) makes house and room calls in most of the Orlando area. **Centra-Care** lists several walk-in clinics in the Yellow Pages, including ones on International Drive (© 407/370-4881), and at Lake Buena Vista near Disney (© 407/934-2273).

Emergencies　Dial © **911** for police, fire departments, and ambulance.

Hospitals　**Sand Lake Hospital,** 9400 Turkey Lake Rd. (© 407/351-8550), is about 2 miles (3.5km) south of Sand Lake Road. From the WDW area, take I-4 east to the Sand Lake Road exit and make a left on Turkey Lake Road. The hospital is 2 miles (3.25km) up on your right. **Celebration Health** (© 407/303-4000), located in the near-Disney town of Celebration, is at 400 Celebration Place. From I-4, take the U.S. 192 exit. At the first traffic light, turn right onto Celebration Avenue. At the first stop sign, take another right.

Kennels　The theme parks board pets for $5 to $6 per day. WDW also offers overnight kennels ($11; $9 for its resort guests) at the Transportation and Ticket Center's kennel near the Polynesian Resort.

Lost Children　Every theme park has a designated spot for parents to reunite with lost children. Ask a park staffer or check at guest services.

Newspapers　Friday's *Orlando Sentinel* has entertainment and dining listings, as does the *Sentinel's* website, **www.orlandosentinel.com**.

Pharmacies　Walgreens, 1003 W. Vine St. (Hwy. 192; © 407/847-5252), operates a 24-hour pharmacy. There's an Eckerd Drugs at 12125 Apopka-Vineland Rd. (© 407/238-9333) that's open until 7pm. There are scores of others in the *Yellow Pages.*

Post Office　The main post office in Lake Buena Vista is at 12541 Hwy. 535, in the Crossroads Shopping Center (© 800/275-8777). It's open Monday through Friday from 9am to 4pm, Saturday from 9am to noon.

Taxes　Florida's 6% sales tax is charged on all goods except most grocery-store items and medicines. Additionally, hotels add another 5% or 6% to your bill for a total of 11% or 12%.

Telephone　If you're making a local call in Orlando, even to someone just across the street, *you must dial the 407 area code followed by the number you wish to call,* for a total of 10 digits.

Tourist Information　See "Visitor Information," earlier in this chapter.

Weather　Call © 321/255-0212 for the local weather forecast.

3 Where to Stay

There are more than 111,000 rooms in the Orlando area, with thousands added annually. While the economy softened the second half of 2001, occupancy is generally high—as much as 90% at Disney, so if you're planning to stay in one of Mickey's resorts, book as far ahead as possible.

The lowest rates are usually available September through November and January through April. High season occurs during holidays and the summer months.

WALT DISNEY WORLD CENTRAL RESERVATIONS OFFICE

To reserve a room or book packages at Disney's resorts, villas, campgrounds, and official hotels, call the **Walt Disney World Travel Company** at © **800/ 828-0228** or contact **Central Reservation Operations** (CRO), P.O. Box 10000, Lake Buena Vista, FL 32830-1000 (© **407/934-7639;** www.disney world.com).

Both can recommend accommodations suited to your price range and specific needs, such as proximity to your favorite park or those with supervised child-care centers. The clerks who answer the telephones can be very helpful but usually won't volunteer information about a better deal or a special *unless you ask.*

DISNEY RESORTS
VERY EXPENSIVE

Disney's Beach Club Resort ⭐   This Cape Cod–style hotel is close enough to Epcot that health-and-fitness types walk to the park, but the Disney Transportation System is there for the rest of us. Stormalong Bay, one of its main draws, is a huge pool with a 3-acre water park. Room views range from the pool to (ugh!) the parking lot, but you'll pay a lot more to see the pool. Some rooms have balconies and can accommodate five people.

1800 Epcot Resorts Blvd. (off Buena Vista Dr., P.O. Box 10000), Lake Buena Vista, FL 32830-0100. © 407/ 934-7639 or 407/934-8000. Fax 407/934-3850. www.disneyworld.com. 583 units. $289–$640 double; $485–$1,995 suites. Extra person $25. Children 17 and under stay free with parents. AE, DC, DISC, MC, V. Free parking; $6 valet. Pets $9 a night. Take I-4 east to the Hwy. 536/Epcot Center Dr. exit and follow the signs. **Amenities:** Restaurant (seafood); grill; 4 lounges; 2 heated outdoor pools; children's pool; 2 lighted tennis courts; Jacuzzi; water-sports equipment; children's club; video arcade; WDW Transportation System; transportation for a fee to non-Disney theme parks; business center; salon; 24-hr. room service; babysitting; guest laundry; no-smoking rooms. *In room:* A/C, TV, dataport, minibar, fridge ($10 a night), hair dryer, iron, safe.

Disney's BoardWalk Inn ⭐⭐⭐   Romantics like staying at this plush 1940s-style "seaside" resort (it's really on a lake), which has clubs and restaurants on a quarter-mile (.5km) boardwalk. The B&B–style rooms sleep four, and some have balconies. The priciest rooms overlook the boardwalk or pool; the less expensive face the parking lot but are sheltered from the boardwalk noise. Hang onto your swimsuit if you hit the pool's famous—or infamous, depending on how you look at it—200-foot (60m) "keister coaster" water slide. The Board-Walk's villas range from studios to units that can sleep up to 12 people.

2101 N. Epcot Resorts Blvd. (off Buena Vista Dr.; P.O. Box 10000), Lake Buena Vista, FL 32830-1000. © 407/934-7639 or 407/939-5100. Fax 407/934-5150. www.disneyworld.com. 378 units. $289–$770 double; $565–$2,275 suites; $289–$1,885 villas. Extra person $25. Children 17 and under stay free with parent. AE, DC, DISC, MC, V. Free parking; $6 valet. Pets $9 a night. Take I-4 to the Hwy. 536/Epcot Center Dr. exit and follow the signs. **Amenities:** 2 restaurants (steak/seafood, Mediterranean); grill; 2 lounges; 3 clubs; 2 outdoor heated pools; kids' pool; 2 lighted tennis courts; croquet; health club; Jacuzzi; children's activity center; arcade; concierge; WDW Transportation System; transportation to non-Disney parks for a fee; business center; shopping arcade; 24-hr. room service; babysitting; guest laundry; valet; no-smoking rooms; concierge-level rooms. *In room:* A/C, TV, dataport, fridge ($10 a night), hair dryer, iron, safe.

Where to Stay in Walt Disney World & Lake Buena Vista

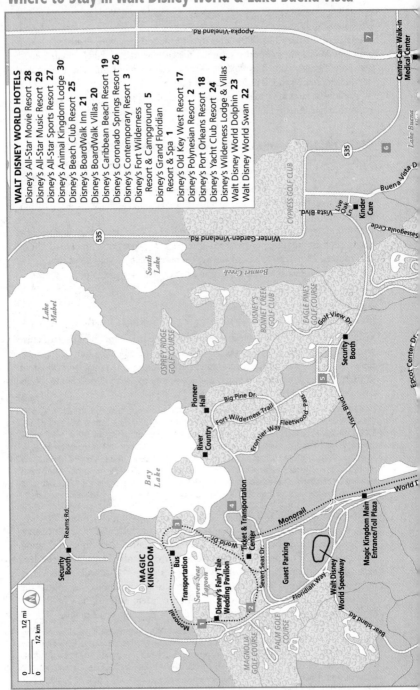

WALT DISNEY WORLD HOTELS
Disney's All-Star Movie Resort **28**
Disney's All-Star Music Resort **29**
Disney's All-Star Sports Resort **27**
Disney's Animal Kingdom Lodge **30**
Disney's Beach Club Resort **25**
Disney's BoardWalk Inn **21**
Disney's BoardWalk Villas **20**
Disney's Caribbean Beach Resort **19**
Disney's Coronado Springs Resort **26**
Disney's Contemporary Resort **3**
Disney's Fort Wilderness
  Resort & Campground **5**
Disney's Grand Floridian
  Resort & Spa **1**
Disney's Old Key West Resort **17**
Disney's Polynesian Resort **2**
Disney's Port Orleans Resort **18**
Disney's Yacht Club Resort **24**
Disney's Wilderness Lodge & Villas **4**
Walt Disney World Dolphin **23**
Walt Disney World Swan **22**

OFFICIAL HOTELS

Best Western Lake Buena Vista Hotel **8**
Courtyard by Marriott **12**
DoubleTree Guest Suites **9**
Hotel Royal Plaza **10**
The Wyndham Palace Resort & Spa **11**

LAKE BUENA VISTA HOTELS

Gaylord Palms **16**
Hawthorn Suites Lake Buena Vista **7**
Holiday Inn Family Suites Resort **15**
Hyatt Regency Grand Cypress **6**
Marriott's Orlando World Center **14**
Summerfield Suites Lake Buena Vista **13**
Villas of Grand Cypress **6**

513

Disney's Contemporary Resort ⭐ Location, Location, LOCATION. The Contemporary is one of three resorts on the monorail system, and it's near the golf courses. Unfortunately, the 15-story, 30-year-old A-frame dates to WDW's infancy, and even a complete renovation in 1999 couldn't restore it to the same luster as some of the top dogs in this price category. The standard rooms are somewhat dull and sleep four. The best views are from the upper floors, which are a tad quieter than those on the lower floors, which are exposed to noisy public areas and the monorail.

4600 N. World Dr. (P.O. Box 10000), Lake Buena Vista, FL 32830-1000. ℰ **407/934-7639** or 407/824-1000. Fax 407/824-3535. www.disneyworld.com. 1,041 units. $234–$525 double; $310–$1,675 suites. Extra person $25. Children 17 and under stay free with parent. AE, DC, DISC, MC, V. Free parking; $6 valet. Pets $9 a night. Take I-4 to the Hwy. 536/Epcot Center Dr. exit and follow the signs. **Amenities:** 2 restaurants (steak, American); food court; 2 lounges; 2 heated outdoor pools; kids' pool; 6 lighted tennis courts; fitness center; Jacuzzi; water-sports equipment; kids' club; concierge; WDW Transportation System; transportation to non-Disney parks for a fee; salon; 24-hr. room service; babysitting; guest laundry; valet; no-smoking rooms; concierge-level rooms. *In room:* A/C, TV, dataport, fridge ($10 a night), hair dryer, iron, safe.

Disney's Grand Floridian Resort & Spa ⭐⭐⭐ *Finds* From the moment you step into the opulent five-story domed lobby, you'll feel as if you've slipped back to an era when a guy named Gatsby was at the top of his game. High tea is served in the afternoon; later, a small band plays music from the 1940s. The Floridian has become the romantic choice for couples, especially honeymooners, who like luxuriating in the first-class spa and health club—the best in WDW. The Victorian-style rooms sleep at least four; virtually all overlook a garden, pool, courtyard, or the Seven Seas Lagoon. This, too, is on the monorail system and close to the Magic Kingdom.

4401 Floridian Way (P.O. Box 10000), Lake Buena Vista, FL 32830-1000. ℰ **407/934-7639** or 407/824-3000. Fax 407/824-3186. www.disneyworld.com. 900 units. $329–$815 double; $810–$2,175 suite. Extra person $25. Children 17 and under stay free with parent. AE, DC, DISC, MC, V. Free parking; $6 valet. Pets $9 a night. Take I-4 to the Hwy. 536/Epcot Center Dr. exit and follow the signs. **Amenities:** 5 restaurants (American, seafood); grill; 3 lounges; 1 heated outdoor pool; kids' pool; 2 lighted tennis courts; health club; spa; water-sports equipment; children's center; arcade; concierge; car-rental desk; WDW Transportation System; transportation to non-Disney parks for a fee; business center; shopping arcade; salon; 24-hr. room service; babysitting; guest laundry; valet; no-smoking rooms; concierge-level rooms. *In room:* A/C, TV, dataport, mini-bar, fridge ($10 a night), hair dryer, iron, safe.

Disney's Old Key West Resort ⭐ This resort has tree-lined, brick walkways edged by white-picket fences reminiscent of Key West's Old Town. Located between Epcot and Downtown Disney West Side, it offers some of the quietest, homiest rooms on WDW property. The rooms come in four sizes (all with a balcony or patio): studios, one- and two-bedroom villas, and grand villas (with beds for 12 and whirlpool tubs). All units have kitchens or kitchenettes.

1510 N. Cove Rd. (off Community Dr.; P.O. Box 10000), Lake Buena Vista, FL 32830-1000. ℰ **407/934-7639** or 407/827-7700. Fax 407/827-7710. www.disneyworld.com. 761 units. $249–$359 studios; $335–$775 1- and 2-bedroom villas; $1,015–$1,410 grand villas. Call for extra adult fees. Children 17 and under stay free with parent. AE, DC, DISC, MC, V. Free parking. Pets $9 a night. Take I-4 to the Hwy. 536/Epcot Center Dr. exit and follow the signs. **Amenities:** Restaurant (American); groceries; 4 heated outdoor pools; kids' pool; 2 lighted and 1 unlighted tennis courts; Jacuzzi; sauna; water-sports equipment; game room; WDW Transportation System; transportation to non-Disney parks for a fee; massage; babysitting; guest laundry; no-smoking rooms. *In room:* A/C, TV, kitchenette or kitchen, fridge, coffeemaker, hair dryer.

Disney's Polynesian Resort ⭐ Just south of the Magic Kingdom, the 25-acre Polynesian is the third resort on the monorail line. Its extensive play areas and themed swimming pools make it a good choice for those traveling with kids. Public areas have canvas cabanas, hammocks, and big swings overlooking a

200-acre lagoon. Rooms are average size, and all but a few accommodate five people. The main drawback is that there isn't much difference between the resort now and when it opened in the 1970s, making it overpriced for what's inside.

1600 Seven Seas Dr. (P.O. Box 10000), Lake Buena Vista, FL 32830-1000. (C) **407/934-7639** or 407/824-2000. Fax 407/824-3174. www.disneyworld.com. 853 units. $299–$540 double; $380–$655 concierge-level; $495–$2,225 suite. Extra person $25. Children 17 and under stay free with parent. AE, DC, DISC, MC, V. Free parking; $6 valet. Pets $9 a night. Take I-4 to the Hwy. 536/Epcot Center Dr. exit and follow the signs. **Amenities:** Restaurant (Pacific Rim); cafe; 2 lounges; 2 heated outdoor pools; kids' pool; water-sports equipment; children's club; arcade; concierge; WDW Transportation System; transportation to non-Disney parks for a fee; shopping arcade; 24-hr. room service; babysitting; guest laundry; valet; no-smoking rooms; concierge-level rooms. *In room:* A/C, TV, fridge ($10 a night), hair dryer, iron, safe.

Disney's Yacht Club Resort ★★ The Yacht Club is a cut above its sister, the Beach Club (see above), because the rooms, views, service, and atmosphere are a bit better. It's also geared more toward adults and families with older children, although young kids are catered to (this *is* Disney). It shares a 25-acre lake, a first-class swimming pool, and magnificent landscaping with the Beach Club. The theme is turn-of-the-20th-century New England. The rooms have space for up to five people, and most have balconies. Stay here and you can walk to Epcot, but you can save shoe leather by using the free buses.

1700 Epcot Resorts Blvd. (off Buena Vista Dr.; P.O. Box 10000), Lake Buena Vista, FL 32830-1000. (C) **407/ 934-7639** or 407/934-7000. Fax 407/924-3450. www.disneyworld.com. 630 units. $289–$495 double; $415–$640 concierge-level; $510–$2,180 suite. Extra person $25. Children 17 and under stay free with paying parent. AE, DC, DISC, MC, V. Free parking; $6 valet. Pets $9 a night. Take I-4 to the Hwy. 536/Epcot Center Dr. exit and follow the signs. **Amenities:** 3 restaurants (steaks, seafood); grill; lounge; 2 heated outdoor pools; kids' pool; 2 lighted tennis courts; Jacuzzi; water-sports equipment; children's center; arcade; concierge; WDW Transportation System; transportation to non-Disney parks for a fee; business center; shopping arcade; salon; 24-hr. room service; babysitting; guest laundry; valet; no-smoking rooms; concierge-level rooms. *In room:* A/C, TV, dataport, minibar, fridge ($10 a night), coffeemaker, iron, safe.

Walt Disney World Dolphin ★★ If Antonio Gaudí and Dr. Seuss had teamed up on an architectural design, they might have created something like this Sheraton resort and its sister, the Walt Disney World Swan (see below). This hotel centers on a 27-story pyramid with two 11-story wings crowned by 56-foot (17m) twin dolphin sculptures that look like the whale in *Pinocchio*. Since it isn't as theme-intensive as the other Disney resorts, it's popular with business travelers and those who prefer their accommodations a little less sugary. Rooms sleep four. The resort has a grotto pool with waterfalls, water slide, and whirlpools. The Swan and Dolphin share a Body by Jake health club. Epcot is the nearest park.

1500 Epcot Resorts Blvd. (off Buena Vista Dr.; P.O. Box 22653), Lake Buena Vista, FL 32830-2653. (C) **800/ 227-1500** or 407/934-4000. Fax 407/934-4884. www.swandolphin.com. 1,509 units. $325–$495 double; $465–$3,100 suite. Extra person $25. Children 17 and under stay free with parent. AE, DC, DISC, MC, V. Free parking; valet $8. Pets $9 a night. Take I-4 to the Hwy. 536/Epcot Center Dr. exit and follow the signs. **Amenities:** 4 restaurants (steak, Mexican, American); grill; 2 lounges; 4 heated outdoor pools; 4 lighted tennis courts; health club; water-sports equipment; children's center; 2 game rooms; concierge; car-rental desk; WDW Transportation System; transportation to non-Disney parks for a fee; shopping arcade; salon; 24-hr. room service; massage; babysitting; guest laundry; valet; no-smoking rooms; concierge-level rooms. *In room:* A/C, TV, dataport, minibar, hair dryer, iron, safe, Nintendo.

Walt Disney World Swan ★★ Not to be outdone by the huge dolphins at its sister resort, this high-rise Westin resort is topped with dual 45-foot (14m) swan statues and seashell fountains. It shares a beach, health club, some restaurants, and other trimmings with the Dolphin (see above). The Swan's rooms are a shade smaller, but they still have room for four. The best room views are from the 11th and 12th floors' Royal Beach Club, the hotel's concierge level; the beach next to the pool offers a great view of Epcot's IllumiNations fireworks.

1200 Epcot Resorts Blvd. (off Buena Vista Dr.; P.O. Box 22786), Lake Buena Vista, FL 32830-2786. ℂ **800/ 248-7926** or 407/934-3000. Fax 407/934-4499. www.swandolphin.com. 758 units. $325–$495 double; $465–$3,100 suite. Extra person $25. Children 17 and under stay free with parent. AE, DC, DISC, MC, V. Free parking; valet $8. Pets $9 a night. Take I-4 to the Hwy. 536/Epcot Center Dr. exit and follow the signs. **Amenities:** 4 restaurants (American, Italian, Pacific Rim); grill; lounge; 4 heated outdoor pools; 4 lighted tennis courts; health club; water-sports equipment; children's center; 2 game rooms; concierge; car-rental desk; WDW Transportation System; transportation to non-Disney parks for a fee; shopping arcade; salon; 24-hr. room service; massage; babysitting; guest laundry; valet; no-smoking rooms; concierge-level rooms. *In room:* A/C, TV, dataport, minibar, hair dryer, iron, safe, Nintendo.

EXPENSIVE

Disney's Animal Kingdom Lodge ✪ Disney did a good job giving its newest resort the feel of an African game-reserve lodge—well, with a little of your imagination. The rooms follow a *kraal* design, a semicircle that gives guests an occasional view of birds, giraffes, and other animals on a 30-acre savanna. Typical rooms are a bit smaller than those in Disney's Very Expensive category, making things slightly more crowded for four. The lodge is adjacent to Animal Kingdom, but most everything else on the property is quite a distance away.

2901 Osceola Pkwy., Bay Lake, FL 32830. ℂ **407/934-7639** or 407/938-4760. Fax 407/352-2792. www. disneyworld.com. 1,293 units. $204–$510 double; $415–$595 concierge; $640–$2,450 suite. Extra person $25. Children 17 and under stay free with parent. AE, DC, DISC, MC, V. Free parking; valet $8. Pets $9 a night. Take I-4 to the Hwy. 536/Epcot Center Dr. exit and follow the signs. **Amenities:** 3 restaurants (African, American); lounge; heated outdoor pool; kids' pool; health club; children's center; arcade; concierge; WDW Transportation System; transportation to non-Disney parks; shopping arcade; limited room service; babysitting; guest laundry; no-smoking rooms; concierge-level rooms. *In room:* A/C, TV, dataport, fridge ($10 a night), hair dryer, iron, safe.

Disney's Wilderness Lodge ✪✪✪ The geyser out back, a mammoth stone hearth in the lobby, and bunk beds for the kids give the Wilderness Lodge a national-park feel. The geyser "blows" periodically throughout the day, and nightly electric water pageants can be seen from the shore. Standard rooms sleep four, and if a view is important to you, those with woods views are best. The nearest park is Magic Kingdom, but the resort is in a pretty remote area.

The **Villas at Disney's Wilderness Lodge** is another Disney Vacation Club (time-share) property that rents vacant rooms. This resort offers a more upscale experience, but you get less kitchen space here than in Old Key West.

901 W. Timberline Dr. (on the southwest shore of Bay Lake just east of the Magic Kingdom; P.O. Box 10000), Lake Buena Vista, FL 32830-1000. ℂ **407/934-7639** or 407/938-3200. Fax 407/824-3232. www.disney world.com. 909 units. $194–$500 lodge; $340–$460 concierge-level; $640–$1,090 suite, $269–$920 villa. Extra person $25. Children 17 and under stay free with parent. AE, DC, DISC, MC, V. Free parking. Pets $9 a night. Take I-4 to the Hwy. 536/Epcot Center Dr. exit and follow the signs. **Amenities:** 2 restaurants (American); 2 lounges; heated outdoor pool; kids' pool; 2 Jacuzzis; water-sports equipment; children's center; arcade; WDW Transportation System; transportation to non-Disney parks for a fee; limited room service; babysitting; guest laundry; no-smoking rooms; concierge-level rooms. *In room:* A/C, TV, fridge ($10 a night), hair dryer, iron, safe.

MODERATE

Disney's Caribbean Beach Resort ✪ The Caribbean Beach isn't as bargain-basement as the All-Star resorts that follow and offers good value for families who don't need a lot of frills or amenities. The units are grouped into five "villages" around a large duck-filled lake. When booking, ask for a recently refurbished room. Even then, your party had better be into togetherness—the bathrooms are tight. The main pool replicates a Spanish-style fort complete with slide. The closest park is Disney–MGM Studios.

900 Cayman Way (off Buena Vista Dr.; P.O. Box 10000), Lake Buena Vista, FL 32830-1000. ℂ 407/934-7639 or 407/934-3400. Fax 407/934-3288. www.disneyworld.com. 2,112 units. $133–$219 double. Extra person $15. Children 17 and under stay free in parents' room. AE, DC, DISC, MC, V. Free parking. Pets $9 a night. Take I-4 to the Hwy. 536/Epcot Center Dr. exit and follow signs. **Amenities:** Restaurant (American); grill; lounge; large heated outdoor pool and 6 smaller ones in the villages; kids' pool; Jacuzzi; water-sports equipment; arcade; WDW Transportation System; transportation to non-Disney parks for a fee; limited room service; babysitting; guest laundry; no-smoking rooms. *In room:* A/C, TV, fridge ($10 a night), hair dryer, iron, safe.

Disney's Coronado Springs Resort ✸   Here's another clone of the Disney moderate-price class. Were it not for exterior gingerbread and inside-the-room decor (in this case, American Southwest), it would be hard to tell one from the other. The Coronado's pool looks like a mini–Mayan temple. Rooms are small-ish, suitable for four people who get along; don't expect to fit more than one into the bathroom at a time. Those nearest the central public area, pool, and lobby tend to be noisier. The nearest park is Animal Kingdom.

1000 Buena Vista Dr., near All-Star Resorts and Blizzard Beach, Lake Buena Vista, FL 32830. ℂ 407/934-7639 or 407/939-1000. Fax 407/939-1001. www.disneyworld.com. 1,967 units. $133–$219 double; $278–$1,050 suite. Extra person $15. Children 17 and under stay free with parent. AE, DC, DISC, MC, V. Free parking. Pets $9 a night. Take I-4 to the Hwy. 536/Epcot Center Dr. exit and follow the signs. **Amenities:** Restaurant (Mexican); grill/food court; 2 lounges; 4 heated outdoor pools; kids' pool; health club; Jacuzzi; sauna; water-sports equipment; 2 arcades; WDW Transportation System; transportation to non-Disney parks for a fee; business center; salon; limited room service; massage; babysitting; guest laundry; no-smoking rooms. *In room:* A/C, TV, dataport, fridge ($10 a night), hair dryer, iron, safe.

Disney's Port Orleans Resort ✸✸ *(Value)*   This resort, resembling turn-of-the-20th-century New Orleans, includes the old Dixie Landings property that was merged into it in 2000. It has the best location, landscaping, and, perhaps, the coziest atmosphere of all resorts in this class. Its Doubloon Lagoon pool has a water slide that curves out of a dragon's mouth. Rooms are big enough for four, but are a tight fit. Port Orleans is east of Epcot and Disney–MGM Studios.

2201 Orleans Dr. (off Bonnet Creek Pkwy.; P.O. Box 10000), Lake Buena Vista, FL 32830-1000. ℂ 407/934-7639 or 407/934-5000. Fax 407/934-5353. www.disneyworld.com. 3,056 units. $133–$219 double. Extra person $15. Children 17 and under stay free with parent. AE, DC, DISC, MC, V. Free parking. Pets $9 a night. Take I-4 to the Hwy. 536/Epcot Center Dr. exit and follow the signs. **Amenities:** 2 restaurants (American); grill/food court; 2 lounges; 6 heated outdoor pools; 2 kids' pools; Jacuzzi; water-sports equipment; 2 arcades; WDW Transportation System; transportation to non-Disney parks for a fee; limited room service; babysitting; guest laundry; no-smoking rooms. *In room:* A/C, TV, fridge ($10 a night), hair dryer, iron, safe.

INEXPENSIVE

Disney's All-Star Movie Resort   Kids love the larger-than-life themes at the All-Star resorts, but adults usually cringe at the visual overload. Giant cartoon characters such as Buzz Lightyear adorn this one and help hide a 21st-century rendition of a 1950s Holiday Inn. The rooms are spartan and very small—the bathrooms are even worse. Like its two siblings, the All-Star Movie Resort is buried in WDW's southwest corner to avoid frightening the higher-paying guests.

1991 W. Buena Vista Dr., Lake Buena Vista, FL 32830-1000. ℂ 407/934-7639 or 407/939-7000. Fax 407/939-7111. www.disneyworld.com. 1,900 units. $77–$124 double. Extra person $10. Children 17 and under stay free with parent. AE, DC, DISC, MC, V. Free parking. Pets $9 a night. Take I-4 east to exit 25B. Follow signs to WDW, then to resort. **Amenities:** Food court; lounge; 2 heated outdoor pools; kids' pool; arcade; WDW Transportation System; transportation to non-Disney parks for a fee; limited room service; babysitting; guest laundry; no-smoking rooms. *In room:* A/C, TV, dataport, fridge ($10 a night), safe.

Disney's All-Star Music Resort *Value* Giant trombones and musical themes from jazz to calypso can't hide the fact that this is a clone of the All-Star Movie Resort. The small rooms are compounded by cramped bathrooms, where opening a door can injure a loved one. The perks? They're at least $50 a night cheaper than other Disney resorts. The closest off-site activities are the Winter Summerland Miniature Golf Course, Blizzard Beach, and Animal Kingdom.

1801 W. Buena Vista Dr. (at World Dr. and Osceola Pkwy.; P.O. Box 10000), Lake Buena Vista, FL 32830-1000. ☏ 407/934-7639 or 407/939-6000. Fax 407/939-7222. www.disneyworld.com. 1,920 units. $77–$124 double. Extra person $10. Children 17 and under stay free with parent. AE, DC, DISC, MC, V. Free parking. Pets $9 a night. Take I-4 to the Hwy. 536/Epcot Center Dr. exit and follow the signs. **Amenities:** Food court; lounge; 2 heated outdoor pools; kids' pool; arcade; WDW Transportation System; transportation to non-Disney parks for a fee; limited room service; babysitting; guest laundry; no-smoking rooms. *In room:* A/C, TV, dataport, fridge ($10 a night), safe.

Disney's All-Star Sports Resort *Value* Yogi Berra said it best: "It's déjà vu all over again." It's a different theme, but the same routine. Rooms are the same size and equipped with the same micro-bathrooms as the All-Stars above. This resort's buildings sport football, baseball, basketball, tennis, and surfing motifs.

1701 W. Buena Vista Dr. (at World Dr. and Osceola Pkwy.; P.O. Box 10000), Lake Buena Vista, FL 32830-1000. ☏ 407/934-7639 or 407/939-5000. Fax 407/939-7333. www.disneyworld.com. 1,920 units. $77–$124 double. Extra person $10. Children 17 and under stay free with parent. AE, DC, DISC, MC, V. Free parking. Pets $9 a night. Take I-4 to the Hwy. 536/Epcot Center Dr. exit and follow the signs. **Amenities:** Food court; lounge; 2 heated outdoor pools; kids' pool; arcade; WDW Transportation System; transportation to non-Disney parks for a fee; limited room service; babysitting; guest laundry; no-smoking rooms. *In room:* A/C, TV, dataport, fridge ($10 a night), safe.

ROUGHING IT, DISNEY-STYLE

Disney's Fort Wilderness Resort & Campground Pines, cypress trees, and fish-filled lakes and streams surround this woodsy 780-acre camping resort. The biggest knock is that it's quite far from Epcot, Disney–MGM Studios, and Animal Kingdom. But it's close to the Magic Kingdom, and if you're a true outdoors type, you'll enjoy the break from some of the Mickey madness. There are 784 campsites for RVs, pull-behind campers, and tents (110/220-volt outlets, grills, and comfort stations with showers and restrooms).

Some sites are open to pets—at a cost of $3 per site, not per pet—which is cheaper than using the WDW overnight kennel, where you pay $9 per pet. The 408 wilderness cabins (actually trailers) are large enough for six people once you pull down the Murphy beds, and they also have kitchens.

3520 N. Fort Wilderness Trail (P.O. Box 10000), Lake Buena Vista, FL 32830-1000. ☏ 407/934-7639 or 407/824-2900. Fax 407/824-3508. www.disneyworld.com. 784 campsites, 408 wilderness cabins. Campsite $34–$80 double; wilderness cabin $224–$314 double. Extra person $2 for campsite, $5 for cabin. Children 17 and under stay free with parent. AE, DC, DISC, MC, V. Free parking. Take I-4 to the Hwy. 536/Epcot Center Dr. exit and follow the signs. **Amenities:** 2 restaurants (American); grill; lounge; 2 heated outdoor pools; kids' pool; 2 lighted tennis courts; water-sports equipment; outdoor activities (fishing, horseback and hay rides, campfires); 2 game rooms; WDW Transportation System; transportation to non-Disney parks for a fee; babysitting; guest laundry; no-smoking homes. *In room:* A/C, TV, VCR (cabins only), kitchen, fridge, coffeemaker, hair dryer (cabins only), outdoor grill.

LAKE BUENA VISTA/OFFICIAL HOTELS

The "official" Disney hotels are located on or around Hotel Plaza Boulevard, on the northeast side of Disney property. Guests enjoy some of the perks of staying in a WDW resort, such as free transportation to Disney parks. You can reserve a room through Central Reservations Operations (☏ **407/934-7639**). But it's best to call the individual hotel or parent chain to check on special deals or packages.

EXPENSIVE

Wyndham Palace Resort ★★ This is the most upscale of the "official" properties and is popular with business as well as leisure travelers. Rooms are a comfortable size and sleep at least four. Many have balconies or patios; ask for one above the fifth floor with a "recreation view." The lobby has overstuffed chairs where you can enjoy quiet conversation and the view. Arthur's 27, the signature restaurant, offers a great panoramic view from the 27th floor. The resort is known for its full-service, European-style spa.

1900 Buena Vista Dr. (just north of Hotel Plaza Blvd.; P.O. Box 22206), Lake Buena Vista, FL 32830. © **800/327-2990** or 407/827-2727. Fax 407/827-6034. www.downtowndisneyhotels.com or www.bvp resort.com. 1,014 units. $199–$398 double; $279–$718 suite. Extra person $20. Children 17 and under stay free with parent. AE, DC, DISC, MC, V. Free parking; valet $10. From I-4, take the Hwy. 535/Apopka–Vineland Rd. exit north to Hotel Plaza Blvd. and go left. At first stoplight, turn right onto Buena Vista Dr. It's the first hotel on the right. **Amenities:** 2 restaurants (continental, steaks); grill; 4 lounges; 3 heated outdoor pools; kids' pool; spa; Jacuzzi; sauna; children's center; arcade; concierge; complimentary bus service to WDW parks; transportation to non-Disney parks for a fee; salon; 24-hr. room service; massage; babysitting; guest laundry; valet; no-smoking rooms; concierge-level rooms. *In room:* A/C, TV w/pay movies, dataport, minibar, coffeemaker, hair dryer, iron.

MODERATE

Accommodations in this category are usually a step above the "moderates" inside WDW.

Best Western Lake Buena Vista Hotel *(Value)* This 12-acre lakefront hotel has nicer rooms and public areas than you might find in others within the chain. Rooms are in an 18-story tower, and all of them come with balconies. The views improve from the eighth floor up, and guests on the west side have a better chance of seeing something Disney. The hotel's 18th-floor lounge offers an excellent view of the Magic Kingdom's fireworks. You can reserve an oversize room (20% larger) or one with a view of WDW fireworks for $10 more a night.

2000 Hotel Plaza Blvd. (between Buena Vista Dr. and Apopka–Vineland Rd./Hwy. 535), Lake Buena Vista, FL 32830. © **800/348-3765** or 407/828-2424. Fax 407/828-8933. www.downtowndisneyhotels.com or www.orlandoresorthotel.com. 325 units. $99–$159 for 4 persons; $199–$319 suite. Fifth person $15. AE, DC, DISC, MC, V. Free parking. From I-4, take the Hwy. 535/Apopka–Vineland Rd. exit north to Hotel Plaza Blvd. and go left. It's the first hotel on the right. **Amenities:** Restaurant (American); grill; heated outdoor pool; kids' pool; guest-services desks; complimentary bus service to WDW parks; transportation to non-Disney parks for a fee; limited room service; guest laundry; no-smoking rooms. *In room:* A/C, TV w/pay movies, coffeemaker, hair dryer, iron, safe, Nintendo.

Courtyard by Marriott *(Value)* This moderately priced member of the Marriott chain is popular with families. The inner and outer glass elevators are a fun ride, the hotel is in a good location, and the price is, well, decent. The guest rooms are clean and can sleep four comfortably. Ask for a room on floors 8 to 14 on the hotel's west side for the best view of the Kingdom and fireworks.

1805 Hotel Plaza Blvd. (between Lake Buena Vista Dr. and Apopka–Vineland Rd./Hwy. 535), Lake Buena Vista, FL 32830. © **800/223-9930** or 407/828-8888. Fax 407/827-4626. www.downtowndisneyhotels.com or www.courtyardorlando.com. 323 units. $99–$229 double. AE, DC, DISC, MC, V. Free parking. From I-4, take the Hwy. 535/Apopka–Vineland Rd. exit north to Hotel Plaza Blvd. and go left. It's the third hotel on left. **Amenities:** Restaurant (American); 2 lounges; 2 heated outdoor pools; kids' pool; Jacuzzi; arcade; guest-services desk; complimentary bus service to WDW parks; transportation to non-Disney parks for a fee; car-rental desks; limited room service; guest laundry; no-smoking rooms. *In room:* A/C, TV w/pay movies, coffeemaker, hair dryer, iron, safe, Nintendo.

DoubleTree Guest Suites ★ *(Kids)* Children have their own check-in desk and theater, and they get a gift upon arrival at this hotel, which is the best of the official hotels for families traveling with little ones. All of the accommodations in this seven-story hotel are two-room suites, large by most standards, and there's space for up to six to catch some *zzz's*. This is the easternmost of the "officials," meaning it's farthest from the other Disney action but closest to (for some within walking distance of) the cheaper free-world shops on Apopka–Vineland Road.

2305 Hotel Plaza Blvd. (just west of Apopka–Vineland Rd./Hwy. 535), Lake Buena Vista, FL 32830. ℂ 800/222-8733 or 407/934-1000. Fax 407/934-1011. www.downtowndisneyhotels.com or www.double treeguestsuites.com. 229 units. $119–$249 double. Extra person $20. Children 17 and under stay free with parent. AE, DC, DISC, MC, V. Free parking. From I-4, take the Hwy. 535/Apopka–Vineland Rd. exit north to Hotel Plaza Blvd. and go left. It's the first hotel on the left. **Amenities:** Restaurant (American); 2 lounges; heated outdoor pool; kids' pool; 2 lighted tennis courts; arcade; concierge; car-rental desk; complimentary bus service to WDW parks; transportation to non-Disney parks for a fee; limited room service; guest laundry; no-smoking rooms. *In room:* A/C, TV, dataport, fridge, microwave, coffeemaker, hair dryer, iron, safe.

Hotel Royal Plaza ✿   The Plaza is one of the boulevard's originals, but renovations over its 25-year history (its most recent makeover was 2 years ago) have kept it in good shape. A favorite with the budget-minded, its hallmark is a friendly staff. The nicely decorated rooms are medium size and have enough space for five. Poolside rooms have balconies and patios; the tower rooms have separate sitting areas, and some offer whirlpool tubs in the bathrooms. If you want a view from up high, ask for a room facing west and WDW.

1905 Hotel Plaza Blvd. (between Buena Vista Dr. and Apopka–Vineland Rd./Hwy. 535), Lake Buena Vista, FL 32830. ℂ 800/248-7890 or 407/828-2828. Fax 407/827-6338. www.downtowndisneyhotels.com or www.orlandotravel.com/hotels/royal.htm. 394 units. $119–$225 double; $159–$675 suite. Extra person $15. Children 17 and under stay free with parent. AE, DC, DISC, MC, V. Free parking; valet $8. From I-4, take the Hwy. 535/Apopka–Vineland Rd. exit north to Hotel Plaza Blvd. and go left. It's the second hotel on the left. **Amenities:** Restaurant (American); lounge; heated outdoor pool; whirlpool; 4 lighted tennis courts; fitness center; guest-services desk; complimentary bus service to WDW parks; transportation to non-Disney parks for a fee; limited room service; laundry; no-smoking rooms. *In room:* A/C, TV w/pay movies and VCR, dataport, minibar, coffeemaker, hair dryer, iron, safe.

OTHER LAKE BUENA VISTA–AREA HOTELS

The hotels in this section are within a few minutes' drive of WDW parks. They offer the location but not the privileges of staying at an "official" hotel.

VERY EXPENSIVE

Gaylord Palms ✿✿✿   Orlando's newest resort is a classy convention spot that appeals to vacationers too. Its entertainment, recreation, dining, and other amenities turn many into willing prisoners of this property—with the exception of time pledged to the theme parks. The 4½-acre octagonal Grand Atrium has a glass dome and a mini-version of the Castillo de San Marcos, the old fort at St. Augustine. The Emerald Bay, a 362-room hotel within the hotel, has an elegant air. Other areas have Key West, St. Augustine, and Everglades themes. If you really need to unwind, try the 20,000-square-foot Canyon Ranch Spa Club. Our biggest gripe: Room-to-room and room-to-hall soundproofing could be better.

6000 Osceola Pkwy., Kissimmee, FL 34747. ℂ 877/677-9352 or 407/586-0000. Fax 407/239-4822. www.gaylordpalms.com. 1,406 units. $269–$460 double. Extra adult $20. Kids under 18 stay free with parent. AE, DC, DISC, MC, V. Free self-parking; valet $12. Take the I-4 Osceola Pkwy. exit east to the hotel. **Amenities:** 3 restaurants (steaks, seafood, Italian); 4 lounges; 2 outdoor heated pools; fitness center; spa; children's center; concierge; tour desk; car-rental desk; free transportation to Disney parks; transportation to non-Disney parks for a fee; business center; shopping arcade; salon; room service; massage; babysitting; dry cleaning; no-smoking rooms; concierge-level rooms. *In room:* A/C, TV w/pay movies, dataport, coffeemaker, hair dryer, iron, safe, PlayStation.

Hyatt Regency Grand Cypress Resort ★★★ *Finds* A favorite of honeymooners and those seeking a resort without Mickey doodads, this romantic getaway's lobby has lush foliage from which macaws wave to passersby. The 18-story atrium has inner and outer glass elevators (ride the outers to the roof for a panoramic rush). The rooms are beautifully decorated and sleep four. The Hyatt shares a golf club and academy, racquet club, and equestrian center with its sister property, The Villas of Grand Cypress (see below); both offer excellent packages aimed at the sports set. The Hyatt's half-acre, 800,000-gallon pool is one of the best in Orlando and features caves, grottoes, waterfalls, and a 45-foot (14m) water slide.

1 N. Jacaranda (off Hwy. 535), Orlando, FL 32836. © 800/233-1234 or 407/239-1234. Fax 407/239-3800. www.grandcypress.com. 750 units. $229–$469 double; $479–$1,500 suite. Extra person $25. Children 17 and under stay free with parent. AE, DC, DISC, MC, V. Free parking; valet $12. Take I-4 to the Hwy. 535/Apopka–Vineland Rd. exit and go north; then turn left at the 2nd light (after the ramp light) onto Hwy. 535. **Amenities:** 4 restaurants (American, seafood, steaks); store; 4 lounges; large heated outdoor pool; 45 holes of golf; 12 tennis courts (5 lighted); equestrian center; 2 racquetball courts; spa; health club; water-sports equipment; children's center; arcade; concierge; free Disney shuttle; transportation to non-Disney parks for a fee; car-rental desk; salon; 24-hr. room service; in-room massage; babysitting; guest laundry; valet; no-smoking rooms; concierge-level rooms. *In room:* A/C, TV, dataport, minibar, hair dryer, iron, safe.

The Villas of Grand Cypress ★★★ *Finds* As long as you're willing to splurge—and we mean *splurge*—this is an exceptional place to set up camp. At its "modest" end, this Mediterranean-inspired resort has junior suites with beds for four, Roman tubs, and patios. Floor plans then progress to elegant one- to four-bedroom villas. All include kitchens, dining rooms, and patios. The resort shares equestrian amenities and golf and racquet clubs with the Hyatt (see above).

1 N. Jacaranda (off Hwy. 535), Orlando, FL 32836. © 800/835-7377 or 407/239-4700. Fax 407/239-7219. www.grandcypress.com. 146 villas. $215–$470 junior suite; $315–$1,880 villa. Extra person included. Children 17 and under stay free with parent. AE, DC, MC, V. Free parking; valet $12. Take I-4 to the Hwy. 535/Apopka–Vineland Rd. exit and go north; then go left at the 2nd light (after the ramp light) onto Hwy. 535. It's on the right. **Amenities:** 2 restaurants (American, continental); 2 lounges; heated outdoor pool; 45 holes of golf; 12 tennis courts (5 lighted); equestrian center; 2 racquetball courts; spa; health club; water-sports equipment; kids' center; arcade; concierge; free Disney shuttle; transportation to non-Disney parks for a fee; car-rental desk; salon; 24-hr. room service; in-room massage; babysitting; guest laundry; no-smoking rooms; concierge-level rooms. *In room:* A/C, TV, dataport, minibar, hair dryer, iron, safe.

EXPENSIVE

Marriott's Orlando World Center ★ Golf, tennis, and spa lovers find plenty to do at this 230-acre resort. The sports facilities are first-class and the largest of its five pools has water slides and waterfalls. The location, only 2 miles (3.25km) from the Disney parks, is another plus. The large, comfortable rooms sleep four, and the higher poolside floors offer views of Mickeyville.

8701 World Center Dr. (on Hwy. 536 between I-4 and Hwy. 535), Orlando, FL 32821. © 800/621-0638 or 407/239-4200. Fax 407/238-8777. www.marriottHotels.com/MCOWC/. 2,111 units. $189–$410 for up to 5; $425–$2,400 suite. Children 17 and under stay free in parents' room. AE, DC, DISC, MC, V. Free self-parking; valet $12. Take I-4 to the Hwy. 535/Apopka–Vineland Rd. exit, go south 1½ miles (2.5km), then right/west on Hwy. 536, and go ⅓ mile (.5km). **Amenities:** 4 restaurants (Japanese, steaks, Italian, American); 2 lounges; 3 heated outdoor pools; heated indoor pool; kids' pool; 18-hole golf course; 8 lighted tennis courts; spa; health club; whirlpool; sauna; concierge; car-rental desk; transportation to all theme parks for a fee; business center; salon; 24-hr. room service; massage; babysitting; guest laundry; no-smoking rooms. *In room:* A/C, TV w/pay movies, dataport, minibar, coffeemaker, hair dryer, iron, safe.

MODERATE

Hawthorn Suites Lake Buena Vista ★ *Value*   One of the features that appeals to us most about this property, which opened in summer 2000, is its floor plan. Standard rooms have a living room with pullout sofa, chair, and TV; full kitchen with dining-room table for four; bathroom with vanity; and bedroom with recliner and TV. Two-bedroom units are also available. The atmosphere is friendly, the service is good, and it's just 3 minutes from Hotel Plaza Boulevard.

8303 Palm Pkwy., Orlando, FL 32836. ℂ 800/269-8303, 800/527-1133, or 407/597-5000. Fax 407/597-6000. www.hawthornsuiteslbv.com. 120 units. $104–$159 for 4–6. AE, DC, DISC, MC, V. Free self-parking. From I-4, take the Hwy. 535/Apopka–Vineland Rd. exit east to Palm Pkwy., then right ¼ mile (.5km) to hotel. **Amenities:** 1 outdoor heated pool; basketball court; exercise room; Jacuzzi; free shuttle to Disney parks; transportation to non-Disney parks for a fee; guest laundry; no-smoking rooms. *In room:* A/C, TV w/pay movies, dataport, kitchen, fridge, coffeemaker, hair dryer, iron, microwave.

Holiday Inn Family Suites Resort ★★ *Finds*   This all-suite property opened in July 1999 and does a fantastic job catering to a diverse clientele. Families appreciate the two-bedroom Kid Suites that feature a second semi-private bedroom equipped with bunk beds and changing themes (from Disney to Coke to the comics). In the Classic Suites, the semiprivate bedroom has a queen-size bed. Others cater to honeymooners and romantics (Sweet Heart Suites with heart-shaped tubs) and movie buffs (Cinema Suites with 60-inch big-screen TVs and DVD players). All suites have small kitchenettes. The resort, voted in 2001 as best Holiday Inn property in North America, has themed activity nights (movies, magic, variety shows, and more). *Note:* If you are child-free, ask to stay in the West Track Courtyard section, which is much quieter.

14500 Continental Gateway (off Hwy. 536), Lake Buena Vista, FL 32821. ℂ 877/387-5437 or 407/387-5437. Fax 407/387-1489. www.hifamilysuites.com. 800 units. $109–$169 Kid Suite; $109–$169 Classic Suite; $129–$189 Cinema Suite; $129–$189 Sweet Heart Suite. AE, DC, DISC, MC, V. Free self-parking. From I-4, take the Hwy. 536/International Dr. exit east 1 mile (1.5km) to the resort. **Amenities:** 1 restaurant (American); lounge; general store; several fast-food counters; 1 large lap pool; 1 family swimming pool; fitness center; 2 Jacuzzis; 3 outdoor Ping-Pong tables; 2 shuffleboard courts; game room; mini-golf course; complimentary recreation center for ages 4–12; kids' library; free transportation to Disney parks; transportation to non-Disney parks for a fee; coin-op washers and dryers; tour desk. *In room:* A/C, TV w/pay movies and VCR (some with Nintendo), dataport, refrigerator, coffeemaker, hair dryer, iron, safe, microwave.

ON U.S. 192/KISSIMMEE

This tin-glitz stretch of highway is dotted with fast-food eateries, burger barns, and T-shirt shops. It's not scenic, but it has fairly inexpensive motels 1 to 8 miles (1.5–13km) from the Disney parks.

EXPENSIVE

Celebration Hotel ★★   Living the yuppie life? Then you'll love this hotel, inspired by the same-name Disney-owned development that surrounds it. Its three-story, wood-frame design is straight out of 1920s Florida. Rooms have *very comfy* beds; to enjoy a soothing view, ask for a lakefront room. The hotel's biggest perk: A location near Disney. The downside: You or your driver must tackle U.S. 192's traffic and construction delays to get to the parks.

700 Bloom St. ℂ 888/499-3800 or 407/566-6000. Fax 407/566-6001. www.celebrationhotel.com. 115 units. $139–$219 for up to 4; $289–$470 suite. AE, DC, DISC, MC, V. Free self-parking; valet $10. Take I-4 to the U.S. 192 exit, go east to the second light, then right on Celebration Ave. and follow the signs. **Amenities:** 1 restaurant (American); lounge; 1 outdoor heated pool; 18-hole golf course; state-of-the-art health-and-fitness center; spa; concierge; free shuttle to Disney parks; transportation to non-Disney parks for a fee; nearby shopping district. *In room:* A/C, TV/Nintendo, dataport, hair dryer, iron, safe.

INEXPENSIVE

Hampton Inn Maingate West Just 4½ years old, this inn hasn't been around long enough to earn the battle scars usually found in U.S. 192 accommodations. While it's more expensive on the front end than the Ramada (below), it's also much more modern and upbeat. The inn is located 1½ miles (2.5km) west of the WDW entrance road.

3000 Maingate Lane, Kissimmee, FL. 34747. © **877/428-4782** or 407/396-6300. Fax 407/396-8989. www.hamptoninnmaingatewest.com. 118 units. $69–$119 double. Extra person $10. Rates include continental breakfast. Children 17 and under stay free in parents' room. AE, DC, DISC, MC, V. Free self-parking. From I-4, take exit 25A onto U.S. 192 west; go 3 miles (5km), then right on Maingate Lane (across the street from Celebration). **Amenities:** 1 outdoor heated pool; guest-services desk; free shuttle to Disney parks; transportation to non-Disney parks for a fee; no-smoking rooms. *In room:* A/C, TV, dataport, coffeemaker, iron.

Ramada Disney Eastgate *Value* Remodeled in 1998, this Ramada is a cut cleaner than many of the chain's standard motels, but no fancier. Standard rooms sleep four but are somewhat cramped. One child eats free for each paying adult. The inn is 4 miles (6km) from Disney.

5150 W. Irlo Bronson Memorial Hwy. (U.S. 192), Kissimmee, FL 34746. © **888/298-2054** or 407/396-1111. Fax 407/396-1607. www.ramada.com. 402 units. $59–$129 double. Extra person $10. Children 17 and under stay free in parents' room. AE, DC, DISC, MC, V. Free self-parking. From I-4, take the U.S. 192 exit east 2½ miles (4km) to the motel. **Amenities:** 1 restaurant (American); lounge; 1 outdoor heated pool; kids' pool; Jacuzzi; arcade; car-rental desk; free shuttle to Disney parks; transportation to non-Disney parks for a fee; limited room service; guest laundry; valet; no-smoking rooms. *In room:* A/C, TV w/pay movies, dataport, coffeemaker, hair dryer, iron, safe, Nintendo.

INTERNATIONAL DRIVE AREA

The hotels and resorts listed here are 7 to 10 miles (11–16km) northeast of the Walt Disney World parks and 1 to 3 miles (1.5–5km) from Universal Orlando and SeaWorld, which makes this zone centrally located for those who want to sample more than one area. The disadvantages: The northern end of International Drive is badly congested. The shops, motels, eateries, and attractions along this stretch can be as tacky as those on U.S. 192, and many of the motels and hotels don't offer free transportation to any of the parks.

VERY EXPENSIVE

Peabody Orlando ★★★ *Finds* The five mallards that march into a lobby fountain every morning at 11am and then back out at 5pm, accompanied by John Philip Sousa's *King Cotton March,* are just part of the appeal of Central Florida's friendliest hotel. The Peabody Orlando is primarily a business and convention destination, but it's one of our top picks in O-Town. It's classy without being stuffy, and if your budget allows the splurge, you won't be disappointed. Rooms sleep up to five, and those on the west side (sixth floor and higher) offer a distant view of Disney and its fireworks displays.

9801 International Dr. (between Bee Line Expwy. and Sand Lake Rd.), Orlando, FL 32819. © **800/732-2639** or 407/352-4000. Fax 407/354-1424. www.peabody-orlando.com. 891 units. $380–$475 standard room for up to 3; $520–$1,600 suite. Extra person $20. Children 17 and under stay free in parents' room. AE, DC, DISC, MC, V. Free self-parking; valet $8. From I-4, take the Sand Lake Rd./Hwy. 482 exit east to International Dr., then south. Hotel is on the left across from the Convention Center. **Amenities:** 3 restaurants (Continental, Northern Italian, American); deli; 3 lounges; 1 outdoor heated pool; kids' pool; 4 lighted tennis courts; fitness center; spa; Jacuzzi; concierge; guest-services desk; business center; shopping arcade; shuttle to WDW and other parks for a fee; 24-hr. room service; massage; valet; no-smoking rooms; concierge-level rooms. *In room:* A/C, TV, dataport, minibar, hair dryer.

Portofino Bay Hotel ★★★ *Finds* Universal's first hotel has the stature of Disney's Grand Floridian. This 4-year-old resort is designed to look like the village of

Portofino, Italy, complete with a harbor and canals that take you via boat to the theme parks. The rooms sleep up to five. The beds have Egyptian-woven sheets, and the pillows are so soft you'll want to take them home. Ask for a view overlooking the piazza and "bay" area. Like many of the Disney properties, the Portofino doesn't just have swimming pools; its beach pool has a fort with a water slide (the villa pool offers several cabanas). The resort's privately run Greenhouse Spa features a state-of-the-art fitness center and full-service spa. *Note:* Guests get no-line access to almost all rides at Universal Studios Florida and Islands of Adventure.

5601 Universal Blvd., Orlando FL. 32819. ☎ **888/322-5541** or 407/503-1000. Fax 407/224-7118. www.loewshotels.com/hotels/orlando_portofino_bay. 750 rooms. $249–$359 double; $450–$2,100 suite. Extra person $25. Children 17 and under stay free in parents' room. AE, DC, DISC, MC, V. Self-parking $6; valet $10. From I-4, take the Kirkman Rd./Hwy. 435 exit and follow the signs to Universal. **Amenities:** 3 restaurants (Northern Italian); deli; 3 lounges; 2 outdoor heated pools (1 for concierge and suite guests only); kids' pool; bocce courts (concierge and suite guests only); fitness center; spa; water-sports equipment; kids' club; arcade; concierge; tour desk; free water-taxi transportation to Universal Studios, Islands of Adventure, and CityWalk; free shuttle to SeaWorld; transportation to WDW parks for a fee; business center; shopping arcade; 24-hr. room service; babysitting; guest laundry; valet; no-smoking rooms; concierge-level rooms. *In room:* A/C, TV, hair dryer, iron, safe.

EXPENSIVE

Hard Rock Hotel ★★   You can't get any closer than this to CityWalk or Universal Studios Florida. Opened in January 2001, this California mission–style resort sports a rock-and-roll theme and rack rates a shade cheaper than the Portofino (above). The Hard Rock is a cut above some of Disney's comparable properties, including Animal Kingdom Lodge. The rooms are very comfortable; the bathrooms aren't big, but, like the rooms at all the Disney resorts, there is a separate dressing area with a sink. Unfortunately, though the rooms are fairly soundproof, a few notes seep through the walls, so ask for one that's away from the lobby area. *Note:* Guests get no-line access to most rides at Universal Studios Florida and Islands of Adventure.

5000 Universal Blvd., Orlando, FL 32819. ☎ **800/232-7827** or 407/363-8000. Fax 407/224-7118. www.hardrock.com/locations/hotels/orlando/. $199–$359 double; $395–$1,575 suite. Extra person $20. Children 17 and under stay free in parents' room. AE, DC, DISC, MC, V. Self-parking $6; valet $10. From I-4, take the Kirkman Rd./Hwy. 435 exit and follow the signs to Universal. **Amenities:** 2 restaurants (American); grill; 2 lounges; 1 outdoor heated pool; kids' pool; fitness center; kids' club; arcade; concierge; free water-taxi transportation to Universal Studios, Islands of Adventure, and CityWalk; free shuttle to SeaWorld; transportation to WDW parks for a fee; shopping arcade; 24-hr. room service; babysitting; guest laundry; valet; no-smoking rooms. *In room:* A/C, TV, hair dryer, iron, safe.

Renaissance Orlando Resort at SeaWorld ★★   This stylish hotel offers large rooms and a great location for theme-park nomads: It's across from Sea-World and about 10 to 15 minutes from Universal and Disney. The lobby charms guests with a 10-story atrium, a pond filled with huge koi, a free-flight aviary, and six glass elevators that overlook the atrium. East-side rooms, especially from the sixth floor up, have a nice view of the Kraken roller coaster at SeaWorld, which is within walking distance (but watch the traffic). North- and south-side rooms have balconies overlooking the atrium.

6677 Sea Harbour Dr., Orlando, FL 32821. ☎ **800/327-6677** or 407/351-5555. Fax 407/351-1991. www.renaissancehotels.com. 778 units. $169–$289 double. Extra person $20. Children 17 and under stay free in parents' room. AE, DC, DISC, MC, V. Free self-parking; valet parking $9. From I-4, the Hwy. 528/Bee Line Expwy. exit east to International Dr., then go south to Sea Harbour Dr. and turn right. **Amenities:** 2 restaurants (seafood, American); grill; 3 lounges; 1 outdoor heated pool; kids' pool; 4 lighted tennis courts; health club; spa; 2 Jacuzzis; sauna; arcade; concierge; tour desk; car-rental desk; transportation to all the parks for a fee; business center; shopping arcade; 24-hr. room service; massage; babysitting; guest laundry; valet; no-smoking rooms. *In room:* A/C, TV w/pay movies, dataport, safe, PlayStation.

Where to Stay & Dine in the International Drive Area

Orlando •

FLORIDA

ACCOMMODATIONS ■
Fairfield Inn
   International Drive **3**
Hard Rock Hotel **2**
La Quinta Inn & Suites
   Convention Center **7**
Peabody Orlando **10**
Portofino Bay Hotel **1**
Radisson Barcelo Hotel **4**
Renaissance Orlando
   Resort at SeaWorld **11**

DINING ◆
Atlantis (in the Renaissance
   Orlando Resort) **11**
B-Line Diner (in the
   Peabody Orlando) **10**
Bahama Breeze **6**
Delfino Riviera (in the
   Portofino Bay Hotel) **1**
Dux (in the Peabody
   Orlando) **10**
Ming Court **9**
The Palm (in the
   Hard Rock Hotel) **2**
Ran-Getsu of Tokyo **8**
Siam Orchid **5**

So You Didn't Book a Room . . .

Coming to Orlando without a reservation isn't a good idea. But if you do, try one of these chains. They're moderate or inexpensive in price and in the budget corridors of Kissimmee/U.S. 192 or International Drive. While we can't vouch for them personally, their names generally mean reliability:

In Kissimmee:

Best Western Eastgate, 5565 W. Irlo Bronson Memorial Hwy., Kissimmee (© **407/396-0707**).

Best Western Kissimmee, 2261 E. Irlo Bronson Memorial Hwy., Kissimmee (© **407/846-2221**).

Comfort Suites Maingate Hotel, 7888 W. Irlo Bronson Memorial Hwy., Kissimmee (© **407/390-9888**).

Comfort Suites Resort Maingate East, 2775 Florida Plaza Blvd., Kissimmee (© **407/397-7848**).

Days Inn East of the Magic Kingdom, 5840 W. Irlo Bronson Memorial Hwy., Kissimmee (© **407/396-7969**).

Days Inn Maingate–West, 7980 W. Irlo Bronson Memorial Hwy., Kissimmee (© **407/997-1000**).

DoubleTree Maingate, 4787 W. Irlo Bronson Memorial Hwy., Kissimmee (© **407/397-0555**).

Howard Johnson Maingate West, 8660 W. Irlo Bronson Memorial Hwy., Kissimmee (© **407/396-4500**).

Quality Suites Maingate East, 5876 W. Irlo Bronson Memorial Hwy., Kissimmee (© **407/396-8040**).

In the International Drive Area:

Days Inn Convention Center/SeaWorld, 9990 International Dr., Orlando (© **407/352-8700**).

Days Inn East of Universal Studios, 5827 Caravan Court, Orlando (© **407/351-3800**).

Days Inn International Drive, 7200 International Dr., Orlando (© **407/351-1200**).

Holiday Inn Express International Drive, 6323 International Dr., Orlando (© **407/351-4430**).

Sheraton Studio City Hotel, 5905 International Dr., Orlando (© **407/ 351-2100**).

Travelodge International Drive, 5859 American Way, Orlando (© **407/345-8880**).

You also can try **Central Reservation Service** (© **407/740-6442;** www.reservation-services.com) and **Discount Hotels of America** (© **407/294-9600;** www.discounthotelsamerica.com).

MODERATE

La Quinta Inn & Suites Convention Center   Opened in 1998, this is one of a handful of upscale, moderately priced motels on Universal Boulevard, which runs parallel to (but isn't as congested as) International Drive. The hotel is aimed at business travelers, but this is Orlando, so families traveling with kids are welcomed with open arms. King rooms come with a fridge and microwave. There are a limited number of two-room suites offering separate living and sleeping areas.

8504 Universal Blvd., Orlando, FL 32819. © **800/531-5900** or 407/345-1365. Fax 407/345-5586. www.laquinta.com. 185 units. $89–$139 double. Extra person $10. Rates include continental breakfast. Children 18 and under stay free in parents' room. AE, DC, DISC, MC, V. Free self-parking. Take I-4 to the Sand Lake Rd./Hwy. 482 exit, go east toward Universal, then right. **Amenities:** 1 outdoor heated pool; exercise room; Jacuzzi; transportation to all theme parks for a fee; guest laundry; no-smoking rooms. *In room:* A/C, TV w/pay movies, dataport, coffeemaker, hair dryer, iron, Nintendo.

Radisson Barcelo Hotel ⭐ Like many I-Drive properties, the Radisson offers a good location for people whose vacations center on Universal Orlando or SeaWorld, and a central location for travelers who also plan to visit Disney. Rooms are brightly decorated, but views are basic. The seventh floor (the highest) will give you a look at SeaWorld to the south. Otherwise, you'll be watching traffic on I-4 or I-Drive.

8444 International Dr., Orlando, FL 32819. © **800/333-3333** or 407/345-0505. Fax 407/352-5894. www.radisson.com/orlandofl_barcelo/. 520 units. $99–$199 double. Extra person $15. Children 17 and under stay free in parents' room. AE, DC, DISC, MC, V. Free self-parking. From I-4, take the Sand Lake Rd/Hwy. 482 exit. Turn right on International Dr., go a half-mile (.75km), and the hotel is on the right. **Amenities:** 1 restaurant (Florida/regional); grill; lounge; 1 outdoor heated pool; lighted tennis court; bocce court; guest-services desk; free shuttle to Universal Orlando and SeaWorld; transportation to Disney parks for a fee; guest laundry; valet; no-smoking rooms. *In room:* A/C, TV w/pay movies, dataport, fridge, coffeemaker, hair dryer, iron, safe, Nintendo.

INEXPENSIVE

Fairfield Inn International Drive ⭐ *Value* If you're looking for I-Drive's best value, it's hard to beat the Fairfield. This one combines a quiet location off the main drag, down-to-earth rates, and a clean, modern motel in one package. The rooms are very comfortable and there are a number of restaurants within walking distance of the hotel.

8342 Jamaican Court (off International Dr. between the Bee Line Expwy. and Sand Lake Rd.), Orlando, FL 32819. © **800/228-2800** or 407/363-1944. Fax 407/363-1944. www.fairfieldinn.com. 135 units. $69–$89 for up to 4. AE, DC, DISC, MC, V. Free self-parking. From I-4, take the Sand Lake Rd./Hwy. 482 exit east 1 block, turn right on I-Dr., then right on Jamaican Court. **Amenities:** 1 outdoor heated pool; guest-services desk; transportation to the parks for a fee; guest laundry; valet; no-smoking rooms. *In room:* A/C, TV w/pay movies, dataport, safe.

AN ORLANDO BED-&-BREAKFAST

The Courtyard at Lake Lucerne ⭐ *Finds* You might feel the sting of Cupid's arrows in this downtown hideaway. The inn has several historic buildings, such as the Art-Deco Wellborn (one-bedroom apartments and a suite) and the I.W. Phillips House, built in 1919 and reminiscent of old Southern homes with large verandas overlooking gardens and a fountain. The property offers a respite from the crowded, run-and-gun world of the resorts or chains, and it's ideal for couples looking for a little quiet time or romance. But if you choose to stay here, you'll need a car or some other kind of transportation because the inn doesn't provide any.

211 N. Lucerne Circle E., Orlando, FL 32801. © **800/444-5289** or 407/648-5188. Fax 407/246-1368. www.orlandohistoricinn.com. 30 units. $89–$225 double. Rates include continental breakfast. AE, DC, MC, V. Free self-parking. Take Orange Ave. south; immediately following City Hall (dome building with fountains and glass sculpture), turn left onto Anderson. After 2 lights, at Delaney Ave., turn right. Take first right onto Lucerne Circle. Be aware of 1-way streets. Follow the brown "historic inn" signs. Children are permitted. **Amenities:** 1 restaurant (American/Southern); no-smoking rooms. *In room:* A/C, TV, kitchen in some, fridge, coffeemaker, microwave.

PLACES TO STAY ELSEWHERE IN ORLANDO

There are two good reasons to choose accommodations away from all of the hustle and hassle of the attractions: Crowds are thinner and, in some cases, prices are lower. On the flip side, if you're heading to the theme parks, your location off the beaten path means that you'll have to deal with a long drive and traffic.

Best Western Mount Vernon Inn *Value*   This is one of the best bargains in town—a place where guests get comfortable rooms and a shield from Mickeyville, which is 25 miles (40km) south. The Colonial-style Mt. Vernon isn't fancy, but its rooms are cozy and the staff is friendly. Some rooms overlook the pool, and a few have refrigerators. Deluxe rooms feature a small sitting area. Families love visiting the city park across the street.

110 S. Orlando Ave., Winter Park, FL 32789 Ⓒ **800/992-3379** or 407/647-1166. Fax 407/647-8011. www.bestwestern.com. 147 units. $79–$119 double. Extra person $6. Children 17 and under stay free in parents' room. AE, DC, DISC, MC, V. Free self-parking. The inn is on U.S. 17–92, between Fairbanks Ave. and Lee Rd. **Amenities:** 1 restaurant (American); lounge; 1 outdoor heated pool; guest laundry; valet; no-smoking rooms. *In room:* A/C, TV, dataport.

Westin Grand Bohemian ✿✿   Downtown's newest jewel opened in spring 2001. Rooms have an Art-Deco look with plenty of chrome, reds or purples, and mirrors. The "Heavenly Beds" (firm mattresses, down blankets, comforters, and with five pillows) are among the best in Orlando. (You can buy one for $2,200!) Upper floors on the east side overlook the pool; those on the north side face downtown. The smoke-free hotel has more than 100 pieces of 19th- and 20th-century American fine art.

325 S. Orange Ave. (across from City Hall). Ⓒ **888/937-8461** or 407/313-9000. Fax 407/313-9001. www.grandbohemianhotel.com. 250 units. $159–$189 for up to 4; $225 and up suite. AE, DC, DISC, MC, V. Valet $12. Take I-4 to the Washington St. exit, merge with W. Robinson/Hwy. 526, then south on Orange. The garage is 2 blocks west on Jackson. **Amenities:** 1 restaurant (international); 1 lounge, 1 coffee shop; 1 heated outdoor pool and spa; fitness center; concierge; shuttle to the theme parks for a fee; business center; 24-hr. room service; guest laundry and dry cleaning; concierge-level rooms. *In room:* A/C, TV w/pay movies, dataport, minibar, coffeemaker, hair dryer, iron, safe, Nintendo.

4 Where to Dine

Orlando has more than its share of fast fooderies and theme eateries. But it also has a growing number of upscale restaurants. Since most visitors spend much of their time at Disney, we're going to focus a lot of energy there. But we won't leave out worthwhile spots that are out of this World. We'll also explore better places to eat at Universal's CityWalk, along International Drive, and elsewhere.

HOW TO ARRANGE PRIORITY SEATING AT DISNEY RESTAURANTS

Priority seating *isn't* a reservation. It's a promise that you'll get the next available table once you arrive. There may be a wait, but if you don't use this system you may have a longer one. To get priority seating at any WDW restaurant, call Ⓒ **407/939-3463.** You can book as far as 60 days in advance of your arrival.

If you're staying on Disney property, you can arrange priority seating at your resort. At Epcot, you can do it at the WorldKey interactive terminals at Guest Relations near Innoventions East, the WorldKey Information Service on the main concourse to the World Showcase, and the restaurant of your choice.

TIPS ON WALT DISNEY WORLD RESTAURANTS

All park restaurants are **no-smoking.**

Magic Kingdom restaurants don't serve alcohol, but those at Animal Kingdom, Epcot, and Disney–MGM Studios do.

Sit-down restaurants in WDW take American Express, Diners Club, Discover, MasterCard, Visa, and the Disney Card.

Unless otherwise noted, *restaurants in the parks require park admission.* Unless you're using WDW transportation, there's also a $6 parking fee.

Nearly all WDW restaurants with sit-down or counter service offer children's menus with items ranging from $4 to $6.

INSIDE THE WALT DISNEY WORLD THEME PARKS

With few exceptions, you won't find Disney's park restaurants winning accolades from *Food & Wine* or *Bon Appétit.* The food at most of them is on par with the food at Universal Orlando—filling and palatable, but overpriced for the quality. The following list includes the Magic Kingdom, Epcot, Disney–MGM Studios, and Animal Kingdom. Get information on all Disney restaurants by calling © 407/939-3463 or visiting www.disneyworld.com.

EPCOT
World Showcase

The World Showcase has the best dining options inside the WDW theme parks, thanks to the cultural cuisine of its 11 nation pavilions. Although many consider a meal here an essential part of the experience, we must point out that the vittles (as in all theme parks) are priced higher than comparable fare in the free world.

The restaurants below are arranged geographically, beginning at the Canada pavilion and proceeding counterclockwise around the World Showcase Lagoon. *Prices are for entrees only* and don't include things like tax, tip, and beverages.

CANADA   Le Cellier Steakhouse has a castlelike ambience accentuated by vaulted stone arches. Red-meat main events (all Midwest, corn-fed) include the usual range of cuts—filet, porterhouse, prime rib, sirloin, and so on. Wash down your meal with a Canadian wine or choose from a selection of Canadian beers. Lunch runs $9 to $18; dinner is $15 to $26.

UNITED KINGDOM   The Tudor-beamed **Rose & Crown** is a cozy pub suggestive of Victorian England. Visitors from the U.K. flock to this spot, where folk music and sometimes-saucy servers entertain you as you feast on a short but joyfully traditional menu including steak-and-mushroom pie and fish and chips. The outdoor dining area overlooks the lagoon and is a good place to see the IllumiNations fireworks display. Lunch is $10 to $14; dinner is $13.75 to $21.

Tips **Special Tastes**

Looking for kosher food? Want to satisfy your vegetarian taste buds? WDW usually can handle those diets and other special ones (people who need fat-free or sugar-free meals, folks who have allergies or a lactose intolerance, for instance), as long as guests give advance notice—usually 24 hours. You can do that when you make priority-seating arrangements (© 407/939-3463) or, if you're staying at a Disney resort, at its guest-services desk. If you're not staying at WDW, call © 407/824-2222.

FRANCE   Chefs de France has an Art Nouveau interior agleam with mirrors and brass chandeliers. Three French chefs designed the menu, which is respectable by park standards but doesn't threaten Orlando's better French restaurants. The dinner entrees include Mediterranean seafood casserole (grouper, scallops, and shrimp dusted with saffron, then allowed to swim in a mild garlic sauce) and a garlicky braised lamb shank. There's an extensive wine list. Lunch is $10 to $19; dinner is $20 to $30.

MOROCCO   Of all the Epcot restaurants, **Marrakesh** 🅰 exemplifies the spirit of the park, yet a lot of guests don't know it's there or ignore it because they're worried that the menu is too exotic. Expect belly dancers to entertain while you feast on options like marinated beef shish kebob, braised chicken with green olives, and a medley of seafood, chicken, and lamb. Most entrees come with couscous (steamed semolina with veggies and, sometimes, other embellishments). The palatial restaurant—with hand-set mosaic tiles, latticed shutters, and a ceiling painted in elaborate Moorish motifs—represents 12 centuries of Arabic design. Lunch costs $12 to $17.50; dinner is $17 to $26.

JAPAN   If you've been to any of the Japanese steak-house chains, you know the drill at **Teppanyaki:** Diners sit around grill tables while white-hatted chefs rapidly dice, slice, stir-fry, and sometimes launch the food onto your plate with amazing skill. Unfortunately, the culinary acrobatics here are better than the cuisine. Lunch is $9 to $21; dinner is $16.50 to $31. The adjoining **Yakitori House** is a bamboo-roofed cafeteria that serves casual fare for under $10.

ITALY   Patterned after Alfredo De Lelio's celebrated ristorante in Rome, **L'Originale Alfredo di Roma** is Epcot's most popular restaurant. Nevertheless, critics say its pasta is overpriced and its servers are carefree. It's hard to take issue with the former when one meatless pasta dish tops the $20 mark—the celebrated fettuccine. On the meatier side of the menu, a smallish veal chop is served with a Chianti-and-truffle sauce, mushrooms, asparagus, and roasted potatoes. There's an extensive Italian wine list. If you want a quieter setting, ask for a seat on the veranda. Lunch costs $10 to $26; dinner runs $17 to $38.

GERMANY   The **Biergarten** simulates a Bavarian village at Oktoberfest. Unfortunately, the festive atmosphere hardly makes up for the bland food. The all-you-can-eat buffet is filled with traditional Bavarian fare (assorted sausages, chicken schnitzel, sauerbraten, spaetzle with gravy, sauerkraut, and a large assortment of trimmings). The lunch buffet is $14 for adults, $6 for kids 3 to 11; dinner is $19 for adults, $8 for children. At **Sommerfest,** a cafeteria, you can purchase bratwurst sandwiches with sauerkraut. All items are under $8.

CHINA   When it comes to decor, **Nine Dragons** shines with carved rosewood furnishings and a dragon-motif ceiling. Some windows overlook the lagoon outside. The food, alas, doesn't match its surroundings. Main courses feature Mandarin, Cantonese, and Szechwan cuisine, but portions are small. You can order Chinese or California wines with your meal. Lunch runs $9.50 to $19; dinners go for $12.50 to $30. If you want something lighter, the open-air **Lotus Blossom Café** sells egg rolls, pork fried rice, and stir-fried chicken and vegetables served over noodles ($4.50–$6.50).

NORWAY   **Akershus** is a re-created 14th-century castle where you can sample a 40-item smorgasbord of *smavarmt* (hot) and *koldtbord* (cold) dishes. The reasonably good entrees usually include such dishes as venison stew, stuffed pork, gravlax, smoked mackerel, and mustard herring. Norwegian beer and aquavit complement a list of French and California wines. The lunch buffet costs $11.95 for adults, $5.25 for children 4 to 9; the dinner buffet is $18.50 for adults, $7.95 for kids. The **Kringla Bakeri og Kafe** has open-face sandwiches, sugar-sprinkled waffles, and fresh-baked Norwegian pastries. All items cost under $8.

MEXICO   It's always night at the **San Angel Inn** 🍴, where candlelit tables set the mood, and the menu delivers reasonably authentic food. One top seller is the *mole poblano* (chicken brought to life with more than 20 spices, carrots, and a hint of chocolate). Another favorite: *filete motuleno* (grilled beef tenderloin served over black beans, melted cheese, pepper strips, and fried plantains. Lunch is $9 to $17; dinners are $17 to $22. The **Cantina de San Angel**, a cafeteria with outdoor seating at umbrella tables overlooking the lagoon, offers tacos, burritos, and other items under $8.

Future World
At the Living Seas pavilion, the mood is half the fun at the **Coral Reef**, where the tables circle a 5.6-million-gallon aquarium that has 4,000 denizens of the not-so-deep. Tiered seating ensures everyone a good view. Menu standards include garlic-roasted shrimp with seafood sausage and pan-seared salmon with garlic-pesto mashed potatoes. Lunch and dinner are $15 to $42.

IN THE MAGIC KINGDOM
In addition to these restaurants, there are plenty of fast-food outlets located throughout the park. But you may find that a quiet, sit-down meal is an essential though brief getaway from the forced-march madness. Don't forget to make priority-seating arrangements.

Fantasyland   Romantics may find it hard to beat the ambience of eating at **Cinderella's Royal Table** 🍴 in Cinderella Castle, the Magic Kingdom's icon. Servers treat you like a lord or lady while fetching you headliners such as spice-crusted salmon, a New York strip, or roasted chicken. Lunch costs $11 to $16; dinner sells for $20 to $26.

Liberty Square   The **Liberty Tree Tavern's** colonial decor and mood are fun, but the food (including the evening character buffet) is basic. Expect roast turkey, marinated flank steak, and honey-mustard ham. Lunch is $10.75 to $17; the buffet is $21 for adults, $10 for kids 3 to 11.

Main Street   Lunch and dinner at **Tony's Town Square Restaurant** are non-descript (and in some cases cardboard-quality) Italian. Evening fare includes garlic-sautéed shrimp, chicken scaloppini, and a grilled pork chop Marsala. Lunch costs $9.50 to $16; dinner is $18.50 to $25.50.

AT DISNEY–MGM STUDIOS
There are more than a dozen places to refuel in this Hollywood-style theme park. The ones listed below are the best of the bunch. Again, priority seating is a must.

Modeled after the Los Angeles celebrity haunt where Louella Parsons and Hedda Hopper held court, the **Hollywood Brown Derby** offers a good time and pricey meal. On the lighter side, try a Cobb salad, invented in the 1930s by Bob Cobb, who owned the one in the other Hollywood. Dinner entrees at Disney's version include pan-seared black grouper and mustard-crusted rack of lamb. The Derby's signature dessert, grapefruit cake with cream-cheese icing, is a perfect meal capper. Entrees go for $14 to $22 at lunch; $17 to $26 at dinner.

The concept behind the **50's Prime Time Café** is intriguing: Build a restaurant based on a 1950s time warp/sitcom psychodrama. The atmosphere delivers with black-and-white TV sets showing "My Little Margie" and servers threatening to withhold dessert if you don't eat all your food. But we won't blame you if you turn up your nose. Although the desserts are good, the meatloaf and pot roast don't deliver. Meals cost $13 to $18.50 at lunch and dinner.

The safest bets at **Mama Melrose's Ristorante Italiano** are the wood-fired flatbreads (grilled pepperoni, portobello mushroom, and four-cheese). The menu is fleshed out with so-so Italian pretenders—chicken Marsala, cioppino, and others. Lunch is $12 to $18; dinner is $15 to $18.

Take the above review for the 50's Prime Time Café, give it a science-fiction spin, and welcome to the **Sci-Fi Dine-In Theater Restaurant.** Diners sit in chrome-plated convertibles with the Hollywood hills as a backdrop and are treated to newsreels, cartoons, and "B" horror flicks. Forget food adjectives such as marinated, smoked, and pan-seared. It's still your basic beef, pork, poultry, tuna, and pasta. Lunches set you back $10 to $16.50; dinners are $15 to $18.50.

IN THE ANIMAL KINGDOM

You'll find only a few dining options in Animal Kingdom, and most of those are grab-and-go places. Nevertheless, there are two spots where you can park yourself.

Expect California fare with an island spin at the **Rainforest Cafe.** Menu offerings tend to be tasty and sometimes creative, but the cafe, like other Disney restaurants, charges more than it should. Dishes include a turkey pita with fried onions, romaine, and tomatoes. The mixed grill has ribs, steak on skewers, barbecued chicken, and peppered shrimp. Lunch and dinner run $10 to $40.

Taste at the **Tusker House** is there, even if quantity and quality aren't. The options are grilled chicken salad in a sourdough-bread bowl; rotisserie or fried chicken; and a chicken, ham, and Swiss cheese sandwich. Prices are $7 to $8.

IN THE WALT DISNEY WORLD RESORTS

Most of these restaurants continue the trend of being above market price, but the food generally is a notch (or more) higher than what you find in the theme parks.

VERY EXPENSIVE

Citricos ✦ NEW FRENCH   The chefs create what the resort calls French, Alsatian, and Provençal cuisine with California and Florida touches. The translation: The oft-changing menu might offer basil-crusted rack of lamb, grilled salmon with fennel ravioli, or pan-seared sea bass with shellfish bouillabaisse.

4401 Floridian Way, in Disney's Grand Floridian Resort & Spa. ℭ 407/939-3463. www.disneyworld.com. Priority seating recommended. Main courses $22–$45. AE, DC, DISC, MC, V. 5:30–10pm Wed–Sun; Chef's Domain seatings 6 and 8:30pm.

Victoria & Albert's ★★★ *Finds* INTERNATIONAL   It's not often we can describe dinner as "an event," but Disney's most elegant restaurant earns that distinction. Dinner is next to perfect—if the portions seem small, we dare you to make it through all seven courses—and the setting is exceptionally romantic. The fare changes nightly, but you might find main events such as Alaskan rockfish with couscous or filet mignon with Vidalia-onion mash. The dining room is crowned by a domed, chapel-style ceiling; 20 exquisitely appointed tables are lit softly by Victorian lamps; and your servers (always named Victoria and Albert) provide service that will have you begging to take them home. There's an extensive wine list. We suggest splurging on the wine pairing.

> (**Moments** The Chef's Table: Best Seat in the World
>
> There's a special dining option at **Victoria & Albert's**. Reserve the **Chef's Table** (far, *far* in advance) and dine in a charming alcove at a candlelit table in the heart of the kitchen! Sip bubbly with the chef while discussing your preferences for a seven- to nine-course menu created for you. The Chef's Table can accommodate up to 12 people a night. It's a leisurely affair, lasting 3 or 4 hours. The price is $115 without wine, $160 per person including five wines. It's so popular that Disney takes reservations 180 days in advance, so reserve *early* (📞 **407/939-3463**).

4401 Floridian Way, in Disney's Grand Floridian Resort & Spa. 📞 **407/939-3463**. www.disneyworld.com. Reservations required. Jackets required for men. Not recommended for children. Prix fixe $85 per person, $35 additional for wine pairing; $115 Chef's Table, $160 with wine. AE, DC, DISC, MC, V. 2 dinner seatings daily, 5:45–6:30pm and 9–9:45pm. Chef's Table 6pm only. Free self- and validated valet parking.

Yachtsman Steakhouse ⭐ SEAFOOD/STEAKS   Even by outside-the-park standards, this is a solid steakhouse. The exhibition kitchen provides a tantalizing peek at steaks, chops, and seafood being grilled over oak and hickory. Options range from a 6-ounce filet to a 12-ounce bourbon-marinated strip to an XXXL 24-ounce T-bone. The menu also has rack of lamb, salmon, and chicken. The Yachtsman has an extensive wine list, and its staff is very cordial.

1700 Epcot Resorts Blvd., in Disney's Yacht Club Resort. 📞 **407/939-3463**. Priority seating is recommended. Main courses $19–$50. AE, DC, DISC, MC, V. Daily 5:30–10pm. Free self- and valet parking.

EXPENSIVE

Artist Point ⭐ *Finds* SEAFOOD/STEAKS   Enjoy a grand view of Disney's Wilderness Lodge while you select from a menu that changes seasonally. You might discover roasted halibut with a basil crust, grilled veal tenderloin with mushrooms, pan-roasted shrimp with capers and tomatoes, or a mixed grill of elk, ostrich, and venison. Expect a reasonably extensive wine list. *Note:* Artist Point isn't as "discovered" as some other WDW resort restaurants (enjoy that while it lasts), which makes for a more relaxed atmosphere.

901 W. Timberline Dr., in Disney's Wilderness Lodge. 📞 **407/939-3463** or 407/824-1081. www.disney world.com. Priority seating recommended. Main courses $18–$32. AE, DC, DISC, MC, V. Daily 5:30–10pm. Free self- and valet parking.

California Grill ⭐⭐⭐ CALIFORNIA   Settle into the 15th floor of the Contemporary Resort and enjoy views of the Magic Kingdom while you drool over menu options prepared in an exhibition kitchen. Headliners change often, but they sometimes include seared yellowfin tuna served rare, roasted striped bass, or grilled pork tenderloin. The Grill has a very nice sushi menu (crab, eel, tuna, and more). This is one of the few spots in WDW that isn't crawling with kids. The list of California wines helps complement the meal and views, but it can be tough to get a table, so make a reservation as far ahead as possible.

4600 N. World Dr., at Disney's Contemporary Resort. 📞 **407/939-3463** or 407/824-1576. www.disney world.com. Reservations recommended. Main courses $20–$30; sushi $10–$30. AE, DC, DISC, MC, V. Daily 5:30–10pm. Free self-parking.

Jiko—The Cooking Place INTERNATIONAL   The Animal Kingdom Lodge's signature restaurant is a nice diversion from the normal Disney restaurants. Jiko's show kitchen turns out a unique menu of international cuisine with

African overtones that might include banana leaf–wrapped shrimp, pan-roasted monkfish, horseradish-crusted salmon, wood-cooked wahoo, and fire-roasted papaya stuffed with beef.

2901 Osceola Pkwy., at Disney's Animal Kingdom Lodge. ✆ **407/939-3463.** www.disneyworld.com. Priority seating recommended. Main courses $16.50–$28.50. AE, DC, DISC, MC, V. Daily 5:30–10pm. Free self-parking.

MODERATE

'Ohana ✿ PACIFIC RIM   Its star is earned on the fun front, but the decibel level will turn some off. As your luau is being prepared over an 18-foot-wide (5m) fire pit, the staff keeps you busy with coconut races, hula lessons, and other shenanigans. Turkey, shrimp, pork loin, and steak fill out the menu. You'll also find lots of trimmings and a full bar with a limited wine selection.

1600 Seven Seas Dr., at Disney's Polynesian Resort. ✆ **407/939-3463** or 407/824-2000. www.disney world.com. Priority seating is strongly encouraged. $21 adults, $10 children 3–11. AE, DC, DISC, MC, V. Daily 7:30–11am and 5–10pm. Free self- and valet parking.

DOWNTOWN DISNEY
VERY EXPENSIVE

Fulton's Crab House ✿ SEAFOOD   Oysters and stone crab claws are the specialties of this fun and fashionable eatery, which is in a replica of a (permanently moored) 19th-century Mississippi riverboat. It's one of the area's best seafood houses, but you might want to bring your banker along for the ride. One popular meal for two combines Alaskan king crab and lobster served over potatoes and creamed spinach. The grilled tuna mignon is delicious—it's served rare with lemon grass dipping sauce, steamed bok choy, and a jasmine rice cake. Fulton's has one of Lake Buena Vista's better wine lists.

1670 Buena Vista Dr., aboard the riverboat docked at Downtown Disney. ✆ **407/934-2628.** Priority seating recommended. Main courses $11–$37 at lunch, $17–$44 at dinner. AE, DC, DISC, MC, V. Daily 11:30am–11pm. Free self-parking; valet parking $6.

EXPENSIVE

Portobello Yacht Club ✿ MEDITERRANEAN   The pizzas here go beyond the routine to *quattro formaggi* (four-cheese, plus sun-dried tomatoes) and *margherita* (Italian sausage, plum tomatoes, and mozzarella). But it's the less casual entrees that pack people into this joint. You may find *costoletta di mai'ale* (marinated roasted pork loin with fennel, carrots, and roasted-garlic whipped potatoes) or *spaghettini alla portobello* (pasta with pieces of Alaskan king crab, scallops, shrimp, and clams in light olive oil, wine, and herbs). The Portobello's cellar is small, but there's a nice selection of wine to match the meals.

1650 Buena Vista Dr., in Pleasure Island. ✆ **407/934-8888.** www.levyrestaurants.com. Priority seating recommended. Main courses $10–$18 at lunch, $16–$50 at dinner; pizzas $9. AE, DC, DISC, MC, V. Daily 11:30am–11pm (dinner served from 4pm). Free self-parking; valet parking $6.

MODERATE

Rainforest Cafe ✿ CALIFORNIA   Don't arrive starving. Waits average 2 hours if you fail to call ahead for priority seating, although even then you'll wait longer than at Animal Kingdom's Rainforest Cafe (p. 532). The menu can be tasty and creative, though somewhat overpriced. Fun dishes include Mojo Bones (pork ribs), Rumble in the Jungle Turkey Pita, and Mixed Grill (ribs, steak skewers, chicken breast, and peppered shrimp).

Downtown Disney Marketplace; near the smoking volcano. ✆ **407/827-8500.** www.rainforestcafe.com. Priority seating. Main courses $11–$40 at lunch and dinner (most under $25). AE, DISC, MC, V. Sun–Thurs 10:30am–11pm; Fri–Sat 10:30am–midnight. Free self-parking.

Wolfgang Puck Café CALIFORNIA   The wait can be distressing and the sticker prices depressing, but the chefs turn out a mean menu of pizza, sushi, and fu-fu food. Possibilities include coriander-crusted tuna, fettucine Wolf-fredo, Puck's pucks (crab cakes), and spicy tuna rolls. The eclectic eatery is often busy and noisy, making conversation difficult. But after enough sake, who cares?

1482 Buena Vista Dr., at Disney's West Side. © 407/938-9653. Reservations not accepted. Main courses $12–$28 (many under $20); pizza and sushi $5–$25. AE, DC, DISC, MC, V. Daily 11am–1am. Free self-parking.

ELSEWHERE IN LAKE BUENA VISTA
VERY EXPENSIVE

Arthur's 27 ⭐ CONTINENTAL   Insiders come for the 27th-floor views of Central Florida sunsets and the Wizard of Disney's fireworks. Those who can afford the high-altitude prices get a restaurant that has the feel of a 1930s supper club minus the cigarette smoke. Some tables are in alcoves facing huge picture windows. Book an 8pm reservation for a table facing the 9pm Disney fireworks. The cuisine is tasty, but unfortunately doesn't live up to the view and prices. The herb-crusted rack of lamb, when ordered medium rare, is pleasing to the eye and taste, but the Chilean sea bass sometimes arrives brittle and liquid enough to be sushi. *Our best advice:* Skip the meal and go for the equally good view of the fireworks in the Top of the Palace Lounge, also on the 27th floor. But arrive early.

1900 Lake Buena Vista Dr., in the Wyndham Palace Resort, just north of Hotel Plaza Blvd. © 407/827-3450. Reservations recommended. Jackets suggested for men. Main courses $31–$48; $62–$68 prix fixe; no kids' menu. AE, DC, DISC, MC, V. Daily 6–10pm. Free self-parking. From I-4, take the Hwy. 535/Apopka–Vineland Rd. exit north to Hotel Plaza Blvd., then left to the Wyndham.

La Coquina ⭐ *Finds* INTERNATIONAL   Expect an imaginative menu at this upscale but casual eatery, the most acclaimed of the Hyatt Regency's five restaurants. The veal tenderloin with sake-glazed prawns is a real winner. Ditto for the sugarcane-seared scallops, which arrive with rice grits and artichokes. As for the mango-glazed duck breast, it's introduced with a shiitake-risotto cake. When making your reservation, request a table with a view of Lake Windsong.

1 Grand Cypress Blvd., in the Hyatt Regency Grand Cypress Resort. © 407/239-1234. Reservations recommended. Jackets suggested for men. Main courses $20–$40; no kids' menu. AE, DC, DISC, MC, V. Daily 6:30–10pm. Free self- and validated valet parking. Take the I-4 Hwy. 535/Apopka-Vineland Rd. exit north to Winter Garden–Vineland Rd./Hwy. 535, then left.

MODERATE

Pebbles ⭐⭐ *Finds* CALIFORNIA   If you want to dine like a gourmet without the hefty price, here's your ticket. Pebbles is a four-restaurant chain that has a reputation for great food, a sexy-if-small wine list, and creative appetizers. The chèvre-coated lamb chops, when available, are worth fighting for. The twin brie filet mignons are a good second. Like many entrees, they come with three-cheese mashed potatoes and zucchini wedges. Pebbles also has locations at 17 W. Church St. (© **407/839-0892**); in Longwood at 2110 W. Hwy. 434 (© **407/ 774-7111**); and in Winter Park at 2516 Aloma Ave. (© **407/678-7001**).

12551 Apopka–Vineland Rd., in the Crossroads Shopping Center. © 407/827-1111. www.pebblesworld wide.com. Reservations not accepted. Main courses $10–$21. AE, DC, DISC, MC, V. Sun–Thurs noon–11pm; Fri–Sat 11am–11pm. Free self-parking. Take the I-4 Hwy. 535/Apopka-Vineland Rd. exit north to the Crossroads Shopping Center on the right.

PLACES TO DINE IN UNIVERSAL ORLANDO

Universal stormed the restaurant scene with the opening of its dining and entertainment venue, CityWalk, in 1999.

VERY EXPENSIVE

Delfino Riviera ⭐ NORTHERN ITALIAN   The signature ristorante in Universal Orlando's Portofino Bay Hotel overlooks the Harbor Piazza and delivers a romantic mood reminiscent of the Italian Riviera—complete with strolling musicians and crooners. It has a chef's table for eight in addition to indoor and terrace dining. The menu changes, but the pasta side might have lobster-champagne risotto, black-olive pasta with monkfish, and pesto-stuffed ravioli. Carnivores can dig into veal roasted with porcini mushrooms, while fish fans delight in sea bass with mushrooms and potatoes in Chianti sauce. The service is snappy and dining areas are quiet enough to allow conversation. Its wine list is one of the best on the I-Drive/Universal Orlando corridor.

5601 Universal Studios Blvd., in the Portofino Bay Hotel. ℂ **407/503-3463.** Reservations recommended. Main courses $25–$47. AE, MC, V. Tues–Sat 5–10pm. Free self-parking; valet parking $8. From I-4, take the Kirkman Rd./Hwy. 435 exit and follow the signs to Universal.

Emeril's ⭐⭐ NEW ORLEANS   It's next to impossible to get short-term reservations for dinner unless you're willing to take your chances with no-shows. But most who wait say the food is worth it. Best bets are andouille-crusted redfish (a moist, white fish with roasted pecan–vegetable relish and meunière sauce) and the quail (yes, they *are* little) stuffed with Louisiana oyster dressing and served with a ragout of vegetables and cornmeal-crusted oysters. If you want some vino with your meal, no problem; the back half of the building is a glass-walled 12,000-bottle above-ground cellar. Prices are high enough that Emeril can afford tons of legroom between tables. If you want a show, we recommend one of eight counter seats, where you can watch chefs working their magic; but to get one, reservations are required *excruciatingly* early.

Note: Lunch costs about half what you'll spend on dinner, and the menu and portions are almost the same. It's also easier to get a midday reservation.

6000 Universal Studios Blvd., in CityWalk. ℂ **407/224-2424.** www.emerils.com/restaurants/orlando. Reservations necessary. Main courses $17–$26 at lunch; $18–$42 at dinner. Daily 11:30am–2:30pm and 5:30–10pm (until 11pm Fri–Sat). AE, DISC, MC, V. Parking $7 (free after 6pm). From I-4, take the Kirkman Rd./Hwy. 435 exit and follow the signs to Universal.

The Palm STEAKS/SEAFOOD   This upscale eatery is the 23rd member of a chain started more than 75 years ago in New York. The food is good, though, as is the case with most Disney restaurants, somewhat overpriced for the value received. Beef and seafood rule a menu headlined by a 36-ounce New York strip steak for two and a 3-pound Nova Scotia lobster. Smaller appetites and budgets can feast on broiled crab cakes, veal piccata, and lamb or pork chops.

5800 Universal Blvd., in the Hard Rock Hotel. ℂ **407/503-7256.** www.thepalm.com. Reservations recommended. Main courses $9–$31 at lunch, $16.50–$45 at dinner (many under $25). AE, DC, DISC, MC, V. Mon–Fri 11:30am–11pm; Sat 5–11pm; Sun 5–10pm. Free self-parking; valet $8. From I-4, take the Kirkman Rd./Hwy. 435 exit and follow the signs to Universal.

MODERATE

Jimmy Buffett's Margaritaville CARIBBEAN   As soon as the parrotheads have enough to drink (no later than 4pm on weekends), the noise makes it futile to try conversation, but most folks come to Margaritaville to sing and get stupid, not to gab. Despite the cheeseburgers in paradise (yes, they're on the menu at $7.95), Jimmy's reasonably tasty victuals lean toward the Caribbean side, including jerk chicken and a Cuban meatloaf survival sandwich.

1000 Universal Studios Plaza, in CityWalk. © **407/224-2155.** www.universalorlando.com. Reservations not accepted. Main courses $8–$19. AE, DISC, MC, V. Daily 11:30am–midnight. Parking $7 (free after 6pm). From I-4, take the Kirkman Rd./Hwy. 435 exit and follow the signs to Universal.

Pastamore Ristorante SOUTHERN ITALIAN This family-style restaurant greets you with display cases brimming with mozzarella and other goodies on the menu. The antipasto primo is a meal unto itself. It includes bruschetta, eggplant Caponata, melon with prosciutto, grilled portobello mushrooms, Italian cold cuts, olives, plum tomatoes, mozzarella, and more. The menu also has traditional features such as veal Marsala, chicken piccata, shrimp scampi, fettuccine Alfredo, lasagna, and pizza. An open kitchen allows diners a view of the chefs at work. You can also eat in a cafe where lighter fare—breakfast and sandwiches—is served from 8am to 2am.

1000 Universal Studios Plaza, in CityWalk. © **407/363-8000.** www.universalorlando.com. Reservations accepted. Main courses $7–$18. AE, DISC, MC, V. Daily 5pm–midnight. Parking $7 (free after 6pm). From I-4, take the Kirkman Rd./Hwy. 435 exit and follow the signs to Universal.

PLACES TO DINE IN THE INTERNATIONAL DRIVE AREA

International Drive has one of the area's larger collections of fast-food joints, but the midsection and southern third also have some of this region's better restaurants. I-Drive is 10 minutes by auto from the Walt Disney World parks.

VERY EXPENSIVE

Atlantis ✦ SEAFOOD/STEAKS/CHOPS This intimate dining room has a warm, woody feel, especially in the booths separated by etched-glass panels. Chef's specials such as a Mediterranean seafood medley (Florida lobster, grouper, shrimp, and scallops) frequently complement menu standards such as grilled sea bass or pan-seared duck and rock shrimp. Sunday's champagne brunch is served in the atrium. Themes change, but the menu often has treats such as quail, duck, lamb chops, Cornish hen, clams, mussels, snapper, sea bass, sushi, and much more. Although pricey, it's one of Orlando's more popular brunches.

6677 Sea Harbour Dr., in the Renaissance Orlando Resort. © **407/351-5555.** www.renaissancehotels.com. Reservations recommended. Main courses $24–$36; Sunday brunch $32 adults, $16 children. AE, DC, DISC, MC, V. Daily 6–10pm. Free self-parking; valet parking $9. From the I-4 Hwy., take the 417/Central Florida Pkwy, exit and follow the signs to SeaWorld.

Dux ✦✦✦ *Finds* INTERNATIONAL The name is a tribute to the Peabody Orlando's resident ducks, who parade ceremoniously in and out of the lobby every day (p. 523), while the food is a tribute to chefs who create a marvelous menu that changes often. It might include oven-roasted grouper with bok choy, mushrooms, and ginger sauce. Hope, too, for a veal chop roasted medium rare with an artichoke-basil fricassee and garlic au jus. Dux is best reserved for a very special night out or a meal on an expense account. It has impeccable service and one of the best wine lists in Orlando.

9801 International Dr., in the Peabody Orlando. © **407/345-4550.** www.peabody-orlando.com. Reservations recommended. Main courses $26–$45. AE, DC, DISC, MC, V. Mon–Sat 6–10pm. Free self- and validated valet parking. From I-4, take the Sand Lake Rd./Hwy. 528 exit east to International Dr., then south. Hotel is on the left across from the Convention Center.

EXPENSIVE

Ran-Getsu of Tokyo JAPANESE   Authentic cuisine including a sushi bar has made Ran-Getsu a popular haunt for moneyed Asian tourists, though some travelers find the prices too high. *Tekka-don,* tender slices of tuna that are mild enough for first-timers, is a refreshing choice on the sushi side; so are platters, such as sashimi, maki rolls, and thinly sliced *chirashi* (rice topped with assorted seafood). *Yosenabe* is a bouillabaisse with an unconventional though savory twist—duck and chicken are added to the seafood mix. Speaking of seafood, *una-ju* delights eel lovers; the filets are grilled in kabayaki sauce. A Japanese drum team usually performs at 7:30 and 9pm, Thursday through Saturday.

8400 International Dr., near Orlando Convention Center. © 407/345-0044. www.rangetsu.com. Reservations recommended. Main courses $14–$35 (most under $25); sushi entrees $14–$41 (most under $25). AE, DC, DISC, MC, V. Daily 5–11:30pm. From I-4, take the Sand Lake Rd./Hwy. 528 exit east to International Dr., then south. Restaurant is on the right.

MODERATE

Bahama Breeze *Value* CARIBBEAN   This spunky chain uses traditional Caribbean food as a base for creative items, such as "fish in a bag" (strips of mahimahi in a parchment pillow flavored with carrots, peppers, mushrooms, and spices) and a B+ *paella* (rice with shrimp, fish, mussels, chicken, and sausage). It's always crowded, so arrive early and be patient. The restaurant doesn't accept reservations and the wait can be up to 2 hours during prime time, from 6 to 8pm.

8849 International Dr. © 407/248-2499. Reservations not accepted. Main courses: full orders $9–$18; half orders $7–$12; sandwiches and salads $8–$11. AE, MC, V. Sun–Thurs 4pm–1am; Fri–Sat 4pm–1:30am. Free parking. From I-4, take exit 29 (Sand Lake Rd./Hwy. 528) east to International Dr., then south. It's on the left.

B-Line Diner ★ AMERICAN   Come to have fun in a chrome-plated '50s-style diner where you can sink into upholstered booths or belly up to the counter. It gets noisy, partly due to an exuberant staff. The round-the-clock menu features comfort foods such as chicken pot pie that's up to what mom made; a ham and cheese sandwich on a baguette; and roast pork with grilled apples, sun-dried cherry stuffing, and brandy-honey sauce. The portions are hearty, but so are the prices for diner fare. There's a full bar.

9801 International Dr., in the Peabody Orlando. © 407/345-4460. www.peabody-orlando.com. Reservations not accepted. Main courses $4–$14 at breakfast, $7–$17 at lunch, $9–$26 (most under $17) at dinner. AE, DC, DISC, MC, V. Daily 24 hr. Free self- and validated valet parking. From I-4, take the Sand Lake Rd./Hwy. 528 exit east to International Dr., then south. Hotel is on the left across from the Convention Center.

Ming Court ★ CHINESE   Local patronage and the diverse menu make this one of O-Town's most popular Chinese restaurants. The lightly battered, deep-fried chicken breast gets plenty of zip from a delicate lemon-tangerine sauce. If you're in the mood for beef, try the grilled filet mignon seasoned Szechwan-style (the topping has toasted onions, garlic, and chili). Portions are sufficient, there's a moderate wine list, and the service is excellent.

9188 International Dr., between Sand Lake Rd. and Bee Line Expwy. © 407/351-9988. www.ming-court.com. Reservations recommended. Dim sum mostly $3–$5; main courses $7–$13 at lunch, $13–$36 at dinner. AE, DC, DISC, MC, V. Daily 11am–2:30pm and 4:30–10:30pm. Free self-parking. From I-4, take the Sand Lake Rd./Hwy. 528 exit east to International Dr., then south. It's on the right, 3 blocks past Bahama Breeze (see above).

Siam Orchid ★ *Finds* THAI   Tim and Krissnee Martsching grow the mint, chilies, cilantro, lemon grass, and wild lime that go into their entrees. The star attractions include Pad Thai (rice noodles tossed with ground pork, garlic, shrimp, crab claws, crab meat, and crushed peanuts in a tongue-twanging sweet sauce) and Royal Thai (a curry with chicken chunks, potato, and onion in yellow curry sauce). Siam Orchid serves sake, plum wine, and Thai beers from a full bar.

7575 Universal Dr. (between Sand Lake Rd. and Carrier Dr.). © 407/351-0821. Reservations recommended. Main courses $11–$21. AE, DC, DISC, MC, V. Mon–Fri 11am–2pm; daily 5–11pm. Free self-parking. From I-4, take the Sand Lake Rd./Hwy. 528 exit east to Universal, then go north to the restaurant (on the left).

PLACES TO DINE ELSEWHERE IN ORLANDO
Here's a look at the best spots beyond the mainstream.

MODERATE
Rolando's ★ *Finds* CUBAN   Big portions and authentic cuisine are the main draws at this mom-and-pop eatery. Our favorites include *arroz con pollo* (chicken with yellow rice), *ropa vieja* (shredded beef), and, if you call a day in advance, *paella* (fish and shellfish served on a bed of rice). Entrees come with yucca or plantains. There's a very limited beer and wine list.

870 E. Hwy. 436/Semoran Blvd., in Casselberry. © 407/767-9677. Reservations accepted. Main courses $4–$6 at lunch, $8–$18 at dinner. AE, DC, DISC, MC, V. Mon–Fri 11am–9:30pm; Sat noon–10pm; Sun noon–8:30pm. Free self-parking. From I-4, take the Hwy. 408/E.–W. Expwy. exit, head east, and make a left on Hwy. 436.

INEXPENSIVE
Bubbaloo's Bodacious BBQ ★ *Value* BARBECUE   This spot serves some of the best barbecue in Florida. Go for the full pork platter that comes with a heaping helping of pork and all the fixin's. The uninitiated should stay away from the "Killer" sauce, which produces a tongue buzz that's likely to last for hours; you might even taste-test the mild sauce before moving up to the hot.

1471 Lee Rd., Winter Park (about 5 min. from downtown Orlando). © 407/628-1212. Reservations not accepted. Main courses $5–$15. AE, MC, V. Mon–Thurs 10am–9pm; Fri–Sat 10am–10:30pm. Free self-parking. Take the I-4 Lee Rd. exit and follow your nose; Bubbaloo's is on the left next to a dry cleaner.

Little Saigon ★ *Finds* VIETNAMESE   Asian immigrants created the demand for this great little eatery that's yet to be discovered by tourists. Try the summer rolls—a soft wrap filled with rice, shrimp, and pork served with a delicious peanut sauce. Head next for the grilled pork and egg over rice and noodles, or barbecued beef with fried egg and rice. The numbered menu isn't translated well, but your server or the manager can help.

1106 E. Colonial Dr./Hwy. 50 (near downtown Orlando). © 407/423-8539. Reservations not accepted. Main courses under $5 at lunch; $5–$8 at dinner. AE, DISC, MC, V. Daily 10am–9pm. Free self-parking. Take the Colonial Dr./Hwy. 50 exit off I-4 and head east. Turn right on Thorton Ave. The parking lot is immediately to the left.

ONLY IN ORLANDO: DINING WITH DISNEY CHARACTERS
Dining with costumed characters is a treat for almost any Disney fan, but it's a special one for those under 10. Some of their favorite 'toons show up to greet them, sign autographs, pose for photos, and interact with the family. These meals aren't low-turnout events, so make priority-seating arrangements (© 407/939-3463) as early as possible, and call for schedules. Prices vary, but generally expect breakfast (most serve it) to be $14 to $16 for adults, $8 to $10 for kids 3 to 11; those that serve dinner charge $19 to $22 for adults, $9 to $13 for kids. Character meals are offered at **Cape May Café** (in Disney's Beach Club Resort), **Chef Mickey's** (at Disney's Contemporary Resort), **Cinderella's Royal Table** (in Cinderella Castle, Magic Kingdom), **Crystal Palace Buffet** (at Crystal Palace,

Magic Kingdom), **Donald's Prehistoric Breakfastosaurus** (in Dinoland U.S.A., Animal Kingdom), **Garden Grill** (in The Land Pavilion at Epcot), **Hollywood & Vine Character Dining** (at Hollywood & Vine, in Disney–MGM Studios), **Liberty Tree Tavern** (in Liberty Square, in the Magic Kingdom), **'Ohana** (at Disney's Polynesian Resort), and **1900 Park Fare** (at Disney's Grand Floridian Resort & Spa).

5 Tips for Visiting Walt Disney World Attractions

Walt Disney World is the umbrella above four theme parks: the Magic Kingdom, Epcot, Disney–MGM Studios, and Animal Kingdom, with around 40 million guests annually.

Besides its theme parks, Disney has an assortment of other venues, including Downtown Disney (Cirque du Soleil and DisneyQuest, Pleasure Island), Blizzard Beach, Typhoon Lagoon, River Country, and more.

TIPS FOR PLANNING YOUR TRIP

Information   Before leaving home, call or write the Walt Disney World Co., Box 10000, Lake Buena Vista, FL 32830-1000 (© **407/934-7639**), for a *Walt Disney World Vacations* brochure and video; both are good planning aids. Also ask if there are special events during your visit. Don't forget to request park maps to get you familiar with the layouts. There are information booths in each park: in the Magic Kingdom at City Hall, in Epcot at Innoventions East near the World Key, and at Guest Services in Disney–MGM Studios and Animal Kingdom.

You also can get information online at **www.disneyworld.com**.

Parking   Cars, light trucks, and vans currently pay $6 (though we expect Disney to follow Universal and SeaWorld and go to $7). Visitors with disabilities can park in special areas near the entrances; ask the parking-lot attendants or call © **407/824-4321.** *Don't forget* to write down where you parked (area and row number), because it's easy to get lost after a long day.

When You Arrive   Grab a park guide map! It not only tells you where the fun is but also lists the daily entertainment schedule. If you want to see certain shows or parades, arrive early to get a good seat. Use this guide and the map to come up with a game plan on where to eat, what to ride, and what to see during your stay.

Best Times to Visit   There isn't a real off-season, but crowds are usually thinner from mid-January to March and from mid-September until the week before Thanksgiving. The busiest days at all of the theme parks are generally Saturdays and Sundays, when the locals visit. Beyond that, Monday, Thursday, and Saturday are pretty frantic in the Magic Kingdom; Tuesday and Friday are hectic at Epcot; Sunday and Wednesday are crazy at Disney–MGM Studios; and Monday, Tuesday, and Wednesday are a zoo at Animal Kingdom. Major holidays attract throngs: from Christmas to New Year's is a frenzied time.

Note: Summer is the worst time to go, because of the crowds, heat, and humidity.

(*Tips*   **A Note about Smoking**

Disney parks prohibit smoking in shops, attractions, restaurants, ride lines, and other areas. Smokers may light up only in designated areas.

Operating Hours   Park hours vary and are influenced by special events and the economy. So call ahead or go to **www.disneyworld.com** to check. Generally, expect Animal Kingdom to be open from 8 or 9am to 5 or 6pm; Epcot to be open from 10am to 9pm; and Magic Kingdom and Disney–MGM to be open from 9am to 5 or 6pm. All may open or close earlier or later.

Tickets   There are several options, from 1-day to multiday tickets. The best choices are 4- and 5-day passes. Some don't save you money—they may even cost more—but they add the flexibility of moving from park to park and returning on the same or multiple days. The following don't include **6% sales tax** unless noted. *Note:* Price hikes are frequent occurrences, so call (© **407/ 824-4321**) or visit WDW's website (**www.disneyworld.com**) for up-to-the-minute fees.

   1-day/1-park tickets, for admission to the Magic Kingdom, Epcot, Animal Kingdom, or Disney–MGM Studios, are $48 for adults, $38 for children 3 to 9. (Ouch!)

   4-Day Park Hopper Passes provide unlimited admission to the Magic Kingdom, Epcot, Animal Kingdom, and Disney–MGM Studios. Adults pay $192; children 3 to 9 pay $152.

   5-Day Park Hopper Plus Passes also include your choice of two admissions to Typhoon Lagoon, River Country, Blizzard Beach, Pleasure Island, or Disney's Wide World of Sports. They sell for $247 for adults and $197 for children 3 to 9.

   Passes for 6 and 7 days are available, too.

Tips **FASTPASS**

Don't want to stand in line as long as the other guests, yet not flush enough to hire a stand-in? Disney parks use a reservation system whereby you go to the primo rides, feed your theme-park ticket into a small ticket-taker machine, and get an assigned time to return. When you reappear at the appointed time, you get into a short line and climb aboard. Here's the drill:

Hang onto your ticket stub when you enter, and head to the hottest ride on your dance card. If it's a FASTPASS attraction (they're noted in the guide map you get when you enter) and there's a line, feed your stub into the waist-level ticket taker. Retrieve your stub and the FAST-PASS stub that comes with it. Look at the two times stamped on the FASTPASS. Come back during that 1-hour window and you can enter the ride with almost no wait. In the interim, go to another attraction or show.

Note: Early in the day, your window may begin 40 minutes after you feed the FASTPASS machine, but later in the day it may be hours. Initially, Disney allowed you to do this on only one ride at a time, but now you can get a pass for a second attraction 2 hours after your first assigned time.

1-day ticket to Typhoon Lagoon or Blizzard Beach is $29.95 for adults, $24 for children 3 to 11. **1-day ticket to River Country** is $15.95 for adults, $12.50 for children 3 to 11.

1-day ticket to Pleasure Island is $21 including tax. Since this is primarily an 18-and-over entertainment complex, there's no bargain price for children.

If you're staying at a WDW resort, you're eligible for a money-saving **Ultimate Park Hopper,** priced according to the length of your stay.

If you're planning an extended stay or going to visit Walt Disney World more than once during the year, **annual passes** ($349 for adults, $297 for children) are another option.

6 The Magic Kingdom

The Magic Kingdom offers 40 attractions, plus restaurants and shops, in a 107-acre package. Its symbol, Cinderella Castle, forms the hub of a wheel whose spokes reach to **seven "lands."**

MAIN STREET, USA

The gateway to the Kingdom, Main Street is designed to resemble a turn-of-the-20th-century American street (okay, so it leads to a 13th-century European castle). Don't dawdle on Main Street when you enter the park; leave it for the end of the day when you're heading back to your hotel.

Walt Disney World Railroad You can board an authentic 1928 steam-powered train for a 15-minute trip clockwise around the perimeter of the park. It's a good way to save shoe leather *if* you're headed from one of its three stations—the park entrance, Frontierland, and Mickey's Toontown Fair—to another, or if you just want to go for a ride with shorter lines.

Behind the Scenes: Special Disney Tours

Disney parks offer several walking tours and learning programs. Times, descriptions, and prices are subject to change. Program and tour details described here represent the information available at press time. It's best to call ahead (℡ **407/939-8687**), to make reservations or get additional information. Unless otherwise noted, *you must also pay* park admission.

- The **Family Magic Tour** explores the nooks and crannies of the Magic Kingdom in a 2-hour scavenger hunt with character greetings at the end. The cost is $20 for kids 3 to 9 and $25 for adults. You must book in advance. The tour begins daily at 11:30am outside City Hall.
- The **Magic Behind Our Steam Trains** (ages 10 and up) is a fun tour for locomotive buffs. Tours are Monday, Thursday, and Saturday at 7:30am; cost is $30 per person.

The following tours are for those 16 and older:

- The 3-hour **Hidden Treasures of the World Showcase** explores the architectural and entertainment offerings at Epcot. The $59 tours begin at 9:45am on Tuesday and Thursday.
- **Gardens of the World**, a 3-hour tour of the extraordinary landscaping at Epcot, is held Tuesday and Thursday at 9:45am and is led by a Disney horticulturist ($59 per person).
- The 4½-hour **Keys to the Kingdom** tour provides an orientation and look at the high-tech systems at the Magic Kingdom. The cost is $58 (lunch is included). It begins daily at 8:30, 9:30, and 10am.
- At the top of the price chain ($199 per person), **Backstage Magic** is a 7-hour, foot and bus tour through areas of Epcot, the Magic Kingdom, and Disney–MGM Studios that aren't seen by mainstream guests. The tour departs at 9:30am weekdays. It's not for everyone, but if you must know how things work, you might find the investment worthwhile. You'll see WDW mechanics and engineers repairing and building animatronic beings from "It's a Small World" and other attractions. You'll peek over the shoulders of cast members who watch closed-circuit TVs to make sure other visitors are surviving the harrowing rides. And at the Magic Kingdom, you'll venture into tunnels used for work areas as well as corridors for the cast to get from one area to the other without fighting tourist crowds. Park admission isn't required.

ADVENTURELAND

Cross a bridge and stroll through an exotic jungle of foliage, thatched roofs, and totems. Amid dense vines and stands of bamboo, drums are beating and swash-buckling adventures are taking place.

Jungle Cruise   In 10 minutes, you sail through an African veldt in the Congo, an Amazon rain forest, the Nile in Egypt, and several other sets. Dozens of animatronic creatures inhabit the hanging vines, cascading waterfalls, and tropical foliage. On the shore, there's a temple guarded by snakes and a Buddha. Most boat captains keep up an amusing patter.

Magic Carpets of Aladdin ✯   The first major ride added to Adventureland since 1971 delights wee ones and some older kids. Its 16 four-passenger carpets circle a giant genie's bottle while camels spit water at riders. The fiberglass carpets spin and move up, down, forward, and back.

Pirates of the Caribbean ✯   It may be politically incorrect, but these pirates chase "wenches" as your boat passes audio-animatronic figures including "yo-ho-hoing" pirates who raid a Caribbean town. After a lot of looting and boozing, the pirates pass out. This ride might be scary for kids under 5.

FRONTIERLAND

From Adventureland, step into the wild and woolly past of the American frontier. The landscape is straight out of the Wild West, with log cabins and rustic saloons.

Big Thunder Mountain Railroad ✯✯   This low-key roller coaster has tight turns and dark descents rather than sudden, steep drops. It's situated in a 200-foot-high (60m), red-stone mountain with 2,780 feet (834m) of track winding through caves and canyons. Your runaway train careens through the ribs of a dinosaur, under a thundering waterfall, past geysers and bubbling mud pots, and over a bottomless volcanic pool. It's tailor-made for kids and grownups who want a thrill but aren't quite up to tackling the big coasters. *Note:* You must be 40 inches or taller to ride.

Country Bear Jamboree ✯✯   The Jamboree is a hoot. It's a 15-minute show featuring audio-animatronic bears belting out rollicking country tunes and crooning plaintive love songs. Trixie, decked out in a satiny skirt, laments lost love in "Tears Will Be the Chaser for Your Wine." Teddi Barra descends from the ceiling in a swing to perform "Heart We Did All That We Could." Big Al moans "Blood in the Saddle," which makes everyone laugh.

Splash Mountain ✯✯✯   Based on Disney's 1946 film *Song of the South*, Splash Mountain takes you flume-style past 26 colorful scenes that include swamps, bayous, caves, and waterfalls. Riders are caught in the schemes of Brer Fox and Brer Bear as they chase the ever-wily Brer Rabbit. Your hollow-log vehicle twists, turns, and splashes, sometimes plummeting in darkness as the ride leads to a 45°, 52-foot-long (16m), 40 mile-per-hour (64kmph) splashdown in a briar-filled pond. *Note:* You must be at least 40 inches tall to ride.

Tom Sawyer Island   Board Huck Finn's raft for a short ride to this island. Kids love exploring Injun Joe's cave, a windmill, and an old mine. There's also a rickety swing, barrel bridges, and sit-downs for weary parents.

LIBERTY SQUARE

This zone depicts 18th-century America. Thirteen lanterns, symbolizing the colonies, hang from the Liberty Tree, an immense live oak. And you might encounter a fife-and-drum corps on the cobblestone streets.

The Diamond Horseshoe Saloon Revue & Medicine Show   Enjoy Dr. Bill U. Later's turn-of-the-20th-century Wild West revue. Jingles plays honky-tonk and Miss Lucille L'Amour and her dance-hall girls do a spirited cancan—all with lots of humor and audience participation. There are several shows daily.

Hall of Presidents ✯✯   Every American president is represented by a lifelike audio-animatronic figure. If you look closely, you'll see them fidget and whisper. The show begins with a film, then the curtain rises on America's leaders and, as each comes into the spotlight, he nods or waves with presidential dignity.

Lincoln rises and speaks, occasionally referring to his notes. Each president's costume reflects his period's fashion, fabrics, and tailoring techniques.

Haunted Mansion 🎯🎯   Once inside, darkness, spooky music, howling, and screams enhance the ambience. The slow-motion ride has bizarre scenes: a ghostly banquet and ball, a graveyard band, a suit of armor that comes alive, luminous spiders, a talking head in a crystal ball, and weird flying objects. At the end, a ghost joins your car. It's more amusing than terrifying. And though the ride has changed little over the years and may be stale for some, it has long lines and a cult following.

FANTASYLAND

The attractions in this happy land are themed after classics such as *Snow White, Peter Pan,* and *Dumbo.* If your kids are 8 and under, you may want to make this and Mickey's Toontown your primary stops in the Magic Kingdom.

Cinderella Castle 🎯   There's not a lot to do, but its status as the Magic Kingdom's 185-foot (56m) icon makes it a must. The namesake character appears sometimes, and Cinderella's Royal Table restaurant is inside.

Cinderella's Golden Carousel 🎯🎯   This beauty was constructed by Italian carvers in 1917 and refurbished by Disney artists, who added 18 hand-painted scenes from Cinderella on a wooden canopy above the horses. The carousel organ plays Disney classics such as "When You Wish Upon a Star."

Dumbo the Flying Elephant 🎯 *Kids*   Here's a very tame kid's ride, in which the cars that are Dumbo clones go around in a circle, gently rising and dipping. If you can stand the lines, it's very exciting for wee ones.

It's a Small World 🎯   If you don't know the song, you will by the end of the ride. It'll crawl into your mind like a brain-eating mite, playing continually as you sail "around the world." Built for the 1964 New York World's Fair, this transplanted ride takes you to countries inhabited by appropriately costumed animatronic dolls singing, incessantly, "It's a small world after all," in tiny doll-like voices remarkably similar to how yours would sound if you sucked on a helium balloon. Every adult ought to pay his or her dues and ride it at least once.

Legend of the Lion King 🎯   This is a good stage show based on Disney's motion-picture musical and combines animation, movie footage, sophisticated puppetry, and high-tech special effects. Whoopi Goldberg and Cheech Marin are among the actors lending voices to the continuous show. It's a fun and entertaining opportunity to rest your feet.

Mad Tea Party *Overrated*   This is a traditional amusement park ride a la Disney, with an Alice in Wonderland theme. Riders sit in big pastel-hued teacups on saucers that careen around a circular platform while tilting and spinning. This can be a pretty nauseating ride if you spin your steering-like wheel enough.

The Many Adventures of Winnie the Pooh   The Many Adventures of Winnie the Pooh features the cute-and-cuddly little fellow along with pals Eyeore, Piglet, and Tigger. You board a golden honey pot and ride through a storybook version of the Hundred-Acre Woods, keeping an eye out for Heffulumps, Woozles, and Blustery Days.

Peter Pan's Flight   Riding in airborne versions of Captain Hook's ship, riders take a flight over nighttime London to Never-Never Land. There, you encounter mermaids, a ticking crocodile, the Lost Boys, Princess Tiger Lilly, Tinker Bell, Hook, and Smee. It's fun (from a '70s perspective, anyway).

Snow White's Scary Adventures Snow White now appears in pleasant scenes, such as at the wishing well and riding off to live happily ever after. The colors and story line are bright, but it still could be scary for kids under 5.

MICKEY'S TOONTOWN FAIR
Where's Mickey? This 2-acre site is a great place for small children to find him and his cronies. Toontown offers a chance to meet Disney characters, including Mickey, Minnie, Donald, and Goofy. There's also a small collection of cottages and candy-striped tents like those at long-gone county fairs.

The Barnstormer at Goofy's Wiseacre Farm ★★ This mini–roller coaster likely inspired Woody Woodpecker's Nuthouse Coaster at Universal Studios Florida (see later in this chapter). It looks and feels like a crop duster that flies off-course and through Goofy's barn. The ride has very little in the dip-and-drop department, but a bit of zip on the spin-and-spiral front. (It even gets squeals from adults.) The 60-second ride has a 35-inch height minimum.

Donald's Boat (S.S. Miss Daisy) ★ Daisy's ship offers a lot of interactive fun, and the "waters" around it feature fountains of water snakes and other wet fun things that earn squeals of joy (and relief on hot days).

Mickey's & Minnie's Country Houses ★ These separate cottages offer a lot of visual fun and some marginal interactive areas for youngsters. Mickey's place features garden and garage playgrounds. Minnie's lets kids play in her kitchen, where popcorn goes wild in a microwave and the utensils play melodies.

TOMORROWLAND
In 1994, WDW decided Tomorrowland (originally designed in the 1970s) was beginning to look like "Yesteryear," so it was revamped with a more futuristic feel.

Astro Orbiter *Overrated* This ride is like those in kiddie carnivals everywhere: Its "rockets" are on arms attached to "the center of the galaxy" and they move up and down. It's tame and lame. Skip it unless you can breeze right through.

Buzz Lightyear's Space Ranger Spin ★ Join Buzz and try to save the universe while flying your cruiser through a world you'll recognize from the original *Toy Story* movie. Kids enjoy using the dashboard-mounted laser cannons as they spin through the sky (filled with gigantic toys instead of stars). If they're good shots, they can set off sight and sound gags with their lasers.

The ExtraTERRORestrial Alien Encounter ★★★ *Star Wars* director George Lucas earned a tidy payday when he added his space-age vision to this attraction, in which a corporation sells transporter services to Earthlings like you. But things go wrong when it tries to transport its CEO and instead an ugly alien lands in your backyard. This carries a legitimate child warning: It's dark, scary, and confining (a shoulder plate locks you in). Special effects include the alien's breath on your neck and a mist of its slime. *Note:* Minimum height is 44 inches.

Space Mountain ★ This cosmic coaster usually has *long* lines (if you don't use FASTPASS), even though it's years past its prime. Once aboard a rocket, you'll climb and dive through the inky, starlit blackness of outer space. The hairpin turns and plunges make it seem as if you're going at breakneck speed, but your car doesn't go any faster than 28 miles per hour (45kmph). If you like dark or semidark thrill rides, you'll be much happier with Rock 'n' Roller Coaster at Disney–MGM Studios. *Note:* Riders must be at least 44 inches tall.

Tips **Swap Meet**

Many attractions at Walt Disney World offer a Ride-Share program for parents traveling with small children. One parent rides while the other stays with the kids; then the adults switch places without having to stand in line again. Notify a cast member if you wish to participate.

The Timekeeper   At the time this was written, Disney had closed, then reopened on a *very* limited basis this multimedia show. It's hosted by a robot/mad scientist (Robin Williams) and his assistant, 9-EYE, a flying, camera-headed 'droid that moonlights as a time-machine test pilot. In this jet-speed escapade, the audience hears Mozart as a young prodigy playing for French royalty, watches da Vinci work, and floats in a hot-air balloon over Red Square.

Tomorrowland Indy Speedway   Younger kids love this ride, especially if their adult companion lets them drive (without a big person, there's a 52-inch height minimum for driving a lap), but teens and other fast starters hate it. The cars go only 7 miles per hour (11kmph) and are loosely locked into lanes.

Walt Disney's Carousel of Progress *Overrated*   Here's another *now-you-see-it, now-you-don't* attraction open on a very limited basis—*if, by the time this book goes to press, at all.* It was "updated" a few years ago, but it still comes up way short in terms of wow power or keeping abreast of progress. That said, it's one of the few surviving things actually designed by Uncle Walt.

PARADES, FIREWORKS & MORE

For up-to-the-moment information, see the entertainment schedule given in the park guidemap that you get when entering the park.

Fantasy in the Sky Fireworks ✷✷✷   This is one of the most explosive displays in Orlando. Disney has pyrotechnics down to an art form, and this is clearly the best way to end your day in the Magic Kingdom. The fireworks go off nightly during peak periods, but only on selected nights the rest of the year.

Share a Dream Come True Parade ✷   Share a Dream is the Magic Kingdom's parade honoring the 100th anniversary of Uncle Walt's birth. Giant gloves and loads of Disney characters march up Main Street and into Frontierland daily. It's scheduled to be at the park at least through Dec. 31, 2002.

SpectroMagic ✷✷ *Moments*   This after-dark display returned in 2001 for a second engagement at WDW, replacing the **Main Street Electrical Parade.** The 20-minute production combines fiber optics, holographic images, old-fashioned twinkling lights, and a soundtrack featuring classic Disney tunes. The parade runs on a *very limited basis.*

7 Epcot

Epcot is an acronym for Experimental Prototype Community of Tomorrow, and it was Walt Disney's dream for a planned residential community. But, after his death, it opened in 1982 as Central Florida's second theme park.

The 260-acre park has two sections, **Future World** and **World Showcase.** It's so large that hiking World Showcase from tip to tip (1⅓ miles/2km) can be exhausting. That's why some folks say Epcot really stands for "Every Person

Comes Out Tired." Depending on how long you intend to linger at each of the 11 countries in World Showcase, this park can be seen in 1 day, but it's better over 2.

FUTURE WORLD

Future World is centered on Epcot's icon, a giant geosphere known as Spaceship Earth (or that big golf ball). Major corporations sponsor its 10 themed areas, and the focus is on discovery, scientific achievements, and tomorrow's technologies in areas running from energy to undersea exploration. Here are the headliners:

Imagination ☆☆ The fountains are magical—they fire "water snakes" that arch into the air and dare kids to avoid their "bite." The 3-D **Honey I Shrunk the Audience** ☆☆ show shrinks you, then terrorizes you with giant mice, a cat, and a 5-year-old who gives you a sound shaking. **Journey into Your Imagination** ☆ was recently renovated and welcomes back an old park favorite—Figment the dinosaur.

Innoventions ☆ House of Innoventions in **Innoventions East** heralds a smart house equipped with a refrigerator that can make your grocery list; a picture frame that can send photos to other smart frames; and a commode outfitted with a seat warmer, automatic lid opener, and a sprayer and dryer that eliminate the need for toilet paper. The exhibits in **Innoventions West** are led by Video Games of Tomorrow, in which Sega showcases games at nearly three dozen game stations.

The Land ☆ The largest of Future World's pavilions looks at our relationships to food and nature. **Living with the Land** ☆ is a 13-minute boat ride through a rain forest, an African desert, and the windswept American plains. **Circle of Life** ☆☆ blends spectacular live-action footage with animation in a 15-minute, 70mm motion picture based on *The Lion King* that delivers a cautionary environmental message. In **Food Rocks** ☆, audio-animatronic mock rock-performers deliver an entertaining message about nutrition.

The Living Seas ☆ This pavilion's 5.7-million-gallon saltwater aquarium has a coral reef and more than 4,000 sea creatures, such as sharks, barracudas, parrotfish, rays, and dolphins. A 2½-minute multimedia preshow about today's ocean technology is followed by a 7-minute film on the formation of the earth and seas as a means to support life. After the films, you enter "hydolators" for a rapid "descent" to the simulated ocean floor, where you get close-up views through acrylic windows of the denizens in a natural coral-reef habitat.

Spaceship Earth *(Overrated)* This large, silvery geosphere is Epcot's icon, but all that awaits inside is a 15-minute yawn of a show/ride that takes you through the history of communications. *Tip:* Skip it.

Test Track ☆☆ Test Track is a long-time-coming marvel that combines GM engineering and Disney imagineering. The line can be more than an hour long, so consider FASTPASS. The pre-ride area (that's theme-park talk for the last part of the line) has a number of exhibits from GM's proving grounds. Once you're in your six-passenger convertible, the 5-minute ride follows what looks like a real highway and includes a brake test, climb, and tight S-curves. There's also a 12-second burst of speed that reaches 65 miles per hour (105kmph) on the straightaway. *Note:* Riders must be at least 40 inches tall.

Universe of Energy ☆ Sponsored by Exxon, the main event is a 32-minute ride, **Ellen's Energy Adventure,** that features comedian Ellen DeGeneres as an energy expert tutored by Bill Nye the Science Guy to be a "Jeopardy!"

> **Tips Coming Soon**
>
> Epcot is working with Compaq and NASA on a new out-of-this-world attraction called **Mission: Space**. Located in the former Horizons pavilion, its headliner will be a motion simulator like those used by astronauts training for missions. (Think g-force and weightlessness.) The $150 million exhibit, scheduled to open in 2003, will include interactive games and programs about space exploration.

contestant. In the process, you learn about energy resources from the dinosaurs to tomorrow, while Ellen becomes a game-show champ.

Wonders of Life ★★   Housed in a vast geodesic dome fronted by a 75-foot-tall (23m) replica of a DNA strand, this pavilion offers some of Future World's most engaging shows and attractions. The *Making of Me* is a captivating 15-minute motion picture combining live action (starring Martin Short) with animation and spectacular in-utero photography to create the sweetest introduction imaginable to the facts of life. (If your kids are under 10, this show may prompt certain questions about reproduction.) In **Body Wars,** you're reduced to the size of a cell in order to join a medical rescue inside the immune system of a human body. The motion simulator takes you on a wild ride through gale-force winds in the lungs and pounding heart chambers. This one isn't a smart choice for those prone to motion sickness or who generally prefer to be stirred rather than shaken. *Note:* Riders must be at least 40 inches tall. In the hilarious, multimedia **Cranium Command** ★★, you tag along with Buzzy, an audio-animatronic brain-pilot-in-training charged with a seemingly impossible task—controlling the brain of a typical 12-year-old boy. Charles Grodin, Jon Lovitz, Bobcat Goldthwaite, George Wendt, Kevin Nealon, and Dana Carvey play the boy's body parts as he encounters preadolescent traumas such as meeting a girl and having a run-in with the principal.

WORLD SHOWCASE

This community of 11 miniaturized nations surrounds a 40-acre lagoon at the park's south end. All of these "countries" have indigenous architecture, landscaping, restaurants, and shops. The nations' cultural facets are explored in art exhibits, dance or other live performances, and innovative films. The employees in each pavilion are natives of that country. The World Showcase opens at noon daily, so there's time for Future World forays if you arrive earlier.

U.S.A.—The American Adventure ★   Housed in a Georgian-style structure, this 29-minute dramatization of U.S. history uses video, rousing music, and a cast of audio-animatronic figures, including narrators Mark Twain and Ben Franklin. You'll see Jefferson writing the Declaration of Independence, Matthew Brady photographing a family being divided by the Civil War, the stock market crash of 1929, the attack on Pearl Harbor, and the *Eagle* heading for the moon.

Canada ★★   The architecture ranges from a mansard-roofed replica of Ottawa's 19th-century, French-style Château Laurier (here called Hôtel du Canada) to a British-influenced stone building modeled after a famous landmark near Niagara Falls. But the highlight is **O Canada!** ★★, a dazzling, 18-minute, 360° CircleVision film that shows Canada's scenic splendor, from a dog-sled race to the thundering flight of thousands of snow geese.

China ✵   Bounded by a serpentine wall that wanders its perimeter, the China pavilion is entered via a triple-arched ceremonial gate inspired by the Temple of Heaven in Beijing, a summer retreat for Chinese emperors. Passing through the gate, you'll see a half-size replica of this ornately embellished red-and-gold circular temple, built in 1420 during the Ming dynasty. Gardens simulate those in Suzhou, with miniature waterfalls, fragrant lotus ponds, bamboo groves, corkscrew willows, and weeping mulberry trees. **Wonders of China** ✵✵ is a 20-minute, 360° CircleVision film that explores 6,000 years of dynastic and communist rule and the breathtaking diversity of the Chinese landscape. It includes scenes of the Great Wall (begun 24 centuries ago!), a performance by the Beijing Opera, the Forbidden City in Beijing, rice terraces of Hunan Province, the Gobi Desert, and tropical rain forests of Hainan Island.

France ✵   This pavilion focuses on La Belle Epoque, a period from 1870 to 1910 in which French art, literature, and architecture flourished. It's entered via a replica of the Pont des Arts footbridge over the "Seine" and leads to a 1/10-scale model of the Eiffel Tower constructed from Gustave Eiffel's original blueprints. **Impressions de France** ✵✵ is an 18-minute film, shown in a theater à la Fontainebleau, that depicts diverse French landscapes enhanced by the music of French composers on a vast, 200° wraparound screen.

Germany   Enclosed by castle walls and towers, this festive pavilion is centered on a cobblestone square with pots of colorful flowers girding a fountain statue of St. George and the Dragon. The adjacent clock tower has glockenspiel figures that herald each hour with quaint melodies. The pavilion's **Biergarten** features a year-round Oktoberfest. Sixteenth-century facades replicate a merchant's hall in the Black Forest and the town hall in Römerberg Square.

Note: Model-train enthusiasts and kids enjoy the exquisitely detailed miniature version of a small **Bavarian town** ✵, complete with working train station.

Italy   One of the prettiest World Showcase pavilions lures visitors over an arched stone footbridge to a replica of Venice's intricately ornamented pink-and-white Doge's Palace. Other highlights include an 83-foot-tall (25m) bell tower, Venetian bridges, and a central piazza enclosing a version of Bernini's Neptune Fountain.

Japan ✵✵   A flaming red *torii* (gate of honor) leads the way to the Goju No To pagoda, inspired by a shrine built at Nara in A.D. 700. In a traditional Japanese garden, cedars, yews, bamboos, willows, and flowering shrubs frame pebbled footpaths, rustic bridges, waterfalls, rock landscaping, and a pond of koi. The Yakitori House is based on the 16th-century Katsura Imperial Villa in Kyoto, considered the crowning achievement of Japanese architecture. Another highlight is the moated **White Heron Castle,** a replica of the Shirasagi-Jo, a 17th-century fortress overlooking the city of Himeji. The drums of **Matsuriza** ✵✵—one of the best performances in the World Showcase—entertain guests daily.

Mexico ✵   You'll hear marimbas and mariachi bands (including **Mariachi Cobre**) as you approach this festive showcase, fronted by a towering Mayan pyramid modeled on the Aztec temple of Quetzalcoatl (God of Life) and surrounded by dense Yucatán jungle landscaping. Upon entering the pavilion, you'll find yourself in a museum of pre-Colombian art and artifacts. Down a ramp, **El Rio del Tiempo** (River of Time) ✵ offers an 8-minute cruise through Mexico's past and present. Passengers get a close-up look at a Mayan pyramid.

Morocco ⭐⭐ Note the imperfections in the mosaic tile in the Koutoubia Minaret, the prayer tower of a 12th-century mosque in Marrakech. They were put there intentionally in accordance with the belief that only Allah is perfect. The **Medina** (old city), entered via a replica of an arched gateway in Fez, leads to Fez House (a traditional Moroccan home) and the narrow, winding streets of the *souk,* a bustling marketplace where all manner of authentic handcrafted merchandise is on display. The Medina's rectangular courtyard centers on a replica of the ornately tiled Najjarine Fountain in Fez, the setting for musical entertainment.

Treasures of Morocco is a daily, 35-minute guided tour (noon–7pm) that highlights this country's culture, architecture, and history.

Norway ⭐ This pavilion is centered on a picturesque cobblestone courtyard. A *stavekirke* (stave church), styled after the 13th-century Gol Church of Halling-dal, features changing exhibits. A replica of Oslo's 14th-century **Akershus Castle,** next to a cascading woodland waterfall, is the setting for the featured restaurant.

Maelstrom ⭐, a ride in a dragon-headed Viking vessel, traverses fjords before trolls cast a spell on you. The boat crashes through a gorge and spins into the North Sea, where you're hit by a storm (don't worry—this is relatively calm). Then passengers disembark at a 10th-century Viking village to view the 70mm film *Norway,* which documents a thousand years of Norwegian history.

United Kingdom The U.K. pavilion takes you to Merry Olde England through **Britannia Square,** a formal London-style park complete with copper-roofed gazebo bandstand, a stereotypical red phone booth, and a statue of the Bard. Four centuries of architecture are represented along quaint cobblestone streets, complete with a traditional British pub. A formal garden with low box hedges in geometric patterns, flagstone paths, and a stone fountain replicates the landscaping of 16th- and 17th-century palaces.

Don't miss **The British Invasion** ⭐⭐, a group that impersonates the Beatles daily except Sundays, and pub pianist Pam Brody (Tues, Thurs, Fri, and Sun).

IllumiNations ⭐⭐⭐ (Moments) Little has changed since Epcot's millennium version ended January 1, 2001. This grand nightcap continues to be a blend of fireworks, lasers, and fountains in a display that's signature Disney. The show is worth the crowds that flock to the parking lot when it's over. *Tip:* Stake your claim to the best viewing areas a half-hour before show time (listed in your entertainment schedule). The ones near Showcase Plaza have a head start for the exits. The Rose & Crown Pub in the U.K. pavilion, above, offers a great view.

8 Disney–MGM Studios

You'll probably spy the Tower of Terror and the Earful Tower—a water tower outfitted with gigantic mouse ears—before you enter this park, which Disney bills as "the Hollywood that never was and always will be." Once inside, you'll find pulse-quickening rides such as the **Rock 'n' Roller Coaster** and movie- and TV-themed shows such as **Who Wants to Be a Millionaire—Play It!** On Hollywood and Sunset boulevards, Art-Deco movie sets remember the golden age of Hollywood. New York Street is lined with miniature renditions of Gotham's landmarks and typical characters, including peddlers hawking knock-off watches. This 110-acre park has some of the best street performing anywhere.

MAJOR ATTRACTIONS & SHOWS

Disney–MGM Studios Backlot Tour ⊛ This 35-minute tram tour takes you behind the scenes for a look at the vehicles, props, costumes, sets, and special effects used in movies and TV shows. But the real fun begins once you reach **Catastrophe Canyon,** where an earthquake causes canyon walls to rumble. A raging oil fire, massive explosions, torrents of rain, and flash floods threaten you and other riders before you're taken behind the scenes to see how filmmakers use special effects to make such disasters.

Beauty and the Beast Live on Stage ⊛ Producers adapted this 30-minute, live show from the same-name movie. Musical highlights from the show include the rousing "Be Our Guest" opening number and the poignant title song featured in the romantic waltz-scene finale. The sets and costumes are lavish, and the production numbers are pretty spectacular. Arrive early to get a good seat.

Fantasmic! ⭐⭐⭐ *Moments* The show is wonderful, but the fireworks, laser lights, and choreography make it a spectacular, 25-minute, end-of-day experience. Mickey comes to life in this extravaganza featuring shooting stars, fireballs, and animated fountains. The cast has 50 performers, a giant dragon, a king cobra, and one million gallons of water, all of which are orchestrated by a sorcerer mouse that looks more than remotely familiar. Throughout, musical scores and characters from Disney classics entertain you.

The Great Movie Ride Film footage and 50 audio-animatronic replicas of movie stars re-create some of the most famous scenes in films on this 22-minute train ride. You'll see the classic airport farewell scene by Bergman and Bogart in *Casablanca;* Brando bellowing "Stellaaaaa"; and Gene Kelly singin' in the rain.

Hunchback of Notre Dame: A Musical Adventure ⊛ This rollicking stage show brings the animated feature's main characters to life, mainly in costumes but sometimes in puppets. Dozens of performers tell the story of Quasimodo, an orphan banished to a church bell tower. Show up 30 minutes early to ensure a good seat during the summer and holiday seasons.

Indiana Jones Epic Stunt Spectacular ⭐⭐⭐ Peek into the world of movie stunts in this 30-minute show that re-creates major scenes from the Indiana Jones films. The show opens on an elaborate Mayan temple backdrop. Indy crashes the party on a rope and, as he searches with a torch for the golden idol, he encounters several booby traps. The set is dismantled to reveal a colorful market where the action includes a sword fight, bullwhip maneuvers, gunfire, and a truck bursting into flame. An explosive finale takes place in a desert scenario. Theme music and an entertaining narrative enhance the show, which helps explain how elaborate stunts are pulled off. Arrive early and sit near the stage for your shot at being an audience participant. Alas, this is a job for adults only.

Jim Henson's Muppet*Vision 3D ⭐⭐⭐ Kermit and Miss Piggy star in this must-see film that marries Jim Henson's puppets with Disney audio-animatronics,

---

Tips **Front-Row Seat**

Make a priority seating reservation for the Hollywood Brown Derby, Mama Melrose's Ristorante Italiano, or Hollywood & Vine and, when you do, ask for the Fantasmic! package (no extra charge). After dinner you'll get preferred seating at the show.

special-effects, 70mm film, and 3-D technology. The coming-at-you action includes flying Muppets, cream pies, cannonballs, high winds, fiber-optic fireworks, bubble showers, even an actual spray of water. Kermit is the host, Miss Piggy sings "Dream a Little Dream of Me," Statler and Waldorf critique the action (which includes numerous mishaps and disasters) from a balcony, and Nicki Napoleon and his Emperor Penguins (a full Muppet orchestra) provide music from the pit. The 25-minute show runs continuously.

The Magic of Disney Animation   You'll see Disney characters come alive at the stroke of a brush or pencil as you tour glass-walled animation studios. Walter Cronkite and Robin Williams explain what's going on via video monitors and star in an 8-minute Peter Pan–themed film about the basics of animation. It's painstaking work: To produce an 80-minute movie, the animation team must do more than 1 million drawings of characters and scenery! Original cels (paintings or drawings on celluloid sheets) from famous Disney movies and some of the many Oscars won by Disney artists are on display. The 35-minute tour also includes a selection of magical moments from Disney's classic films.

Playhouse Disney—Live on Stage! *(Kids)*   Younger audiences (2–5) love this 20-minute show where they meet characters from *Bear in the Big Blue House, The Book of Pooh,* and others. It encourages preschoolers to dance, sing, and play along with the cast. It happens several times a day. Check your schedule.

Rock 'n' Roller Coaster ★★★ *(Moments)*   Want the best thrill ride WDW has to offer? Then tackle this fast-and-furious coaster. You sit in a 24-passenger "stretch limo" customized with 120 speakers that blare Aerosmith at 32,000 watts as you blast from 0 to 60 miles per hour (97kmph) in 2.8 seconds, then fly into the first gut-tightening inversion at 5Gs. It's a real launch (sometimes of lunch) followed by a wild ride through a make-believe California freeway system in the semidarkness. The ride lasts 3 minutes, 12 seconds, about the running time of Aerosmith's hit "Sweet Emotion." *Note:* Riders must be at least 48 inches tall.

Sounds Dangerous Starring Drew Carey   Drew provides laughs while dual audio technology provides some hair-raising effects during this 12-minute show at ABC Sound Studios. You'll feel like you're right in the middle of the action of a TV pilot that features undercover police work and plenty of amusing mishaps. Even when the picture disappears and the theater is plunged into darkness, you continue on a chase that shows off 3-D sound effects.

Star Tours   Cutting-edge when it opened, this galactic journey based on the original *Star Wars* trilogy (George Lucas collaborated on the ride) is now a couple of rungs below the latest technology but still fun. You board a 40-seat "spacecraft" for an otherworldly journey that greets you with sudden drops, crashes, and oncoming laser blasts as it careens out of control. *Note:* Riders must be at least 40 inches tall.

The Twilight Zone Tower of Terror ★★★ *(Moments)*   Disney continues to finetune this ride into a true stomach-lifter. As legend has it, during a violent storm on Halloween night 1939, lightning struck the Hollywood Tower Hotel, causing an entire wing and an elevator full of people to disappear. And you're about to meet them as you star in a special episode of *The Twilight Zone.* After various spooky adventures, the ride ends in a dramatic climax: a 13-story free-fall in stages. At 199 feet (60m), it's surely the tallest ride in WDW, and it's a grade above Doctor Doom's Fearfall at Islands of Adventure (see later in this chapter). *Note:* You must be at least 40 inches tall to ride.

Voyage of the Little Mermaid ⚝ Hazy lighting creates an underwater effect in a reef-walled theater and helps set the mood for a charming musical show that combines live performers with puppets, film clips, and more. Sebastian sings the movie's theme, "Under the Sea"; Ariel shares her dream of becoming human in "Part of Your World"; and Ursula, the tentacled one, belts out "Poor Unfortunate Soul." The 17-minute show is a great place to rest and sing along.

Who Wants to Be a Millionaire—Play It! ⚝ Contestants can't win $1 million, but they can win points used to buy prizes ranging from collectible pins to a leather jacket or a trip to New York to meet Regis Philbin. Based on Disney-owned ABC TV's game show, the theme-park version features lifelines (such as asking the audience or calling a stranger on two phones set up in the park). Contestants get a shot at up to 15 multiple-choice questions in the climb to the top. Games run continuously in the 600-seat studio. Audience members play along on keypads. The fastest to answer qualifying questions become contestants.

9 Animal Kingdom

Disney's fourth major park combines animals, elaborate landscapes, and a handful of rides to create yet another reason that many guests don't venture outside this World.

Animal Kingdom is a 500-acre park for animals, a conservation venue as much as an attraction. It's easy for most of the animals to escape your eyes here. Busch Gardens (335 acres) has fewer places for hide-and-seek, so it's easier to see them there if you want to make the 3-hour round trip (there's a $5 shuttle service; ✆ **800/221-1339**). Animal Kingdom wins the battle of the shows with **Tarzan Rocks!** and **Festival of the Lion King,** but Busch wins hands-down the battle of thrill rides with five roller coasters.

THE OASIS

With its garden entrance and chirping birds, this painstakingly landscaped point of entry has streams, grottoes, and waterfalls that set the tone for the rest of the park. It's a good place to see wallabies, iguanas, tree kangaroos, otters, and macaws, if you get here early or stay late. But it's mainly a pass-through zone.

SAFARI VILLAGE

Like Cinderella Castle in the Magic Kingdom, the 14-story **Tree of Life** ⚝⚝ is the park's central landmark. WDW artisans built the tree, which has 8,000 limbs, 103,000 leaves, and 325 mammals, reptiles, amphibians, bugs, birds, Mickeys, and dinosaurs in its trunk, limbs, and roots. Teams of artisans worked for a year creating its sculptures, and it's worth a walk around its roots, especially on the way to see "It's Tough to Be a Bug!" (see below).

It's Tough to Be a Bug! ⚝⚝ Once you pass the Tree of Life, grab your 3-D specs and settle into a creepy-crawly seat. This show's special effects are pretty impressive. It's not a good one for very young kids (it's dark and loud) or bug haters, but for others it's a fun, sometimes poignant look at life from a smaller perspective. Near the conclusion, a stinkbug truly awakens your senses.

Discovery Island Trails The trails offer a leisurely stroll through the root system of the Tree of Life and a chance to see real, not-so-rare critters, such as otters, flamingos, tamarins, lemurs, tortoises, ducks, storks, and cockatoos.

Tips   Stay Tuned

Dinoland U.S.A. is scheduled to get a new ride, **Primeval Whirl,** a carnival-style twin roller coaster with spinning, rider-controlled cars. The small coaster should debut in summer 2002.

DINOLAND U.S.A.

Enter by passing under "Olden Gate Bridge," a 40-foot (12m) Brachiosaurus reassembled from fossils. Speaking of which, until late summer 1999, this land had three paleontologists working on the very real skeleton of "Sue," a Tyrannosaurus Rex found in South Dakota. Her new home is at Chicago's Field Museum, but Dinoland has a replica cast from her 67-million-year-old bones.

The Boneyard ✹ *Kids*   Kids love the chance to slip, slither, slide, and slink through this giant playground, where they can discover the real-looking remains of Triceratops, T-rex, and other vanished giants. It's also a great place for parents to take a break from the pavement pounding of a day in the park.

Dinosaur   Formerly called Countdown to Extinction, this ride hurls you through darkness in CTX Rover "time machines" that pass an array of snarling (though somewhat hokey) dinosaurs. Young children may find the dinos and darkness a bit frightening. *Note:* You must be 40 inches or taller to climb aboard.

Tarzan Rocks! ✹   Phil Collins's soundtrack and a cast of 27 very live performers (tumblers, dancers, and in-line skating daredevils) put on quite a show during this 28-minute production. The costumes and music are spectacular, second in Animal Kingdom only to "Festival of the Lion King" (see below).

TriceraTop Spin   This is a mini-thrill for youngsters that will bore adults and teenagers. Cars that look like cartoon dinosaurs are attached to arms that circle a hub while moving up and down and all around.

CAMP MINNIE-MICKEY

Characters and one of the best theme-park shows in town are the main attractions in this small area of Animal Kingdom.

Character Greeting Trails ✹ *Moments*   This is a must-do for people traveling with children. A variety of Disney characters, from Winnie the Pooh and Pocahontas to Timon and Baloo, have separate trails where you can meet and mingle. Mickey, Minnie, Goofy, and Pluto also make appearances.

Festival of the Lion King ✹✹✹ *Finds*   Almost everyone in the audience comes alive when the music starts in this rousing, 28-minute show in Lion King Theater. The festival celebrates nature's diversity, with a talented troupe of singers, dancers, and life-size critters that lead the way to an inspiring sing-along that gets the crowd caught up in the fun. The action is onstage as well as moving around the audience. Make sure to arrive at least 20 minutes early.

AFRICA

Enter through the town of Harambe, a run-down representation of an African coastal village on the edge of the 21st century. A central marketplace is surrounded by structures built of coral stone and thatched with reed by craftspeople from Africa.

Kilimanjaro Safaris ★★★ Animal Kingdom doesn't have many rides, so calling this the best may sound like a qualified endorsement. But the animals make it a winner as long as your timing is right. They're scarce at midday most times of year (in cooler months you may get lucky), so *ride this one as close to the park's opening or closing as you can.* Your vehicle is a very large truck that takes you through a simulated African landscape. These days, you might see black rhinos, hippos, antelopes, crocodiles, wildebeests, zebras, and lions that, if your timing is good, might offer a half-hearted roar toward some gazelles that are safely out of his reach.

Pangani Forest Exploration Trail ★★ *(Moments)* Hippos, tapirs, ever-active mole rats, and some other critters often are on the trail for your viewing, but the real prize is getting a look at the gorillas. One area houses a family including a 500-pound silverback; the other has five bachelors. They're not always cooperative, especially in hot weather when they tend to spend most of the day in shady areas out of view. Those who come early, stay late, are patient, or make return visits can be rewarded with a close look at some special creatures.

Rafiki's Planet Watch *(Overrated)* Board an open-sided train near Pangani Forest Exploration Trail for the trip to the back edge of the park, which has three attractions. **Conservation Station** offers a behind-the-scenes look at how Disney cares for animals. You'll pass nurseries and veterinarian stations. But these facilities need to be staffed to be interesting, and that's not always the case. **Habitat Habit!** is a trail with small animals such as cotton-top tamarins. The **Affection Section's** petting zoo has goats and pot-bellied pigs.

ASIA

Disney's Imagineers did a good job of creating the mythical kingdom of **Anandapur.** The intricately painted artwork out front helps make the lines seem to move a tad faster.

Flights of Wonder *(Overrated)* This bird show is a low-key break from the madness and has a few laughs, but it's not much different from the other bird shows you'll find throughout Florida, except for some new faces.

Kali River Rapids ★★ This is a good raft ride—slightly better, we think, than Congo River Rapids at Busch Gardens in Tampa, but not quite as good as Popeye & Bluto's Bilge-Rat Barges at Islands of Adventure (p. ###). Its churning water mimics real rapids, and some optical illusions will have you wondering if you're about to drop over the falls. You *will* get wet. *Note:* There's a 38-inch height minimum.

Maharajah Jungle Trek ★ With this exhibit, Disney keeps its promise to provide up-close views of animals. If you don't show up in the midday heat, you may see Bengal tigers through the thick glass, while nothing but air divides you from dozens of giant fruit bats (wing spans up to 6 ft./1.75m) in another habitat.

10 Other WDW Attractions

TYPHOON LAGOON ★★★

A storm-stranded fishing boat—the *Miss Tilly*—sits atop 95-foot-high (29m) Mount Mayday and overlooks this Disney water park. Every few minutes the boat blows its stack, shooting a 50-foot (15m) geyser into the air. It has several other attractions.

Castaway Creek's rafts and inner tubes glide along a 2,100-foot-long (630m) river that circles most of the park and includes a rain forest, caves, and grottoes. At **Water Works,** jets of water spew from shipwrecked boats.

Ketchakiddie Creek is for 2- to 5-year-old guests. An innovative water playground, it has bubbling fountains to frolic in, mini–water slides, a pint-sized "white-water" tubing run, spouting whales and squirting seals, rubbery crocodiles to climb on, grottoes to explore, and waterfalls to loll under.

At **Shark Reef,** guests get free equipment and instructions for a 15-minute swim through this very small snorkeling area that includes a simulated reef populated by parrotfish, rays, and small sharks.

Typhoon Lagoon 🏄🏄, the park's 2.75 million–gallon wave pool, launches **big breakers** every 90 seconds. A foghorn warns you when, in case you want to head for cover. Young children can wade in the lagoon's more peaceful tidal pools—**Blustery Bay** or **Whitecap Cove.** There's also a 2½-hour **surfing program** (pre-park opening, Tues and Fri, $125, minimum age 8; © **407/ 939-7529).**

Humunga Kowabunga consists of three 214-foot (64m) Mount Mayday slides that propel you down the mountain on a serpentine route through waterfalls and bat caves and past nautical wreckage before depositing you into a bubbling catch pool. *Note:* You must be 48 inches or taller to ride this. **White-Water Rides** at Mount Mayday is the setting for three white-water rafting adventures—**Keelhaul Falls, Mayday Falls,** and **Gangplank Falls**—all offering steep drops coursing through caves and passing lush scenery.

Typhoon Lagoon is open from 10am to 5pm, with extended hours during holiday periods and summer (© **407/560-4141;** www.disneyworld.com). A 1-day ticket is $29.95 for adults, $24 for children 3 to 9.

BLIZZARD BEACH 🏄🏄🏄

Disney's newest water park is a 66-acre "ski resort" in the midst of a tropical lagoon centering on the 90-foot (27m) Mount Gushmore.

Its 2,900-foot-long (870m) **Cross Country Creek** is a lazy tube run, but watch out for the cave, where you'll get splashed with melting ice. **Runoff Rapids** offers another tube job. This one lets you careen down one of three twisting, turning runs through semidarkness.

Ski-Patrol Training Camp, designed for preteens, features a rope swing, a T-bar hanging over the water, the wet and slippery **Mogul Mania** slide, and an ice-floe walk along slippery floating icebergs.

Snow Stormers has three flumes descending from the top of Mount Gushmore, following a switchback course through slalom-type gates.

Summit Plummet 🏄🏄 is one of the most breath-defying adventures in any water park. Read every speed, motion, vertical-dip, wedgie, and hold-onto-your-breast-plate warning before hopping on. This starts slow, with a lift ride to the 120-foot (36m) summit. But it finishes as the world's fastest body slide—a test

DisneyQuest

The reaction to DisneyQuest's virtual video arcade ★★★ is usually the same, whether it's from kids who are just reaching the video-game age, teens who are firmly hooked, or adults who never outgrew Pong. Almost everyone leaves saying, "Awesome!"

This five-level arcade has everything from nearly old-fashioned pinball to virtual games and rides. Here's a sampling:

- **Aladdin's Magic Carpet Ride** puts you astride a motorcycle-like seat while you fly through the 3-D Cave of Wonders.
- **Invasion: An Extraterrestrial Alien Encounter** finds you trying to save colonists from intergalactic bad guys. One member of your group flies the module as the other three fire an array of weapons at the uglies.
- **Pirates of the Caribbean: Battle for Buccaneer Gold** outfits you and three mates in 3-D helmets so you can battle pirate ships virtual reality–style. One of you plays captain, steering the ship, while the others use cannons to blast the black hearts into oblivion.
- **Songmaker** lets you step into a phone booth–size recording studio to make your own CD (it costs $10 extra to buy it).
- Try the **Mighty Ducks Pinball Slam** if you're a pinball fan. It's an interactive, life-size game in which you ride platforms and use body English to score points.
- If you have an inventive mind, stop in **The Create Zone** ★★, where Bill Nye the Science-Turned-Roller-Coaster Guy helps you create the ultimate loop-and-dipster, which you then can ride in a lifelike simulator.
Note: Heavy crowds after 1pm can cut into your fun time.

DisneyQuest (✆ **407/828-4600;** www.disneyworld.com) is located in Downtown Disney West Side. The admission ($29 for adults, $23 for children 3–9) gives you unlimited play from 11:30am to 11pm.

of your courage and swimsuit—that virtually goes straight down and has you moving sans vehicle at 60 miles per hour (97kmph) into the catch pool. *Note:* It has a 48-inch height minimum.

Teamboat Springs is this World's longest white-water raft ride, twisting down a 1,200-foot (360m) series of rushing waterfalls.

Tike's Peak is a kiddie version of Mount Gushmore. It has short water slides, animals to climb aboard, a snow castle, a squirting ice pond, and a fountain play area for young guests.

Blizzard Beach is open from 10am to 5pm, with extended hours during some holiday periods and summer (✆ **407/560-3400;** www.disneyworld.com). A 1-day ticket is $29.95 for adults, $24 for children 3 to 9.

RIVER COUNTRY

Yes, another (and we promise, the last) water park in Disney. This Fort Wilderness Resort mini park is themed after Tom Sawyer's swimming hole. Kids scramble over boulders that double as diving platforms for a 330,000-gallon pool. Two 16-foot (5m) slides provide access to the pool. Attractions on **Bay Lake,** equipped with ropes and ships' booms for climbing, include two flumes—one 260 feet (78m) long, the other 100 feet (30m)—that corkscrew through Whoop-N-Holler Hollow. **White Water Rapids** carries inner-tubers along a winding, 230-foot-long (69m) creek with a series of chutes and pools, while **The Ol' Wading Pool** is a smaller version of the swimming hole designed for younger children.

River Country is open from 10am to 5pm most of the year (with extended hours during holidays and summer). A 1-day admission to River Country is $15.95 for adults, $12.50 for children (© **407/824-4321;** www.disneyworld. com). *Note:* River Country is usually closed from just after Labor Day until early March. A WDW insider has informed us, however, that Disney is currently mulling plans to close the park permanently, so call before you go to make sure it's open.

Fantasia Gardens & Winter Summerland Miniature Golf ⭐⭐   Hippos, ostriches, and alligators decorate the **Fantasia Gardens** course, where the Sorcerer's Apprentice presides over the final hole. This course is a good bet for beginners and kids. Seasoned mini-golfers probably will prefer the second 18-hole course, **Fantasia Fairways,** which is a scaled-down golf course complete with sand traps, water hazards, tricky putting greens, and holes ranging from 40 to 75 feet (12–23m).

Santa Claus and his elves provide the theme for **Winter Summerland,** which offers two more 18-hole courses. The winter course takes you from an ice castle to the North Pole. The summer course is pure Florida, from sandcastles to surf-boards to a visit with Santa on the "Winternet."

Tickets are $9.76 for adults and $7.78 for kids 3 to 9. Both courses are open from 10am to 10pm daily. For information about Fantasia Gardens, call © **407/ 560-8760.** For information on Winter Summerland, call © **407/560-3000.** Find both on the Internet at **www.disneyworld.com.**

DISNEY'S WIDE WORLD OF SPORTS ⭐

This 200-acre complex has a 7,500-seat baseball stadium, 10 other baseball and softball fields, six basketball courts, a dozen lighted tennis courts, a track-and-field complex, a golf driving range, and six sand volleyball courts.

Organized programs and events include:

- The **NFL Experience.** Ten drills test your running, punting, passing, and receiving skills. You can dodge cardboard defenders and run pass patterns while a machine shoots you passes. Depending on your stamina and the size of the crowds, the experience lasts 45 minutes to several hours. It's included in general admission (see below).
- The **Atlanta Braves** play 18 spring-training games beginning in early March. Tickets cost $11.50 and $19.50. For tickets call © **407/839-3900.**
- The **NFL, NBA, NCAA, PGA,** and **Harlem Globetrotters** also host events, sometimes annually and sometimes more frequently, at the complex. Admission varies by event.

General admission is $8.70 for adults and $6.71 for kids 3 to 9. Disney's Wide World of Sports is open daily, from 10am to 5pm. It's on Victory Way, just north of U.S. 192 (west of I-4). For information, call © **407/828-3267** or 407/939-1500.

RICHARD PETTY DRIVING EXPERIENCE 🏎

Epcot's Test Track is for sissies. Here's the real thing: The Petty team gives you a chance to drive a 600-horsepower, Winston-Cup car. How real is it? Expect to sign a two-page waiver that features words like *dangerous* and *calculated risk* before you climb in. At one end of the spectrum, you can ride shotgun for a couple of laps at 145 miles (233km) per hour ($90). At the other, spend from 3 hours to 2 days learning how to drive this machine yourself and race fellow daredevils in 8 to 30 laps of excitement ($350–$1,200). *Note:* You must be 18 years old to do this. Hours and seasons vary. For reservations, call © **800/237-3889.**

11 What to See & Do Beyond Disney: Universal Orlando, SeaWorld & Other Orlando Attractions

There are so many attractions in Orlando that it's impossible to see half of them unless you're here 14 days or longer. But the following should help you finish picking your A-Team.

UNIVERSAL STUDIOS FLORIDA

Even with fast-paced, grown-up rides such as Twister, Terminator, and Men in Black Alien Attack, Universal Studios Florida is fun for kids. And as a plus, it's a working motion-picture and TV studio, so occasionally there's filming being done at Nickelodeon's sound stages or elsewhere in the park. **Hanna-Barbera characters** such as Yogi Bear, Scooby Doo, and Fred Flintstone usually are on hand to greet visitors, as is a talented group of actors portraying a wide range of characters.

TICKET PRICES   A **1-day ticket** costs $49.95 (plus 6% sales tax) for adults, $40.95 for children 3 to 9. A 2-day, two-park unlimited-access Escape Pass is $94.95 for adults, $81.95 for children 3 to 9; a 3-day, two-park pass is $109.95 for adults, $96.95 for children 3 to 9.

THE FLEXTICKET   The cheapest way to see Universal, SeaWorld, *and* Wet 'n Wild is with one of these passes. With FlexTicket, you pay one price to visit the participating parks during a 14-day period. A four-park pass to Universal Studios Florida, Islands of Adventure, Wet 'n Wild, and SeaWorld is $169.95 for adults and $134.95 for children 3 to 9. A five-park pass, which adds Busch Gardens in Tampa, is $202.95 for adults and $164.95 for kids. The **FlexTicket** can be ordered through Universal (© **407/363-8000;** www.universalorlando. com). FlexTickets can be purchased at any of the participating parks.

PARKING   Parking is $8 for cars, light trucks, and vans. Valet is $14.

MAJOR ATTRACTIONS

Back to the Future: The Ride ★★   Blast through the space-time continuum in a flight simulator built to look like the movie's famous DeLorean car. You'll blaze a trail through volcanic tunnels, collide with glaciers, thunder through caves and canyons, and briefly get swallowed by a dinosaur in a multisensory adventure. You twist, turn, dip, and dive—all the while feeling like you're really flying. This is similar to but *more intense* than Body Wars at Epcot (earlier in this chapter). *Note:* It's bumpy and might not be a good idea if you're prone to dizziness or motion sickness. Riders must be at least 40 inches tall.

Beetlejuice's Rock 'n' Roll Graveyard Revue   Dracula, Wolfman, Frankenstein, and Beetlejuice stage a rock musical with loud and lively pyrotechnic special effects and MTV-style choreography. It carries Universal's PG-13 rating, meaning it may not be suitable for some preteens.

A Day in the Park with Barney *Kids* Set in a parklike theater-in-the-round, this 25-minute musical stars the Purple One, Baby Bop, and BJ. It uses song, dance, and interactive play to deliver an environmental message. This could be the highlight of the day for preschoolers. However, for many adults, it can have serious, brain-eating effects.

Earthquake—The Big One *✸* Not long after you climb on a BART train in San Francisco, there's an earthquake that's 8.3 on the Richter scale! As you sit helplessly trapped, concrete slabs collapse around you, a propane truck bursts into flames, a runaway train hurtles your way, and the station floods.

E.T. Adventure *✸* Soar with E.T. on a mission to save his ailing planet, passing through the forest and into space aboard a bicycle. You'll also meet some new characters that Steven Spielberg created for the ride, including Botanicus, Tickli Moot Moot, Horn Flowers, and Tympani Tremblies.

The Funtastic World of Hanna-Barbera *✸ Kids* This spaceship/motion-simulator offers a surprisingly wild ride as pilot Yogi Bear tries to save Elroy Jetson from Dick Dastardly. Its brain-scrambling motion is similar to Back to the Future (above), although this one's a bit tamer. At press time, it was likely that Universal would close this ride in favor of one based on the movie *Jimmy Neutron: Boy Genius*. *Note:* There's a 40-inch height minimum.

Jaws *✸* As your boat heads into a 7-acre, 5 million-gallon lagoon, a dorsal fin cuts across the surface. Then, what goes with the fin—a 3-ton, 32-foot-long (10m), mechanical great white shark—attacks. The wall of flame that surrounds your boat truly causes you to feel the heat in this $45 million attraction. *Note:* The effects of this ride are more spectacular after dark.

Kongfrontation King Kong is back and everyone must evacuate The Big Apple, so it's all aboard a tram. Police helicopters hover overhead, putting you directly in the line of fire; then the tram malfunctions; and, of course, you encounter Kong—40 feet tall (12m) and 12,000 pounds. He belches banana breath into your face and dangles you over the East River. The big ape executes 46 movements, including simulated noogies on top of your tram. *Note:* Insiders say Kong may soon be replaced by an indoor roller coaster based on the movie *The Scorpion King*.

Men in Black Alien Attack *✸✸✸* Board a six-passenger cruiser, buzz the streets of New York, and use your "zapper" to splatter up to 120 bug-eyed targets. You have to contend with return fire and light, noise, and clouds of liquid nitrogen (aka fog) that can spin you out of control. Your laser tag–style gun fires infrared bullets. The 4-minute ride relies on 360° spins rather than speed for its thrill factor. At the end, a giant roach (30 ft./9m tall with 8-ft./2.5m fangs and 20-ft./6m claws) swallows you. Fortunately, it explodes. Unfortunately, the blast douses you with bug guts (okay, it's only warm water) as you blast your way out. *Note:* Guests must be at least 42 inches tall for this $70 million ride.

Nickelodeon Studios *✸* You'll tour the sound stages where Nick shows are produced. You'll also view concept pilots, visit the kitchen where Gak and green slime are made, and try new Sega video games. This 45-minute behind-the-scenes walking tour is a fun escape from the hustle of the midway. A child volunteer gets slimed, but it's only green applesauce or a reasonable facsimile.

Terminator 2: 3-D Battle Across Time *✸✸✸ Finds* James Cameron, who directed the movie, supervised this $60 million production, which features Arnie and other original cast members (on film). It combines three huge screens with technical effects and live action on stage, including a custom-built Harley and six 8-foot-tall (2.5m) cyberbots. *Note:* The crisp 3-D effects are among the best in any Orlando park, but Universal has given this show a PG-13 rating, too.

Twister . . . Ride It Out ★ Two million cubic feet of air per minute (that's enough to fill four full-size blimps) create an ominous funnel cloud, five stories tall. And the roar of a freight train, at rock-concert level, fills the theater as cars, trucks, and a cow fly by while the audience watches just 20 feet (6m) away. Crowds sometimes applaud when it's all over. *Note:* This show also has a PG-13 rating.

The Wild, Wild, Wild West Stunt Show ★ Actors demonstrate falls, gun and whip fights, dynamite explosions, and other Wild West staples in this 18-minute show that's a real hit with Far East visitors, who are intrigued by America's Wild West. *Warning:* Heed the splash zone or you will get very wet.

Woody Woodpecker's Nuthouse Coaster ★★ *Kids* This kiddie coaster will thrill some moms and dads, too. Although only 30 feet (9m) at its peak, it offers quick, banked turns. The ride lasts only about 60 seconds and waits can be 30 minutes or more, but few kids will want to miss the experience. It's much like The Barnstormer at Goofy's Wiseacre Farm in the Magic Kingdom (p. 542). *Note:* The coaster has a 36-inch height minimum.

ADDITIONAL ATTRACTIONS

The Boneyard is an oft-changing area where you can see props used in a number of Universal movies. **Alfred Hitchcock: The Art of Making Movies** is a tribute to the "master of suspense." At press time, Universal was planning to close this attraction in favor of *Shrek and Donkeys Scary-Tale Adventure*, a 4-D fractured fairytale based on the hit movie *Shrek*. The **Gory, Gruesome & Grotesque Horror Make-up Show** offers behind-the-scenes looks at transformation scenes from such movies as *The Fly* and *The Exorcist* (shows from 11am). **Lucy, A Tribute** is a remembrance of America's queen of comedy, and the **Blues Brothers** launch their foot-stomping revue five times a day.

Back at Woody Woodpecker's KidZone, **Fievel's Playland** is a playground with a house to climb and a water slide for small fry. **Curious George Goes to Town** has water- and ball-shooting cannons, while **Animal Planet Live!** is a 20-minute multimedia show with critters as its stars.

ISLANDS OF ADVENTURE

At 110 acres, Universal's second theme park (opened in 1999) is the same size as its big brother, Universal Studios Florida, but it seems larger. Roller coasters roar above pedestrian walkways and water rides slice through the park. It is, bar none, *the* Orlando theme park for thrill-ride junkies.

A few words of caution: *Nine of the park's 14 major rides have height restrictions.* Dueling Dragons and the Incredible Hulk Coaster, for instance, deny access to anyone under 54 inches. And many of the same rides may not be suitable for those who are tall enough but are pregnant or have health problems, physical restrictions, or a tendency toward motion sickness.

TICKET PRICES A **1-day ticket** costs $49.95 (plus 6% sales tax) for adults, $40.95 for children 3 to 9. A 2-day, two-park unlimited-access Escape Pass is $94.95 for adults, $81.95 for children 3 to 9; a 3-day, two-park pass is $109.95 for adults, $96.95 for children 3 to 9.

THE FLEXTICKET See "The FlexTicket" information earlier in this section, under Universal Studios Florida (p. 560).

PARKING Parking is $8 for cars, light trucks, and vans. Valet is $14.

MAJOR ATTRACTIONS
Port of Entry
This park gateway has five shops, four restaurants, and the **Island Skipper Tours,** which ferries passengers to **Jurassic Park.**

Seuss Landing *(Kids)*
The main attractions here are aimed at youngsters. But anyone who loved the good Doctor as a child will enjoy the nostalgic fun.

The Cat in the Hat *✦✦*   Seuss fans recognize the giant candy-striped hat looming over the entrance to this ride, and probably the chaotic journey. Comparable to, but a lot spunkier than It's a Small World at WDW, The Cat in the Hat puts you in a spinning couch that travels through 18 scenes from the famous book, retelling the tale of a day gone very much awry.

One Fish, Two Fish, Red Fish, Blue Fish *✦*   This kiddie charmer is similar to the Dumbo ride at WDW (including the ridiculously long line). Here, your controls let you move your funky fish up or down 15 feet (4.5m) as you spin around on an arm attached to a hub. Watch out for "squirt posts," which spray unsuspecting riders who don't follow the rhyme (and some who do).

Caro-Seuss-El *✦✦✦ (Moments)*   Forget tradition. Try a not-so-normal carousel that gives you a chance to ride whimsical characters from Dr. Seuss, including Cowfish, elephant birds, and Mulligatawnies.

If I Ran the Zoo *✦✦*   This 19-station interactive play land features flying water snakes and a chance to tickle the toes of a Seussian animal. Kids can also spin wheels, explore caves, fire water cannons, climb, slide, and otherwise burn off excited energy that most adults can't remember ever having.

Marvel Super Hero Island
Thrill junkies love the twisting, turning, stomach-churning rides on this island filled with building-tall murals of Marvel Super Heroes.

The Amazing Adventures of Spider-Man *✦✦✦ (Moments)*   The original web master stars in this very moving ride. Passengers wearing 3-D glasses squeal as their 12-passenger cars twist and spin, plunge, and soar through a comic-book universe. There's a simulated 400-foot (120m) drop that feels an awful lot like the real thing. *Note:* Expectant mothers or those with heart, neck, or back problems shouldn't get on. Those who ride must be at least 40 inches tall.

Doctor Doom's Fearfall *✦*   Look! Up in the sky! It's a bird, it's a plane . . . uh, it's you falling 150 feet (45m), if you're courageous enough to climb aboard. The screams that can be heard far from the ride's entrance add to the anticipation. You're fired to the top, with feet dangling, and dropped in intervals, leaving your stomach at several levels. The fall isn't quite up to the Tower of Terror's at Disney–MGM Studios, but it's still frightful. *Note:* Expectant mothers or those with heart, neck, or back problems shouldn't ride. Minimum height is 52 inches.

Incredible Hulk Coaster *✦✦✦ (Moments)*   Expect a ride that launches you from a dark tunnel and hurtles you into the lower ozone while accelerating from 0 to 40 miles per hour (64kmph) in 2 seconds. While that's only two-thirds the speed of Rock 'n' Roller Coaster at Disney–MGM Studios, the Hulk has more action. You spin upside down 128 feet (38m) from the ground, feel weightless, and careen through the center of the park. Coaster-lovers will be pleased to know this ride, which lasts 2 minutes and 15 seconds, includes seven inversions and two deep drops. The 32-passenger coasters glow green at night (riders who ignore all the warnings occasionally turn green as well). *Note:* Expectant mothers or those with heart, neck, or back problems shouldn't ride. Riders must be at least 54 inches tall.

Storm Force Accelatron   You and the X-Men's super heroine, Storm, try to defeat the evil Magneto by converting human energy into electrical forces. To do that, you need to spin faster and faster. In addition to some upset stomachs, the spiraling creates a thunderstorm of sound and light that gives Storm all the power she needs to blast Magneto into the ever after (or until the next riders arrive). *Note:* This ride is sometimes closed during off-peak periods.

Toon Lagoon
More than 150 life-size cartoon images let you know you've entered an island dedicated to your favorites from the Sunday funnies.

Dudley Do-Right's Ripsaw Falls ★★   Dudley's staid red hat can be deceiving: The ride that lies under it has a lot more speed and drop than onlookers think. Six-passenger logs launch you into a 75-foot (23m) dip at 50 miles per hour (81kmph). You *will* get wet on this ride. *Note:* Once again, expectant mothers or folks with heart, neck, or back problems should go elsewhere. Riders must be 44 inches or taller.

Me Ship, The Olive ★   This three-story boat is family-friendly from bow to stern. Kids can toot whistles, clang bells, or play the organ. Sweet Pea's Playpen is fun for young guests. Adults and kids 6 and up love Cargo Crane, which lets you drench riders on Popeye & Bluto's Bilge-Rat Barges (see below).

Popeye & Bluto's Bilge-Rat Barges ★★★   These rafts are like the ones on Kali River Rapids at WDW's Animal Kingdom (see the "Animal Kingdom" section, earlier in this chapter), but they're faster and bouncier. Adding to the fun, you'll be squirted by water cannons fired from Me Ship, The Olive (above). The rafts bump, churn, and dip 14 feet (4m) at one point, as you travel a *c-c-cold* white-water course. You will get *soaked*! Again, expectant mothers or people with heart, neck, or back problems shouldn't get in line. Riders must be at least 42 inches tall.

Toon Trolley Beach Bash   Beetle Bailey and other favorites from the Sunday comics will have you rockin' and rollin' in the streets as they sing and make you laugh during this several-times-a-day, surfing-safari-and-limbo show.

Jurassic Park
All of the basics and some of the high-tech wizardry from Stephen Spielberg's wildly successful films are incorporated in this lushly landscaped tropical locale that includes a replica of the visitor center from the *Jurassic Park* movie.

Camp Jurassic ★★ *Kids*   This play area has everything from lava pits with dino bones to a rain forest. Watch out for the spitters that lurk in dark caves. The multilevel play area has plenty of places for kids to crawl, explore, and spend energy. But keep an eye on young ones: It's easy to get confused in the caverns.

Jurassic Park Discovery Center ★   Here's an amusing, educational pit stop that offers life-size dinosaur replicas and interactive games. The sequencer lets you combine your DNA with a dinosaur's. "Beasaur" allows you to see and hear as "they" did. The highlight is watching a velociraptor "hatch" in the lab.

Jurassic Park River Adventure ✭✭✭   After you enjoy a leisurely raft tour along a faux river, things get dicey. A T-Rex thinks you look like a tasty morsel, and spitters launch "venom" your way. The only way out: an 85-foot (26m) plunge in your log-style life raft. It's steep and quick enough to lift your fanny out of the seat. (Spielberg designed it, but on a test run insisted on getting out before the drop.) Expect to get wet. *Note:* Expectant mothers or those with heart, neck, or back problems shouldn't ride. Guests must be at least 42 inches tall.

Pteranodon Flyers ✭ *(Kids)*   The ride's metal frames and simple seats are flimsy, the landing is bumpy, and you'll swing from side to side 25 feet (7.5m) up, which makes some riders queasy. Unlike some sky rides, this one lets your feet dangle from the two-seat flyer and there's only a restraining belt between you and the ground. *That said, it's a kids' ride*—single passengers must be between 36 and 56 inches tall; adults can climb aboard only when accompanying someone that size.

Triceratops Discovery Trail   Meet a "living" dinosaur and learn from its "trainers" about the care and feeding of a 24-foot-long (7m), 10-foot-high (3m) Triceratops. It responds to touch, and its movements include realistic blinks, breathing, and flinches. *Note:* This exhibit is at least seasonally closed.

The Lost Continent

Universal has created a foreboding mood in this section of the park, whose entrance is marked by menacing stone griffins.

Dueling Dragons ✭✭✭ *(Moments)*   Designers created two roller coasters that roar at each other. Coaster crazies love the intertwined set of leg-dangling racers that climb to 125 feet (38m), invert five times, and three times come within 12 inches of each other as the dragons test your bravery and bowels. There's a special (longer!) line for the front seat. *Note:* Expectant moms or those with heart, neck, or back problems shouldn't ride. Riders must be at least 54 inches tall.

Eighth Voyage of Sindbad *(Overrated)*   The mythical sailor is the star of a stunt show that includes six water explosions and 50 pyrotechnic effects, including a 10-foot (3m) circle of flames. It's pretty corny and doesn't come close to the Indiana Jones stunt show at Disney–MGM Studios.

The Flying Unicorn ✭✭   The Unicorn is a small roller coaster that travels through a mythical forest. It's like Woody Woodpecker's Nuthouse Coaster at Universal Studios Florida and The Barnstormer at Goofy's Wiseacre Farm in the Magic Kingdom (see earlier in this chapter). That means a fast, corkscrew run sure to earn squeals, but probably not at the risk of losing lunch.

The Mystic Fountain ✭ *(Finds)*   Those who notice it have fun at this "smart" fountain, which especially delights kids. It can "see," "hear," and talk, leading to a lot of kibitzing with those who stand before it and take the time to kibitz back.

Poseidon's Fury ✭   The park's best show (given the lack of competition, that's something of a back-handed compliment) has changed a couple of times, but it still revolves around a battle between the evil Poseidon, god of the sea, and Zeus, king of the gods. Speaking of revolving, you'll pass through a small room that has a 42-foot (13m) vortex where 17,500 gallons of water swirl around you, barrel-roll style, and see the gods hurl fireballs at each other.

SEAWORLD

This 200-acre marine-life park explores the mysteries of the deep by combining conservation awareness with entertainment. The stars of the park are **Shamu,** a killer whale, and his ever-expanding family, which includes baby Orcas.

TICKET PRICES A **1-day ticket** costs $49.95 for ages 10 and over, $40.95 for children 3 to 9, plus 6% sales tax.

THE FLEXTICKET See "The FlexTicket" information earlier in this section, under Universal Studios Florida (p. 560).

PARKING Parking is $7 for cars, light trucks, and vans.

MAJOR ATTRACTIONS

Clyde & Seamore Take Pirate Island 🌟 A lovable sea lion and otter, with a supporting cast of walruses and harbor seals, appear in this fish-breath comedy with a swashbuckling conservation theme. It's corny, but fun.

Intensity Water-Ski Show 🌟🌟🌟 *Moments* This ski show has evolved over more than 15 years. It's a hyper-competition involving some of the most skilled and daring athletes on water. The 20-person team includes world-class skiers, wake-boarders, and stunt men and women performing nonstop aquabatics.

Journey to Atlantis 🌟🌟 Taking a cue from Disney Imagineers, SeaWorld created a story to go with its $30 million water coaster. But what really matters is the drop—a wild plunge from 60 feet (18m) with lugelike curves. *Note:* Riders must be at least 46 inches tall and pregnant women as well as folks with heart, neck, or back problems should find something else to do.

Key West at SeaWorld The big attractions are the hands-on encounters with harmless Southern diamond and cownose rays; Sea Turtle Point, the home of threatened and endangered species; and Dolphin Cove, where you can feed smelt to the namesakes. *Warning:* It's real easy to spend $20 feeding these cute critters.

Key West Dolphin Fest Atlantic bottlenose dolphins perform flips and high jumps, twirl, swim on their backs, and give rides to trainers. The tricks are impressive, but it's like any other dolphin show. If you go, see this before Shamu. He puts these little mammals to shame.

Kraken 🌟🌟🌟 SeaWorld's deepest venture into thrill rides starts slow but ends with speed. Its floor-less, open-sided 32-passenger trains plant you on a pedestal high above the track. You climb 151 feet (45m), fall 144 feet (43m), hit 65 miles per hour (105kmph), go underground three times (spraying bystanders with water), and make seven loops during a 4,177-foot-long (1,253m) course. It may be the longest 3 minutes and 39 seconds of your life. *Note:* Kraken has a 54-inch height minimum.

Manatees: The Last Generation? 🌟 Underwater viewing stations, innovative cinema techniques, and interactive displays combine for a tribute to these gentle marine mammals. While this isn't as good as seeing them in the wild, it's as close as most folks get, and it's a much roomier habitat than the tight quarters their kin have at The Living Seas in Epcot (p. 548).

Penguin Encounter *Overrated* Sadly, this is a very superficial encounter that transports you by moving sidewalk through Arctic and Antarctic displays. You'll get a glimpse of penguins as they preen, socialize, and swim at bullet speed in their 22° habitat. You'll also see puffins and murres in a similar, separate area.

Shamu's Happy Harbor ⭐   This 3-acre play area has a four-story net tower with a 35-foot-high (11m) crow's nest, water cannons, remote-controlled vehicles, nine slides, a submarine, and a water maze. Most kids love it.

The Shamu Adventure ⭐⭐⭐ *(Moments*   Everyone comes to SeaWorld to see the big guy and his friends—the stars of this well-choreographed show. The whales (up to 25 ft./7.5m and 10,000 pounds) really dive into their work. When you hear the warning that Hurricane Shamu is approaching, it's time for those sitting in the first 14 rows to hightail it. Those who don't are drenched with *icy water* as the Orcas race around the pool, creating a huge wave that rolls over the edge and into the audience. Veteran animal handler Jack Hanna also makes a video appearance on the big overhead monitors.

Terrors of the Deep   Remember Shark Encounter? SeaWorld has added other species—220 in all. Pools out front have small sharks and rays (feeding isn't allowed). The interior aquariums have big eels, poisonous lionfish, menacing barracudas, and bug-eyed pufferfish. *Note:* This isn't a tour for the claustrophobic— you walk through a tube, beneath millions of gallons of water.

Wild Arctic ⭐   Enveloping guests in the beauty, exhilaration, and danger of a polar expedition, Wild Arctic combines a high-definition adventure film with flight-simulator technology to display breathtaking Arctic panoramas. After a hazardous flight over the frozen north, visitors emerge into an exhibit where you can see a playful polar bear or two, beautiful beluga whales, and walruses performing aquatic ballets. Kids and those prone to motion sickness may find the ride bumpy. There's a separate line if you want to skip the flight.

ADDITIONAL ATTRACTIONS

Other features at SeaWorld include **Pacific Point Preserve,** a 2½-acre natural setting that duplicates the rocky home of California sea lions and harbor seals. **Tropical Rain Forest,** a bamboo and banyan-tree habitat, is the home of cockatoos and other birds. At the 5½-acre **Anheuser-Busch Hospitality Center,** indulge in free samples of Anheuser-Busch beers and then stroll through the stables to watch the famous Budweiser Clydesdale horses being groomed.

DISCOVERY COVE: A DOLPHIN ENCOUNTER

Anheuser-Busch spent $100 million building SeaWorld's sister park, which debuted in 2000. That's 10 times less than Universal's Islands of Adventure (above), but the admission is as much as four times higher. There are two options: Pay $219 per person ($229 after March 1, 2003) plus 6% sales tax— ages 6 and up—if you want to swim with a dolphin; $119 ($129 after March 1) if you can skip that luxury.

The **dolphin encounter** ⭐⭐⭐ stars an amazing group of 28 of these mammals. They do tricks and take guests on brief but thrilling rides. The experience lasts 90 minutes, 35 to 40 minutes of which is spent in the lagoon with a dolphin. The rest is used as a classroom experience on these remarkable mammals.

Here's what you get for your money, with or without the dolphin encounter:

- A limit of *no more than 1,000 other guests a day.* (The average daily attendance at Disney's Magic Kingdom is 41,000.)
- Lunch (fajitas, salmon, stir fry, pesto chicken pasta, salad, or sandwich), a towel, locker, and snorkeling gear. Souvenir photos are $17 a pop.
- Other 9am-to-5:30pm activities include a chance to swim near (but on the other side of Plexiglas from) **barracudas and black-tip sharks.** There are no

barriers, however, between you and the gentle rays and brightly colored tropical fish in the 1.3 million-gallon coral reef. The 3,300-foot-long (990m) Tropical River is a great place to swim or float in a mild current—it goes through a cave, two waterfalls, and a 100-foot-long (30m), 30-foot-high (9m) aviary where you can take a stroll, becoming a human perch. There also are beaches for tanning.

- Seven days of **unlimited admission** to SeaWorld (park admission normally costs $49.95 a day for adults, $40.95 for children 3–9).

Get more information on Discovery Cove by calling ☎ **877/434-7268** or go to **www.discoverycove.com**. If you want to try it, make a reservation as far in advance as possible. Despite the price, it reaches its capacity almost every day.

12 Other Area Attractions

We've covered the monster parks. Now, we're going to explore some of the best smaller attractions. Many of these require less than a day (or a fortune) to see, so we'll note how much time and money to budget. **Add 6% sales tax** to the prices below unless otherwise noted.

IN KISSIMMEE

Kissimmee's tourist strip is 10 to 15 minutes west of Disney.

Florida Splendid China   Crowds are reasonably small at this 76-acre attraction, partly due to a lack of publicity but mainly because it lacks the pizzazz of the big parks. Highlights include replicas of China's 4,200-mile (6,762km) Great Wall, the Forbidden City's 9,999-room Imperial Palace, and the Mongolian mausoleum of Genghis Khan. The Mysterious Kingdom of the Orient is a 90-minute dance-and-acrobatic show held nightly except Monday in the Golden Peacock Theater. (Separate tickets are $16.) Allow 4 to 5 hours to tour the park.

3000 Splendid China Blvd. (off Irlo Bronson Memorial Hwy./U.S. 192). ☎ **800/244-6226** or 407/396-7111. www.floridasplendidchina.com. Admission $28.88 adults, $18.18 children 5–12 including tax. Daily from 9:30am; closing hr. vary seasonally (call ahead). Free parking. From I-4 take the U.S. 192 west exit and turn left at the Florida Splendid China dragons.

Flying Tigers Warbird Restoration Museum   This is a working restoration facility and museum that allows visitors to see, smell, and touch the history many have only heard or read about. With B-17 Flying Fortress (among many others) restoration projects underway year round, as well as dozens of flyable WWII and vintage airplanes on exhibit and memorabilia and armament displays, you'll like it here if you're a fan of vintage flying machines and their restoration. Admission includes a guided tour. The museum also has a restoration school and available daily flights in an authentic WWII Warbird for an extra charge.

231 N. Hoagland Blvd. (south of U.S. 192). ☎ **407/933-1942.** www.warbirdmuseum.com. Admission $9 adults (plus tax), $8 seniors 60 and over and children 8–12 (plus tax). Free for children 7 and under. Mon–Sat 9am–5:30pm; Sun 9am–5pm. Free parking. Take U.S. 192 east of Disney to Kissimmee, then turn right (south) on Hoagland.

Gatorland ⭐   Founded in 1949 with only a handful of alligators living in huts and pens, Gatorland now houses thousands of alligators and crocodiles on its 70-acre spread. There are three shows. **Gator Wrestlin'** uses the old "put-them-to-sleep" trick, but it's more of an environmental awareness program. **The Gator Jumparoo** is a crowd-pleaser in which one of these big reptiles lunges

4 or 5 feet (1.25–1.5m) out of the water to snatch a dead chicken from a trainer's hand. And **Jungle Crocs** is a showcase of toothy carnivores. Plan to spend 4 to 5 hours here.

14501 S. Orange Blossom Trail (U.S. 441; between Osceola Pkwy. and Hunter's Creek Blvd.). ℂ **800/ 393-5297** or 407/855-5496. www.gatorland.com. Admission $17.93 adults, $8.48 children 3–12 including tax. Open daily at 9am; closing times vary. Free parking. From I-4, take the Osceola Pkwy. exit east to U.S. 17/92/441 and go left/north. Gatorland is 1½ miles (2.5km) on the right.

Water Mania   You can boogie board or body surf in the continuous-wave pools, float lazily along an 850-foot-long (255m) river, enjoy a white-water tube run on **Riptide,** and spiral down the **Twin Tornadoes** water slide. If you dare, ride the **Abyss,** an enclosed tube slide that corkscrews through 380 feet (114m) of darkness, exiting into a splash pool. There's a water playground for kids, a miniature golf course, and a picnic area, too. Allow 4 to 5 hours here.

6073 W. Irlo Bronson Memorial Hwy./U.S. 192 (just east of I-4). ℂ **800/527-3092** or 407/396-2626. www.watermania-florida.com. Admission $17 ages 3–adult. Mar–Oct daily 10am–5pm. Parking $5. From I-4, take U.S. 192 east about ½ mile (.75km).

ON INTERNATIONAL DRIVE

Like Kissimmee attractions, these are a 10- to 15-minute drive from the Disney area and 5 to 10 minutes from Universal Orlando.

Peabody Ducks ℛ *(Moments*   One of the best shows in town is short and sweet, but, more importantly—*free.* The Peabody Orlando's five mallards march into the lobby each morning, accompanied by John Philip Sousa's "King Cotton March" and their own red-coated duck master. They spend the day splashing in a marble fountain. Then, in the afternoon, they march back to the elevator and up to their 4th-floor "penthouse." Donald Duck never had it this good. Allow 1 hour.

9801 International Dr. (between the Bee Line Expwy. and Sand Lake Rd.). ℂ **800/732-2639** or 407/352-4000. Free admission. Daily at 11am and 5pm. Free self-parking; valet parking $8. From I-4, take the Sand Lake Rd./Hwy. 528 exit east to International Dr., then south. Hotel is on the left across from the Convention Center.

Ripley's Believe It or Not! Odditorium *(Overrated*   Do you crave weird science? The oddities here include a two-headed kitten, a three-quarter–scale model of a 1907 Rolls-Royce made of 1 million matchsticks, and a Tibetan flute created from human bones. Allow 2 hours.

8201 International Dr. (1½ blocks south of Sand Lake Rd.). ℂ **800/998-4418** or 407/363-4418. www.ripleys.com/orlando2.htm. Admission $15 adults, $13 seniors, $10 children 4–12. Daily 9am–1am. Free parking. From I-4, exit onto Sand Lake Rd. and then turn right on International Dr.

Titanic—Ship of Dreams *(Overrated*   Didn't get enough with the movie? This exhibit has some 200 artifacts (a deck chair, life jacket, etc.), movie memorabilia, actors, and a replica of the great ship's grand staircase. Allow 1 or 2 hours.

8445 International Dr. (3 blocks south of Sand Lake Rd.). ℂ 407/248-1166. www.titanicshipofdreams.com. Admission $17 adults, $13 children 6–12. Free parking. Daily 10am–9pm. Take I-4 to the Sand Lake Rd./Hwy. 528 exit and turn left on International Dr. and go ¾ mile (1.25km). It's in the Mercado.

Wet 'n Wild ℛℛ   Orlando's favorite non-Disney water park offers 25 acres of fun including: **Fuji Flyer,** a six-story, four-passenger toboggan run through 450 feet (135m) of banked curves; **The Surge,** one of the longest (580 ft./174m of curves) and fastest multipassenger tube rides in the Southeast; and **Black Hole,** a two-person, spaceship-style raft that makes a 500-foot (150m), twisting, turning voyage through darkness (all three require that kids 36–48 inches tall be accompanied by an adult). You also can ride **Raging Rapids,** a simulated white-water run with a waterfall plunge; **Blue Niagara,** a 300-foot-long (90m), six-story loop-and-dipster that also has a plunge (48-inch height min.); **Knee Ski,** a cable-operated knee-boarding course that's open in warm-weather months only (56-inch height min.); and **Mach 5,** a trio of twisting, turning flumes. The park also has a large kids' area with mini-versions of the big rides. Plan on a full day here.

In addition to the admission prices below, Wet 'n Wild is part of the multiday **FlexTicket package** that includes admission to Universal Orlando (which owns this attraction), SeaWorld, and Busch Gardens in Tampa. See "The FlexTicket" information earlier in this section, under Universal Studios Florida (p. 560).

6200 International Dr. (at Universal Blvd.). © **800/992-9453** or 407/351-9453. www.wetnwild.com. Admission $31 adults, $25 children 3–9. Hr. vary seasonally, weather permitting. You can rent tubes ($4), towels ($2), and lockers ($5); all require a $2 deposit. Parking is $6 for cars, light trucks, and vans. From I-4, take the Universal Orlando exit and follow the signs.

ELSEWHERE IN ORLANDO

Orlando has some cultural attractions that are 45 minutes north of Disney.

Harry P. Leu Gardens *Value*   This 50-acre garden offers a respite from themepark razzle-dazzle. Paths lead through camphors, oaks, palms, cicadas, and camellias—the latter represented by one of the world's largest collections, 50 species and 2,000 plants that bloom October through March. There's also an extensive rose garden. Orlando businessman Harry P. Leu, who donated his 49-acre estate to the city in the 1960s, created the gardens. There are free 20-minute tours of his house, built in 1888. It takes about 2 hours to see everything.

1920 N. Forest Ave. (between Nebraska St. and Corrine Dr.). © **407/246-2620.** www.ci.orlando.fl.us/departments/leu_gardens/. Admission $4 adults, $1 children grades K–12. Daily 9am–5pm, later in summer and during holidays; museum tours 10am–3:30pm (closed during July). Free parking. Take I-4 to the Princeton St. exit and go east, then right on Mills Ave. and left on Virginia Dr. Look for the gardens on your left, just after you go around a curve.

Orlando Museum of Art *★*   This local heavyweight handles some of the most prestigious traveling exhibits in the nation. It hosts special exhibits throughout the year, but even if you miss one it's worth a stop to see the rotating permanent collection of 19th- and 20th-century American art, pre-Columbian art dating from 1200 B.C. to A.D. 1500, and African art. Allow 2 to 3 hours.

2416 N. Mills Ave. (in Loch Haven Park). © **407/896-4231.** www.omart.org. Admission $6 adults, $5 seniors and students, $3 children 4–11. Tues–Sat 10am–5pm; Sun noon–5pm. Free parking. Take the I-4 Princeton St. exit east and follow signs to Loch Haven Park.

Orlando Science Center *★★ (Finds*   The four-story center has 10 exhibit halls that explore everything from swamps to the plains of Mars. One of the big attractions is the **Dr. Phillips CineDome,** a 310-seat theater that presents films, planetarium shows, and laser-light displays. **KidsTown** has a pint-size park and construction site. **Science City** includes a power plant, and **123 Math Avenue** uses puzzles and other things to make learning fun. Allow 3 to 4 hours.

777 E. Princeton St. (between Orange and Mills aves., in Loch Haven Park). © **888/672-4386** or 407/514-2000. www.osc.org. Basic admission (exhibits only) $9.50 adults, $8.50 seniors 55 and older, $6.75 children 3–11; additional prices for CineDome film and planetarium show. Tues–Thurs 9am–5pm; Fri–Sat 9am–9pm; Sun noon–5pm. Parking available in a garage across the street for $3.50. Take the I-4 Princeton St. exit east and cross Orange Ave.

A SIDE TRIP TO CYPRESS GARDENS

Cypress Gardens ★★   FDR was in his first term when this foundation tourist attraction opened in 1936. Water-ski shows and flowers are still its bread and butter, but a lot has changed over the years.

At **Carousel Cove,** kids ride ponies and an ornate carousel. **Cypress Junction** is outfitted with a model railroad that travels 1,100 feet (330m) of track with up to 20 trains, visiting miniature places such as New Orleans and Mount Rushmore. You can rise 153 feet (46m) in **Island in the Sky** for a panoramic vista of the gardens and a beautiful chain of Central Florida lakes. And **Do You Know Your Animals?** features a show-and-tell with coatimundis, ring-tailed lemurs, muntjac deer, colorful macaws, and a 15-foot (4.5m) albino python affectionately called Banana Boy.

On the water, the **Greatest American Ski Team** keeps a legendary tradition going strong with standards such as ramp jumping, the aqua-maid ballet line, human pyramid, flag line, and slapstick comedy. Shows change, but they usually combine yesterday with modern magic acts. On the frozen-water front, **Moscow on Ice** presents *Skate the States,* a tribute to some of the U.S.A.'s finest.

Wings of Wonder is a conservatory with 1,000 brilliant butterflies in a Victorian-style, free-flight aviary. The **Birdwalk Aviary** has 40 to 50 hand-raised lories and lorikeets that welcome visitors by landing on their shoulders.

Allow a full day to see Cypress Gardens.

2641 S. Lake Summit Dr. (Hwy. 540 at Cypress Gardens Blvd., 40 miles/64km southwest of Disney World), Winter Haven. ☎ **800/282-2123** or 863/324-2111. www.cypressgardens.com. Admission $35 (plus 6% tax) adults, $20 children 6–17. Parking $6. Daily 9:30am–5pm, later during some periods. Take I-4 west to U.S. 27 south, and proceed west to Hwy. 540.

WINTER PARK

This is a great half-day stop. In addition to the two attractions described below, you can browse through the posh boutiques that line Park Avenue.

Audubon of Florida—National Center for Birds of Prey ★ *Finds*   In addition to being a rehabilitation center—one of the biggest and most successful in the Southeast—this is a great place to get to know rehabilitated winged wonders that roost here and earn their keep by entertaining the relatively few visitors who come. You can get a close look at hams like Elvis, the blue suede shoe–wearing American kestrel; Daisy, the polka-dancing barn owl; and Trouble, an eagle born with a misaligned beak. *Note:* The center reopened in spring 2002 after a $2 million, 4-year expansion. Allow 2 hours.

1101 Audubon Way, Maitland. ☎ **407/644-0190.** www.adoptabird.org. Recommended donation $5 adults, $4 children 3–12. Tues–Sun 10am–4pm. From Orlando, go north on I-4 to Lee Rd., turn right/east, and at the first light (Wymore Rd.) go left, then right/east at the next light (Kennedy Blvd.). Continue ½ mile (.75km) to East Ave., turn left, and go to the stop sign at Audubon Way. Turn left, and the center is on the right.

Charles Hosmer Morse Museum of American Art ★ *Value*   Louis Comfort Tiffany left a fingerprint on this museum, which has 40 vibrantly colored windows and 21 paintings of his. There are also non-Tiffany windows by Frank Lloyd Wright, paintings by John Singer Sargent and Maxfield Parrish, and photographs by Tiffany and other 19th-century artists. Allow 2 hours.

445 Park Ave. N. ☎ **407/645-5311.** www.inusa.com/tour/fl/orlando/morse.htm. Admission $3 adults, $1 children 12–17. Tues–Sat 9:30am–4pm; Sun 1–4pm. Take I-4 to Fairbanks Ave. and exit east to Park Ave., and go left for 4 traffic lights.

13 Staying Active

SPORTS ACTIVITIES

Disney and the surrounding areas have plenty of recreational options. The following are open to everyone, no matter where you're staying.

BICYCLING

Bike rentals (singles, multi-speeds, tandems, and bikes with training wheels or baby seats) are available from the **Bike Barn** (© 407/824-2742) at Fort Wilderness Resort and Campground. Rates are $7.54 per hour, $20.75 per day. Fort Wilderness offers good bike trails.

BOATING

With a ton of man-made waterways, WDW owns a navy of pleasure boats. **Capt. Jack's** at Downtown Disney rents Water Sprites, canopy boats, and 20-foot (6m) pontoon boats ($22–$35 per half hour). For information, call © 407/828-2204.

FISHING

Disney has a variety of fishing excursions, but true anglers won't find them a challenge. The excursions can be arranged 2 to 90 days in advance by calling © 407/824-2621. The cost is $160 to $185 for up to five people for 2 hours. Bait is extra. Outside Disney, **A Pro Bass Guide Service** offers guided trips along some of central Florida's most picturesque rivers and lakes. Hotel pickup is available (© 800/771-9676 or 407/877-9676; www.probassguideservice. com). The cost is $225 for two people per half day, $325 for a full day.

GOLF

Disney operates five 18-hole, par-72 golf courses and one 9-hole, par-36 walking course. The rates are $105 to $170 per 18-hole round for resort guests ($5 more if you're not staying at a WDW property). For tee times and information, call © 407/824-2270 up to 7 days in advance (up to 30 days for guests of the Disney resort and official properties). Call © 407/934-7639 about golf packages.

Beyond Mickey's shadow, **Golfpac** (© 800/327-0878 or 407/260-2288; www.golfpacinc.com) is an organization that packages golf with accommodations and arranges tee times at more than 40 Orlando-area courses. **Tee Times USA** (© 800/465-3356; www.teetimesusa.com) and **Florida Golfing** (© 866/833-2663; www.floridagolfing.com) are two others offering package information and course reservations.

HAY RIDES

Wagons depart **Pioneer Hall** at Disney's Fort Wilderness at 7 and 9:30pm for 45-minute old-fashioned hay rides with singing, jokes, and games. The cost is $8 for adults, $4 for children ages 3 to 10. An adult must accompany children under 12. No reservations; it's first-come, first-served. Call © 407/824-2832.

HORSEBACK RIDING

Disney's Fort Wilderness offers 45-minute guided trail rides daily. The cost is $30.19 per person. Children must be at least 9. Maximum weight limit is 250 pounds. For information, call © 407/824-2832.

The **Villas of Grand Cypress' Equestrian Center** offers 45-minute walk-trot trail rides for $45. A 30-minute private lesson is $55; an hour lesson is $100. Call © 407/239-4700 and ask for the equestrian center.

SWIMMING

The **YMCA Aquatic Center** has a full fitness center, racquetball courts, and an indoor Olympic-size pool. Admission is $10 per person, $25 for families. It's at 8422 International Dr. For information, call © **407/363-1911.**

TENNIS

There are 22 lighted tennis courts throughout Disney properties. Most are free. If you're willing to pay, courts can be reserved at Disney's **Contemporary** and **Grand Floridian** resorts by calling © **407/824-2270.** Both charge $18 per hour. Lessons are also available.

SPECTATOR SPORTS

Central Florida has a number of venues for inactive sportsters.

ARENA FOOTBALL

The **Orlando Predators** play from April to August. Game tickets ($7.50–$40) are often available the day of the game at the **TD Waterhouse Centre,** 600 W. Amelia St., between I-4 and Parramore Avenue (© **407/447-7337**).

BASEBALL

The **Atlanta Braves** play 18 spring-training games at Disney's Wide World of Sports beginning in early March. Tickets are $11.50 to $19.50. Call © **407/839-3900** for more information. From April to September, the **Orlando Rays,** the Tampa Bay Devil Rays' Class AA Southern League affiliate, play their 70 home games at the same complex. Tickets through **Ticketmaster** (© **407/839-3900**) sell for $5 to $8.

BASKETBALL

The **TD Waterhouse Centre,** 600 W. Amelia St., between I-4 and Parramore Avenue, is the home of the **Orlando Magic,** which plays 41 of its games here from October to April. Call © **407/896-2442** or check out **www.nba.com/magic.** Single-game tickets are $25 to $175. On the women's side, the WNBA's **Orlando Miracle** has a 16-game home stand beginning in early June on the same court. Tickets are $8 to $34. Call © **407/916-9622** or surf over to **www.wnba.com/miracle/.**

14 Shopping

Some of us get as much pleasure from shopping as a good meal or show. But if you're going to ring registers in the theme parks, expect to pay top dollar. So plan a day out of the parks and be as savvy here as you are back home.

On International Drive, look for **Pointe Orlando,** a complex with three dozen stores including FAO Schwarz and Banana Republic (© **407/248-2838**). Also on International Drive, **Festival Bay** (© **407/345-1311**) has a 20-screen theater, Bass Pro Shop, skateboard park, and several restaurants.

There are several factory outlets, but their publicized discounts of 25% to 75% are often a mirage. You can avoid being taken by knowing suggested retail prices, so you can decide whether you're making a killing. **Belz Factory Outlet World,** 5401 W. Oak Ridge Rd. (at the north end of International Dr.; © **407/354-0126;** www.belz.com), and **Orlando Premium Outlets,** 8200 Vineland Ave. (© **407/238-7787;** www.PremiumOutlets.com), are two of the better ones.

Florida Mall, 8001 S. Orange Blossom Trail (© **407/851-6255;** www.shopsimon.com), which offers Saks, Dillards, and 200 more stores; and **Mall at**

Value **A Disney Bargain?**

Little-known, surplus-property auctions are the best bargain in Disney. In addition to castoffs from the parks and resorts, routine items are available, from well-worn lawn mowers to never-used stainless-steel pots. If you're looking for a unique piece of Disney, the auctions are held four to six times a year—always on a Thursday, when Disney workers get paid. You might even run into furniture from Miss Piggy's dressing room. Call ② **407/824-6878** for information, dates, and directions.

Millennia, scheduled to open in October 2002 near Universal Orlando (Bloomingdale's, Macy's, Neiman Marcus, Tiffany's) are the best of the malls.

Old-stuff buffs love **Antique Row** on Orange Avenue in downtown Orlando. This collection of two dozen shops is about as far away as you can get from the manufactured fun of Disney. Headliners include **Flo's Attic** (② **407/895-1800**), which sells traditional antiques. **Wildlife Gallery** (② **407/898-4544**) has pricey, original works of wildlife art, including sculptures. And the **Fly Fisherman** (② **407/898-1989**) sells—no surprise here—fly-fishing gear. Sometimes, you can spot people taking casting lessons in the park across the street.

15 Walt Disney World & Orlando After Dark

Central Florida has plenty for night owls to do. Parties last into the wee hours at **Pleasure Island, Downtown Disney, CityWalk,** and other hot spots.

DISNEY DINNER SHOWS

Hoop-Dee-Doo Musical Revue ★ *Moments*   As WDW's most popular show, Hoop-Dee-Doo requires priority-seating reservations as early as possible. The reward: You can feast on an all-you-can-eat barbecue (fried chicken, smoked ribs, salad, corn on the cob, baked beans, freshly baked bread, strawberry shortcake, and coffee, tea, beer, sangria, or soda). While you stuff yourself silly, performers in 1890s garb lead you in a foot-stomping, hand-clapping high-energy show that includes jokes you haven't heard since second grade.

3520 N. Fort Wilderness Trail (at WDW's Fort Wilderness Resort and Campground). ② **407/939-3463.** www.disneyworld.com. Reservations required. Adults $47.80, kids 3–11 $24.81, including tax and gratuity. Free parking. Show times 5, 7:15, and 9:30pm daily.

Polynesian Luau Dinner Show ★ *Moments*   Almost as popular as the Hoop-Dee-Doo, the luau presents a delightful 2-hour show that's a favorite among kids. They're invited on stage as part of an evening that includes hyperactive entertainers from New Zealand, Hawaii, and Tahiti, who perform hula, warrior, ceremonial, and fire dances on a flower-filled stage. Arrive early for a preshow featuring crafts (lei making, hula lessons, and more). The all-you-can-eat meal includes island fruits, roasted chicken and pork, fried rice, vegetables, potatoes, tropical ice-cream sundaes, coffee, tea, beer, wine, and soda.

1600 Seven Seas Dr. (at Disney's Polynesian Resort). ② **407/939-3463.** www.disneyworld.com. Reservations required. Adults $47.80, kids 3–11 $24.81, including tax and gratuity. Free parking. Show times 5:15 and 8pm Tues–Sat.

MORE DINNER SHOWS

These shows won't win any culinary awards (the food is frequently overcooked), but the entertainment is tons of fun.

Arabian Nights   If you're a horse fancier, this show is a must. It stars Arabians and other breeds. Most nights, it begins with a ground trainer working one-on-one with a black stallion and progresses to Wild-West trick riders, chariot races, a little slapstick comedy, and bareback daredevils. Dinner includes prime rib, vegetables, potatoes, salad, and dessert.

6225 W. Irlo Bronson Memorial Hwy. (U.S. 192), Kissimmee. ✆ **800/553-6116** or 407/239-9223. www.arabian-nights.com. Reservations recommended. Adults $42, children 3–11 $26. Shows daily at 7:30pm. Free parking.

Medieval Times   Guests pig out on barbecued ribs, roast chicken, soup, appetizer, potatoes, dessert, and beverage. But because this is the 11th century, you eat with your fingers from metal plates while mounted knights run around the arena, jousting and clanging to please the fair ladies. Arrive 90 minutes early and see the Medieval Village, a re-created Middle Ages settlement.

4510 W. Irlo Bronson Memorial Hwy. (U.S. 192), Kissimmee. ✆ **800/229-8300** or 407/396-1518. www.medievaltimes.com. Reservations recommended. Adults $42, children 3–11 $26. The shows usually are at 8 or 8:30pm, but sometimes there's an earlier one. Free parking.

ENTERTAINMENT MECCAS
AT DISNEY

PLEASURE ISLAND   This 6-acre complex has nightclubs, restaurants, shops, and movie theaters where during the day you can enjoy for free whatever's open. At night, for a single admission price ($21 including tax; ✆ **407/ 934-7781**), you can go club hopping and rock into the wee hours every night of the week. The mood is festive, especially at midnight, when the New Year's Eve party gets started. *Note:* At night, this is primarily an adult venue. Here's the lineup:

Adventurers Club   The most unique of Pleasure Island's clubs, Adventurers occupies a multistory building chock-full of artifacts like 1940s aviation photos, hunting trophies, shrunken heads, Buddhas, and a mounted "yakoose"—a half yak, half moose that occasionally speaks, whether you've been drinking or not. In the Mask Room, the 100 or so masks move their eyes, jeer, and make bizarre pronouncements. Improv comedy takes place throughout the evening in the salon. We could easily hang out here all night, sipping potent tropical drinks in the library or the bar, where elephant-foot bar stools rise and sink mysteriously.

BET Soundstage ✪   This club grooves with traditional R&B and the rhyme of hip-hop. If you like the BET Cable Network, you'll love it. Boogie on an expansive dance floor or kick back on the terrace. The club sometimes has concerts for a separate charge. Call ✆ **407/934-7666.**

Mannequins Dance Palace ✪✪   Housed in a vast dance hall with a small-town movie-house facade, Mannequins is supposed to be a converted mannequin warehouse (remember, you're still in Disney World). This high-energy club has a big, rotating dance floor, and its popularity makes it one of the toughest nightspots to get into. It offers three levels of bars and hangout space that are festooned with elaborately costumed mannequins and moving scenery suspended from the overhead rigging. A deejay plays contemporary tunes filtered

---

Moments **Not Your Ordinary Circus**

Cirque du Soleil, the famous no-animals circus, is located in Downtown Disney West Side. At times, it seems as if all 64 performers are onstage simultaneously, especially during the intricately choreographed trampoline routine. Trapeze artists, high-wire walkers, an airborne gymnast, a posing strongman, mimes, and two zany clowns cement a show called **La Nouba** ★★★ (it means "live it up") into a five-star performance.

But, in a world of pricey attractions, this is one of the pricier. The 90-minute show costs $67 for adults and $39 for children 3 to 9 (plus 6% tax). Shows are at 6 and 9pm, Wednesday through Sunday, though times and days rotate and there's sometimes a matinee. Call ✆ **407/939-7600** or check out **www.cirquedusoleil.com** for details.

---

through speakers that could wake the dead, and there are high-tech lighting effects. You must be 21 to get in, and they're *very* serious about it.

The Pleasure Island Jazz Company   This big, barnlike club features contemporary and traditional live jazz. Most performers are locals, but about once a month there's a big name, such as Kenny Rankin or Maynard Ferguson.

Rock 'n' Roll Beach Club   Live bands play classic rock from the 1960s through the 1990s. There are bars on all three floors. The first level has a dance floor; the others offer arcade-style games, pizza, and more.

Motion   Pleasure Island's newest dance club features Top-40 tunes and alternative rock. This club replaced the Wildhorse Saloon.

DOWNTOWN DISNEY WEST SIDE

Bongo's Cuban Café. *(Overrated*   Created by Cuban-American singer Gloria Estefan and her husband, Emilio, the cafe is Disney's version of old Havana. There are mosaic bar stools shaped like bongo drums, and a Desi Arnaz look-alike might show up to sing a few tunes. There's no dance floor to speak of, but you could cha-cha on an upstairs patio that overlooks the rest of West Side. It's a great place to sit back and enjoy the view while basking in the Latin rhythms. But the food is lacking. Downtown Disney West Side. ✆ 407/828-0999. www.bongoscubancafe.com. No reservations. No cover charge. Daily 11am–2am. Free parking.

House of Blues   Past performers have included Jethro Tull, Quiet Riot, Duran Duran, and others. The three-tier, barnlike building may be a little difficult for those with disabilities to maneuver in, but there really isn't a bad seat in the house. The atmosphere is dark, perfect for the oft-featured bluesy sounds that raise the rafters. The dance floor is big enough to boogie without doing the bump with a stranger. You can dine in the adjoining restaurant ($9–$24) on baby-back ribs, blackened chicken, jambalaya, Orleans-style shrimp, and Cajun meatloaf. There's also a Sunday gospel brunch. Downtown Disney West Side. ✆ 407/934-2583. www.hob.com. Cover charges vary by event/artist. Free parking.

CITYWALK

Located between Islands of Adventure and Universal Studios Florida, this 30-acre club-and-restaurant district (✆ 407/363-8000; www.citywalk.com) is five times larger than Pleasure Island. Alcohol is prominently featured, so an adult should accompany all children and free-flowing peers.

You can walk the district for free or visit individual clubs for the cover charges in the following listings. CityWalk also offers two **party passes.** A pass to all clubs costs $7.95 plus tax. For $11.95 plus tax, you can add a movie at Universal Cineplex (✆ **407/354-5998**) to the basic club access. *Note:* Daytime parking in the Universal Orlando garages costs $7, but parking is free after 6pm.

Bob Marley—A Tribute to Freedom This hybrid bar/restaurant has a party atmosphere that makes the food more appealing as the night wears on. The clapboard building is said to be a replica of Marley's home in Kingston. Jamaican food—meat patties, jerk red snapper, and, of course, the brew of champions, Red Stripe—is served amid portraits of the original Rastamon. If you try an Extreme Measure, have a designated driver. Reggae bands, local and national, perform on a microdot-sized stage. ✆ 407/224-2262. Cover charge $4.25 after 8pm, more on special nights. Sun–Fri 4pm–2am; Sat 2pm–2am.

CityJazz The cover includes the **Downbeat Jazz Hall of Fame** (which has memorabilia from Louie Armstrong and other greats) as well as the **Thelonious Monk Institute of Jazz,** a performance venue that's also the site of jazz workshops. The two-story, 10,500-square-foot building has more than 500 pieces of memorabilia representing Dixieland, swing, bebop, and jazz. On the food, look for tapas, sushi, and more. ✆ 407/224-2189. Cover charge $3.25 (more for special events). Sun–Thurs 8:30pm–1am; Fri–Sat 8:30pm–2am.

the groove This club is Universal's answer to Mannequins at Pleasure Island, though it's not as popular and, therefore, has less of a waiting list. There's a high-tech sound system that will blow your hair back and a spacious dance floor in a room gleaming with chrome. A deejay plays tunes most nights, featuring the latest in hip-hop, jazz-fusion, techno, and alternative music. Bands occasionally play the house, too. The decor touches five entertainment eras, reaching from vaudeville to the millennium. Each area has a unique design, bar, and specialty drink to fit its ambience. ✆ 407/363-8000. Cover charge $5.25. Must be 21 to get in. Sun–Wed 9pm–2am; Thurs–Sat 9pm–3am.

Hard Rock Cafe/Hard Rock Live The cafe side is the chain's standard—a theme restaurant with memorabilia and other tributes to rock's greats. The difference is that this one has the first concert hall with the Hard Rock name on the door. Call ahead to find out what acts are featured. Tickets for big-name performers sell fast. ✆ 407/351-7625; www.hardrock.com. No cover in the cafe; concerts range from $6–$150. Cafe daily 11am–midnight.

Jimmy Buffett's Margaritaville Music from the maestro drifts through the building, and live tunes are performed on a small stage inside later in the evening. A Buffett sound-alike also strums on the back porch. Inside, there are three themed bars: The Volcano erupts margarita mix; the Land Shark has fins hanging from the ceiling; and the 12 Volt, is, well, a little electrifying—we'll leave it at that. If you opt for dinner among the palm trees, go for the true Key West experience. Early in the day that means a cheeseburger (in paradise, of course); later, it's one of several kinds of fish (pompano, sea bass, dolphin). ✆ 407/224-2155. Cover $4.75 after 10pm. Daily 11:30am–2am.

Latin Quarter This two-level restaurant/nightclub offers you a chance to absorb the salsa-and-samba culture and cuisine of 21 Latin nations. If you don't know how to move your hips, there's a dance instructor to lend a hand. The music ranges from merengue to Latin rock. The sound system is loud enough to blow you into the next county, but before that happens you can leave on your own to peruse a Latin American art gallery. © **407/363-5922.** Cover charge $5–$10 Thurs–Sat after 10pm. 11am–2am.

Motown Cafe Orlando   Try finger food and sandwiches ($8–$15.50), or just enjoy the canned music of Motown greats like Smokey Robinson and the Supremes. A live band frequently plays. © **407/363-8000.** www.motown.com. Cover charge $5.25 after 9pm Mon–Thurs, after 10pm Fri–Sat. Sun–Thurs 11:30am–11pm; Fri–Sat 11am–2am.

Pat O'Brien's *Overrated*   Just like the French Quarter, which is home to the original Patty O's, drinking, drinking, and more drinking are the highlights here. Enjoy dueling Baby Grands and a flame-throwing fountain while you suck down the drink of the Big Easy, a Hurricane. There's a limited menu of sandwiches and treats like jambalaya and shrimp Creole ($6–$12). © **407/363-8000.** Cover charge $2.25 after 9pm. Daily 4pm–2am.

HOT SPOTS IN DOWNTOWN ORLANDO

There are dozens of clubs and restaurants along Orange Avenue, the main street in downtown Orlando. A free bus called **Lymmo** runs in a designated lane that connects many of the nighttime spots, but Lymmo stops running about 11pm.

Cairo   One of the newer arrivals downtown, this popular dance club has bars on three levels, lots of 1970s retro clothes and kids trying to look older than their age. Reggae arrives on weekends. 22 S. Magnolia Ave. (1 block off Orange Ave.), Orlando. © **407/422-3595.** www.cairo-nightclub.com. Cover charge $5–$10. Fri–Sun 10pm–3am. Free street parking.

Cricketers Arms Pub   Regardless of whether you're British or just a fun lover, this pub is a place to party. As the name implies, cricket (as well as soccer) matches are shown on the telly. Live blues and soft-rock bands are featured, too, mainly on weekends. The revelry offers a good excuse to try a pint or two of any of 17 imports. The menu offers steak-and-ale pie and bangers and mash, among others ($6–$12). 8445 International Dr. © **407/354-0686.** No cover for music; $10 for soccer. Daily 11am–2am. Free parking.

8 Seconds ★ *Finds*   Sure, there's a bar and dance floor inside, but what's outside really sets this place apart. A rodeo pen next to the parking lot features "Buckin' Bull Nights" with live bull riding. Rising country stars occasionally hold concerts here. 100 W. Livingston Ave. © **407/839-4800** or 407/843-5775. Cover charge $5 for 21 and older; $7 for 18–21. Fri–Sat 8pm–2am. Parking in city lot $3.

Howl at the Moon Saloon   Your best bet is to hit this joint on a full moon—even if you're too shy to cock your head back and *howllll* with the best of them when the club's dueling pianos march through classic rock tunes from the 1950s to the 1990s. 55 W. Church St. © **407/841-9118.** www.howlatthemoon.com. Cover charge Wed–Sat $2–$4. Daily 6pm–2am. Metered-lot parking runs about $1 an hour.

Sak Comedy Lab   Locals perform at this 200-seat club that has 8 to 10 performances weekly (usually Tues, Thurs, and Sat). Favorites include the Duel of Fools, where two teams face off in improvised scenes based on suggestions from the audience, and Lab Rats, where students play in improv formats. 380 W. Amelia St. © **407/648-0001.** www.sak.com. Admission $5–$13. Shows usually at 8 and 10pm, plus midnight Sat. Parking $5.

Northeast Florida

by Bill Goodwin

Northeast Florida traces its history to 1513, when the Spaniard Juan Ponce de León, who later undertook a quixotic quest for the Fountain of Youth, sighted this coast and landed somewhere between present-day Jacksonville and Cape Canaveral. Observing that the land was "very pretty to behold with many refreshing trees," he named it La Florida, or "the flowery land." In 1565 the Spanish established a colony at St. Augustine, making it the country's oldest permanent settlement.

If those early colonists were to come back to life, they would feel right at home in St. Augustine, where the streets of the restored Old City look much as they did in Spanish times. But they would surely be astonished at what they would see elsewhere in Northeast Florida.

To the south, their eyes would pop open with disbelief at today's "Space Coast," where rockets blast off from the Kennedy Space Center at Cape Canaveral. Nearby in Cocoa Beach, they would see another of our curiosities: surfers. And in Daytona Beach, they would hear the deafening roar of the stock cars and motorbikes that make this beach town the "World Center of Racing."

Heading north along the coast, they would come to the rich folks' haven of Ponte Vedra Beach, where golf definitely takes precedence over manual labor. And they would marvel at sprawling Jacksonville, Florida's largest metropolis and a thriving example of today's New South.

Up near the Georgia border, they'd cross a bridge to Amelia Island, where exclusive resorts take full advantage of 13 miles (21km) of beautiful beaches. Amelia's Victorian-era town, Fernandina Beach, would seem modern to them; to us, it's a quaint and historic retreat.

1 Cocoa Beach, Cape Canaveral & the Kennedy Space Center

46 miles (74km) SE of Orlando, 186 miles (299km) N of Miami, 65 miles (105km) S of Daytona

The "Space Coast," the area around Cape Canaveral, was once a sleepy place where city dwellers escaped the crowds from the exploding urban centers of Miami and Jacksonville. But then came the NASA space program. Today, the region produces and accommodates its own crowds, especially hordes of tourists who come to visit the Kennedy Space Center and enjoy the area's 72 miles (116km) of beaches (this is, after all, the closest beach to Orlando's mega-attractions) and excellent fishing, surfing, and golfing.

Thanks to NASA, this is also a prime destination for nature lovers. The space agency originally took over much more land than it has needed to launch rockets. Rather than sell off the unused portions, it turned them over to the

Canaveral National Seashore and the Merritt Island National Wildlife Refuge (www.nbbd.com/godo/minwr), which have preserved them in their pristine natural states.

A handful of the major Caribbean-bound cruise ships depart from the man-made Port Canaveral. The south side of the port is lined with seafood restaurants and marinas, which serve as home base for gambling ships and the area's deep-sea charter and group fishing boats.

ESSENTIALS

GETTING THERE   The nearest airport is **Melbourne International Airport** (© **321/723-6227;** www.mlbair.com), 22 miles (35km) south of Cocoa Beach, which is served by **Continental** (© **800/525-0280**) and **Delta** (© **800/221-1212**); but **Orlando International Airport,** about 35 miles (56km) to the west, is a much larger hub with many more flight options and generally less expensive fares (see "Getting There," in chapter 12). It's an easy 45-minute drive from the Orlando airport to the beaches via the Bee Line Expressway (Fla. 528)—it can take almost that long from the Melbourne airport. **Comfort Travel** (© **800/567-6139** or 407/799-0442) or the **Cocoa Beach Shuttle** (© **407/784-3831**) will take you from the Orlando airport to the beaches for about $20 per person.

VISITOR INFORMATION   For information about the area, contact the **Florida Space Coast Office of Tourism,** 8810 Astronaut Blvd., Suite 102, Cape Canaveral, FL 32920 (© **800/872-1969** or 321/868-1126; fax 321/868-1139; www.space-coast.com). The office is in the Sheldon Cove building, on Fla. A1A a block north of Central Boulevard and is open Monday through Friday from 8am to 5pm.

The office also operates an information booth at the Kennedy Space Center Visitor Complex (see below).

GETTING AROUND   A car is essential in this area, so rent one at the airport. **Space Coast Area Transit** (© **321/633-1878;** www.ridescat.com) operates buses, but routes tend to be circuitous and therefore extremely time-consuming.

SEEING THE SPACE & ASTRONAUT ATTRACTIONS

In addition to the two attractions below, Brevard College's **Astronaut Memorial Planetarium and Observatory,** 1519 Clearlake Rd., Cocoa Beach (© **321/634-3732;** www.brevard.cc.fl.us/~planet), south of Fla. 528, has its own International Hall of Space Explorers, but its big attractions are sound and light shows in the planetarium. Call or check their website for schedules and prices.

Astronaut Hall of Fame ⭐ *Kids*   Children will enjoy a playful visit to this hands-on museum at the mainland end of NASA Causeway (Fla. 405). In addition to honoring our space voyagers, the museum has artifacts from the space program and several interactive exhibits. A flight simulator and a G-Force Trainer will subject you to four times the pull of gravity, and the "3-D 360" will flip you around 360°. Most kids eat this stuff up; we adults need a relatively strong stomach! A tamer moonwalk uses swings to let you experience a degree of weightlessness, and a Mars mission ride will take you on a simulated trip to the red planet. That full-size replica of a space shuttle you see by the highway actually holds a theater with a multimedia presentation. The rooftop observation deck is a grand place to watch a shuttle launch if you can't get into the Kennedy Space Center (see below).

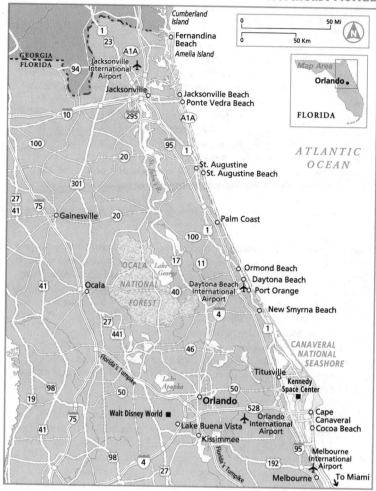

You can park your kids here for a week in the museum's **Space Camp** (℗ **800/ 63-SPACE;** www.spacecamp.com). They will come home trained to be junior astronauts; you will have had a quiet stay at the beach.

6225 Vectorspace Blvd., Titusville. ℗ **321/269-6100.** www.astronauthalloffame.com. Admission $13.95 adults, $12.95 seniors, $9.95 children 6–12, free for kids under 6. Daily 9am–5pm.

John F. Kennedy Space Center ★★★ Whether you're a space buff or not, you'll appreciate the sheer grandeur of the facilities and technological achievements displayed at NASA's primary space-launch facility. Astronauts departed Earth at this site in 1969 en route to the most famous "small step" in history—humankind's first voyage to the moon—and today's space shuttles still regularly lift off from here on their latest missions.

Since all roads other than Fla. 405 and Fla. 3 are closed to the public in the space center, you must begin your visit at the **Kennedy Space Center Visitor**

Tips **Out to Launch**

If you'd like to see a shuttle launch at the **Kennedy Space Center,** first call ℭ **321/867-4636** or check NASA's official website (www.ksc.nasa.gov) for a schedule of upcoming takeoffs. You can buy launch tickets at the Kennedy Space Center Visitor Complex (ℭ **321/449-4444**) or online at www.ksctickets.com. If you can't get into the space center, other good viewing spots are on the rooftop observation deck of the **Astronaut Hall of Fame** (ℭ **321/269-6100**; www.astronauthalloffame.com), on the causeways leading to the islands, and on U.S. 1 as it skirts the waterfront in Titusville. The **Holiday Inn Riverside–Kennedy Space Center,** on Washington Avenue (U.S. 1) in Titusville (ℭ **800/HOLIDAY** or 321/269-2121; www.holidayinnksc.com), also has a clear view of the launch pads across the Indian River.

Complex. A bit like a themed amusement park, this privately operated complex has been undergoing an ambitious $130 million renovation and expansion, so check to see that they have not changed their tours and exhibits before going. Call beforehand to see what's happening on the day you intend to be here, and arrive early to plan your visit. You'll need at least 2 hours to see the highlights on the bus tour through the space center, up to 5 hours if you linger at the stops along the way, and a full day to see and do everything here. Buy a copy of the Official Tour Book; it's easier to use than the rental cassette tapes, and you can take it home as a colorful souvenir (though some of our readers think you don't need any extra information since the bus tours are narrated and the exhibits have excellent descriptions).

The visitor complex has real NASA rockets and the actual Mercury Mission Control Room from the 1960s. Exhibits look at early space exploration and where it's going in the new millennium. There are space-related hands-on activities aimed at kids, a daily "Encounter" with a real astronaut, several dining venues, and a shop selling a variety of space memorabilia and souvenirs. IMAX movies shown on 5½-story-high screens are informative and entertaining.

While you could spend your entire day at the visitor complex, you must take a **KSC Tour** to see the actual space center where rockets and shuttles are prepared and launched. Plan to take the bus tour early in your visit. Be sure to hit the restrooms before boarding the bus—there's only one out on the tour. The buses depart every 10 minutes, and you can reboard as you wish. They stop at the LC-39 Observation Gantry, with a dramatic 360° view over launch pads where space shuttles blast off; the International Space Station Center, where scientists and engineers prepare additions to the space station now in orbit; and the impressive Apollo/Saturn V Center, which includes artifacts, photos, interactive exhibits, and the 363-foot-tall (109m) Saturn V, the most powerful rocket ever launched by the United States.

It's worth the extra cost to take the **NASA Up Close** tour. These 90-minute excursions are better than the regular bus tours since they are narrated by program experts and go to the space shuttle launch pads, the shuttle landing facility, the massive Vehicle Assembly Building (where shuttles are prepared for launch), and other places normally restricted to NASA personnel. They generally take you along the same route the astronauts follow on launch days.

Only 25 persons are allowed on board the NASA Up Close tour, and the last bus leaves 4 hours before closing, so call ahead for departure times and reservations.

NASA Pkwy. (Fla. 405), 6 miles (10km) east of Titusville, ½ mile (.75km) west of Fla. 3. ✆ **321/449-4444** for general information, 321/449-4444 for guided bus tours and launch reservations. www.kennedyspacecenter.com. Admission $26 adults, $16 children 3–11. Annual passes $44 adults, $28 children 3–11. Add $20 per person for NASA Up Close guided tour. Audio tours $5 per person. All tours and movies free for children under 3. Daily 9am–5:30pm. Shuttle-bus tours daily 9:45am–2:15pm. Closed Christmas and some launch days.

BEACHES & WILDLIFE REFUGES

To the north of the Kennedy Space Center, **Canaveral National Seashore** ★★★ is a protected 13-mile (21km) stretch of barrier-island beach backed by cabbage palms, sea grapes, palmettos, marshes, and Mosquito Lagoon. This is a great area for watching herons, egrets, ibis, willets, sanderlings, turnstones, terns, and other birds. You might also glimpse dolphins and manatees in Mosquito Lagoon. Canoeists can paddle along a marked trail through the marshes of Shipyard Island, and you can go backcountry camping November through April (permits required—see below).

The main **visitor center** is at 7611 S. Atlantic Ave., New Smyrna Beach, FL 32169 (✆ **321/867-4077** or 321/867-0677 for recorded information), on Apollo Beach, at the north end of the island. The southern access gate to the island is 8 miles (13km) east of Titusville on Fla. 402, just east of Fla. 3. A paved road leads from there to undeveloped **Playalinda Beach** ★★★, one of Florida's most beautiful. It's now officially illegal, but nude sunbathing has long been a tradition here (at least for those willing to walk a few miles to the more deserted areas). The beach has toilets but no running water or other amenities, so bring everything you will need. The seashore is open daily from 6am to 8pm during daylight saving time, daily from 6am to 6pm during standard time. Admission fees are $5 per motor vehicle, $1 for pedestrians or bicyclists. National Park Service passports are accepted. Backcountry camping permits cost $10 for up to six persons and must be obtained from the New Smyrna Beach visitor center (see above). For advance information, contact the seashore headquarters at 308 Julia St., Titusville, FL 32796 (© **321/867-4077** or 321/267-1110; www.nps.gov/cana).

Its neighbor to the south and west is the 140,000-acre **Merritt Island National Wildlife Refuge** ★★, home to hundreds of species of shorebirds, waterfowl, reptiles, alligators, and mammals, many of them endangered. Stop and pick up a map and other information at the visitor center, on Fla. 402 about 4 miles (6km) east of Titusville (it's on the way to Playalinda Beach). The center has a quarter-mile-long (.5km) boardwalk along the edge of the marsh and has displays showing the animals you may see here. You can see them from the 6-mile-long (10km) Black Point Wildlife Drive or one of the nature trails through the hammocks and marshes. The visitor center is open Monday through Friday from 8:30am to 4:30pm, Saturday and Sunday from 9am to 5pm (closed Sun Apr–Oct). Admission is free. For more information and a schedule of interpretive programs, contact the refuge at P.O. Box 6504, Titusville, FL 32782 (© **321/861-0667**; www.nbbd.com/godo/minwr).

Note: Those parts of the national seashore and the wildlife refuge near the Kennedy Space Center close 3 days before a shuttle launch and usually reopen the day after a launch.

Other beach areas here include **Lori Wilson Park,** on Atlantic Avenue at Antigua Drive in Cocoa Beach (© **321/868-1123**), a fine municipal facility that preserves a stretch of beach backed by a forest of live oaks. It's home to a small but interesting nature center, and it has restrooms by the beach. The park is open daily from sunrise to sunset; the nature center, Monday through Friday from 1 to 4pm.

The beach at **Cocoa Beach Pier,** on Meade Avenue east of Fla. A1A (© **321/ 783-7549**), is a popular spot, especially with surfers, who consider this the East Coast's surfing capital. The rustic pier was built in 1962 and has 842 feet (253m) of fishing, shopping, and food and drinks overlooking a wide, sandy beach (see "Where to Dine," below). Because this is not a public park, there are no restrooms other than the ones in the restaurants on the pier.

The privately owned **Jetty Park,** 400 E. Jetty Rd. (© **321/783-7111;** fax 321/783-5005; www.portcanaveral.org/floridafun/recreation.htm), at the south entry to Port Canaveral, has lifeguards, a fishing pier with bait shop, a children's playground, a volleyball court, a horseshoe pitch, picnic tables, a snack bar, a grocery store, restrooms and changing facilities, and the area's only campground. From here you can watch the big cruise ships as they enter and leave the port's narrow passage. The park is open daily from 7am to 10pm, and the pier is open 24 hours for fishing. Admission is $3 per car, $7 for RVs. The 150 tent and RV campsites (some of them shady, most with hookups) cost $17 to $26 a night, depending on location and time of year. No pets are allowed.

OUTDOOR ACTIVITIES

ECOTOURS Funday Discovery Tours (© 321/725-0796; www.funday tours.com) offers a variety of day trips, including backcountry kayaking, airboat and swamp-buggy rides, dolphin-watching cruises, bird-watching expeditions, and personalized tours of the Kennedy Space Center and Merritt Island National Wildlife Refuge. Reservations are required, so call, check the website, or pick up a copy of their list of trips from the visitor center (see "Essentials," above).

FISHING Head to Port Canaveral for catches like snapper and grouper. Jetty Park (© 321/783-7111), at the south entry to the port, has a fishing pier equipped with a bait shop (see "Beaches & Wildlife Refuges," above). The south bank of the port is lined with charter boats, and you can go deep-sea fishing on the *Miss Cape Canaveral* (© 321/783-5274 or 321/648-2211 in Orlando; www.misscape.com), one of the party boats based here. All-day voyages departing daily at 8am cost $60 for adults, $50 for seniors, $30 students 11 to 17, and $30 for kids 6 to 10, including breakfast, lunch, soft drinks, gear, and bait.

GOLF You can read about Northeast Florida's best courses in the free *Golfer's Guide,* available at the tourist information offices and in many hotel lobbies. See "The Active Vacation Planner," in chapter 2, for information about ordering copies.

In Cocoa Beach, the municipal **Cocoa Beach Country Club,** 500 Tom Warringer Blvd. (© 321/868-3351), has 27 holes of championship golf and 10 lighted tennis courts set on acres of natural woodland, rivers, and lakes. Greens fees are about $40 in winter, dropping to about $35 in summer, including cart.

On Merritt Island south of the Kennedy Space Center, **The Savannahs at Sykes Creek,** 3915 Savannahs Trail (© 321/455-1377), has 18 holes over 6,636 yards bordered by hardwood forests, lakes, and savannahs inhabited by a host of wildlife. You'll have to hit over a lake to reach the seventh hole. Fees with cart are about $35 in winter, less in summer.

The best nearby course is the Gary Player–designed **Baytree National Golf Club,** 8010 N. Wickham Rd., a half-mile (.75km) east of I-95 in Melbourne (© 321/259-9060), where challenging marshy holes are flanked by towering palms. This par-72 course has 7,043 yards with a unique red-shale waste area. Fees are about $90 in winter, dropping to about $50 in summer, including cart.

SURFING Rip through some occasionally awesome waves at the **Cocoa Beach Pier** area or down south at **Sebastian Inlet.** Get outfitted at Ron Jon Surf Shop and learn how with the store's **Cocoa Beach Surfing School** ★, 150 E. Columbia Lane (© 321/452-0854; www.ronjons.com/surfschool). They offer equipment and lessons for beginners or pros at area beaches. Be sure to bring along a towel, flip-flops, sunscreen, and a lot of nerve.

WHERE TO STAY

The hotels listed below are all in Cocoa Beach, the closest resort area to the Kennedy Space Center, about a 30-minute drive to the north. Closest to the space center and Port Canaveral is the **Radisson Resort at the Port,** 8701 Astronaut Blvd. (Fla. A1A) in Cape Canaveral (© 800/333-3333 or 321/784-0000; fax 321/784-3737). It isn't on the beach, but you can relax in a lushly landscaped courtyard with a waterfall cascading over fake rocks into an outdoor heated pool. This comfortable, well-equipped hotel caters to business travelers and passengers waiting to board cruise ships departing nearby Port Canaveral.

The newest chain motels in Cocoa Beach are the **Hampton Inn Cocoa Beach**, 3425 Atlantic Blvd. (© **877/492-3224** or 321/799-4099; www.hamptoninncocoabeach.com), and **Courtyard by Marriott**, 3435 Atlantic Blvd. (© **800/321-2211** or 321/784-4800). Opened in 2000 and 2001, respectively, they stand side-by-side and have access to the beach via a pathway through a condominium complex.

The **Florida Space Coast Office of Tourism** (see "Essentials," earlier in this chapter) publishes a booklet of the area's Superior Small Lodgings. See "Tips on Accommodations," in chapter 2, for information about this excellent program.

The area has a plethora of rental condominiums and cottages. **King Rentals Inc.,** 102 W. Central Blvd., Cape Canaveral, FL 32920 (© **888/295-0934** or 321/784-5046; www.kingrentals.com), has a wide selection in its inventory.

Given the proximity of Orlando, the generally warm weather all year, and business travelers visiting the space complex, there is little if any seasonal fluctuation in room rates here. They are highest weekends, holidays, and during special events, such as space-shuttle launches.

Tent and RV camping is available at **Jetty Park** in Port Canaveral (see "Beaches & Wildlife Refuges," above).

You'll pay a 4% hotel tax on top of the Florida sales tax here.

Cocoa Beach Hilton   Instead of balconies or patios from which you can enjoy the fresh air and view down the shore, the rooms at this seven-story Hilton have smallish, sealed-shut windows, and only 16 of them actually face the beach. That and other architectural features make it seem more like a downtown commercial hotel transplanted to a beachside location. Nevertheless, it's one of the few upscale beachfront properties here. No doubt you will run into a crew of name-tagged conventioneers, since it's especially popular with groups. Despite their lack of fresh air, the rooms are spacious and comfortable.

1550 N. Atlantic Ave., Cocoa Beach, FL 32931. © **800/HILTONS** or 321/799-0003. Fax 321/799-0344. 296 units. $79–$179 double. AE, DC, DISC, MC, V. **Amenities:** Restaurant (American); 2 bars; heated outdoor pool; exercise room; game room; water-sports equipment rentals; business center; limited room service; laundry service; coin-op washers and dryers; concierge-level rooms. *In room:* A/C, TV, dataport, coffeemaker, hair dryer, iron.

DoubleTree Hotel Cocoa Beach Oceanfront ⭐   This six-story hotel was extensively remodeled and upgraded in 1998, and although not as upscale as the Cocoa Beach Hilton (see above), it's the pick of the full-service beachside hotels here. All rooms have balconies with ocean views and easy chairs, and 10 suites have living rooms with sleeper sofas and separate bedrooms. A charming dining room facing the beach serves decent Mediterranean fare and opens to a bi-level brick patio with water cascading between two heated swimming pools. Conference facilities draw groups.

2080 N. Atlantic Ave., Cocoa Beach, FL 32931. © **800/552-3224** or 321/783-9222. Fax 321/799-3234. www.cocoabeachdoubletree.com. 148 units. $125–$179 double; $185–$275 suite. AE, DC, DISC, MC, V. **Amenities:** Restaurant (Mediterranean); bar; 2 heated outdoor pools; exercise room; game room; limited room service; laundry service; coin-op washers and dryers; concierge-level rooms. *In room:* A/C, TV, dataport, coffeemaker, hair dryer, iron.

Econo Lodge of Cocoa Beach *Value*   About half of the spacious rooms at this Econo Lodge—more charming than most members of this budget-priced chain—face a tropical courtyard with a V-shaped swimming pool by which stands a sign bearing the names of the seven original astronauts, who built and owned this motel in its original incarnation as the Cape Colony Inn. It was the center of activities in those 1960s days, with helicopters bringing in the likes of anchorman Walter Cronkite and that genie herself, actress Barbara Eden. Today a variety of comfortable and clean units here include standard motel rooms and four suites with living rooms and kitchenettes. Amenities vary greatly, so tell the reservation clerk which features you require. Regardless of amenities, rooms facing the courtyard are preferable to those fronting the surrounding parking lots. For drinks, try the indoor sports bar or the poolside tiki hut.

1275 N. Atlantic Ave. (Fla. A1A, at Holiday Lane), Cocoa Beach, FL 32931. © **800/553-2666** or 321/783-2252. Fax 321/783-4485. 128 units. $45–$105 double. AE, DC, DISC, MC, V. Pets accepted, no fee. **Amenities:** Restaurant (Chinese); 2 bars; heated outdoor pool; coin-op washers and dryers. *In room:* A/C, TV, kitchen (suites only), fridge, coffeemaker.

Holiday Inn Cocoa Beach Oceanfront Resort *(Kids)*   Set on 30 beachside acres, this sprawling family-oriented complex offers a wide variety of spacious hotel rooms, efficiencies, and apartments. A few suites even come equipped with bunk beds and Nintendo games for the kids. Most are in 1960s-style motel buildings flanking a long central courtyard with tropical foliage surrounding tennis courts. Only those rooms directly facing the beach or pool have patios or balconies; the rest are entered from exterior corridors.

1300 N. Atlantic Ave. (Fla. A1A, at Holiday Lane), Cocoa Beach, FL 32931. © **800/206-2747** or 321/783-2271. www.holidayinnsofcentralflorida.com. Fax 321/783-8878. 500 units. $69–$159 double. AE, DC, DISC, MC, V. **Amenities:** 2 restaurants (American); 2 bars; heated outdoor pool; 2 tennis courts; exercise room; Jacuzzi; water-sports equipment rentals; game room; concierge; limited room service; laundry service; coin-op washers and dryers. *In room:* A/C, TV, dataport, coffeemaker, hair dryer, iron.

The Inn at Cocoa Beach ★★   Despite having 50 units, an intimate bed-and-breakfast ambience prevails at this seaside inn, far and away the most romantic place to stay in the area (which is why it draws so many couples). The inn began as a beachfront motel but underwent a transformation under current owner Karen Simpler, a skilled interior decorator. She has furnished each unit with an elegant mix of pine, tropical, and French country pieces. Rooms in the three- and four-story buildings are much more spacious and have better sea views from their balconies than the "standard" units in the original two-story motel wing (all but six units here have balconies or patios). The older units open to a courtyard with a swimming pool tucked behind the dunes. Highest on the romance scale are two rooms with Jacuzzi tubs, double showers, and easy chairs facing gas fireplaces. Guests are served a deluxe continental breakfast in a room opening to a beachside lawn and are treated to evening wine-and-cheese socials.

4300 Ocean Blvd., Cocoa Beach, FL 32932. © **800/343-5307** or 321/799-3460. Fax 321/784-8632. www.theinnatcocoabeach.com. 50 units. $145–$295 double. Rates include continental breakfast. AE, DISC, MC, V. No children under 12 accepted. **Amenities:** Bar (guests only); heated outdoor pool; sauna; massage; laundry service. *In room:* A/C, TV, dataport.

WHERE TO DINE

On the **Cocoa Beach Pier,** at the beach end of Meade Avenue, you'll get a fine view down the coast to accompany the seafood offerings at **Atlantic Ocean Grill** (© 321/783-7549) and the mediocre pub fare at adjacent **Marlins Good Times Bar & Grill** (same phone). The restaurants may not justify spending an entire evening on the pier, but the outdoor, tin-roofed **Boardwalk Tiki Bar** ⊛, where live music plays most nights, is a prime spot to have a cold one while watching the surfers or a sunset.

Bernard's Surf/Fischer's Seafood Bar & Grill ⊛ SEAFOOD/STEAKS
Photos on the walls testify that many astronauts—and Russian cosmonauts too—come to these adjoining establishments to celebrate their landings. It all

started as Bernard's Surf, which has been serving standard steak-and-seafood fare in a nautically dressed setting since 1948. Bernard's offers house specials such as filet mignon served with sautéed mushrooms and béarnaise sauce, but your best bets are chargrilled fish supplied by the Fischer family's own boats. The fresh seafood also finds its way into Fischer's Seafood Bar & Grill, a friendly, *Cheers*-like lounge popular with the locals. Fischer's menu features fried combo platters, shrimp and crab-claw meat sautéed in herb butter, and mussels with a wine sauce over pasta, to mention a few worthy selections. Fischer's also provides sandwiches, burgers, and other pub fare, and it has the same 25¢ happy-hour oysters and spicy wings as a branch of **Rusty's Seafood & Oyster Bar** (see below), also part of this complex.

2 S. Atlantic Ave. (at Minuteman Causeway Rd.), Cocoa Beach. ✆ 321/783-2401. Reservations recommended in Bernard's, not accepted in Fischer's. Bernard's main courses $14–$35. Fischer's main courses $9–$16; sandwiches and salads $4–$8. AE, DC, DISC, MC, V. Bernard's Mon–Fri 4–10pm; Fri–Sat 4–11pm. Fischer's Mon–Fri 11am–10pm; Fri–Sat 11am–11pm. Closed Christmas.

The Mango Tree ★★ CONTINENTAL   Gourmet seafood, pastas, and chicken are served in a plantation-home atmosphere with elegant furnishings in this stucco house, the finest dining venue here. Goldfish ponds inside and a waterfall splashing into a Japanese koi pond out in the lush tropical gardens provide pleasing backdrops. Start with finely seasoned Indian River crab cakes, then go on to the chef's expert spin on fresh tuna filets, roast Long Island duckling, tournedos with peppercorn-mushroom sauce, and other excellent dishes drawing their inspiration from the continent.

118 N. Atlantic Ave. (Fla. A1A, between N. 1st and N. 2nd sts.), Cocoa Beach. ✆ 321/799-0513. Reservations recommended. Main courses $15–$39. AE, MC, V. Tues–Sun 6–10pm.

Rusty's Seafood & Oyster Bar *Value* SEAFOOD   This lively sports bar beside Port Canaveral's man-made harbor offers inexpensive chow ranging from very spicy seafood gumbo to a pot of seafood that will give two people their fill of steamed oysters, clams, shrimp, crab legs, potatoes, and corn on the cob. Raw or steamed fresh oysters and clams from the raw bar are first-rate and a very good value, as is a lunch buffet on weekdays. Seating is available indoors or out, but the inside tables have the best view of fishing boats and cruise liners going in and out of the port. Daily happy hours from 3 to 6pm see beers drafted at 59¢ a mug, and tons of raw or steamed oysters and spicy Buffalo wings go for 25¢ each. It's a busy and sometimes noisy joint, especially on weekend afternoons, but the clientele tends to be somewhat older and better behaved than at some other pubs along the banks of Port Canaveral. There's another **Rusty's** in the Bernard's Surf/Fischer's Seafood Bar & Grill restaurant complex in Cocoa Beach (see above). It has the same menu.

628 Glen Cheek Dr. (south side of the harbor), Port Canaveral. ✆ 321/783-2033. Main courses $7–$18; sandwiches and salads $4–$6; lunch buffet $6. AE, DC, DISC, MC, V. Sun–Thurs 11am–11:30pm; Fri–Sat 11am–12:30am (lunch buffet Mon–Fri 11am–2pm).

THE SPACE COAST AFTER DARK

For a rundown of current performances and exhibits, call the **Brevard Cultural Alliance's Arts Line** (✆ 321/690-6819). For live music, walk out on the **Cocoa Beach Pier,** on Meade Avenue at the beach, where **Oh Shuck's Seafood Bar & Grill** (✆ 321/783-7549), **Marlins Good Times Bar & Grill** (✆ 321/783-7549), and the alfresco **Boardwalk Tiki Bar** ★ (same phone as Marlins) have bands on weekends, more often during the summer season. The tiki bar is a great place to hang out over a cold beer all afternoon and evening.

2 Daytona Beach ✦✦

54 miles (87km) NE of Orlando, 251 miles (404km) N of Miami, 78 miles (126km) S of Jacksonville

Daytona Beach is a town with many personalities. It is at once the "World's Most Famous Beach," the "World Center of Racing," a mecca for tattooed motorcyclists and pierced spring-breakers, *and* the home of a surprisingly good art museum. The city and developers are also spending millions of dollars to turn the somewhat seedy beachfront area (complete with the requisite t-shirt and souvenir shops), around the famous Main Street Pier, into Ocean Walk Village, a redevelopment area of shops, entertainment, and resort facilities.

Daytona Beach has been a destination for racing enthusiasts since the early 1900s when "horseless carriages" raced on the hard-packed sand beach. One thing is for sure: Daytonans still love their cars. Recent debate over the environmental impact of unrestricted driving on the beach caused an uproar from citizens who couldn't imagine it any other way. As it worked out, they can still drive on the sand, but not everywhere, and especially not in areas where sea turtles are nesting.

Today, hundreds of thousands of race enthusiasts come to the home of the National Association for Stock Car Auto Racing (NASCAR) for the Daytona 500, the Pepsi 400, and other races throughout the year. The Speedway is also home to DAYTONA USA, a state-of-the-art motor-sports entertainment attraction worth a visit even by nonracing fans.

Be sure to check the "Florida Calendar of Events," in chapter 2, to know when the town belongs to college students during spring break, hundreds of thousands of leather-clad motorcycle buffs during Bike Week, or racing enthusiasts for big competitions. You can't find a hotel room, drive the highways, or enjoy a peaceful vacation when they're in town.

ESSENTIALS

GETTING THERE   **Continental** (✆ 800/525-0280; www.continental.com) and **Delta** (✆ 800/221-1212; www.delta.com) fly into the small, pleasant, and calm **Daytona Beach International Airport** (✆ 386/428-8030; http://flydaytonafirst.com), 4 miles (6km) inland from the beach on International Speedway Boulevard (U.S. 92), but you usually can find less expensive fares to **Orlando International Airport,** about an hour's drive away (see "Getting There," in chapter 12). **Daytona-Orlando Transit Service (DOTS)** (✆ 800/231-1965 or 386/257-5411; www.dots-daytonabeach.com) provides van transportation to or from Orlando International Airport. Fares are about $27 for adults one-way, $49 round-trip; children 11 and under are charged half. The service brings passengers to the company's terminal at 1034 N. Nova Rd., between 3rd and 4th Streets, or to beach hotels for an additional fee.

If you're intent on flying into the Daytona Airport, know that there are no airport shuttles at the Daytona Airport. The ride from here to most beach hotels via **Yellow Cab Co.** (✆ 386/255-5555) costs between $7 and $15.

Alamo (✆ 800/327-9633), **Avis** (✆ 800/331-1212), **Budget** (✆ 800/527-0700), **Dollar** (✆ 800/800-4000), **Hertz** (✆ 800/654-3131), and **National** (✆ 800/CAR-RENT) have booths at the Daytona airport. **Enterprise** (✆ 800/325-8007) is in town. If it suits you, why not rent a Harley? This is Daytona, after all. Contact **Daytona Harley-Davidson** (✆ 386/253-2453; www.daytonahd.com).

Amtrak (✆ 800/USA-RAIL; www.amtrak.com) trains stop at Deland, about 15 southwest of Daytona Beach, with connecting bus service from Deland to the beach.

VISITOR INFORMATION The **Daytona Beach Area Convention & Visitors Bureau,** 126 E. Orange Ave. (P.O. Box 910), Daytona Beach, FL 32115 (© **800/854-1234** or 386/255-0415; www.daytonabeach.com), can help you with information on attractions, accommodations, dining, and events. The office is on the mainland just west of the Memorial Bridge. The information area of the lobby is open daily from 9am to 5pm. The bureau also maintains a branch at DAYTONA USA, 1801 W. International Speedway Blvd. (open daily 9am–7pm), and a kiosk at the airport.

GETTING AROUND Although Daytona is primarily a driver's town, VOTRAN, Volusia County's public transit system (© **386/761-7700;** http://votran.org), runs a **free shuttle** around the Main Street Pier/Ocean Walk Village area and a pay **trolley** along Atlantic Avenue on the beach, Monday through Saturday from noon to midnight. Trolley fares are $1 for adults, 50¢ for seniors and children 6 to 17, and free for kids under 6 riding with an adult. VOTRAN also runs **buses** throughout downtown and the beaches.

For a taxi, call **Yellow Cab** (© 386/255-5555) or **Southern Komfort Cab** (© 386/252-2222).

Over at the beach, **Scooters & Cycles,** 2020 S. Atlantic Ave. (Fla. A1A; © **386/253-4131**), rents both.

A VISIT TO THE WORLD CENTER OF RACING

Daytona International Speedway/DAYTONA USA ★★ You don't have to be a racing fan to enjoy a visit to the **Daytona International Speedway,** 4 miles (6km) west of the beach. Opened in 1959 with the first Daytona 500, this 480-acre complex is the keynote of the city's fame. The track presents about 9 weekends of major racing events annually, featuring stock cars, sports cars, motorcycles, and go-karts, and is used for automobile and motorbike testing and other events nearly every other day of the year. Its grandstands can accommodate more than 150,000 fans. Big events sell out months in advance (tickets to the Daytona 500 in Feb can be gone a year ahead of time), so get your tickets and hotel reservations as early as possible.

Start your visit at the **World Center of Racing Visitors Center,** in the NASCAR office complex at the east end of the speedway. Admission to the center is free, and you can walk out and see the track during nonrace days (there's a small admission to the track during qualifying races leading up to the main events). Entertaining 25-minute guided tram tours of the facility (garage area, pit road, and so on) depart from the visitor center and are well worth taking.

The visitor center houses a large souvenir shop, a snack bar, and the phenomenally popular **DAYTONA USA,** a 60,000-square-foot, state-of-the-art interactive motor-sports entertainment attraction. Here you can learn about the history, color, and excitement of stock car, go-kart, and motorcycle racing in Daytona. In Daytona Dream Laps, one of its newest "rides," you get the feel of what it's like to zoom around the track in a Daytona 500 race from a 32-seat motion simulator. If that doesn't get your stomach churning, hop inside your own 80-percent scale NASCAR car in Acceleration Alley, buckle up, and roar up to 200 mph in a spectacular simulator that combines motion, video, projection, and sound for the ultimate virtual reality-like racing experience. On the milder side, you can participate in a pit stop on a NASCAR Winston Cup stock car, see the actual winning Daytona 500 car still covered in track dust, talk via video with favorite competitors, and play radio or television announcer by calling the

finish of a race. An action-packed IMAX film will put you in the winner's seat of a Daytona 500 race.

To really experience what it's like, you can actually make (for $99) three laps around the track in a stock car from May to October with the **Richard Petty Driving Experience Ride-Along Program** (© **800/BE-PETTY;** www.1800bepetty.com). Neither you nor racing legend Petty does the driving—other professionals will be at the wheel—but you'll see just how fast an average 115 miles per hour (185kmph) speed really is.

Allow at least 3½ hours to see everything and bring your video camera.

1801 W. International Speedway Blvd. (U.S. 92, at Bill France Blvd.). © **386/253-RACE** for race tickets, 386/253-7223 for information, or 386/947-6800 for DAYTONA USA. www.daytonaintlspeedway.com and www.daytonausa.com. Speedway admission free except on race days; tram rides $7. DAYTONA USA admission $16 adults, $13 seniors, $8 children 6–12. Combination DAYTONA USA–tram tour $20 adults, $17 seniors, $14 children 6–12. Tram rides and DAYTONA USA admission free for children under 6. Speedway daily 9am–7pm; trams depart every 30 min. 9:30am–5pm except during races and special events. DAYTONA USA daily 9am–7pm (later during race events). Closed Christmas.

HITTING THE WORLD'S MOST FAMOUS BEACH

The beautiful and hard-packed beach here runs for 24 miles (39km) along a skinny peninsula separated from the mainland by the Halifax River. The bustling hub of activity is at the end of Main Street, near the Adam's Mark Daytona Beach Resort, where you'll find the **Main Street Pier,** which was the longest wooden pier on the East Coast until Hurricane Floyd washed away about a third of its 1,006 feet (302m) in 1999. Out here you'll find a restaurant, bar, bait shop, beach-toy concessions, a chairlift running its entire length, and views from the 180-foot-tall (54m) Space Needle. Admission as far out as the restaurant and bar is free (at about a third of the way, this is far enough for a good view down the beach), but you'll have to pay $1 to walk out beyond there, more if you fish (see "Outdoor Activities," below). Beginning at the pier, the city's famous ocean-side **Boardwalk** is lined with restaurants, bars, and T-shirt shops, as are the 4 blocks of Main Street nearest the beach. The city's Ocean Walk Village redevelopment project begins here and runs several blocks north.

There's another busy beach area at the end of **Seabreeze Boulevard,** which has a multitude of restaurants, bars, and shops.

Couples seeking greater privacy usually prefer the northern or southern extremities of the beach. Especially peaceful is **Ponce Inlet,** at the very southern tip of the peninsula, where there is precious little commerce or traffic to disturb the silence.

OUTDOOR ACTIVITIES

AMUSEMENT PARKS   Part of the Ocean Walk Village redevelopment project, **Adventure Landing,** 601 Earl St., west of Atlantic Avenue (© **386/258-0071;** www.adventurelanding.com), is a multifaceted amusement center offering indoor and outdoor activities to keep you and especially the kids entertained—and thoroughly wet. You enter into a cacophony of deafening noise and music in a huge electronic games arcade. Outside there are pools, slides, and waterfalls, plus go-kart rides and a 27-hole mini-golf course. Admission is free to the games area, but water-park entry costs about $20 for anyone over 48 inches tall, $17 for anyone shorter, and free for kids under 3. Ask about a discounted "night splasher" (4–8pm) pass. Open daily during the summer, from 10am to midnight.

Tips **Driving on the Beach**

You can drive and park directly on sections of the sand along 18 miles (29km) of the beach during daylight hours and at low tide (Hurricane Floyd and other recent storms have greatly reduced the beach's width). Watch for signs warning of sea turtles nesting. There's a $5 per vehicle access fee.

CRUISES Take a leisurely cruise on the Halifax River aboard the 14-passenger, 25-foot (7.5m) *Fancy*, a replica of an 1890s-style fantail launch. It's operated by **A tiny Cruise Line River Excursions,** 425 S. Beach St., at Halifax Harbor Marina (© **386/226-2343**). Captain Jim regales passengers with river lore and points out dolphins (which are more commonly spotted in the mornings), manatees, herons, diving cormorants, pelicans, egrets, osprey, oyster beds, and other natural phenomena during his 2-hour midday cruise. In the afternoon, you can see the man-made estates along the river. Cruises range from $9.50 to $15 for adults, $6 to $8 for children 4 to 12, and free for children 3 and under. Weather permitting, the midday cruises depart year-round (with a brief hiatus during the holidays), Monday through Saturday at 11:30am. The 1-hour tour of riverfront homes is at 2pm and of historic downtown at 3:30pm; there are no Monday cruises in winter months. Call for reservations. Romantic sunset cruises are also available.

FISHING The easiest and least-expensive way to fish offshore for marlin, sailfish, king mackerel, grouper, red snapper, and more is with the **Critter Fleet,** 4950 S. Peninsula Dr., just past the lighthouse in Ponce Inlet (© **800/338-0850** or 386/767-7676; www.critterfleet.com), which operates two party boats. One goes on all-day trips (about $55 adults, $35 kids under 12), while the other makes morning and afternoon voyages (about $35 adults, $25 kids under 12). The fares include rod, reel, and bait. Call for schedules, prices, and reservations.

Deep-sea charter-fishing boats are available from the Critter Fleet and from **Sea Love Marina,** 4884 Front St., Ponce Inlet (© **386/767-3406** or 407/293-2050 in Orlando).

Save the cost of a boat and fish with the locals from the **Main Street Pier,** at the ocean end of Main Street near the Adam's Mark Daytona Beach Resort (© **386/253-1212**). Admission for fishers is $3.50 for adults, $2 for kids under 12. Bait and fishing gear are available, and no license is required.

GOLF More than 25 courses await you within 30 minutes of the beach, and most hotels can arrange starting times for you. **Golf Daytona Beach,** 126 E. Orange Ave., Daytona Beach, FL 32114 (© **800/881-7065** or 386/239-7065; fax 386/239-0064; www.golf-daytona.com), publishes an annual brochure describing the major courses. It's available at the tourist information offices (see "Essentials," above).

Two of the nation's top-rated links for women golfers are at the **LPGA International** ★★, 1000 Championship Dr. (© **386/274-5742;** www.lpgainternational.com): Those are the Champions course designed by Rees Jones, and the Legends course designed by Arthur Hills. Both boast 18 outstanding holes. LPGA International is a center for professional and amateur women golfers (workshops and teaching programs), and the pro shop carries a great selection of ladies' equipment and clothing. Greens fees with a cart are usually about $75, less in summer. You do not have to be female to play here.

A Lloyd Clifton–designed course, the centrally located 18-hole, par-72 **Indigo Lakes Golf Course,** 2620 W. International Speedway Blvd. (© **386/ 254-3607;** www.indigolakesgolf.com), has flat fairways and large bunkered Bermuda greens. Fees here are about $55 in winter, including a cart, less in summer.

The semiprivate South Course at **Pelican Bay Country Club,** 550 Sea Duck Dr. (© **386/788-6494;** www.pelicanbaygolfclub.com), is one of the area's favorites, with fast greens to test your putting skills. Fees are about $40 with cart in winter, less in summer (no walking allowed). The North Course here is for members only.

The city's prime municipal course is the **Daytona Beach Country Club,** 600 Wilder Blvd. (© **386/258-3119**), which has 36 holes. Winter fees here are about $20 to walk, $30 to share a cart. They drop $3 in summer.

HELICOPTER RIDES Take a helicopter ride around the Daytona area to see the city from a different point of view. **Air Florida** (© **386/257-6993;** www.airfloridahelicopters.com) offers rides starting at $20, leaving from the pier and across from the Daytona Farmer's and Flea Market (see below).

HORSEBACK RIDING **Shenandoah Stables,** 1759 Tomoka Farms Rd., off U.S. 92 (© **386/257-1444**), offers daily trail rides and lessons. Call for prices and schedules.

SPECTATOR SPORTS The **Daytona Cubs** (© **386/872-2827;** www.daytonacubs.com), a Class A minor-league affiliate of the Chicago Cubs, play baseball April through August at Jackie Robinson Ballpark, on City Island downtown. A game here is a treat, since the park has been restored to its classic 1914 style by the designers of Baltimore's Camden Yards and Cleveland's Jacobs Field.

WATER SPORTS Water-sports equipment, as well as bicycles, beach buggies, and mopeds, can be rented along the Boardwalk, at the ocean end of Main Street (see "Hitting the World's Most Famous Beach," above), and in front of major beachfront hotels. For jet-ski rentals, contact **Daytona High Performance— MBI,** 925 Sickler Dr., at the Seabreeze Bridge (© **386/257-5276**).

MUSEUMS & ATTRACTIONS

Halifax Historical Museum ★ Located on Beach Street, Daytona's original riverfront commercial district on the mainland side of the Halifax River (see "Shopping," below), this local history museum is worth a look just for the 1912 neoclassical architectural details of its home, a former bank (you can still see the old vault). A mural of Old Florida wildlife graces one wall, the stained-glass ceiling reflects the sunlight, and across the room an old gold-metal teller's window still stands. The Halifax's eclectic and interesting collection includes Native American artifacts, more than 10,000 historic photographs, possessions of past residents (such as a ball gown worn at Lincoln's inauguration), and, of course, model cars. A noteworthy race exhibit opens annually in mid-January as a stage-setter for Race Week.

252 S. Beach St. (just north of Orange Ave.). © 386/255-6976. www.halifaxhistorical.org. Admission $4 adults, $1 children 11 and under; free Sat for children. Tues–Sat 10am–4pm.

Klassix Auto Attraction True aficionados of the car will enjoy a visit to this attraction, which showcases Corvettes—a model from every year since 1953—and historic vehicles from every motor sport. The rest of us will head to the original "Batmobile" from the 1960s *Batman* TV series, the car from *The Flintstones* series, the "Dragula" owned by the *Munsters*, and "Greased Lightning" from the movie *Grease*. A 1950s-style soda shop and gift shop are also on the premises.

2909 W. International Speedway Blvd., at Tomoka Farms Rd., just west of I-95. ⓒ 386/252-3800. Admission $8.50 adults, $4.25 children 7–12, free for children under 7. Daily 9am–6pm.

Marine Science Center *Kids* This new (opened in June 2002) center has interior displays (with exhibits on mangroves, mosquitoes, marine mammal bones, shells, artificial reefs, dune habitats, and pollution solutions), a 5,000 gallon aquarium, as well as educational programs and activities. Though the exhibit area is rather small, there's more than enough information for a child to digest at one time. Perhaps the most interesting part of the center is the space reserved for the rehabilitation of endangered and threatened sea turtles (once they're "fixed," the healthy turtles are set back into nature). You can watch them in any of 7 turtle tanks—look for the ones who need life jackets to stay afloat!

100 Lighthouse Dr., Ponce Inlet. ⓒ 386/304-5545. www.marinesciencecenter.com. $3 adults, $1 children 5–12, free for children under 5. Tues–Sat 10am–4pm; Sun noon–4pm; closed Mondays. See directions for Ponce de León Inlet Lighthouse & Museum (below).

Museum of Arts and Sciences ⭐⭐ An exceptional institution for a town Daytona's size, this museum is best known for its Cuban Museum, with paintings acquired in 1956, when Cuban dictator Fulgencio Batista donated his private collection to the city. Among them is a portrait of Eva ("Evita") Perón, said to be the only existing painting completed while she was alive (it hangs near the lobby, not in the Cuban Museum). The Dow Gallery displays Smithsonian-quality examples of American decorative arts, and the Bouchelle Study Center for the Decorative Arts contains both American and European masterpieces. Other rooms worth visiting include the Schulte Gallery of Chinese Art; Africa: Life and Ritual, with the largest collection of Ashante gold ornaments (these are stunning) in the United States; and the Prehistory of Florida gallery, with the skeleton of a 13-foot-tall (4m), 130,000-year-old giant ground sloth. A recent addition is the unique collection of the late Chapman S. Root, a Daytona philanthropist and a founder of the Coca-Cola empire; among the Root memorabilia is the mold for the original Coke bottle as well as many other changing exhibitions (the collection is very large). The Root family's two private railroad cars are also on display. The planetarium presents 30-minute shows of what the night sky will look like on the date of your visit. Even though this is a first-class art museum, except for the skeleton and the model railroads, children are apt to be bored here.

1040 Museum Blvd. (off Nova Rd./Fla. 5A between International Speedway Blvd. and Bellevue Ave.). ⓒ 386/255-0285. www.moas.org. Museum $7 adults, $2 children and students with ID, free for children 5 and under. Planetarium shows $3 adults, $2 children and students. Tues–Fri 9am–4pm; Sat–Sun noon–5pm. Planetarium shows Tues–Fri 2pm; Sat–Sun 1 and 3pm. Closed Thanksgiving, Christmas Eve, Christmas Day. Take International Speedway Blvd. west, make a left on Nova Rd. (Fla. 5A), and look for a sign on your right.

Ponce de León Inlet Lighthouse & Museum ⭐⭐ This National Historic Landmark is well worth a stop even if you're not a lighthouse enthusiast. The 175-foot (53m) brick-and-granite structure is the second-tallest lighthouse in the United States, second only to the beacon at Cape Hatteras, North Carolina.

Built in the 1880s, the lighthouse and the graceful Victorian brick buildings surrounding it have been restored (it's one of the only light stations in the United States to have all its original buildings still standing). There are no guided tours, but you can walk through the 12 areas which feature different exhibits (lighthouse lenses, historical artifacts, and a film of early car racing on the nearby beach) and around the tugboat *F. D. Russell,* now sitting high-and-dry in the sand. Use common sense if you climb the 203 steps to the top of the lighthouse; it's a grinding ascent, but the view from up there is spectacular.

4931 S. Peninsula Dr., Ponce Inlet. ℂ 386/761-1821. www.ponceinlet.org. Admission $5 adults, $1.50 children under 12. Memorial Day–Labor Day daily 10am–8pm; rest of year daily 10am–4pm. Follow Atlantic Ave. south, make a right on Beach St., and follow the signs.

SHOPPING

On the mainland, Daytona Beach's main riverside drag, **Beach Street,** is one of the few areas in town where people actually stroll. The street is wide and inviting, with palms down its median and decorative wrought-iron archways and fancy brickwork overlooking a branch of the Halifax River that separates downtown from City Island, home of municipal offices and the lovingly restored Jackie Robinson Ballpark (see "Spectator Sports," above). Today, Beach Street between Bay Street and Orange Avenue offers antiques and collectibles shops, art galleries, clothiers, a magic shop, the local historical museum (see "Museums," above) and several good cafes. 154 S. Beach St. is the home of the **Angell & Phelps Chocolate Factory** (ℂ 800/969-2634), which has been making candy for more than 75 years. Come here to watch the goodies being made (and get a free sample!) or just to buy some of the handmade treats.

"Hog" riders will find several shops to their liking along Beach Street, north of International Speedway Boulevard, including the **Harley-Davidson Store,** 290 Beach St., at Dr. Mary McLeod Bethune Boulevard (ℂ 386/253-2453), a 20,000-square-foot retail outlet and diner serving breakfast and lunch. It's one of the nation's largest dealerships. In addition to hundreds of gleaming new and used Hogs, you'll find as much fringed leather as you've ever seen in one place.

The **Daytona Farmer's and Flea Market,** on Tomoka Farms Road at the junction of I-95 and U.S. 92, a mile west of the Speedway (ℂ 386/252-1999; www.daytonafleamarket.com), is huge, with 1,000 covered outdoor booths plus 100 antiques and collectibles vendors in an air-conditioned building. Most of the booths feature new (though not necessarily first rate) wares along the lines of socks, sunglasses, luggage, handbags, jewelry, and the like. It's open year-round Friday through Sunday from 8am to 5pm. Admission and parking are free.

Also keep an eye on the Ocean Walk Shoppes (ℂ 877/845-WALK), whose upscale boutiques should be complete in early 2003.

WHERE TO STAY

Room rates here are among the most affordable in Florida. Some properties have as many as 20 rate periods during the year, but generally they are somewhat higher from the beginning of the races in February all the way to Labor Day. They skyrocket during major events at the Speedway, during bikers' gatherings, and during college spring break (see "Florida Calendar of Events," in chapter 2), when local hotels fill to the bursting point. Even if you can find a room then, there's often a minimum-stay requirement.

Hundreds of hotels and motels line Atlantic Avenue along the beach, many of them family owned and operated. The Daytona Beach Area Convention & Visitors Bureau (see "Essentials," earlier in this chapter) distributes a brochure that lists **Superior Small Lodgings** for Daytona Beach, Deland, and New Smyrna Beach. See "Tips On Accommodations," in chapter 2, for information about this excellent program. All of the small motels listed below are members.

If you're going to the races and don't care about staying on the beach, some upper-floor rooms at the new **Hilton Garden Inn Daytona Beach Airport,** 189 Midway Ave. (© 877/944-4001 or 386/944-4000), actually overlook the international speedway track. Unlike most members of Hilton's Garden Inn chain, this one has a restaurant.

Thousands of rental condominiums line the beaches here. Among the most luxurious is the new, 150-unit condominium hotel **Ocean Walk Resort,** 300 N. Atlantic Ave., Daytona Beach, FL 32118 (© 800/649-3566 or 386/323-4800; www.oceanwalkresort.com), which is part of the Ocean Walk Village redevelopment. Near the Main Street Pier, it's in the center of the action and has one and two bedroom apartments with fully equipped kitchens, washers and dryers, and all of the usual hotel amenities, plus a wondrous computer golf simulator, a "lazy river" in the outdoor pool, an island putting green, and much more—including the gaudiest lobby we've ever seen. One of the largest rental agents is **Peck Realty,** 2340 S. Atlantic Ave., Daytona Beach Shores, FL 32118 (© 800/44-PECK or 386/257-5000; www.peckrealty.com).

In addition to the 6% state sales tax, Volusia County levies a 4% tax on hotel bills.

Adam's Mark Daytona Beach Resort ⭐ Already Daytona's largest beachfront hotel, the Adam's Mark recently added another 310 units as part of the Ocean Walk Village development plans. With extensive on-site meeting facilities and the city's Ocean Center convention complex across the street, that means lots of big groups stay here. It's also in the middle of the beach action, right on the city's Boardwalk and a block north of the busy Main Street Pier (see "Hitting the World's Most Famous Beach," earlier in this chapter). One of Daytona's best-equipped properties, it's designed so every room has an ocean view.

100 N. Atlantic Ave. (Fla. A1A, between Earl St. and Auditorium Blvd.), Daytona Beach, FL 32118. © 800/444-ADAM or 386/254-8200. Fax 386/253-0275. www.adamsmark.com. 746 units. $105–$165 double. AE, DC, DISC, MC, V. Valet parking $8; free self-parking. **Amenities:** 3 restaurants (American); 3 bars; heated outdoor pool; exercise room; Jacuzzis; sauna; water-sports equipment rentals; bike rental; game room; concierge; limited room service; massage; babysitting; laundry service; coin-op washers and dryers; concierge-level rooms. *In room:* A/C, TV, dataport, coffeemaker, hair dryer, iron.

Daytona Beach Hilton Oceanfront Resort ⭐⭐ Far enough south to escape the maddening crowds at Main Street, the Hilton is among the best choices here. It welcomes you in an elegant terra-cotta–tiled lobby with comfortable seating areas, a fountain, and potted palms. The large guest rooms are grouped in pairs and can be joined to form a suite; only one of each pair has a balcony. Oceanfront rooms are preferable, but all have sea and/or river views. A few also have kitchenettes. The surprisingly good Blue Water lobby restaurant is one of Daytona's most beautiful; patio dining is an option.

2637 S. Atlantic Ave. (Fla. A1A, between Florida Shores Blvd. and Richard's Lane), Daytona Beach, FL 32118. © 800/525-7350 or 386/767-7350. Fax 386/760-3651. 214 units. $116–$359 double. AE, DC, DISC, MC, V. **Amenities:** Restaurant (American); bar; heated outdoor pool; Jacuzzi; exercise room; water-sports equipment rentals; game room; salon; limited room service; babysitting; laundry service; coin-op washers and dryers; concierge-level rooms. *In room:* A/C, TV, dataport, kitchen, coffeemaker, hair dryer, iron.

Old Salty's Inn The most unusual of the many mom-and-pop beachside motels here, Old Salty's is a lush tropical enclave carrying out a *Gilligan's Island* theme, with old motors, rotting boats, life preservers, and a Jeep lying about, and the TV series' main characters depicted in big murals painted on the buildings. The two-story wings flank a courtyard festooned with palms and banana trees (you can pick one for breakfast). Facing this vista, the bright rooms have microwaves, refrigerators, and front-and-back windows to let in good ventilation. The choice units have picture windows overlooking the beach. There are gas grills and rocking chairs under a gazebo out by a heated beachside swimming pool.

1921 S. Atlantic Ave. (Fla. A1A, at Flamingo Ave.), Daytona Beach Shores, FL 32118. ✆ **800/417-1466** or 386/252-8090. Fax 386/947-9980. www.oldsaltys.com. 19 units. $53–$121 (double rooms–efficiencies and suites, depending on the time of year). AE, DISC, MC, V. **Amenities:** Heated outdoor pool; free use of bikes; coin-op washers and dryers. *In room:* A/C, TV, kitchen, fridge, coffeemaker, hair dryer, iron.

The Plaza Resort & Spa ★★   Remodeled to the tune of $26 million (the original 7-story hotel was built in the early 20th century) in 2000, these elegant adjoining 7- and 13-story buildings now hold some of Daytona Beach's best rooms (in a much more tasteful atmosphere than many of the neighboring hotels)—provided you don't need a large bathroom. The choice units are the corner suites, which have sitting areas and two balconies overlooking the Atlantic; some even have a Jacuzzi. All units have balconies and microwave ovens (an on-premises convenience store sells frozen dinners). The renovations also saw the opening of the full-service **Ocean Waters Spa** ★★ (✆ **386/267-1660;** www.oceanwatersspa.com), Daytona's only such facility. There are 16 treatment rooms and a soothing menu of facials, massages, and wraps.

600 N. Atlantic Ave. (at Seabreeze Ave.), Daytona Beach, FL 32118. ✆ **800/767-4471** or 386/255-4471. Fax 386/253-7543. www.plazaresortandspa.com. 323 units. $69–$449 doubles–suites. AE, DC, DISC, MC, V. **Amenities:** Restaurant (seafood/sushi); bar; heated outdoor pool; exercise room; spa; Jacuzzi; water-sports equipment rentals; game room; business center; limited room service; massage; babysitting; laundry service; coin-op washers and dryers; concierge-level rooms. *In room:* A/C, TV, dataport, fridge, coffeemaker, hair dryer, iron.

Radisson Resort Daytona Beach ★   This 11-story, all-modern Radisson sits beachside a half-mile north of the Main Street Pier and around the corner from restaurants and bars on Seabreeze Boulevard. The rooms here are among the most spacious on the beach and have angled balconies facing the beach (your neighbor's air conditioner exhausts onto your balcony, however, which can create noise and heat when you're sitting out there). About a third have small additional rooms with wet bars with microwaves and refrigerators.

640 N. Atlantic Ave. (Fla. A1A, between Seabreeze and Glenview Blvds.), Daytona Beach, FL 32118. ✆ **800/355-1721** or 386/239-9800. Fax 386/253-0735. www.daytonaradisson.com. 206 units. $99–$169 double. AE, DC, DISC, MC, V. **Amenities:** Restaurant (American); bar; heated outdoor pool; exercise room; water-sports equipment rentals; limited room service; babysitting; coin-op washers and dryers; concierge-level rooms. *In room:* A/C, TV, dataport, fridge, coffeemaker, hair dryer, iron.

Shoreline All Suites Inn & Cabana Colony Cottages *Value*   The Shoreline All Suites Inn, built in 1954 but substantially modernized, features one- and two-bedroom suites that occupy two buildings separated by a walkway leading to the beach. Most have small bathrooms with scant vanity space and—shall we say—intimate shower stalls. Every unit has a full kitchen, plus there are barbecue grills on premises. For a change of scenery, consider the fine little cottage complex at the Shoreline's sister property, the **Cabana Colony Cottages** ★. All 12 of the cottages were built in 1927 but were upgraded by owner-managers Frank and Barbara Molnar. They aren't much bigger than a motel room with a kitchen, but they're light and airy and are attractively furnished with white wicker pieces. The cottages share a heated beachside swimming pool with the Shoreline.

2435 S. Atlantic Ave. (Fla. A1A, at Dundee Rd.), Daytona Beach Shores, FL 32118. ✆ 800/293-0653 or 386/252-1692. Fax 386/239-7068. www.daytonashoreline.com. 32 units, including 12 cottages. $59–$139 suites–cottages. Rates include continental breakfast. Golf packages available. AE, DISC, MC, V. **Amenities:** Heated outdoor pool; coin-op washers and dryers. *In room:* A/C, TV/VCR, kitchen, coffeemaker.

The Villa Bed & Breakfast ✿ You'll think you're in Iberia upon entering this Spanish mansion's great room with its fireplace, baby grand piano, terra-cotta floors, and walls hung with Mediterranean paintings. Also downstairs are a sun room equipped with a TV and VCR, a formal dining room, and a breakfast nook where guests gather at their leisure to start the day. The lush backyard surrounds a swimming pool and a covered, four-person Jacuzzi. Upstairs, the nautically themed Christopher Columbus room has a vaulted ceiling and a small balcony overlooking the pool. The largest quarter here is the King Carlos suite, the original master bedroom with a four-poster bed, entertainment system, refrigerator, rooftop deck, dressing area, and bathroom equipped with a four-head shower. The Queen Isabella room has a portrait of the queen over a queen-size bed, and the Marco Polo room has Chinese black-lacquer furniture and Oriental rugs evoking the great explorer's adventures.

801 N. Peninsula Dr. (at Riverview Blvd.), Daytona Beach, FL 32118. ✆ and fax 386/248-2020. www.thevillabb.com. 4 units (all with bathroom). $85–$250 double. Rates include continental breakfast. AE, MC, V. No children or pets accepted. **Amenities:** Heated outdoor pool; Jacuzzi. *In room:* A/C, TV, hair dryer, no phone.

WHERE TO DINE

Daytona Beach has a few interesting dining venues, but not many are likely to leave an indelible memory. A profusion of fast-food joints line the major thoroughfares, especially along Atlantic Avenue on the beach and along International Speedway Boulevard (U.S. 92) near the racetrack. Restaurants come and go in the Beach Street district on the mainland, and along Main Street and Seabreeze Boulevard on the beach. A casual restaurant serves burgers and chicken wings and lots of suds out on the Main Street Pier.

The local **Shells** seafood restaurant is on the beach at 200 S. Atlantic Ave. (✆ 386/258-0007), a block north of International Raceway Boulevard. See p. 455 for details about this inexpensive chain.

There are two other outlets of chain restaurants that are worth a special mention. **Buca di Beppo** (a boisterous, fun, and loud restaurant serving "immigrant southern Italian specialties" family style) is open for dinners only, until 10pm (11pm on Fri and Sat). Expect to take home leftovers, as the portions are huge—but don't worry, you'd want to anyway: The food is surprisingly good, especially for a "theme" restaurant (2514 W. International Speedway Blvd.; ✆ **386/ 253-6523;** www.bucadibeppo.com). **Stonewood Tavern & Grill** (100 S. Atlantic Ave. in Ormand Beach; ✆ **386/671-1200;** www.stonewoodgrill.com) is a casual but upscale restaurant with a nice but dark mahogany interior, good American food, and excellent service. Also only open for dinner, you won't be disappointed with their menu of steaks, seafood, and the like, voted one of the best places to dine in Central Florida by Zagat in 2001.

AT THE BEACHES

Anna's Italian Trattoria ✿ SOUTHERN ITALIAN Originally from Sicily, the Triani family makes all the pastas at their simple yet comfortable trattoria, which offers more-formal dining than Rosario's equally good *ristorante* on the mainland (see below). The star here isn't the pasta, however; it's risotto alla Anna, an Italian version of Spanish paella. Portions are hearty; main courses come with soup or salad and a side dish of angel-hair pasta or a vegetable, and a bit of between-courses sorbet to cleanse the palate. There's a good selection of Italian wines to complement your meal. Everything is cooked to order; be patient.

304 Seabreeze Blvd. (at Peninsula Dr.). © **386/239-9624.** Reservations recommended. Main courses $10–$17. AE, DISC, MC, V. Tues–Sun 5–10pm. Closed 1 week in June.

Down the Hatch ★ *Value* SEAFOOD   Occupying a 1940s fish camp on the Halifax River, Down the Hatch serves up big portions of fresh fish and seafood (note its shrimp boat docked outside). Inexpensive burgers and sandwiches are available, too, and you can start your day here with a Belgian waffle, French toast, or a country-style breakfast while taking in the scenic views of boats and shorebirds through the big picture windows—you might even see dolphins frolicking. At night, arrive early to catch the sunset over the river, and also to beat the crowd at this very popular place. In summer, light fare is served outside on an awninged wooden deck.

4894 Front St., Ponce Inlet. © **386/761-4831.** Call ahead for priority seating. Main courses $9–$25 (most $10–$16); breakfast $2–$5; burgers and sandwiches $3–$6.50; early-bird menu (served 11am–5pm) $6–$8. AE, MC, V. Daily 7am–10pm. Closed 1st week in Dec. Take Atlantic Ave. south, make a right on Beach St., and follow the signs.

Ocean Deck Restaurant & Beach Club *Value* SEAFOOD/PUB FARE   Known by spring-breakers, bikers, and other beachgoers as Daytona's best "beach pub" since 1940, the Ocean Deck also is the best restaurant in the busy area around the Main Street Pier. Opening to the sand and surf, the downstairs reggae bar is as sweaty, noisy, and packed as ever (a band plays down there nightly from 9pm–2:30am). The upstairs dining room can be noisy, too, but both you and the kids can come here for some good food, reasonable prices, and great ocean views. You can choose from a wide range of seafood, chicken, sandwiches, and the best burgers on the beach, but don't pass up the mahimahi, first broiled with peppery Jamaican spices and then finished off on a grill, a bargain at $9. There's valet parking after dark, or you can park free at the lot behind the Ocean Deck's Reggae Republic surf shop, a block away on Atlantic Avenue.

127 S. Ocean Ave. (at Kemp St.). © **386/253-5224.** Main courses $8–$16; salads and sandwiches $5–$8. AE, DISC, MC, V. Daily 11am–2am (bar to 3am).

ON THE MAINLAND

The Cellar AMERICAN   An excellent place for a ladies' lunch, this tearoom occupies the basement of a Victorian home built in 1907 as President Warren G. Harding's winter home (he spent election eve here in 1920) and now is listed in the National Register of Historic Places. It couldn't be more charming, with low ceilings, back-lit reproduction Tiffany windows, fresh flowers everywhere, linen tablecloths and napkins, and china teacups. If you can play the piano, help yourself to the baby grand. A wide-ranging lunch menu offers the likes of the house signature chicken salad as a platter or croissant sandwich, a quiche du jour, crab-cake sandwich, vegetarian lasagna, or chicken pot pie. In the warm months, there's outdoor seating at umbrella tables on a covered garden patio.

220 Magnolia Ave. (between Palmetto and Ridgewood Aves.). © **386/258-0011.** Soups, salads, sandwiches $6–$9. AE, DISC, MC, V. Mon–Fri 11am–3pm.

The Dancing Avocado Kitchen ⚘ VEGETARIAN   A healthy place to start your day, or have lunch while touring downtown, this store-front establishment purveys a number of vegetarian omelets, burritos, salads, personal-size pizzas, and hot and cold sandwiches such as an avocado Reuben. A few chicken and turkey items are on the menu, but the only red-meat selection is a hamburger. You can dine outside or inside the store with vegetable drawings on its brick walls and ceiling fans suspended from black rafters. No smoking.

110 S. Beach St. (between Magnolia St. and International Speedway Blvd.). ☎ 386/947-2022. Breakfast $2–$4.50; sandwiches, salads, pizzas $4–$7. AE, DC, DISC, MC, V. Mon–Sat 8am–4pm.

Frappes North ★★ CREATIVE AMERICAN/FUSION   It's worth the 6-mile (10km) drive north to Bobby and Meryl Frappier's sophisticated, hip establishment, at which they provide this area's most entertaining cuisine. Several chic dining rooms—one has beams extending like spokes from a central pole—set the stage for an inventive, ever-changing "Menu of the Moment" fusing a multitude of styles. Ingredients are always fresh, and the herbs come from the restaurant's garden. Outstandingly presented with won-ton strips and a multihued rice cake, my Southeast Asian–style pompano in a piquant peanut sauce was a memorable dish. Bobby and Meryl always have at least one vegetarian (though not necessarily nondairy) main course. Lunch is a steal here, with dinner-size main courses at a fraction of the dinnertime price. The restaurant is in a store front on the mainland stretch of Granada Boulevard, Ormand Beach's main drag.

123 W. Granada Blvd. (Fla. 40; between Ridgewood Ave. and Washington St.), Ormand Beach. ☎ 386/615-4888. Reservations recommended. Main courses $15–$25. AE, MC, V. Mon–Thurs 11:30am–2:30pm and 5–9pm; Fri 11:30am–2:30pm and 5–10pm; Sat 5–10pm. From the beaches, drive 4 miles (6km) north on Fla. A1A to left on Granada Blvd. (Fla. 40); cross Halifax River to restaurant on right.

McK's Dublin Station AMERICAN/IRISH   Worth knowing about because it serves food after midnight, this upscale Irish tavern has a highly eclectic menu. The pub fare includes club sandwiches, burgers, a tasty mahimahi wrap, and a few main courses of steaks, fish, and chicken. The food isn't exceptional, but it's perfectly acceptable after a few Bass ales. The service is sometimes rushed, but usually pleasant.

218 S. Beach St. (between Magnolia St. and Ivy Lane). ☎ 386/238-3321. Reservations not accepted. Main courses $6–$13; salads and sandwiches $5–$7. AE, MC, V. Mon–Wed 11am–9pm; Thurs–Sat 11am–10pm (bar open later).

Rosario's ★★ SOUTHERN ITALIAN/TUSCAN   A Victorian boarding house with lace curtains on high windows makes an incongruous setting for this lively Italian restaurant. Originally from Florence, Italy, gregarious Rosario offers pastas with the familiar Bolognese and marinara sauces, but his nightly specials are much more intriguing, drawing inspiration from ancient Tuscan recipes. If the mixed grill of squirrel, pheasant, rabbit, and quail in a hunter's sauce doesn't appeal, you can always opt for Rosario's trusty grouper Livornese. There's music in the cozy bar Thursday through Saturday nights.

In Live Oak Inn, 448 S. Beach St. (at Loomis Ave.). ☎ 386/258-6066. Reservations recommended. Main courses $12–$21. MC, V. Tues–Sat 5–10pm.

DAYTONA BEACH AFTER DARK

Check the Daytona Beach *News-Journal* (www.n-jcenter.com) Friday edition for its weekly "Go-Do" and the Sunday edition for the "Master Calendar" section, which both list upcoming events. Other good sources are *Happenings Magazine* and *Backstage Pass Magazine,* two tabloids available at the visitor center (see "Essentials," earlier in this chapter) and in many hotel lobbies.

THE PERFORMING ARTS   The city-operated **Peabody Auditorium,** 600 Auditorium Blvd., between Noble Street and Wild Olive Avenue (© **386/ 255-1314**), is Daytona's major venue for serious performance, including concerts by the local Symphony Society (© **386/253-2901**). Professional actors perform Broadway musicals during winter and summer at the **Seaside Music Theater,** 176 N. Beach St., downtown (© **800/854-5592** or 386/252-6200; www.seasidemusictheater.org).

Under the city auspices, the **Oceanfront Bandshell** (© **386/258-3169**), on the boardwalk next to the Adam's Mark Hotel, hosts a series of free big-name concerts every Sunday night from early June to Labor Day. It's also the scene of raucous spring-break concerts.

THE CLUB & BAR SCENE   In addition to the following, the sophisticated **Clocktower Lounge** at the Adam's Mark Daytona Beach Resort (see "Where to Stay," earlier in this chapter) is worth a visit.

Main Street and **Seabreeze Boulevard** on the beach are happening areas where dozens of bars (and a few topless shows) cater to leather-clad bikers.

A popular beachfront bar for more than 40 years, the **Ocean Deck Restaurant & Beach Club,** 127 S. Ocean Ave. (© **386/253-5224;** see "Where to Dine," above), is packed with a mix of locals and tourists, young and old, who come for live music and cheap drinks. Reggae or ska bands play after 9:30pm. There's valet parking after dark, or leave your vehicle at Ocean Deck's Reggae Republic surf shop on Atlantic Avenue.

3 St. Augustine: America's First City ★★

105 miles (169km) NE of Orlando, 302 miles (486km) N of Miami, 39 miles (63km) S of Jacksonville

With its 17th-century fort, old city gates, horse-drawn carriages clip-clopping along narrow streets, historic buildings, and reconstructed 18th-century Spanish Quarter, St. Augustine seems more like a picturesque European village than a modern American city. This is, after all, the oldest permanent European settlement in the United States (no, it wasn't Jamestown in 1607 or the Pilgrims at Plymouth Rock in 1620). A group of French Huguenots settled in 1562 near the mouth of the St. Johns River, in present-day Jacksonville. Three years later, a Spanish force under Pedro Menéndez de Avilés arrived on the scene, wiped out the Huguenot men (de Avilés spared their women and children), and established a settlement on the harbor he named "St. Augustín."

The colony survived a succession of attacks by pirates, Indians, and the British over the next 2 centuries. The Treaty of Paris, ending the French and Indian War, ceded the town to Britain in 1763, but the British gave it back 20 years later. The United States took control when it acquired Florida from Spain in 1821.

Tourism is St. Augustine's main industry these days; but despite the daily invasion (with good reason—there are a plethora of interesting attractions), it's an exceptionally charming town, with good restaurants, an active nightlife, and shopping bargains. Give yourself 2 days here just to see the highlights, longer to savor this historic gem: St. Augustine is one of those places that actually lives up to most of the sickly sweet and sentimental promotional literature written about it.

ESSENTIALS

GETTING THERE   The Daytona Beach airport is about an hour's drive south of St. Augustine, but services are more frequent—and fares usually lower—at Jacksonville's international airport, about the same distance north. Amtrak's nearest train station is in Jacksonville. See "Essentials," in sections 2 and 4 of this chapter, for details.

VISITOR INFORMATION   Before you go, contact the **St. Augustine, Ponte Vedra & The Beaches Visitors and Convention Bureau,** 88 Riberia St., Suite 400, St. Augustine, FL 32084 (*©* **800/OLD-CITY** or 904/829-1711; fax 904/829-6149; www.visitoldcity.com), and request the *Visitor's Guide,* detailing attractions, events, restaurants, accommodations, shopping, and more.

The **St. Augustine Visitor Information Center** is at 10 Castillo Dr., at San Marco Avenue, opposite the Castillo de San Marcos National Monument (*©* **904/825-1000**). There are numerous ways to see the city, depending on your interest and time, and this is a good place to make your plans. For $1, you can watch "Struggle to Survive," a 42-minute video about the town's difficult first 14 years (history buffs will enjoy it; otherwise, it's a good way to kill an hour on a rainy day). However, the free 22-minute orientation video is more helpful in planning your visit. Once you've looked through their extensive information and made a plan, you can buy tickets for sightseeing trains and trolleys, which include discount admissions to the attractions (see "Getting Around," below). The center is open daily, from 8:30am to 5:30pm.

GETTING AROUND   Once you've parked at the visitor center, you can walk or take one of the sightseeing trolleys, trains, or horse-drawn carriages around the historic district. The trolleys and trains follow 7-mile (11km) routes, stopping at the visitor center and at or near most attractions between 8:30am and 5pm daily. You can get off at any stop, visit the attraction, and step aboard the next vehicle that comes along. Several vehicles make continuous circuits along the route throughout the day; you won't ever have to wait more than 15 or 20 minutes. If you don't get off at any attractions, it takes about 1 hour and 10 minutes to complete the tour. They don't all go to the same sights, so speak with their agents at the visitor center in order to pick the right one for you. You can buy tickets there or from the drivers. The companies also sell **discounted tickets** to some attractions.

St. Augustine Historical Tours (*©* **800/397-4071** or 904/829-3800) operates the green-and-white, open-air buses (and enclosed buses when it rains, a definite advantage). You can park your car at the headquarters (the Authentic Old Jail and the Florida Heritage Museum at the Authentic Old Jail, which are also stops on the tour). The bus tours cost $15 for adults, $5 for kids 6 to 12,

---

Tips Where to Park in "St. Aug"

On-street parking is nonexistent in St. Augustine's historic district, and metered parking lots are difficult to find and often full. Your best bet is to park in the large lots behind the visitor center on Castillo Drive. The $3 fee is good for 2 consecutive days, so you may leave and return at will. Most of the top historic attractions are within walking distance of the center, as it is virtually across the street from the Old City Gates.

free for kids under 6. They also run twice-nightly (7 and 8:30pm) "Ghosts & Gravestones" tours that are theatrical and mildly amusing/interesting ($16 adults, $6 kids).

St. Augustine Sightseeing Trains (© 800/226-6545 or 904/829-6545; www.redtrains.com) cover all the main sites except the Authentic Old Jail and the Florida Heritage Museum at the Authentic Old Jail, but its red open-air trains are small enough to go down more of the narrow historic-district streets. $12 for adults, $5 for kids 6 to 12, free for kids under 6, and tickets are good for 3 consecutive days. The company also sells package tickets for your convenience.

You may also want to see the sights from the back of a horse-drawn carriage. **Colee's Carriage Tours** (© 904/829-2818) has been showing people around town since 1877. The carriages line up on Avenida Menendez, south of Castillo de San Marcos National Monument. Slow-paced, entertainingly narrated 1-hour rides past major landmarks and attractions are offered from 8am to midnight. Private tours and hotel and restaurant pickups are available. Carriage tours cost $15 for adults, $5 for kids 6 to 12, free for kids under 6.

For more personalized tours, call **Tour St. Augustine** (© 800/797-3778 or 904/825-0087), which offers guided walking tours around the historical area. Tours range from $10 per person for 1 hour.

You can also search for old spirits with the nightly **Ghost Tours of St. Augustine** ★★ (© 888/461-1009 or 904-461-1009; www.ghosttoursofstaugustine. com), in which guides in period dress lead you through the historic district or to the St. Augustine Lighthouse; tickets are $8 per person, children under 6 free. They also have 1-hour ghost cruises on the river in a 72-foot (22m) tall-mast schooner. They cost $28 per person including soft drinks and snacks. Call for schedule and reservations.

The Sunshine Bus Company (© 904/823-4816) runs public bus routes Monday through Saturday from 6am to 7pm. The north-south line runs between the St. Augustine Airport on U.S. 1 and the historic district via San Marco Avenue and the Greyhound bus terminal on Malaga Street. Rides cost $1 per person. Call for exact schedule.

For a taxi, call **Yellow Cab** (© 904/824-6888).

Solano Cycle, 61 San Marco Ave., at Locust Avenue (© 904/825-6766), 2 blocks north of the visitor center, rents bicycles, mopeds, and scooters. Bikes cost $12 a day; scooters and mopeds, $30 to $40 a day. Open daily from 10am to 6pm.

SEEING THE TOP HISTORIC ATTRACTIONS

St. George Street from King Street north to the Old City Gate (at Orange St.) is the heart of the historic district. Lined with a plethora of restaurants and boutiques selling everything from T-shirts to antiques, these 4 blocks get the lion's share of the town's tourists. You'll have much less company if you poke around the narrow streets of the primarily residential neighborhood south of King Street.

Most of the town's attractions do not have guided tours, but most do have docents on hand to answer questions.

Be sure to drive through the parking lot of the Howard Johnson Express Inn, at 137 San Marco Ave., to see a gorgeous and stately Live Oak tree ★★ that is at least 600 years old and then continue east to Magnolia Avenue ★★, which is a spectacularly beautiful street with a lovely canopy of old magnolia trees.

St. Augustine

WHERE TO STAY ■
Bayfront Westcott House
  Bed & Breakfast Inn **28**
Best Western
  Spanish Quarter Inn **8**
Carriage Way
  Bed and Breakfast **13**
Casa Monica Hotel **23**
Casablanca Inn
  on the Bay **16**
Kenwood Inn **27**
Monterey Inn **14**
Ponce de León Hotel,
  Golf & Conference
  Resort **1**
Victorian House **26**

WHERE TO DINE ◆
A1A Ale Works **20**
The Bunnery Bakery
  & Café **17**
Gypsy Cab Co. **18**
La Parisienne **15**
Raintree **6**
The Spanish Bakery **11**

ATTRACTIONS ●
Authentic Old Jail **3**
Castillo San Marcos
  National Monument **9**
Colonial Spanish
  Quarter **12**
Florida Heritage Museum
  at the Authentic
  Old Jail **3**
Fountain of Youth
  Archaeological Park **4**
Government House
  Museum **22**
Lightner Museum **24**
Mission of Nombre
  de Dios **5**
The Oldest House **30**
The Oldest Store
  Museum **25**
The Oldest Wooden
  Schoolhouse
  in the USA **10**
Old St. Augustine Village
  Museum **29**
Ripley's Believe It Or Not!
  Museum **7**
Spanish Military
  Hospital **21**
St. Augustine Alligator
  Farm and
  Zoological Park **19**
St. Augustine Lighthouse
  & Museum **19**
World Golf Village **2**

Castillo de San Marcos National Monument ★★   One of the two best attractions here, America's oldest and best-preserved masonry fortification took 23 years (1672–1695) to build. It is stellar in design, with a double drawbridge entrance (the only way in or out) over a 40-foot (12m) dry moat. Diamond-shaped bastions in each corner, which enabled cannons to set up a deadly cross-fire, contained domed sentry towers. The seemingly indestructible Castillo was never captured in battle, and its coquina (limestone made from broken sea shells and corals) walls did not crumble when pounded by enemy artillery or violent storms throughout more than 300 years. Today, the old bombproof storerooms surrounding the central plaza house exhibits documenting the history of the fort, a national monument since 1924. You can also tour the vaulted powder magazine, a dank prison cell (supposedly haunted), the chapel, and guard rooms. Then, climb the stairs to get a great view of the Mantanzas Bay. A self-guided tour map and brochure are provided at the ticket booth. If available, the 20- to 30-minute ranger talks are well worth attending. There are popular torch-light tours of the fort in winter (call for schedule).

If you like forts, you should also check out **Fort Mantanzas,** built on an island in the 1740s to warn St. Augustine of enemy attacks from the south (which were out of reach of the Castillo de San Marcos). For more information, call ✆ **904/471-0116** or visit www.nps.gov/foma/. The monument is open daily from 8:30am to 5:30pm, and both admission to the fort and the ferry ride to the island are free, though donations are accepted.

1 E. Castillo Dr. (at San Marco Ave.). ✆ **904/829-6506.** www.nps.gov/casa. Admission $5 adults, $2 children 6–16, free for children under 6 with an adult. Fort daily 8:45am–4:45pm; grounds daily 5:30am–midnight.

Colonial Spanish Quarter and Spanish Quarter Museum ★★   The city's colonial architecture and landscape have been re-created in this 2-square-block history park, which interprets St. Augustine's history circa 1750. Once inside the museum, you can take a 20-minute guided tour of the **DeMesa-Sanchez House** (ca. 1740–60), the only authentic colonial-era structure in the compound (the others are reproductions). Elsewhere, interpreters (as craftsmen, storekeepers, and more) in 18th-century attire are on hand to help you envision the life of early inhabitants. If you have to make a choice of one or the other, the Old St. Augustine Village Museum (see below) covers more history.

33 St. George St. (between Cuna and Orange sts.). ✆ **904/825-6830.** Admission $6.50 adults, $5.50 seniors, $4 students 6–18, free for children 5 and under; or $13 per family. Daily 9am–5:30pm (last entry at 4:30pm).

Government House Museum   This museum is neither as informative nor as entertaining as the Old St. Augustine Village Museum or the Colonial Spanish Quarter (see below and above), but a walk through it will give you a quick overview of the Old City's history. Spanish coins, pottery, and other items unearthed during archaeological digs are the most interesting exhibits.

48 King St. (at St. George St.). ✆ **904/825-5079.** www.historicstaugustine.com. Admission $2.50 adults, $2 seniors, $1 children. Daily 9am–5pm.

Lightner Museum ★★   Henry Flagler's opulent Spanish Renaissance–style Alcazar Hotel, built in 1889, closed during the Depression and stayed vacant until Chicago publishing magnate Otto C. Lightner bought the building in 1948 to house his vast collection of Victoriana. The building is an attraction in itself and makes a gorgeous museum, centering on an open palm courtyard with an arched stone bridge spanning a fishpond. The first floor houses a Victorian village, with shop fronts representing emporia selling period wares. A Victorian

Science and Industry Room displays shells, rocks, minerals, and Native American artifacts in beautiful turn-of-the-20th-century cases. Other exhibits include stuffed birds, an Egyptian mummy, steam-engine models, and amazing examples of Victorian glassblowing. Plan to spend about 90 minutes exploring it all, and be sure to be here at 11am or 2pm, when a room of automated musical instruments erupts in concerts of period music. The imposing building across King Street was Henry Flagler's opulent rival resort, the Ponce de León Hotel. It now houses **Flagler College,** which runs tours from May through August of its magnificent Tiffany stained glass windows, Spanish-Renaissance architecture, and gold-leafed Maynard murals. ($4 adults, $1 kids under 12; call ℭ **904/ 823-3378** or visit www.flagler.edu/news_events/tours.html for more information.) Across Cordova Street stands another competitor of the day, the 1888-vintage Casa Monica Hotel (see "Where to Stay," later in this chapter).

75 King St. (at Granada St.). ℭ 904/824-2874. www.lightnermuseum.org. Admission $6 adults, $2 college students with ID and children 12–18, free for children 11 and under. Daily 9am–5pm (last tour 4pm).

Old St. Augustine Village Museum ★★   Operated by Daytona Beach's excellent Museum of Arts and Sciences (see p. 595), this museum brings to life each period of the city's history, from Spanish colonial times to the late 19th century. The buildings here (an entire block of 10 restored homes—built between 1790 and 1910—plus formal gardens) are original (and on their original building sites), the oldest of which was built in 1790 and owned (for a year in the early 19th century) by Achille Murat, Napoleon's exiled nephew (original letters from the French emperor are among the many fascinating exhibits). Many of the houses have varying exhibits inside, though since this museum is a work in progress, some are also closed, temporarily, until refurbishments are complete. The reconstructed Star General Store sells preserves and other Victorian-era goods. You'll need 2 hours to see it all, including the 30-minute guided tour. Admission is good all day, so if you miss the start of a tour, you can leave and come back.

250 St. George St. (entry on Bridge St. between St. George and Cordova sts.). ℭ 904/823-9722. www.old staug-village.com. Admission $7 adults, $6 seniors, $5 children under 12. Daily 9am–5pm. Guided tours on the hr. 10am–4pm.

The Oldest House ★★   Archaeological surveys indicate that a dwelling stood on this site as early as the beginning of the 17th century. What you see today, called the Gonzáles-Alvarez House (named for two of its prominent owners), evolved from a two-room coquina dwelling built between 1702 and 1727. The rooms are furnished to evoke various historical eras. Admission also entitles you to explore the adjacent **Manucy Museum of St. Augustine History,** where artifacts, maps, and photographs document the town's history from its origins through the Flagler era a century ago. Both are owned and operated by the St. Augustine Historical Society. Allow about 30 minutes.

14 St. Francis St. (at Charlotte St.). ℭ 904/824-2872. www.oldcity.com/oldhouse. Admission $5 adults, $4.50 seniors 55 and over, $3 students, free for children under 6; or $12 families. Daily 9am–5pm; tours depart every half-hr. (last tour at 4:30pm).

The Oldest Store Museum ★★   The C&F Hamblen General Store was St. Augustine's one-stop shopping center from 1835 to 1960, and the museum on its premises today replicates the emporium at the turn of the last century. On display are more than 100,000 items sold here in that era, many of them gleaned from the store's attic. They include high-button shoes, butter churns, spinning wheels, 1890s bathing suits, barrels of dill pickles (you can purchase one), and medicines that were 90% alcohol. Some 19th-century brand-name products shown here are still available today, among them Hershey's chocolate, Coca-Cola, Ivory soap, and Campbell's soups. It all makes for about 30 minutes of fascinating browsing.

4 Artillery Lane (between St. George and Aviles sts. behind Trinity Episcopal Church). ☎ 904/829-9729. www.oldcity.com/oldstore. Admission $5 adults, $4.50 seniors over 60, $1.50 children 6–12, free for children 5 and under. Mon–Sat 10am–4pm; Sun noon–4pm.

The Oldest Wooden Schoolhouse in the U.S.A. ★ *Kids* One of three structures here dating from the Spanish colonial period of more than 2 centuries ago, this red-cedar and cypress structure is held together by wooden pegs and handmade nails, its hand-wrought beams still intact. The last class was held here in 1864. Today, the old-time classroom is re-created using cheesy animated pupils and teacher, complete with a dunce and a below-stairs "dungeon" for unruly children, which will make your kids count their lucky stars that they weren't in school back then.

14 St. George St. (between Orange and Cuna sts.). ☎ 888/OLD-SCHL or 904/824-0192. www.oldestschool-house.com. Admission $2.75 adults, $2.25 seniors 55 and over, $1.75 children 6–12, free for children 5 and under. Daily 9am–5pm (later during summer).

Spanish Military Hospital This clapboard building is a reconstruction of part of a hospital that stood here during the second Spanish colonial period from 1784 to 1821. A 20-minute guided tour will show you what the apothecary, the administrative offices, the patients' ward, and the herbarium probably looked like in 1791. The ward and a collection of actual surgical instruments of the period will enhance your appreciation of modern medicine.

3 Aviles St. (south of King St.). ☎ 904/825-6830. Admission $2.50 adults, $2 seniors, $1.50 children. Mon–Sat 10am–5pm; Sun noon–5pm.

MORE HISTORIC ATTRACTIONS

Authentic Old Jail This compact prison, a mile north of the visitor center, may be authentic, but it is not particularly historic. It was built in 1890 and served as the county jail until 1953. The sheriff and his wife raised their children upstairs and used the same kitchen facilities to prepare the inmates' meals and their own. Among the "regular" cells, you can also see a maximum-security cell where murderers and horse thieves were confined, a cell housing prisoners condemned to hang (they could see the gallows being constructed from their window), and a grim solitary-confinement cell—with no windows or mattress. A restaurant serves inexpensive lunch fare.

167 San Marco Ave. (at Williams St.). ☎ 904/829-3800. Admission $5 adults, $4 children 6–12, free for children 5 and under. Daily 8:30am–5pm.

Florida Heritage Museum at the Authentic Old Jail After you've seen the Authentic Old Jail, you can spend another 30 minutes wandering through this commercial museum documenting 400 years of Florida's past, focusing on the colorful life of Henry Flagler, the Civil War, and the Seminole Wars. Highlights are an extraordinary collection of toys and dolls, mostly from the 1870s to the 1920s; and a replica of a Spanish galleon filled with weapons, pottery, and treasures complementing display cases filled with actual gold, silver, and jewelry recovered by treasure hunters. A typical wattle-and-daub hut of a Timucuan Indian in a forest setting illustrates the lifestyle of St. Augustine's first residents.

167 San Marco Ave. (at Williams St.). ☎ 904/829-3800. Admission $5 adults, $4 children 6–12, free for children 5 and under. Admission free with purchase of Old Town Trolley Tour. Daily 8:30am–5pm.

Fountain of Youth Archaeological Park *(Overrated)*   Never mind that Juan Ponce de León never did find the Fountain of Youth, this 25-acre archaeological park bills itself as North America's first historic site. Smithsonian Institution archaeological digs have established that a Timucuan Indian village existed on this site some 1,000 years ago, but there's no evidence that Ponce de León visited here during his 1513 voyage of discovery. You can wander around the not-so-interesting grounds yourself, but you'll learn more on a 45-minute guided tour or a planetarium show about 16th-century celestial navigation. *Be warned:* this place could be a secondary dictionary definition for the phrase tourist trap (not to mention the water from the fountain smells and tastes *awful*). Nevertheless, the grounds are lovely and the non-fountain exhibits are ok, which is good, because people feel the need to come here, even though they know it's basically a waste of time.

11 Magnolia Ave. (at Williams St.). ℂ **800/356-8222** or 904/829-3168. Admission $5.75 adults, $4.75 seniors, $2.75 children 6–12, free for children 5 and under. Daily 9am–5pm.

Mission of Nombre de Dios   This serene setting overlooking the Intracoastal Waterway is believed to be the site of the first permanent mission in the United States, founded in 1565. The mission is a popular destination of religious pilgrimages. Whatever your beliefs, it's a beautiful tree-shaded spot, ideal for quiet meditation.

27 Ocean Ave. (east of San Marco Ave.). ℂ **904/824-2809.** Free admission; donations appreciated. Daily 8am–5:30pm.

Old Florida Museum ★★ *(Kids)*   This mostly outdoors museum gives you the chance to experience historic Florida, with many hands-on activities (shelling and grinding corn, pumping water, writing with a quill pen, and so on) that kids will enjoy (as will their parents). Showcasing daily living activities, everyday objects (games, weapons, tools, and more), and recreational pastimes, the museum is able to demonstrate how 3 different eras of people in the area—the native Timucuan Indians, Colonial Spaniards, and American Pioneers—lived, worked, and played during the 16th through early-20th centuries.

254-D San Marco Ave. ℂ **800/813-3208** or 904/824-8874. www.oldfloridamuseum.com. Adults $5, kids $3. Daily 10am–5pm.

St. Augustine Lighthouse & Museum ★   This 165-foot-tall (50m) structure, Florida's first official lighthouse, was built in 1875 (with a signature black and white spiral stripe and red lantern) to replace the old Spanish lighthouse that had stood at the inlet since 1565. Sitting in a shady grove of live oaks, the lightkeeper's Victorian cottage was destroyed by fire in 1970 but was meticulously restored to its Victorian splendor. Also new is a Victorian-style visitor center that houses a museum explaining the history of both the lighthouse and the area. You should be in good physical condition (children must be at least 7 yr. old *and* 4 ft. tall) to climb the 219 steps to the top of the lighthouse, where you can see 19 nautical miles on a clear day.

81 Lighthouse Ave. (off Fla. A1A east of the Bridge of Lions). ℂ **904/829-0745.** www.stauglight.com. Admission to museum and tower $6.50 adults, $5.50 seniors, $4 children 7–11, free for kids under 7 and all active-duty and retired military personnel. Daily 9am–6pm. Follow Fla. A1A south across Bridge of Lions; take last left before turnoff to Anastasia State Park.

OTHER ENTERTAINING ATTRACTIONS

Marineland   This, the world's first oceanarium (1938), is located 15 minutes south of St. Augustine and is on the National Register of Historic Places. Here you can see dolphins, sea lions, penguins, flamingoes, and a myriad of other ocean life or you can snorkel or scuba in the 450,000 gallon oceanarium with some of them, if you make reservations. Though the facility is not presently in spectacular condition, Marineland is in the process of renovating, rebuilding, and revitalizing back into the modern first-class attraction it was when it first opened.

9600 Ocean Shore Blvd. ② **877/326-7539.** www.marineland.net. Admission $14 adults, $9 children. Dolphin encounter $120. Scuba diving $65 (need your own equipment); snorkeling $35 (just need a bathing suit). Dolphin photo $9.35; Dolphin touch and feed $19.95. Wed–Mon 9:30am–4:30pm. South of St. Augustine, on A1A.

Ripley's Believe It or Not! Museum *Kids*   This is the original Ripley's museum, housed in an architecturally interesting converted 1887 Moorish Revival residence—complete with battlements, massive chimneys, and rose windows. Like the Ripley's in a dozen other U.S. cities, the exhibits run the gamut, from a Haitian voodoo doll owned by Papa Doc Duvalier to letters carved on a pencil with a chain saw by Ray "Wild Mountain Man" Murphy.

19 San Marco Ave. (at Castillo Dr.). ② **904/824-1606.** www.staugustine-ripleys.com. Admission $9.95 adults, $7.95 seniors, $5.95 children 5–12, free for children 4 and under. June 8–Labor Day daily 9am–9pm; day after Labor Day–June 7 9am–7pm.

St. Augustine Alligator Farm and Zoological Park ★★ *Kids*   You can't leave Florida without seeing at least one real live gator, and there are more than 2,700 gators and crocodiles—including some rare white gators—on display at this century-old attraction. In fact, it houses the world's only complete collection of every species (22) of crocodilians, a category that includes alligators, crocodiles, caimans, and gavials. Other creatures living here include geckos, prehensile-tailed skinks, lizards, snakes, tortoises, monkeys, and exotic birds. There are ponds and marshes filled with a variety of ducks, geese, swans, herons, egrets, ibises, wood storks, and other native wading birds as well as a petting zoo with pygmy goats, potbellied pigs, miniature horses, mouflon sheep, and deer. Entertaining (and educational) 20-minute alligator and reptile shows take place hourly throughout the day, and spring through fall you can often see narrated feedings. There's also a taxidermied (and famous) giant crocodile from New Guinea named Gomek on display.

999 Anastasia Blvd. (Fla. A1A), east of Bridge of Lions at Old Quarry Rd. ② **904/824-3337.** www.alligator-farm.com (check for discounts). Admission $14.25 adults, $8.50 children 3–10, free for children under 3. Daily 9am–5pm; summer hours 9am–6pm.

HITTING THE BEACH

There are several places to find sand and sea: in **Vilano Beach,** on the north side of St. Augustine Inlet; and in **St. Augustine Beach,** on the south side (the inlet dumps the Matanzas and North rivers into the Atlantic). Be aware, however, that erosion has almost swallowed the beach from the inlet as far south as Old Beach Road in St. Augustine Beach. The U.S. Army Corps of Engineers is reclaiming the sand, but in the meantime, hotels and homes here have rock seawalls instead of sand bordering the sea.

Erosion has made a less noticeable impact on the beautiful **Anastasia State Park** ★★, on Anastasia Boulevard (Fla. A1A) across the Bridge of Lions and just past the Alligator Farm, where the 4 miles (6km) of beach (on which you can drive and park) are still backed by picturesque dunes. On its river side, the area faces a lagoon flanked by tidal marshes. Available here are shaded picnic areas

Where Golf Is King

Passionate golf fans can easily spend a day at the **World Golf Hall of Fame** ⭐ ((C) **904/940-4123**), a state-of-the-art museum honoring professional golf, its great players, and the sport's famous supporters (including comedian Bob Hope and singer Dinah Shore). It's the centerpiece of **World Golf Village,** which is a complex of hotels, shops, offices, and 18-hole golf courses (see "Cruises, Fishing, Golf, Sailing & Water Sports" below). There's an IMAX screen next door.

Museum admission is $10 adults, $9 seniors and students, $6 children 5 to 12. IMAX movie tickets range from $7 to $10 adults, $6 to $9 seniors and students, $5 to $8 children 3 to 12. Combination tickets to the museum and one IMAX movie cost $15 for adults, $13 seniors and students, $10 children 5 to 12. Throw in a round on the putting green and you'll pay $21 for adults, $18 seniors and students, and $14 for children 5 to 12. Admission and movies are free for children under 5. The museum is open daily from 10am to 6pm (IMAX movies to 8pm on Fri and Sat).

You don't have to play the real courses, because the village is built around a lake with a "challenge hole" sitting out in the middle, 132 feet (40m) from the shoreline. You can hit balls at it or play a round on the nearby putting course. The Walkway of Champions (whose signatures appear in pavement stones) circles the lake and passes a shopping complex whose main tenant is the two-story **Tour Stop** ((C) **904/ 940-0422**), a purveyor of pricey apparel and equipment.

You can stay at the luxurious **World Golf Village Renaissance Resort,** 500 S. Legacy Trail, St. Augustine, FL 32092 ((C) **800/228-9290** or 904/940-8000; www.worldgolfrenaissance.com).

The village is at exit 95A off I-95. For more information, contact World Golf Village, 21 World Golf Place, St. Augustine, FL 32092 ((C) **904/940-4000;** www.wgv.com).

with grills, restrooms, windsurfing, sailing and canoeing (on a saltwater lagoon), a nature trail, and saltwater fishing (for bluefish, pompano, and whiting from the surf; sea trout, redfish, and flounder—a license is required for out-of-state residents). In summer, you can rent chairs, beach umbrellas, and surfboards. There's good bird-watching here, too, especially in spring and fall; pick up a brochure at the entrance. The 139 wooded campsites are in high demand all year. They have picnic tables, grills, and electricity. Admission to the park is $3.25 per vehicle and $1 for bicyclists and pedestrians. Campsites cost $16 per night plus $2 for electricity. For camping reservations, call (C) **800/326-3521** or go to the website at www.reserveamerica.com. The day-use area is open daily from 8am to sunset. You can bring your pets. For more information, contact Anastasia State Park, 1340A Fla. A1A S., St. Augustine, FL 32084 ((C) **904/ 461-2033;** www.floridastateparks.org/district3/anastasia).

All St. Augustine beaches charge a fee of $3 per car at official access points from Memorial Day to Labor Day; the rest of the year you can park free, but there are no lifeguards on duty and no toilet facilities on the beach.

CRUISES, FISHING, GOLF, SAILING & WATER SPORTS

For additional outdoor options, contact the St. Augustine, Ponte Vedra & The Beaches Visitors and Convention Bureau (see "Essentials," earlier in this section) and ask them to send you a copy of their *Outdoor Recreation Guide*.

CRUISES The Usina family has been running **St. Augustine Scenic Cruises** (© **800/542-8316** or 904/824-1806; www.scenic-cruise.com) on Matanzas Bay since the turn of the last century. They offer 75-minute narrated tours aboard the double-decker *Victory III*, departing from the Municipal Marina just south of the Bridge of Lions. You can sometimes spot dolphins, brown pelicans, cormorants, and kingfishers. Snacks, soft drinks, beer, and wine are sold on board. Departures normally are at 11am and 1, 2:45, and 4:30pm daily except Christmas, with an additional tour at 6:15pm from April 1 to May 21 and Labor Day to October 15; May 22 to Labor Day there are two additional tours, at 6:45 and 8:30pm. Call ahead—schedules can change during inclement weather. Fares are $10.50 adults, $8.50 seniors, $7 juniors ages 13 to 18, $5 children 4 to 12, free for children under 4. If you're driving, allow extra time to find parking on the street.

You can also take the free ferry to Fort Mantanzas on Rattlesnake Island. There are often dolphins in the water as you make the trip, and the fort is interesting if you have the time. Ferries take off from 8635 Highway A1A, South (follow A1A south out of St. Augustine for about 15 miles). Call © **904/471-0116** or visit www.nps.gov/foma/ for more information.

FISHING You can fish to your heart's content at **Anastasia State Park** (see "Hitting the Beach," above). You can also cast your line off **St. Johns County Fishing Pier,** on the north end of St. Augustine Beach (© **904/461-0119**). The pier is open 24 hours daily and has a bait shop with rental equipment that is open from 6am to 10pm. Admission is $2 ($1 children under 2) for fishing, 50¢ per person for sightseeing.

For full-day, half-day, and overnight **deep-sea fishing** excursions (for snapper, grouper, porgy, amberjack, sea bass, and other species), contact the **Sea Love Marina,** 250 Vilano Rd. (Fla. A1A north), at the eastern end of the Vilano Beach Bridge (© **904/824-3328;** www.sealovefishing.com). Full-day trips on the party boat *Sea Love II* cost about $50; half-day trips, $35. No license is required, and rod, reel, bait, and tackle are supplied. Bring your own food and drink.

GOLF The area's best golf resorts are in Ponte Vedra Beach—about a half-hour's drive north on Fla. A1A, closer to Jacksonville than St. Augustine (see "Where to Stay," in section 4, later in this chapter, for details).

At World Golf Village, 12 miles (19km) north of St. Augustine at exit 95A off I-95 (see the box, "Where Golf Is King," above), **The Slammer & The Squire** and **The King & The Bear** (© **904/940-6088;** www.wgv.com) together offer 36 holes amid a wildlife preserve. Locals say they're not as challenging as their greens fees, about $100 in summer, $165 in winter, including cart. For those not schooled in golf history, the "Slammer" is in honor of Sam Sneed; the "Squire" is for Gene Sarazen; the "King" is Arnold Palmer, and the "Bear" is Jack Nicklaus. Palmer and Nicklaus actually collaborated in designing their course.

Nicklaus also had a hand in the stunning course at the **Ocean Hammock Golf Club** ★★ (© **386/477-4653;** www.oceanhammock.com), on Fla. A1A in Palm Coast, about halfway between St. Augustine and Daytona Beach. Opened in late 2000 with six of its holes actually skirting the beach, it is the first truly ocean-side course built in Florida since the 1920s.

There are only a few courses in St. Augustine, including a rather-flat 18 at the **Ponce de León Hotel, Golf & Conference Resort** (see "Where to Stay," below) and the **St. Augustine Shores Golf Club,** 707 Shores Blvd., off U.S. 1 (© **904/ 794-4653**). The latter is a par-70 course featuring 18 holes, lots of water, a lighted driving range and putting green, and a restaurant and lounge. Greens fees usually are under $30, including cart.

SAILING   You can spend 3 to 4 hours under sail with Captain Paul Kulik on board his *Voyager* (© **904/347-7183;** www.villavoyager.com), a 22-foot-wide (7m) trimaran, which departs the Municipal Marina next to the Bridge of Lions. The cruises cost $35 per person, including lunch, soft drinks, and beer. The boat can carry a maximum of six guests, so call for reservations and schedule.

WATER SPORTS   Jet skis and surfing and windsurfing equipment can be rented at **Surf Station,** 1020 Anastasia Blvd. (Fla. A1A), a block south of the Alligator Farm (© **904/471-9463**); at **Raging Water Sports,** at the Conch House Marina Resort, 57 Comares Ave. (© **904/829-5001**), which is off Anastasia Avenue (Fla. A1A) halfway between the Bridge of Lions and the Alligator Farm; and at **Watersports of St. Augustine,** at Sea Love Marina, 250 Vilano Rd. (Fla. A1A north), at the eastern end of the Vilano Beach Bridge (© **904/ 823-8963**).

SHOPPING

The winding streets of the historic district are home to dozens of **antiques stores** and **art galleries** stocked full of original paintings, sculptures, bric-a-brac, fine furnishings, china, and other treasures. Brick-lined **Aviles Street,** 1 block from the river, has an especially good mix of shops for browsing, as does **St. George Street** south of the visitor center and the Uptown area on **San Marco Avenue** a few blocks north of the center. The **Alcazar Courtyard Shops** at the Lightner Museum (© **904/824-2874**) has a good selection of antiques shops (see "Seeing the Top Historic Attractions," earlier in this section). The visitor center has complete lists of art galleries and antiques shops; or contact the **Antique Dealers Association of St. Augustine,** 60 Cuna St., St. Augustine, FL 32084 (no phone), and **Art Galleries of Saint Augustine** (© **904/829-0065** or 904/825-4577).

Experience chocolate heaven at **Whetstone Chocolates,** 2 Coke Rd. (Fla. 312), between U.S. 1 and the Mickler O'Connell Bridge (© **904/825-1700**). Free tours of the store and factory usually take place Monday through Saturday from 10am to 5:30pm, but call to make sure of the factory's schedule. Whetstone has a retail outlet at 42 St. George St. in the historic district.

Outlet shoppers will find plenty of good hunting 7 miles (11km) northwest of downtown on Fla. 16 at I-95 in the **St. Augustine Outlet Mall** (© **904/ 825-1555**), on the west side of I-95; and the enclosed, air-conditioned **Belz Factory Outlet World** (© **904/826-1311;** www.belz.com), on the east side of the Interstate. Stores in both malls are open Monday through Saturday from 9am to 9pm, Sunday from 10am to 6pm.

WHERE TO STAY

There are plenty of moderate and inexpensive motels and hotels in St. Augustine. Most convenient to the historic district is the 40-room **Best Western Spanish Quarter Inn,** 6 Castillo Dr. (© **800/528-1234** or 904/824-4457; fax 904/829-8330), directly across the street from the visitor center. It's completely surrounded by an asphalt parking lot but does have a swimming pool and hot tub.

Almost all accommodations increase their prices on weekends, when the town is most crowded with visitors. St. Johns County charges a 9% tax on hotel bills.

HOTELS & MOTELS

Casa Monica Hotel ★★ This hotel was built in 1888 as a luxury hotel by Bostonian and YMCA founder Franklin W. Smith. (Unfortunately, Smith never really opened it, since the furniture he'd purchased for the hotel never made it to St. Augustine, thanks to Henry Flagler who owned the railroad the furniture was to be shipped on as well as the neighboring—and thus competing—hotel. In a bind and losing too much money, Smith finally sold the hotel to Flagler, for 25 cents on the dollar for what he originally spent, and the furniture mysteriously appeared almost immediately!) This Spanish-Moorish-style building (look for the atmospheric, arched, old-time carriage entrance near the present garage) was also used as the St. Johns County Courthouse from the 1960s until 1997.

Now totally restored, it's easily the best hotel here, with top-notch rooms and services. Most of the lovely guest quarters are spacious and fully modern hotel rooms, with Iberian-style armoires, wrought-iron headboards, and tapestry drapes. "Premium" rooms have sitting areas with sofas and easy chairs. All units have big bathrooms equipped with high-end toiletries and either a huge walk-in shower or a combination tub-shower. Much more interesting are the "signature suites" installed in the building's two tile-topped towers and fortresslike central turret. Each of these one- to four-bedroom units is unique. One in the turret has a half-round living room with gun-port windows overlooking the historic district, while a three-story town-house model in one of the towers has a huge whirlpool bathroom on its top floor. The 95 Cordova restaurant, which serves regional fare, has an excellent wine list, great service, and is beautifully decorated. However, though a lot of people swear the food served there is the best in the city, we couldn't find much to our taste. A player piano provides music in the adjoining bar. Guests here can pay $15 a day to use the swimming pools, restaurants, and other facilities at an exclusive oceanfront club in Ponte Vedra Beach.

95 Cordova St. (at King St.), St. Augustine, FL 32084. ☎ 800/648-1888 or 904/827-1888. Fax 904/819-6065. www.casamonica.com. 138 units. $149–$239 double. Packages available. AE, DC, DISC, MC, V. Valet parking $8; limited free self-parking 2 blocks from hotel. **Amenities:** Restaurant (American, with several additional influences); marketplace, bar; heated (and cooled) outdoor pool; access to nearby health club; exercise room; Jacuzzi; bike rental; children's programs; concierge; business center; limited room service; babysitting; coin-op washers and dryers. *In room:* A/C, TV, dataport (high-speed access), fridge, coffeemaker, hair dryer, iron.

Monterey Inn *Value* For the price, you can't find a better choice than this modest, wrought iron–trimmed motel overlooking the Matanzas Bay and close to the attractions and nightlife of the Old City. Three generations of the Six family have run this simple two-story motel, and they keep the 1960s building and grounds always clean and functional. Rooms are not especially spacious but they are comfortable.

16 Avenida Menendez (between Cuna and Hypolita sts.), St. Augustine, FL 32084. ☎ 904/824-4482. Fax 904/829-8854. www.themontereyinn.com. 59 units. $49–$99 double. AE, DC, DISC, MC, V. **Amenities:** Heated outdoor pool. *In room:* A/C, TV, dataport, hair dryer.

Ponce de León Hotel, Golf & Conference Resort Located 2½ miles (4km) north of the historic district, this 400-acre complex, until recently known as the Radisson Ponce de León Golf & Conference Resort, primarily appeals to golfers, who can play a round on its Donald Ross–designed par-72 course before heading off to see the sights. Although it's been in business since Henry Flagler built a resort here in 1916, today's establishment is a modern motel. Rooms are in one- and two-story buildings spread out in a virtual forest of palms, magnolias, centuries-old live oaks, and clumps of sawgrass, with a large swimming pool in the center. The units all have balconies or patios. Minisuites are good for families, with trellises separating small sitting rooms from sleeping areas. The Fairway Grill, with its big window walls overlooking the golf course and the marshes beyond, offers breakfast, lunch, and dinner. On weekend evenings you can join conferences unwinding in the lounge for live entertainment in a cozy bar overlooking the greens. Other activities include a putting green; volleyball, shuffleboard, croquet, bocce ball, and basketball courts; and a horseshoe pitch.

4000 U.S. 1 N., St. Augustine, FL 32095. © **800/228-2821** or 904/824-2821. Fax 904/824-8254. www.theponce.com. 193 units. $69–$149 double. Golf, family, and other packages available. AE, DC, DISC, MC, V. **Amenities:** Restaurant (American); bar; heated outdoor pool; golf course; 6 tennis courts; varied sports facilities; Jacuzzi; limited room service; laundry service. *In room:* A/C, TV, dataport, coffeemaker, hair dryer, iron.

BED-&-BREAKFASTS

St. Augustine has more than two dozen bed-and-breakfasts in restored historic homes. They all provide free parking, complimentary breakfast, 24-hour refreshments, and plenty of atmosphere (the St. Francis Inn has a spectacular walled courtyard), but most accept neither young children nor guests who smoke (check before booking). Those listed below are in the historic district. For more choices, contact **St. Augustine Historic Inns,** P.O. Box 5268, St. Augustine, FL 33085-5268 (no phone; www.staugustineinns.com), for descriptions of its member properties.

Bayfront Westcott House Bed & Breakfast Inn ⋆   Overlooking Matanzas Bay, this two-story, wood-frame house offers rare opportunities for an uncluttered view from the porch, the second-story veranda, and a shady courtyard. The rooms—some with bay windows, two-person whirlpool tubs, and working fireplaces—are exquisitely furnished and immaculate. Yours might have authentic Victorian furnishings and a brass bed made up with a white quilt and lace dust ruffle.

146 Avenida Menendez (between Bridge and Francis sts.), St. Augustine, FL 32084. © **800/513-9814** or 904/824-4301. Fax 904/824-4301. www.westcotthouse.com. 9 units (all with bathroom). $95–$250 double. Rates include full breakfast. AE, DISC, MC, V. **Amenities:** Access to nearby health club; free bicycles; Jacuzzi; massage. *In room:* A/C, TV, hair dryer.

Carriage Way Bed and Breakfast *(Value)*   Primarily occupying an 1883 Victorian wood-frame house fronted by roses and hibiscus, this bed-and-breakfast isn't fancy or formal, but it is comfortable, relaxed, and a good value. Rooms in the main house are furnished with simple antique reproductions, including many four-poster beds. One room even retains its original fireplace. A console TV, books, magazines, and games are provided in a homey parlor. For more privacy, two more rooms are down the street in "The Cottage," a one-story clapboard house built in 1885. It has its own living room and kitchen, and both the Miranda and the Ashton Rooms have claw-foot bathtubs. Miranda also sports a two-person Jacuzzi, and Ashton has its own small back porch.

70 Cuna St. (between Cordova and Spanish sts.), St. Augustine, FL 32084. ℂ **800/908-9832** or 904/829-2467. Fax 904/826-1461. www.carriageway.com. 11 units (all with bathroom). $85–$190 double. Rates include full breakfast. AE, DISC, MC, V. **Amenities:** Free use of bikes. *In room:* A/C, dataport.

Casablanca Inn on the Bay   This 1914 Mediterranean-style white-stucco house faces the bay, although only a few of the rooms actually offer views. The most stunning are the two second-floor suites with bay-front balconies, generously sized hammocks, and private porches. The furnishings—a mix of turn-of-the-last-century American oak, European, and Victorian pieces—are of a higher quality than those at many other inns. One modern convenience is a cassette player with a small selection of classical tapes. This may be appreciated, especially if you are on a ground-floor room that unfortunately suffers from the noise of the street and the next-door bar and grill. Breakfast is served alfresco on the porch or in a glass-enclosed conservatory. Six units have neither TVs nor telephones.

24 Avenida Menendez (between Hypolita and Treasury sts.), St. Augustine, FL 32084. ℂ **800/826-2626** or 904/829-0928. Fax 904/826-1892. www.casablancainn.com. 20 units (all with bathroom). $125–$350 double. Rates include full breakfast. AE, DISC, MC, V. **Amenities:** Access to nearby health club; free use of bikes. *In room:* A/C, TV (18 units), no phone (6 units).

Kenwood Inn   This inn is unusual because of its relatively large outdoor space, which includes a swimming pool, a lushly landscaped sun deck, and a secluded garden courtyard (complete with a fishpond and neat flower bed under a sprawling pecan tree). This Victorian wood-frame house with graceful verandas has served as a boardinghouse or inn since the late 19th century. Everything from the carpeting to the linens to the china is first-class. Rooms are larger and more private than most other accommodations in converted single-family homes. Some rooms have neither televisions nor telephones.

38 Marine St. (at Bridge St.), St. Augustine, FL 32084. ℂ **800/824-8151** or 904/824-2116. Fax 904/824-1689. www.oldcity.com/kenwood. 14 units (all with bathroom). $95–$175 double; bridal suite $225. Rates include continental breakfast. DISC, MC, V. **Amenities:** Outdoor pool; free use of bikes. *In room:* A/C, TV, fax, dataport, kitchen, minibar, fridge, coffeemaker, hair dryer, iron.

Victorian House *(Kids)*   This bed-and-breakfast occupies an 1897-vintage Victorian residence, complete with wraparound porch and an adjoining old store, now dubbed the "Carriage House." The latter is divided into four units, one of which has a kitchenette. What's unusual is that children are welcome to stay in the Carriage House units, all of which have TVs and private entrances. Kids are not welcome to stay in the main house, whose rooms lack TVs. Country Victorian antiques adorn all units here, but none of the units has a telephone.

11 Cadiz St. (between Aviles and Charlotte sts.), St. Augustine, FL 32084. ℂ **877/703-0432** or 904/824-5214. Fax 904/824-7990. www.victorianhouse-inn.com. 8 units (all with bathroom). $90–$175 double. Rates include full breakfast. AE, DISC, MC, V. **Amenities:** Free bikes. *In room:* A/C, TV (4 units), kitchen (1 unit), no phone.

WHERE TO DINE

In a town with as much tourist traffic as St. Augustine, there are, of course, a fair number of "tourist trap" restaurants. But on the whole, the food in St. Augustine, even at the popular eateries, is fairly priced and of good quality.

The historic district has a branch of Tampa's famous **Columbia** restaurant, at 98 St. George St., at Hypolita Street (© **904/824-3341**). Like the original in Ybor City (p. 457), this one sports Spanish architecture, including intricate tile work and courtyards with fountains.

A1A Ale Works ⊕ SEAFOOD   You can't miss this two-story Victorian-style building on the waterfront opposite the Bridge of Lions. One of the city's most popular watering holes, the noisy downstairs bar offers nightly entertainment, which sometimes filters upstairs into the restaurant. Despite the noise potential, the kitchen turns out a surprisingly good blend of new-world Floribbean, Cuban, Caribbean, and Latino styles, in a nice setting with big windows and outside balcony seating overlooking the river and Bridge of Lions. Most of the seafood is very fresh, and the sauces are made to order. The spicy ahi stick appetizer (sushi grade tuna, pickled ginger, and sesame seeds wrapped in a wonton skin, cooked rare, served over Caribbean slaw and topped with a wasabi and siracha aioli) is as good as it gets, and you shouldn't leave without trying it. Don't overlook the nightly specials, either, especially the fresh fish. The house brew ranges from a very light lager to a nonalcoholic root beer.

1 King St. (at Avenida Menendez). © 904/829-2977. Call for preferred seating. Main courses $12–$20; sandwiches $7–$9. AE, DC, DISC, MC, V. Sun–Thurs 11am–10:30pm; Fri–Sat 11am–11pm. Late-night menu served downstairs.

The Bunnery Bakery & Café ⊕ Value BAKERY/DELI   Alluring aromas waft from this bakery and cafe in the heart of the historic district. It's lovely to come here for breakfast or for a fresh pastry and hot cup of latte, cappuccino, or espresso anytime you need a break from sightseeing. At lunch, plop yourself into one of the colorful booths and indulge in soup, salads, burgers, panini, or a croissant stuffed with walnut-and-pineapple chicken salad. Order at the counter; the staff will call your number when it's ready.

121 St. George St. (between Treasury and Hypolita sts.). © 904/829-6166. Breakfast $3–$7; sandwiches and salads $3.50–$7.50. No credit cards. Daily 8am–6pm. Closed New Year's Day, Easter, Thanksgiving, Christmas Eve, Christmas.

Gypsy Cab Co. ⊕⊕ Value NEW AMERICAN   Billing itself as a temple of "urban cuisine," owner-chef Ned Pollack's high-energy establishment, with gaudy purple neon stripes outside and bright, art-filled dining rooms inside, offers the town's most interesting culinary experience. Ned's creative menu changes daily, although a hearty black-bean soup is a constant winner. I had expertly cooked shrimp with artichokes sautéed with scallions, mushrooms, and julienned carrots and served with a pleasantly peppered white-wine and butter sauce—a delightful combination of flavors. Grouper in a tomato-basil sauce, strip steak under a peppercorn sauce, and Cayman Island–style pork were among the other offerings. The house salad dressing is so good they sell it by the bottle. Also worshipped here during autumn: Beaujolais nouveau, by the glass or bottle. Lunch is served in the Gypsy Bar & Grill next door, which has live music Tuesday and Wednesday nights and serves as a comedy club from Thursday to Saturday evenings (© **904/808-1305**).

828 Anastasia Blvd. (Fla. A1A, at Ingram St., east of the Bridge of Lions). © 904/824-8244. Reservations not accepted. Main courses $12–$20. AE, DC, DISC, MC, V. Mon–Thurs 11am–4pm and 4:30–10pm; Fri 11am–4pm and 4:30–11pm; Sat 11am–4pm and 4:30–11pm; Sun 10:30am–4pm and 4:30–10pm.

La Parisienne ★★ CONTEMPORARY FRENCH   Despite its name, this lovely dining room evokes the French countryside, with a rough-hewn beamed-pine ceiling, lace-curtained windows, and ladder-back chairs. Changing seasonally, the menu always features fresh seafood, and in fall you'll see venison and quail. If they're offered, begin with pan-seared sea scallops in a citrus sauce; then go on to steak au poivre with a Cognac-cream sauce, roast rack of lamb Provençal, or the day's treatment of fresh local fish. A fixed-price, five-course menu offers a choice of meat or seafood appetizers and main courses plus cheeses and dessert. The weekend brunch menu offers beignets, eggs Benedict, and scrambled eggs with smoked salmon.

60 Hypolita St. (between Spanish and Cordova sts.). ℂ **904/829-0055.** Reservations recommended. Main courses $19–$28; 5-course prix fixe menu $58. AE, DISC, MC, V. Tues–Fri 5–9pm; Sat–Sun 11am–3pm and 5–9pm.

Raintree ★ INTERNATIONAL   Even if you don't have a full meal at this romantic 1879 Victorian house (about half a mile north of the historic district), the tempting variety of hot crepes and an exemplary crème brûlée is worth a visit. Sweetness works its way onto the main menu, too, starting with fruit salsa with the blue–crab-cake appetizer and progressing to the likes of cashew-encrusted pork tenderloin mignonettes with a champagne and frothed-blackberry butter sauce. More-traditional main courses include beef Wellington and rack of New Zealand lamb. It's all very good, though not as exciting as at Gypsy Cab Co. or as expertly prepared as at La Parisienne (see above). The list of more than 300 vintages has won *Wine Spectator* awards.

102 San Marco Ave. (at Bernard St.). ℂ **904/824-7211.** Reservations recommended. Main courses $15–$23; dessert bar $5.50. AE, DC, MC, V. Sun–Thurs 6–9:30pm; Fri–Sat 6–10pm. Courtesy car provides transportation from/to downtown hotels.

The Spanish Bakery COLONIAL   Occupying a reconstructed 17th-century kitchen building, this little family-operated establishment bakes almond, lemon, and cinnamon cookies, using recipes from the Spanish colonial period, when a lack of refrigeration limited the use of milk and eggs. A couple of these crunchy morsels, eaten at the picnic tables outside, make a fine snack while you're touring the historic district. Or you can have lunch here, choosing from daily specials such as spicy Spanish-style chili over rice.

Rear of 42½ St. George St. (between Cuna and Orange sts.). ℂ **904/471-3046.** Reservations not accepted. Lunch specials $5; cookies and rolls 40¢–50¢ each. No credit cards. Daily 9:30am–3pm. Closed Thanksgiving, Christmas.

ST. AUGUSTINE AFTER DARK

Especially on weekends, the Old Town is full of strollers and partiers making the rounds to the dozens of active bars, clubs, and restaurants. For up-to-date details on what's happening in town, check the local daily, the *St. Augustine Record* (www.staugustine.com), or the irreverent *Folio Weekly* (www.folioweekly.com).

The best-looking crowd in town can be found at the **A1A Ale Works** (see "Where to Dine," above). Twenty-something hipsters and middle-aged partiers mingle at this handsome New Orleans–style microbrewery and restaurant. Thursday through Saturday nights, downstairs at the bar, on a crowded window-front stage, you'll find live music, often light rock and R&B tunes.

Ann O'Malley's, 23 Orange St., near the Old City Gate (ℂ **904/825-4040**), is an Irish pub, open day and night until 1am. Besides the selection of ales, stouts, and drafts, this is one of the only spots in town where you can grab a late-night bite.

Also popular with locals, **Mill Top Tavern,** 19½ St. George St., at the Fort (© **904/829-2329**), is a warm and rustic tavern housed in a 19th-century mill building (the waterwheel is still outside). Weather permitting, it's an open-air space. There's music every day from 1pm until 1am.

At **Scarlett O'Hara's,** 70 Hypolita St., at Cordova Street (© **904/824-6535**), a catacomb of cozy rooms with working fireplaces in a rambling, 19th-century wood-frame house is the setting for live rock, jazz, and R&B bands nightly. Sporting events are aired on a large-screen TV.

Across the river, the **Gypsy Bar & Grill,** part of the Gypsy Cab Co. restaurant, 828 Anastasia Blvd. (© **904/824-8244**), has live music Tuesday and Wednesday nights, then transforms itself into a comedy club Thursday through Saturday evenings (© **904/808-1305**).

You can also take one of the many ghost tours that are offered nightly.

4 Jacksonville

36 miles (58km) S of the Georgia border, 134 miles (216km) NE of Orlando, 340 miles (547km) N of Miami

Once infamous for its smelly paper mills, the sprawling metropolis of Jacksonville—residents call it "Jax," from its airport abbreviation—is now one of the South's insurance and banking capitals. Development was rampant throughout Duval County during the 1990s, with hotels, restaurants, attractions, and clubs springing up, especially in suburban areas near the interstate highways. Nevertheless, there are shady older neighborhoods to explore, 20 miles (32km) of Atlantic Ocean beaches upon which to sun and swim, many championship golf courses to play, and an abundance of beautiful and historic national and state parks to roam.

Spanning the broad, curving St. Johns River, downtown Jacksonville is a vibrant center of activity during weekdays and on weekend afternoons and evenings, when many locals return to the restaurants and bars of Jacksonville Landing and Southbank Riverwalk, two dining-and-entertainment complexes facing each other across the river that have helped to revitalize downtown.

ESSENTIALS

GETTING THERE   Jacksonville International Airport, on the city's north side about 12 miles (19km) from downtown (© **904/741-2000;** www.jaxairports.org), is served by **Air Canada** (© 888/247-2262), **AirTran** (© 800/AIR-TRAN), **American** (© 800/433-7300), **Continental** (© 800/525-0280), **Delta** (© 800/221-1212), **Midway** (© 800/446-4392), **Northwest** (© 800/225-2525), **Southwest** (© 800/435-9792), **United** (© 800/241-6522), and **Metro Jet** and **US Airways** (© 800/428-4322).

You can get visitor information about Jacksonville, St. Augustine, and Amelia Island at the **First Coast Welcome Center,** on the lower level by the baggage area (© **904/741-4902**). Open daily from 9am to 9pm.

Alamo (© 800/327-9633), **Avis** (© 800/331-1212), **Budget** (© 800/527-0700), **Dollar** (© 800/800-4000), **Enterprise** (© 800/325-8007), **Hertz** (© 800/654-3131), and **National** (© 800/CAR-RENT) have rental-car booths at the airport.

Gator City Taxi (© **904/741-0008** at the airport or 904/355-TAXI elsewhere) provides cab service. Fares for up to four persons are about $20 to downtown, $38 to $45 to beach hotels, $55 to $65 to St. Augustine, and $40 to Amelia Island. **Express Shuttle** (© **904/353-8880** or 904/355-2583) provides van service to and from hotels and resorts throughout the area. Per-person fares

---

(**Fun Fact** Once a Cow Town

Although Jacksonville claims to be the capital of Florida's historic "First Coast," the city dates its beginnings from an early-1800s settlement named Cowford, because cattle crossed the St. Johns River here. It changed its name in 1822 to honor General Andrew Jackson, who had forced Spain to cede Florida to the United States 2 years earlier.

---

are about $17 to downtown Jacksonville, $22 to $28 to the beaches, $57 to $67 to St. Augustine, and $35 to Amelia Island.

There's an **Amtrak** station in Jacksonville at 3570 Clifford Lane, off U.S. 1, just north of 45th Street (© **800/USA-RAIL;** www.amtrak.com).

VISITOR INFORMATION Contact the **Jacksonville and the Beaches Convention & Visitors Bureau,** 201 E. Adams St., Jacksonville, FL 32202 (© **800/733-2668** or 904/798-9111; fax 904/789-9103; www.jaxcvb.com), for maps, brochures, calendars, and advice. The bureau is open Monday through Friday from 8am to 5pm. It operates information booths at the airport (see above) and in the upstairs food court of **Jacksonville Landing** (see "Exploring the Area," below). The latter is open Monday through Saturday from 10am to 7pm, Sunday 12:30 to 5:30pm. The bureau also has a walk-in information office in **Jacksonville Beach** at 403 Beach Blvd., between 3rd and 4th streets (© **904/242-0024**), which is open Monday through Saturday from 10am to 6pm.

GETTING AROUND You can get around downtown Jacksonville via the **Skyway,** an elevated and completely automated train that runs down Hogan Street from the Florida Community College Jacksonville campus through downtown and across the river via the Acosta/Fla. 13 bridge to the Southbank Riverwalk. The Skyway operates Monday through Friday from 6am to 11pm, Saturday from 10am to 11pm, and Sunday only for special events. Skyway rides cost 35¢. **The Trolley** connects with the Skyway and runs east-west through downtown, primarily along Bay Street. It's free and operates Monday through Friday from 6:30am to 7pm. Get maps and schedules from the convention and visitors bureau or at the visitor information booth at Jacksonville Landing (see above). Both are operated by the **Jacksonville Transportation Authority** (© **904/630-3100;** www.ridejta.net), which also provides local bus service.

Otherwise, you're better off having a car if you want to explore this vast area. You can hail a **taxi** downtown if you spot one, although it is usually best to call **Gator City Taxi** (© **904/355-8294**) or **Yellow Cab** (© **904/260-1111**) for a pickup. Fares are $1.25 when the flag drops, and 25¢ for each ⅕ mile thereafter.

Out at the beaches, the **St. Johns River Ferry** (© **904/241-9969**) shuttles vehicles across the river between Mayport, an Old Florida fishing village on the south side, and Fort George on the north shore. The boats depart Mayport on the hour and the half-hour Monday through Friday from 6am to 10pm, weekends from 6:20am to 10pm. One-way fare is $2.75 per two-axle private vehicle, 50¢ for pedestrians and bicyclists. Even if you have to wait 30 minutes for the next ferry, the 5-minute ride greatly shortens the trip between the Jacksonville beaches and Amelia Island. I always stop for lunch at Singleton's Seafood Shack in Mayport (see "Where to Dine," later in this chapter).

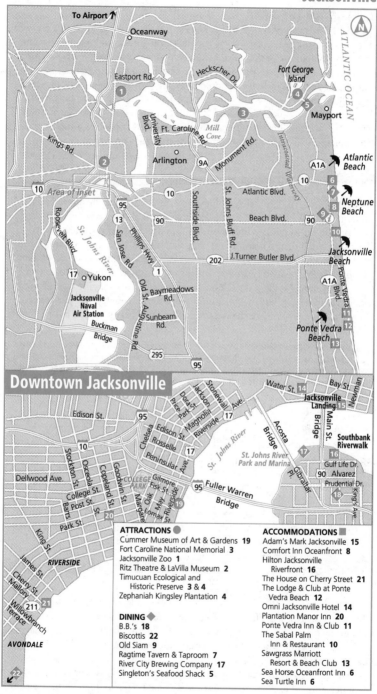

Jacksonville

To Airport ↑

Oceanway

Eastport Rd.

1

Heckscher Dr.

Fort George Island

4

5

Mayport

University Blvd.

Ft. Caroline Rd.

Mill Cove

3

Kings Rd

2

Arlington

9A

Monument Rd.

A1A

Atlantic Beach

ATLANTIC OCEAN

10

Area of inset

95

13

90

Southside Blvd.

St. Johns Bluff Rd.

Atlantic Blvd.

6

10

7

8

Neptune Beach

Beach Blvd.

90

9

i

10

St. Johns River

San Jose Rd

Phillips Hwy.

202

J.Turner Butler Blvd.

Jacksonville Beach

Roosevelt Blvd.

17

Yukon

Old St. Augustine Rd.

1

Baymeadows Rd.

A1A

Ponte Vedra Blvd.

Jacksonville Naval Air Station

Sunbeam Rd.

11

12

Buckman Bridge

295

95

Ponte Vedra Beach

13

Downtown Jacksonville

Edison St.

95

Jackson St.

Pearl St.

Stonewall

Ave.

Water St.

14

Bay St.

Newnan

Jacksonville Landing

15

10

Stockton St.

Osceola St.

Chelsea

Edison St.

Rosselle

Magnolia

Riverside

17

Peninsular

17

Acosta Bridge

Main St.

Southbank Riverwalk

St. Johns River

Main St. Bridge

Dellwood Ave.

Goodwin St.

Copeland St.

COLLEGE PARK

Gilmore

Fisk St.

St. Johns River Park and Marina

17

Gibraltar Pl.

Gulf Life Dr.

16

College St.

Post St.

Barrs St.

95

Fuller Warren Bridge

90

Alvarez

Prudential Dr.

Park St.

Margaret

Oak

May

Lomax

Riverside

19

20

King St.

RIVERSIDE

18

King's Ave.

James St.

Cherry St.

Mallory

211

21

Willowbranch Terrace

AVONDALE

22

ATTRACTIONS ●
Cummer Museum of Art & Gardens **19**
Fort Caroline National Memorial **3**
Jacksonville Zoo **1**
Ritz Theatre & LaVilla Museum **2**
Timucuan Ecological and
    Historic Preserve **3 & 4**
Zephaniah Kingsley Plantation **4**

DINING ◆
B.B.'s **18**
Biscottis **22**
Old Siam **9**
Ragtime Tavern & Taproom **7**
River City Brewing Company **17**
Singleton's Seafood Shack **5**

ACCOMMODATIONS ■
Adam's Mark Jacksonville **15**
Comfort Inn Oceanfront **8**
Hilton Jacksonville
    Riverfront **16**
The House on Cherry Street **21**
The Lodge & Club at Ponte
    Vedra Beach **12**
Omni Jacksonville Hotel **14**
Plantation Manor Inn **20**
Ponte Vedra Inn & Club **11**
The Sabal Palm
    Inn & Restaurant **10**
Sawgrass Marriott
    Resort & Beach Club **13**
Sea Horse Oceanfront Inn **6**
Sea Turtle Inn **6**

621

EXPLORING THE AREA

Cummer Museum of Art & Gardens ★★ Built on the grounds of a private Tudor mansion, this modestly sized but outstanding museum is worth a visit for anyone who appreciates the visual arts. The permanent collection encompasses works from 2000 B.C. to the present. It's especially rich in American Impressionist paintings and includes an impressive collection of 18th-century porcelain and 18th-century and early-19th-century Japanese Netsuke ivory carvings. Don't miss the stunning Italian and English gardens set on the scenic St. Johns River. The museum hosts temporary and traveling exhibits and sponsors a multitude of activities during the year, so call to see what's on tap.

829 Riverside Ave. (between Post and Fisk sts.). ✆ **904/356-6857**. www.cummer.org. Admission $6 adults, $4 seniors over 65 and military, $3 students, $1 children under 5; free Tues after 4pm. Tues and Thurs 10am–9pm; Wed and Fri–Sat 10am–5pm; Sun noon–5pm.

Jacksonville Landing Resembling New York City's South Street Seaport, Boston's Faneuil Hall, and Baltimore's Inner Harbor, this glass-and-steel complex on the north bank of the river serves as the focus of downtown activity. There are more than 65 stores here, but shopping is secondary to dining and entertainment. You can choose from about half a dozen full-service restaurants, plus an inexpensive food court with indoor and outdoor seating overlooking the river. The Landing is the scene of numerous special events, ranging from arts festivals to baseball-card shows, and outdoor rock, blues, country, and jazz concerts on weekends. Call or check the website to find out what's going on during your stay.

2 Independent Dr. (between Main and Pearl sts.), on the St. Johns River. ✆ **904/353-1188**. www.jackson villelanding.com. Free admission. Mon–Thurs 10am–8pm; Fri–Sat 10am–9pm; Sun noon–5:30pm; bars and restaurants open later. From I-95, take exit 107 downtown to Main St., go over the Blue Bridge, and turn left at Bay St. Then go 2 blocks and make a left on Laura St., which dead-ends at the Landing. Park on east side of complex.

Jacksonville Zoo ★ *Kids* Between downtown and the airport, this environmentally sensitive zoo is well on its way to becoming one of the country's best. While the zoo's new Wild Florida area presents local fauna including black bears, red wolves, Florida panthers, and alligators, the main exhibits feature an extensive and growing collection of lions, rhinos, elephants, antelopes, Nile crocodiles, cheetahs, monkeys, western lowland gorillas, and other African wildlife. You'll enter the 73-acre park through the authentic thatched roof built in 1995 by 24 Zulu craftsmen. Whether you go on foot or by tram, allow at least 2 hours to tour this vast and lush zoo. When you arrive, ask about current animal shows and special events. Strollers and wheelchairs are available for rent.

8605 Zoo Pkwy. ✆ **904/757-4462** or 904/757-4463. www.jaxzoo.org. Admission $8 adults, $6.50 seniors, $5 children 3–12, free for children under 3. Daily 9am–5pm. Closed Thanksgiving, Christmas. Take I-95 north to Heckscher Dr. (exit 124A) and follow the signs.

Ritz Theatre & LaVilla Museum From 1921 to 1971, the Ritz Theatre was the center of cultural life in LaVilla, an African-American neighborhood so vibrant that it was known as the Harlem of the South. Many entertainers played the Ritz before moving on to the Apollo Theater in the real Harlem. Most of LaVilla's small, clapboard "shotgun" houses (so called because you could fire a shotgun through the central hallway and not hit anything) have been torn down in anticipation of urban renewal, but the Ritz has been rebuilt and is once again a center of the city's cultural life. Only the northwest corner of the building, including the Ritz sign, is original, but the new 426-seat theater captures the spirit of vaudevillian times. Off the lobby, LaVilla Museum recounts local African-American history and exhibits the works of black artists.

829 N. Davis St. (between State and Union sts.). ℂ **904/632-5555.** Admission $4 adults, $2 seniors and children 18 and under. Tues–Fri 10am–6pm; Sat 10am–2pm; Sun 2–5pm. From downtown, take Main St. north, turn left (west) on State St. to theater and museum at Davis St.

Southbank Riverwalk   Bordering the St. Johns River directly opposite the Jacksonville Landing (see above), this 1¼-mile (2km) wooden zigzag boardwalk is usually filled with joggers, tourists, folks sitting on benches, and lovers walking hand-in-hand, all of them watching the riverboats, the shorebirds, and downtown's skyline reflected on the water. At 200 feet (60m) in diameter, the **Friendship Fountain** near the west end is the nation's largest self-contained fountain; it's especially beautiful at night when illuminated by 265 colored lights. Nearby, you'll pass military memorials, a small museum dedicated to the city's history, and the **Museum of Science & History of Jacksonville (MOSH),** at Museum Circle and San Marco Boulevard (ℂ **904/396-MOSH;** www.themosh.org). The latter is an interactive children's museum focusing on science and the history of Northeast Florida. One of its stars is an Allosaurus dinosaur skeleton. It also has a small planetarium, whose shows are included in admission to the museum: $6 adults, $4.50 seniors, $4 children 3 to 12, free for children under 3. Open Monday through Friday from 10am to 5pm, Saturday from 10am to 6pm, Sunday from 1 to 6pm. The Riverwalk is the scene of special MOSH programs, seafood fests, parties, parades, and arts-and-crafts festivals.

On the south bank of the St. Johns River, flanking Main St. Bridge between San Marco Blvd. and Ferry St. ℂ **904/396-4900.** Take I-95 north to Prudential Dr. exit, make a right, and follow signs.

AN UNUSUAL BREED OF NATIONAL PARK
Named after the American Indians who inhabited Central and North Florida some 1,000 years before European settlers arrived, the **Timucuan Ecological and Historic Preserve** offers visitors an opportunity to explore untouched wilderness, historical buildings, and informative exhibits on the area's natural history. Unusual for a national park, this 46,000-acre preserve hasn't been hacked off from the rest of the community and drawn within arbitrary boundaries. The result is a vast, intriguing system of sites joined by rural roads alongside tumbledown fish camps, trailer parks, strip malls, condominiums, and stately old homes.

Admission to all park facilities is free (donations accepted). The visitor centers at Fort Caroline National Memorial and Zephaniah Kingsley Plantation are open daily from 9am to 5pm except New Year's Day, Thanksgiving, and Christmas. The Theodore Roosevelt natural area is open daily from 7am to 5pm during Eastern Standard Time, daily from 7am to 8pm during daylight savings time. Closed Christmas.

SOUTH OF THE RIVER
The preserve's prime attractions are 14 miles (23km) northeast of downtown on the south bank of the St. Johns River. Your starting point is the **Fort Caroline National Memorial** ✪, 12713 Ft. Caroline Rd. (ℂ **904/641-7155;** www.nps.gov/timu), which serves as the preserve's visitor center. This was the site of the 16th-century French Huguenot settlement that was wiped out by the Spanish who landed at St. Augustine. This two-thirds–size replica shows you what the original was like. You can see archaeological artifacts and two very well-produced half-hour videos highlighting the area.

The fort sits at the northwestern edge of the 600-acre **Theodore Roosevelt Area,** a beautiful woodland and marshland rich in history that has been undisturbed since the Civil War. On a 2-mile (3km) hike along a centuries-old park trail, you'll see a wide variety of birds, wildflowers, and maritime hammock forest. Bring binoculars if you have them, since such birds as the endangered wood stork, great and snowy egrets, ospreys, hawks, and painted buntings make their home here in spring and summer. On the ground, you might catch sight of a gray fox or raccoon. You may also want to bring a blanket and picnic basket to spread out under the ancient oak trees that shade the banks of the wide and winding St. Johns River. After the trail crosses Hammock Creek, you're in ancient Timucuan country, where their ancestors lived as far back as 500 B.C. Farther along is the site of a cabin in the wilderness that belonged to the reclusive brothers Willie and Saxon Browne, who lived without the modern conveniences of indoor plumbing or electricity until the last brother's death in 1960.

If you're here on a weekend, take the fascinating 1½-hour guided tours of the fort and Theodore Roosevelt Area, offered every Saturday and Sunday (when weather and staffing permit). Call the fort for details and schedules.

The **Ribault Monument,** on St. Johns Bluff about a half mile east of the fort, was erected in 1924 to commemorate the arrival in 1562 of French Huguenot Jean Ribault, who died defending Fort Caroline from the Spanish. It's worth a stop for the dramatic view of the area.

To get here from downtown, take Atlantic Boulevard (Fla. 10) east, make a left on Monument Road, and turn right on Fort Caroline Road; the Theodore Roosevelt Area is entered from Mt. Pleasant Road, about 1 mile (1.5km) southeast of the fort; look for the trail-head parking sign and follow the narrow dirt road to the parking lot.

NORTH OF THE RIVER
On the north side of the river, history buffs will appreciate the **Zephaniah Kingsley Plantation** ✪, at 11676 Palmetto Ave. on Fort George Island (© **904/ 251-3537**). A winding 2½-mile (4km) dirt road runs under a canopy of dense foliage to the remains of this 19th-century plantation. The National Park Service maintains the well-preserved two-story clapboard residence, kitchen house, barn/carriage house, and remnants of 23 slave cabins built of "tabby mortar"— oyster shell and sand. Exhibits in the main house and kitchen focus on slavery as it existed in the rice-growing areas of Northern Florida, Georgia, and South Carolina. You can see it all on your own, but 40-minute ranger-guided tours are the best way. They are usually given at 1pm Monday through Friday, 1 and 3pm on weekends, but call to confirm. Allot some extra time to explore the grounds. A well-stocked book and gift shop will keep you even longer. The plantation is open daily from 9am to 5pm, except Christmas.

To get here from I-95, take Heckscher Drive (Fla. 105) east and follow the signs. From Fort Caroline, take Fla. 9A north over the St. Johns River to Heckscher Drive east. The plantation is about 12 miles (19km) east of Fla. 9A, on the left. From the beaches, take Fla. A1A to the St. Johns River Ferry and ride it from Mayport to Fort George; the road is half a mile east of the ferry landing.

HITTING THE BEACH
You can fish, swim, snorkel, sail, sunbathe, or stroll on the sand dunes (at least Mar–Nov, since winter can get downright chilly here). All of these activities are just a 20- to 30-minute drive east of downtown at Jacksonville's four beach communities.

Escaping Intolerance

Zephaniah Kingsley, the white man who from 1817 to 1829 owned the plantation that is now part of the Timucuan Ecological and Historic Preserve, held some seemingly contradictory views on race. Although he owned more than 200 slaves, he believed that "the coloured race were superior to us, physically and morally." He married a Senegalese woman—one of his former slaves—and in 1837 moved his mixed-race family to what is now the Dominican Republic to escape what he called the "spirit of intolerant injustice" in Florida.

Atlantic Boulevard (Fla. 10) will take you to **Atlantic Beach** and **Neptune Beach.** The boulevard divides the two towns, and where it meets the ocean, you'll come to **Town Center,** a quaint community with a number of shops, restaurants, pubs, and a few inns.

Beach Boulevard (U.S. 90) dead-ends at **Jacksonville Beach,** where you'll find beach concessions, rental shops, and a fishing pier. This is also the most popular local surfing beach.

To the south, J. Turner Butler Boulevard (Fla. 202) leads from I-95 to the boundary between Jacksonville Beach and Ponte Vedra Beach. A right turn there will take you to **Ponte Vedra Beach** (pronounced here as Ponti *Vee*-dra). This ritzy, golf-oriented enclave actually is in St. Johns County (St. Augustine), but it's so much closer to Jacksonville that I've included it in this chapter.

OUTDOOR ACTIVITIES & SPECTATOR SPORTS

CRUISES   **Jacksonville River Cruises** (© 800/711-3470 or 904/396-2333; www.rivercruise.com) operates sightseeing, dinner, and dancing cruises on the stern-wheel paddleboats *The Lady St. Johns* and *The Annabelle Lee.* They usually dock at the Radisson Riverwalk Hotel on the Southbank Riverwalk. Prices range from $22 to $45, and schedules vary greatly by season, so call ahead or check the website.

FISHING   The least-expensive way to fish for red snapper, grouper, sea bass, small sharks, amberjack, and more, 15 to 30 miles (24–48km) offshore in the Atlantic Ocean, is aboard the *King Neptune,* a 65-foot (20m) air-conditioned deep-sea party boat. The full-day trips depart at 7:30am daily from Monty's Marina, 4378 Ocean St. (Fla. A1A), half a mile south of the Mayport Ferry landing (© **904/246-7575**), and return at 4:30pm. Price is $50 per person, including all bait and tackle. You don't need a license, but reservations are required.

GOLF   The Jacksonville area offers a great variety of golf courses, some of which are ranked among the top in the country. In Ponte Vedra Beach, the Sawgrass Marriott Resort sits on the most famous course, the **TPC at Sawgrass** ✦✦✦, home of the Players Championship in March. Ranked among the nation's top courses, its island hole is one of the most photographed in the world. Nearby are the Ocean and Lagoon courses at the Ponte Vedra Inn & Club. See "Where to Stay," below, for information about the resorts.

Top courses open to the public include the **Golf Club of Jacksonville,** at 10440 Tournament Lane (© **904/779-0800**), which is managed by the PGA Tour. It's a great bargain, with greens fees ranging from $30 to $40. The

semiprivate **Cimarrone,** at 2690 Cimarrone Blvd. (© **904/287-2000**), is a fast
and watery course with greens fees ranging from $30 to $50.

On your way out to the beach, the semiprivate **Windsor Parke Golf Club,**
at 4747 Hodges Blvd., at Turner Butler Boulevard (© **904/223-GOLF**), is one
of the most challenging and scenic courses in Jacksonville. Designed by Arthur
Hill, the 6,740 yards of green are surrounded by towering pines and lots of
water. Fees are usually less than $45 and include a cart, even on the weekends.
Nonmembers should call 4 or 5 days in advance for tee times.

Be on the lookout for the free *Golfer's Guide* in visitor centers and hotel lobbies (see "The Active Vacation Planner," in chapter 2, for information about
ordering copies).

HORSEBACK RIDING   For a scenic ride along the sand and dunes (or lessons), call **Sawgrass Stables,** 23900 Marsh Landing Pkwy., off Fla. A1A in
Ponte Vedra Beach (© **904/285-3791**). Call for rates and reservations. **SPEC-
TATOR SPORTS**   The 73,000-seat **Alltel Stadium,** 1 Stadium Place, at East
Duval and Haines Streets (© **904/630-3901** for information, or 904/353-3309
to charge tickets), hosts the annual Florida-Georgia football game every October, and other college football games September through December. It also is the
home field of the National Football League's **Jacksonville Jaguars** (© **800/
618-8005** or 904/633-2000 for ticket information; www.jaguars.com). One of
the stadium's biggest draws is the **Toyota Gator Bowl,** usually on New Year's
Day (see "Florida Calendar of Events," in chapter 2).

Adjacent to the stadium, the 10,600-seat **Jacksonville Veterans Memorial
Coliseum,** 1145 E. Adams St. (© **904/630-3900** for information, or
904/353-3309 to charge tickets), hosts National Hockey League exhibition
games, college basketball games, ice-skating exhibitions, wrestling matches, and
various family shows.

SHOPPING & BROWSING

Jacksonville has plenty of shopping opportunities, including an upscale mall,
The Avenues Mall, south of town at 10300 Southside Blvd., as well as a number of flea markets, including the **Beach Boulevard Flea and Farmer's Market**
on Beach Boulevard (Fla. 90; © **904/645-5961**). More than 600 vendors show
up daily from 9am to 5pm to sell their wares in a partially covered facility.

San Marco Square, at San Marco and Atlantic boulevards, south of the river,
is a quaint shopping district in the middle of a stunning residential area. Shops
in meticulously refashioned Mediterranean-revival buildings sell antiques and
home furnishings, as well as clothing, books, and records.

Another worthwhile neighborhood to explore is the **Avondale/Riverside** historic district southwest of downtown on St. Johns Avenue between Talbot
Avenue and Boone Park, on the north bank of the river. More than 60 boutiques, antiques stores, art galleries, and cafes line the wide, tree-lined avenue.

Nearby, the younger set hangs out at **Five Points,** on Park Street at Avondale
Avenue, where used-record stores, vintage clothiers, coffee shops, and funky art
galleries stay open late.

Like St. Augustine, Jacksonville is a mecca for chocoholics, particularly **Peterbrooke Chocolatier Production Center,** 1470 San Marco Blvd., on San Marco
Square (© **904/398-4812**). If you've never tried chocolate-covered popcorn or
pretzels, this is the place. Open Monday through Friday from 10am to 5pm.
Peterbrooke also has a retail shop on St. Johns Avenue in Avondale.

WHERE TO STAY

I've arranged the accommodations listed below geographically, in and around downtown first, followed by the beach scene. The suburbs have dozens more to choose from, especially along I-95. Many are clustered south of downtown in the **Southpoint** (exit 101, Turner Butler Blvd./Fla. 202) and **Baymeadows** (exit 101, Baymeadows Rd./Fla. 152) areas. These locales have a multitude of chain restaurants, and you can hop on the highways and zoom to the beach or downtown—although you aren't really at either one if you stay out here.

Rates in the downtown hotels are higher midweek when rooms are in demand by business travelers. Beach accommodations are somewhat less expensive in the cold months from December through March.

IN JACKSONVILLE

Prudential Drive in the Southbank Riverwalk area is home to the **Radisson Riverwalk Hotel** (℃ **800/333-3333** or 904/396-5100), the **Hampton Inn Central** (℃ **800/HAMPTON** or 904/396-7770), and the all-suites **Extended Stay American Downtown** (℃ **800/EXT-STAY** or 904/396-1777; www.extendedstay.com).

Adam's Mark Jacksonville ★★   This 18-story hotel opened its doors in 2001 on a choice location a block east of Jacksonville Landing. This definitely is a convention hotel, with a whopping 110,000 square feet of meeting space, a showy lobby, two big restaurants, and a sports bar, all opening to a riverside promenade. Most of the guest rooms are relatively small; in fact, those with two double beds have room for little else, so opt for a king-bed room or a suite. Although none has a balcony, about half have sliding glass doors (be careful!). The swimming pool is on the rooftop, where a tiki bar serves refreshments in summertime.

225 Coastline Dr., Jacksonville, FL 32202. ℃ **800/444-ADAM** or 904/633-9095. Fax 904/633-9988. www.adamsmark.com. 966 units. $139–$259. AE, DC, DISC, MC, V. Valet parking $12; self-parking $8. **Amenities:** 2 restaurants (Italian/American); 4 bars; heated outdoor pool; exercise room; Jacuzzi; sauna; concierge; activities desk; business center; limited room service; laundry service; concierge-level rooms. *In room:* A/C, TV, dataport, coffeemaker, hair dryer, iron.

Hilton Jacksonville Riverfront ★   On the Southbank Riverwalk, this 10-story tower is famous for its Elvis Presley Suite, where "the King" purportedly stayed half a dozen times between 1955 and 1976 when this establishment was known as the Jacksonville Hotel. If you can afford its $300-a-night price tag, you will see some of Elvis's million-seller gold records mounted on the walls and can watch some of his movies on the suite's two VCRs. It and the other units have dark-wood furniture and smallish marble-tiled bathrooms. Riverfront rooms have balconies (those on the west end catch traffic noise from the Main St. Bridge). A branch of Ruth's Chris Steakhouse here offers extraordinarily tender beef.

1201 Riverplace Blvd. (at Main St. on Southbank Riverwalk), Jacksonville, FL 32207. ℃ **800/HILTONS** or 904/398-8800. Fax 904/398-9170. www.jacksonvillehilton.com. 292 units. $116–$180 double. AE, DC, DISC, MC, V. Valet parking $8; self-parking $7. **Amenities:** 2 restaurants (American); 2 bars; heated outdoor pool; exercise room; Jacuzzi; concierge; business center; limited room service; laundry service; concierge-level rooms. *In room:* A/C, TV, dataport, coffeemaker, hair dryer, iron.

The House on Cherry Street ★   This colonial-style, wood-frame house, on the St. Johns River in the Riverside neighborhood, is ideal for a romantic B&B vacation. French doors open to a delightful screened-in back porch furnished with rocking chairs; it overlooks an expanse of tree-shaded lawn (where guests play croquet) leading to the river (where they play with kayaks and canoes). You might select the Rose or the Duck room, both with canopied four-poster beds and river views. Ducks are rather a theme here, with hundreds of antique decoys on display. All accommodations offer adjacent sitting rooms and ceiling fans and have fresh flowers, books, and magazines. No smoking is permitted inside.

1844 Cherry St. (on the St. Johns River), Jacksonville, FL 32205. © 904/384-1999. Fax 904/384-5013. www.1bbweb.com/cherry/. 4 units (all with bathroom). $85–$115 double. Rates include full breakfast. AE, MC, V. No small children accepted. **Amenities:** Free use of bikes; canoes; kayaks. *In room:* A/C, TV, hair dryer, no phone.

Omni Jacksonville Hotel ⭐   Located directly across the street from the Times-Union Center for the Performing Arts (see "Jacksonville After Dark," later in this chapter) and a block west of Jacksonville Landing, the Omni enjoys a more convenient location than the Hilton across the river. It caters primarily to a corporate clientele who fill the meeting facilities during the week. Most rooms are of moderate size, with the pick being the Florida suites, which have sitting areas with river or city views. The pool is on the rooftop here. The reasonably priced Juliette's Restaurant & Bistro provides a locally famous pasta bar. Your pet can stay with you here, for a hefty fee.

245 Water St. (between Pearl and Hogan sts.), Jacksonville, FL 32202. © 800/THE-OMNI or 904/355-OMNI. Fax 904/791-4809. www.omnihotels.com. 354 units. $145–$190 double. Weekend rates available. AE, DC, DISC, MC, V. Valet parking $10; self-parking $12. Pets accepted ($50 fee). **Amenities:** Restaurant (American); bar; heated outdoor pool; small exercise room; Jacuzzi; concierge; business center; limited room service; laundry service; concierge-level rooms. *In room:* A/C, TV, dataport, minibar, coffeemaker, hair dryer, iron.

Plantation Manor Inn ⭐   The setting for many weddings and special events, this three-story plantation-style bed-and-breakfast in the historic Riverside district is 2 blocks from the river, 10 minutes from downtown, and a short drive to Avondale's shopping and dining. Its homey interior, outfitted with a mix of thrift-store antiques, features glossy pine floors and gorgeous cypress paneling, wainscoting, and carved moldings. Breakfast, including freshly baked muffins and breads, is served in a lovely dining room with a working fireplace. When the sun is shining, take the morning meal on a brick patio, a delightful setting with ivy-covered walls, flower beds, and garden furnishings under the shade of a massive oak tree. The patio also contains a lap pool and whirlpool spa. On the second floor you can enjoy a big wraparound porch with seating amid potted geraniums, hibiscus, and bougainvillea. All but one of the rooms here have shower-only bathrooms.

1630 Copeland St. (between Oak and Park sts.), Jacksonville, FL 32204. © 904/384-4630. Fax 904/387-0960. www.plantationmanorinn.com. 9 units (all with bathroom). $145–$175 double. Rates include full breakfast. AE, DC, MC, V. **Amenities:** Outdoor pool; Jacuzzi. *In room:* A/C, TV, hair dryer.

AT THE BEACHES

A dozen modest hotels line Jacksonville Beach's 1st Street, along the Atlantic Ocean. Completely renovated in 1998, the **Comfort Inn Oceanfront,** 1515 N. 1st St., 2 blocks east of Fla. A1A (© **800/654-8776** or 904/241-2311; fax 904/249-3830; www.comfortinnjaxbeach.com), is one of the better values. Its rooms all have balconies or screened patios, and guests can enjoy a large pool with four rock waterfalls and a palm-fringed sun deck, a secluded grotto whirlpool, an exercise room, a gift/sundries shop, and a multicourt sand-volleyball park.

If you'd like to rent an old-fashioned cottage or a luxurious condominium in the affluent enclave of Ponte Vedra, contact **Ponte Vedra Club Realty,** 280 Ponte Vedra Blvd., Ponte Vedra Beach, FL 32082 (℃ **800/278-8171** or 904/285-6927; fax 904/285-5218; www.pvclubrealty.com). The company has more than 100 properties in its rental inventory, about 75% of them on the ocean. Its renters get a discount on use of facilities at The Lodge & Club at Ponte Vedra Beach and at the Ponte Vedra Inn & Club (see below).

The Lodge & Club at Ponte Vedra Beach ★★ One of Florida's more romantic hotels, this long, two-story Mediterranean-style building sits right along the beach, affording every unit an ocean view from its own private balcony or patio. The guest quarters have considerable charm, with gorgeous artwork on their walls, two-person settees recessed in front of windows looking out to the beach, and huge bathrooms with two-person tubs and separate showers. The "preferred" rooms and all of the suites also have gas fireplaces, and ceiling fans hang from vaulted ceilings in the upstairs units. The suites also come with sleeper sofas and kitchenettes, making them suitable for small families. Down by the beach, one swimming pool with a hot tub is reserved for couples, while families can use two other pool areas. Guests here have access to all facilities of the Ponte Vedra Inn & Club (see below), including the spa, tennis center, and two golf courses. Restricted to guests of the two properties, the bright Innlet Dining Room serves fine continental cuisine with an ocean view, and afternoon tea daily in the adjoining lounge, where a pianist performs by the fireplace at night. The poolside Oasis Bar & Grill is open daily during summer, weekends the rest of the year.

607 Ponte Vedra Blvd. (at Corona Rd.), Ponte Vedra Beach, FL 32082. ℃ 800/243-4304 or 904/273-9500. Fax 904/273-0210. www.pvresorts.com. 66 units. $190–$430 double. Packages available. AE, DC, DISC, MC, V. **Amenities:** 2 restaurants (Continental/American); 2 bars; 3 heated outdoor pools; health club (with lap pool); access to nearby spa; Jacuzzi; sauna; water-sports equipment rentals; bike rental; concierge; business center; 24-hr. room service; babysitting; laundry service. *In room:* A/C, TV, fax, dataport, minibar, kitchen (suites only), coffeemaker, hair dryer, iron.

Ponte Vedra Inn & Club ★★ This luxurious 300-acre private country club and spa is a great place to pamper yourself between rounds of golf or games of tennis. The inn is ultra-elegant from the moment you drive up to its manicured front lawn, which doubles as a putting green. A gorgeous on-premises spa offers oceanview massage, a salon, herbal and seaweed wraps, facials, hydrotherapy, fitness training, and much more. A new three-story building in front of the original 1937 clubhouse contains an expansive lobby downstairs and spacious, upscale guest rooms upstairs. Across the road, the condominiums are in two-story buildings along the beach. They all have furnished patios or balconies and are individually decorated; some have four-poster or sleigh beds. Ceiling fans are among the numerous in-room amenities. The larger units have full kitchens, and microwave ovens and small refrigerators are available upon request. In addition to the inn's two 18-hole golf courses, its excellent tennis center, and fully equipped gym with six-lane Olympic pool, guests can use the three beachside swimming pools and other facilities at the nearby Lodge & Club at Ponte Vedra Beach (see above).

200 Ponte Vedra Blvd. (off Fla. A1A), Ponte Vedra Beach, FL 32082. ℃ 800/234-7842 or 904/285-1111. Fax 904/285-2111. www.pvresorts.com. 221 units. $200–$600 suite. Packages available. AE, DC, DISC, MC, V. **Amenities:** 3 restaurants (American); 3 bars; indoor pool; golf courses; tennis courts; health club and spa; water-sports equipment rentals; bike rental; children's programs (summer only); concierge; business center; 24-hr. room service; massage; babysitting; laundry service; coin-op washers and dryers. *In room:* A/C, TV, dataport, kitchen (some units), minibar, coffeemaker, hair dryer, iron.

The Sabal Palm Inn & Restaurant   Bed-and-breakfast lovers will find a comfortable and charming home in this Victorian-era house set on a residential street just half a block from the beach. Bay windows shed plenty of light in the first-floor formal parlor and dining room, occupied by a French restaurant serving breakfast to houseguests and lunch and dinner to all comers. One apartment-size unit, complete with kitchen, runs the entire length of the house on the first floor. Two other guest units are at the top of a central stairway, from which a door leads to a porch with a fine view of the Jacksonville Fishing Pier. Two more guest units are upstairs. One is a suite with a monstrous bathroom with both shower stall and claw-foot tub, and its own stairway to the backyard. Another apartment-size suite upstairs has a kitchen. Beside the house is a small swimming pool with a sun deck.

115 5th Ave. S. (between 1st and 2nd sts.), Jacksonville Beach, FL 32250. ✆ **877/725-6466** or 904/241-4545. Fax 904/241-2407. 5 units (all with bathroom). $75–$110 double. Rates include full breakfast. AE, DISC, MC, V. **Amenities:** Restaurant (French); outdoor pool; free bicycles; limited room service; laundry service. *In room:* A/C, TV, dataport, kitchen (2 units), fridge, coffeemaker, hair dryer, iron.

Sawgrass Marriott Resort & Beach Club ★★   One of the nation's largest golf resorts, this duffer's paradise is virtually surrounded by 99 holes, including the Pete Dye–designed **TPC at Sawgrass** ★★★, home of the annual Players Championship in March. In fact, this course has appeared on every critic's "best of" list since it opened in 1980. Overlooking the TPC's picturesque 13th hole, the seven-story hotel sits beside one of the lakes that make the course so challenging. The view augments the gourmet fusion cuisine served in the Augustine Grille, the hotel's signature restaurant. The guest rooms in the hotel are comfortable but of modest size. Best for families are the fully equipped one- and two-bedroom "villa suites" (condominium apartments) on or near a golf course, which offer large furnished patios or balconies. Especially luxurious are the one- to three-bedroom beachfront units, which sport huge kitchens, living rooms with working fireplaces, full dining rooms, and large screened wooden decks. A complimentary shuttle takes guests to the ocean-side Cabana Beach Club for snacks and meals.

1000 PGA Tour Blvd. (off Fla. A1A between U.S. 210 and J. Turner Butler Blvd.), Ponte Vedra Beach, FL 32082. ✆ **800/457-GOLF**, 800/228-9290, or 904/285-7777. Fax 904/285-0906. www.sawgrassmarriott.com. 508 units. $109–$350 double. Golf packages available. AE, DC, DISC, MC, V. Free self-parking; valet parking $12. **Amenities:** 6 restaurants (Fusion/American); 4 bars; 3 outdoor pools (2 heated); 5 golf courses; 17 tennis courts; 2 health clubs; Jacuzzi; water-sports equipment rentals; bike rental; children's programs; game room; concierge; activities desk; business center; limited room service; babysitting; laundry service; coin-op washers and dryers; concierge-level rooms. *In room:* A/C, TV, dataport, kitchen (condos only), minibar, coffeemaker, hair dryer, iron.

Sea Horse Oceanfront Inn *Value*   One of the anchors of quaint Town Center, this older but well-run beachfront motel offers clean, spacious rooms with ocean views from balconies or patios. Families will appreciate the six units here with kitchenettes, not to mention a big beachfront lawn with pool, shuffleboard, picnic tables, and a barbecue grill. And young couples will enjoy proximity to some of Jacksonville's top nightspots. If you have a large family or group, consider the vast and lovely third-floor penthouse—it has a big living room and dining area, full kitchen, separate bedroom as well as sofa beds, and huge balcony furnished with a dining table and chaise lounges. A coffee shop adjoins the motel, and Town Center's restaurants and bars are across the street.

120 Atlantic Blvd. (at beach end of Atlantic Blvd.), Neptune Beach, FL 32266. ✆ **800/881-2330** or 904/246-2175. Fax 904/246-4256. www.seahorseresort.com. 38 units. $89–$129 double; $200–$225 penthouse suite for up to 6. AE, DC, DISC, MC, V. **Amenities:** Bar; heated outdoor pool. *In room:* A/C, TV, dataport, kitchen (6 units).

Sea Turtle Inn ★★ Completely gutted and restored in 1999 and 2000, this elegant, eight-story beachfront hotel is much more upscale than the Sea Horse Oceanfront Inn, which it faces across Atlantic Boulevard (despite their shouting-distance proximity, one technically is in Atlantic Beach; the other, in Neptune Beach). The guest units are spacious except for their faux-marble—but somewhat cramped—bathrooms. Choice units on the beachfront have balconies, but the majority of rooms don't face the beach or have balconies. Plantains Restaurant is a fine spot for an alfresco beachside meal, and it has live music on weekends. There's a lounge in the restaurant and a summertime tiki bar beside the swimming pool by the beach.

1 Ocean Blvd. (at beach end of Atlantic Blvd.), Atlantic Beach, FL 32233. © 800/874-6000 or 904/249-7402. Fax 904/247-1517. www.seaturtle.com. 193 units. $119–$209 double. AE, DC, DISC, MC, V. **Amenities:** Restaurant (American); 2 bars; outdoor pool; access to nearby health club; water-sports equipment rentals; limited room service; babysitting; laundry service; coin-op washers and dryers. *In room:* A/C, TV, fax, dataport, minibar, fridge, coffeemaker, hair dryer, iron.

WHERE TO DINE

The convention and visitors bureau's annual guide (see "Essentials," earlier in this section) contains a complete list of restaurants. For more choices, check listings in the "Shorelines" and "Go" sections of Friday's *Florida Times-Union* (www. jacksonville.com) and in *Folio Weekly* (www.folioweekly.com), the free local alternative paper available at restaurants, hotels, and nightspots all over town. I have concentrated here on restaurants in downtown Jacksonville and at the beaches.

IN DOWNTOWN JACKSONVILLE

Southbank Riverwalk is the city's up-and-coming mecca for eating out. In addition to B.B.'s and the River City Brewing Company, both reviewed below, the area has riverfront branches of **Ruth's Chris Steakhouse,** in the Hilton Jacksonville Riverfront, 1201 Riverplace Blvd. (© **904/396-6200**); **Morton's of Chicago,** 1510 Riverplace Blvd. (© **904/399-3933**); and **The Chart House,** in the Radisson Riverwalk Hotel, 1515 Prudential Dr. (© **904/398-3353**). Also expensive, the **Wine Cellar,** 1314 Prudential Dr. (© **904/398-8989**), offers very good continental fare and has a wine list to justify its name.

You will also find a plethora of good cafes and restaurants in the San Marco Square and Avondale neighborhoods, to break up your shopping excursions.

Don't forget that on the north side of the river, **Jacksonville Landing** has several full-service restaurants and an inexpensive food court with outdoor seating (p. 622).

B.B.'s ★★ ECLECTIC South of the Southbank Riverwalk, this bistro son of Biscottis (see below) is one of the city's hottest restaurants. You'll find local yuppies congregating at the big marble-top bar on one side of the sometimes noisy Art-Deco dining room, especially during weekday "wine-downs" featuring beer and wine specials and discounted appetizers (the mozzarella bruschetta is a big hit both here and at Biscottis), from 4 to 7pm. There's a small but inventive selection of sandwiches, salads, and individual-size pizzas available all day. Featuring local seafood, the nightly main-course specials run the gamut from roasted sea bass with citrus couscous to seared scallops with lemon grass–scented rice, sun-dried tomatoes, and lobster butter. Save room for the famous desserts, available for inspection in the chiller case near the open kitchen. Saturday brunch sees the likes of yummy Benedict-style crab cakes and flaming bananas Foster.

1019 Hendricks Ave. (between Prudential Dr. and Home St.). © 904/306-0100. Call for priority seating. Main courses $12–$22; sandwiches and salads $5–$8; pizzas $6–$8. AE, DC, DISC, MC, V. Mon–Thurs 11am–10:30pm; Fri 11am–midnight; Sat 10am–midnight (Sat brunch 10am–2pm).

Biscottis ★★ *Value* ECLECTIC   This brick-walled little gem in the trendy Avondale neighborhood might have come out of New York's East Village. Start your day here with a pastry and cup of joe. For lunch and dinner, daily specials like pan-seared tuna or pork loin are always fresh and beautifully presented. The huge and inventive salads are especially good: Try the Oriental version with chicken breast, orange slices, roasted peppers, and creamy sesame dressing. Pizzas, too, are served with wonderfully exotic and delicious toppings—ever try guacamole and black beans on your slice? And by all means, don't leave without sampling the wonderful desserts. On warm days choose a tiny sidewalk table for great people-watching. If the wait's too long here, several other choices ranging from a neighborhood diner to expensive haute cuisine line these 2 blocks of St. Johns Avenue in Avondale.

3556 St. Johns Ave. (between Talbot and Ingleside aves. in Avondale). ✆ **904/387-2060.** Main courses $9–$17; sandwiches and salads $5–$8; pizzas $7–$8.50. AE, DC, DISC, MC, V. Tues–Thurs 7am–10pm; Fri 7am–midnight; Sat 8am–midnight; Sun 8am–3pm.

River City Brewing Company ★★ NEW AMERICAN/LOUISIANA Occupying a prime location on the Southbank Riverwalk, this gorgeous restaurant and microbrewery has dramatic waterfront and skyline views. For an even better vantage point, sit outside on the enormous covered deck. The quality of the cuisine very nearly lives up to the vista, especially the "hanging" coconut shrimp served with a sweet Mandarin-orange sauce. For a main course, try the Cajun chicken linguine with mushrooms and ham in a spicy cream sauce, or pretzel-encrusted mahimahi with a mustard-cream sauce. While you can easily drop a bundle in the main dining room, you can devise an inexpensive, simpler meal in the Brew Haus, a large sports bar that opens to the big covered deck and the riverbank. Bands play on the deck weekend evenings. Sunday brunch brings incredible buffets with decadent desserts.

835 Museum Circle (on Southbank Riverwalk). ✆ **904/398-2299.** Main courses $15–$18; sandwiches and salads $5–$11; Sun brunch buffet $20 adults, $15 seniors, $12 children 3–12. AE, DC, DISC, MC, V. Dining room Sun–Thurs 11am–3pm and 5–10pm; Fri–Sat 11am–3pm and 5–11pm; Sun 10:30am–2:30pm and 5–10pm. Pub and deck (light fare) Sun–Thurs 3–10pm (bar to midnight); Fri–Sat 3–11pm (bar to 2am). Closed Christmas. Valet parking available on weekends.

AT THE BEACHES

In addition to the Ragtime Tavern & Taproom (see below), you'll have several dining (and drinking) choices in the brick storefronts of Town Center, the old-time beach village at the end of Atlantic Boulevard. Among the best is the oceanfront **Plantains,** in the Sea Turtle Inn (p. 631).

Old Siam ★★ THAI   The best of several Thai restaurants here, this sophisticated little cafe serves fine cuisine and a good selection of wines to match the fare's spicy yet subtle flavors. The signature dish is a seafood special: shrimp, sea scallops, mussels, squid, and crab claws in a red chili sauce accented with sweet basil. The "number 3" spice level (out of 6) touched my tongue but did not overwhelm the other seasonings. Standard favorites like Pad Thai are light and perfectly balanced with sweet and slightly sour fish sauce.

1716 N. 3rd St. (Fla. A1A, in Holiday Plaza shopping center, between 16th and 17th aves. N.), Jacksonville Beach. ✆ **904/247-7763.** Main courses $10–$23. AE, DISC, MC, V. Mon–Thurs 5–10pm; Fri–Sat 5–11pm; Sun 5–9:30pm.

Ragtime Tavern & Taproom ★★ SEAFOOD/CAJUN   In the heart of Town Center, this lively sister of St. Augustine's A1A Ale Works offers six hand-crafted brews, including a refreshing pilsner known as Dolphin's Breath. You can imbibe at one of two bars on either end of the building. In between, a rabbit warren of dining rooms provides fine enough fare to keep it filled with local professionals right through the cool winter months. A variety of appetizers includes conch fritters and coconut shrimp. For a main course, you can select from seared sesame-coated yellowfin tuna (the best dish here if you like rare fish) or several other treatments of fish, shrimp, chicken, and pastas. Save room for some New Orleans–style beignets for dessert. Also from the Big Easy, po'boy sandwiches are served at all hours. Good local bands play here Thursday through Sunday evenings.

207 Atlantic Blvd. (at 1st Ave.), Atlantic Beach. ℂ **904/241-7877.** Call to get on waiting list. Main courses $11.50–$22; sandwiches and salads $6–$8. AE, DC, DISC, MC, V. Sun–Thurs 11am–10:30pm; Fri–Sat 11am–11pm (bar open later).

Singleton's Seafood Shack ★★ (Value SEAFOOD This rustic fish camp has been serving every imaginable kind of fresh-off-the-boat seafood since 1969. And rustic it is, constructed primarily of unpainted, well-weathered plywood nailed to two-by-fours. Unlike most other fish camps that tend to overwork the deep fryer, the fried standbys like conch fritters, shrimp, clam strips, oysters, and squid actually retain their seafood taste! In fact, the fried shrimp are among the best I've had anywhere. Singleton's also offers other preparations such as blackened mahimahi and Cajun shrimp. Best bets at lunch are the fried shrimp or oyster po'boy sandwiches covered in crispy onion rings. At dinner your Styrofoam plate will come stacked with a choice of side items like black beans and rice, marvelous horseradishy coleslaw, fries, and hush puppies. They do have a selection of chicken dishes here, but I'd stick with the seafood.

4728 Ocean St. (Fla. A1A, at St. Johns River Ferry landing), Mayport. ℂ **904/246-4442.** Main courses $11–$18; sandwiches $2–$7. AE, DISC, MC, V. Sun–Thurs 10am–9pm; Fri–Sat 10am–10pm.

JACKSONVILLE AFTER DARK

In addition to the spots recommended below, check the listings in the "Shorelines" and "Go" sections of Friday's *Florida Times-Union* (www.jacksonville.com) and *Folio Weekly* (www.folioweekly.com), the free local alternative paper, available at restaurants, at hotels, and all over town. Another source is www.jax events.com.

THE PERFORMING ARTS With the 73,000-seat **Alltell Stadium,** at East Duval and Haines Streets (ℂ **904/630-3900**); the 10,600-seat **Jacksonville Veterans Memorial Coliseum,** 1145 E. Adams St. (ℂ **904/630-3900** for information or 904/353-3309 to charge tickets); the 3,200-seat **Florida Times-Union Center for the Performing Arts,** 300 Water St., between Hogan and Pearl streets (ℂ **904/630-3900**); and the revitalized **Ritz Theatre** (ℂ **904/ 632-5555;** see "Exploring the Area," earlier in this chapter), Jacksonville has plenty of seats for concerts, touring Broadway shows, dance companies, and big-name performers. Call or check the sources above for what's playing.

THE BAR SCENE You will find several libation options downtown at **Jacksonville Landing** (see "Exploring the Area," above), including a lively waterfront **Hooters** (ℂ **904/356-5400**), plus free outdoor rock, blues, country, and jazz concerts every Friday and Saturday night except during winter. There's also live music on weekends across the river at the **River City Brewing Company** (see "Where to Dine," earlier in this chapter).

Out at Town Center, at the ocean end of Atlantic Boulevard, one of several popular spots is **Ragtime Tavern & Taproom** (see "Where to Dine," earlier in this chapter), where local groups play live jazz and blues Wednesday through

Sunday nights. Weekends, especially, the place is really jumping and the crowd is young, but it's lively rather than rowdy. Across the street is the **Sun Dog Diner,** at 207 Atlantic Blvd. (© **904/241-8221**), with nightly acoustic music and decent diner food. If these don't fit your mood, walk around Town Center until you find something you like.

5 Amelia Island ★★

32 miles (52km) NE of Jacksonville, 192 miles (309km) NE of Orlando, 372 miles (599km) N of Miami

With 13 beautiful miles (21km) of beach and a quaint Victorian town, Amelia Island is a charming getaway about a 45-minute drive northeast of downtown Jacksonville. Overall, this skinny barrier island, 18 miles (29km) long by 3 miles (5km) wide, has more in common with the Low Country of Georgia (across Cumberland Sound from here) and South Carolina. In fact, it's more like St. Simons Island in Georgia or Hilton Head Island in South Carolina than other beach resorts in Florida.

Amelia itself has five distinct personalities. First is its southern end, an exclusive real-estate development built in a forest of twisted, moss-laden live oaks. Here you will find world-class tennis and golfing at two of Florida's most luxurious resorts. Second is modest **American Beach,** founded in the 1930s so that African Americans would have access to the ocean in this then-segregated part of the country. Today it's a modest, predominately black community tucked away among all that south-end wealth. Third is the island's middle, a traditional beach community with a mix of affordable motels, cottages, condominiums, and a seaside inn. Fourth is the historic bay-side town of **Fernandina Beach** ★★★, which boasts a 50-square-block area of gorgeous Victorian, Queen Anne, and Italianate homes listed in the National Register of Historic Places. And fifth is lovely **Fort Clinch State Park,** which keeps developers from turning the island's northern end into more ritzy resorts.

The town of Fernandina Beach dates from the post–Civil War period, when Union soldiers who had occupied Fort Clinch began returning to the island. In the late 19th century, Amelia's timber, phosphate, and naval-stores industries boomed. Back then, the town was an active seaport, with 14 foreign consuls in residence. You'll see (and occasionally smell) the paper mills that still stand near the small seaport here. The island experienced another economic explosion in the 1970s and 1980s, when real-estate developers built condominiums, cottages, and two big resorts on the island's southern end. In recent years, Fernandina Beach has seen another big boom, this time in bed-and-breakfast establishments.

ESSENTIALS

GETTING THERE   The island is served by **Jacksonville International Airport** (see "Essentials," in section 4, earlier in this chapter). Skirting the Atlantic in places, the scenic drive here from downtown Jacksonville is via Fla. A1A and the St. Johns River Ferry. The fast, four-lane way is via I-95 north and the Buccaneer Trail (Fla. A1A) east.

VISITOR INFORMATION   For advance information, contact the **Amelia Island–Fernandina Beach–Yulee Chamber of Commerce,** 102 Centre St. (P.O. Box 472), Fernandina Beach, FL 32035 (© **800/2-AMELIA** or 904/277-0717; fax 904/261-6997; www.ameliaisland.org). The chamber's visitor information center, in the old train station at the bay end of Centre Street, is open Monday through Friday from 9am to 5pm, Saturday from 10am to 2pm.

Amelia Island

FLORIDA

ACCOMMODATIONS ■
Amelia Island Plantation **11**
Beachside Motel Inn **9**
Elizabeth Pointe Lodge **2**
Fairbanks House **8**
Florida House Inn **4**
Hampton Inn & Suites **6**
The Ritz-Carlton
  Amelia Island **10**

ATTRACTIONS ●
Amelia Island Museum of
  History **7**
Fort Clinch State Park **1**
Little Talbot Island
State Park **12**

DINING ◆
Beach Street Grill **3**
Brett's Waterway Cafe **5**
Marina Restaurant **5**

GETTING AROUND There's no public transportation on this 13-mile-long (21km) island, so you'll need a vehicle. An informative and entertaining way to tour the historic district is on a 30-minute ride with **Old Towne Carriage Company** (© **904/277-1555**), whose horse-drawn carriages leave from the waterfront on Centre Street between 6:30 and 9pm. Advance reservations are essential. Rides cost $15 for adults, $7.50 for kids under 13, with a minimum of $55 per ride. The carriage company closes for 2 months during the winter when the horses are put out to pasture.

Another excellent way to see the town is on a walking tour sponsored by the Amelia Island Museum of History (see the "An Old Jail Turned Historic Museum," section, below).

HITTING THE BEACH

Thanks to a reclamation project, the widest beaches here are at the exclusive enclave on the island's southern third. Even if you aren't staying at one of the swanky resorts there, you can enjoy this section of beach at **Peters Point Beach Front Park,** on Fla. A1A, north of the Ritz-Carlton. The park has picnic shelters and restrooms. North of the resort, the beach has public-access points with free parking every quarter mile or so. The center of activity is **Main Beach,** at the ocean end of Atlantic Avenue (Fla. A1A), with good swimming, restrooms, picnic shelters, showers, a food concession, and a playground. There's lots of free parking, and this area is popular with families.

The beach at **Fort Clinch State Park** ★★, which wraps around the island's heavily forested northern end, is backed by rolling dunes and is filled with shells and driftwood. A jetty and pier jutting into Cumberland Sound are popular with anglers. There are showers and changing rooms at the pier. Elsewhere in the park, you might see an alligator—and certainly some of the 170 species of birds that live here—by hiking the Willow Pond nature trail. Rangers lead nature tours on the trail, usually beginning at 10:30am on Saturday. There are also 6 miles (10km) of off-road bike trails here. Visit the remarkably well-preserved **Fort Clinch.** Construction began in 1847 on the northern tip of the island and was still underway when Union troops occupied it in 1862. The fort was abandoned shortly after the Civil War, except for a brief reactivation in 1898 during the Spanish-American War. Reenactors gather the first full weekend of each month to re-create how the Union soldiers lived in the fort in 1864. Rangers are on duty at the fort year-round, and they lead candlelight tours on Friday and Saturday evenings during summer, beginning about an hour after sunset. The candlelight tours cost $3 per person. You can arrange guided tours at other times for an extra fee. The park entrance is on Atlantic Avenue near the beach. Entrance fees are $3.25 per vehicle with up to eight occupants, $1 for pedestrians and bicyclists. Admission to the fort costs $2, free for children under 5. The park is open daily from 8am to sunset; the fort, daily from 9am to 5pm. For a current schedule of tours and events, contact the park at 2601 Atlantic Ave., Fernandina Beach, FL 32034 (© **904/277-7274;** www.floridastateparks.org/district2/fortclinch).

The park has 62 **campsites,** some behind the dunes at the beach (no shade out there), most in a forest along the sound side. They cost $20.67 per night with electricity, $18.53 without, including tax. Pets cost an extra $2 a night. You can reserve a site up to 11 months in advance (a very good idea in summer) by calling © **800/326-3521** or going to the website (www.reserveamerica.com).

Pets on leashes are allowed on all the island's public beaches and in Fort Clinch State Park.

OUTDOOR ACTIVITIES

BOATING, FISHING, SAILING & KAYAKING The **Amelia Island Charter Boat Association,** at Tiger Point Marina on 14th Street north of the historic district (✆ **800/229-1682** or 904/261-2870), can help arrange deep-sea fishing charters, party-boat excursions, and dolphin-watching and sightseeing cruises. Other charter boats dock at Fernandina Harbor Marina, downtown at the foot of Centre Street.

Voyager Adventures, based at Fernandina Harbor Marina, 3977 1st Ave. (✆ **904/321-1244;** fax 904/321-2505; www.voyageradventures.com), has several cruises aboard the *Voyager,* a 100-foot (30m) replica of a 19th-century gaff-rigged packet schooner. A prime destination is Cumberland Island, across the sound in Georgia (the late John F. Kennedy Jr. was married over there without a single member of the paparazzi being present). The half-day trips cost $35 for adults, $16 for kids under 12. Also based at the marina, **Windward Sailing School** (✆ **904/261-9125;** www.windwardsailing.com) will teach you to skipper your boat. Call these companies for details and reservations.

You have to be careful in the currents, but the backwaters here are great for kayaking, whether you're a beginner or a pro. Ray and Jody Hetchka of **Kayak Amelia** ★★ (✆ **888/30-KAYAK** or 904/321-0697; www.kayakamelia.com) have beginner- and advanced-level trips on the back bays, creeks, and marshes. Half-day trips go for about $50 per person, all-day $95. Reservations are required.

GOLF If you're not staying in a resort with a golf course (see "Where to Stay," below), try the new 18-hole **Royal Amelia Golf Links** (✆ **904/491-8500;** www.royalamelia.com), or the older and less expensive 27-hole **Fernandina Municipal Golf Course** (✆ **904/277-7370**).

HORSEBACK RIDING You can go riding on the beach with **Kelly Seahorse Ranch** (✆ **904/491-5166**), near Little Talbot Island State Park. Rides cost $35 per person, and reservations are required. There are pony rides for kids, too. The ranch is open daily from 10am to dark.

AN OLD JAIL TURNED HISTORIC MUSEUM

Amelia Island Museum of History ★ Housed in the Nassau County jail, built of brick in 1878, this award-winning local museum explains Amelia Island's fascinating history, from Timucuan Indian times through its possession by France, Spain, Great Britain, the United States, and the Confederacy (the island changed flags eight times). Only an upstairs photo gallery is open for casual inspection, so plan to take the 1-hour, 15-minute docent-led tour.

The museum also offers excellent **walking tours** of historic Centre Street on Thursday and Friday September through June. These depart at 3pm from the chamber of commerce (see "Essentials," above) and cost $8 for adults, $3 for students. You can't make a reservation; just show up. Longer tours of the entire 50-square-block historic district can be arranged with 24-hour notice; these cost $10 per person, with a minimum of four persons required.

233 S. 3rd St. (between Beech and Cedar sts.). ✆ **904/261-7378.** www.ameliaislandmuseumofhistory.org. Admission by donation. Tours $4 adults, $2 students. Mon–Fri 10am–5pm; Sat 10am–4pm. Tours Mon–Sat 11am and 2pm.

SHOPPING

Stroll down **Centre Street** in downtown Fernandina Beach, with its vintage store fronts and charming boutiques. Quality antiques shops, consignment shops, and bookstores line the wide boulevard ending at the marina. Be sure to go around the corner and poke your head into the **Island Art Association Gallery,** 18 N. 2nd St. (© **904/261-7020**), a co-op exhibiting works by local artists.

On the south end of the island on Fla. A1A, **Palmetto Walk,** under a canopy of live oaks, and the **Village Shops,** at the entrance to Amelia Plantation, are other good shopping bets.

WHERE TO STAY

More than two dozen of the town's charming Victorian and Queen Anne houses have been restored and turned into B&Bs. For a complete list, contact the chamber of commerce (see "Essentials," above) or the **Amelia Island Bed & Breakfast Association** (© **888/277-0218;** www.ameliaislandinns.com). You can tour all the B&Bs during an island-wide open house the first weekend in December.

A number of agencies will book vacation properties ranging from affordable cottages to magnificent mansions. Contact **Amelia Island Lodging Systems,** 584 S. Fletcher Ave., Fernandina Beach, FL 32034 (© **800/872-8531** or 904/261-4148; fax 904/261-9200; www.amelialodgings.com), which even has two lighthouse replicas for rent. Or try **Lodging Resources, Inc.,** at the Elizabeth Pointe Lodge, 98 S. Fletcher Ave., Fernandina Beach, FL 32034 (© **904/277-4851;** fax 904/277-4851; lodging@worldnet.att.net), which also has a lighthouse in its inventory.

Your best **camping** option here is **Fort Clinch State Park** (see "Hitting the Beach," above).

Amelia Island Plantation ✮✮   This huge real-estate development occupies 1,250 lush beachfront acres that encompass manicured, emerald golf greens as well as a breathtaking coastal wilderness of marshes and lagoons. The resort is so spread out that a free tram runs around the grounds every 15 minutes. Unless you're here to attend a convention, choose this rustically elegant resort for its natural beauty and its outstanding sports offerings. Most notable are the three consistently top-rated championship golf courses open to resort guests; they comprise 54 holes bordering the ocean, swamps, marshes, and woodlands. The **Long Point** ✮✮ course, a breathtakingly beautiful 18-holer, has two par-3s in a row bordering the ocean. Ranked among the nation's top 50 by *Tennis* magazine, the plantation's 27 tennis courts host many professional tournaments, including the annual Bausch & Lomb Championships. A new 13,200-square-foot spa has 25 treatment rooms and offers a rejuvenating array of massages, facials, peels, herbal wraps, and hydrotherapies. Along with the adjoining convention center, the six-story, Mediterranean-style **Amelia Inn & Beach Club** serves as the resort's focal point and holds its 249 spacious, upscale hotel rooms. Traditionally furnished, the rooms boast patios or balconies facing the sea across a row of dunes. All of the inn's rooms are no-smoking. The other accommodations here are one- to three-bedroom privately owned condominium apartments (or "villas" in Florida-speak). All but a few have balconies or patios. Each is uniquely decorated with an eclectic mix of high-end furnishings, and all offer living and dining areas (VCRs can be rented) and fully equipped kitchens. The inn's dining room, though not on a par with The Grill at the nearby Ritz-Carlton, offers exceptional and expensive New American cuisine, with stunning ocean views. An adjoining lounge offers dancing and entertainment.

6800 First Coast Hwy., Amelia Island, FL 32035-3000. © **800/874-6878** or 904/261-6161. Fax 904/277-5945. www.aipfl.com. 249 units, 400 condo apts. $135–$335 double; $185–$945 condo. Packages available. AE, DC, DISC, MC, V. Free self-parking; $10 valet parking. **Amenities:** 4 restaurants (American); 4 bars; 1 heated indoor pool; 26 outdoor pools; 3 golf courses; 23 tennis courts; health club and spa; Jacuzzi; sauna; water-sports equipment rentals; bike rental; children's programs; game room; concierge; business center; shopping arcade; salon; limited room service; massage; babysitting; laundry service. *In room:* A/C, TV, dataport, kitchen (condos only), minibar (Amelia Inn only), coffeemaker, hair dryer, iron.

Beachside Motel Inn *(Value)* This family-run property—the only motel beside the beach here—is clean and well maintained. The white-and-blue, two-story, 1970s stucco building sits on a beautiful stretch of public but uncluttered beach. The rooms, many with ocean views, are spacious and furnished with standard motel furnishings. Many long-term visitors return each season to stay in the efficiencies, which have fully equipped kitchens. An outdoor pool is surrounded by lounge chairs and a spacious deck that overlooks the ocean. The hotel is convenient to lots of sports activities and restaurants.

3172 S. Fletcher Ave. (Fla. A1A, south of Simmons Rd.), Fernandina Beach, FL 32034. © 904/261-4236. www.beachsidemotel.com. 20 units. $65–$129 double; $89–$169 efficiency. Rates include continental breakfast. Weekly discounts available. AE, DISC, MC, V. **Amenities:** Outdoor pool. *In room:* A/C, TV, kitchen (efficiencies only).

Elizabeth Pointe Lodge ★★ You'd swear that this three-story, Nantucket-style shingled beauty, sitting right on the beach, was a lovingly maintained Victorian home—but you'd be wrong. Built in 1991 by B&B gurus David and Susan Caples, it's has big-paned windows that look out from the comfy library (with stone fireplace) and dining room to an expansive front porch and the surf beyond. Antiques and reproductions, handmade quilts, and other touches lend the 20 rooms in the main building a turn-of-the-20th-century cottage ambience. They all have oversize bathtubs. Four other rooms are in the Harris Lodge next door, and the two-bedroom, two-bathroom Miller Cottage is also available.

98 S. Fletcher Ave. (just south of Atlantic Ave.), Fernandina Beach, FL 32034. © 800/772-3359 or 904/277-4851. Fax 904/277-6500. www.elizabethpointelodge.com. 24 units, 1 cottage. $160–$240 double; $270 cottage. Rates include buffet breakfast and evening social hr. Packages available. AE, DISC, MC, V. **Amenities:** Restaurant (American); bar; access to nearby health club; Jacuzzi; water-sports equipment rental; bike rental; 24-hr. room service; laundry service. *In room:* A/C, TV, dataport, hair dryer, iron.

Fairbanks House ★ Having all the amenities and almost as much privacy as a first-class hotel in a superbly refurbished 1885 Italianate home, the Fairbanks House is a top B&B choice in the historic district. Many rooms and all the cottages offer private entrances for guests who prefer not to walk through the main house. Room no. 3, in the back of the house on the main floor, is one of the finest rooms, with a private entrance, large sitting room, plush king-size bed, period antiques, porcelain, oil paintings, and fresh flowers. Occupying the entire top floor, the two-bedroom Tower Suite has plenty of room to spread out, plus 360° views and its own whirlpool tub. Five other units here have whirlpool tubs. Note that Fairbanks is the only B&B on the island with a swimming pool. No smoking indoors or out.

227 S. 7th St. (between Beech and Cedar sts.), Fernandina Beach, Amelia Island, FL 32034. © 800/261-4838 or 904/277-0500. Fax 904/277-3103. www.fairbankshouse.com. 9 units, 3 detached cottages (all with bathroom). $160–$275 double; $210 cottage. Rates include full breakfast. Packages available. AE, DISC, MC, V. **Amenities:** Heated outdoor pool. *In room:* A/C, TV, dataport, kitchen (cottage only), minibar, fridge, coffeemaker, hair dryer, iron.

Florida House Inn ★ *(Value)* Built near a railroad in 1857, this clapboard Victorian building is Florida's oldest operating hotel. Ulysses S. Grant stayed here, as did Cuban revolutionary José Martí; and the Rockefellers and Carnegies broke bread at the boardinghouse-style dining room that still provides family-style, all-you-can-eat traditional Southern fare. You can rock away on the two gingerbread-trimmed front verandas (Grant made a speech from the upstairs porch) or on a back porch overlooking a brick courtyard shaded by a huge oak tree. The 11 rooms in the original building, all up to modern standards, are loaded with antiques. Most have working fireplaces, and some have claw-foot tubs. Four rooms are in a wing added in 1998; one of these has log-cabin walls, and the others are done country-style. All have fireplaces and whirlpool tubs.

20 S. 3rd St. (between Centre and Ash sts.), Fernandina Beach, FL 32034. ✆ 800/258-3301 or 904/261-3300. Fax 904/277-3831. www.floridahouse.com. 15 units. $79–$179 double. Rates include full breakfast. AE, DISC, MC, V. Pet dogs accepted ($10 nightly fee). **Amenities:** Restaurant (Southern); bar; coin-op washers and dryers. *In room:* A/C, TV, coffeemaker, hair dryer, iron.

Hampton Inn & Suites ★★   When plans were announced a few years ago to build this four-story hotel in the center of the historic district, they created quite a stir among preservationists. But the all-woman hotel firm of Miriam Taylor & Co. put those fears to rest by designing one of the most unusual Hampton Inns I've ever seen. Although there's only one building, the exterior looks like a row of different structures, all in the styles and sherbet hues of the Victorian store fronts lining Centre Street. Above a curving staircase rising in the two-story Victorian-style lobby, quadrants of an unusual ceiling clock have been painted to represent the 4 centuries of Fernandina Beach's history. Wooden floors taken from an old Jacksonville church, slatted door panels evocative of 19th-century sailing schooners, and many other touches add to the Victorian ambience. About half of the guest rooms are near the top of the romance scale: king beds, gas-burning fireplaces, and two-person whirlpool tubs. (If honeymooning in a Hampton Inn has never crossed your mind, you haven't seen the luxurious, two-room bridal suite here.) The standard suites are large enough for families, and the other standard rooms are adequately equipped for business travelers, making this a good choice for everyone. About a third of the units have balconies. Those higher up on the west side have fine views over the river and marshes. The only drawback: Trains slowly rumble by on the west side a few times a day.

19 S. 2nd St. (between Centre and Ash sts.), Fernandina Beach, FL 32034. ✆ 800/HAMPTON or 904/491-4911. Fax 904/491-4910. 122 units. $114–$179 double. Rates include extensive breakfast buffet. AE, DC, DISC, MC, V. **Amenities:** Outdoor pool; exercise room; Jacuzzi; business center; babysitting; laundry service; coin-op washers and dryers. *In room:* A/C, TV, dataport, fridge, coffeemaker, hair dryer, iron.

The Ritz-Carlton Amelia Island ★★★ *Kids*   Sprawling over 13 acres of stunning beachfront, this member of the world-renowned chain offers glitzier and grander accommodations than its neighbor, the Amelia Island Plantation. Millions of dollars' worth of museum-quality art and furnishings decorate the public areas, and the staff provides prompt and flawless service. But this Ritz-Carlton is downright relaxed compared with some of its siblings. The Ritz-Kids program makes well-heeled families feel just as much at home as the conventioneers who flock here to meet and make use of the extensive recreational facilities, including a beautiful and challenging 18-hole championship golf course. The spacious guest rooms—all with oceanfront or oceanview balconies or patios—have many extra amenities such as scales, cosmetic mirrors, and phones in their magnificent marble bathrooms. Concierge-level guests enjoy a stunning lounge with a working fireplace. Leading the hotel's restaurants, **The Grill** offers an ocean view to go with its exceptional seafood. A gourmet takeout shop sells the oft-requested Ritz dressings, condiments, and sauces, in addition to salads, sandwiches, and decadent desserts.

4750 Amelia Island Pkwy., Fernandina Beach, FL 32034. ☎ 800/241-3333 or 904/277-1100. Fax 904/261-9064. 449 units. $199–$409 double; $269–$549 suite. Golf, tennis, and other packages available. AE, DC, DISC, MC, V. Valet parking $15; no self-parking. **Amenities:** 3 restaurants (American); 3 bars; heated indoor and outdoor pools; golf course; 9 tennis courts; health club and spa; water-sports equipment rentals; bike rental; children's programs; game room; concierge; business center; salon; 24-hr. room service; massage; babysitting; laundry service; concierge-level rooms. *In room:* A/C, TV, dataport, minibar, coffeemaker, hair dryer, iron.

WHERE TO DINE

You'll find several restaurants, pubs, and snack shops along Centre Street, between the bay and 8th Street (Fla. A1A), in Fernandina Beach's old town. Two good dining options stand opposite the Hampton Inn & Suites on South 2nd Street, between Centre and Ash streets: the hip **Joe's 2nd Street Bistro** (☎ 904/ 321-2558) and the more formal but still relaxed **Le Clos** (☎ 904/261-8100). Joe's serves fine international fare in an old store, while Le Clos provides provincial French fare in a charming old house. Both are open for dinner only, and reservations are recommended. Drop by during the day for a look at the menus posted outside each.

And don't forget **The Grill** at the Ritz-Carlton Amelia Island, where great food and impeccable service come at a high price. Also, the **Florida House Inn** (see "Where to Stay," above) serves boardinghouse-style, all-you-can-eat lunches and dinners Tuesday through Saturday from 11:30am to 2:30pm ($7 per person) and from 5:30 to 9pm ($12 per person).

Beech Street Grill ★★ REGIONAL NEW AMERICAN   Almost on a par with The Grill in the Ritz-Carlton, the Beech Street Grill pleases all palates with a rich menu of fish, chicken, and meat choices, including seasonal game dishes like roasted venison loin in a black-currant sauce with sweet-potato-and-onion hash. Nightly fish specialties are always exceptional (some can be pricier than printed menu options). A Parmesan-encrusted red snapper with a mustard-basil sauce is superb. Seared tuna is always perfect, too. The dense and tasty crab cakes and the chewy steamed dumplings are great choices for starters, as is the huge mixed-green salad with mustard-basil vinaigrette, toasted pecans, and blue cheese. Housed in a century-old landmark home and in a newer wing to one side, five dining rooms offer a lively atmosphere. The upstairs features a pianist.

801 Beech St. (at 8th St./Fla. A1A), Fernandina Beach. ☎ 904/277-3662. Reservations strongly recommended. Main courses $19.50–$27.50. AE, DC, DISC, MC, V. Daily 6–10pm.

Brett's Waterway Cafe SEAFOOD/STEAKS   You'll pay for the view, but this friendly waterfront cafe at the foot of Centre Street is the only place in town to dine while watching the boats coming and going on the river—and to sip a drink while watching the sun setting over the marshes between here and the mainland. In fine weather you can grab a table outside by the docks. One of the best dishes is shrimp broiled with a sun-dried-tomato cream sauce. The nightly fresh fish specials are well prepared, and there are steaks and chops. At lunch, try the bacon, lettuce, and fried-green-tomato sandwich.

1 S. Front St. (at Centre St., on the water), Fernandina Beach. ☎ 904/261-2660. Main courses $15–$26. AE, MC, V. Mon–Sat 11:30am–2:30pm and daily 5:30–9:30pm.

Marina Restaurant *Value* AMERICAN   Occupying a brick store built in the 1880s, this quintessential small-town restaurant has been feeding Low Country fare to the locals since 1965. A lot of the seafood here is fried and broiled, but you can order crab-stuffed shrimp or flounder as well as grouper topped with scallops and a garlicky wine sauce. Budgeteers love the $10-and-under list of

Southern favorites such as country-fried steak, breaded veal cutlet, grilled pork chops, and fried chicken. Meatloaf with a tomato-and-basil gravy, stuffed bell peppers with a Greek-style tomato sauce, and other lunchtime specials come with three fresh country-style vegetables, which are themselves worth the price of the meal. Hearty breakfasts feature eggs, omelets, French toast, and hotcakes.

101 Centre St. (at Front St.), Fernandina Beach. ℂ 904/261-5310. Main courses $8–$19; breakfast $2–$6; sandwiches $5–$9. DC, MC, V. Daily 7–10am and 11:30am–9pm.

AMELIA ISLAND AFTER DARK

This romantic island goes to bed early. If you tire of the lounges in the island's resorts, check out the **Palace Saloon,** 117 Centre St., at 2nd Street (ℂ **904/261-6320**). It claims to be Florida's oldest watering hole (open since 1878). Complete with a pressed-tin ceiling and a 40-foot-long (12m) mahogany bar, it once hosted the Carnegies and the du Ponts. Some nights you'll find live local blues or rock. It's open daily from 11am until the last patrons leave.

Another popular local watering hole, **O'Kane's Irish Pub & Eatery,** 318 Centre St., at 4th Street (ℂ **904/261-1000**), has live music until midnight Monday through Thursday, until 1:30am on weekends.

Northwest Florida: The Panhandle

by Bill Goodwin

If you like beaches, you'll love Florida's northwestern Panhandle. Thanks to quartz washed down from the Appalachian Mountains, the beaches here along the Gulf of Mexico consist of dazzlingly white sand that is so talcumlike that it actually squeaks when you walk across it. And walk across it you can, for some 100 miles (161km) of these incomparable sands are protected in state parks and the gorgeous Gulf Islands National Seashore.

Pensacola, Destin, Fort Walton Beach, and Panama City Beach have long been summertime beach meccas for families, couples, and singles from the adjoining states of Georgia and Alabama—a geographic proximity that lends this area the languid charm of the Deep South. Indeed, Southern specialties like turnip greens and cheese grits appear frequently on menus here.

But there's more to the northwestern Panhandle than beaches and Southern charm. Championship catches of grouper, amberjack, snapper, mackerel, cobia, sailfish, wahoo, tuna, and blue marlin have made Destin one of the world's fishing capitals. In the interior near Pensacola, the Blackwater, Shoal, and Yellow Rivers teem with bass, bream, catfish, and largemouth bass, and also offer some of Florida's best canoeing and kayaking adventures.

The area is also steeped in history. Rivaling St. Augustine as Florida's oldest town, picturesque Pensacola carefully preserves a heritage derived from Spanish, French, English, and American conquests. Famous for its oysters, Apalachicola saw the invention of the air conditioner, a moment of great historical note in Florida. And Tallahassee, seat of state government since 1824, has a host of 19th-century buildings and homes, including the majestic Old State Capitol.

EXPLORING NORTHWEST FLORIDA BY CAR

Both I-10 and U.S. 98 link Tallahassee and Pensacola, some 200 miles (322km) apart. The fastest route is I-10, but all you'll see is a huge pine forest divided by two strips of concrete. Plan to take U.S. 98, a scenic excursion in itself. Although it can be traffic-clogged in the beach towns during summer, U.S. 98 has some beautiful stretches out in the country, particularly as it literally skirts the bay east of Apalachicola and the Gulf west of Port St. Joe. It's also lovely along skinny Okaloosa Island and across the high-rise bridge between Fort Walton Beach and Destin. From the bridge you'll see the brilliant color of the gulf and immediately understand why they call this the Emerald Coast.

1 Pensacola ★★

191 miles (308km) W of Tallahassee, 354 miles (570km) W of Jacksonville

Native Americans left pottery shards and artifacts in the coastal dunes here centuries before Tristan de Luna arrived with a band of Spanish colonists in 1559. Although his settlement lasted only 2 years, modern Pensacolans claim that de Luna made their town the oldest in North America. Pensacola actually dates its permanence from a Spanish colony established here in 1698, however, so St. Augustine wins this friendly feud, having been permanently settled in 1565.

France, Great Britain, the United States, and the Confederacy subsequently captured (and in one case recaptured) this strategically important deep-water port. They left Pensacola with a charming blend of Old Spanish brickwork, colonial French balconies reminiscent of New Orleans, magnificent Victorian mansions built by British and American lumber barons, and its motto, "City of Five Flags."

West of town, the excellent National Museum of Naval Aviation at the U.S. Naval Air Station celebrates the storied past of navy and marine corps pilots who trained at Pensacola. The Blue Angels, who are based here, demonstrate the high-tech present with thrilling exhibitions of precision flying in the navy's fastest fighters.

Also on the Naval Station, historic Fort Barrancas looks across the bay to Perdido Key and Santa Rosa Island, which reach out like narrow pinchers to form the harbor. Out there, powdery white-sand beaches beckon sun-and-surf lovers to their spectacular gulf shores, which include Pensacola Beach, a small family-oriented resort, and most of Florida's share of Gulf Islands National Seashore, home of historic Fort Pickens.

ESSENTIALS

GETTING THERE Pensacola Regional Airport (© 850/436-5005; www.flypensacola.com), on 12th Avenue at Airport Road, is served by **AirTran** (© 800/AIR-TRAN), **Continental** (© 800/525-0280), **Delta** (© 800/221-1212), **Northwest** (© 800/225-2525), and **US Airways** (© 800/428-4322).

Alamo (© 800/327-9633), **Avis** (© 800/331-1212), **Budget** (© 800/527-0700), **Dollar** (© 800/800-4000), **Enterprise** (© 800/325-8007), **Hertz** (© 800/654-3131), and **National** (© 800/CAR-RENT) have rental-car operations here.

Taxis wait outside the modern terminal. Fares are approximately $11 to downtown, $15 to Gulf Breeze, and $20 to Pensacola Beach.

The **Amtrak** transcontinental *Sunset Limited* stops in Pensacola at 980 E. Heinberg St. (© **800/USA-RAIL;** www.amtrak.com).

VISITOR INFORMATION The **Pensacola Visitor Information Center,** 1401 E. Gregory St., Pensacola, FL 32501 (© **800/874-1234** or 850/434-1234; fax 850/432-8211; www.visitpensacola.com), gives away helpful information about the Greater Pensacola area, including maps of self-guided tours of the historic districts, and sells a detailed street map of the area. The office is at the mainland end of the Pensacola Bay Bridge and is open daily from 8am to 5pm (until 4pm Sat and Sun Oct–Mar).

For information specific to the beach, contact the **Pensacola Beach Chamber of Commerce,** 735 Pensacola Beach Blvd. (P.O. Box 1174), Pensacola Beach, FL 32561 (© **800/635-4803** or 850/932-1500; fax 850/932-1551;

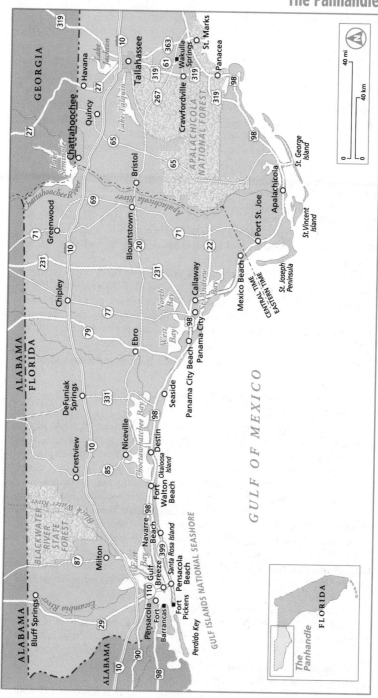

The Panhandle

645

www.visitpensacolabeach.com). The chamber's offices and visitor center are on the right as you drive onto Santa Rosa Island across the Bob Sikes Bridge. They're open daily from 9am to 5pm.

GETTING AROUND   To see the historic sights in town, park at the Pensacola visitor center (see above) and take the **Five Flags Trolley** (© 850/436-9383). The one-way East Bay (Blue) Line runs Monday through Friday from 9am to 4pm between the visitor center and downtown. The Palafox (Red) Line runs Monday through Friday from 7am to 6pm north-south along Palafox Street between the waterfront and North Hill Preservation District. Both pass through Historic Pensacola Village. The 25¢ fare includes a transfer between the two lines. The visitor center has free route maps.

A free **Tiki Trolley** operates along the full length of Pensacola Beach Memorial Day weekend through Labor Day weekend, Friday and Saturday from 10am to 3am, Sunday from 10am to 10pm.

Both trolleys are operated by **Escambia County Area Transit System (ECAT)** (© **850/595-3228;** www.ecat.pensacola.com), which also runs public buses around town Monday through Saturday—but not to the beach. Call for schedules.

If you need a cab, call **Airport Express Taxi** (© 850/572-5555), **Crosstown Cab** (© 850/456-TAXI), **Pensacola Red & Gold Taxi** (© 850/505-0025), or **Yellow Cab** (© 850/433-3333). Fares are $1.50 at flag fall, plus $1.40 a mile.

You can rent bicycles and scooters from **Floats-N-Spokes,** 500 Quietwater Beach Rd. (© **850/934-RIDE**), in Pensacola Beach. Bike fees range from $5 an hour to $15 a day. Scooters go for $30 an hour to $90 a day.

TIME   Pensacola is in the **central time zone,** 1 hour behind Miami, Orlando, and Tallahassee.

HITTING THE BEACH: GULF ISLANDS NATIONAL SEASHORE & MORE

Stretching eastward 47 miles (76km), from the entrance to Pensacola Bay to Fort Walton Beach, skinny **Santa Rosa Island** is home to the resorts, condominiums, cottages, restaurants, and shops of **Pensacola Beach,** the area's prime vacation spot. This relatively small and low-key resort began life a century ago as the site of a beach pavilion, or "casino" as such facilities were called back then; and the heart of town—at the intersection of Pensacola Beach Boulevard, Via de Luna, and Fort Pickens Road—is still known as **Casino Beach.** This lively area at the base of the town's water tank sports restaurants, snack bars, a games arcade for kids, a mini-golf course, public restrooms, walk-up beach bars with live bands blaring away, an indoor sports bar, and an outdoor concert pavilion with summertime entertainment. And the shops, restaurants, and bars of **Quietwater Boardwalk** are just across the road on the bay side of the island. If you want an active beach vacation, it's all here in one compact zone.

One reason Pensacola Beach is so small is that most of Santa Rosa Island is included in the **Gulf Islands National Seashore** ✲✲✲. Jumping from island to island from Mississippi to Florida, this magnificent preserve includes mile after mile (150 to be exact) of undeveloped white-sand beach and rolling dunes covered with sea grass and sea oats. Established in 1971, the national seashore is a protected environment for more than 280 species of birds.

The most interesting part of the seashore is at **Fort Pickens** (© 850/934-2635), on the western end of Santa Rosa Island, about 7 miles (11km) west of Pensacola Beach. Built in the 1830s to team with Fort Barrancas in guarding

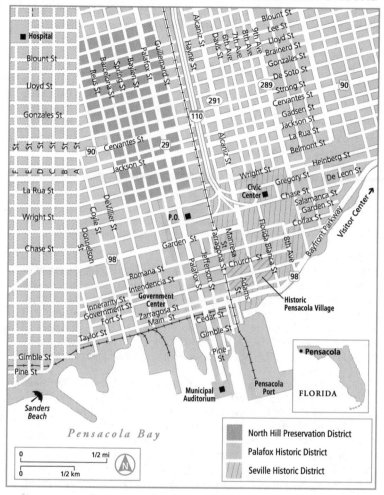

Pensacola's harbor entrance, this huge brick structure saw combat during the Civil War, but it's best known as the prison home of Apache medicine man Geronimo from 1886 to 1888. The visitor center has a small museum featuring displays about Geronimo, coastal defenses, and the seashore's ecology. Plan to be here at 2pm, when rangers lead 1-hour guided tours of the fort (the schedule can change, so call the fort to make sure). Seven-day admission permits (that's the minimum you can get) to the Fort Pickens area are $8 per vehicle, $3 per pedestrian or bicyclist, free for holders of National Park Service passports. The fort and museum are open March through October daily from 9:30am to 5pm, November through February daily from 8:30am to 4pm. Both are closed on Christmas.

The Fort Pickens area has 200 **campsites** (135 with electricity) in a pine forest on the bay side of Santa Rosa Island. Nature trails lead from the camp through Blackbird Marsh and to the beach. A small store sells provisions. Sites cost $15 a night without power, $20 a night with it, and you have to pay the admission fee to the Fort Pickens area. Golden Age and Golden Access card-holders get a 50% discount. Call ℰ **800/365-2267** for reservations (enter code GUL), or 850/934-2621 for recorded information. You can make reservations up to 5 months in advance.

The national seashore's headquarters are in the 1,378-acre **Naval Live Oaks Area,** on U.S. 98, a mile east of Gulf Breeze (ℰ **850/934-2600**). This former federal tree plantation is a place of primitive beauty, with nature trails leading through the oaks and pines to picnic areas and a beach. Pick up a map at the headquarters building, which has a small museum and a gorgeous view through the pines to Santa Rosa Sound. Picnic areas and trails are open from 8am to sun-set all year except Christmas. Admission is free. The visitor center is open daily from 8am to 5:30pm.

The national seashore also maintains historic **Fort Barrancas** on the U.S. Naval Air Station west of town. See the "Pensacola's Other Fort," box, on p. 652, for details.

For more information, contact the **Gulf Islands National Seashore,** 1801 Gulf Breeze Pkwy., Gulf Breeze, FL 32561 (ℰ **850/934-2600;** www.nps.gov/guis).

OUTDOOR ACTIVITIES

FISHING   Red snapper, grouper, mackerel, tuna, and billfish are abundant offshore all along the Panhandle. The easiest way to drop a line into the gulf is off the new **Pensacola Beach Gulf Fishing Pier,** on Fort Pickens Road in Pen-sacola Beach (ℰ **850/934-7200;** www.fishpensacolabeachpier.com). At 1,471 feet (441m), it's the longest fishing pier on the gulf coast. The pier is open 24 hours a day year-round. Fees to fish are $6.50 per day for adults, $5.50 seniors, $3.50 for children 6 to 12. Bait and equipment cost extra. Observers can watch for $1 per person.

Fishing-charter services are offered at Pensacola Beach by the *Chulamar* (ℰ 850/434-6977), *Lively One* (ℰ 850/932-5071), *Boss Lady* (ℰ 850/932-0305 or 850/477-4033), *Entertainer* (ℰ 850/932-0305), *Exodus* (ℰ 850/626-2545 or 850/932-0305), and *Lady Kady* (ℰ 850/932-2065 or 850/932-0305). Expect to pay between $350 and $750 for one to four passengers, depending on the length of your trip. You may be able to save by driving to Des-tin, where party boats charge less per person (see "Outdoor Activities," in sec-tion 2, below). Sightseeing and evening cruises here go for about $50 per person.

GOLF   The Pensacola area has its share of Northwest Florida's numerous championship golf courses. Look for free copies of *Gulf Coast Tee Time* (www.teetimeweb.com), an annual directory describing all of them, at the visi-tor information offices and in many hotel lobbies (see "The Active Vacation Planner," in chapter 2, for information about ordering copies). Reasonably priced golf packages can be arranged through many local hotels and motels.

Among this region's best courses is **Marcus Pointe,** on Marcus Pointe Boule-vard off North W Street (ℰ **800/362-7287** or 850/484-9770), which has hosted the Nike Tour, the American Amateur Classic, and the Pensacola Open. *Golf Digest* magazine has described this wide-ranging, 18-hole course as a "great value," and it is: Greens fees with cart are about $40 to $50, depending on the season.

The Moors, on Avalon Boulevard north of I-10 (ℰ **800/727-1010** or 850/995-4653), also has greeted the Nike Tour and is home to the Emerald Coast Classic, a PGA Seniors event. Pot bunkers here make you think you're playing in Scotland. Greens fees are about $30 without cart. The Moors also has a lodge with eight luxury rooms.

Florida's Canoe Capital

About 20 miles (32km) northeast of Pensacola via U.S. 90 is the little town of Milton, the official "Canoe Capital of Florida" (by an act of the state legislature, no less). It's a well-earned title, because the nearby Blackwater River, Coldwater River, Sweetwater Creek, and Juniper Creek are all perfect for canoeing, kayaking, tubing, rafting, and paddleboating.

The Blackwater is considered one of the world's purest sand-bottom rivers. It has remained a primordial, backwoods beauty, thanks chiefly to Florida's largest state forest (183,000 acres of oak, pine, and juniper) and **Blackwater River State Park** ★★, 7720 Deaton Bridge Rd., Holt, FL 32564 (ℂ 850/983-5363; www.floridastateparks.org/district1/blackwater), where you can closely observe plant life and wildlife along nature trails. The park has facilities for fishing, picnicking, and camping. Admission is $2 per day per vehicle, $1 for pedestrians or bicyclists. Campsites cost $8 per night per person ($10 with electricity), plus $2 per pet with tags and vaccination papers. For camping reservations call ℂ 800/326-3521 or go to the website (www.reserveamerica.com).

Adventures Unlimited, Route 6, Box 283, Milton, FL 32570 (ℂ 800/239-6864 or 850/623-6197; fax 850/626-3124; www.adventuresunlimited.com), is a year-round resort with day and overnight canoeing, kayaking, and rafting expeditions. Special arrangements are made for novices. Canoe trips start at $16 per person, kayaking adventures from $22. Inner tubes start at $6. Campsites cost $15 a night, $20 with electricity. The resort also has 14 cottages on the Coldwater River ($39–$129 a night), and bed-and-breakfast accommodations at the Wolfe Creek Old School House Inn (eight rooms, all with bathrooms, $79–$109 double). Two-night minimum stays are required; 3 nights on holidays. Call for the trips schedule and reservations for trips, accommodations, and camping.

Blackwater Canoe Rental, 10274 Pond Rd., Milton, FL 32570 (ℂ 800/967-6789 or 850/623-0235; www.blackwatercanoe.com), also rents canoes, kayaks, floats, tubes, and camping equipment. It has day and overnight camping trips by canoe or kayak, or inner tubes ranging from $9 to $19 per person and overnight excursions ranging from $19 to $28 per person. Tents, sleeping bags, and coolers are available for rent.

Others worth considering are the **Lost Key Golf Club,** on Perdido Key (ℂ 850/492-1300), one of the area's more difficult courses; **Scenic Hills,** on U.S. 90 northwest of town (ℂ 850/476-9611), whose rolling fairways are unique for this mostly flat area; the 36-hole **Tiger Point,** 1255 Country Club Rd. east of Gulf Breeze by Santa Rosa Sound (ℂ 850/932-1330), overlooking the water (the 5th-hole green of the East Course actually sits all by itself on an island); **Hidden Creek,** 3070 PGA Blvd., in Navarre between Gulf Breeze and Fort Walton Beach (ℂ 850/939-4604); **Creekside Golf Course,** 2355 W. Michigan Ave. (ℂ 850/944-7969); and **Osceola Municipal Golf Course,** 300 Tonawanda, off Mobile Highway (ℂ 850/456-2761).

In addition, **The Sportsman Golf Resort,** 1 Doug Ford Dr. (© 850/ 492-1223; www.sportsmanresort.com), on the mainland north of Perdido Key, has accommodations available for visiting golfers. It was the home of the PGA Pensacola Open from 1978 to 1987, when it was known as the Perdido Bay Golf Resort. Greens fees range from $55 to $65.

WATER SPORTS Visibility in the waters around Pensacola can range from 30 to 50 feet (9–15m) deep inshore to 100 feet (30m) deep 25 miles (40km) offshore. Although the bottom is sandy and it's too far north for coral, the battleship USS *Massachusetts,* submerged in 30 feet (9m) of water 3 miles (5km) offshore, is one of some 35 artificial reefs where you can spot loggerhead turtles and other creatures. There are also good snorkeling sites just off the beach; get a map from the Gulf Islands National Seashore (see the "Hitting the Beach: Gulf Islands National Seashore & More" section above).

Scuba Shack, 711 S. Palafox St. (© 850/433-4319), is Pensacola's oldest dive shop, offering sales, rentals, classes, and diving and fishing charters on the *Wet Dream,* moored behind the office. **Divers Den,** 512 N. 9th Ave. (© 850/ 438-0650; www.diversden.com), also offers trips, equipment rental, and PADI instruction. **Gulf Breeze Dive Pros,** 297B Gulf Breeze Pkwy. (U.S. 98), in Gulf Breeze (© 850/934-8845), offers rentals, all levels of instruction, and diving excursions on the 30-foot (9m) *Easy Dive.* The *Chulamar,* at Pensacola Beach (© 850/434-6977), and the *Lo-Baby,* in Gulf Breeze (© 850/934-5285), both make arrangements for diving excursions.

Key Sailing Center, 500 Quietwater Beach Rd., on the Quietwater Beach Boardwalk (© 850/932-5550; www.keysailing.com), and **Radical Rides,** 444 Pensacola Beach Blvd., near the Bob Sikes Bridge (© 850/934-9743), rent Hobie Cats, pontoon boats, WaveRunners, jet skis, and windsurfing boards.

EXPLORING HISTORIC PENSACOLA

Adjacent to the Historic Pensacola Village, the city's **Vietnam Memorial,** on Bayfront Parkway at 9th Avenue, is known as the "Wall South," since it is a three-quarter–size replica of the national Vietnam Veterans Memorial in Washington, D.C. Look for the "Huey" helicopter atop the wall.

Civil War Soldiers Museum ✿ Founded by Dr. Norman Haines Jr., a local physician who grew up discovering Civil War relics in Sharpsburg, Maryland, this store-front museum in the heart of the Palafox Street business district emphasizes how ordinary soldiers lived during that bloody conflict. The doctor's collection of military medical equipment and treatment methods is especially informative. A 23-minute video tells of Pensacola's role during the Civil War. The museum's bookstore carries more than 600 titles about the war.

108 S. Palafox St. (south of Romana St.). © 850/469-1900. www.cwmuseum.org. Admission $5 adults, $2.50 children 6–12, free for children 5 and under. Tues–Sat 10am–4:30pm. Closed New Year's Day, Thanksgiving, Christmas Eve, Christmas Day.

Historic Pensacola Village ✿✿ Bounded by Government, Taragona, Adams, and Alcanz Streets, this original part of Pensacola resembles a shady English colonial town—albeit with Spanish street names—complete with town green and **Christ Church,** built in 1832 and resembling Bruton Parish in Williamsburg, Virginia. Some of Florida's oldest homes, now owned and preserved by the state, are here, and the village has charming boutiques and interesting restaurants. During summer, costumed characters go about their daily chores and demonstrate old crafts, and University of Florida archaeologists unearth the old Spanish commanding officer's compound at Zaragosa and Tarragona Streets. Among the landmarks you can visit are the **Museum of Industry,** the **Museum of Commerce,** the French Creole–style **Charles Lavalle House,** the elegant **Victorian Dorr House,** the French Colonial–Creole **Quina House,** and **St. Michael's Cemetery** (land was deeded by the king of Spain). Another fascinating site is the **Julee Cottage Black History Museum,** 204 E. Zaragosa St. Built around 1790, this small house was owned by Julee Panton, a freed slave who ran her own business, invested in real estate, and loaned money to slaves so they could buy their freedom. Today the museum recalls her life and deeds. Start your tour by buying tickets at **Tivoli House,** 205 E. Zaragosa St., just east of Tarragona Street, where you can get free maps and brochures. Try to take one of the 90-minute guided walking tours of the village, which will take you through Christ Church and other buildings not otherwise open to the public.

Admission to the village includes the **T.T. Wentworth Jr. Florida State Museum,** 330 S. Jefferson St. (© **850/595-5989**), at Church Street downtown, a classic yellow-brick building housing exhibits of Western Florida's history and a special hands-on Discovery Museum for children.

205 E. Zaragosa St. (east of Tarragona St.). © 850/595-5985. www.historicpensacola.org. Admission $6 adults, $5 seniors, $2.50 children 4–16, free for children 3 and under. Mon–Fri 10am–4pm; 60-min. guided tours 11am and 1pm. Closed New Year's Day, Thanksgiving, Christmas Eve, Christmas Day, all other state holidays.

National Museum of Naval Aviation ★★★
The U.S. Navy and Marine Corps have trained at the sprawling U.S. Naval Air Station since they began flying airplanes early in the last century. Celebrating their heroics, this truly remarkable museum has more than 100 aircraft dating from the 1920s to the space age. There's even a torpedo bomber flown by former President George Bush during World War II. Both children and adults can sit at the controls of a jet trainer, and the mock-ups of aircraft carrier conning towers and hanger decks are realistic. You can almost feel the tug of gravity while watching the Blue Angels and other naval aviators soaring about the skies in the stunning *Magic of Flight,* one of two IMAX films shown at the museum. If the movie doesn't get your stomach churning, then a 15-minute ride in the museum's flight-motion simulator will. Using high-tech video and real motion, it simulates a high-speed, low-level mission in the navy's F-18 Hornet jet fighter. All guides are retired naval and marine corps aviators, which adds a personal touch to the hour-long museum tours. Allow at least half a day here, and save 20 minutes for a Flight Line bus tour of more than 40 aircraft parked outside the museum's restoration hangar.

Radford Blvd., U.S. Naval Air Station. © 850/452-3604. www.naval-air.org. Free admission. IMAX movies $6.25 adults; $5.75 seniors, military, and children 6–13; free for children under 6. Add $3 for second movie. Flight-motion simulator rides $3.50 per person. Daily 9am–5pm. Guided tours daily at 9:30 and 11am, and 1 and 2:30pm. Flight Line bus tours daily every 30 min. 10am–noon and 1–4pm. IMAX movies on the hr. daily 10am–4pm. Flight-motion simulator every 15 min. 9am–4:45pm. Closed New Year's Day, Thanksgiving, Christmas. Enter naval station either at the Main Gate at the south end of Navy Blvd. (Fla. 295) or at the Back Gate on Blue Angel Pkwy. (Fla. 173) and follow the signs. No passes are required.

Pensacola Historical Museum
To learn more about Pensacola's diverse, five-flag history, spend a few minutes at this local museum in the Arbona Building, a commercial structure built about 1882. An archaeological dig of the Spanish commanding officer's compound across Zaragosa Street has a boardwalk

Pensacola's Other Fort

Standing on Taylor Road near the National Museum of Naval Aviation, **Fort Barrancas** ★★ (© 850/455-5167) is definitely worth a visit while you're at the naval station. This imposing brick structure sits on a bluff overlooking the deep-water pass into Pensacola Bay. The Spanish built the water battery in 1797. Linked to it by a tunnel, the incredibly intricate brickwork of the fort's upper section was constructed by American troops between 1839 and 1844. Entry is by means of a drawbridge across a dry moat, and an interior scarp gallery goes all the way around the inside of the fort. Meticulously restored and operated by the National Park Service as part of Gulf Islands National Seashore, the fort is open March through October, daily from 9:30am to 4:45pm; November through February, daily from 8:30am to 3:45pm. Ranger-led, 1-hour guided tours are well worth taking. The schedule changes seasonally, so call for the latest information. Admission and the tours are free.

The **Pensacola Lighthouse** (© 850/455-2354), opposite the museum entrance on Radford Boulevard, has guided ships to the harbor entrance since 1825. Except for occasional guided tours (call the lighthouse or the Pensacola visitor centers for a schedule), the lighthouse is not open to the public, but you can drive right up to it. The nearby **Lighthouse Point Restaurant** (© 850/452-3251) offers bountiful, all-you-can-eat luncheon buffets and magnificent bay views for about $5.50 per person Monday through Thursday and $6.25 per person on Fridays; it's open Monday through Friday from 10:30am to 2pm (closed both Sat and Sun), and reservations are not required.

with explanatory signposts. The museum is operated by the Pensacola Historical Society, which has a resource center and library at 117 E. Government St. (© 850/434-5455).

115 E. Zaragosa St. (between Tarragona and Jefferson sts.). © 850/433-1559. www.pensacolahistory.org. Admission $1. Mon–Sat 10am–4:30pm.

Pensacola Museum of Art   Housed in what was the city jail from 1906 to 1954, this museum showcases a fine collection of European and American decorative glass, some African tribal art, and minor works by Salvador Dalí, John Marin, Thomas Hart Benton, Lynda Benglis, Milton Avery, and Alexander Calder, among others.

407 S. Jefferson St. (at Main St.). © 850/432-6247. Admission free on Tues; other days $2 adults, $1 students and active-duty military, free for children under 6. Tues–Fri 10am–5pm; Sat 10am–4pm.

HISTORIC DISTRICTS

In addition to Historic Pensacola Village in the Seville Historic District (see below), the city has two other preservation areas worth a stroll. The Pensacola Visitor Information Center provides free walking-tour maps (see "Essentials," earlier in this chapter).

PALAFOX HISTORIC DISTRICT   Running up Palafox Street from the water to Wright Street, the Palafox Historic District is also the downtown business district. Beautiful Spanish Renaissance and Mediterranean-style buildings stand from the early days, including the ornate Saenger Theatre. In 1821 General Andrew Jackson formally accepted Florida into the United States during a ceremony in Plaza Ferdinand VII, now a National Historic Landmark. His statue commemorates the event.

The Palafox district is home to the **Pensacola Historical Museum;** the **Pensacola Museum of Art,** in the old city jail; and the **T.T. Wentworth Jr. Florida State Museum** (see "Exploring Historic Pensacola," above).

NORTH HILL PRESERVATION DISTRICT   Another entry in the National Register of Historic Places, the North Hill Preservation District covers the 50 square blocks north of the Palafox Historic District bounded by Wright, Blount, Palafox, and Reus streets. Descendants of Spanish nobility, timber barons, British merchants, French Creoles, buccaneers, and Civil War soldiers still live in some of the more than 500 homes. They are not open to the public but are a bonanza for anyone interested in architecture. In 1863 Union troops erected a fort in Lee Square, at Palafox and Gadsden streets. It later was dedicated to the Confederacy, complete with a 50-foot-high (15m) obelisk and sculpture based on John Elder's painting *After Appomattox.*

A NEARBY ZOO WITH LIONS & TIGERS

The Zoo *Kids*   Situated in a 50-acre forest 15 miles (24km) east of Pensacola, this environmentally sensitive zoo has more than 700 exotic animals—including tigers, lions, rhinos, and lowland gorillas—living in landscaped habitats. Japanese gardens, a giraffe-feeding tower, and a petting farm make for a fun visit. A Safari Line train chugs through a 30-acre wildlife preserve with free-ranging herds, and youngsters also will love riding the wild animals instead of horses on a merry-go-round.

5701 Gulf Breeze Pkwy. (U.S. 98), Gulf Breeze. © 850/932-2229. www.the-zoo.com. Admission $9.95 adults, $8.95 seniors, $6.95 children 3–11, children 2 and under free. Train rides $3 per person. Carousel rides $1 per person. Apr–Oct daily 9am–5pm. Nov–Mar daily 9am–4pm. Closed day before Thanksgiving, Thanksgiving, Christmas Eve, Christmas Day.

SHOPPING

Sightseeing and shopping can be combined in Pensacola's Palafox and Seville Historic Districts, where many shops are housed in renovated centuries-old buildings. The **Quayside Art Gallery,** on Plaza Ferdinand at the corner of Zaragosa and Jefferson Streets (© **850/438-2363;** www.quaysidegallery.com), is the largest cooperative gallery in the Southeast. More than 100 artists display their works here, and the friendly staff will direct you to other nearby galleries.

North T Street between West Cervantes Street and West Fairfield Drive has so many antiques dealers and small flea markets that it's known as Antique Alley. Other dealers have booths in the **Ninth Avenue Antique Mall,** 380 N. 9th Ave. between Gregory and Strong streets (© **850/438-3961**). Get a complete list of local antiques dealers from the Pensacola Visitor Information Center (see "Essentials," earlier in this chapter).

Browsers will enjoy poking through the 400 dealer spaces covering 45 acres at the **Flea Market,** on U.S. 98, opposite The Zoo, 15 miles (24km) east of Pensacola (© **850/934-1971**). It's open on Saturday and Sunday from 9am to 5pm. Admission is free.

WHERE TO STAY

The Pensacola Visitor Information Center (see "Essentials," earlier in this chapter) publishes a complete list of rental condominiums and cottages. Among the leading rental agents are **Gulf Coast Accommodations,** 400 Quietwater Beach Rd., Box 12, Pensacola Beach, FL 32561 (© **800/239-4334** or 850/932-9788; fax 850/932-3449; www.innisfree.com); and **Tristan Realty,** P.O. Box 1611, Gulf Breeze, FL 32562 (© **800/445-9931** or 850/932-7363; fax 850/932-8361; www.tristanrealty.com).

The **Fort Pickens Area** of Gulf Islands National Seashore is your best bet here for camping (see "Hitting the Beach: Gulf Islands National Seashore & More," earlier in this chapter).

Escambia County adds 11.5% tax to all hotel and campground bills.

The accommodations listed below are arranged by geographic area: downtown Pensacola and Pensacola Beach. Bear in mind that Pensacola Beach is at least a 15-minute drive from downtown.

DOWNTOWN PENSACOLA

The University Mall complex at I-10 and Davis Highway, about 5 miles (8km) north of downtown, has a host of chain motels, and there's an ample supply of inexpensive restaurants on Plantation Road and in the adjacent mall. Another good bet is the 1998-vintage **Hampton Inn Airport,** 2187 Airport Blvd. (© **800/HAMPTON** or 850/478-1123; fax 850/478-8519). This area is not as congested as that around University Mall. The inn runs a free shuttle to nearby Cordova Mall and its adjacent chain restaurants.

Several of the town's Victorian homes have been turned into luxurious bed-and-breakfasts. Among the best is **Springhill Guesthouse,** 903 N. Spring St. (© **800/475-1956** or 850/438-6887; www.bbonline.com/fl/springhill), whose wraparound porch faces the extraordinary Hopkins' Boarding House across the street (see "Where to Dine," below).

Crowne Plaza Pensacola Grand Hotel Opposite the Civic Center in the Seville Historic District near the southern end of I-110, this unique hotel has turned the historic L&N Railroad Depot into a grand lobby with bar, restaurants, lounges, meeting rooms, and a cozy library. You'll see such turn-of-the-20th-century accouterments as an ornate railroad clock, original oak stair rails, imported marble, ceramic mosaic-tile floors, and old-fashioned carved furniture. An unimpressive 15-story glass-and-steel tower behind the depot holds the rooms and suites, which are popular primarily with business travelers and groups.

200 E. Gregory St. (at Alcanz St.), Pensacola, FL 32501. © 800/348-3336 or 850/433-3336. Fax 850/432-7572. www.pensacolagrandhotel.com. 212 units. $110–$135 double; $250–$408 suite. AE, DC, DISC, MC, V. **Amenities:** Restaurant (American); bar; outdoor pool; exercise room; business center; limited room service; laundry service; concierge-level rooms. *In room:* A/C, TV, dataport, fridge (suites only), coffeemaker, hair dryer, iron.

New World Inn Near the scenic bay and in the historic district, this urban version of a comfortable country inn is part of a meeting facility known as New World Landing. From the colonial-style lobby, a grand staircase leads to high-ceilinged and spacious rooms and suites artistically decorated with antiques. The rooms depict aspects of Pensacola's rich history: Four of them flaunt Spanish decor, four are très chic French style, four portray Early Americana, and four focus on Olde England.

600 S. Palafox St. (at Pine St.), Pensacola, FL 32501. ℂ 850/432-4111. Fax 850/432-6836. www.new-worldlanding.com. 16 units. $85–$105 double; $120 suite. Rates include continental breakfast. AE, MC, V. **Amenities:** Access to nearby health club; laundry service. *In room:* A/C, TV, dataport.

PENSACOLA BEACH

Best Western Resort Pensacola Beach   This casual motel on the gulf front is notable for bright, clean, and extra-spacious accommodations, complete with refrigerators, coffeemakers, microwaves, and wet bars. Outside corridors lead to all rooms. Although none has its own balcony or patio, units facing the beach have great views; the less expensive "inland" rooms don't. Two swimming pools and a children's playground are on the beach. Chan's Market Cafe (see "Where to Dine," below) sits in the parking lot.

16 Via de Luna Dr., Pensacola Beach, FL 32561. ℂ **800/934-3301** or 850/934-3300. Fax 850/934-4366. www.pensacolabeach.com/bestwestern. 123 units. Summer $149–$189 double; off-season $79–$149 double. Rates include continental breakfast. Golf packages available. AE, DC, DISC, MC, V. **Amenities:** 2 outdoor pools; water-sports equipment rentals; game room. *In room:* A/C, TV, dataport, fridge, coffeemaker, hair dryer, iron.

Clarion Suites Resort & Convention Center ⊛   This most unusual of Pensacola Beach's resorts resembles a village of tin-roofed, pastel-sided cottages. The attractively decorated accommodations are one-bedroom suites that can accommodate four people. The best units are those directly facing the beach. They have balconies or patios, while the others do not.

20 Via de Luna Dr., Pensacola Beach, FL 32561. ℂ **800/874-5303** or 850/932-4300. Fax 850/934-9112. www.clarionsuitesresort.com. 86 units. Summer $127–$178 up to 4 persons; off-season $84–$140 up to 4 persons. Rates include continental breakfast. AE, DC, DISC, MC, V. **Amenities:** Heated outdoor pool; water-sports equipment rentals; coin-op washers and dryers. *In room:* A/C, TV, dataport, kitchen, coffeemaker, hair dryer, iron.

The Dunes ⊛   This eight-story beachfront tower has spacious rooms, all with gorgeous gulf or bay vistas. All rooms have a gulf-facing balcony, and the penthouse suites have their own whirlpool tubs. The extra-large suites can accommodate small families. The Dunes has a restaurant and bar (both with lovely views of the gulf), so you don't have to go out for lunch or dinner unless you want to. There's a jogging trail, a bike path, and an undeveloped dune preserve next door.

333 Fort Pickens Rd., Pensacola Beach, FL 32561. ℂ **800/83-DUNES** or 850/932-3536. Fax 850/932-7088. www.theduneshotel.com. 76 units. Summer $115–$175 double; $295–$345 suite. Off-season $85–$115 double; $255–$305 suite. Packages available. AE, DISC, MC, V. **Amenities:** Restaurant (American); bar; heated outdoor pool; access to nearby health club; water-sports equipment rentals; limited room service; laundry service. *In room:* A/C, TV, dataport, coffeemaker, hair dryer, iron.

⟨*Tips*⟩ When Room Rates Are Lowest

Room rates at all Panhandle beaches are highest from mid-May to mid-August, and premiums are charged at Easter, Memorial Day, July 4, and Labor Day. Hotel or motel reservations are essential during these periods. There's another high-priced peak in March, when thousands of raucous college students invade during spring break. Economical times to visit are April (except Easter) and September—the weather is warm, most establishments are open, and room rates are significantly lower than during summer. The least-expensive rates occur during winter, but many attractions and some restaurants may be closed then.

Five Flags Inn (Value) Sitting between the Holiday Inn Express and The Dunes, this basic but friendly motel looks like a jail from the road, but don't be fooled. Big picture windows look from the rooms out to the swimming pool (heated Mar–Oct) and to the gorgeous white-sand beach, which comes right up to the property. Although the accommodations are small, the rates are a bargain for clean, gulf-front rooms.

299 Fort Pickens Rd., Pensacola Beach, FL 32561. ℭ **850/932-3586.** Fax 850/934-0257. www. fiveflagsinn.com. 49 units. Summer $95 double; off-season $55–$75 double. AE, DC, DISC, MC, V. **Amenities:** Heated outdoor pool. *In room:* A/C, TV, hair dryer, iron.

Hampton Inn Pensacola Beach ✦ This pastel, four-story hotel sits right by the gulf next to the action on Casino Beach. The bright lobby opens to a wooden sun deck with beachside swimming pools on either side (one is heated). Half the oversize rooms have balconies overlooking the gulf; these are more expensive than rooms on the bay side, which have nice views but no outside sitting areas.

2 Via de Luna, Pensacola Beach, FL 32561. ℭ **800/320-8108** or 850/932-6800. Fax 850/932-6833. www.hamptonbeachresort.com. 181 units. Summer $149–$189 double; off-season $89–$149 double. Rates include continental breakfast and local phone calls. AE, DC, DISC, MC, V. **Amenities:** Bar; 2 outdoor pools; access to nearby health club; exercise room; water-sports equipment rentals; laundry service, coin-op washers and dryers. *In room:* A/C, TV, dataport, fridge, coffeemaker, hair dryer, iron.

Holiday Inn Express Pensacola Beach This nine-story hotel boasts terrific views from its brightly furnished upper-floor rooms. Although it received a major facelift in 1998, it's one of the oldest hotels in the area, which means the rooms aren't as large as those at other new properties such as the Hampton Inn. There is adequate space for a king-size bed, but rooms with two double beds are relatively cramped. They all have private balconies, however, with the most expensive rooms facing directly onto the gulf.

165 Fort Pickens Rd., Pensacola Beach, FL 32561. ℭ **800/465-4329** or 850/932-5361. Fax 850/932-7121. www.pensacolabeach.com/holiday. 150 units. Summer $120–$150 double; off-season $70–$140 double. Rates include continental breakfast. AE, DC, DISC, MC, V. **Amenities:** Heated outdoor pool; coin-op washers and dryers. *In room:* A/C, TV, dataport, coffeemaker, hair dryer, iron.

WHERE TO DINE
PENSACOLA

Hopkins' Boarding House ✦✦✦ (Value) SOUTHERN You'll get a delicious peek into the past when you dine at this extraordinary Victorian boardinghouse in the heart of the North Hill Preservation District. Outside, ancient trees shade a wraparound porch with old-fashioned rocking chairs in which to await the next available place at the large dining tables inside. It's all-you-can-eat family-style, so you could be seated next to the mayor or a mechanic, since everyone in town dines here. Platters are piled high with staples of down-home Southern cooking: black-eyed peas, collard greens, and other seasonal vegetables from nearby farms. Tuesday is famous as Fried Chicken Day, and you're likely to be served fried fish on Friday. Yankees should sample the piping-hot grits accompanying each bountiful breakfast (slop on some butter to give them taste). In true boardinghouse fashion, you'll bus your own dishes and pay on the way out. No alcoholic beverages are served, but the "already-sweet" ice tea is great.

900 N. Spring St. (at Strong St.). ℭ **850/438-3979.** Breakfast $3.50–$8; lunch and dinner full meals $8. No credit cards. Tues–Sun 7–9:30am and 11:15am–2pm; Tues and Fri 5:15–7:30pm.

Jamie's ★★ TRADITIONAL FRENCH   Occupying a restored Victorian home in Historic Pensacola Village, the town's classiest and most romantic restaurant enhances the dining experience with an Art Deco ambience augmented by glowing fireplaces, gleaming antiques, and subdued background music. The excellent fare is traditional French. Roast leg of lamb and tournedos of beef are good choices from the regular menu, but don't overlook the seafood specials.

424 E. Zaragosa St. (between Alcanz and Florida Blanca). © 850/434-2911. Reservations recommended at both lunch and dinner. Main courses $19–$28. AE, DISC, MC, V. Mon–Sat 11:30am–2pm and 5:30–9:30pm.

Marina Oyster Barn ★ *Value* SEAFOOD   Exuding the ambience of the quickly vanishing Old Florida fish camps, this plain but clean restaurant at the Johnson-Rooks Marina is to seafood what the Hopkins' Boarding House is to grits. It has been a local favorite since 1969, for both its view and its down-home–style seafood. Freshly shucked oysters, served raw, steamed, fried, or Rockefeller, are the main feature; but the seafood salad here is also first-rate, and the fish, shrimp, and oysters are breaded with cornmeal in true Southern fashion. The daily luncheon specials give you a light meal at a bargain price.

505 Bayou Blvd. (on Bayou Texar). © 850/433-0511. Main courses $4–$12; sandwiches $2.50–$5.50; lunch specials $3.75–$6.50. AE, DISC, MC, V. Tues–Sat 11am–9pm (lunch specials 11am–2pm). Go east on Cervantes St. (U.S. 90) across the Bayou Texar Bridge, then take first left on Stanley Ave., and left again to the end of Strong St.

McGuire's Irish Pub ★ STEAKS/SEAFOOD   Every day is St. Patrick's Day at this lively and popular Irish pub, complete with corned beef and cabbage, Irish stew, and other such Dublin delicacies. Super-size steaks are the best offerings here, however, as are hickory-smoked ribs and chicken. You can also order seafood, including a hearty bouillabaisse with shrimp, red snapper, clams, mussels, and oysters. Big burgers come with a choice of more than 20 toppings, from smoked Gouda cheese to sautéed Vidalia onions. You can watch your ale being brewed in copper kettles and dine in a cellarlike room with 8,000 bottles of wine on display. More than 125,000 dollar bills line the bar's walls and ceilings. Live music is offered most nights.

600 E. Gregory St. (between 11th and 12th aves.). © 850/433-6789. Main courses $16–$25; snacks, burgers, and sandwiches $8–$12. AE, DC, DISC, MC, V. Daily 11am–2:30am.

Skopelos on the Bay ★ SEAFOOD/STEAKS/GREEK   Perched on a bluff overlooking the bay, this family-owned restaurant has been famous hereabouts since 1959 for its great views and creative seafood dishes, such as the scamp Cervantes (scamp is a deepwater fish with white, flaky meat). Other seafood selections range from broiled scallops to Mediterranean-style grouper prepared with a sauce of tomato and roasted eggplant. The menu also features charcoal-grilled steaks and chicken and roast leg of lamb. Befitting the owner's Greek heritage, roast lamb is served with moussaka, dolmades, titopita, and spanakopita. In warm weather, opt for an outside table with bay view.

670 Scenic Hwy. (U.S. 90 east, at E. Cervantes St.). © 850/432-6565. Reservations recommended. Main courses $15–$27. AE, DISC, MC, V. Tues–Thurs and Sat 5–10:30pm; Fri 11:30am–2:30pm and 5–10:30pm.

PENSACOLA BEACH

Chan's Market Cafe *Value* AMERICAN   The aroma of pastries in the oven permeates this pleasant little cafe and bakery, which shares quarters with a liquor store in the parking lot of the Best Western Pensacola Beach. It's the best place on the beach for a breakfast of freshly baked croissants or bagels. Lunches and dinners feature economical specials such as meatloaf, barbecued chicken, pot roast, and grilled fish, all served with a choice of Southern-style veggies. Or you can order a heaping sandwich on one of Chan's large, flaky croissants.

16 Via de Luna. ℂ 850/932-8454. Breakfast/lunch/snacks $3–$7; meals $5–$10. AE, DISC, MC, V. Daily 7am–9pm.

Flounder's Chowder House ⭐ SEAFOOD   Inside, this restaurant radiates piousness, with decor featuring stained-glass windows from an old New York convent and confessional-booth walls from a New Orleans church. Outside on the sandy beach by the bay is a totally different story, however, for in summer this is one of the most popular reggae bars here (see "Pensacola After Dark," below). The food is pretty good, with steamed Maine lobster and chargrilled tuna, grouper, and mahimahi leading the list. If you're lucky, a big smoker grill outside will be producing more fish and some exceptional ribs. Burgers, salads, and sandwiches are offered all day. A glass of champagne accompanies a sumptuous bay-side Sunday brunch.

800 Quietwater Beach Rd. (at Via de Luna and Fort Pickens Rd.). ℂ 850/932-2003. Reservations not accepted. Main courses $15–$21; burgers and sandwiches $8–$10. AE, DC, DISC, MC, V. Sun–Thurs 11am–midnight (to 11pm in winter); Fri–Sat 11am–2am (to 11pm in winter).

PENSACOLA AFTER DARK

For what's going on, pick up the daily *Pensacola News Journal* (www. pensacolanewsjournal.com), especially its Friday entertainment section. Another good source is the *Pensacola Downtown Crowd* (www.burchellpublishing. com/downtown.asp), a free publication available at the Pensacola Visitor Information Center (see "Essentials," earlier in this chapter).

THE PERFORMING ARTS   Pensacola has a surprisingly sophisticated array of entertainment choices for such a relatively small city. For a schedule of upcoming events, get a copy of *Vision,* a bimonthly newsletter published by the Arts Council of Northwest Florida (ℂ **850/432-9906;** www.artsnwfl.org). Also pick up **Sneak Preview,** a calendar of events at the Pensacola Civic Center and the Saenger Theater. Both publications are available at the Pensacola Visitor Information Center (see "Essentials," earlier in this chapter). Tickets for all major performances can be purchased from **Ticketmaster** (ℂ **800/488-5252** or 850/433-6311; www.ticketmaster.com).

The highlight venue here is the ornate **Saenger Theatre** ⭐, 118 S. Palafox St., near Romano Street (ℂ **850/444-7686;** www.saengertheatre.com), a painstakingly restored masterpiece of Spanish baroque architecture that the locals call the Grande Dame of Palafox. The variety of presentations includes the local opera company and symphony orchestra, Broadway musicals, and touring performers. The 10,000-seat **Pensacola Civic Center,** 201 E. Gregory St., at Alcanz Street (ℂ **850/432-0800;** www.pensacolaciviccenter.com), hosts a variety of concerts, exhibitions, and conventions. Call ahead for the current schedule.

THE CLUB & BAR SCENE   Pensacola's downtown nighttime entertainment center is **Seville Quarter,** 130 E. Government St., at Jefferson Street (ℂ **850/434-6211;** www.rosies.com), in the Seville Historic District. This restored antique-brick complex with New Orleans–style wrought-iron balconies is actually a collection of pubs and restaurants whose names capture the ambience: Rosie O'Grady's Goodtime Emporium, Lili Marlene's Aviator's Pub, Apple Annie's Courtyard, End o' the Alley Bar, Phineas Phogg's Balloon Works

The Last Great Road House

Sitting precisely on the Florida-Alabama state line on Perdido Key, about 15 miles (24km) west of downtown Pensacola, the **Flora-Bama Lounge,** 17401 Perdido Key Dr. (© **850/492-0611;** www.florabama.com), is almost a shrine to country music. Billing itself as the "Last Great American Road House," this slapped-together gulf-side pub is famous for its special jam sessions from noon until way past midnight on Saturday and Sunday. Flora-Bama is the prime sponsor and a key venue for the Frank Brown International Songwriters' Festival during the first week of November. If you've never attended an Interstate Mullet Toss, catch the fun here during the last weekend of April. The raw oyster bar is popular all the time. Granted, the joint can get a bit rough from time to time, but you won't soon forget the great gulf views while sipping a cold one at the Deck Bar. The Flora-Bama is open daily from 8:30am to 2:30am.

(a dance hall, not a balloon shop), and Fast Eddie's Billiard Parlor (which has electronic games, too). The pubs all serve up libations, food, and live entertainment from Dixieland jazz to Country and Western. Get a monthly calendar at the information booth next to Rosie O'Grady's. Open daily from 11am to 2am.

Every night is party time at **McGuire's Irish Pub,** the city's popular Irish pub, brewery, and eatery (see "Where to Dine," above). Irish bands appear nightly during summer, on Saturday and Sunday the rest of the year.

Nightlife at the beach centers around **Quietwater Boardwalk,** Via de Luna at Fort Pickens Road (no phone), a shopping/dining complex on Santa Rosa Sound. With the lively beach and reggae bar at **Flounder's Chowder House** just a few steps away, it's easy to barhop until you find a band and crowd to your liking. Across Via de Luna at Casino Beach is **The Dock** (© 850/934-3316), which has beachside live bands nightly during summer, on weekends off-season. You can catch all the games here at **Sidelines Sports Bar & Restaurant** (© 850/934-3660). See "Where to Dine," above, for details about Chan's and Flounder's.

2 Destin & Fort Walton Beach ★★

40 miles (64km) E of Pensacola, 160 miles (258km) W of Tallahassee

Sitting on a round harbor off East Pass, which lets broad and beautiful Choctawhatchee Bay flow into the Gulf of Mexico, Destin is justly famous for its fishing fleet, the largest in the state. It's also Northwest Florida's fastest-growing and most upscale vacation destination, with a multitude of high-rise condominiums, the huge Sandestin luxury resort, several excellent golf courses, and some of Northwest Florida's best restaurants and lively nightspots. By and large, Destin attracts a more affluent crowd than does Fort Walton Beach, its more down-to-earth neighbor.

Although Fort Walton Beach has its own gorgeous strip of white sand over on Okaloosa Island, it is a "real" city whose economy is supported less by tourism than by sprawling Eglin Air Force Base. Covering more than 700 square miles, Eglin is the world's largest air base and is home to the U.S. Air Force's Armament Museum and the 33rd Tactical Fighter Wing, the "Top Guns" of Operation Desert Storm in 1991.

To the east of Destin, development is picking up steam along the beaches of southern Walton County. Still, this picturesque area has mostly cottages nestled among rolling sand dunes covered with sea oats. Here you'll find Grayton Beach State Park, which sports one of America's finest beaches, and the quaint village of **Seaside** ★★, which served as the set for Jim Carrey's movie *The Truman Show.* Seaside was built on a lovely stretch of beach in the 1980s—but with Victorian architecture that makes it look a century older. The village's gulf-side honeymoon cottages make for one of Florida's most romantic retreats; and the village has interesting shops and art galleries, a stamp-size post office, and a resident population of artists, writers, and other creative folks, who permit only their own cars in their relatively expensive little enclave. Don't worry, there are parking spaces for tourists on the one main road through Seaside, but you can't drive into the village itself unless you live there.

ESSENTIALS

GETTING THERE   Flights arriving at and departing from **Okaloosa Regional Airport** (© 850/651-7160; www.co.okaloosa.fl.us/airport.html) actually use the enormous strips at Eglin Air Force Base. The terminal is on Fla. 85 north of Fort Walton Beach and is served by **Delta** (© 800/221-1212), **Northwest/KLM** (© 800/225-2525), and **US Airways** (© 800/428-4322).

Avis (© 800/331-1212), Budget (© 800/527-0700), Hertz (© 800/654-3131), and National (© 800/CAR-RENT) have rental cars at the airport, and Enterprise (© 800/325-8007) is in town.

Top Class Shuttle Service (© 888/SHUTTLE or 850/830-7229) and **Airport Shuttle Service** (© 850/897-5238) provide van transportation to and from the airport. Fares are based on a zone system: $12 to $15 to Fort Walton Beach, $25 to Destin, and $32 to $35 to Sandestin and southern Walton County.

The Sunset Limited transcontinental service on **Amtrak** (© 800/USA-RAIL; www.amtrak.com) stops at Crestview, 26 miles (42km) north of Fort Walton Beach.

VISITOR INFORMATION   For advance information about both Fort Walton Beach and Destin, contact the **Emerald Coast Convention and Visitors Bureau,** P.O. Box 609, Fort Walton Beach, FL 32549 (© 800/322-3319 or 850/651-7131; fax 850/651-7149; www.destin-fwb.com). The bureau shares quarters with the **Okaloosa County Visitors Welcome Center** in a tin-roofed, beachside building on Miracle Strip Parkway (U.S. 98) on Okaloosa Island at the eastern edge of Fort Walton Beach. Stop there for brochures, maps, and other information. The welcome center is open Monday through Friday from 8am to 5pm, Saturday and Sunday from 10am to 4pm.

The **Destin Area Chamber of Commerce,** 4484 Legendary Dr., Destin, FL 32541 (© 850/837-6241; fax 850/654-5612; www.destinchamber.com), gives away brochures and sells maps of the area. The chamber resides in an office complex at the entry to Regatta Bay Golf & Country Club, on U.S. 98, one half mile (.75km) east of the Mid-Bay Bridge. It's open Monday through Friday from 9am to 5pm. Closed holidays.

For information about the beaches of South Walton, contact the **South Walton Tourist Development Council,** P.O. Box 1248, Santa Rosa Beach, FL 32459 (© 800/822-6877 or 850/267-1216; fax 850/267-3943; www.beachesofsouth walton.com). Its **visitor center** is at the intersection of U.S. 98 and U.S. 331 in Santa Rosa Beach (© 850/267-3511). Open daily from 8:30am to 5:30pm.

Tips How to Find a Street Address

Don't worry about getting lost, since most of what you'll want to see and do in Destin and Fort Walton Beach is either on, or no more than a few blocks from, U.S. 98, the area's main east-west drag. Finding a street address is another matter, however, for even many local residents don't fully comprehend the post office's bizarre naming and numbering system along U.S. 98.

In Fort Walton Beach, U.S. 98 is known as the "Miracle Strip Parkway," with "southwest" and "southeast" addresses on the mainland and "east" addresses on Okaloosa Island.

In Destin, U.S. 98 is officially known as "Highway 98 East" from the Destin Bridge east to Airport Road, and street numbers get progressively higher as you head east from the bridge. East of Airport Road, however, the post office calls U.S. 98 the "Emerald Coast Parkway"—although locals still say a place is on "98 East." The highway also is known as the Emerald Coast Parkway in Walton County, but the street-numbering system changes completely once you pass the county line.

Adding to the confusion in Destin, "Old Highway 98 East" is a short spur from Airport Road to the western side of Henderson Beach State Park, and "Scenic Highway 98 East" parallels the real U.S. 98 along the beach from the eastern side of Henderson Beach to Sandestin.

In other words, call and ask for directions if you're not sure how to find an establishment here.

GETTING AROUND   The Okaloosa County Tourist Development Authority (© **850/651-7131**) operates a free **Island Shuttle** trolley during the summer months along the entire length of Santa Rosa Boulevard on Okaloosa Island. The two trolleys run every 30 minutes Sunday through Thursday from 7am to 10pm, Friday and Saturday from 7am to 1am. They also connect the island to the Uptown Bus station, on Eglin Parkway NE on the Fort Walton Beach mainland.

For a cab in Fort Walton Beach, call **Charter Taxis** (© 850/863-5466), **Checker Cab** (© 850/244-4491), **Crosstown Taxi** (© 850/244-7303), **JC's Cab** (© 850/865-0578), **Veterans Cab Co.** (© 850/243-1403), or **Yellow Cab** (© 850/244-3600). In Destin, call **Destin Taxi** (© 850/654-5700). Fares are based on a zone system rather than meters, with a $4 minimum. Trips within Fort Walton Beach or Destin should range from $4 to $8.

TIME   The area is in the central time zone, an hour behind Miami, Orlando, and Tallahassee.

HITTING THE BEACH

DESTIN   Like an oasis in the middle of Destin's rapid development, the 208-acre **Henderson Beach State Park** ★★, east of Destin Harbor on U.S. 98, allows easy access to swimming, sunning, surf fishing, picnicking, and seabird-watching along its 1½ miles (2.5km) of beach. There are restrooms, outdoor showers, and surf chairs for persons with disabilities. The area is open daily from 8am to sunset. Admission is $2 per vehicle, $1 for pedestrians and cyclists. Several good restaurants are just outside the park's western boundary. The park has 30 campsites in a wooded setting. They cost $16 per night, plus $2 for electricity, and can be reserved up to 11 months in advance. Pets on leashes are allowed in the park, including the beach and campground. For camping reservations call © **800/326-3521** or go to the website (www.reserveamerica.com). For more information, contact the park at 1700 Emerald Coast Pkwy., Destin, FL 32541 (© **850/837-7550;** www.floridastateparks.org/district1/hendersonbeach).

The **James W. Lee Park,** between Destin and Sandestin on Scenic Highway 98, has a long white-sand beach overlooked by covered picnic tables, an ice-cream parlor, and a moderately priced seafood restaurant with great views.

FORT WALTON BEACH   Do your loafing on the white sands of **Okaloosa Island,** joined to the mainland by the high-rise Brooks Bridge over Santa Rosa Sound. Most resort hotels and amusement parks are grouped around the Gulfarium marine park on U.S. 98, east of the bridge. Here you'll find **The Boardwalk,** a collection of tin-roofed beachside buildings that have a games arcade for the kids, a saloon for adults, covered picnic areas, a summertime snack bar, and a seafood restaurant. Just to the east, you can use the restrooms, cold-water showers, and other free facilities at **Beasley Park,** home of the Okaloosa County Visitor Welcome Center.

Across U.S. 98, the Okaloosa area of the **Gulf Islands National Seashore** has picnic areas and sailboats for rent on Choctawhatchee Bay, plus access to the gulf. Admission to this part of the national seashore is free.

SOUTHERN WALTON COUNTY   Sporting the finest stretch of white sand on the gulf, **Grayton Beach State Park** ★★★, on County Road 30A, also has 356 acres of pine forests surrounding scenic Western Lake. There's a boat ramp and a campground with electric hookups on the lake. Get a leaflet at the main gate for a self-guided tour of the nature trail. Pets are not allowed anywhere in the recreation area. The area is open daily from 8am to sunset. Admission is $3.25 per vehicle with up to eight occupants, $1 per pedestrian or bicyclist. Campsites cost $14 from March to September, $8 from October to February. Add $2 for electricity. For camping reservations call © **800/326-3521** or go to the website (www.reserveamerica.com). For information, contact the park at 357 Main Park Rd., Santa Rosa Beach, FL 32459 (© **850/231-4210;** www.floridastateparks.org/district1/graytonbeach).

Seaside has free public parking along County Road 30A and is a good spot for a day at the beach, a stroll or bike ride around the quaint village, and a tasty meal at one of its restaurants.

OUTDOOR ACTIVITIES

BOATING & BOAT RENTALS   Pontoon boats are highly popular for use on the back bays and on Sunday-afternoon floating parties in East Pass. Several companies rent them, including **Best Boat Rentals** (© 850/664-7872) on Okaloosa Island in Fort Walton Beach; and **Adventure Pontoon Rentals** (© 850/837-3041), **B&J Boat Rentals** (© 850/243-4488), **East Pass Watersports** (© 850/654-4253), and **Premier Powerboat Rentals** (© 850/837-7755), all on Destin Harbor. Expect to pay about $70 for a half day, $120 for a full day. Premier Powerboat Rentals also has speedboats for rent.

CRUISES   The *Emerald Magic* (© **888/654-1685** or 850/837-1293; www.moodysinc.com) and the *Southern Star* (© **888/424-7217** or 850/837-7741; www.dolphin-sstar.com) have daily dolphin and sunset cruises June through August, by arrangement the rest of the year. The *Emerald Magic* is operated by Moody's, on U.S. 98 at Destin Harbor (see "Fishing," below), while the *Southern Star* docks in Destin at the Harbor Walk Marina, behind the Lucky Snapper Restaurant. The *Emerald Magic* charges $15 for adults, $7.50 for kids 3 to 12. The *Southern Star* costs $2 more for adults, 50¢ less for children.

FISHING   Billing itself as the "World's Luckiest Fishing Village," Destin has Florida's largest charter-boat fleet, with more than 140 vessels based at the marinas lining the north shore of Destin Harbor, on U.S. 98 east of the Destin Bridge. Arranging a trip is as easy as walking along the Destin Harbor waterfront, where you will find the booking booths of several agents, such as **Boardwalk Fishing Charters** (© 800/242-2824 or 850/837-2343; www.harborwalkfishing.com), **Pelican Charters** (© 850/837-2343), **Harbor Cove Charters** (© 850/837-2222), and **Fishermen's Charter Service** (© 850/654-4665). Rates for private charters range from about $400 to $900 per boat, depending on the length of the voyage.

A less-expensive way to try your luck is on a larger group-oriented party boat such as those operated by **Moody's,** at 194 U.S. 98 east on Destin Harbor (© 888/654-1685 or 850/837-1293; www.moodysinc.com). Moody's charges $35 per person ($30 off-season) for its half-day runs (morning is the best time to fish). Children 8 to 12 and nonfishing sightseers are charged half price. Other party boats are the *Destin Princess* (© 888/837-5088 or 850/837-5088), *Emmanuel* (© 850/837-6313), the *Lady Eventhia* (© 850/837-6212), and three craft operated by **Olin Marler's Deep Sea Fishing Fleet** (© 850/837-7095), all based at Destin Harbor.

You don't have to go to sea to fish from the catwalk of the 3,000-foot (900m) **Destin Bridge** over East Pass. The marinas and bait shops at Destin Harbor can provide gear, bait, information, and a fishing license. In Fort Walton Beach, you can cast a line off **Okaloosa Island Fishing Pier,** 1030 Miracle Strip Pkwy. E. (U.S. 98; © 850/244-1023). The pier is open 24 hours a day. Adults pay $6.50 to fish; children pay $3.50. Observers pay $1. Bait and equipment rentals are available.

GOLF   The area takes great pride in having more than 250 holes of golf. For advance information on all area courses, contact the **Emerald Coast Golf Association,** P.O. Box 304, Destin, FL 32540 (© 850/654-7086). Also look for *Gulf Coast Tee Time,* the free annual directory published in Pensacola (see "Outdoor Activities," in section 1, earlier in this chapter). It's available on the Web at www.teetimeweb.com. Be sure to inquire whether your choice of accommodations in this area offers golf packages, which can represent significant savings.

On the mainland, nonresidents are welcome to play at the city-owned **Fort Walton Beach Golf Club,** on Lewis Turner Boulevard (C.R. 189) north of town (© 850/862-3314 or 850/862-0933; www.fwb.org/golf/index.htm). The club has two 18-hole courses—the **Pines** (© 850/833-9529) and the **Oaks** (© 850/833-9530)—plus a pro shop. Greens fees at both courses are about $30 year-round, including a cart.

In Destin, scenic **Indian Bayou Golf and Country Club,** off Airport Road (© 850/837-6191), has three 9-hole courses with large greens and wide fairways. They look easy, but watch out for water hazards and strategically placed hidden bunkers! Greens fees, including cart, are about $60.

In southern Walton County, **Sandestin Golf and Beach Resort** on U.S. 98 East (© 850/267-8211 for tee times) is the largest facility here (see "Where to Stay," below). Its 63 holes are spread over three outstanding championship courses. The Baytowne and Links courses overlook Choctawhatchee Bay. Fees for 18 holes are about $70 for resort guests, $90 for nonguests.

Some of the 27 championship holes at **Emerald Bay Golf Club,** 2 miles (3.25km) east of the Mid-Bay Bridge on U.S. 98 (© **850/837-5197;** www.emeraldbaydestin.com), run along Choctawhatchee Bay; the water adds both beauty and challenges to the otherwise wide and forgiving fairways. Greens fees are about $75 with cart.

In southern Walton County, the semiprivate **Santa Rosa Golf & Beach Club,** off County Road 30A in Dune Allen Beach (© **850/267-2229;** www.santarosaclub.com), offers a challenging 18-hole course through tall pines looking out to vistas of the gulf. The club has a pro shop, a beachside restaurant, a lounge, and tennis courts. Fees are about $65 in summer, $50 off-season. The **Seascape Resort & Conference Center,** 100 Seascape Dr. (© **850/837-9181**), off County Road 30A, features a Joe Lee–designed 18-hole course winding through woods and around lakes, with a premium placed on accuracy rather than power. The center also has tennis courts, accommodations, a restaurant, a bar, and a pro shop.

In Niceville, a 20-minute drive north via the Mid-Bay Bridge, nonguests may play golf (four 9-hole courses) or tennis (21 courts) at the **Bluewater Bay Resort** (© **850/897-3613;** www.bwbresort.com), which also has condominiums for rent.

Call ahead for reservations and current fees at all these clubs, and ask about afternoon and early-evening specials.

SAILING   **Sailing South** (© **850/837-7245;** www.sailingsouth.com), on U.S. 98 at Destin Harbor, has half-day cruises aboard the 72-foot (22m) schooner *Daniel Webster Clements.* The 1½-hour morning cruise goes in search of dolphins to watch and costs $15 for adults and $12 for kids under 12. The 2½-hour afternoon cruises stop for swimming and snorkeling virtually under the Destin Bridge; these cost $35 for adults and $18 for kids under 12. It also offers sunset cruises and 3-day voyages. The 54-foot (16m) schooner *Nathaniel Bowditch* (© **850/650-8787;** www.bowditchsailing.com) will take you on half-day shelling excursions, while the *Blackbeard* (© **850/837-2793;** www.blackbeardsailing.com) concentrates on dolphin-watching cruises.

SCUBA DIVING & SNORKELING   At least a dozen dive shops are located along the beaches. Considered one of the best, **Scuba Tech Diving Charters** has two locations in Destin: at 301 U.S. 98 E. (© **850/837-2822;** www.scubatech nwfl.com) and at 10004 U.S. 98 E. (© **850/837-1933**), about a half mile west of the Sandestin Beach Resort.

WATER SPORTS   Hobie Cats, WaveRunners, jet boats, jet skis, and parasailing are available all along the beach. The largest selection of operators, including **Boogies** (© **850/654-4497**), is at the marinas just east of the Destin Bridge, behind Hooter's and Fat Tuesday's pubs. **Paradise Water Sports** (© **850/664-7872**) rents equipment and offers parasailing rides at seven locations along U.S. 98 in both Destin and Fort Walton Beach.

EXPLORING THE AREA

Eden Gardens State Park   Evoking images from *Gone With the Wind,* the garden's magnificent 1895 Greek Revival–style Wesley Mansion has been lovingly restored and richly furnished. It stands overlooking scenic Choctawhatchee Bay and is surrounded by immense moss-draped oak trees and the Eden Gardens, resplendent with camellias, azaleas, and other typical Southern flowers. Your visit won't be complete without a guided tour of the house, so avoid coming here on a Tuesday or Wednesday. Picnicking is allowed on the plantation grounds.

181 Eden Gardens Rd. (off C.R. 395), Point Washington. ℂ 850/231-4214. www.floridastateparks.org/district1/edengardens. Grounds and gardens $2 per vehicle; mansion tours $1.50 adults, 50¢ children 12 and under. Gardens and grounds daily 8am–sunset; 45-min. mansion tours on the hr. Thurs–Mon 9am–4pm.

Florida's Gulfarium *Kids*   One of the nation's original marine parks features ongoing 25-minute shows with dolphins, California sea lions, Peruvian penguins, loggerhead turtles, sharks, sting rays, moray eels, and alligators. There are fascinating exhibits, including the Living Sea, with special windows for viewing undersea life. During one of the shows, a scuba diver explains the sea life while swimming among the various creatures.

1010 Miracle Strip Pkwy. (U.S. 98) on Okaloosa Island. ℂ 850/244-5169. www.gulfarium.com. Admission $16 adults, $14 seniors, $10 children 4–11, free for children 3 and under. Mid-May to Labor Day, daily 9am–6pm (park closes 8pm). Sept to mid-May, daily 9am–4pm (park closes 6pm).

Indian Temple Mound and Museum   This ceremonial mound, one of the largest ever discovered, dates from A.D. 1200. The museum showcases part of its collection of more than 6,000 ceramic artifacts from southeastern American Indian tribes, the nation's largest such collection. Exhibits depict the lifestyles of the four tribes that lived in the Choctawhatchee Bay region for 12,000 years.

139 Miracle Strip Pkwy. SE, on the mainland. ℂ 850/833-9595. www.fwb.org/html/fwbmuseum01.htm. Park free; museum $2 adults, $1 children 6–17, free for children 5 and under. Park daily dawn–dusk. Museum Sept–May Mon–Fri 11am–4pm, Sat 9am–4pm; June–Aug Mon–Sat 9am–4:30pm, Sun 12:30–4:30pm.

U.S. Air Force Armament Museum ★★   Although this fascinating museum is not on a par with Pensacola's National Museum of Naval Aviation, you'll love it if you're into warplanes. Located on the world's largest air force base, it traces military developments from World War II through the Korean and Vietnam Wars to Operation Desert Storm. On display are reconnaissance, fighter, and bomber planes, including the SR-71 Blackbird spy plane.

100 Museum Dr., off Eglin Pkwy. (Fla. 85) at Eglin Air Force Base, 5 miles (8km) north of downtown. ℂ 850/882-4062. Free admission. Daily 9:30am–4:30pm. Closed federal holidays.

SHOPPING

The third-largest "designer" outlet mall in the United States, **Silver Sands Factory Stores** ★★, on U.S. 98 between Destin and Sandestin (ℂ **800/510-6255** or 850/864-9780; www.silversandsfactorystores.com), has upscale stores such as Anne Klein, Donna Karan, J. Crew, Brooks Brothers, Hartmann luggage, Coach leather, Bose electronics, and so on. Shops are open Monday through Saturday from 10am to 9pm (to 7pm Jan–Feb), Sunday from 10am to 6pm (noon–6pm Jan–Feb). The fine food court here, **Morgan's Market** (ℂ **850/654-3320**), serves a varied menu. There are electronic games for kids and a sports bar for adults.

Over at the Sandestin Beach Resort on U.S. 98, you can window-shop in **The Market at Sandestin,** where boutiques purvey expensive clothing, gifts, and Godiva chocolates.

WHERE TO STAY

The area has a vast supply of condominiums and cottages for rent. One good-value example is Venus Condos, listed below. The tourist-information offices (see "Essentials," earlier in this chapter) will provide lists of others for rent. The largest rental agent is **Abbott Realty Services,** 3500 Emerald Coast Pkwy.,

Destin, FL 32541 (© **800/336-4853** or 850/837-4853; fax 850/654-2937; www.abbott-resorts.com). It publishes a magazine-size annual brochure picturing and describing its many properties throughout the area.

There are several commercial campgrounds here, but the best camping is at **Henderson Beach State Park** in Destin and at **Grayton Beach State Park** in south Walton County (see "Hitting the Beach," earlier in this chapter).

State and local governments add 9% to all hotel and campground bills.

DESTIN

A former Comfort Inn, the local **Motel 6,** 405 U.S. 98 E. (© **800/466-8356** or 850/837-0007; fax 850/837-5325; www.motel6.com), sitting across the highway from the harbor, has rooms that are generally larger than those at many other members of this cut-rate chain. There's also an outdoor swimming pool on the premises, which makes it a more attractive place to stay.

Best Western SummerPlace Inn   Located across U.S. 98 from the Hampton Inn Destin (see below), this four-story, Spanish-motif building offers innlike rooms and suites decorated with wildlife prints. A few suites have hot tubs in their living rooms (you won't get those at the Hampton Inn). The more expensive gulf-side units have balconies (those facing the bay do not). Larger units have microwave ovens and refrigerators. Doors open from an indoor pool, a whirlpool, and an exercise room to an outdoor pool. You'll have to negotiate your way across busy U.S. 98 to reach the gulf.

14047 Emerald Coast Pkwy. (U.S. 98, at Airport Rd.), Destin, FL 32541. © **888/BEACH-99** or 850/650-8003. Fax 850/650-8004. 72 units. Summer $115–$175; off-season $45–$99. Rates include continental breakfast and local telephone calls. AE, DISC, MC, V. **Amenities:** Indoor and outdoor pools; exercise room; Jacuzzi; business center; coin-op washers and dryers. *In room:* A/C, TV, dataport, fridge, coffeemaker, hair dryer.

Hampton Inn Destin   This pink, two-story building sits at the junction of the new and old U.S. 98s, about 200 yards west of Henderson Beach State Park and near a covey of restaurants just outside the recreation area and another bunch of them across U.S. 98. There's a beach a short walk away on the old highway, which means you don't have to fight the traffic on U.S. 98 to reach the gulf. External corridors lead to the standard motel-style rooms and the suites with two rooms and kitchenettes. A gazebo-like sitting area offers shade next to a heated outdoor pool and hot tub.

1625 Hwy. 98 E. (at Old Hwy. 98 and Airport Rd.), Destin, FL 32541. © **800/HAMPTON** or 850/654-2677. Fax 850/654-0745. www.hamptoninndestin.com. 104 units. Summer $129–$149 double; $160–$180 suite. Off-season $69–$89 double; $99 suite. Rates include continental breakfast. AE, DC, DISC, MC, V. **Amenities:** Heated outdoor pool; Jacuzzi; coin-op washers and dryers. *In room:* A/C, TV, dataport, kitchen (suites only), fridge, coffeemaker, hair dryer, iron.

Henderson Park Inn ★★   At the end of Old U.S. 98 on the undeveloped eastern edge of the Henderson Beach State Park, this shingle-sided, Cape Hatteras–style bed-and-breakfast is the area's most romantic get-away-from-it-all escape without screaming kids (children and pets are not accepted). Individually decorated in a Victorian theme, the rooms have high ceilings, fireplaces, Queen Anne furniture, and gulf views from private balconies. Most have Jacuzzis and some have canopy beds. The main building (16 rooms are in a separate shingle-sided structure next door) sports a beachside veranda complete with old-fashioned rocking chairs in which to sit and admire the glorious sunsets. Guests are treated to a Southern-style buffet breakfast and to beer and wine at the nightly before-dinner social hour in the wonderful Veranda Restaurant (reservations recommended), which opens to the wraparound porch of the main building. Guests are provided with complimentary beach umbrellas and chairs.

2700 Scenic Hwy. 98 E. (P.O. Box 30), Destin, FL 32541. ℂ 800/336-4853 or 850/837-4853. Fax 850/654-0405. www.hendersonparkinn.com. 35 units. Summer $189–$334 double; off-season $95–$189 double. Rates include full breakfast and evening cocktails. Packages and weekly rates available. AE, DISC, MC, V. No children or pets accepted. **Amenities:** Restaurant (American); bar; heated outdoor pool; Jacuzzi; limited room service; laundry service. *In room:* A/C, TV, dataport, fridge, coffeemaker, hair dryer, iron.

Holiday Inn of Destin *Kids*   Many guest rooms in this family-friendly gulf-front resort are in a round high-rise building, but get one facing south or east because a tall condominium next door blocks southwest-facing units from enjoying the spectacular gulf views from their balconies. Better yet, request a room in the older, four-story building, where the rooms are more spacious and many open directly onto the beach. Others open to walkways in an enclosed "Holidome" sporting a comfortable mezzanine lounge with indoor pool and billiard and Foosball tables (plenty here to keep the kids occupied).

1020 Hwy. 98 E. (P.O. Box 577), Destin, FL 32541. ℂ 877/837-6181 or 850/837-6181. Fax 850/837-1523. www.holidayinndestin.com. 233 units. Summer $145–$220 double; off-season $75–$125 double. AE, DC, DISC, MC, V. **Amenities:** Restaurant (American); bar; 3 heated pools (1 indoor, 1 children's); exercise room; Jacuzzi; sauna; children's programs; game room; babysitting; laundry service; coin-op washers and dryers. *In room:* A/C, TV, dataport, fridge, coffeemaker, hair dryer, iron, safe.

FORT WALTON BEACH

The managers of Venus by the Sea (see below) also run the new **Sea Crest Condominiums,** located next door at 895 Santa Rosa Blvd. (ℂ **800/476-1885** or 850/301-9600; fax 850/301-9205; www.seacrestcondos.com). The 112 units in this seven-story building aren't as spacious as those in Venus, but they're considerably more luxurious, and those on the higher floors have great views toward the west. The complex has indoor and outdoor pools (actually one pool; you can swim under a glass partition between them), and it sits next to a county park with a boardwalk leading over the dunes to the beach.

   Among other chain motels here is the new **Hampton Inn Ft. Walton Beach,** 1112 Santa Rosa Blvd. (ℂ **800/HAMPTON** or 850/301-0906; www. hamptoninnfwb.com). It's adjacent to the Radisson Beach Resort and shares its facilities (see below).

Four Points By Sheraton *Kids*   This beachfront resort sports spacious rooms decorated with vivid, tropical colors. The older, motel-style wings here surround a lush tropical courtyard with a whirlpool, heated swimming pool, and bar. With their balconies overlooking the beach, the choice units are in a newer, seven-story gulf-side building with a second swimming pool and bar. Some rooms have kitchenettes. A summertime children's program helps make this a good if not perfect family choice.

1325 E. Miracle Strip Pkwy. (U.S. 98), Fort Walton Beach, FL 32548. ℂ 800/874-8104 or 850/243-8116. Fax 850/244-3064. www.sheraton4pts.com. 216 units. Summer $115–$245 double; off-season $76–$175 double. Rates include full breakfast. AE, DC, DISC, MC, V. **Amenities:** 2 restaurants (American); bar; 2 heated outdoor pools; exercise room; Jacuzzi; water-sports equipment rentals; children's programs; game room; limited room service; babysitting; laundry service; coin-op washers and dryers. *In room:* A/C, TV, dataport, fridge, coffeemaker, hair dryer, iron.

Marina Motel   This family-operated, self-described "fisherman's motel" may be pedestrian-looking, but it has clean, comfortable rooms and apartments directly across U.S. 98 from the magnificent public beach at Beasley Park. A low-slung, brick-fronted motel block holds most of the rooms. Other units are in two-story stucco structures near a marina whose 560-foot (168m) pier is home to charter-fishing boats. Two one-bedroom apartments at the end of the complex overlook the marina and bay. All units here have refrigerators and microwaves; 16 have full kitchens. If traffic is too busy to cross U.S. 98 to the beach (there are no nearby overpasses or traffic lights), you can sun at the motel's little bay-side beach or take a dip in its roadside pool.

1345 E. Miracle Strip Pkwy. (U.S. 98), Fort Walton Beach, FL 32548. ✆ **800/237-7021** or 850/244-1129. Fax 850/243-6063. www.marinamotel.net. 38 units. Summer $67–$87 double; $115–$125 apt. Off-season $39–$63 double; $65–$92 apt. AE, DC, DISC, MC, V. **Amenities:** Outdoor pool; coin-op washers and dryers. *In room:* A/C, TV, kitchen (efficiencies and apartments only), fridge, coffeemaker, iron.

Radisson Beach Resort   A glass-enclosed elevator climbs up through a soaring, six-story lean-to atrium lobby to rooms with spectacular gulf views from their standing-room-only balconies at this resort. Beach lovers are more likely to appreciate the units in an older two-story motel building that have sitting-room patios or balconies facing the gulf. Other units in the older building open to a lush courtyard surrounding a pool. In the atrium, a tropically adorned cafe serves breakfast, lunch, and dinner, and a bar has nightly entertainment during summer.

1110 Santa Rosa Blvd. (at U.S. 98), Fort Walton Beach, FL 32548. ✆ **800/333-3333** or 850/243-9181. Fax 850/664-7652. www.radissonresort.com. 287 units. Summer $129–$189 double; off-season $89–$129 double. Packages available. AE, DC, DISC, MC, V. **Amenities:** Restaurant (American); 2 bars; 3 outdoor pools (1 children's); 2 lighted tennis courts; exercise room; water-sports equipment rentals; limited room service; babysitting; laundry service. *In room:* A/C, TV, dataport, coffeemaker, hair dryer, iron.

Ramada Plaza Beach Resort ⟨⟩   This big resort boasts the prettiest outdoor areas in northwest Florida, with waterfalls cascading over lofty rocks and a romantic grotto bar, all surrounded by thick tropical foliage. Although there is another swimming pool, a large sun deck, and a bar out by the beach, this gorgeous courtyard would have even more charm if it weren't cut off from the gulf by a six-story block of hotel rooms. The guest rooms and the one-bedroom suites in this beachfront building are the best here, with gulf or courtyard views from balconies or patios. The least-expensive units, in the adjacent building, overlook a parking lot. On-site dining options include a barbecue shack out in the tropical forest. The Boardwalk beach pavilion and restaurants are next door. There's also a cozy lobby lounge with sports TVs.

1500 E. Miracle Strip Pkwy. (U.S. 98), Fort Walton Beach, FL 32548. ✆ **800/874-8962** or 850/243-9161. Fax 850/243-2391. www.ramadafwb.com. 335 units. Summer $120–$185 double; $280–$350 suite. Off-season $70–$140 double; $160–$270 suite. AE, DC, DISC, MC, V. **Amenities:** 3 restaurants (American); 3 bars; 2 outdoor pools (1 heated); exercise room; Jacuzzi; water-sports equipment rentals; children's programs; game room; limited room service; coin-op washers and dryers. *In room:* A/C, TV, dataport, fridge, coffeemaker, hair dryer, iron.

Venus by the Sea ⟨⟩ (Value   Offering considerably more space than a hotel would at these rates, this pleasant, three-story enclave on western Okaloosa Island was built in the 1970s and has been immaculately maintained ever since. Each of the one-, two-, and three-bedroom units has a long living/dining/kitchen room, with a rear door leading to a balcony or to a patio opening to a grassy courtyard. The beach is a short walk across the dunes, and you can stroll along the undeveloped beach at an Eglin Air Force Base auxiliary facility about 200 yards away. The same management also operates the new and much more luxurious **Sea Crest Condominiums** next door (see above), and guests here can use the indoor-outdoor pool there.

885 Santa Rosa Blvd., Fort Walton Beach, FL 32548. © **800/476-1885** or 850/301-9600. Fax 850/301-9205. www.venuscondos.com. 45 units. Summer $110–$180 apt.; off-season $50–$135 apt. Weekly and monthly rates available. Ask for off-season specials. MC, V. **Amenities:** Outdoor pool; tennis court; coin-op washers and dryers. *In room:* A/C, TV/VCR, kitchen, coffeemaker, iron.

SOUTHERN WALTON COUNTY

If you want to stay near Sandestin Golf and Beach Resort (see below) without paying its prices, there's a modern **Sleep Inn** a mile west at 5000 Emerald Coast Pkwy. (U.S. 98; © **800/627-5337** or 850/654-7022).

Hilton Sandestin Beach & Golf Resort ★★ *Kids* This all-suites beachside resort, housed in two adjacent towers, is the top full-service hotel here. It's nicely situated on the grounds of Sandestin Golf and Beach Resort (see below) and shares its golf and tennis facilities. The elegant Elephant Walk restaurant is next door. "Executive suites" in one wing are equipped primarily for business travelers and conventioneers (lots of meeting space here), while the spacious "junior suites" in the old wing are geared to families, with a special area for children's bunk beds. Parents can send the kids off to a supervised summertime program (including movies) while pampering themselves at the full-service spa.

4000 Sandestin Blvd. S., Destin, FL 32541. © **800/445-8667** or 850/267-9500. Fax 850/267-3076. www.sandestinresort.hilton.com. 598 suites. Summer $250–$395 suite; off-season $150–$335 suite. Golf and tennis packages available. AE, DC, DISC, MC, V. **Amenities:** 2 restaurants (American); 2 bars; indoor and outdoor pools; golf course; tennis courts; health club, spa; Jacuzzi; water-sports equipment rentals; children's programs; game room; concierge; activities desk; car-rental desk; business center; shopping arcade; salon; 24-hr. room service; massage; babysitting; laundry service; coin-op washers and dryers; concierge-level rooms. *In room:* A/C, TV, dataport, minibar, coffeemaker, hair dryer, iron.

Sandestin Golf and Beach Resort ★★ Known until recently as The Resort at Sandestin, this luxurious real-estate development is one of Florida's biggest sports-oriented resorts. It sprawls over 2,300 acres complete with a spectacular beach 5 miles (8km) west of Destin, plus a marina. It's notable for its 81 holes of championship golf and its tennis clinic (both with instruction available), plus a fully equipped sports spa and health center. An array of handsomely decorated accommodations overlooks the gulf or Choctawhatchee Bay, the golf fairways, lagoons, or a nature preserve. The hotel rooms and suites are in the Bayside Inn. They all have kitchenettes and balconies, but you'd be wise to opt for one of the much more spacious junior suites or one-, two-, and three-bedroom condominium apartments, which are in high- and mid-rise buildings either on the gulf or along the manicured fairways. The privately owned condominiums are individually decorated and come with full kitchen and patio or balcony, and many have washers and dryers. Most amenities are a short walk or bike or free tram ride away, and a tunnel runs under U.S. 98 to connect Sandestin's gulf and bay areas. Among the relatively limited on-site dining options is the romantic **Elephant Walk** (© **850/267-4800**), located on the gulf; it serves up different, gourmet-quality choices for dinner every evening.

9300 Emerald Coast Pkwy. W. (U.S. 98), Destin, FL 32541. © **800/277-0800** or 850/267-8000 in the U.S., or 800/933-7846 in Canada. Fax 850/267-8222. www.sandestin.com. 175 units, 620 condo apts. Summer $155–$210 double; $210–$560 condo apt. Off-season $85–$190 double; $105–$395 condo apt. Packages and weekly/monthly rates available. Rates include health club, bicycle, boogie board, canoe, and kayak use; 1-hr. tennis daily; discounts on other amenities. AE, DC, DISC, MC, V. **Amenities:** 3 restaurants (American); 3 bars; 9 heated outdoor pools; 4 golf courses; 18 tennis courts; spa; Jacuzzis; water-sports equipment rentals; children's programs; game room; concierge; shopping arcade; salon; limited room service (hotel only); massage; babysitting; laundry service; coin-op washers and dryers. *In room:* A/C, TV, dataports, kitchen, coffeemaker, hair dryer, iron.

SEASIDE

If you decide to rent a home or a **romantic honeymoon cottage** 🏠🏠 in this quaint village, contact the **Seaside Cottage Rental Agency,** P.O. Box 4730, Seaside, FL 32459 (℃ **800/277-8696** or 850/231-1320; fax 850/231-2293; www.seasidefl.com). The agency has several hundred cottages in its rental inventory, from one to six bedrooms. The beachside honeymoon cottages are one of Florida's best getaways for newlyweds or anyone else looking for a romantic escape.

Josephine's French Country Inn at Seaside 🏠🏠   With its six large Tuscan columns reminiscent of an elegant Virginia mansion, Josephine's is an elegant country inn, with mahogany four-poster beds, lace comforters, rich furnishings, and marble bathtubs. Most guest rooms also have fireplaces. Conveniences like wet bars, microwaves, and small refrigerators are neatly incorporated into the design so that they don't conflict with the nostalgic charm. Sumptuous breakfasts are served either in-room (beside the fireplace or on your private veranda) or in the gracious dining room. The Guest House offers four suites, two with gulf views. Each has a fireplace, kitchen, and full bathroom. No smoking is allowed inside, nor are pets. With rich mahogany furniture and a wealth of period accouterments, the dining room here is one of the region's finest places for a gourmet romantic dinner. Glowing with candlelight, this intimate room seats only 22 people (by reservation only). Josephine's Maryland-style crab cakes are consistently delicious.

County Rd. 30A (P.O. Box 4767), Seaside, FL 32459. ℃ **800/848-1840** or 850/231-1940. Fax 850/231-2446. www.josephinesinn.com. 9 units (all with bathroom). Year-round $200 double; $250 suite. Rates include gourmet breakfast. Weekly rates available. AE, DISC, MC, V. **Amenities:** Restaurant (American); bar; free use of bikes. *In room:* A/C, TV, dataport, kitchen (in some suites) fridge, coffeemaker, hair dryer, iron.

WHERE TO DINE

Except for the strip on Okaloosa Island, a plethora of national fast-food and family chain restaurants line U.S. 98.

DESTIN

If you didn't catch a fish to be grilled at Fisherman's Wharf (see below), you can buy one to brag about from **Sexton's Seafood,** 602 Hwy. 98 E. opposite Destin Harbor (℃ **805/837-3040**). It's the best market here.

AJ's Seafood & Oyster Bar SEAFOOD   Jimmy Buffett tunes set the tone at this fun, tiki-topped establishment on the picturesque Destin Harbor docks, where fishing boats unload their daily catches right into the kitchen. Obviously, the best items here are grilled or fried fish, but raw or steamed Apalachicola oysters also lead the bill of fare. You can sample a bit of everything with a "run of the kitchen" seafood patter. AJ's is most famous for its topside Club Bimini, a "meet bar" featuring reggae music and limbo contests every summer evening (you may want to have dinner elsewhere if you're not in the partying mood). At lunch, picnic tables on the covered dock make a fine venue with a view across the harbor.

116 Hwy. 98 E., Destin Harbor. ℃ **850/837-1913.** Main courses $12–$19; sandwiches and salads $6–$8. AE, DISC, MC, V. Apr–Sept Sun–Thurs 11am–10pm, Fri–Sat 11am–midnight (bar until 4am). Off-season daily 11am–9pm.

Back Porch 🦐 SEAFOOD   This cedar-shingled seafood shack offers glorious beach and gulf views from its long porch. The popular, casual restaurant originated charcoal-grilled amberjack, which you'll now see on menus throughout Florida. Other fish and seafood, as well as chicken and juicy hamburgers, also come from the coals. Monthly specials feature crab, lobster, and seasonal fish. Come early, order a rum-laden Key Lime Freeze, and enjoy the sunset. The Back

Porch sits with a number of other restaurants near the western boundary of the Henderson Beach State Park.

1740 Old Hwy. 98 E. ✆ **850/837-2022.** Main courses $12–$20; sandwiches, burgers, and pastas $6.50–$8.50. AE, DC, DISC, MC, V. Apr–Sept daily 11am–11pm. Off-season daily 11am–10pm. From U.S. 98, turn toward the beach at the Hampton Inn.

Callahan's Island Restaurant & Deli ★ *Value* AMERICAN/DELI The best place in the area for picnic fare, this family-operated deli offers burgers, excellent Reubens, and other made-to-order sandwiches, pastas, and nightly specials such as charcoal-grilled chicken and grilled pork chops. A long refrigerator case across the rear holds a variety of top-grade cheeses, deli meats, steaks, and chops (choose your own cut, and the chef will chargrill it to order). Tables and booths are set up garden fashion, adding an outdoorsy ambience to this pleasant store-front establishment. Locals like to do lunch here. Breakfast is served only on Saturday mornings.

950 Gulf Shore Dr. (2 blocks south of U.S. 98). ✆ **850/837-6328.** Main courses $8–$16; sandwiches, burgers, and salads $3.50–$6.50. DISC, MC, V. Mon–Fri 10am–9pm; Sat 8am–9pm.

Ciao Bella Pizza *Finds* PIZZA/SOUTHERN ITALIAN This urbane little parlor offers more than just very good 12-inch pizzas; chef Gugliemo Ianni also whips up excellent salads and pastas, which he displays on a cafeteria-style steam table, just like they do in his native Italy. Afterwards enjoy some creamy gelato.

29 Hwy. 98 (in Harborwalk Center near Destin Bridge). ✆ **850/654-9815.** Main courses $8–$11; pizza $8–$17. AE, DISC, MC, V. Mon–Sat noon–10pm; Sun 3–10pm.

Donut Hole SOUTHERN Available around the clock, breakfasts at this popular spot highlight eggs Benedict, hot fluffy biscuits under sausage gravy, Belgian waffles, and freshly baked doughnuts. Lunch sees fresh deli sandwiches, half-pound burgers, and big salads. The rough-hewn building has booths and counter seating. Be prepared to wait on the deck, especially on weekends. Daily specials such as half a Southern fried chicken with three country-style vegetables and dessert are a bargain. There's another Donut Hole, open daily from 6am to 10pm, on U.S. 98 East in southern Walton County 2½ miles (4km) east of the Sandestin Beach Resort (✆ **850/267-3239**).

635 U.S. 98 E., Destin. ✆ **850/837-8824.** Breakfast $4–$7.50; sandwiches, salads, and burgers $4.50–$6.50; main courses $6.50–$8. No credit cards. Daily 24 hr. Closed 2 weeks before Christmas.

Fisherman's Wharf Seafood House SEAFOOD Have that fish you caught filleted, bring it here, and the chef will chargrill it at this atmospheric restaurant next to a charter fleet marina (the restaurant hosts most of Destin's fishing competitions). If you had no luck, and didn't stop by Sexton's Seafood on the way here to buy a few filets (see above), you can select from the restaurant's fresh-off-the-boat catch for grilling, broiling, frying, or blackening. Charcoal grilling is the house specialty—my triggerfish filet was white and flaky but still moist. All main courses include a trip to the salad bar, rice pilaf, baked potato, or roasted vegetables. Although this building dates from 1996, it evokes an Old Florida fish camp, with rough-hewn wood walls and double-hung windows looking out to a large harborside deck, a venue during the warmer months for two bars, an oyster bar, live music, and great sunsets.

210D Hwy. 98 E., Destin Harbor. ✆ **850/654-4766.** Main courses $11–$18; sandwiches and burgers $7–$9; cook-your-catch $6 lunch, $8 dinner. AE, DC, DISC, MC, V. Summer daily 11am–11pm (deck bar open later). Off-season daily 11am–9pm.

Harbor Docks SEAFOOD/JAPANESE   The harbor views are spectacular from indoors or outdoors at this casual, somewhat-rustic establishment. You can order your fill of fried fish, but specialties such as the daily catch sautéed with artichoke hearts are far more enjoyable. Asian influences include a sushi bar and hibachi table, which are open for dinner, and a few Thai specialties that grace the lunch menu. Except during winter, hearty fishermen's breakfasts are cooked by the owners of the Silver Sands, a popular local haunt that burned down several years ago. The bar here is popular with charter-boat skippers, and frequent live entertainment keeps the action going on the outdoor deck at night.

538 U.S. 98 E., Destin Harbor. ✆ 850/837-2506. Reservations accepted only for hibachi table. Main courses $16–$23; sushi $4.50–$8. AE, DC, DISC, MC, V. Feb–Oct daily 5:30–10:30am and 11am–11pm; Nov–Jan daily 11am–11pm. Sushi bar daily 5–10pm.

Harry T's Boat House *Kids* AMERICAN   To honor the memory of trapeze artist "Flying Harry T" Baben, his family opened this lively spot on the ground floor of Destin Harbor's tallest building. Standing guard is the stuffed Stretch, Harry's beloved giraffe. Other decor includes circus memorabilia and relics from the luxury cruise ship *Thracia,* which sank off the Emerald Coast in 1927; Harry T was presented with the ship's salvaged furnishings and fixtures for personally leading the heroic rescue of its 2,000 passengers. The tabloid-style menu offers traditional seafood, steaks, chicken, and pasta dishes. Kids eat for 99¢ until 7pm and at Sunday brunch. Watch for clowns and other children's entertainment at least 1 night a week. Both the dining room and the downstairs lounge (with live entertainment Fri and Sat nights) enjoy harbor views.

320 U.S. 98 E., Destin Harbor. ✆ 850/654-4800. Main courses $10.50–$20; sandwiches and salads $10–$12. AE, DISC, MC, V. Summer Mon–Sat 11am–2am; Sun 10am–2am. Off-season Mon–Sat 11am–11pm; Sun 10am–11pm. Bar open later. Sun brunch year-round 10am–3pm.

Marina Cafe 🌟🌟 NEW AMERICAN   Destin's finest restaurant provides a classy atmosphere with soft candlelight, subdued music, and walls of glass overlooking the harbor. The changing menu always offers nouveau preparations of seafood. Pizzas are topped with the likes of spicy cayenne rock shrimp, roasted corn, and onion marmalade, and pastas might feature fusilli with roast chicken, sun-dried tomatoes, goat cheese, broccoli, pine nuts, and an herb-and-balsamic-vinegar broth. Any main course will be an exciting combination of flavors, too. If it's offered, try the grouper coated with crab and horseradish and served with herb-roasted potatoes and wild-mushroom parsnip and asparagus ragout. Enjoy the outdoor deck for drinks and appetizers.

404 Hwy. 98 E., Destin Harbor. ✆ 850/837-7960. Reservations recommended. Main courses $17–$29; pizza and pasta $9–$17. AE, DC, DISC, MC, V. Daily 5–11pm. Closed first 3 weeks in Jan.

McGuire's Irish Pub & Brewery STEAKS/SEAFOOD   Like Pensacola's original McGuire's (listed above), this younger sibling sports thousands of dollar bills stuck on the ceilings and walls, plus Notre Dame football schedules, a prominent logo of the Boston Celtics, and other memorabilia recalling Irish-American lore. This is Destin's most popular hangout, and local professionals congregate at the big oak bar in the center of the dining room, especially when live entertainment starts at 9pm Tuesday through Sunday. You can opt for a table on either side of the bar or up on a rooftop deck. Dining here is almost secondary to the see-and-be-seen scene, although the tender chargrilled steaks and giant hamburgers are worthy antidotes to a big appetite.

33 Hwy. 98 E., Destin Harbor (in Harborwalk Center near Destin Bridge). ✆ 850/650-0000. Main courses $16–$25; snacks, burgers, and sandwiches $8–$12. AE, DC, DISC, MC, V. Mon–Sat 11am–2am; Sun 11am–1am.

FORT WALTON BEACH

Big City Coffeehouse and Cafe COFFEE/PASTRIES/DELI For a caffeine fix, an inexpensive breakfast or lunch, or afternoon tea, head to Tina and Jim Ivanchukov's bright yellow-and-purple cafe on the mainland near the Brooks Bridge. In addition to offering gourmet coffees, the owners make great salads such as herb-roasted chicken with apples, walnuts, and tarragon dressing (sold by the pound), and sandwiches served on homemade focaccia bread.

201 Miracle Strip Pkwy. SE (U.S. 98). © 850/664-0664. Sandwiches and salads $5.50–$8.50. MC, V. Mon–Fri 7am–7pm; Sat–Sun 8am–5pm.

Caffè Italia ★★ NORTHERN ITALIAN Nada Eckhardt is from Croatia, but she met her American husband, Jim, while working at a restaurant named Caffè Italia in northern Italy. The Eckhardts duplicated that establishment in this 1925 Sears & Roebuck mail-order house tucked away on the waterfront. You can dine on the patio with a view of the sound through sprawling live oak trees (one table is set romantically under its own gazebo) or dine inside, where Nada has installed floral tablecloths and photos from the old country. A limited but fine menu includes excellent pizzas; pasta dishes such as tortellini with tomatoes, chicken, and peas in Alfredo sauce; northern Italian risotto with either asparagus or smoked salmon; and meat and seafood dishes to fit the season. Don't expect to make a full meal by ordering only a pasta here, because meals are served in the authentic Italian fashion, with a small portion of pasta preceding the seafood or meat course. On the other hand, you can quickly fill up on the seasoned, pizza-dough breadsticks served with olive oil for dipping. The cappuccino here is absolutely first-rate, as are the genuine Italian desserts.

189 Brooks St., on the mainland in the block west of Brooks Bridge. © 850/664-0035. Reservations recommended. Main courses $15–$18; pizza and pasta $8–$13. AE, DC, DISC, MC, V. Sun and Tues–Fri 11am–10pm; Sat 5–11pm. Closed Thanksgiving, Christmas.

Pandora's Restaurant & Lounge ★ STEAKS/PRIME RIB/SEAFOOD The front part of this unusual restaurant is a beached yacht now housing the main-deck lounge. Below is a beam-ceilinged dining room aglow with lights from copper chandeliers. Try for the private Bob Hope booth, where you can dine below two of the great comedian's golf clubs (he used to come here to raise money for a local air force widows' home). Anything from the charcoal grill is excellent, including the wonderful bacon-wrapped scallops offered as an appetizer. Several varieties of freshly caught fish are among the main-course choices, but steaks and prime rib keep the locals coming back for more. The tender beef is cut on the premises and grilled to perfection. The delicious breads and pies are homemade. Live entertainment and dancing are an added attraction in the lounge Wednesday through Saturday, as are free snacks during happy hour from 5 to 7pm weekdays. There's another Pandora's in Grayton Beach at the corner of Fla. 283 and County Road 30A (© **850/231-4102**).

1120B Santa Rosa Blvd. © **850/244-8669.** Reservations recommended. Main courses $12–$25. AE, DISC, MC, V. Sun–Thurs 5–10pm; Fri–Sat 5–10:30pm.

Staff's Seafood Restaurant SEAFOOD/STEAKS Considered the first Emerald Coast restaurant, Staff's started as a hotel in 1913 and moved to this barnlike building in 1931. Among the display of memorabilia are an old-fashioned phonograph lamp and a 1914 cash register. Staff's tangy seafood gumbo has gained fame for this casual, historic restaurant. One of the most popular main dishes is the "seafood skillet," sizzling with broiled grouper, shrimp, scallops, and crab meat drenched in butter and sprinkled with cheese. All main courses are served with heaping baskets of hot, home-baked wheat bread from a secret 70-year-old recipe, a salad, and dessert. A pianist plays at dinner year-round.

24 SW Miracle Strip Pkwy. (U.S. 98), on the mainland. © 850/243-3526. Main courses $13–$30. AE, DISC, MC, V. Summer daily 5–11pm. Off-season Mon–Thurs 5–9pm; Fri–Sat 5–10pm.

SOUTHERN WALTON COUNTY

A good budget choice here is **Morgan's Market** (© **850/654-3320**), the food court at Silver Sands Factory Stores (see "Shopping," earlier in this chapter).

Criolla's ★★★ *(Value)* INTERNATIONAL One of Florida's finest restaurants, Johnny Earles' charming establishment derives its name from the archaic word *criollo*, signifying persons of pure Spanish descent born in the New World. The attractive decor, combining New Orleans with the Caribbean, features potted palms, whirling ceiling fans, and tropical island paintings. The menus change seasonally, but many fish dishes carry the wonderful aroma of smoke from a wood-fired grill (the bacon-wrapped swordfish is always a winner). Be sure to ask about a special four-course, fixed-price dinner, which draws inspiration from such warm spots as the Caribbean, Central America, and Tahiti. It's also worth asking in advance about special events featuring visiting chefs and spotlighting excellent vineyards (the wine cellar here has won awards).

170 E. Scenic Hwy. 30A, ¼ mile (.5km) east of C.R. 283, Grayton Beach. © 850/267-1267. Reservations recommended. Main courses $19–$31. AE, DISC, MC, V. Jan–Feb and Oct–Dec Tues–Sat 5:30–10pm; Mar–Apr and Sept Mon–Sat 5:30–10pm; May–Aug daily 5:30–10pm.

SEASIDE

Several cafes and sandwich shops in Seaside's gulf-side shopping complex offer inexpensive snacks to beachgoers.

Bud and Alley's ★★ SEAFOOD/STEAKS/MEDITERRANEAN Set among the gulf-side dunes, Seaside's first restaurant is still number one. The freshest seafood can be selected from seasonal menus featuring an innovative selection of Basque, Italian, Louisianan, and Floridian dishes prepared by owners and accomplished chefs Scott Witcoski and Dave Raushkolb. You can dine indoors or out, on the screened porch, or under an open-air gazebo where you'll hear the waves splashing against the white sands. The roof deck, open in season, serves appetizers and light meals and is a fabulous spot to watch the sun set on the Gulf of Mexico. Jazz is usually in the spotlight on weekends. On New Year's Eve, everyone in town and from miles around celebrates at Bud and Alley's. Call ahead to see whether a noted guest chef is cooking or a special wine-tasting dinner is scheduled. No smoking.

County Rd. 30A, in the beachside shops. © 850/231-5900. Reservations recommended. Main courses $19–$27; lunch $7.50–$14. MC, V. Apr–Sept Sun–Thurs 11:30am–3pm and 5:30–9:30pm; Fri–Sat 11:30am–3pm and 5:30–10pm. Oct–Mar Sun–Thurs 5:30–9pm; Fri–Sat 5:30–9:30pm.

DESTIN & FORT WALTON BEACH AFTER DARK

Most resorts spotlight live entertainment during the summer season, including the Radisson Beach Resort and the Ramada Plaza Beach Resort in Fort Walton Beach, and the Sandestin Hilton Beach & Golf Resort and Sandestin Golf and Beach Resort in southern Walton County (see "Where to Stay," earlier in this chapter). It's a good idea to inquire ahead to be sure of what's scheduled, especially during the slow season October through February.

For other ideas and listings of what's happening, pick up a copy of the weekly *Walton Sun* newspaper.

DESTIN   Several Destin restaurants offer entertainment nightly during summer, on weekends off-season. The dockside **AJ's Club Bimini,** 116 U.S. 98 E. (© **850/837-1913**), has live reggae under a big thatch-roofed deck. A somewhat older, if not more sober, crowd gathers for entertainment at the big harborside deck at **Fisherman's Wharf,** on U.S. 98 East (© **850/654-4766**); **The Deck,** on U.S. 98 East at the Harbor Docks restaurant, overlooking the harbor (© **850/837-2506**); and **Harry T's Boat House** (© **850/654-6555**), also on the harbor; and for Irish tunes nightly year-round at **McGuire's Irish Pub & Brewery** (© **850/650-0000**), in the Harborwalk Shops on U.S. 98 just east of the Destin Bridge. See "Where to Dine," earlier in this chapter, for details about the restaurants. The **Grande Isle Sky Bar,** above Grazti Italian Restaurant, 1771 Old Hwy. 98 (© **850/837-7475**), draws the after-dinner crowd from the Back Porch and other adjacent restaurants.

Twenty-somethings are attracted to the dance club, rowdy saloon, Jimmy Buffett–style reggae bar, and sports TV and billiards parlor all under one roof at the acclaimed **Nightown,** 140 Palmetto St. (© **850/837-6448;** www.nightown. com), near the harbor on the inland side of U.S. 98 East. One admission covers it all. Nearby, **Hogs Breath Destin,** 541 Hwy. 98 E. (© **850/837-5991**), is another lively pub with bands playing beach music.

Out toward Sandestin, **Fudrucker's Beachside Bar & Grill,** 20001 Hwy. 98 E. (© **850/654-4200**), opposite the Henderson Beach State Park, offers double the fun with two summertime stages. There's another Fudrucker's at 108 Santa Rosa Blvd. on Okaloosa Island in Fort Walton Beach (© **850/243-3833**).

FORT WALTON BEACH   Country music and dancing fans will find a home at the **Seagull,** on Miracle Strip Parkway (U.S. 98) opposite the Gulfarium (© **850/243-3413**). The generations of air force pilots who have hung out here call it the "Dirty Gull." Its main rival for the country set is the **High Tide Oyster Bar,** at Okaloosa Island off the Brooks Bridge (© **850/244-2624**).

3 Panama City Beach

100 miles (161km) E of Pensacola, 100 miles (161km) SW of Tallahassee

Panama City Beach has long been known as the "Redneck Riviera," since it's a summertime mecca for millions of low- and moderate-income vacationers from nearby Southern states. It still has a seemingly unending strip of bars, amusement parks, and old-fashioned motels. But this lively and crowded destination now also has luxury resorts and condominiums to go along with its 20-plus miles (32km) of white-sand beach, golf courses, fishing, boating, and fresh seafood.

Panama City Beach is the most seasonal resort in Northwest Florida, since many restaurants, attractions, and even some hotels close between October and spring break in March. Spring break is a big deal here; MTV even sets up shop in Panama City Beach for annual beach-party broadcasts.

ESSENTIALS

GETTING THERE   The commuter arms of **Delta** (© 800/221-1212), **Northwest/KLM** (© 800/225-2525), and **US Airways** (© 800/428-4322) fly into **Panama City/Bay County International Airport** (© 850/763-6751; www.pcairport.com), on Lisenby Avenue, north of St. Andrews Boulevard, in Panama City.

Alamo (℡ 800/327-9633), **Avis** (℡ 800/331-1212), **Budget** (℡ 800/527-0700), **Enterprise** (℡ 800/325-8007), **Hertz** (℡ 800/654-3131), and **National** (℡ 800/CAR-RENT) have rental-car offices here.

Taxi fares to the beach range from about $12 to $25.

The Sunset Limited transcontinental service on **Amtrak** (℡ **800/USA-RAIL;** www.amtrak.com) stops at Chipley, 45 miles (72km) north of Panama City.

VISITOR INFORMATION   For advance information, contact the **Panama City Beach Convention & Visitors Bureau,** P.O. Box 9473, Panama City Beach, FL 32417 (℡ **800/PC-BEACH** in the U.S., 800/553-1330 in Canada, or 850/233-6503; fax 850/233-5072; www.800pcbeach.com). It operates a visitor information center in the city hall complex, 17001 Panama City Beach Pkwy. (U.S. 98), at Fla. 79. The center is open daily from 8am to 5pm; closed New Year's Day, Thanksgiving, and Christmas.

GETTING AROUND   A **trolley** (℡ **850/769-0557**) runs five times a day Monday through Friday year-round along Thomas Drive and on Front Beach Road as far west as Fla. 79. Rides cost 50¢. Call for the schedule. For taxis, call **Yellow Cab** (℡ **800/763-0211** or 850/763-4691) or **AAA Taxi** (℡ **850/785-0533**). Fares at the beach are $2.50 for the first ⅔ mile plus 25¢ a mile thereafter, or $5 to $10 for rides within Panama City Beach. **Classic Rentals,** 13226 Front Beach Rd. (℡ **850/235-1519**), rents bicycles, scooters, and motorcycles. Call for prices and reservations.

TIME   The Panama City area is in the central time zone, 1 hour behind Miami, Orlando, and Tallahassee.

HITTING THE BEACH: ST. ANDREWS STATE PARK

A nearly unbroken strand of fine white sand fronts all 22 miles (35km) of Panama City Beach, but the highlight for many here is **St. Andrews State Park** ★★★, at the east end of the beach. With more than 1,000 acres of dazzling white sand and dunes, this preserved wilderness demonstrates what the area looked like before motels and condominiums lined the beach. Lacy, golden sea oats sway in the refreshing gulf breezes, and fragrant rosemary grows wild. Picnic areas are on both the gulf beach and the Grand Lagoon. Restrooms and open-air showers are available for beachgoers. For anglers, there are jetties and a boat ramp. A nature trail reveals wading birds and perhaps an alligator or two. And drive carefully here, for the area is home to foxes, coyotes, and a herd of deer. Overnight camping is permitted (see "Where to Stay," below). On display is a historic turpentine still that was formerly used by lumbermen to make turpentine and rosin, both important for caulking the old wooden ships.

The park's 176 RV and tent **campsites** are among the state's most beautiful, especially the 40 situated in a pine forest right on the shores of Grand Lagoon. They are very popular, so reservations are highly recommended—and absolutely essential in summer (call ℡ **800/326-3521** or go to the website www.reserveamerica.com). Sites cost $17 to $23 March through September. They drop to $10 to $14 October through February.

Park admission is $4 per car with two to eight occupants, $2 for single-occupant vehicles, and $1 for pedestrians and cyclists. The area is open daily from 8am to sunset. Pets are not allowed in the park. For more information or for camping reservations, contact the park at 4607 State Park Lane, Panama City, FL 32408 (℡ **850/233-5140;** www.floridastateparks.org/district1/standrews).

A few hundred yards across an inlet from St. Andrews State Park sits pristine **Shell Island** ★★, a 7½-mile-long (12km), 1-mile-wide (1.5km) barrier island that's accessible only by boat. This uninhabited natural preserve is great for shelling and also fun for swimming, suntanning, or just relaxing. Visitors can bring chairs, beach gear, coolers, food, and beverages. The best way to get there is on the park's **Shell Island Shuttle** (© 800/227-0132 or 850/233-5140; www.shellislandshuttle.com), which runs every 30 minutes daily from 9am to 5pm in summer, weekends from 10am to 3pm in spring and fall. Fares are $9.50 for adults, $5.50 for children 11 and under, plus admission fees to the state recreation area (see above). A special snorkel package costs $17.95, including shuttle ride and equipment. Kayak rentals cost $35 a day for a single-seat boat, $45 for a double seater.

Several cruise boats go to Shell Island, including the glass-bottomed *Captain Anderson III,* which cruises there from Captain Anderson's Marina, 5500 N. Lagoon Dr., at Thomas Drive (© 850/234-3435). It charges $10 for anyone over age 12, $8 for kids. The *Glass Bottom Boat* (© 850/234-8944) stops at Shell Island as part of its "sea school" trips from Treasure Island Marina, 3605 Thomas Dr. at Grand Lagoon (see "Cruises," under "Outdoor Activities," below).

OUTDOOR ACTIVITIES

BOATING   A variety of rental boats are available at the marinas near the Thomas Drive bridge over Grand Lagoon. These include the **Captain Davis Queen Fleet,** based at Captain Anderson's Marina, 5500 N. Lagoon Dr. (© 800/874-2415, or 850/234-3435 from nearby states); **the Panama City Boat Yard,** 5323 N. Lagoon Dr. (© 850/234-3386); the **Passport Marina,** 5325 N. Lagoon Dr. (© 850/234-5609); the **Port Lagoon Yacht Basin,** 5201 N. Lagoon Dr. (© 850/234-0142); the **Pirates Cove Marina,** 3901 Thomas Dr. (© 850/234-3839); and the **Treasure Island Marina,** 3605 Thomas Dr. (© 850/234-6533).

Many resorts and hotels provide beach toys for their guests' use. WaveRunners, jet boats, inflatables, and other equipment can be rented from **Panama City Beach Sports** (© 850/234-0067), **Raging Rentals** (© 850/234-6775), and **Lagoon Rentals** (© 850/234-7245).

CRUISES   You'll have your choice of numerous cruises here, from sailing to visiting the dolphins aboard noisy jet skis. The visitor information center (see "Essentials," above) has information about them all—and discount coupons for many.

One of the most comprehensive outings here is aboard the *Glass Bottom Boat,* based at Treasure Island Marina, 3605 Thomas Dr., at Grand Lagoon (© 850/234-8944). Its 3-hour, narrated "sea school" cruise includes underwater viewing, dolphin watching, bird feeding, and a 1-hour stop for swimming at Shell Island. Along the way, the crew picks up and rebaits a crab trap and explains the creatures brought up in a shrimp net. The boat has a snack bar and an air-conditioned cabin. The trips cost about $15 for adults and $8 for children. Call for cruise times and reservations.

Children get a kick out of the make-believe swashbucklers on the *Sea Dragon* (© 850/234-7400; www.piratecruise.net), an 80-foot-long (24m) replica of a pirate ship that goes on 2-hour cruises from its dock next to the Treasure Ship on Thomas Drive at Grand Lagoon. The trips cost $16, $13 for seniors, $12 for children 3 to 12, and free for children under 3. Call for seasonal schedules and reservations.

FISHING The least-expensive way to try your luck fishing is with **Captain Anderson's Deep Sea Fishing,** at Captain Anderson's Marina on Thomas Drive at Grand Lagoon (© **800/874-2415** or 850/234-5940). The captain's party-boat trips last from 5 to 12 hours, with prices ranging from about $30 to $50 per person, including bait and tackle. Observers can go along for half price.

More expensive are the charter-fishing boats that depart daily from March to November from the marinas mentioned in "Boating," above.

You won't get seasick casting your line from the **M. B. Miller County Pier,** 12213 Front Beach Rd. (© **850/233-3039**), or the **Dan Russell Municipal Pier,** 16101 Front Beach Rd. (© **850/233-5080**).

GOLF **Marriott's Bay Point Resort Village,** 4200 Marriott Dr., off Jan Cooley Road (© **850/234-3307;** www.baypointgolf.com), offers 36 holes of championship play, including the Bruce Devlin–designed **Lagoon Legends** ★★ course, rated as one of the country's most difficult. Both it and the Club Meadows course have clubhouses, putting greens, driving ranges, clinics, and private instruction. Greens fees with cart range from about $50 in summer to $80 in winter, depending on the day of the week. See "Where to Stay," below.

The **Edgewater Beach Resort,** 11212 U.S. 98A (© **850/235-4044**), also has a 9-hole resort course, and its guests have access to **The Hombre,** 120 Coyote Pass, 3 miles (5km) west of the Hathaway Bridge off Panama City Beach Parkway/U.S. 98 (© **850/234-3573**), a par-72 championship course that is home to the Nike Panama City Beach Classic. Fifteen of its 18 holes have water hazards (the unforgiving 7th hole sits on an island). Greens fees are about $65 in summer, $60 in winter, including cart.

The course at the semiprivate **Holiday Golf Club,** 100 Fairway Blvd. (© **850/234-1800**), sports lake-line fairways and elevated greens. Greens fees with cart are about $45 in summer, $35 in winter. You can play at night on a lighted 9-hole, par-29 executive course.

The least-expensive place to play here is the flat and forgiving **Signal Hill,** 9516 N. Thomas Dr. (© **850/234-3218**), where you'll pay about $20 to walk 18 holes in summer, $15 in winter. Add about $10 per person for a cart.

SCUBA DIVING & SNORKELING Although the area is too far north for extensive coral formations, more than 50 artificial reefs and shipwrecks in the gulf waters off Panama City attract a wide variety of sea life. The largest local operator is **Hydrospace Dive Shop,** 6422 W. Hwy. 98 (© **850/234-3036;** www.hydrospace.com). Others include **Panama City Dive Center,** 4823 Thomas Dr. (© **850/235-3390;** www.pcdivecenter.com); **Emerald Coast Divers,** 5121 Thomas Dr. (© **800/945-DIVE** or 850/233-3355); **West End Dive Center,** 17320 Panama City Beach Pkwy. (© **850/235-7873**); and **Pete's Scuba Center,** 9007 Front Beach Rd. (© **800/401-DIVE** or 850/230-8006). These companies lead dives, teach courses, and take snorkelers to the grass flats off Shell Island.

EXPLORING THE AREA

Gulf World Marine Park *Kids* This landscaped tropical garden and marine showcase features shows with talented dolphins, sea lions, penguins, and more. Not to be upstaged, parrots perform daily, too. Sea turtles, alligators, and other critters also call Gulf World home. Scuba demonstrations, shark feedings, and underwater shows keep the crowds entertained. Allow about 3½ hours to see it all, including the shows.

15412 Front Beach Rd. (at Hill Ave.), Panama City Beach. ℭ 850/234-5271. www.gulfworldmarinepark. com. Admission $19.42 adults, $13.40 children 5–11, free for children under 5. Summer daily 9am–4pm; off-season daily 9am–2pm.

Museum of Man in the Sea   Owned by the Institute of Diving, this small museum exhibits relics from the first days of scuba diving, historical displays of the underwater world dating from 1500, and treasures recovered from sunken ships, including Spanish treasure galleons. Hands-on exhibits explain water and air pressure, light refraction, and why diving bells work. Both kids and adults can climb through a submarine and see live sea animals in a pool. Videos and aquariums explain the sea life found in St. Andrew Bay.

17314 Panama City Beach Pkwy. (at Heather Dr., west of Fla. 79), Panama City Beach. ℭ 850/235-4101. Admission $5 adults, $2.50 children 6–16, free for children 5 and under. Daily 9am–5pm. Closed New Year's Day, Thanksgiving, Christmas.

ZooWorld Zoological & Botanical Park ★ *Kids*   Sitting in a pine forest, this educational and entertaining zoo is an active participant in the Species Survival Plan, which helps protect endangered species by employing specific breeding and housing programs. Among the 350 guests here are orangutans and other primates, lions, tigers, leopards, and alligators and other reptiles. Also included are a walk-through aviary, a bat exhibit, and a petting zoo.

9008 Front Beach Rd. (near Moylan Dr.), Panama City Beach. ℭ 850/230-1243. Admission $10.95 adults, $8.95 seniors, $6.95 children 3–11, free for children under 3. Daily 9am–5:30pm (to 4:30pm in winter).

AMUSEMENT PARKS

An exciting, 105-foot-high (32m) roller coaster is just one of the 30 rides at the **Miracle Strip Amusement Park,** 12000 Front Beach Rd., at Alf Coleman Road (ℭ 850/234-5810; www.miraclestrippark.com). Little ones will love the traditional carousel. Nine acres of fun include nonstop live entertainment and tons of junk food. Adjoining is **Shipwreck Island Water Park** (ℭ 850/234-0368; www.shipwreckisland.com), which offers a variety of water amusements, including the 1,600-foot-long (480m) winding Lazy River for tubing and a daring 35-mile-per-hour (56kmph) Speed Slide. The Tad Pole Hole is exclusively for young kids. Lounge chairs, umbrellas, and inner tubes are free, and lifeguards are on duty. Admission to either park is less than $20, and combination tickets are available. Both are open weekends from mid-March until Memorial Day, then daily to mid-August, and weekends from then to Labor Day weekend. Hours and prices change from year to year, so call for the latest.

SHOPPING

An attraction in itself is the main branch of **Alvin's Island Tropical Department Store,** 12010 Front Beach Rd. (ℭ 850/234-3048), opposite the James I. Lark Sr. Visitors Information Center. It not only sells a wide range of beach gear and apparel, but also has cages containing colorful parrots, tanks with small sharks, and an enclosure with alligators. The sharks are fed at 11am daily; the gators get theirs at 4pm (the older ones are too lethargic to eat during the cool winter months).

WHERE TO STAY

There are scores of motels along the beach here, ranging from small mom-and-pop operations to sizable members of national chains. The annual guide distributed by the Panama City Beach Convention & Visitors Bureau has a complete list (see "Essentials," earlier in this chapter).

The most modern of the chain motels are the recently renovated **Howard Johnson Resort Hotel,** 9400 S. Thomas Dr. (© **800/654-2000** or 850/ 234-6521), and the **Four Points by Sheraton,** 9600 S. Thomas Dr. (© **888/ 625-5144** or 850/234-6511), both part of the redeveloped Boardwalk Beach Resort area, a center of beach action.

Panama City Beach also abounds with condominium complexes, such as the Edgewater Beach Resort listed below. Among the many rental agents are **Arvida Realty Services,** 726 Thomas Dr., Panama City Beach, FL 32408 (© **800/ 621-2462** or 850/235-4075; fax 850/233-2833; www.panamabeachrentals. com); and **Condo World,** 8815A Thomas Dr. (P.O. Box 9456), Panama City Beach, FL 32408 (© **800/232-6636** or 850/234-5564; fax 850/233-6725; www.condoworld.net).

The best camping is at the lovely sites in **St. Andrews State Park,** one of this area's major attractions (see "Hitting the Beach," above).

Rates at even the most expensive properties here drop precipitously during winter, when the town rolls up the sidewalks. Bay County adds 3.5% tax to all hotel and campground bills, bringing the total add-on tax to 9.5%.

Beachcomber by the Sea ☆   Watercolors by local artist Paul Brent grace every unit in this eight-story all-suites resort, built and opened in 1998 at the junction of Front Beach Road and Fla. 79. They also have balconies overlooking a gulf-side swimming pool and hot tub bordered by a concrete deck accented by areas of palm trees. The well-equipped suites come in two sizes. The larger editions have living rooms with sleeper sofas, bedrooms with either king-size or two double beds, and their own phones and TVs. Bathrooms and kitchenettes separate the living rooms and bedrooms. The suites are similar to those at the Flamingo Motel & Tower (see below), except that here they have air conditioners in both the living rooms and the bedrooms. The smaller units are more like motel rooms, but they have microwaves. Two of the smaller units also have whirlpool tubs. There's no restaurant here but several are nearby, and complimentary continental breakfast is available in the lobby each morning. Spring-breakers are not welcome.

17101 Front Beach Rd., Panama City Beach, FL 32413. © **888/886-8916** or 850/233-3600. Fax 850/233-3622. www.beachcomberbythesea.com. 96 units. Summer $99–$229; off-season $99–$129. Rates include continental breakfast. Packages available. AE, DISC, MC, V. **Amenities:** Heated outdoor pool; access to nearby health club; Jacuzzi; game room; coin-op washers and dryers. *In room:* A/C, TV, dataport, kitchen, fridge, coffeemaker, hair dryer, iron.

Edgewater Beach Resort ☆☆   One of the Panhandle's largest condominium resorts, this sports-oriented facility enjoys a beautiful beachfront location and 110 tropically landscaped acres. Units in five gulf-side towers enjoy commanding views of the emerald gulf and gorgeous sunsets from their private balconies. A pedestrian overpass leads across Front Beach Road to low-rise apartments and town homes fringing ponds and the fairways of the resort's own 9-hole golf course. A daytime shuttle runs around the resort to swimming pools, whirlpools, the tennis center, and the golf course (guests also get privileges at the 18-hole Hombre Golf Club, ¼ mile [.5km] north). The Shoppes at Edgewater restaurants are across the road.

11212 Front Beach Rd. (P.O. Box 9850), Panama City Beach, FL 32407. © **800/874-8686** or 850/235-4044. Fax 850/235-6899. www.edgewaterbeachresort.com. 500 units. Summer $150–$400 condo; off-season $70–$175 condo. $5-per-day, per-unit amenities fee. Weekly rates and maid service available. AE, DC, DISC, MC, V. **Amenities:** 2 restaurants (American); 2 bars; 11 heated outdoor pools; 9-hole golf course; 11 tennis courts; health club; Jacuzzi; water-sports equipment rentals; children's programs; concierge; car-rental desk;

limited room service; babysitting; coin-op washers and dryers. *In room:* A/C, TV, dataport, kitchen, coffeemaker, hair dryer, iron.

Flamingo Motel & Tower ★ *Value*   Reggie, Rebecca, and Dana Lancaster take great pride in the gorgeous tropical garden surrounding a heated swimming pool and a large sun deck overlooking the gulf at their well-maintained motel. The brightly decorated rooms have either full kitchens or refrigerators and microwave ovens. They can sleep two to six people, some in separate bedrooms. Kitchenette rooms in a two-story motel block across the road are less appealing but will accommodate six to eight. Budget-conscious families can opt for lower-priced rooms, accommodating two to four. Next door, the seven-story Flamingo Tower contains 49 suites, all sporting living rooms with sofa beds and dining tables; bedrooms with ceiling fans and their own TVs; kitchens; and balconies overlooking the gulf and a beachside swimming pool and hot tub. These suites have air-conditioning units in their living rooms but not in their bedrooms (the ceiling fans will come in handy during the hot, humid summer months). Some older units here have shower-only bathrooms. The Dan Russell fishing pier is only half a mile away, and Gulf World Marine Park and Shuckums Oyster Pub & Seafood Grill are virtually across the road (see "Exploring the Area," above, and "Where to Dine," below). College spring-breakers are not welcome.

15525 Front Beach Rd., Panama City Beach, FL 32413. © 800/828-0400 or 850/234-2232. Fax 850/234-1292. www.flamingomotel.com. 117 units. Summer $79–$139; off-season $39–$99. AE, DISC, MC, V. **Amenities:** 2 heated outdoor pools; access to nearby health club; Jacuzzi; water-sports equipment rental; coin-op washers and dryers. *In room:* A/C, TV, kitchen, fridge, coffeemaker.

Georgian Terrace   Located right on the beach, this two-level motel offers clean, cozy apartments with knotty-pine paneling. Opening to the beach, all units have full kitchens and private, enclosed sun porches. Some units have desktop computers with high-speed Internet connections, and the "home theater" suite comes equipped with a 54-inch TV and a Surround Sound system. A greenhouse-enclosed heated pool area with lush tropical plantings and attractive lounge chairs makes this place a good pick off-season. There's a rare stretch of undeveloped beach almost next door. The mother-son team of Karen and Wes Grant make sure that everyone feels at home here.

14415 Front Beach Rd., Panama City Beach, FL 32413. © 888/882-2144 or 850/234-2144. Fax 850/234-8413. www.georgianterrace.com. 28 units. Summer $89–$149 double; off-season $39–$89 double. MC, V. **Amenities:** Heated indoor pool. *In room:* A/C, TV, dataport, kitchen, coffeemaker.

Holiday Inn SunSpree Resort ★   One building removed from the Edgewater Beach Resort and across the road from the Shoppes at Edgewater, this 15-story establishment is the top full-service gulf-front hotel here. It's designed in an arch, with all rooms having balconies looking directly down on the beach, where a heated, foot-shaped swimming pool and wooden sun deck are separated from the beach by a row of palms and Polynesian torches, which are lighted at night. The hotel has won architectural awards for its dramatic lobby with a waterfall and the Fountain of Wishes (coins go to charity). The attractive, spacious guest rooms feature full-size ice-making refrigerators, microwave ovens, and two spacious vanity areas with their own lavatory sinks.

11127 Front Beach Rd., Panama City Beach, FL 32407. © 800/633-0266 or 850/234-1111. Fax 850/235-1907. www.holidayinnsunspree.com. 342 units. Summer $185–$225 double; off-season $75–$129 double. AE, DC, DISC, MC, V. **Amenities:** 2 restaurants (American); 2 bars; heated outdoor pool; exercise room; Jacuzzi; water-sports equipment rentals; game room; concierge; limited room service; babysitting; laundry service; concierge-level rooms. *In room:* A/C, TV, dataport, fridge, coffeemaker, hair dryer, iron, safe.

Marriott's Bay Point Resort Village ★★ *Value* Not only is this luxurious vacation miniworld ranked among the nation's top golf and tennis resorts, but it's an extraordinarily good value for Florida, as well. Although guests pay extra for most activities, its room rates are among the top steals in the state. They would be higher if the property were beside the gulf; instead, it's the centerpiece of a manicured real-estate development sprawling over 1,100 acres on a peninsula bordered by St. Andrew Bay and the Grand Lagoon. Situated beside the lagoon, the luxurious, vivid-coral stucco hotel is surrounded by gardens, palm trees, oaks, and magnolias. From the glamorous three-story lobby, window walls look out to scenic water views and two swimming pools (one in its own glass-enclosed building). Furnished in dark woods, the Marriottesque rooms are spacious and luxurious, and all have balconies or patios. The highlights for duffers are the Lagoon Legends and the Club Meadows golf courses (see "Outdoor Activities," earlier in this chapter). Water sports here are at Grand Lagoon Beach, reached by the hotel's long pier. There's a free shuttle to the gulf beaches.

4200 Marriott Dr., Panama City Beach, FL 32408. © **800/874-7105** or 850/236-6000. Fax 850/236-6158. www.marriottbaypoint.com. 356 units. Summer $119–$209 double; off-season $109–$169 double. Packages available. AE, DC, DISC, MC, V. From Thomas Dr., take Magnolia Beach Rd. and bear right on Dellwood Rd. to resort complex. **Amenities:** 2 restaurants (American); 2 bars; 3 heated outdoor pools; 1 indoor pool; 2 golf courses; 4 tennis courts; health club; Jacuzzi; water-sports equipment rental; bike rental; concierge; business center; limited room service; massage; babysitting; laundry service; coin-op washers and dryers; concierge-level rooms. *In room:* A/C, TV, dataport, fridge, coffeemaker, hair dryer, iron.

Sunset Inn This very-well-maintained establishment, off Thomas Drive between Chicksaw and Snapper Streets near the east end of the beach, is right on the gulf but away from the crowds. The spacious beachside motel rooms accommodate families in one- and two-bedroom apartments with kitchens, while across the street stands a block of refurbished efficiencies and a new building with tropically furnished one- and two-bedroom condominiums. The condominiums are the most expensive units here, but the units with patios or balconies right on the beach will better suit sun-and-sand lovers. Some of the older units have shower-only bathrooms.

8109 Surf Dr., Panama City Beach, FL 32408. © **850/234-7370.** Fax 850/234-7370, ext. 303. www.poteau.com/sunset/suninn.htm. 62 units. Summer $65–$155 double; off-season $50–$125 double. Weekly and monthly rates available. AE, DISC, MC, V. **Amenities:** Heated outdoor pool; coin-op washers and dryers. *In room:* A/C, TV, kitchen, fridge, coffeemaker.

WHERE TO DINE

Except for fast-food joints, there aren't many national-chain family restaurants in Panama City Beach (you'll find those along 15th and 23rd sts. over in Panama City). One local chain worth a meal is the **Montego Bay Seafood House,** which offers a wide range of fairly inexpensive munchies, sandwiches, burgers, and seafood main courses. Branches are at the "curve" on Thomas Drive (© **850/234-8687**); at the intersection of Thomas Drive and Middle and Front Beach Roads (© **850/236-3585**); and in the Shoppes at Edgewater, Front Beach Drive at Beckrich Road (© **850/233-6033**).

Pay attention to the restaurant hours here, because some places are closed during the winter months. Even if they're open, many will close early when business is slow. Call ahead to make sure the restaurant you want to go to is open.

Billy's Steamed Seafood Restaurant *Value* SEAFOOD More a lively raw bar than a restaurant, Billy and Eloise Poole's casual spot has been serving the best crabs in town since 1982. These are hard-shell blue crabs prepared

Maryland style: steamed with spicy Old Bay Seasoning. Unlike crab houses in Baltimore, however, Billy and Eloise remove the crab's top shell, clean out the "mustard" (intestines), and cut the crabs in two for you; all you have to do is "pick" the meat. Don't worry, they'll show you. Other steamed morsels include shrimp (also with spicy seasoning), oysters, crabs, and lobster served with corn on the cob and garlic bread. Order anything from the briny deep here, but pass over other items.

3000 Thomas Dr. (between Grand Lagoon and Magnolia Beach Rd.). ℂ 850/235-2349. Main courses $5.50–$16; sandwiches $2.50–$5.50. AE, DISC, MC, V. Daily 11am–9pm.

Boar's Head Restaurant ☆ STEAKS/SEAFOOD   An institution since 1978, this shingle-roofed establishment appears from the road to be a South Seas resort. Inside, its impressive beamed ceiling, stone walls, and fireplaces create a warm, almost–English tavern atmosphere suited to the house specialties: tender, marbled prime rib of beef and perfectly cooked steaks. Beef eaters don't have the Boar's Head to themselves, however, because the coals are also used to give a charred flavor to salmon, grouper, and yellowfin tuna. Other cooking styles are offered, too, including a combination of lobster, shrimp, and scallops in a cream sauce over angel-hair pasta. And venison, quail, and other game dishes find their way here during winter. An extensive wine list has won awards, and a cozy tavern to one side has live music, usually Wednesday through Saturday evenings.

17290 Front Beach Rd. (just west of Fla. 79). ℂ 850/234-6628. Main courses $16–$27. AE, DC, DISC, MC, V. Summer daily 4:30–10pm. Off-season Sun–Thurs 4:30–9pm; Fri–Sat 4:30–10pm.

Cajun Inn LOUISIANA CAJUN   This lively, family-owned restaurant with high-backed wooden booths brings the Big Easy to the Gulf. Offerings include jambalaya, seafood étouffée, peppered shrimp or crayfish, and Cajun-style blackened fish. Po'boy sandwiches stuffed with fried oysters or shrimp are a specialty. You won't get gourmet New Orleans cuisine at these prices, but your tongue will have plenty of spice to savor. Dine inside or outside. There's live music on weekends.

817 Azalea Ave. (near Front Beach Rd./Middle Beach Rd. intersection). ℂ 850/233-0403. Main courses $12–$17; sandwiches $6–$11. AE, DC, DISC, MC, V. Daily 11am–10pm.

Canopies ☆☆ SEAFOOD/STEAKS   This area's most elegant restaurant and purveyor of its finest cuisine occupies a 1910-vintage gray clapboard house with a magnificent view of St. Andrew Bay. Dining is outside on the patio or on an enclosed veranda, and the dark, cozy bar in the old living room invites before- or after-dinner drinks. The menu changes monthly but always offers the consistently excellent creamy she-crab soup under a flaky croissant dome. Other selections could include sushi-quality yellowfin tuna in a sherry-soy sauce served over a haystack of leeks; a "trio" of tuna, salmon, and grouper with a citrus-butter sauce served with a mandarin-orange salsa and Vidalia-onion mashed potatoes; and sautéed grouper with lump crab meat in a sherry-butter sauce. Forget the crab cakes. Landlubbers can partake of award-winning beef, veal, lamb, pork, and game dishes. White-chocolate mousse is among several wonderful sweet endings.

4423 W. Hwy. 98, Panama City (1 mile [1.5km] east of Hathaway Bridge on U.S. 98). ℂ 850/872-8444. Reservations recommended. Main courses $18–$26; early-bird specials $11. AE, DC, DISC, MC, V. Daily 5–10pm. Early-bird specials 5–6pm.

⌐ **Fun Fact** **"We Shuck 'Em, You Suck 'Em"**

That's the motto at **Shuckums Oyster Pub & Seafood Grill,** 15614 Front Beach Rd. at Powell Adams Drive (© **850/235-3214**). Comedian Martin Short made this noisy, lively, and smoky pub famous when he tried unsuccessfully to shuck oysters at its bar during the making of an MTV spring-break special. The original bar where Short tried to shuck is virtually papered over with dollar bills signed by old and young patrons who have been flocking here since 1967. The obvious specialty is fresh Apalachicola oysters, served raw, steamed, or baked with a variety of toppings. Otherwise, the menu consists of pub fare and mediocre seafood main courses. Shuckums is open daily during the summer from 11am to 2am. It closes during the off-season at 9pm during the week, at midnight on weekends.

Captain Anderson's Restaurant & Waterfront Seafood Market SEAFOOD   Since 1953 this famous restaurant has been attracting early diners, who come to watch the fishing fleet unload the catch of the day at the busy marina on Grand Lagoon. It's so popular, in fact, that you may have to wait 2 hours for a table during the peak summer months; three bars are there to help you pass the time. The Captain's menu is noted for grilled local fish, crab-meat–stuffed jumbo shrimp, and a heaped-high seafood platter. The food isn't as interesting as at Hamilton's Seafood Restaurant & Lounge across the road (see below), but the local atmosphere makes it worth a visit while you're here.

5551 N. Lagoon Dr. (at Thomas Dr.). © **850/234-2225.** Main courses $11–$35. AE, DC, DISC, MC, V. Summer Mon–Sat 4–10pm; off-season Mon–Sat 4:30–10pm. Closed Nov–Jan.

Hamilton's Seafood Restaurant & Lounge ℛ SEAFOOD   Proprietor Steve Stevens continues in the tradition of his noted Mississippi-born, restaurateur father. The attractive blond-wood and knotty-pine restaurant lies on Grand Lagoon. The baked oysters Hamilton appetizer—a rich combination of oysters, shrimp, and crab meat—almost left me too full for a main course. Several other dishes are unique to Hamilton's, such as spicy snapper étouffée and a Greek-accented shrimp Cristo. Mesquite-grilled fish and steaks are also house specialties, and vegetarians can order a coal-fired vegetable kebab served over angel-hair pasta. The Lagoon Saloon makes the wait for a table go by quickly, and you can select from an extensive selection of well-chosen California and French wines.

5711 N. Lagoon Dr. (at Thomas Dr.). © **850/234-1255.** Main courses $13–$22. AE, DISC, MC, V. Summer daily 4–10pm. Off-season Mon–Thurs 5–9pm; Fri–Sat 5–9:30pm. Closed 1 week in Jan.

SPECIAL DINING EXPERIENCES

You've got to see the **Treasure Ship,** at Treasure Island Marina, 3605 S. Thomas Dr. at Grand Lagoon (© **850/234-8881;** http://thetreasureship.com), to believe it. This amazing 2 acres of ship space claims to be the world's largest land-based Spanish galleon and a reputed replica of the three-masted sailing ships that carried loot from the New World to Spain in the 16th and 17th centuries. You can get anything from an ice-cream cone to peel-it-yourself shrimp to a sophisticated dinner in the restaurant and bar here, which are open daily at 4:30pm; closed during the winter months. Call to make sure it's open when you want to go.

Lady Anderson **dinner-dance cruises** are a romantic evening escape; they're available March through October. This modern, three-deck ship boards at

Captain Anderson's Marina, 5550 N. Lagoon Dr. (© **800/360-0510** or 850/234-5940; www.ladyanderson.com), Monday through Saturday evenings, with the cruises lasting from 7 to 10pm. Buffet dinners are featured, followed by live music for dancing Monday, Wednesday, Friday, and Saturday nights; gospel music on Tuesday and Thursday. Dinner-dance tickets cost $39.50 for adults, $37.50 seniors, $22.50 for children 6 to 11, and $14.50 for children 2 to 5. Gospel music cruises go for $34.50 for adults, $33 for seniors, $22.50 for children 6 to 11, and $14.50 for children 2 to 5. Tips are included. Summertime reservations should be made well in advance.

PANAMA CITY & PANAMA CITY BEACH AFTER DARK

THE PERFORMING ARTS   The Rader family and a cast of 20 perform year-round in the **Ocean Opry Show,** 8400 Front Beach Rd., Panama City Beach (© **850/234-5464;** www.theoceanoprymusicshow.com), the area's answer to the Grand Ole Opry. There's a show every night at 8pm during the summer, less frequently off-season. Popcorn, hot dogs, and soft drinks are available. Admission is about $20 for adults, half price for children. Prices jump to $30 or more when stars like Kitty Welles, B.J. Thomas, and the Wilkensons are in town, usually during winter. The box office opens at 9am Monday through Saturday, and reservations are recommended but not required.

THE CLUB & BAR SCENE   The **Breakers,** 12627 Front Beach Rd. (© **850/234-6060**), is the area's premier supper club, with unsurpassed gulf views and music for dining and dancing. You'll swear The King has risen from the grave as "Elvis Presley" and other impersonators of **Clutch Rock 'n' Roll Cafe** perform here. The show is worth the $10 to $15 per-person cover charge. The beachfront **Harpoon Harry's Waterfront Cafe** is part of the same complex.

Romantic lounges with live entertainment are at the **Treasure Ship,** 3605 S. Thomas Dr. (© **850/234-8881**), where comedian-hypnotist Mike Harvey performs during summer in the top-floor Captain's Quarters; and at the **Boar's Head,** 17290 Front Beach Rd. (© **850/234-6628**). See "Where to Dine" and "Special Dining Experiences," above, for more information.

The 20-something crowd likes to boogie all night at beach clubs such as **Schooners,** 5121 Gulf Dr. (© **850/235-9074**), where every table has a gulf view; **Spinnaker's,** on the beach at 8795 Thomas Dr. (© **850/234-7882**); **Club La Vella,** a bikini-contest kind of place and one of Florida's largest nightclubs, also on the beach at 8813 Thomas Dr. (© **850/234-3866**); and **Sharkey's on the Gulf,** 15201 Front Beach Rd. (© **850/235-2420**). The clubs often stay open until 4am in summer while their bands play on. **Pineapple Willie's Lounge,** beachside at 9900 S. Thomas Dr. (© **850/235-0928**), is open from 11am until 2am, serving ribs basted with Jack Daniel's and spotlighting live entertainment during summer and a host of sports-TVs year-round.

4 Apalachicola ⭐⭐

65 miles (105km) E of Panama City, 80 miles (129km) W of Tallahassee

Sometimes called Florida's Last Frontier, **Apalachicola** makes a fascinating day trip from Panama City Beach or Tallahassee, as well as a destination in its own right. The long, gorgeous beaches on **St. George Island,** 7 miles (11km) from town, are among the nation's best. Justifiably famous for Apalachicola oysters, the bays and estuaries are great for fishing and boating. And if you love nature, the area is also rich in wildlife preserves.

The charming little town of Apalachicola (pop. 2,600) was a major seaport during autumns from 1827 to 1861, when plantations in Alabama and Georgia shipped tons of cotton down the Apalachicola River to the gulf. The town had a racetrack, an opera house, and a civic center that hosted balls, socials, and gambling. The population shrank during the mosquito-infested summer months, however, when yellow fever and malaria epidemics struck. It was during one of these outbreaks that Dr. John Gorrie of Apalachicola tried to develop a method of cooling his patients' rooms. In doing so, he invented the forerunner of the air conditioner, a device that made Florida tourism possible and life a whole lot more bearable for locals.

Apalachicola has traditionally made its living primarily from the gulf and the lagoonlike bay protected by a chain of offshore barrier islands. Today, this area produces the bulk of Florida's oyster crop, and shrimping and fishing are major industries. The town has also been discovered by a number of urban expatriates, who have moved here, restored old homes, and opened interesting antiques and gift shops (there aren't many towns this size where you can buy Crabtree & Evelyn products).

ESSENTIALS

GETTING THERE The nearest airport is 65 miles (105km) to the west at Panama City Beach (see "Essentials," in section 3, earlier in this chapter). From there you'll have to rent a car or take an expensive taxi ride. The Tallahassee airport is about 85 miles (137km) to the northeast (see "Essentials," in section 5, later in this chapter). **Croom's Transportation** (© **888/653-8132**) has airport shuttle service between Tallahassee and Apalachicola. Call for fares and schedule.

The scenic way to drive here is via the gulf-hugging U.S. 98 from Panama City Beach, or via U.S. 319 and U.S. 98 from Tallahassee. From I-10, take exit 21 at Marianna, then follow Fla. 71 south to Port St. Joe, and then take U.S. 98 east to Apalachicola.

VISITOR INFORMATION The **Apalachicola Bay Chamber of Commerce,** 99 Market St., Apalachicola, FL 32320 (© **850/653-9419;** fax 850/653-8219; www.baynavigator.com), supplies information about the area from its office on Market Street (U.S. 98) between Avenue D and Avenue E. The chamber is open Monday through Friday from 9:30am to 5pm.

TIME The town is in the eastern time zone, like Orlando, Miami, and Tallahassee (it's 1 hr. ahead of Panama City Beach and the rest of the Panhandle). Many shops are closed on Wednesday afternoon, when Apalachicolans go fishing.

BEACHES, PARKS & WILDLIFE REFUGES

Some experts consider the 9 miles (14km) of beaches in **St. George Island State Park** ✮✮✮ to be among America's best. This pristine nature preserve occupies the eastern end of St. George Island, about 15 miles (24km) east of Apalachicola. A 4-mile-long (6km) paved road leads through the dunes to picnic areas, restrooms, showers, and a boat launch. An unpaved trail leads another 5 miles (8km) to the island's eastern end, but be careful: It's easy to get stuck in the soft sand, even in a four-wheel-drive sport-utility vehicle. From a hiking trail leading from the campground out a narrow peninsula on the bay side, you can see countless terns, snowy plovers, black skimmers, and other birds. Entry costs $2 for a vehicle with one occupant, $4 for vehicles with up to eight occupants, and $1 for pedestrians and bicyclists. Campsites cost $15 February through

August, $8 September through January. Add $2 for electricity. Primitive camping (take everything with you, including water) costs $3 a night per adult, $2 for children. The park is open daily from 8am to sunset. Pets are allowed. For more information, contact the park at 1900 E. Gulf Beach Dr., St. George Island, FL 32328 (© **850/927-2111;** www.floridastateparks.org/district1/stgeorge).

There are no facilities whatsoever at the **St. Vincent National Wildlife Refuge,** southwest of Apalachicola. This 12,358-acre barrier island has been left in its natural state by the U.S. Fish and Wildlife Service, but visitors are welcome to walk through its pine forests, marshlands, ponds, dunes, and beaches. In addition to native species like bald eagles and alligators, the island is home to a small herd of sambar deer from Southeast Asia. Red wolves are bred here for reestablishment in other wildlife areas. Access is by boat only. **St. Vincents Island Shuttle Service** (© **850/229-1065;** www.stvincentisland.com), at Indian Pass, 21 miles (34km) west of Apalachicola via U.S. 98 and County Roads 30A and 30B, will take you to the island in a pontoon boat. If you bring your bike, they'll drop you on one end of the island and pick you up later at the other. Call for prices and reservations, which are required.

The refuge headquarters, at the north end of Market Street in town, has exhibits of wetland flora and fauna. It's open Monday through Friday from 8am to 4:30pm. Admission is free. For more information, contact the refuge at P.O. Box 447, Apalachicola, FL 32329 (© **850/653-8808**).

The huge **Apalachicola National Forest** begins a few miles northeast of town. It has a host of facilities, including canoeing and mountain-bike trails. See section 5, later in this chapter, for details.

OUTDOOR ACTIVITIES

CRUISES   Jeanni McMillan of **Journeys of St. George Island** ✦ (© **850/927-3259;** www.sgislandjourneys.com) takes guests on narrated nature cruises to the barrier islands and on canoe and kayak trips in the creeks and streams of the Apalachicola River basin. She also has night hikes with blue-crab netting, shelling excursions, and fishing and scalloping trips, plus excursions tailored exclusively for children. Prices range from $25 to $75 per person. Reservations are required, so call her to find out what she's offering when you'll be in town. Jeanni also rents canoes, kayaks, sailboats, and sailboards.

An easier way to see the marshes, swamps, and shallow-water rivers is via a nature cruise with **EcoVentures, Inc.** (© **850/653-2593;** www.apalachicola tours.com). It uses the *Osprey,* a 40-foot (12m), all-weather boat that can carry up to 32 passengers. Fares are $20 for adults, $10 for children under 16. Call for schedule and reservations.

You can go afternoon or sunset sailing on the bay for hours on Captain Jerry Weber's 40-foot (12m) sloop *Wind Catcher* (© **850/653-3881**). The 2½-hour voyages cost $35 for adults, $20 for children under 16, including snacks and soft drinks. Reservations are essential.

FISHING   You can't go oystering, but fishing is excellent in these waters, where trout, redfish, flounder, tarpon, shark, drum, and other fish abound. The chamber of commerce (see "Essentials," above) can help arrange charters on the local boats, many of which dock at the Rainbow Inn on Water Street. For guides, contact **Robinson Brothers Guide Service** (© **850/670-8896;** fax 850/653-3118; www.flaredfish.com) or **Boss Guide Services** (© **850/653-8139**).

EXPLORING THE TOWN

Start your visit by picking up a map and a self-guided tour brochure from the chamber of commerce (see "Essentials," above), and then stroll around Apalachicola's waterfront, business district, and Victorian-era homes.

Along Water Street, several tin warehouses evoke the town's seafaring days of the late 1800s, as does the 1840s-era **Sponge Exchange** at Commerce Street and Avenue E. A highlight of the residential area, centered around Gorrie Square at Avenue D and 6th Street, is the Greek Revival–style **Trinity Episcopal Church,** built in New York and shipped here in 1837. At the water end of 6th Street, Battery Park has a children's playground. A number of excellent art galleries and gift shops are grouped on Market Street, Avenue D, and Commerce Street.

The showpiece at the **John Gorrie Museum State Park** , Avenue D at 6th Street (© **850/653-9347;** www.floridastateparks.org/district1/johngorrie), is a display replica of Doctor Gorrie's cooling machine, a prototype of today's air conditioner. It really does work. The park is open Thursday through Monday from 9am to 5pm; closed New Year's Day, Thanksgiving, and Christmas. Admission is $1, free for children 6 and under.

The **Estuarine Walk,** at the north end of Market Street on the grounds of the Apalachicola National Estuarine Research Reserve (© **850/653-8063**), contains aquariums full of fish and turtles, and displays of various other estuarine life. It's open Monday through Friday from 8am to 5pm. Admission is free.

WHERE TO STAY

Built in 1997, the 42-room **Best Western Apalach Inn,** 249 Hwy. 98 W. (© **800/528-1234** or 850/658-9131; fax 850/653-9136; www.apalachicola. com/bestwestern), a mile west of downtown, is the only national chain hotel here.

Apalachicola River Inn The town's only waterfront accommodation, this two-story motel's rough-hewn exterior timbers make it look like one of the neighboring warehouses. Recently spiffed up, units in the main building all have views across a marina to Apalachicola Bay. Those on the second floor are larger and have their own balconies, making them preferable to the smaller downstairs units, whose doors open directly onto the marina's boardwalk. Most of the upstairs rooms have shower-only bathrooms. Two rooms and a two-bedroom apartment in a building next door have whirlpool tubs. Facing the river, Caroline's Restaurant serves breakfast, lunch, and seafood dinners (it's a bit pricey at dinner but a fine spot for an alfresco, dockside lunch). The Roseate Spoonbill Lounge, over the restaurant, is *the* local watering hole, with a grand view and music on an outdoor deck on weekends.

123 Water St., Apalachicola, FL 32320. © 850/653-8139. Fax 850/653-2018. www.apalachicolariverinn. com. 26 units. $85–$95 double; $110–$160 suite. AE, DC, DISC, MC, V. Pets accepted in smoking rooms ($10 nightly fee). **Amenities:** Restaurant (American); bar. *In room:* A/C, TV.

Coombs House Inn The most luxurious accommodation here, this large bed-and-breakfast occupies two Victorian homes. The main house was built in 1905 by a lumber baron, and it shows: Polished black cypress paneling lines the entire central hallway and grand parlor. Each of the 10 guest rooms in the main house is tastefully decorated, with lots of Victorian reproductions. Outstanding is the Coombs Suite, with bay windows, a sofa, a four-poster bed, and its own whirlpool. The "Love Bungalow" has its own private entrance. Less grand but still impressive are eight rooms in another restored Victorian, known as the

"Coombs House East," half a block away. One of these rooms has a whirlpool tub and bidet, and there's an apartment in the carriage house over there. One room in each house is equipped for guests with disabilities. A major truck route, U.S. 98, runs along the north side of both houses; request a south room to escape the periodic road noise. Guests are treated to complimentary wine receptions on weekends.

80 6th St., Apalachicola, FL 32320. © 850/653-9199. Fax 850/653-2785. www.coombshouseinn.com. 18 units (all with bathroom). $89–$225 double. Rates include full breakfast. DISC, MC, V. **Amenities:** Access to nearby health club; free use of bikes. In room: A/C, TV, dataport, fridge (3 units), hair dryer.

Gibson Inn ★★ Built in 1907 as a seaman's hotel and gorgeously restored in 1985, this cupola-topped inn is such a brilliant example of Victorian architecture that it's listed on the National Register of Historic Inns. No two guest rooms are alike (some still have the original sinks in the sleeping areas), but all are richly furnished with period reproductions. Nonguests are welcome to wander upstairs and peek into unoccupied rooms (whose doors are left open). Reservations are advised during summer and spring and fall weekends, and as much as 5 years ahead for the seafood festival in November. Grab a drink from the bar and relax in one of the high-back rockers on the old-fashioned veranda. The dining room serves excellent seafood and is open to all comers, so don't expect this to be private like a bed-and-breakfast; instead, you'll find yourself in a reborn, absolutely charming turn-of-the-20th-century hotel.

51 Ave. C, Apalachicola, FL 32320. © 850/653-2191. Fax 850/653-3521. www.gibsoninn.com. 30 units (all with bathroom). $85–$100 double; $100–$130 suite. AE, MC, V. **Amenities:** Restaurant (American); bar. In room: A/C, TV.

Rancho Inn On the western edge of the historic district, this older, Spanish-look motel has been spiffed up by owners Mark and Mary Lynn Rodgers, who keep it clean and well maintained. Although simple when compared to the more expensive properties here, the rooms are spacious and comfortable, and all have microwave ovens and fridges. Restaurants are within walking distance.

240 Hwy. 98 W., Apalachicola, FL 32320. © 850/653-9435. Fax 850/653-9180. www.ranchoinn.com. 32 units. $50–$150 double. AE, DISC, MC, V. Pets accepted ($6 fee). **Amenities:** Outdoor pool; bicycle rental. In room: A/C, TV, dataport, fridge, coffeemaker.

WHERE TO DINE

Townsfolk still plop down on the round stools at the marble-topped counter to order Coca-Colas and milkshakes at the **Old Time Soda Fountain & Luncheonette,** 93 Market St. (© **850/653-2006**). This 1950s relic was once the town drugstore. It's open Monday through Saturday from 10am to 5pm.

The Boss Oyster ★ SEAFOOD You've heard about the aphrodisiac properties of Apalachicola oysters. Well, you can see if those properties are real at this rustic, dockside eatery, whose motto is "Shut Up and Shuck." In fact, this is one of the best places in Florida to try the bivalves raw, steamed, or under a dozen toppings ranging from capers to crab meat. They'll even steam three dozen of them and let you do the shucking. Steamed shrimp also are offered, as are delicious po'boy sandwiches. Most main courses come from the fryer, so consider this joint a great local experience, not fine dining. Sit at picnic tables inside, on a screened porch, or out on the dock.

125 Water St. (between Aves. C and D). © 850/653-9364. Main courses $17–$22; oysters $4.50–$13.50; sandwiches and baskets $7–$10. AE, DC, DISC, MC, V. Apr–Sept Sun–Thurs 11:30am–10pm; Fri–Sat 11:30am–11pm. Oct–Mar Sun–Thurs 11:30am–9pm; Fri–Sat 11:30am–10pm.

Chef Eddie's Magnolia Grill ★★★ CONTINENTAL/CAJUN   One of the top places to dine in Northwest Florida, Boston-bred chef-owner Eddie Cass's pleasant restaurant offers nightly specials ranging from classic French rack of lamb and beef Wellington to fresh local seafood with New Orleans–style sauces. You will long remember Eddie's mahimahi Pontchartrain with cream and artichoke hearts. The dry-aged, oak-grilled New York sirloin steak stuffed with roasted oysters, peppers, and artichoke hearts and served with a Merlot bordelaise sauce is another memorable feast. Start with a bowl of spicy seafood gumbo, a consistent hit during the Florida Seafood Festival. No smoking inside.

99 11th St. (between Aves. E and F). ℂ 850/653-8000. Reservations recommended. Main courses $12–$24. MC, V. Mon–Sat 6–9:30pm.

The Owl Cafe ★★ SEAFOOD   Ensconced on the first floor of a two-story clapboard commercial building in the heart of downtown, this sophisticated restaurant ranks only behind Chef Eddie's Magnolia Grill as having the best cuisine in town. Go for the nightly fresh seafood specials or opt for the terrific grouper with garlic, capers, and artichokes. Now paneled in rich wood, the walls are adorned with the works of noted local photographer Richard Bickel.

15 Ave. D (at Commerce St.). ℂ 850/653-9888. Reservations recommended. Main courses $12–$25. MC, V. Mon–Sat 11:30am–3pm and 5:30–10pm.

Tamara's Cafe Floridita   FLORIBBEAN/LATIN AMERICAN   Tamara Suarez's store-front cafe offers a change of pace. Before settling in Apalachicola, Tamara was a TV producer in Venezuela, and her black-bean soup comes directly from the old country. Otherwise, you'll find Latino spices accentuating Floribbean fare, such as a creamy jalapeño sauce putting a little fire into pecan-encrusted grouper, and homemade mango chutney sweetening grouper stuffed with crab meat. Her paella is a winner, too.

17 Ave. E (at Commerce St.). ℂ 850/653-4111. Reservations recommended. Main courses $12–$22. MC, V. Tues–Sun 5–10pm and Wed–Sun 11:30am–2:30pm.

APALACHICOLA AFTER DARK

Nocturnal diversions are scarce in this small town, but you can catch summer-stock performances of plays like "Same Time Next Year" in the lovingly restored, 1912-vintage **Dixie Theatre,** 21 Ave. D (ℂ **850/653-3200**). Tickets range from $2 to $12.

Locals like to have their after-work drinks in the fine old bar at the **Gibson Inn** and then hit the **Roseate Spoonbill Lounge,** in the Apalachicola River Inn (see "Where to Stay," above), where bands play on weekend evenings.

5 Tallahassee

163 miles (262km) W of Jacksonville, 191 miles (308km) E of Pensacola, 250 miles (403km) NW of Orlando

Tallahassee was selected as Florida's capital in 1823 because it was halfway between St. Augustine and Pensacola, then the state's major cities. That location puts it almost in Georgia; in fact, Tallahassee has more in common with Macon than with Miami. There's as much Old South ambience here as anywhere else you're likely to visit in Florida. Here, you'll find lovingly restored 19th-century homes and buildings, including the 1845 Old Capitol. They all sit among so many towering pines and sprawling live oaks that you'll think you're in an enormous forest. The trees form virtual tunnels along Tallahassee's five official Canopy Roads, which are lined with historic plantations, ancient Native

Downtown Tallahassee

American settlement sites and mounds, gorgeous gardens, quiet parks with picnic areas, and beautiful lakes and streams. And the nearby Apalachicola National Forest is a virtual gold mine of outdoor pursuits.

While tradition and history are important here, you'll also find the modern era, beginning with the New Capitol Building towering 22 stories over downtown. Usually sleepy Tallahassee takes on a very lively persona when the legislature is in session and when the powerful football teams of Florida State University and Florida A&M University take to the gridiron.

If you're inclined to give your credit cards a workout, the nearby town of Havana is Florida's antiquing capital.

ESSENTIALS

GETTING THERE   **Tallahassee Regional Airport** (✆ 850/891-7802; http://talgov.com/citytlh/aviation), 10 miles (16km) southwest of downtown on Southeast Capital Circle, is served by **AirTran** (✆ 800/AIR-TRAN), **Delta** (✆ 800/221-1212), **Northwest/KLM** (✆ 800/225-2525), and **US Airways** (✆ 800/428-4322).

Alamo (✆ 800/327-9633), **Avis** (✆ 800/331-1212), **Budget** (✆ 800/527-0700), **Dollar** (✆ 800/800-4000), **Enterprise** (✆ 800/325-8007), **Hertz** (✆ 800/654-3131), **National** (✆ 800/CAR-RENT), and **Thrifty** (✆ 800/367-2277) have rental cars here.

You can take a taxi to downtown for about $12.50.

Amtrak's transcontinental train the Sunset Limited stops in Tallahassee at 918½ Railroad Ave. (✆ **800/USA-RAIL;** www.amtrak.com).

VISITOR INFORMATION   For information in advance, contact the **Tallahassee Area Convention and Visitors Bureau,** 200 W. College Ave. (P.O. Box 1369), Tallahassee, FL 32302 (✆ **800/628-2866** or 850/413-9200; fax 850/487-4621; www.seetallahassee.com). The bureau's excellent quarterly visitor's guide has descriptions (including hours and admission fees) of just about everything going on here.

Go to the **Tallahassee Area Visitor Information Center,** 106 E. Jefferson St. across from the capitol (✆ **850/413-9200**), for free street and public-transportation maps, brochures, and pamphlets outlining tours of the historic districts and the Canopy Roads. The center is open Monday through Friday from 8am to 5pm, Saturday from 9am to noon.

For statewide information, a **Florida Welcome Center** is in the west foyer of the New Capitol Building (see below).

GETTING AROUND   Operated by TALTRAN, the city's public-transportation agency (✆ **850/891-5200;** www.state.fl.us/citytlh/taltran), the free **Old Town Trolley** is the best way to see the sights of historic downtown Tallahassee. You can get on or off at any point between Adams Street Commons, at the corner of Jefferson and Adams streets, and the Governor's Mansion (see the exact route on the "Downtown Tallahassee" map). The trolley runs Monday through Friday every 20 minutes between 7am and 6:30pm.

TALTRAN also provides city bus service from its downtown terminal at Tennessee and Adams streets. Both the ticket booth there and at the Tallahassee Area Visitor Information Center have route maps and schedules.

For taxi service, call **Yellow Cab** (✆ **850/580-8080**) or **City Taxi** (✆ 850/562-4222). Fares are $1.60 at flag fall, plus $1.50 per mile.

TIME   Tallahassee is in the eastern time zone, like Orlando, Miami, and Apalachicola. It's 1 hour ahead of the rest of the Panhandle.

EXPLORING THE CITY
THE CAPITOL COMPLEX

Florida's capitol complex, on South Monroe Street at Apalachee Parkway, dominates the downtown area and should be your first stop after the Tallahassee Area Visitor Information Center, just across Jefferson Street.

The **New Capitol Building** (© 850/488-6167), a $43 million skyscraper, was built in 1977 to replace the 1845-vintage Old Capitol. State legislators meet here from March to May. The chambers of the house and the senate have public viewing galleries. For a spectacular view, take the elevators to the 22nd-floor **observatory,** where on a clear day you can see all the way to the Gulf of Mexico. You can also view works by Florida artists while up there. The New Capitol is open Monday through Friday from 8am to 5pm.

Directly in front of the skyscraper is the strikingly white **Old Capitol** ☆ (© 850/487-1902; http://dhr.dos.state.fl.us/museum/m_sites.html). With its majestic dome, this "Pearl of Capitol Hill" has been restored to its original beauty. An eight-room exhibit portrays Florida's political history. Turn-of-the-20th-century furnishings, cotton gins, and other artifacts are also of interest. The Old Capitol is open Monday through Friday from 9am to 4:30pm, Saturday from 10am to 4:30pm, and Sunday and holidays from noon to 4:30pm. Admission is free to both the old and the new capitols.

Across Monroe Street from the Old Capitol are the twin granite towers of the **Vietnam Veterans Memorial,** honoring Florida's Vietnam vets. Next to it, facing Apalachee Parkway, the **Union Bank Museum** (© 850/487-3803) is housed in Florida's oldest-surviving bank building. For a while, it was the Freedman's Savings and Trust Company, which served emancipated slaves. It's worth a brief visit. Admission is free. It's open Monday through Friday 9am to 4pm.

The Old Town Trolley will take you to the lovely Georgian-style **Governor's Mansion,** north of the capitol at Adams and Brevard Streets (© 850/488-4661). Enhanced by a portico patterned after Andrew Jackson's columned antebellum home in Tennessee, the Hermitage, and surrounded by giant magnolia trees and landscaped lawns, the mansion is furnished with 18th- and 19th-century antiques and collectibles. Tours are given when the legislature is in session from March to May. Call for schedules and reservations.

Located adjacent to the Governor's Mansion, **The Grove** was home to Ellen Call Long, known as "The Tallahassee Girl," the first child born after Tallahassee was settled.

HISTORIC DISTRICTS

Although modern buildings have made inroads into the downtown area, Tallahassee makes an ongoing effort to preserve many of its historic homes and buildings.

Many of them are concentrated in three historic districts within an easy walk north of the capitol complex. The information center in the New Capitol (see "Essentials," above) distributes free brochures of walking tours that cover the three areas. Taken together, the tours are about 4 miles (6km) long and should take half a day. Most interesting is the Park Avenue District, 3 blocks north of the capitol complex, which you can see in about 1 hour.

Tours With A Southern Accent (© 850/513-1000) offers 2-hour walking and van tours of downtown for $20 per person, free for children under 5. Call for schedules and reservations.

ADAMS STREET COMMONS This 1-block-long winding brick and land-scaped area along Adams Street begins on the north side of the capitol complex (it's between Jefferson St. and College Ave.) and retains an old-fashioned town-square atmosphere. Restored buildings include the Governor's Club, a 1900s Masonic lodge, and Gallie's Hall, where Florida's first five African-American college students received their Florida A&M University diplomas in 1892. Restaurants, shops, and Gallie Alley are also here. Adams Street crosses Park Avenue 3 blocks north of the capitol complex. This is a good place for lunch at one of several cafes that cater to downtown office workers.

PARK AVENUE HISTORIC DISTRICT The 7 blocks of Park Avenue between Martin Luther King Jr. Boulevard and North Meridian Street are a lovely promenade of beautiful trees, gardens, and outstanding old mansions. This broad avenue, with a shady median strip lined with moss-bearded live oaks, was originally named 200 Foot Street and then McCarty Street, but was later renamed Park Avenue to satisfy a snobbish Anglophile society matron who didn't want an Irish name imprinted on her son's wedding invitations.

Several Park Avenue historic homes are open to the public, including the **Knott House Museum,** at Calhoun Street (see "Museums, Art Galleries & Archaeological Sites," below). **The Columns,** at Duval Street, was built in the 1830s and is the city's oldest surviving building (it's the home of the Tallahassee Chamber of Commerce). **The First Presbyterian Church,** at Adams Street, built in 1838, is the city's oldest church and has been an important African-American historic site since slaves were welcome to worship here without their masters' consent. **The Walker Library,** between Monroe and Calhoun streets, was one of Florida's first libraries, dating from 1903 (it's home to Springtime Tallahassee, which sponsors the city's top special event). Just north of Park Avenue on Gadsden Street, the **Meginnis-Monroe House** contains the Lemoyne Art Gallery (see "Museums, Art Galleries & Archaeological Sites," below).

At Martin Luther King Jr. Boulevard, the **adjacent Old City Cemetery** and **Episcopal Cemetery** contain the graves of Prince Achille Murat, Napoleon's nephew, and Princess Catherine Murat, his wife and George Washington's grand-niece. Also buried here are two governors and numerous Confederate and Union soldiers who died at the Battle of Natural Bridge during the Civil War. The cemeteries are important to African-American history since a number of slaves and the first black Florida A&M graduates are interred here. The visitor information center in the New Capitol has a cemetery walking-tour brochure.

CALHOUN STREET HISTORIC DISTRICT Affectionately called "Gold Dust Street" in the old days, the 3 blocks of Calhoun Street between Tennessee and Georgia streets, and running east on Virginia Street to Leon High School, sport elaborate homes built by prominent citizens between 1830 and 1880. A highlight here is the **Brokaw-McDougall House,** in front of Leon High School at the eastern end of Virginia Street, which was built in 1856.

MUSEUMS, GALLERIES & ARCHAEOLOGICAL SITES

Black Archives Research Center and Museum Housed in the columned library built by Andrew Carnegie in 1908, and located on the grounds of the Florida Agricultural and Mechanical University (FAMU), this fascinating research center and museum displays one of the nation's most extensive collections of African-American artifacts, as well as such treasures as a 500-piece

Ethiopian cross collection. The archives contain one of the world's largest collections on African-American history. Visitors here can listen to tapes of gospel music and of elderly people reminiscing about the past. FAMU was founded in 1887, primarily as a black institution. Today it's acclaimed for its business, engineering, and pharmacy schools.

Martin Luther King Jr. Blvd. and Gamble St., on the Florida A&M University campus. 🕿 **850/599-3020.** www.famu.edu. Free admission. Mon–Fri 9am–4pm. Closed major holidays. Parking lot next to building.

Florida State University Museum of Fine Arts   A permanent, 3,000-piece collection here features 16th-century Dutch paintings, 20th-century American paintings, Japanese prints, pre-Colombian artifacts, and much more. Touring exhibits are displayed every few weeks.

250 Fine Arts Building, Copeland and Call Sts. (on the FSU campus). 🕿 **850/644-6836.** www.fsu.edu/. Free admission. Sept–Apr Mon–Fri 9am–4pm, Sat–Sun 1–4pm; May–July Mon–Fri 9am–4pm. Closed Aug.

Foster Tanner Art Center   The focus in this gallery is on works by local, national, and international African-American artists, with a wide variety of paintings, sculptures, and more.

Florida A&M University (between Osceola and Gamble Sts., off Martin Luther King Jr. Blvd.). 🕿 **850/ 599-3161.** www.famu.edu. Free admission. Mon–Fri 9am–5pm.

Knott House Museum ("The House That Rhymes") ⭐   Adorned by a columned portico, this stately mansion was constructed in 1843, probably by a free black builder named George Proctor. Florida's first reading of the Emancipation Proclamation took place here in 1865. In 1928 it was purchased by politician William Knott, whose wife Louella wrote eccentric rhymes about the house and its elegant Victorian furnishings, including the nation's largest collection of 19th-century gilt-framed mirrors, and about social, economic, and political events of the era. Attached by satin ribbons to tables, chairs, and lamps, her poems are the museum's most unusual feature. The house is in the Park Avenue Historic District and is listed in the National Register of Historic Places. It's preserved as it looked in 1928, when the Knott family left it and all of its contents to the city (it's now administered by the Florida Museum of History). The museum gift shop carries Victorian greeting cards, paper dolls, tin toy replicas, reprints of historic newspapers, and other nostalgic items.

301 E. Park Ave. (at Calhoun St.). 🕿 **850/922-2459.** http://dhr.dos.state.fl.us/museum/m_sites.html. Free admission. Wed–Fri 1–4pm; Sat 10am–4pm. 1-hr. tours depart on the hour.

Lemoyne Art Gallery ⭐   This restored 1852 antebellum home is listed on the National Register of Historic Places and is a lovely setting for fine art. Known as the **Meginnis-Monroe House,** the gallery itself is named in honor of Jacques LeMoyne, a member of a French expedition to Florida in 1564. Commissioned to depict the natives' dwellings and map the seacoast, LeMoyne was the first European artist known to have visited North America. Exhibits here include permanent displays by local artists, traveling exhibits, sculpture, pottery, and photography—everything from the traditional to the avant-garde. The gardens, with an old-fashioned gazebo, are spectacular during the Christmas holiday season. Programs of classical music are combined with visual arts during the year; check in advance for the current schedule.

125 N. Gadsden St. (between Park Ave. and Call St.). 🕿 **850/222-8800.** www.lemoyne.org. Admission $1, free for children 12 and under. Tues–Sat 10am–5pm; Sun 1–5pm. Closed holidays.

Mission San Luís de Apalachee ★★   A Spanish Franciscan mission named San Luís was set up in 1656 on this hilltop, already a principal village of the Apalachee Indians. From then until 1704, it served as the capital of a chain of Spanish missions in Northwest Florida. The mission complex included a tribal council house, a Franciscan church, a Spanish fort, and residential areas. Based on extensive archaeological and historical research, the council house and the 10-by-50-foot (15m) thatch-roofed church have been reconstructed. They are both open to the public. So is a reconstruction of the 50-foot (15m) by 110-foot (33m) thatch-roof mission church. Interpretive markers are located across the 60-acre site, and self-guided tour brochures are available at the visitor center. Call for a schedule of ranger-led guided tours on weekends.

2021 Mission Rd. (between W. Tennessee and Tharpe sts.). © 850/487-3711. http://dhr.dos.state.fl.us/bar/san_luis/. Admission free. Tues–Sun 10am–4pm. Closed Thanksgiving, Christmas. From downtown, take Tennessee St. (U.S. 90) west to entrance on right past Ocala St.

Museum of Florida History ★   An 11-foot-tall (3.25m) mastodon greets you at the official state history museum, where you look back 12,000 years to the first Native Americans to live in Florida (mastodons were very much alive back then). Ancient artifacts from Native American tribes are exhibited, plus such relics from Florida's past as a reconstructed steamboat and treasures from 16th- and 17th-century sunken Spanish galleons. Inquire about guided tours and special exhibits. There's an interesting museum gift shop. Visitor parking is available in the garage around the corner on St. Augustine Street between Bronough and Duvall streets.

Lower level of R.A. Gray Building, 500 S. Bronough St. (at Pensacola St.). © 850/248-6400. http://dhr.dos.state.fl.us/museum/. Admission free (suggested donation $3 adults, $1 children). Mon–Fri 9am–4:30pm; Sat 10am–4:30pm; Sun and holidays noon–4:30pm. Closed Thanksgiving, Christmas.

PARKS & NATURE PRESERVES

Maclay State Gardens ★★   In 1923 New York financier Alfred B. Maclay and his wife, Louise, began planting the floral wonderland that surrounded their winter home on Lake Hall, on Tallahassee's northeastern outskirts. After her husband's death in 1944, Louise continued his dream of an ornamental garden to delight the public. In 1953 the land was bequeathed to the state of Florida. The more than 300 acres of flowers feature at least 200 varieties; 28 acres are devoted exclusively to azaleas and camellias. The surrounding park offers nature trails, canoe rentals, boating, picnicking, swimming, and fishing. The high blooming season is January through April, with the peak about mid-March. Beyond the house and gardens, the state park also includes Lake Overstreet, around which wind 5½ miles (9km) of hiking, biking, and horseback-riding trails, making this a major venue for those outdoor activities.

3540 Thomasville Rd. (U.S. 319, north of I-10). © 850/487-4556. www.floridastateparks.org/district1/maclaygardens. Admission to park $3.25 per vehicle with up to 8 passengers, $1 for pedestrians and cyclists. May–Dec admission to gardens free; Jan–Apr $3 adults, $1.50 children under 12. Gardens daily 8am–sunset. Maclay House daily 9am–5pm Jan–Apr; closed May–Dec.

TRAVELING THE CANOPY ROADS

Graced by canopies of live oaks draped with Spanish moss, the St. Augustine, Miccousukee, Meridian, Old Bainbridge, and Centerville Roads are the five official Canopy Roads leading out of Tallahassee. Driving is slow on these winding, two-lane country roads (the locals only reluctantly are turning some limited sections of them into four-lane highways); some of them are canopied for as much as 20 miles (32km). Take along a picnic lunch, since there are few places to buy a meal along these tranquil byways.

The visitor information center in the New Capitol provides a useful driving guide map of the Canopy Roads and Leon County's country lanes (see "Essentials," earlier in this chapter).

If you have time for only one, take **Old Bainbridge Road,** which leads to the Lake Jackson Mounds State Archaeological Site in the northwest suburbs and then on to Havana, Florida's antiquing capital (see "Shopping," below).

SHOPPING

Antiques hounds flock to the little village of **Havana** ★★, 12 miles (19km) northwest of I-10 on U.S. 27. Havana used to make its living from shade-grown tobacco, and when that industry went into decline in the 1960s, the town went with it. Things turned around 20 years later, however, when Havana began opening art galleries and antiques, handcrafts, and collectibles shops. Today these are housed in lovingly restored, turn-of-the-20th-century brick buildings along Havana's commercial streets. Just drive into town on Main Street (U.S. 27), turn left on 7th Avenue, find a parking place, and start browsing. You'll have plenty of company on weekends.

Bradley's Country Store, about 8 miles (13km) north of I-10 on Centerville Road (© **850/893-1647;** www.bradleyscountrystore.com), sells more than 80,000 pounds a year of homemade sausage, both over the counter and from mail orders. You can also buy coarse-ground grits, country-milled corn meal, hogshead cheese, liver pudding, cracklings, and specially cured hams. This friendly store, which is on the National Register of Historic Places, is also a sightseeing attraction with self-guided tours. It's open Monday through Friday from 8am to 6pm, Saturday from 8am to 5pm.

OUTDOOR ACTIVITIES & SPECTATOR SPORTS

BIKING & IN-LINE SKATING   The 16-mile (26km) **Tallahassee–St. Marks Historic Railroad Trail State Park** (© **850/922-6007;** www.floridastateparks.org/district1/stmarkstrail) is the city's most popular bike route. Constructed with the financial assistance of wealthy Panhandle cotton-plantation owners and merchants, this was Florida's oldest railroad, functioning from 1837 to 1984. Cotton and other products were transported from Tallahassee to St. Marks for shipment to other cities. In recent years the tracks were removed and 16 miles (26km) of the historic trail were improved for joggers, hikers, bicyclists, and horseback riders. A paved parking lot is at the north entrance, on Woodville Highway (Fla. 363) just south of Southeast Capital Circle. See "Side Trips from Tallahassee," later in this chapter, for more about what you can see in the St. Marks area.

At press time, the park was in the process of negotiating a contract for a bike-rental concessionaire to be located at the north end of the trail. Call the park for more information.

The **Apalachicola National Forest** also has extensive mountain-biking trails (see "Side Trips from Tallahassee," later in this chapter), and there are 5½ miles (9km) of trails at **Maclay State Gardens** (see "Parks & Nature Preserves," above).

GOLF   Play golf at outstanding Hilaman Park, 2737 Blair Stone Rd., where the **Hilaman Park Municipal Golf Course** features 18 holes (par-72), a driving range, racquetball and squash courts, and a swimming pool. Rental

---

(**Fun Fact** *Semi-Tough:* **The Prequel**

Burt Reynolds played defensive back for Florida State University's football team in 1957 and is still an avid 'Noles booster.

---

equipment is available at the club, and there's a restaurant too (© **850/ 891-3935** for information and fees). Compared with most courses in Florida, greens fees are a steal: about $25 on weekdays, $30 on weekends, including cart (they're about $13 and $17, respectively, if you walk). The park also includes the recently renovated **Jake Gaither Municipal Golf Course,** at Bragg and Pasco Streets (© **850/891-3942**), with a 9-hole, par-35 fairway and a pro shop. Call for fees.

The leading golf course is at the **Killearn Country Club and Inn** (© **800/ 476-4101** or 850/893-2186), which once hosted the Sprint Classic. Moss-draped oaks enhance the beautiful 27-hole championship course, which is for members with reciprocal privileges only.

SPECTATOR SPORTS   Tallahassee succumbs to football frenzy whenever the perennially powerful Seminoles of **Florida State University** (FSU) take to the gridiron. Call © **850/644-1830** (www.seminoles.com) well in advance for tickets. Even when the Seminoles play on the road, everything except Tallahassee's many sports bars comes to a stop while fans watch the games on TV.

The **Florida A&M University** (FAMU) Rattlers are cheered on by the school's high-stepping, world-famous Marching 100 Band. Call © **850/ 599-3230** or check the website at www.famu.edu/athletics for FAMU schedules and tickets.

Both FSU and FAMU have seasonal basketball, baseball, tennis, and track schedules. Call the numbers above for information.

WHERE TO STAY

There is no high or low season here, but every hotel and motel for miles around is completely booked during FSU and FAMU football weekends from September to November, and again at graduation in May. Reserve well in advance or you may have to stay 60 miles (97km) or more from the city. For the schedules, call FSU or FAMU (see "Spectator Sports," above).

Most hotels are concentrated in three areas: downtown Tallahassee, north of downtown along North Monroe Street at exit 29 off I-10 (where you'll find most chains), and along Apalachee Parkway east of downtown.

Tax on all hotel and campground bills is 10% in Leon County.

Cabot Lodge North (*Value*   A clapboard plantation-style house with a tin roof and a partially screened wraparound porch provides Southern country charm to distinguish this friendly motel from its nearby competitors. Guests can relax in straight-back rockers on the porch or on comfy sofas and easy chairs by a fireplace in the living room. Although the guest rooms in the two-story motel buildings out back don't hold up their end of the atmosphere factor, they're still quite satisfactory at these rates, and they give quick access to the outdoor swimming pool. Guests can enjoy a complimentary continental breakfast buffet and evening cocktails.

2735 N. Monroe St., Tallahassee, FL 32303. © **800/223-1964** or 850/386-8880. Fax 850/386-4254. www.cabotlodge.com. 160 units. $66–$80 double. Rates include continental breakfast, evening reception, and local phone calls. AE, DC, DISC, MC, V. **Amenities:** Outdoor pool; access to nearby health club; laundry service. *In room:* A/C, TV, dataport, hair dryer (king-size bedrooms only).

Courtyard by Marriott   Just a mile east of the Old Capitol, this comfortable member of the business-traveler–oriented chain encloses a landscaped courtyard with a swimming pool and gazebo. About half of the rooms face the courtyard; the others face parking lots. They are a bit cramped for families but ideal for singles and couples. The marble-floored lobby features a lounge with fireplace, honor bar, and a dining area open for a breakfast buffet only. Several chain restaurants are within walking distance or a short drive away. The Parkway Shopping Center is also across the road.

1018 Apalachee Pkwy., Tallahassee, FL 32301. © **800/321-2211** or 850/222-8822. Fax 850/561-0354. 154 units. Mon–Thurs $120 double; Fri–Sun $70 double. AE, DC, DISC, MC, V. **Amenities:** Restaurant (breakfast only); bar; heated outdoor pool; exercise room; Jacuzzi; laundry service, coin-op washers and dryers. *In room:* A/C, TV, dataport, coffeemaker, hair dryer, iron.

DoubleTree Hotel   Most of the media covering the Bush-Gore 2000 election case before the Florida Supreme Court stayed at this 16-story hotel, one of the tallest buildings in town. The best thing about it is the location, just 2 blocks north of the Capitol Building at Park Avenue, and the views from the spacious rooms, especially those on the upper floors. It's usually booked solid by politicians and lobbyists during legislative sessions March through May.

101 S. Adams St., Tallahassee, FL 32301. © **800/222-TREE** or 850/224-5000. Fax 850/513-9516. 243 units. $89–$159 double. AE, DC, DISC, MC, V. **Amenities:** Restaurant (American); bar; outdoor pool; exercise room; limited room service; laundry service; concierge-level rooms. *In room:* A/C, TV, dataport, coffeemaker, hair dryer, iron.

Governors Inn ★★   Vice President Gore's lawyers stayed at this elegant, richly furnished inn just half a block north of the Old Capitol in the Adams Street Commons historic district. The building was once a livery stable, and part of its original architecture has been preserved, including the impressive beams. The guest rooms are distinctive, with four-poster beds, black-oak writing desks, rock-maple armoires, and antique accouterments. Of the suites, each one named for a Florida governor, one has a whirlpool bathtub; another has a loft bedroom with wood-burning fireplace. Complimentary continental breakfast and afternoon cocktails are presented in the pine-paneled Florida Room, and a restaurant across the street provides limited room service.

209 S. Adams St., Tallahassee, FL 32301. © **800/342-7717** in Florida, or 850/681-6855. Fax 850/222-3105. 40 units. $129–$149 double; $159–$229 suite. Rates include continental breakfast and evening cocktails. AE, DC, DISC, MC, V. **Amenities:** Access to nearby health club; limited room service; laundry service. *In room:* A/C, TV, dataport.

Quality Inn & Suites *Value*   In contrast to most Quality Inns, there's real charm here. In fact, an almost English country-inn atmosphere prevails in the classy, marble-lined lobby and spacious guest rooms, which are furnished with sofas and reclining wing chairs. A complimentary continental breakfast is served in a lounge with views of the inn's swimming pool, and guests can partake of a

---

Fun Fact   Count Them Out

Demand for hotel rooms during the weekends of Florida State University football games is so great that the high-powered lawyers representing Vice President Gore and Texas Governor George W. Bush had to vacate their rooms when the University of Florida Gators came to play the 'Noles during the 2000 election dispute.

free wine bar Monday through Thursday evenings. A nearby restaurant will deliver food, and several fast-food and family-style restaurants are within a short walk.

2020 Apalachee Pkwy., Tallahassee, FL 32301. ☎ **800/228-5151** or 850/877-4437. Fax 850/878-9964. www.qualityinn.com. 100 units. $79 double; $99 suite. Rates include full breakfast, evening drinks, and local phone calls. AE, DC, DISC, MC, V. **Amenities:** Outdoor pool; access to nearby health club; Jacuzzi; business center; limited room service; laundry service. *In room:* A/C, TV, dataport, fridge, coffeemaker, hair dryer, iron, safe.

Radisson Hotel Tallahassee   President George W. Bush's legal team stayed at this seven-story hotel about a half mile north of the capitol complex. The inn-like lobby with reproduction antiques strikes an elegant ambience, but the regular guest rooms are rather small (this hotel was built in the 1950s as a college dormitory), and air-conditioning units eat up about a third of each unit's window. The spacious suites are much better choices; they are equipped with four-poster beds, whirlpool bathtubs, and wet bars. The pleasant Plantation Dining Room is open daily for breakfast, lunch, and dinner, and the lobby lounge provides libations.

415 N. Monroe St. (at Virginia St.), Tallahassee, FL 32301. ☎ **800/333-3333** or 850/224-6000. Fax 850/222-0335. www.radisson.com/tallahasseefl. 119 units. $111 double; $150–$197 suite. Weekend rates available. AE, DC, DISC, MC, V. **Amenities:** Restaurant (American); bar; exercise room; sauna; limited room service; laundry service; concierge-level rooms. *In room:* A/C, TV, dataport (high-speed Internet access), coffeemaker, hair dryer, iron.

WHERE TO DINE

Numerous budget-priced fast-food and family chain restaurants lie along Apalachee Parkway and North Monroe Street. For inexpensive seafood, the local **Shells** is at 2136 N. Monroe St., at Universal Drive (☎ **850/385-2774**). See p. 455 for details about the Shells chain.

Anthony's ☆ SOUTHERN ITALIAN   Locals come to see and be seen at Dick Anthony's elegantly relaxed trattoria, which supplies them with the city's best Italian cuisine. Among his specialties is *pesce Venezia,* spinach fettuccine tossed in a cream sauce with scallops, crab meat, and fish. Chicken piccata and chicken San Marino are also favorites, and Dick's thick, juicy steaks are always popular with beef eaters. A wall-size wine cupboard features choices from Italy and the United States by the bottle or glass. Espresso pie leads the dessert menu.

1950 Thomasville Rd., at Bradford Rd. in the Betton Place Shops. ☎ **850/224-1447.** Reservations recommended. Main courses $12–$21. AE, DC, DISC, MC, V. Daily 5–9pm.

Bahn Thai THAI/CANTONESE   Lamoi (Sue) Snyder and progeny have been serving the spicy cuisine of her native Thailand at this store front since 1979. In deference to local Southerners, who may never have sampled anything spicier than cheese grits, much of her menu is devoted to mild Cantonese-style Chinese dishes. More adventurous diners, however, flock here to order such authentic tongue-burners as *yon voon-sen,* a combination of shrimp, chicken, bean threads, onions, lemon grass, ground peanuts, and the obligatory chili peppers. Sue's specialty is her deliciously sweet, slightly gingered version of Penang curry. You can ask her to turn down the heat in her other Thai dishes. Come at lunch and sample it all from the all-you-can-eat buffet—a real bargain.

1319 S. Monroe St. (between Oakland Ave. and Harrison St.). ☎ **850/224-4765.** Main courses $6–$15. Lunch buffet $6.50. DISC, MC, V. Mon–Thurs 11am–2:30pm and 5–10pm; Fri 11am–2:30pm and 5–10:30pm; Sat 5–10:30pm.

Barnacle Bill's Seafood Restaurant SEAFOOD   There's always plenty of action at this noisy, very casual spot, a favorite of the journalists and talking heads who covered the Gore-Bush election contest. Freshly shucked Apalachicola oysters are the stars at the enormous tile-topped raw bar in the middle of the room, but the menu offers a mélange of seafood to please the palates of the singles, couples, and families who flock here. The cooking is simple and usually done by Florida State University students working part-time jobs. Best bets are charcoal-grilled mahimahi, tuna, amberjack, and grouper. For a smoked sensation, try the mahimahi and amberjack cured on the premises. During nice weather, guests can sit at outdoor tables under a lean-to tent. A downstairs bar serves the regular seafood items plus sushi, deli sandwiches, and salads.

1830 N. Monroe St. (north of Tharpe St.). © 850/385-8734. Main courses $8–$17 (most $10–$12); sandwiches and salads $5–$9. AE, DC, DISC, MC, V. Sun–Thurs 11am–11pm; Fri–Sat 11am–midnight.

Chez Pierre 🐸🐸 TRADITIONAL FRENCH   You become an instant Francophile in Florida at this chic restaurant in a beautifully restored 1920s brick home. French-born chef Eric Favier and his American wife and partner, Karen Cooley, offer traditional French cuisine either inside the house—where the walls are adorned with changing, for-sale works by local artists—or outside on a large deck nearly shaded by live oaks draped with Spanish moss. Opening to the deck, a bistro-style bar provides a light-fare menu between lunch and dinner. Chez Pierre offers daily specials to take advantage of fresh produce. Among the winners are rack of lamb, a version of Provençal-style ratatouille, and crab cakes with a luscious mustard and thyme demi-glacé. French table wines are moderately priced, and California house wines are also served. Live music regularly accompanies dining. No smoking except on the front porch, where stogies and brandy can be enjoyed while lounging in wicker chairs. Book as early as possible for Bastille Day (July 14), which sees a grand fete here.

1215 Thomasville Rd. (at 6th Ave.). © 850/222-0936. Reservations recommended. Main courses $15–$23. AE, DC, DISC, MC, V. Mon–Sat 11am–10pm; Sun 11am–9pm.

Food Glorious Food 🐸🐸 *(Value)* AMERICAN/INTERNATIONAL   Very unusual and very healthy sandwiches, salads, and pastas make Susan Turner's deli/cafe one of the town's favorite lunch and early-dinner spots. Items displayed in a cold case change daily but always include gazpacho, a variety of gourmet salads, inventive sandwiches, a daily quiche, and plenty of tempting pastries and cookies. Main courses feature the likes of pineapple jerk chicken, Cuban chicken, and several pastas. You can get your selection to go or dine at a few tables inside or, in good weather, on the outside courtyard.

In Betton Place Shops, 1950 Thomasville Rd. at Bradford Rd. © 850/224-9974. Reservations not accepted. Main courses $9–$20; sandwiches and salads $5.50–$11. AE, DC, MC, V. Mon–Thurs 11am–8pm; Fri–Sat 11am–9pm (table service 11am–3pm). Closed July 4, Thanksgiving, Christmas.

Kool Beanz Cafe 🐸🐸 ECLECTIC   The coolest cafe in town, this noisy emporium of trendy cooking draws lots of patrons in their late 20s and early 30s who appreciate exciting blends of flavors. The joint is dimly lit but painted in bright pastels from the Caribbean. You'll find many island-style items on the constantly changing menu, including Jamaican jerk grouper served with black beans, rice, and a sweet tropical-fruit relish. You may want to get here early because more-inventive items like the seared but rare tuna crusted with spice and served with a terrific roasted-peanut sauce will sell out early, as will the curried lamb shank and the pork tenderloin marinated with orange molasses.

921 Thomasville Rd. (at Williams St.). ℂ **850/224-2466.** Main courses $12–$16. AE, DISC, MC, V. Mon–Fri 11am–2:30pm and 5:30–10pm; Sat 5:30–10pm.

TALLAHASSEE AFTER DARK

Check the "Limelight" section of Friday's *Tallahassee Democrat* (www.tallahasseedemocrat.com) for weekend entertainment listings.

As a college town, Tallahassee has numerous pubs and nightclubs with live dance music, not to mention a multitude of sports bars. Pick up a copy of *Break* and other entertainment tabloids at **Barnacle Bill's Seafood Emporium** or other entertainment venues.

The major performing-arts venue is the **Tallahassee–Leon County Civic Center,** 505 W. Pensacola St. (ℂ **800/322-3602** or 850/222-0400; www.tlccc.org), which features a Broadway series, concerts, and sporting events including Florida State University (FSU) collegiate basketball games. Special concerts are presented by the **Tallahassee Symphony Orchestra** (www.tso live.org) at FSU Ruby Diamond Auditorium, at College Avenue and Copeland Street (ℂ **850/224-0462**). **The FSU Mainstage/School of Theatre,** at the Fine Arts Building on Call and Copeland streets (ℂ **850/644-6500;** www.fsu.org), presents excellent productions from classic dramas to comedies.

SIDE TRIPS FROM TALLAHASSEE

The following excursions are generally on the way to Apalachicola, so if you're headed that way, plan to make a detour or two.

WAKULLA SPRINGS 👫👫

The world's largest and deepest freshwater spring is 15 miles (24km) south of Tallahassee in the 2,860-acre **Edward W. Ball Wakulla Springs State Park** 👫👫 , on Fla. 267 just east of its junction with Fla. 61. Edward Ball, a financier who administered the du Pont estate, turned the springs and the moss-draped surrounding forest into a preservation area. Divers have mapped an underwater cave system extending more than 6,000 feet (1,800m) back from the spring's mouth. Wakulla has been known to dispense an amazing 14,325 gallons of water per second at certain times. Mastodon bones, including those of Herman, now in Tallahassee's Museum of Florida History, were found in the caves. The 1930s *Tarzan* movies starring Johnny Weissmuller were filmed here.

A free 10-minute orientation movie is offered at the park's theater at the waterfront. You can hike or bike along the nature trails, and swimming is allowed, but only in designated areas. It's important to observe swimming rules since alligators are present.

If the spring water is clear enough, 30-minute glass-bottom–boat sightseeing trips depart every 45 minutes daily, from 9:45am to 5pm during daylight saving time, 9:15am to 4:30pm the rest of the year. Even if the water is murky, you're likely to see alligators, birds, and other wildlife on 30-minute riverboat cruises, which operate during these same hours. Either boat ride costs $4.50 for adults, half-price for children under 13.

Entrance fees to the park are $3.25 per vehicle with up to eight passengers, $1 for pedestrians and bicyclists. The park is open daily from 8am to dusk.

For more information, contact the park at 550 Wakulla Springs Dr., Wakulla Springs, FL 32305 (ℂ **850/224-5950;** fax 850/561-7251; www.florida stateparks.org/district1/wakullasprings).

Where to Stay & Dine

Wakulla Springs Lodge   On the shore of Wakulla Springs, this dated but charming lodge is distinctive for its magnificent Spanish architecture and ornate old-world furnishings, such as rare Spanish tiles, black-granite tables, marble floors, and ceiling beams painted with Florida scenes by a German artist (supposedly Kaiser Wilhelm's court painter). The guest rooms are simple by today's standards (you'll get a marble bathroom and phone but no TV). By all means, ask for a room in the front, so you'll have a lake view. You don't have to be a lodge guest to enjoy the warm, smoky ambience of the great lobby with its huge stone fireplace and arched windows looking onto the springs, or to enjoy reasonably priced meals featuring Southern cuisine in the lovely Ball Room (reservations recommended). The fountain (a 60-ft.-long marble drugstore-style counter for old-fashioned ice-cream sodas) provides snacks and sandwiches.

550 Wakulla Park Dr., Wakulla Springs, FL 32305. 📞 **850/224-5950.** Fax 850/561-7251. 27 units. $79–$99 double. AE, DISC, MC, V. **Amenities:** Restaurant (Southern). *In room:* A/C.

THE ST. MARKS AREA

Rich history lives in the area around the little village of **St. Marks,** 18 miles (29km) south of the capital at the end of both Fla. 363 and the Tallahassee–St. Marks Historic Railroad Trail State Park (p. 697).

After marching overland from Tampa Bay in 1528, the Spanish conquistador Panfilo de Narvaez and 300 men arrived at this strategic point at the confluence of the St. Marks and Wakulla Rivers near the Gulf of Mexico. Since their only avenue back to Spain was by sea, they built and launched the first ships made by Europeans in the New World. Some 11 years later, Hernando de Soto and his 600 men arrived here after following Narvaez's route from Tampa. They marked the harbor entrance by hanging banners in the trees, then moved inland. Two wooden forts were built here, one in 1679 and one in 1718, and a stone version was begun in 1739. The fort shifted among Spanish, British, and Native American hands until General Andrew Jackson took it away from the Spanish in 1819.

Parts of the old Spanish bastion wall and Confederate earthworks built during the Civil War are in the **San Marcos de Apalache Historic State Park,** reached by turning right at the end of Fla. 363 in St. Marks and following the paved road. A museum built on the foundation of the old marine hospital holds exhibits and artifacts covering the area's history. The site is open Thursday through Monday from 9am to 5pm; closed New Year's Day, Thanksgiving, and Christmas. Admission to the site is free; admission to the museum costs $1, free for children 6 and under. For more information, contact the site at 1022 DeSoto Park Dr., Tallahassee, FL 32301 (📞 **850/925-6216** or 850/922-6007; www.floridastateparks.org/district1/sanmarcos).

De Soto's men marked the harbor entrance in what is now the **St. Marks Lighthouse and National Wildlife Refuge** 🐾, P.O. Box 68, St. Marks, FL 32355 (📞 **850/925-6121**). Operated by the U.S. Fish and Wildlife Service, this 65,000-acre preserve occupies much of the coast from the Aucilla River east of St. Marks to the Ochlockonee River west of Panacea and is home to more species of birds than anyplace else in Florida except the Everglades. The visitor center is 3½ miles (5.75km) south of U.S. 98 on Lighthouse Road (Fla. 59); turn south off U.S. 98 at Newport, about 2 miles (3.25km) east of St. Marks. Stop at the center for self-guided-tour maps of the roads and extensive hiking trails, some of them built atop levees running through the marshland.

> **Tips   A Ramshackle Riverside Lunch**
>
> Tallahasseeans love to drive or bike down to St. Marks and have a water-side lunch at **Posey's Oyster Bar,** at the end of Fla. 363 (© **850/925-6172**). Some nighttime patrons at this ramshackle wooden restaurant and bar can get rowdy, especially when Country-and-Western bands are playing on weekends, but it's a fine place for freshly shucked oysters or smoked mullet during the day. Be sure to walk all the way through the dining rooms to the bar beside the St. Marks River. Posey's opens daily at 11am.

The 80-foot-tall (24m) **St. Marks Lighthouse,** 8 miles (13km) south of the visitor center, was built in 1842 of limestone blocks 4 feet (1.25m) thick at the base. The nearby beach is a popular crabbing spot.

Admission to the refuge is $4 per vehicle, $1 for pedestrians and bicyclists (federal Duck Stamps and National Park Service passports accepted). The refuge is open daily from sunrise to sunset; the visitor center, Monday through Friday from 8am to 4pm and Saturday and Sunday from 10am to 5pm (closed all federal holidays). Contact the refuge for information about seasonal tours and hunting.

In 1865, during the final weeks of the Civil War, Federal troops landed at the lighthouse and launched a surprise attack on Tallahassee. The Confederates quickly assembled an impromptu army of wounded soldiers, old men, and boys as young as 14. This ragtag bunch fought the Federal regulars for 5 days at what is now the **Natural Bridge Battlefield State Historic Site.** Surprisingly, the old men and boys won. As a result, Tallahassee remained the only Confederate state capital east of the Mississippi never to fall into Yankee hands. The historic site is on County Road 2192, 6 miles (10km) east of Woodville on the St. Marks River, halfway between Tallahassee and St. Marks. Follow the signs from Fla. 363 and go to the end of the pavement. It's open daily from 8am to sunset and admission is free. For more information, contact the San Marcos de Apalache Historic State Park (see above) or check www.floridastateparks.org/district1/naturalbridge.

APALACHICOLA NATIONAL FOREST

The largest of Florida's three national forests, this huge preserve encompasses 600,000 acres stretching from Tallahassee's outskirts southward to the Gulf Coast and westward some 70 miles (113km) to the Apalachicola River. Included are a variety of woodlands, rivers, streams, lakes, and caves populated by a host of wildlife. There are picnic facilities with sheltered tables and grills, canoe and mountain-bike trails, campgrounds with tent and RV sites, and a number of other facilities, some of them especially designed for visitors with disabilities.

The **Leon Sinks Area** is closest to Tallahassee, 5½ miles (9km) south of Southeast Capital Circle on U.S. 319 near the Leon–Wakulla County line. Nature trails and boardwalks lead from one sinkhole (a lake formed when water erodes the underlying limestone) to another. The trails are open daily from 8am to 8pm.

A necessary stop before heading into this wilderness is the **Wakulla Area Ranger District,** 57 Taft Dr., Crawfordville, FL 32327 (© **850/926-3561;** fax 850/926-1904; www.southernregion.fs.fed.us/florida/forests/apalachicola.htm), which provides information about the forest and its facilities and sells topographical and canoe trail maps. The station is off U.S. 319, about 20 miles (32km) south of Tallahassee and 2 miles (3.25km) north of Crawfordville. It's open Monday through Thursday from 8am to 4:30pm, Friday from 8am to 4pm.

Index

HIT THE ROAD WITH FROMMER'S DRIVING TOURS!

Booked seat 6A, open return.

Rented red 4-wheel drive.

Reserved cabin, no running water.

Discovered space.

:h over 700 airlines, 50,000 hotels, 50 rental car companies and
00 cruise and vacation packages, you can create the perfect get-
ay for you. Choose the car, the room, even the ground you walk on.

Travelocity.com
A Sabre Company
Go Virtually Anywhere.

You Need
A Vacation.

700 Airlines, 50,000 Hotels, 50 Rental Car
Companies, And A Million Ways To Save Money.

Travelocity.com
A Sabre Company
Go Virtually Anywhere.